CRIME AND JUSTICE IN AMERICA

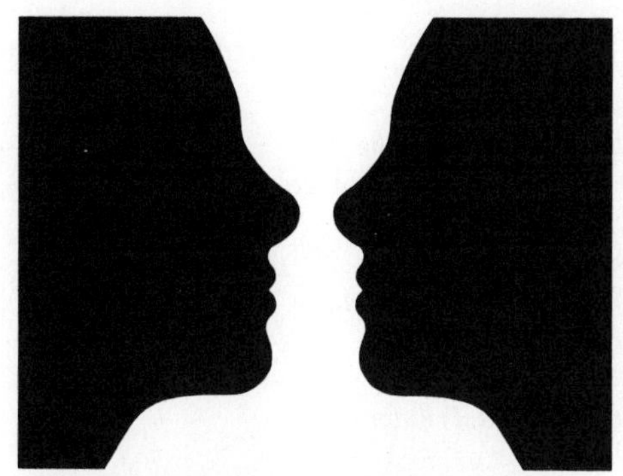

CRIME AND JUSTICE IN AMERICA

A HUMAN PERSPECTIVE

LEONARD TERRITO
University of South Florida

JAMES HALSTED
University of South Florida

MAX BROMLEY
University of South Florida

WEST PUBLISHING COMPANY
St. Paul New York Los Angeles San Francisco

Chapter opening photos:

1 *UPI/Bettman*
2 *UPI/Bettman*
3 *Wide World Photos*
4 *David Farr/Imagesmythe Inc.*
5 *Wide World Photos*
6 *Robert Eckert/EKM-Nepenthe*
7 *Tony O'Brien/Criminal Justice Pictures*
8 *H. Armstrong Roberts*
9 *Robert Eckert/EKM-Nepenthe*
10 *Supreme Court Historical Society*
11 *Jim Shaffer*
12 *UPI/Bettman*
13 *Robert Burke/Tampa Tribune*
14 *Wide World Photos*
15 *Tony O'Brien/Criminal Justice Photos*
16 *BI Incorporated*
17 *Tim Jewett/EKM-Nepenthe*
18 *Courtesy of the Detroit, Michigan, Police Department*

PRODUCTION CREDITS
Copy Editor: Pat Lewis
Composition: Parkwood Composition Service, Inc.
Interior Design: Linda Beauvais
Cover Design: Linda Beauvais

50 West Kellogg Boulevard
P.O. Box 64526
St. Paul, MN 55164-1003

Printed in the United States of America
96 95 94 93 92 91 8 7 6 5 4 3 2

LIBRARY OF CONGRESS
Library of Congress Cataloging-in-Publication Data

Territo, Leonard.
Crime and justice in America: a human perspective / Leonard Territo, Max Bromley, Jim Halsted.–2nd ed.
p. cm.
Rev. ed. of: Crime and justice in America: a human perspective / Harold J. Vetter, Leonard Territo. c1984.
ISBN 0-314-45798-4
1. Criminal justice, Administration of—United States. 2. Crime and criminals—United States. I. Bromley, Max. II. Halsted, Jim. III. Vetter, Harold J., 1926– Crime and justice in America. IV. Title.
HV9950.V47 1989
364'.973—dc19 88-22000
CIP

Dedicated to our parents and the special women in our lives.

B. Robert and Yolanda Territo, Hal and Virginia Halsted, and Max and Faye Bromley

and

Chris, Teri, and Debbie

CONTENTS

PREFACE

The theme and direction of this second edition is similar to that of our first edition; namely, to introduce the reader to the study of crime and justice in America. Our focus continues to be the "Human Perspective" as it applies to the major components of the criminal justice system. However, as former students ourselves, more years ago than we care to remember, we too, often found ourselves bored to tears with some of our reading assignments. We wanted to write a book that would not only meet the highest academic standards of our colleagues, but one which was also interesting and informative. In order to help us to accomplish this objective, we have used generous numbers of case studies, newspaper articles, photos, and examples from our own experiences as police administrators, correctional administrators, and trial attorneys.

The criminal justice discipline is a dynamic one with changes occurring rapidly and there are important issues today that were not even minor issues a few years ago. For example, one highly charged and complex problem deals with the arrest and incarceration of persons with AIDS. There has been a virtual explosion of new research on this topic to assist police officers and correctional officers in dealing with such individuals. This very new and important topic has been given considerable attention in the second edition. Some of the other new and interesting topics included are: an expanded discussion of inherited criminality; the expansion of the victims rights movement; law enforcement accreditation; criminal profiling; the conservative direction of recent Supreme Court decisions; suicide in jails; corrections in the private sector; electronically monitored home confinement; crimes against the elderly; and drug screening of police officers.

In addition, we have replaced some of the previous issue papers with more current ones. Some of these new issue papers discuss domestic terrorism in the 1980s, investigative grand juries, male and female correctional officers, and castration of sex offenders.

In short, we believe we have written a book that the reader will find interesting, informative, and yes, even entertaining. It continues to be our judgment that it is better to tell a story than to belabor an abstraction and it is this consideration that has guided our selection, organization, and presentation of topics in this book.

LEARNING FEATURES

In addition to the basic content of the text, there are several distinctive features found in each chapter.

Cases. These are interspersed throughout the chapter and are short summaries of actual criminal cases which pertain to the content of the text.

Articles. These are excerpts from press accounts of criminal activities and their consequences. They provide a valuable perspective on the criminal justice system from outside the system.

Summaries. The chapter summaries are intended to help the student see the chapter contents in a nutshell.

Issue Papers. These are longer press and professional journal articles on important issues facing criminal justice professionals.

Discussion and Review. These are questions which give the student practice in thinking about the material covered and give the instructor suggestions for generating class discussion.

Glossaries. The glossaries found at the end of the chapter for easy reference define key terms from each chapter.

SUPPLEMENTS

An instructor's manual with test bank and transparency masters is available to instructors. The manual was written by the authors of the text. The test bank contains questions in a multiple choice format. Also in the instructor's manual are 181 transparency masters.

A student's study guide, written by Leda Thompson, is available for purchase. It contains for each chapter Learning Objectives, a Chapter Summary, a list of Key Terms and Concepts, a Fill in the Blank Review, and a Self Test with true/false, multiple choice, matching, and essay questions.

LT
JBH
MLB

ACKNOWLEDGEMENTS

In the first edition of this book, our good friend, colleague, mentor, and teacher, Dr. Harold J. Vetter, was the senior author. He was not involved with the second edition, but a substantial portion of his writing from the first edition remains. We, therefore, want to thank him collectively for his significant contributions to this book.

In the transition from the first to the second edition of any book, it is imperative that colleagues in the profession be given an opportunity to review the earlier edition and to make suggestions and recommendations for improvement. A number of individuals were particularly helpful to us in this endeavor and we wish to thank them for their time and effort. These individuals were: Nick Cobun, Coastal Carolina Community College; John Gray, Tidewater Community College; Alex Greenberg, Niagra Community College; Leon Hoffman, Grossmont College; John Kocher, Lane Community College; Walter Niederberger, Albuquerque Technical Vocational Institute; Harold Smith, Northern Arizona University; and Larry Strauser, Lycoming College.

Dr. Charles R. (Mike) Swanson, University of Georgia, generously provided us with material we used in the chapter on jails and detention as well as information on the role of the court administrator used in our chapter dealing with the courts.

Our good friends and colleagues, Dr. Richard Dembo and Dr. Kathleen Heide, University of South Florida, were most generous with their time and research materials. Their contributions were of invaluable assistance in updating our juvenile justice chapter.

Chief Jim Sewell, of the Gulfport, Florida Police Department, generously allowed the use of his law enforcement critical life events scale for inclusion in our discussion of police stress. Other individuals who made significant contributions in the police chapters were as follows: Darrel W. Stephens, Executive Director of the Police Executive Research Forum; John E. Eck, Gerard Murphy, also with the Police Executive Research Forum; Ken Medeiros, Executive Director of the Commission on Accreditation for Law Enforcement Agencies, Inc.; Garry Mendez of the National Urban League; and Lt. Ross Lundstrom of the St. Paul, Minnesota Police Department.

Dr. Simon Dinitz, Department of Sociology, Ohio State University, graciously allowed us to use major portions of his paper titled "Are Safe and Humane Prisons Possible?" in chapter 14—Social, Political and Racial Forces in American Prisons.

Dr. David Agresti, PRIDE of Florida, supplied us with several photos which appear in the corrections chapter. Photos were also contributed by our longtime friend, Robert L. Smith, Director of Public Safety, Tampa, Florida, as well as Margaret C. Hambrick, Warden, Federal Correctional Institution, Butner, North Carolina; Robert J. Henderson, Superintendent, Auburn Correctional facility, Auburn, New York; Frank W. Wood, Warden, Minnesota Correctional facility, Oak Park Heights, Minnesota; Harold J. Miller, Warden, United States Penitentiary, Marion, Illinois; Dean J. Leech, Executive Assistant, and Michael Aun, Information Officer, U.S. Department of Justice, Federal Prison System. Our good friend, Jeff Crawford of the Florida Department of Health and Rehabilitative Services, in West Palm Beach, Florida also supplied several photographs of juvenile justice correctional facilities used in our juvenile justice chapter. Additional photos were supplied by Chief Cornelius J. Behan and E. Jay Miller of the Baltimore County Police Department, Towson, Maryland, Leon Swartzman of Passaqequa New York, Thomas Deakin, Editor of the FBI Law Enforcement Bulletin, Inspector Nathaniel Topp of the Detroit, Michigan Police Department, and Chief Curtis McLane of the Tampa Police Department, Tampa, Florida.

Bobbie Deck, Indiana University, Pennsylvania was kind enough to supplement our issue paper which addresses the socialization of correctional officers with an entire new section dealing with female correctional officers working in male correctional facilities.

Paul Hogan, former editor of the *Tampa Tribune,* who has always been very kind in the past and allowed us to reprint news stories and photos appearing in the *Tampa Tribune,* continued his generosity with this second edition.

Contributions to ideas, encouragement and support were also forthcoming from Phyllis Daniels, Jim Shriner, David Wickham, Bruce Underwood, and Jan DeCosmo.

Typing and numerous other clerical services were provided by a battery of people who collectively made innumerable contributions. Many thanks to Marianne Bell, Mike Copeland, Nita Desai, Maggie Deutsch, Gregg

Gronlund, Jerry Hren, Sharon Johnson-Hamilton, Robin Kester, Marian Pittman, Cecile Pulin, Peter Selle, and Wayne Wlodawsky.

We also wish to thank our editor, Peter Marshall and his editorial assistant, Jane Bacon, for their guidance, support and encouragement. William Gabler, our production editor, was always a pleasure to work with and made, what can be, a tedious task much easier for all of us.

Special thanks are also in order for our creative Promotion Manager, Beth Hoeppner, who was always responsive to our suggestions and ideas.

Lastly, we wish to thank all the publishers who so willingly shared their work with us. Without their cooperation, this book could not have had the strong human perspective that we wanted.

LT
JBH
MLB

CHAPTER

1

Crime and Justice in America

CHAPTER OUTLINE:

CRIME IN AMERICAN HISTORY

Apprehension about crime has been present in every period of American history. Riots and mob violence erupted in American cities during the Civil War. Rival gangster mobs battled in the streets in the Roaring Twenties. The bank-robbing exploits of Bonnie and Clyde marked the Great Depression. In fact, "crime waves" and "the crime problem," are nothing new. As the President's Commission on Law Enforcement and Administration of Justice noted:

> A hundred years ago contemporary accounts of San Francisco told of extensive areas where "no decent man was in safety to walk the streets after dark; while at all hours, both night and day, his property was jeopardized by incendiarism and burglary." Teenage gangs gave rise to the word "hoodlum"; while in one central New York City area, near Broadway, the police entered "only in pairs, and never unarmed . . ." "Alarming" increases in robbery and violent crimes were reported throughout the country prior to the revolution. And in 1910 one author declared that "crime, especially in its more violent forms, and among the young is increasing steadily and is threatening to bankrupt the Nation" (*Challenge of Crime in a Free Society* 1967, p. 19).

Still, attitudes toward crime and the treatment of criminals have varied over the years.

Crime has been viewed as a sin, as an illness, as a result of individual flaws, and as a consequence of societal failure. Over the centuries criminals have been banished, beheaded, impaled, burned, flogged, mutilated, chained to oars as galley slaves, impressed into military service, exiled, and imprisoned. The intent was usually to punish the offender. However, as the ideas of sin and crime came together in Western religion, punishment took on a new dimension: penance. No longer was punishment meted out solely to get even with the offender; rather, through the punishment, the offender was to find a path to reformation and redemption.

Spiritual redemption as an approach to the reform of the criminal was a dominant theme in corrections during the colonial period and in the first two decades of the nineteenth century. It was abandoned when it proved incapable of producing desired changes in people. Its decline was hastened by the growing urbanization and industrialization of the United States in the early and middle 1800s. For all practical purposes, spiritual reform for the criminal was largely discarded by the 1850s, although some of its influence endured—including its influence today within corrections. Although penitentiaries have not been very successful in reforming criminals, imprisonment has persisted as a punishment.

In the twentieth century, yet another approach to criminal reform evolved: rehabilitation was redefined as a medical, or psychiatric, problem. As a result, criminals have been operated on, given drugs, trained for jobs, counseled in groups or as individuals, conditioned, counterconditioned, and otherwise "treated" in attempts to modify their mental states or behavior.

Although attitudes and treatments change, crime persists. Crime may have been as frequent around the time of the Revolution as it is today. In the nineteenth century, both the cities and the frontier were dangerous; and immigrants were frequently blamed for increases in crime. From 1900 to the 1930s, violent crime soared, with labor battles and racial violence contributing to the toll. Then, from about 1933 until the early 1960s, "the

United States, perhaps for the first time in its history, enjoyed a period in which crime rates were either stable or declining and in which fear of crime was relatively low" (Silberman 1978, p. 30). This domestic peace contrasted with America's past and its future.

Thus, crime is not a new, and not a peculiarly American, problem; crime is timeless and universal. But it is not crime in foreign countries that Americans fear; it is crime in their own communities. The concern is not whether crime is more prevalent or less prevalent than it was in some earlier period; people are afraid of crime *right now*. Social reality is largely what a society believes about itself. If the members of a society believe they are unsafe in their homes, workplaces, and public areas, apprehension and insecurity become an important part of social reality. Has this happened in the United States, where society sees itself as beleaguered by crime?

When people perceive themselves to be threatened by crime, they take measures to protect themselves, their families, and their property. Feeling like hunted animals, people are "curfewed by their own fear" (Conklin 1975, p. 3). In daily life, fear of crime may take an even greater toll than crime itself. Individuals and communities often respond to the threat of crime by seeking refuge behind deadbolts, guard dogs, electronic alarms, closed-circuit television cameras, and security guards.

THE PSYCHOLOGICAL AND SOCIAL IMPACTS OF CRIME

Measuring the impact of crime in terms of economic factors is somewhat analogous to the assessing seriousness of an accident based on the total medical bill. Tangible possessions such as money and property can be replaced, even though their loss may impose a crushing burden. But the psychological and social costs of crime, because they involve subjective factors and intangibles, can constitute a far more serious problem.

Fear and Its Consequences

Fear is a basic ingredient of any psychological or social reaction to crime. It is a gut reaction that produces marked changes in individual behavior. The most intense fear is of the crimes least likely to occur: murder, assault, and forcible rape. Ironically, the perpetrator in such crimes is often a family member, close friend, or personal acquaintance. Nevertheless, what people fear most is violence at the hands of a stranger. Fear of an unknown assailant is prominent in both individual and collective responses to crime. Fear of strangers generalizes to fear of strange places, and people eventually see even public streets as unsafe. When fear of public places peaks, people avoid areas perceived as potentially hazardous. Consequently, normal activity is interrupted in various areas, removing one deterrent to criminal activity. Areas thus avoided are then increasingly frequented by persons bent upon crime.

The Impact of Criminal Violence

Official crime reports generally distinguish between crimes against property and crimes against the person. However, this distinction ignores, or at least minimizes, the fact that property crimes inevitably affect a victim adversely beyond *observable* losses of goods or money. For example, Bard and Ellison (1974) emphasize that victims of burglary, armed robbery, assault and robbery, and rape suffer significant psychological consequences.

The psychological impact of burglary on an individual is often disregarded, because the only visible consequence to the victim may be a property loss covered by insurance. What is often not recognized, however, is that people regard their homes or apartments as extensions of themselves. A person's home is more than his or her castle: it is a physical projection of the self. Moreover, in an urban-industrial society in which privacy is at a premium, the home is the only place that offers individuals security and a place to escape from the pressures of everyday life. Furthermore, every home uniquely represents the personality of its occupants. When a home is burglarized, occupants are often far more upset about the actual intrusion into the home than about the loss of property. The burglary represents a violation or intrusion into a part of the self.[1] In armed robbery, not only is personal property lost, but the victim is also deprived of self-determination while the crime is in progress. The victim's fate rests in the unpredictable hands of the robber.

In addition to loss of self-determination and personal property, assault and robbery involve an injury inflicted on the body; and the body can be regarded as the "envelope of self." The injury causes both physical and psychological pain. As Bard and Ellison suggest, "victims are left with the physical evidence reminding them that they were forced to surrender their autonomy and also the fact that they have been made to feel like less than adequate people . . . a visible reminder of their helplessness to protect or defend themselves" (1974, p. 71).

Short of homicide, forcible rape is the ultimate violation of self. Rape victims are deprived of self-determination and often suffer external physical injury.

Further, the offender intrudes internally into the victim's body. As far as the victim is concerned, it makes no difference which body orifice is breached; it is the act of forceful entry into the body that causes the trauma. This forceful intrusion is one of the most trying crises a victim can sustain, particularly in view of the moral taboos surrounding the sexual function. In many cases, a rape victim is not physically injured, but suffers catastrophic psychological injury.

Assault on the Quality of Life

Each of us experiences the impact of economic crime whenever we make a purchase in a supermarket or department store. The costs of offenses such as shoplifting and employee pilferage are inevitably transmitted to the consumer in the form of increased prices, adding appreciably to the burden of inflation. But the harm of economic crime goes even deeper, extending to our social and economic institutions. The Chamber of Commerce of the United States assesses the damage this way: "A major long-term impact of white-collar crime is loss of public confidence in business, industry, and the professions and debasement of competition" (1974, p. 7). Edelhertz gives specific examples of how white-collar crimes affect our system of competition:

> . . . every stock market fraud lessens competition in the securities market. Every commercial bribe or kickback debases the level of business competition, often forcing other suppliers to join in the practice if they are to survive. The business which accumulates capital to finance expansion by tax evasion places at a disadvantage the competitor who pays his taxes and is compelled to turn to lenders (for operating and expansion capital). The pharmaceutical company which markets a new drug based on fraudulent test results undercuts its competitors who are marketing a properly tested drug, and may cause them to adopt similar methods. Competitors who join in a conspiracy to freeze out their competition, or to fix prices, may gravely influence the course of our economy, in addition to harming their competitors and customers (1970, p. 9).

In addition to debasing competition, indifference to ethical practices can retard economic growth. For example, many companies refuse to conduct business in one particular state in which payoffs to government officials are expected (Chamber of Commerce of the United States 1974). When such abuses become flagrant, public pressure sometimes results in legislation or regulations that adversely affect the innocent as well as the guilty. The Chamber of Commerce reports that, in reaction to numerous verified abuses, a district attorney in one county has essentially banned door-to-door sales. The policy is supported by local business people who fear that the unethical practices of some door-to-door sellers will undermine the public trust in local business, thus reducing the patronage of those businesses. Unfortunately, the policy makes life nearly impossible for ethical companies that employ honest door-to-door sellers.

In a broader sense, white-collar crime affects the entire moral climate of our country. When people in positions of community leadership—corporate executives and government officials, for example—receive light penalties for offenses, our criminal justice system is undermined. And conventional offenders are provided with an opportunity to rationalize their own misconduct.

DEFINING AND CLASSIFYING CRIMES

In colonial America, religious offenses such as blasphemy were punished as crimes. In the 1920s, it was a crime to drink Scotch. Today, it is illegal in the state of Wisconsin to sing in a bar; in Louisiana, it is illegal to appear drunk at a meeting of a literary society. Thus, crime is not synonymous with evil or deviance. A society may punish for many kinds of wrong or abnormal behavior by informal sanctions—disapproval, verbal abuse, ostracism (casting the offender out of the group). *Crimes,* however, are only those acts that violate *laws,* (i.e., formal, official, written statements of norms). No matter how reprehensible an act or the omission of an act may be, a crime has not been committed unless a specific law has been violated. Moreover, the violation must be either intentional or negligent.

Laws vary greatly with time, place, and circumstance, but they are remarkably similar in their definition of the most serious crimes, felonies. A *felony* is an offense serious enough to merit strong punishment; in the United States, felonies are punishable by one year or more in prison. Criminal homicide, forcible rape, burglary, and aggravated assault—just to name a few—are all felonies. Lesser offenses are called *misdemeanors,* generally defined in the United States as crimes for which the sentence is confinement in a county jail for less than one year; a fine may also be assessed. Drunkenness, vagrancy, disorders of the peace, and small-scale gambling are all misdemeanors.

Conventional Crimes

The most serious felonies are crimes against the person: criminal homicide, forcible rape, robbery, and aggravated assault. These four crimes arouse the greatest public emotion and concern. They are the "headline" crimes that create fear and incite demands for tougher and more vigorous law enforcement. However, most felonies are directed not against persons, but against property. Property crimes—burglary, larceny-theft, motor vehicle theft, arson—exclude crimes of violence.

Other offenses not commonly thought of as violent crimes or crimes against the person have the potential for violence. For example, an act of shoplifting can result in physical injury if a store employee tries to restrain the shoplifter and is attacked. Similarly, a homeowner who is awakened by a burglar may end up as a murder victim rather than a victim of breaking and entering. An arson may turn into a crime against the person if a security guard is in a building when it is torched. Thus, what starts as a crime against property may, as a consequence of circumstances, become a different crime—a crime against the person. Nevertheless, in recent years property offenses have made up the bulk of the more than 13 million crimes reported annually.

The government, for reasons long criticized by criminologists, collects data on eight offenses that make up the FBI's Crime Index: criminal homicide, forcible rape, robbery, aggravated assault, burglary, larceny-theft, motor vehicle theft, and arson. As is pointed out in Chapter 3, the Crime Index provides information on "crime in the streets"; however, it fails to provide adequate coverage of "crime in the suites" (i.e., the highly profitable, large-scale property crimes perpetrated by corporations and businesses). Official statistics also fail to report accurately on "workplace crimes"—the auto mechanic who performs unneeded repairs or the microwave repairer who replaces a transistor and charges for a new mag tube; annual losses from these offenses dwarf by comparison losses from conventional crimes such as shoplifting and burglary.

Economic Crimes

Criminologist Edwin Sutherland introduced the idea of white-collar crime to direct attention to crimes of the "upper world," in contrast to conventional crimes committed by the lower classes. He defined **white-collar crime** as offenses committed by "a person of respectability and high social status in the course of his occupation" (1949, p. 9). Other criminologists find Sutherland's definition too narrow. For one thing, many so-called white-collar crimes are committed by persons *outside* their occupations; for example, people file fraudulent claims for unemployment insurance, or they falsify income tax returns. For another, Sutherland's definition fails to account for businesses in which crime is the central activity—businesses such as fraudulent land-sale companies, pyramid clubs, and bogus home-improvement companies.

Today, Sutherland's white-collar crimes are often considered as part of a broader category, economic crimes. **Economic crimes** are illegal acts "committed by nonphysical means and by concealment or guile, to obtain money or property, or to obtain business or personal advantage" (Edelhertz 1970, p. 3). These crimes include:

1. *Personal crimes.* Crimes committed by persons operating on an individual, *ad hoc* basis (credit purchases with no intention to pay; individual income tax violations; credit card frauds; bankruptcy frauds; and social security frauds).
2. *Abuses of trust.* Crimes committed in the course of their occupations by workers operating inside business, government, or other establishments, in violation of their duty of loyalty or fidelity to employer or client (commercial bribery and kickbacks; embezzlement; securities fraud; employee theft; and padding of payroll and expense accounts).
3. *Business crimes.* Crimes incidental to, and in furtherance of, business operations, but that are not the central purpose of the business (antitrust violations; tax violations; food and drug violations; commercial espionage; and deceptive advertising).
4. *Con games.* White-collar crime committed as a business or as the central activity of a business (medical and health frauds; phony contests; diploma mills; charity and religious frauds; insurance frauds; and coupon redemption frauds).

After many years of neglect (since the 1940s, when Sutherland coined the phrase "white-collar crime"), economic crime is now receiving the attention it is due from the criminal justice system. One reason for this attention is that consumer advocacy has raised the public consciousness about economic crime. Complaints about the rudeness, stridency, and partizan zeal of groups such as "Nader's Raiders" can probably be considered testimonials to the effectiveness of their activities—and an indication that many of their barbs have hit the mark. Civil rights activism has also aroused indignation over gross disparities between sentences handed out to the poor and minorities for conventional property crimes and sentences given to middle-class or affluent whites for white-collar crimes.

Watergate drew attention to the minimal sentences often received by persons convicted of nonconventional property crimes, in contrast to the more severe sentences meted out to conventional offenders. Watergate and its aftermath may have indirectly created public pressure for more effective prosecution and more stringent sentencing for economic crimes. In addition, continuing revelations about abuses of political morality (such as irregularities and illegal practices in campaign funding) may have prompted a closer scrutiny of possibly collusive relationships between political leaders and leaders of business and industry. Henceforth, we may witness a closer examination of the political-industrial connection. Concern is already growing over inappropriate appointments to federal regulatory agencies and over the propriety of high-level appointees leaving government to assume positions of responsibility in businesses and industries they once regulated.

Advocates of ecology and environmental protection have contributed greatly to increasing public awareness of economic crime. Ever since the offshore oil spill that blackened the beaches of Santa Barbara, organizations like the Sierra Club and Common Cause have pressured the government relentlessly for the passage of legislation—or for the effective enforcement of existing legislation—to prevent further despoliation of irreplaceable natural resources. These efforts have focused on the concept of corporate accountability.

In the final reckoning, our current economic difficulties may have more to do with increased national concern for white-collar crime than any other factor. Traditional American indifference to economic crime and its perpetrators may prove to be one of the luxuries of the affluent society of the 1950s and 1960s, a luxury headed for extinction along with cheap gasoline and the eight-cylinder family automobile. Now that official scrutiny has turned toward economic crime, a return to public apathy is unlikely, even if our national fortune takes a turn for the better. It may be increasingly difficult for the white-collar criminal to make a dishonest dollar.

Syndicated (Organized) Crime

Organization is the keynote of syndicated crime. In fact, **organized crime** is the more familiar expression for the illegal activities of syndicate criminals. Syndicated crime is a continuing and self-perpetuating conspiracy that relies heavily on fear and corruption. The roots of syndicated crime reach far back into our national history, with almost every nationality and ethnic group having been represented in the ranks at one time or another. The latter fact has given rise to the hotly disputed concept of **ethnic succession,** which maintains that immigrant arrivals used syndicated crime to attain wealth and power before finding safer and more attractive opportunities in legitimate business.

Among the principal revenue sources for syndicated crime are the illegal importation and distribution of drugs—chiefly cocaine, heroin, and marijuana—and gambling, which has an estimated annual take of billions of dollars. Another lucrative activity is loan-sharking, a low-risk, high-return enterprise. Syndicated crime has also infiltrated legitimate business, where it is involved in bankruptcy fraud, the manipulation of stocks and bonds, land fraud, and union racketeering (Pace and Styles 1983).

Political Crimes

Traditionally, the term **political crime** refers to offenses against governments: treason, sedition, rebellion, and assassination. In the post-Watergate and Abscam era, however, the term is used increasingly to cover offenses committed by agents of the government against individuals, groups, the general public, and even foreign governments. Roebuck and Weeber (1978) have identified seven categories of political crimes:

1. Domestic intervention by government (Watergate; the FBI investigation of the Reverend Martin Luther King).
2. Foreign intervention by government (the Vietnam War; CIA intervention in Chile).
3. Intervention against the government (the Weathermen faction of the Students for a Democratic Society; the Symbionese Liberation Army; The Order; Arayan Nation).
4. Domestic surveillance (FBI wiretaps and bugging; surveillance by the Internal Revenue Service).
5. Domestic confrontation (Kent State; the suppression of the Attica insurrection).
6. Evasion and collusion by the government (Kennedy's denial of the Bay of Pigs incursion; the Nixon administration's cover-up of the Watergate break-in; Iran-Contra Affair).

7. Evasion and collusion against government (income tax evasion; draft resistance; military desertion).

Two points should be made regarding political crimes. First, ordinary crimes can be invested with political meaning and used symbolically to express dissent toward an existing political structure. Political dissent that leads to crimes against the government can be viewed as *principled deviance* (Clinard and Quinney 1973), because it often represents a deliberate violation for the purpose of demonstrating the unfairness of a law. The violation can be an isolated, individual act, but it is more often a group action.

Second, the distinctions between political crimes and more conventional crimes are easily blurred when legal codes are applied punitively for politically motivated social control. As Roebuck and Weeber observe, "There may be nothing inherently illegal in an act; but the actor is criminalized when persons in power attach the illegal label to his behavior" (1978, p. 20). Thus, political dissenters may be arrested for disorderly conduct, trespassing, parading without a permit, or violating fire ordinances.

The political crime that has received the most attention from the media, if not from criminologists, is terrorism. *Terrorism* and *terrorist* are terms of limited usefulness, at best, and are prone to causing confusion. Terrorism includes both violent acts and threats of violence. It lumps together acts committed by criminals, psychotics, self-proclaimed patriots, and others with extreme ideological convictions. It makes no distinctions between acts carried out by individuals, groups, or even governments. It encompasses the capture of an airliner and its passengers; the explosion of a bomb in a crowded shopping center; the murder of a prominent person or government official; and the seizure of a public building and its occupants. Such actions are carried out with the objective of focusing attention on a cause or grievance; in accomplishing this aim, little heed is given to the victims of the terrorist act. Victims may be carefully selected according to plan, or they may simply be caught in the path of random violence.

Incidents of violence and horror that directly affect only a few people can nonetheless have a psychological impact on millions. Terrorist acts prompt costly, and sometimes disruptive, security precautions, and they can lead to repressive retaliation and the erosion of civil liberties. Some even challenge the accepted international order among sovereign nations.

Consensual Crimes

Organized crime is profitable because many people are willing, even anxious, to buy illegal goods and services. The buyers, too, are breaking the law. Who are the victims of organized crime? Gambling, prostitution, and deviant drug use are illegal, but it is often difficult to pinpoint the victims. Thus, these activities are often called **victimless crimes**—illegal acts in which all parties *choose* to be involved. Other victimless crimes include some types of pornography, deviant sexual acts among consenting adults, and vagrancy.

Some people argue that these crimes are *not* victimless, that they harm a broad range of people and society in general. Because social norms are violated, the offenses might instead by called **public-order** or **consensual offenses.** At any rate, many people question whether these acts—even if they are shameful, immoral, or harmful—should be defined as crimes. Two arguments are often made for decriminalizing activities such as marijuana use, pornography, and prostitution. First, critics argue that criminal sanctions against these activities constitute an unwarranted intrusion into privacy and an indefensible extension of the government's authority. In other words, is it the government's business what sexual activities consenting adults engage in? Is it the government's business if you gamble? Second, some critics claim that enforcing laws against these activities overburdens the police, the courts, and the prisons, and increases problems in the criminal justice system.

THE ADMINISTRATION OF JUSTICE

As the fear of crime intensifies, the debate grows over how crime might be decreased or prevented. The agents of the **criminal justice system**—police, prosecutors, courts, and corrections—are the main actors in the fight against crime. The police are responsible for detecting and apprehending people who violate the criminal law; prosecutors decide whether circumstances warrant prosecution; the courts decide guilt or innocence and sentence those who are convicted or plead guilty; the corrections component carries out the sentence of the court.

As described above, the administration of justice sounds neat, orderly, and systematic. Unfortunately, it is none of these things—least of all, systematic. Until recently, criminologists and practitioners of criminal justice jokingly referred to the "criminal injustice nonsystem." Now that investigative reporters and television documentaries have introduced the public to some of the idiosyncrasies of "justice American-style," such characterizations are no longer private.

The comedian Lenny Bruce once observed that "in the Halls of Justice, all of the justice is in the halls." The quip summons up a picture of lawyers and clients huddled in the drafty corridors of the mildewed county courthouse, haggling over the details of a bargained plea. Bruce was not trying to be funny: his comment was based on his own experiences within the criminal justice system (as a frequent violator of public-order statutes and drug laws). And as a rough description of how justice is administered in the United States, the remark is not without accuracy.

Some difficulty lies in the term "criminal justice system," itself. The term is a convenient fiction—an abstraction with no counterpart in reality. The American criminal justice system is not a single system but a hodgepodge of separate systems, subsystems, institutions, and procedures. Throughout the tens of thousands of towns, cities, and states in the United States, and in the federal government, there are many different types of criminal justice systems. The systems may appear similar in that they all apprehend, prosecute, convict, and try to correct lawbreakers; but no two systems are exactly alike, and very few are linked together in any comprehensive way. The popular myth that depicts the criminal justice system as a monolithic structure is described by the National Advisory Commission on Criminal Justice Standards and Goals:

> The contemporary view is to consider society's institutionalized response to crime as the criminal justice system and its activities as the criminal justice process. This model envisions interdependent and interrelated agencies and programs that will provide a coordinated and consistent response to crime. The model, however, remains a model—it does not exist in fact. Although cooperation between the various components has improved noticeably in some localities, it cannot be said that a criminal justice "system" really exists (*Corrections* 1973, pp. 5–6).

The situation is even more complicated, however. In another report entitled *Criminal Justice System,* the commission asserts that "there are two criminal justice systems in the United States today, one of which is visible and controversial, the other of which is submerged and usually ignored" (1973, p. 1). Identifying these systems as Criminal Justice Systems 1 and 2, the report continues:

> Criminal Justice System 1 is known well. It is the traditional series of agencies that have been given the formal responsibility to control crime: police and sheriffs' departments, judges, prosecutors and their staffs, defense offices, jails and prisons, and probation and parole agencies. Criminal Justice System 1 is an overt system, the one seen each day in operation, the one customarily understood and referred to in crime and delinquency literature. Even in this report, the phrase "criminal justice system" usually refers to Criminal Justice System 1.
>
> But there are broader implications of the term. . . . Many public and private agencies and citizens outside of police, courts, and corrections are—or ought to be—involved in reducing and preventing crime, the primary goal of criminal justice. These agencies and persons, when dealing with issues related to crime reduction and prevention, plus the traditional triad of police, courts, and corrections, make up a larger criminal justice system, a system which this Commission calls Criminal Justice System 2.
>
> A State legislature, for example, becomes part of this larger criminal justice system when it considers and debates any proposed law that might affect, even remotely, any area of criminal justice activities. So also the executive agencies of the State, educational administrative units, welfare departments, youth service bureaus, recreation departments, and other public offices become a part of Criminal Justice System 2 in many of their decisions and actions. Moving outside the State and local governments, community organizations, . . . neighborhood action groups, and employers may also be important functionaries in the second system (p. 1).

The attitude expressed by the commission has been noted less formally elsewhere, evidence that coping with crime and its consequences has become everyone's business. Unfortunately, as the commission notes in *Criminal Justice System, "many public agencies and private citizens refuse even to acknowledge that they have a role in reducing crime" (p. 1). Moreover the effectiveness of Criminal Justice System 1 is lessened by intramural conflicts among the police, courts, and correctional agencies.*

If cooperation is poor among members of Criminal Justice System 1 it is markedly worse with respect to interactions involving members of Criminal Justice System 2. Many courts, law enforcement agencies, and correctional facilities have few (or no) working relationships with various private and public organizations that might provide valuable services to their clients. Worse, most agencies have no clear policy for obtaining such assistance, even if there is an awareness of its availability.

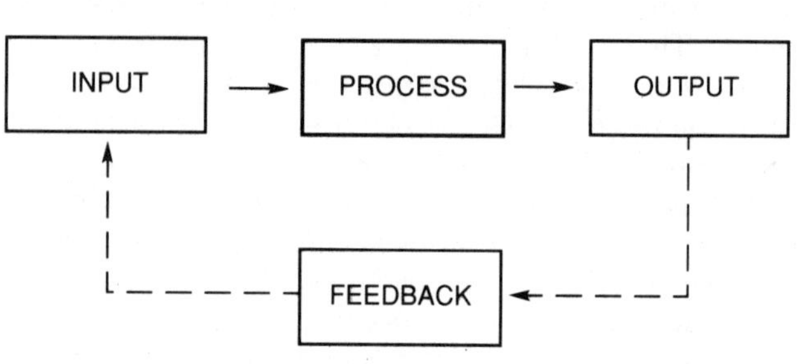

FIGURE 1.1
Linear process model. From A. Coffey, E. Eldefonso, and W. Hartinger, *An Introduction to the Criminal Justice System and Process* (Englewood Cliffs, N.J.: Prentice-Hall, 1974), p. 9, by permission of the authors and the publisher.

SYSTEM AND PROCESS: THE ROLE OF DISCRETION AND ACCOMMODATION

The word *system* connotes an orderly arrangement of parts according to some plan or design. The basic idea is that relationships among parts or components in a system are deliberate, rather than haphazard. Further, the word implies that the arrangement exists to achieve some goal or purpose. A major operating characteristic of systems is that what affects the function of one part can potentially affect other parts, as well as the entire system.

In recent years, a field has developed called *systems analysis*. Systems analysts use sophisticated mathematical and statistical procedures to study organizational structures, operations, and problems. The field draws on contributions from many other areas of inquiry—communications research, information theory, and cybernetics, to name a few. Although the methods employed by systems analysts are rather complex and rigorous, some of the key concepts—such as the *linear process model*—are easy to understand and apply. This model, shown in Figure 1.1, schematizes a continuum, an orderly progression of events from input to output. Its developers—Coffey, Eldefonso, and Hartinger—describe systems this way: "The input is what the system deals with; the process is *how* the system deals with the input; and the output is the *results* of the process. . . ." (1974, p. 9). If this model is applied to the criminal justice system, *input* refers to selected law violations (i.e., reported crimes); *process* refers to the activities of the police, courts, and corrections; and output refers to the outcome (i.e., success or failure) of the process.

The linear process model can be applied to components of the criminal justice system, as well as to the total system. For example, as shown in Figure 1.2, the probation subsystem receives, as input, cases selected by

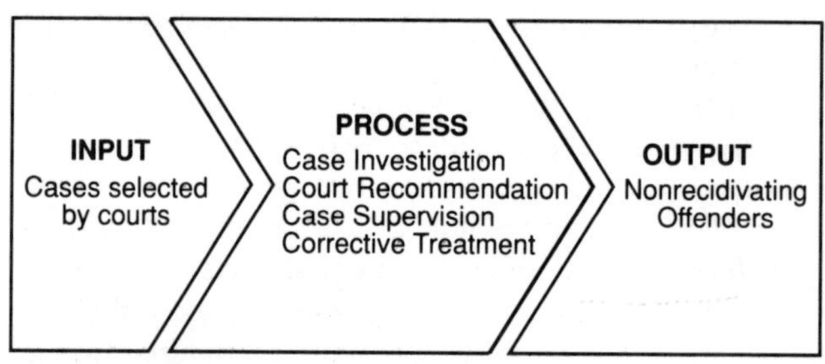

FIGURE 1.2
The probation subsystem of corrections. From A. Coffey, E. Eldefonso, and W. Hartinger, *An Introduction to the Criminal Justice System and Process* (Englewood Cliffs, N.J.: Prentice-Hall, 1974), p. 11, by permission of the authors and the publisher.

the courts. The goal of probation is to produce an output of individuals who will not repeat their criminal activities. This goal is to be met through presentence investigation of the offender's background and supervision within the community, without resorting to incarceration.

The linear process model reinforces the idea that whatever is done in one subsystem has direct and indirect effects upon other subsystems. For example, increased arrests by the police result in more work for prosecutors, courts, and corrections. If the corrections component of the criminal justice system is ineffective because of excessive work loads, released offenders may commit more crimes and again be apprehended by the police. This circular process is the focus of much controversy among representatives from various components of the criminal justice system. Repeat offenders are known as **recidivists.**

A major difficulty with the linear process model is that, by directing attention to the administration of justice as a system, it diverts attention from the real way justice is administered in thousands of daily transactions—namely, through discretion and accommodation. *Discretion* refers to the exercise of choice by those charged with the responsibility for and authority to carry out various tasks assigned by the laws of municipal, county, state, and federal governments. From the traffic officer who can choose between issuing a warning or citation, to the members of the parole board who can decide whether to release an offender from prison next week, next month, or next year, practitioners in all components of the criminal justice system are armed with discretionary powers. Needless to say, although these powers are susceptible to influence and are often misused or abused, they are an indispensable requirement of the criminal justice system.

Accommodation refers to give-and-take interactions among practitioners in the criminal justice system in the daily business of administering justice. These interactions take place within the context of a bureaucracy whose members fill a variety of work roles. The system sets objectives with regard to equity and justice, but individual practitioners within the system have other—often competing—objectives related to job performance and efficiency. Thus, police departments are interested in "clearing" cases by arresting suspected offenders, while prosecutors are concerned about a backlog of cases. At the same time, judges complain about crowded dockets, and correctional authorities worry about overcrowding in jails and prisons. Consequently, many decisions are made through give-and-take discussions that appear to accused persons to be less than just and equitable, however conducive the decisions may be to administrative efficiency.

It is nearly impossible to overstate the importance of discretion and accommodation in the criminal justice system in the United States. Models and analogies tend to leave people with a feeling that there is some "right way" for justice to be administered, with any deviation from the prescribed path being tantamount to a miscarriage of justice. Even interactions between practitioners in the system are subject to distortion and misinterpretation. For example, when one of the authors was participating in a study of inmates on Florida's death row, he asked prisoners if they believed they had received a fair trial. With rare exceptions, the answer was no—under the circumstances, a predictable answer. But when asked why they felt their trials had been unfair, inmate after inmate replied in roughly this way: In recesses during the trial, the defense attorney (usually a public defender or court-appointed lawyer) talked in a friendly way and joked or laughed with the prosecutor's staff, leading the convicts to doubt their attorney's dedication (Lewis et al. 1979).

The administration of justice is not a series of abstract operations or processes that take place according to a blueprint or a computer program: it is a series of human interactions. Defense counsels negotiate with assistant prosecutors to reduce charges against defendants; judges confer with probation officers over presentence reports to determine if justice is better served by incarcerating offenders or letting them go. Objectives are balanced between what is needed and required for the well-being of the offender and what is needed and required for the welfare and protection of society. The tool for balance is compromise through accommodation.

ASSESSING CRIMINAL JUSTICE NEEDS FOR THE 1990s

Leaders of the criminal justice system agree that the most important issue facing them today and in the immediate future is prison and jail overcrowding.[2] That is the most significant finding of a survey of top state and local officials conducted several years ago by the National Institute of Justice (NIJ). The NIJ study covered all areas of the country, including both small and large agencies. Scientific polling techniques were applied to the criminal justice system as a whole—to attorneys general, police chiefs, chief justices, corrections directors, district attorneys, judges, sheriffs, wardens, pubic defenders, court administrators, probation and parole directors, and heads of state criminal justice agencies. The results give a snapshot of the challenges facing the criminal justice system.

"The findings show a system under great stress," says James K. Stewart, director of NIJ. "Some areas of the criminal justice system are making adaptations that work to the disadvantage of other parts of the system. We need to focus our resources on the overcrowding problem, but if we deal with it on a piecemeal basis, we will not be meeting the needs of the whole system."

The survey, part of the institute's National Assessment Program, was designed to help NIJ officials plan its activities most effectively. In conducting the survey, researchers for Abt Associates, a research firm based in Cambridge, Massachusetts, contacted nearly 2,400 administrators. More than 61 percent responded, an excellent rate. Follow-up telephone conversations were held with 117 respondents to obtain further information about their problems. The officials appreciated the contact: "You mean someone actually read what I wrote on the survey?" one asked.

Researchers from NIJ and Abt said that consensus on the importance of the overcrowding problem was impressive, since it came in response to the open-ended question, "What do you feel is the most pressing problem confronting your State's criminal justice system today?" Although it is not surprising that corrections officials focused on overcrowding, leaders of other agencies shared their concern. Police officials named overcrowding twice as often as any other problem; prosecutors cited it three times as often. Of the six groups in the survey (corrections, police, prosecutors, public defenders, courts, and probation and parole), only public defenders failed to give overcrowding top priority.

While corrections officials have to deal directly with the idleness and potential violence associated with overcrowding, representatives of other agencies said they felt its effect as well. Police, prosecutors, and probation officers said that serious offenders were being placed on probation instead of being incarcerated. Parole officials often have to cope with mass releases under early parole programs; one Pennsylvania county had to provide 250 person-months of additional supervision for early-release parolees without any increase in staff.

Overcrowded institutions are the end product of a tidal wave of cases that has flooded all agencies in the criminal justice system. When asked to name the most pressing problem facing their own agency, administrators generally cited their version of the same phenomenon. Variations on the response "Too large a caseload" were given by prosecutors, public defenders, court officials, and heads of probation and parole departments. Police talked about having too few officers.

The rising caseloads come at a time when state and local governments are cutting back on expenditures because of economic conditions. Of the different groups, only the prosecutors came close to rating their financial resources "adequate." A majority of other officials—ranging from 64 percent of corrections officials to 68 percent of probation and parole officials—rated their resources "inadequate." The squeeze was illustrated by a suburban county in Michigan where the felony caseload of the public defender's office had gone up 300 percent from 1977 to 1983, but the staff had been cut 25 percent in the past three years.

Other conclusions drawn from the survey:

- *Drugs and crime.* Narcotics problems were a prime concern among police and prosecutors. They said they lacked the sophisticated resources needed to reduce either usage or trafficking. Most agreed with the sentiments expressed by an Indiana police chief: "If you cut down on drug crimes, you would cut down on other problems as well."
- *Crime prevention.* Police had hope for prevention programs, especially those aimed at keeping school-age youngsters from getting involved with drugs.
- *Information processing.* Many officials saw computers as a tool that can help them cope with the increased volume of cases, but they need help in adapting computers to their needs.
- *Crime control policy.* Professionals in all areas worried about the lack of consensus among agencies on how to deal with the crime problem, and about the lack of coordination in their activities. Public defenders rated this the top problem facing the criminal justice system, and it ranked second or third among the concerns of other officials.
- *Research.* Research got mixed reviews. Some officials were antagonistic, saying that all available funds should go for immediate needs. Others said the problem lay in implementing what was already known. Some were enthusiastic and offered suggestions for both basic and applied research topics.
- *Training.* Officials in all fields put great value on training as an aid to retaining qualified staff. Many mentioned programs sponsored by other national agencies such as the National Center for State Courts, the National Institute of Corrections, and the National College of Criminal Defense.

Some sought regional training centers, saying the time and expense of traveling to a distant location can be prohibitive.

Police

From their responses, police officials seem frustrated: just when police services are in greatest demand, they do not have enough officers. More than half cited this as their most pressing problem. Shortage of personnel was cited by 31.2 percent, and another 20.3 percent spoke of the difficulty of recruiting, selecting, and training police officers. Big-city chiefs reported they were swamped by calls for service, and needed help in managing them. The largest jurisdictions tended to see their financial problems as the greatest; 92.4 percent of those from areas with populations of more than 1 million said their funds were inadequate.

When asked what they would do with a hypothetical $100,000 budget, police officials said they would invest almost twice as much in beefing up narcotics investigation and prevention as in the next areas of concern (burglaries, robberies, and community crime prevention). Many respondents said state and federal cutbacks had hurt narcotics enforcement. "We used to just funnel information to the State police, but now we have to start investigating by ourselves," said one small-town chief. Heads of small departments said they needed assistance in undercover work, since their own officers were too well known locally to conduct these touchy operations. Officials in Texas, Florida, California, and Oregon said they did not have the resources to cope with increased smuggling by airplanes and boats.

More than half the respondents suggested drug-prevention programs in schools as a priority. Efforts to reduce drug usage through heavy penalties, treatment programs, and undercover operations have fallen short, they said. As one state police official put it, "The target has to be the potential users, and they are grade-school children."

Prosecutors

District attorneys and attorneys general shared police officials' concern about narcotics, describing this program area as most in need of improvement. Prosecutors sought technical assistance and training for their staffs in areas such as the rules of evidence, use of wiretaps, and tracking money in large transactions. They also complained of lack of funds for investigation, both for their own investigators and for police; they would use increased funds to conduct surveillance, to provide "buy money" for undercover agents, and to purchase needed equipment, ranging from airplanes and boats to body recorders and videotape equipment.

Prosecutors did not agree on the type of drug problems that posed the greatest threat. While some were concerned with major trafficking in heavy narcotics, prosecutors from smaller jurisdictions more often cited marijuana.

When asked for ideas on combating illicit drugs, prosecutors expressed an interest in forfeiture laws that would enable the states to seize the assets of major traffickers. But they saw progress as requiring long-term effort. One prosecutor said that private agencies in his state had given funds to several counties to hire agents for occasional "sweeps" of narcotics offenders, but added that these tactics failed to exert the continuous pressure that is needed.

Prosecutors also showed significant interest in learning to use computers, in victim/witness programs, and in specialized types of prosecutions, such as those targeting career criminals.

Courts

Among judges and administrators of court systems, excessive caseloads were mentioned as the major problem by 36 percent of the respondents, three times as many as mentioned the next concern. A state chief justice attributed the growth of court cases to "legislative changes and an increasingly litigious society prompting more cases than the courts can handle with existing staffing policies and facilities." To keep up with the pressure, the respondents saw the greatest hope in computers for case management: docketing court appearances, generating subpoenas, notifying jurors, and monitoring traffic fines (one area that was "falling through the cracks," several officials said). But finding the right computer and the right software was a difficult task. Court officials cited problems in meshing their computers with those of state government. Often, they said, the needs of a small jurisdiction could be met by a microcomputer, but these were sometimes not compatible with state hardware. The basic recordkeeping needs of a small county are often different from those of the state, which needs to collect and aggregate statistics of greater complexity. Many respondents sought technical assistance from software development and modification.

The second greatest concern among judges was for counsel for indigent defendants—not exclusively out of concern for criminals' rights, some judges noted, but because adequate defense resources result in more efficient court operations and in the long run save taxpayers money.

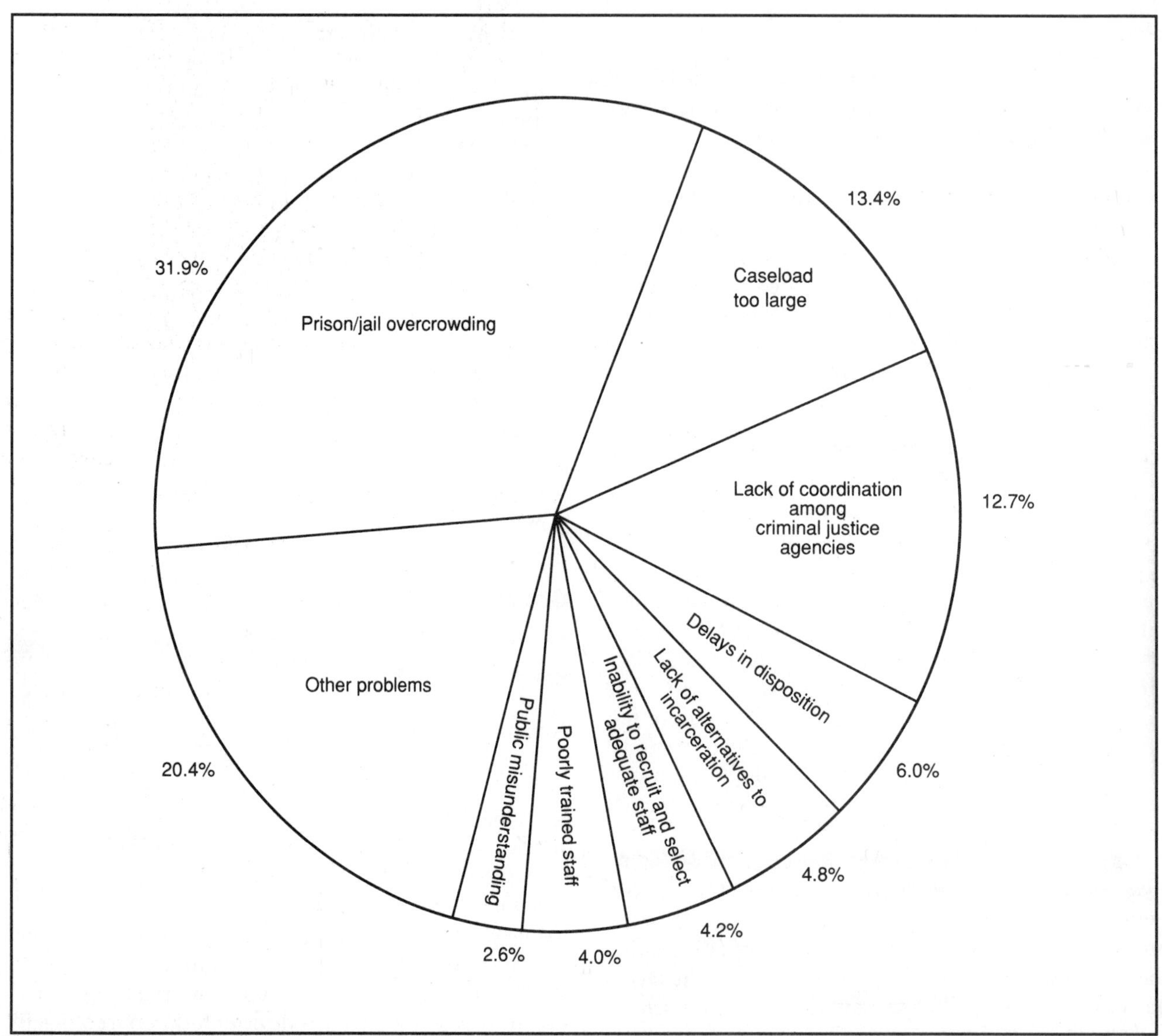

FIGURE 1.3
Most pressing problems for State criminal justice systems. From S. Gettinger, *Assessing Criminal Justice Needs* (Washington, D.C.: U.S. Department of Justice, National Institute of Justice, June 1984), p. 93.

Public Defenders

Those in charge of providing counsel for indigents often seemed, from their questionnaires and interviews, to feel alone. One defender in Arizona even questioned whether public defenders were part of the criminal justice system. Many said that police and prosecutors had far more resources for prosecution than public defenders had for defense. Their problems were illustrated by their low response rate (49 percent), which seemed to be due to heavy schedules of in-court appearances and a lack of secretarial help. Of 78 respondents, not one rated financial resources "very adequate."

When asked what their biggest problem was, more than 43 percent cited heavy caseloads; the next concern, pubic misunderstanding, got 6.9 percent. Defenders attributed their growing caseloads to growing populations, higher crime rates, and the state of the economy, which forces people to use public defenders instead of private attorneys. The problems seemed to be most acute in smaller jurisdictions. Sometimes, in addition to high caseloads, geography presented a problem; in Minnesota, for example, one investigator was solely responsible for all cases in seventeen rural counties.

The defenders saw their most critical need as improving the quality of representation in felony cases. They sought funds for expert witnesses, for legal research, and for investigators. Several respondents were concerned with the quality of training available and said they had difficulty attracting and retaining experienced attorneys.

Institutional Corrections

Among wardens, sheriffs, jail chiefs, and directors, the pressures of finding room for burgeoning inmate populations overwhelmed all other worries. It was mentioned three times as often as any other pressing problem. Every respondent from a system that held more than 15,000 inmates named overcrowding as his or her biggest headache.

Most of the other concerns voiced by the administrators stemmed from overcrowding: huge caseloads for staff members (15.4 percent mentioned it); other staffing problems (9.3 percent); and the lack of programs for inmates (5 percent). The officials complained of difficulties recruiting and training staff; one warden noted, "My best people work long hours to subsidize the State."

When asked to allocate a hypothetical $100,000 budget, the officials' most critical need was "facility design and security"; they allocated 21.8 percent of the budget to it. "Institutions tend to be too secure, or pretty but too loose," remarked one South Carolina official. The next level of financial commitment (11.7 percent of the total) went to staff recruitment, selection, and training.

How could things be improved? "More money" was a typical response, a not surprising sentiment since more than two-thirds of the respondents reported their resources as somewhat to very inadequate. But recognizing that NIJ did not have funds for direct support, several officials asked for help in areas such as evaluating building materials and providing technical assistance on design of buildings.

Probation and Parole

The problem of too large caseloads was mentioned three times as often as the next problem (lack of consensus in the criminal justice system) by probation and parole officials. One California county has laid off 119 agents in the past three years. Tougher laws (such as drunk-driving statutes) had sent more offenders their way, and prison overcrowding had forced judges to increase the use of probation, officials said. More serious offenders were being put back on the streets on probation, and more parolees were coming out of the prisons under early-release programs; officials sought help in learning to deal with these types of individuals.

Respondents often expressed faith in the potential of probation and parole. As one parole official put it, "Most criminal problems can be worked out in a free society rather than in institutions if alternatives are given the appropriate resources." But finding those resources has become more and more difficult; some 80 percent of state probation and parole directors rated their financial resources inadequate. Some officials have geographical problems: in Wyoming, only forty agents cover a state in which six counties are each larger than Massachusetts.

The probation and parole officials would put most of their hypothetical $100,000 budget into direct services. They wanted help in starting work-release or education-release programs, restitution and community-service programs, and volunteer systems that involve families, employers, and friends of probationers. They noted a need for programs to deal with special types of clients: juveniles, the retarded, alcoholics, and drug abusers. Training was mentioned as a need by 65 percent of the respondents; several noted that there is no national training center for probation and parole officials as there is for other areas of the criminal justice system.

SUMMARY

The problems of crime and how to cope with crime rank high as a national priority. Although earlier periods in our history may have been more lawless and violent than today, crime is still a major concern for many people. And though losses due to crimes of the "upper world" ("crimes in the suites") and syndicated crime far exceed losses due to conventional crimes such as larceny and burglary, it is "crime in the streets" that people fear most. Frustration and anger result when newspaper and television accounts imply that police waste valuable time and resources enforcing laws against consensual crimes such as gambling and prostitution.

As defined by the National Advisory Commission on Criminal Justice Standards and Goals, we have two criminal justice systems: Criminal Justice System 1, a formal, official, and highly visible system, and Criminal

Justice System 2, an unofficial, less visible network of public and private agencies. The goal of System 2 is to reduce or prevent crime.

The concluding portion of this chapter was devoted to assessing criminal justice needs for the 1990s. Although leaders in the criminal justice system generally agreed that one of the most important issues facing them today and in the immediate future is prison and jail overcrowding, this was certainly not the only serious problem they found. For example, police officials were frustrated by the fact that just when police services are in greatest demand, they do not have enough officers. More than half of the respondents cited this as their most pressing problem.

District attorneys expressed considerable concern about narcotics and also cited the need for technical assistance and training for their staffs in areas such as the rules of evidence, use of wiretaps, and tracking money in large transactions.

Among judges and administrators of court systems, excessive caseloads were mentioned as the major problem by 36 percent of the respondents. Three times as many cited this problem as mentioned the next concern.

When public defenders were asked what their biggest problem was, more than 43 percent cited heavy caseloads. And lastly, probation and parole respondents also indicated that too large caseloads were their major problem.

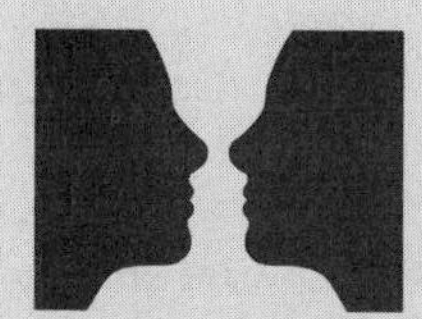

ISSUE PAPER
HIGH-TECH CRIME—A GLIMPSE AT A POSSIBLE FUTURE

Police and criminals constantly compete with one another to exploit the fruits of science and technology. Chemistry, physics, and other branches of the natural sciences contribute to *criminalistics,* the generic term for the science and technology of criminal investigation. Laboratory applications of scientific developments in these fields have produced an array of investigative techniques ranging from ballistics and toxicology to voice print identification and handwriting analysis. The expert witness is often a medical specialist or a person with a doctorate in one of the sciences; many of the larger metropolitan police agencies retain such experts on staff.

The competition is by no means one-sided, however. Criminals are alert to new products and possibilities. When the cordless electric drill was introduced, burglars started using them to gain ready access to residential and commercial buildings. Helicopters have been used in prison breaks, and two convicts escaped from a federal maximum security prison at Marion, Illinois, by neutralizing an electronic security system with a device made in the prison workshop.

Few areas of scientific and technological development can match the impact of the computer revolution. Already the computer has begun to reshape the world. And there is every reason to believe that it will also revolutionize crime. The advent of the computer made the crime of embezzlement easier to commit and harder to detect. The theft of computer time has created new variants on the older common-law crimes of larceny and trespass. Thus computers, a valuable resource to business, industry, and government, provide matchless opportunities for criminal exploitation. Electronic data processing (EDP) crimes are wide ranging, because computer data banks generally contain information that encompasses the full scope of a business operation. Consequently, computer abuse "can take the form of embezzlement, misappropriation of computer time, theft of programs, and illegal acquisition of such proprietary information as marketing plans and forecasts, product design, secret manufacturing processes, and confidential technical data" (Chamber of Commerce of the United States 1974, p. 20). Whatever the cost of computer crime—and it has been estimated in the billions of dollars—it seems likely that such crime will increase. More than 3 percent of the total work force in the United States is now employed in computer-related jobs. And the figure continues to grow.

EDP crimes require much more sophistication and technical skill than more commonplace forms of theft. The typical "electronic criminal" is male, highly moti-

FIGURE 1.4
The computer criminal. Courtesy Donna Ward for *Science News.*

vated, bright, energetic, and generally young (eighteen to thirty years old) (Parker and Nycum 1974). He is often the master of a technical expertise that borders on esoterica. In fact, he may find it difficult to explain the details of his crime to someone with less detailed knowledge of computer operations (Farr 1975).

The following case suggests con games:

> At Citibank cash dispensers in New York City and surrounding suburbs, an imaginative con man's scheme depleted accounts of $92,000—with the unwitting assistance of the victims. The scheme worked like this: the con man, posing as a customer, stands between two cash terminals and pretends to be talking on the service phone. A legitimate customer comes in and inserts his card into one of the terminals, only to be told by the con man that the machine isn't working. The customer withdraws his card, leaving the first machine activated, and inserts his card into the second machine. The con man looks on surreptitiously as the customer enters his personal identification number and completes his transaction. Then, still holding the phone, the con man enters the same number and a withdrawal order on the first machine. To complete the theft, he must get the legitimate customer to insert the card once more into the first machine, and he does this by claiming that customer service thinks there is something wrong with his card. Three hundred seventy-four customers cooperated, and the courteous, well-spoken man got away with their money (Coniff 1982, p. 62).

The persuasive power of the mere mention of the term "computer" works to the advantage of the electronic con man. Farr (1975) relates the case of a woman in Cincinnati, Ohio, who paid for purchases in several shops by check, identifying herself in each instance by presenting her bank card. While chatting with a neighbor en route to the parking lot, the woman was stopped by a man who accused her of passing a phony check: " 'We've had a negative report on your bank check card from the computer.' " The magic word "computer" implied that an infallible machine had discovered an act of wrongdoing. While the flustered woman and her friend waited in the parking lot, the man took her checkbook, bank card, and enough money to cover the last check she had written. " 'This will show your good faith,' " he told her. " 'Perhaps I can clear up the matter for you.' "

After waiting for nearly half an hour for the man to return, the two women went into the store to check on the whereabouts of the bank card and checkbook. As soon as the store manager heard their story, he advised them to contact the bank and the police. By the time the victim reported the matter to the bank, however, the con man and his accomplices had purchased goods worth $170 with her checks. The woman commented sadly, " 'My bank covered the loss because I informed them immediately. But I was so upset by being conned that I had nightmares about it for more than a month' " (p. 3).

Kidnapping—by Computer

R. Coniff Science Digest

At age 24 and with 6 arrests on his record, Masatoshi Tashiro was one of Tokyo's petty thieves, no more, no less. It wasn't likely that he would commit the Crime of the Century. Not of *this* century, anyway. But Tashiro did make himself a harbinger of the way criminals will work, and (to his chagrin) of the way criminals will be foiled, in the electronic world of the year 2000. He did it by computerizing the ancient crime of kidnapping, a centuries-old felony.

It started with a cash-card account, which he opened under a false name and address at a major Tokyo bank. With this magnetically coded card, depositors could make withdrawals as large as $1,000 at a time from any of 348 automatic cash dispensers located throughout Japan. Tashiro made several test withdrawals. By phoning the bank afterward, he determined that it took the computer system at least 20 minutes to tell the bank which cash dispenser station he had used. That crucial lag would be his getaway time.

Tashiro chose as his victim the four-month-old daughter of a well-known Japanese movie actor. The abduction itself was conventional—a break-in and escape while the family slept—but the ransom demand was brilliantly original. The parents were to deposit $16,500 in Tashiro's cash-card account; he gave them the account number and the false name as calmly as if he were making a real-estate deal.

His reasoning quickly became apparent to the police. They might be able to cover 348 cash dispenser stations, but they would not know the one from which the kidnapper was operating until the computer told them so at least 20 minutes too late. Under the circumstances, the missing child's parents had little choice except to deposit the ransom money. First, though, the police made a countermove; they had the bank computer reprogrammed. Its new instructions were to trace any withdrawal from the ransom account instantly. When Tashiro made his first withdrawal, word flashed immediately to the central computer and from there, by radio, back to the stakeout team. The kidnapper was arrested as he strolled out of the dispenser station with the card and the cash in his hands. Shortly afterward, police recovered the missing baby from his home.

The relationship between computers and feelings of frustration or even rage has been demonstrated both in the United States and abroad. In Olympia, Washington, someone fired shots into the computer at the State Unemployment Office; in Johannesburg, South Africa, a similar incident occurred with a tax-processing computer; and antiwar demonstrators in Melbourne, Australia, "shotgunned to death" an American-made computer, leaving it a total loss (Swanson and Territo 1980).

The nature of evidence in computer offenses creates special difficulties from the standpoint of detection and investigation. For example, a single computer tape may contain more information than an entire shelf of books. This not only makes evaluation more difficult, but it also allows evidence to be destroyed easily and information to be "booby-trapped" (if an investigator tries to retrieve booby-trapped material, the material is automatically lost). For example, when the perpetrators of the famous Equity Funding swindle—which fabricated 64,000 phony insurance policies worth $1 billion—were caught, they had a computer program available that could have erased all of the evidence against them.

The problems of computer crime have prompted a search for new and increasingly sophisticated approaches to computer security. One approach is to code or encrypt information so that only people with keys can unscramble the data. Such systems are available to protect stored information, and even the owners of personal computers can buy encryption devices to keep their private affairs private. But, as Peterson (1982) points out, there is no absolute security in electronic safeguards: in the end, the human element is the ultimate weakness. Quoting a well-known expert in the field, Peterson claims that "the most effective way to break into a secure computer system is with a bribe . . . or by introducing a pretty woman or handsome man to the right computer operator" (p. 14.).

R. Coniff, "Twenty-First Century Crime-Stoppers," *Science Digest* 90 (1982): 61, by permission of the author and the publisher.

DISCUSSION AND REVIEW

1. What evidence is there to suggest that fear of crime is widespread in America?
2. Is violent crime more prevalent today than one hundred years ago?
3. Which crimes are the most expensive for our society? Are these the same crimes people fear most?
4. Discuss Edelhertz's fourfold classification of white-collar and economic crimes. Do you believe it is more effective to sentence white-collar criminals to prison than to levy fines or use alternatives to imprisonment?
5. Why has political crime become an issue in recent years? What kinds of illegal activity are included by Roebuck and Weeber under this heading?
6. Why are some consensual or public-order offenses referred to as "victimless" crimes? Are they really without victims?

7. Distinguish between Criminal Justice System 1 and Criminal Justice System 2, as defined by the National Advisory Commission on Criminal Justice System Standards and Goals. What are the major components of System 1?
8. Why is discretion so important in the criminal justice system?
9. What major criminal justice needs for the 1990s were identified by police, prosecutors, courts, public defenders, officials from corrections, and probation and parole officials?
10. Is crime by computer a new kind of criminal activity or merely a variation on older crimes?

■ GLOSSARY

Consensual crime Illegal acts in which the parties willingly participate in a transaction involving the sale or gift of desired goods or services (e.g., gambling or prostitution).

Criminal justice system The complex of institutions and agencies responsible for controlling crime. The system includes the police, the prosecution, the courts, and corrections.

Economic crime Illegal acts committed by nonphysical means and by concealment or guile to obtain money or property, to avoid the payment or loss of money or property, or to obtain business or personal advantage. *See also* White-collar crime.

Ethnic succession A concept asserting that each group of immigrants to the United States used organized (syndicated) crime to acquire wealth and power before gaining a foothold in legitimate business.

Organized crime A business that provides illegal, but desired, goods and services for the noncriminal public. Also known as *syndicated crime.*

Political crime Illegal acts against the government (e.g., treason, sedition, or rebellion) or illegal acts committed by agents of government against individuals, groups, or the general public.

Public-order offense An illegal act in which the offender engages in behavior that is not markedly different from conventional behavior (e.g., gambling or public intoxication) and which differs from many other crimes only to the extent that it usually involves only the offender. *See also* Consensual crime, Victimless crime.

Recidivist From the French *récidiver* ("to repeat"); a *recidivist* is an individual who shows commitment to criminality by repeated arrests and convictions.

Victimless crime Illegal acts between consenting adults (e.g., prostitution or homosexual behavior) that are presumed not to cause any direct harm, loss, or injury to anyone and in which there is no "victim" in the ordinary sense (as there is in robbery or burglary). *See also* Public-order offense, Consensual crime.

White-collar crime Originally used to designate offenses committed by "a person of respectability and high social status in the course of his occupation" (Sutherland 1949). The term is now being replaced by more specific terms such as *economic crime, occupational crime,* and *corporate crime.*

■ REFERENCES

Bard, M., and Ellison, K. "Crisis Intervention and Investigation of Forcible Rape." *Police Chief* 41 (1974): 68–74.

Chamber of Commerce of the United States. *White Collar Crime: Everyone's Problem, Everyone's Loss.* Washington, D.C.: Chamber of Commerce of the United States, 1974.

Chandler, R. *The Long Goodbye.* Boston: Houghton, Mifflin, 1954.

Clark, B. "Is Law Enforcement Headed in the Right Direction?" *Police* 12 (1968): 31–34.

Clinard, M. B., and Quinney, R. *Criminal Behavior Systems: A Typology.* New York: Holt, Rinehart and Winston, 1973.

Coffey, A., Eldefonso, E., and Hartinger, W. *An Introduction to the Criminal Justice System and Process.* Englewood Cliffs, N.J.: Prentice-Hall, 1974.

Coniff, R. "Twenty-First Century Crime-Stoppers." *Science Digest* 90 (1982): 60–65.

Conklin, J. E. *The Impact of Crime.* New York: Macmillan, 1975.

Edelhertz, H. *The Nature, Impact, and Prosecution of White Collar Crime.* Washington, D.C.: U.S. Government Printing Office, 1970.

Farr, R. *The Electronic Criminal.* New York: McGraw-Hill, 1975.

Gettinger, S. *Assessing Criminal Justice Needs.* Washington, D.C.: U.S. Department of Justice, National Institute of Justice, June 1984.

Kaplan, J. *Criminal Justice: Introductory Cases and Materials.* Mineola, N.Y.: Foundation Press, 1973.

Law Enforcement Assistance Administration (LEAA). *Manpower Survey of the Criminal Justice System: Executive Summary.* Washington, D.C.: U.S. Government Printing Office, 1978.

Lewis, P. L.; Mannle, H.; Vetter, H. J.; and Allen, H. E. "A Post-Furman Profile of Florida's Condemned: A Question of Discrimination in Terms of the Race of the Victim and a Comment on *Spinkelink* v. *Wainwright.*" *Stetson Law Review* 9 (1979): 1–45.

Morris, N. *The Future of Imprisonment.* Chicago: University of Chicago Press, 1974.

National Advisory Commission on Criminal Justice Standards and Goals. *Corrections.* Washington, D.C.: U.S. Government Printing Office, 1973.

National Advisory Commission on Criminal Justice Standards and Goals. *Corrections.* Washington, D.C.: U.S. Government Printing Office, 1973.

National Advisory Commission on Criminal Justice Standards and Goals. *Criminal Justice System.* Washington, D.C.: U.S. Government Printing Office, 1973.

Office of Juvenile Justice and Delinquency Prevention (OJJDP). *A National Assessment of Serious Juvenile Crime and the Juvenile Justice System: The Need for a Rational Response.* Washington, D.C.: U.S. Government Printing Office, 1980.

Pace, D. F., and Styles, J. C. *Organized Crime: Concepts and Control.* Englewood Cliffs, N.J.: Prentice-Hall, 1983.

Parker, D. B. *Crime by Computer.* New York: Scribner's, 1976.

Parker, D. B., and Nycum, S. "The New Criminal." *Datamation* (January 1974): 56–58.

Peterson, I. "Computer Crime: Insecurity in Numbers." *Science News* 122 (1982): 12–14.

President's Commission on Law Enforcement and Administration of Justice. *The Challenge of Crime in a Free Society.* Washington, D.C.: U.S. Government Printing Office, 1967.

President's Commission on Law Enforcement and Administration of Justice. *Task Force Report: The Police.* Washington, D.C.: U.S. Government Printing Office, 1967.

Roebuck, J., and Weeber, S. C. *Political Crime in the United States: Analyzing Crime By and Against Government.* New York: Praeger, 1978.

Silberman, C. E. *Criminal Violence, Criminal Justice.* New York: Random House, 1978.

Sutherland, E. H. *White Collar Crime,* New York: Dryden Press, 1949.

Swanson, C. R., and Territo, L. "Computer Crime: Dimensions, Types, Causes, and Investigation." *Journal of Police Science and Administration* 8 (1980): 304–11.

Wright, J. D., and Rossi, P. E. "Weapons and Violent Crime." Research project conducted for the National Institute of Justice, U.S. Department of Justice, Washington, D.C., as reported in *Police and Security Bulletin* (January 1982): 3.

■ NOTES

1. "The self is an abstract concept: sometimes called ego. It is the sum of what and who a person feels he is. A large part of the concept of self involves the body and the way in which one feels about the body, but it also includes such extensions of self as clothing, automobile, and home. For example, this may be expressed in such ways as: 'that's just the sort of home I expect him to have' " (Bard and Ellison 1974, p. 70).

2. This section was adapted from Stephen Gettinger, *Assessing Criminal Justice Needs* (Washington, D.C.: U.S. Department of Justice, National Institute of Justice, June 1984).

CHAPTER

2

Crime, Deviance, and the Criminal Law

SEVERAL

Laws and Orders

MADE AT A

GENERAL COURT

Held at Boston, February the *4th* 16$^{79}_{80}$.

EDWARD RAWSON Secretary.

CHAPTER OUTLINE:

Legal scholars define a "crime" as an act or an omission that is prohibited by law for the protection of the public, the violation of which is prosecuted by the state in its own name and is punishable by incarceration (Model Penal Code, section 1.014). Criminal justice authorities and criminologists, however, are apt to find fault with such a definition. For one thing, crime is relative (i.e., behaviors covered by laws and statutes are not fixed and unchanging, but vary according to time, place, and circumstance). What the law says is illegal today may not be the same as what the law said was illegal yesterday—or what it may say is illegal tomorrow. Moreover, legal definitions of crimes would be unduly restrictive, because they would limit the study of criminal behavior to those persons who have been *officially adjudicated* (judged) "criminal" or "delinquent"; hence, much behavior that may be relevant to understanding and explaining criminal behavior might never be examined.

A significant point to understand here is that the definition of criminal behavior is derived from the social process and has little to do with the individual criminal. While recognizing the need on legal grounds to deal with crime as law-violating behavior, criminal justice professionals and criminologists find it worthwhile to consider criminal conduct as part of a much broader spectrum of *deviant behavior*. Deviance involves behavior that varies or diverges from social *norms*—the rules that regulate conduct within a group or society. Most people tend to be "socially invisible" within their communities; deviance means, among other things, that an individual or group becomes visible to the majority when the deviant behavior elicits a societal reaction.

NORMS AND SOCIALIZATION

The *norms* of a society may be simple or elaborate, but their purpose is the same: to protect the society against disruption and to safeguard its basic structure and values. Members of a society internalize the norms through a complex process of social learning known as *socialization.*

The principal agency of socialization, and the basic unit of society, is the family. Much of a culture is transmitted to children by informal learning within the family. Speech patterns, customs, and social values are acquired through communication between the generations. As an individual develops and matures, peer-group associations assume increasing importance in socialization, often becoming a source of sharp conflict with parental norms (especially during the adolescent years).

Informal learning from interactions with family and peer-group members is augmented by formal school learning. As agents of socialization, schools rank almost as high as the family and peer groups as a medium of societal perpetuation.

Social Sanctions

Norms are acquired and maintained by a system of reward and punishment. When parents approve of their children's actions, they reward them with a smile, a caress, a murmur of praise, or a tangible reward of candy, cookies, or money. When children misbehave, parents mete out punishment ranging from a scolding to physical chastisement.

Rewards and punishments are incorporated into the normative structure as *social sanctions.* Sanctions may contain proscriptive or prescriptive elements. *Proscriptions* are statements of forbidden behavior (e.g., murder, rape, kidnapping, treason, and other rebellions against group authority). *Prescriptions* are statements of encouraged or reinforced behavior (e.g., getting married, raising children, holding down a steady job, paying taxes, and other forms of conduct that foster the common welfare).

Figure 2.1 illustrates how social sanctions promote "proper" behavior. Behavior toward the center of the continuum of social behavior is controlled by social norms called *folkways.* These social rules are usually enforced by *mild disapproval* (a cold stare, raised eyebrows, a reproving glance) or *mild encouragement* (a smile, applause, an approving glance). Behavior that threatens the existence of the group or is seen as necessary to the perpetuation of the group is controlled by a set of stronger norms called *mores.* Mores are enforced by more rigorous or severe expressions of social disapproval (verbal abuse, beatings, temporary ostracism) or by greater encouragement (monetary rewards, praise, testimonials, promotions).

Normative Variation

Norms do not set out a blueprint for behavior; at best, they provide a rough sketch. As Williams points out, "The institutionalized norms of social conduct never fully define concrete action. A norm is a standard (not necessarily explicit) for the course that action *should* follow, not a description of the action that actually occurs" (1970, p. 413). Norms are general; the situations within which behavior occurs, specific. Hence, behavior can vary considerably around a standard.

Note also that modern societies are composed of diverse subcultures with different norms and standards.

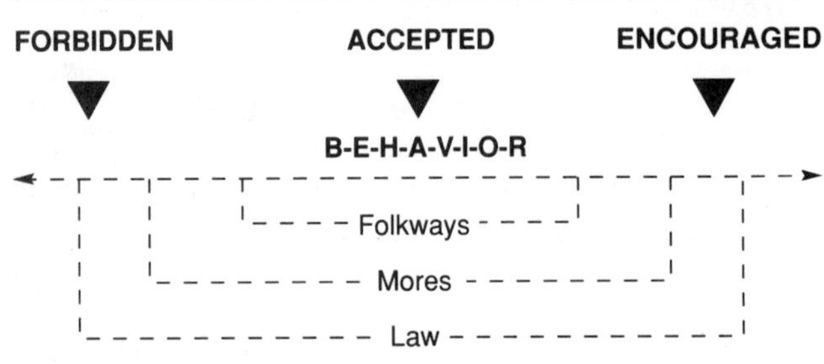

FIGURE 2.1
Continuum of social behavior.

Thus, behavior that deviates from presumably general or universal norms often involves a subcultural conflict.

SOCIAL VALUES AND LAW

In primitive or preliterate societies, rules governing normative behavior are perpetuated by word of mouth and passed from leader to leader. Eventually, normative expectations evolve into formal statements of proper behavior that are written and codified as laws. These formal statements, which usually express the most important societal values at the time, relate to objects, conditions, or states that are considered desirable and good and for which people are willing to expend time and energy to own or achieve.

The Value Consensus and Value Conflict Models

The relationship between social values and laws has been interpreted in two sharply differing ways: the *value consensus model* and the *value conflict model.* The basic premise of the value consensus model is that the criminal law reflects societal values that extend beyond the interests of particular individuals or groups and can therefore be considered an expression of the social consciousness of the entire society. According to this perspective, law develops through the efforts of a unified society to preserve and protect social values. Toward this purpose, the law relies on the deliberations and rational decisions of governing bodies (such as congresses or parliaments) that incorporate the principal authority of the society (Hall 1947).

In contrast, the value conflict model sees dissension rather than consensus, diversity rather than homogeneity—and a perennial struggle for power. As stated by Chambliss:

> Conventional myths notwithstanding, the history of criminal law is *not* a history of public opinion or public interest being reflected in criminal law legislation. On the contrary, the history of the criminal law is everywhere the history of legislation and appellate-court decisions which in effect (if not in intent) reflect the interests of the economic elites who control the production and distribution of the major resources of the society (1973, p. 430).

Economic power bestows political power, a fact related in this wry twist on the Golden Rule: "Them that has the gold makes the rules." According to the value conflict model, "the rules" (i.e., the law) become a tool used by the dominant class to maintain and enhance its power over the weak. Law is used by the state "and its elitist government to promote and protect itself" (Quinney 1974, p. 24). One way this is done through criminal law is controlling enforcement so that certain groups are singled out and labeled as "criminals" and "members of the dangerous classes."

It is difficult to accept either the value consensus or the value conflict model as an exclusively accurate characterization of the social processes underlying the development of criminal law. Despite Quinney's assertion that the standards for what ought to be considered criminal conduct are a reflection of various group and class definitions, it appears that a consensus on crimes against the person cuts across class lines in our society. Disagreement is more likely to be found with regard to laws proscribing gambling, abortion, prostitution, and homosexual behavior between consenting adults—the offenses often designated as victimless crimes.

The Value Divergence Model

A third position, called the *value divergence model,* recognizes the contributions of both the value conflict and value consensus models. It emphasizes that the United States is not a cultural monolith but a mosaic of diverse subcultures held together by shared beliefs and social values. It further maintains that the aggregate is stronger than the forces of divisiveness. Yet seldom in our pluralistic society can any body of statutes claim the support and allegiance of a majority of social groups.

Political scientist Stanley J. Makielski, in *Pressure Politics in America,* deals with the processes by which an *interest group*—"a collection of more than two people who interact on the basis of a commonly shared concern" (1980, p. 17)—is transformed into a *pressure group* that turns to the political system to press its demands. He defines *interests* as "the cement that binds a group together and the motivating power which impels a group into politics" (p. 21); these economic, social, or ideological interests are the base for structuring the policy concerns that characterize various groups. More importantly, the various *ways* in which pressure groups gain access through persuasion, mutual interest, established relationships, domination, or outright purchase provide the key to how such groups influence legislative activity to bring statutory changes in the law.

DEVIANCE

Deviance is not a fundamental property of human behavior; rather, it is an attribute of certain kinds of conduct. It is a discretionary term in that it can be ascribed to almost any behavior departing from customary standards or expectations. For example, a student who attends a college commencement ceremony in the headgear of a sorcerer's apprentice rather than a traditional mortarboard is acting in a deviant manner. So was the woman in this example:

How Sweet It Is!

SANTA CRUZ, California (AP)—A 30-year-old woman, spurned in love, disguised herself as a chocolate Easter bunny Friday and tried to hop into her neighbor's heart, but wound up under psychiatric observation instead, police said.

A city police officer, who asked not to be identified, said he was investigating a complaint of a disturbance at a man's home when he spotted what looked like a tall, chocolate rabbit coming "hippity-hoppity" out of the yard.

After a closer look, the officer discovered it was a female neighbor who had covered her nude body with chocolate glaze.

The man told the officer he had called police because of the woman's romantic advances over the last few months.

From *The Tampa Tribune,* 5 April 1980.

Schur states that human behavior is deviant "to the extent that it comes to be viewed as involving a personally discreditable departure from a group's normative expectations and elicits interpersonal or collective

FIGURE 2.2
On aspect of deviant behavior is that it differs from the behavior expected in a particular situation. Courtesy Ellis Herwig/Stock Boston.

reactions that serve to isolate, treat, correct, or punish individuals engaged in such behavior" (1971, p. 24). This definition asserts that a deviant's behavior is regarded negatively by others and that the response to the behavior has the effect of either changing or suppressing the behavior or punishing the person who exhibits it.

Deviance is also a matter of degree: cheating on an income tax return and committing armed robbery are both viewed as deviant behavior; but the robber is much more likely to be condemned and punished than the tax violator. As emphasized in Schur's statement, normative violations do not have equally adverse effects on an individual's identity. Large sectors of society are tolerant of, or even sympathetic toward, tax violators; but robbery is universally condemned as a violent crime. People who commit such crimes are apt to be scarred for the rest of their lives.

Schur's definition also identifies possible reactions of individuals or groups to those who engage in deviant behavior. Reactions vary according to how serious a threat to basic social values the deviance is perceived as being, whether the deviance is viewed as voluntary or something beyond the doer's control, and whether the behavior ceases to be objectionable to a large minority, or even a majority, of people in the society. During the 1960s and 1970s, for example, alcoholism came to be viewed by both the courts and the general public as a disease. Although public drunkenness continued to be subject to criminal sanctions, the movement of alcoholism from the category of criminality to the category of illness allowed people to be treated rather than punished. Other acts—such as participation in labor unions, divorce, and doing business on Sunday—have undergone a shift from condemnation, to tolerance, and finally to public approval.

In summary, the deviance of an act or an individual is relative, changeable, and a matter of degree, depending on the public's perception of, and response to, the behavior. The analysis of social definitions of, and responses to, these types of behavior has come to be known as the *labeling perspective.*

LAW IN HISTORICAL PERSPECTIVE

Durant (1950) identifies four stages in the development of law: (1) personal revenge; (2) fines; (3) courts; and

(4) assumption by the state of the obligation to prevent and punish wrongdoing. Revenge is embodied in the ancient principle of **lex talionis (talion law),** a phrase apparently devised by Cicero. Talion law, or "law of equivalent retaliation," was incorporated in the Babylonian Code of Hammurabi (circa 1800 B.C.), in Roman law, and in the Mosaic demand of "an eye for an eye and a tooth for a tooth." As Durant points out, talion law "lurks behind most legal punishments even in our own day" (1950, p. 27).

In operation, talion law does not *demand* retaliatory justice by depriving the perpetrator of an eye for one lost by the victim; rather, it limits the victim's legitimate claim to *no more* than an eye for the lost eye—not a tooth, an ear, or an arm as well. Durant claims that the Abyssinians were so meticulous in this form of justice that when a boy fell from a tree, fatally injuring his companion below, judges decided that justice could only be satisfied by allowing the bereaved mother to send another of her sons to the same tree to fall upon the offender's neck. Hence, in less sophisticated societies, crime and criminal activity were attributed to the offender's bad nature. Implicit in revenge was the notion of seeking redress. Aided by family or friends, or alone, a victim would pay back his attacker. A certain pleasure was also associated with a revenge—"It's sweeter than honey," said Homer. Although revenge provided an immediate solution to criminality, it also led to lawlessness and blood-letting feuds (Schafer 1969).

The concept of equivalent retaliation is present today in the idea of penalties being proportionate to the gravity or severity of the offense (i.e., "letting the punishment fit the crime"). A modern version of talion law is now in effect in the Islamic republic of Iran.

In the second stage of the development of law, the physical assault of talion law was replaced by fines, or the award of the appropriate damages as a means to secure equivalent retaliation. This principle is used today in some criminal cases and in cases involving civil injuries. The famous trial lawyer Melvin Belli once presented an artificial leg to a jury in a personal injury suit; he asked members of the jury how much money they would consider adequate payment for a lost limb.

Fines or settlements paid to avert personal revenge require some deliberation and adjudication of offenses and damages. Courts—a third natural development of the law—were established in response to this need. Early courts were not always judgment seats as we know them today; many were boards of voluntary conciliation. And if an offended party was dissatisfied with a court verdict, he or she was still free to seek personal revenge.

The Talion Law, Muslim Style

In an effort to rid Iranian society of undesirable foreign influences, Islamic fundamentalists led by the Ayatollah Khomeini have returned to the kind of criminal sanctions advocated by the Koran (the holy book of Islam) and the sayings of the Prophet Mohammed. As a result, a 199-article bill known as the Law of Punishment was passed by the Iranian parliament in 1981 to establish severe penalties for murder, assault, sodomy, adultery, and drunkenness.

The bill goes to great lengths to specify fair retaliation. For example, Article 62 states: "The equality of body parts applies in the Law of Punishment. This means that for the punishment of someone who cuts the right hand off someone else, only the right hand of the offender should be cut off. If the offender does not have a right hand, then the left hand can be cut off, and if he has neither right nor left hands, then one of his legs can be severed." For knife wounds and similar injuries, the bill specifies that punishment should be "in the same place, the same length and width and if possible the same depth." It empowers an Islamic court judge to order hair shaved to obtain "good implementation."

In Kerman, in southeastern Iran, two middle-aged women and two men—a young farmer and a worker with six children—were found guilty of prostitution, adultery, sodomy, and rape. First they were visited by Iranian clergymen, washed and clothed in white and masked with ceremonial "hoods of the dead." Then workmen buried them in earth up to their chests, and rocks, ranging in size from nuts to baseballs, were assembled not far away. The presiding judge threw the first stone; then, five onlookers bombarded each of the condemned persons with rocks. Fifteen minutes later, all four were pronounced dead.

Based on material reported in "Q'sas—The Law of Punishment," *Tampa Tribune*, November 12, 1982, p. 11A, and "Death by stoning for sex crimes," *Newsweek*, July 14, 1980, p. 40.

In the Middle Ages, disputes were settled through *trial by ordeal,* a practice that persisted into the twentieth century in the form of duels. Durant believes that "the primitive mind resorted to an ordeal not so much on the medieval theory that a diety would reveal the culprit as in the hope that the ordeal, however unjust, would end a feud that might otherwise embroil the tribe for generations" (1950, p. 28). Trials by ordeal were often referred to as "ordeals of God."

Trial by Ordeal

In trial by ordeal, a primitive means of determining guilt or innocence, accused persons were submitted to dangerous or painful tests believed to be under divine or supernatural control. Escape from death or injury was ordinarily taken to be a vindication of the innocence of the accused as reflected by the judgment of God (*judicium Dei*). The most common forms of ordeal were the wager of battle (or trial by combat), in which the winner was held to be innocent; the ordeal of fire, in which the accused walked barefoot over hot coals or carried a red-hot iron in his or her hand; and trial by cold water (often applied to witches), in which the accused was immersed in water and pronounced guilty if he or she floated.

Another ordeal was the corsned trial, which involved placing hallowed bread (corsned) into the mouth of the accused; if the individual swallowed the wafer, he or she was freed from punishment. In the trial of the cross, accuser and accused were placed before a cross with their arms extended; the first person to move his hands or let his arms drop was considered guilty. In the judgment of the bier, used in murder trials, the corpse of the victim was placed on a bier and the accused was required to touch the body; if blood flowed or foam appeared at the mouth of the victim, the suspect was judged guilty.

Despite attempts to curb or abolish trial by ordeal in Europe, the practice continued into the fourteenth century. In England, forms of ordeal other than trial by combat were abolished by Henry III in the year 1219, following their condemnation by Pope Innocent III in 1216. However, the "ducking stool"—used to subject suspected witches to trial by water—was still used in colonial America as late as the seventeenth century.

The fourth advance in law, according to Durant, was the assumption by the state of the obligation to punish wrongdoing and protect the citizen. Crimes came to be regarded as offenses against the state, because their commission adversely affected the community. The state enlarged its domain of authority from merely settling disputes to making an effort to prevent them.

American law is deeply indebted to the English **common law.** Laws began to be written in England as early as 680 A.D. Eventually, English law came to a combination of tribal rules, Roman law, and the customs of invaders from northern France, Scandinavia, and what was later to become the modern state of Germany.

When the Normans invaded England from France in the eleventh century, they found among the defeated Anglo-Saxons a well-developed and workable system for maintaining public order and administering justice. The system had evolved over a lengthy period and was based on a body of common law derived from the customs of collective experience of Anglo-Saxon society. A principal feature was its reliance on precedents to continually refine and develop suitable legal responses to meet the needs of a growing and dynamic society.

The Norman ruler, William the Conqueror, imposed his own representatives on the existing system to consolidate his power and authority. Under the royal justices appointed by William, state law became common law—called such because it originated in the customary practices of the realm and was common to all of England. Common law was firmly embedded in custom and tradition, but it continued to evolve through the process of judicial decision making.

Common law is judge-made law, molded, refined, examined, and changed in a collection of actual decisions handed down from generation to generation in the form of reported cases. Judges drew their decisions from existing principles of law, which reflected the living values, attitudes, and ethical ideals of the English people. In practice, these judges relied on their own past actions, which they modified under the pressure of changing times and changing patterns of litigation (Friedman 1973).

Civil law derived from Roman antecedents and even earlier attempts by Sumerian and Babylonian societies to provide formal rules for human conduct. Nearly two millenia before the birth of Christ, a Babylonian monarch named Hammurabi formulated a code that enunciated a series of offenses and accompanying penalties. The historical significance of the Code of Hammurabi rests in its effort to standardize the relationship between crime and punishment. From such beginnings, civil law evolved as a system based on written and legislated codes.

American criminal law combines features of both civil and common law in that it includes both written codes and judge-made law based on precedents. *Statutory law*—that is, statutes enacted by state legislatures and the Congress—is a major source of criminal law in the United States. These laws are usually compiled in codes that sort or classify statutes under separate headings. State codes are usually subject to revision at annual legislative sessions. The criminal laws of any state are found in the state penal code. Thus, to find out how Florida defines the crimes of kidnapping and indecent exposure, and the penalties imposed for them, you would look in the newest version of the Florida Penal Code, as provided in the Florida Statutes Annotated §§ 787.01 and 800.02:

As an offshoot of statutory law, *administrative law* is comprised of rulings by government agencies at the federal, state, and local levels. The legislative or executive branch invests a body such as a board of health with the authority to establish regulations governing specific policy areas (e.g., social problems or safety and health standards). Although much of the content of administrative law is not targeted directly at criminal behavior, direct violations of the rules of certain governmental agencies are dealt with in criminal courts. For

CHAPTER 787
KIDNAPPING; FALSE IMPRISONMENT; CUSTODY OFFENSES

787.01	**Kidnapping**
787.02	**False imprisonment**
787.03	**Interference with custody**
787.04	**Felony to remove children from state or conceal children contrary to court order**

787.01 Kidnapping

(1)(a) "Kidnapping" means forcibly, secretly, or by threat confining, abducting, or imprisoning another person against his will and without lawful authority, with intent to:

1. Hold for ransom or reward or as a shield or hostage.
2. Commit or facilitate commission of any felony.
3. Inflict bodily harm upon or to terrorize the victim or another person.
4. Interfere with the performance of any governmental or political function.

(b) Confinement of a child under the age of 13 is against his will within the meaning of subsection (1) if such confinement is without the consent of his parent or legal guardian.

(2) Whoever kidnaps a person is guilty of a felony of the first degree, punishable by imprisonment for a term of years not exceeding life or as provided in § 775.082, § 775.083, or § 775.084.

CHAPTER 800
CRIME AGAINST NATURE; INDECENT EXPOSURE

800.01	Repealed
800.02	Unnatural and lascivious act
800.03	Exposure of sexual organs
800.04	Lewd, lascivious or indecent assault or act upon or in presence of child

800.01 Repealed by Laws 1974, c. 74-121, § 1, eff. Oct. 1, 1974

800.02 Unnatural and lascivious act

Whoever commits any unnatural and lascivious act with another person shall be guilty of a misdemeanor of the second degree, punishable as provided in § 775.082 or § 775.083.

800.03 Exposure of sexual organs

It shall be unlawful for any person to expose or exhibit his sexual organs in any public place or on the private premises of another, or so near thereto as to be seen from such private premises, in a vulgar or indecent manner, or so to expose or exhibit his person in such place, or to go or be naked in such place. Provided, however, this section shall not be construed to prohibit the exposure of such organs or the person in any place provided or set apart for that purpose. Any person convicted of a violation hereof shall be guilty of a misdemeanor of the first degree, punishable as provided in § 775.082 or § 775.083.

FIGURE 2.3
Florida Penal Code §§ 787.01 and 800.02. From *Florida Statutes Annotated* (St. Paul, Minn.: West Publishing Co., 1981).

example, the scheduling of drugs by the Drug Enforcement Administration is a set of administrative rules. These have been adopted by many criminal statutes in the federal government as well as in several states.

The meaning and intent of criminal statutes are tested and interpreted within the context of specific cases. The courts are generally bound to follow the criminal law as it has been jurisdictionally determined in prior cases. This is one of the principal components of criminal law and is referred to as the law of precedent. Thus, criminal law can be created by judges in their rulings on statutory laws. Known as *case law,* this kind of law is heavily influenced by the principle of *stare decisis* ("let the decision stand")—the rule that requires judges to follow precedent in judicial interpretations. The legal principles of precedent and *stare decisis* promote stability and certainty in the process of making legal decisions. Without these principles, as Eldefonso and Coffey observe, "the defendant in a civil or criminal case would never know whether or not his activities were lawful" (1981, p. 36). Nevertheless, prior decisions are sometimes overruled by the higher authority of a court of appeals, thus reversing or modifying existing case law.

FIGURE 2.4
John A. Walker, Jr., a retired army Navy communications expert, is escorted to court for a hearing on espionage charges that he sold secrets to the Soviet Union for seventeen years. He was convicted and is currently serving his sentence in a federal prison. Wide World Photos.

CLASSIFICATION OF CRIMES

Crimes are legally classified as either felonies, misdemeanors, or treason. In general, felonies are more serious crimes and are punishable by death or imprisonment of a year or more in state prison. Misdemeanors are less serious and are punishable by fines usually not exceeding one thousand dollars, or by a term of up to one year in city or county jail. A few states provide a fourth classification for certain offenses—"highest misdemeanors." In terms of seriousness, these offenses lie between felonies and misdemeanors. Although still technically misdemeanors, they often provide a maximum sentence in excess of one year incarceration. Some states, such as North Carolina, have a two year maximum for misdemeanors. "Violations" are offenses for which punishments do not include imprisonment.

The felony-misdemeanor distinction is crucial to the criminal justice system and process. As Robin points out, the classification of a crime as a felony or a misdemeanor will affect the following (1980, p. 10):

1. The conditions under which the police can make an arrest and the degree of force that will be authorized
2. The "charges" the prosecutor will ultimately press
3. The care exercised by the trial judge in accepting a guilty plea and admitting evidence into the record
4. The availability of procedural and constitutional safeguards
5. The quality of counsel and the conduct of the court
6. The determination of which court will have trial jurisdiction
7. The sentence that can be imposed

8. The type of institution to which an offender may be committed
9. The conditions of release from incarceration
10. The size of the jury
11. Whether a jury verdict must be unanimous

These factors have significant consequences for the defendant; in some cases, the outcome may be a matter of life or death.

Common law originally separated crimes that were "wrong in themselves" (***mala in se***) from those that were wrong because they were prohibited (***mala prohibita***). The latter are acts forbidden by statute but which otherwise do not shock the conscience of the community. Crimes involving gross immorality or depravity such as murder, mayhem, armed robbery, rape, and arson are essentially evil and are considered *mala in se* offenses. *Mala prohibita* offenses include crimes such as driving under the influence of alcohol, being disorderly, driving on the wrong side of the road, breach of the peace, running a red light, and polluting the air and water.

Other classifications of crime include "crimes against nature," which, in the broadest sense, include carnal knowledge of an animal, sodomy, fellatio, cunnilingus, and intercourse in any position other than face to face (even between legally married partners). The reference to these acts as "crimes against nature" does not, of course, represent an indictment from nature itself; rather it is a value judgment by a legislative body as to what is "natural." For example, if we can repose any confidence in the many investigations of sexual behavior—from Alfred Kinsey to Masters and Johnson—we must conclude that a sexual experience regarded as "unnatural" in one segment of society may actually be the norm in another group.

Violations of the "natural law" are often confused with crimes against nature. The natural law consists of sets of standards, ideals, limitations, and sanctions imposed upon individuals by higher spiritual authority. This law is believed to be binding even in the absence of human-made law.

Another classification of crime, "crimes against humanity," was developed at the end of World War II and used by the Allies in the trials of Nazi leaders at Nuremberg. The Nazi crimes (which included genocide) were seen as being of such magnitude and severity that the offenders should be compelled to answer to all of humanity, rather than to a specific country or jurisdiction. Years later, European peace groups applied this same concept to President Lyndon B. Johnson and members of his administration, trying them *in absentia* for alleged war crimes in Vietnam.

An offense can also be classified as a *private wrong*, called a "civil injury" or *tort*, or a *public wrong*, which falls under the rubric of criminal law. A public wrong is a violation of public order for which the community may take action. The punishment imposed is for the protection of the community, not for the redress of individual injury. In contrast to criminal law, the **civil law** is a set of rules that determines private rights and liabilities. In civil cases a single individual brings a law suit against another individual whereas in the criminal law the state initiates the court action against the accused. Private parties must seek redress through a civil court action. When an individual or organization sues another to obtain a remedy or recompense for an alleged injury, the case is a civil action. When the state prosecutes an individual or organization for violating a legislative statute, the case is usually a criminal action.

In some cases, a single offense may give rise to both civil and criminal action. Assault and battery, for example, may result in a civil action by the victim to secure damages for injuries; and the state may file criminal charges to punish the guilty party by a fine or imprisonment.

SUBSTANTIVE CRIMINAL LAW

In our brief historical sketch of the antecedents of American criminal jurisprudence, we referred rather informally to "criminal law." It is time to abandon this casual usage in favor of the more exact designation *substantive criminal law*, as distinguished from *criminal procedure*. Substantive criminal law is concerned with acts, mental states, and accompanying circumstances or consequences that constitute the necessary features of crimes. It identifies particular kinds of behavior (acts or omissions) as wrongs against society or the state and prescribes punishments to be imposed for such conduct. Any references in this book to "criminal law" are actually references to "substantive criminal law."

Criminal procedure (as discussed later in this chapter) sets forth the *rules* that direct the application and enforcement of substantive criminal law. That is, criminal procedure lays the steps that officials—police, prosecutors, judges, corrections personnel, and others—must take in the administration of justice, from arrest to conviction and beyond.

FIGURE 2.5
After World War II, Nazi leaders were charged with crimes against humanity for the atrocities of the Holocaust. Although laws prohibiting crimes against humanity were not "on the books" when the Nazis committed the atrocities, many people said that the laws were derived from the natural law. Wide World Photos.

Foundations of Criminal Law

Anglo-American criminal law is founded upon seven basic principles traditionally observed by legislatures and the courts in formulating and interpreting the substantive criminal law. These principles are interlocking. The criminal law recognizes the existence of the same essential ingredients in every crime. Thus for a particular behavior to be considered criminal and, as such, to be penalized by the state, all of these seven principles must be present: (1) legality; (2) actus reus; (3) mens rea; (4) concurrence of actus reus and mens rea; (5) harm; (6) causation; and (7) punishment. Hall summarized these principles as follows: "The harm forbidden in a penal law must be imputed to any normal adult who voluntarily commits it with criminal intent, and such a person must be subjected to the legally prescribed punishment" (1947, p. 18).

LEGALITY A crime is defined legally as "an intentional act or omission in violation of a criminal law, committed without defense or justification and sanctioned by the state as a felony or misdemeanor" (Tappan 1966, p. 10). The idea that there can be no crime unless a law exists that has been violated is embodied in the ancient Latin saying *Nullum crimen sine lege*—"no crime without a law." Legality is one of the most venerated concepts in Anglo-American law.

ACTUS REUS The term *actus reus,* which means the "guilty act," refers to the forbidden act itself. Criminal law uses this term to describe the physical crime and/or the commission of the criminal act. Thoughts alone do not constitute a crime. One can legally wish an enemy dead, fantasize a rape, or harbor thoughts about income tax evasion—as long as the thoughts do not result in an action (*actus reus*) to bring about the desired result. However, it is necessary to distinguish mere thoughts from *speech,* because a crime can be committed by an act of speech under our legal system. For example, because we consider individuals acting together to be a greater threat to society than a lone offender, we regard an *agreement* by two or more persons to commit a crime as an act of *criminal conspiracy.* Nevertheless, approximately half of the states require (by statute) that an act be committed *in furtherance of the conspiracy* (LaFave and Scott 1972, pp. 476–78). Other crimes that can be committed by acts of speech include perjury and solicitation.

MENS REA A further requirement of criminal conduct is the presence of the "guilty mind" (***mens rea***) of the accused. This requirement is also called the criminal intent of the crime. For the prosecution, proving the criminal intent is more complex than proving the *actus reus* because it demands an evaluation of the psychology and motives of the defendant. For example, a bus driver who fails to stop at an intersection and causes a collision with an automobile entering from a cross street would not be charged with a crime if it could be proven that he was unaware his brakes were defective—that he had done everything he could to avert the accident. Similarly, a person who unknowingly buys stolen goods from a local merchant is not guilty of the criminal offense of receiving stolen property, because the element of intent is missing. On the other hand, a person who drives a sports car at ninety miles an hour in a residential area and kills a young child may well be convicted of manslaughter, because her behavior constitutes a reckless disregard for associated risks. In an actual case, a nightclub owner was found criminally negligent and convicted of manslaughter for failing to provide adequate fire escapes, resulting in the death of many patrons during a fire. In affirming the owner's conviction, the court held that more than mere negligence was necessary, i.e., that "a grave danger to others must have been apparent." As the court stated, "even if a particular defendant is so stupid (or) so heedless . . . that in fact he did not realize the grave danger," he is guilty of manslaughter "if an ordinary normal man under the same circumstances would have realized the gravity of the danger" (*Commonwealth* v. *Welansky* [55 N.E.2d 902(1944)], as cited in LaFave and Scott 1972, pp. 212–13).

The concept of *mens rea* is based on the assumption that people have the capacity to control their behavior and the ability to choose between alternative courses of conduct. Traditionally, the *mens rea* of the crime means the defendant intended to commit the prohibited act. In addition, states of mind such as malice, criminal knowledge, recklessness, negligence, and criminal purpose are considered to be the *mens rea* of certain crimes.

Generally, two types of *mens rea* are recognized in the criminal law: general intent and specific intent. General intent consists of voluntarily intending to do the prohibited act. Accordingly, the only state of mind that is required is the intent to commit the act constituting the crime. The offender need not have intended to violate the law, nor need he have been aware that the law made his act criminal. Also, the defendant's general intent does not have to be specifically proven. The courts allow the jury to infer from the fact that the defendant engaged in the prohibited conduct that he voluntarily intended to commit the act. A specific intent is the *mens rea* of only certain crimes. Crimes like burglary and larceny require that in addition to a general intent, the offender must intend to do something further or to cause consequences beyond those that must have been committed in order to complete the crime. For example, the *mens rea* of burglary is the "intent to commit a felony inside another's home." Were the intent of burglary just a general intent, the state would merely need to prove that the defendant intended to break and enter the home. Since burglary has a specific intent, however, the state is required to prove that the defendant intended to engage in more serious activity.

Offenses that involve no mental element but consist of only forbidden acts or omissions are classified as **strict-liability offenses.** Thus, a statute may simply indicate that someone who does or omits a certain act, or who brings about a certain result, is guilty of a crime. Such statutes are justified on the grounds that although there is a need to control the behavior in question, convictions would be difficult to obtain if the prosecution had to prove fault. Examples of laws imposing liability without fault include liquor and narcotics laws, pure-food laws, and traffic laws. Since these offenses require no *mens rea,* even an accidental violation of statute is proscribed. Accordingly, the accused cannot claim in court that she made an "innocent mistake." Innocent mistakes result in convictions of persons who commit strict liability crimes. An excellent example is the crime of statutory rape. This crime often begins when the offender picks up a female who is under age at a bar (she usually must be under eighteen years of age). Indeed, the crime is committed even if the young woman advises the offender that she is twenty-two years old. If the two later engage in sexual intercourse, the offender is guilty of statutory rape. Since this crime contains no *mens rea,* the fact that he honestly believed she was over eighteen is irrelevant. Also irrelevant is the fact that the victim fully consented to the intercourse.

The law recognizes that some groups of people are unable to attain the requisite mental state for crime. Children, mental defectives, and, in some cases, those diagnosed as insane are exempt from criminal responsibility because they are unable to appreciate the nature and quality of their behavior. Mens rea is also considered lacking when people act under coercion, defending themselves or others, or act under statutory authority (e.g., the police officer acting in the line of duty).

CONCURRENCE OF ACTUS REUS AND MENS REA Another basic premise of criminal law is that the act and the mental state must *concur* for a crime to have been committed. The act and the mental state are not concurrent if they are separated by a considerable gap in time. A lack of concurrence between mental state and act is a strong argument that the mental state did not activate or cause the act.

HARM An additional requirement in the criminal law is that only conduct that is harmful in some way can be considered criminal. This idea is reflected in the concept of due process, which holds that a criminal statute is unconstitutional if it bears no reasonable relationship to the matter of injury to the public. It is important to recognize, however, that criminal harm is not restricted to *physical* injury. In cases of libel, perjury, and treason, no physical injury is inflicted. Thus, the criminal law must deal with intangibles, such as harm to institutions, public safety, autonomy of women, and reputation. In essence, criminal harm signifies loss of value, because an individual who commits a crime does something contrary to community values (Hall 1947).

CAUSATION Causation relates to crimes that require that a defendant's conduct produce a given result. Crimes such as perjury or forgery are defined so that the crime consists of both the act itself and the intent to cause the harmful result—without regard to whether that result in fact occurs. On the other hand, offenses such as intent-to-kill murder and intent-to-injure battery require a specific result. In such cases, the defendant's conduct must be the "but for" cause of the result, and the harm that actually occurs must be similar enough to the intended result that the defendant can be held responsible.

In many instances, it is difficult for the prosecution to probe a causal connection between intent and harm. For example, if A, with intent to kill, drives a knife into the heart of B, a prosecutor would have no particular difficulty demonstrating that A's action was the cause of B's death. However, the matter of intended harm varies according to person, manner, and type of harm. For example, suppose that A shoots B and—believing B is dead—leaves B's body on the interstate. B is killed when C—who doesn't see B lying on the road—runs over her. Will A be convicted of B's murder? Only if it can be demonstrated that A's conduct was a substantial factor in bringing about B's death or that what happened to B was a foreseeable consequence of A's behavior.

The rule of causation has also been applied generally in cases of *felony murder*. At issue is whether an offender can be held responsible for unintended deaths that result from the perpetration of a crime. For example, suppose A sets out to rob storeowner B. During the robbery, B, acting to protect his property, fires at A and accidentally

Case 2.1

Angry with Carol for stealing the affections of her boyfriend, Bob, Alice plans to kill both Carol and Bob with poisoned lemonade. But when she goes to Bob's apartment to invite the couple for a picnic, she finds they have eloped. Ten years later, at an intersection in Denver, Bob (who is color blind) runs a traffic light. He and Carol are killed instantly when their Honda motorcycle is totaled in a collision with a Cherokee Chief (with ski rack) driven by—none other than—Alice.

Is Alice guilty of murder? No. There was no concurrence between the intent and the harmful conduct. Fate delivered the couple into Alice's hands.

kills a customer. The robbery foiled, A runs out of the store and a police officer shoots at him, killing a bystander. Is A responsible for either or both of these deaths? In general, the courts have ruled that if the death is a natural and forseeable consequence of the offense, the offender is liable (LaFave and Scott 1972, pp. 263–264). Thus, A could be prosecuted for both deaths in this example.

PUNISHMENT Under the American legal system, citizens must not only be warned as to what conduct is forbidden, but they must also be made aware of the consequences of their actions. Thus, the law stipulates the sanctions for every crime.

Characteristics of Criminal Law

Sutherland and Cressey (1978) identify four characteristics that distinguish criminal law from other rules affecting human conduct: (1) politicality; (2) specificity; (3) uniformity; and (4) penal sanction.

POLITICALITY Criminal laws are enacted, modified, and repealed by duly elected legislative bodies. Yet in a pluralistic society with no system of universally shared social values, what is defined as criminal behavior during a given period depends largely on what conduct politically influential and powerful groups perceive as a threat to their values. Since the turn of the century, for example, prohibition has been enacted and repealed; abortion, gambling, and pornography laws have been liberalized; and laws dealing with the possession and sale of marijuana and other drugs have been enacted and modified. This element of change and influence is known as the *politicality* of criminal law.

SPECIFICITY *Specificity* means that laws must be stated in terms that clearly indicate what conduct is expected. For example, statutes that specify punishment for commonly understood offenses such as rape or robbery are usually quite clear, but a statute that prohibits "immoral acts" in general would be difficult to interpret. Any law that requires or prohibits the commission of an act in terms so vague that people of normal intelligence must guess at the meaning violates an essential requirement of due process. The courts refer to this as **substantive due process.** This right protects us from being punished by unreasonably vague or arbitrary laws. In the criminal justice process, substantive due process requires that the criminal statute must not be so vague and uncertain that "men of common intelligence must necessarily guess at its meaning and differ as to its application" (Lewis and Peoples 1978). Certain criminal statutes and local ordinances are consistently judged to be so vague as to violate substantive due process. For example, laws that make it unlawful to "wander the street at night without lawful business" or to "treat contemptuously the American flag" have been declared unconstitutional for violating due process. A long-standing objection to some statutes for juvenile offenses is that terms such as "incorrigible" or "ungovernable" are used without definition.

UNIFORMITY "Justice" is often portrayed as a blindfolded woman who weighs evidence for the guilt or innocence of those standing before her. The ideal in American criminal jurisprudence is that *uniformity* will prevail—that all persons adjudged by the law will be treated equally, regardless of their ethnic or national origins, religious convictions or affiliations, or social standing. The theory is noble, but in practice "some people are more equal than others."

PENAL SANCTION As we have already seen, criminal statutes must not only give people fair warning of what behavior to avoid, but they must also convey some idea of the penalties incurred when laws are violated. In the broadest terms, the goal of punishment is to protect society, for the first duty of any government is to safeguard the lives and property of its citizens. No society that tolerates unrestrained theft and violence can endure for long. Given the propensity toward aggressive and predatory behavior in many human societies, few laws without penalty would be honored by observance.

For example, a recent law passed in Mississippi requires that all persons having reasonable suspicion that child abuse has occurred must report the abuse to local authorities. Initially, this law was hailed as a step forward in protecting helpless children. The problem with this law, however, is that it does not authorize any penal sanctions for those who have reasonable suspicion that child abuse has occurred and do *not* report it. Hence, without penal sanctions, the law becomes nonenforceable. Nonenforceable laws normally do not regulate social behavior in an optimum manner.

CRIMINAL PROCEDURE

The U.S. Constitution is the most authoritative source of criminal procedure in our country. We are introduced as school children to the first ten amendments to the Constitution, known collectively as the Bill of Rights. Most Americans know that the Bill of Rights contains certain safeguards for American citizens. These safeguards are embodied in such phrases as the right to "Assistance of Counsel," the protection from "unreasonable searches and seizures," and "the right against self-incrimination." But we are less likely to know that safeguards for the rights of the accused were not applicable to state courts until the passage of the Fourteenth Amendment in 1868. Prior to the Fourteenth Amendment, the Bill of Rights applied directly only to proceedings in federal courts. In fact, even after the enactment of the Fourteenth Amendment, it took years before many of the safeguards in the Bill of Rights were applied to the states. Most of the rights of the accused were not guaranteed constitutionally in state criminal courts until the 1960s.

The Fourteenth Amendment

The Fourteenth Amendment to the U.S. Constitution declares, in part, that "no State shall make or enforce any law which shall abridge the privileges or immunities of citizens of the United States, nor shall any State deprive any person of life, liberty, or property, without due process of law; nor deny any person within its jurisdiction the equal protection of the laws. . ." Together with the Thirteenth and Fifteenth amendments, which were passed just after the Civil War, the Fourteenth Amendment extended citizenship to former slaves and guaranteed them the same protections of law provided for other citizens by the Constitution. But the due process and equal protection phrases of the Fourteenth Amendment were not immediately applied to civil rights. As late as the 1940s, state courts and the U.S. Supreme Court employed these features of the Fourteenth Amendment primarily to protect business corporations from government regulation.

In 1884, in the case of *Hurtado* v. *California* (110 U.S. 516), the Supreme Court rejected the "shorthand doctrine," which sought to bind the states to a blanket application of the Bill of Rights. The subsequent judicial history of the Fourteenth Amendment involved a continuing debate within the U.S. Supreme Court between proponents of a piecemeal application of the due process and equal protection provisions and those justices who supported viewpoints that inclined toward total incorporation.

The Supreme Court has never made clear exactly what constitutes due process. Both the definition and significance of due process seem to be flexible and continually changing. One thing seems certain. Procedural due process of law has always meant at least that an accused person in criminal cases in both state and federal courts in the United States must be accorded certain rights to ensure he or she receives a fair trial. Table 2.1 highlights the major positions that have been taken within the

TABLE 2.1
Basic Interpretations of the Due Process Clause of the Fourteenth Amendment*

Ordered liberty (fundamental fairness)	The due process clause applies only to those "traditional notions" of due process, such as freedom of religion, speech, and press and procedural rights, that are "implicit in the concept of ordered liberty." The Fourteenth Amendment incorportes none of the guarantees of the Bill of Rights as such.
Total incorporation	The due process clause includes *all* rights found in the Bill of Rights, but limits the inclusion to *only* those rights enumerated therein. No unenumerated rights are recognized.
Total incorporation plus (ultraincorporation)	The due process clause encompasses *all* of the specific guarantees of the Bill of Rights *plus* any additional fundamental unenumerated rights that are properly classified as essential to "fairness and individual liberty" (e.g., the right of privacy).
Selective incorporation	Combines aspects of both "ordered liberty" and "total incorporation" interpretations of the Fourteenth Amendment. Accepts the basic premise that the due process clause encompasses *all* rights that are "fundamental to the American system of justice." Recognizes that *not all* rights enumerated in the Bill of Rights are necessarily fundamental (e.g., grand jury indictments). However, this view also recognizes that other rights may be fundamental even though not specifically enumerated in the Bill of Rights (e.g., the right to terminate a pregnancy).
Neo-incorporation	A "half-way house" between the ordered liberty and traditional incorporation approaches. According to this view, the fact that a procedural right is incorporated into the Bill of Rights does *not* make federal procedures binding on state criminal trials (e.g., unanimous jury verdicts required in federal criminal trials, but not in state criminal trials).

* Implicit in these traditional incorporation views is the idea that once any Bill of Rights' guarantee is "incorporated," it limits state authority in precisely the same way that the Bill of Rights directly limits federal authority. This is not true for neo-incorporation.

Adapted from P. W. Lewis and K. D. Peoples, *The Supreme Court and the Criminal Process—Cases and Comments* (Philadelphia: W. B. Saunders, 1978), p. 102, by permission of the publisher.

Supreme Court or by legal scholars in interpreting the meaning and significance of due process.

From 1961 to 1969—a period often referred to as the "due process revolution"—the U.S. Supreme Court took an activist role, becoming a giver of the law rather than just an interpreter. Under Chief Justice Earl Warren, the court expanded the meaning of the due process requirement; it moved from the old policy that a state must afford "fundamental fairness" to an accused toward insisting on absolute compliance by state and local officials with a vast majority of the provisions in the Bill of Rights. As Swanson and Territo (1983) point out, the Warren court's activist role in extending the provisions of the Bill of Rights to criminal proceedings in the states (via the due process clause of the Fourteenth Amendment) may have been a policy decision.

Some statistics illustrate the magnitude of the revolution. The Supreme Court normally writes about 115 opinions in any term. During the 1938–39 term, only five of the cases appeared under the heading of criminal law; three decades later, however, during the height of the due-process revolution, about one-fourth of all decisions related to criminal law.

Among the key Supreme Court decisions in the due-process revolution were *Mapp* v. *Ohio* (367 U.S. 643 [1961]), *Gideon* v. *Wainwright* (372 U.S. 355 [1963]), *Escobedo* v. *Illinois* (375 U.S. 902 [1964]), and *Miranda* v. *Arizona* (384 U.S. 436 [1966]). These cases focused on the three vitally important areas of search and seizure, the privilege against self incrimination and the right to counsel. Collectively, the cases constitute a watershed period in the administration of criminal justice in the United States.

In the mid 1970s, the ongoing debate concerning the application of due process continued. More conservative political leaders emphasized that crime control rather than protection of an accused's individual liberties created the greater social good. When Earl Warren retired in 1969, Warren Burger was appointed the fifteenth Chief Justice of the United States. The resignations of Justices Black and Harlan (who were replaced by Lewis Powell and William Rehnquist in 1971) also altered the direction of the due process revolution. Later, with the resignation of William O. Douglas and the addition of John Paul Stevens, Richard Nixon's and Gerald Ford's appointees remade the philosophy of the Supreme Court. Liberals feared the protections announced by the Court during the 1960s might be reversed. Most legal scholars now agree that the Burger court of the 1970s and 1980s (now the Rehnquist court) has interpreted the meaning of the due process clause in a far more conservative manner than did the Warren court. Constitutional expert Yale Kamisar writes,

> A Warren court admirer probably would say that the new court did retreat on any number of search and seizure fronts but that it held firm on others and even advanced on some. In the confession area, again viewed from the prospective of a Warren court supporter, the Burger Court did inflict substantial damage, especially in earlier years, but much less than it had been threatening to do (Kamisar 1983).

Any examination of the Bill of Rights from a criminal justice perspective must include both the due process revolution of the Warren court and the somewhat conservative retreat of the Burger/Rehnquist Courts. Remaining through all these changes and interpretations, however, are the Fourth, Fifth, Sixth and Eighth Amendments' guarantees of specific rights and the historical interpretations attached to them.

The Fourth Amendment: Search and Seizure

The Fourth Amendment to the Constitution guarantees people the right "to be secure in their persons, houses, papers, and effects, against unreasonable searches and seizures." A search is any governmental intrusion against a person's reasonable and justifiable expectation of privacy. A seizure is the exercise of control by a government agent over a personal thing. Generally, a search warrant is required before a search may lawfully be conducted. This requirement seems central to the Fourth Amendment protection against unreasonable searches and seizures. However, the Supreme Court has stated through the years that searches may be conducted without a warrant and are constitutional if the search qualifies under one of the six exceptions to the search warrant requirement. These exceptions include the following: a search incident to a lawful arrest, searches of moving automobiles, seizures of contraband or instrumentalities of crime that the police discover in plain view, the stop and frisk exception, searches conducted when the owner voluntarily and intelligently gives his or her consent, and searches made when police are in hot pursuit of a dangerous suspect and in specific danger zones such as a crime scene.

In 1914 the Supreme Court, in the case of *Weeks* v. *United States* (232 U.S. 383), established the so-called Exclusionary Rule to govern the operation of the federal courts. According to the Exclusionary Rule, evidence

obtained as a result of an unreasonable or illegal search is not admissible in a federal criminal prosecution. In *Weeks,* the Court argued that the government must not be encouraged to commit illegal acts by gaining a conviction from illegally seized evidence. The Court suggested that without this rule the police would not be deterred from conducting unconstitutional searches and seizures against private citizens.

The Exclusionary Rule curbed, but did not eliminate, abuse of the Fourth Amendment. Evidence obtained illegally by state law enforcement officers continued to find its way into federal prosecutions on the grounds that no federal official had participated in violating the defendant's rights. This type of federal-state search and seizure became known as the "silver platter" doctrine, a name that originated in Justice Frankfurter's decision in *Lustig* v. *United States* (338 U.S. 74 [1949]). Frankfurter held that "the crux of that doctrine is that a search is a search by a federal official if he had a hand in it; it is not a search by a federal official if evidence secured by state authorities is turned over to the federal authorities on a silver platter." The Supreme Court condemned this practice with regard to criminal investigations in *Elkins* v. *United States* (364 U.S. 206 [1960]). Writing for the majority, Justice Stewart held that the "silver platter" doctrine constituted an "inducement to subterfuge and evasion" (p. 222).

In *Mapp* v. *Ohio,* the Exclusionary Rule was extended to the state courts, a reversal of the 1949 decision of *Wolf* v. *Colorado* (338 U.S. 25); the latter decision had permitted the states to establish their own procedural safeguards against unreasonable search. On May 23, 1957, Cleveland police officers entered the home of Doll Ree Mapp without a search warrant, saying that they were looking for a suspect in a recent bombing. The police claimed they thought he was hiding in Mapp's house. She demanded to see a search warrant. One of the officers held up a piece of paper (later it turned out not to be a search warrant) whereupon Mapp grabbed it and tucked it into her blouse. A struggle ensued and the officer recovered the paper. Then, Mapp was handcuffed and led to her bedroom while the officers searched the other rooms in her home. Finally, they went into the basement where they found some obscene material in a trunk. At trial, no search warrant was produced, yet the Supreme Court of Ohio upheld the conviction because the evidence was not taken from the defendant's person by the use of coercion or offensive physical force. Ms. Mapp successfully appealed her case to the U.S. Supreme Court.

In *Mapp* v. *Ohio,* the court held that

> . . . all evidence obtained by searches and seizures in violation of the Constitution is, by that same authority, inadmissible in a state court. Since the Fourth Amendment's right of privacy has been declared enforceable against the States through the Due Process clause of the Fourteenth Amendment, it is enforceable against them by the same sanction of exclusion as is used against the Federal Government . . .(p. 655).

An even broader extension of the Exclusionary Rule is the doctrine known as the "fruit of the poisonous tree." This doctrine prohibits the admission of evidence obtained *as a result* of an "illegal or initially 'tainted' admission, confession, or search" (Kerper 1972, p. 316). Assume, for example, that the police employed coercive methods to extract a confession from a suspect who names a second party as an accomplice in the illegal sale of narcotics. Using a properly executed search warrant, the police search the residence occupied by the second party and confiscate a quantity of heroin. In this case, the fact that the search was authorized by legal warrant does not validate the admission of the heroin as evidence, because the police obtained the information leading to the search and seizure in an unauthorized, or "tainted," manner.

Many law enforcement officials maintain that the chief purpose of the Exclusionary Rule is to punish police "misconduct" involving disregard of the Fourth Amendment. Although no one defends the proposition that police officers should be free to disregard the Constitution in pursuit of a conviction, it is argued that the Exclusionary Rule punishes good-faith mistakes made by honest, conscientious officers. Such mistakes include writing the wrong address on an affidavit or warrant or writing an incomplete description of premises to be searched.

In 1980, a federal appellate court recognized an exception to the Exclusionary Rule. In *United States* v. *Williams* (622 F.2d 830 [5th Cir. 1980]), the court held that

> . . . evidence is not to be suppressed under the exclusionary rule where it is discovered by officers in the course of actions that are taken in good faith and in the reasonable, though mistaken, belief that they are authorized. We do so because the exclusionary rule exists to deter wilful or flagrant actions by police, not reasonable, good-faith ones.

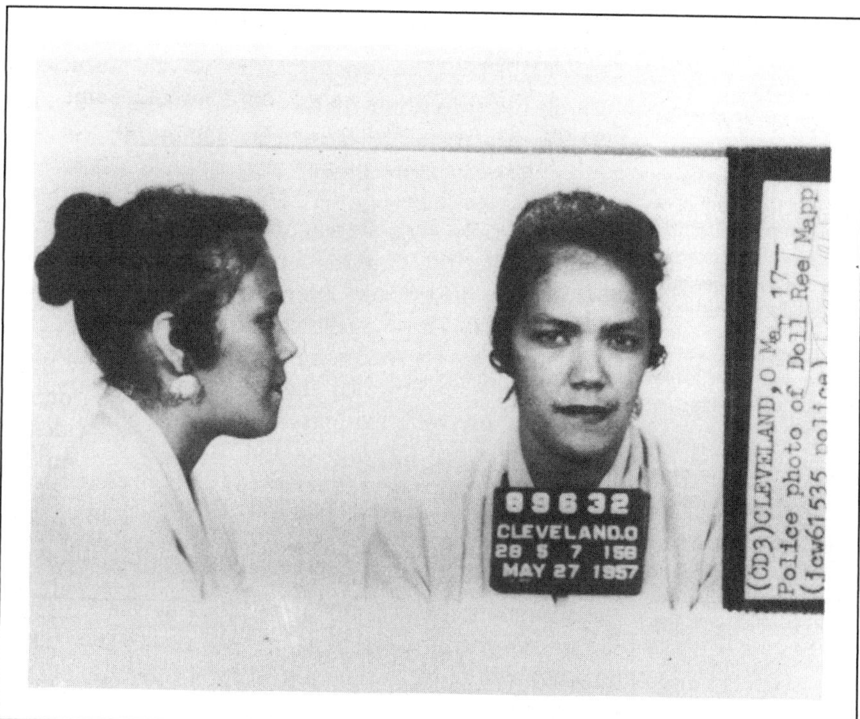

FIGURE 2.6
Mugshot photo of Doll Ree Mapp.
Wide World Photos.

> Where the reason for the rule ceases, its application must cease also (p. 840).

In another crucial case, *United States* v. *Leon* (52 U.S.L.W. 5155 [1984]), the Court ruled that evidence seized by police on the basis of a search warrant issued by a detached and neutral magistrate *can* be used in court even though the judge who issued the warrant may have relied on evidence that was insufficient to establish probable cause. In *Leon,* the Court articulated, again, the "good faith exception" to the exclusionary rule by insisting that evidence obtained on a less-than-adequate search warrant still is admissible in court if the police officer acted in good faith in obtaining court approval of the search. However, the Court warned that if the officer deliberately misleads the judge or uses a warrant that the police know is deficient, then the Exclusionary Rule can still be enforced.

Civil libertarians believe that good faith exceptions to the Exclusionary Rule will result in wholesale abuses by the police. An opposing view is offered by a group called Americans for Effective Law Enforcement (AELE):

> Visions of police harrassment of innocent persons in their homes at 3:00 A.M., however dramatic, are not in issue. The "real" issue is the good faith mistake of a professionally trained officer, or an unnoticed minor error, or the retroactive effect of an overturned court precedent, or even a 3-to-2 decision that a particular law or procedure is "unconstitutional." Defense attorneys, who sometimes constitute the largest group of state legislators, have a vested interest in perpetuating the status quo.
>
> The real goal of criminal justice should be the encouragement of professional law enforcement and to obtain convictions of the guilty. A search for technicalities does not further that end. The good faith exception, however, encourages police professionalism and still punishes intentional misconduct or an indifferent attitude to the rights of society. Good faith legislation is the modification of a rigid rule that in no way affects its principal purpose (1982, p. 3).

The AELE believes that most problems raised by opponents of the good faith exception can be resolved by statute. The organization has proposed a model statute in that regard, maintaining that the courts should be given as much direction and as little discretion as possible.

AELE MODEL STATE STATUTE

Adopted by *Americans for Effective Law Enforcement, Inc.*, 14 July 1982.

Exclusionary Rule Limitations: Admissibility of evidence obtained as a result of an unlawful search or seizure.

A. If a party in a proceeding, whether civil or criminal, seeks to exclude evidence from the trier of fact because of the conduct of a peace officer in obtaining the evidence, the proponent of the evidence may urge that the peace officer's conduct was taken in a reasonable, good faith belief that the conduct was proper and that the evidence discovered should not be kept from the trier of fact if otherwise admissible.

B. No court shall suppress evidence which is otherwise admissible in a civil or criminal proceeding if the evidence was seized in good faith or as a result of a technical violation.

C. "Evidence" means contraband, instrumentalities or fruits of a crime, or any other evidence which tends to prove a fact in issue.

D. "Good faith" means whenever a peace officer obtains evidence:
   1. Pursuant to a search warrant obtained from a neutral and detached magistrate, which warrant is free from obvious defects other than non-deliberate errors in preparation and the officer reasonably believed the warrant to be valid; or
   2. Pursuant to a warrantless search, when:
      a. The officer reasonably believed he possessed probable cause to make the search, and
      b. The officer, possessed at least a reasonable suspicion that the person or premises searched, possessed or contained items of an evidentiary nature, and
      c. The officer reasonably believed there were circumstances excusing the procurement of a search warrant; or
   3. Pursuant to a search resulting from an arrest, when:
      a. The officer reasonably believed he possessed probable cause ot make the arrest, and
      b. The officer reasonably believed there were circumstances excusing the procurement of an arrest warrant, or
      c. The officer procured or executed an invalid arrest warrant he reasonably believed to be valid; or
   4. Pursuant to a statute, local ordinance, judicial precedent or court rule which is later declared unconstitutional or otherwise invalidated; and
   5. The officer has completed a law enforcement academy or other approved prerequisite curriculum and any mandatory subsequent training or instruction in Constitutional law and criminal procedure, where required by the [State Peace Officers' Standards and Training Commission].

E. This section shall not adversely affect the rights of any plaintiff to seek special damages against a peace officer or a governmental entity, provided that the trier of fact in such civil action determines that the officer or entity conducted an unlawful search or seizure.

F. [Appropriate savings and severability clause].

FIGURE 2.7
AELE Model State Statute.

The Fifth Amendment: Self-Incrimination

Among the provisions of the Fifth Amendment is the right of protection against self-incrimination: "No person . . . shall be compelled in any criminal case to be a witness against himself . . . ." This right goes to the very heart of the adversary system of criminal justice, because it implies that the state must prove the guilt of the accused. It has its greatest relevance in the matter of interrogation and how confessions are elicited from suspects. In *Brown* v. *Mississippi* (297 U.S. 278 [1936]), the Supreme Court ruled that confessions secured by physical abuse were inadmissible in state courts. In the cases of *Escobedo* v. *Illinois* and *Miranda* v. *Arizona,* the Court added that to secure the validity of confessions suspects must be notified of their rights against self-incrimination and to representation by counsel during an interrogation.

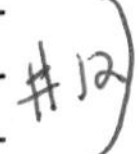

Escobedo's conviction was reversed by the Supreme Court on the ground that he was denied his Sixth Amendment right to have his attorney present during the interrogation. While Danny Escobedo was being interviewed for a second time at a Chicago police station, his attorney arrived. The police would not permit him to see his client. Escobedo's attorney and Escobedo repeatedly requested to see each other, but both were continuously denied the privilege. Escobedo was told he could not consult with his attorney until the police had finished the questioning. During the interrogation, Escobedo made a statement that later would be construed as a voluntary confession of a crime.

In March 1963, Ernesto Miranda was arrested in Arizona for kidnapping and rape. After being identified by the victim and questioned by police for several hours, Miranda signed a confession that included a statement that his confession was made voluntarily. Over the objections of his attorney, the confession was admitted into evidence and Miranda was found guilty. The Supreme Court of Arizona affirmed the conviction and held that Miranda's constitutional rights had not been violated in obtaining the conviction; the court said its decision was in accordance with the earlier *Escobedo* ruling because Miranda had not specifically requested counsel. The U.S. Supreme Court, in reversing the Arizona decision, attempted to clarify its intent in the *Escobedo* case by spelling out specific guidelines to be followed by police before interrogating persons in custody and using their statements as evidence. The guidelines require that after

FIGURE 2.8
Danny Escobedo walks from the courthouse with his wife. Wide World Photos.

a suspect is taken into custody for an offense and prior to any questioning by law enforcement officers, the suspect must be advised of certain rights if there is intent to use his or her statements in court. These guidelines, as they have been incorporated into the "Miranda warning," have become familiar to many Americans by their frequent reiteration on police shows on television. A copy of the warning, reproduced from a card carried by urban law enforcement officers, is shown in Figure 2.10.

The Miranda story had a violent ending. On the night of Saturday, 13 January 1976, Miranda became involved in a fight over a card game in a skid row bar in Phoenix, Arizona. He was stabbed twice by one of the men he had beaten—an illegal alien from Mexico named Fernando Zamora Rodriguez—and was dead on arrival at the hospital. One assumes that the police officer who arrested Rodriguez remembered to read him his Miranda rights!

The Burger/Rehnquist Courts diluted some of the significance from these decisions. In a series of consecutive cases the Court ruled that the violation of the Miranda requirements does not effect the admissibility of a confession. If the confession impeaches the credibility of the defendant when he or she takes the stand in his or her own defense, the confession is admissible (*Harris* v. *New York* [401 U.S. 222 (1971)]. *Miranda* warnings need not be read to grand jury witnesses before they testify (*United States* v. *Mandujano* [425 U.S. 564 (1976)]. In *Nix* v. *Williams* (467 U.S. 431 [1984]), the Court held that confessions that would have been inevitably discovered by the police can be admitted even though they violate the *Miranda* rule.

Attacking the *Miranda* decision even has become political. Attorney General Edmund Meese, voicing the general political view of the Reagan administration, declared that the *Miranda* decision was "wrong." Meese expressed his desire to limit its scope. "The thing is," said Meese, "you don't have many suspects who are innocent of the crime."

The Fifth Amendment also says that no person shall "be subject for the same offense to be twice put in jeopardy of life or limb." This is our constitutional prohibition against **double jeopardy.** The prohibition means essentially that if the defendant is found not guilty at trial, or is placed in jeopardy for a significant portion of the trial, he or she cannot be tried again for the same offense even if overwhelming evidence that proves his or her guilt is discovered afterwards.

Yet in 1985, the Supreme Court ruled in *Heath* v. *Alabama* 474 U.S. 82 (1985) that two states may prosecute a defendant for the same criminal act without violating the Fifth Amendment. Larry Heath was tried in Alabama and in Georgia for hiring two men to kidnap and kill his pregnant wife. She was kidnapped from their home in Alabama and later shot to death in Georgia. At the time, Georgia did not have the death penalty. In order to avoid possible execution, Heath decided to plead guilty in Georgia. However, to his surprise, he was subsequently tried and convicted of the exact same charges in Alabama and sentenced to death. Heath argued that the second conviction violated his constitutional right against double jeopardy. However, the Burger Court voted seven to two in upholding the Alabama conviction. The Court stated that each state is a separate sovereign and that the defendant committed separate offenses against the law in each state. Hence Heath's two

FIGURE 2.9
Ernesto Miranda (right) with his attorney, John Flynn. The U.S. Supreme Court's reversal of Miranda's conviction established guidelines for police to follow in the interrogation of suspects. United Press International.

convictions were ruled an exception to the double jeopardy clause.

The Sixth Amendment: Right to Counsel

No prison is without its share of "jailhouse lawyers," men and women who have become familiar with the law from first-hand experience. In the days when the right to an attorney was not available in court, much less behind the jailhouse walls, these jailhouse lawyers helped put cases together for appellate review. With time on their hands and great personal interest in their cases, these men and women paved the way for the prisoners of today. Perhaps the most famous appeal was made by Clarence Earl Gideon. An indigent prisoner in Florida

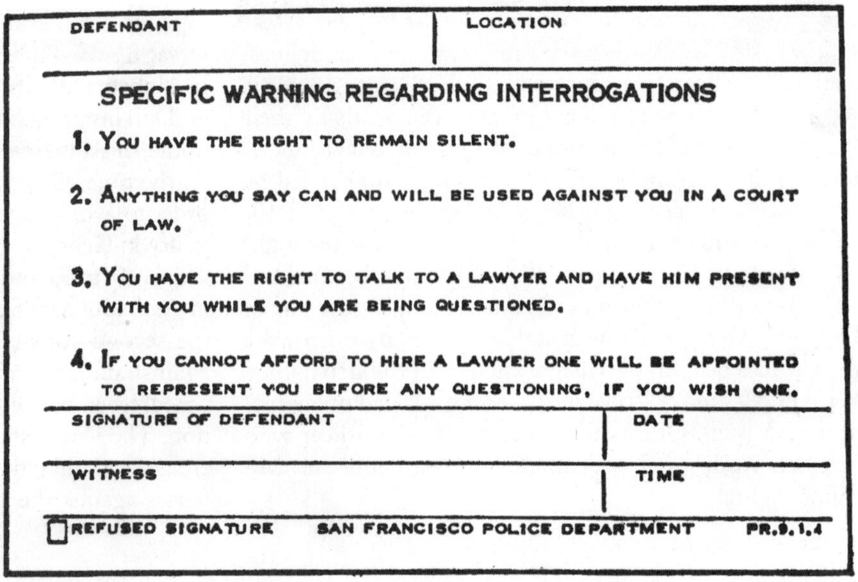

FIGURE 2.10
Card listing Miranda warnings given to arrested individuals. United Press International.

DEFENDANT | LOCATION

SPECIFIC WARNING REGARDING INTERROGATIONS

1. YOU HAVE THE RIGHT TO REMAIN SILENT.
2. ANYTHING YOU SAY CAN AND WILL BE USED AGAINST YOU IN A COURT OF LAW.
3. YOU HAVE THE RIGHT TO TALK TO A LAWYER AND HAVE HIM PRESENT WITH YOU WHILE YOU ARE BEING QUESTIONED.
4. IF YOU CANNOT AFFORD TO HIRE A LAWYER ONE WILL BE APPOINTED TO REPRESENT YOU BEFORE ANY QUESTIONING, IF YOU WISH ONE.

SIGNATURE OF DEFENDANT | DATE

WITNESS | TIME

☐ REFUSED SIGNATURE SAN FRANCISCO POLICE DEPARTMENT PR.9.1.4

FIGURE 2.11
Police photo of Fernando Zamora Rodriguez after his arrest for the slaying of Ernesto Miranda in 1976. United Press International.

State Prison at Raiford, Gideon was described by journalist Anthony Lewis in *Gideon's Trumpet* (1966, pp. 5–6):

> Gideon was a fifty-one-year-old white man who had been in and out of prisons much of his life. He had served time for four previous felonies, and he bore the physical marks of a destitute life: a wrinkled, prematurely aged face, a voice and hands that trembled, a frail body, white hair. He had never been a professional criminal or a man of violence; he just could not seem to settle down to work, and so he had made his way by gambling and occasional thefts. Those who had known him, even the men who had arrested him and those who were now his jailers, considered Gideon a perfectly harmless human being, rather likeable, but one tossed aside by life. Anyone meeting him for the first time would be likely to regard him as the most wretched of men.
>
> And yet a flame still burned in Clarence Earl Gideon. He had not given up caring about life or freedom; he had not lost his sense of injustice. Right now he had a passionate—some thought almost irrational—feeling of having been wronged by the State of Florida, and he had the determination to try to do something about it.

Gideon submitted his petition to the U.S. Supreme Court as a pauper under a special federal statute. The statute makes great allowances for those unable to afford the expense of counsel and administrative technicalities. For example, it is usually necessary to submit *forty* typewritten copies of a petition; Gideon submitted *one,* handwritten in pencil on lined yellow sheets. Although he did not have counsel in 1961 when he stood trial for breaking into a pool hall, he *did* have counsel before the Supreme Court when his petition was heard in the 1962–63 term. Abe Fortas, one of Washington's most successful lawyers (and later a Supreme Court justice) was appointed as Gideon's attorney for the case. In its decision in *Gideon* v. *Wainwright* (372 U.S. 335) the Court stated:

> In deciding as it did—that "appointment of counsel is not a fundamental right, essential to a fair

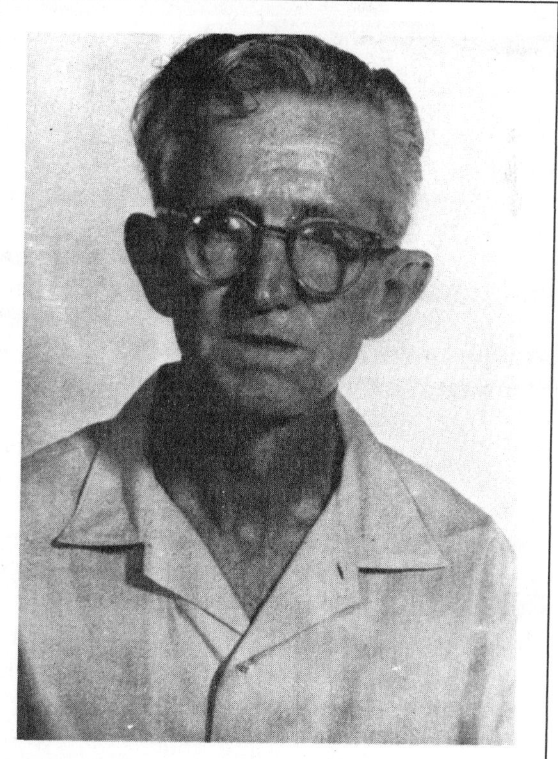

FIGURE 2.12
Clarence Earl Gideon, who argued that his constitutional right to a fair trial was denied when he was refused an attorney. Wide World Photos.

> trial"—the Court in *Betts* made an abrupt break with its own well-considered precedents. In returning to these old precedents, sounder we believe than the new, we but restore constitutional principles established to achieve a fair system of justice. Not only these precedents but also reason and reflection require us to recognize that in our adversary system to hire a lawyer, cannot be assured a fair trial unless counsel is provided for him (p. 341).

As if to emphasize the Supreme Court's finding, Gideon was acquitted when he was finally retried with counsel. The right to counsel has since moved rapidly in both directions along the continuum of criminal justice. In decision after decision, the Supreme Court has ruled in favor of the right to counsel at a "critical stage" in the defendant's case. This "critical stage" has been extended from initial police contact, to the preparation of briefs for appeal, to assistance in preparing transcripts of a trial. It also included pre-trial custody interrogations, preliminary hearings, guilty pleas and the sentencing portion of the trial. The right to counsel has moved into the prison as well as the courtroom. A milestone case decided in the 1967–68 term, *Mempa* v. *Rhay* (389 U.S. 128 [1967]), extended a limited right to counsel to state probation revocation hearings; these hearings were previously considered as essentially administrative. The Court held in *Mempa* that the application of a deferred sentence was a "critical point" in the proceeding.

Although the *Gideon* case extended the right to counsel to every defendant charged with a felony, the right to counsel was extended further in 1972. Even a person charged with a misdemeanor must be afforded counsel which results in imprisonment *Argersinger* v. *Hamlin* (407 U.S. 25 [1972]; *Scott v. Illinois* 440 U.S. 367 [1979]). The effect of this case was to ensure that defendants who are poor at least have some of the same protections in criminal courts as defendants who have money.

The Sixth Amendment also guarantees that in all criminal prosecutions the accused has the right to a "speedy and public trial, by an impartial jury." The Supreme Court has held that the right to a jury trial applies to crimes in which the defendant is subject to a possible term of imprisonment of six months or more. Although the federal government requires that every defendant have a twelve-member jury, in *Williams* v. *Florida* (399 U.S. 78 [1970]), the Supreme Court declared the use of the six-member jury is constitutional in all but capital cases. However, the Court ruled that a five-member jury, which was used in the trial of a defendant named Ballew in Georgia in 1978, violates the Sixth Amendment (*Ballew* v. *Georgia* [435 U.S. 223 (1978)]).

The Sixth Amendment also provides that a defendant in a criminal trial has the right "to be informed of the nature and the cause of the accusation; to be confronted with the witnesses against him"; and "to have a compulsory process for obtaining witnesses in his favor." These rights essentially ensure that the defendant's attorney will have the right to cross-examine the key witnesses used by the prosecution, and will be allowed to present the defendant's own witnesses at trial.

The Eighth Amendment

The Eighth Amendment states that "Excessive bail will not be required nor excessive fines imposed, nor cruel and unusual punishment inflicted." The right to bail is one of the rights in the Bill of Rights that the Supreme Court has not declared to be a "due process right." Hence, defendants prosecuted in state courts do not have a constitutional right to bail. However, every state has some type of law that ensures state defendants the right to bail in certain cases. In 1987, the Supreme Court ruled that an accused in federal court may be denied bail if the prosecution demonstrates by clear and convincing evidence that his or her release on bail would cause a danger to the public. Critics argue that this decision delivers a "crushing blow" to the presumption of innocence enjoyed in the United States for two centuries (*United States* v. *Salerno* [107 S.Ct. 2095 (1987)]).

The cruel or unusual punishment clause in the Eighth Amendment has been used throughout the years to prevent the use of torture and excessive physical punishment on prisoners, which was common in early European history. In addition, at one time in American history, this clause was interpreted to overturn the legality of the death penalty (in 1972) only to have the courts restore it later. Many laws affecting the regulation of prisons, including the elimination of isolation and segregation, have been enacted under this provision. Indeed, most prisoners' rights, including the right to moderate discipline and to express their grievances, have come from litigation based on this clause.

The Rule of Law

In the past several decades, the U.S. Supreme Court has made more changes in criminal procedure than were made in nearly 200 years. Critics of the Court object that the changes have resulted in the "coddling of criminals" and that they reflect a permissiveness detrimental to the rights of law-abiding citizens. However, the Supreme Court has not created any new rights for criminals; rather, it has *moved toward equalizing the rights of rich and poor suspects*. The major consequence of the due process revolution has been to extend to the poor, the illiterate, and the ignorant some of those rights that have long been enjoyed by middle-class or upper-class defendants. But the revolution remains unfinished. Although the Court may have equalized rights on paper, many barriers still effectively bar the poor from the full benefits of due process and equal protection under the law.

SUMMARY

To understand the problem of crime, one must examine the broader issue of deviance from societal norms. Societies attempt to contain deviance through controls (sanctions) that range from informal disapproval to the use of the police powers of the state. Antisocial attitudes, eccentricities, and various kinds of atypical behavior may all be studied for their potential value in helping to illuminate the factors involved in criminal conduct. All criminal acts are deviant, but not all deviant acts are criminal. Thus, only those deviant acts that legislative bodies have defined by statute as criminal may legitimately be considered crimes.

American criminal law as analyzed in this chapter combines the features of two systems: common law, which develops continually based on interpretation of precedents, and civil law, based on specific codes that are written and legislated. These systems are the basis of *substantive criminal law,* laws that define the necessary elements of crimes and specify the penalties for commission.

Depending on the punishment, offenses are classified as felonies or misdemeanors. Felonies are punishable by death or imprisonment. Misdemeanors are punishable by fines or relatively brief periods of incarceration.

Procedural criminal law focuses on how the criminal law is enforced, how evidence is collected, and what rights are guaranteed to persons accused of crimes. Contrary to popular belief, the Bill of Rights of the U.S. Constitution has not always provided such guarantees to people tried in state criminal courts. Not until the "due process revolution" of the 1960s were such rights made applicable to the states by means of the Fourteenth Amendment. Some people believe that the due process revolution made it possible for criminals to escape punishment; others maintain that the revolution increased the fairness of the criminal justice process by extending to the poor rights long enjoyed by the well-to-do.

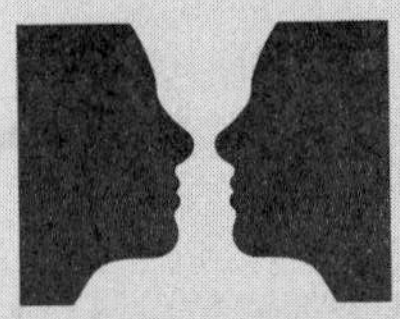

ISSUE PAPER

SHOULD CONSENSUAL CRIMES BE DECRIMINALIZED?

To demonstrate the futility of attempting to "legislate morality," consensual crimes are often compared with more conventional offenses against person and property. If by "legislating morality" we mean the enactment of statutes that provide legal sanctions for deviations from normative standards of conduct, then legislating morality is precisely what the criminal law seeks to do. Distinctions between legal order and moral order appear to rest primarily on the means by which conformity to normative standards is sought, rather than upon the standards themselves. Both law and morality reflect attempts to influence behavior in a desired direction.

In offenses such as robbery and rape, there is little or no conflict between morality and law, because these actions are proscribed both by moral codes and by legal statutes. But behaviors under the heading of consensual crime are sometimes proscribed by one set of rules and not the other. As a Catholic bishop visiting Boston reputedly told a Protestant minister, "Gambling in moderation is not a sin." "That may be true," the minister replied, "but in this state it is a crime."

Although few people seriously question the need for legal sanctions against offenses such as robbery and rape, many people do have serious reservations about sanctions against gambling, prostitution, homosexual behavior involving consenting adults, and abortion. In the latter case, it is argued that criminal sanctions for such behaviors constitute an unwarranted intrusion upon privacy and an indefensible extension of governmental authority into matters more properly dealt with by *informal* social sanctions. The American Law Institute, in its *Model Penal Code: Proposed Official Draft* (1964), recommended that most consensual crimes be abolished. The earlier Wolfenden Report (Committee on Homosexual Offenses and Prostitution 1964), which addressed the specific issue of consensual adult homosexuality, stated that society should not seek to equate "the sphere of crime with that of sin" and that "there must remain a realm of private morality and immorality which is, in brief and crude terms, not the law's business" (p. 24).

An intense and continuing controversy surrounds the conceptualization and legal status of "crimes against public order," societal reactions to such offenses, and the difficulties these crimes create for law enforcement, the courts, and corrections. The criminal justice system is often in the unenviable position of having to carry out conflicting policies and enforce statutes that are vague, overlapping, or even contradictory. At the same time, criminal justice personnel are subject to heated criticism for their inability to perform tasks that verge on the impossible.

Although opposition to consensual-crime laws is manifold and varied, objections concentrate on the following issues (Schur and Bedau 1974, p. 9):

1. Consensual criminal laws are essentially nonenforceable.
2. Apart from their failure to achieve desired ends, such laws appear to increase or worsen social ills rather than reduce them.
3. Attempts at enforcement preempt a great deal of the time, energy, and money available for other law enforcement activity.
4. Police are forced to adopt legally and morally questionable techniques in the investigation of the offenses.
5. The efforts at banning such transactions may actually encourage the growth of an illicit traffic and raise the price of the goods and services in question.
6. Some of these laws may produce *secondary crime* (i.e., other than the proscribed behavior itself) and all of them create new "criminals," many of whom are otherwise law-abiding individuals.
7. The administration of consensual crime laws is arbitrary and discriminatory; certain segments of society feel their impact a great deal more than others.
8. The largely discretionary nature of the enforcement of these laws—along with the above features of consensual-crime laws—invites corruption and exploitation and may throw the entire criminal justice system into disrepute.

Finally, there is the issue of the disposition of consensual criminals. It is difficult to fashion a compelling argument to support punishment for the drug addict; detoxification seems a more promising approach to the public inebriate than a "revolving door" of arrest-sentencing-incarceration-rearrest. The punitive response has had little success in dealing with gambling and prostitution, and the treatment approach has not yielded much gain except for a minority of self-professed compulsive gamblers or women for whom prostitution is symptomatic of serious emotional maladjustment. And even if we were able, through techniques currently available, to alter the behavior of individuals who voluntarily practice homosexual lifestyles, there are no grounds in law or morality to proceed with behavior modification without the consent of the individual. Thus, the issue of disposition may provide the most cogent and convincing arguments for the decriminalization of consensual crimes.

Winston Churchill, in volume 3 of *History of the English-Speaking Peoples* (1959), noted that the English Puritans during the Protectorate of Oliver Cromwell, like their American counterparts in Massachusetts, devoted themselves to the suppression of vice.

> All betting and gambling were forbidden. In 1650 a law was passed making adultery punishable by death, a ferocity mitigated by the fact that nothing would convince the juries of the guilt of the accused. Drunkenness was attacked vigorously and great numbers of alehouses were closed. Swearing was an offense punishable by a graduated scale of fines. Christmas excited the most fervent hostility of these fanatics. Parliament was deeply concerned at the liberty which it gave to carnal and sensual delights. Soldiers were sent around London on Christmas Day before dinnertime to enter private houses without warrants and seize meat cooking in all kitchens and ovens. Everywhere was prying and spying.
>
> All over the country the Maypoles were hewn down, lest old village dances around them should lead to immorality or at least to levity. Walking abroad on the Sabbath, except to go to church, was punished, and a man was fined for going to a neighbouring parish to hear a sermon. It was even proposed to forbid people sitting at their doors or leaning against them on the Sabbath. Bearbaiting and cockfighting were effectually ended by shooting the bears and wringing the necks of the cocks. All forms of athletic sports, horse racing, and wrestling were banned, and sumptuary laws sought to remove all ornaments from male and female attire (pp. 240–41).

The stifling effects of these innumerable petty tyrannies extended into every corner of life and made Cromwell's Protectorate despised and hated as no English government has ever been hated, before or since.

Despite its addiction to Old Testament rhetoric, Cromwell's government was a military dictatorship, with most of the characteristics of similar regimes in the twentieth century. In a dictatorship, deviance from official norms is harshly, even ruthlessly, suppressed. Dissenters may be sent to labor camps or mental hospitals. Conflicts between law and morality exhibit few of the properties associated with consensual crime in our own society. For example, it is difficult to imagine the existence of an erotic-minorities movement or C.O.Y.O.T.E. in Soviet Russia. (C.O.Y.O.T.E.—Cast Off Your Old Tired Ethics—is a group favoring legal prostitution.)

In a relatively open, pluralistic society composed of groups with divergent traditions, customs, beliefs, and values, conflicts between the law and the moral views of some groups are inevitable. And although agreement on some issues is possible among groups with diverse moral and ethical convictions, certain key issues allow little or no room for compromise. It is on issues of this kind that groups are likely to seek the support of legal sanctions as a backstop for morality.

Legal scholar Herbert L. Packer has identified six conditions that ought to be present if criminal sanctions are to be imposed against conduct that engenders societal disapproval (1968, p. 296):

1. The conduct must be regarded by most people as socially threatening and must not be condoned by any significant segment of society.
2. Subjecting the conduct to criminal penalties must not be inconsistent with the goals of punishment.
3. Suppressing the conduct will not inhibit other socially desirable behavior.
4. The conduct can be dealt with through evenhanded and nondiscriminatory law enforcement.
5. Controlling the conduct through the criminal

process will not expose the process to severe qualitative or quantitative strain.

6. No reasonable alternatives to the criminal sanction exist for dealing with the conduct.

We might ask whether any or all of these conditions are met by the behaviors now designated as consensual crimes.

The most reasonable conclusion about consensual crime seems to be that laws that cannot be enforced should not be enacted; the corollary to this proposition is that behavior subject to nonenforceable laws should not be legally proscribed. This does not necessarily imply, however, that certain behaviors that fit Packer's specifications should, or can be, exempt from adverse public opinion or other types of social disapproval. As Geis reminds us, "To the extent that a society thrusts from its core nonconformists and then takes harsh measures to repress them, it will create a resistant force in its midst" (1972, p. 260). As an alternative, he suggests that "the most efficacious method of dealing with deviancy is to ignore, to the furthest point of our tolerance, those items which we find offensive" (p. 261). This recommendation is made in the belief that an unwillingness to isolate the deviant individual allows an opportunity for the operation of those societal values that may renew the deviant individual's "stake in conformity."

■ DISCUSSION AND REVIEW

1. Is *deviant* behavior more appropriate as an object of study by criminal justice professionals than the more specific study of criminal and delinquent behavior? Explain your answer.
2. How do we distinguish between *prescription* and *proscription* as forms of social sanction?
3. Compare the value consensus and value conflict models of criminal law.
4. Define and discuss *substantive criminal law* and *criminal procedure*. What are the major sources of criminal law?
5. What four characteristics of criminal law distinguish it from other rules governing human conduct?
6. What are *felonies* and how do they differ from *misdemeanors?* Why is the distinction important in the administration of justice?
7. How do crimes differ from *torts?*
8. What are the provisions of the Fourteenth Amendment that contributed so significantly to the "due process revolution"?
9. How did the Burger/Rehnquist Courts retreat somewhat from due process revolution of the Warren Court?
10. What is the Exclusionary Rule? What is considered a "good faith exception" to the Exclusionary Rule?
11. What was the significance of the U.S. Supreme Court's decision in *Gideon v. Wainwright?*
12. Explain the nature and scope of the Fifth Amendment protections against self-incrimination and double jeopardy.

GLOSSARY

Actus reus The conduct that constitutes a specific crime.

Civil law A set of rules that determines private rights and liabilities.

Crime An act or omission that is prohibited by law for the protection of the public, the violation of which is prosecuted by the state in its own name and is punishable by incarceration.

Common law The body of legal fact and theory that developed in England over a period of centuries and became uniform throughout the country as judges followed precedents (previous court decisions) in handling new, but similar, cases. Distinguished from code law, which seeks to lay down legal principles in the form of statutes.

Double jeopardy When a defendant is found not guilty at trial or is placed in jeopardy for a significant portion of the trial, he or she cannot be tried again for the same offense.

Lex talionis (talion law) The "law of equivalent retaliation," which asserts that an injured party if entitled to "an eye for an eye," but no more than an eye. The aggrieved party is entitled to appropriate retaliation in kind or measure.

Mala in se Latin for "evil in itself." Refers to crimes that are considered intrinsically wrong, regardless of existing legal sanctions (e.g., murder, rape, robbery).

Mala prohibita Refers to criminal acts that are wrong because they are prohibited by law, (i.e., declared wrong by legislative action, e.g., traffic violations, sale of liquor on Sunday).

Mens rea The "guilty mind" or criminal intent required for an accused person to be held responsible for criminal actions; the state of mind at the time a crime occurs.

Search Any governmental intrusion into a person's reasonable expectation of privacy.

Stare decisis Latin for "let the decision stand." Means that court decisions on points of law are binding on future cases that are substantially the same (i.e., where the totality of circumstances does not vary).

Strict-liability crimes Offenses such as statutory rape and bigamy that require no proof of a *mens rea* for conviction.

Substantive due process Fifth and Fourteenth Amendments rights not to be punished by unreasonably vague or arbitrary laws.

REFERENCES

American Law Institute, *Model Penal Code: Proposed Official Draft*. Philadelphia: American Law Institute, 1964.

Americans for Effective Law Enforcement. *Impact*. (July 1982): 1–4.

Chambliss, W. J. "Elites and the Creation of Criminal Law." *Sociological Readings in the Conflict Perspective*. Edited by W. J. Chambliss. Reading, Mass.: Addison-Wesley, 1973.

Churchill, W. L. S. *A History of the English-Speaking Peoples*. The Age of Revolution, vol. 3. New York: Dodd Mead, 1959.

Cole, G. F. *The American System of Criminal Justice*. Belmont, Calif.: Brooks/Cole, 1982.
Committee on Homosexual Offenses and Prostitution. *The Wolfenden Report*. New York: Lancer Books, 1964.
"Death by Stoning for Sex Crimes." *Newsweek*. 14 July 1980, p. 40.
Durant, W. *Our Oriental Heritage*. New York: Simon and Schuster, 1950.
Eldefonso, E.,and Coffey, A. R. *Criminal Law: History, Philosophy, and Enforcement*. New York: Harper and Row, 1981.
Friedman, L. M. *A History of American Law*. New York: Simon and Schuster, 1973.
Geis, G. *Not the Law's Business*. Washington, D.C.: U.S. Government Printing Office, 1972.
Hall, J. *General Principles of Criminal Law*. Indianapolis, Ind.: Bobbs-Merrill, 1947.
Kamisar, Y. "The Warren Court (Was It Really So Defense-Minded?), The Burger Court (Is It Really So Prosecution-Oriented?) and the Policy Investigation Practices." *The Burger Court*. Edited by Vincent Blasi. New Haven, Conn.: Yale University Press, 1983.
Kerper, H. B. *Introduction to the Criminal Justice System*. St. Paul: West Publishing, 1972.
LaFave, W. R., and Scott, A. W. *Criminal Law*. St. Paul: West Publishing, 1972.
Lewis, A. *Gideon's Trumpet*. New York: Random House, 1966.
Lewis, P. and Peoples, K. *The Supreme Court and the Criminal Process—Cases and Comments*. Philadelphia: W. B. Saunders, 1978.
Makielski, S. J. *Pressure Politics in America*. Lanham, Md.: University Press of America, 1980.
Packer, H. *The Limits of the Criminal Sanction*. Palo Alto, Calif.: Stanford University Press, 1968.
Perkins, R. M. *Criminal Law*. Mineoloa, N.Y.: Foundation Press, 1969.
Quinncy, R. *Critique of Legal Order: Crime Control in Capitalist Society*. Boston: Little, Brown, 1974.
"Q'sas—The Law of Punishment." *Tampa Tribune*. 12 November 1982, p. 11A.
Robin, G. D. *Introduction to the Criminal Justice System*. New York: Harper and Row, 1980.
Roby, P. A. "Politics and Criminal Law: Revision of the New York State Penal Law on Prostitution." *Social Problems* 17 1969): 83–109.
Schafer, S. *Theories in Criminology; Past and Present Philosophies of the Crime Problem*. New York: Random House, 1969.
Schur, E. M. *Labeling Deviant Behavior: Its Sociological Implications*. New York: Harper and Row, 1971.
Schur, E. M., and Bedau, H. A. *Victimless Crime: Two Sides of a Controversy*. Englewood Cliffs, N.J.: Prentice-Hall, 1974.
Sutherland, E. H., and Cressey, D. R. *Criminology*. Philadelphia: Lippincott, 1978.
Swanson, C. R. and Territo, L. *Police Administration: Structures, Processes, and Behavior*. New York: Macmillan, 1983.
Tappan, P. *Crime, Justice, and Correction*. New York: McGraw-Hill, 1966.
Williams, R. M. *American Society*. New York: Alfred A. Knopf, 1970.

■ CASES

Argersinger v. *Hamlin* 407 US. 25, 92 S.Ct. 2006, 32 L.Ed.2d 530 (1972).
Ballew v. *Georgia* 435 U.S. 223, 98 S.Ct. 1029, 55 L.Ed.2d 234 (1978).

Brown v. *Mississippi* 297 U.S. 278, 56 S.Ct. 461, 80 L.Ed. 682 (1936).
Commonwealth v. *Wealensky* 316 Mass. 383, 55 N.E.2d 902 (1944).
Elkins v. *United States* 364 U.S. 206, 80 S.Ct. 1437, 4 L.Ed.2d 1669 (1960).
Escobedo v. *Illinois* 375 U.S. 902, 84 S.Ct. 203, 11 L.Ed.2d 143 (1964).
Gideon v. *Wainwright* 372 U.S. 335, 83 S.Ct. 792, 9 L.Ed.2d 799 (1963).
Harris v. *New York* 401 U.s. 222, 91 S.Ct. 643, 28 L.Ed.2d 1 (1971).
Heath v. *Alabama* 474 U.S. 82, 106 S.Ct. 433, 88 L.Ed.2d 837 (1985).
Hurtado v. *California* 110 U.S. 516, 4 S.Ct. 111, 4 S.Ct. 292, 28 L.Ed. 232 (1884).
Lustig v. *United States* 338 U.S. 74, 69 S.Ct. 1372, 93 L.Ed. 1819 (1949).
Mapp v. *Ohio* 367 U.S. 643, 81 S.Ct. 1684, 6 L.Ed.2d 1081 (1961).
Mempa v. *Rhay* 389 U.S. 128, 88 S.Ct. 254, 19 L.Ed.2d 336 (1967).
Miranda v. *Arizona* 384 U.S. 436, 86 S.Ct. 1602, 16 L.Ed.2d 694 (1966).
Nix v. *Williams* 467 U.S. 431, 104 S.Ct. 2501, 81 L.Ed.2d 377 (1984).
Scott v. *Illinois* 440 U.S. 367, 99 S.Ct. 1158, 59 L.Ed.2d 383 (1979).
United States v. *Leon* 52 U.S.L.W. 5515, 104 S.Ct. 3405, 82 L.Ed.2d 677 (1984).
United States v. *Mandujano* 425 U.S. 564, 96 S.Ct. 1768, 48 L.Ed. 212 (1976).
United States v. *Salerno* ______U.S.______, 107 S.Ct. 2095 (1987).
United States v. *Williams* 622 F.2d 830 (5th Cir. 1980).
Weeks v. *United States* 232 U.S. 383, S.Ct. 341, 58 L.Ed. 652 (1914).
Williams v. *Florida* 399 U.S. 78, 90 S.Ct. 1893 (1970).
Wolf v. *Colorado* 338 U.S. 25, 69 S.Ct. 1359, 93 L.Ed. 1782 (1949).

CHAPTER

3

The Nature and Distribution of Crime

CHAPTER OUTLINE:

The average citizen, by listening to the radio, viewing television, or reading the daily newspaper, is frequently exposed to reports about the community crime rate. Yet few people realize that news reports about the crime rate refer to only eight categories of crime: murder and nonnegligent manslaughter (**criminal homicide**); aggravated assault; forcible rape; robbery; burglary; larceny-theft; motor vehicle theft; and arson. The **crime rate** in an area is defined as the number of these offenses that occur per 100,000 inhabitants.

Crimes reported to the police extend beyond these eight categories, but only these eight are included in the crime rate or crime index reported in the **FBI Uniform Crime Reports.** The solution of crimes involving these eight offenses is an index by which the public and media can evaluate the efficiency of police departments; other indices can be used to evaluate police efficiency, but for better or for worse, this one is used most often by the media in news reports.

This chapter discusses the crime reporting system in the United States, examines each of the eight index crimes, defines and describes the elements of these crimes, and, when applicable, provides case studies of each crime. The accuracy of offenses reported to the FBI by local police is examined, and the problems of underreporting by victims and the manipulation of statistics by police are discussed. We also examine recommendations for changes in the Uniform Crime Reporting Program that address these and other criticisms of the system. Additionally, we compare the National Crime Survey (NCS), conducted by the Bureau of Justice Statistics, with the Uniform Crime Reporting Program. Finally, we will look at what crime does to victims and to society and will discuss the price of crime for victims as individuals and for the nation as a whole.

THE UNIFORM CRIME REPORTING PROGRAM

Using crime statistics contributed by over 16,000 law enforcement agencies across the United States, the Uniform Crime Reporting (UCR) Program provides periodic assessments of crime in the nation as measured by offenses that come to the attention of the law enforcement community. The program's primary goal is to generate reliable criminal statistics for use in law enforcement administration, operation, and management. However, data from the program are also used by other criminal justice professionals, legislators, and scholars who have an interest in the crime problem. In addition, the statistics furnish the general public with an indication of fluctuations in crime levels.

The Committee on Uniform Crime Records of the International Association of Chiefs of Police (IACP) initiated the voluntary national data collection effort in 1930. That same year, Congress appointed the FBI as the national clearinghouse for statistical information on crime. Since then, a large volume of data based on uniform classifications and reporting procedures has been obtained from the nation's law enforcement agencies.

To provide a more complete picture of crime in the United States, the Committee on Uniform Crime Records of the IACP chose to use data on offenses coming to the attention of law enforcement agencies; these data are more readily available than any other reportable

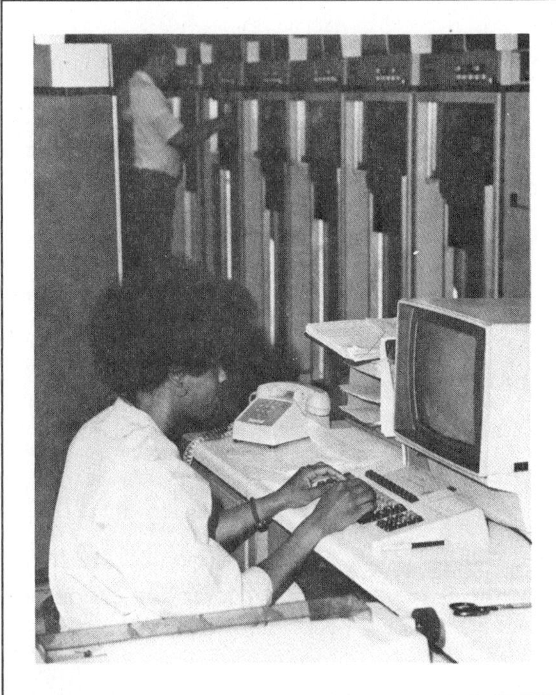

FIGURE 3.1
Uniform Crime Reports data can be retrieved in the form of summary tabulations by the FBI's main computer system. Courtesy *FBI Law Enforcement Bulletin.*

crime information. Seven offenses, because of their seriousness, frequency of occurrence, and likelihood of being reported to police, were initially selected to compute an index for evaluating fluctuations in crime volume. These crimes, known as the crime-index offenses, were murder and nonnegligent manslaughter, forcible rape, robbery, aggravated assault, burglary, larceny-theft, and motor vehicle theft. By congressional mandate, arson was added as the eighth index offense in late 1978.

To provide nationwide uniformity in the reporting of data, standard definitions have been adopted for all offenses. Standardization is needed to eliminate variations in the definitions of offenses in different parts of the country. Without regard for local statutes, reporting agencies are required to submit data in accordance with the UCR definitions. Because punishment for some offenses varies among the state codes, the program does not distinguish between felonies and misdemeanors.

The IACP's Committee on Uniform Crime Records still serves in an advisory capacity to the FBI on the operation of the UCR program. In this connection, the IACP, through surveys of law enforcement records and crime reporting systems, has an active role in the program. In June 1966, the National Sheriffs' Association (NSA) established a Committee on Uniform Crime Reporting to serve in an advisory role to the NSA membership and to the national UCR program. This committee actively encourages sheriffs throughout the country to fully participate in the program. Committees on uniform crime reporting within state law enforcement associations are also active in promoting interest in the UCR program. These committees foster widespread and more intelligent use of uniform crime statistics and lend assistance to the agencies that contribute data.

Contributors to the UCR program compile and submit their data in one of two ways: directly to the FBI or through state UCR programs. Contributors that submit directly to the FBI are provided with continuing guidance and support from the national program. At present, there are forty-one operational state-level UCR programs; these programs have increased the coverage of agencies by instituting mandatory state reporting requirements, by providing more direct and frequent service to participating agencies, and by making information readily available at the state level. Thus, state programs have greatly increased the efficiency of operations at the national level.

When a state develops a UCR program, the FBI ceases to collect data directly from individual law enforcement agencies within that state. Instead, information from within the state is forwarded to the national program by the state collection agency. The state systems are developed to ensure the consistency and comparability of data submitted to the national program and to provide for regular and timely reporting of national crime data. Toward these goals, the following conditions must be met:

1. A state program must conform to the standards, definitions, and information in the FBI Uniform Crime Reports. However, states are not prohibited from collecting data beyond the scope of the national program.
2. The state criminal justice agency must have a proven, effective, and mandatory statewide program with acceptable quality control procedures.
3. Coverage within a state by a state agency must be at least equal to the coverage attained by FBI Uniform Crime Reports.
4. The state agency must have adequate field staff to conduct audits and to assist contributing

agencies in keeping records and following established reporting procedures.

5. The state agency must furnish to the FBI all of the detailed data regularly collected by the FBI in the form of duplicate returns, computer printouts, or magnetic tapes.
6. The state must have the proven ability (tested over time) to supply all the statistical data required to meet the publication deadlines for the FBI Uniform Crime Reports.

If a state agency does not comply with these requirements, the national program may reinstitute direct collection of data from law enforcement agencies within the state (Federal Bureau of Investigation 1986, pp. 1–2).

To fulfill its responsibilities to the UCR program, the FBI edits and reviews incoming reports for completeness and quality, contacts (when necessary) individual contributors within the states (coordinating such contacts with the state agencies), and conducts training programs on state recordkeeping and reporting procedures.

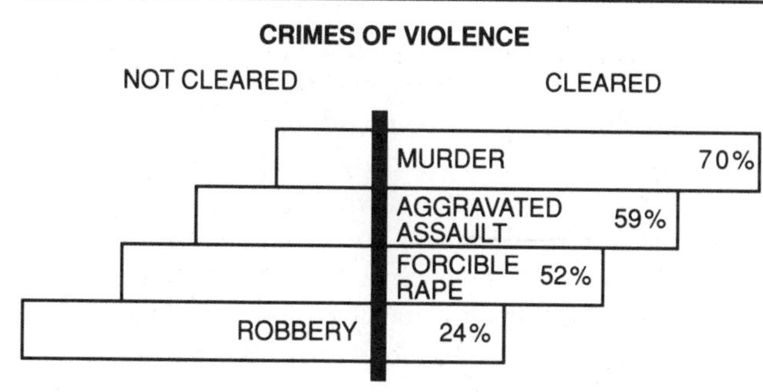

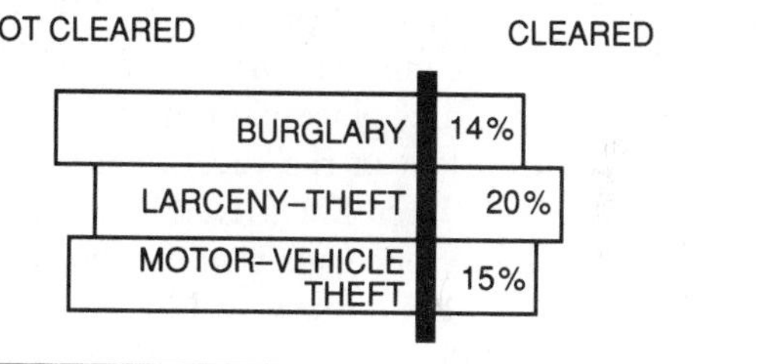

FIGURE 3.2
Crimes cleared by arrest, 1986. Data from Federal Bureau of Investigation, *Crime in the United States, FBI Uniform Crime Reports* (Washington, D.C.: U.S. Government Printing Office, 1986), p. 155.

CRIME TRENDS

The eight index crimes are frequently divided into two categories: violent crimes and crimes against property (Federal Bureau of Investigation 1986, pp. 1–50).[1]

Violent Crimes

The violent crimes among the index crimes are murder and nonnegligent manslaughter, aggravated assault, forcible rape, and robbery.

Murder and Nonnegligent Manslaughter Murder and nonnegligent manslaughter are defined in the UCR program as the willful (nonnegligent) killing of one human being by another. The classification of these offenses, as in all crime-index offenses, is based solely on police investigation—as opposed to determination by a court, medical examiner, coroner's jury, or other judicial body. Not included under this classification are deaths caused by negligence, suicide, or accident; justifiable homicides (the killing of felons by law enforcement officers in the line of duty or by private citizens); and attempted murder or assault with the intent to murder (classified as aggravated assaults).

Murder consistently has the highest solution rate, or **clearance rate,** of the eight index crimes (see Figure 3.2). This high rate often surprises the average citizen, who assumes incorrectly that criminal homicides are seldom solved. Such a misconception is understandable however, considering the media attention given to murders that go unsolved for a long time. One merely has to recall the Boston strangler murders, the Hillside murders in Los Angeles, the murder of black children in Atlanta, or the murder of two Florida State University coeds in the Chi Omega Sorority House in Tallahassee, Florida.

The latter crimes can be accurately called media events, and both the print and the electronic media expend considerable time, money, and effort to assure that the grisly details of the crimes are brought to public attention. However, most criminal homicides are less "newsworthy"; most involve individuals who live together, work together, play together, or socialize together. Such homicides are rarely carefully planned, are frequently spontaneous, and often have witnesses. This poor planning and the ineptness of assailants partially explains the high clearance rate. In addition, criminal homicides of any type are normally investigated more intensively than other index crimes.

Consider the two murder cases involving acquaintances on page 56.

Case 3.1

Bill and Lonnie were next-door neighbors and regularly argued about the parking places in the street in front of their homes. Each man lived in his own single-family home, and each usually parked his car on the city street directly in front of his home when the parking place was vacant. Lonnie usually got home from work earlier than Bill, and if the parking place in front of his own home was taken, he would park in front of Bill's home. Bill's parking place was on the city street, so neither man had a legal right to the spot.

One evening Lonnie returned home from work, found the parking place in front of his home taken, and parked in the vacant spot in front of Bill's home. When Bill arrived home and saw that Lonnie had once again parked in front of his home, he went directly to Lonnie and confronted him. Bill was verbally abusive, profane, and threatened to "beat Lonnie's ass" if he didn't move his car. Lonnie agreed and both men then walked toward the car. When they reached it, Bill punched Lonnie in the face, knocking him to the pavement. He told Lonnie never to park in his spot again. Lonnie got up, got into his car, and drove away. The assault was witnessed by both families, including the children. (Bill was six feet four inches tall and weighed 225 pounds, Lonnie was five feet four inches tall and weighed 140 pounds.)

The following morning as Bill was exiting his home, Lonnie approached him with a razor sharp pocketknife that he had opened but concealed in his pocket. Lonnie told Bill he should not have hit him the evening before, then pulled the knife out of his pocket and cut Bill's throat. Bill fell to the pavement and bled to death. This assault was witnessed by both families, as well as by some neighbors seated on their porches. After the attack, Lonnie fled on foot. He was arrested several hours later in a nearby saloon after police were advised by neighbors that the saloon was his regular hangout.

These cases illustrate that—although tragic—murders involving acquaintances are rarely difficult to solve and almost impossible to prevent.

Case 3.2

Dave and Al, who worked together at a construction site, went to a restaurant near the site to have lunch. After examining the menu, they agreed to order the special of the day, which was actually a meal for two. One of the conditions of the special was that they would have to share one large crock of soup. The men disagreed about the type of soup they wanted, and became involved in a loud and heated argument about the matter. After several minutes, Dave pulled a pistol out of his pocket and shot and killed Al. Dave made no effort to leave the restaurant. The police were called, and Dave surrendered quietly.

An alarming turn of events in the past decade has been the increase of criminal homicides. The ten-year trend showed the 1986 total 8 percent above the 1977 level. The clearance rate for criminal homicides decreased from 84 percent in 1971 to 70 percent in 1986, in part because of an increase in homicides that involve total strangers and are committed during the commission of crimes such as burglaries, robberies, and rape. The latter homicides are infinitely more difficult to solve, and the clearance rate will likely continue to decrease as the rate of this type of crime continues to increase. The following case, although eventually solved, fits into the category of criminal homicides, committed during other crimes.

Case 3.3

Suzanne, 26, a technician at a burn treatment center attended a musical show at a nearby university. On her way home she drove into a grocery store parking lot and mistakenly locked her car with the keys inside. Two young men helpfully unlocked the car, asked for a short lift—then forced her to drive to her apartment where they beat and raped her for several hours. The men who were later arrested after an extensive investigation advised police that they drove 50

Case 3.3 continued

miles to an isolated desert area and hurled Suzanne off a cliff. They heard her moaning and climbed down to her side. She pleaded with them to leave her alone because she said "I'm dying anyway." The response was swift. "Damn right you are" one of the men said and picked up a large rock and crushed her head to still her sounds (Magnuson 1981, p. 19).

Aggravated Assault Aggravated assault is an unlawful attack by one person upon another for the purpose of inflicting severe or aggravated bodily injury. The crime usually involves a weapon or some means likely to produce death or great bodily harm. Attempted assaults are included in this category; if a gun, knife, or other weapon is used that could and probably would result in serious personal injury if the crime was successfully completed, it is not necessary that an injury result.

In view of the alarming increase in criminal homicides in this country, it is not surprising to find a similar increase in the occurrence of aggravated assault. There were 177 assault victims per 100,000 inhabitants in 1971, 346 assault victims per 100,000 inhabitants in 1986. Many aggravated assaults stop short of criminal homicide simply because an assailant's bullet or knife misses its target or does not strike a vital organ.

Although many victims and assailants in aggravated assaults are involved in close relationships, just as victims and assailants in criminal homicides are, there is considerable difference in the clearance rates for these crimes—70 percent for criminal homicide and 59 percent for aggravated assault in 1986. The low clearance rate for aggravated assault can be attributed in part to less intensive police investigation of such crimes, especially when injuries are not serious. Also, it is not uncommon for assault victims to be uncooperative with the police—for one of the following reasons:

1. The assailant is a husband or boyfriend who is the breadwinner of the family, or is a wife or girlfriend who cares for the disputant's children. An arrest would undo an arrangement that benefits the victim.
2. The victim considers the offense to be a personal matter and wants to settle the dispute privately.
3. The victim believes that he or she got what he or she deserved, and therefore does not want the assailant to be punished.
4. The victim fears revenge if charges are pursued.

An uncooperative victim creates both legal and investigative difficulties. All states consider felony assaults to be crimes against the people of the state; thus, the

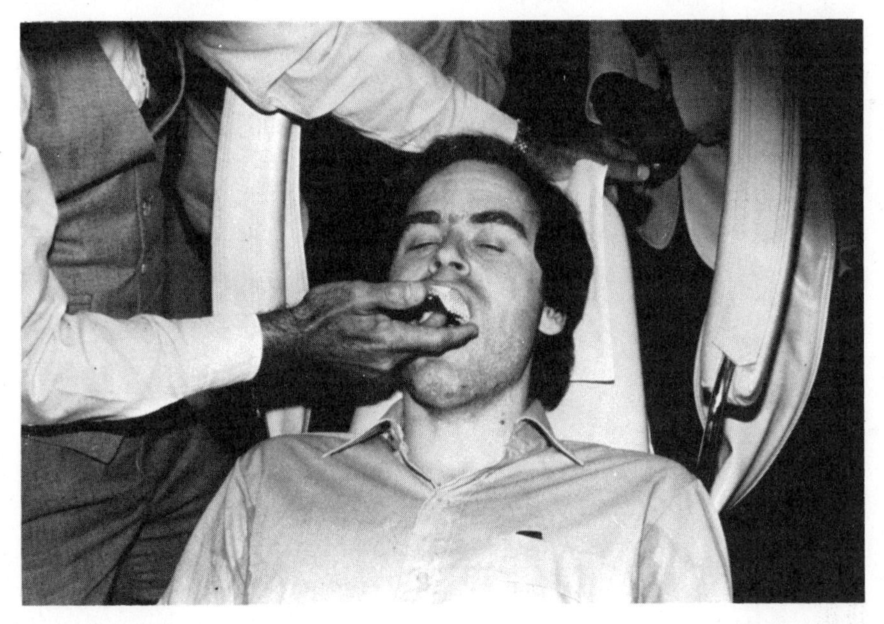

FIGURE 3.3
Forensic dentist obtaining dental impressions of Ted Bundy before his trial for the murder of two Florida State University coeds. Teeth marks, proven to be Bundy's, were found on one of the victims. Courtesy Ken Katsaris, former Sheriff, Leon County (Florida) Sheriff's Office.

state is legally the aggrieved party. Technically, the victim has no legal right to decide whether an assailant will or will not be prosecuted. Rather, the decision is made by the prosecutor; and many prosecutors are reluctant to pursue prosecution in felony assaults involving uncooperative victims. This is especially true when a victim's injuries are not critical and when the parties involved are related. This tendency not to prosecute is not commonly known among victims, however. Thus, a victim feloniously assaulted by a spouse may fear for that person's arrest and may be uncooperative or may fabricate a story about how the offense occurred.

Faced with an uncooperative victim, an officer's job is to get that victim to provide facts about the crime. This can be done, but the victim generally has to be convinced that no legal action will be taken against the assailant. The laws vary from state to state, but in many jurisdictions informal arrangements have been worked out between the prosecutor's office, the courts, and the police department to give police the authority (under carefully controlled conditions) to have a victim sign a **waiver of prosecution.** A waiver includes the name of the assailant, a statement of the victim's total satisfaction with the investigation by the police, and a statement of the victim's desire not to have the state prosecute (Figure 3.4).

Some people object strenuously to the practice of using waivers, because they believe that nonprosecution

FIGURE 3.4
Waiver of prosecution form. Courtesy Hillsborough County Sheriff's Office, Tampa, Florida. (Adapted with permission.)

WALTER C. HEINRICH, SHERIFF
HILLSBOROUGH COUNTY SHERIFF'S OFFICE
2008 E. 8TH AVENUE
TAMPA, FLORIDA 33605

STATE OF FLORIDA
COUNTY OF HILLSBOROUGH

CASE NO.: ____________
DATE: ____________

I, ______________________, the undersigned, do hereby:

WAIVER OF PROSECUTION

[INITIALS] request the HILLSBOROUGH COUNTY SHERIFF'S OFFICE not to prosecute [NAME] regarding my complaint. I am satisfied with the manner in which the investigation was conducted and release the Sheriff's Office of any responsibility regarding this complaint. I request that any further investigation not be pursued.

signed this ________ day of ________, 19__, at ________ o'clock __M.

____
(AUTHORITY/RELATION)

____
DEPUTY

WITNESSES:

____

____

____

Courtesy Hillsborough County Sheriff's Office, Tampa, Florida. (Adapted with permission.)

tends to encourage assaults. This position assumes that persons who commit assaults and are not punished are encouraged to commit similar assaults in the future. Nevertheless, overcrowded court dockets and the difficulties associated with prosecuting cases with reluctant victims obviate any preventive or punitive benefits that might be derived from the prosecution of all assaults.

Many state and local governments have statutes and ordinances that make it unlawful to withhold intentionally information relating to a crime or to provide false and misleading information about the crime. A victim who is uncooperative or who is suspected of not being completely truthful is usually advised of such laws and the penalties associated with them (Swanson, Chamelin, and Territo 1988, p. 279).

Forcible Rape Forcible rape is defined in the UCR program as the carnal knowledge of a female, forcibly and against her will. Assault or attempts to commit rape by force or threat of force are included in this category, but statutory rape (without force) and other sex offenses are not.

Although the number of rapes increased dramatically between 1971 and 1986—40 per 100,000 females in 1971, 73 per 100,000 females in 1986—evidence still suggests that rape is one of the most underreported violent crimes. As victimization studies reveal, victims have specific reasons for not reporting rapes (*Rape Victimization Study,* 1975; President's Commission on Law Enforcement and the Administration of Justice 1967):

1. Lack of belief in the ability of the police to apprehend the suspect
2. Concern that they would receive unsympathetic treatment from the police and would have to go through discomforting procedures
3. Desire to avoid the embarrassment of publicity
4. Fear of reprisal by the rapist
5. Apprehension, based on television programs or newspaper reports, that they would be further "victimized" by court proceedings

Unfortunately, some complaints about the treatment of rape victims are justified; but efforts are being made to correct these deficiencies in the system. For example, women's groups are working with local police departments to educate the public, especially women, about the crime of rape and to correct misinformation presented in television programs and the news media.

The failure of victims to report rapes seriously diminishes the ability of the police to protect other women. In an effort to combat the problems of rape and the nonreporting of rape, many police departments have implemented rape prevention programs. One hazard of such programs is that if they are successful there could be an initial increase in the number of rapes reported to the police—thus conveying an impression that the program has failed. Therefore, prior to launching a rape prevention program, a police department should make the public and the news media aware of the possibility of increased reporting.

FIGURE 3.5
Women's karate class at California State University. Ben Martin/ *TIME Magazine.*

Reported rape, like murder, frequently involves individuals who know each other casually or even very well. For this reason, rape has a fairly high clearance rate.

ROBBERY Robbery is the taking, or the attempt to take, anything of value from the care, custody, or control of a person or persons by force, by threat of violence, by violence, or by putting the victim in fear. Because of the face-to-face confrontation between perpetrator and victim, the potential for violence is always present in a robbery; and when violence does occur, injuries can range from minor harm to loss of life. Because of its personal and often violent nature, robbery is feared greatly by the public. This fear may well be heightened by perceptions of police inability to deal effectively with the offense (only one in every four reported robberies is solved). And the robbery rate is increasing—from 187 victims per 100,000 inhabitants in 1971 to 225 victims per 100,000 inhabitants in 1986. In 1986 robberies accounted for 36 percent of violent crimes reported to UCR.

As already mentioned, the crime of robbery requires that force or threat of force be directed against the physical safety of the victim. Thus, a threat to expose a victim as a homosexual or an embezzler would not satisfy this element of the crime. Proof that force was used—or, at the very least, that threats were made to cause the victim to fear imminent bodily harm—is essential for the successful prosecution of robberies. However, the force used in a robbery to separate victims from their property does not have to be great. When a victim *is* seriously injured, the injury is usually enough to convince an investigator or a jury that force was used. However, difficulties do arise when a victim who claims to have been robbed under the threat of force exhibits no injury. (The taking of property *without* force is the crime of *larceny*.)

In some cases, the difference between a crime classified as a robbery and one classified as a larceny is marginal. Often the force element of robbery can be satisfied only by determining whether a victim attempted to resist the force used, and to what extent that resistance took place. A typical purse-snatching case is an example: it is generally accepted by courts that a woman who puts her purse next to her on the seat of a bus without keeping her hand on it, or loosely holds it in her hand, is not the victim of robbery if someone quickly grabs the purse and runs (neither the purse nor the woman resisted); however, if the woman were clutching her bag tightly and someone manages to grab it from her, after even a slight struggle or tug-of-war, sufficient force and resistance have occurred to constitute robbery. A good rule to follow is that the removal of an article without more force than is absolutely necessary to remove it from its original resting place constitutes larceny. If any additional force, no matter how slight, is used, the crime is considered robbery.

In addition, the force or threat of force in robbery must precede or accompany the taking. Force applied *after* the taking does not constitute robbery. Thus, victims who, realizing that their property has been stolen, encounter force when attempting to recover that property, are not robbery victims if their property was originally taken without force. When force is not used but a threat to the physical well-being of the victim is substituted, it is not necessary that the victim be frightened to the point of panic. It is enough that he or she is reasonably apprehensive and aware of the potential for injury (Swanson, Chamelin, and Territo 1988, pp. 344–45).

Robbery has a low clearance rate for several reasons: physical evidence may not be found; the on-scene time of perpetrators is limited; and witnesses are usually shaken, so that their information runs the gamut from minimal to completely erroneous. Physical descriptions are the most common evidence in robbery, but the descriptions are of limited use because the robbers are usually some distance away by the time the police arrive (Swanson, Chamelin, and Territo 1988, pp. 350–351).

Crimes against Property

Among the eight index crimes, the four crimes against property are burglary, larceny-theft, motor vehicle theft, and arson.

BURGLARY Burglary is the unlawful entry of a structure to commit a felony or theft. The use of force is not a requirement for burglary. In the FBI Uniform Crime Reports, burglary is divided into three classifications: forcible entry, unlawful entry without force, and attempted forcible entry.

Two important aspects of burglary are its frequency and economic impact. Nationally, if reported burglaries were distributed evenly in time, a burglary would occur every ten seconds (Federal Bureau of Investigation 1986, p. 6). The offense accounts for about 28 percent of all reported property crimes. Two-thirds of all burglaries are residential burglaries, the rest being attacks on various commercial establishments. Between 1982 and 1986 there was a downward trend in the rate of both residential and nonresidential burglaries (see Figure 3.6). The total annual loss due to burglaries is $3.1 billion, with an average loss of $960 per burglary (Federal Bureau of Investigation 1986, p. 25).

Burglaries are not the product of modern society; the tomb of the Egyptian pharaoh Tutankhamen was broken into shortly after his death, and churches and abbeys were constantly victimized in the Middle Ages. Burglary does, however, change with time. Types that flourished even in the recent past have disappeared today: for example, the transom, coal-slide, and dumbwaiter burglaries are virtually extinct. Another rapidly vanishing species is the so-called step-over burglary. Apartment dwellers often place screening or other coverings on windows that open onto fire escapes, but they don't cover the windows next to the escapes. A step-over burglar crosses from the fire escape to the ledge and enters an unprotected window. This technique has declined since the advent of interior fire escapes.

Although burglars tend to come from lower socioeconomic classes and are often not well educated, there have been notable exceptions. Burglaries have been com-

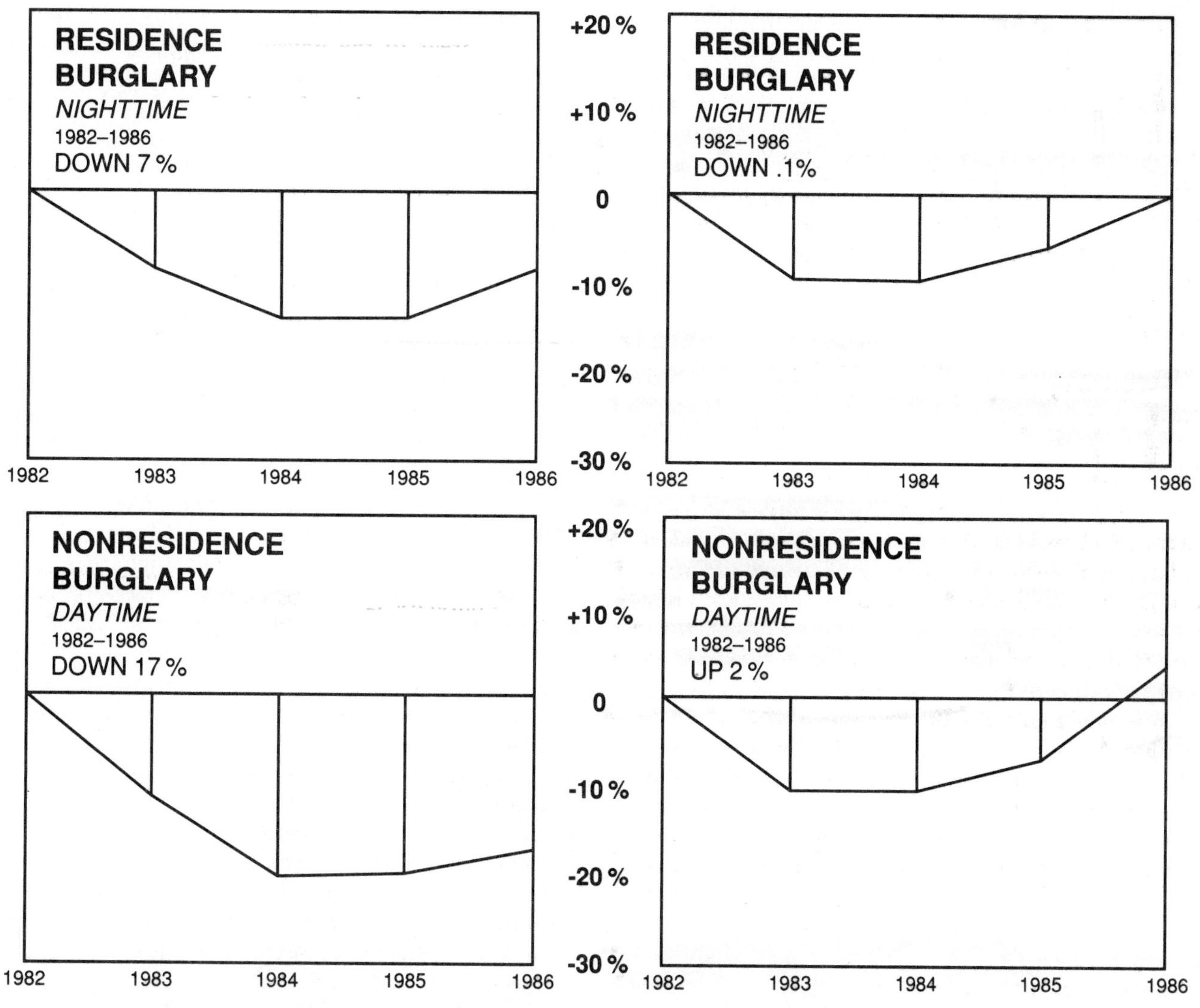

FIGURE 3.6
Percentage changes in number of day and nighttime burglaries, 1982–86. Data from Federal Bureau of Investigation. *Crime in the United States, FBI Uniform Crime Reports* (Washington, D.C.: U.S. Government Printing Office, 1986), p. 26.

mitted by professors, probation officers, and psychiatrists. A South Carolina psychiatrist who held a law degree and earned up to $100,000 a year was once arrested, and the arresting officers recovered $500,000 in stolen property, linking the psychiatrist to 150 burglaries in a single county.

Burglars can be classified according to several variables, such as preferences for premises to be attacked and types of property they will or will not take. But the most useful classification is skill. Burglars range from the amateur to the professional, but most are unskilled at their crime.

Professional burglars may commit only four or five offenses each year. Despite the infrequency of their acts, however, they are important to the police because of the large value of cash or property taken and their intimate knowledge of sophisticated fencing systems. In addition to the "big score," the hallmark of the professional is thorough planning preceding each burglary. Professionals refuse to place themselves in jeopardy for anything other than sizable gain, and they do so only after weeks or months of painstaking study of a target. Because they know exactly what they want in advance, professionals do not ransack a premises. Thus, a stolen article may not be missed for some time. Working nationally—or, at the highest professional level, internationally—the professional burglar often operates for a long time without being arrested (Swanson, Chamelin, and Territo 1988, pp. 365, 366).

LARCENY-THEFT Larceny is the unlawful taking, carrying, leading, or riding away of property from the possession or constructive possession of another without the use of force or fear. It includes crimes such as shoplifting, pocket-picking, purse snatching, motor vehicle theft, theft of parts and accessories for motor vehicles, and bicycle theft (Figure 3.7).

Larcenies made up 55 percent of the eight index crimes in 1986. Studies indicate that many offenses in this category, particularly when the value of stolen goods is low, never come to the attention of the police because victims do not report the thefts. In other cases, merchants and business owners are not aware of the total value of the thefts that occur; this is a common problem in the crime of shoplifting.

Most larcenies—38 percent in 1986—consist of thefts of parts, accessories, and contents of motor vehicles (Federal Bureau of Investigation 1986, p. 31). And there is reason to believe that organized crime is now involved extensively in this type of crime. In November 1979, the Senate Permanent Investigations Subcommittee held

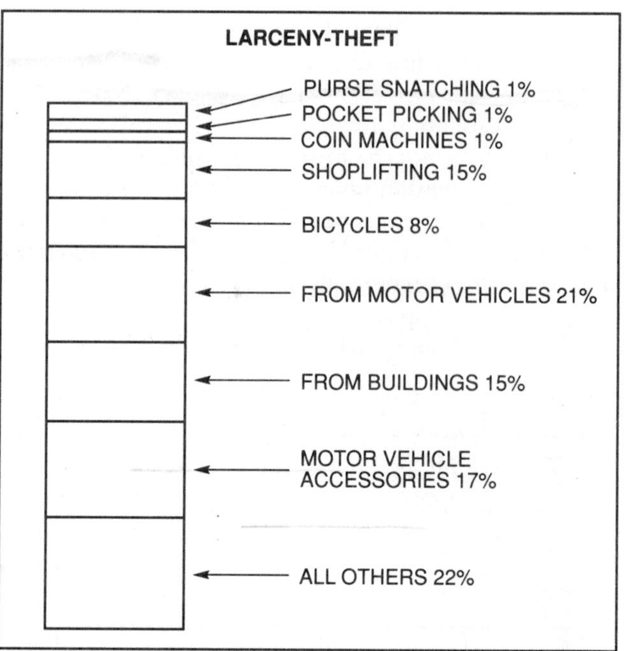

FIGURE 3.7
Percentage breakdown of larceny, 1986. Data from Federal Bureau of Investigation, *Crime in the United States, FBI Uniform Crime Reports* (Washington, D.C.: U.S. Government Printing Office, 1986), p. 31.

hearings to look into this problem, and a number of interesting findings emerged. For example, it was found that although a 1966 law aimed at making cars more theft resistant had been effective against teenage joy riding, the law had not stopped professional auto thieves.

The Senate subcommittee also looked into the operations of **chop shops**—garages that strip stolen cars of usable parts and sell the parts to auto repair shops. In a legitimate business, an auto repair shop will call a salvage yard to get a part. Yard owners generally have large inventories of parts obtained at auctions (insurance companies auction wrecks not worth repairing). If the yard does not have the part, it can call upon a network of other yards across the country. In an illegal operation, however, a salvage yard responds to the request for a part and offers a lower-than-cost price and a delivery date. The dishonest yard owner then contacts a thief and instructs him or her to steal the car or truck from which the part is needed. The stolen vehicle is dismantled in a chop shop in a matter of hours, and the part is delivered to the yard owner who requested it. The high cost of replacing parts for automobiles—$23,000 to buy separately what went into a $5,100 car—is considered a prime factor in the emergence of chop shops ("Senate

FIGURE 3.8
Inside a chop shop. Automobiles, some of them still bearing license plates, have been partially disassembled. When this photo was taken, several of the vehicles shown had not yet been reported stolen. Courtesy Samuel J. Rozzi, Commissioner of Police, Nassau County (New York).

Probing Car Theft Industry," *Atlanta Journal,* 26 November 1979, p. 24).

Bicycle Theft The enormous increase in the use of bicycles for sport, transportation, and exercise has not occurred without some serious side effects for the police. The theft of bicycles, especially the more sophisticated and expensive ones, has reached almost epidemic proportions in some areas. Nationally, bicycle theft accounts for 8 percent of all larceny crimes (Federal Bureau of Investigation 1986, p. 31).

Despite this situation, however, many bike owners are not sufficiently aware of the problem. As a result, they fail to lock their bicycles or they use inexpensive, minimum-security locks that only slightly deter thieves. Additionally, parking facilities for bicycles are generally in short supply and are easily compromised. Increasingly, people are buying more expensive ten-speed bicycles, starting in price at $150. This high value makes the bicycles particularly attractive to thieves. Also, the increasing demand for multigeared models makes the disposal of stolen bicycles easier; potential customers can be found almost anywhere.

In a recent national survey conducted in the fifty largest cities and on 200 college campuses, the following facts were revealed: on college campuses, 88 percent of stolen bicycles are locked; in cities, the average is 74 percent. The thief's favorite tool for locked bicycles is the bolt cutter; other tools employed include hacksaws, hammers, pry bars, lock pliers, and vise grips.

Shoplifting The National Retail Merchants Association indicates that twelve cents of every dollar spent by consumers is an incremental cost due to shoplifting. Shoplifting accounts for 15% of all larceny crimes (Federal Bureau of Investigation 1986, p. 31). The techniques employed in shoplifting are legion and the appearance and types of shoplifters innumerable.

MOTOR VEHICLE THEFT Motor vehicle theft is the theft or attempted theft of a motor vehicle. This definition excludes the taking of a motor vehicle for temporary use by someone with lawful access. There were 1,224,137 motor vehicle thefts in 1986, accounting for 9 percent of all index crimes (Federal Bureau of Investigation 1986, p. 34). These thefts are generally grouped into four categories: joy riding, theft of vehicles for use in other crimes, thefts for transportation, and professional thefts (Swanson, Chamelin, and Territo 1988, p. 410).

Joy Riding Car thefts for joy riding constitute the majority of motor vehicle thefts. The perpetrators are usually teenagers—fifteen to nineteen years old—who steal a car on a dare, as initiation into a gang, or for parts and accessories. Youths arrested for car theft are often repeat offenders.

Theft of Vehicles for Use in Other Crimes Criminals who plan to commit a crime often steal a vehicle that can be abandoned immediately after the crime and that cannot be traced. The perpetrator usually steals the vehicle as close to the time of the primary crime as possible; this minimizes the possibility that the vehicle theft will be reported to the police, and that a pickup order will be broadcast for the car while the thief is en route to, or departing from, the scene of the primary crime.

Thefts for Transportation Thefts for transportation generally involve transients, hitchhikers, and runaways. Stolen cars are abandoned when the thief reaches his or her destination or runs out of gas (Horgan 1974, p. 185).

Professional Thefts The professional auto thief steals with the specific intent of making a profit, either by dismantling the vehicle for parts or by altering it for resale. Evidence suggests that organized crime is behind the growing steal-to-order car theft industry ("Senate Probing Car Theft Industry," *Atlanta Journal,* 26 November 1979, p. 24).

ARSON **Arson** is defined as any willful or malicious burning or attempt to burn—with or without intent to defraud—a dwelling, house, public building, motor vehicle, aircraft, or personal property of another. Only fires determined through investigation to have been willfully or maliciously set are classified as arsons. Fires of suspicious or unknown origin are excluded. Because arson was not added to the list of index offenses until 1978, limited historical data are available for the crime.

CRIME DATA MANIPULATION

Although most police departments report crimes accurately to the FBI, **crime data manipulation** does sometimes occur—and for various reasons. For example, a police chief may want to convey the impression to citizens and superior that everything is under control and that the police department is doing an effective job. Another chief, angry about potential budget reductions and personnel cutbacks, may manipulate statistics or reporting procedures to convey the impression that crime is increasing dramatically and that cutbacks will worsen the problem. And a sheriff preparing for reelection who is concerned about the effect of rising crime on his or her reputation may urge deputies to discourage citizens from making crime reports or may instruct deputies to reclassify serious crimes as less serious offenses. As Patrick Murphy, president of the Police Foundation in

Drug Fighters Take to Street

By Paul Clancy
USA TODAY

Beefed-up police pressure on street-level drug buyers and sellers is cutting crime in big-city neighborhoods.

While a USA TODAY survey found urban crime rose last year, a new Harvard study says cities that commit up to 15 percent of police resources to street drug sweeps have 30 percent drops in robberies and burglaries.

Another result: Once-fearful residents reclaim neighborhoods. A two-year push in the Bronx, N.Y., cut murders, burglaries and robberies.

But dealers keep moving and returning, so police and citizen groups have to keep up the pressure. Said Bronx resident Nilda Osario: "It's like a disease; it keeps on spreading."

Elsewhere:

- Washington, D.C., police last week restored their effective but costly Operation Clean Sweep after residents objected to plans to end it.
- Baltimore's decentralized police efforts and a 24-hour hot line bring an average of 41 drug arrests a day, up 33 percent over last year.

  Said narcotics chief Michael Fannon: "If the criminal element sees this community means business, they won't be as blatant."
- Los Angeles drug arrests rose 22 percent this year when neighborhood groups took their complaints from City Hall to the state Legislature. "They know how to put pressure on us," said Deputy Police Chief Jesse Brewer.
- In Miami, demand for illegal drugs has declined as police teams focused on buyers and sellers and left big investigations to federal task forces.

  "We're beginning to see the first signs of decline in cocaine use," said Miami-Dade narcotics chief Arthur Nehrbass, though "it won't show up in studies for a long time."

Crime Up In Many USA Cities

Crime was on the rise in 1986 in most of the USA's biggest cities, a USA TODAY survey shows. These 16 cities reported an average 8 percent increase. Among reasons cited: more handguns, drugs and prison overcrowding.

Source: City police departments; researched by Tracy Walmer and Wendy Marlow, USA TODAY

How crime rose or dropped

City	Crimes reported in 1986	Changed from 1985
Baltimore	66,273	+0.2%
Boston	68,958	+1.3%
Chicago	294,471	+5.6%
Dallas	153,927	+18.9%
Honolulu	46,455	+10.5%
Houston	168,150	+7.9%
Indianapolis	29,642	No change
Jacksonville, Fla.	63,571	+21.9%
Los Angeles	245,268	+10.3%
New York	635,199	+5.6%
Phoenix, Ariz.	89,377	+8.3%
San Antonio, Texas	100,231	+19.9%
San Diego	79,746	+17.5%
San Francisco	56,637	−3.3%
San Jose, Calif.	38,842	−3.2%
Washington, D.C.	66,152	+8.4%

Change by crime category

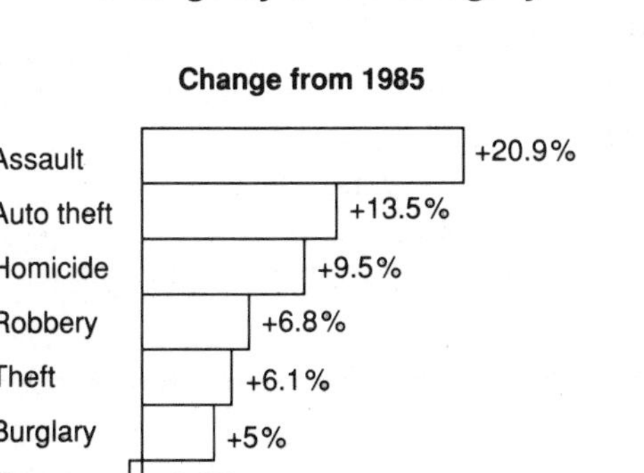

Breakdown of '86's 2.2 million crimes in cities surveyed

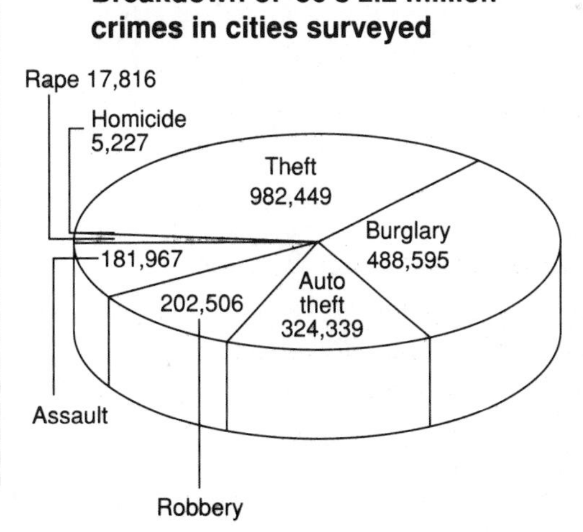

FIGURE 3.9
Crime Up in Many USA Cities. Crime was on the rise in 1986 in most of the USA's biggest cities, a USA TODAY survey shows. These 16 cities reported an average 8 percent increase. Among reasons cited: more handguns, drugs and prison overcrowding. Source: City police departments; researched by Tracy Walmer and Wendy Marlow, USA TODAY.

Crime Rises at 'Alarming' Rate in Cities

By Sam Meddis
USA TODAY

Crime was up in 1986 in most of the USA's biggest cities, a USA TODAY survey shows.

Of 16 major cities with available statistics, 13 saw overall increases in all crime categories except for rape—suggesting that crime is swinging up after drops in the early 1980s.

Where crime rate rose most: Jacksonville, Fla.; San Antonio, Texas; Dallas; San Diego; Honolulu; and Los Angeles.

"Everything I see and hear certainly points to an increased level of crime—and in some areas of the country, an alarming increase," said Jerald Vaughn, head of the 14,000-member International Association of Chiefs of Police.

He cites:

- Accessibility of handguns, drugs and prison crowding.
- Our popular culture—in TV, films and news media—that promotes a "seeming addiction to violence."

The FBI Saturday releases its preliminary report on crime in 1986. In the first half of last year, the FBI found that crimes reported to police increased 8 percent.

New increases surprise crime experts who had predicted that the aging of the Baby Boomers—beyond the crime-prone ages of 14–21—would result in lower crime rates until the 1990s.

James Fox, criminologist at Northeastern University, says that while there are fewer young people, they may be committing more crime: "Proportionately, there's a lot more bad kids than you had before."

City police cite factors:

- In Los Angeles—which had a 10.3 percent increase—police spokesman Bill Frio points to police shortages and gang activity.
- San Antonio police spokesman Jimmy Kopeck blames early releases from overcrowded prisons: "It really impresses in the criminal's mind that there's no deterrent."

Residents of Bronx Wear Down Dealers

By Paul Clancy
USA TODAY

BRONX, N.Y.—Residents' years of marching and badgering public officials are finally paying off—drugs and related crime are being forced out of some New York City neighborhoods.

"We have shown that we can take back our neighborhoods," said Barbara Grant, watching over preschoolers at a playground.

A report by the Northwest Bronx Community and Clergy Coalition shows that drug arrests more than doubled from 1984 to 1986, and related crime is down.

Residents:

- Marched on the police station and the mayor's house and went by the busload to Albany and Washington, D.C. Police eventually stepped up anti-drug efforts.
- Monitored arrests to make sure dealers were prosecuted.
- Put signs on crack houses and pressured landlords to evict dealers.

Dealers haven't gone far.

Standing on Mosholu Parkway North, David McKenzie pointed to a man leaning against a building.

"That's one of them," he said. Immediately, the man vanished around the corner.

But it's getting harder for dealers to do business in McKenzie's neighborhood. He and neighbors confront people who come into their building to buy or sell drugs.

"They got the message that we're not playing," he said.

Washington, D.C., commented in a recent news article, "When I was a rookie in the 72nd precinct in Brooklyn, no police commander worth his salt would admit he couldn't control crime—and proved it by controlling statistics" (Magnuson 1981, p. 17).

Independent Audit Demanded Following Charges That Chicago Police Manipulated Crime Statistics

Law Enforcement News

The Chicago Crime Commission has called for an independent audit of the Chicago Police Department's crime statistics after a television news report last month accused the department of covering up the true numbers of crime in the city.

In a four-part series, station WBBM-TV in Chicago alleged that Chicago police falsify reports and violate FBI standards for crime reporting in an effort to make the city appear safer.

The report said that Chicago police kill nearly half of the reports of rape it receives and nearly a third of the robbery and burglary reports. It said the percentage of reports the department declares unfounded is six times that of police in eight other cities surveyed.

Police superintendent Richard Brzeczek has promised to launch an internal investigation of the charges, saying anyone found guilty of falsifying reports will be fired.

He denied assertions that the manipulation of crime statistics is condoned by police management and said comparisons between the "unfounded" rates in Chicago and other cities is invalid because of differences in how reports are taken in various police departments.

But Brzeczek's promise of an internal audit has not satisfied the Crime Commission. Executive Director Patrick Healy said the commission will continue to push for an independent investigation.

"An independent, objective review must occur," he said. "The Chicago Crime Commission plans to take on the responsibility of keeping the issue before the Chicago community until such an audit occurs."

The WBBM-TV report focused on how Chicago police handle reports of robberies, burglaries, and rapes. Reporter Pam Zekman alleged that anywhere from 44 to 57 percent of robbery cases reported during her eight-month investigation were "literally wiped off the books." She also said nearly half of the rape cases reported during that time were not counted, and that one out of every three burglaries reported were not counted.

She said the manipulation of crime statistics occur in three ways.

The first, she said, is that police declare large numbers of crime reports unfounded, many times because the person making the complaint reportedly could not be found. Zekman located and interviewed three crime victims who claimed that the crimes they reported had been declared unfounded although no attempt was made to contact them.

Zekman claimed that Chicago police declared 9,000 robbery reports unfounded last year, one out of every three reported. She said New York, Los Angeles and St. Louis declared fewer than one out of a hundred unfounded.

But Brzeczek said comparing those statistics is "like comparing apples and oranges." He said police in other cities may exercise more discretion before taking the report, making their decisions about what reports are unfounded in a less formal way that would not show up in unfounding statistics.

Zekman also reported that Chicago police play down crime rates by reclassifying many crimes as less serious offenses. She said police killed 16,000 burglary reports last year, half of them by declaring the reports unfounded and half by reclassifying them to less serious crimes.

Police also changed or omitted evidence on crime reports to make the reports appear unfounded or less serious, Zekman alleged. She interviewed two rape victims who say medical evidence that supported their claims was omitted from the reports and their cases dropped. A burglary victim claimed that the report of a break-in at her home was changed to say the door had been left open although the door frame showed damage from the burglar's forced entry.

Brzeczek said he has no knowledge of such manipulation of reports, but that he will investigate the charges. "If it's something that some people are doing, we'll stop it," he said.

John Dineen, president of the Chicago Fraternal Order of Police, said the television reports of falsifying information on crime reports exaggerate the problem, but said he is concerned with the number of crimes that are reclassified as less serious offenses or dropped.

"If the administration continually downgrades crime, it hurts," Dineen said. "When you get a television station saying that the police department is taking burglaries and making thefts out of them, and that sort of thing, the public has to begin to wonder."

Dineen said he thinks crimes are reclassified because "no city wants to be known as a city where crime is high. No one wants that onus put on them."

But Brzeczek said the department is not playing down crime to improve the city's image and denied that manipulating the reports is "standard operating procedure," as one officer asserted in the television reports.

"It absolutely is not," Brzeczek said. "This is not something that has come down from the top."

The superintendent said that if the internal audit shows that there is a systemic problem with declaring reports unfounded or reclassifying them, he will consider hiring an outside auditor.

Brzeczek said he believes the internal audit will root out any problem. "If the internal audit can't be trusted, then you're saying I can't be trusted, and if I can't be trusted, they better find somebody else for this job."

But Healy said an independent audit must be made because any inaccuracy in crime figures would create "a myriad of problems" for the Chicago criminal justice system.

He said playing down crime could mean that city government hasn't properly allocated its resources for dealing with crime, that citizens are operating with an incorrect perception of the danger they're in, that citizens will stop calling police to report crime if they feel they are getting no response, and that city officials can't accurately measure the effectiveness of the department.

"The accurate reporting of incidences of crime is central to protection of any community," Healy said.

Brzeczek challenged the Crime Commission's procedure in handling the problem. He said the commission called for an independent audit before meeting with him to discuss the television report.

"I think they should have sat down with me to talk it over before issuing their press release," he said.

Law Enforcement News Vol. VIII, No. 22, 27 December 1982.

Another technique used by police departments to manipulate crime data is a practice referred to as **clearing the books.** Although not regularly engaged in by police departments, the practice is not as uncommon as one might think. Certainly, in those communities where the practice is employed, there is a distorted picture of the crime problem and the ability of the police to solve crime.

Case 3.4

Frank, a twenty-six-year-old previously convicted burglar, was arrested by police inside an appliance store he had broken into. There was little doubt in Frank's mind that he was going to be convicted and sent back to prison. The detectives who interrogated him realized his desperate plight and seized upon the opportunity to improve their own difficulties with a dramatically increasing burglary rate.

The detectives approached Frank with a "deal" that they described as mutually beneficial. If Frank would accept responsibility for approximately fifty unsolved burglaries, they would put in a "good word" for him with the local prosecutor, judge, and parole and probation officer who would eventually be doing his presentence investigation. Frank, of course, would only be charged with the crime he actually committed. Frank agreed, and as the detectives promised, they put in a "good word" with the appropriate people. In turn, Frank was given a lighter sentence than he might normally have received.

OTHER CRITICISMS OF THE UCR PROGRAM

#9)

In addition to the criticism of data manipulation by law enforcement agencies, the Uniform Crime Reporting Program has been criticized over the years on several issues. We describe a few of the problems here.

Nonmandatory Nature of the Program

Historically, law enforcement agencies' contributions to the UCR system of crime data gathering have been voluntary. Therefore, almost by definition, the UCR system does not *reflect* all crimes reported to police agencies in the United States, let alone those crimes that go unreported. This situation creates some obvious problems for researchers and law enforcement personnel.

Incomplete Crime Categories

As explained earlier in this chapter, the UCR crimes index is divided into two categories (violent crimes and crimes against property). The crimes included in the index are murder, aggravated assault, forcible rape, robbery, burglary, larceny-theft, motor vehicle theft, and arson. Critics argue that although these categories may still be relevant for the most part in the 1980s, shouldn't crimes such as major drug activities, white collar violations, serial murder, and domestic terrorism be added to the index? The latter examples are clearly relevant to national concerns about crimes today, yet they are not defined for UCR reporting purposes.

UCR Hierarchy Rule

For years the UCR hierarchy rule has been the subject of severe criticism. When a crime is recorded for UCR purposes, only the most serious crime appearing in the UCR hierarchy is scored. For example, if an individual broke into a person's home, raped a woman, and stole jewelry, only the most serious crime in the UCR hierarchy (rape) would be scored for UCR purposes. Many critics argue that, because of this rule, UCR information on the actual level of criminal activity is incomplete at best.

Lack of Information on Part II Crimes

As explained earlier, the nation's crime rate, as defined by the FBI Uniform Crime Reports, includes only the eight "index" or Part I offenses. Unfortunately, Part II crimes, or "other" offenses, are recorded for UCR purposes *only* when an arrest is made. Some examples of Part II crimes include simple assaults, forgery, fraud, embezzlement, buying, receiving or possessing stolen goods, vandalism, sex offenses, violation of narcotic drug laws, gambling, and driving under the influence. Critics suggest that some of the Part II offenses should be elevated to the status of index offenses. Some police officials argue that their personnel spend a significant amount of time on Part II offenses such as forgery, driving under the influence, and vandalism, yet the public and media generally are only familiar with index-type offenses that define the annual "crime rate."

FUTURE OF THE UCR PROGRAM

Although UCR data have been widely used by law enforcement agencies, researchers, government policymakers, and the media, many criticisms of the program have arisen from the same sources. Many think the system needs to be expanded to cover a wider range of offenses and provide more detailed information on the nature of criminal incidents. Some indicate that the system needs to provide greater analytic flexibility, while others suggest that published reports should have more analysis and interpretation. Many question the accuracy of UCR data; UCR statistics appear to disagree in some ways with those of related sources, such as the National Crime Survey, but the form of UCR data prevents meaningful comparison or reconciliation between different crime series. At the same time, the data processing capabilities of state programs and large police and sheriffs' agencies have begun to outpace the antiquated methods of the UCR national program. Based on the extensive criticism and the rapidly changing data processing environment, the IACP three times called for a review of the UCR program. In response, the Bureau of Justice Statistics and the Federal Bureau of Investigation formed a joint task force, which in 1982 contracted with Abt Associates, Inc. to determine what, if any, changes should be made to the current national UCR program (Poggio et al. 1985, pp. 1–3).[2]

The study encompassed all aspects of the program, including its objectives and intended user audience, data items, reporting mechanisms, quality control, publications and user services, and relationships with other criminal justice data systems.

The study relied on extensive outreach to obtain the views of all interested parties. A Steering Committee composed of leading criminal justice researchers and practitioners regularly reviewed the study's progress, as did the Joint UCR Committee of the International Association of Chiefs of Police and the National Sheriffs' Association. Moreover, the views of collectors and users of UCR data were solicited through on-site visits and surveys of law enforcement agencies and state UCR programs, interviews with criminal justice researchers, and a national conference of UCR experts. The law enforcement agency survey drew 3,400 responses. From all these sources a remarkable consensus emerged on desirable improvements to be made.

Overview of the Recommended UCR System

The proposed new UCR program differs from the existing one in two fundamental ways. First, rather than sending only monthly summary statistics to the national program, state or local agencies will submit individual records for each incident and each arrest that occurred during the month. This conversion to unit-record reporting provides the flexibility that is needed to incorporate additional data elements into the system, and it will enhance the accuracy and usefulness of UCR data. Second, two levels of reporting will be established: most contributors will provide basic offense and arrest information similar to that currently reported, while a comparatively small sample of agencies will report much more extensive information. All large agencies will be expected to participate in the second reporting level, together with a nationally representative sample of smaller agencies. Two-level reporting meets the need for increased depth and scope of regional and national statistics about crime while minimizing the burden imposed on contributors and agencies that process the data.

Table 3.1 summarizes the distinctions between the two levels of reporting (in the columns labeled Level I and Level II components) and compares them with the current system. Aside from the change to submitting individual records of incidents and arrests, Level I reporting is substantially the same as the present UCR program: only minor changes are proposed in the types of offenses reported to the national program, the definitions of offenses, and the detailed data elements. Level II reporting is expanded to cover many types of offenses not previously included in the UCR program; over twenty new data items will be added for each offense, and additional information about Level II component agencies and their jurisdictions will be collected annually. Nearly all the information planned for inclusion in Level II reporting is already collected by major city, county, and state agencies with advanced crime data processing capabilities.

In addition to the changes shown in Table 3.1, the proposed new system includes improvements in procedures for assuring the quality of UCR data, an expanded series of publications, enhanced analysis capabilities and user services, and better compatibility with National Crime Survey data and Offender-Based Transaction Statistics.

The benefits of the new system will be readily apparent to legislators and other government officials, members of the public, criminal justice researchers, the media, and the contributing law enforcement agencies. The recommended UCR system will provide law enforcement and the public with far more compelling and accurate local, regional, and national statistics on crime conditions and the activities of law enforcement agencies in relation to crime. It will permit UCR information to be combined with information from other sources, thereby presenting a more complete picture of crime and the criminal justice system's response to crime than ever before possible. This will include the ability to identify the actual extent of injury and loss and the risk of victimization, to distinguish crimes that are preventable and defensible through police action, and to identify the circumstances of crimes and hence the potential for defensive actions by the public and police.

THE NATIONAL CRIME SURVEY

Within the last decade, the U.S. Department of Justice, Bureau of Justice Statistics initiated a program to learn more about crimes and the victims of crime. The program called the National Crime Survey (NCS) was established to measure crimes *not* reported to police as well as those that are reported. Except for homicide (which is well reported in police statistics) and arson (which is difficult to measure using survey techniques), the NCS measures the same crimes as the UCR, but counts attempted as well as completed crimes (Rand, Kaus, and Taylor 1983, p. 6).[3]

Some of the more important differences between UCR and NCS programs, which are thought to account for most of the differences in the resulting statistics, are as follows (see also Table 3.2):

- The UCR counts only crimes coming to the attention of the police. The NCS obtains information on both reported and unreported crime.
- The UCR counts crimes committed against all people and all businesses, organizations, government agencies, and other victims. NCS

TABLE 3.1
Comparison of Current and Recommended UCR Systems

CHARACTERISTIC	CURRENT SYSTEM	RECOMMENDED SYSTEM	
		LEVEL I COMPONENT	LEVEL II COMPONENT
Target percentage of agencies	100	93–97	3–7
Type of reporting	Summary	Unit-record	Unit-record
Offense types for which offense data are collected	Criminal homicide, forcible rape, robbery, assault, burglary, larceny-theft, motor-vehicle theft, and arson	Criminal homicide,[a] forcible sexual offense, robbery, assault, burglary, larceny-theft, motor vehicle theft, and arson	All offenses
Handling of attempted crimes	Included in counts; not distinguished from actual (completed) crimes[b]	Include in counts; distinguish from actual crimes	Include in counts; distinguish from actual crimes
Use of hierarchy rule	Yes	No[c]	No[c]
Classification of offense	Part I and Part II offenses as defined by the UCR program	Current Part I definitions, with sharper definitions of aggravated assault and rape category broadened to include all forcible sexual offenses; refined Part II definitions	Current Part I definitions, with sharper definitions of aggravated assault and rape category broadened to include all forcible sexual offenses; refined Part II definitions; detailed data allow alternative classifications as well
Collection of detailed incident data	Limited	Limited, but including type of victim (individual, business, or other) and resident/nonresident status	Extensive, including victim type, victim characteristics, victim-offender relationship, use of force/weapon, type of weapon, nature/extent of injury, day of week/time of day, type of location, resident/nonresident status of victim
Cross-referencing of cleared offenses to arrests[d]	No	Yes	Yes
Agency and jurisdictional characteristics	Number of employees; population size	Number of employees; population-at-risk data	Extensive set of characteristics

[a] Negligent manslaughter is excluded.

[b] Except for attempted rapes and attemped forcible entry for burglaries; attempted homicides are counted as aggravated assaults.

[c] Except to determine the *primary* offense, which is recorded first.

[d]An offense is cleared by arrest when at least one person is arrested, charged with commission of the offense, and turned over to the court for prosecution.

Adapted from Eugene C. Poggio et al., *Blueprint for the Future of the Uniform Crime Reporting Program* (Washington, D.C.: Bureau of Justice Statistics, Federal Bureau of Investigation, 1985), p. 3.

counts only crimes against persons age twelve or older and against their households.

- The two programs, because they serve different purposes, count crime differently, in some instances. For example, a criminal robs a victim and steals someone else's car to escape. UCR only counts the robbery, the more serious crime. NCS could count both; one as a personal crime and one as a household crime.
- Each program is subject to the kinds of errors and problems typical of its method of data collection; consequently, these errors may serve to widen or narrow the differences in the counts produced by the two programs. For example, many analysts believe that the rise in the number of rapes reported to police stems largely from the special programs established by many police departments to treat victims of rape more sympathetically.

TABLE 3.2
Comparison of the UCR and NCS Systems

	UNIFORM CRIME REPORTS	NATIONAL CRIME SURVEY
Offenses measured:	Homicide Rape Robbery (personal and commercial) Assault (aggravated) Burglary (commercial and household) Larceny (commercial and household) Motor vehicle theft Arson	Rape Robbery (personal) Assault (aggravated and simple) Household burglary Larceny (personal and household) Motor vehicle theft
Scope:	Crimes reported to the police in most jurisdictions; considerable flexibility in developing small-area data	Crimes both reported and not reported to police; all data are for the Nation as a whole; some data are available for a few large geographic areas
Collection method:	Police department reports to FBI	Survey interviews: periodically measures the total number of crimes committed by asking a national sample of 60,000 households representing 135,000 persons over the age of 12 about their experiences as victims of crime during a specified period
Kinds of information:	In addition to offense counts, provides information on crime clearances, persons arrested, persons charged, law enforcement officers killed and assaulted, and characteristics of homicide victims	Provides details about victims (such as age, race, sex, education, income, and whether the victim and offender were related to each other) and about crimes (such as time and place of occurrence, whether or not reported to police, use of weapons, occurrence of injury, and economic consequences)
Sponsor:	Department of Justice Federal Bureau of Investigation	Department of Justice Bureau of Justice Statistics

Adapted from U.S. Department of Justice, Bureau of Justice Statistics, *Report to the Nation on Crime and Justice* (Washington, D.C.: Government Printing Office, 1983), p. 6.

BJS Says Crime Drops; the UCR Isn't So Sure

The nation's top two agencies for gathering and analyzing crime statistics are once again in disagreement on the question of whether crime increased last year.

Figures collected by the FBI's Uniform Crime Reporting Program indicate that crime increased by 8 percent during the first half of 1986, while the Bureau of Justice Statistics reportedly [sic] recently that the nation's crime rate has remained virtually the same since 1985.

The UCR's reported increase in crime showed sharp jumps in the South and Southwest, due in part to drug trafficking and abuse and the early release of felons from overcrowded prisons.

In Texas, according to the UCR, crime jumped 14.9 percent. Increases of 11.5 percent in Florida and 11.0 percent in Oklahoma were also reported, including upward trends in auto theft, larceny, and burglary.

On the other hand, the National Victims' Survey conducted by BJS says crime has remained static for the past two years, holding at a level that is the lowest since the survey began in 1973.

Unlike the UCR, which records only serious crimes reported to police, the BJS survey interviews about 100,000 people, who may or may not have reported victimization to police.

BJS director Steven R. Schlesinger said that the discrepancy between the UCR and his agency's report might be attributable to an increase in the number of people who report crimes to the police.

Thirty-seven [percent] of all crimes and 50 percent of violent crimes were reported to police last year, according to the victims' survey. "For the first time in the survey's history we now have fully one-half of all violent crimes being reported to law enforcement officials," Schlesinger said.

According to BJS figures, the number of personal and household crimes fell by 2 percent last year. While that figure could have been caused by sampling variations and is not considered statistically significant, it included a sharp—and reportedly consequential—decrease of 9 percent in the rate of assaults. Assaults dropped from 24 per 1,000 persons in 1985 to 22 per 1,000 in 1986, the lowest assault rate the survey has ever recorded.

Schlesinger said that if the current trend continues, "the final rate for 1986 will be the lowest since 1973."

Law Enforcement News, 12 May 1987, p. 3. Reprinted with permission.

WHAT CRIME DOES TO VICTIMS AND SOCIETY

There is always a danger when studying crime of overlooking the tragic impact it has on individual victims and society. Victims are too often lumped into a "victim profile," where they become part of a "crime trend." People who study crime should never lose sight of the fact that crime has tragic effects on people and their families and an equally important and profound effect upon the way we live and interact as a society. The following news story provides valuable insight into this aspect of crime.

What Crime Does to the Victims and Society

By John Leo. Reported by Steven Holmes and Christopher Redman/Detroit, with other U.S. bureaus TIME

Miami was host to a convention of travel agents last week. The city fathers, anxious to show how safe Miami really is, blanketed the better areas with extra police. Outside an elegant restaurant in Coconut Grove, four visitors witnessed a mugging. It was not an especially dramatic incident, and the visitors were not hurt or even involved. Yet afterward all four sat at their table, unable to eat because of their rage and fear. Incidents like that are common these days and so is a common feeling: no matter how many police are around, the feral youngsters who account for most U.S. crime seem to be able to strike when and where they wish. Says Criminal Justice Planner Bruce Hamersley of Miami: "The stability of the community has been destroyed. We are now living in a period where uncertainty is the rule rather than the exception."

Last September's *Figgie Report on Fear of Crime* warned that "Americans have today become afraid of one another. Confronted with this frightening new challenge, American ability to act is rendered ineffective. Fear of violent crime seems to have made the country helpless, incapable of dealing with the sources of its fear." More important, perhaps, the report says that fear "may be one of the key factors impeding society's ability to cope successfully with those problems."

That fear is measurable in the ways in which Americans are adapting to the new realities of crime—the gun sales, the overbooked karate classes, the rush to buy burglarproof locks for doors and windows. It can also be seen in the ways in which Americans have consciously changed the pattern of their lives. Wealthy businessmen, fearful of kidnapping, who drive to work by different routes each day. Ordinary citizens who learn to walk the streets turning their heads from side to side to check on who might be behind them. Joggers learn to carry at least $20 in "mugger's money," to avoid being shot.

The feeling that all citizens are vulnerable to crime is especially strong among the elderly. Says James Gilsinan, a criminologist at St. Louis University: "The elderly feel a loss of power, of control, of decision making in most facets of their lives. The feeling that they are victims in other areas spills over into crime as well. The elderly stay in a lot, and when they do go out they tend to be in group situations"—which, Gilsinan points out, reduces their chances of being victimized.

Some of the adjustments in life-styles can be quirky. Mimi Warren, 26, of Philadelphia, has developed her own "waiting for a bus behavior." If she sees anyone near a bus stop at night, she breaks into sunny chatter, on the theory that even if the person is a mugger, the conversation will reduce her chances of being attacked. Hilary Stephenson, 38, also of Philadelphia, parks illegally outside her house at night because she would rather pay the parking tickets than walk four blocks from her garage. When she was lost in an unfamiliar part of town, she purposely drove the wrong way down a one-way street to attract a policeman's attention rather than stop and ask for directions. She arranges to call a friend after arriving home from an evening out, with the understanding that the friend will summon police if there is no call. Says Stephenson, who is divorced and lives alone: "With the collapse of the nuclear family, you've got all these singles tucked away in little boxes. I think we must become each other's family."

To be sure, some people make a loud point of taking no precautions, often on the ground that criminals should not have the power to impose a quivering form of life on anyone. Former Attorney General Griffin Bell refuses to get a burglar alarm for his expensive home in northwest Atlanta. Nevenka Charia, 56, a sales clerk in New Orleans, is adamant about not changing her daily patterns out of fear of crime. "I refuse to restrict myself in my movements, day and night, or stay locked up in this house. That's not living at all." But she bought a handgun last December, and on Jan. 8, shot and killed one of two men who attacked her late at night in front of her house. She had never fired a gun before, and is now taking lessons. "It's difficult to say to anyone that they should have a gun," says Charia. "But I'll say this: by all means, fight back, resist, don't be afraid."

Police strongly disagree with her view, but people are beginning to fight back, sometimes in an organized way. At least three times in recent months, groups of subway riders in New York City have grappled with muggers and held them for police. In Memphis last month, Robert Druien, 31, happened to be in Union Planters National Bank during a robbery. He chased the robber to his car, was knocked down when the robber put the car suddenly into reverse, but then got up and joined three other citizens in a car chase through the midtown area. They got their man. Druien hit him in the face and sat on him until police arrived. In Wilmington, Del., after a woman was found dead and mutilated last year, residents of a high-rise apartment complex launched a "crime-watch program," monitoring a police radio scanner and looking out the window for signs of trouble. Richmond has a well-organized program in which neighbors agree to watch one another's homes and report suspicious behavior to police via CB radios.

"People are struggling to find a way to deal with the crime problem," says Catherine Bacharach, who has helped organize volunteer anti-crime groups in Philadelphia with federal funds. "I see the rage and anger as healthy when it's channeled in a positive direction. My sense is that people who work in the system have recognized the need to work with community groups."

Not all officials feel that way. New York City authorities are ambivalent about the Guardian Angels, a group of unarmed red-bereted youngsters, mostly black and Hispanic, who patrol the subways. Though they clearly make riders feel safer, Mayor Edward Koch has labeled them "paramilitary," and the powerful transit police union regards them as amateurs. More muscular kinds of vigilante groups have begun to pop up and around the country. Frank J. Shaw, 60, a retired union organizer and one of the new breed of vigilantes, is a folk hero in Panorama City, Calif. His 40-member citizens' patrol cruises the area by car, armed with floodlights and Mace, staying in touch by CB radio. "We're not flag-waving heroes. We are angry," says Shaw. "We can put blindfolds on, close the shades, turn on the television and be in another world that we hope doesn't close in on us. Or we can face up to reality."

Part of the new reaction to crime is more attention to the victims of violent crimes. As psychologists have warned for years, a victim's lingering fear can be chronic and crippling. Ann McCaughey saw a hand reaching in the window of her Boston apartment one night. She screamed and the hand withdrew. Now she does not sleep well and the slightest noise at night can make her hyperventilate. Says her boyfriend: "It really gets to you. You don't forget." The couple are planning to move. "Being victimized is disabling, even when the crime is unsuccessful," says McCaughey's friend.

As a counselor to rape victims in southern New York State, Registered Nurse Bonnie Hollenbeck began to notice some of the hidden effects of rape and other sexual abuse—confusion, low self-esteem and an impaired ability to function in the adult world. Says Hollenbeck: "Many of these women have failed to establish a connection between their history as victims of sexual crimes and their current difficulties." She and a few colleagues have set up a volunteer crisis counseling group to move in quickly after an assault to help the victim deal with anger, depression and grief.

J. Richard Ciccone, a University of Rochester psychiatrist, thinks all victims of violent crime need that kind of help: the trauma of a beating, a stabbing or a rape requires a period of mourning, just like the death of a loved one. Says he: "Victims who do not receive appropriate understanding and treatment often fall into chronic depression, lose their ability to make their way in the world and become reclusive shadows of their former selves." Though blaming the victim often happens in rape cases, Ciccone warns that many families manage to heap blame on all victims of violence, increasing grief and guilt by saying something like "I warned you never to go into that bar." Unless society begins to do more, he warns, the epidemic of crime will be paralleled by an epidemic of psychiatric problems in victims.

In Jackson Park Highlands, an integrated neighborhood near the University of Chicago, people have begun showing up in court to support crime victims and witnesses. "There is a strong sense of community among those engaged in criminal activity," says Louise Schiff, who works with the program. "You go to court and the defendant's relatives and friends are all there. I think a person who has been victimized deserves support too." Nearby Evanston, Ill., has a more formal victim-witness program, funded through the police budget. The unit assigns social workers and other professionals to guide a victim through emotional recovery and legal complaint. Says Police Chief William C. McHugh: "It helps in a lot of ways."

Experts agree that there tends to be less crime in cohesive, closely knit communities with shared values and a strong sense of neighborhood. But artificially instilling this community spirit into a mobile society is difficult. Some psychologists believe that Americans are becoming dehumanized by crime—not just by the reality but by the fear of it, and the pervasiveness of violent scenes in newspapers and on television. Some social scientists believe that public paranoia has led not only to demands for the restoration of capital punishment and long prison sentences but also to such ugly phenomena as the resurgence of the Ku Klux Klan. "The country is becoming more conservative and punitive," says John Matthews, a sociologist for the Houston police. Indeed, some in authority envision a day when the public will want crime stopped—and will not much care how. "Frustration and fears are very natural reactions when people feel their lives are being shaped by forces beyond their control," says California Supreme Court Justice Rose Elizabeth Bird. She believes there is "great power" in such anger, but great danger as well.

SUMMARY

In this chapter we wanted to accomplish a number of objectives. First, we attempted to familiarize the reader with the crime reporting system in the United States. The Uniform Crime Reporting Program is a voluntary system established in 1930 by the International Association of Chiefs of Police, with the FBI serving as the national clearinghouse. With crime statistics voluntarily contributed by over 16,000 law enforcement agencies throughout the country, the UCR program provides periodic assessments of crime in the United States. Data from the program are widely used by criminal justice professionals, legislators, and scholars who have an interest in the crime problem.

Second, we examined the eight index crimes and defined and described the elements of each and, when applicable, provided case examples of each crime. These eight crimes are frequently divided into the following two broad categories: violent crimes (murder and nonnegligent manslaughter, aggravated assault, forcible rape, and robbery) and crimes against property (burglary, larceny, motor vehicle theft, and arson).

Murder and nonnegligent manslaughter have the highest clearance rate of all index crimes. This is the case in part because a high percentage of these offenses are spontaneous and poorly planned, and in part because these crimes normally receive more intensive investigative efforts by police than the other index crimes. However, the solution rate for this category of crimes has decreased from 84 percent in 1971 to 70 percent in 1986. A major reason for this is that an increasing percentage of these crimes involve total strangers and are committed during the commission of other crimes such as burglaries, robberies, and rapes. Crimes involving strangers are typically more difficult to investigate and solve.

Aggravated assault, like murder and nonnegligent manslaughter, involves a high percentage of people who live together, work together, play together, or socialize together. Aggravated assaults also have a fairly high clearance rate—59 percent—but one quite a bit lower than the solution rate for criminal homicide. The nature of the injuries and close relationship between the victims and assailants are part of the reason. For example, if the victim's injuries are not serious, (nonlethal, or will not cause permanent injury) and if the victim and assailant know each other, there is a tendency for police not to conduct highly intensive investigations. In such cases the victim is also likely to be reluctant to cooperate with the police, thus hampering police investigative efforts.

Forcible rapes reported to the police have increased dramatically during the past decade. In 1971 the rate was 40 per 100,000 females in the United States, and in 1986 it was 73 per 100,000 females in the United States. According to a number of victimization studies, rape is one of the most underreported violent crimes. Reluctance on the part of victims to report rapes stems from their expectations of how they will be treated by the criminal justice system. The perceptions that most citizens have about the way victims are handled come largely from the news media and from highly dramatic television programs, both of which often focus on mistreatment of the victim by the police, prosecutors, and courts. Fortunately, a variety of educational and preventive programs sponsored by police and private groups are modifying some of these distorted perceptions.

Robbery, the last in the category of violent crimes, has the lowest solution rate, 25 percent. This low solution rate results because physical evidence at the scene of the robbery is rarely present, the on-scene time of the perpetrator is limited, and witnesses are usually of little value because they are usually quite frightened and nervous at the time of the offense. Because of its personal and often violent nature, robbery is one of the crimes most feared by the public.

Two important aspects of the crime of burglary are its frequency and economic impact. Burglary comprises 28 percent of all reported property crimes, with an annual estimated loss of $3.1 billion. Burglars tend to come from lower socio-economic classes and are usually not well educated, but notable exceptions include a professor of sociology, a probation officer, police officers in several cities, and, in one case, a psychiatrist.

Although burglars are classified according to a number of variables, the most useful classification is skill. This continuum ranges from amateur to professional, with most burglars falling into the former category.

Larceny, another crime of property, involves a variety of specific offenses including shoplifting, pocket picking, purse snatching, thefts from motor vehicles, theft of motor vehicle parts and accessories, and bicycle theft. This type of crime comprises 55 percent of the total index crime and a clearance rate of only 20 percent.

Motor vehicle theft, which comprises 9 percent of the index crime, and which has a clearance rate of 15 percent, is generally divided into four types of theft by police. These are theft by joy riders, theft of vehicle for use in other crimes, theft for transportation, and theft by professional auto thieves.

Arson was added to the index crimes in 1978 because of the growing severity of the problem at the national level.

The third objective of this chapter was to discuss some of the problems related to gathering crime data and some of the changes that have been suggested for the UCR. We also briefly discussed the National Crime Survey (NCS) and how it differs from the UCR.

Lastly we wanted to provide the reader with some insights into the effects of crime on both the victim and society. The individual cases discussed in the *Time* magazine article assisted in accomplishing this objective.

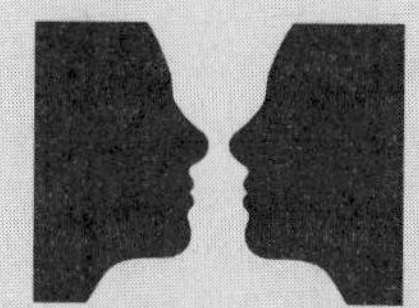

ISSUE PAPER
GUN CONTROL

Firearms and Violence

Americans own a greater number and variety of firearms than do the citizens of any other Western democracy, and they also use their guns against one another much more often. This special significance of firearms in American life has led to a protracted and acrimonious conflict about gun control. Gun control laws in the United States have not achieved the levels of public safety that their supporters had hoped for. Firearms continue to multiply, and deaths from guns have increased since the early 1960's to roughly 30,000 per year. From the failure of existing gun control laws, opponents conclude that controls cannot work, while proponents declare that existing laws must be better enforced or different kinds of controls tried.

The central task of firearms controls through public law is to reduce the hundreds of thousands of occasions each year when guns are used illegitimately without unduly disrupting the millions of occasions when guns are used legitimately—including hunting, target sports, self-defense, and collecting. A perfect gun control law would eliminate the unlawful use of guns and leave all legitimate users undisturbed. Real world choices involve harder tradeoffs.

What exactly is the "gun problem"? Advocates of control begin by pointing out that more than 20 percent of all robberies and about 60 percent of all homicides are committed with firearms. Their opponents reply that the vast majority of the country's 130 million firearms are not involved in violence, and that crime rather than firearms is the real problem. "Guns don't kill people," they assert, "people kill people."

Serious assault with a gun is, according to the best estimates, three to five times as likely to cause death as a similar attack with a knife, the next most dangerous weapon. And gun robberies are three to four times as likely to result in the death of a victim as are other kinds of robbery.

Firearms are often discussed as a general category, without distinguishing among handguns, rifles, and shotguns. In some respects that approach is appropriate because a rifle or a shotgun, if used in an attack, is at least as dangerous as a handgun. Even a superficial study of statistics on firearms and violence, however, suggests that the handgun presents special problems. The handgun—small, easy to conceal, and relatively unimportant in hunting—accounts for about one-fourth of the privately owned firearms in the country, but it is involved in three-fourths of all gun killings. In the big cities, handguns account for more than 80 percent of gun killings and virtually all gun robberies.

Even though the most common reason for owning a handgun is for household self-defense, studies suggest that loaded household handguns are more likely to kill family members than to save their lives. A Detroit study found that more people died in 1 year from handgun accidents alone than were killed by home-invading robbers or burglars in 4½ years. The discovery that self-defense handguns are from this standpoint a poor investment suggests that rejecting handgun ownership makes sense from a safety perspective, even if other families retain their guns. But if unilateral disarmament is rational, why do people not give up their guns voluntarily, and why do handguns continue to proliferate in the cities?

To some extent, urban gun ownership for self-defense results from misinformation about the risk of accidental death and the usefulness of guns in defense of the home. However, it is foolish to think that millions of American families keep handguns merely because they have not read the statistics, or to suppose that showing them data will change their minds. The risk of accidental or homicidal death from a loaded gun in the home—although greater than the chance that the gun will save lives—is nevertheless small. In the majority of homes with handguns, the only real use of the gun may be to make its owner feel safer. People will reject statistics that show otherwise because, even if their guns do not give them any real measure of protection, they have no other way to deal with their fears.

Gun Control Strategies

Simply because the problems are real does not mean that the solutions are easy. Indeed, the extent of the gun problem in the United States should be a warning that reducing gun violence will be difficult and expensive. There are already more than 20,000 gun laws in the Nation to match the thousands of gun killings. Why should gun laws decrease the rate of criminal killings when criminals, by definition, do not obey laws?

A number of different types of gun control strategies have been attempted and proposed. How are these various laws supposed to work, and is it likely that they will?

A number of different types of gun control strategies have been attempted and proposed. How are these various laws supposed to work, and is it likely that they will?

1. *Place and manner restrictions.* Most of the gun laws in the United States attempt to separate illegitimate from legitimate gun use by regulating the "place and manner" in which firearms may be used. They prohibit the carrying of firearms within city limits or in a motor vehicle, the carrying of concealed weapons on one's person, or the discharging of a firearm in a populated area. Such laws attempt to reduce firearm violence by authorizing the police to intervene before violence or crime actually takes place. Since there are obvious limits to the ability of police to prevent firearm violence and to discover persons who violate place and manner laws, these laws may deter at most a limited amount of gun violence.
2. *Stiffer penalties for firearm violence.* Members of the National Rifle Association have been among the most vocal supporters of laws that increase prison sentences, or make them mandatory, for persons committing crimes with guns. Such laws do not make it harder for potential criminals, or anyone else, to obtain guns, but they are intended to reduce gun crime by making punishments for crimes with guns so severe that potential criminals either will commit the crime without a gun or will not commit the crime at all. More than half of the States have laws providing for longer sentences for criminals who carry or use a gun while committing a felony.

In order to reduce the number of gun crimes, such laws would have to deter persons who would not be deterred by the already stiff penalties for gun crimes. Can the threat of additional punishment succeed? Perhaps the robber could be deterred from using a gun if the punishment for gun robbery were several times greater than that for nongun robbery.

Many gun owners doubt that such plans will work because "when guns are criminal, only criminals will have guns." Moreover, they argue, if handguns are illegal, criminals will switch to other kinds of guns, a development that will not reduce gun crime but will spur efforts to confiscate all kinds of civilian firearms.

Both of these arguments have some force, but they must be balanced against important facts about the relationship between guns and violence in the United States. First, guns are more lethal than other weapons. Thus, substantially reducing the number of handguns should reduce the number of homicides resulting from accidental weapon use and the use of a weapon to settle an argument, even though some criminals will undoubtedly continue to use handguns. Second, it appears to be harder than one might suspect for the handgun robber or attacker to switch to a rifle or other "long" gun. For this reason, the average handgun is many times more likely to kill than the average long gun. States that try to restrict handguns find that their major problem becomes not the long gun but the illegal handgun.

The real difficulty in restricting the handgun is how to reduce the number of such guns in circulation enough to make headway against gun violence, and, if it can be done, how long this will take and what its cost will be. It is possible, by law, to put a stop to the manufacture of handguns at any time, but even if this were done, some of the 35 million handguns in the civilian inventory would still be killing people in the 21st century. Under the best conditions, collecting the vast arsenal of civilian handguns would be neither easy nor swift. Americans do not live under the best of conditions—the very crime rate that makes many people want gun control also makes gun control extremely difficult to achieve. How many citizens would turn in their guns when the law took effect? How long would it take to remove the guns from the streets, where they do the most harm? Should urban households be left fearfully defenseless? Is it desirable to add yet another victimless and unenforceable crime—possession of a handgun—to the depressingly long list of such crimes that have already accumulated? These are not easy questions to answer.

Finding appropriate gun control strategies also involves constitutional considerations and the balance between Federal and State responsibility for crime control. The second amendment to the United States Constitution provides for a right of the people to bear arms, and many State constitutions contain similar provisions. While there is dispute as to what that provision of the second amendment means, it has never been held to invalidate Federal or State gun control legislation. Nonetheless, the "right to bear arms" is frequently invoked as a reason to avoid restrictions on legitimate gun ownership and use.

The traditional division of authority for crime control between the Federal Government and the States also limits the extent of Federal involvement in gun control. Street police work is the province of local government in the United States. Gun control laws that require police enforcement must be carried out by municipal police.

But whatever gun control strategies are tried, it seems that local initiatives must have State and national support if they hope to achieve their goals. When jurisdictions pass strict laws against certain kinds of gun sales and resales, guns leak in from other jurisdictions that do not have the same controls. Moreover, the existing Federal law designed to assist States and localities has not been adequately enforced.

Any gun control policy will be something of an experiment in the coming years. It is not known how effective any law can be when there are so many guns in circulation and so much pressure to keep them there.

References

Cook, Philip. 1983. "The Influence of Gun Availability on Violent Crime Patterns." In *Crime and Justice: An Annual Review of Research,* vol. 4, edited by Michael Tonry and Norval Morris. Chicago, Illinois: The University of Chicago Press.

Newton, George D., Jr., and Franklin E. Zimring. 1969. *Firearms and Violence in American Life: A Staff Report Submitted to the National Commission on the Causes and Prevention of Violence.* Washington, D.C.: National Commission on the Causes and Prevention of Violence.

Wright, James D., Peter H. Rossi, and Kathleen Daly. 1983. *Under the Gun: Weapons, Crime, and Violence in America.* New York: Aldine Publishing Company.

This article was written by Franklin E. Zimring for the National Institute of Justice "Crime File" series. It appeared as a study guide to accompany the videotape *Gun Control,* 1987.

DISCUSSION AND REVIEW

1. What are the two categories that encompass the eight index crimes?
2. Why is the clearance rate for murder higher than the clearance rate for the other index crimes?
3. Why is the clearance rate for aggravated assault lower than the clearance rate for murder, even though both crimes often involve close relationships between victims and assailants?
4. Why is rape one of the most underreported violent crimes?
5. What is the difference between robbery and larceny?
6. What are "chop shops"?
7. What are the four categories of motor vehicle theft?
8. Why would a law enforcement agency manipulate crime data?
9. What are some of the traditional criticisms of the UCR system?

GLOSSARY

Aggravated assault Unlawful attack by one person upon another for the purpose of inflicting severe or aggravated bodily injury.

Arson The willful and malicious setting of fires.

Burglary Unlawful entry of a structure to commit a felony or theft.

Chop shop Garages that strip stolen cars of usable parts for sale to auto repair shops.

Clearance rate Solution rate (percent) for crimes reported to the police.

Clearing the books Efforts by police to improve clearance rates by getting people already charged with a crime to confess to other crimes they have not committed.

Crime data manipulation Falsification of crime data submitted to the FBI Uniform Crime Reports by state and local police.

Crime rate Number of index crimes committed per 100,000 inhabitants.

Criminal homicide The willful, nonnegligent, killing of one human being by another.

FBI Uniform Crime Reports Annual reports distributed by the FBI and based upon crime data provided by state and local police.

Forcible rape The carnal knowledge of a female, forcibly and against her will.

Larceny Theft of property without force or fear.

Motor vehicle theft Theft or attempted theft of a vehicle for nontemporary use.

NCS Acronym for the National Crime Survey; conducted by the Bureau of Justice Statistics, the NCS obtains both reported and unreported crime information.

Part II crimes Nonindex crimes in the UCR system. For example, forgery, vandalism, and driving under the influence.

Robbery Theft or attempted theft by use of force, violence, or threat of violence, or by putting the victim in fear.

Waiver of prosecution A desire on the part of a crime victim to have the state not prosecute the assailant.

REFERENCES

Coleman, J. C. *Abnormal Psychology and Modern Life.* 6th ed. Glenview, Ill.: Scott, Foresman, 1980.

Federal Bureau of Investigation. *Crime in the United States.* FBI Uniform Crime Reports. Washington, D.C.: U.S. Government Printing Office, 1971.

Federal Bureau of Investigation. *Crime in the United States.* FBI Uniform Crime Reports. Washington, D.C.: U.S. Government Printing Office, 1981.

Federal Bureau of Investigation. *Crime in the United States.* FBI Uniform Crime Reports. Washington, D.C.: U.S. Government Printing Office, 1986.

Horgan, J. J. *Criminal Investigation.* New York: McGraw-Hill, 1974.

Kukla, R. J. *Gun Control.* Harrisburg, Pa.: Stackpole Books, 1973.

Magnuson, E. "The Curse of Violent Crime." *Time,* 23 March 1981, pp. 16–21.
"National Strategy to Reduce Crime." *The National Commission on Criminal Justice Standards and Goals,* Washington, D.C.: Government Printing Office, 1973.
Oster, Patrick, R. "How One State's Gun Control Is Working." *U.S. News and World Report,* 30 August 1976, p. 35.
Poggio, Eugene C.; Kennedy, Stephen D.; Chaiken, Jan M.; and Carlson, Kenneth, E. *Blueprint for the Future of the Uniform Crime Reporting Program.* Washington, D.C.: U.S. Department of Justice, Bureau of Justice Statistics, Federal Bureau of Investigation, 1985.
Pope, C. E. *Crime Specific Analysis: The Characteristics of Burglary Incidents.* Washington, D.C.: U.S. Government Printing Office, 1977.
President's Commission on Law Enforcement and the Administration of Justice. *Task Force Report: Crime and Its Impact.* Washington, D.C.: U.S. Government Printing Office, 1967.
Rand, Michael R.; Klaus, Patsy A.; and Taylor, Bruce M. "The Criminal Event." In Marianne W. Zawitz, Ed., *Report to the Nation on Crime and Justice—The Data.* Washington, D.C.: U.S. Department of Justice, Bureau of Justice Statistics, 1983.
Rape Victimization Study. San Francisco: Queens Bench Foundation, 1975.
"Senate Probing Car Theft Industry." *Atlanta Journal,* 26 November 1979, p. 24.
Swanson, C. R.; Chamelin, N. C.; and Territo, L. *Criminal Investigation.* 4th ed. New York: Random House, 1988.
Turner, C. W.; Layton, J. R.; and Simons, L. S. "Naturalistic Studies of Aggressive Behavior: Aggressive Stimuli, Victim Visibility, and Horn-honking," *Journal of Personality and Social Psychology,* 31 (1975): 1098–1107.
Williams, J. S., and McGrath, J. *Social Psychological Dimension of Gun Ownership.* Washington, D.C.: U.S. Government Printing Office, 1975.

■ NOTES

1. The discussion of UCR classifications of crimes against property and violent crimes was adapted from Federal Bureau of Investigation, *Crime in the United States,* FBI Uniform Crime Reports (Washington, D.C.: U.S. Government Printing Office, 1986), pp. 1–50.
2. The discussion of future trends in the UCR program was adapted from Eugene C. Poggio et al., *Blueprint for the Future of the Uniform Crime Reporting Program.* (Washington, D.C.: U.S. Department of Justice, Bureau of Justice Statistics, Federal Bureau of Investigation, 1985), pp. 1–3.
3. The discussion of the comparison of NCS and UCR crime data was adapted from Michael R. Rand, Patsy A. Klaus, and Bruce M. Taylor, *Report to the Nation on Crime and Justice—The Data.* (Washington, D.C.: U.S. Department of Justice, Bureau of Justice Statistics, 1983), p. 6.

CHAPTER

4

Factors and Theories in Criminality: The Search for the Criminal

CHAPTER OUTLINE:

Before the eighteenth century, criminal behavior was simply treated as moral degeneracy or "badness," without much consideration given to the reasons for its occurrence. Medieval interpretations attributed a wide range of abnormal behaviors to demonic possession—an "explanation" that could be extended to include at least some forms of criminally deviant behavior. Offenders were to be rescued from the clutches of the Devil by being made to suffer horrible punishments. These drastic measures usually met with success, but the unfortunate offenders were often freed from possession at the expense of their lives. The Supreme Court of the state of North Carolina, as recently as 1862, endorsed the notion of demonic possession when it declared, "To know the right and still the wrong pursue proceeds from a perverse will brought about by the seductions of the Evil One" (Sutherland and Cressey 1978, p. 54).

More recently, the causes of crime have been looked for both within and outside the offender. Physiology and heredity, mental disorders, personality characteristics, poverty and frustration, and the criminal justice system itself—all of these factors and others have been examined as possible causes of criminal behavior. As this chapter shows, it is nearly impossible with our present knowledge to rule out any of these factors as an explanation for at least some kinds of criminality.

ECONOMIC FACTORS

Attempts to relate crime to economic conditions have taken several approaches. The oldest approach attributes criminality to relative poverty, i.e., to how poor a person is compared with others in society who are better off economically. A second approach—the one most common to modern industrial societies—links crime to affluence. A third perspective, rooted in the works of Marx and Engels and incorporated today in the doctrine of radical criminology, views crime as the result of social circumstances produced by capitalism. Changing social beliefs and convictions have led to shifts in emphasis from one of these perspectives to another.

Understanding the relationship between crime and economic factors is complicated by the lack of precise measures of either crime or economic conditions. It may be possible to measure the economic situation in relatively simple agricultural communities such as those found in Third World countries, but it is far more difficult to do so in a society such as ours with a complex economic structure. Although one industry can serve as the economic barometer of a simple society, economic change in a complex society must be measured by a diversified index that considers all major industries. The development of such a device is a task that continues to baffle even the most expert economists.

FIGURE 4.1
Left, Demon riding the tail of a woman's cloak. *Right,* Casting out demons by torture. These fifteenth-century woodcuts illustrate a moral tract that attributed misconduct to demonic possession. From Alan C. Kors and Edward Peters, *Witchcraft in Europe: 1100–1700: A Documentary History* (Philadelphia: University of Pennsylvania Press, 1972).

Criminologists Sutherland and Cressey (1978) surveyed studies of crime and economic conditions both in the United States and abroad, dating back to the turn of the century. Their conclusions are as follows:

1. During periods of economic depression, the general crime rate does not rise significantly.
2. There is a slight, yet inconsistent, tendency for serious crime to increase during periods of economic depression and to decline in periods of prosperity.
3. Violent property crimes tend to increase during periods of depression. Nonviolent property crimes (such as larceny) show an extremely slight—but not consistent—tendency to rise during such periods.
4. Some studies show that drunkenness increases during periods of prosperity; yet other studies indicate that there is no correlation between drunkenness and economic conditions.
5. There is no consistent evidence that crimes against the person are affected by changes in the business cycle.
6. Juvenile delinquency has a tendency to rise during periods of prosperity and to decline in periods of depression.

Poverty is also associated with certain social conditions that may be of greater significance than economic need as a cause of crime (Sutherland and Cressey 1978). Poverty areas in our modern cities typically occur in segregated, low-rent districts in which people are exposed to criminal behavior. And poverty usually means high unemployment with no future potential for work, loss of social status, loss of respect, feelings of powerlessness, and the attitude that there is "little to lose."

Working parents in poor areas are often away when their children are awake, and they are irritable and fatigued when at home. And approximately 43 percent of poor families are headed by women (Poplin 1978); this situation in particular adversely affects the attitudes of male children toward family responsibilities and work. Typically, a disproportionate number of children in poor areas drop out of school at an early age because they see little value in education. As a result, the jobs they hold are generally low paying, unskilled, and uninteresting, with little chance for economic advancement. Thus the cycle continues. Because the vast majority of conventional offenders come from poverty areas, it must be concluded that poverty contributes to the crime problem.

The idea of **radical criminology** takes this conclusion one step further. Radical criminologists see criminality as primarily an expression of class conflict. Behavior designated as "criminal" by the ruling classes is viewed as the inevitable product of a fundamentally corrupt and unjust society, and law enforcement agencies are seen as the domestic military apparatus used by the ruling classes to maintain themselves in power. Because the causes of crime are thought to lie within society and its legal system, it is held that crime will persist until both are changed.

Radical criminology encompasses the views of a number of contemporary criminologists whose ideas derive directly from, or have been heavily influenced by, Marxist thought. These writers have presented their approaches under a variety of designations: "new criminology," "critical criminology," "Marxist criminology," or "conflict criminology." The basic tenets of the position are outlined by Quinney (1974, p. 16):

1. American society is based on an advanced capitalist economy.
2. The state is organized to serve the interests of the dominant economic class, the capitalist ruling class.
3. Criminal law is an instrument of the state and the ruling class to maintain and perpetuate the existing social and economic order.
4. Crime control in capitalist society is accomplished through a variety of institutions and agencies established and administered by a government elite, representing ruling-class interests, for the purpose of establishing domestic order.
5. The contradictions of advanced capitalism—the disjunction between existence and essence—require that the subordinate classes remain oppressed by whatever means necessary, especially through the coercion and violence of the legal system.
6. Only with the collapse of capitalist society and the creation of a new society based on socialist principles will there be a solution to the crime problem.

Radical criminologists divide the fundamental inequities of the American criminal justice system into two categories: discriminatory treatment on the basis of class, and discriminatory treatment on the basis of race. Although race discrimination is fading somewhat in parts of the system, it is still a significant factor in the administration of justice. Class discrimination is becoming more widespread than ever today, as economic deterioration widens the gap between classes. Class and race are not, of course, mutually exclusive, as demonstrated by the position of poor blacks in the process of justice.

Radical theorists reject the concept of individual guilt and responsibility for illegal acts committed by the working class against the persons and property of the bourgeoisie. They see these crimes as wholly justified acts of rebellion by slaves against masters. This view makes the bulk of property crimes "political" crimes—morally acceptable and, indeed, almost mandatory in view of the criminal nature of society itself. Assaults and property crimes by the proletariat against members of their own class are not justified by radical theory but are understood as inevitable social distortions produced by a capitalist society that breeds racial distrust among the poor, protects the person and property of the bourgeoisie more effectively than the person and property of workers, and produces poverty and alienation.

Critics of radical criminology question the adequacy of class conflict as an explanation for a wide range of criminal behavior. As McCaghy states:

> The theory's application is actually limited to explaining legal reaction against behaviors threatening established economic interests. Thus there is no pretense at explaining such facets of the crime problem as a school janitor sexually molesting a ten-year-old student, parents brutally beating a baby because "it won't stop crying," or two friends trying to stab each other in a dispute over a fifty cent gambling debt (1976, p. 96).

He further observes that the conflict perspective is not a statement of facts or of empirically verified relationships; it is a perspective that directs attention to a *possible* interpretation of the facts.

BIOLOGICAL FACTORS

An ancient and persistent notion holds that character is closely linked to physique. In Shakespeare's *Julius Caesar* (act 1, scene 2), the protagonist entreats Marc Antony:

> *Let me have men about me that are fat*
> *Sleek-headed men and such as sleep o' nights:*
> *Yon Cassius has a lean and hungry look;*
> *He thinks too much; such men are dangerous.*

In the nineteenth century, a physician named Cesare Lombroso gave this notion an intriguing twist. He suggested that criminal behavior could be explained by **atavism**—by the idea that criminals are throwbacks to some earlier, more primitive forerunner of modern humans. The proof of his contention? Lombroso believed that "born criminals" could be identified by certain "stigmata of degeneracy," such as pointed ears, sloping forehead, receding chin, close-set and shifty eyes, and other physical abnormalities.

Lombroso's speculations were never proven, but later "Lombrosians" pointed to still other physical characteristics thought to be associated with criminality. Some believed that a particular body type (such as a tough, muscular physique) was characteristic of criminals; others said that criminals had glandular imbalances or abnormalities of the nervous system. To date, however, these speculations have not held up under close study. No one has identified a physical characteristic reliably found among criminals but not among noncriminals, although, as explained in the following sections, there is some evidence that certain physical characteristics and physiques appear more frequently among criminals than noncriminals.

Still, many people believe that biology plays some role in the development of criminal behavior. Decades ago, researchers compiled family histories to show that crime "ran" in families, concluding that some people were "born" criminals, that crime was the result of "bad seed." However, because behavior is linked to upbringing, as well as to genes, family histories alone cannot prove that criminality is inherited.

Research on Chromosomes

The strongest evidence for the theory of inherited criminality comes from studies of chromosomes where a particular abnormality of the chromosomes is found disproportionately among male criminals (Herrnstein 1987).[1] Gender and gender characteristics are determined by one of the twenty-three pairs of chromosomes that contain the human genetic endowment. For genetically normal females, the sex-determining pair consists of two ordinary-sized chromosomes, called XX because of their microscopic appearance. Males normally have an XY pair

Do Criminals Have "Roots"? The Infamous Jukes and Kallikaks

Studies of the famed lineages of the Juke family by Richard Dugdale in the 19th century and the Kallikak family in the early 20th century by Henry H. Goddard supported the claim that some individuals were "born criminals" and that "bad genes" could be passed from generation to generation. Although Dugdale did not invent the Jukes, he often used his imagination when the facts failed to bolster his theory of the hereditary causes of crime. When information about individuals was difficult to obtain, Dugdale resorted to the characterizations such as "supposed to have attempted rape," "reputed sheep stealer but never caught," "hardened character."

Goddard studied the descendants of two clans of the Kallikak family. Although both clans descended from the same Revolutionary War soldier, Martin Kallikak, the "bad" Kallikaks were attributed to the soldier's union with a feebleminded girl. There is little evidence that these families committed actual crime. In fact, Goddard found only three official cases of crime. All of the supposedly "good" Kallikaks descended from the soldier's marriage with a Quaker woman. Since none of the good Kallikaks seem to have inherited any "bad genes" something rather strange must have occurred in the lineages, for we know that a certain number of the good offspring should have shown some "degenerate" traits.

Alberta J. Nassi and Stephen I. Abramowitz, "From Phrenology to Psychosurgery and Back Again: Biological Studies of Criminality," *American Journal of Orthopsychiatry* 46 (1976): 595–96, Reprinted by permission of the authors and the publisher.

FIGURE 4.2
Cesare Lombroso combined ideas from phrenology and organic evolution to develop the concept of the "born criminal." This sketch compares the head of a minister (*left*) with the head of a murderer to show a biological basis for criminality. Chiolini Photo Agency.

instead, of which one of the chromosomes (the Y) is smaller. For less than one-tenth of 1 percent of the male population, however, there is an extra Y chromosome, so that instead of a sex-determining pair, there is a sex-determining triplet of chromosomes, **XYY**. The extra Y chromosome may turn up unpredictably in any social class or ethnic group or family setting. Such men are taller than average and have other minor physical characteristics. They also have a ten to twenty times greater tendency to break the law than do genetically normal men from comparable populations.

Even with their elevated criminal tendencies, there are too few XYY men to affect overall crime rates much. However, they illustrate the power of genetic influences on criminal behavior, for any effect that the extra chromosomes have on behavior is genetic by definition. Some, but evidently not all, of the elevated risk of criminal behavior among XYY males has been traced to the lower IQ scores they have been shown to have. The implication that IQ scores are to a degree controlled by genes and correlated with crime is briefly discussed in a later section (Herrnstein 1987).

RESEARCH ON TWINS AND ADOPTIONS Another approach to the biological basis of criminality is to compare identical and fraternal twins. Identical twins, arising as they do from a single fertilized ovum, share identical genes. Fraternal twins arise from two fertilized ova and have the same genetic overlap as ordinary sisters and brothers. Traits for which identical twins are more similar than fraternal twins are likely to involve genes. Familiar examples are height, weight, and general appearance, all of which are typically more similar for identical twins. From the results of about a dozen studies in Europe, Asia, and the United States, criminality can be added to the list. An identical, as contrasted with a fraternal, twin with a criminal record has approximately twice the likelihood of having a co-twin with a record, too. Identical twins are also more alike than fraternal twins in the frequency of criminal behavior they admit to in anonymous questionnaires. The differential resemblance of identical and fraternal twins is generally considered to be strong, though it is not by itself conclusive evidence of genetic involvement in criminal behavior.

The other main source of evidence comes from studies of children adopted early in life and of their biological and adopting parents. For example, the criminal convictions among a sample of more than 4,000 Danish boys were more dependent on their biological, as compared to their adoptive, parents' criminality. The more serious an offender a biological parent was, the greater the risk of criminality for his or her child, particularly for property crimes. Adopted boys who had a chronically criminal biological parent (three or more convictions) were three times more likely to become criminal than those whose biological parents were not criminal. The risk for the child depended neither on whether the child or the adopting parents knew about the biological parents' criminal records nor on whether the biological parents committed their crimes before or after the child was adopted. Swedish and American studies have confirmed the main conclusions and have extended them to female adopted children.

The bits of evidence may be individually disputed but, taken together, the case for some genetic involvement in criminal behavior cannot plausibly be rejected. On the average, offenders are distinctive in physical constitution (to be discussed in a later section), they are more likely to have chromosomal abnormality, and they tend to occur in families with other offenders whether or not they were raised by their criminal relatives. Unwholesome environments are surely among the significant predictors of crime; they are just not the only predictors. But genes do not cause crimes as such. Rather, the evidence suggests a more complex chain of connections: genes affect psychological traits, which in turn affect the likelihood of breaking the law. Intelligence and personality are the two traits most strongly implicated in this chain (Herrnstein 1987).

RESEARCH ON IQ Many studies have shown that the offender population has an average IQ of about 91–93, compared to the average IQ of 100 for the population at large. Since the general population includes an unknown fraction of offenders, the IQ gap between offenders and nonoffenders can only be estimated, but a conservative value is about 10 points. Different categories of offender have different average IQs, some lower and some higher than 91–93. In general, however, the common offenses—the impulsive violent crimes and the opportunistic property crimes—are most often committed by people in the low normal and borderline retarded range.

Since test scores and crime rates are both correlated with socioeconomic status, it is sometimes suggested that status, rather than test score, is the critical variable in explaining criminal behavior. But the evidence says otherwise. At each socioeconomic level, offenders tend to have lower IQ test scores; among people with the same scores, people from lower socioeconomic levels commit more crime. Thus, both cognitive ability (intelligence) and socioeconomic status (environment) contribute to the likelihood of criminal behavior, and there is some reason for concluding that ability contributes more.

IQ test items call on cognitive abilities of various sorts, each of which can be described as verbal or nonverbal. A vocabulary test is obviously verbal; a test of speed and accuracy in assembling the pieces of a jigsaw puzzle is nonverbal. Spatial reasoning is nonverbal; arithmetical reasoning is usually considered verbal. Tests are usually constructed so that the average person has equal verbal and nonverbal scores, but offenders average lower verbal than nonverbal scores. Even among groups of offenders and nonoffenders matched for age, overall IQ, ethnic background, and socioeconomic status, offenders have lower verbal scores than nonoffenders (and higher nonverbal scores, so as to equalize overall scores for the two groups). Low verbal scores may create a risk for criminal behavior because they impair a person's ability to formulate and follow internal standards of conduct, or because they lead to failure and frustration in school and on the job, or for all those reasons.

A large scientific literature indicates that the abilities measured by IQ tests are partly genetic. Verbal abilities are at least as heritable as nonverbal. The IQs of children raised in foster homes correlate more closely with those of their biological parents than with their foster parents'. Identical twins have more similar IQs than fraternal twins. In general, people who are more closely related by blood have more similar test scores. Estimates of the heritability of intelligence, by serious students of the subject, range from about 40 percent to 80 percent. This does not mean that intelligence is immune to influence by the environment, but it helps explain the evidence for an inherited biological factor in criminal behavior. Since crime correlates with IQ, and IQ is partly inherited, a heritable susceptibility to criminal behavior follows.

RESEARCH ON BODY TYPES AND PHYSIQUE In the 1930s, Earnest A. Hooton, an American anthropologist, compared standard physical measurements of over 10,000 male prisoners with those of noncriminals of corresponding ages and ethnic ancestries from corresponding regions of the country. Hooton discovered that criminals were, on the average, physically distinctive in small but statistically significant ways. In some samples, he also found small physical differences between groups of criminals convicted for different crimes. The physical correlates were things like particular ear shapes or eye colors or relative sizes of parts of the body or hair distributions—all in all, minor attributes that had no clear or obvious connection to crime besides the correlation itself.

What mattered to Hooton was not what the physical correlates of crime were as much as that there were correlates at all. From his evidence that criminals were physically distinctive, Hooton argued for a biological susceptibility to crime that also happened to show up in otherwise irrelevant physical characteristics, such as the shape of one's ear. Thus the physical correlate was a form of evidence, albeit indirect, of biological involvement in the tendency to break the law (Hooton 1939).

More such evidence began to accumulate in the 1940s, after the physician William H. Sheldon developed a new system for classifying human physiques. A person's body build, in this system, is represented by three numbers for the three "dimensions" of physique—that is, endomorphy (soft, round), mesomorphy (large boned, muscular), and ectomorphy (linear, fragile). Each dimension is assigned a score on a 7-point scale (4 being the midpoint); the value for any individual is derived from objective measurements of the body, ideally after adjusting for age, health, and nutritional status. The average male's physique is approximately 4.0–4.0–3.5 (for endomorphy, mesomorphy, and ectomorphy, respectively); the average female's, approximately 5.0–3.0–3.5. Extreme values along any of the dimensions are relatively rare: for example, the 4–6–1 body type, which is highly mesomorphic and very weakly ectomorphic, is estimated to occur only twice per 1,000 males. This also happens to be one of the physiques disproportionately susceptible to criminal behavior.

Several studies by Sheldon and by others reported that male and female offenders were more mesomorphic and less ectomorphic, on the average, than nonoffenders who were matched for age, IQ, socioeconomic status, or ethnic ancestry. A small amount of evidence suggests that criminal recidivists have more atypical physiques (even more mesomorphy and less ectomorphy) than criminals in general. The third dimension, endomorphy, does not reliably correlate with criminal behavior. Not everyone who has high mesomorphy and low ectomorphy commits crimes, or vice versa. Indeed, it is likely that other pursuits besides crime attract the same sorts of body builds.

Physique, as measured in Sheldon's system, is a constitutional variable, not greatly affected by environment or experience; hence it is likely to be dependent on one's genes. Its correlation with criminal behavior implies that criminal tendencies involve genes to some extent. Sheldon and others have found that physique is correlated, although imperfectly, with personality and temperament. The mesomorphic component is typically associated with, among other traits, high activity levels, restlessness, a craving for adventure and danger, and aggressiveness; the ectomorphic component, with introspectiveness, self-consciousness, inhibition, rich inner psychic experience, and a capacity for delayed gratification. Mesomorphy unleavened by ectomorphy is therefore likely to be accompanied by a taste for uninhibited, aggressive excitement and by deficits in internal feelings and forbearance. Such a combination of personality traits has been directly associated with criminal tendencies (Sheldon, Stevens, and Zucker 1940).

Nutrition

In 1968, Linus Pauling—twice the recipient of the Nobel Prize—coined the term **orthomolecular psychiatry.** He suggested that mental illness and behavior disorders are caused mostly by abnormal reaction rates in the body as a result of constitutional defects, faulty diet, and abnormal concentrations of essential elements. Pauling recommended that treatment of behavior disorders include the establishment of an optimal chemical state for the brain and nervous system. He attracted nationwide interest with his vigorous advocacy of massive doses of vitamin C as a remedy for the common cold.

Supporters of the orthomolecular approach maintain that various kinds of delinquent and criminal behavior are not psychosocial reactions but indications of metabolic or biochemical imbalances. That is, an adolescent youth may engage in violent behavior not because he or she is the unfortunate victim of maternal rejection, a broken home, or peer pressures, but because he or she is suffering from faulty diet, inadequate nutrition, or the presence of some toxic substance in the body (such as mercury), which adversely affects general health and functioning.

As a case in point, hyperactivity in youngsters—a syndrome characterized by restlessness, distraction, excessive physical activity, and aggressive behavior—is often regarded as antisocial or delinquent. Yet it has been suggested that hyperactivity is principally caused by nutritional deficiencies, and low blood sugar (hypoglycemia). Both of these conditions may be systematically related to the "junk food" that youngsters in this country consume in large quantities and that are loaded with the processed sugar, starches, and toxic additives that produce orthomolecular imbalances. As Thornton, James, and Doerner observe:

> Children who are hyperative often become labeled as problem cases by parents and teachers. Unable to concentrate and learn, these youth can grown into adulthood lacking a wide variety of knowledge and skills. Thus, they are prime candidates for truancy and dropping out of school, activities conducive to delinquent behavior (1982, p. 82).

Most criminologists agree that nutritional and biochemical factors influence behavior. There is much less agreement, however, as to what extent and in what specific ways these factors are involved in delinquent and criminal behavior. Arguments that low blood sugar is mainly responsible for crimes such as rape, robbery, arson, assault, and homicide, or that nearly all convicted murderers suffer from hypoglycemia or vitamin deficiencies, must be considered hypotheses that await confirmation through controlled research. Until the evidence is in, the criminological community is obliged to maintain an attitude of cautious interest toward orthomolecular claims about the causes of crime.

Epilepsy

Epilepsy—the "falling sickness" of classical reference—refers to a group of heterogenous, complex, and controversial disorders characterized by the recurrence of convulsive attacks or seizures. An alleged relationship between epilepsy and violent behavior has long been one of the popular myths relating criminality to mental illness. Batchelor feels it is more accurate to speak of epilepsies as symptoms rather than disorders: "The essential feature is not the convulsive seizure or the disturbance of consciousness, but the episodic sudden disturbance of function in the central nervous system" (1969, p. 420). Experimental studies involving brain stimulation have shown that some seizures closely resembling epileptic attacks can be elicited by electrical means.

Epilepsy has been known from antiquity, and behavioral pathologists are fond of compiling lists of world-famous figures who have been afflicted. With Alexander of Macedon, Julius Caesar, and Napoleon heading the parade, one might wonder if epilepsy and visions of world conquest go hand in hand. However, there are enough gifted artists, writers, and musicians in the tally—Maupassant, van Gogh, and Byron, for instance—to dispel that idea.

The major types of epilepsy are grand mal, petit mal, Jacksonian, and psychomotor epilepsy. Grand mal, the most common and dramatic of epileptic reactions, is characterized by severe motor convulsions and an interruption or loss of consciousness. Petit mal, which is rare in adults over twenty-one, causes a fleeting disruption of consciousness that may go unrecognized for a long time. Jacksonian seizures, which resemble grand mal attacks in most respects, begin with a spasmodic muscular contraction in an arm or leg and usually extend to involve an entire side of the body.

Psychomotor epilepsy (or "psychic equivalents") also represents a disruption of consciousness; but the epileptic often manages to carry out some fairly complicated patterns of behavior. Among such patterns—according to standard views—are violence and aggression, up to and including mass murder (Suinn 1970). It is almost traditional in discussions of epilepsy and violence to cite the case of the Flemish painter Vincent van Gogh, who sliced off one of his own ears with a razor, carefully packed it in cotton, and presented it to a prostitute in a provincial French bordello. Van Gogh is believed to have carried out this act of self-mutilation during one of his psychomotor **fugues.**

On examination, the murderous reputation of the psychomotor epileptic is largely folklore. For example, Turner and Merlis (1962) report that only 5 out of 337 epileptics whose case records they examined exhibited antisocial behavior during their seizures. Rodin (1973) found no instances of aggressive or violent behavior in 57 patients with psychomotor epilepsy who were photographed during seizures; and he found only 34 examples of aggressive actions in 700 case histories.

Brain-Wave Studies

The **electroencephalograph** (EEG) is an instrument that picks up electrical activity in brain cells by means of electrodes attached to the scalp. This activity is recorded in oscillating patterns called *brain waves* by a machine connected to the electrodes. EEG studies have been used to investigate criminals since the early 1940s (Mednick and Volavka 1980). Over the years, research has indicated a rather high incidence of brain-wave abnormalities among antisocial personalities, especially in the slow-wave activity in the temporal lobe of the brain. Hare suggests that such anomalies might be a reflection of abnormal functioning of inhibitory mechanisms in the central nervous system and that "this malfunction makes it difficult to learn to inhibit behavior that is likely to lead to punishment" (1970, pp. 33–34).

Mednick, Volavka, Gabrielli, and Itil (1981) conducted a longitudinal study of 265 Danish youngsters born on approximately the same date. Seventy-two children with schizophrenic parents were matched with 72 children of "psychopathic fathers or character disorder mothers" for whom psychiatric hospitalization records were available. The control subjects were 121 children whose parents had never been hospitalized. All of the subjects were given exhaustive tests to measure psychological, neurological, and social-familial factors.

EEG results significantly discriminated delinquents from nondelinquents, although the findings did not support the hypothesis that delinquents exhibit a developmental lag. However, the fact that the testing was done well before the individuals exhibited delinquent behavior—

and was therefore *predictive*—led Mednick (1979) to suggest that the EEG might be used in testing to help prevent delinquency.

Skin-Conductance Studies

When people are upset, anxious, fearful, or otherwise emotionally aroused, their palms perspire. This perspiration increases the electrical conductivity of the skin, which can be measured as the **galvanic skin response** (GSR). Individuals with high levels of emotional arousal tend to show significantly higher levels of GSR reactivity than those who exhibit lower levels of anxiety, fear, or anger.

In an early study by Lykken (1957), psychopathic offenders showed low arousal as measured by the GSR and had low anxiety scores on questionnaires. Lykken concluded that psychopathic individuals have fewer inhibitions about committing antisocial behavior because they experience little anxiety over their actions. Subsequent research has consistently affirmed this finding in skin-conductance measures with criminals, especially violent offenders (Hare 1970; Lippert 1965).

Toward a Biosocial Theory of Criminality

Mednick states that no research to date has provided conclusive evidence that genetic factors take precedence over environmental factors as a cause of criminality:

> Given the nature of the genetic and environmental facts, it is still an appropriate a priori hypothesis that *heredity and environment always interact in a dynamic fashion to bring about and shape criminal behavior,* and that both the mutual interaction and the mutual strength of the two factors form a continuous dimension from all persons and situations (1977, p. 88).

He further points out that criminality can only be studied meaningfully from a genetic perspective if it is closely associated with a "well-defined somatic or psychological state" (ibid., p. 88).

Has biocriminological research identified any such somatic or psychological states? In Mednick's judgment, the evidence from nearly thirty years of investigation indicates that deviance in the autonomic nervous system has been demonstrated to reliably differentiate antisocial individuals. Lykken (1957) reports abnormally diminished reactivity of the autonomic nervous system (ANS) and slow recovery in psychopathic offenders (as measured by the GSR). Skin-conductance measures afford a convenient method for measuring ANS activity at the surface of the body.

In 1967, Hare reported that psychopathic inmates at a maximum security prison were sluggish ANS responders. Ten years later, he found that inmates who had committed additional serious crimes exhibited the slowest recovery rates (Hare and Schalling 1978). Thus, abnormally diminished ANS reactivity and slow recovery have predictive validity in forecasting serious criminality. Further research by Bell, Mednick, Gottesman, and Sergeant (1977)—in a study of electrodermal responses of children with criminal and noncriminal fathers—demonstrated that ANS reactivity is hereditary.

Mednick has attempted to formulate a theory to explain how ANS deviance may help to account for some types of crime and some percentage of criminals. His approach seeks to understand the possible interaction of biological and social factors in the socialization process. He assumes that law-abiding behavior must be learned; that the learning of law-abiding behavior involves certain environmental conditions and individual abilities; and that the lack of any of these conditions might be responsible for some forms of antisocial behavior. An essential part of socialization involves learning to inhibit antisocial or asocial behavior such as aggression. Typically, this learning occurs when aggressive acts are followed by punishment. The child learns to avoid further punishment by suppressing or inhibiting the disapproved behavior. Fear reduction is a "powerful, naturally occurring reinforcement" in this passive-avoidance learning sequence. That is, the individual both avoids punishment and reduces fear by *learning not to do something* for which he or she was previously punished.

According to this approach, four conditions must be present for the child to learn to inhibit antisocial behavior effectively:

1. A censuring agent (typically the family or peers).
2. An adequate fear response.
3. The ability to learn the fear response in anticipation of an asocial act.
4. Fast dissipation of fear to quickly reinforce the inhibiting response.

The fourth point is critical: to be effective, reinforcement must be delivered immediately following the relevant response. The fear response, in turn, is largely controlled by the autonomic nervous system. As Mednick points out:

> If child A has an autonomic nervous system that characteristically recovers very quickly from fear, then he will receive a quick and large reinforcement and learn inhibition quickly. If he has an autonomic nervous system that recovers very slowly, he will receive a slow, small reinforcement and learn to inhibit aggression very slowly, if at all. This orientation would predict that (holding constant critical extraindividual variables such as social status, crime training, and poverty level), those who commit asocial acts would be characterized by slow autonomic recovery. The slower the recovery, the more serious and repetitive the asocial behavior predicted (1977, p. 51).

These predictions have been empirically demonstrated by research.

The central idea of Mednick's formulation has been expressed again and again in different, and less precise, language by theorists of other persuasions. Intrapsychic theorists characterize the antisocial personality as "lacking in conscience" or being "deficient in superego," while sociologically oriented theorists stress environmental factors that may lead to "defective socialization."

It is also noteworthy that Mednick refers to his formulation as a *biosocial* theory. Geneticists have cautioned repeatedly that genes are not directly responsible for the personality or characteristics of an individual; their influence is manifested only through a chain of metabolic processes and interactions with other genes and—most importantly—through interactions with the environment. Montagu states that genes "do not determine anything—they simply influence the morphological and physiological expression of traits" (1968, p. 46). It should not be assumed that a certain chromosome structure or deviation predestines fate. Again, as Montagu points out, "Unchangeability and immutability are not characteristics of the genetic system as a whole" (ibid., p. 46). Mednick's biosocial theory is consistent with this position.

PSYCHOLOGICAL FACTORS

If your household has been looted to your last remaining dime,
By some gentleman recruited from the serried ranks of crime,
Do not think that he was stealing that his pockets he might fill,
But remember he was feeling rather ill . . .
Men who rob you of your treasures, or who beat you out of spite,
Men who think that theft's a pleasure, and that murder's a delight,
Men who with their shell games venture to entrap the guileless hick,
Should be never named with censure; they are sick.

James J. Montague (1873–1941)
Who Can Blame Him?

Psychiatry is a branch of medicine; psychology is a behavioral science. Psychiatrists tend to interpret criminality within a *clinical* perspective. Criminal behavior is viewed as a personality disturbance or even a type of mental illness (as James Montague's satirical verses suggest). Thus, dealing with criminality is seen as a task requiring treatment or psychotherapy.

Psychologists, on the other hand, interpret criminality or criminal conduct as a problem in the acquisition or learning of behaviors that conform to the same principles governing the learning of any other kind of behavior, prosocial or antisocial. According to this perspective, coping with criminality is a matter of exchanging variables that help maintain and reinforce criminal behavior for other variables that reinforce noncriminal behavior. The laboratory is regarded as more promising than the clinic for finding explanations for criminality.

A bridge between psychiatry and psychology has been supplied by *psychoanalysis*, the body of concepts originally developed by Sigmund Freud and subsequently elaborated on and modified by Alfred Adler, Otto Rank, Karen Horney, Erik Erikson, and others. The imaginative terms and ideas used by psychoanalysts to describe the structure and dynamics of personality, its origins and development, and its sources of conflict, frustration, and motivation gave psychiatry and psychology a common vocabulary for communication. Psychiatrists readily adopted the psychoanalytic theories that bore upon maladaptive behaviors identified as neurosis, psychosis, and character disorders; psychologists expended considerable effort attempting to reproduce, under laboratory conditions, such processes as repression ("motivated forgetting") and regression. Most importantly, psychoanalysis provided a theoretical framework for interpreting crime and delinquent behavior in terms of the same processes used to explain mental illness. The contributions of psychoanalytic criminology are discussed in this chapter.

Differences between psychiatrists and psychologists are not absolute; some psychiatrists (e.g., William Glasser) reject the "mental illness" model as a valid basis for interpreting deviant behavior, including criminality; and not all psychologists endorse the learning-theory perspective on criminal behavior. Nevertheless, the distinctions between psychiatry and psychology are extremely important to an understanding of their respective approaches to criminological theory. Unfortunately, the differences are often blurred or even ignored by some contemporary thinkers.

Criminality as Mental Illness

Psychiatry has been defined as "that branch of medicine whose special province is the study, prevention, and treatment of all types and degrees of mental ill health however caused" (Slater and Roth 1969, p. 6). Professional practitioners of this medical specialty have been invested with the responsibility for managing "mental ill-health" or "mental illness." The deviant behavior covered by such labels encompasses a broad range of conduct perceived as bizarre, threatening, objectionable, or merely hard to understand—including everything from the "transient situational maladjustment" of an individual experiencing the pangs of grief to the strange grimaces and antic behavior of a person labeled "schizophrenic." The psychiatrist, as a member of the medical profession, employs a vocabulary and a set of concepts that bear a strained relationship to the physical-disease models they emulate. Thus, a deviant individual becomes a "patient," the deviant behavior becomes the "symptom," and the determinants of the behavior become the "underlying pathology."

The "internal sickness" (or medical) model of criminality further strains the analogy between deviance and disease. This approach asserts that the commission of the crime is symptomatic of an offender's psychological maladjustment and an indication of a need for professional help. Halleck, in his historical review of American psychiatry and the criminal, states that the criminal offender has been a source of interest to the psychiatrist

> . . . because he bears many startling resemblances to those we call mentally ill. When incarcerated (and sometimes before) the offender proved to be a miserable, unhappy person who could be observed to suffer in the same way as the mental patient. Psychoanalytic psychiatry taught us that those psychological mechanisms which produced neurotic suffering were also operant in individuals who demonstrated criminal behavior. These observations fostered psychiatry's hopes of contributing to the understanding and alteration of criminal behavior (1965, pp. 1–2).

In this passage, Halleck treads a thin line: he does not actually say that criminals *are* mentally ill, only that they bear "startling resemblances" to those who are.

Mental health and mental illness cannot be described with any of the objectivity and precision that characterize diagnoses of physical illness. Rather, as a 1973 study by Rosenhan demonstrates, psychiatric diagnoses are subject to severe problems of reliability and validity.

Psychodiagnosis and Pseudodiagnosis

Psychologist David Rosenhan of Stanford University conducted a study in which eight normal people—a psychiatrist, graduate student, painter, housewife, pediatrician, and three psychologists—gained admittance as pseudopatients to twelve public and private mental hospitals at various locations in the United States. Each person contacted a hospital and complained of hearing voices that seemed to say "empty" and "hollow" and "thud." Apart from accompanying indications of being nervous and ill at ease during the initial interview, the behavior of the pseudopatients was normal. They gave a fictitious name and occupation to the diagnostician; otherwise all of the life history information they provided was authentic.

Eleven of the twelve admissions received a diagnosis of schizophrenia and one was identified as manic-depressive psychosis. These diagnostic assessments were arrived at primarily on the basis of the reported auditory hallucinations. The pseudopatients spent an average of 19 days per hospitalization, according to Rosenhan, and together they received over 2,100 pills. At discharge the diagnosis was "schizophrenia in remission." In nearly every instance, the first persons to become aware of the true identify of the pseudopatients were the real patients.

If Rosenhan had reported merely that his study had found low validity for psychiatric judgments of mental illness, it is doubtful that his article would have attracted much attention in professional circles. Instead, by making the very extreme claim that the validity of judgments of mental illness is zero, his article was given an extraordinary reception.

From David Rosenhan, "On Being Sane in Insane Places," *Science* 179 (1973): 250–58.

According to one view, mental illness can best be understood as a label representing societal reactions to behavior that deviates from (or in some cases, conforms to) normative standards based on cultural values. It is held that the term "mental illness" is loosely and indiscriminately applied to psychosocial problems such as crime, promiscuity, marital infidelity, political fanaticism, general unhappiness, and discontent—even to the behavior of those who manage to make themselves disliked. Those who endorse this viewpoint maintain that the term seems at times to be used as a ready explanation for almost any kind of behavior that does not make sense to the observer, reveals no clear or reasonable motivation, or merely disturbs our sensibilities.

Psychoanalysis and Criminality

The founder of psychoanalysis, Sigmund Freud, had no direct contact with any criminals during his lifetime, and in his extensive writings—twenty-four volumes of *Collected Works*—there are few references to crime. Freud did not formulate a theory of criminality; psychoanalysis was intended to be a theoretical system for explaining *all* behavior. Specific applications of psychoanalytic theory were made by Freud's followers or by neo-Freudians (those who had fallen away from orthodoxy in their psychoanalytic doctrines). Such applications usually took the form of extended analyses of individual cases.

Much of psychoanalysis has entered into the mainstream, to the extent that terms such as "superego" and "Oedipus complex" have entered into pop art and culture—even into our everyday language. We speak casually of "ego trips," of "Freudian slips," and of "psychoanalyzing" our friends and relatives. Indeed, the influence of psychoanalysis in our culture and language is so pervasive that it often goes unrecognized.

PERSONALITY STRUCTURE AND DYNAMICS Freud conceived that the development of each individual is dependent upon three types of factors: innate, instinctual forces; biologically determined stages of development; and environmental influences. Although all three categories were viewed as important, Freud believed the sex instinct, to which he applied the term *psychosexual development,* to be the central factor in human development. As an infant matures, the sex instinct moves from one area of the body to another, causing a series of stages, each denoted by a primary *erogenous zone,* the major area of sexual satisfaction during a stage. According to this theme, psychosexual development can be divided into three periods: infantile sexuality (from birth to approximately five years), latent phase, and puberty. Infantile sexuality can further be divided into the oral, anal, and phallic periods, the latter culminating in the Oedipus complex, and the "family romance" in which the child wishes to have intimate relations with the parent of the opposite sex and harbors antagonism toward the parent of the same sex.

Freud postulated that personality is governed by three dynamic systems, which he named id, ego, and superego. The *id* consists of instinctual sexual and aggressive drives—the substratum of personality from which all other systems develop. It operates by the "pleasure principle," seeking tension reduction through the discharge of impulses. The *ego* develops as a control system that seeks to satisfy drives through contact with reality. It functions to control the impulsiveness of the id so that drive satisfaction can be obtained; however, it operates within the limits imposed on the individual by society. The ego has control over all cognitive and intellectual functions. The *superego* is the moral element of personality: it represents all the internalized demands from parents and society.

The defense of repression is the most basic means by which the ego can control id impulses. Through repression, the ego forces emerging id impulses to remain unconscious and not function in reality. Because the direct expression of primitive impulses is forbidden by social norms, the superego and the id generally oppose one another. The struggle between the id and the superego is often an intense encounter, and anxiety is one of the by-products. Anxiety is a warning signal to the ego to take the needed steps to keep emerging impulses from overthrowing the system. Repression provides the ego with a direct mechanism for anxiety reduction: the primitive impulse is forced back into the unconscious, and the delicate balance between the id and the superego is maintained.

CRIMINALITY AND THE UNCONSCIOUS Behavior, as viewed within the psychoanalytic framework, is functional in the sense that it operates to fulfill certain needs or drives and has consequences for other aspects of personality. But Freud's emphasis on the importance of unconscious factors in mental life adds an element of complexity to the interpretation of behavior. Freud and later psychoanalysts assume that much, if not most, of the behavior exhibited by an individual possesses meaning that lies outside the range of the individual's awareness. Thus, the observable behavior of a person must be considered as merely an outward, or *symbolic,* expression of underlying (i.e., unconscious) drives and impulses. This principle implies that a focus upon the criminal action itself (manifest function) defeats any attempt to understand the etiology of the crime. Says Feldman:

> . . . like any other behavior, criminal behavior is a form of self-expression, and what is intended to be expressed in the act of crime is not only unobservable in the act itself, but also may even be beyond the awareness of the criminal actor himself. So, for example, an overt criminal act of stealing may be undertaken for the attainment of purposes which are far removed from, and even contrary to, that of simple illegal aggrandizement; indeed, it may even be, as shall be seen in the sequel, that the criminal, in stealing, seeks not material gain but self-punishment. The etiological basis of a criminal act can, therefore, be understood only in terms of the functions, latent as well as manifest, which the act was intended to accomplish (1969, p. 434).

FIGURE 4.3
A teenager's fascination with knives and guns may express hidden antisocial impulses and fantasies that can emerge later as violent behavior.

Although the specific cause of a given criminal act must be looked for in the life history of the individual offender, the general etiological formula for psychoanalytic criminology asserts that criminal behavior is an attempt to maintain or restore psychic balance. But this formula has a major flaw: neurosis is explained the same way. Therefore, what factor or factors can be identified that dispose an individual toward criminality rather than toward some other emotional or mental disorder?

One interpretation that neatly bypasses this issue is that criminality is actually a *form* of neurosis. Unfortunately, empirical data fail to support any contention that the criminal is a neurotic individual compulsively driven toward self-punishment. On the contrary, criminal offenders appear to use every effort and resource to elude capture. Moreover, empirical evidence suggests that "neurotic" personality characteristics are found in the criminal population to approximately the same degree they are found in the noncriminal population.

Equally dubious is the view of the criminal as an antisocial character who seeks immediate gratification, lives entirely in the present; and is unable to withstand tedium and monotony. Many kinds of criminal behavior require extensive training in specific skills or in systematic planning. Indeed, professional, syndicated, and white-collar crimes seem to exemplify the operation of Freud's "reality principle," (i.e., the capacity to defer or postpone gratification in order to achieve a larger gratification at some later time).

By failing to give appropriate emphasis to the fact that patterned criminality is not the spontaneous creation of the individual offender, psychoanalytic criminology minimizes the crucial importance of social learning. According to Feldman,

> . . . this learning process requires the individual's participation in the formation and maintenance of relationships with others who dispose of the necessary knowledge and put it to use. It is in the context of these relationships that the individual learns his criminality and adopts for himself distinctive criminalistic attitudes and percepts. Presumably, the experiences of such a learning process must have an effect on the personality of the individual undergoing them. Yet, this reciprocating influence of criminal experience on the personality of the criminal appears to have no consideration in psychoanalytic criminology (ibid., p. 441).

Once again, the question is raised, Which comes first in the causal sequence, the personality characteristics or the criminal experience? Psychoanalytic criminology assumes it is the personality that produces involvement in criminal activity, but no systematic procedure to verify this view is available.

In addition to the problems mentioned in these criticisms, psychoanalytic criminology possesses some serious flaws when judged as a formal theory. Psychoanalytic constructs tend to be global and all-inclusive in nature and loaded with "surplus meaning"; rarely, if ever, are they anchored in explicit, observable events. Nevertheless, such constructs have become the "facts" of psychoanalysis, upon which even more speculative and elaborate concepts have been based.

Most research generated by psychoanalytic theory is not directed at modifying the theory based on new information; rather, the goal is usually to demonstrate the essential validity of the basic postulates and assumptions of the theory. Because of the ambiguity and lack of operational specificity of the constructs in the system, however, no hypothesis derived from psychoanalytic theory can be either clearly confirmed or clearly refuted. Thus, critics of psychoanalysis have charged that the theory and its proponents do not conform to the widely accepted canons of empirical verification and refutation implicit in the scientific method.

The Search for a Criminal Personality

Instead of pursuing criminality as a mental illness, some psychiatrists and psychologists have tried to identify a criminal personality. They have sought to discover some cluster of personality traits distinctive to criminal offenders, in general, or to particular categories of offenders. One approach has been to examine the results of personality tests administered to both criminals and noncriminals, with the aim of finding significant differences between them. Another approach has been to look at the incidence of psychiatrically diagnosed disorders in the criminal population. Neither method has yielded conclusive results, however. And both kinds of research present an additional serious problem: the chicken-egg dilemma. Even if investigators *did* find that certain personality traits were characteristic of criminal offenders,

for example, it would still be necessary to ask which came first—the traits or the criminal behavior.

The most recent claim about the discovery of a criminal personality was advanced by Samuel Yochelson and Stanton Samenow in *The Criminal Personality* (1977). Based on a fifteen-year study of 255 criminals, the volume proposes that people become criminals early in life on the basis of choice, not accident, and that the criminal personality results more from inborn characteristics than from acquired ones. However, critics of the book have had some unkind things to say about the authors' lack of objectivity and their general disregard for accuracy. Thus, the issue of whether a criminal personality exists remains unresolved.

Learning Theory and Criminality

Common sense affirms the belief that aggressiveness can be taught to those who do not exhibit it in their normal behavior. From time immemorial, this belief has guided and structured basic training for military recruits. In addition to close-order drill, military etiquette, and the use and maintenance of weapons and equipment, recruits are exposed to situations intended to inculcate aggressiveness. Paul Bäumer, the protagonist of Erich Maria Remarque's classic novel *All Quiet on the Western Front* (1929), reminisces about the training he received as a recruit in the German Army in World War I:

> We were trained in the army for ten weeks and in this time more profoundly influenced than by ten years of school. . . . At first astonished, then embittered, and finally indifferent, we recognized that what matters is not the mind but the boot brush, not intelligence but the system, not freedom but drill. . . . We became hard, suspicious, pitiless, vicious, tough—and that was good; for these attributes had been entirely lacking in us. Had we gone into the trenches without this period of training most of us would certainly have gone mad. Only thus were we prepared for what awaited us . . . (pp. 20–25).

Novelist John Masters—writing in *Bugles and a Tiger* (1962)—reflected similarly about the training he received one world war later, as a cadet in the Royal Military College at Sandhurst, England, in the early 1930s.

However, it is one thing to assert that a given response or pattern of behavior is learned; it is quite a different matter to describe with precision and in detail how such behavior is acquired, maintained, or modified. Yet significant advances toward accomplishing the latter objective have been made by psychologists during the past several decades. Through systematic observation of the ways in which behavior is acquired, maintained, altered, or eliminated under controlled conditions, researchers have formulated the following principles (adapted from Suinn 1970):

1. The association between a stimulus and a response is strengthened each time the response

is followed by reinforcement. This is known as *acquisition.*

2. The association is weakened each time the response occurs and is *not* followed by reinforcement. This is known as *extinction.* Thus, disuse alone does not lead to extinction.
3. A response to a given stimulus may be seen to recur after complete extinction when the stimulus is re-presented. This phenomenon is known as *spontaneous recovery.*
4. Once a specific-response habit has been acquired, another stimulus that is similar in some way to the original stimulus can also elicit the learned response. This is called *stimulus generalization.*
5. Responses that occur just prior to a reinforced, learned response will also be strengthened, those nearest in time being strengthened the most. This is called the *gradient of reinforcement.*
6. Responses nearer to the time of a reinforcement tend to occur before their original time in the response sequence and to crowd out earlier, useless behaviors. This is known as the development of *anticipatory responses.*
7. Drives can act as cues and elicit specific, learned responses, or as responses and be elicited by certain cues and strengthened by reinforcement.

Learning Theory and Behavior Modification

A program that applies learning theory with the aim of modifying criminal behavior is referred to as a **contingency management program.** A contingency, as Lillyquist notes, "is something that may or may not occur; the management aspect involves increasing the chances that it *will* occur" (1980, p. 232). In contingency management in a correctional setting, the aim is to increase the probability of occurrence of certain kinds of desired behaviors by reinforcing the behaviors when they occur. Participation in educational or vocational training programs, money management, nonaggressive behavior, and successful interviewing (for employment) are some of the behaviors that have been dealt with in contingency management programs (Brauckmann et al. 1975). Reinforcement can range from verbal praise ("Good job"; "That's fine"; "You're really getting a handle on this stuff") to release from prison. Tangible reinforcement such as candy, soft drinks, cigarettes, and snacks might be augmented with access to desired activities—such as watching television, making phone calls, and getting extra visits from family members.

TOKEN ECONOMIES An action that has no reinforcing value of its own will tend to acquire reinforcing qualities if it becomes associated with a reinforcer: it will become valuable as a medium of exchange. This principle of secondary reinforcement is basic to the idea of a **token economy.** A token is a secondary reinforcer that, like money, can be exchanged for goods or services according to a standard scale. In addition to the advantages of ease and convenience, the principal benefit of using tokens as a medium of exchange is that the system encourages stability and continuity of behavior. According to Lillyquist:

> A person in a social learning program that uses television watching and soda sipping as reinforcers is not always desirous of these rewards because appetites for all things wax and wane. But desirable behavior can be maintained if it can be made contingent on the presentation of a token that promises *future* reinforcement when the person is more in the mood for it (1980, pp. 232–33).

Token economies are particularly well suited to institutional settings, where behavior management is easier than in a free-response environment. In fact, the earliest token-economy programs were established in mental hospitals and institutions for the mentally retarded.

AVERSIVE CONDITIONING OF DEVIANT SEXUAL BEHAVIOR **Aversive conditioning,** a form of behavior modification, is the reduction or elimination of certain patterns of behavior by associating them with unpleasant or noxious stimuli. Variations of this method have been used to alter an individual's sexual behavior by teaching him or her to dislike and avoid stimuli that he or she regards as a source of abnormal sexual excitation. That is, the individual himself (or herself) must consider a behavior as deviant and be willing to cooperate in eliminating it; otherwise, the aversive conditioning will not work and will be considered punishment.

Nausea-inducing drugs were used extensively in early experiments in aversive conditioning. The drugs were usually given by injection to induce vomiting during an undesirable behavior. This procedure, often unpleasant and traumatic, was designed to condition the sexual deviate to feel nausea whenever he or she subsequently tried to carry out the undesirable behavior. Electric shock later replaced drugs as an aversive stimuli. In the following example, an electric shock was administered to the subject, a male transvestite, through the soles of his feet. In later experiments with aversive conditioning for deviant sexual behavior, electrical shocks were applied directly to the genital organs.

> The electric grid was made from a 4 feet by 3 feet rubber mat with a corrugated upper aspect. Tinned copper wire, one-tenth of an inch thick, was stapled lengthwise in the grooves of this mat at approximately half-inch intervals. . . . A manually operated G.P.O. type generator . . . produced a current of approximately 100 volts a.c. when resistance of 10,000 ohms and upwards were introduced on to the grid surface. Two rapid turns of the generator handle were sufficient to give a sharp and unpleasant electric shock to the feet and ankles of the person standing on the grid. . . . Treatment sessions were administered every half-hour, each session consisting of 5 trials with one minute's rest between each trial. A total of 400 trials was given over 6 days (average 65 to 75 per day). . . . The patient utilized his own clothing, which was not interfered with in any way, except that slits were cut into the feet of his nylon hose to enable a metal conductor to be inserted into the soles of his black court shoes. He commenced dressing up at the beginning of each trial and continued until he received a signal to undress irrespective of the number of garments he was wearing at the time. This signal was either a shock from the grid or the sound of the buzzer which was introduced at random into half the 400 trials. The shock or buzzer recurred at regular intervals until he had completely undressed.
>
> (Reprinted from J. C. Barker, "Behaviour Therapy for Transvestism: A Comparison of Pharmacological and Electrical Aversion Techniques," *British Journal of Psychiatry* 111 [1965]: 271, by permission of the author and the publisher.)

Science fiction is replete with stories of a nightmarish future in which people are depersonalized and dehumanized. Consider Ayn Rand's *Anthem* (1961), about a world so collectivized that the very concept of self is lost and has to be rediscovered; Huxley's *Brave New World* (1978), with its test-tube genetics and mind-altering drugs; and George Orwell's *1984* (1949), with Newspeak, thought crime, and the omnipresent eye of Big Brother watching, watching, watching. Such a future seemed already upon us in 1970 when *Psychology Today* published an article making the following claim:

> I believe the day has come when we can combine sensory deprivation with drugs, hypnosis, and astute manipulation of reward and punishment to gain almost absolute control over an individual's behavior. . . . We have the techniques to do it. . . . I foresee the day when we could convert the worst criminal into a decent respectable citizen in a matter of a few months—or perhaps even less time than that (McConnell 1970, p. 4).

Two years later, Schwitzgebel (1972) reported that Anectine (succinylcholine chloride) was being used in the aversive conditioning of alcoholics in California; Anectine produces a sensation of suffocation. The program in which this approach was used was singled out by Jessica Mitford in her influential book *Kind and Unusual Punishment* (1974) as an example of the outrages perpetrated in the name of correctional treatment.

Behavior modification has further been criticized for making excessive claims about results, for using inmates as guinea pigs, and for opening the way for "behavior modification programs" that are actually thinly disguised programs for furthering institutional objectives at the expense of inmates. In 1974, the Law Enforcement Assistance Administration banned federal support from any and all programs using behavior modification. The ban has never been lifted.

Perhaps in response to spirited attacks from critics, proponents of behavior modification have experienced a noticeable waning in enthusiasm among their own ranks; and the techniques they use are now more sophisticated and humane. As Lazarus observes, "Behavior therapists do not deny consciousness . . . do not treat people like Pavlovian dogs . . . and are not ignorant of the part played by mutual trust and other relationship factors among our treatment variables" (1977, p. 553). Nevertheless, as a defense, many institutional authorities have dropped the term "behavior modification" from the names of their programs, knowing that the term carries with it many of the characteristics of aversive conditioning.

SOCIOLOGICAL THEORIES

Sociological theories about what causes crime deal with criminality in its collective, rather than individual, aspects. That is, the sociologist seeks to answer questions such as what factors are responsible for the higher crime rates among urban black males than among rural black males? Or, how can we account for the steep increase in violent crimes that has taken place in the United States during the past decade? Sociological explanations do not deny the importance of motivation in criminal acts, but they seek to tie that motivation to societal arrangements external to the individual. According to Nettler:

> A strictly sociological explanation is concerned with how the *structure* of a society or its *institutional practices* or its *persisting cultural themes* affect the conduct of its members. Individual differences are denied or ignored, and the explanation of collective behavior is sought in the patterning of social arrangements that is considered to be both "outside" the actor and "prior" to him. That is, the social patterns of power or of institutions which are held to be determinative of human action are also seen as having been in existence *before* any particular actor came on the scene. They are "external" to him in the sense that they will persist with or without him. In lay language, sociological explanations of crime place the blame on something social that is prior to, external to, and compelling of a particular person (1974, p. 138).

Thus, Nettler identifies two sociological explanations of criminality, one *structural* and one *subcultural*. Both explanations assume that *culture conflict* is the principal source of crime; they differ, as Nettler indicates, in their evaluation of conflict and, therefore, in the societal response they prescribe.

The Structural Approach

The French sociologist Emile Durkheim (1858–1917) was among the first social scientists to point out the "normality" of crime. Human behavior is not inherently "normal" or "pathological"; certain forms of conduct simply are labeled as such by important or influential groups within society. Thus, in a society of saints, singing too loud in church might be punished as severely as theft would be punished in a prison society of thieves. In Durkheim's view, a society totally exempt from crime is unthinkable.

One of Durkheim's major contributions to the understanding of deviant behavior stems from his efforts to show how suicide relates to an individual's lack of integration into stable social groups. He proposed that many suicides result from **anomie**, a social condition of "normlessness" in which people experience an acute lack of meaningful rules and purpose in their lives.

The concept of anomie was extended by the American sociologist Robert K. Merton (1957) to explain deviant behavior in modern Western societies. Merton considered socially deviant behavior to be as much a product of the social structure as is conformist behavior, and he attempted to determine how the sociocultural structure of society pressures people toward deviance. Merton sought an answer to the question, Why does the frequency of deviant behavior vary with the social structure?

Societal structure is composed of various elements, but two are essential to Merton's analysis: (1) culturally defined goals (those objectives defined as legitimate for everyone); and (2) the regulatory norms that define and control the means to achieve goals. Merton maintained that deviant behavior can be regarded sociologically as a symptom of dissociation between culturally prescribed aspirations and socially accepted avenues for realizing those aspirations.

In American society, wealth is a basic symbol of success. Money obtained illegally can be spent just as easily as hard-earned money and can be translated into the visible signs of success: expensive cars, clothes, jewelry, and luxurious apartments. Merton felt that American society placed a heavy emphasis on wealth without a corresponding emphasis on the use of legitimate means to reach this goal. Individual adaptation to this situation may take several forms, including *conformity, innovation, ritualism, retreatism,* or *rebellion.*

Merton pointed out that the greatest pressure toward deviant behavior is experienced by people in the lower class. Cloward and Ohlin, in a work appropriately entitled *Delinquency and Opportunity* (1960), expanded this idea to explain urban gang delinquency:

> The disparity between what lower-class youth are led to want and what is actually available to them is the source of a major problem of adjustment. Adolescents who form delinquent subcultures, we suggest, have internalized an emphasis on conventional goals. Faced with limitations on legitimate avenues of access to these goals, and unable to revise their aspirations downward, they experience intense frustrations; the exploration of nonconformist alternatives may be the result (p. 86).

This view holds that delinquency is partly *adaptive,* because it is instrumental in the attainment of desired goals, and also partly *reactive,* because it is prompted by a resentment of being deprived of things the delinquents believe should be theirs.

The Subcultural Approach

"Subculture" is a term social scientists use to refer to variations within a society on how cultural themes, patterns, artifacts, and traditional ideas are incorporated and expressed within various groups. Subcultures are presumed to have some stability and endurance. In addition, they can differ widely in the magnitude and direction of their deviation from the general culture. When the norms of a subculture impose standards of conduct different from those prescribed by the general culture, the resulting conflict can contribute to criminal behavior.

A principal advocate of the subcultural approach to delinquency is Walter B. Miller (1958). Miller does not go so far as to say that the lower class in the United States is a criminal class, but he does maintain that delinquency is the result of an "intensified response" of some children to "focal areas of concern" found in lower-class culture. Youths who conform to values of the lower class find themselves in inevitable conflict with the prevailing middle-class mores and the law.

Miller identifies six focal areas of concern for the lower class, discussed here in the order of their importance. *Concern over trouble* means avoiding entanglements with official authorities or agencies of the middle class. *Toughness* (bravery, body tattooing, absence of sentimentality) is viewed as the result of upbringing in female-dominated (matriarchal) homes. There is an almost obsessive concern with masculinity, and hostility toward homosexuality is expressed in "queer" baiting. The third concern, *smartness,* is defined as the ability to obtain a maximum amount of money or goods with a minimum of effort.

Traditionally, the deadening routine of lower-class life has led its members to seek relief in alcohol or evangelism; thus, Miller's delinquents seek *excitement* in "booze, bands, and broads." And related to the belief among the lower class that goal-directed efforts are futile is the concept of *fate.* Many lower-class persons see themselves as subject to a destiny over which they have no control. This attitude serves as an inhibitor to initiative and as a compensation for failure. Miller regards the lower-class emphasis on *autonomy* ("doing your own thing") as an expression of ambivalence toward authority (e.g., resenting external controls while actively seeking out a restrictive environment such as the military). The life-style is summed up in the proverb, "Trouble is what life gets you into."

Cohen (1955, 1966) has tried to explain the development of a *delinquent subculture*—an antisocial way of life that has become traditional in a society. According to Cohen, a subculture develops when people with a common problem of adjustment become involved in effective interaction. The problems central to the delinquent subculture appear to be problems of status: lower-

FIGURE 4.4
The anti-establishment behavior of some gangs reflects a subcultural form of delinquency. Courtesy Michael Weisbrot.

class children are denied status in middle-class culture. The delinquent subculture deals with such problems by providing status criteria that youngsters *are* able to meet. Specifically, the subculture functions simultaneously to combat internal stress in the individual (as represented by feelings of insecurity and low self esteem) and to deal with the representatives of middle-class culture. It does so by erecting a counterculture that offers alternative status criteria in direct opposition to those of the middle class, to the extent that they impart a "non-utilitarian, malicious, and negativistic" quality to the subculture (Cohen 1955, p. 25).

SOCIOPSYCHOLOGICAL THEORIES

The sociological theories discussed in the preceding section sought to explain how people in certain social groups are subjected to pressures that produce a tendency toward criminality. As noted, however, the theories fail to account for the fact that most people exposed to such pressures *do not* become delinquent or criminal, while others not exposed *do*. This inconsistency is of major interest to sociopsychological theorists.

Sociopsychological explanations of crime center on the symbolic interactions through which people acquire the skills, techniques, values, orientations, and self-concepts essential to the criminal role. Theorists recognize that not all crime results from progressive involvement in deviant behavior; some crimes occur because of the attractions and provocations of isolated situations.

Differential Association

A well-known and widely used intelligence test asks, Why should we avoid bad company? The answer—supplied by common sense and experience—is that this is the way to keep out of trouble with the law. Criminologist Edwin H. Sutherland reached the same conclusion more than a half century ago. The basic idea of Sutherland's theory of *differential association* is that people *learn* to become criminals through communication, through prolonged, intimate contact with people who are criminals themselves or who are, at least, strongly inclined to violate the law.

What, exactly, do people have to learn to become criminals? For one thing, they may learn techniques. Says Sutherland, "I worked for several years with a professional thief and had been greatly impressed by his statement that a person cannot become a professional thief merely by wanting to be one; he must be trained in personal association with those who are already professional thieves" (1973, p. 17). More importantly, in Sutherland's view, a person acquires the drives, rationalizations, attitudes, and motives that support criminal activity. These are learned in face-to-face relationships in primary groups such as the family, gang, or play group. Criminal motives and attitudes, Sutherland stresses, precede the actual commission of criminal acts.

Containment Theory

Walter C. Reckless (1973) agrees with Sutherland that some environments pressure people to engage in criminal action. Other individuals grow up in environments in which family, friends, and the community exert pressures to obey the law. Reckless calls the latter kind of pressure *outer containment*. At the same time, however, people learn to self-regulate their behavior as they grow up. This self-control, which Reckless calls *inner containment*, is a key factor in determining whether a person will stay within the bounds of accepted norms, values, and laws. Reckless hypothesizes that people with a poor self-concept—a negative or ill-defined view of themselves—engage in more criminal behavior than do people with favorable self-concepts. Critics of containment theory, however, point out that it is impossible to determine whether a poor self-concept is a *cause* or a *result* of criminal conduct. Moreover, the theory leaves unanswered the crucial question of why a poor self-concept would leave someone vulnerable to criminality.

The Labeling Perspective

When applied to crime, the labeling perspective focuses on the processes by which people are labeled as deviant and on the consequences of such processes. It switches our concern from the causes of crime and delinquency to the processes that amplify and encourage criminal and delinquent patterns. That is, once a person has been labeled as criminal or delinquent by some official agency, he or she is much more likely to be singled out for further attention by school authorities, the police, and the courts. And since misery loves company, youngsters or adults who have been labeled in this way tend to seek the company of others who have undergone the same treatment. As a result, offenders are increasingly estranged from the influence of noncriminal or nondelinquent groups.

The labeling perspective can thus be seen as a complement to other explanations of the origins and development of criminal behavior. The idea has spurred efforts to remove as many criminals as possible—and as soon as possible—from the juvenile and criminal justice systems.

SORTING IT ALL OUT

Despite some progress, we are still groping to identify the causes of crime. One thing, however, seems abundantly clear: crime in general, as emphasized by the passages quoted earlier from the President's Commission on Law Enforcement and Administration of Justice, cannot be accounted for by a single factor or theory. Sunday-supplement journalists are fond of "explaining" crime and delinquency as the result of poverty, broken homes, failure of the schools, or "bad company." But "crime" is a term that embraces vastly different acts—from the vicious murders of black children in Atlanta to the greed of congressmen convicted of taking bribes in the Abscam scandal.

Increasingly, efforts to explain crime will be directed toward discovering what causes *specific* criminal or delinquent acts. Solutions to the problems posed by crime and delinquency, however, will not come automatically with the discovery of the causes of criminality. What criminologists have said about the causes of crime have affected crime policies indirectly at best. As Robert Rhodes observes:

> It is one thing to know the causes of crime; it is quite another to know how criminal justice agencies can act on these causes. . . . Where criminologists do agree on the social factors correlated with criminal behavior, family instability, lower-class behavior . . . or whatever, their conclusions lend themselves to suggesting alterations of the social structure far beyond the capacity of the criminal justice system (1977, p. 260).

SUMMARY

The relationship between economic factors and criminality is extremely complex. Poverty can bring about crime, but its social conditions may be more important than the economic circumstances in producing crime. To the radical or critical criminologist, criminality is one of the consequences of the class struggle in a capitalist society. Criminal law and the criminal justice system are viewed as tools used by the power elites to maintain the status quo and exclude the poor and disenfranchised from sharing power and wealth.

The nature-nurture issue has never dropped entirely from criminology theories since the time of Lombroso.

FIGURE 4.5
Boys who are disruptive and aggressive are likely to be singled out as having behavior problems. Hiroji Kubota.

But genetic studies of criminality have progressed considerably since the turn of the century, when investigators traced the genealogies of families distinguished by unusually high percentages of criminals, lunatics, and mental defectives.

The strongest evidence for a view of inherited criminality has come from the studies of chromosomes with a particular abnormality of the chromosomes being found disproportionately among male criminals. Men with the XYY combination of chromosomes (XY being normal) have a ten to twenty times greater tendency to break the law than do normal men.

Research on the study of identical and fraternal twins also suggests some evidence of linkage between genetics and criminality. Studies in a dozen countries in Europe, Asia, and the United States suggest that identical as contrasted with fraternal twins with a criminal record are twice as likely to have a co-twin with a record. The differential resemblance of identical and fraternal twins is generally considered to be strong though not by itself conclusive.

In a study of the criminal connections of more than 4,000 adopted Danish boys, it was determined that they were more dependent on their biological as compared to their adoptive parents' criminality. The more serious an offender a biological parent was, the greater the risk of criminality for his or her child, particularly for property crimes. Adopted boys who had a chronically criminal biological parent (three or more convictions) were three times more likely to become criminal than those whose biological parents were not criminal.

In the study of the relationship between IQ and criminality, many studies have shown that the offender population has an average IQ of about 91–93 compared to the IQ of 100 for the population at large. In general, the most common offenses, impulsive violent crimes and opportunistic property crimes, are most often committed by people in the low normal and borderline retarded range.

Psychiatrists have interpreted crime as a syndrome or category of mental illness. Psychologists, on the other hand, have tended to view criminality as behavior that is acquired in the same way as other patterns of learned behavior, i.e., through reinforcement. The psychiatric approach has fostered two lines of inquiry: (1) the search for a "criminal personality," and (2) the assessment of psychiatric disorders among criminals. Both of these areas of research have failed to provide results that confirm the theories on which they are based. Neither clinical observations nor psychological tests have identified any cluster of psychological traits distinctive to the criminal. With the exception of alcoholism, drug addiction, and sociopathy or psychopathy—terms often defined with reference to the criminal behavior they are supposed to explain—psychiatric disorders appear to occur with about the same frequency in both criminal and noncriminal populations.

Approaches to criminality using learning theories, developed chiefly from laboratory studies of animal and human subjects, have provided some of the clearest theoretical accounts of how criminal behavior may be acquired, maintained, and changed. Attempts to modify criminal behavior by means of "psychotechnology," however, have generated intense opposition. Outrage over certain projects that seemed to reduce human beings to the level of animal subjects led in 1974 to the withdrawal of federal support from all projects involving "behavior modification." Current programs have dropped the language of psychotechnology and show a great deal of restraint in their claims and methods.

Sociological theories of criminality are directed toward finding answers to questions about collective rather than individual criminal behavior. There are two approaches to the exploration and interpretation of social factors in crime causation. The structural approach looks at the influence of social patterns of power or institutions on criminality. The subcultural approach emphasizes the role of conflict between the norms of the larger society and those characteristic of lower-class or ethnic subcultures. The latter approach maintains that when the norms of the subculture impose standards of conduct different from those prescribed by the larger culture, the resulting normative conflict can become the major source of criminal behavior.

Sociopsychological theories of criminality examine the processes by which people become delinquents or criminals, and the differential response factors that help explain why some people who are exposed to adverse environmental conditions engage in crime and delinquency while others do not. Sutherland's differential association theory suggests that crime is learned principally in primary groups. Reckless's containment theory attempts to consider both social and cultural factors (outer containment) and individual factors (inner containment) and the way these factors interact to produce crime and delinquency. Finally, the labeling perspective focuses on societal reactions to deviant behavior. The imposition of a deviant label may result in increasing, rather than decreasing, tendencies to engage in criminal behavior. According to this approach, formal treatment of deviant behavior may do more harm than good.

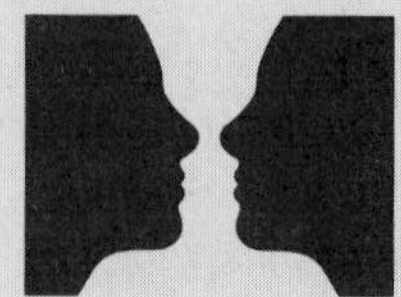

ISSUE PAPER

MIND HUNTERS

By Bruce Porter

When the New York police finally called the FBI into the case in October of 1979, the investigation was beginning to stall. The nude body of a 26-year-old special-education teacher had been found on the roof of the Bronx public housing project where she lived. She had been badly beaten about the face and strangled with the strap of her purse. Her nipples had been cut off, and scrawled on the inside of her thigh in ink was: "Fuck you. You can't stop me."

"We get a lot of murders, but not this type of mutilation," says homicide detective Thomas Foley, who was in a quandary as to what kind of suspect to look for. "Frankly, I didn't see where the FBI could tell us anything, but I figured there was no harm in trying." A few days after delivering pictures of the murder scene and a copy of the autopsy report to the FBI Academy in Quantico, Virginia, Foley got back a description of the probable killer. He would be a white man, probably 25 to 35 years old, who knew the victim and either lived or worked nearby, possibly in her apartment building. He would be a high-school dropout, live by himself or with a single parent, and own an extensive collection of pornography. What's more, in all probability he would already have been interviewed by the police.

It took Foley and other detectives 10 more months of digging before they were ready to turn the case over to the district attorney for prosecution. By then they had found out that the murderer was indeed 32 years old and a high-school dropout who knew the victim and lived on the fourth floor of her building. The police had already questioned the young man's father—with whom he shared both an apartment and a pornography collection. Detectives had lost interest in the youth after they were told that he had been in a mental hospital at the time of the killing. But because he fit the sketch so closely, detectives checked the hospital and discovered that security was lax enough to permit patients to come and go more or less at will. This led them to concentrate on the young man, and eventually they built up enough evidence to convict him of the murder and send him off to prison for 25 years to life. "What the FBI description did," says Foley, a 10-year veteran of the force, "was to keep me on course."

The sketch not only provided the key that broke the case, but also, in its uncanny accuracy, gave New York detectives an eye-opening illustration of the latest weapon in the FBI arsenal: psychological profiling. What's more, it persuaded Foley and his colleagues to join a growing number of policemen across the country who think that when it comes to solving certain kinds of crime, profiling can provide crucial help. "They had him so right that I asked the FBI why they hadn't given us his telephone number, too," says Lieutenant Joseph D'Amico, Foley's boss and head of the homicide squad for the New York City Housing Police.

The FBI agrees to provide profiles in only a narrow selection of crimes—mainly multiple rape or child molesting, or so-called "motiveless" murders, in which the nature of the killing points to major psychological abnormality in the killer. One reason that such cases are chosen for profiling is that deviant crimes lend themselves much more readily to the technique than do the mundane varieties. "The more bizarre the crime scene," says agent John Douglas, who helped work up the Bronx profile, "the easier it is to tell what kind of person did it."

Another reason is that bizarre crimes have increased significantly in recent years. Twenty years ago, according to the FBI, the rule of thumb was that in more than 80 percent of murder cases, the killer had some kind of previous relationship with the victim. The motive was passionate anger or a desire for revenge, and a quick canvass of the neighborhood usually turned up a list of likely suspects.

Recently, though, the 80 percent figure has dropped to 72 percent in part because many more murders were either "stranger murders," in which killer and victim had never seen each other before the crime, or murders in which the killer was listed as "unknown." Many such cases are felony murders—killings that occur as outgrowths of robbery or some other crime, and are motivated by the need to escape. But in an increasingly large number of "stranger" homicides, the killer seems driven to murder not by some "rational" reason or easily understood emotion, but by a serious psychological disorder. The FBI estimates that as many as 25 percent of killings may now fall into this category. Indeed, according to Sergeant Richard Ruffino of the Bergen

County, New Jersey, Missing Persons Bureau, who runs a nationwide clearinghouse that identifies murder victims, some 5,000 people turn up each year in the category of unidentified bodies that appear to be those of murder victims.

Overwhelmingly, the victims of bizarre murder are women or children; the killers are almost invariably men. They are usually intraracial—blacks killing blacks and whites killing whites. And the list of victims killed by a single murderer often runs into double figures. Authorities believe that Wayne Williams killed 27 children and young men in Atlanta. Gerald Eugene Stano confessed to killing 34 women in Florida. John Wayne Gacy killed 33 boys in Chicago. The Zodiac killer, as yet uncaught, is said to be responsible for as many as 40 killings in San Francisco. Coral Eugene Watts admitted killing only 13 women in Texas, but police elsewhere are convinced that he has killed as many as 60 others.

"These are the cases usually considered unsolvable," says Roger Depue, chief of the FBI's Behavioral Science Unit, whose handful of profilers have time to help local police in only about 300 to 400 cases each year.

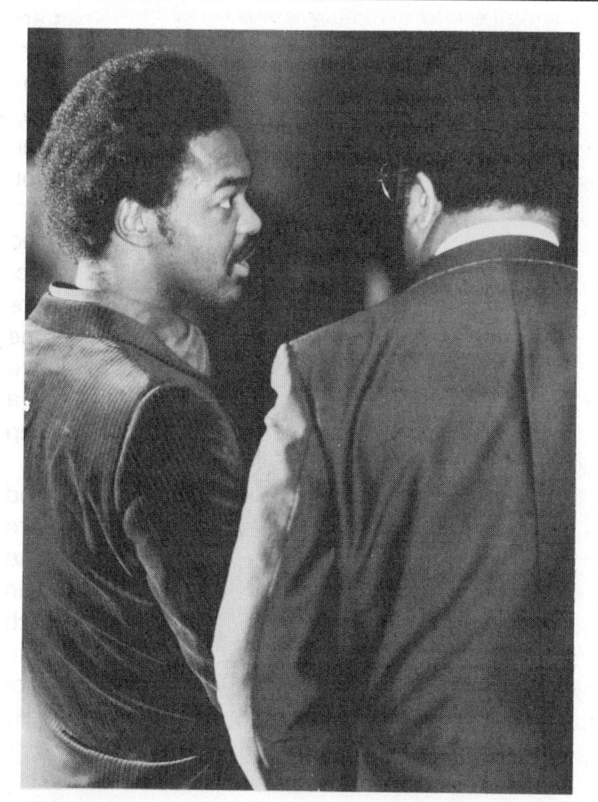

FIGURE 4.6
Coral Eugene Watts confessed to killing 13 women. UPI/Bettman Newsphotos.

FIGURE 4.7
Gerald Eugene Stano admitted killing 34 women. UPI/Bettman Newsphotos.

Using psychology to catch criminals hardly qualifies as a recent discovery. Its literary origin goes back at least to 1841 and the publication of "The Murders in the Rue Morgue" by Edgar Allan Poe. His detective, C. Auguste Dupin, demonstrated the ability to follow the thought pattern of a companion while the pair strolled

In real life, undoubtedly the most ingenious piece of profiling was performed in the late 1950s by a Greenwich Village psychiatrist named James A. Brussel to help the police catch the Mad Bomber of New York.

The bomber turned out to be George Metesky, a disgruntled ex-employee of the local utility company. Metesky had set off 32 devices over an eight-year period. After poring over letters written by the bomber and looking at pictures of bomb scenes, Brussel theorized that the criminal was an Eastern European man, 40 to 50 years old, who lived with a maiden aunt or sister in a Connecticut city. He hated his father but loved his mother, something Brussel divined from the way Metesky rounded out the sharp points in his W's so that they resembled cartoon versions of a woman's breasts. Brussel diagnosed him as a paranoiac who was meticulous in his personal habits; when he was found, Brussel said, he would be wearing a double-breasted suit—buttoned.

When Metesky was captured shortly thereafter in Waterbury, Connecticut, the portrait turned out to be an extraordinary likeness, right down to the suit. (Metesky actually lived with *two* maiden sisters.) But other profiles by independent psychiatrists and psychologists—in contrast to those by FBI agents—have not always proved helpful. Some are so vague as to point to practically anyone. In the worst cases, psychological profiles can severely hamper an investigation by sending the police off in the wrong direction. During the 1960s, a committee of psychiatrists and psychologists set up to help catch the Boston Strangler portrayed him as not one man but two, each of whom lived alone and probably worked as a schoolteacher. One of them, the committee said, was a homosexual. The person who later confessed to being the strangler was one man, Albert DeSalvo. He lived with his wife and two children, was employed as a construction worker, and would never have been found by any of the policemen assigned to search the city's homosexual community.

"I don't think psychiatrists or psychologists have any business pretending to be experts in profiling criminal suspects," says Park Elliott Dietz, an associate professor at the University of Virginia Schools of Law and Medicine and chief psychiatrist for the prosecution during the assassination trial of John W. Hinckley Jr. "What's different about the FBI's effort is that they process a crime scene through an experienced investigative brain."

In working up its profiles, the FBI pays microscopic attention to autopsy reports and to maps and photographs of the crime scene. How the victim was treated reveals a lot about the killer. "A person who covers up the body with clothing, or hides it, is saying that he feels

FIGURE 4.8
George Metesky, the Mad Bomber of New York City. When captured, he was wearing a double-breasted suit—just as predicted by a psychological profiler. UPI/Bettman Newsphotos.

FIGURE 4.9
Boston Strangler Albert DeSalvo. In his case, profiling went awry. UPI/Bettman Newsphotos.

pretty bad about what he's done," says FBI agent Douglas, who has a master's degree in educational psychology from the University of Wisconsin and has profiled some 450 murderers. "If he moves the body so it will easily be found, this may show that he has some feeling for the person. He doesn't want them exposed to the elements. He wants them to have a funeral and decent burial."

Profilers pay particular attention to the manner in which a person was killed, the kind of weapon that was used, and something the bureau calls "post-offense behavior," or what the killer did to the victim after he or she was dead. Sex murders typically are stabbings, strangulations, or beatings, rather than shootings. If the killer brought along his own weapon, it points to a stalker, someone fairly well organized, even cunning, who came from another part of town and probably drove a car. If the killer used whatever weapon was available—a knife from the kitchen or a lamp cord—it points to a more impulsive act, a more disorganized personality. It also means that the person probably came on foot and lives nearby.

Was there a lot of beating about the face? The general rule is that a brutal facial attack, as in the case of the murder in the Bronx, means that the killer knew the victim; the more brutal the attack, the closer the relationship. Was the victim killed immediately in a blitz style of assault? This usually indicates a younger killer, someone in his teens or early 20s, who feels threatened by his victims and needs to render them harmless right away. On the other hand, if the killer showed mastery of the situation, if he killed slowly and methodically, it points to a more sadistic personality, a man in his late 20s or 30s.

Equally significant is what the killer does right after the murder. Does he seem to be hanging around the scene, enjoying himself, going through the victim's things, setting the body up in a ritualistic position? Or does he kill and run? And has he taken something? Killers often carry away an artifact, such as a bracelet or compact, to use afterward as a way to recreate the experience in memory. Certain kinds of killers also keep diaries and scrapbooks about their crimes.

Even evidence that at first seems contradictory and confusing can be exceedingly helpful in pointing to a culprit. Two years ago a 22-year-old woman was abducted one night from a babysitting job in a small town in Pennsylvania. Her body was found several days later at the local garbage dump. When Douglas eventually got the photographs and autopsy report, he saw evidence that pointed to two totally different personalities. On the one hand, the fact that the victim was murdered in a fierce, blitz-style attack, and had been mutilated after death, pointed to a disorganized, frightened killer who was able to carve her up only after she was no longer alive. On the other hand, the girl was murdered at one location, then taken by car to the dump, something that Douglas felt could be done only by an organized, calculating killer. There was also evidence of postmortem rape. Again, judging from similar cases, Douglas reasoned that this act was probably not done by a disorganized man.

In the end, Douglas told the nonplussed chief of police that he should be looking for two killers rather than one. And that's the way it turned out. One of them—the man responsible for the frenzied attack—was the girl's live-in boyfriend; the other was his brother, who organized the transportation of the body from the original scene of the crime to the dump.

As for the methods it uses to interpret crime scenes, the FBI relies less on deep psychological insight than on statistical probabilities, plain common sense, and the experience gained from looking at hundreds of similar cases. In the matter of the nude body in the Bronx, Douglas was at once virtually certain that since the girl was white, so was the killer. This is because in the overwhelming majority of mutilation murders, the killer is the same race as his victim. Douglas settled on an age for the murderer—the mid-20s to early 30s—from the fact that the crime scene demonstrated a kind of methodical organization. The girl's earrings had been unscrewed from her lobes, not torn off, and were placed neatly on either side of her head. The body had been carefully spread-eagled so that it took the form of a Chai, a Jewish good-luck charm. Experience told Douglas that this kind of measured conduct would have been highly unusual in an impulsive teenager or someone in his early 20s. Neither was it probable that the killer was an older man, in his late 30s or 40s. The urge to commit brutal sex murders tends to surface at an early age, and the chances that a person could commit a number of such murders over a span of years without being captured would be slim. "If he were in his 40s," Douglas said, "he'd probably be in jail now."

The killer's other characteristics emerged from similar chains of reasoning. The FBI knows from its crime statistics that killers of this nature tend to come from broken homes and that they can rarely sustain a lasting relationship with a woman. This led to the inference that the Bronx murderer lived by himself or with a single parent. Douglas came up with what the police considered the most important lead—that the killer lived or worked near the crime scene—from looking at the leisurely way in which he seemed to have conducted himself at the scene. "He spent a lot of time there, which tells us he was fairly familiar with the surroundings," Douglas says. "He knew it well enough so that he felt he could do whatever he wanted and no one would disturb him." And if the killer lived near the crime scene, this meant that the police had very probably already talked to him, since standard procedure calls for interviewing every resident in the area.

How the FBI gets each piece of the puzzle seems understandable enough. But a completed profile can astound even the most seasoned investigator. The oldest and one of the best-known profilers at the agency is Howard Teten, a 20-year veteran of the FBI and now director of its Institutional Research and Development Unit. Teten is famous for his ability to come up with detailed descriptions of killers on the scantiest of information.

Teten began doing profiles in 1970; at that time, he taught a course at the FBI Academy in applied criminology, and students from various police departments would bring him their cases. On one occasion, a California policeman telephoned about a baffling case involving the multiple stabbing of a young woman. After hearing just a quick description of the murder, Teten told him he should be looking for a teenager who lived nearby. He would be a skinny kid with acne, a social isolate, who had killed the girl as an impulsive act, had never killed before, and felt tremendous guilt. "If you walk around the neighborhood knocking on doors, you'll probably run into him," Teten said. "And when you do, just stand there looking at him and say, 'You know why I'm here.' " Two days later, the policeman called back to say that he had found the teenager as Teten had said he would. But before the officer could open his mouth, the boy blurted out: "You got me."

Along with poring over crime-scene photographs, the FBI uses data from basic research among murderers themselves. Last year, the Behavioral Science Unit received a $128,000 grant from the National Institute of Justice for the purpose of building a file of taped interviews with at least 100 notorious mass murderers and assassins, and computerizing the similarities in their cases. This is the first methodical study ever made of so many killers. So far the bureau has talked with 36 of them, from Charles Manson and Richard Speck to David Berkowitz, Sirhan Sirhan, and Arthur Bremer, the man who tried to kill George Wallace. Agents even visited the criminally insane ward of the Mendota Mental Health Institute in Madison, Wisconsin, to see 77-year-old Ed Gein, the "Ghoul of Plainfield," whose nocturnal excavations in the graveyard of a small Wisconsin town supposedly provided Alfred Hitchcock with his inspiration for the movie *Psycho.*

What the agency hopes to gain from the interviews is insight into how criminals actually work—something that, for all the academic research in crime, remains largely uncharted territory. How do killers approach their victims? What do they talk to them about before killing them? How do they react right after the murder? In the case of one man who abducted children from shopping malls and then murdered them, the FBI was particularly interested in how he had persuaded his victims to come away with him. The answer: He would wrap his arm in a bandage and sling, then get children to help him carry a load of packages to his car, which would be waiting in a deserted area of the parking lot.

"When we went to New York to talk to the 'Son of Sam,' David Berkowitz," says Robert K. Ressler, the agent in charge of the project, "he told us that on the nights when he couldn't find a victim to kill he would go back to the scene of an old crime to relive the crime and to fantasize about it. Now that's a heck of a piece of information to store somewhere to see whether other offenders do the same thing."

In writing up its profiles, the FBI steers clear of psychiatric terminology and couches everything in plain English. For one thing, local policemen tend to regard the mental-health professions, and their language,

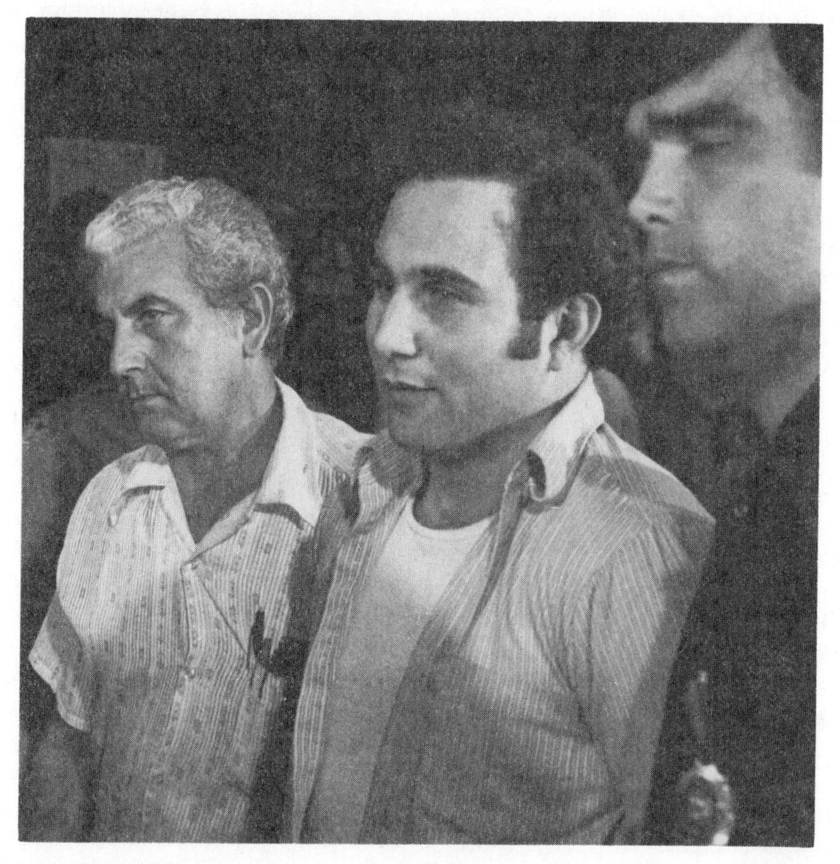

FIGURE 4.10
David Berkowitz, the Son of Sam killer who found his victims in lovers' lanes. UPI/Bettman Newsphotos.

with considerable suspicion. For another, psychiatric language is not terribly helpful in catching criminals. "It's much more useful for the police to know a person's age, race, and marital status than read a precise diagnosis from the American Psychiatric Association's *Diagnostic and Statistical Manual of Mental Disorders,*" says Dietz, the Hinckley psychiatrist. Besides, the FBI isn't particularly interested in a murderer's psychology or motives. "We don't get hung up on why the killer does the things he does," says FBI agent Roy Hazelwood. "What we're interested in is that he *does* it, and that he does it in a way that leads us to him."

The agency warns local policemen not to take any profile too literally—not to limit their investigation to people who exhibit the characteristics in the sketch. A profile is supposed to describe a general type of person, not point to a certain individual. And there is always the possibility that an FBI profile could be dead wrong. Hazelwood, for instance, holds the dubious distinction in the agency of having drawn perhaps the most inaccurate profile on record. He did it in a Georgia case in which a stranger showed up at a woman's door one day and for no apparent reason punched her in the face and shot her little girl—not fatally, as it turned out—in the stomach. Hazelwood told the local police to look for a man who came from a broken home, had dropped out of high school, held a low-skilled job, hung out in honky-tonk bars, and lived far from the crime scene. When the culprit was finally caught, he turned out to have been raised by both of his parents, who had stayed married for 40 years. He had a college degree and had earned above-average grades. He held an executive job in a large bank, taught Sunday school and regularly attended church, never touched a drop of alcohol, and lived in a neighborhood close to the scene of the crime. "I keep that profile around," says Hazelwood, "as a reminder that we're still in the stage where profiling is an art rather than a science."

Along with helping the police narrow down an investigation, profiles are also frequently used to lure killers into the open. The police refer to this as a "pro-active," as opposed to "reactive," technique—and it often requires getting cooperation from the local press. When the FBI determines that a killer is jumpy or under a great deal of stress as a result of his crimes, it encourages the local police to promote newspaper stories saying that the investigation is getting closer and closer to a solution—even if it's getting nowhere at all. "You never want to let the guy off the hook psychologically," Douglas says. "You put enough stress on him and it can cause a change in his behavior so he'll give you something to go on."

When the profile suggests that the killer is experiencing strong feelings of guilt over his crime, the pro-active tactic might be to encourage a newspaper story on the anniversary of the crime, perhaps a sympathetic piece about the victim's family. "What you're trying to do here is to draw the person psychologically back to the victim," Douglas says. The police might also be told to watch the cemetery where the victim is buried, or even place a listening device on the tombstone. Several killers have been caught when they went back to put flowers on the grave.

Some professionals in the mental-health field get a little queasy over the use of psychological approaches to create or compound stress rather than relieve it. Dietz, for instance, occasionally consults with the FBI on profiling, and has joined with agents in publishing papers on crime in professional journals. But when it comes to planning pro-active strategy, he begs off on the ground that the tactic could lead a suspect to kill himself. "It is generally unethical," he says, "for a physician to apply medical knowledge that can result in direct harm to a human being."

The general police reaction to the possibility of a suspect's suicide is "good riddance." And the police argue that whatever the moral complications, pro-active techniques are justified by the deaths they may prevent. If the police aren't careful, however, such techniques can prove to be dangerous. In one Western state, the FBI profile of the killer who stabbed a girl 84 times was presented over a local "crime-stopper" television program, together with vivid pictures from the crime scene. The police, however, had not thought to stake out the girl's home. Shortly after the program, the killer returned to the house and smeared blood over the wall of the girl's room. Had her mother not been out at the time, she might well have met the same fate as her daughter.

The FBI has recently been using psychological profiles in the later as well as the earlier stages of investigations. The agency instructs local policemen in the best techniques for interrogating different kinds of suspects—whether, for instance, to take them to the station in the daytime and use bright lights and hard grilling, or whether to see them at night and approach them in a softer manner.

The agency has also begun advising prosecutors during trials on how to cross-examine the accused on the stand. During the prosecution of Wayne Williams for two of the Atlanta killings, Douglas sat next to Assistant District Attorney Jack Mallard during most of the trial. The problem, from the prosecutor's point of view, was that in the beginning, Williams appeared too cool and composed—hardly the picture of a man capable of murderous outbursts. "We were concerned," Douglas recalls, "that the jury was seeing him as a creditable type of person." Douglas therefore advised Mallard to keep Williams on the stand as long as possible and to rattle him with detailed questions about the killings. "It's difficult for him here in the courtroom where he's not in control and where all the flaws in his personality are coming out. The longer you can keep him up there, the more he'll become agitated and the greater the chance that he'll create an outburst," Douglas explained.

FIGURE 4.11
Wayne Williams, who was tried for two of the 27 Atlanta killings of children and young men. FBI profiling helped to break his composure on the witness stand. UPI/Bettman Newsphotos.

That's exactly what happened. As Mallard bored into how the victims were strangled—"What did it feel like, Wayne, when you wrapped your hands around their throats?" he asked. "Did you panic, Wayne?"—Williams became increasingly uneasy. Suddenly, he interrupted the cross-examination, pointed a finger at the District Attorney, and called him a "fool." Then he went off into a rambling tirade during which his manner of talking changed from calm, educated English into street slang. "You could see the jury suddenly look up in astonishment," says Douglas. "They were shocked; here was a completely different side of his personality coming out."

As for the future of profiling, the FBI says that the system will soon be computerized, so that a policeman anywhere in the country can punch the characteristics of a bizarre murder into a terminal and get back an educated guess as to who did it. The killer will be categorized on the basis of whether he fits into an "organized," "disorganized," or "mixed" personality type. And his characteristics, such as age, race, and how near he lived to the crime scene, will be given numerical weight, depending on how frequently they showed up in similar crimes of the past. No one, of course, is willing to say how the computer can factor intuition and instinct into its analysis. But the day does not seem far off when the police will be able to identify a criminal by the psychic loops and whorls he left at the scene, just as quickly and as surely as if he had covered the wall with fingerprints.

■ DISCUSSION AND REVIEW

1. Summarize the conclusions of Sutherland and Cressey in their review of research on crime and economic conditions. What are some of the factors that contribute to the complexity of the relationship between crime and economics in an industrial country like the United States?

2. How do radical criminologists view the influence of economics on crime?
3. Are there any explanations other than genetics as to why crime might "run in families"?
4. What are some of the physical characteristics and behavioral differences of men who possess the XYY chromosome combination?
5. What was learned about genetically linked criminal tendencies as a result of the studies of identical twins and adoptions?
6. How do the IQ scores of the offender population compare with the population at large?
7. William H. Sheldon, a physician in the 1940s, developed a new system for classifying human physiques into three body builds. What are these three body builds and which type is disproportionally susceptible to criminal behavior?
8. Why does Mednick refer to his theory of criminality as a "biosocial" theory? What is the significance of social learning in Mednick's formulation?
9. What are the principal weaknesses and shortcomings of the psychiatric approach to criminality as mental illness?
10. Why might you be skeptical about the prospect of identifying a "criminal personality"? What are the conclusions of research on this issue?
11. In Rosenhan's study of normal people who faked mental illness to gain entry to a mental hospital, who first became aware that the entrants were pseudopatients?
12. Why is it easier to set up and operate a token economy *within* an institution than outside one?
13. Describe Barker's attempt to treat transvestism by means of conditioning.
14. How does Merton explain the relationship between social structure and deviant behavior?
15. Why has the solution rate for murders dropped so dramatically in the past twenty years?

■ GLOSSARY

Anomie A state of normlessness in society that may be caused by decreased homogeneity and that is conducive to crime and other deviant behavior.

Atavism From the Latin *atavus,* meaning ancestor. Term that implies that certain "born criminals" are an evolutionary throwback to an earlier, more primitive, human form.

Aversive conditioning Treatment in which a person is aversively (negatively) stimulated until he or she performs a certain behavior, at which time the stimulation is discontinued. The effect is positive reinforcement for stopping an undesirable behavior.

Contingency management program Treatment in which desirable behavior is reinforced by reward.

Criminal personality A hypothetical constellation or cluster of traits and characteristics that distinguish criminals from noncriminals.

Electroencephalograph (EEG) An instrument that picks up electrical activity in brain cells by electrodes attached to the scalp. Activity is recorded in oscillating patterns called *brain waves* by a machine connected to the electrodes. The visual recording that results is called an *electroencephalogram.*

Epilepsy A group of nervous disorders characterized by recurring attacks of motor, sensory, or psychic disturbances, sometimes accompanied by convulsive movements and loss of consciousness.

Fugue A pathological amnesic condition during which an individual is apparently conscious of his or her actions; upon a return to normal, however, the sufferer has no recollection of those actions.

Galvanic skin response (GSR) The *GSR* is a component of the polygraph, or "lie detector," apparatus. The apparatus measures minute changes in electropotential on the surface of the skin to provide an index of emotional responses such as anxiety.

Orthmolecular psychiatry Doctrine based on the belief that various kinds of deviant behavior, including delinquent and criminal activity, are systematically related to abnormal reaction rates in the body as a result of constitutional defects, faulty diet, and abnormal concentrations of essential elements.

Radical criminology An approach to crime based on the assumption that criminal law reflects the power of elite groups in society and is manifested by the use of the criminal justice system to maintain control of the production and distribution of wealth. Also known as "critical criminology."

Token economy A method of reinforcement often used in institutional settings. People are rewarded for constructive social behavior with tokens that can be exchanged for desired objects or activities.

XYY syndrome A chromosomal abnormality in males (the presence of an extra Y chromosome). Men with this abnormality have a ten to twenty times greater tendency to break the law than do genetically normal men.

■ REFERENCES

Barker, J. C. "Behaviour Therapy for Transvestism: A Comparison of Pharmacological and Electrical Aversion Techniques." *British Journal of Psychiatry* 111 (1965): 268–276.

Batchelor, I. R. C. *Henderson and Gillespie's Textbook of Psychiatry.* London: Oxford University Press, 1969.

Bell, B.; Mednick, S. A.; Gottesman, I. I.; and Sergeant, J. "Electrodermal Parameters in Young Normal Male Twins." In *Biosocial Bases of Criminal Behavior,* edited by S. A. Mednick and K. O. Christiansen. New York: Gardner Press, 1977.

Braukmann, C.; Fixen, D.; Phillips, E.; and Wolf, M. "Behavioral Approaches to Treatment in the Crime and Delinquency Field." *Criminology* 13 (1975): 299–331.

Chorover, S. L. "Big Brother and Psychotechnology." *Psychology Today* 7 (1973): 43–54.

Cloward, R. A., and Ohlin, L. E. *Delinquency and Opportunity*. Glencoe, Ill.: Free Press, 1960.

Cohen, A. K. *Delinquent Boys*. Glencoe, Ill.: Free Press, 1955.

Cohen, A. K. "The Delinquency Subculture." In *Juvenile Delinquency: A Book of Readings,* edited by R. Giallombardo. New York: Wiley, 1966.

Feldman, D. "Psychoanalysis and Crime." In D. R. Cressey and D. Ward, eds., *Delinquency, Crime, and Social Process*. New York: Harper and Row, 1969.

Halleck, S. L. "American Psychiatry and the Criminal: A Historical Review." *American Journal of Psychiatry* 121 (1965): 1–21.

Hare, R. D. *Psychopathy: Theory and Research*. New York: Wiley, 1970.

Hare, R. D., and Schalling, D., eds. *Psychopathic Behavior*. New York: Wiley, 1978.

Herrnstein, R. *Biology and Crime*. Washington, D.C.: U.S. Department of Justice, National Institute of Justice, 1987.

Hooten, E. A. *Crime and Man*. Cambridge, Mass.: Harvard University Press, 1939.

Hooton, E. A. *The American Criminal*. Cambridge, Mass.: Harvard University, 1939.

Huxlely, A. *Brave New World*. New York: Harper and Row, 1978.

Lazarus, A. "Has Behavior Therapy Outlived Its Usefulness?" *American Psychologist* 32 (1977): 550–54.

Lillyquist, M. J. *Understanding and Changing Criminal Behavior*. Englewood Cliffs, N.J.: Prentice-Hall, 1980.

Lippert, W. W. "The Electrodermal System of the Psychopath." Ph.D. dissertation, University of Cincinnati, 1965.

Lykken, D. T. "A Study of Anxiety in the Sociopathic Personality." *Journal of Abnormal and Social Psychology* 55 (1957): 6–10.

Mark, V., and Ervin, F. *Violence and the Brain*. New York: Harper & Row, 1970.

Mark, V. H., Sweet, W. H., and Ervin, F. R. "Role of Brain Disease in Riots and Urban Violence." *Journal of the American Medical Association* (1967): 201, 217.

Masters, J. *Bugles and a Tiger*. New York: Viking Press, 1962.

McCaghy, C. H. *Deviant Behavior: Crime, Conflict, and Interest Groups*. New York: Macmillan, 1976.

McConnell, J. "Stimulus/Response: Criminals Can Be Brainwashed—Now." *Psychology Today* 3 (1970): 14–18, 74.

Mednick, S. A. "A Biosocial Theory of the Learning of Law-Abiding Behavior." In *Biosocial Bases of Criminal Behavior,* edited by S. A. Mednick and K. O. Christiansen. New York: Gardner Press, 1977.

Mednick, S. A. "Biosocial Factors and Primary Prevention of Antisocial Behavior." In *New Paths in Criminology,* edited by S. A. Mednick and S. G. Shoham. Lexington, Mass.: Lexington Books, 1979.

Mednick, S. A., and Volavka, J. "Biology and Crime." In *Crime and Justice: An Annual Review of Research,* edited by N. Morris and M. Tonry. Chicago: University of Chicago Press, 1980.

Mednick, S. A.; Volavka, J.; Gabrielli, W. F.; and Itil, T. M. "EEG as a Predictor of Antisocial Behavior." *Criminology* 19 (1981): 219–29.

Merton, R. K. *Social Theory and Social Structure*. Glencoe, Ill.: Free Press, 1957.

Miller, Walter B. "Lower-Class Culture as a Generating Milieu of Gang Delinquency." *Journal of Social Issues* 14 (1958): 5–19.

Mitford, Jessica. *Kind and Unusual Punishment: The Prison Business*. New York: Random House, 1974.

Montagu, A. "Chromosomes and Crime." *Psychology Today* 2 (1968): 43–49.
Nettler, G. *Explaining Crime.* New York: McGraw-Hill, 1974.
Orwell, G. *Nineteen Eighty-Four.* New York: Harcourt Brace, 1949.
Poplin, D. E. *Social Problems.* Glenview, Ill.: Scott, Foresman, 1978.
President's Commission on Law Enforcement and Administration of Justice. *The Challenge of Crime in a Free Society.* Washington, D.C.: U.S. Government Printing Office, 1967.
Quinney, R. *Critique of Legal Order: Crime Control in Capitalist Society.* Boston: Little, Brown, 1974.
Rand, A. *Anthem.* New York: New American Library, 1961.
Reckless, W. C. *The Crime Problem.* New York: Appleton-Century-Crofts, 1973.
Remarque, E. M. *All Quiet on the Western Front.* Boston: Little, Brown, 1929.
Rhodes, Robert P. *The Insoluble Problems of Crime.* New York: Wiley, 1977.
Rodin, E. "Psychomotor Epilepsy and Aggressive Behavior." *Archives of General Psychiatry* 28 (1973): 210–13.
Schwitzgebel, R. "Limitations on the Coercive Treatment of Offenders." *Criminal Law Bulletin* 8 (1972): 267–320.
Sheldon, W. H.; Stevens, S. S.; and Zucker, W. B. *The Variation of Human Physique.* New York: Harper, 1940.
Slater, E., and Roth, M. *Clinical Psychiatry.* London: Balliere and Tindall, 1969.
Stephens, G. "Crime in the Year 2000." *The Futurist* 25 (1981): 48–52.
Suinn, R. M. *Fundamentals of Behavior Pathology.* New York: Wiley, 1970.
Sutherland, E. H. *On Analyzing Crime.* Chicago: University of Chicago Press, 1973.
Sutherland, E. H., and Cressey, D. R. *Criminology.* Philadelphia: Lippincott, 1978.
Thornton, W. E.; James, J. A.; and Doerner, W. G. *Delinquency and Justice.* Glenview, Ill.: Scott, Foresman, 1982.
Turner, W. J., and Merlis, S. "Clinical Correlations between Electroencephalography and Antisocial Behavior." *Medical Times* 90 (1962): 505–11.
Yochelson, S., and Samenow, S. E. *The Criminal Personality.* A Profile for Change, vol. 1. New York: Jason Aronson, 1977.

NOTES

1. This discussion of research on chromosomes, twins and adoptions, body type and physique, and IQ was adopted from Richard Herrnstein, *Biology and Crime* (Washington, D.C.: U.S. Department of Justice, National Institute of Justice, 1987).

CHAPTER

5

The Victims of Crime

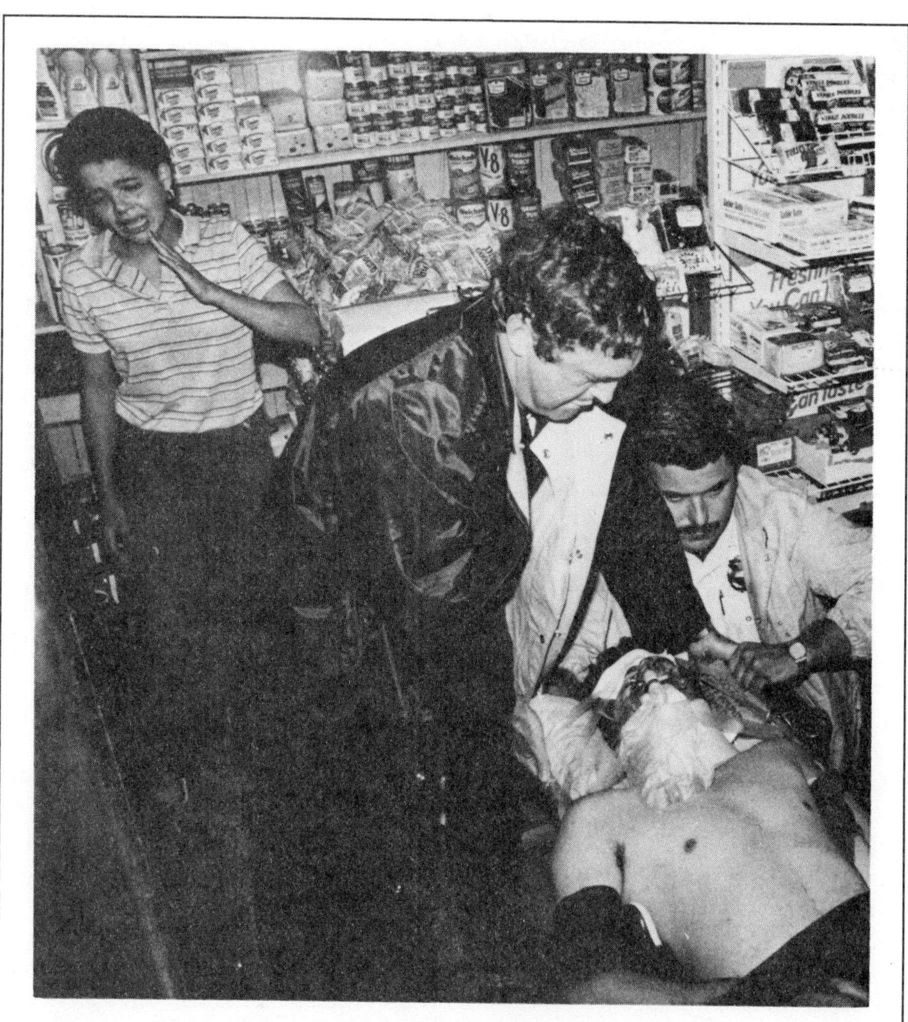

CHAPTER OUTLINE:

Crime victims can hardly be blamed for feeling that the American system of criminal justice has totally neglected them in its exaggerated concern for the rights of offenders. Not only do victims suffer financial losses, but they are also often forced to pay for the treatment of their injuries. In contrast, the criminal receives free medical attention. Public funds pay for the prosecution, and if the criminal has no money, public funds also pay for the defense.

Further, victims may be threatened with reprisal by defendants who are freed on bail or on their own recognizance. Victims can be intimidated by domineering defense attorneys and forced to take days off from work to appear as witnesses in hearings that are postponed again and again. Rarely are they notified of court dates, and no one bothers to keep them posted about the results of plea bargaining. Months may pass before they are able to recover stolen property being held as evidence.

A report of the President's Task Force on Victims of Crime (1982) outlined a series of proposals that, if implemented, might begin to redress these long-standing inequities. Recommendations ranged from training persons who deal with crime victims to be more courteous and sensitive to modifying the Exclusionary Rule and abolishing parole. The task force also supported state and federal legislation to require that victim statements be presented to the court before sentencing, that victims and witnesses be protected from intimidation, and that victims of sexual assault not be compelled to pay for physical examinations or for medical kits used to collect evidence.

Another recommendation was that federal funding be provided for victim **compensation:** "It is simply unfair that victims should have to liquidate their assets, mortgage their homes or sacrifice their health or education or that of their children while the offender escapes responsibilities for the financial hardship he has imposed" (p. 79).

The task force also recommended that hospitals should be required to give emergency treatment to crime victims without regard to their ability to pay; payment should be collected from state compensation funds. Further, judges should order offenders to make **restitution** to victims whenever possible, even when the offender is sent to prison, and should then make sure the payments are actually made. Judges should also give as much weight to the interests of the victims as to the interests of the defendants when ruling on continuances. There should also be more referral and counseling services for victims, involving not only social agencies but also the mental health community and the ministry. Prosecutors should ensure that victims are informed about the progress of the case, and victims should get police protection if they are being harassed.

The task force also made several highly controversial proposals: that bail be denied to persons judged to be clearly dangerous; that parole be abolished (because it undercuts the courts and is unfair to victims, and because parole boards lack accountability); and that the Exclusionary Rule regarding evidence be abolished. The task force concluded that the Exclusionary Rule "does not work, severely compromises the truth-finding process, imposes an intolerable burden on the system and prevents the court from doing justice" [p. 28]. Finally, the task force proposed an amendment to the Constitution that would add the following statement to the Sixth Amendment: "Likewise, the victim in every criminal prosecution shall have the right to be present and to be heard at all critical stages of judicial proceedings" (p. 114).

Increasing concern for the crime victim within the criminal justice system and the agencies of local, state, and federal governments has been paralleled by a revival of criminologists' interest in the victim. Although criminologists have contributed to what (as Edelhertz and Geis [1974] point out) has been "gracelessly dubbed" over a period of more than two centuries as the field of **victimology**—*the systematic study of criminal-victim relationships—the crime victim has never occupied a position of prominence in the field of criminology. Recently, however, attention has been directed toward various groups within society that are especially prone to victimization by criminal offenders—the elderly, children, and the poor.*

Another player in the crime problem who has been insufficiently researched is the bystander. The **Good Samaritan** who intervenes to prevent a potential victim from harm by a criminal predator and the bystander who watches passively as someone is assaulted mark two extremes of participant-observer behavior that pose interesting and significant problems for society and the criminologist. The notorious case of Catherine Genovese, who was murdered outside her New York apartment while neighbors listened to her screams but did not help her, focused national attention on bystander behavior during violent crimes.

GOVERNMENTAL EFFORTS TO ASSIST VICTIMS

The Federal Victim and Witness Protection Act of 1982 is designed to protect and assist victims and witnesses of federal offenses by (1) making it a felony to threaten or intimidate a victim or witness, (2) providing for inclusion of a victim impact statement in presentence reports, (3) furnishing explicit authority for federal trial courts to order offenders to make restitution to victims, and (4) requiring judges to state on the record the reasons for not ordering restitution. The legislation directs the federal government to exercise a leadership role in the victim-witness movement and to provide a model for legislation by state and local governments (Finn 1987).[1]

The Comprehensive Crime Control Act of 1984 brought about major reforms throughout the federal criminal justice system. From tightening bail procedures to strengthening the government's hand against organized crime, this twenty-three-chapter law marked the most sweeping change in the history of the federal justice system. One of its provisions, the Victims of Crime Act, authorized the disbursement of up to $100 million to the states for their programs. The act helps states that compensate a victim for financial losses that result from crime. It also offers funds to enhance victim services, which are vitally important as victims wind their way through the justice system and try to recover from their life-shattering experiences. It is important to note that the money for this program comes from the fines of federal criminals—not from the pockets of innocent taxpayers (U.S. Department of Justice 1986).[2]

In 1982, thirty-seven states had victim compensation programs, which paid roughly $50 million to victims. Some worked well; others were only programs on paper. As more people became aware of the tremendous financial burden a crime can impose, many states improved their responses. Now forty-three states and the District of Columbia offer compensation to victims and their survivors; they paid $68 million in 1984. In addition to making awards to victims, more states are now able to offer assistance for other victim expenses such as mental health counseling and property loss. California, for example, is doubling the maximum payment allowable per claim. New York is enhancing its coverage for essential property loss. Independent organizations in Massachusetts, Arizona, and California are raising private funds to help victims with emergency financial needs (see Table 5.1).

Some state legislation regarding victims of crimes now allows for the introduction of **Victim Impact Statements** at the sentencing stage of the criminal justice process. These statements are used to inform the sentencing judge of the physical, financial, and emotional impact of the crime on the victim or the victim's survivors. In 1987, as described in the article on page 119, the U.S. Supreme Court narrowed the use of Victim Impact Statements in death penalty cases by setting aside the death penalty of a convicted murderer.

The state of California actually has a Victim's Bill of Rights, which specifies that the victim or next of kin if the victim is dead may appear personally or by counsel at the sentencing proceeding to express their views. According to a study conducted by the National Institute of Justice, very few (less than 3 percent) of the victims actually exercised their right to appear at sentencing (Villmoare and Neto 1987). The researchers in this study found that many of the victims who exercised their right to speak at the sentencing did so to find out what was happening in their cases. However, the vast majority of victims surveyed by Villmoare and Neto indicated they felt the right of the victim to appear at sentencing was very important.

TABLE 5.1
State Legislation Mandating the Fair Treatment of Crime Victims

	Pre-1982	As of July 1985
Enacting comprehensive laws that include a majority of the reforms below	4	31
Requiring a victim impact statement at sentencing	8	39
Victim allocution at sentencing	3	19
Permitting victim input into key prosecutorial decisions	1	10
Opening parole hearings	6	19
Abolishing parole	5	8
Requiring that victim be notified of crucial developments in case	2	27
Keeping victim counseling records confidential	6	20
Not disclosing addresses and phone numbers of victims	0	5
Allowing hearsay at preliminary hearings	23	26
Assuring prompt property return	4	20
Protecting victims from intimidation and harassment	4	27
Providing separate and secure waiting rooms	1	17
Checking people who work with children for a history of sex offense convictions	1	20
Mandating restitution to victims as part of sentence	8	29
Providing funds for services to all victims of crime	7	28
Preventing criminals from profiting from the sale of their stories	14	32
Victim compensation	37	43

Adapted from U.S. Department of Justice, *President's Task Force on Victims of Crime—Four Years Later* (Washington, D.C.: U.S. Government Printing Office, 1986), p. 4.

THE VICTIM IN HISTORICAL PERSPECTIVE

Redress of injury was once the responsibility of the victims themselves, their immediate families, or others bound to them by blood or tribal loyalties. Thus, the beginnings of social control are apparent in the transition from the individual quest for retaliation to the identification of injuries sustained by the victim with the interests of the victim's family or social group. This idea of familial or blood relationships is central to the concept of the "blood feud." Consanguinity implied a responsibility on the part of the individual's relatives to act on his or her behalf in seeking compensation or vengeance for injuries sustained as the result of a criminal act.

Court Limits Murder Case Testimony

By Tony Mauro USA TODAY

The anguished testimony of victims' families can't be used in deciding whether to sentence a murderer to death, the Supreme Court said Monday.

Ruling 5–4 in the brutal 1983 killing of an elderly couple in west Baltimore, Md., the court set aside the death penalty for John Booth, convicted of murder in the case.

A Maryland law allowing the couple's survivors to testify about their loss "can serve no other purpose than to inflame the jury and divert it from deciding the case on the relevant evidence," wrote Justice Lewis Powell for the majority.

The court limited its ruling to death penalty cases. Only Nebraska and Maryland have such laws, said the NAACP Legal Defense Fund. All states except Alabama, Hawaii and Tennessee allow victims' testimony in other criminal cases.

"It's a horrifying ruling," said Shirley Butler of Los Angeles, who founded Loved Ones of Homicide Victims after two sons were slain. "It takes away all your rights, your ability to tell the courts what you've lost. All the rights go to the defendant."

"We're all for victims' rights, but you can't have punishment based on the social worth of the victim," said the NAACP defense fund's Tanya Coke.

Alexander von Auersperg, president of the Sunny von Bulow National Victims Advocacy Center, said the decision won't "roll back the gains."

"We will work even harder now," said von Auersperg, von Bulow's son.

With the increase in population and the growth of the organs of social control, however, it became necessary for the rest of society to set limits on the blood feud. An obvious problem with the private vendetta was the lack of effective means to bring a particular dispute to conclusion. Once started, vendettas tended to become perpetual: each injury spawned a search for vengeance in the form of a counterinjury, and an endless cycle of retaliation and counterretaliation was thus inflicted on society. By transferring this concept from the individual to the nation, and from one society to the international scene, it is possible to see in the vendetta a similarity to the modern arms race and the need for imposing stringent limitations upon weapons and armaments.

Talion Law

Talion law (*lex talionis*), discussed in Chapter 2, represented an early effort by society to constrain the widening circle of damage caused by the blood feud. Central to this law was the concept of "equivalent retaliation." An individual who had suffered injury or loss of property was entitled to a fair and just recompense—one that did not exceed the original injury or loss. Thus, talion law was an effort toward social defense (i.e., toward the imposition of curbs upon parties to the vendetta to protect and maintain the social organization of the tribe or clan).

Early Forms of Compensation

Additional efforts to mitigate the depredations of the blood feud resulted in the idea of compensation—the payment of damages to placate the victim and to satisfy, at least partially, the desire for vengeance. But compensation has not always been equal to the damage: Fry (1951) notes that the Law of Moses required fourfold restitution for stolen sheep and fivefold restitution for cattle; and Schafer (1968) observes that the eighteenth-century B.C. Code of Hammurabi—which was notorious for its deterrent cruelty—sometimes demanded as much as thirty times the value of the damage caused. Says Schafer, "The criminal's obligation to pay was enforced not in the interest of the victim, but rather for the purpose of increasing the severity of the criminal's punishment" (p. 12).

In time, a tariff system was introduced that set appropriate levels of recompense in relation to the type and extent of injuries inflicted upon the victim. But the system generally did not apply to rape or murder, which were seen as too serious to be compensated for, except in terms of in-kind retaliation. On occasion, however, even homicide was atoned for by a fine in livestock large enough to humiliate the offender and thus appease the desire for revenge.

In one form or another, the system of compensation has prevailed in many cultures of the world. In the Germanic tribes, most injuries were punished by fines called *faida*, meaning "the feud commuted for money." In the development of Anglo-Saxon law, the *bot* (a money payment used to atone for criminal action) came into use, although some classes of particularly serious offenses had no bot—that is, they were "botless" or "bootless." The amount of restitution to be provided in the form of bot was determined by the nature of the crime and the age, sex, or rank of the injured party. Rank was established by a system of *wergilds*, which outlined a hierarchy among the injured parties: a free-born man was worth more than a slave, a man was worth more than a woman, and an adult was worth more than a child. Out of these distinctions developed a complicated system of regulations that constituted the earliest codified law of the Anglo-Saxons.

With the establishment of the king as a strong central authority, the conception of crime changed, as did the methods used to deal with lawbreakers. A crime was defined as an offense against the king's peace and was consequently dealt with by public authority. The dominant way of handling offenders shifted away from compensation and restitution to various methods of corporal punishment and, more recently, to incarceration.

Decline in concern for the victim and for compensation or restitution seems to have been widespread in Western civilization. But this trend was opposed by various individuals and by international prison congresses from the middle of the nineteenth century until well into the twentieth century. Schafer (1977) points out that at the International Prison Congress held in Stockholm, Sweden, in 1878, Sir George Arney, chief justice of New Zealand, proposed a return to the ancient practice of requiring an offender to make reparation to the victim. And participants in the International Penal Association Congress at Christiania, Sweden, in 1895, agreed that modern law does not sufficiently consider the reparation due to injured parties; that, in the case of petty offenses, time should be given for indemnification; and that prisoners' earnings in prison might be used for reparation (Schafer 1977, p. 18).

Four years later (in 1899), the problem of victim compensation was extensively discussed at the International Prison Congress in Paris. One of the principal questions on the agenda was, Is the victim of a delict sufficiently armed by modern law to enable him to obtain indemnity from the person who has injured him? Despite this early interest among criminologists, however, the victim's case at the turn of the century was still not advanced with much success.

By the middle of the twentieth century, interest in the idea of compensation to crime victims had been renewed. This phenomenon, which may be seen as part of a more general concern for civil rights and the rights of minorities, has led to a renewed emphasis by criminologists on the victim's role in the criminal-victim relationship.

THE CRIMINAL-VICTIM RELATIONSHIP

Hans von Hentig published *The Criminal and His Victim: Studies in the Sociobiology of Crime* in 1948. Hentig advanced the notion that victims themselves often contribute significantly to their own victimization. He suggested that the relationship between the perpetrators and victims of some crimes may be more complex than is recognized by our criminal laws.

Hentig saw the relationship between criminal and victim as one of mutuality. To speak of mutuality is to raise questions about the distinctness of such categories as "victims" and "criminals." As Hentig points out, although the "mechanical outcome of a criminal action may be profit to one party, harm to another, the psychological interaction between the criminal and victim, carefully observed, will not submit to this kindergarten label" (p. 384).

Victim Precipitation of Crime

As already noted, some people—by virtue of age, sex, infirmity, or similar factors—can be considered potentially more vulnerable to various crimes than are people who do not possess such characteristics. The concept of **victim precipitation,** however, goes considerably beyond victim proneness by postulating that certain personality or behavioral characteristics or certain aspects of relationships may contribute directly to victimization. That is, according to victim precipitation, the blame for various criminal acts is *shared* by the criminal offender and the victim.

In his classic study of murder, criminologist Marvin Wolfgang (1958) introduced the concept of victim-precipitated homicide. According to this concept, certain actions of homicide victims (such as brandishing a weapon or striking the first blow) help to bring about the victim's own death. One out of four of the victims in Wolfgang's study met this criterion. Wolfgang maintains that, in at least some cases, two potential offenders come together in a potential homicide situation, and it is pure chance that one becomes a victim, and the other a perpetrator.

It is widely believed that some rape victims are responsible, either consciously or by default, for their own victimization—that by word, provocative behavior, dress, or manner, the victim gives the offender the impression that she (or he) is available for sexual liaison. Amir defines victim-precipitated rape this way:

> The term "victim precipitation" describes those rape situations in which the victim actually, or so it was deemed, agreed to sexual relations but retracted before the actual act or did not react strongly enough when the suggestion was made by the offender(s). The term applies also to cases in risky situations marred with sexuality, especially when she uses what could be interpreted as indecency in language and gestures, or constitutes what could be taken as an invitation to sexual relations (1971, p. 266).

According to Amir, 19 percent of the 646 rapes he studied in Philadelphia were victim precipitated; but a study conducted by the National Commission on the Causes and Prevention of Violence (1970) showed that less than 5 percent of rapes that occurred in seventeen U.S. cities could be categorized as victim precipitated.

The issue of victim precipitation in both homicide and forcible rape is complex, delicate, and highly controversial. The law is far from clear on the relative culpability of the victim in many cases. The principle of causation in criminal law is often expressed as *sine qua non* ("without which not"), meaning that the harm would not have resulted but for the act of the defendant. But what about the act of the *victim?*

It is easy to imagine a situation in which a woman's acceptance of overtures toward intimacy may result in encouraging the man to make overtures that she is unready or unwilling to accept. Her "message" may be completely misinterpreted by the other party. Whatever she intended, it is very unlikely that she was encouraging the man to proceed to the extremity of sexual assault. Nevertheless, a sequence of events of this kind might help explain—not justify, but explain—how a rape transpired. And although most circumstances do not excuse an offender's behavior, they may influence the disposition of the case by supporting a reduced charge or a reduced sentence—or the complete withholding of prosecution.

VICTIMIZATION STUDIES

The official counting of crimes is susceptible to many errors. A major reason for inaccuracy in official crime statistics is that people are reluctant, for a variety of reasons, to report that they have been victimized. Fortunately, victimization studies provide supplemental crime data. Victimization surveys and investigations ask people to indicate the frequency and types of crimes that have been perpetrated against them. In addition to gathering information on selected crimes of violence and theft, these surveys also collect data on the characteristics of victims and the circumstances surrounding criminal acts—including victim-offender relationships, characteristics of offenders, victim self-protection, extent of victim injuries, time and place of occurrence, economic consequences to victims, use of weapons, whether the police were called, and reasons advanced for *not* calling the police.

The first nationwide victimization studies were conducted for the President's Commission on Law Enforcement and Administration of Justice. The best known of these studies—a broad-based, well-designed survey conducted by the National Opinion Research Center in 1966—involved interviews in ten thousand households throughout the continental United States. Based on this survey, researchers estimated that the rate of victimization for index crimes was more than twice the rate reported in the FBI's Uniform Crime Reports.

Another series of victimization studies was carried out in twenty-six American cities between 1972 and 1974 (U.S. Department of Justice 1974, 1975a, 1975b). Decker (1977) combined the data from these studies and compared them with FBI crime data for the same years. As shown in Table 5.2, he found that victims reported almost three times as many index offenses as were recorded in the Uniform Crime Reports. The figures from these two sources are not totally comparable, of course, but they do suggest that victimization studies may be a more accurate indicator of increases in crime, because they are not subject to the same reporting and recording problems that affect the FBI's Uniform Crime Reports.

More recent victimization studies conducted by the federal government reflect the following nationwide crime trends. One-fourth of the nation's households were touched by a crime of violence or theft in 1986, the same proportion as in 1985 and well below the one-third of all households touched by crime in 1975, the first year for which measure is available. There were no measurable differences in 1986 from 1985 in the percentages of households touched by any of the crime measured: rape, robbery, assault, personal theft, household burglary, household theft, and motor vehicle theft.

The term "household" refers to a dwelling unit (usually a house or apartment) and the people who occupy it. A household is considered "touched by crime" if during the year it experienced a burglary, auto theft, or household theft or if a household member was raped, robbed, or assaulted, or was a victim of personal theft, no matter where the crime occurred (Rand 1987).

In general, victimization surveys confirm that groups disproportionately involved in the perpetration of

TABLE 5.2
Difference of Means Test for Official and Survey Estimates of Crime

	Mean Rate (Per 100,000)				
	VIC	*UCR*	*t Value*	*Degrees of Freedom*	*Significance*
Rape	137	50	8.05	25	*
Robbery	1621	582	9.98	25	*
Aggravated assault	766	360	5.28	25	*
Larceny	9581	2737	8.92	25	*
Burglary	6187	2065	13.64	25	*
Motor vehicle theft	1073	1186	−1.68	25	0.10
Violent crime rate	2525	993	9.94	25	*
Property crime rate	16954	5875	10.94	25	*
Overall crime rate	19478	6868	11.11	25	*

*Significant beyond 0.0005.

Reproduced from S. H. Decker, "Official Crime Rates and Victim Surveys: An Empirical Comparison," *Journal of Criminal Justice* 5 (1977): 51, by permission of the author and publisher.

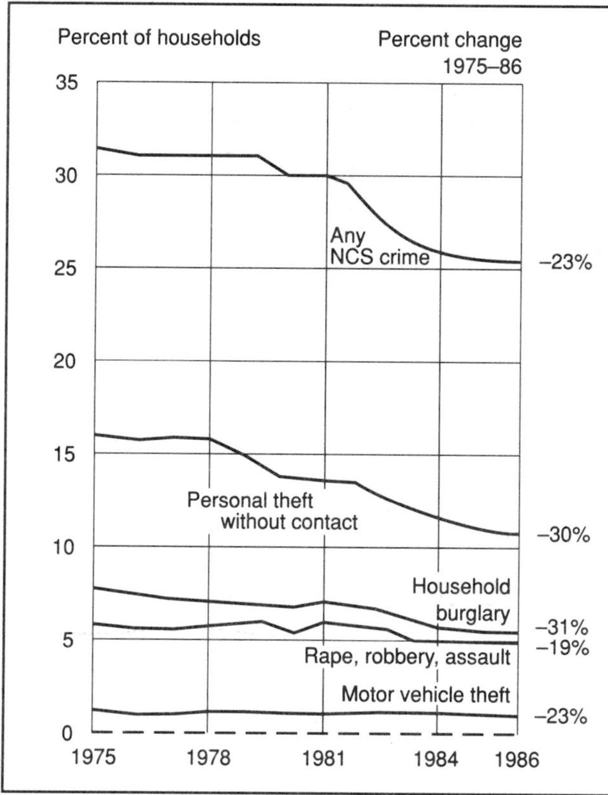

FIGURE 5.1
Households touched by selected crimes of violence and theft, 1975–86. Adapted from Michael R. Rand, *Households Touched by Crime, 1986.* (Washington, D.C.: U.S. Department of Justice, Bureau of Justice Statistics, 1987), p. 1.

crimes—the young, males, the poor, and blacks—are also the groups most likely to be victimized (both by crimes against the person and crimes against property). In addition, residents of the central city—our urban ghettos—are much more vulnerable to crime victimization than people who live in nonmetropolitan areas or suburbs. Among commercial victims, retail stores suffer the highest rates of burglary and robbery.

Personal crimes of violence usually involve members of the same race. Although the fear of crime is often fear of the violent crimes committed by strangers, the National Crime Survey, which measured violent crimes between 1982 and 1984, found that almost 40 percent occurred among friends, acquaintances, or relatives. Other findings of that victimization survey are as follows (Timrots and Rand 1987, p. 1).

- Among violent crimes, robbery was most likely to be committed by a stranger; homicide, least likely.
- Most violent crimes by strangers (70 percent) were committed against males; most crimes by relatives (77 percent) were committed against females.
- Spouses or ex-spouses committed over half of all crimes by relatives and about two-thirds of all crimes by relatives against women.
- Crimes by strangers were more often committed by two or more offenders than were crimes by nonstrangers.
- Stranger-to-stranger crimes more often involved a weapon but less often resulted in an attack than nonstranger crimes. Crimes by relatives involved an attack and injury more often than crimes by either strangers or acquaintances.
- Of those injured, victims of stranger crimes and victims of crimes by acquaintances were more likely to require medical attention than victims of crimes committed by relatives.

The value of information obtained from victimization studies depends on the accuracy and reliability of the survey techniques. A key issue is the adequacy of the sample on which the results are based. Other factors include the fallibility of memory of the crime victims and the truthfulness—or lack of it—that characterizes survey responses.

Early victimization studies (those conducted for the President's Commission on Law Enforcement and Administration of Justice in 1966) were criticized because approximately one quarter of the people who were approached refused to be interviewed, thus introducing an immediate bias into the sample. The National Opinion Research Center's study was challenged because only one available adult in each household was questioned—a method that produced an overrepresentation of women and older persons (the people most likely to be at home during the day). These problems were overcome in later surveys in which everyone over the age of twelve in a household was interviewed; these surveys obtained nearly 100 percent participation of eligible persons and eliminated the excessive reliance on the responses of a single individual in a household.

Victims do not always remember crimes that were perpetrated against them during a given time period. And in some cases, they may not even be aware that they *were* victims (e.g., in such offenses as fraud, embezzlement, or buying stolen property). It is also possible that victimization figures are inflated by respondents who give false reports to justify illegal tax deductions or spurious insurance claims. Unfortunately, there is no easy way to gauge the extent of such overreporting.

TABLE 5.3
Victim-Offender Relationship for Selected Violent Crimes, 1982–84

VICTIM-OFFENDER RELATIONSHIP	VIOLENT CRIME TOTAL	RAPE	ROBBERY	AGGRAVATED ASSAULT	SIMPLE ASSAULT
Percent of victimizations					
Total	100%	100%	100%	100%	100%
Nonstranger**	39%	40%	20%	39%	46%
Relative	8	4	4	7	9
Spouse	3	1*	1	3	4
Ex-spouse	2	1*	1	1	2
Parent	–	1*	–*	1	–
Child	–	–*	–*	–	–
Brother/sister	1	–*	1	1	1
Other relative	2	2*	1	1	2
Acquaintance	31	35	15	30	36
Boyfriend/ex-boyfriend	3	7	2	3	3
Girlfriend/ex-girlfriend	1	–*	–	1	1
Friend/ex-friend	6	6	3	7	7
Other person well known but not related	6	6	2	6	8
Casual acquaintance	14	16	7	14	16
Stranger	57%	55%	77%	56%	52%
Completely unknown	46	49	71	44	39
Known by sight only	11	7	6	12	13
Relationship not ascertained	3%	4%	3%	5%	2%
Number of victimizations					
Total	19,999,000	504,000	3,715,300	5,289,600	10,490,200
Nonstranger**	7,879,500	202,700	743,800	2,082,100	4,851,000
Relative	1,502,400	21,200	148,200	389,900	943,200
Spouse	574,200	4,400*	46,500	153,400	369,900
Ex-spouse	322,600	5,600*	41,200	72,500	203,300
Parent	91,500	2,600*	13,800	35,600	39,500
Child	52,900	0*	6,300*	21,500	25,100
Brother/sister	157,900	0*	20,100	34,500	103,300
Other relative	303,000	8,700	20,200	72,300	202,100
Acquaintance	6,114,000	174,200	562,900	1,610,300	3,766,600
Boyfriend/ex-boyfriend	638,300	33,700	86,600	152,900	365,100
Girlfriend/ex-girlfriend	193,100	1,500*	17,300	52,800	121,500
Friend/ex-friend	1,283,100	29,500	126,400	344,900	782,200
Other person well known but not related	1,197,600	29,300	67,800	306,400	794,100
Casual acquaintance	2,802,000	80,200	264,700	753,500	1,703,600
Stranger	11,488,000	279,100	2,847,800	2,952,100	5,409,000
Completely unknown	9,291,400	245,300	2,629,800	2,333,900	4,082,500
Known by sight only	2,196,600	33,800	218,000	618,300	1,326,500
Relationship not ascertained	631,600	22,200	123,800	255,400	230,300

Note: Detail may not add to total because of rounding.

*Represents 10 or fewer sample cases.

**Nonstranger totals include crimes for which detailed relationship was not ascertained.

– Less than 0.5%.

Adapted from Anita D. Timrots and Michael R. Rand, *Violent Crimes by Strangers and Nonstrangers* (Washington, D.C.: U.S. Department of Justice, Bureau of Justice Statistics, 1987), p. 2.

A recent report produced by the U.S. Department of Justice took a slightly different approach to victimization and attempted to estimate the likelihood that a person would become the victim of a crime during his or her *lifetime*. The report also attempted to predict the likelihood of a household being victimized during a twenty-year period. This contrasted with conventional one-year periods of measuring crimes and victimization.

For example, the report found that based on 1975–84 annual victimization rates, an estimated five out of six people will be victims of the violent crimes of rape, robbery, and assault, either attempted or completed, during their lives. According to the same study, virtually everyone will be the victim of personal theft at least once during his or her life. In general, the potential for victimization decreases the older one gets (Koppel 1987, p. 3). These estimates of lifetime victimization have obvious implications for both individuals and the criminal justice system (see Table 5.4).

TABLE 5.4
Lifetime Likelihood of Victimization, by Age

	Percentage of Persons Who Will Be Victimized by Crime Starting at Various Ages			
	Total	Number of Victimizations		
	One or More Victimizations	One	Two	Three or More
Violent Crimes*				
Current age				
12 years old	83%	30%	27%	25%
20	72	36	23	14
30	53	35	13	4
40	36	29	6	1
50	22	19	2	—
60	14	13	1	—
70	8	7	—	—
Robbery or assault resulting in injury				
Current age				
12 years old	40%	30%	7%	2%
20	30	25	4	1
30	19	17	2	—
40	11	11	1	—
50	7	6	—	—
60	4	4	—	—
70	2	2	—	—
Personal theft				
Current age				
12 years old	99%	4%	8%	87%
20	98	9	16	73
30	93	19	25	48
40	82	31	19	33
50	64	37	19	8
60	43	32	9	2
70	24	21	3	—

Note: Data are based on average victimization rates measured by the National Crime Survey for 1975–84. All crimes include attempts.
—Less than 0.5 percent.
*Includes rape, robbery, and assault.

From Herbert Koppel, *Lifetime Likelihood of Victimization* (Washington, D.C.: U.S. Department of Justice, Bureau of Justice Statistics, 1987), p. 3.

TREATMENT OF VICTIMS

Restitution

Restitution sometimes involves partial or complete payments voluntarily offered by adult criminal offenders—particularly for white-collar crimes—to allay prosecution or to mitigate the sentence. More commonly, however, it involves offender-restitution-to-the-victim schemes that consider both punishment and offender rehabilitation. Such schemes have been adopted experimentally in the United States in recent years, primarily by juvenile courts.

Restitution by adult offenders, either as a condition of probation or voluntarily offered, has been largely limited to cases of fraud, embezzlement, forgery, and other white-collar offenses. As MacNamara and Sullivan observe, "On more than one occasion such offers of restitution and their acceptance come perilously close to the compounding of felonies" (1974, p. 224). These authors also note that court-ordered restitution directed by juvenile court judges against juvenile offenders or their parents has often been less concerned with restoring the victim than with teaching the offender a lesson. In cases involving vandalism against schools, churches, and public property, there is usually little relationship between the amount of restitution—usually paid in services rather than in money—and the actual extent of damage.

A noteworthy attempt at offender repayment to the crime victim is being made at the Minnesota Restitution Center, a community-based correctional program operated by the Minnesota Department of Corrections (1976). The program is offered to selected property offenders sentenced to the Minnesota State Prison, the State Reformatory for Men, and the Minnesota Institution for Women. Participating offenders make restitution to the victim or victims of their crimes. Eligibility for the program is established in a thorough screening designed to eliminate offenders that have a history of drug dependency, severe psychiatric problems, or assaultive offenses, and intelligent individuals who have adequate social skills but have chosen to live outside the law and have not demonstrated any consistent attempt at lawful employment. Once selected for the program, an offender works out a restitution plan with the victim. He or she then becomes a resident of Restitution House until full restitution is made. During this period, the offender must pay for room and board and contribute to the support of his or her own family.

Being a Crime Victim

Most crime victims experience physical suffering, financial loss, or emotional distress. Physical injuries occur in nearly one-third of all violent crimes. Financial losses include destruction of property, loss of money and other valuables, loss of income, medical expenses, and reha-

FIGURE 5.2
A Minnesota inmate signing a restitution contract. Courtesy Bill Powers/*Corrections Magazine.*

bilitation costs. Victims may also feel obliged to incur substantial expenses in efforts at self-defense—such as installing burglar alarm systems.

Emotional distress, often the most important consequence of victimization, can include feelings of fear, anger, shame, self-blame, helplessness, and depression. Sometimes long-term emotional disabilities also result—including sleeplessness, loss of concentration, and fear of being left alone.

Crime victims often receive insensitive or callous treatment from the criminal justice system:

- There may be insensitive questioning.
- There may be innuendos that the victim was somehow at fault. (There is a dilemma here—often the police do not know who was at fault and whether the apparent victim was the aggressor or somehow provoked the offender; aggressive questioning may be a necessary investigative technique.)
- The victim may have difficulty learning what is happening with the case.
- Property may be kept as evidence for a long time or may never be returned.
- Wages may be lost for time spent testifying in court.
- Time may be wasted as victims appear for court proceedings only to have the case postponed or dismissed.
- Victims may experience indifference to their fear of retaliation if they cooperate with the authorities.
- Victims may be anxious about testifying in open court and fearful of being questioned by defense attorneys (Finn 1987).[3]

Delivery of Victim Services

In response to a growing public concern for the plight of victims of criminal offenses, a variety of programs have been developed in recent years to provide victim services. Such programs address both immediate and long-term goals, and services range from crisis intervention by police officers in the emergency treatment of victims to the mobilization of community support for crime prevention activities. An interesting proposal by Dussich (1972) is to establish a community ombudsman to assist crime victims by intervening in the crisis and directing the victim to community resources. Victim service programs can be seen as a formalization of community support and action formerly supplied by neighborhood residents.

Dussich (1975) has also thoroughly analyzed various victim service models and their efficacy. In these analyses, Dussich focused on the objectives or functions—categorized as *primary* or *secondary*—of each model. The primary function of each model, he discovered, is to deliver a broad range of services to crime victims on behalf of the respective agencies that host the programs. These services include

1. Assuming immediate responsibility for the victim at the scene of the crime
2. Referring or transporting the victim to emergency medical or social service facilities
3. Providing the victim with a companion for a period immediately following the crime
4. Addressing the victim's family situation
5. Protecting the victim from unnecessary exploitation by the media, the police, and the courts
6. Thorough follow-up and assurance of adequate delivery of public assistance services
7. Assisting victims with their responsibilities to the court as key witnesses
8. Counseling victims to prevent revictimization
9. Using information from victim contacts to plan community crime prevention activities
10. Developing public awareness programs to refine the goals of victim services
11. Coordinating victim volunteer programs to supplement existing manpower needs
12. Assisting the families of victims with aftermath arrangements (e.g., insurance, funerals, compensations)
13. Conducting victimization surveys to pinpoint high victimization areas
14. Providing the victim with information about the progress of the case and his or her role and responsibilities in the legal process

Secondary functions of victim service include encouraging victims to report crimes to the police and gathering information from victims to assist in police crime prevention (functions specific to the *police model*), and, in the case of the *district attorney model*, notifying victim-witnesses about court appearances and helping them adjust their schedules to the court's schedule. Additional secondary functions—such as maintaining a hot line for crime victims in need of immediate help or providing victims with a community services directory of key resources—are appropriate to all models.

Dussich notes that victim service programs may be located administratively within a police agency, the office of the public prosecutor, a hospital, or various other agencies (including the office of the county manager, a religious mission, a private agency, or a volunteer agency). "The phenomenon of manifest self-interest occurs in all models. The host agency, in large part, determines *what* the priorities are, and *how* they will be carried out" (1975, p. 7). Thus, a program within a police agency offers the advantage of quick referral; yet many victims shy away from anything associated with the police and are likely to refuse services from this source. Similarly, programs within the office of the public prosecutor gain from identification with the prestige and authority of the judicial process; on the other hand, however, the tendency of the prosecution to stress the victim's role as a *witness,* rather than as a *victim,* and the lack of proximity to referral services are distinct disadvantages.

The religious mission is a ready-made, caring agency that is already staffed and funded and offers the advantages of the dedication of its personnel and its acceptance within the community. In general, private agencies are more flexible than publicly funded programs in the delivery of services. Unfortunately, however, such agencies are apt to suffer from difficulties in gaining access to the processes of the criminal justice system. "Referrals to these programs . . . are made reluctantly and subsequent referrals made by the program to other community resources are given low priority" (Dussich 1975, p. 9). Volunteer programs also suffer the disadvantage of being outside the formal criminal justice system—despite community support and a high level of motivation and enthusiasm among volunteer participants. Like private agencies, volunteer agencies are extremely restricted in their ability to make lasting changes within the system.

The value of any program, Dussich observes, is measured by its ability to deliver services to its clients. He identifies the two most relevant functions of a victim services program as victim restoration and crime reduction. The three critical factors in victim restoration are physical recuperation from assault, emotional readjustment from trauma, and improvement of living conditions altered by the victimization. In terms of crime reduction, target areas include increased crime reporting, increased offender conviction, increased offender responsibility, and crime prevention. Dussich remarks that the specialized handling of these services is developing into a new profession called "victim advocacy." The main mission of the victim advocate is to "address the plight of victims locally and generate new techniques, strategies, and systems for humanizing the way victims are dealt with by the criminal justice system" (1975, p. 1).

Dussich's belief that the role of victim advocate must be legitimized and institutionalized is perhaps best exemplified by his proposal to establish victim ombudsmen in the community. It is abundantly clear from Dussich's review of victim service models that the variety of services required by victims cannot be encompassed by any single public or private agency. Thus, we will probably witness a period of experimentation, of trial and error, in which victim service models and programs will be judged in terms of their results. In any event, we will probably end up with a number of programs in various host agencies within the public and private sectors, supported by both private and federal funding.

BYSTANDERS AND GOOD SAMARITANS

An event that occurred in New York City in 1964 raised disturbing questions about the social climate of the large city and the response of urban Americans to citizens who fall victim to crime. In the early morning hours of 13 March 1964, a young woman named Catherine Genovese was stabbed to death outside her apartment in a middle-class neighborhood of Queens. Thirty-eight of her neighbors witnessed at least part of the attack, but none of them went to her aid or even called the police until after she was dead. *New York Times* editor Abe Rosenthal, author of the book *Thirty-Eight Witnesses,* observes that most of the witnesses were "neither defiant or terribly embarrassed nor particularly ashamed. The underlying attitude or explanation seemed to be fear of involvement of any kind" (1964, pp. 78–79). Witnesses defended their inaction with such statements as, "I was tired," "We thought it was a lover's quarrel," "I didn't want my husband to get involved," and "I don't know."

The publicity surrounding the Genovese case provoked speculation—lay and professional—on the motives of the thirty-eight neighbors and the significance of the entire episode. The obvious question—Why didn't someone help?—was asked repeatedly. And researchers Milgram and Hollander (1970) asked the more significant question, "Why *should* anyone have helped? Why should anyone have taken the trouble to go to the aid of the victim or even to call the police?

There are no easy answers to these questions. However, it is believed that a number of social conditions that characterize urban industrial life set up barriers to bystander action. Because most interaction in modern society takes place on an impersonal level, a positive response to another person's plight requires an expression of care and concern that is atypical of the way people respond in most situations (Shaskolsky 1970). In addition, the middle class is not socialized to deal with or use violence, even when it is called for or justified by the circumstances. Within a highly specialized society such as ours, extraordinary situations are assumed to be the concern of specialists—in this case, the police. Often, however, people fail even to summon the police, a failure that has been attributed to the reluctance of bystanders to intervene in situations in which they have no personal mandate and which may cause them embarrassment, resentment, and possible physical danger. In addition, people may take refuge in the belief that the police have already been summoned or in the feeling that the police would be unable to do anything anyway (McCall 1975).

Latané and Darley (1970) have studied the circumstances under which bystanders *do* take action to aid a victim. They indicate that the intervention process involves a sequence of five decisions: the bystander (1) notices that something is happening; (2) interprets the event as an emergency; (3) assumes some degree of personal responsibility for helping; (4) decides the appropriate form of assistance to be given; and (5) implements the intervention. McCall maintains that the most critical factor in bystander response is the assumption of personal responsibility. Research indicates that this action is *inversely* related to the number of persons present in a given situation (Latané and Darley 1970). That is, the more persons that witness a situation, the less likely it is that any one of them will act to help the victim. Latané and Darley suggest four reasons why this occurs (1970, p. 125):

1. Other bystanders inhibit the potential helper by serving as an audience to his or her actions.
2. Other bystanders guide behavior; if they are inactive, the potential helper will also be inactive.
3. The interactive effect of the two processes of guidance and inhibition will be much greater than either alone; if each bystander sees other bystanders momentarily frozen by audience inhibition, each may be misled into thinking that the situation must not be serious.
4. The presence of other people dilutes the responsibility and urge to act felt by any single bystander (this is referred to as diffusion of blame or responsibility).

Conklin points out that the American system of law does not generally require a witness to an emergency to help the victim if the predicament is not caused by the witness. In fact, says Conklin, "Anglo-American law warns witnesses that they face certain risks if they try to help a victim and fail; sometimes they may be sued for harming the victim as a result of errors they commit during their rescue attempt. Our legal system thus discourages bystander aid to victims" (1975, p. 217).

In nations such as France and Germany, however, affirmative action by witnesses is *required* by the law under certain conditions. But American law not only fails to require such assistance, it also provides relatively little opportunity for a witness to collect for injuries suffered during a rescue attempt. Thus, there are no incentives to help a victim. Rather, in its failure to absolve the well-intentioned rescuer from a civil suit by a victim or a victim's dependents, the law actually *discourages* altruistic behavior by a prospective helper. Fear of legal repercussions may inhibit willingness to help even in situations that do not involve a threat of physical injury.

One of the major obstacles to the passage of Good Samaritan legislation is that there is no organized effort to support such laws. In addition, the public does not completely understand that, despite their status as specialists, the police require a great deal of public cooperation to function effectively. In addition, police officers, physicians, and firefighters tend to be critical of citizens for amateurish attempts to render aid in emergencies.

Despite these obstacles, however, Conklin feels that Good Samaritan legislation is needed:

> Knowing the people are not legally obligated to help victims or to intervene in a crime may make potential offenders more likely to commit a crime. This will reinforce public fears and make Good Samaritan laws even more difficult to pass. Still, the absence of such laws is not the major reason that people do not respond to victims in distress, although such laws might occasionally influence behavior. The presence of a law, even if unenforced

> and lacking strong impact on behavior, might create confidence that *others* would help. This could increase social solidarity and make people more willing to walk the streets at night because of the feeling that they could depend on others to help in an emergency. This view might be inaccurate, but it still could be self-fulfilling if it leads people to spend more time on the street, since potential criminals might be less willing to commit crimes in the sight of others. For such an effect to occur, a potential offender would have to feel that there was some chance of being interfered with or reported to the police by witnesses (pp. 222–23).

Until or unless the behavior of people in public places is supported by such legislation, this observation by Alan Barth will probably hold true:

> Let us bear in mind . . . that the original Good Samaritan extolled by St. Luke was fortunate in not arriving on the scene until after the thieves had set upon the traveler, robbed him, and beaten him half to death. The Samaritan cared for him and showed him great kindness, but he did not put himself in peril by doing so. Perhaps this is about as much as can be reasonably asked by the ordinary mortal man (1966, p. 163).

SPECIAL CATEGORIES OF VICTIMS

In the recent years much attention has been drawn to four general categories of criminal victimization. Each category is significant enough to merit recognition and a response from the public at large and from practitioners within the criminal justice system.

Domestic Violence Victims

About one-fourth of all homicides and serious assaults are domestic. Minor violence, which usually precedes serious injuries, is far more pervasive. Although it is hard to measure, "family" violence is probably the most widespread form of violence in the country and can occur in all social classes and income groups. The recent resignation of a high federal official under pressure of publicity about his admitted wife beating illustrates both the presence of the problem among the well-to-do and the new morality that refuses to tolerate such conduct. Most of the cases to which police are called involve poorer people. Whether this is because lower income people are likelier to call the police, because lower income people are likelier to be victims of family violence, or because of other factors, is unclear. In a study in Minneapolis, a city with about 5 percent unemployment, about 60 percent of the males in the households to which police were called were unemployed (Sherman 1987).[4]

Handling a violent domestic incident has never been an easy matter for police, and for years arrest was unusual as long as the police themselves were not assaulted or insulted. In the late 1960s the police became more involved in the conflict itself and tried to act as mediators or counselors. The U.S. Department of Justice provided funds to police departments to support training for police officers in techniques of counseling and mediation.

By the mid-1970s, however, the innovative mediation approaches came under criticism because, it was argued, they did not provide sufficient punishment for the spouse abuser and the child abuser. Advocates of victims demanded that police arrest offenders, and they filed lawsuits in New York City and elsewhere to enforce their demand. Although these suits had some impact, in 1984 a survey of big city police departments found that only 10 percent encouraged officers to make arrests in domestic violence cases, while 40 percent still encouraged mediation and 50 percent had no policy at all. If extreme action is desired, many police would rather not make an arrest; they prefer to order an informal separation or to tell the offender to leave the house for the night.

There are many possible explanations why police traditionally have not arrested assailants in domestic violence cases. One of the most important is that for many domestic violence incidents, the police have legal authority to make an arrest only if they witness the incident or if they have obtained an arrest warrant from a judge. This is because the law treats much domestic violence as a misdemeanor, a less serious offense. Only for felonies, the more serious offenses, may an arrest be made without a warrant or without witnessing the alleged criminal conduct. Only in twenty-eight states are police allowed to make arrests in misdemeanor domestic violence cases in which they did not witness the disputed conduct.

Even where police can make arrests on their own authority, they are often afraid the arrest will backfire, producing more violence rather than less. They decide not to arrest out of fear that the offender will return to the victim and inflict even more harm.

In explaining why arrests in domestic violence cases are not more common, police also cite the frequent change of heart victims have the day after the assault and their refusal to cooperate with a criminal prosecution—both reasons for dropping the charges. Police argue that it is pointless to make an arrest if there will be no court-imposed punishment to produce a deterrent effect, and there often cannot be court-imposed punishment unless the victim cooperates.

Many police also consider the risk of injury to themselves if they make an arrest. Academies have taught, and most police believe, that domestic "disturbance" calls are among the most dangerous tasks police face. But recent statistics compel us to ask if that is true.

A major experiment was recently conducted by the Police Foundation in Minneapolis to learn whether mediation, separation, or arrest works best at reducing subsequent violence against the victim. The premise was that police practice should be guided by knowledge about the actual effects of using one policy instead of another (Sherman and Berk 1984).

The experiment was conducted by police officers who agreed to give up their discretion in domestic assault cases and to take whatever action was dictated by a random system of employing arrest in some cases, mediation in others, and so on. This method attempts to ensure that those arrested, those advised, and those ordered out of the house were roughly comparable in average age, education, income, rate of offending, percentage who were black or white, and whether they were intoxicated. Otherwise, the police would have arrested only the most "serious" offenders, who might then have had the highest rate of repeat violence—not because they were arrested, but because they were unusually violent people.

After the police completed their work on a case, Police Foundation researchers contacted the victims and attempted to interview them every two weeks for the next six months. The main focus of the interviews was to discover if the offenders had repeated their assault. Repeat violence was also measured by tracking, for six months, all of the official records of repeat contacts between police and offenders (or victims). Under both methods of measurement, the arrested offenders were about half as likely to commit repeat violence as the nonarrested offenders. The official records showed that about 18 percent of all offenders repeated their violence, while only 10 percent of the arrested offenders repeated it. Findings from the interviews with victims were similar.

In the city of Atlanta domestic violence cases are handled differently than in Minneapolis. Atlanta's program employs a special unit, the **Domestic Crisis Intervention Unit,** to handle domestic violence calls. Police working in this unit receive extensive training in mediation and use it in most simple assault cases, although they may arrest if this seems appropriate. In the Atlanta system, arrest is usual for felony cases, but there is no strict arrest policy, the preference being to give police discretion in individual cases.

One strength of the Atlanta program is the provision for longer term treatment through a network of social service agencies working together. Social workers play an important role in the program, particularly in the follow-up treatment. Referrals for treatment of offenders may come through court orders after arrest. See Figures 5.3 and 5.4 for samples of forms used by police in domestic violence cases.

Victims of domestic violence may receive counseling and other support from public or private groups within the community. For example, The Spring, a not-for-profit corporation in Hillsborough County, Florida, which is organized to serve abused women and their children, offers the following kinds of assistance.

Founded in 1977 to serve abused women and their children, The Spring has sheltered more than 3,000 victims of domestic violence. It provides the following services:

- Confidential twenty-four-hour hotline offering information and referral and crisis management.
- Safe shelter for abused women and their children.
- Confidential outpatient counseling.
- Help in obtaining such community services as legal help, medical services, and housing information; help includes transportation to all appointments.
- A children's program, including the following:
  - A safe, confidential public school.
  - A pre-school program.
- Counseling with mothers to help them understand the effects of a violent home and how to keep their children safe.
- After care and support services.
- Battery repair, which involves group treatment for men who want to make changes.
- Information and referral for violent men.

Children as Victims

It is a sad commentary on modern society that children, like adults, become victims of crime. Any crime that can be committed against an adult can be perpetrated as easily (if not more so) upon a child. What is perhaps even more appalling is the fact that so little is known about the incidence and types of crimes committed against

Toughening Up: Spouse Abuse Arrests Grow

The number of police departments that deal with cases of minor domestic assault by arresting one of the parties quadrupled from 1984 to 1986, with one-third of those having changed their policy as a direct result of the 1982 Minneapolis experiment on domestic violence, according to the Crime Control Institute.

A telephone survey conducted last year by the institute showed that 46 percent of responding police departments in cities of more than 100,000 residents said arrest was their preferred policy in domestic violence cases. In 1985, only 31 percent of those departments had an arrest policy and in 1984, only 10 percent preferred arrest in such cases.

The institute reported that during 1984 and 1985, almost half of all urban police departments gave officers no policy guidelines in cases of minor domestic violence. Pressure on police departments to make arrests in these cases, stemming from several highly publicized lawsuits and media events, resulted in changes of policy.

However, half of all urban departments still fail to encourage arrest, the institute's report pointed out. Thirty-five percent of the 176 departments surveyed in 1986 still allow police complete discretion regarding whether to arrest, mediate, separate the parties or take other action. Sixteen percent of the departments encourage mediation and 5 percent recommend separation.

Those departments that were among the first to change their policies to a preference for arrest were those that had previously encouraged mediation. Mediation was the leading policy in 1984, with 38 percent of the responding departments advocating this approach. That figure dropped to 17 percent in 1985, mirroring the percentage increase in the number of departments preferring arrest.

Those departments allowing full officer discretion in domestic violence incidents have dropped from 49 percent of the total in 1984 to 34 percent in 1986.

"For the first time, officer discretion is clearly declining in the area of domestic violence and being replaced with clear policy guidelines and restraints upon responding officers," the study noted.

A policy that limits or eliminates officer discretion tends to get a mixed reaction among police, however.

According to James K. Stewart, director of the National Institute of Justice, while police generally do not like change, "when confronted with some hard evidence they are willing to go ahead and make that change."

The Minneapolis experiment and other efforts that limit discretion are not without difficulties. Stewart said, "because police said, 'Look, I'm there and if I decide that this person ought to go to jail because of the violence, or shouldn't go to jail because of a lack of sufficient evidence or because the partner contributed a lot to the episode, then I want to use my discretion.'

"They're a lot like judges," Stewart said. "They have the authority to do that and they don't like to give that up."

The study found that the percentage of police departments reporting actual arrests in cases of domestic violence increased from 24 percent in 1984 to 47 percent in 1986.

The increase is due to several factors, the institute asserted. On the one hand, the institute said, police agencies in growing numbers are following the advice of the Attorney General's Task Force on Family Violence and keeping separate statistics on domestic assault cases.

The Minneapolis Domestic Violence Study, changes in state laws, liability lawsuits and the spotlight of media attention have also contributed to the changes in policy.

The Minneapolis study, conducted from 1981 to 1982 by the Police Foundation, found that arrest was more effective than two non-arrest alternatives in reducing the likelihood of repeat domestic violence over a six-month, follow-up period.

The impact of the Minneapolis study was underscored in the institute's new report where it was noted that two-thirds of those police departments surveyed had heard of the Minneapolis experiment, and 78 percent of those correctly identified the research findings of the study.

Reprinted from *Law Enforcement News.* With permission. 3/10/87 edition, pp. 8, 13.

Lock 'em Up, Split 'em Up, Calm 'em Down: How 176 Police Departments Are Dealing with Cases of Domestic Violence.

Arrest

Cities with a preferred policy of arresting one party in a domestic dispute.

Allentown, Pa.	Huntington Bch., Calif.	Reno, Nev.
Arlington, Tex.	Jersey City, N.J.	Richmond, Va.
Atlanta	Knoxville, Tenn.	Riverside, Calif.
Bakersfield, Calif.	Lansing, Mich.	Sacramento, Calif.
Berkeley, Calif.	Las Vegas	St. Louis
Boston	Lexington, Ky.	St. Paul, Minn.
Bridgeport, Conn.	Lincoln, Neb.	Salem, Ore.
Buffalo, N.Y.	Long Beach, Calif.	San Diego
Cedar Rapids, Iowa	Los Angeles	San Francisco
Chicago	Madison, Wisc.	San Jose, Calif.
Colo. Springs, Colo.	Mesa, Ariz.	Santa Ana, Calif.
Columbus, Ohio	Miami	Seattle
Concord, Calif.	Milwaukee	Simi Valley, Calif.
Dallas	Minneapolis	South Bend, Ind.
Dayton, Ohio	Newark, N.J.	Spokane, Wash.
Denver	Newport News, Va.	Springfield, Ill.
Duluth, Minn.	New York	Stamford, Conn.
Elizabeth, N.J.	Oakland, Calif.	Stockton, Calif.
El Paso, Tex.	Orlando, Fla.	Sunnyvale, Calif.
Eugene, Ore.	Pasadena, Calif.	Tacoma, Wash.
Flint, Mich.	Paterson, N.J.	Tampa, Fla.
Fort Wayne, Ind.	Peoria, Ill.	Tempe, Ariz.
Fort Worth, Tex.	Philadelphia	Toledo, Ohio
Fresno, Calif.	Phoenix, Ariz.	Tulsa, Okla.
Garden Grove, Calif.	Portland, Ore.	Waterbury, Conn.
Gary, Ind.	Pueblo, Colo.	Youngstown, Ohio
Hartford, Conn.		

Separation

Cities with a preferred policy of removing either the violent spouse or the victim.

Amarillo, Tex.	Baton Rouge, La.	Irving, Tex.
Anaheim, Calif.	Columbus, Ga.	Lubbock, Tex.
Anchorage, Alaska	Indianapolis	Wichita, Kan.

children. We do not even know the true magnitude of the problem.

There is no single data source to consult for statistics on crimes committed against children. Although several sources provide partial information, attempts to develop a composite are confounded by variations in definitions and reporting practices. For example, sources define the end of childhood at different ages, varying from twelve to sixteen to eighteen to twenty-one. Some sources provide only "snapshot" views of crimes occurring during a brief time period and have not been routinely updated. Existing sources are also limited in the types of crimes

Mediation

Cities with a preferred policy of attempting to resolve the dispute with the couple.

Abilene, Tex.	Corpus Christi, Tex.	Modesto, Calif.
Albany, N.Y.	Erie, Pa.	Norfolk, Va.
Austin, Tex.	Glendale, Calif.	Salt Lake City, Utah
Baltimore	Grand Rapids, Mich.	San Antonio, Tex.
Beaumont, Tex.	Hampton, Va.	Shreveport, La.
Birmingham, Ala.	Houston	Springfield, Mass.
Boise, Idaho	Jackson, Miss.	Tucson, Ariz.
Chattanooga, Tenn.	Little Rock, Ark.	Waco, Tex.
Chesapeake, Va.	Louisville, Ky.	Washington, D.C.

Officer discretion

Cities with no preferred policy of dealing with domestic disputes; matter is usually left to the discretion of the officer responding.

Akron, Ohio	Hialeah, Fla.	Pittsburgh
Albuquerque, N.M.	Hollywood, Fla.	Portsmouth, Va.
Alexandria, Va.	Honolulu	Providence, R.I.
Ann Arbor, Mich.	Huntsville, Ala.	Raleigh, N.C.
Arlington, Va.	Independence, Mo.	Roanoke, Va.
Aurora, Colo.	Jacksonville, Fla.	Rochester, N.Y.
Charlotte, N.C.	Kansas City, Kan.	Rockford, Ill.
Cincinnati	Kansas City, Mo.	St. Petersburg, Fla.
Cleveland	Lakewood, Colo.	San Bernardino, Calif.
Columbia, S.C.	Livonia, Mich.	Savannah, Ga.
Davenport, Iowa	Macon, Ga.	Springfield, Mo.
Des Moines, Iowa	Memphis, Tenn.	Sterling Hts., Mich.
Detroit	Mobile, Ala.	Syracuse, N.Y.
Durham, N.C.	Montgomery, Ala.	Topeka, Kan.
Evansville, Ind.	Nashville, Tenn.	Torrance, Calif.
Ft.Lauderdale, Fla.	New Haven, Conn.	Virginia Beach, Va.
Fremont, Calif.	New Orleans	Warren, Mich.
Fullerton, Calif.	Oklahoma City	Winston-Salem, N.C.
Garland, Tex.	Omaha, Neb.	Worcester, Mass.
Greensboro, N.C.	Oxnard, Calif.	Yonkers, N.Y.
	Pasadena, Tex.	

Source: Crime Control Institute

Reprinted from *Law Enforcement News*. With permission. 3/10/87 edition, p. 13.

for which they collect data on child victims. Admittedly, the available data are sketchy, but they do suggest that children become victims of crime more often than some may care to believe.

The FBI's Uniform Crime Reports (UCR) publishes crime statistics contributed by nearly 16,000 law enforcement agencies covering 97 percent of the American population. Although the UCR offers the most compre-

DOMESTIC VIOLENCE VICTIM INFORMATION FORM

Date: ______________________ Police Case # ______________________________

Defendant: __________________________________ Hm. Phone # ______________

Address: ____________________________________ Wk. Phone # ______________
City/Zip

Victim: _____________________________________ Hm. Phone # ______________

Victim Not in Safe Home: ________ Address: __________________________________

Victim is in Safe Home: ________ Wk. Phone # ______________

Bellevue Police Officers have responded to this call to investigate the crime of domestic violence. Domestic Violence is any crime or act of violence committed by one cohabitant against another, including — but not limited to — assault, burglary, trespass, kidnapping and unlawful imprisonment. Without intervention, domestic viomence will escalate in frequency and intensity.

It may be possible to avoid a trial in this case if charges are filed. At the arraignment on the charges, the judge may sign a Stipulated Order of Continuance if both parties agree to cooperate with guidelines set forth by the court and if the defendant meets other conditions and qualifications.

☐ The above named defendant has been arrested for ______________________ and will not be released on personal recognizance prior to arraignment, but might be released after posting a bail or bond. You as the victim need to be present at arraignment for an explanation of the nature of a Stipulated Order of Continuance and what procedures are involved. **Phone the City Prosecutor (455-6822) on the first business morning following this incident to find out the date and time of the arraignment.**

☐ This case will be reviewed by the City Prosecutor and charges may be filed. If the defendant receives a summons to appear in court as a result of this incident, you as the victim will be subpoenaed to be present at the arraignment. At that time, the judge may sign a Stipulated Order of Continuance allowing both parties to meet specific conditions in order to avoid a trial. For the victim, assistance is available through the Eastside Domestic Violence Program (451-8233). Assistance is also available for the defendant through Bellevue Probation (455-6956).

FIGURE 5.3
Domestic Violence Victim Information Form. Courtesy of the Bellevue Washington Police Department.

DOMESTIC VIOLENCE
DEFENDANT INFORMATION FORM

Date: ______________________ Police Case Number: ______________

☐ You have been arrested for ______________________. At your arraignment, you may be allowed to enter into a Stipulated Order of Continuance. If eligible, you will begin an 11-month program that bypasses part of the court process (trial-sentencing). If all conditions of the Stipulated Order of Continuance are met, the prosecutor will then dismiss the charge(s), thereby closing the case, and you will not have to go through a trial.

☐ Your involvement in this case will be reviewed by the City Prosecutor for the filing of charges. If criminal charges are filed, you may be allowed to enter a Stipulated Order of Continuance at your arraignment. If eligible, you will begin an 11-month program that bypasses part of the court process (trial-sentencing). If all conditions of the Stipulated Order of Continuance are met, the prosecutor will then dismiss the charge(s), thereby closing the case, and you will not have to go through a trial.

Conditions:

1. Your criminal record will be considered (juvenile. misdemeanor and felony matters), and might disqualify you.
2. You must intend to plead guilty to the charge or state it if the evidence were presented in court, there would be a substantial likelihood of a guilty verdict.
3. You must be willing to pay probation costs.
4. You must agree to follow and pay for the conditions set forth in the program prepared by the counselor, which may include but is not limited to, one or more of the following: alcohol, drug or anger management and (no cost) community service.
5. You may not be eligible for this program if you suffer from chronic problems of alcoholism, drug addiction or mental illness.
6. You must cooperate throughout the period of continuance and compliance must be evident, having no criminal arrests during the program.
7. The counselor may reject your application for a Stipulated Order of Continuance if it is determined that you are ineligible, based on the above criteria.
8. The prosecutor will review all applications and has the discretion to reject any application, even though an applicant may meet the general criteria.

If you believe you are eligible for this program and wish to apply, call Bellevue Probation Department, 455-6956 within three (3) days of your arrest date. (Bellevue Probation Department, 10856 N.E. 2nd Pl., Bellevue, WA.

I have received a copy of this document and it has been explained to me. I understand that a trial may be avoided in this case if I qualify and if I cooperate with all conditions set forth in the Stipulated Order of Continuance.

____
Defendant's Signature

______________________ ______________________
Date/Time Defendant's Name Printed

____
Investigating Officer

FIGURE 5.4
Domestic Violence Defendant Information Form. Courtesy of the Bellevue Washington Police Department.

hensive picture of reported crime in the United States, it provides almost no information on crimes against children. With the exception of murder, UCR statistics are not reported by victim age (Whitcomb, Shapiro, and Stellwagen 1985).[5]

No one knows the proportion of crimes against children that is reported to law enforcement or child protection authorities. Indeed, even the child's most trusted confidante may be unaware that something has happened. Very young children may simply lack the verbal capacity to report or the knowledge that an incident is inappropriate or criminal. Older children may be embarrassed. Many child victims are threatened into silence. When they do confide in trusted adults, their reports may be dismissed as fantasy or outright lies.

The Child Abuse and Neglect Prevention Act of 1974 required that every state designate an agency to receive reports of alleged abuse of children (including sexual abuse) by parents or caretakers. Most states designated their departments of social services, but there is great variation and controversy as to whether and when reports must also be made to police. This problem is compounded by a general reluctance among police to work with social workers, and vice versa. In many communities around the country, efforts are underway to encourage greater cooperation between police and child protection workers. This trend may result in more cases being brought for prosecution.

There are several reasons why some child sexual abuse cases, particularly intrafamilial cases, do not result in criminal prosecution. Cases that involve juvenile perpetrators are typically pursued in juvenile court. Some offenders are "diverted" into a supervised treatment program, and prosecution is deferred pending its outcome. Sometimes prosecutors and families choose not to subject a child to the perceived trauma of the criminal justice process.

From the prosecutor's perspective, victim and offense characteristics are perfectly sound reasons to decline a case. But what happens to the children when their cases are not prosecuted? Victims of stranger abuse may feel that no one believed them, and they may fear being victimized again. These children are sometimes at an advantage, because with counseling and a supportive family, they may overcome some of the long-range effects of victimization. Victims of intrafamily abuse, however, are not so lucky. When their cases are not prosecuted in the criminal courts, the best they can hope for is a favorable outcome of juvenile court intervention. Perhaps the offender will obey a no-contact order. Perhaps he or she will be amenable to treatment. But in many cases, removing child victims from their homes and placing them in foster care is necessary as a last resort of the juvenile courts. This may feel like punishment to the child and leaves habitual offenders free to molest others.

ASSISTANCE FOR CHILD VICTIMS Like it or not, allegations of child sexual abuse have become newsworthy. The fallout of all this publicity has been mixed. On the negative side, children and their families are needlessly thrust into the public eye and subjected to insensitive probing and scrutiny by reporters anxious for a "scoop." On the positive side, the heightened media attention has raised our awareness of the child's plight in the criminal justice system. Interest runs especially high in the potential for introducing modern technology to alleviate the stress on child victims. Videotape and closed circuit television, in particular, have received much media play, and legislators have been pressured to adopt these controversial measures with limited opportunity for reflection and study.

Some research has concluded that too much attention is presently directed to legislative reforms permitting innovative practices that benefit only a handful of the growing number of children enmeshed in the criminal justice system. This viewpoint holds that a large portion of the effort now devoted to statutory reform might be more productively focused toward alternative techniques that are less dramatic, yet equally—or even more—effective. In other words, creative exploitation of resources that are already available might achieve many of the same goals without threatening the structural premises of American law.

The following are some of the recommendations that have been made for the purpose of assisting child victims in prosecution:

- *Aids to communication.* By now most prosecutors should be familiar with the anatomically complete dolls that therapists use to help child victims explain what happened to them. And every prosecutor should be conscious of the need to scale down his or her vocabulary to meet the child's level.
- *Modifying the physical environment.* Providing a smaller chair for child witnesses, sitting at their level, and wearing business clothes rather than formal courtroom attire are simple things judges have done to help child witnesses feel more at ease.

- *Preparing the child.* Many prosecutors and victim advocates spend a great deal of time preparing child witnesses for the experience of testifying. They brief children on the roles of people in the courtroom and the range of possible outcomes. They introduce them to a judge. They take them for a tour of the courtroom, show them where their support person and the defendant will be, and let them sit on the witness chair and speak into the microphone. They explain the proceedings and let the children ask questions—this may be the only opportunity to find out what worries each child as an individual.

Many feel that by supporting the child through all the pretrial activities—by reducing the number of interviews or continuances, for example—and thoroughly preparing the child for the courtroom experience, prosecutors are more likely to have a strong witness at trial. At some point, such precautions may be provided to every child coming into the system, not only those whose cases actually come to trial or whose emotional well-being is severely threatened by the prospect of testifying. By applying these precautions across the board, drastic interventions—like closed circuit television and videotaped depositions in lieu of live testimony—may only be necessary in the most extraordinary cases. These measures should not, indeed, cannot be seen as panaceas.

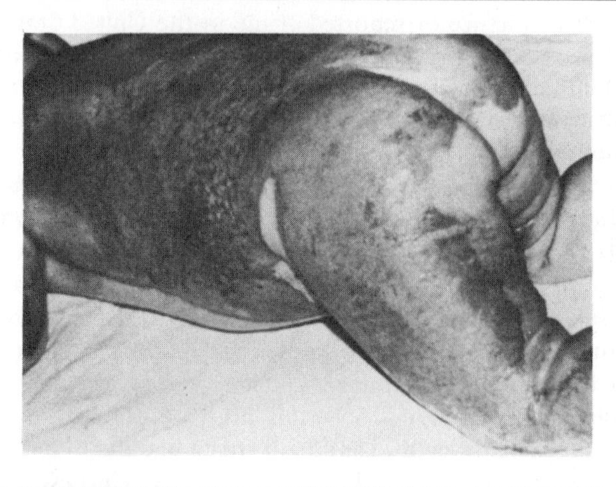

FIGURE 5.5(a)
Child scalded with hot water for soiling his diaper. Courtesy Tampa Police Department.

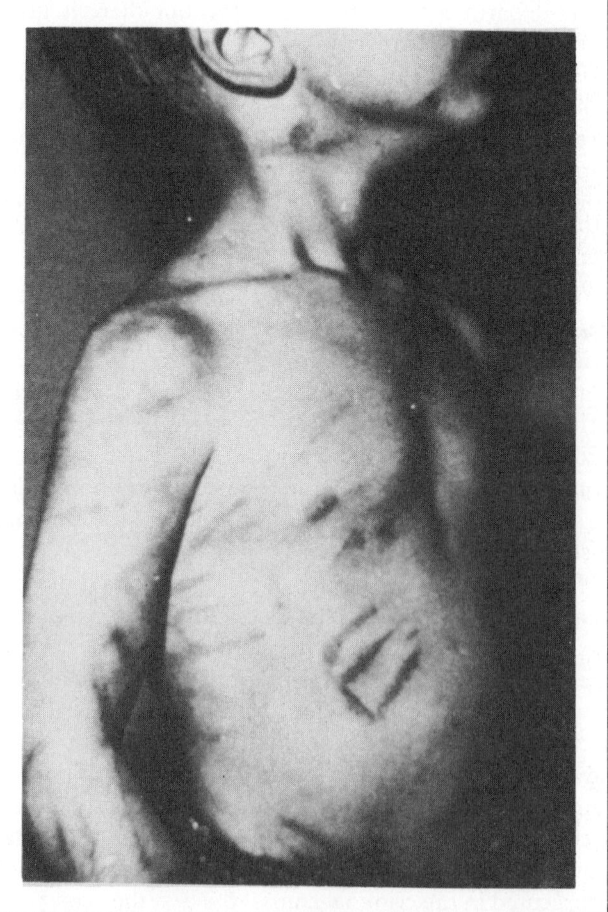

FIGURE 5.5(b)
Boy beaten with buckle end of a belt. Courtesy Tampa Police Department.

Victims of Drunk Driving Accidents

Drunk driving is one of the most serious public health and safety problems facing the American people and their policymakers. In a two-year period, 50,000 Americans die as a result of drunk driving—almost as many American lives as were lost in the entire ten years of the Vietnam War. Conservative estimates place the annual economic loss from drunk driving accidents at $21 billion to $24 billion for property damage alone.

In the past, state laws dealing with drunk driving ran the gamut of sanctions from release with warning, through moderate to heavy fines, to suspension and revocation of licenses, and—rarely—to incarceration. Enforcement, too, varies considerably from one jurisdiction to the next (National Institute of Justice 1984).[6]

Citizens groups such as Mothers Against Drunk Driving (MADD) have become very active and persuasive in the victims advocacy movement regarding drunk driving accidents.

Surviving victims, including family members, of alcohol-impaired crashes suffer serious physical, psychological, and financial damage as a result of their victimization. In December 1983, the Presidential Commission on Drunk Driving, as well as judges attending a conference on Victim's Rights at the National Judicial College, made clear recommendations regarding this badly neglected issue.

No state has a "Drunk Driving Victim's Bill of Rights." It is unlikely that a state legislature would enact a bill for such specific victims. However, some states now have a "Victim's Bill of Rights" as a more generic safeguard. Some rights exist in the form of statutory laws, rules, and regulations. Some exist but are not of much practical value to the victim (MADD 1985).

Groups such as MADD state that, just as the offender has the right to a fair trial and suitable defense, so should victims, as law-abiding citizens, have equal or enhanced rights. MADD, whose goal is to enact state Bills of Rights that will not reduce the rights guaranteed defendants, but which will assure the rights of victims, maintains that these rights should be afforded the victims of alcohol-impaired crashes. They encourage citizen groups to contact governmental representatives as advocates for nonexistent victims' rights in these cases. The results of a direct mail survey regarding drunk driving and victims' issues that was conducted by MADD appear in Table 5.5.

TABLE 5.5
MADD Survey Results

1. Should MADD launch a national advertising campaign against drunk driving?

   Yes–22,793 (75%) No–3,995 (13%) Undecided–3,432 (12%)

2. Should MADD give high priority to youth education programs about the hazards of drunk driving?

   Yes–27,768 (92%) No–1,156 (4%) Undecided–1,296 (4%)

3. On which grade levels should MADD youth educational programs focus?

   Grammar School–8,349 (28%) Middle School–12,421 (41%)
   High School–7,919 (26%) Undecided–1,531 (5%)

4. What types of public policies do you want MADD to support?

Stiffer penalties for drunk drivers	20,103	(67%)
Lower legal blood alcohol content limits for drivers	635	(2%)
Stricter enforcement of laws	7,266	(24%)
Banning open containers of alcohol in vehicles	492	(1%)
Victim rights and assistance	1,142	(4%)
Undecided	582	(2%)

5. Do you favor use of sobriety check points to catch drunk drivers?

   Yes–24,103 (80%) No–4,230 (14%) Undecided–1,887 (6%)

6. Are there enough anti-drunk driving messages in the media?

   OK–10,050 (33%) Too Many–62 (.2%) Too Few–18,502 (61%)
   Undecided–1,606 (5.8%)

7. Should MADD conduct a national campaign for people to pledge they won't drink and drive?

   Yes–9,769 (32%) No–12,296 (41%) Undecided–8,155 (27%)

8. Should MADD develop a "Memorial Gift in Lieu of Flowers" program for friends and relatives of victims of drunk drivers?

   Yes–18,137 (60%) No–4,596 (15%) Undecided–7,487 (25%)

9. Are you still MADD enough to fight?

   Yes–24,219 (80.3%) No–224 (.7%) Undecided–5,777 (19%)

Adapted with permission from *MADD National Newsletter* (Winter/Spring 1987): 7.

Elderly Victims

BY CATHERINE J. WHITAKER, PH.D.
BJS STATISTICIAN

Data from the National Crime Survey (NCS) show that between 1980 and 1985 the elderly, those age 65 and older, had the lowest victimization rates of any age group of the U.S. population age 12 and older. In a number of respects, however, crimes committed against the elderly are often more serious than crimes against younger people.

Major findings of this report include the following:

- Elderly violent crime victims were more likely than younger victims to face offenders armed with guns (16% vs. 12%).
- Elderly violent crime victims were more likely than younger victims to report that the offenders were total strangers (62% vs. 47%).
- The elderly were more likely than victims under age 65 to be victimized by a violent crime at or near their own homes (45% v. 22%). Those 75 and older were the most likely of any age group to be victimized in this location (55%).
- About 46% of elderly victims of violent crime were attacked, and 29% were injured, about the same proportions as victims under 65.
- Among the elderly, violent crime victims age 75 and older were more likely to be injured and to receive medical care for their injuries than victims age 65–74.
- The elderly were less likely than younger victims to attempt to protect themselves during a crime incident (52% vs. 72%).
- Among victims who reported financial losses, the elderly reported large losses ($250 or more) about as often as did younger victims.
- Among the elderly, certain groups were more vulnerable to crime than others: Males, blacks, separated or divorced persons, and urban residents generally had the highest victimization rates.
- Those age 75 and older had similar victimization rates to those age 65–74 for robbery and personal larceny with contact but lower rates for assaults, personal larceny without contact, and household crimes.

Victimization rates

The elderly were less likely than younger persons to be victims of crime. Teenagers and young adults under age 25 had the highest victimization rates. Older age groups generally had lower rates, and, for most types of crime, the elderly had the lowest rates of all. For example, the robbery rate for persons under age 25 was about 4 times higher than the rate for the elderly (11 vs. 3 robberies per 1,000 persons in each age group). The assault rate for those under 25 was about 17 times higher than the rate for the elderly. Persons age 25–49 had a robbery rate that was more than twice as high and an assault rate that was about 8 times higher than the comparable rates for the elderly.

The exception to this pattern of lower victimization rates for older age groups was personal larceny with contact (nonforcible purse snatching and pocket picking). The rate of this crime for the elderly was not measurably different from the rates for the other age groups.

From *Elderly Victims* (Bureau of Justice Statistics, U.S. Department of Justice, 1987) p. 1.

Older Persons as Victims

Older persons are frequently the victims of crime and are often very fearful of such occurrences. Individuals over sixty years of age comprise a significant segment of our population. A generally higher standard of living in this country, the control of many diseases in younger persons, advancements in medical technology, and better overall health care all are likely to lead to continued increases in the numbers of this age-specific group.

Older Americans as potential victims of crimes create additional challenges for the criminal justice system. For example, some criminals seem to specialize in the following categories of crimes against older persons:[7]

- *Home improvement con-artists.* These criminals offer home repairs at a very low price without a written estimate. Frequently, they use inferior

ovide poor workmanship at a
er than the verbal quote. The
eft with no choice but to pay.
er citizens receive notice they have
receive letters offering miracle
ses. The actual "prize" or "cure" is
yet the older persons find out only
with their cash.
ud. A bogus insurance agent contacts
id requires jewelry to be turned over
sal due to increasing insurance rates.
is never seen again or is replaced with

Thieves know when monthly pension
to arrive and burglarize mail boxes in

izens are also vulnerable to street crimes such
e snatches, pickpocketing, and personal attacks.
ggers and robbers again are often aware of when checks arrive and wait for an opportunity to attack an older victim outside banks and shopping areas.

Once an elderly person has been victimized, he or she is in need of additional attention by the criminal justice system components. Emotional and psychological support is necessary. This is of particular importance if the older person lives alone or does not have other family nearby. The financial losses that an older victim might suffer may represent a significant portion of his or her total income or monthly allotment.

At present, the criminal justice system is not adequately prepared to meet the specific needs of older victims of crimes. As this particular segment of American society grows, it can only be a matter of time until more adequate resources are allocated towards preventing crimes against the elderly and to assist after a victimization has occurred. The state of Florida, which has a sizable elderly population, has been active in developing public education programs geared towards older victims. A poster used in their program appears in Figure 5.6 on page 142.

VICTIM SPECIAL INTEREST GROUPS

Several special interest groups have become troubled by the psychological and financial burdens that crime imposes on its victims. Women's groups particularly are concerned about the double trauma of rape victims, who are first assaulted by the rapist and then are often handled insensitively by the criminal justice system. In 1975 and 1976, social service providers and criminal justice personnel organized a National Organization for Victim Assistance (NOVA) to promote a victim-oriented perspective in the adminstration of criminal justice (Finn 1987).[8]

The National Organization for Victim Assistance is a private, nonprofit, membership organization committed to the recognition of victim rights. NOVA's work is guided by four purposes.

1. Getting public policies to support victim rights and services.
2. Helping individual victims deal with the crime and its aftermath.
3. Assisting local victim service programs nationwide.
4. Responding to its national membership (NOVA 1987).

Advocacy groups such as NOVA and MADD do not seek to reduce the protection afforded the defendant by the courts, nor do they attempt to pressure law enforcement officers, prosecutors, and judges to "bend the rules." Rather, they work to improve the treatment of victims and witnesses in order to create a balance between the consideration shown to them and the attention paid to defendants.

UNRESOLVED VICTIM—CRIMINAL JUSTICE SYSTEM ISSUES

As this discussion has shown, more services for victims are becoming available, and victims are playing a larger role in the American criminal justice system, as a result of the research that has led to many of today's innovations in the treatment of victims. But much remains to be learned about ways to make these reforms as effective and as efficient as possible. The following are only a few of the issues that future research might address (Davis 1987).[9]

More information is needed on the effect of service programs for victims. Some specific questions that might be addressed include:

- Which counseling techniques work best for which victims?
- Can we learn something about which techniques might be most effective by studying differences in coping styles between victims who do and those who do not recover quickly after the crime?
- Can police officers, whose behavior seems to significantly shape how victims react to their

What yo

don't know...

You're nev

too old

to be a victim

Happy Birthday

Older Floridians Can...

HELP! STOP CRIME

Can hurt you!

Find out how to protect yourself from criminals.

DATE: __________ TIME: __________

PLACE: ____________________

Older Floridians Can... HELP! STOP CRIME

Attorney General's Office • Tallahassee, Florida 32301

FIGURE 5.6
Courtesy of the Florida Attorney General's Office.

experience, be trained successfully in techniques to alleviate victims' trauma?

- Do programs designed to aid victims in the court process promote greater willingness of victims to cooperate with officials?
- Are compensation programs aiding those victims with the greatest needs or are such victims often excluded due to lack of information or overly complex application procedures?

Secondly, more research is needed about the role of the victim in the criminal justice system. Current research on victim impact statements will yield important information on the administrative effects of such statements. But we still need to learn about other basic issues involving the use of impact statements:

- How many victims actually want the opportunity to make a statement?
- Does the opportunity to make a statement promote the healing of psychological wounds?
- Do victims view the opportunity to make impact statements as meaningful involvement in the criminal justice process? If so, do impact statement opportunities increase satisfaction with the criminal justice system? What new incentives can be developed to increase victim participation?

Research might provide useful answers to questions on other victim-related issues as well. For instance:

- Do elderly and child victims have special psychological or material needs that are currently not being addressed?
- What are the benefits and impediments to having the private sector ease victims' financial burden through employee counseling and referrals and provision of paid leave for medical treatment or court appearances?

These and perhaps other significant victim assistance issues remain to be reviewed in the future.

SUMMARY

Victims of crime and their relationships with criminals were briefly explored in this chapter. Beginning with a historical sketch of the ways in which various societies in the past have dealt with the victim of crime, the pioneering work of Hentig and Mendelsohn in the development of victim typologies was discussed, and some consideration was given to the issues of victim compensation and restitution. The federal and state responses to victim's needs were discussed. Models for the delivery of victim services were also briefly examined. Victimization surveys and their significance for the assessment of crime were treated in some detail, and the chapter also included several observations on the bystander who remains a passive witness to someone else's victimization.

Also discussed were the following categories of victimization: domestic violence, children, the victims of drunk driving accidents, and older victims. The criminal justice system response to these special categories of victims was highlighted. Finally, an overview of some unresolved victim-criminal justice system issues was provided.

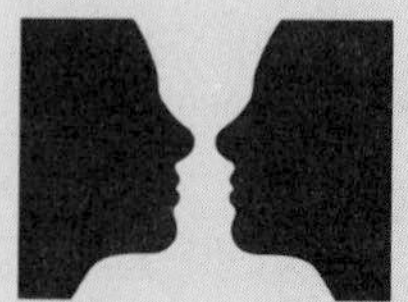

ISSUE PAPER
A LARGER SLICE OF JUSTICE—CRIME VICTIMS FIGHTING BACK

In January 1983, a federal judge in New York upheld a jury award of $30,000 to the parents of Bonnie Joan Garland, a twenty-year-old Yale University student who was bludgeoned to death by her boyfriend, Richard Herrin, when she told him she was breaking off their relationship. Herrin was found guilty of manslaughter and sentenced to eight to twenty-five years. Outraged by the sentence, Ms. Garland's parents filed a $3.3 million suit against Herrin in 1979, seeking damages for wrongful death. The resulting judgment against Herrin in 1983 held that he had recklessly caused the Garlands severe emotional distress. Says Bonnie's mother, "Now a criminal can't say, 'I have no responsibility for the damage I've done you' " (Beach 1983, p. 40).

In Denver, a young woman named Stacey Johnson was approached late at night in a suburban parking lot by a man who asked her to help him get his truck started. After driving around in a fruitless search for jumper cables, the two returned to the lot, where without warning, the man stabbed Ms. Johnson seven times, putting her in the hospital for a month. Her assailant, a twenty-eight-year-old named Gary Tucker, was eventually sentenced to eight years for attempted murder. Ms. Johnson filed a civil suit against him for $6 million in damages. Jurors raised the sum to $8 million. "I wanted to punish him," said Ms. Johnson, "I wanted to strike back" (ibid.).

In St. Louis the police finally apprehended two men accused of burglarizing a physician's office five times in a single year. The men pled guilty to a lesser charge, were fined $50 apiece, and were placed on two years' probation. The irate physician filed a suit for $200,000 in punitive damages. His attorney said that the suit was intended to "put the word out on the street that potential burglars are taking risks not only with the authorities but also with the people being victimized" (Rottenberg 1980, p. 22).

These people—the grief-stricken parents of a murdered girl, the assault victim, and the physician—are among the growing number of crime victims turning to the civil courts when the criminal courts fail to provide satisfaction. Regardless of financial awards for damages, such action relieves these victims of feelings of helplessness and frustration that occur when the criminal justice system seems more concerned with the rights of criminals than with the rights of the victims. As an attorney in Wyoming says, "Such cases are as close to basic historical justice as man has ever known" (Beach 1983, p. 40).

The satisfaction of suing a criminal like Herrin may be purely symbolic, however. As F. Lee Bailey has observed, violent crimes are not ordinarily committed by the wealthy. Nevertheless, there are exceptions, and government is making it easier for victims to lay hold of their assailants' assets. Several states have passed "Son of Sam" laws (named for David Berkowitz, the multiple "lover's lane" slayer) that require criminals to put into state-controlled escrow funds any profits made from books or recounts of their crimes. These funds are used to satisfy claims from victims or their survivors. The widow of a man stabbed to death by Jack Henry Abbott, protégé of Norman Mailer and author of *In the Belly of the Beast* (1981), has already sued for damages under New York's "Son of Sam" law.

When the criminal has no money, some victims gain tangible satisfaction by suing a "third party" whose carelessness or negligence was responsible for the crime. For example, in 1979, a widow sued the state

FIGURE 5.7
Joan and Paul Garland, parents of Bonnie Garland, were awarded $30,000 by a federal jury for emotional distress they suffered when their daughter was beaten to death. Wide World Photos.

FIGURE 5.8
Richard Herrin, *left,* convicted murderer of Bonnie Garland. Courtesy *N.Y. Daily News.*

of Washington after her husband was slain by a prison inmate participating in a "Take a Lifer to Dinner" program. The court held that the warden and the state were negligent in allowing a man with a record of forty felonies and seventeen escape attempts to leave the prison grounds. The widow collected $186,000 (Rottenberg 1980). And a couple in California sued the California Youth Authority after their son was assaulted by a youth who had been released from jail without receiving the psychiatric treatment ordered as a condition of his release. The case was settled out of court for more than $200,000.

All such cases are not directed against government agencies, however. A Denver secretary who was sexually assaulted in her apartment was awarded a total of $350,000 from her assailant and the building developer. Her attacker was an employee who obtained a master key as a result of the developer's carelessness. In July 1976, singer Connie Francis, who was the victim of a rape in a motel in Westbury, New York, was awarded $2.5 million by a Brooklyn federal court jury. Her lawsuit against Howard Johnson charged that the motel chain had been negligent in failing to provide adequate door locks and other security measures.

Despite the skepticism of F. Lee Bailey, attorney Frank Carrington, an official of the Crime Victims Legal Advocacy Institute and a member of the Presidential Task Force on Victims of Crime, believes that civil litigation can be effective as a new weapon for crime victims. Carrington goes even further in suggesting that victim advocate groups should seek state funds to finance such lawsuits, just as defendants receive free legal counsel. Says Carrington:

> The idea of state assistance in filing victims' rights lawsuits is certainly novel. Moreover, it would appear to stand up under analysis. We have seen the growth of any number of state-funded human rights and civil rights boards and commissions charged with the laudable task of enforcing the civil rights of our citizens. Why, then should not the government get into the business of enforcing the rights of victims of crime? (1981, p. 311).

Why not, indeed? As Carrington himself observes, the victims of crime in the United States are long overdue for their day in civil court.

FIGURE 5.9
Connie Francis and her husband, Joseph Garzilli, outside federal court in Brooklyn, New York, during the civil trial involving her lawsuit against Howard Johnson Lodges. Wide World Photos.

ISSUE PAPER

BERNARD GOETZ: VIGILANTE OR HERO?

Just how far victims (or potential victims) should be allowed to go in terms of providing for their personal protection is a matter of serious debate in American society. In December 1984, Bernhard Goetz shot several black youths on a subway. He maintained they were trying to rob him. The youths stated they were only "panhandling" for money to play video games. Subsequently, Goetz was tried on attempted murder charges, but was convicted only of a weapon's possession violation. Was Goetz a vigilante or hero? The Goetz story is chronicled in the following articles.

Goetz: 'Fade into Woodwork'— Acquitted of murder, guilty of weapons

By Stephan Stern and Timothy McQuay USA TODAY

Bernhard Goetz was acquitted Tuesday of trying to murder four youths in a New York City subway he said were trying to rob him.

Juror Michael Axelrod: "He was looking to stop the threat."

Goetz was convicted only of a weapons charge. Possible sentence [sic] ranges from probation to seven years.

Mayor Ed Koch accepted the verdict, but warned:

"We're saying to those who might think to engage in (vigilantism), we'll come down as hard as we possibly can."

Goetz' shooting of the black youths on a subway train Dec. 22, 1984, sparked a furor across the USA. Some called Goetz, 39, a hero; others called him the "subway vigilante."

The youths say they were panhandling for $5 to play video games.

The 12-person jury included five crime victims, two blacks. Some jurors asked for Goetz' autograph after the verdict.

Goetz was freed on $50,000 bail to await sentencing Sept. 4. He left the court without comment.

Said Barry Slotnick, Goetz' lawyer: "This has been a terrible chapter in his life . . . all he wants to do is fade into the woodwork."

Said prosecutor Gregory Waples: "My feelings about the case are my own."

"I think the decision emanated out of a climate of racism," said the Rev. Herbert Daughtry of the House of Lords Pentecostal Church in Manhattan.

The verdict, he said, "gives a license to people to take lives."

Goetz Verdict Divides NYC

Where They Are at Case's Close

The file closing on the December 1984 shooting shows:

- **Bernhard Goetz,** 39, has no plans to leave New York City, where he works as a self-employed electronics engineer. He was free on $5,000 bail throughout the legal proceedings. He's become adept at saying little, avoiding the media. Goetz wants to be "an anonymous stranger in the city of New York," said his lawyer Barry Slotnick.
- **Troy Canty,** 21, who asked Goetz for $5 on the subway train, is completing two years at a drug rehabilitation center. He is a cooking school student and wants to be a chef. He has been arrested at least a half-dozen times for criminal mischief and petty theft. One of the bullets fired by Goetz missed his heart by an inch.
- **Barry Allen,** 21, is doing 1½ years to four years in prison for violating probation by snatching a gold chain from a woman.
- **James Ramseur,** 21, is doing 8⅓ to 25 years for pistol whipping, robbing, raping and sodomizing a pregnant teen-ager on a Bronx rooftop on May 5, 1986.
- **Darrell Cabey,** 21, is paralyzed from the waist down and is in a wheelchair. Also suffers brain damage. Goetz told Cabey, "You look all right, here's another," and shot him a second time in the spine while Cabey was seated. His lawyer,

FIGURE 5.10
Bernard Goetz, *left,* leaving court escorted by a Guardian Angel. Wide World Photos.

William Kunstler, says Cabey "does not remember who Goetz is."

'Message to criminals,' but others fear racism

By Keith Greenberg and Timothy McQuay USA TODAY

NEW YORK—Riders on the No. 2 subway train in lower Manhattan—the route where Bernhard Goetz did battle in 1984—were divided Tuesday on whether justice was done.

"I've seen robberies and fights on the trains. I would have protected myself like he (Goetz) did," said cashier Ronaldo Carmona, 19.

But graphic designer James Stone, 20, said, "If it was a black man who shot four white people, he wouldn't get off—for any reason."

Worried banker Steve Seckeres, 24: "Your first reaction is, someone should react. Then you think, what if you were sitting there and someone started shooting."

The debate raged throughout the city.

Outside court, a man held a sign saying: "Congratulations! Bernie Goetz wins one for the good guys."

But bus driver Demesmin Deupuy, 36, said he worried that "it might happen to me too. Anybody might decide they don't like the way I look and start shooting a gun off."

Ron Kuby, a lawyer for Darrell Cabey, who was shot by Goetz, warned, "A lot of people will follow in his footsteps . . . It further cheapens the value of black life."

"I hope the jury will have the opportunity to be on the subway train when the next Bernie Goetz acts out his rage."

But Roy Innis of the Congress of Racial Equality didn't see New York streets as an impending OK Corral.

"I'm smiling. This is a victory for the people. The right signal was sent to the criminals. They have no friends with the people on the juries."

Curtis Sliwa of the street-patrol Guardian Angels said: "I doubt the verdict means people frightened by black youths will take license in violently defending themselves."

Civil rights leader Al Sharpton said, "It sends a social signal that you can bear arms and then based on your own imagination use deadly force."

Jury not strangers to impact of crime

Special for USA TODAY

NEW YORK—More than half the jury that acquitted Bernhard Goetz has been touched by crime.

James Hurley, 29, the foreman, a financial analyst. He was robbed of less than $10 on the subway in 1981.

Catherine Brody, 59, an English professor. Two youths in a Brooklyn subway station tried to mug her in 1986.

D. Wirth Jackson, 74, a retired civil engineer. He is the victim of several burglaries. In one, an intruder threatened to shoot his wife.

Carolyn Perimuth, 31, a financial journalist. Her mother was mugged.

Diana Serpe, 33, airline sales agent. Her car was stolen five years ago.

Robert Leach, mid-50s, a city bus driver for 14 years. He has a bus driver friend who was attacked and beaten.

Francisco Figueroa, 32, computer operator. His apartment was burglarized 3½ years ago.

Other jurors: Ralph Schriempf, 62, Michael Axelrod, 34, James Mosely, early 20s, Mark Lesly, 27, Erniece Dix, 23.

CHRONOLOGY OF THE GOETZ CASE

Special for USA TODAY

Dec. 22, 1984: A tall, blond, bespectacled white man shoots four black youths on a Manhattan subway train and escapes on foot through a tunnel.

Dec. 31, 1984: Goetz surrenders in Concord, N.H.

Jan. 3, 1985: Goetz is arraigned in New York on attempted-murder and weapons-possession charges.

Jan. 8, 1985: Goetz is released on bail; the victims refuse to waive immunity and say they won't testify before a grand jury.

Jan. 25, 1985: A grand jury indicts Goetz on only weapons-possession charges.

February 1985: Victims' lawyers file civil suits against Goetz. Civil rights groups protest grand jury action.

Feb. 25, 1985: Federal authorities launch a probe.

March 27, 1985: A second grand jury indicts Goetz on attempted-murder, reckless-endangerment, assault and weapons charges.

Dec. 12, 1986: Jury selection starts in Goetz's trial.

April 27, 1987: The trial begins.

June 12, 1987: The jury begins deliberations.

June 16, 1987: Goetz is acquitted of all charges except third-degree weapons possession.

DISCUSSION AND REVIEW

1. Discuss how the Federal Victim and Witness Protection Act of 1982 is designed to protect and assist victims and witnesses of federal offenses.
2. How did early societies attempt to provide compensation or restitution to the victims of crime?
3. Discuss von Hentig's contributions to victimology. How did he view the criminal-victim relationship?
4. Why is the concept of victim precipitation so controversial? In your judgment, is the concept adequately supported by the evidence?
5. What are victimization surveys and why are they important?
6. Summarize the major findings of victimization studies. What are some of the principal limitations of these findings?
7. Discuss the Minnesota Restitution Center's approach to victim restitution. Is this an adequate and effective model for establishing similar centers elsewhere in the country?
8. List and describe ways in which crime victims may receive insensitive or callous treatment from the criminal justice system.

9. What are the main functions of a victim services delivery system? Can these services be handled better by a single, unified system or by a diversity of programs?
10. What are some of the issues raised by the bystander responses in the murder of Catherine Genovese?
11. What is your position (pro or con) on Good Samaritan legislation? Defend your stand.
12. Discuss the Police Foundation experiment conducted in Minneapolis regarding the handling of domestic violence cases. What were the results?
13. Discuss the role of the civil courts in providing redress for crime victims. Should the state help fund civil lawsuits as Frank Carrington suggests?
14. List and discuss three recommendations that have been made to assist in the prosecution of cases when the victims are children.

GLOSSARY

Compensation Action taken by the state to restore some or all of the losses sustained by a crime victim.

Domestic Crisis Intervention Unit A police unit that has received extensive mediation training and is used to respond to domestic violence situations. There is often a link with a social worker or social services network.

Good Samaritan doctrine The concept that a person who sees another person in imminent and serious peril through the negligence of another cannot be charged with contributory negligence (as a matter of law) in risking his or her own life or serious injury in attempting to effect a rescue (provided the attempt is not recklessly or rashly made).

MADD Mothers Against Drunk Driving. A citizens group that strongly advocates victims rights in drunk driving accidents. Also a powerful lobby group for legislative change regarding drinking laws.

Victim impact statement These statements are used to inform the sentencing judge of the physical, financial, and emotional impact of the crime on the victim or the victim's survivors.

Victim precipitation The direct, immediate, and positive contribution of a victim to the occurrence of the crime. The term is used primarily to refer to crimes against the person (homicide, rape, and assault).

Victimology A growing body of fact and theory that reflects the systematic study of crime victims, their relationship with criminals, and programs intended for assistance and reparation.

REFERENCES

Abbott, J. H. *In the Belly of the Beast: Letters from Prison.* New York: Random House, 1981.

Amir, M. *Patterns in Forcible Rape*. Chicago: University of Chicago Press, 1971.

Barth, A. "The Vanishing Samaritan." In *The Good Samaritan and the Law,* edited by J. M. Ratcliffe. New York: Doubleday, 1966.

Beach, B. H. "Getting Status and Getting Even." *Time,* 7 February 1983, p. 40.

Brooks, J. "How Well Are Criminal Injury Compensation Programs Performing?" *Crime and Delinquency* 21 (1975): 50–56.

Bureau of Justice Statistics. *Victim/Witness Legislation: An Overview*. Washington, D.C.: U.S. Department of Justice, 1984.

Carrington, F. "Victim Rights Litigation—A Wave of the Future?" In *Perspectives on Crime Victims,* edited by B. Galaway and J. Hudson. St. Louis: C. V. Mosby, 1981.

Conklin, J. E. *The Impact of Crime*. New York: Macmillan, 1975.

Davis, R. C. "Crime Victims: Learning How to Help Them." Washington, D.C.: U.S. Department of Justice, National Institute of Justice, 1987.

Decker, S. H. "Official Crime Rates and Victim Surveys: An Empirical Comparison." *Journal of Criminal Justice* 5 (1977): 47–54.

Dussich, J. P. J. "The Victim Ombudsman." *Governor's Council on Criminal Justice*. Tallahassee, Fla.: State of Florida, 1972.

Dussich, J. P. J. "Victim Service Models and Their Efficacy." A paper presented to the International Advanced Study Institute on Victimology and the Needs of Contemporary Society. Bellagio, Italy, July 1–12, 1975.

Edelhertz, H., and Geis, G. *Public Compensation to Victims of Crime*. New York: Praeger, 1974.

Finkelhor, D.; Gelles, R. J.; Hotaling, G. T.; and Straus, M. A., eds. *The Dark Side of Families*. Beverly Hills, Cal.: Sage, 1984.

Finn, P. *Crime File Study Guide—Victims*. Washington, D.C.: U.S. Department of Justice, National Institute of Justice, 1987.

Finn, P., and Lee, B. *Serving Crime Victims and Witnesses*. Washington, D.C.: U.S. Department of Justice, 1985.

Fry, M. *The Arms of the Law*. London: Gollancz, 1951.

Galaway, B., and Hudson, J., eds. *Perspectives of Crime Victims*. St. Louis: C. V. Mosby, 1981.

Garner, J. H., and Clemmer, E. C. *Danger to Police in Domestic Disturbances: A New Look*. Washington, D.C.: U.S. Department of Justice, National Institute of Justice, 1986.

Hentig, H. von. *The Criminal and His Victim: Studies in the Sociobiology of Crime*. New Haven, Conn.: Yale University Press, 1948.

Koppel, H. *Lifetime Likelihood of Victimization*. Washington, D.C.: U.S. Department of Justice, Bureau of Justice Statistics, 1987.

Kratcoski, P. C., and Walker, D. B. *Criminal Justice in America*. Glenview, Ill.: Scott Foresman, 1978.

LaFave, W. R., and Scott, A. W. *Criminal Law*. St. Paul, Minn.: West, 1972.

Latané, B., and Darley, J. *The Unresponsive Bystander: Why Doesn't He Help?* New York: Appleton-Century-Crofts, 1970.

McCall, G. J. *Observing the Law: Application of Field Methods to the Study of the Criminal Justice System*. Rockville, Md.: National Institute of Mental Health, 1975.

MacNamara, D. E. J., and Sullivan, J. J. "Composition, Restitution, Compensation: Making the Victim Whole." In *Victimology,* edited by I. Drapkin and E. C. Viano, Lexington, Mass.: Lexington Books, 1974.

MADD. *See* Mothers Against Drunk Driving.

Milgram, S., and Hollander, P. "The Murder They Heard." In *Violence: Causes and Solutions,* edited by R. Hartogs and E. Artzt. New York: Dell, 1970.

Minnesota Department of Corrections. *The Minnesota Restitution Center*. Minneapolis, Minn.: State of Minnesota, 1976.

Mothers Against Drunk Driving. *Victims Rights in Alcohol Impaired Cases.* Hurst, Texas: Mothers Against Drunk Driving, 1985.

National Commission on the Causes and Prevention of Violence. *Crimes of Violence.* Washington, D.C.: U.S. Government Printing Office, 1970.

National Institute of Justice. *Jailing Drunk Drivers Impact on the Criminal Justice System.* Washington, D.C.: U.S. Department of Justice, 1984.

National Organization for Victim Assistance. *Help Victims of Crimes Information Brochure.* Washington, D.C.: NOVA, 1987.

NOVA. *See* National Organization for Victim Assistance.

Pagelow, M. D. *Family Violence.* New York: Praeger, 1984.

President's Task Force on Victims of Crime. *Final Report, December 1982.* Washington, D.C.: U.S. Government Printing Office, 1982.

Rand, M. R. *Households Touched by Crime, 1986.* Washington, D.C.: U.S. Department of Justice, Bureau of Justice Statistics, 1987.

Rosenthal, A. M. *Thirty-Eight Witnesses.* New York: McGraw-Hill, 1964.

Rottenberg, D. "Crime Victims Fighting Back." *Parade,* 16 March 1980, pp. 21–23.

Schafer, S. *The Victim and His Criminal.* New York: Random House, 1968.

Schafer, S. *Victimology: The Victim and His Criminal.* Reston, Va.: Reston, 1977.

Shaskolsky, L. "The Innocent Bystander and Crime." *Federal Probation* 34 (1970): 44–48.

Sherman, L. *Crime File Study Guide—Domestic Violence.* Washington, D.C.: U.S. Department of Justice, National Institute of Justice, 1987.

Sherman, L. W., and Berk, R. A. *The Minneapolis Domestic Violence Experiment.* Washington, D.C.: The Police Foundation, 1984.

Timrots, A. D., and Rand, M. R. *Violent Crime by Strangers and Nonstrangers.* Washington, D.C.: U.S. Department of Justice, Bureau of Justice Statistics, 1987.

U.S. Department of Justice. *President's Task Force on Victims of Crime—Four Years Later.* Washington, D.C.: U.S. Government Printing Office, 1986.

U.S. Department of Justice, Law Enforcement Assistance Administration, National Criminal Justice Information and Statistics Service. *Crimes and Victims: A Report of the Dayton-San Jose Pilot Surveys of Victimization.* Washington, D.C.: U.S. Government Printing Office, 1974.

________. *Criminal Victimization Surveys in the Nation's Five Largest Cities.* Washington, D.C.: U.S. Government Printing Office, 1975a.

________. *Criminal Victimization Surveys in Thirteen American Cities.* Washington, D.C.: U.S. Government Printing Office, 1975b.

________. *Criminal Victimization in the United States, 1975.* Washington, D.C.: U.S. Government Printing Office, 1977.

________. *Criminal Victimization in the United States, 1978.* Washington, D.C.: U.S. Government Printing Office, 1980.

________. *Criminal Victimization of California Residents.* Washington, D.C.: U.S. Government Printing Office, 1981.

Villmoare, E., and Neto, V. V. *Research in Brief—Victim Appearances at Sentencing under California's Victims' Bill of Rights.* Washington, D.C.: U.S. Department of Justice, National Institute of Justice, 1987.

Whitcomb, D.; Shapiro, E. R.; and Stellwagen, L. D. *When the Victim Is a Child: Issues for Judges And Prosecutors.* Washington, D.C.: U.S. Department of Justice, National Institute of Justice, Office of Development, Testing and Dissemination, 1985.

Wolfgang, M. E. *Patterns of Criminal Homicide.* Philadelphia: University of Pennsylvania Press, 1958.

Young, M. A. *The Victim Service System: A Guide to Action.* Washington, D.C.: The National Organization for Victim Assistance, 1983.

STATUTES

The Federal Victim and Witness Protection Act of 1982, Public Law 97-291.
The Victims of Crime Act of 1984, Public Law 98-473.

NOTES

1. The information regarding the Federal Victim and Witness Protection Act was adapted from Peter Finn, *Crime File Study Guide—Victims* (Washington, D.C.: U.S. Department of Justice, National Institute of Justice, 1987), pp. 1–3.
2. The discussion of the Comprehensive Crime Control Act of 1984 and state victim compensation programs was adapted from a U.S. Department of Justice report entitled, *President's Task Force on Victims of Crime—Four Years Later,* (Washington, D.C.: U.S. Department Printing Office, 1986), pp. 1–5.
3. See reference citation in note 1.
4. The information regarding the victims of domestic violence was adapted from Lawrence Sherman, *Crime File Study Guide—Domestic Violence* (Washington, D.C.: U.S. Department of Justice, National Institute of Justice, 1987), pp. 1–3.
5. The discussion of children as victims and the recommended responses by the criminal justice system was adapted from Debra Whitcomb, Elizabeth R. Shapiro, and Lindsey D. Stellwagen, *When the Victim Is a Child: Issues for Judges and Prosecutors* (Washington, D.C.: U.S. Department of Justice, National Institute of Justice, Office of Development, Testing and Dissemination, 1985), pp. 1, 4, 5, 6, 111, 112, 115.
6. The discussion of the vast number of drunk driving accidents in the United States and victims rights in alcohol-related accidents was adapted from National Institute of Justice, *Jailing Drunk Drivers Impact on the Criminal Justice System* (Washington, D.C.: U.S. Department of Justice, 1984), p. 1, and Mothers Against Drunk Driving, *Victims Rights in Alcohol Impaired Crashes* (Hurst, Texas: Mothers Against Drunk Driving, 1985). The following individuals on the National Institute of Justice staff contributed to the NIJ document: Fred Heinzelmann, Ph.D., W. Robert Burkhart, Bernard A. Gropper, Ph.D., Cheryl V. Martorana, Louis Felson Mock, Maureen O'Connor, and Walter Phillip Travers. Permission was obtained from MADD for use of their materials.
7. Much of the information regarding categories of crimes committed against older persons was provided courtesy of the Florida Attorney General's Help Stop Crime Program.
8. The discussion of victim special interest groups was adapted from Finn, *Crime File Study Guide—Victims* (see note 1).
9. The discussion of additional unresolved victims issues was adapted from Robert C. Davis, "Crime Victims: Learning How to Help Them" (Washington, D.C.: U.S. Department of Justice, National Institute of Justice, 1987), p. 6.

CHAPTER

6

Police Operations and the Crime Laboratory

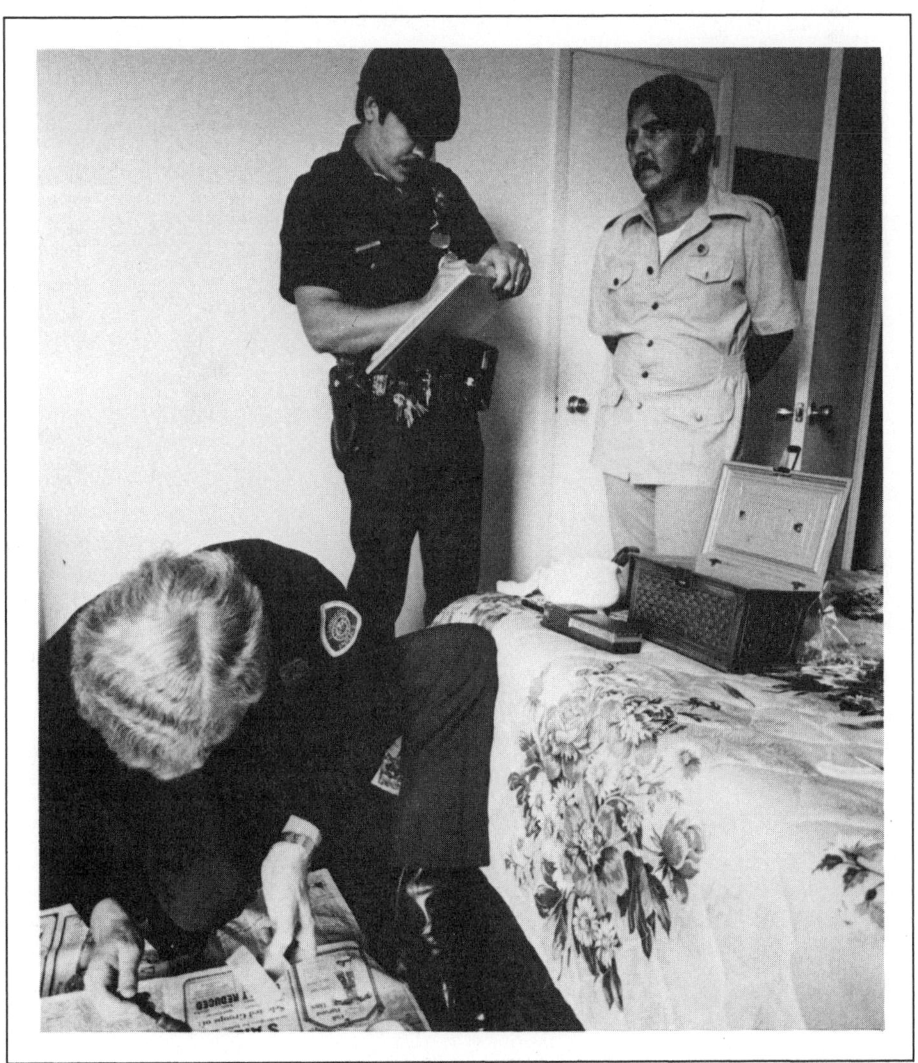

CHAPTER OUTLINE:

The conventional approach to police operations is to describe briefly the many tasks performed by the various units of a police department. In this chapter, we instead focus on four major components of police operations—namely, the patrol bureau, the traffic bureau, the detective bureau, and the crime laboratory. When possible, we go beyond merely describing the tasks performed by these units and attempt to address issues not usually discussed in general criminal justice books.

In our discussion of the patrol bureau, we look at two specific problems common to most major patrol bureaus: first, the desire of many patrol officers to be transferred from patrol bureaus, and second, the use of the patrol bureau as a manpower pool for specialized units.

We examine the sources of these problems and recommend some ways to reverse them, or at least slow them down. We also review some nontraditional methods of performing the patrol function and discuss the patrol officer's role in handling mentally disabled persons.

Next the team policing efforts that were so popular in the 1970s are examined. In addition, we outline the implications of the Kansas City Patrol Experiment, which sought to determine the effectiveness of the traditional strategy of routine patrol with conspicuously marked vehicles. One of the patrol strategies that grew out of the results of the Kansas City Patrol Experiment is Directed Patrol, which is also discussed in this chapter.

Our discussion of traffic bureaus focuses on traffic quotas, the impact of traffic-law enforcement on community relations, and the possible variations among the traffic-law enforcement policies of municipal police departments and sheriff's departments. Our discussion of detective bureaus seeks to dispel some of the stereotypes associated with detectives and to provide a realistic portrait of detective work. We also review the findings and policy recommendations of the *Rand Criminal Investigation Study* (Greenwood 1979), the first analytical scrutiny of police investigators nationwide. Later the Police Executive Research Forum (PERF) conducted another study on criminal investigations, which has also been included.

The purposes, capabilities, limitations, and use of the crime laboratory in criminal investigations are examined next. In the last section of the chapter, we discuss computerized criminal information files, specifically the NCIC system.

POLICE DEPARTMENTS IN THE UNITED STATES

Often members of the public form their opinions about police agencies in the United States by watching the electronic news media or reading national newspaper headlines. Popular television police shows also play a significant part in shaping citizen beliefs about the size, operation, and functions of police departments across the country. To many individuals, the Los Angeles, New York or Chicago police departments are the models that come to mind when they think of the police "role."

In reality there is no single "model" police agency in the United States. Instead the thousands of police departments in existence vary widely. Many police agencies are somewhat small in number of personnel (less than twenty), are not highly specialized in terms of officer assignments (patrol, detective, crime scene technician), and may perform functions the public does not readily associate with law enforcement (serving eviction notices, providing money escorts, delivering minutes of town council meetings, and so forth).

There are also numerous types of law enforcement agencies, which reflect their governmental level. For example, on the federal level are agencies such as the Federal Bureau of Investigation, the Secret Service, and the Drug Enforcement Agency. Each of these federal agencies operates under mandates set forth in federal legislation and is responsible for enforcing specific federal laws that range from investigating bank robberies (FBI) to protecting the president (Secret Service).

Some states have state police (responsible for general policing and investigations), highway patrol (responsible for enforcing motorist-related laws), or state investigation bureaus. Such state investigation bureaus usually do not employ uniformed officers, but investigate major crimes as required by statute or when requested by local agencies.

Local governments may have township police, city police, county sheriff's departments, or some combination of agencies that are responsible for enforcing local ordinances and laws. Some small towns or municipalities may "contract" for law enforcement services with the local sheriff's department or the state police. This practice can be very cost effective if the local government tax base is too small to support its own law enforcement agency. Some small localities may employ a police officer during certain hours of the day or night and rely on the county sheriff's department or state police to provide after-hours assistance and law enforcement service.

In many areas of the country a category of **"special purpose" police** agency may exist. Some examples of special purpose police agencies include university police, airport police, harbor police, park police, transit authority police, housing authority police, and school system police. All such agencies were established to provide "special purpose" law enforcement services for somewhat unique communities or constituents. For example, the emergence of university police departments reflects the desire of legislative bodies, campus trustees, or similar governing groups to have professional police services within a campus setting, without having to rely on city or country agencies exclusively.

The jurisdiction of most "special purpose" police agencies is limited to specific geographic boundaries, which may in fact fall within a larger overall jurisdiction. For example, a public housing project within a city or

an airport within a county may have its own police agency. Generally, there is an operating agreement or "mutual aid pact" between the smaller special purpose agency and the larger municipal/county police department; the agreement establishes who is responsible for handling various kinds of investigations and incidents.

Despite the wide variety of police agencies across the country, some general statements apply to most municipal or county departments: They serve law enforcement and order-maintenance functions; officers must meet required formal training standards; the majority of personnel working in police agencies are "sworn" officers as opposed to civilians; and the largest percentage of "sworn" personnel are assigned to the uniformed patrol bureau.

Evolution of Policing in America

Many of the roots of modern American policing may be found in the model established by Sir Robert Peel in 1829, when the British Parliament agreed to the formation of a metropolitan police force in London. Many of Peel's principles of effective policing such as organizing police along military lines, distributing crime news to the public, training police officers, and hiring them on a probationary basis are still present in today's law enforcement agencies in this country.

Organized policing as we now think of it came to America around the mid-1800s. Most authorities agree that the first unified (day and night) police force in America was established in New York City in 1844, although cities such as Chicago, New Orleans, and others quickly followed. By the early 1900s, most major American cities had police forces, and states such as Pennsylvania and New York also had state police departments.

THE PATROL BUREAU: BACKBONE OR MANPOWER TOOL?

The first assignment for almost all police officers graduating from police academies, regardless of the size of the agency, is with the patrol bureau. This assignment—for better or worse—is the foundation upon which all other police experiences are formed. Skolnick, commenting on the similarity of experiences among American police officers, states that

> the policeman's working personality is most highly developed in his constabulary role of the man on the beat. For analytical purposes that role is sometimes regarded as an enforcement specialty, but in the general discussion of the policemen as they comport themselves while working, the uniformed cop is seen as the foundation for the policeman's working personality. There is a sound organizational basis for making this assumption. The police, unlike the military, draw no caste distinction in socialization even though their order of rank title approximates the military. Thus one cannot join a local police department as, for instance, a lieutenant, as a West Point graduate joins the Army. Every officer must serve an apprenticeship as a patrolman. This feature of police organizations means that the constabulary role is the primary one for all police officers and that whatever the special requirements of roles in law enforcement specialties they are carried out with a common background of constabulary experience (1966, pp. 43–44).

The rookie officer is usually assigned to work directly with a senior patrol officer, who bears the title **field training officer,** or *coach*. Because their job is to "break in" rookies, these senior officers are often very influential in the professional development of the new officers placed under their tutelage. The amount of time a rookie and a senior officer spend together is a function of the policy of the organization, the pace at which the new officer masters certain skills, and the needs of the organization.

One of the earliest, if not the first formally recognized, field training program was established in the San Jose, California Police Department in 1972. The program was developed as a result of an incident in which an inadequately trained new officer negligently operated a police vehicle, causing the death of a citizen. Today the San Jose field training program is held in high regard and is widely emulated throughout the country.

In a survey of field training programs in police departments across the United States, McCampbell found a number of common factors (McCampbell 1986, pp. 1–7).[1]

The trend in law enforcement training is toward the use of field training programs, and the trend is relatively recent: 67 percent (122 agencies) reported that their programs are less than ten years old. Agencies of every size in all sections of the country have some form of a program. Sixty-four percent (1983) of all respondents reported that they have a field training program (see Table 6.1).

However, a substantial portion reported that they do not use field training programs. Of these agencies, al-

TABLE 6.1
Departments with field training programs.

Agency Size (number of sworn officers)	Agencies That Received a Questionnaire N	%	Respondents N	%	Respondents with Programs N	%
300 plus	277	100	142	51	107	75
200–299	109	100	40	37	29	73
100–199	35	10	27	77	14	52
50–99	84	10	34	41	18	53
25–49	83	5	45	54	15	33
Total	588		288	49%	183	64%

Adapted from Michael S. McCampbell, *Field Training for Police Officers: State of the Art* (Washington, D.C.: National Institute of Justice, November 1986), p. 3.

most one-half reported that they provide on-the-job training with a senior officer combined with additional classroom instruction in lieu of field training; many others reported using only on-the-job training with a senior officer.

Characteristics of Agencies Using Field Training Programs

Agencies that have developed field training programs share a number of characteristics. Most appear to have

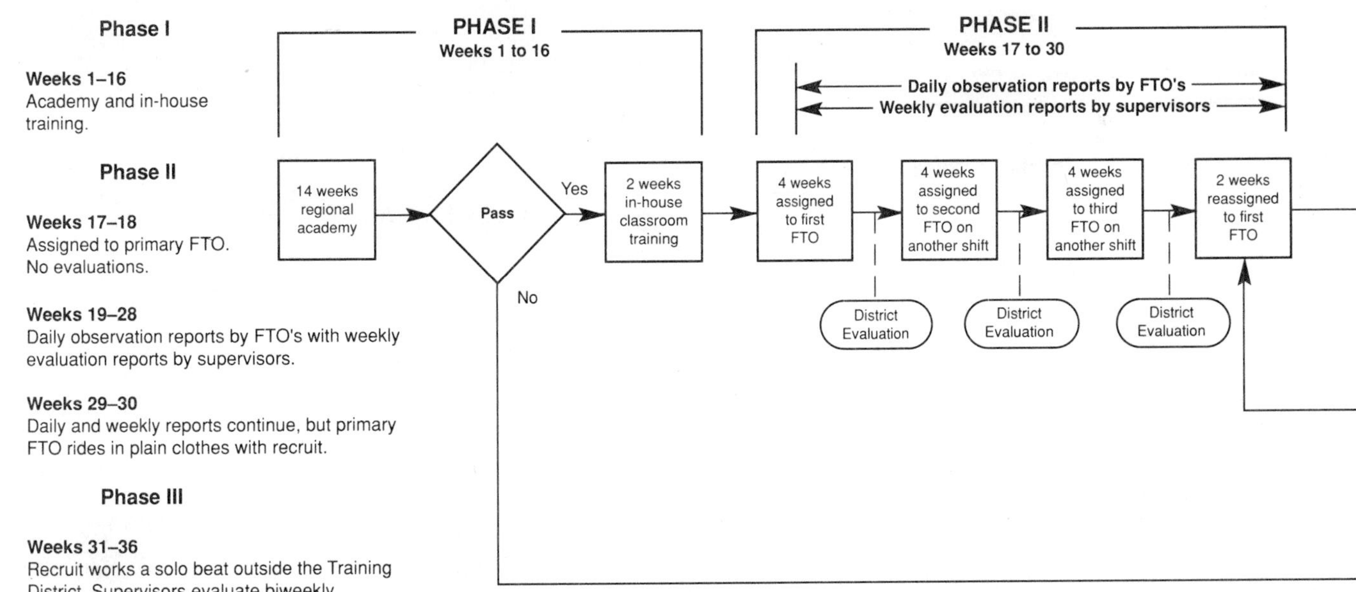

FIGURE 6.1
The San Jose field training program. Adapted from *Field Training for Police Officers: State of the Art* (Washington, D.C.: National Institute of Justice, November 1986), pp. 4, 5, 6.

implemented the programs in response to perceived personnel problems and the need to improve the recruit training process. A large percentage of the programs use the San Jose Police Department field training program as a model.

Field training programs appear to have reduced the number of civil liability complaints filed against law enforcement agencies. Field training programs also seem to be associated with a decrease in equal employment opportunity complaints.

Recruit evaluation is an important part of most field training programs. The majority of agencies reported using daily evaluation of recruits. Additionally, the vast majority reported using standardized evaluation guidelines and indicated that they could dismiss recruits based on poor performance.

The field training officer (FTO) is the single most critical position in field training programs. Agencies reported devoting considerable time and resources to selecting, training, and retaining FTOs. Most agencies in this study reported that their FTOs received special training prior to assuming their duties. However, less than one-half of the agencies reported that their FTOs receive extra pay. The costs associated with field training programs appear to depend mainly upon whether FTOs receive extra compensation, either as salary supplements or overtime pay.

The study identified the major benefits of field training programs as standardization of the training process and better documentation of recruit performance. Better documentation improves the agency's ability to make informed decisions about recruit retention.

In all field training programs, training is divided into identifiable phases; the personnel who train recruits are specially selected and trained; training and evaluation techniques are standardized and evaluation by FTOs occurs regularly; and programs are used to continue the personnel selection process.

Generally, the study suggested that field training programs could be enhanced by upgrading the quality of the FTOs, primarily through improved FTO selection, training, and compensation.

Patrol Bureau Assignments

The part of a community to which a new officer is assigned depends upon the personnel needs of the patrol bureau and the philosophy of the chief administrator or #2)

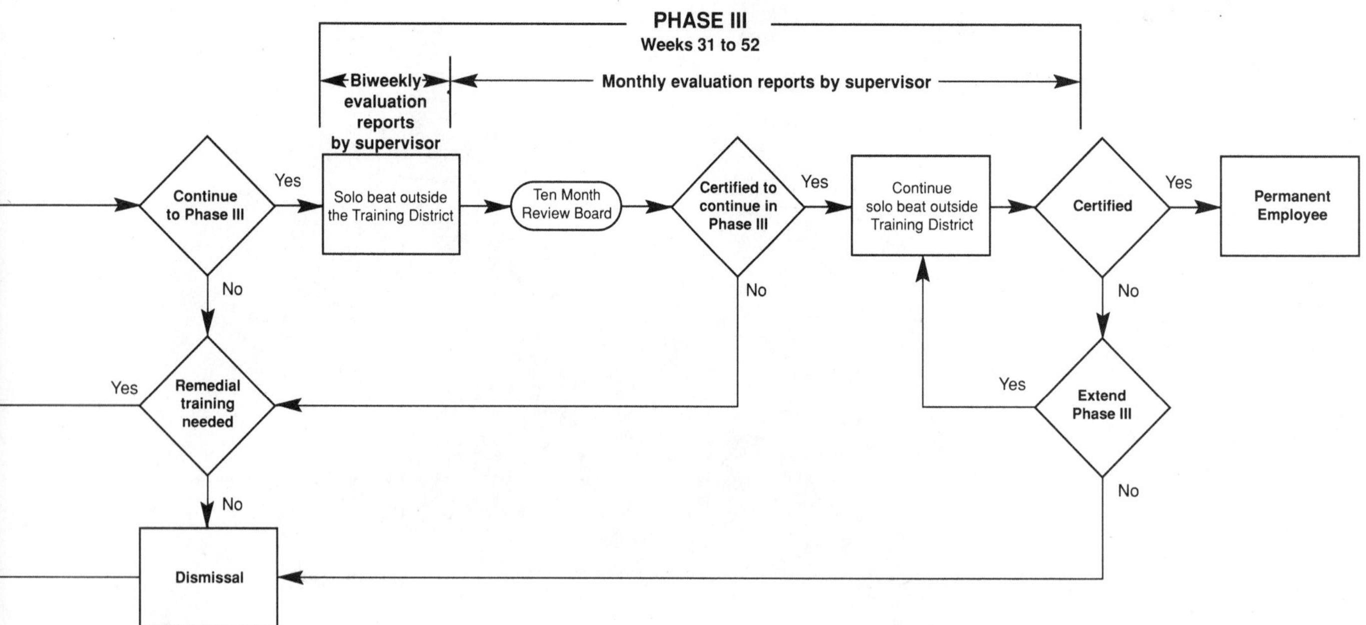

bureau commander. For example, one administrator might favor assigning rookie officers to high-crime areas to accelerate their experience and to allow an assessment of their ability to function under stress. This type of intensive exposure to police problems might also reduce the time a new officer has to spend under the direct supervision of a senior partner. Other administrators assign rookie officers to areas with few serious crime problems, allowing the officers to gain experience at a slower rate and in a less hostile environment.

Most patrol bureaus contain some interesting organizational contradictions that can have a negative impact on bureau operations. For example, chief administrators frequently espouse the position that the patrol bureau is the "backbone" of the agency, but they then proceed to transfer the best and brightest officers away from that bureau to other assignments, such as the detective bureau, vice squad, or training academy. This practice, which is common to many police departments, can create serious personnel problems. If continued with regularity, the practice guarantees that the "backbone" of the police department will be composed primarily of inexperienced officers and those who are average, or even below average, in ability and motivation.

Why would a police administrator employ a policy that depletes a primary operating unit of its finest people? There are several answers to this question. First, an administrator may not really believe in the importance of the patrol bureau. Second, he or she may not believe that the patrol bureau is sufficiently stimulating, rewarding, or challenging enough to keep the best, brightest and most able officers satisfied. Such officers are therefore provided with higher status and more challenging positions to keep them from resigning or becoming dissatisfied and bored with their patrol assignments. A chief of police who clings to these beliefs probably has instituted policies that do indeed make an assignment to the patrol bureau unchallenging and lacking in status. For instance, if a police chief believes that patrol officers should have no responsibility for inves-

FIGURE 6.2
Patrol officers discuss career development opportunities with their captain. Courtesy Greensboro (North Carolina) Police Department.

tigating even the most routine criminal offenses and that all segments of an investigation should be conducted by a detective, then that chief has eliminated for the patrol officer one of the most interesting and challenging functions of police work—namely, criminal investigation.

Another problem in patrol bureaus is that many officers wish to be transferred to other bureaus. The environment of most patrol bureaus probably contributes to this situation. By necessity, patrol bureaus operate twenty-four hours a day, every day of the year; and because of this schedule, officers assigned to patrol must work more weekends, nights, and holidays than many of their counterparts in other bureaus. This work schedule increases the possibility that days off will be spent making court appearances; and shift-related problems may be particularly troublesome to officers whose spouses work at regular daytime jobs with weekends off. Schedule conflicts do not promote domestic harmony and have been cited by many police officers as a prominent cause of marital discord.

The normal working day of a patrol officer is not filled with glamorous and exciting crime-fighting activities like those depicted on popular television programs. Instead, days are spent on routine patrol or performing noncriminal services for the public. However, in spite of this routine, the patrol officer's job is often far more dangerous than most people imagine. Patrol officers are the ones who are called to respond to crimes in progress or crimes that have just been committed. Such assignments increase the possibility that a criminal will still be at the scene of the crime or in the immediate area, thereby increasing the potential for physical and armed confrontation. Thus, the job of the patrol officer has often been described as one consisting of both hours of boredom (especially on the midnight shift) and moments of terror.

Patrol officers also spend much of their day in contact with the human dregs of our society. They have to deal with drunks who have soiled themselves but who still must be searched before being transported to jail; with teenage gangs who are arrogant, disrespectful, and openly contemptuous; with prostitutes, pimps, petty thugs; and with child abusers. Patrol officers are called upon to intercede in domestic disputes in which combating couples often turn on the officers trying to settle the dispute peacefully. With all of these problems—on top of the incredible number of written reports that patrol officers must complete—a job in the patrol bureau can be highly stressful both physically and psychologically. (Police stress is discussed in detail in Chapter 7.) Thus, in spite of efforts by many progressive administrators to improve supervision and working conditions and to give greater recognition to patrol bureau officers, the ambition of many of these officers is first to become a detective and later to move into management, with its higher status, better hours, and higher pay.

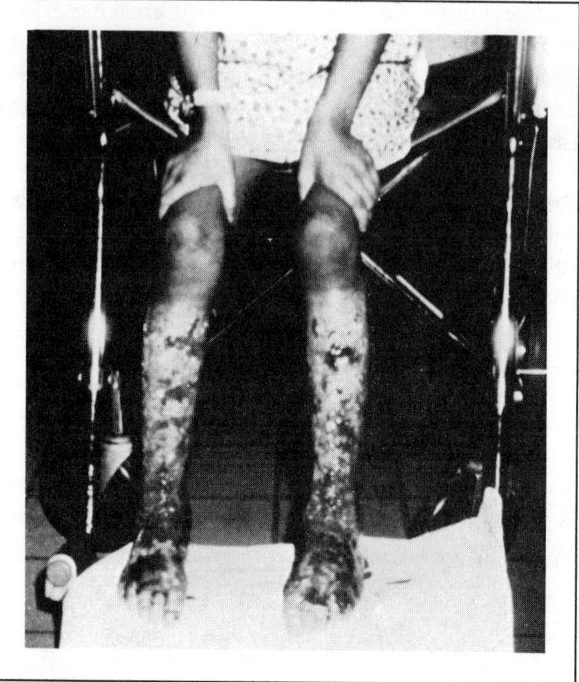

FIGURE 6.3
Victim of child abuse. The victim was immersed in scalding hot water by one of her parents for misbehaving. Courtesy of the Tampa (Florida) Police Department.

Patrol officers know that the financial rewards and professional status in most police departments are reserved for managers. Persons who serve as patrol officers for twenty years and then retire are frequently considered to be "not very successful" by their peers, regardless of their accomplishments. This is a serious problem, because the organization of most police departments makes it impossible for more than 10 to 20 percent of all officers to rise above the rank of patrol officer. Thus, because of the built-in limitations of organizations, the expectations and ambitions of many officers cannot be met.

One can find among the ranks of any police department many individuals who have neither the interest nor the aptitude to become managers; yet these same individuals feel compelled to pursue managerial positions, because such positions offer the only route for achieving some degree of professional stature and monetary reward. It is apparent that new organizational models

must be considered to provide realistic and cost-effective alternatives. One possibility is a dual-career system that allows police officers to follow either a nonmanagerial, **professional officer track** or a **professional police management track** (Figures 6.4 & 6.5).

A two-track system would provide a realistic and workable alternative to management. An officer could remain within the patrol ranks in a nonmanagerial role, yet still enjoy some of the professional and monetary rewards of the organization. Table 6.2 outlines some of the recommended training and educational components that can be built into the system to assure individual development, along with quality control. Thus, all police officers would know precisely what they must do to move up the professional police officer track or the professional police management track. This dual-track model may not be appropriate in its present form to meet the needs of some police departments, but it does provide a conceptual basis from which alternative models can be developed.

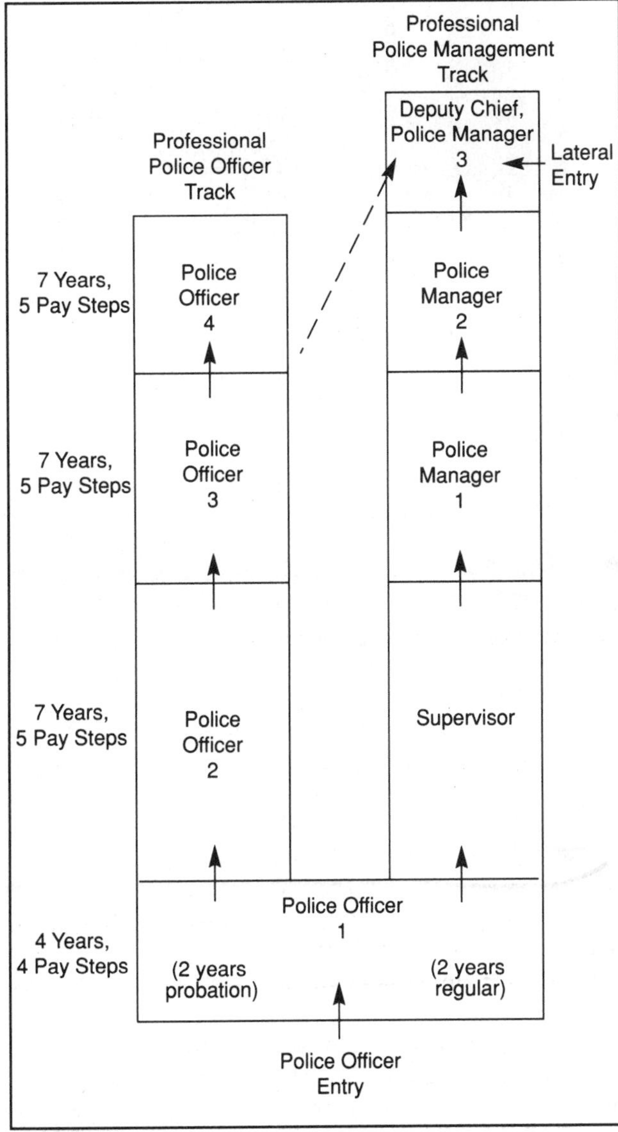

FIGURE 6.4
Professional career tracks in the police department. Adapted from P.M. Whisenand, *Police Career Development* (Washington, D.C.: U.S. Government Printing Office, September 1973), p. 8.

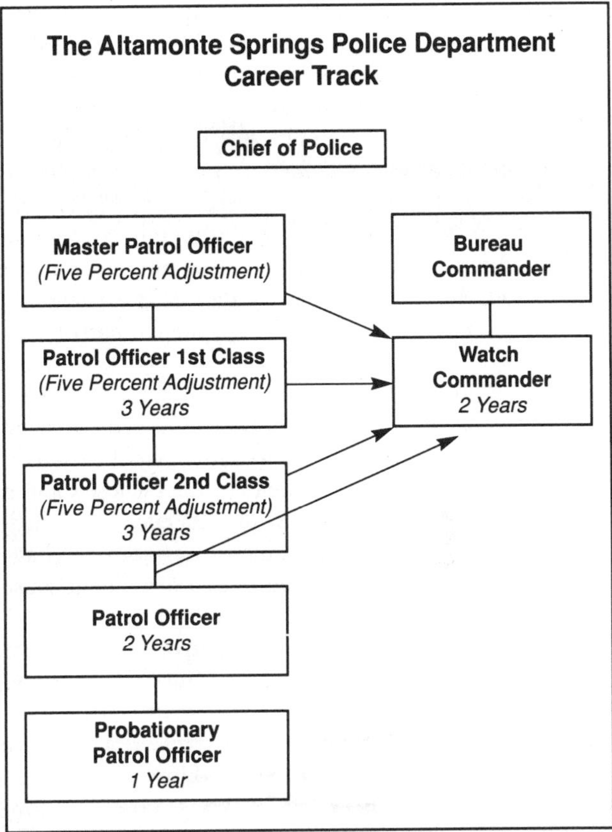

FIGURE 6.5
How one department operationalized the dual-career path concept. Altamonte Springs, Florida Police Department.

Activities of the Patrol Bureau

No two patrol bureaus perform identical tasks, although some tasks are basic to all bureaus, regardless of size. In general, patrol duties are not spelled out in great detail, except when patrol officers are assigned to a specific call for police service. Thus, the catchall phrase "routine patrol and observation" is interpreted in different ways by individual departments, supervisors, and

TABLE 6.2
Training and Education for Professional Career Tracks

Training Step	Training Requirement	Police Official	Police Management
5	Bachelor's degree and proven ability are the minimum qualifications. Exempt positions can be filled from one or more of the ladders or laterally from outside the agency.		Deputy chief, police manager 3
4	Bachelor's degree, 3160 training points, and seven years as a police officer 3 needed to be eligible for the three-day in-service selection and training program. If selected, a two-week in-service training program must be completed. Each person must earn 80 training points annually.	Police officer 4	Police manager 4
3	Ninety college hours (semester), 2150 training points, and seven years as a police officer 2 needed to be eligible for the three-day in-service selection and training program. If selected, a two-week in-service training program must be completed. Each person must earn 80 training points annually.	Police officer 3	Police manager 1
2	Sixty college hours (semester) and 1140 training points needed to be eligible for the three-day in-service selection and training program. If selected, a two-week in-service training program must be completed. Each person must earn 80 training points annually (1 point = 1 training hour; 15 points = 1 semester hour; 10 points = 1 quarter unit).	Police officer 2	Supervisor
1	Six-month basic academy and 24 college hours (semester).	Police officer 1	
Entry	High school diploma and the passing of other job-related tests.	Police officer entry	

Adapted from P. M. Whisenand, *Police Career Development* (Washington, D.C.: U.S. Government Printing Office, September 1973), p. 15.

patrol officers. For example, some patrol officers on the day shift who do not have a specific assignment might decide to concentrate on traffic enforcement; others might decide to patrol a residential area that has had a recent rash of daytime burglaries. The same variations in preference may also exist in the evening and midnight shifts; some officers might patrol a main street or business district to prevent robberies, and others might patrol a warehouse district to prevent burglaries.

Ideally, the type of routine patrol and observation engaged in by patrol officers should be the result of a collaborative effort between the patrol supervisor and the patrol officer, based on the crime data for a given patrol area. Unfortunately, such an effort is often the exception rather than the rule. Some innovative police departments have developed programs in which patrol officers who work days and are not on call are encouraged to conduct crime prevention checks of homes and businesses in their districts that are susceptible to burglaries and robberies. Such efforts usually result in more productive use of patrol time than when each officer is allowed to "do his or her own thing."

NONCRIME CALLS FOR SERVICE Between 80 and 90 percent of all calls for police service are of a noncriminal nature. Many of these calls involve possession and repossession of property, landlord and tenant disputes, property-line arguments, animal control, and noise at parties. Thus, patrol officers must be knowledgeable about the civil law as well as the criminal law. Even calls for service that are clearly civil in nature must be handled promptly and tactfully, because they can quickly escalate into violent confrontation between disputants or between a disputant and an officer.

New research done on behalf of the National Institute of Justice may cause policymakers to reexamine the issue of violence against police officers who respond to domestic disputes. Many officers have been warned that intervention in domestic disturbances is the single most common cause of police deaths. National Institute of Justice researchers Joel Garner and Elizabeth Clemmer (1986, pp. 1–8) found, however, that "domestic disturbances" actually comprise only a small part of the "disturbance" category of police responses and, when separated from other disturbances, fewer deaths are actually associated with these assignments (see Figure 6.6).[2] The following article illustrates the potential for violence in domestic disturbances.

It should also be noted that many police departments have started maintaining very accurate records on res-

Tampa Man Holds Police at Bay

TAMPA—A Tampa man was arrested Saturday morning after barricading himself and a 9-month-old child in their home for about six hours, according to a Sheriff's Office spokesman.

Michael Leroy Hoops, 21, was charged with spouse battery. He is being held in the county jail. Bond has been set at $1,000.

According to administrative deputy P. J. Guarino, officers responded to a domestic complaint at the suspect's residence about 7:45 P.M. Friday.

During a domestic argument, his wife, 19, was struck in the face by her husband, reports said. She fled the residence and ran to a neighbors, leaving her husband and their 9-month-old child in the home, Guarino said.

The suspect then armed himself with a shotgun and barricaded the residence, police said.

The Sheriff's Office Crisis Management Team and the Emergency Response Team responded to a call from his wife, and they were able to move the child from the home through a window of the residence, Guarino said.

At approximately 1:45 A.M. members of the Emergency Response Team entered the residence and arrested Hoops, who was charged with spouse battery.

A .22-caliber rifle, a shot gun and a pellet gun were retrieved from the residence. There were no injuries during the incident, Guarino said.

The Tampa Tribune, Northside Edition, 4 May 1987.

idences that have frequently requested a police response to domestic disturbances, thus affording police officers with additional information relative to their self-protection prior to arriving at the scene. It is also safe to say that officers will, in all likelihood, continue to respond to domestic disturbances with a significant degree of anxiety, based upon their perceptions.

ATTENDANCE AT PUBLIC GATHERINGS Patrol officers are frequently assigned to work at large public gatherings such as political rallies and sporting events. Their presence is needed to assure peaceful assembly and to provide protection for those wishing to exercise their rights to peaceful assembly and free speech. Sometimes arrests are made at events (see Figure 6.7). An officer's presence may also prevent unlawful activity on the part of individuals or the crowd as a whole. A recent trend is for sponsors of an event to hire off-duty patrol officers, especially if the sponsors are private enterprises or individuals. For example, many sports authorities and convention centers now employ off-duty officers to work the interior and exterior of their facilities during special events and to control traffic into and out of parking areas.

BENEVOLENT AND COMMUNITY SERVICES Patrol officers are frequently called upon to perform tasks not in their job descriptions. They are called upon to deliver babies, to give advice to families about marital problems and problems with adolescent children, to help

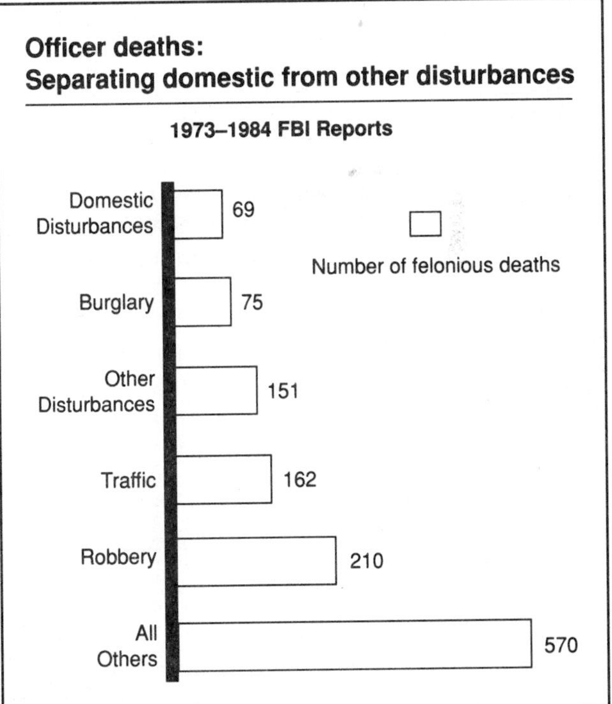

FIGURE 6.6
Domestic disturbances are actually responsible for fewer officer deaths than are other categories. Adapted from Joel Garner and Elizabeth Clemmer, *Danger to Police in Domestic Disturbances—A New Look* (Washington, D.C.: U.S. Department of Justice, National Institute of Justice, November 1986), p. 55. Data compiled from *Law Enforcement Officers Killed and Assaulted.* 1983, 1984, 1985.

FIGURE 6.7
District of Columbia police officers take into custody a protestor who was taking part in a demonstration concerning AIDS. Wide World Photos.

Case 6.1

In one city, the head librarian of the public library contacted the city manager and asked for police assistance in recovering overdue books. The city manager agreed to help and ordered the police chief to have patrol officers go to the homes of violators (children, in some cases) and pick up books. If no one was at home, the officers were to leave a written warning on the door that arrest for larceny could result if the books were not returned immediately. Needless to say, the patrol officers were not thrilled with this task; some were, in fact, quite embarrassed by it.

In another city, officers were instructed to turn on (at dusk) the Christmas tree lights in front of the homes of several influential citizens. The lights were also to be turned off at sunrise.

people who have lost the keys to their homes or automobiles, to inform people about accidents and deaths, and to deliver blood from one hospital to another. A constant complaint heard from patrol officers is that they should not have to perform so many nonpolice functions; such tasks do nothing to enhance the image of officers in the eyes of the public or in the eyes of the officers themselves. However, having reliable personnel available twenty-four hours a day to perform such services is simply too tempting for some government officials. The following example (Case 6.1) illustrates this point.

PRELIMINARY INVESTIGATIONS The patrol officer is on duty and available for all incidents that call for police service, including crimes and accidents. A patrol bureau that is adequately staffed and has properly trained its officers is in the best position to handle the **preliminary investigation** of all types of crimes. As the first police officer to arrive at the scene of a crime, the patrol officer must care for any injured persons and must apprehend the criminal if he or she is still in the immediate area. The patrol officer takes immediate steps to preserve the crime scene, then establishes communication with the dispatcher to broadcast a description of the wanted person and to request additional assistance if needed.

Because he or she has been on the scene from the beginning, the patrol officer usually continues with the initial investigation—collecting evidence, cataloging and filing it, and preparing the necessary reports. When all leads are exhausted and further investigation would take the officer out of his or her assigned district for a long period of time, the follow-up work is usually taken over by an investigator and other specialists (Adams 1971, pp. 15–16).

However, many small departments cannot afford the expense of employing full-time investigators to conduct the follow up investigations. Therefore, in these departments a more experienced patrol officer or supervisor will usually assume the role of investigator. Likewise, many small agencies allow their patrol officers to

conduct most investigations in their entirety, which provides them with additional incentive and experience.

ARRESTS Another of the many duties of the patrol officer is to arrest those who violate the law. This activity is one of the officer's primary objectives at the crime scene. Once an officer makes an arrest, several methods may be used to introduce the arrestee into the criminal justice system. These methods are defined by the laws, the courts, and the procedural manuals of various agencies. In most cases, the arrestee is taken to jail and "booked" or processed and then given an opportunity to post bail to assure his or her appearance in court at a later date (Adams 1971, p. 17).[3] The article on page 167 describes street arrests.

TRAFFIC DIRECTION AND CONTROL Safe and efficient movement of pedestrians and vehicles through a community is the patrol officer's responsibility even if another division of the police department exists strictly

FIGURE 6.8
Two officers take a suspect into custody. Courtesy of Baltimore County Police Department Towson, Maryland.

Police Crack Down on Heroin Market in Lynn, Massachusetts

In 1983, a virtual drug bazaar operated each day just four blocks from the downtown business district of Lynn, Massachusetts. Drug dealers openly competed for business, sending "runners" out to hawk their wares to both pedestrians and drivers passing by. The easy and consistent availability of high-potency drugs made Lynn the preferred place to buy heroin for drug users all over the North Shore of Massachusetts.

Lynn, with a population of 80,000, had the second highest crime rate of all Massachusetts cities and a police department whose sworn strength had fallen by about one-third due to fiscal pressures. Understaffed, it had no resources it could dedicate solely to narcotics work.

Chronic complaints from residents and merchants brought Lynn's drug trade to the attention of the newly organized county Drug Task Force. When it began operations in September 1983, the Task Force's objective was to make the streets of Lynn an unattractive place for heroin buyers and sellers to meet. And, it was hoped, retail heroin enforcement would lead not only to a reduction of drug sales but also to a reduction in the area's property crime.

The National Institute of Justice assessed the results of the Task Force effort. By every available measure, the heroin market in Lynn shrank substantially. What was a bustling street drug market became placid and ordinary looking, with no report of substitute drug markets developing.

In the first 10 months, 186 arrests were made on a total of 227 charges. Ninety-six defendants were convicted or pleaded guilty, including 10 on felony heroin charges. Nominal minimum sentences on all charges totaled 110 years.

The effect on non-drug crime was also dramatic. A year after the enforcement effort began, robberies dropped 18.5 percent and reported burglaries were down 37.5 percent compared to the previous 12 months. A year later, even after drug enforcement manpower in Lynn was reduced due to a shift in personnel, reported burglaries remained at their new, lower level. Reported robberies declined still further, to a level 30 percent below the 1983–84 period.

Two Types of Enforcement

In many cities, police departments have assigned retail drug traffic enforcement to a separate vice or narcotics unit staffed by detectives. Traditionally, those units have been devoted to catching the "kingpins" of the drug trade and have accorded little value to street arrests. At the same time, policies designed to ensure rapid response to calls for service and to prevent corruption have insulated retail drug markets from the uniform patrol force.

The two types of enforcement—one for high-level drug dealers, the other for street dealers and users—produce different effects on the drug trade.

If risk increases due to more vigorous enforcement, some high-level dealers may quit, cut back, or refuse to expand when the opportunity arises. This shift will generate higher prices. Higher prices mean users may commit more crime just to meet the cost of the drug.

When street-level enforcement becomes more vigorous, though, heroin buyers are likely to face increased difficulty in "scoring" (as well as increased risk of arrest for possession) rather than just higher dollar prices. Thus, street-level enforcement increases the time and risk involved in buying heroin rather than its money price. In Lynn, the increase in transaction time and risk cut both drug and non-drug crime.

While the Lynn results indicate the impact enhanced street enforcement can have, some questions remain. Is the drug trade and related crime really decreased or just displaced to other locations by street-level enforcement? What about the scale, timing, and duration of such efforts? Police managers need to think through the possible resource needs for launching retail drug enforcement efforts. Further analysis of the Lynn program data and evaluation of a similar effort in Lawrence, Massachusetts, will help answer some of these questions.

(This summary was drawn from the report *Bringing Back Street-Level Heroin Enforcement* by Mark A. R. Kleiman, who is a Research

Fellow in Criminal Justice at the Kennedy School of Government, Harvard University. He is evaluating the Lynn and Lawrence programs for the National Institute of Justice.)

From *NIJ Reports* (March/April 1987), p. 6.

for traffic control. (See the discussion on traffic bureaus later in this chapter.)

COURT TESTIMONY Testifying in court is the patrol officer's final step in the investigative process. When an officer receives a call, he or she responds, then conducts the investigation, arrests the offender, processes the evidence, completes reports, and presents evidence and testimony in court.

Nontraditional Patrol

For the last thirty years, the majority of police officers assigned to the patrol bureau conducted their business out of patrol cars. Although there is little doubt that the ability to cover large geographic areas has been enhanced by motorized police vehicles, there is a growing concern among law enforcement officials that too much emphasis has been placed on officers themselves being in the cars.

What seems to be missing in many towns and cities is face-to-face interaction between police officers and their communities. If officers are required to respond to calls for service, take appropriate action, and return immediately to their cars to continue "patrol," there is little opportunity for officers and citizens to get to know one another. Furthermore, the patrol officer has virtually no opportunity to learn what has gone on prior to his or her response and even less chance to be empathetic.

In an effort to develop more positive police-community interaction, and to reduce the overdependence on vehicular patrol, some police departments have utilized alternative **nontraditional modes of patrol,** such as the following:

1. *Park and walk.* Officers are assigned to specific geographic areas and are required to park their patrol cars several times a day and conduct foot patrol for a period of time.
2. *Bicycle patrol.* Officers are provided with ten-speed bikes and assigned to a geographic zone for patrol purposes. Officers respond to calls for service and provide a conspicuous presence in areas that cannot be accessed by cars.
3. *Golf-cart patrol.* Officers are assigned to patrol (usually) business districts or parking lots in four-wheeled golf carts. Again golf carts allow these officers to interact readily with the public and to be available to calls for service (see Figure 6.9).
4. *Horse patrol.* Some cities have gone back to purchasing horses for use in patrol by select officers. The officers are highly visible and can interact quite easily with the community (see Figure 6.10).

Municipalities have also recognized the positive value of assigning some officers in certain geographic locations to foot patrol for their entire shift. They find that an officer on foot patrol is able to improve communications through frequent, positive contact and develop meaningful linkages between the community and its government.

For example, in the Flint, Michigan Police Department, a specific program of foot patrol was implemented

FIGURE 6.9
Golf cart converted for use as a "nontraditional" means of patrol. Courtesy of the University of South Florida Police Department.

FIGURE 6.10
Deputies from the Hillsborough County Sheriff's Office patrol parking lot at Mall. Courtesy of *The Tampa Tribune,* Northside Edition, 30 November 1987.

and evaluated. In Flint, Michigan, the foot patrol officer is expected to serve as a catalyst for community crime prevention programs and is seen as the "linkage" person to governmental services for neighborhood residents (Trojanowicz et al., 1985).[4]

In Flint, Michigan, the foot patrol officer is expected to perform several functions in addition to taking incident reports and investigating crimes. Foot patrol officers are expected to get to know the people in the areas to which they are assigned as well as becoming familiar with the problems in those areas. Some of the problems might not be thought of as "criminal" in nature. For example, foot patrol officers in Flint might hear complaints about garbage service. Flint foot patrol officers will in turn contact the sanitation department for appropriate assistance, thereby serving as a "link" to the appropriate governmental service.

Flint foot patrol officers are expected to serve as catalysts for involving their citizens in crime prevention efforts. These officers routinely conduct public education programs on crime prevention, develop community newsletters with crime prevention tips, and make house

or business visits to encourage good crime prevention techniques.

Generally, when evaluated, the Flint Foot Patrol Program was found to be successful. Among the indicators of success were the fact that crime was down; that residents surveyed responded positively to foot patrol; that residents reported feeling safer in their neighborhoods; and that police-community relations appeared to have improved.

Handling the Mentally Disabled

One of the more difficult tasks performed usually, although not always, by uniformed police officers is dealing with those persons who are mentally disabled. Traditionally, police officers have been inadequately trained in this area and are provided with insufficient policy guidelines on how to respond to this type of individual when required to do so. Types of mental disorders, recognizing and handling the mentally ill, the proper exercise of discretion, local laws, commitment procedures, and rights of the mentally ill are among the issues facing a police officer when confronted with a person displaying mental disabilities.

Gerard Murphy conducted a survey of how police departments addressed these issues. Although the survey's findings suggest that the majority of the departments contacted were in need of substantial improvement, it also revealed that a smaller number had responded with some success and ingenuity to the problems created by deinstitutionalization. Three of these, inspected onsite, not only had devised relatively effective responses, but had done so in ways that differed markedly from one another (1986, pp. x–xv).[5]

MODEL PROGRAMS In Galveston, Texas, for example, the Sheriff's Department created a special unit staffed twenty-four hours daily by peace officers who also are certified emergency medical technicians and mental health specialists. These mental health deputies will go to the scene of the incident if called by the responding deputy. Otherwise, the responding deputy transports the subject to a central location for screening by the mental health deputy who assumes responsibility for the disposition. Since 1975 the unit has reduced jail admissions by 99 percent and reduced the rate of involuntary hospitalization admissions to the lowest in Texas and one of the lowest in the nation.

In Madison, Wisconsin, the Police Department has not set up its own specialized unit. Instead, every patrol officer receives comprehensive and in-depth training in managing the mentally ill. All officers are expected to reach a disposition by themselves. Nevertheless, in particularly difficult cases, round-the-clock assistance is available from the country mental health staff. The mental health staff also provides feedback to patrol officers regarding the outcome of their referrals. A sworn officer with special training in handling of the mentally ill facilitates coordination of police and county mental health services and serves as an in-house resource for the department.

Birmingham, Alabama, lacks a service comparable to the county mental health center in Madison. The city does, however, operate a twenty-four-hour program of emergency services for persons in difficulty to which the Birmingham police can turn for assistance. Staffed by community service officers with training in social work, the program provides the police with on-site assistance and takes responsibility for case disposition. The program is reported to have reduced both repeat calls and the time patrol officers must stay on the scene, and has improved these officers' understanding of mental illness and the role of mental health services.

MODEL PROGRAM ELEMENTS The three programs just discussed differ in the respective roles played by police and mental health services, in the method by which interagency coordination is achieved, and in the amount of resources invested in handling mentally ill cases. These differences, in turn, are by-products of normal variations in communities' needs, resources, and priorities. However, each also incorporates a number of elements that appear to be essential to the effectiveness of any program involving the police in the handling of mentally disturbed persons:

- Each program maintains a twenty-four-hour, on-site response capability, so there is less "slippage" in resolving cases involving the mentally ill.
- Each program maintains twenty-four-hour access to the needed resources, which also forestalls delays in resolution.
- Each program either provides trained mental health professionals (police or civilian) or provides line officers with thorough and appropriate training, which is necessary for the expeditious and appropriate handling of cases.
- Each program clearly delineates the separation of duties and responsibilities among the key actors from different agencies.
- Each program has developed procedures that

reduce the time officers need to spend handling mentally ill persons.

- Each program includes close and regular liaison between the participating agencies to ensure that operational information is shared, feedback is provided, and minor problems are addressed.

Team Policing

The 1960s were a time of considerable strain on our police forces; it was a period marked by urban upheavals, a burgeoning crime problem, and the due process revolution (Phelps, Swanson, and Evans 1979).[6] As the public's anxiety grew, so did the demand for more effective police service. The police responded by attempting to provide more of their traditional services; this approach was perceived as unsatisfactory and unresponsive by many communities, however. By the late 1960s, the gulf between the police and their communities was large, a situation antithetical to the proposition that maximum citizen cooperation is fundamental to crime control in a free society. Recognizing this problem, police departments started the concept of team policing to "reduce isolation and induce community support in the war on crime" (National Advisory Commission on Criminal Justice Standards and Goals 1973, p. 154).

Team policing consists of five elements: (1) combining all line functions of patrol, traffic, and investigation into a single unit under common supervision; (2) blending generalists (such as patrol officers) and specialists, (such as homicide investigators) into teams; (3) establishing geographical stability by the continuous assignment of particular teams to particular areas; (4) making teams responsible for the delivery of all police services in their area; and (5) maximizing communication between team members and neighborhood residents (Sherman, Milton, and Kelly 1973, pp. 4–6). Differences between this approach and traditional policing are found in the categories of size, supervision, scheduling, assignments, coordination, community interface, planning, and service orientation (Block and Specht 1973).

TEAM SIZE In the traditional organization, patrol officers are grouped by precincts or large divisions; a precinct or division usually contains 100 to 250 officers. Teams typically consist of only 20 to 40 officers.

TEAM SUPERVISION Team policing relies upon professional supervision characterized by the delegation of most decision making to the patrol officers. Mistakes are viewed as a learning, rather than a fault-finding, exercise; supervisors are open to suggestions and criticisms from subordinates; and interpersonal communications occur in an atmosphere of trust and confidence. In contrast, traditional supervision tends to centralize decision making; its stated preference for close supervision in the field subtly incorporates a depreciated view of the capabilities of subordinates, thereby discouraging a rich source of contributions.

SHIFT SCHEDULES Traditional patrol service is delivered on eight-hour tours of duty, with around-the-clock responsibility vested only in the precinct or division commander. This approach often produces unevenness in the style, level, and type of services offered. In contrast, team commanders are responsible for all police services around the clock.

PERMANENCY OF ASSIGNMENTS The prevailing method of assigning patrol officers is to rotate geographical areas, precincts, or assignments. Team policing, because it depends upon a detailed knowledge of an area and upon maximum interaction with citizens, uses fairly stable assignments.

BLENDING SPECIALISTS AND GENERALISTS- Team policing blends specialists and generalists together under the unified leadership of the team commander. The traditional method of patrol services leaves the patrol officer—a generalist—in need of support ser-

FIGURE 6.11
An investigator and a uniformed officer feed information into a computer. Courtesy Cincinnati Police Division.

vices from specialists in other bureaus; the latter situation often results in bureaucratic fencing over prerogatives and credit and fragmenting of the organizational effort.

COMMUNITY INTERFACE Many police departments started community relations programs in the 1960s in an effort to lessen racial tension. Some departments did conduct meaningful programs, but others used them as a window dressing for public relations campaigns. The existence of such programs often created the attitude among patrol officers that community relations was solely, or primarily, the responsibility of a particular unit, rather than the responsibility of the entire department. In team policing, community relations is viewed as an essential, on-going effort of all officers, stressing the need for friendly contacts and attendance at neighborhood meetings.

DECENTRALIZED PLANNING Traditional policing relies upon planning that is heavily centralized; innovation—such as may occur—flows from the top of the organization down. Team policing, on the other hand, emphasizes decentralized planning, with key contributions coming from team commanders and subordinates, subject to review and approval by senior officials.

SERVICE ORIENTATION Team policing is proactive; maximum positive interaction with the community produces the knowledge and support necessary for crime prevention programs. Traditional policing is heavily, although not exclusively, reactive—responding to calls after the fact. It makes use of programs that are often abrasive to the neighborhood, such as aggressively conducted field interrogations or stop-and-frisk encounters.

THE RESPONSE TO TEAM POLICING Efforts to implement team policing occasionally meet with resistance from within departments. Team policing represents change, which is often threatening to senior officers. Patrol officers who see themselves as enforcers view certain elements of team policing as an attempt to make social workers out of them—a serious attack upon their perceived role. Other officers resist the idea out of a concern that informal contact with the community offers too much potential for corruption. Finally, it is argued that team policing may significantly alter the organizational structure and existing career paths; officers with a strong military orientation or heavy career investment may subvert team policing because they believe it threatens their vested interest.

The Kansas City Patrol Experiment

From 1 October 1972 to 30 September 1973, the Kansas City Police Department, with the support of the Police Foundation, conducted a study to determine if routine patrol with conspicuously marked vehicles had any measurable impact upon crime or the public's sense of security. As noted in a report on the study, "police patrol strategies have always been based on two unproven but widely accepted hypotheses: first, that visible police presence prevents crime by deterring potential offenders; second, that the public's fear of crime is diminished by such police presence" (Kelling et al. 1974, p. 42).

The study was conducted within fifteen beats in a thirty-two-square-mile area with a 1970 resident population of 148,395 (Figure 6.12). (*Beats* are limited geographical areas that are ordinarily patrolled by marked vehicles operated by one or two uniformed officers.) The beats were designated as reactive, proactive, or control areas. **Reactive beats** did not have preventive patrols; officers entered these areas only upon a citizen's request for service. When not responding to calls, officers in reactive units patrolled adjacent proactive beats or the boundaries of their own beats. In **proactive beats,** routine preventive patrol was intensified to two to three times its usual level. A normal amount of patrolling was conducted in *control beats*. The following trends were noted in the evaluation of the experiment:

1. The amount of reported crime in reactive, control, and proactive beats showed only one significant statistical variation: the number of incidents in the category "other sex crimes," which excludes rape and includes such offenses as exhibitionism and molestation, was higher in reactive areas than in control areas. However, project evaluators felt that this statistical significance was probably random.
2. No statistically significant differences were found among the three types of areas with regard to fluctuations in crimes that were not officially reported to the police.
3. There was no statistically significant difference in arrests among the three types of beats.
4. Citizen fear of crime was not significantly altered by changes in the level of routine preventive patrol.
5. Variations in the level of patrolling did not significantly alter the security measures taken by citizens or businesses.
6. Little correlation was found between the level of

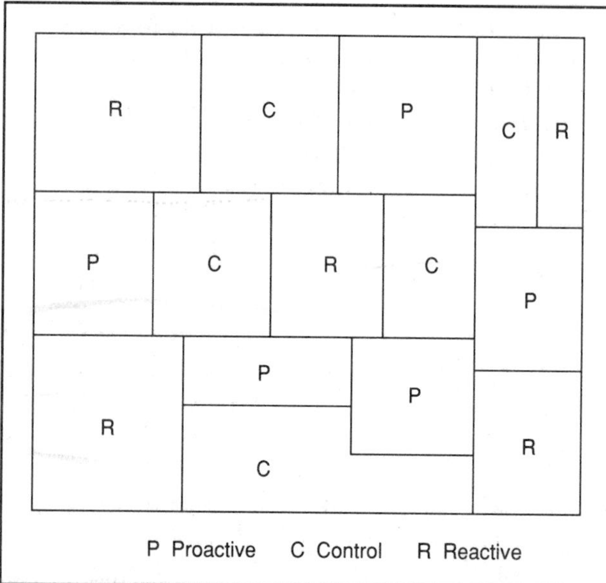

FIGURE 6.12
Schematic representation of the fifteen-beat experimental area of the Kansas City Patrol Experiment. From George L. Kelling et al., *The Kansas City Patrol Experiment* (Washington, D.C.: Police Foundation, 1974), p. 9.

patrol and the attitudes of citizens and businesspersons toward the policing.

7. The time taken by police to answer calls was not significantly altered by variations in the level of routine preventive patrol.
8. Level of patrol had no significant effect upon the incidence of traffic accidents.

The interpretations and findings of the Kansas City Patrol Experiment are highly controversial. Upon learning of the study, some local leaders felt that further increases in police manpower were not warranted and that decreases might even be justified. However, such persons failed to consider that just because the prevailing method of preventing crime—routine preventive patrol—was not effective, it did not follow that no strategy of prevention would work. The findings do suggest that administrators might be able to move into team policing—diverting significant manhours from routine patrol to community interface—without increasing the crime rate. This bridge between the Kansas City Patrol Experiment and team policing is tenuous, however.

Directed Patrol

Since the Kansas City Patrol Experiment, police administrators have reviewed numerous ways to improve the overall productivity of their patrol officers. One promising technique is frequently called *directed patrol.* This type of program attempts to define priorities for patrol officers and to encourage the productive use of uncommitted, random patrol time (Gay, Schell, and Schack 1977, pp. 1–7).[7] The details of this operational concept are as follows.

Two operational mechanisms have been combined to greatly enhance the value of visible patrol. First, crime analysis has been used to specify carefully the time and locations of directed saturation patrol so that police visibility is concentrated in areas of high criminal activity. In most cases, patrols have focused upon areas where the suppressible crimes of robbery, burglary, auto theft, and larceny as well as traffic accidents, vandalism and order maintenance constitute significant problems.

A second, but no less significant factor, in directed patrol has been the high priority given to directed saturation assignments. Directed assignments take precedence over all other patrol activities except emergency calls, which represent 10–15 percent of the entire patrol call workload in most departments. The high priority assigned to directed patrol assignments ensures that officers will have an opportunity to plan and complete these patrols. Perhaps the principal achievement of directed patrol is that it has enabled departments to achieve a level of saturation patrol without increasing the number of personnel assigned to patrol operations.

DIRECTED PATROL TECHNIQUES The development of a saturation patrol program involves several steps.

1. *An analysis of order maintenance, crime, and traffic problems must be undertaken to identify patterns of activity.* This analysis provides the basis for determining the time (day, hour) and location (street, block) for deploying directed patrol assignments, as well as method of operation and suspect information when it is available.
2. *Directed patrol tactics that can be used to address crime and order maintenance problems must be developed and documented.* In most cases, directed deterrent tactics seek to capitalize upon high visibility by using a combination of vehicle and foot patrols as well as traffic and pedestrian stops. These activities should be carefully focused upon crime targets and possible suspects.
3. *Written instructions for patrol officers to follow in implementing the directed patrol assignment*

must be prepared and distributed. Officer assignment sheets often contain a brief description of the problem, including the level of crime, method of operation descriptions, and information about known suspects and vehicle descriptions. In addition, the assignment contains the objective of the directed patrol assignment, time needed to complete assignment, and detailed instructions about what the officer should do and how it should be done (see Figure 6.13). Similar kinds of instructions may be developed for residential

DIRECTED TRAFFIC ASSIGNMENT: BLAIR AVENUE

Problem

Blair Avenue between Arbor and Madison has experienced 18 accidents during May, most occurring during evening rush hours. The intersection of Blair and Madison is a major problem. Traffic congestion is particularly heavy between 7–11 P.M.. In addition, citizens have complained about numerous standing and moving violations.

Objectives

Reduce the number of traffic accidents on Blair Avenue by pin-pointing traffic problems and directing traffic, especially during rush hour. Officer will also strictly enforce parking codes and be observant for moving violations.

General Instructions

Sergeants will have discretion in activating this assignment. Activity should be implemented primarily during the evening rush hours Monday through Friday and during Friday and Saturday evenings. Sergeants are requested to note changes in traffic patterns which might necessitate modification of this directed traffic assignment. This directed assignment takes approximately one hour.

Location	Activity
Arch Street & Blair Avenue	*Park* in North driveway of Hal's Service Station for 15 minutes. If necessary, *leave car and assist traffic* entering Blair Avenue from Arch Street and McDonald's.
Franklin Street & Blair Avenue	*Park* in exit driveway of Thrifty's for ½ hour. *Leave car to check for parking violations.* Walk to Franklin Street to assist with traffic. If necessary, clear traffic at Post Office driveway.
George Street & Blair Avenue	*Park* near the driveway of Citco station on the north side of George Street for 15 minutes. *Monitor traffic problems* caused by the shopping center at the corner of George and Blair. *Direct traffic and issue citations,* if necessary.

FIGURE 6.13
An officer assignment sheet from a directed patrol program. From William G. Gay, Theodore H. Schell, and Stephen Schack, *Improving Patrol Productivity: Vol. 1, Routine Patrol Prescription Package* (Washington, D.C.: U.S. Government Printing Office, 1977), p. 111.

burglary, street robbery, auto theft, and, in fact, any problem encountered by the police.

4. *Strict guidelines for the implementation and cancellation of directed saturation patrol assignments are prepared and enforced.* Whether directed patrol assignments are made by dispatch personnel or patrol supervisors, departments will have to establish strict control over the initiation and completion of directed assignments. Patrol administrators have found, for example, that unless strict guidelines are followed, dispatch personnel, first-line supervisors, and officers can effectively block implementation of saturation patrols and other directed activities.
5. *It is necessary to develop and implement feedback procedures so that officers who are not involved in the preparation of directed assignments can impact the planning process.* Although first-line supervisors may not always be involved in the analytical and design steps that lead to directed saturation patrol, they often give input to the planning process and have responsibility for modifying these patrols to better meet street conditions. In addition, a feedback mechanism is a useful tool in familiarizing officers with systematic patrol planning.

It is safe to say that police operations have benefited from techniques such as directed patrol, which developed as a result of research such as the Kansas City Patrol Experiment.

THE TRAFFIC BUREAU

Traffic is the most pervasive problem confronting police agencies. Every person who drives and every vehicle on the street is part of the problem. Because the responsibility for congestion control, traffic-law enforcement, and accident prevention cannot be fixed on any single unit, traffic duty must be shared to some degree by every uniformed member of a police force. The degree to which an officer may be held accountable for traffic duties is dictated by the extent of the traffic problem.

In cities where traffic constitutes a significant problem, specific duties may be assigned to a traffic bureau to concentrate efforts. The existence of traffic specialists does not relieve the patrol officers of all responsibility

for traffic, but it does free them to adjust their traffic responsibilities in relation to their other duties.

Activities of the Traffic Bureau

As in most areas of police activity, police departments vary as to how they structure their traffic organizations. However, most traffic bureaus are responsible for traffic control, accident investigation, and traffic-law enforcement. Some bureaus also have a safety division concerned primarily with traffic safety education. The traffic bureau shares it responsibilities with the patrol bureau, relieving the patrol officer of traffic duties that are time consuming or immobilizing, and it provides the initiative and guidance for the traffic program of the department. Traffic programs are designed by traffic specialists to concentrate on the specific needs of an area (Caldwell 1972, p. 48).

TRAFFIC CONTROL Officers working in traffic control usually concentrate on relieving congestion by controlling intersections, parking, and emergency traffic. Intersection control requires measures to ensure a safe and continuous flow of vehicular and pedestrian traffic. Traffic signals alone cannot regulate traffic flow; officers must ensure that traffic signals are obeyed and that intersections are kept clear. Intersection control is usually needed only during peak traffic. Traffic-control officers also serve as a vital source of information to citizens, thus providing a rare and needed source of contact between the police and the public.

Some traffic-control officers use three-wheel motorcycles or scooters to increase mobility in congested traffic. Officers on motorcycles can patrol heavily travelled arteries, enforcing tow-away zones and removing obstacles such as stalled vehicles and illegally parked cars. Their mobility allows them to relieve congestion occasioned by changing traffic patterns throughout the day. They may also have to direct traffic at the scene of an accident or a fire, thus allowing regular patrol officers to return to their duties and the accident investigator to concentrate on the details of the investigation (Caldwell 1972, pp. 48–49).

ACCIDENT INVESTIGATION Investigating traffic accidents is a vital function of the traffic bureau. Accident investigation requires skills and time commitments that preclude categorical assignment to the regular patrol officer. The extent of patrol involvement in accident investigation is determined by the demands for other patrol services.

Accident investigation is usually the responsibility of an investigator skilled in reconstructing accident scenes. Acting as evidence technicians, investigators must be able to determine why an accident occurred, how it occurred, and the extent of culpability of the parties involved. They arrive at answers by examining damages, interviewing witnesses and participants, and reviewing physical evidence. They must also render first aid and obtain medical assistance for the injured and prevent accidents from becoming worse by removing involved vehicles from moving traffic. When the investigation is complete, they must prepare a report to provide data for accident prevention efforts.

Accident investigation reports are often a vital part of civil litigation relating to accidents. The goal of such litigation is to fix civil liability for accidents and to allow injured parties to recover part of their financial losses. The accident investigator is often called as a witness in such cases (Caldwell 1972, pp. 49–50). Report data is also used by traffic engineers to correct roadway defects and by traffic researchers to determine the types of traffic violations associated with deaths and injuries.

TRAFFIC-LAW ENFORCEMENT Probably no other function performed by the police causes more ill will between police and the public than traffic-law enforcement. Even if community leaders, public officials, and the media lend strong support to enforcement, support is rarely found among the millions of people who receive traffic tickets each year. No particular insight is needed to understand this phenomenon; tickets can result in fines, mandatory attendance at driver education programs, and penalty points that can eventually lead to license suspension and increases in insurance premiums. Even when fairly imposed, such penalties rarely engender good will toward the police. (We do not mean to suggest, however, that traffic-law enforcement be eliminated or curtailed. But we do believe that sometimes the police may engage in practices that create more ill will than is necessary.)

SELECTIVE TRAFFIC ENFORCEMENT Contrary to popular belief, the major purpose of traffic-law enforcement is *not* to fill the coffers of city, county, or state governments: it is to prevent accidents. However, this fact is rarely known by the public and is sometimes not fully appreciated by the police. The following case illustrates this point.

What should have been done or could have been done differently in the case just described? First, the super-

Case 6.2

After having its traffic engineering department conduct a comprehensive traffic-flow study on one of its major streets, a Florida city decided to increase the speed limit on that street from thirty miles per hour to forty-five miles per hour. New speed signs were installed, but someone failed to increase the timing of one of the caution lights on a traffic signal at a major intersection. One keen-eyed motorcycle officer who noted this failure realized that motorists travelling forty-five miles per hour would have great difficulty stopping for a traffic signal that had its caution light timed to accommodate vehicles traveling at thirty miles per hour.

Based on this discovery, the officer proceeded to engage in a practice referred to professionally as "off-street observation" and informally as "bird-dogging" (the informal term is undoubtedly subject to regional variations). He wrote an average of three tickets per day for red-light violations all within a period of one hour—and thus was well on his way to meeting his quota of five citations per shift (quotas are discussed later in this chapter). His supervisor never questioned him about the inordinate number of citations given at this one intersection every day for three weeks.

As one might expect, the number of traffic accidents at this intersection also started to increase. One of the engineers employed by the city's traffic engineering department to analyze accident trends noted the dramatic increase in accidents at this intersection and, upon checking further, realized to his surprise and shock that the timing mechanism on the traffic signal had not been adjusted. The timing was quickly changed, and, as expected, traffic accidents decreased dramatically. The motorcycle officer who had been so judiciously observing this intersection lamented bitterly that his "fishing hole" had dried up. This officer and his supervisor either never learned or had forgotten that the purpose of traffic-law enforcement is accident prevention.

visor had a responsibility to check data on accident patterns occurring in his area. These data were available from the traffic engineering department. Personnel should have then been deployed to high-accident areas to enforce violations that appeared to be contributing to accidents (a strategy known as **selective traffic enforcement**). In this case, the timing problem should have been promptly reported to the traffic engineering department. Traffic tickets given in high-hazard areas are certainly no more welcome than those given at safer intersections, but this type of enforcement does do more toward reducing accidents and protecting life and property than does the random issuance of tickets merely to meet a quota.

THE QUOTA SYSTEM: MYTH OR REALITY Citizens frequently ask the question, Do police departments have a traffic ticket quota? The answer in some cases is an emphatic yes; but in the final analysis, the decision to use a **quota system** depends upon the philosophy of the chief of police, command officers, and lower-level supervisors. Further, the decision can be affected by officer assignments. For example, if a police department has a traffic bureau, officers assigned to the bureau will devote most of their time to traffic responsibilities, including traffic-law enforcement. However, in patrol bureaus that have numerous other responsibilities besides traffic responsibilities, the emphasis on traffic-law enforcement may vary considerably. Police departments do not, as a rule, document how many traffic tickets they expect their officers to write; but the expected number is rarely zero. Most officers are fully aware of what is expected of them by their departments or supervisors.

WHO GETS THE MONEY? In most cases, money derived from traffic fines does not go to the agencies that enforce the traffic laws; rather, it goes into a general fund at the city, county, or state level. On occasion, a small surcharge (of one or two dollars) imposed along with a regular fine is diverted to the police department for training purposes. However, contrary to popular belief, law enforcement agencies that issue traffic citations rarely derive much financial benefit from their activities. The fee system that was common in this country about twenty years ago—in which officers got a percentage of fines—is virtually nonexistent today.

Traffic Enforcement Policies: Police Departments and Sheriff's Departments

Any comparison of law enforcement agencies must be prefaced with the knowledge that because of variations

Patrol Officer Says Firing is Ticket Related

Leesburg, Fla. (AP)—A Florida Highway Patrol trooper says he was fired after 15 years on the force because he didn't write enough speeding tickets.

P. M. Taylor, 47, said the emphasis of the Florida Highway Patrol troopers has shifted from safety to writing speeding tickets.

Sgt. N. H. Duttenhaver, his supervisor, denied that the patrol has a ticket quota and said Taylor had not "been in keeping with department expectations."

Taylor said troopers in the Leesburg station each wrote between 25 and 80 tickets last month. He wrote 19, he said.

Taylor was suspended once this year for substandard quality of work, which Taylor also attributes to a dearth of ticket writing.

Taylor has filed two grievances with the Employee Improvement Committee, the first in February when he was suspended and the second on March 5.

The Tampa Tribune-Times, 11 April 1982.

in size, community expectations, geographical differences, and managerial philosophies, only broad generalizations can be made. However, there are some basic differences between the enforcement policies of police and sheriff's departments.

For example, with few exceptions, police chiefs are appointed to their positions; sheriffs are elected. Thus, sheriffs are generally very sensitive about enforcement practices that might jeopardize their tenure in office. This is not to suggest that sheriffs encourage their deputies to ignore such violations as drunk driving, reckless driving, or drag racing; this is certainly not the case. But in many cases, high premiums may not be placed on the strong enforcement of less serious violations, and warnings may be issued in place of regular tickets for minor traffic infractions.

THE DETECTIVE BUREAU

Three common stereotypes influence the public's perception of investigative effectiveness in the detective bureau: the media stereotype, the historical stereotype, and the critical stereotype. Some combination of these three provides the basis for current investigative policies in most police departments (Greenwood and Petersilia 1975).[8]

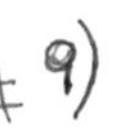

The *media image* of working detectives—an image pervasive on television—is that of clever, imaginative, perseverant, streetwise cops who consort with glamorous women or handsome men and duel with crafty criminals. They and their partners roam cities for days or weeks trying to break a single case that is ultimately solved by means of the investigator's deductive powers. This is the image that many investigators prefer—although perhaps with some concessions. Most investigators concede that criminals are rarely as crafty or diabolical as depicted in the media, but they may not quarrel with the media portrayal of their own capabilities. Some current investigative practices are used mainly to preserve a media-like image or to give victims the services they expect because of that image. For example, activities such as dusting for fingerprints, showing mug shots, or questioning witnesses are sometimes done without any hope of developing leads; rather, they are done simply for public relations.

FIGURE 6.14
Motorcycle officer as viewed by a traffic violator. Courtesy Fairfax County (Virginia) Police Department.

The *historical stereotype* is the image held by older police administrators of the special status of detectives in earlier times (Smith 1960). Not so many years ago, various illicit activities such as vice, gambling, prostitution, and speakeasies were openly tolerated by city governments. These illegal, but accepted, enterprises created problems for the city police. How could they control such institutions without driving them completely out of business?

Police dealings with illegal institutions were frequently handled by detectives. The detectives ensured that the businesses were run in an orderly fashion and that "undesirables" were driven out. By this delicate balance the detectives often won the favor of the business leaders and politicians involved in the illegal activities. Such political connections elevated the detective to a position of respect and influence.

The police in general also benefited by allowing these illegal enterprises to continue. When serious crimes did occur or when public pressure was brought to bear on the police to deal with a particular problem, the illegal activities provided a valuable source of information for detectives. Not surprisingly, thieves and con men were often the customers of the vice and gambling operations, or at least had close contact with the people engaged in these businesses. If the police wanted information on a particular criminal activity, they could solicit information as a favor or extort it by threatening the safety of the illegal operations. Thus, the "effectiveness" of detective operations frequently depended on close contacts with a select group of potential informers.

Another role played by detectives of the past was that of dispensers of street-corner justice. Good cops were expected to maintain order without resorting to the courts. They did this by persuasion, by making threats, and, if necessary, by using physical force. Only when it was clear that their presence alone would not deter crime did the police bring a suspect in for criminal proceedings. Detectives played this role because they were less visible than uniformed patrol officers. Because of their experience, they were expected to be more diplomatic in handling these incidents (part of the detective's basic working knowledge was an understanding of which individuals could be treated roughly without getting the department into trouble). Detectives who could handle delicate situations without causing a commotion were highly valued by police and city administrators.

Another method once available to detectives was the third-degree or extended interrogation. However, this type of activity has been limited by the Supreme Court decision on interrogations in *Miranda* v. *Arizona* (86 S.Ct. 1602 [1966])—which increased the enforcement of civil liberties—and by the rise of community review boards. It is no longer acceptable for detectives to arrest suspects and keep them in custody simply for investigative purposes. Neither is it permissible to use physical or psychological force to extort a confession or to get information about other suspects in a case.

The *critical stereotype* of investigative effectiveness is expressed in several studies that analyze how detectives go about their work. One of the earliest critics of investigative practices and detectives was Raymond Fosdick (1921). After visiting police departments in all of the major cities of the United States, he criticized detectives for lack of civil service standards in selection; lack of training; poor coordination with patrol operation; lack of effective supervision; and lack of ordinary "business systems" for handling administrative work. More recently, analysts have made these arguments:

1. Police agencies do not routinely collect and summarize data that can be used to determine the effectiveness of investigative activities. Clearance and arrest statistics, in particular, are unsuitable because they fail to distinguish outputs of investigative efforts from those of other units in the department. Used alone, clearance data are also extremely unreliable indicators of police performance because of their subjective nature.
2. The solution rate of crimes appears to be insensitive to the number of cases assigned to each detective. This implies that detectives can accurately predict which cases can be solved and work on only those, or that some cases solve themselves.
3. A high proportion of cases are closed when a patrol officer makes an arrest at the scene of the crime.
4. Investigators make little use of physical evidence such as fingerprints or tool marks.

Uncomplimentary views of detectives have also been espoused by progressive police chiefs who have seen reforms and new initiatives in every other area of policing except the detective bureau. In such departments, an appointment to the detective bureau is no longer viewed as the best path to promotion. In other departments (the Los Angeles Police Department, for example), independent detective bureaus no longer exist, and investigators are assigned directly to local operations commanders. Many progressive police chiefs are candidly critical of the old, freewheeling style of detective work.

They see detectives as trying to preserve the freedom and prerequisites of their jobs without making any effort to adapt to the shifting community and legal climate in which they work.

Activities of the Detective Bureau

A realistic view of investigative activities can be conveyed by describing how a typical case is handled, variations that frequently occur in the typical pattern, departmental policies that govern how cases are handled, and the supporting activities police perform to increase the likelihood of identification and apprehension.

INCIDENT REPORT AND PRELIMINARY INVESTIGATION Most cases involving the discovery of major felonies are initiated by a citizen who calls the police to report the crime or by a police patrol unit that responds to evidence that a crime is in progress. In either case, the first police representative on the scene is usually a uniformed patrol officer. The patrol officer's duties are to provide aid to the victim, to secure the crime scene for later investigation, and to document the facts of the crime. In a few departments, investigators may be dispatched simultaneously with the patrol unit to begin an investigation of the crime, but in most departments, investigation by detectives does not take place until after a patrol unit files a report. The patrol officer's initial report usually contains the basic facts of the crime—the identity of the victim, a description of the suspect, the identity and location of any potential witnesses, a description of the crime scene, and any pertinent statements by witnesses or the victim. This report is passed on to the detective unit, which then continues the investigation.

Patrol units are generally under considerable pressure to cut short their investigations and get back on patrol. Thus, detectives, rather than patrol officers, are usually responsible for developing potential leads and continuing an investigation. In a few departments, however, patrol officers are encouraged to use their own initiative to continue an investigation perhaps by conducting house-to-house checks or using other means to track down suspects.

EVIDENCE COLLECTION AND PROCESSING Studies show that many crime scenes contain physical evidence linking a suspect with the crime. To collect this evidence (primarily fingerprints), many departments use trained **evidence technicians** whose sole task is to process crime scenes. Technicians may be dispatched at the time of the crime report, or they may be sent out following the initial report if the responding patrol officer feels that usable evidence might be found. Their job is to examine the crime scene, lift any latent fingerprints, and submit a report of their results to the responsible unit.

In most departments, latent fingerprints are not used unless an investigator asks the print examiner to compare them with the inked prints of a specific suspect. Occasionally, a print examiner may conduct a "cold" search, comparing lifted prints with files of known or suspected offenders.

SCREENING AND CASE ASSIGNMENT Every morning, incident reports are assembled from the previous day and distributed to the appropriate investigative unit. The assignment of an investigator to a case is determined by the organizational pattern of the department; for example, assignments might be made by crime specialty (e.g., robbery, burglary, sex offenses) or by geographic area. Specialization might be so detailed that assignment personnel can direct an incident report to the specific investigator who will handle that case. Otherwise, the report goes to a unit supervisor who assigns the case to a detective in his or her unit, based on previous assignments or individual work loads. Each detective usually receives one or two new cases a day. Work loads are lower for detectives who handle crimes against the person, higher for those who handle minor property crimes.

In some departments, formal "solvability factors" and the judgment of the unit supervisor are used to determine if a specific case should be followed up by an investigator or suspended until new facts develop. Generally, however, every case is assigned to a responsible investigator, with some minimal attempt at follow-up expected. This minimal effort is usually an attempt to contact the victim to obtain facts in addition to those recorded in the incident report. Although most investigators have twenty or thirty open cases on their desks at any one time, only two or three cases are really considered active. Workload data shows that most cases are closed within the first day of activity, and very few remain active after two or three days.

FOLLOW-UP (LATENT) INVESTIGATION New cases assigned to an investigator generally fall into one of three categories. Cases that receive first priority are those in which the investigative steps are obvious, based on the facts in the incident report. These are the cases in which the victim names a suspect, gives a license number, identifies where the suspect can be found, or indicates additional witnesses who were not interviewed by the responding patrol officer.

Second in priority are those cases that require attention not because of obvious leads, but because of the seriousness of the offense or its notoriety in the press or in the community. Investigators want to avoid charges by the community that they are not doing their job, and they may simply be outraged by an offense and want to help the victim. Cases of the lowest priority are routine cases that offer no additional leads. In all departments, these cases are given only perfunctory treatment.

The first task of investigators when they come to work is to plan their activities for the day. Part of the morning is usually devoted to reviewing new cases, finishing paperwork, processing prisoners who were taken into custody the night before, and making required court appearances. Late morning and afternoon are usually free for conducting interviews or street patrol. The use of this "free" time is usually determined by a detective's own judgment; this judgment is based on a sense of priority about each case, the difficulty or attractiveness of conducting various interviews, transportation difficulties, and the activities of fellow investigators.

Investigators rarely take detailed written notes during interviews. Rather, they record only telephone numbers, addresses, nicknames, and other basic information for the official case folder. Transcripts of witness statements are made only in the most serious cases.

CLEARANCE AND ARREST A major demand on an investigator's time occurs when a suspect is taken into custody—usually as a consequence of patrol activity. When an arrest occurs, an effort is often made to clear other crimes similar to the one for which the suspect was arrested. Such is the responsibility of the investigator. If the suspect is willing, the investigator may talk to him or her about similar offenses; if the suspect is not willing to talk, investigators may use their own judgment about whether the suspect might be involved in other cases. If a suspect has been identified by a victim (as often occurs in sex crimes or robberies), previous victims may be brought in to view the suspect in a lineup.

All results of a **follow-up (latent) investigation** are conveyed to the prosecutor in written reports. In many jurisdictions, prosecutors require investigators to consult them about the facts of a case at the time of filing. If an investigator helps solve a case, he or she may also have to testify in court.

FILE MAINTENANCE In addition to regular investigative activities, most departments expend resources to develop leads or identify suspects by alternative means. For example, all departments maintain a variety of information files that serve as sources of investigative leads. These files may include a file of crimes by type, location, or time period; a file of the addresses, descriptions, and modus operandi of known offenders; files of mug shots (usually organized by crime type and basic descriptors); files containing the fingerprints of all past arrestees; intelligence files with the names of individuals suspected of particular criminal activity; files of stolen or pawned property; and **field interrogation files** that indicate where and why certain individuals or vehicles were stopped, along with a description of the person and his or her vehicle (Figure 6.15). In addition, an increasing number of police agencies have highly developed crime analysis units that provide valuable information to investigators to help them narrow and focus their efforts. (Factors used in **crime analysis** are summarized in Tables 6.3 and 6.4 on pages 182, 183).

In some departments, special details or strike forces are operated to provide investigative leads that never come through in normal incident reports. The most common example of such activity is a pawnshop detail that routinely inspects items taken in by pawnshops and compares them with lists of stolen property. Another type of strike force—typically called a "sting" operation"—uses investigators to buy stolen property in an attempt to identify fences and burglars. In other cases, investigators are assigned temporarily as decoys in high-crime areas.

SELECTION, TRAINING, AND SUPERVISION Before becoming an investigator, an officer usually has to spend three to five years on patrol. Selection for investigative units is not based strictly on civil service criteria; rather, more aggressive patrol officers are often selected—presumably because an officer who makes a large number of arrests has the initiative and insight to make a good investigator.

Investigators usually get all their new training on the job. When new recruits join a detective bureau, they are given some investigative training to help them in their work, but there are rarely any special training classes. And only a few departments offer continuing education for detectives on investigative assignments.

Most investigators operate out of detective bureaus separate from the patrol bureau, except in jurisdictions where investigators are integrated into a patrol-team concept (team policing). At any rate, detective bureaus as an institution have only administrative significance: each investigator or investigator pair operates independently. Supervisors are concerned primarily with vacation schedules, the timeliness of reports, and the tidiness of paperwork, and they do not usually enter into sub-

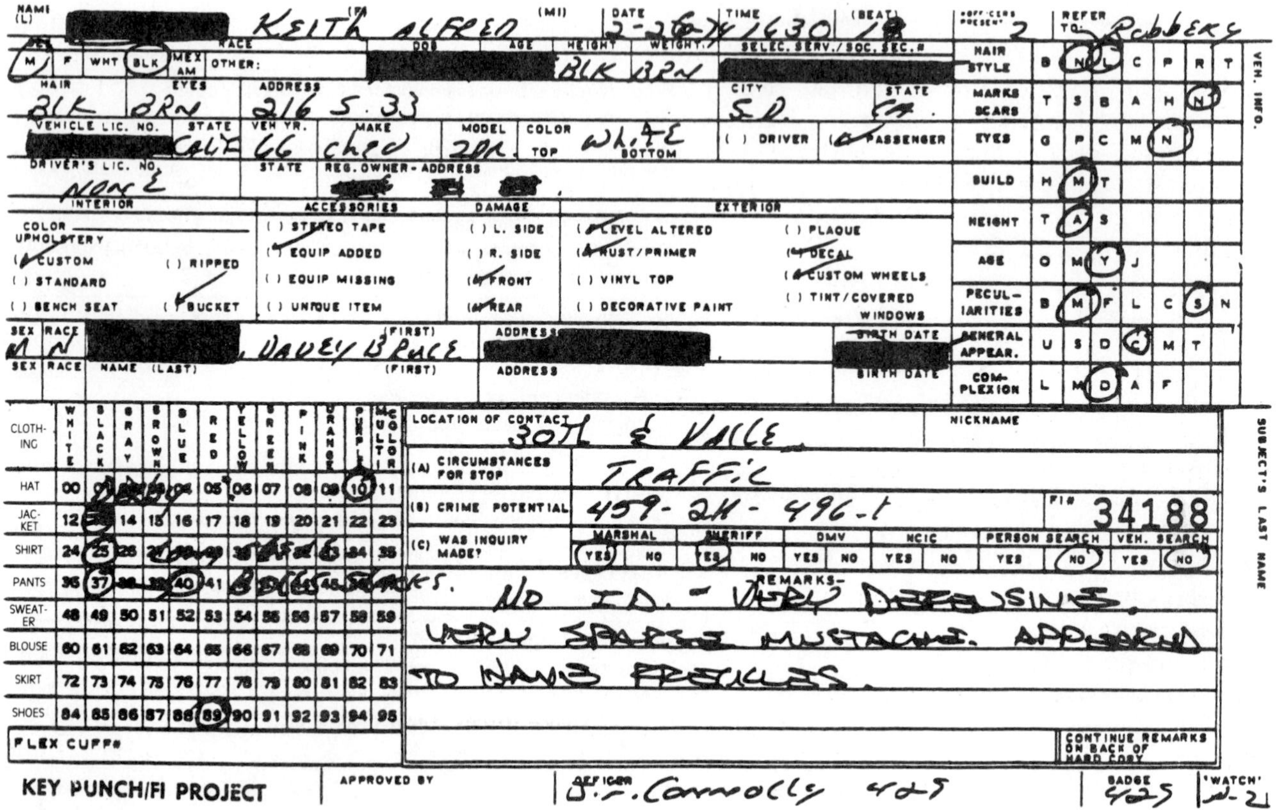

NAME (L) (F) KEITH ALFRED (MI) | DATE 2-26-74 | TIME 1630 | (BEAT) | OFFICERS PRESENT 2 | REFER TO: Robbery

SEX M F | RACE WHT BLK MEX AM OTHER: | DOB | AGE | HEIGHT | WEIGHT | SELEC. SERV./SOC. SEC. #

HAIR BLK | EYES BRN | ADDRESS 216 S. 33 | CITY S.D. | STATE CA.

VEHICLE LIC. NO. | STATE CALIF | VEH YR. 66 | MAKE Chev | MODEL 2Dr. | COLOR TOP White BOTTOM | ( ) DRIVER | (✓) PASSENGER

DRIVER'S LIC. NO. NONE | STATE | REG. OWNER - ADDRESS

INTERIOR: COLOR UPHOLSTERY (✓) CUSTOM ( ) STANDARD ( ) BENCH SEAT ( ) RIPPED (✓) BUCKET

ACCESSORIES: ( ) STEREO TAPE (✓) EQUIP ADDED ( ) EQUIP MISSING ( ) UNIQUE ITEM

DAMAGE: ( ) L. SIDE ( ) R. SIDE (✓) FRONT (✓) REAR

EXTERIOR: (✓) LEVEL ALTERED (✓) RUST/PRIMER ( ) VINYL TOP ( ) DECORATIVE PAINT ( ) PLAQUE (✓) DECAL (✓) CUSTOM WHEELS ( ) TINT/COVERED WINDOWS

HAIR STYLE B N L C P R T | MARKS SCARS T S B A H N | EYES G P C M N | BUILD H M T | HEIGHT T A S | AGE O M Y J | PECULIARITIES B M F L C S N | GENERAL APPEAR. U S D C M T | COMPLEXION L M D A F

VEH. INFO.

SEX M RACE N NAME (LAST) DAVEY BRUCE (FIRST) ADDRESS BIRTH DATE

SEX RACE NAME (LAST) (FIRST) ADDRESS BIRTH DATE

CLOTHING	WHITE	BLACK	GRAY	BROWN	BLUE	RED	YELLOW	GREEN	PINK	ORANGE	PURPLE	MULTICOLOR
HAT	00	01	02	03	04	05	06	07	08	09	10	11
JACKET	12	13	14	15	16	17	18	19	20	21	22	23
SHIRT	24	25	26	27	28	29	30	31	32	33	34	35
PANTS	36	37	38	39	40	41	42	43	44	45	46	47
SWEATER	48	49	50	51	52	53	54	55	56	57	58	59
BLOUSE	60	61	62	63	64	65	66	67	68	69	70	71
SKIRT	72	73	74	75	76	77	78	79	80	81	82	83
SHOES	84	85	86	87	88	89	90	91	92	93	94	95

FLEX CUFF#

LOCATION OF CONTACT 30th & Valle | NICKNAME

(A) CIRCUMSTANCES FOR STOP Traffic

(B) CRIME POTENTIAL 459 - 211 - 496.1 | FI# 34188

(C) WAS INQUIRY MADE? MARSHAL YES NO | SHERIFF YES NO | DMV YES NO | NCIC YES NO | PERSON SEARCH YES NO | VEH. SEARCH YES NO

REMARKS- ...SLACKS. NO I.D. - VERY DEFENSIVE. VERY SPARSE MUSTACHE. APPEARED TO HAVE FRECKLES.

CONTINUE REMARKS ON BACK OF HARD COPY

SUBJECT'S LAST NAME

KEY PUNCH/FI PROJECT | APPROVED BY | OFFICER J. F. Connolly 425 | BADGE 425 | WATCH II-2

FIGURE 6.15
Field interrogation report. Courtesy San Diego (California) Police Department.

stantive decisions about cases. In departments in which investigators are encouraged to spend a good deal of their time on the street, supervisors may be only vaguely aware of what their people are doing on a day-to-day basis.

The Rand Criminal Investigation Study

Several years ago, the Rand Corporation was awarded a grant by the National Institute of Law Enforcement and Criminal Justice to undertake a nationwide study of criminal investigations in major metropolitan police agencies. The purposes of the study were to describe how police investigations were organized and managed and to assess the contribution of various activities to overall police effectiveness. Prior to the Rand study, police investigators had not been subject to the type of scrutiny that was being focused on other types of police activity. Most police administrators knew little about the effectiveness of the day-to-day activities of their investigative units, and even less about the practices of other departments (Greenwood 1979).[9]

THE STUDY DESIGN The Rand study concentrated on the investigation of index offenses—serious crimes against unwilling victims—as opposed to vice, narcotics, gambling, or traffic offenses. Information on current practices was obtained by a national survey of all municipal and county police agencies employing more than 150 officers or serving jurisdictions with a population in excess of 100,000. Interviews and observations were conducted in more than twenty-five departments selected to represent different investigative styles. Data on the outcome of investigations were obtained from FBI Uniform Crime Report tapes; from samples of completed cases, which were coded for the study; and from internal evaluations or statistics compiled by individual departments. Data on the allocation of investigative efforts were obtained from a computerized work-load file maintained by the Kansas City Police Department.

Data from the national survey and the Uniform Crime Reports were combined for the purpose of analyzing relationships between departmental characteristics and apprehension effectiveness. Case samples were analyzed to determine how specific cases were solved.

TABLE 6.3
Universal Factors for Crime Analysis

Crime Type	Burglary (class: business-commercial, residential, other)
	Robbery (class: armed vs. not armed)
	Auto theft (automobile, commercial vehicle, motorcycle, etc.)
	General larceny (thefts from autos, auto accessories, scrap metal, dock, etc.)
	Fraud (forgery, credit cards, confidence games, etc.)
	Rape and sex crimes (forcible rape, child molesting, indecent exposure)
	Aggravated assault and murder
Geography	Location offense occurred
	Street address or intersection
	Block
	Subreporting area or census tract
	Reporting area, patrol area, or beat
	Zone, precinct, or district
Chronology	Specific time offense occurred
	Time span in which offense occurred (day or night)
	Day of week
	Week of year
	Month of year
Victim Target	Person (sex, age, race, etc.)
	Structure (single dwelling house, apartment, high rise, etc.)
	Premise (commercial, industrial, public, etc.)
	Purpose (sales, service, manufacturing, etc.)
	Victim's knowledge of suspect
Suspect	Name
	Age
	Race
	Height
	Weight
	Clothing and unusual characteristics
Suspect Vehicle Description	License number
	Make
	Model and year
	Color
	Damage
Property Loss Description	Serial number of property loss
	Make of property loss (brand name, etc.)
	Model of property loss
	Type of property loss
	Use of the property

Adapted from George A. Buck et al., *Police Crime Analysis Unit Handbook* (Washington, D.C.: U.S. Government Printing Office, 1973), p. 33.

POLICY RECOMMENDATIONS The first recommendation of the Rand study was that post-arrest investigation activities be coordinated more directly with prosecutors—either by assigning investigators to prosecutors' offices or by allowing prosecutors to exert more guidance over the policies and practices of investigators. The purpose of the recommendation was to increase the percentage of cases that could be prosecuted.

Secondly, it was suggested that patrol officers be given a larger role in conducting preliminary investigations, both to provide an adequate basis for case screening and to eliminate redundant efforts by an investigator. Most cases can be closed on the basis of the preliminary investigation, and patrol officers can be trained to conduct such investigations adequately. Expanding the role of the patrol officer is consistent with other trends toward

TABLE 6.4
Crime-Specific Factors for Crime Analysis

Residential Burglary	Type of premise attacked (house, exterior or interior apartment, etc.) Occupied vs. unoccupied Point of entry (window, door, etc.) Method of entry (pry door or window, wrench door, break window, etc.) Presence of physical evidence (latent prints, etc.)
Commercial Burglary	Type of business attacked (television store, clothing store, savings and loan, etc.) Alarm information (no alarm, alarm defeated, method, etc.) Point of entry (window, door, roof, wall, floor, vent, etc.) Method of entry (window smash, lock in-break out, peel wall, etc.) Safe attack method (rip, punch, peel, burn, drill, grind, etc.)
Robbery	Type of victim business (diner, bar taxi, savings and loan, gas station, etc.) Victim personal descriptors (sex, race, age, occupation, etc.) Weapon used (handgun, shotgun, knife, club, etc.) Suspect mask and type (facial area covered) Suspect statement during commission; particular M.O.
Theft from Person	Exact location of victim (sidewalk, park, hallway, bar, etc.) Victim personal descriptors (sex, race, age, etc.) Victim condition after attack Suspect particular M.O. (approach, flight, statements, etc.) Object of theft (cash, checks, credit cards, jewelry, etc.)
Auto Theft	Area stolen vs. area recovered Exact last location (on-street, parking lot, carport, sales lot, etc.) Make, year, and model of vehicle Degree of strippage and parts Presence or absence of physical evidence
Larceny	Type of victim property (business, personal, use, purpose, etc.) Location of property (left unattended, in vehicle, etc.) Specific property taken and market potential Suspect particular M.O. Presence or absence of physical evidence
Forgery	Check and credit card specifics (how obtained, type, etc.) Type of business or person victimized Document descriptors (commercial, personal, etc.) Type of identification used Confidence game specifics (ploy used, etc.)
Rape, Sex Offenses	Victim personal descriptors (age, race, sex, occupation, etc.) Location of encounter vs. location of departure Suspect statement during commission Suspect actions or M.O. Weapon or degree of force used
Aggravated Assault and Murder	Relationship between victim and suspect Victim personal descriptors Motive Weapon used Physical evidence

Adapted from George A. Buck et al., *Police Crime Analysis Unit Handbook* (Washington, D.C.: U.S. Government Printing Office, 1973), p. 35.

FIGURE 6.16
Drug abusers, captured in a New York City police surveillance photograph, enter a building to buy illegal drugs. Photo by Leon Schwartzman.

geographic decentralization and job enrichment. A third recommendation was that additional resources be devoted to processing latent prints and that improved systems be developed for organizing and searching print files.

Finally, the study recommended that, with regard to follow-up investigations for cases that a department elected to pursue, a distinction should be drawn between those cases that require only routine clerical processing and those that require special investigative or legal skills. The former could be handled by lower-level clerical personnel, the latter by a separate bureau.

IMPACT OF THE STUDY The Rand study was widely covered in the popular media and was the subject of heated controversy within the police profession. Many police officials, especially those who had not come up through the detective ranks, were sympathetic to the study in that it supported their own impressions of how investigators functioned. Others criticized it for "telling us what we already knew." Many police chiefs were hostile because the study was being used by city officials as an excuse to cut police budgets, and others refused to accept the findings because of the limited number of departments that were studied.[10]

Although there have not been any major attempts to replicate or extend the findings of the Rand study, several reports have been published with consistent findings. Bloch and Weidman's analysis of the investigative practices of the Rochester, New York, Police Department (1975) and Greenberg's efforts to develop a felony investigation decision model (Greenberg et al. 1977) both resulted in findings supportive of the idea that preliminary investigations conducted by patrol officers pro-

duce the majority of arrests and can provide adequate information for screening cases. A report by the Vera Institute (1977) on felony arrests in New York City indicates that a substantial portion of felony arrests for street crimes involve offenders who are known to their victims.[11] A report by Forst (1978) on the disposition of felony arrests in Washington, D.C., demonstrates the importance of physical evidence and multiple witnesses in securing convictions for felony street crimes.

The PERF Study: Solving Crimes

In 1983 the Police Executive Research Forum (**PERF**) conducted a study of the roles played by patrol officers and detectives in the investigation of robbery and burglary cases. Some of the findings and implications of that study are reviewed in the following paragraphs (Eck 1983).[12]

Police detectives and patrol officers contribute equally to the solution of robbery and burglary cases. But the investigation of such cases rarely consumes more than four hours, spread over as many days, and three-quarters of the investigations are suspended within two days for lack of leads. In the remainder of cases, the follow-up work by detectives is a major factor in determining whether suspects will be identified and arrested. However, detectives and patrol officers alike rely too heavily on victims, who seldom provide information leading to an arrest, and make too little use of those sources of information most likely to lead to arrest—witnesses, informants, their own colleagues, and police records.

FIGURE 6.17
New York detective dressed as a woman, working as a decoy in an area with a high incidence of assaults and thefts against women. Copyright New York News Inc. Reprinted by permission.

Those were the major findings of PERF's two-year study of criminal investigations of burglary and robbery in three jurisdictions: DeKalb County, Georgia; St. Petersburg, Florida; and Wichita, Kansas. The findings demonstrate that investigations are not necessarily as wasteful or mismanaged as earlier studies suggested, perhaps because those studies stimulated management improvements. The findings show, in addition, that the follow-up investigations by detectives are more valuable in identifying and arresting suspects than the earlier research suggested. Finally, PERF's research points the way toward a series of management changes.

PRELIMINARY INVESTIGATIONS: SOME RECOMMENDATIONS One recommendation of the PERF study was that greater emphasis should be put on collecting physical evidence when such evidence can be used. Physical evidence is seldom used to identify an unknown suspect but is valuable in corroborating identifications made through other means. Although most agencies lack the resources to send trained evidence technicians to all crime scenes, only a few have developed policies defining when technicians should or should not be sent. As a result, technicians are overused, the quality of their work declines, and more evidence is collected than can be used.

Consequently, a second recommendation made by PERF was that guidelines should be developed for the use of evidence technicians in routine cases such as robberies and burglaries without serious injuries or extremely high losses. The criteria should take into account the fact that physical evidence is not likely to be useful unless the suspect is identified by other means.

A third recommendation was that greater effort should be devoted to canvassing neighborhoods for witnesses. Although the importance of witnesses in identifying suspects and leading to arrests and convictions is well established, patrol officers often fail to canvass neighborhoods near crime scenes in order to find witnesses. Relying solely on victims and those witnesses immediately avail-

DeKalb County Police Burglary Screening Decision Model

Weight (Circle)	*Information Element*	
	1. Suspect information	
10	A. Positive Identification	
8	B. Tentative Identification	
6	C. Poor Identification	
	2. Vehicle Information	
10	A. Positive Identification (tag and/or other)	
8	B. Definitive Description	
6	C. Poor Description	
	3. Estimate Time Between Incident—Report	
4	A. Less than one hour	
3	B. One to twelve hours	
2	C. Twelve hours and over	
	4. Method of Reporting	
2	A. Witness and/or victim	
1	B. Officer on-view	
	5. Information Received →	SECTION 5 TO BE USED *ONLY* IF INFORMATION AVAILABLE AT CODING *OR* TO ACTIVATE AN INACTIVE CASE
	A. Confidential Informant and/or victim	
10	1. Definitive Information	
8	2. Possible Information	
6	3. Poor Information	
	B. Information shared from other investigator and/or agency	
10	1. Definitive Information	
8	2. Possible Information	
6	3. Poor Information	
	6. Modus Operandi	
5	A. Definitive pattern	
4	B. Possible pattern	
3	C. Poor pattern	
	7. Fingerprints	
10	A. Identified with suspect	
1	B. Without suspect	
______	TOTAL CUT POINT FOR CASE ACTIVATION IS 10	

Case: Active
Inactive (Circle)

Other factors not listed which cause the case to be active.

(Specify) ______________________________

NOTE: *This scale is to be used as a guideline only and is not intended to override nor interfere with the good judgment of a supervisor in assigning cases where there may be considerations not included in this scale.*

CASE NUMBER __________ INVESTIGATOR ______________

DATE __________ SCREENER ______________

FIGURE 6.18

A sample case screening device used by supervisors to assign burglary case investigations. From John E. Eck, *Solving Crimes: The Investigation of Burglary and Robbery* (Washington, D.C.: Police Executive Research Forum, 1983), p. 80.

able at the crime scene obstructs the effectiveness of further investigative efforts. It is crucial that patrol officers conducting preliminary investigations routinely search for potential witnesses who are not at the crime scene when officers arrive.

PERF also suggested that patrol officers should use department records more extensively. Checking department records was found to be an especially productive activity for patrol officers, but they did so with varying frequency in the agencies studied. Officers may believe they are tied to their vehicles and that records are difficult and time-consuming to locate. Police managers should design record systems that enhance radio and telephone accessibility for patrol officers.

Finally, PERF recommended that patrol officers should make greater use of informants. Informants have been found to be particularly useful in identifying suspects and bringing about arrests. Nonetheless patrol officers rarely use them, perhaps because the officers are untrained in the skills of cultivating informants. Patrol managers should make greater efforts to provide the necessary training and encouragement to help patrol officers develop informants.

IMPROVING MANAGEMENT OF FOLLOW-UP INVESTIGATIONS The PERF study also made a series of recommendations to improve the management of follow-up investigations; these recommendations fall into three categories: regulating case flow, monitoring investigative activities, and assessing performance.

One recommendation was that the flow of cases should be regulated to ensure that resources are applied to the cases where they will yield the greatest return. A second recommendation was that investigations should be monitored to ensure that resources are used effectively. A third recommendation was that supervisors employ measures of productivity to determine how well investigative units are meeting their goals.

FINDINGS DIFFER FROM EARLIER RESEARCH The major difference between PERF's findings and those of earlier researchers concerns the role of detectives and the value of follow-up investigations. Earlier studies tended to emphasize the importance of patrol officers and preliminary investigations while downgrading the worth of follow-up investigations. The PERF study reaches the quite different conclusion that patrol officers and detectives contribute equally important work toward the solution of cases.

THE CRIME LABORATORY

To understand the role of crime laboratories, we must first understand the relationship of crime laboratories to the scientific community and to the functions of the criminal justice system (Swanson, Chamelin, and Territo 1988, p. 223).[13] There are two distinct activities in laboratory work: the gathering of evidence at the scene of the crime (usually done by evidence technicians or investigators) and the scientific analysis of evidence (which usually occurs in the laboratory). The effectiveness of the latter activity depends on the efficiency of the first operation.

The terms **forensic science** and **criminalistics** are often used interchangeably to denote the same function. Forensic science is that part of science applied to answering legal questions. Criminalistics is a branch of forensics that deals with the study of physical evidence related to a crime (Safersteen 1981, p. 1–3); a crime may be reconstructed from evidence obtained in such studies. Criminalistics is interdisciplinary in nature, drawing upon mathematics, physics, chemistry, biology, and anthropology. The case on page 188 illustrates the services offered by physical anthropologists.

The late Paul L. Kirk, a noted leader in the criminalistics movement in the United States, once remarked, "Criminalistics is an occupation that has all the responsibilities of medicine, the intricacy of the law, and the universality of science" (Kirk 1963, p. 238). One myth associated with the occupation is that its function is identification. In scientific terms, identification simply means the placing of an item in a class with other items. However, this definition is often totally insufficient for the criminalist, who must actually pinpoint the source and identity of evidence so that it can be distinguished from anything that is even remotely similar. The ability of the criminalist to do this depends largely on the resources and technology available. Because all of the needed technology does not exist at the present time, there are many things the criminalist cannot do to assist the investigator. For this reason, it is essential that the investigator have an understanding of the capabilities and limitations of crime laboratories (Federal Bureau of Investigation 1981, p. 2).

Capabilities, Limitations, and Use of a Crime Laboratory

The President's Commission on Law Enforcement and Administration of Justice notes that crime laboratories

Personality Reconstructed from Unidentified Remains

The badly decomposed remains of a human were found in an isolated wooded area adjacent to an industrial park. The crime scene investigation disclosed that the skeletal remains had been dragged a few feet from the location and it was suspected that this dislocation of the remains resulted from animal activities. An intensive search produced only a few strands of hair, a medium-sized sweater, and a few pieces of women's jewelry. The physical remains were taken to the medical examiner's office where the time of death was estimated to be three-to-six weeks prior to the discovery of the body. A subsequent review of missing-person reports for the pertinent time period produced no additional clues.

With the question of the victim's identify still unresolved, the remains were forwarded to the Curator of Physical Anthropology at the Smithsonian Institute in Washington, D.C. Based upon an examination of the skeletal remains, it was concluded that the skeleton was that of a Caucasian female approximately 17 to 22 years of age, who was of less than average stature. She had broader than average shoulders and hips, and was believed to be right-handed. Her head and face were long; the nose high bridged. Also noted was the subcartilage damage to the right hip joint, a condition which had probably caused occasional pain and suggested occupational stress. An irregularity of the left clavicle (collarbone) revealed a healed childhood fracture.

Local police officials then began a social and personality profile of the deceased based upon an analysis of the physical evidence obtained through the crime scene search and related photographs, medical examiner's reports, and reports from the FBI laboratory. In addition, aided by a physical anthropologist from the Smithsonian Institute, a police artist was able to sketch a photograph. The sketch was then published in a local newspaper and police officials immediately received calls from three different readers who all supplied the same name of a female whom they all knew. They advised that she resembled the sketch and they further advised that she had been missing for approximately four months.

A search of the local police files disclosed that the individual with this name had been previously photographed and fingerprinted. These prints were compared with the badly decomposed prints from one of the victim's fingers and a positive identification was made.

Further investigation by the police determined the victim was 20 years of age. Associates related that, when she was working as a nightclub dancer, she occasionally favored one leg. It was further determined that she had suffered a fracture of the left clavicle at age six.

D. G. Cherry and J. L. Angel, "Personality Reconstruction from Unidentified Remains," *FBI Law Enforcement Bulletin* 49 (1977): 12–15.

are the oldest and strongest link between science and technology and criminal justice (1967, p. 17). However, the growth of scientific criminal investigation in the American justice system has not been harmonious and has not been based upon a national consensus about the purpose and function of crime laboratories. Instead, most crime laboratories developed in response to a particular need in a community or region. The areas of scientific concentration in particular laboratories were, and still are, based on those needs, but have also been influenced by the interests and expertise of the people who operate them.

Not all crime laboratories have the same capabilities. Some can do much more than others, and some build up expertise in particular areas. The way in which some types of physical evidence is collected varies according to the test procedures a laboratory applies. Thus, it is important for police investigators to familiarize themselves with the capabilities of the crime laboratories in their jurisdictions, as well as with the requirements of the national forensic science laboratories. Regardless of variances in capability, all crime laboratories in the United States have a basic mission to reduce or eliminate uncertainty in the criminal investigation and to supply facts for supposition (Fox and Cunningham 1973, p. 1).

Today, there are over 300 laboratories in the United States that serve criminal justice agencies. Not all of

FIGURE 6.19
Left to right: Skull of murdered woman; police artist's sketch of victim based on information provided by a physical anthropologist; police photograph of victim found in local police files. Courtesy *FBI Law Enforcement Bulletin.*

these laboratories are publicly funded, and many have primary functions other than criminalistics. For example, private medical or hospital laboratories occasionally perform services for local police agencies.

Most crime laboratories do not have unlimited resources either in equipment, instrumentation, or human expertise to perform the vast array of scientific examinations normally identified with the FBI Crime Laboratory or the laboratories of major metropolitan law enforcement agencies. Specific laboratories may thus specialize and concentrate their analyses in one or two of the following areas: firearms identification, chemical analysis, drug analysis, photography, document examination, toxicology, microscopy, or biology.

The American Society of Crime Laboratory Directors was formed in 1974 in an attempt to solve problems caused by the varying specializations and concerns of laboratories and to settle disagreements over their purpose, function, and services. The organization provides a means for laboratory directors to discuss mutual problems and work out solutions that provide the qualitative and quantitative level of service needed to support law enforcement efforts (Field et al. 1977).

Measures of Effectiveness

The effectiveness of a crime laboratory can be measured in terms of three criteria: quality, proximity, and timeliness (Field et al. 1977). It is widely understood, if not accepted, that it is unrealistic administratively and budgetarily for most police departments in the United States to staff and maintain a crime laboratory. However, police agencies that desire and would utilize such a facility should not be denied the opportunity to have laboratory services at their disposal. Past experience indicates that police investigators rarely seek laboratory assistance when a facility is not convenient. In some cases, technicians or investigators must travel unreasonable distances to obtain laboratory services. Evidence submission decreases sharply as the distance from the crime scene to the laboratory increases (National Advisory Commission on Criminal Justice Standards and Goals 1973, p. 302). The solution to this problem lies in adequate planning on the state level to provide needed services to agencies throughout the state.

Studies indicate that a unified statewide system can best serve the needs of the law enforcement community by providing a parent, or core, laboratory on the state level that can deliver commonly needed laboratory services. In addition, a series of regional or satellite laboratories (strategically located) should be equipped to respond to less sophisticated analytical needs and to serve as a screening agency when more sophisticated analyses are required. Texas, for example, has a central laboratory under the auspices of the Texas Department of Public Safety in Austin, with field laboratories in Dal-

Drug Detection through Hair Analysis: Developing Future Capabilities

Since all drug testing methods have inherent limitations, the National Institute of Justice is interested in developing new screening capabilities that complement those already available. Urinalysis provides an objective and efficient large-scale tool for rapidly screening criminal justice populations for drug use. Its power to detect is limited, however, to drugs consumed within the previous 2 to 3 days. Analysis of a few strands of human hair, on the other hand, offers the potential to detect drugs absorbed by the growing hair over a much longer period.

Hair analysis promises a complementary type of drug detection for various criminal justice and forensic applications. At present, however, it is still in the developmental stage and may be a few years from wide-scale field applications.

An NIJ pilot study will explore whether present laboratory capabilities can be transferred into operational environments. The research will monitor a sample of Los Angeles parole and probation clients over a 1-year period for compliance with abstinence from serious drugs as a condition of release. The results obtained with radioimmunoassay of hair (RIAH) will be compared to those obtained from urine samples.

Monitoring Methods

Current drug detection methods primarily monitor two types of effects. The first are *short-term behavioral impacts* on speech, eye movements, and coordination of motion. These stem from the effects of drugs or alcohol on the brain and typically start within several seconds or minutes after the drug or alcohol is consumed. They are generally over within a few hours. Drunk driving and violent assaults are the most common instances where offenders are likely to be apprehended and tested while these effects are still present.

A second type of possible indicators of drug usage are the *short-term metabolic effects* evidenced in changes in the breath, blood, and urine. These effects begin within about a half-hour and end within 2 to 4 days for heroin or cocaine. Other drugs such as marijuana and PCP may be detectable in trace amounts for up to 2 to 3 weeks. But the body's processing eliminates so much within a few days that urine tests become impractical beyond that period.

A third set of possible diagnostic indicators exists. *Long-term organic effects* result when drug molecules are absorbed by growing body tissues such as hair and nails. Drugs become detectable within the hair about 3 to 4 days after consumption. Thus, hair analysis cannot reveal recent usage. But after 3–4 days, the portion of the growing hair nearest the scalp has entrapped detectable drug molecules that remain for the entire life of the hair shaft. As the hair grows, it records the individual's pattern of drug consumption much as a recorded tape retains a pattern of the signals imposed on it. Hair on the head grows about one-half inch per month. A 2–3 inch strand of hair, for example, would contain a record of the last 4–6 months of drug usage. Any body hair is potentially usable in tests, but hair on the head offers the advantages of relatively rapid growth and minimal intrusiveness.

The techniques of hair analysis are essentially the same as those of radioimmunoassay of urine and offer the same general detection sensitivity. Because hair analysis involves additional steps, however, it is inherently more time consuming and more costly per test. But detecting a probationer's abstention or drug usage over a prolonged period, for example, may require only periodic sampling—testing hair every month or two rather than conducting much more frequent urine tests. The result may be not only greater reliability but reduced expense for long-term monitoring.

Hair analysis capabilities could also minimize some concerns associated with urinalysis:

- Hair samples can be readily obtained from either sex in public without violating privacy and without the invasiveness related to blood or urine as monitoring mediums.
- Subjects cannot claim they are "unable" to provide a sample while being observed.

- subjects cannot attempt to avoid detection by "flushing" the system with large quantities of fluids to dilute urine samples or by "staying clean" for a few days or weeks before a scheduled test.

Hair analysis also means that additional samples can be acquired and tested. This retesting capability would be valuable to confirm a positive result, as is now done with positive urine samples. It also would permit acquisition of a totally new sample to verify or refute original test findings. This would overcome, in ways not now possible, the legal and operational challenges presented by offenders' claims of "That's not my sample," "Somebody must have put something in it," and "I haven't taken anything at any time."

For the long term, it appears that present laboratory-based hair analysis methods will be refined and made more amenable to larger scale applications. When this occurs, hair analysis will become a technique complementary to urinalysis, expanding the criminal justice system's ability to detect and monitor illicit drug abuse.

From *NIJ Reports*, SNI 202 (March/April 1987) p. 5.

las, Tyler, Houston, Corpus Christi, Midland, El Paso, Lubbock, and Waco. The Division of Consolidated Laboratory Services in Richmond, Virginia, serves as a parent laboratory with regional facilities located in Norfolk, Roanoke, and Fairfax. Other states using the regionalized concept are Alabama, California, Florida, Georgia, and Illinois. Regional laboratories should be located within fifty miles of any agencies they routinely serve (ibid., p. 302). Local laboratories that serve large cities can also serve as regional laboratories for nearby agencies.

Much of the current case load in crime laboratories consists of analyses of suspected or known samples of narcotics and dangerous drugs (Peterson 1974, p. 6). Even in areas where officers carry and are trained to use test kits available on the commercial market, laboratory analyses are conducted to provide conclusive evidence. Although many laboratory tests serve only to corroborate evidence, the analysis of suspected narcotics or dangerous drugs can be a key factor in successful prosecution—particularly in the early stages of judicial proceedings. Thus, the results of laboratory examinations must be made available to investigators as quickly as possible. The National Advisory Commission on Criminal Justice Standards and Goals (1973) recommends that laboratories operate round the clock when needed to handle existing case loads and that, whenever possible, analyses be completed within twenty-four hours after submission (ibid., p. 302). Of course, adequate budgeting and staffing of qualified personnel are required for such prompt action.

The FBI Crime Laboratory

Of the approximately 400 employees of the FBI Crime Laboratory, the majority possess specialized technical expertise acquired through education and training. The facilities of the laboratory are available without charge to all state, county, and municipal law enforcement agencies in the United States.

Only two provisions must be met concerning the submission of evidence to the FBI Crime Laboratory. First, the evidence must be connected with an official investigation of a criminal matter and the laboratory report must be used only for official purposes related to that investigation or to a subsequent criminal prosecution. Laboratory investigations and reports cannot be used in connection with civil proceedings. The second provision is that the FBI facility not be asked to make examinations if any evidence in the case has been or will be subjected to the same type of examination by another laboratory; this policy eliminates duplication of effort and ensures that evidence is received in its original condition, thus enabling laboratory personnel to interpret their findings properly and to present meaningful testimony and evidence in court. (The FBI will furnish—at no cost to local law enforcement agencies—the experts needed to testify in state or federal courts in connection with the results of their examinations.)

The FBI Crime Laboratory provides a comprehensive array of forensic services to law enforcement. Blood and other body fluids are identified and characterized in serology examinations; hairs, fibers, fabric, tape, rope, and wood are analyzed in microscopic examinations; poisons, paint, ink, tear gas, dyes, paper, blood, and urine are analyzed in chemical examinations; and soils and combinations of mineral substances (such as safe insulation, concrete, plaster, mortar, glass, ore, abrasives, gems, industrial dusts, and building materials) are analyzed in mineralogy examinations.

FIGURE 6.20
Examiners in the Serology Unit of the FBI Crime Laboratory prepare blood samples for analysis and record data. Courtesy of the FBI.

In addition, firearms examiners may be called upon to determine if firearms are operating properly or to determine gunpowder shot patterns. Bullets or cartridge cases may also be examined to assist in ascertaining the type of weapon used in a crime. The basic principles of firearms examination are also used to identify telltale marks left at crime scenes by punches, hammers, axes, pliers, screwdrivers, chisels, wrenches, and other objects. The explosives specialist can analyze fragments of explosives to determine the original composition and possible sources of raw materials.

The job of the FBI Metallurgy Unit is to restore obliterated or altered numbers on items such as firearms, sewing machines, watches, outboard motors, slot machines, automobiles, tools, and other metallic items. Tests can determine the possible causes of metal separation and can show if two or more pieces of metal are related in any way, or if production specifications for metals have been met.

Based on handwriting examinations by highly trained experts over many years, it is commonly agreed that no two individuals write exactly alike. Even though there can be some superficial resemblances in writing as a result of similar training, the complexity of writing is such that individual peculiarities and characteristics still appear. These characteristics can be detected by a documents expert.

The FBI Identification Division, an entity separate from the Laboratory Division, was established by an Act of Congress on 1 July 1924. The act combined the fingerprint records of the National Bureau of Criminal Identification and the Leavenworth Penitentiary—a total of 810,188 prints—into a file that serves as the national repository of criminal identification data. The file now contains over 173 million civil and criminal prints representing 64 million persons; and approximately 24,000 prints are received each day for processing. The Fugitive Program of the Identification Division goes through the file and places Wanted notices on the prints of people wanted by law enforcement agencies. Over 200,000 fugitive notices are now on file, with an average of 1,500 added each month.

FIGURE 6.21
An examiner in the FBI Microscopic Analysis Unit searches a pill box for hairs and fibers. A technician in the background removes debris from a garment. Courtesy of the FBI.

The Identification Division also maintains two important reference files in its Latent Fingerprint Section. One file contains known prints of persons who have committed certain types of major crimes—such as bank robbery, bank burglary, bank larceny, kidnapping, extortion, interstate transportation of obscene materials, major theft, or check fraud. The second file, the National Unidentified Latent File, contains unidentified latent prints taken from the scene of major crimes investigated by the FBI.

COMPUTERIZED FILES

An innovation in law enforcement that has been critical to the efficiency and effectiveness of police operations has been the development of computerized criminal information. Large and small police departments have come to rely heavily on computerized information that now includes such items as a persons "wanted status, whether a vehicle or other property has been stolen, prior criminal history on persons, and the like. Today, even officers making a routine traffic stop are aware of the types of information that the National Crime Information Center (NCIC) makes available and further coordinates with parallel state crime computer systems (Woodard 1986).[14]

The NCIC Network

The NCIC is a nationwide computerized information system established in 1967 to make an automated file of documented criminal justice information available to criminal justice agencies throughout the country. The NCIC computer equipment is located at FBI headquarters in Washington, D.C. Connecting terminals are located throughout the United States, Canada, Puerto Rico, and the U.S. Virgin Islands, in police departments, sheriff's offices, state police facilities, federal law enforcement agencies and other criminal justice agencies. The system provides virtually uninterrupted service twenty-four hours a day, seven days a week.

The FBI is responsible for the operation of the computer center located in Washington, D.C., including equipment, programming, and personnel costs. In addition, the costs of telecommunications lines and modems that link the NCIC computer to federal agencies and to central Control Terminal Agencies (CTAs) in each state are borne by the FBI. Telecommunications lines and equipment that link criminal justice agencies within each state to the state's control terminal are provided by the states and by participating criminal justice agencies. Each state's Control Terminal Agency is responsible for the observance of NCIC rules and policies by the CTA and all the agencies it services.

Local agencies that do not have an NCIC terminal (including many small rural agencies throughout the country) can access NCIC through an agency that does have terminal access. Dispatchers with terminal access can inquire for and respond by radio to law enforcement officers on the street. Some agencies utilize mobile terminals—vehicle-mounted terminals that enable officers to inquire directly from their units into NCIC and state data banks. To ensure prompt responses to users, NCIC and the state CTAs have established response-time standards that require responses to be returned within seconds.

Contents of the NCIC Files

The NCIC hot files contain identifying information about wanted and missing persons, stolen vehicles, and identifiable stolen property of several types. The information is entered into the system by the originating agency—the agency holding the arrest warrant, the missing person report, or the theft report. Originating agencies are primarily responsible for the validity, timeliness, accuracy, and completeness of the data they enter. The FBI and the Control Terminal Agencies have established policies and implemented procedures that are designed to help maintain the integrity and quality of the NCIC system records.

Types of files in the NCIC system include wanted persons, missing persons, stolen vehicles, stolen license plates, stolen guns, stolen boats, stolen securities, stolen articles, and unidentified persons (see Table 6.5).

NCIC Quality Control Procedures

Since the information contained in the hot files is extremely sensitive, there is good reason to take care to ensure that the records are accurate, complete, and timely. This is important both from the standpoint of law enforcement officials, who must rely upon the information in making critical decisions affecting their safety and the rights of citizens with whom they deal, and from the point of view of persons whose names and identifying data are contained in the records and who may be subjected to detention or arrest as a result of reliance upon the information. In an effort to promote record quality and integrity, NCIC system rules include detailed procedures designed to ensure that information entered into the files is accurate and complete and that records are

TABLE 6.5
NCIC Daily Hot Files Inquiries

	Average Daily Hot Files Inquires 403,230*	
File	**No. Inquiries**	**Percentage**
Wanted and Missing Persons	216,453	53.68
Stolen Vehicles and License Plates	167,435	41.52
Stolen Articles	9,045	2.24
Stolen Guns	8,688	2.15
Stolen Boats	1,208	.30
Stolen Securities	355	<.10
Unidentified Persons	46	<.10

*September 1985

Source: Federal Bureau of Investigation

Adapted from Paul L. Woodard, *Criminal Justice "Hot" Files* (Washington, D.C.: U.S. Government Printing Office, November 1986), p. 20.

corrected when found to be inaccurate and are removed from the system when they are no longer valid. These procedures are reflected both in the day-to-day use of the system for entering records and making inquiries, as well as in a systematic quality control program implemented by NCIC personnel and the state control terminal operators.

System-Use Procedures

System-use procedures, which are incorporated in the rules governing use of the NCIC system, are intended to ensure that user agencies enter only accurate, complete, and timely information; that inquiring agencies confirm the accuracy and validity of information received from the system (by contacting the entering agency) before relying upon it; that records are removed from the system when wanted or missing persons have been located or when stolen vehicles or property have been recovered; and that records are canceled when they are no longer valid, such as when warrants are served or withdrawn.

SUMMARY

In this chapter we departed somewhat from the traditional approach taken in most introductory books in addressing the topic of police operations. Rather than taking a broad-brush approach and briefly touching on many facets of police operations, we instead focused primarily on four areas: the patrol bureau, traffic bureau, detective bureau, and crime laboratory. We selected these areas because they are the ones that are frequently of greatest interest to the general public, the

BJS Warns of Sloppy Use of NCIC 'Hot Files' by Police

Computerized "hot files" on missing persons and stolen vehicles, maintained by the FBI's National Crime Information Center (NCIC), have led to wrongful arrests and property seizures through sloppy handling, according to a study by the Bureau of Justice Statistics.

The NCIC, which as of last August held approximately 8 million records of wanted or missing persons and stolen property, was queried over 400,000 times a day by agencies in both the U.S. and Canada as of September 1985.

The files included records on more than 2 million stolen or recovered guns, 1.4 million stolen articles, 1.2 million stolen vehicles, 616,000 stolen license plates, 249,000 wanted persons, 53,000 missing persons (mostly juveniles), 26,000 stolen boats, 1,300 unidentified persons and 253 Canadian warrants, according to the BJS report.

The files also contain information such as whether an individual is wanted for a criminal offense and whether they may be armed and dangerous, making the records invaluable to the street officer.

However, the report warned that even a small percentage of inaccuracy in maintaining the files "may result in the potential for thousands of

inaccurate hits each year and possibly a large number of wrongful arrests and wrongful seizures of vehicles and other property."

While no data have been collected on the number of wrongful actions, research showed over a dozen recent court cases involving issues of personal liability or challenges to the admissibility of evidence seized in connection with arrests based on faulty NCIC information or state system responses.

Most states, the report said, should institute quality controls over the files to avert such problems. While most states have enacted "specific authority for a designated state agency to maintain a statewide criminal history record system," said the study, only a small number have statutory provisions designed to insure the quality of information in those files.

An important step toward assuring that information in the files is current would be to enact a provision which would require the timely cancellation of wanted person reports and stolen vehicle records when they are no longer valid, so that improper information is not entered or continued in the NCIC, said the report.

Reprinted with permission from *Law Enforcement News*, a publication of John Jay College of Criminal Justice. *Law Enforcement News* 4/28/87 pp. 3, 7.

ones with which most citizens are likely to have contact, and the ones for which the most stereotypes and misinformation exist.

The largest of the police operations bureaus and the one to which almost all new police officers are assigned is the patrol bureau. It forms the initial base upon which all future police experiences are built. When first assigned to the patrol bureau, the rookie officer typically works under the direct tutelage of a senior officer before being permitted to work alone. The patrol bureau, for better or for worse, regularly serves as a manpower pool for the other more specialized and prestigious assignments. The residual effect of this practice is a disproportionate number of patrol officers who are either relatively inexperienced or are not considered to be among the best and the brightest officers. This tendency is reinforced by the desire of many patrol officers to be transferred to other bureaus because of the difficulties associated with the environment of the patrol officer's work and the clientele they serve. We suggested the creation of a more varied gradation of classifications within the patrol officer ranks. This could reduce the need to either seek transfer or strive for a supervisory position as the sole route upward. Patrol officers might be content to remain in the patrol ranks if it offered them greater status and financial rewards.

The use of team policing in the patrol bureau was begun as a way to reduce the isolation of the police from the community and to induce the support of citizens in their efforts to reduce crime. The results of the Kansas City Patrol Experiment raised serious questions about the value of marked patrol units in reducing crime and their value in reducing the public's fear of crime. Many patrol administrators have taken the information from the Kansas City Patrol Experiment and developed innovative approaches such as directed patrol in order to better meet public needs and to make good use of patrol resources.

We hope our discussion of the traffic bureau provided the reader with greater understanding about the specific functions performed by this bureau and the relationship between enforcement, education, engineering, and traffic accidents. Traffic officers have an obligation to engage in the selective enforcement of traffic violations and not to write tickets arbitrarily just to meet some quota or to keep their sergeant happy.

The third section of this chapter discussed the detective bureau. What detectives do in their attempts to solve crimes is a crucially important part of policing. Of the three bureaus discussed, this one is surrounded by the most mystique and the most stereotypes. We have sought to convey a realistic impression of the methods that are employed in the selection, training, and supervision of detectives.

The most comprehensive study ever undertaken to analyze the day-to-day effectiveness and activities of detectives was done by the Rand Corporation in 1973. Basically, the study recommended closer post-arrest cooperation between the police and prosecutor's office, giving patrol officers greater responsibility in conducting preliminary investigations, improving the processing of latent fingerprints, improving the system to facilitate fingerprint searches, and, lastly, when a follow-up investigation is deemed justifiable, differentiating between those that need only clerical processing and those which need high level investigation or legal skills. The Police Executive Research Forum (PERF) conducted additional research on preliminary and follow-up investigations in the 1980s. The information obtained in PERF's study

differed somewhat from earlier findings and is now being used by those who manage criminal investigations in police departments.

In the final portion of this chapter we discussed the crime laboratory and examined some of the major functions it can perform. There is a great deal of interest among criminal justice students and the public about the laboratory component of police work. Criminal investigations, like almost every other facet of our lives, have been beneficially affected by the technological explosion in the past twenty years.

We also included an overview of computerized criminal history information, specifically, the use of the National Crime Information Center (NCIC) by law enforcement.

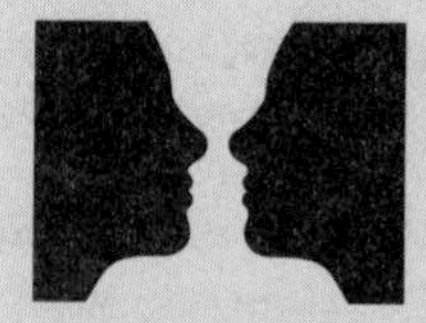

ISSUE PAPER

DOMESTIC TERRORISM IN THE 1980's

By John W. Harris, Jr., M.A. FBI Law Enforcement Bulletin

The United Freedom Front . . . the Armed Forces of the National Liberation . . . the Armed Resistance Unit . . . the EPB-Macheteros. These are some of the names that have become synonymous with terrorist activity in the United States and Puerto Rico during the 1980's. These groups are domestic; they are not funded, directed, controlled, or supported by foreign sources. They, and other groups of similar philosophies and ideologies, are responsible for more than 125 terrorist incidents and numerous other terrorist-related acts since 1980. Bombings, armed robberies, murders, and arsons are some of the criminal acts that have been attributed to them.

The 1980's followed 2 turbulent decades when domestic terrorist and extremist political activity in the United States reached levels not previously recorded in American history. The 1960's, for example, were dominated by violence generated by racial hatred, campus unrest, and urban disorders. The 1970's were dominated by antiwar and anti-imperialist attitudes which resulted in a wave of terrorist bombings. Many of the issues and values that impacted on these times changed little and once again have become factors in the 1980's. Although the majority of the individuals responsible for the post-1980 terrorism were not directly responsible for the violence of the 1960's and 1970's, many can trace either their group's beginnings or their own individual involvement in a movement to this period.

Perspectives

At the beginning of the 1980's there was a certain attitude among law enforcement about the threat of terrorism in the United States. This was based upon the most recent activity, or lack of activity, by the various domestic terrorist factions.

The early-to-mid-1970's were marked by the bombing attacks by such leftist groups as the Weathermen or Weather Underground Organization and the New World Liberation Front. By the end of the decade, however, these activities had become sporadic at best (six terrorist incidents in 1978, one in 1979, and none in 1980). Most of those responsible for the terrorism from these elements were either in custody or they had disappeared and their locations and activities were unknown. Once regarded as a most serious domestic security threat, the "white left," because of a lack of identifiable terrorist activity, was considered to have all but ceased to exist as a problem by 1980. This same opinion was held of black and right-wing elements, neither of which was known to have been actively engaged in terrorist activities during the latter part of the 1970's and into 1980.

In contrast, violence-prone, pro-independence elements of the Puerto Rican independence movement were considered the most viable domestic security threat at the beginning of the 1980's. Approximately 100 terrorist incidents were attributed to Puerto Rican elements in the United States and Puerto Rico between 1977 and 1979, and there were 12 such incidents in 1980. Also considered a threat, but less so than the Puerto Ricans, were the Jewish terrorists, who were responsible for 16 terrorist incidents in 1978 and one in 1979.

But appearances are not always as they seem. The fact is that all factions—right and left, black and white—were very much active during the late 1970's and into the 1980's, even though not all were involved in identifiable terrorist activities such as bombings. Left-wing elements, for example, had begun to reorganize. Sometimes black and white extremists worked together committing robberies. In addition, some right-wing groups that became of interest to law enforcement during the 1980's were organized during the late 1970's.

It was not until late 1981, however, that law enforcement began to refocus its thinking in domestic terrorism because of one event. On October 20, 1981, a Brinks Armored Car Service truck was robbed of more than $1.5 million at a bank in Nanuet, NY. A Brinks guard was killed and another wounded during the robbery. Participants in this crime included black males, who actually committed the robbery, and white males and females, who acted in support roles. The suspects fled the scene in a van but abandoned it nearby for a U-Haul truck. Other suspects accompanied the robbers in a tan Honda automobile.

Police stopped the truck near the entrance to the New York State Thruway in Nyack, NY, to question the driver. Several black males jumped from the back of the truck firing automatic weapons; two police officers were killed and another was wounded. One suspect who had been in the cab of the U-Haul, a white female, was arrested at the scene. Other suspects escaped on foot or in commandeered vehicles.

The Honda and another car sped away from the shooting scene and were pursued by police. During the chase, the Honda crashed and its occupants, a black male, a white male, and a white female, were arrested. The other car was later found abandoned.

The individuals arrested on October 20th were identified as Kathy Boudin (at Nyack), and Judith Clark, David Gilbert, and Samuel Brown (in the Honda). Another suspect, Samuel Smith, was killed in a gun battle with New York City Police Department officers 3 days later, and a second suspect, Nathaniel Burns, was arrested. Several safehouses in the New York City metropolitan area were searched as a result of leads generated by these arrests. Weapons, bombing components, radical literature, and other items were recovered at some of these. Others were implicated in the robbery, including Mutulu Shakur, Marilyn Jean Buck, Donald Weems, Sylvia Baraldini, and Susan Rosenberg, among others.

This event changed many opinions in the law enforcement community toward leftist terrorist activity. It showed that many of the radicals from the 1970's, who had disappeared and were thought to no longer be involved in the "movement" were, in fact, still very much active. It also showed that black and white elements were cooperating. Members or associates of earlier groups, such as the Weather Underground, the Black Liberation Army, and the Black Panther Party, and contemporary groups, such as the May 19th Communist Organization and the Republic of New Afrika, were associated with the events of October 20, 1981. Many of the individuals associated with the Brinks robbery were also connected to other armed robberies in the New York City metropolitan area and elsewhere.

White Leftists

During the 1980's, white leftist terrorism again became a factor after several years of relative inactivity. Since 1981, leftist terrorists have been responsible for 21 bombings or attempted bombings. The most active period was during 1983 and 1984 when white leftists claimed 16 of the 26 terrorist acts committed in the United States.

The radical left bases much of its philosophy on the teachings of such historical revolutionaries as Karl Marx, Lenin, and Chairman Mao. They perceive that many ills exist in the United States, both socially and politically, which they blame on the U.S. Government. They also view the Government as being capitalist, militaristic, and imperialistic.

The solution, according to the radicals, is to destroy the cause of these problems—the system—by any means possible. A violent popular uprising, a revolution, must occur. They realize, however, that they cannot accomplish this alone. The New Left Movement advocates violent revolution, as opposed to nonviolent change by working within the system. To this end, the radicals, who often view themselves as urban guerrillas, have instituted an armed campaign against the state. These philosophies are little different from those espoused by the leftist groups of the 1960's and 1970's.

These radicals have chosen symbolic targets for their attacks—military facilities, corporate establishments, the U.S. Capitol Building. Through communiques, New Left groups have claimed credit for attacks, as well as provided reasons for them, thus delivering a message to the American people: Opposition to South African apartheid policies and to American corporate and governmental support of that regime, opposition to American military presence in Latin America, opposition to American corporate exploitation in Southern Africa and other parts of the world, etc. There is little difference between these demands and those of the 1970's. The reasons for the attacks have basically remained the same; only the names and places have changed.

The New Left terrorist organization most active during the 1980's was the United Freedom Front (UFF). This group, which was organized in early 1981, claimed responsibility for 10 bombings and 1 attempted bombing between December 1982, and September 1984. The UFF was comprised of four white males and three white females. A black male was also a member of the group, prior to the onset of its bombing campaign. All of the UFF members had ties to radical, movements of the 1960's and 1970's. Several members were also engaged in armed attacks against the system during the 1970's.

In addition to the bombings, UFF members were implicated in and/or convicted of other criminal acts, in-

cluding the murder of a New Jersey State policeman in December 1981, and the attempted murders of two Massachusetts State policemen in February 1982. The group also reportedly committed armed bank robberies from Connecticut to Virginia to sustain themselves. They lived under a variety of false identities and usually resided in rural areas, moving regularly. Prior to a criminal act—a bombing or a robbery—group members conducted lengthy and extensive surveillances of the target and surrounding areas. There are no indications that the UFF was connected to other leftist terrorist or extremist groups, except through ideology.

Following intense investigation, five of the UFF members were located and arrested in the Cleveland, OH, area during November 1984. The remaining two members were arrested in Norfolk, VA, during April 1985. Automatic shoulder weapons, handguns, bombing components, and communiques were found in the group's safehouses. Trials have been held in New York and Massachusetts and convictions have been handed down. Other trials are anticipated in the future.

In addition to the UFF, other New Left groups were actively engaged in bombings between January 1983, and February 1985. These included the Red Guerrilla Resistance (four bombings), the Armed Resistance Unit (three bombings), and the Revolutionary Fighting Group (one bombing). Although the identities of all group members are not known, all three groups may be one and the same.

Several other New Left organizations active during the 1980's are the Prairie Fire Organizing Committee (PFOC) and the May 19th Communist Organization (M19CO). The history of these groups dates back into the 1970's to the Weather Underground Organization (WUO), which broke apart in 1976 because of internal dissension. Some former WUO members wanted to continue the struggle alone and adopted the PFOC name, which had been the name of an aboveground WUO support organization. These individuals resided principally on the west coast. Other former WUO members wanted to interact with other radical elements in the struggle and adopted the M19CP name. These individuals were generally located on the east coast. Neither group was more radical than the other, as both were still deeply committed to the cause. Each had aboveground members whose activities generally were nonviolent, and underground members whose identities and activities were not known to law enforcement. Other former Weathermen, including Bernardine Dohrn, Kathy Wilkerson, and Bill Ayers, resurfaced to face charges.

At the beginning of the 1980's, neither the M19CO nor PFOC were known to be involved in criminal activities, but it soon became apparent that some reputed members were involved in criminal conduct. Susan Rosenberg, for example, was a participant in the October 20, 1981, Brinks robbery, during which she and her associates acted in a support role. A fugitive, she and M19CO member Timothy Blunk were arrested in New Jersey during November 1984, in possession of weapons and explosives. Although the explosives were linked to dynamite used by a Puerto Rican group in bombings during December 1982, an exact connection between the two factions has not been determined. Blunk and Rosenberg were convicted on charges of violating Federal weapons statutes during May 1985.

Also during May 1985, M19CO associates Marilyn Buck, Linda Evans, and Laura Whitehorn were arrested in New York City and Baltimore, MD. Materials seized at a safehouse in Baltimore included bombing components, weapons, false identifications, and a target list and surveillance notes for possible bombings.

Neither the M19CO nor the PFOC has claimed credit for a terrorist act. During the 1980's, members of these groups have participated in legal political activities, such as attending rallies and demonstrations and supporting captured leftist terrorists.

Puerto Rican Leftists

The actions of Puerto Rican terrorists revolve around attempts to gain independence for Puerto Rico through violence. They consider their activities to be acts of war, and when captured, they consider themselves to be prisoners of war.

The wave of attacks by Puerto Rican groups during the 1970's has carried over into the 1980's. Since 1980, Puerto Rican terrorists in the United States and Puerto Rico have been responsible for more than 70 terrorist incidents. Included in these are bombings, assassinations, armed robberies, and rocket attacks. Targets have been military facilities and personnel (especially in Puerto Rico), U.S. Government facilities, and corporate interests. Seventeen of these attacks occurred in the continental United States.

The Puerto Rican group most active in the continental United States during the 1980's has been the Armed Forces of the National Liberation, or FALN. Since 1974,

this group has been responsible for more than 100 terrorist attacks in the United States; however, the group has claimed only 10 bombings since 1980. All of these occurred in 1982, when the last FALN-claimed acts occurred. The FALN was also responsible for takeovers at campaign offices of former President Jimmy Carter and Vice President George Bush during March 1980.

Eleven FALN members were arrested in Evanston, IL, during April 1980, planning an armored truck robbery. An FALN leader, Oscar Lopez, was arrested in Glenview, IL, during May 1981. He was subsequently convicted of seditious conspiracy, armed robbery, and weapons violations. Four other FALN members were arrested during June 1983, in connection with a plan to free Oscar Lopez from jail. Following these arrests, several FALN safehouses were located and searched. Dynamite, weapons, bombing materials, and bulletproof vests were seized. A second plot to free Lopez during 1985 was interdicted and resulted in indictments of several persons, including Donna Jean Willmott and Claude Marks, who are Top Ten fugitives.

Another Puerto Rican organization that has been active in the United States during the 1980's is the National Liberation Movement, or MLN. This is an aboveground support group for the FALN. MLN members have been involved in legitimate political activities, such as staging and attending pro-independence Puerto Rican rallies and demonstrations and showing support for jailed FALN members. They have not been involved in known terrorist related activities.

Terrorist groups in Puerto Rico, in contrast, have been far more active committing violent acts than have those in the continental United States. Between 1968 and 1978, for example, slightly more than 200 attacks occurred in Puerto Rico. Since 1980, 56 of the more than 70 terrorist acts committed by Puerto Rican groups occurred in Puerto Rico, approximately 75 percent of the total number of Puerto Rican terrorist incidents since 1980.

Of these 56 terrorist acts committed in Puerto Rico since 1980, nearly 40 have been credited to two groups—the EPB-Macheteros and the Organization of Volunteers for the Puerto Rican Revolution (OVRP). Both of these groups emerged during 1978, when they claimed joint credit for a theft of explosives from a public works warehouse in Puerto Rico.

Most of the attacks attributed to the Macheteros and the OVRP were conducted alone; however, several acts were committed together or with other groups. A majority of the attacks were bombings or attempted bombings; others included shootings, robberies, and two light antitank weapon (LAW rocket) attacks. While Puerto Rican interests have been targeted in most of these incidents, U.S. Government facilities and military facilities and personnel have been attacked with greater frequency since 1983.

Possibly the most spectacular attack to occur in Puerto Rico during the 1980's took place on January 12, 1981. The EPB-Macheteros destroyed nine A-7D Corsair Attack jet fighters at the Puerto Rican Air National Guard base in San Juan. Damage was estimated at approximately $50 million. The Macheteros claimed credit for the attack in a communique, and they sent a video tape, showing members constructing the explosive devices, to a local television station.

Two other attacks by the Macheteros used a light antitank weapon. During October 1983, the group claimed credit for an attack against the Federal building in Puerto Rico, in support of the people of Grenada. During January 1985, the Macheteros and the OVRP claimed joint credit for a similar attack against the U.S. courthouse in Old San Juan.

During September 1983, a $7.2 million robbery occurred at the Wells Fargo terminal in West Hartford, CT. An employee at the terminal, Victor Gerena, eluded capture and reportedly was granted asylum in Cuba. Gerena is currently a Top Ten fugitive. Nearly 2 years later, during August 1985, 17 persons were indicted for their role in the robbery. All were leaders or members of the Macheteros or they were associated with the group in some other way. On August 30, 1985, 14 of those indicted were arrested in Puerto Rico, Mexico, Massachusetts, and Texas; 18 Macheteros safehouses in Puerto Rico were also raided and 37 searches were conducted of houses, automobiles, etc. Numerous documents, weapons, and bombing paraphernalia were found.

Until the August arrests, the EPB-Macheteros was considered the most significant terrorist threat in Puerto Rico. The group's ability to operate was severely disrupted because of the arrests, but it was not completely broken. The group has been credited with eight terrorist attacks in 1986. All but one was jointly claimed with the OVRP and the Armed Forces of National Revolution (FARP); however, the Macheteros' name may have been included in these as a statement of solidarity. These attacks occurred on October 28, 1986, at various military installations and facilities throughout Puerto Rico.

Two bombs detonated and three other live devices were rendered safe. Five additional devices had functioned but did not detonate, due to inadequate main charges. The Macheteros initially claimed credit for the attacks in a telephone call and provided instructions to locate a communique which attributed the attacks to the FARP/OVRP/Macheteros. On November 4, 1986, the Macheteros also provided authorities with the location of a device that was found and rendered safe.

Because the OVRP jointly claimed credit for the October 28th attacks, for two other attacks in 1986, for two attacks in 1985 (one jointly claimed with the Macheteros), and for five attacks during December 1984, this group is currently considered the most significant terrorist threat in Puerto Rico.

Black Groups

There have been three terrorist incidents attributed to domestic black groups in the United States during the 1980's. All of these 1983 acts were the result of a religious rivalry. In addition, at least one other terrorist incident was prevented by arrests in 1984, and a possible terrorist plot was prevented during August 1986. Some black groups, however, have been involved in criminal activities, such as murder and armed robbery.

The three terrorist incidents were attributed to the group Fuqra, a black Islamic religious sect headquartered in Detroit, MI. In order to further its religious goals, Fuqra seeks to purify Islam by eliminating rival religious sects, such as the Ahmaddiya Movement in Islam (AMI). During August 1983, several terrorist acts occurred against the AMI in Detroit: The AMI secretary was killed; firebombs were thrown at the home of the AMI treasurer but the bombs did not ignite; and an AMI temple was burned. Fuqra was implicated in these attacks because the bodies of the arsonists, Fuqra members, were found at the temple. They had become trapped setting the blaze and died. The gun used to kill the AMI secretary was found on one of the bodies.

In addition, a possible terrorist plot involving a black street gang was prevented in August 1986, when several members of the street gang, the El Rukns, were arrested in Chicago. Group members had in their possession numerous weapons, including an inert light antitank weapon that had been sold to them during an undercover operation. This group, which has loose ties to black Islam, is a violent criminal organization involved in narcotics trafficking and other illegal enterprises. Some group members allegedly have met with operatives of the Libyan Government. The El Rukns apparently were seeking to commit a terrorist act in return for money. No act, however, has yet occurred.

Black religious cult-type groups, such as the Yahweh Church or Black Hebrews, have also been active in criminal activity during the 1980's. The Yahweh Church is a national organization headquartered in Miami, FL. Its leader is Hulon Mitchell, Jr., also known as "God" and "Moses Israel." This is a violent, black supremacist organization that claims that whites are devils and that a race war will occur in the near future. The group advocates the violent elimination of all forms of government in the United States, as well as white society. Mitchell has stated that all who speak out or act against the church should be beheaded.

Much of the activity of the group is directed toward fundraising, distributing propaganda, etc. Some members, however, have reportedly been involved in murders, beatings, and arson attacks. Arrests have been made in connection with some of these crimes.

In contrast are other black groups which are politically oriented, such as the Republic of New Afrika (RNA). The RNA calls for the creation of an independent black nation out of Alabama, Georgia, Louisiana, Mississippi, and South Carolina. The group itself is set up as a shadow government with a president, a vice president, a minister of defense, a minister of justice, etc. Another RNA goal is that the U.S. Government pay all black citizens $10,000 for their ancestors' slave labor. The RNA publicly espouses the peaceful attainment of these goals; however, RNA leaders also publicly advocate support of revolutionary groups which preach violence. There have been no terrorist acts claimed by the RNA.

A militant group with views similar to those of the RNA is the New Afrikan Freedom Fighters. During October 1984, nine persons associated with this group were arrested in New York City. They had been planning to blow up police cars and then kill police officers as they ran out of a nearby police station. This was to be a diversion to effect the escape of Nathaniel Burns, a participant in the October 1981, Brinks robbery. Searches of their safehouses yielded weapons, ammunition, and explosives. During August 1985, eight of the nine were convicted of various firearms violations and other charges.

Another militant faction with views similar to the RNA is the New Afrikan People's Organization (NAPO). The stated objective of this group is to win independence

for New Afrika and establish a socialist republic. This, according to the organization, can be accomplished through a people's war. Several RNA leaders and key members are NAPO national leaders.

Some members and/or associates of black leftist groups were involved in the October 1981, Brinks robbery. Marilyn Jean Buck, for example, the only white Black Liberation Army member, was a participant. Chokwe Lumumba, the RNA minister of justice, has been the defense attorney for several defendants in the Brinks robbery case. Jeral Wayne Williams, also known as Mutulu Shakur, who reportedly directed the robbery, was an RNA member. An FBI Top Ten fugitive, Shakur was captured during February 1986. Another RNA member, Cheri Dalton, is currently a fugitive wanted in connection with the October 1981, robbery.

Right Wing

Right-wing terrorism has become an area of focus for law enforcement during the 1980's. Although belief in the white supremacist and antigovernment views of the far right is not illegal, the commission of violent acts to further these views is criminal. These acts have included bombings, armed robberies, assaults, and murder. Much of the rhetoric of the extreme right is particularly volatile and corrosive and is a motivating factor in this violence.

Unlike leftist terrorists, the terrorists of the far right do not leave communiques to claim credit or provide explanations. Therefore, an act that initially appears to be criminal may, in fact, be terrorist related. Although numerous violent acts have been committed by right extremists, the total number of terrorist incidents directly attributed to this faction has been few—two shootings (1981 and 1983) and four bombings and an attempted bombing (1986).

A basic belief of many right-wing extremists is the superiority of the white race. According to this view, blacks, other nonwhites, and Jews are inferior racially, mentally, physically, and spiritually. Much of this is based upon a racist, anti-Semitic religion, the Christian Identity Movement. This religion teaches that the white race is God's chosen race and that whites, not Jews, are the true descendants of Israel. Jews, instead, are of Satan's bloodline. According to Identity doctrine, the Bible is a history and guidebook of the white race that began with Adam. The appearance of the white race on earth (some 7,400 years ago) postdated black, Asiatic, and all other races.

One of the leaders of this philosophy is the Rev. Richard Butler of the Aryan Nations, Church of Jesus Christ Christian, which is headquartered near Hayden Lake, ID. His sermons, Identity propaganda, and other white hate and neo-Nazi literature and materials are distributed nationally from Hayden Lake by members of the group. Aryan Nations members maintain contacts with other far right groups. Symbols, such as double lightning bolts and swastikas, which were used by Hitler's Nazi regime, are often worn by members of the Aryan Nations and other right-wing neo-Nazi extremist groups.

Many followers of the Identity religion live on compounds in isolated areas. Bible readings are conducted and religious instructions are held. Paramilitary and survivalist training also occurs, however, and weapons and foodstuffs are often stored in preparation for the racial and social upheavals that, according to Identify doctrine, will precede the Second Coming of Christ. Some of the groups that are located on compounds include the Aryan Nations in Idaho; the Covenant, the Sword, the Arm of the Lord in Arkansas; and Elohim City in Oklahoma. Another group, the National Alliance, a less religious-oriented organization than the others, is also located on a compound in West Virginia. A several-day Aryan Nations Congress has been held at the Aryan Nations compound for all but one of the past several years. It is attended by members of a number of far right groups.

In addition to racist views, many right-wing groups also espouse antigovernment sentiments. They refer to the Government as the Zionist Occupation Government or ZOG because they view it as being controlled by Jewish interests. Members of these groups engage in paramilitary and survivalist training, believing that the United States is headed toward a moral or economic collapse or a communist takeover.

The most violent far right group active during the 1980's has been the Order, an offshoot of the Aryan Nations. Another name for the group is Bruders Schweigen or Silent Brotherhood. This group was founded by Robert Mathews, who was an Aryan Nations member. Order members were also members of other right-wing organizations and had become disenchanted with their respective groups' lack of action to further the cause. Among the groups represented in the Order were the National Alliance; various chapters of the Ku Klux Klan; and the Covenant, the Sword, the Arm of the Lord.

The Order was loosely based on a book, *The Turner Diaries,* written by National Alliance leader William Pierce under the pseudonym Andrew Macdonald. It is a futuristic account of racial warfare in the United States. In the book, an elite and clandestine force, the Order, spearheads efforts to destroy the U.S. Government to replace it with one based on white supremacy.

Members of the Order have been involved in numerous criminal activities since 1983, mostly in the northwestern United States. Included among these acts are counterfeiting; armed robberies with proceeds totaling more than $4 million; assaults on Federal officers; bombings, including those against a Jewish synagogue and a Catholic priest; and the murders of a suspected informant, a Missouri State patrol officer, and a Denver, CO, talk show host.

Between October 1984, and March 1986, 38 members of the Order were arrested. On December 7, 1984, Robert Mathews was killed on Whidbey Island, WA, resisting arrest. Shoulder weapons, handguns, hand grenades and other explosives, money, ammunition, and possible target lists were recovered at various safehouses and other locations.

Another group that was involved in criminal activity is the Covenant, the Sword, the Arm of the Lord (CSA). Beginning in 1980, some CSA members were involved in bombings, arsons, robberies, and the murder of a black Arkansas State policeman. During April 1985, the CSA compound was raided by Federal authorities. Military surplus equipment, shoulder weapons, a heavy machine gun, money, handguns, and grenades and other explosives were found in a search of the compound. A total of five persons were arrested, including four Order members, two of whom were fugitives, and CSA leader James Ellison. Other CSA members were arrested at a later time. Of the CSA and Order members arrested, all either pled guilty to charges or were convicted in Federal or State courts. As a result, the threat posed by these two groups has significantly decreased.

Another far right-wing faction of interest to law enforcement during the 1980's are the tax protest and antigovernment groups. Organizations such as the Sheriff's Posse Comitatus (SPC) and Arizona Patriots view Federal and/or State authority with suspicion. They espouse parochial as opposed to national interests, and they desire that there be as little government involvement as possible in their lives. They advocate nonpayment of taxes and regard Federal and State laws as unconstitutional. The SPC, for example, views the local sheriff as the only legitimate law enforcement authority and the only legal elected authority, and it regards the justice of the peace as the highest court in the country.

The SPC, however, is the only tax protest group to which a terrorist incident has been attributed. This occurred during February 1983, in North Dakota when SPC members fired upon authorities attempting to arrest Gordon Kahl, an SPC leader, for tax evasion. A U.S. marshal and a deputy U.S. marshal were killed. Kahl himself was killed during June 1983, by authorities trying to arrest him in Arkansas. A county sheriff was also killed at this time. Other SPC members have been arrested for weapons violations and assault. This group, which has autonomous chapters or adherents throughout the country, continues to be a threat because of its penchant for violence.

A favorite target of these antigovernment groups is the Internal Revenue Service (IRS). The leader and several members of the group Committee of States were arrested during October 1986, in Arizona, California, and Nevada by IRS agents for threats made against IRS personnel. On December 15, 1986, eight members/associates of the Arizona Patriots, including its leader, were arrested in connection with a proposed armored truck robbery and other offenses.

Other white supremacist groups active during the 1980's include the White Patriot Party, the National Alliance, the National Socialist White People's Party, the Christian Patriots Defense League, the Ku Klux Klan, and others. These groups hold many of the same racist and antigovernment values as the Posse Comitatus groups and the Aryan Nations, including the desire to create a separate nation out of five Northwestern States. They are engaged largely in demonstrating and distributing propaganda and they participate in paramilitary and survivalist training. Members, however, have been known to engage in destroying property and making threats against blacks, Jews, and others they regard as inferior. The leader of the North Carolina-based White Patriot Party, Frazier Glenn Miller, Jr., and his second-in-command were convicted of criminal contempt charges in July 1986, for engaging in paramilitary training. The WPP was dissolved but some members reformed it as the Southern National Front.

A number of arrests involving right-wing extremists occurred in the spring of 1987. During April, Federal indictments were returned against Richard Butler of the Aryan Nations, Robert Milos of the Mountain Church

of Michigan, and 13 others, representing such organizations as the Order, the SPC; various factions of the Ku Klux Klan, and the CSA. Among the charges in the indictments were seditious conspiracy, interstate transportation of stolen money, and attempted murder of a Federal official. Seven of the individuals listed in the indictments were already in prison on other charges; seven others, including Butler and Miles, were arrested on April 24, 1987; and one other individual, Louis Beam, remains at large, a Top Ten fugitive.

In addition to these arrests, on April 15, 1987, Glenn Miller, formerly of the WPP, mailed copies of a letter than he had written to other right-wing extremists. In this letter, he declared war on ZOG and stated that he had gone underground. On April 30, 1987, Miller and three others were arrested in Ozark, MO; Miller was charged with violating terms of his parole. Among the materials recovered were weapons, including rifles, shotguns, and crossbows; pipebombs; homemade military-type hand grenades; ammunition; gas masks; money; and bombing paraphernalia.

Jewish Extremists

During the 1980's, approximately 20 terrorist incidents and numerous other acts of violence, including extortion and threats, have either been claimed by or attributed to militant Jewish terrorists. Groups claiming credit for these attacks have been the United Jewish Underground, the Jewish Defense League, the Jewish Defenders, and the Jewish Direct Action. Included in these attacks were smoke bombings, fire bombings, and pipe bombings. As a result of these acts, three persons were killed and many more were injured.

Persons, organizations, or other elements deemed anti-Semitic, or overly supportive of Arab efforts determined not to be in the interests of Israel, are targets of the Jewish terrorists. In the past, Soviet Government interests in the United States have been attacked in protest of the U.S.S.R.'s treatment of Soviet Jews, Arab interests have been attacked because of the anti-Israeli policies of various Arab states, and alleged ex-Nazi's have been attacked because of their reported participation in atrocities against the Jewish people during World War II. The two most recent incidents attributed to Jewish terrorists involved the throwing of a tear gas canister during the performance of a Soviet dance troupe in New York City in September 1986, and an arson at Avery Fisher Hall in New York City prior to a performance by a Soviet symphony orchestra in October 1986. Most of the attacks by the Jewish terrorists have occurred in the New York City metropolitan area; however, attacks have also occurred in California, Washington, DC, and elsewhere.

A major pro-Jewish group in the United States is the Jewish Defense League (JDL). The slogan "Never Again" is the slogan of the JDL. This is a national organization with chapters in numerous American cities. Leaders of the organization have publicly advocated, encouraged, and applauded the use of violence against the enemies of the Jewish people. Although terrorist attacks have been claimed on behalf of the JDL, the violence appears to have been committed by a few of the more militant and hardcore members; the entire JDL organization should not be construed as being involved in these criminal acts.

Conclusion

During the 1980's, there have been approximately 125 terrorist acts attributed to domestic groups in the United States; of these, more than 50 occurred in Puerto Rico. Most of the activity took place early in the decade. For example, 74 terrorist incidents occurred between 1980 and 1982 but only 51 have taken place since. Puerto Rican groups accounted for 41 incidents during 1981 and 1982 but only 20 thereafter. White leftist groups accounted for 16 of their 21 incidents during 1983 and 1984 but none since. Between 1982 and 1985, the total number of incidents by domestic groups decreased from 35 to 7. During 1985 this figure rose to 17; however, it can be explained in that there were two instances of multiple bombings that accounted for 11 of the 17 total incidents.

Much of this decreased domestic terrorist activity is the result of arrests made by Federal authorities, often coordinated with State and local officials through joint terrorism task forces. Nearly 100 fugitive terrorists, including several FBI Top Ten fugitives, have been apprehended during the 1980's; many have received lengthy prison sentences. This success has greatly diminished the operations of some terrorist organizations. In at least one instance, the entire group was arrested (the United Freedom Front). In other instances, the leadership structure and/or membership of a group was removed; many groups have had to reconstruct membership or leadership elements as a result.

The groups that commit terrorism, however, are far from being eliminated. Many support elements exist which, if given the proper circumstances, could become more deeply committed to their cause. Certainly, the issues that have generated terrorist activity remain. So long as these issues exist, terrorism, in the form of violent criminal acts to achieve these goals, will remain. The desire for Puerto Rican independence will surely generate future criminal acts by a fanatical few; the values of the left will largely continue unaltered, although specific issues may change; and the white supremacist attitudes of the far right will not likely fade.

Terrorism is cyclic in nature. Activities occur because of certain issues; when the issues fade or the terrorists are arrested, the activities will generally subside. But different issues will arise and different terrorists will come forth to commit new acts. And so the cycle continues.

This Issue Paper first appeared in an article by John W. Harris in the *FBI Law Enforcement Bulletin* (October 1987): 1–9.

DISCUSSION AND REVIEW

1. What is the role of the field training officer?
2. What factors are involved in assigning a rookie officer to a particular geographical region of a city?
3. Why would a police administrator employ a policy that depletes the department's patrol bureau of its finest people?
4. Why do many patrol officers want to be transferred out of the patrol bureau?
5. What are the five basic elements of team policing?
6. How does a directed patrol program work?
7. Briefly describe the three major functions of traffic bureaus.
8. What variations sometimes exist between the traffic-law enforcement policies of police departments and sheriff's departments?
9. Describe the media image of the working detective.
10. How are detectives generally selected, trained, and supervised?
11. What policy recommendations were made based on the Rand Criminal Investigation Study?
12. What was the major difference between PERF's research on criminal investigations and that conducted earlier?
13. Define the terms *forensic science* and *criminalistics*.
14. The effectiveness of a crime laboratory can be measured in terms of three criteria. What are they?
15. What two provisions have to be met by a police agency submitting evidence to the FBI Crime Laboratory?

GLOSSARY

Crime analysis factors Variables that a police department can study in an attempt to focus its investigation and patrol efforts. Examples include crime type, geography, victim target, suspect, and suspect vehicle description.

Criminalistics A branch of forensic science that deals with the study of physical evidence related to crime.

Evidence technician A person trained to process and search crime scenes for fingerprints, tool marks, expended cartridge shells, and other physical evidence.

Field interrogation files Files that contain information on certain individuals or vehicles stopped by the police. Information includes where a vehicle or person is stopped, along with the description of the person or of the driver and his or her vehicle.

Field training officer A senior patrol officer selected to "break in" rookie officers. Also known as a "coach."

Follow-up (latent) investigation The portion of an investigation following the preliminary investigation.

Forensic science That part of science applied to answering legal questions.

NCIC NCIC is a nationwide computerized criminal justice information system established in 1967 to make an automated filing system of documented criminal justice information available to criminal justice agencies throughout the country.

Nontraditional patrol An effort on the part of some police departments to reduce dependence on vehicular patrol and develop more positive police-community relations. Some examples are foot, park and walk, bicycle, golfcart, and horse patrol.

PERF The Police Executive Research Forum.

Preliminary investigation The investigation generally performed by the first officer on the scene of a crime. Includes caring for any injured persons, apprehending the criminal if he or she is still in the immediate area, protecting the crime scene, and establishing communications with the dispatcher to broadcast descriptions of wanted persons.

Proactive beat An area patrolled regularly by the police. Patrols are dispatched *before* citizens call for help.

Professional officer track A career track that leads to upward mobility within the nonmanagerial ranks of the police department.

Professional police management track A career track that leads to upward mobility within the supervisory and managerial ranks of the police department.

Quota system A system requiring officers to write a specified number of traffic tickets in a given time period.

Reactive beat An area that is not patrolled until a request comes in for police service.

Team policing A system that combines all line functions (patrol, traffic, and investigation) into a single unit comprised of teams under common supervision.

Selective traffic enforcement The direction of enforcement efforts to areas experiencing the most traffic accidents. Such areas are monitored closely during peak accident periods.

Special purpose police Types of departments established to provide "special purpose" law enforcement services for somewhat unique communities or

constituents. Some examples of special police agencies include university police, airport police, harbor police, and park police.

■ REFERENCES

Adams, T. F. *Police Patrol: Tactics and Techniques.* Englewood Cliffs, N.J.: Prentice-Hall, 1971.

Bloch, P., and Weidman, D. *Managing Criminal Investigations: Prescriptive Package.* Washington, D.C.: U.S. Government Printing Office, 1975.

Block, P. B., and Specht, D. *Neighborhood Team Policing.* Washington, D.C.: U.S. Government Printing Office, 1973.

Caldwell, H. *Basic Law Enforcement.* Pacific Palisades, Calif.: Goodyear, 1972.

Eck, J. E. *Solving Crimes: The Investigation of Burglary and Robbery.* Washington, D.C.: Police Executive Research Forum, 1983.

Federal Bureau of Investigation Academy. "The Terrorist Organizational Profile: A Psychological Evaluation." Mimeographed. Washington, D.C.: Federal Bureau of Investigation, 1978.

Federal Bureau of Investigation. *Handbook of Forensic Science.* Washington, D.C.: U.S. Government Printing Office, 1981.

Field, K. S.; Schroeder, O., Jr.; Curtid, I. J.; Fabricant, E. L.; and Lipskin, B. A. *Assessment of the Personnel of the Forensic Science Profession.* Assessment of the Forensic Sciences Profession, vol. 2. Washington, D.C.: U.S. Government Printing Office, 1977.

Forst, B. *What Happens After Arrest.* Washington, D.C.: U.S. Government Printing Office, 1978.

Fosdick, R. *American Police Systems.* New York: Century, 1921.

Fox, R. H., and Cunningham, C. L. *Crime Scene and Physical Evidence Handbook.* Washington, D.C.: U.S. Government Printing Office, 1973.

Garner, J., and Clemmer, E. *Danger to Police in Domestic Disturbances—A New Look.* Washington, D.C.: U.S. Department of Justice, National Institute of Justice, November 1986.

Gay, W. G.; Schell, T. H.; and Schack, S. *Improving Patrol Productivity;* Vol. 1, *Routine Patrol Prescription Package.* Washington, D.C.: U.S. Department of Justice, National Institute of Law Enforcement and Criminal Justice, July 1977.

Greenberg, B.; Elliot, C. V.; Kraft, L. P.; and Proctor, H. S. *Felony Investigation Decision Model: An Analysis of Investigative Elements of Information.* Washington, D.C.: U.S. Government Printing Office, 1977.

Greenwood, P. W. *An Analysis of the Apprehension Activities of the New York City Police Department.* New York: The New York City Rand Institute, 1970.

Greenwood, P. W., and Petersilia, J. *The Criminal Investigation Process: A Dialogue on Research Findings,* vol. 1, Washington, D.C.: U.S. Government Printing Office, 1977.

Greenwood, P. W. *The Rand Criminal Investigation Study: Its Findings and Impacts To Date.* Santa Monica, Calif.: The Rand Corporation, 1979.

"Introduction to Terrorism and Intelligence Manual." Portland, Oregon Police Department, 1976.

Jenkins, B. *The Study of Terrorism: Definitional Problems.* Santa Monica, Calif.: Rand Corporation, 1980.

Kelling, G. L.; Pate, T.; Dieckman, D.; and Brown, C. E. *The Kansas City Preventive Patrol Experiment.* Washington, D.C.: Police Foundation, 1974.

Kirk, P. L. "The Ontegency of Criminalistics." *Journal of Criminal Law, Criminology and Police Science* 54 (1963): 235–238.

Langan, P. A., and Innes, C. A. *Preventing Domestic Violence Against Women.* Washington, D.C.: U.S. Department of Justice, Bureau of Justice Statistics, 1986.

McCampbell, M. S. *Field Training for Police Officers: State of the Art.* Washington, D.C.: U.S. Department of Justice, National Institute of Justice, November 1986.

Mickolus, E. "Statistical Approaches to the Study of Terrorism." In *Terrorism: An Interdisciplinary Perspective,* edited by Y. Alexander and S. Finger. New York: McGraw-Hill, 1977.

Murphy, G. R. *Special Care—Improving the Police Response to the Mentally Disabled.* Washington, D.C.: Police Executive Research Forum, 1986.

National Advisory Commission on Criminal Justice Standards and Goals. *Police.* Washington, D.C.: U.S. Government Printing Office, 1973.

National Institute of Law Enforcement and Criminal Justice. *The Criminal Investigation Process: A Dialogue on Research Findings.* Washington, D.C.: U.S. Government Printing Office, 1977.

Peterson, J. L. *The Utilization of Criminalistics Services by the Police: An Analysis of the Physical Evidence Recovery Process.* Washington, D.C.: Law Enforcement Assistance Administration, National Institute of Law Enforcement and Criminal Justice, 1974.

Phelps, T. R., Swanson, C. R., and Evans, K. R. *Introduction to Criminal Justice.* Santa Monica, Calif.: Goodyear, 1979.

President's Commission on Law Enforcement and Administration of Justice. *Task Force Report: Science and Technology.* Washington, D.C.: U.S. Government Printing Office, 1967.

Rosenblum, M. "Terrorism Impossible to Eliminate." *The Tampa Tribune,* 21 November 1982.

Safersteen, R. *Criminalistics: An Introduction to Forensic Science.* 2d ed. Englewood Cliffs, N.J.: Prentice-Hall, 1981.

Sherman, L. W.; Milton, C. H.; and Kelly, T. V. *Team Policing.* Washington, D.C.: Police Foundation, 1973.

Skolnick, J. *Justice without Trial.* New York: Wiley, 1966.

Smith, B. *Police Systems in the United States.* New York: Harper & Row, 1960.

Swanson, C. R., Chamelin, N. C., and Territo, L. *Criminal Investigation,* 4th ed. New York: Random House, 1988.

Trojanowicz, R. C., et al. *An Evaluation of the Neighborhood Foot Patrol Program in Flint, Michigan.* East Lansing, Mich.: Michigan State University, School of Criminal Justice, 1985.

Vera Institute of Justice. *Felony Arrests: Their Prosecution and Disposition in New York City's Courts.* New York: Vera Institute of Justice, 1977.

Wolf, J. "Anti-Terrorism: Operations and Controls in a Free Society." In *Critical Issues in Law Enforcement,* 3d ed., edited by H. W. Moore, Jr. Cincinnati, Ohio: Anderson, 1981.

Woodard, P. L. *Criminal Justice "Hot" Files.* Washington, D.C.: U.S. Department of Justice, Bureau of Justice Statistics, November 1986.

■ NOTES

1. The discussion of field training programs was adapted from Michael S. McCampbell, *Field Training for Police Officers: State of the Art* (Washington, D.C.: U.S. Department of Justice, National Institute of Justice, November 1986), pp. 1–7.

2. The discussion of these research findings was adapted from Joel Garner and Elizabeth Clemmer, *Danger to Police in Domestic Disturbances—A New Look*

(Washington, D.C.: U.S. Department of Justice, National Institute of Justice, November 1986), pp. 1–8.

3. For a further discussion of police patrols, see George L. Kirkham and Lauren A. Wollan, Jr., *Introduction to Law Enforcement* (New York: Harper & Row, 1980): George Eastman and Esther Eastman, eds., *Municipal Police Administration* (Washington, D.C.: International City Management Association, 1982); and Samuel G. Chapman, ed., *Police Patrol Readings* (Springfield, Ill.: Charles C. Thomas, 1970).

4. For a complete discussion of the Flint, Michigan Police Department Foot Patrol Program see Robert C. Trojanowicz, et al., *Neighborhood Foot Patrol Program in Flint, Michigan* (East Lansing, Mich.: Michigan State University, School of Criminal Justice, 1985), pp. 1–93.

5. The discussion of police programs designed to handle the mentally disabled was adapted with permission from Gerard R. Murphy, *Special Care—Improving Police Response to the Mentally Disabled* (Washington, D.C.: Police Executive Research Forum, 1986), pp. x–xv.

6. The discussion of team policing and the Kansas City Patrol Experiment, as well as the accompanying references, were adapted and modified, with permission, from T. R. Phelps, C. R. Swanson, and K. R. Evans, *Introduction to Criminal Justice* (Santa Monica, Calif.: Goodyear, 1979), pp. 171–75.

7. The information regarding directed patrol was adapted from William G. Gay, Theodore H. Schell, and Stephen Schack, *Improving Patrol Productivity;* vol. 1, *Routine Patrol Prescription Package* (Washington, D.C.: U.S. Department of Justice, National Institute of Law Enforcement and Criminal Justice, July 1977), pp. 1–7.

8. This discussion of the detective bureau and the accompanying references were adapted and modified, with permission, from Peter W. Greenwood and Joan Petersilia, *The Criminal Investigation Process: A Dialogue on Research Findings,* vol. 1 (Washington, D.C.: U.S. Government Printing Office, 1977), pp. 5–11.

9. This summary and the accompanying references were adapted, with permission, from Peter W. Greenwood, *The Rand Criminal Investigation Study: Its Findings and Impacts To Date* (Santa Monica, Calif.: The Rand Corporation, July 1979), pp. 3–7.

10. For more detailed information about objections to the findings of the Rand study, see Daryl F. Gates and Lyle Knowles, "An Evaluation of the Rand Corporation Analyses," *The Police Chief* (July 1976): 20–24, 74, 77.

11. The Vera researchers noted that in 56 percent of *all* felony arrests for crimes against the person, the victim had a prior relationship with the offender. In turn, 87 percent of these cases—as compared with only 29 percent of cases involving strangers—resulted in dismissals because the complainants refused to cooperate with the prosecutor. Once complainants "cool off," they are not interested in seeing the defendants prosecuted. Consequently, the Vera report recommends the use of neighborhood justice centers, rather than the courts, as the appropriate place to deal with most cases that involve prior relationships between victims and perpetrators.

12. The review and discussion of the PERF criminal investigation study was adapted with permission from John E. Eck, *Solving Crimes: The Investigation of Burglary and Robbery* (Washington, D.C.: Police Executive Research Forum, 1983), pp. xii–xxxi.

13. This discussion of the crime laboratory and the accompanying references were modified and adapted, with permission, from C. R. Swanson, Neil C. Chamelin, and Leonard Territo, *Criminal Investigation,* 4th ed. (New York: Random House, 1981), pp. 223–40.

14. The discussion of computerized criminal information files and the NCIC system was adapted from Paul L. Woodard, *Criminal Justice "Hot" Files* (Washington, D.C.: U.S. Department of Justice, Bureau of Justice Statistics, November 1986), pp. 1–23.

CHAPTER

7

Trends, Issues, and Problems in Law Enforcement

CHAPTER OUTLINE:

This chapter focuses on numerous topics that are of paramount concern and interest to criminal justice students, citizens, and police: professionalism in law enforcement; affirmative action and equal employment opportunities in policing; officer health; police use of deadly force; nontraditional policing; law enforcement's response to violence in America; the emergence of private security in this country and its relationship to public policing; and some specific technological trends that will assist law enforcement in the future decades.

The discussion on professionalism focuses on the new law enforcement accreditation process, the rationale for college standards for police officers, and a program called the police corps that is being implemented in various locations across the country.

The discussion of affirmative action and equal employment opportunities examines the recruitment of minorities and women. We address some of the reasons that minority recruitment has met with little or no enthusiasm in the minority community and look at what some police departments have done to overcome this problem. Further, we examine why women sometimes encounter unique difficulties in police work and suggest some ways police administrators can minimize these difficulties. We also address the allegations of some white, male officers that affirmative action programs and court-mandated "quotas" discriminate against them in the promotional process.

In the discussion of officer health, we examine the unique features of police work that generate stress. We look at stress-related problems such as alcoholism and suicide and discuss some of the ways these problems can be minimized. We also examine the issue of drug screening of applicants and current employees by police agencies.

In the discussion of the police use of deadly force, we review the latest trends in the management of force by police agencies as well as the case law and subsequent standards relative to the deadly force issue evolving from the Supreme Court's decision in *Tennessee* v. *Garner*.

Our review of law enforcement's response to serious crimes of violence focuses on the National Center for

the Analysis of Violent Crime (NCAVC), the Violent Criminal Apprehension Program (VICAP), and criminal profiling. All three programs demonstrate collaborative efforts to apprehend violent criminals and prevent future acts.

The growth of the private security field coupled with diminishing public police resources is also discussed. In the future there will be even greater interaction and sharing of responsibilities between private and public policing.

Finally, we discuss several innovations in technology that are being utilized and further developed to aid law enforcement. Specifically, we review computer-aided dispatch, and automated fingerprint programs.

PROFESSIONALISM

Solutions to whatever ails law enforcement have consistently been sought in the "professionalization" of policing. Thus, the term *professional* has acquired almost mystical properties in the law enforcement community. Police officers praise a fellow officer's performance by calling it "professional." Well-organized, smoothly run police departments are complimented for their "professionalism." Conduct unbecoming a police officer is criticized as being "unprofessional."

In part, the preoccupation with professionalism among police officers and administrators is directly related to a comparison of salaries and perceived position of various professions within the criminal justice system. The police perceive themselves to be near the bottom of the occupational totem pole. In almost any comparison of prestige and income with prosecutors, defense counsels, judges, physicians, psychiatrists, and expert witnesses (usually with earned doctorates), the police officer comes up short.

Law Enforcement Agency Accreditation

Within the last decade, the law enforcement profession has attempted for the first time to develop and implement recognized standards as has been done in the fields of medicine and law. One such attempt has resulted in a comparative effort to develop a formal accreditation process for law enforcement agencies to meet agreed-upon standards and a commission to administer the process (Commission on Accreditation for Law Enforcement Agencies, Inc., 1984, pp. 1–2).[1]

The Commission on Accreditation for Law Enforcement Agencies, Inc., was formed in 1979 to develop a set of law enforcement standards and to administer a voluntary accreditation process. Through accreditation, law enforcement agencies at the state, county, and local level can demonstrate that they meet professional criteria. The twenty-one-member commission reflects broad representation of state, county, and local law enforcement practitioners, including police chiefs and sheriffs from departments of varying sizes. The commission also includes representatives from the public and private sectors, such as state, county, and city administrations, labor, academia, and the courts.

The commission was formed through the combined efforts of the International Association of Chiefs of Police (IACP), National Organization of Black Law Enforcement Executives (NOBLE), National Sheriffs' Association (NSA), and the Police Executive Research Forum (PERF). Executive members of these four groups supervise 80 percent of the law enforcement community in the United States. Originally supported by grants from the Department of Justice, the commission operates primarily with fees paid by agencies applying for accreditation and encourages financial assistance from foundations and corporations to help defray part of these fees.

The commission is a nonprofit, tax-exempt corporation, founded by law enforcement executives. The commission is not obligated to any governmental unit—local, state, or federal. The commission derives its general standard-setting authority from agencies that *voluntarily* apply for accreditation.

Since 1979, nearly 1,000 standards have been researched and tested to address the diversity of law enforcement responsibilities. Involvement and support from a wide range of law enforcement practitioners have been key factors in the development and review of accreditation standards that are rigorous yet practical. The standards were drafted by the IACP, NOBLE, NSA, and PERF. The proposed standards then were sent for review and comment to over 350 state, county, and local law enforcement agencies.

The standards are the key element in the accreditation program. In measurable terms, they define policies and procedures essential to providing the highest quality protection to the public and to the individual officer.

Like hospital and educational accreditation, law enforcement accreditation is a process of improvement and change. Primarily a management tool, accreditation provides police chiefs and sheriffs with a structure by which they can upgrade the quality of their agencies' service to the public.

BENEFITS OF ACCREDITATION Accreditation represents a commitment to excellence and professionalism. Accreditation, according to some law enforcement practitioners, provides the following benefits:

- Nationwide recognition of professional excellence.
- Community understanding and support.
- Employee confidence; esprit.
- State and local government officials' confidence.
- State-of-the-art, impartial guidelines for evaluation and change, when necessary.
- Proactive management systems; policies and procedures documented.
- Liability insurance costs contained or decreased.
- Liability litigation deterred.
- Coordination with neighboring agencies and other parts of the criminal justice system.
- Access to the latest law enforcement practices.

Many law enforcement officials believe that an agency, once accredited, can provide its community with accurate budget justifications, reduced possibility of vicarious liability, and better relationships with other criminal justice system representatives.

Accreditation is for a five-year period, during which the agencies submit annual reports to the commission, testifying to their continued compliance with the standards by which they were initially accredited. The reaccreditation process involves procedures similar to those required in the original accreditation process.

Higher Education and Law Enforcement

Formal education has traditionally been the path to both self-improvement and increased status in a particular line of work. With the passage of the Omnibus Crime Bill in 1968, public funds were made available to police personnel to pursue a college degree at federal expense—or with a partial federal subsidy. Because many officers and administrators took advantage of this assistance, today's law enforcement personnel are, on the average, much better educated than they were twenty years ago.

The Rationale for Collegiate Standards

Do college graduates make better police officers than people who lack a college education? This question is deceptively simple. What specific criteria, for example, are involved in defining "better"? Higher arrest rates? Fewer citizen complaints? Faster promotion? In a police department with extremely low productivity in terms of arrests and clearance rates, one might expect that the infusion of college-educated officers would lead to increased productivity. If increased productivity was one of the goals of college recruiting, and if the behavior of officers was directed toward this end, then higher arrest and clearance rates certainly *would* indicate the success of higher educational requirements. However, arrest and clearance rates are often highly inflated and counterproductive. That is, arrests are made in many situations that lend themselves to alternative solutions; other arrests are made based on insufficient evidence; and some crimes are cleared based on dubious criteria. If such arrests and solutions are attributed to the competence of agency personnel—and they often are—then the infusion of college-educated officers might well result in a *reduction* in arrests and clearance rates (even though such reductions are usually thought of as indicators of poor performance). Similarly, the crime rate might rise or fall depending upon the perceived ability of officers to establish community rapport and thus increase crime reporting.

In short, the success of any police program—including the implementation of higher personnel standards—is extremely difficult to assess. The appropriateness of a particular measure of productivity depends upon the individual agency and the characteristics of the situation. Hence, efforts to establish the credibility of higher educational standards for the police are plagued by a lack of agreement about what constitutes "good" or "bad" performance.

In some police departments, rewards are based primarily upon the ability to make arrests. In other agencies, notoriety may be obtained by becoming involved in a gun battle or making a "big bust" (note that college education contributes little to one's ability to perform either of these endeavors). On the other hand, an officer who properly refers a criminal offender to psychiatric care may go unrecognized or may even be negatively rewarded. Consider the following two situations involving officers from the same police department.

In the first case, two officers were fired upon by a man with a handgun but they did not return the fire. Instead they implored the man to throw the gun down, then chased him into a house and seized him as he reached for a loaded shotgun. Command personnel were on the scene immediately, but no commendation or verbal compliment ensued. The following month, a case occurred that involved another mental subject, a man armed with a rifle. The subject fired the rifle, then approached a police car. When he would not halt, the man was shot and killed by the two responding officers. Both of these

officers received letters of commendation from the chief of police for bravery in the line of duty. The point here is not that the officers in the second incident did not deserve the letter; they held their fire for as long as they thought was reasonable. However, the officers in the first incident also acted bravely and responsibly. Thus, it appears that, at least in some police departments, rewards are available only to those involved in spectacular shootings and arrests.

Determining Enhanced Productivity

The problem of determining enhanced productivity is complicated by inappropriate expectations. What we fail to recognize about police training and educational programs is that some of the tasks of the patrol officer can be learned adequately only through experience. The police role involves knowledge of dozens of formulas and forms and scores of "ways of doing things." No amount of formal classroom instruction will, for instance, prevent a police recruit from being "had" a few times by con artists on the street. Some sociologists observe that a significant body of knowledge in the police service can be characterized by the term **street wisdom.** It is unfortunate that far too many administrators, and even some educators, look only to formal educational programs to enhance an officer's ability to apply street wisdom. This approach will simply not work. As a matter of fact, certain deficiencies with regard to street wisdom might be expected from middle-class college graduates. One aspect of street wisdom is a knowledge of the value systems, jargon, and customs of lower socioeconomic classes; middle-class college graduates do not normally possess such knowledge. However, experience can quickly remedy the situation.

Another serious problem in the effort to justify higher educational standards for police is that it is difficult to establish precisely what level of improved performance justifies the imposition of higher standards. That is, it is not enough merely to require that collegiate police officers perform at a higher level than noncollegiate officers. Rather, it must be established that increased productivity justifies the expense of higher salaries frequently associated with higher education. Such a determination would be difficult enough to make if police productivity could be easily measured or the goals of the police service were agreed upon by those in the field. Such is not the case, however.

The problem of determining "significant" productivity differences is compounded by the fact that the patrol officer's task is often limited in scope. If the task is merely to write traffic tickets, to shine spotlights through broken windows, or to arrest drunks, then arguments for higher educational standards are weak. However, if the task is defined at a higher level, then any standard less than an undergraduate degree might be inappropriate.

If a job involves only routine and mundane tasks, college graduates cannot be expected to perform significantly better than anyone else. In fact, a college graduate with high expectations who works at a routine or mundane job, may be even less motivated than an officer without a college background. Thus, the full potential of increased educational standards in police work will be realized only when the police task is adjusted to complement the educational background of recruits.

Applying Collegiate Ability to the Crime Problem

Information from two sources—a preventive-patrol study conducted in Kansas City, discussed in Chapter 6, and motivation studies conducted in the last twenty years—can be used to support arguments for expanding the responsibility given to patrol officers. The Kansas City Patrol Experiment questions the value of patrol officers in crime control, since the officers often spend much of their time cruising around without specific direction or purpose. If this view is accepted as valid or is confirmed by additional research, then it behooves us to explore alternatives to current patrol patterns. For the most part, such alternatives involve the reallocation of resources to address particular offenders or classes of offenses.

For example, a principal motivation for team policing (as discussed in Chapter 6) is that it allows more effective use of the patrol officer. In team policing, patrol officers have some investigative responsibility and they are responsible for establishing community contacts to aid in the control of criminal conduct. Thus defined, the police task is anything but mundane. And if we attribute any validity to the Kansas City Patrol Experiment study, then patrol officers' tasks should be changed to direct energies toward more complex activities that have greater potential for contributing to crime reduction.

More compelling reasons for expanding the role of the patrol officer come from motivational studies. These studies indicate that three characteristics of employment contribute substantially to the motivation of personnel, thus increasing productivity. The first characteristic is a management style that moves the emphasis from the supervision of processes to the supervision of goals. Such a difference in style was characterized by Douglas

McGregor in *The Human Side of Enterprise* (1960). The second characteristic is summarized by the term **participative management.** Research shows that whenever employees are allowed to participate in decisions about the procedures and policies that affect their work, motivation and productivity increase substantially. Participative management involves the delegation of policy-making responsibility to operational personnel. It is best described by Rensis Likert in *New Patterns of Management* (1961). The third employment characteristic related to increased motivation is the responsibility and complexity of the work. As the latter two factors increase, motivation and productivity increase also. The term **job enrichment** is used to describe this phenomenon.

Thus, research indicates that we need to alter the nature of the patrol officer's task dramatically. Police performance should be measured by the attainment of goals rather than by adherence to rules and regulations; patrol officers should be involved in the policy-making process; and the responsibilities assigned to the patrol officer should be significantly expanded. As this occurs, the police role will increasingly require professional skills, rather than the skills of a craftsman.

The importance of highly motivated personnel cannot be exaggerated. A misconception that must be overcome is the illusion that patrol units function as tightly controlled, carefully directed units of a crime strike force. The illusion is perpetuated by frequent reference to fighting the "war on crime"—as if patrol units were analogous to army units fighting military battles. In fact, however, in any jurisdiction at any time, there are as many independent police units as there are patrol officers on the street.

Close field supervision of patrol units randomly moving throughout a jurisdiction is difficult. This difficulty was illustrated in one agency in which a patrol officer started a contest to determine who could drive the farthest outside the jurisdiction without being discovered. The record set was 60 miles—120 miles round trip. Although such contests are certainly not typical, the case illustrates that there is little supervisory contact with patrol officers in most jurisdictions. Because such contact is usually initiated by a radio call to set up a time and place to meet, patrol officers are generally free to do as they please. Unfortunately, that sometimes entails idleness and looking after nonpolice business.

Because supervision of patrol officers is so difficult, we must depend on the officers to internalize certain values that will direct them toward crime reduction. The desired value system is characterized as "professional"; that is, we expect police officers to be self-motivated. Unfortunately, many police agencies today are characterized by a "labor-versus-management" attitude among patrol officers and police managers. Almost all patrol officers work at some other job before joining the police agency. In most cases, the jobs held previously by officers without a college background were **working-class jobs.** The behavioral norm pervasive in such employment is that if one has free time when a supervisor is not watching, that time can be used to do anything that does not contribute to the goals of the "company." Anyone who does otherwise is regarded as a "rate buster." If we recruit patrol officers from these ranks, we should expect precisely what we get. If we expect self-motivation from police personnel, then we must draw those personnel from an employment pool that does not perceive the goals of management as existing only to be subverted.

Educational Upgrading: A Second Rationale

Traditional police training programs emphasize the more mechanical aspects of law enforcement. By necessity, these programs deal with subjects such as preservation of crime scenes, proper collection of evidence, motor vehicle codes, and physical and firearms training. Unfortunately, some training academies have not taken the time, and too often do not have the qualified staff, to educate officers about social conflict or human behavior. Robert E. McCann, Director of Training for the Chicago Police Department, comments that "the training programs we have established teach officers how to behave for the twenty percent of the time that they have to operate in a crime situation; and eighty percent of their time we scarcely touch as far as training is concerned."

Peter P. Lejins has documented how an educational background might enhance an officer's ability to handle situations involving social conflict:

> Among the frequent disturbances to which a police officer is called are family conflicts, which often reach the level of disturbances of the peace, fights, assault and manslaughter. It stands to reason that an officer who has been exposed to some educational experience in the area of family relationships, the types of family conflict and the way they run their course, would approach this type of disturbance with a much broader and sounder perspective than someone equipped with many conventional folklore stereotypes permeated by punitive, disciplinary or ridiculing impulses . . . .

> An even more obvious example is a disturbance anchored in the area of ethnic relations and ethnic tensions. Exposure to the university-level study of ethnic relations, contributing an historical and broader perspective . . . again suggests itself, and again one would expect that such study would tend to diminish the effect of prejudice, racial and ethnic stereotypes, erroneous and often exaggerated, rumors, etc. . . .
>
> Still another example is the handling of disturbances for which mentally abnormal people are responsible. The use of conventional and straightforward evaluations of behavior as being or not being a violation of law, and the use of conventional law enforcement steps to arrest and secure the violator for action by the criminal justice system, would often cause unnecessary harm to the perpetrator, who is viewed by contemporary society as a sick person, and to the community itself, by injecting what basically amounts to an improper solution of the problem. . . .
>
> Whatever has been said with regard to the above three categories of disturbances could be properly restated with regard to the handling of drunks and drug addicts. . . .
>
> And finally, let us take the so-called area of civil rights and contemporary struggles for them, which often express themselves in disturbances and so-called riots. Here again the quick and sharp discernment between permissible actions in terms of freedom of speech, and freedom of demonstration, and actions that violate the individual rights of others and have all the characteristics of plain criminal acts, presupposes alert and sophisticated individuals. Persons without any higher education, acquired either in their college-age period or subsequently by means of adult education and in-service training, can hardly be cast in the role of the wise law enforcement officer who manages to lessen the tensions between ideologically antagonistic mobs, protects the rights of innocent bystanders and would-be victims, and contains the amount of violence . . . (1970, pp. 13–16).

It is true that many police officers perform mundane tasks such as directing traffic, issuing parking tickets, conducting permit inspections, and driving tow trucks. Such tasks obviously do not require college training. However, many routine tasks are rapidly being turned over to civilian employees and other governmental agencies. Thus, police officers are going back to more essential tasks, which include social control in a period of increasing social turmoil, preservation of our constitutional guarantees, and exercise of broad discretion—sometimes in life and death situations. The Education and Training Task Force of the Police Foundation comments that "the job defining the delicate balance between liberty and order, of applying wisdom, of being flexible, of using discretion and, most particularly, of seeing the mundane and trivial in a broader legal and moral context is an intellectually and psychologically awesome one" (1972). If the tasks performed by police are those normally performed by professionals, and if other professionals normally prepare for their roles by academic study, then so ought the police to prepare.

Thus, the police function, as it relates to conflict resolution and order maintenance in urban society, involves both social work and law enforcement techniques. Whether these techniques are employed at an appropriate time and in an appropriate way can mean the difference between successful and unsuccessful resolution of conflict. Unsuccessful resolution extols a human cost whether criminal behavior results or not.

The self-concept of the police officer as a crime fighter inhibits the ability of officers to resolve situations that can be handled by social counseling. This situation is the basis for a second rationale for educational upgrading—that college-educated individuals are more able to cope with role conflict, and a college education provides officers with a social perspective and abilities more conducive to conflict resolution.

The Police Corps Concept

Despite the increase in violent and property crimes being experienced in many parts of the country, the size of many city police forces have been reduced or remained the same. In *The New Police Corps,* Adam Walinsky et al. provide the following graphic examples:

> Public order has collapsed in large part because the police have not grown in numbers nearly commensurate with the exploding rate of crime. In 1948 for every violent crime reported in an American city there were 3.22 police officers. Put another way, a city with a police force of two thousand men might expect to deal with about seven hundred violent crimes a year. Thirty years later, in 1978, the ratio of police officers to violent crimes was 0.5 to 1. Thus a police force of two thousand would be confronted with four thousand violent crimes a year. *We are allocating to each*

violent crime one-sixth of the police power that we allocated thirty years ago [emphasis in the original].

This sixfold effective reduction in our police forces is typical of New York cities such as Rochester, where a force barely larger than the five hundred men of thirty years ago must now cope with about 2,500 violent crimes—as opposed to less than 400 in the late 1940's. But in many areas of New York the case is worse. In Buffalo, in 1951, a force of 1,229 men was faced with 361 reported violent felonies. By 1981 a force reduced to 1,053 men had to cope with 3,277 reported violent felonies, nine times the figure of thirty years before.

In New York City the facts are even more crushing. The City is the nerve center of the State; it is the City that places us at the center of the world. What we have allowed to happen in New York City defies description. In 1951, a City police force of over 19,000 was asked to cope with 15,812 violent crimes—less than one per serving officer. But in 1981, a police force of barely 22,000 was confronted with the incredible total of 157,026 violent crimes—more than seven violent crimes for every serving officer. Indeed, these numbers are a dramatic understatement of the problem. We had 157,026 reported violent crimes. But as our people have lost faith, more and more crimes are not reported. A recent Gannett poll indicates that *one out of every four* [emphasis in the original] City households has been the victim of a street robbery within the last year (Walinsky et al., pp. 2–3).[2]

One innovation established in various parts of the country in an attempt to address the serious depletion in human resources in police agencies, has been the establishment of Police Corps made up of college students.

In the Police Corps concept, college students receive training in law enforcement before they graduate. While in college they receive monetary compensation. Just as in military ROTC programs, the students owe a time commitment to their respective communities to serve as police officers. The following newspaper accounts provide two examples of the relative success of the Police Corps concept.

AFFIRMATIVE ACTION AND EQUAL EMPLOYMENT OPPORTUNITIES

The traditional argument for increasing minority recruitment on the police force is that such recruitment increases the effectiveness of the force. Police officers

Police Corps Plan Getting Cautious Look

BY JENNIFER BROWDY

The New Police Corps, a plan to remedy the police manpower shortage affecting many departments, is being studied cautiously by a number of cities and states, although at least two police organizations have already voiced reservations or outright opposition to the plan.

The Police Corps idea, proposed by Adam Walinsky, a former chairman of the New York State Commission of Investigation, would attempt to alleviate the shortage of police officers by offering young people four-year college scholarships in any field of study in exchange for three years service as sworn police officers when they finish school.

Last year, the National Institute of Justice awarded a grant to the Center for Research on Institutions and Social Policy (CRISP) in New York for a feasibility study of the Police Corps concept. The study is being conducted in seven states where public officials have expressed an interest in the concept: New York, New Jersey, Pennsylvania, Massachusetts, California, Florida and Texas.

CRISP has sent questionnaires to 5,000 police departments in the seven states, asking what their needs and resources are, if they would be willing to accept a Police Corps, and if so, how they would use such a group. Additional questionnaires were sent to high school and college students in each of the seven states to find out whether they would be interested in participating in a Police Corps program.

Ellen Spilka, coordinator of the national office of CRISP, said the report detailing the results of the surveys would be available this spring. A cost-analysis of the proposal is also being conducted under the NIJ grant.

Meanwhile, Norman Darwick, executive director of the International Association of Chiefs of Police, said that while his organization is "interested in exploring any concept to augment police departments," he has "serious reservations" about the Police Corps project. He said

he is "uncomfortable" with such aspects of the proposal as funding, recruitment, structure, operation and long-term benefits.

In New York State, where the proposal has sparked considerable interest, many law enforcement officials have expressed opposition to the idea, saying it would be costly and a problem to implement.

The Police Corps proposed for New York would place its members under the control of the State Police, while assigning them to various local police departments. Harlin McEwen, president of the New York State Association of Chiefs of Police, said it was "poor police management" to have officers trained and employed by one agency while assigned to another.

New York State Police Superintendent Donald Chesworth agreed. "It's good to have people discussing the problem of police service," he said. "But this idea is impractical. It would be difficult to implement."

Chesworth said it would be difficult to come up with adequate training and supervision for the Police Corps, and it would cost "a phenomenal amount of money." He also expressed concern that there was no adequate method for insuring that the Police Corps members fulfill their service obligations.

One of McEwen's principal objections to the proposal was that the Police Corps members would not be career officers. "We believe our first priority must be to adequately train career-minded recruits and career personnel before we support a funding program for persons who are perhaps only interested in finding a way to pay for their college education," he said.

Calling the Police Corps a "revolving door training program," McEwen said that by the time a Police Corps officer is properly trained and seasoned, he or she would be leaving the force.

The cost of getting a Police Corps program going in New York has been estimated at $800 million, although some law enforcement officials, such as State Police Supt. Chesworth, believe the real figure will ultimately be much higher. State government officials have talked about imposing a new tax to raise the necessary money. But according to David Langdon, a spokesman for State Assembly Speaker Stanley Fink, it is doubtful that the State Legislature will make any move to get the program underway in fiscal 1985.

"It's not included in the governor's budget proposal," Langdon said, "and it's doubtful that there will be room for it in this year's budget, given that no one is interested in raising taxes. I expect it will be put on hold for at least another year," he said.

Another obstacle facing adoption of the Police Corps program in New York is a competing plan that has the backing of the New York City Police Department.

The Police Cadet Program, which would offer a criminal justice education to persons on the New York City police eligibility list, was conceived by Dr. Gerald W. Lynch, president of John Jay College of Criminal Justice, and Philip Caruso, president of the New York City Patrolmen's Benevolent Association. Backers of the cadet proposal have begun soliciting expressions of interest from those on the eligibility list, and are currently working to convince the mayor of New York City and the governor of New York State to put up the necessary funds.

According to Lynch, the Criminal Justice Educators' Association of New York may be lining up in the Police Cadet camp. "They have actually become quite positive," Lynch said, "because they see that, for criminal justice education, this is the plan."

The educators' association is currently conducting a series of hearings on the merits of both the Police Cadet and Police Corps proposals.

Reprinted from *Law Enforcement News*. February 27, 1984, pp. 1, 6.

. . . But San Jose's Chief Likes What He Sees in Plan

While jurisdictions around the country are haggling over the Police Corps proposal, San

Jose, Calif., Police Chief Joseph McNamara has come out decidedly in favor of the idea. In fact, he plans to implement it in his department sometime next fall.

"It's going to be a real shot in the arm for policing," he said. "It's the best innovation to come along in decades."

Support for the idea has come from the San Jose police themselves, from city officials, from potential Police Corps members and the community, McNamara said. While he is presently negotiating with the police union over the proposal, he expressed confidence that rank-and-file officers will be pleased with the program once it's put into effect.

McNamara listed four major arguments in support of the Police Corps concept. "One, it'll give the city a chance to maintain the high salaries of our career officers while providing more sworn officers. Two, it will be a boost for the morale of the rank-and-file, because it puts them on a par with military officers and the ROTC program. Three, most of the Police Corps will be the offspring of cops. And four, the volunteers will go back into the community and make it that much better."

San Jose, a city of 700,000, has 915 sworn officers and a total of 1,200 personnel, giving it one of the highest citizen/police ratios in the country, according to McNamara. He expects to add 40 Police Corps members in the first year of the program, and increase the corps to a maximum of 120. "We'll never have more than 10 or 11 percent of our sworn strength as Police Corps," he said.

San Jose plans to implement the program without any financial backing from the state. City officials expect to save $16,000 on each Police Corps officer as compared with the cost of training and maintaining a career police officer, which is estimated at $52,000 a year.

McNamara said there has been "a groundswell of public approval" in the city for the concept. There has also been a great deal of interest expressed by students, and McNamara said he is expecting "a deluge of applications." The San Jose Police Corps may serve as a pilot program for the rest of the nation's police departments, McNamara said, optimistically predicting that the concept would "sweep the country" after people see how well it works.

BY JENNIFER BROWDY

Reprinted from Law Enforcement News. February 27, 1984, pp. 1, 6.

Facing the Growing Trend of Cops and College Credits

BY GERALD W. LYNCH

In New York City, Police Commissioner Benjamin Ward establishes a program to attract college graduates to the police force. In Atlanta, Public Safety Commissioner George Napper recommends that minimal educational requirements for entry-level police officers be raised to two years of college. In Dallas, the Police Department successfully fights a court battle to defend its mandatory minimum college requirement.

Why are police leaders from such different cities encouraging college education for their officers? Why do cops need college?

Every national commission on violence and crime in America for the last 20 years has concluded that college education can improve police performance, a conclusion that may jar the thinking of many outside law enforcement.

We know that considerably less than half of a police officer's time is spent on anything to do with the apprehension of criminals. Often, a police officer practices a kind of front-line crisis intervention, arriving in the midst of a violent domestic dispute, calming a psychotic individual or cooling the heated emotion of a street fight. Every day, police officers make quick decisions in emergency situations—to defuse tensions, to influence behavior, and sometimes to use force.

The police officer must be capable of grasping not only the legal issues in his work, but must have an understanding of human nature, of the

social problems he confronts daily and of the thinking of those whose attitudes toward the law are not his own. A college education, regardless of the area of study, can help crystallize raw experience, dispel prejudice and heighten tolerance for ambiguity.

There are obvious public benefits from more humane policing, and college educated police officers are less authoritarian than their non-college-educated counterparts, according to studies published in the *Journal of Criminal Law, Criminology and Police Science.* In a Rand Corporation study of the New York City Police Department (1973), the level of education of an individual police officer was found to be the most powerful predictor of civilian complaints about assaults on suspects, abuse of authority and religious or racial prejudice. Civilians complained three times more often about non-college graduates than they did about college graduates. College graduates also performed better by the disciplinary standards established by the NYPD. College graduates violated the department's internal regulations concerning insubordination, negligent use of a revolver and absenteeism significantly less often than did non-college-educated officers. The Rand study demonstrates that policing is improved when the broad understanding and maturity that college education can bring rationalizes police use of discretion, including, most critically, the rare decision to use a gun.

The number of training hours required of police officers has not increased dramatically since 1967, when officers nationwide were required, on the average, to have 200 hours of training before hitting the streets, armed and in uniform. But before we allow a physician to set up shop, we require him to have had an average of 11,000 hours of training, and lawyers an average of 9,000. The New York City Police Academy puts recruits through a training program more rigorous than that of many cities, but the fact remains that it takes just six months to travel the path from civilian to officer. Every city takes an enormous risk when it puts a person on the street armed with a gun and the authority and discretion to use it. We should take every step to insure that those vested with that authority are as prepared for it as possible.

Almost 15 years ago, the National Advisory Committee on Criminal Justice Standards and Goals warned: "There are few professions today that do not require a college degree. Police, in their quest for greater professionalism, should take notice." The high school diploma or equivalency has for two generations most commonly been the highest level of education required by police departments around the country. When those requirements were established, a high school diploma indicated a superior level of education, but that is no longer true. In 1946, less than half of the 17-year-old population had completed high school. But by 1984, 70 percent of blacks and 83 percent of whites under age 24 had graduated from high school. Further, more than half of recent high school graduates go on to college. The number of black students enrolled in college programs has risen 118 percent since 1970.

Police should represent the communities they work in, and as a whole, Americans have achieved consistently higher levels of education since World War II. As Dallas Police Chief Billy Prince told Law Enforcement News last year, "You may not have to go to college to be a police officer, but there's no question that it makes you much better than you could be without it. It opens your mind. You fit into the world better."

In New York City last year, Mayor Edward I. Koch and Police Commissioner Ward initiated a pioneering police recruitment program specifically designed to attract college graduates to the police force. The program, called the Police Cadet Corps, provides scholarships and practical training in police work to college sophomores committed to joining the police force after graduation. Eventually, the department hopes to make the Police Cadet Corps its principal method of recruitment. So far, Commissioner Ward calls the program "a resounding success."

The first group of 130 police cadets, drawn from a pool of 1,500 applicants, began work last summer. Under the supervision of the precincts' community service officers, police cadets

organized tenant and block associations, distributed crime-prevention information to community residents, escorted senior citizens and assisted in precinct youth programs. When the police cadets join the department as fully-sworn officers, they will be uniquely prepared by their combination of college education, practical police training and a long-range supervised apprenticeship.

The New York City Police Cadet Corps, the first recruitment program of its kind, has already received national acclaim. But New York and Atlanta are not alone in recognizing the benefits that attracting college graduates can bring, and in acting on that conviction. A 1986 study conducted by the Police Executive Research Forum and the Newport News Police Department found that more than two-thirds of the 65 departments surveyed offered economic incentives to their officers to further their educations beyond high school. Twenty-one police departments out of 122 surveyed in 1981 required at least one year of college education for entry-level officers. Police chiefs, who often set the tone for their departments, have made rapid educational achievements in the last 15 years. By 1982, 56.8 percent of police chiefs nationwide had bachelor's degrees, in contrast to only 14.2 percent in 1971.

Legal hurdles that may have at one time discouraged other cities from instituting college requirements may no longer exist. The U.S. Court of Appeals upheld in 1986 a requirement by the City of Dallas that entry-level police recruits have completed 45 college credits. The court let stand a U.S. District Court ruling, *Brenda Davis* v. *City of Dallas,* which held that "the educational requirements bear a manifest relationship to the position of police officer" because police are entrusted with the "lives and well-being" of the public. The precedent-setting decision opens the way for more cities to set requirements similar to the one in Dallas, to the one proposed for Atlanta, and for programs similar to the Police Cadet Corps in New York City.

Reprinted from *Law Enforcement News.* March 10, 1987, pp. 8, 13.

cannot be effective in a hostile environment—an environment where they are unfamiliar with the culture of the community or where they feel alien, frightened, belligerent, or awkward. Citizens will not cooperate with them, will not report crimes, and will not aid in their investigations. One solution to this problem is to assign police officers that have the same ethnic background as the residents. Thus, Hispanics police Hispanics and blacks police blacks. Evidence shows that racial or ethnic similarity on the police force can indeed improve community relations and reduce tensions. Dozens of cities—including Detroit, Baltimore, Washington, D.C., and New Orleans—have improved community relations by staffing troubled areas with police of the same racial or ethnic character as the neighborhood population (Wasserman, Gardner, and Cohen 1973, p. 41).

Recruitment of Minorities

One of the difficulties that even well-intentioned police administrators encounter in attempting to assign officers based on ethnic or racial background is the lack of sufficient personnel to fill such assignments. And minority recruitment, although not nearly as difficult as some contend, is not a simple matter. After decades of exclusion, suspicion, and discrimination, a passive "open-door" policy of recruitment is not enough. Peer-group pressure—strong among young blacks—will work against it. So will fear of failure, nonacceptance, and even outright discrimination. Furthermore, job opportunities for minorities in other fields are often more attractive than those offered by the police department.

In spite of such obstacles, however, minority recruitment can be improved. First, a department must initiate a strong recruitment program. Recruitment left to a civil service board will probably not be successful. Such boards have many other responsibilities, and few have the time or skills needed to attract the kind of candidates police departments require. Thus, the department itself must assume the major responsibility.

The department must also demonstrate a commitment to internal equal opportunity. Applicants are being asked to commit themselves to a new career, and they need to know that the department recruiting them is dedicated to helping them advance. Many departments—such as those in Boston, New Orleans, Dayton, New York City, Miami, and St. Louis—have demonstrated such commitment by appointing qualified minority individuals, both from within and outside the department, to high positions. Most of these departments are also taking the

important step of removing discrimination from their promotional systems.

The most effective recruiters of minority applicants are successful minority officers. Such officers should be asked to direct or assist in the development of the recruitment program, and they should be given the on-duty time to do so—along with whatever other support might be required. Appearances at high schools, community groups, veterans centers, and other gathering places for minority individuals of suitable age have been especially helpful. In addition, recruiting officers should encourage other officers to be alert for qualified applicants. The patrol car itself can be an excellent recruiting tool if officers are willing to expend the effort and are encouraged to do so. Some cities, such as St. Louis, provide up to five days paid vacation to any officer who successfully recruits a new officer. The response to such programs has been positive.

Targeting individuals as prospective officers can be accomplished in much the same manner as the department "targets" an individual criminal. Potential applicants can be assigned to individual police officers, who then visit the applicants' homes, maintain regular contact with them, and help them prepare for their examinations, maintain their determination through the waiting period, and get through training and probation. This technique has been used successfully in private industry and by the Massachusetts State Police (Wasserman, Gardner, and Cohen, 1973, p. 41).

It has often been said that minority recruitment is unsuccessful because police departments refuse to lower their standards for minorities. One of the difficulties in discussing personnel standards is that the issue is seen in terms of "raising" or "lowering" requirements. Code words like these really do not address the issue. Higher or lower standards are not at stake; rather, the goal is to establish standards that are relevant to the functions for which they are designed (Territo, Swanson, and Chamelin 1977, pp. 40–47).

Recruitment of Women

Not so many years ago, it was common for police administrators to dismiss the idea that women could adequately perform the functions within the exclusive domain of male officers—patrol work, nonfamily crime investigations, motorcycle riding, and so on. However, legislative, administrative, and judicial action have long since resolved the question of whether women should be permitted to perform these functions, and women have put to rest questions about their ability to handle such tasks. Empirical evidence supports the proposition that carefully selected and carefully trained females are as effective as carefully selected and carefully trained males. And although not all women are suited for police work, neither are all men. This is not to suggest, however, that women have been universally and enthusiastically accepted by their male counterparts—only that their employment and career advancement opportunities have improved immeasurably in the past decade.

The first women assigned to all-male operating units are faced with unique problems. These women are subject to psychological pressures that are not encountered by men and that will not be faced by those women who follow them months or years later. For example, the first female officer in a department must often perform her duties in an atmosphere of disbelief on the part of supervisors and peers who doubt her ability to deal physically and emotionally with the rigors of street work. And it must be remembered that peer acceptance is one of the greatest pressures operating within the police organization (Washington 1981, p. 142). The desire to be identified as a "good officer" is a strong motivating force, and a failure to achieve that goal in one's own eyes—as well as in the eyes of one's peers—can be devastating and demoralizing.

For the rookie female officer, attaining the approval of her peers can be an even more frustrating task than it is for her male counterparts. Like them, she must overcome doubts about her own ability to perform her duties effectively; but unlike the men, she must also overcome prejudice stemming from societal influences that depict the female as the "weaker sex" (Washington 1981, p. 143). And she will very likely receive little support from her family, friends, and male companions.

Administrators can take several steps to facilitate the entry of females into their operating units. For example, when policewomen are first introduced into patrol activities, the move should be discussed in advance with male patrol officers, emphasizing that female officers will be given neither preferential treatment nor preferential assignments. Also, field training officers and supervisors of rookie female officers should be individuals who will fairly and accurately assess performance without considering sex. A chief administrator should also issue a general order outlining the administrative expectations of women assigned to previously all-male units. For example, one chief of police issued a written order with nineteen guidelines to set the stage for the entry of women into the patrol force. Some of these guidelines were that women should be given the same assignments, privileges, and considerations as men; no special scout

cars or special assignments should be created for women; women should be given a full range of assignments, including assignments to scout cars, foot beats, station duty, and traffic duty; and women should be considered for certification to patrol alone when they have the necessary experience (Washington, D.C., Police Department 1972). A written order will affirm a chief's full support of women in patrol work and have an undeniable impact on the treatment of female patrol officers (Block, Anderson, and Gervais 1973).

Reverse Discrimination

Departments that enjoy a high degree of success in recruiting minority and women officers sometimes encounter an unfortunate and unanticipated side effect when these officers are later promoted or placed in desirable assignments: white, male officers resent being passed over for promotions or desirable assignments because of the department's affirmative action goals. This problem is referred to as **reverse discrimination.** Traditionally, police officers have been told that promotions and assignments are given based on level of performance, promotional examinations, education, and years of experience. Now they are being told that sex, race, and ethnic background are also factors. And although such policies are in keeping with legally mandated federal guidelines and federal court edicts and are the most expeditious way to rectify years of blatant discrimination, it should not come as a surprise that some resentment occurs on the part of those officers who are passed over specifically because of sex, race, or ethnic origin.

One of the side effects associated with this problem is that personal antagonisms are created between white, male officers and officers given preferential treatment. Further, even when a clearly superior officer from a special class is promoted, there will be those who will denigrate the officer's professional accomplishments and attribute the promotion solely to sex, race, or ethnic background.

Supreme Court OK's Alabama Trooper Quotas

Overruling the Reagan Administration's stance in opposition to minority hiring and promotional quotas, the United States Supreme Court last month upheld a Federal District Court ruling requiring the state of Alabama to promote one black state trooper for each white one promoted in an effort to compensate for dramatic past discrimination against blacks.

The 5-to-4 decision was made in the light of the Alabama State Police's long history of discrimination and resistance to court-ordered change. The decision upheld by the Supreme Court in *United States* v. *Paradise* dates back to 1983 and 1984 when a lower court ruled that as long as qualified blacks were available, promotions had to be made one-for-one until the state adopted acceptable promotional procedures.

Blacks had been totally excluded from the state police until a 1972 court order forced their hiring.

It was the "pervasive, systematic and obstinate discriminatory conduct of the department [that] created a profound need and a firm justification for the race-conscious relief ordered by the district court," according to Justice William J. Brennan. Brennan's opinion was joined by Justice Thurgood Marshall, Harry A. Blackmun and Lewis F. Powell, Jr.

Citing decisions issued last year, Brennan said, "It is now well-established that government bodies, including courts, may constitutionally employ racial classifications essential to remedy unlawful treatment of racial or ethnic groups subject to discrimination."

Dissenting from the court's ruling were Chief Justice William H. Rehnquist and Associate Justice Antonin Scalia, both of whom have consistently opposed racial quotas as a means of compensating for past discrimination.

The promotional quota upheld by the Court was decried as "wholly arbitrary" and "profoundly illegal" by U.S. Solicitor General Charles Fried. Through a spokesman, Fried said he was disappointed by the Court's decision and that he agreed with dissenting Justices.

Like Fried, Justice Sandra Day O'Connor said that while Alabama was guilty of an "egregious history of discrimination," the lower court's order was not "narrowly tailored" enough to stand up to the criteria handed down by the Court last year.

The promotional quota, said O'Connor, put an undue burden on white troopers seeking promotion.

"The one-for-one promotion quotas used in this case far exceeded the percentage of blacks in the trooper force, and there is no evidence in the record that such an extreme quota was necessary," wrote O'Connor.

However, it was Justice Brennan who prevailed with his view that since 25 percent of the people qualified to be state troopers are black, a temporary use of the one-for-one "catch-up" quota for promotions was justified because it would help speed up the day when blacks occupy 25 percent of the department's upper echelons.

The 50-percent quota "does not disrupt seriously the lives of innocent individuals," concurred Justice Powell, although some promotions of white troopers may be delayed. The plan is not as harsh, he said, as requiring the layoff of white troopers before less-senior blacks.

Reprinted from *Law Enforcement News*. March 31, 1987, pp. 3, 13.

OFFICER HEALTH

As a result of some of the unique factors associated with their job, police officers often feel isolated from other parts of society. Police officers are taught early in their academy training to be suspicious of nonpolice persons and to be overly cautious and aware of the potential for danger. Likewise, the authority that law enforcement in our society represents often makes officers the target of minority groups who have legitimate grievances (e.g., poor housing and unemployment), yet the officers are not empowered to address those problems. Individual officers may, with some justification, be depicted in the media as brutal, corrupt, or bigoted. Many law enforcement officers, however, feel they are all unjustly labeled when such events occur. Consequently, further isolation from society in general may result wherein the police develop their own subculture. As Skolnick (1966, p. 52) stated, "Set apart from the conventional world, the policeman experiences an exceptionally strong tendency to find his social identity within his occupational milieu."

Some of the potential emotional and mental health problems that officers in the police subculture may face are categorized in the article opposite.

Historically, business and industry in the United States have been slow to identify and provide for the needs of workers. Largely because of labor unions, however, the U.S. worker has attained a variety of benefits, ranging from increased wages to comprehensive medical care to retirement programs. The evolution of mental health compensation as a significant management issue occurred through a combination of union pressures and simple economics. A healthy, well-adjusted worker means increased efficiency and higher production from the corporation. As a consequence, **job stress** "has moved from the nether world of 'emotional problems' and 'personality conflicts' to the corporate balance sheet. . . . Stress is now seen as not only troublesome but expensive" (Slobogin 1977, p. 48).

Police work is highly stressful. It is one of the few occupations in which employees continually face physical dangers and may be asked to put their lives on the line at any time. The police officer is exposed to violence, cruelty, and aggression and must often make critical decisions in high-pressure situations.

If You Ever Have to Kill a Man, Never Look at his Face

UNITED PRESS INTERNATIONAL

MEMPHIS, TENN.—Eight years ago, patrolman John Thomas Cursey, 33 killed two holdup men during a liquor store robbery.

He shot one when the man turned on him with a gun, and the other when he ran. The second man did not die instantly.

"I heard him gasping for breath as he died," Cursey recalled. From this, he learned a lesson: "If you ever have to kill a man, never look at his face."

A few days after the killings, Cursey's buddies presented him with a fifth of whiskey. Over the label, they pasted a police photo of one of the dead bandits sprawled on the liquor store floor.

Six months later, Cursey was an alcoholic. He relived the killings night after night in his dreams. His wife left him and in 1976 the police department fired him because of his "uncontrollable" drinking. He couldn't hold a job.

Thurday, the city of Memphis' pension board awarded Cursey a lifetime disability pension of $5,500 a year—the first it has ever granted for psychological injuries.

Cursey, who reportedly collapsed in tears at the hearing, could not be reached for comment.

E. W. Chapman, Memphis' police director, said the board's decision was an indication that more and more people "have reached the realization that the psychological strain of being in police work is immense."

In an interview two years ago, Cursey recalled that the department had put 20 men on stakeout after a series of liquor store heists.

"The lieutenant called in eight of us and stood us up in front of him while he said, 'I want you to go out and kill those bastards. Don't come back until you've killed 'em.' "

It was February 3, 1970, when two men entered the liquor store where Cursey was watching from a back room. One, armed with a pistol, demanded cash. He struck the storekeeper over the head and Cursey burst in and leveled his shotgun at them.

"The guy with the pistol turned and started to aim at me. That was when I cut loose on him. I had to do it. It was either him, or me, or the manager." The man died instantly and the second robber was wounded.

"The other robber hesitated a moment and I begged him to give up. I said 'Please don't run or I'll have to kill you.' " He ran and I shot him just as he went out the door." He died 30 minutes later.

A psychologist, Dr. Lindley Davis Hutt, Jr., told the pension board Cursey was "what I would describe as a stable, hard working, family-oriented type of fellow with a good circle of friends," Hutt said. "His reaction to the incident was very severe anxiety and depressive neuroses, insomnia and a lack of concentration."

Stress produces many varied psychophysiological disturbances that, if intense and chronic enough, can lead to demonstrable organic disease. It can also result in physiological disorders and emotional instability, manifested in alcoholism, broken marriages, and, in the extreme, suicide. Three-fourths of all heart attacks suffered by police officers are caused by job-related stress. As a result, courts have ruled that a police officer who suffers a heart attack (even off duty) is entitled to worker's compensation (Washington Crime News Service 1975). Thus, even a superficial review of the human, organizational, and legal impacts of stress-related health problems should sensitize every police administrator to the need for preventing, treating, and solving these problems.

Job Stress

Stressors in law enforcement have been identified by various methods (Stratton 1978). Researchers such as Kroes (1974; 1976), Eisenberg (1975), Reiser (1970; 1972; 1974; 1976), and Roberts (1975) have all studied occupational stress in law enforcement. And although these researchers do not group stressors into identical categories, they do follow similar patterns. Thus, most of the stressors can be grouped into four categories: (1) organizational practices and characteristics; (2) criminal justice system practices and characteristics; (3) public practices and characteristics; and (4) police work itself.

Kroes, Margolis, and Hurrell (1974) asked 100 Cincinnati patrol officers about the elements of their jobs that they believed were stressful. Foremost on the list were the courts (scheduling appearances and leniency), police administration (undesirable assignments and lack of backing in ambiguous situations), faulty equipment, and community apathy. Items listed less frequently were changing shifts, relations with supervisors, nonpolice work, other officers, boredom, and pay.

A later survey of twenty police chiefs in the southeastern United States confirmed these findings (Somodevilla et al. 1978, p. 6). When asked about situations they believed were stressful for line personnel, the chiefs listed lack of administrative support, role conflicts, public pressure and scrutiny, peer group pressures, the courts, and imposed role changes.

Working with the San Jose Police Department, one researchers (Eisenberg 1975) identified numerous sources of physiological stress that reflected his personal observations and feelings experienced as a patrol officer for approximately two years. Some of these stress sources were poor supervision; absence or lack of career development opportunities; inadequate reward systems; offensive administrative policies; excessive paperwork; poor equipment; unfavorable court decisions; ineffective cor-

rections agencies (inability to rehabilitate or warehouse criminals); misunderstood judicial procedures; inefficient courtroom management; distorted press accounts of police incidents; unfavorable public attitudes; derogatory remarks by neighbors and others; adverse government decisions; ineffective referral agencies; role conflict; adverse working conditions; exposure to people suffering physical and mental anguish; concern over the consequences and appropriateness of their own actions; and fear of serious injury, disability, or death.

One researcher (Sewell 1983) actually developed a Law Enforcement Critical Life Events Scale, which he administered to two sessions of the FBI National Academy, each of which contained 250 officers from departments throughout the country. Sewell also chose a Virginia county police department for comparison and analysis.

The Law Enforcement Critical Life Events Scale developed by Sewell established a ranking system whereby officers would rate events from most to least stressful. Sewell's research indicated that the events requiring the greatest amount of readjustment were those relating to the categories of violence, threat of violence, personnel matters, and ethical concerns (see Table 7.1).

TABLE 7.1
Law Enforcement Critical Life Events Scale

Event	Value
1. Violent death of a partner in the line of duty	88
2. Dismissal	85
3. Taking a life in the line of duty	84
4. Shooting someone in the line of duty	81
5. Suicide of an officer who is a close friend	80
6. Violent death of another officer in the line of duty	79
7. Murder committed by a police officer	78
8. Duty-related violent injury (shooting)	76
9. Violent job-related injury to another officer	75
10. Suspension	72
11. Passed over for promotion	71
12. Pursuit of an armed suspect	71
13. Answering a call to a scene involving violent non-accidental death of a child	70
14. Assignment away from family for a long period of time	70
15. Personal involvement in a shooting incident	70
16. Reduction in pay	70
17. Observing an act of police corruption	69
18. Accepting a bribe	69
19. Participating in an act of police corruption	68
20. Hostage situation resulting from aborted criminal action	68
21. Response to a scene involving the accidental death of a child	68
22. Promotion of inexperienced/incompetent officer over you	68
23. Internal affairs investigation against self	66
24. Barricaded suspect	66
25. Hostage situation resulting from a domestic disturbance	65
26. Response to "officer needs assistance" call	65
27. Duty under a poor supervisor	64
28. Duty-related violent injury (non-shooting)	63
29. Observing an act of police brutality	62
30. Response to "person with a gun" call	62
31. Unsatisfactory personnel evaluation	62
32. Police-related civil suit	61
33. Riot/crowd control situation	61
34. Failure on a promotional examination	60
35. Suicide of an officer	60
36. Criminal indictment of a fellow officer	60
37. Improperly conducted corruption investigation of another officer	60

TABLE 7.1 continued
Law Enforcement Critical Life Events Scale

Event	Value
38. Shooting incident involving another officer	59
39. Failing grade in police training program	59
40. Response to a "felony-in-progress" call	58
41. Answering a call to a sexual battery/abuse scene involving a child victim	58
42. Oral promotional review	57
43. Conflict with a supervisor	57
44. Change in departments	56
45. Personal criticism by the press	56
46. Investigation of a political/highly publicized case	56
47. Taking severe disciplinary action against another officer	56
48. Assignment to conduct an internal affairs investigation on another officer	56
49. Interference by political officials in a case	55
50. Written promotional examination	55
51. Departmental misconduct hearing	55
52. Wrecking a departmental vehicle	55
53. Personal use of illicit drugs	54
54. Use of drugs by another officer	54
55. Participating in a police strike	53
56. Undercover assignment	53
57. Physical assault on an officer	52
58. Disciplinary action against partner	52
59. Death notification	51
60. Press criticism of an officer's actions	51
61. Polygraph examination	51
62. Sexual advancement toward you by another officer	51
63. Duty-related accidental injury	51
64. Changing work shifts	50
65. Written reprimand by a supervisor	50
66. Inability to solve a major crime	48
67. Emergency run to "unknown trouble"	48
68. Personal use of alcohol while on duty	48
69. Inquiry into another officer's misconduct	47
70. Participation in a narcotics raid	47
71. Verbal reprimand by a supervisor	47
72. Handling of a mentally/emotionally disturbed person	47
73. Citizen complaint against an officer	47
74. Press criticism of departmental actions/practices	47
75. Answering a call to a sexual battery/abuse scene involving an adult victim	46
76. Reassignment/transfer	46
77. Unfair administrative policy	46
78. Preparation for retirement in the near future	46
79. Pursuit of a traffic violator	46
80. Severe disciplinary action to another officer	46
81. Promotion with assignment to another unit	45
82. Personal abuse of prescription drugs	45
83. Offer of a bribe	45
84. Personally striking a prisoner or suspect	45
85. Physical arrest of a suspect	45
86. Promotion within existing assignment	44
87. Handling a domestic disturbance	44
88. Answering a call to a scene involving the violent non-accidental death of an adult	44
89. Change in supervisors	44
90. Abuse of alcohol by another officer	44
91. Response to a silent alarm	44

TABLE 7.1 continued
Law Enforcement Critical Life Events Scale

Event	Value
92. Change in the chief administrators of the dept.	43
93. Answering a call to a scene involving the accidental death of an adult	43
94. Move to a new duty station	43
95. Fugitive arrest	43
96. Reduction in job responsibilities	43
97. Release of an offender by the prosecutor	41
98. Job-related illness	41
99. Transfer of partner	40
100. Assignment to night shift duty	40
101. Recall to duty on day off	39
102. Labor negotiations	39
103. Verbal abuse from a traffic violator	39
104. Change in administrative policy/procedure	38
105. Sexual advancement toward you by a citizen	37
106. Unfair plea bargain by a prosecutor	37
107. Assignment to a specialized training course	37
108. Assignment to stakeout duty	37
109. Release of an offender on appeal	37
110. Harassment by an attorney in court	37
111. Administrative recognition (award/commendation)	36
112. Court appearance (felony)	36
113. Annual evaluation	35
114. Assignment to decoy duty	35
115. Assignment as partner with officer of the opposite sex	35
116. Assignment to evening shift	35
117. Assignment of new partner	34
118. Successful clearance of a case	34
119. Interrogation session with a suspect	33
120. Departmental budget cut	33
121. Release of an offender by a jury	33
122. Overtime duty	29
123. Letter of recognition from the public	29
124. Delay in a trial	28
125. Response to a "sick or injured person" call	28
126. Award from a citizens group	27
127. Assignment to day shift	26
128. Work on a holiday	26
129. Making a routine arrest	26
130. Assignment to a two-man car	25
131. Call involving juveniles	25
132. Routine patrol stop	25
133. Assignment to a single-man car	25
134. Call involving the arrest of a female	24
135. Court appearance (misdemeanor)	24
136. Working a traffic accident	23
137. Dealing with a drunk	23
138. Pay raise	23
139. Overtime pay	22
140. Making a routine traffic stop	22
141. Vacation	20
142. Issuing a traffic citation	20
143. Court appearance (traffic)	19
144. Completion of a routine report	13

Reproduced from the *Journal of Police Science and Administration,* Vol. 11, No. 1, pp. 113–14, with permission of the International Association of Chiefs of Police, P.O. Box 6010, 13 Firstfield Road, Gaithersburg, Maryland 20878.

Potential exposure to life-threatening health problems such as AIDS during a tour of duty may also contribute to officer stress as the following article explains.

AIDS and Law Enforcement

Acquired Immunodeficiency Syndrome (AIDS) is an increasingly serious public health problem in the United States and worldwide. Moreover, it is an extremely emotional issue that has engendered a great deal of fear and misinformation. AIDS affects the criminal justice system in two important ways. First, AIDS risk groups are probably overrepresented among suspects and offenders with whom the justice system deals every day. As a result, many law enforcement officers and other staff have become concerned that they are at increased risk of acquiring the AIDS virus through contact with suspects and offenders. Such fear and concern may adversely affect the level and quality of service delivered by a law enforcement agency. Second, because law enforcement officers are regularly in contact with intravenous drug users, prostitutes and others who are at high risk of being infected and infecting others, they may serve a vital educational function in the community. If they are armed with accurate information and sound judgment, law enforcement officers may be able to encourage behavioral change that will reduce the transmission of the AIDS virus.

In order to deal effectively with the AIDS issue, law enforcement agencies must address it in a forthright manner, preferably before fear and misinformation have a chance to affect service delivery. Regular education and training that present the facts about AIDS in clear, concise terms are absolutely essential. Obviously, agencies must have the facts about AIDS before they can present them to their staff and to citizens. Accurate medical knowledge is a prerequisite for rational policy decisions.

From Theodore M. Hammett, *AIDS and the Law Enforcement Officer: Concerns and Policy Responses* (Washington, D.C.: U.S. Department of Justice, 1987).

Alcoholism

Alcoholism in government and industry is not only widespread but is also extremely costly—a fact established by many independent researchers. Some 6.5 million employed workers in the United States today are alcoholics. Loss of productivity because of alcoholism has been computed at $10 billion (Dishlacoff 1976, p. 32).

Although precise figures are not available, department officials report informally that as many as 25 percent of their officers have serious alcohol problems (Hurrell and Kroes 1975, p. 241). These problems manifest themselves in a number of ways: higher than normal absentee rates prior to and immediately before regular days off, complaints of insubordination by supervisors, complaints by citizens of misconduct in the form of verbal and physical abuse, intoxication during regular working hours, involvement in traffic accidents while under the influence of alcohol on and off duty, and reduced overall performance.

It has been suggested that police work is especially conducive to alcoholism. Because police officers frequently work in an environment where social drinking is common, it is relatively easy for them to become social drinkers. The nature of the work and the environment in which it is performed are the stress stimuli (ibid.). Traditionally, however, police departments adhere to the "character flaw" theory of alcoholism. This philosophy calls for the denunciation and dismissal of an officer with an alcohol problem; to recognize the officer's alcoholism as a symptom of underlying problems would reflect negatively on the department. But this approach does not consider that alcoholism may result from the extraordinary stress of the job and that eliminating the officer does not do away with the source of the stress (ibid.).

There is no single "best way" for a police department to assist an officer with a drinking problem, but some agencies have enjoyed a fair degree of success in their efforts. For example, the Denver Police Department now utilizes a closed-circuit television system to reach officers who are problem drinkers and to encourage them to join an in-house program. The in-house program is designed to persuade the problem drinkers—after they have been sufficiently educated about their problem—to enter the Mercy Hospital Care Unit for recovering alcoholics (Dishlacoff 1976, p. 39).

Dishlacoff concludes that it is the responsibility of the individual police agency and its administrators to recognize and accept alcoholism as a disease and to create a more relaxed atmosphere and an in-house program to disseminate information about the problem. Police chiefs should neither tolerate nor ignore the unsatisfactory performance, excessive cost, and near-certain progressive deterioration of the individual officer (to the point of

AIDS BULLETIN

for your bulletin board

HOW AIDS IS SPREAD

The AIDS virus is spread by an exchange of body fluids. Some infected body fluids have a higher risk of spreading the virus than others.

HIGHER RISK BODY FLUIDS	LOWER RISK BODY FLUIDS*
Blood	Saliva
Semen	Urine
Vaginal Secretions	Feces
	Tears
	Sweat

* The AIDS virus can theoretically be transmitted by these contacts but there is no evidence that this actually occurs. The AIDS virus is not found in the sweat of infected persons.

INFECTION PATHS

FLUID EXCHANGE TYPE	EXAMPLE RISK BEHAVIOR
Blood - to - blood	Sharing hypodermic needles
Semen - to - blood	Unprotected oral, anal or vaginal sex
Vaginal secretions - to - blood	Unprotected vaginal or oral sex

AIDS IS NOT SPREAD BY

- Shaking hands
- Sneezing or coughing
- Food handling
- Sharing living quarters, transportation or work area
- Social kissing
- Breathing
- Mosquito bites

DEFENSIVE TACTICS AGAINST AIDS

- Δ Be informed about AIDS, particularly how to prevent the spread of the virus.
- Δ Use safer sex practices. Select partners carefully, use a condom, and restrict the number of partners.
- Δ Follow departmental infection control procedures rigorously.
- Δ Your skin is an effective barrier against the virus. Keep all cuts, scrapes and irritations bandaged. Replace bandages frequently to keep wound clean.
- Δ Always use a CPR mask with a disposable check valve when giving CPR.
- Δ Use safer search procedures. Use gloves, don't put your hands where you can't see; have subject empty pockets or purse; use a pencil to move contents of pockets or purses.
- Δ Carry all protective equipment (infection control items) when on duty. Always keep available all items recommended by your department.
- Δ Use protective equipment and disinfectants for clean up when appropriate.
- Δ Properly dispose of contaminated non-evidence items. Follow department procedures for handling evidence.
- Δ De-escalate conflicts, when possible, to reduce the risk of injuries to your skin.

PROTECTIVE EQUIPMENT AND WHEN TO USE IT

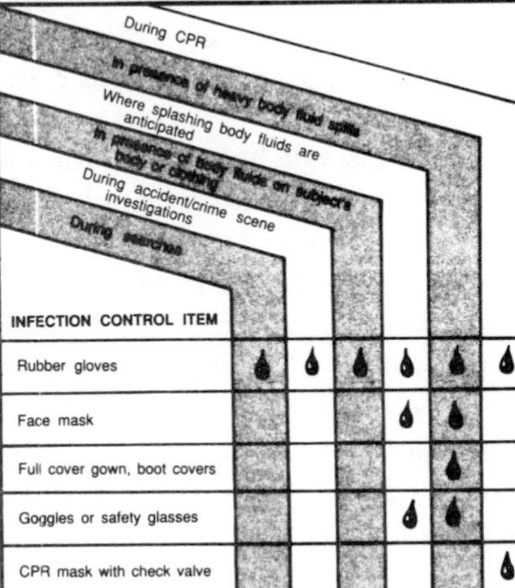

SITUATION

INFECTION CONTROL ITEM	During searches	During accident/crime scene investigations	In presence of body fluids on subject's body or clothing	Where splashing body fluids are anticipated	In presence of heavy body fluid spills	During CPR
Rubber gloves	●	●	●	●	●	●
Face mask				●	●	
Full cover gown, boot covers					●	
Goggles or safety glasses				●	●	
CPR mask with check valve						●

WHAT TO DO IN CASE OF ACCIDENTAL EXPOSURE TO BODY FLUIDS

BODY FLUID EXPOSURE TO YOUR . . .	RECOMMENDED FIRST TREATMENT	SEEK MEDICAL HELP	INJURY REPORT REQUIRED
Clothing	Wash clothes in water and soap	no	no
Skin (healthy intact skin)	Wash area with water and soap	no	no
Broken skin (existing cuts, scrapes, and irritations)	Wash wound with water and soap	yes	yes
Mouth	Wash with water	yes	yes
Nose	Wash with water	yes	yes
Eyes	Flush with water	yes	yes
Ears (in canal)	Flush with water	yes	yes
Fresh injuries (punctures, cuts, scrapes)	Vigorously wash with water and soap	yes	yes

AIDS HOTLINE • 1-800-352-AIDS

FIGURE 7.1
Sample training bulletin on AIDS used for police officers. *AIDS Information for Officers.* Courtesy of the Florida Department of Law Enforcement, 1988.

FIGURE 7.2
Wife of a Cincinnati police officer at her husband's burial. The officer and his partner were killed by a robbery suspect. Courtesy *The Cincinnati Post.*

unemployability) that occur if the illness goes unchecked (ibid.). If drinking affects an officer's health, job, or family, immediate action is essential: the officer is probably an alcoholic.

Reports from the Denver Police Department indicate that the department has benefitted greatly from its alcohol abuse program. Some of the benefits are (ibid.):

1. Retention on staff of most officers who suffer from alcoholism

2. Solution of complex and difficult personnel problems
3. Realistic and practical extension of the police agency's program into the entire city government
4. Improved public and community attitudes for officers and their families
5. Elimination of the dangerous and antisocial behavior of officers in the community
6. Full cooperation with rehabilitation efforts from police associations and unions that represent officers
7. Development of a preventive influence on moderate drinkers

Police Department Drug Testing

A significant issue facing police departments in the 1980s and into the 1990s is that of drug use by officers. The personal and legal ramifications are significant for officers, departments, and the communities they serve (McEwen, Manili, and Connors 1986, pp. 1–5).[3]

The availability and widespread use of illegal drugs is a cause of national alarm today. Reports of drug abuse come from every segment of our society. Thus it should come as no surprise that the police have not been immune to the contagion of drug abuse. Police officers experience stress and trauma in their jobs, and some may turn to drugs as a means of coping.

Drug use by police officers is now an important issue for every police chief in the nation. The problem is receiving national media attention because of its potential threat to the integrity of law enforcement and the safety of the community.

To learn how police departments are addressing this problem, the National Institute of Justice sponsored a telephone survey of thirty-three major police departments. The survey was conducted by Research Management Associates, Inc., of Alexandria, Virginia. Of the thirty-three departments surveyed, twenty-four had drug-testing programs. These departments explained their testing procedures, selection process, and the procedures that were used after a positive test. They also discussed whether treatment programs were available, and whether random testing had ever been considered. Departments provided information on the types of tests conducted, the administration of the tests, the procedures used to establish chain of custody, and the costs of the tests.

Key findings from the survey indicated that

- 73 percent of the departments surveyed were conducting drug-screening tests of applicants.
- Virtually all departments had written policies and procedures for conducting tests when there was reason to suspect that officers were using illegal drugs.
- 21 percent said they were considering mandatory testing of all officers.

- 24 percent indicated that treatment (rather than dismissal) would be appropriate for officers under some circumstances, generally depending on the type of drug and severity of the problem.

These results show that many police managers are taking steps to make their departments as drug-free as possible.

Further impetus for action has come from the International Association of Chiefs of Police (IACP), which in 1986 developed a model drug-testing policy for local police departments to consider in identifying and dealing with the use of illegal drugs by police officers. The policy calls for

- Testing applicants and recruits for drug or narcotics use as part of their pre-employment medical exams.
- Testing a current employee when documentation indicates that the employee is impaired or incapable of performing assigned duties, or experiences reduced productivity, excessive vehicle accidents, high absenteeism, or other behavior inconsistent with previous performance.
- Testing a current employee when an allegation involves the use, possession, or sale of drugs or narcotics, or the use of force, or there is serious on-duty injury to the employee or another person.
- Requiring current sworn employees assigned to drug, narcotics, or vice enforcement units to submit to periodic drug tests.

Many police departments already have policies along these lines. The IACP's endorsement of these steps may encourage other departments to take similar action to deal with employee drug abuse.

TESTING POLICE APPLICANTS AND EMPLOYEES

Drug tests have become a key factor of many police department programs to detect and deter the use of illicit substances by employees. Testing may occur as part of the screening process for applicants, as a requirement during the probationary period, as a condition of accepting a transfer, promotion, or assignment to a sensitive position, when officers are suspected of drug use because of behavior or work performance, or as part of a required annual physical.

Testing Applicants Table 7.2 shows the policies of the police departments in the survey that had some type of drug-testing program. Of the twenty-four departments, fifteen conducted tests of job applicants, and in all fifteen departments applicants were rejected when the tests were positive. The survey did not request information on the percentage of applicants rejected. However, local newspapers have reported that 20 to 25 percent of the applicants for uniformed positions in some large urban departments have shown positive urinalysis results.

In Texas, a recently enacted state law places greater emphasis on law enforcement's responsibility to hire drug-free employees. Specifically, the law states that a person may not become a peace officer, jailer or guard of a county jail, or a reserve law enforcement officer unless the person is "examined by a licensed physician and is declared in writing by the physician to show no trace of drug dependency or illegal drug usage after a physical examination, blood test, or other medical test." In disputed cases, an applicant may be ordered to submit to an examination by a state-appointed physician for certification that he or she is not dependent on drugs and does not use illegal drugs.

TABLE 7.2
Job Categories and Events Tested in Surveyed Police Departments (N = 24)

Job Category and Event Tested	Number of Departments	Percentage
Job applicant	15	62.5%
Probationary officers	5	20.8
Officers seeking transfer to sensitive jobs	3	12.5
Officers in sensitive jobs	4	16.7
Officers suspected of drug use	18	75.0
After auto accidents	2	8.3
Scheduled testing	1	4.2

Adapted from J. Thomas McEwen, Barbara Manili, and Edward Connors, *Employee Drug Testing Policies in Police Departments* (Washington, D.C.: U.S. Department of Justice, National Institute of Justice, 1986), p. 3.

Testing Probationary Officers Testing probationary officers is a standard procedure in some police departments. The New York City Police Department recently administered urinalysis tests for drugs, including marijuana, to more than 5,000 probationary officers. Only eighteen officers (0.35 percent) showed positive results. Although the probationary officers knew they would be tested three times between their recruitment date and the end of their eighteen-month probationary period, they did not know the exact dates of testing.

Testing Officers in Sensitive Jobs Some departments require testing as a condition for transfers or promotions to sensitive jobs such as vice and narcotics, internal affairs, SWAT teams, and data processing. Officers may be asked to sign an agreement that, as part of accepting a new position, they will take periodic drug tests to demonstrate freedom from drug dependency and abuse. In these instances, the testing is considered voluntary and is a condition of seeking and accepting a new position.

Testing Tenured Officers Departments test tenured officers for several reasons. In many instances officers can be required to submit to a test when they are suspected of drug use. Suspicion can occur as a result of a job performance review, a specific incident (such as a traffic accident or shooting), or an internal affairs investigation.

Periodic testing of tenured officers may also be a precondition for employment. For example, Boston Transit police officers agree to allow periodic testing when they are hired, and one department in the survey includes a drug test as part of an officer's annual physical.

Scheduled versus Random Testing One of the most controversial issues involves random testing of officers. Union opposition to random testing of tenured officers is almost universal, and the courts have tended to support the position that random tests violate the Fourth Amendment rights of employees.

Scheduled testing, such as testing as part of the annual physical exam for all employees, has not been as severely criticized as random testing. Scheduled testing allows an employee to stop using drugs temporarily just prior to the tests, but it may still deter some officers from using drugs. It has the additional advantage of becoming an expected, routine part of the physical examination, which reduces objections based on privacy tests.

There is little question that drug use by and drug testing of police officers will continue to be one of the most critical issues faced by departments and their communities for years to come.

Suicide

Suicide as a problem for police officers can best be understood by examining the differences between younger and older officers. Suicide among young officers is not particularly common, but when it does occur it is often associated with divorce or other family problems. Among older police officers, however, suicide is more common and is often related to alcoholism, physical illness, or impending retirement (Schwartz and Schwartz 1975, p. 136). And although hard data are not readily available, some researchers speculate that suicides immediately after retirement are not uncommon. It is widely known within police departments that police officers do not adjust well to retirement. It is not surprising to see newly retired officers become depressed and allow their physical condition to deteriorate. Like individuals in other occupations, police officers in general do not plan realistically for retirement. However, unlike other occupations, police officers are often deeply involved with their work up until the actual day of retirement. It is a shock to suddenly be estranged from a job that has occupied a major portion of one's life and has been the source of many social activities (ibid., p. 136). Such losses can be devastating for retiring or retired officers. But unfortunately, most police departments—unlike many major industries—have not yet addressed the problem.

One study concludes that male officers are more likely to kill themselves than men in other occupations (Lester 1970, p. 17). For example, the annual suicide rate for members of the New York City Police Department from 1960 to 1967 was 21.7 officers per 100,000; the annual rate from 1950 to 1965 was 22.7 per 100,000. Both rates were higher than the suicide rate of 16.7 per 100,000 for all males in the United States during the same periods (Friedman 1967). In reported suicide rates for males in various occupations in the United States in 1950, police officers had the second highest rate out of thirty-six occupations: 27.6 per 100,000 per year. Only self-employed manufacturing managers and proprietors had a higher rate; at 10.6 per 100,000 clergymen had the lowest rate (Labovitz and Hagedorn 1971).

Six possible reasons have been identified for the high suicide rates among police (Nelson and Smith 1970):

1. Police work is a male-dominated profession, and males have a higher suicide rate than females.
2. Firearms are available, and officers know how to use them.

3. Police suffer psychological repercussions from being constantly exposed to death.
4. Long and irregular working hours make strong friendships difficult and strain family ties.
5. Officers are constantly exposed to public criticism and a dislike for "cops."
6. Judicial contradictions, irregularities, and inconsistent decisions tend to negate the value of police work.

Some authorities believe that aggressive behavior does not stem from internal drives, but from societal frustration. In this sense, suicide and homicide are different manifestations of the same phenomenon. As acts of aggression, suicide and homicide cannot be differentiated with respect to the source of the frustration that generates the aggression. Homicide occurs when aggression legitimized by the aggressor is directed outward. Suicide, or self-oriented aggression, occurs when outward expression of frustration is deemed inappropriate (Henry and Short 1954, p. 15).

In one study of the suicides of twelve Detroit police officers who killed themselves between February 1968 and January 1976, Danto found that the group consisted of

> . . . young men, married and for the most part, fathers . . . with backgrounds of unskilled employment prior to their police appointment or military service, high school education or better, and some stable family life as measured by parents who were married and who had created families. The majority of the officers were white and had not been employed as police officers for many years. . . .
>
> The officers who committed suicide . . . used firearms and fatally shot their heads and abdomens. Carbon monoxide was the second most common cause of death and many of the suicides, regardless of method, occurred in an automobile. . . .
>
> The officers of the Detroit Police Department who committed suicide were different from the New York Police Department suicides. The Detroit group was younger, had less service time with the department, had a lower suicide rate within a police department, and less physical illness and police medical consultation histories, and fewer were single. In some respects they were similar: many had a history of alcohol abuse and dependency, had picked primarily firearms as their suicide method, and had suffered marital disharmony prior to their deaths.
>
> Neither study proves that the police officer is any more prone to choose his profession because of its opportunities to express aggression than anyone else in society. The rising suicide and homicide rates for nonpolice persons should attest to that (1978, p. 36).

The most upsetting problem for the suicidal male officer is his marriage. Officers sometimes commit suicide following the death of a significant person, or they kill themselves at a location near the persons they care for. To some extent, marital problems may be connected to the job, because hours are erratic and subject to change and officers are subjected to dangers not always understood by civilians.

Police suicide should be viewed from a psychological basis that emphasizes both the unique and multideterminant aspects of an individual's behavior and the societal influences on that behavior. The human being is a frustrated and status-oriented social animal who is not isolated from peers. In fact, in many ways the American police officer is like a health professional. As part of their life's work, officers frequently are in contact with the behaviorally different and socially ill citizens of our cities. When they themselves suffer unrelenting anguish, they often fear the loss of their jobs if they seek treatment (and perhaps realistically so) because of parochial attitudes toward mental health in many departments. Unfortunately, however, the closest analogy between the police and health professionals is the reluctance to get a fellow worker into treatment, probably because they feel it is none of their business. But a troubled police officer, like a troubled health professional, is of no use to the public or to the profession if he or she does not seek treatment (Heiman 1975).

Coping with Health Problems

There are many ways to reduce stress and to cope with health problems on the police force. The following methods and programs have been recommended in recent years (International Association of Chiefs of Police 1978, p. 3):

1. Using efficient preemployment screening to weed out persons who cannot cope with high stress
2. Increasing practical training for police on the subject of stress, including the simulation of high-stress situations
3. Increasing support from police executives with regard to the stress-related problems of patrol officers

4. Instituting mandatory alcoholic rehabilitation programs
5. Providing immediate consultation to officers involved in traumatic events such as justifiable homicides
6. Providing complete false-arrest and liability insurance to keep officers from worrying about their decisions
7. Providing psychological services to police officers and their families

Whatever the methods, a firm commitment is required from both the individual officer and the department. Any effort to increase effectiveness in coping with stress will be less successful in the absence of close cooperation between these parties.

USE OF DEADLY FORCE

No aspect of police work elicits more passionate concern or more divided opinion than the use of deadly force. Many community groups and minority organizations believe that police killings of civilians are excessive and often unjustifiable. Police agencies, on the other hand, are sometimes apprehensive and angry about unprovoked assaults on patrol officers (Wilson 1980, p. 16).

Few would argue with the idea that police officers have the right to use deadly force to protect their own lives or the lives of innocent persons. In many states, however, the law and departmental policies allow officers discretion that goes far beyond the simple edicts of self-defense or the defense of others. Many laws and policies are still modeled after English common law, which allows a police officer to use deadly force to apprehend someone reasonably believed to have committed a felony. The rationale for this formula is based on the fact that, until the early 1800s in both the United States and England, virtually all felonies were punishable by death. A felon was someone who, by his or her act, had forfeited the right to life (Milton et al. 1977, p. 39).

Recommendations that restrict police discretion in the use of deadly force are becoming increasingly common in law enforcement agencies. For example, the research findings and reports of the Police Foundation (Milton et al. 1977) and the International Association of Chiefs of Police (Matulia 1982) indicate that these groups sup-

FIGURE 7.3
Firearms training on a police shooting range. Courtesy Sergeant Robert Phillips and Deputy Martin Wolinski, Erie County (New York) Sheriff's Department.

port the present trend in many cities to limit the use of deadly force to situations involving self-defense, defense of others, and the apprehension of suspects involved in violent or potentially deadly felonies.

In addition to humanitarian reasons, there are legal, political, and social reasons for controlling police use of deadly force. For example, commissions established to study the causes of urban rioting have pointed out that the event that triggers violence is often the shooting of a young, minority male by a police officer (Kerner 1968).

One Killed, Seven Injured in Miami Melee

MIAMI—A rock-and-bottle-throwing mob, angered over the shooting of an armed black man by police, besieged a pool hall and trapped two officers inside for 30 minutes Tuesday night before they were rescued, authorities said.

Hospital officials said one man was shot to death in the incident, and seven others were injured, four with gunshot wounds. Two other motorists said they were hurt when rocks crashed through the windshield of their car in the street violence.

At least three police cars were set on fire and other scattered blazes were burning in the Overtown area, a predominantly black section of Miami. Crowds estimated at up to 150 blacks milled the streets during the disturbance, which was quelled within an hour, said Miami Police Chief Kenneth Harms.

"The situation is well under control and well in hand," Harms said at an 11 P.M. news conference. Nine people were arrested on "assorted charges," he said, and up to 200 officers had ringed the troubled area at one time.

United Press International reported that after Harms spoke to reporters, police said they had killed one of a band of looters trying to break into National Freezers Inc. in Overtown after someone opened fire on them.

The disturbance began shortly after the two police officers, whom Harms identified only as Hispanic males, entered a pool hall called the Game Room about 6:30 p.m., the police chief said.

One of the officers "saw a bulge" on a pool hall customer, Harms said, and when he asked what it was, the man replied: "That's a gun."

As the officer moved to arrest the man, he moved suddenly and "the officer's gun discharged," Harms added. Police spokesman Jack Sullivan said earlier that the man was shot in the head.

Shortly afterward, a crowd of about 150 people surrounded the pool hall and "became hostile and refused to let the officers exit," he said.

The man shot by police was identified as Neville Johnson Jr., 21. He was listed in critical condition at Jackson Memorial Hospital.

Another man whose identify wasn't released was killed by a gunshot wound to the chest, said hospital spokeswoman Betty Baderman.

"Eight victims have been brought to the hospital, four with gunshot wounds," she said.

Among the wounded were four black males, one white female and three white males, the spokeswoman said.

Shortly after 8 P.M., 15 squad cars assembled at a northwest Miami intersection and officers buckled on riot helmets and hefted billyclubs in preparation for an assault into the area, Sullivan said.

Miami City Commissioner J. L. Plummer said three special weapons teams in combat gear and the entire shifts from the central and south precincts, totaling more than 100 officers, were moved into an 84-block area around the beseiged building before the officers were freed.

At about 9:30 P.M., most of the uniformed officers had been pulled out of the area as public safety officials met to discuss the disturbance.

The police chief said a full review of the shooting would be conducted. City Commissioner Miller Dawkins said, "If anything is found wrong, we will act accordingly."

Several vehicles outside the pool hall, including unmarked police cars and television news vans, were set afire by the mob.

About 50 officers were pulled back to protect Miami police headquarters and a gunshop near the tense area. Traffic was detoured away from the 72-block warehouse district.

From *The Tampa Tribune,* 29 December 1982.

FIGURE 7.4
Violence erupted in the Overtown section of Miami after the shooting of a black man by police officers. Courtesy Wide World Photos.

Financial liability might also result from the use of deadly force. Deaths occurring from police action often result in substantial judgments against financially hard-pressed cities.

Managing the Use of Force

Police departments, which are ultimately held responsible for the actions of their employees, are required to ensure that their officers have received adequate training and supervision in various means of force that they might employ. The St. Paul, Minnesota Police Department in 1985 designed a research study on the use of force by its employees. Officers were required to identify on a report form both the specific amount of force they have used in a situation and the level of force that they encountered when attempting to take an individual into custody (Lundstom and Mullan 1987, pp. 6–9).[4] See Figure 7.5

The St. Paul study found that in 11,989 custody situations, officers encountered significant resistance 1,750 times during the year, or nearly 5 times per day. Of all those cases, only 1 percent resulted in injuries to suspects that required outpatient medical treatment; five individuals were hospitalized overnight; two died.

This type of validated statistical information should be admissible and defensible in any civil suit where the quality of overall department training is questioned. It can also be presented to community groups as part of any package describing department performance.

SHOOTING CONTROL TECHNIQUES One of the few areas in which the deadly force research data do seem to offer beleaguered police leaders some meaningful guidance is on the question of what shooting control techniques help limit problematic violence. Among many techniques, the following show promise (Geller 1987, p. 3):[5]

USE OF FORCE

1. PAGE____ OF____ | CITY OF ST. PAUL | DEPARTMENT OF POLICE | 2. C.N.

DAY	DATE	MO.	YEAR	TIME	LAST NAME (Suspect)	FIRST NAME	MID. INTL.	OFFENSE

ARREST MADE ☐ YES ☐ NO

I. LEVEL OF RESISTANCE

(May check more than one)

____ 1. No force, no handcuffs.
____ 2. No force, suspect handcuffed.
____ 3. Unarmed suspect resisted control, had to be physically handled with minimal force, no blows were struck, all parties remained standing.
____ 4. Number 3, plus at least one more officer was needed for assistance.
____ 5. Unarmed suspect resisted control, officer or suspect fell to the ground or blows were struck, no police weapons were used.
____ 6. Number 5, plus at least one more officer was needed for assistance.
____ 7. Unarmed suspect resisted control, police weapon(s) used.
____ 8. Number 7, plus at least one more officer was needed for assistance.
____ 9. Suspect armed with club or similar weapon and threatened or attacked officer.
____ 10. Suspect armed with knife or similar weapon and threatened or attacked officer.
____ 11. Suspect used motor vehicle to assault one or more officers.
____ 12. Suspect armed with firearm threatened officer.
____ 13. Suspect armed with firearm shot at officer.
____ 14. Other ____________________

II. POLICE WEAPONS USED

(May check more than one)

____ 1. None.
____ 2. Fist or hands.
____ 3. Federal Streamer.
____ 4. Standard baton.
____ 5. Riot Baton.
____ 6. Flashlight.
____ 7. Canine.
____ 8. STUN gun.
____ 9. Service revolver pointed at suspect.
____ 10. Service revolver fired.
____ 11. Shotgun pointed at suspect.
____ 12. Shotgun fired.
____ 13. Chemical munitions.
____ 14. Capture nets, restraints, or similar.
____ 15. Concussion grenades.
____ 16. C.I.R.T. special firearms.
____ 17. Other ____________________

III. EFFECT OF FORCE/RESISTANCE ON SUSPECT/POLICE

(Check one in suspect column, may check more than one in police column)

Suspect Police

____ ____ 1. No visible injury, no complaint of pain.
____ ____ 2. No visible injury, complaint of minor pain, no medical treatment required.
____ ____ 3. Minor visible injury (redness, swelling, abrasion), no medical treatment required.
____ ____ 4. Injury requiring outpatient medical treatment (stitches, x-rays, doctor's exam).
____ ____ 5. Injury requiring overnight hospitalization.
____ ____ 6. Died.
____ ____ 7. STUN guns only.
____ a. No effect.
____ b. Suspect submitted to arrest after seeing STUN gun demonstrated.
____ c. Suspect immobilized with no side effects.
____ d. Suspect immobilized with side effects.

REPORTING OFFICER #1	Employee #	REPORTING OFFICER #2	Employee #	TYPIST	SUPV.	P.O.	CODE CLERK	CARD

REC____ COORD____ SYSTEMS____

FIGURE 7.5
Form used by the St. Paul Police Department when officers use force in arrest situations. Courtesy of the St. Paul, Minnesota Police Department.

- Policies narrowing officer shooting discretion.
- Violence-reduction training to help officers abide by a "shoot only as a last resort" policy.

- Use of modern communications equipment and interagency cooperative arrangements that enable officers to summon whatever assistance they may need.
- Protective equipment, such as lightweight soft body armor suitable for routine wear by officers, and so-called "less lethal weapons," including TASER's (electronic dart guns), stun guns (compact cattle prods), rubber bullets, and other similar devices.
- Strong personnel policies, supervision of line officers, and fair but firm accountability up the chain of command for inappropriate officer aggressiveness and for deficient firearms training, procedures, and practices.
- Counseling for officers who desire help in dealing with job and other stresses and with postshooting trauma.
- "Cultural awareness" training to sensitize officers to ethnic, religious, or other group traits that might have a bearing on the officer's appraisal of a suspect's dangerousness and on the officer's ability to reduce it.

- Departmental reward systems that honor equally both an officer's decisiveness in using deadly force when necessary and his or her ability to resolve situations by less violent means when that option is available.

Big-city departments that have employed a number of these techniques together have produced positive results: fewer controversial shootings by officers, fewer serious injuries of officers, no increase in the crime rate, and no decline in officers' aggressiveness in making arrests.

This and other evidence convinced the U.S. Supreme Court in March 1985 to decide, by a 6–3 vote, that more than half the states' laws and many law enforcement agencies' regulations on police use of deadly force were unconstitutionally permissive. In *Tennessee* v. *Garner,* for the first time, a national minimum standard was imposed. Although ambiguities remain, the ruling prohibits police from shooting at unarmed, nonviolent, fleeing felony suspects. The Supreme Court heard and rejected the argument that a criminal suspect forfeits his or her right to live by committing a crime and disobeying a lawful police order to surrender. The Court reasoned that there must be proportionally reasonable balance between the alleged criminal conduct and the governmental response.

THE CONTINUING DEBATE Even after *Garner,* state laws and departmental shooting policies are likely to remain fairly diverse, although within narrower bounds. No longer can these provisions leave officers virtually untethered, as in the extreme case of one small American town whose only gun-use guidance to its officers was the homily, "Never take me out in anger, never put me away in disgrace." The range of firearms policies hereafter is likely to be from "defense-of-life" regulations, which permit shootings only to defeat an imminent threat to the officer's or another person's life, on the one extreme, to approaches on the other end that, permit shooting at currently nonviolent, fleeing suspects whom the officers reasonably believe committed a felony involving the threat but not the use of violence. Both approaches are currently employed by many police departments.

COMMISSION ON ACCREDITATION USE OF FORCE STANDARDS Most recently, the Commission on Accreditation for Law Enforcement, Inc., has established use-of-force standards, which agencies must meet in order to achieve national accreditation. The standards and a short statement of their purpose or intent are as follows (Commission on Accreditation for Law Enforcement Agencies, Inc., 1985. pp. 1–2, 1–3):[6]

1.3 Use of Force

1.3.1 A written directive states personnel will use only the force necessary to effect lawful objectives.

Commentary: The directive should encompass the use of all types and kinds of force (whether deadly or nondeadly) and all types and kinds of weapons. The directive may be issued in the form of a policy, rule, or order.

1.3.2 A written directive states that an officer may use deadly force only when the officer reasonably believes that the action is in defense of human life, including the officer's own life, or in defense of any person in immediate danger of serious physical injury.

Commentary: The purpose of this standard is to provide officers with guidance in the use of force in life and death situations and to prevent unnecessary loss of life. Definitions of "reasonable belief," and "serious physical injury" should be included in the directive.

1.3.3 A written directive specifies that use of deadly force against a "fleeing felon" must meet the conditions required by standard 1.3.2.

Commentary: A "fleeing felon" should not be presumed to pose an immediate threat to life in the absence of actions that would lead one to believe otherwise, such as a previously demonstrated threat to or wanton disregard for human life.

1.3.8 A written directive establishes criteria for authorizing the carrying of nonissued, personal firearms.

Commentary: The intent of this standard is to ensure that poor quality or inherently dangerous firearms are not used by officers. A firearm meeting accepted criteria should, furthermore, be expected to be in satisfactory working condition. The directive should address areas such as caliber, barrel length, type of weapon, identification of weapon, whether the officer is qualified to use the weapon, and policy concerning on-and off duty use of the weapon.

1.3.9 A written directive requires that a written report be submitted whenever an officer discharges a firearm, other than in training or for recreational purposes.

Commentary: The intent of this standard is to ensure that officers who accidentally or intentionally discharge a weapon submit a written report of the incident. The officer involved (if physically able) should be required

to submit the report within a specified time period. The report should set forth all circumstances surrounding the incident. If the facts of the incident support a conclusion that the shot was the result of negligence, the officer should be required to undergo firearms certification training again.

1.3.10 A written directive requires that only officers demonstrating a proficiency in the use of agency-authorized firearms, in addition to authorized side arms, be allowed to carry such weapons.

Commentary: The intent of this standard is to cover the carrying of weapons such as shotguns, tear gas guns, or automatic rifles. Demonstrated proficiency includes achieving minimum scores on a prescribed course, attaining and demonstrating a knowledge of the laws concerning the use of firearms, and being familiar with recognized safe-handling procedures for the use of these weapons.

1.3.11 A written directive requires each sworn officer to qualify at least annually with any firearm that the officer is authorized to use.

Commentary: The written directive should describe the score required for qualification, target type, timing, distance, and other conditions. Qualification should involve not only the actual firing of the weapon but also a passing score on a "what, when, where, and how" type of written test based on the training provided.

1.3.12 A written directive requires that only weapons and ammunition meeting agency-authorized specifications be used in the performance of duty.

Commentary: Control should be maintained for reasons of safety and civil liability.

1.3.13 A written directive requires a written report be submitted whenever an officer:

- *takes an action that results in (or is alleged to have resulted in) injury or death of another person; and/or*
- *applies force through the use of nonlethal weapons.*

Commentary: The standard is intended to require a written record of the circumstances surrounding injury or death that results from, or is alleged to result from, actions by officers. The report should address use of physical force, use of lethal and nonlethal weapons, or any other action resulting in injury or death, including traffic accident. The standard is not intended to document the display of weapons by officers.

1.3.14 The agency has a procedure for reviewing incidents in which there is application of force through the use of a weapon by agency personnel.

Commentary: The standard provides for latitude in categorizing cases to be reviewed through different procedures. The procedure should include reviewing incidents in which agency personnel discharge a firearm, whether on or off duty. This standard does not apply to firearms training, hunting, or participation in legitimate sporting events.

1.3.15 The procedures required in standard 1.3.14 include a report of findings to the agency's chief executive officer.

Commentary: The report of findings should include the relevant facts and circumstances surrounding the incident, and a conclusion as to whether the discharge violates an agency directive.

1.3.16 A written directive requires the removal of any officer from line-duty assignment, pending administrative review, whose use of force results in a death.

Commentary: The purpose of this standard is twofold: (1) to protect the community's interest when officers may have exceeded the scope of their authority in the use of deadly force; and (2) to shield officers who have not exceeded the scope of the authority from possible confrontations with the community.

As the following article describes, some departments such as the New York City Police Department are considering alternatives to the use of deadly force.

New York Police Select Restraints For Emergencies: Alternatives Are Sought to Use of Deadly Force

By ESTHER IVEREM

New York City police officials, in an effort to equip the department with something more powerful than a nightstick but less deadly than a gun, have chosen five devices to be used in dangerous situations.

The department has been studying alternatives to deadly force after several highly publicized cases in which suspects—particularly those

who were emotionally disturbed—were killed in confrontations with the police or while in police custody.

In each of the 75 police precincts in the city, one patrol car will be designated to carry the five devices, Commissioner Benjamin Ward announced yesterday at a news conference at Police Headquarters. Some of the devices are weapons, others are protective objects.

Sergeants to Use Devices

All of the devices have been tested by the department, and some have been used by the Emergency Services Unit and in a few test precincts. Under new guidelines that are still being prepared, only sergeants will be allowed to use the devices.

The sergeant's patrol car, carrying the devices, could be summoned either by a dispatcher who receives a report of an emergency involving a violent person or by a police officer who happens into such a situation.

These are the devices that will be available to New York City police sergeants:

- A hand-held electronic gun called a taser that shoots two darts, discharging a mild electrical shock to the body.
- A stun device, similar to the taser, but one that must touch the person to be effective.
- A canister similar to a fire extinguisher that can immobilize people with water pressure.
- A 17-pound plastic riot shield, five feet high and 32 inches across, that can withstand blows from a sledgehammer or other blunt objects.
- Padded Velcro retraint straps that can be used to bind ankles, legs or arms when a handcuffed suspect continues to create danger by thrashing or kicking.

Stun devices are being tried by police departments in dozens of cities, said Lester Shubin, the program manager for standards at the National Institute of Justice, a research division of the Justice Department in Washington.

Large water cannons are commonly used in Germany and elsewhere in Europe to disperse crowds, he said. New York police officials said their small water canister and the heavy plastic shield had been developed by the Emergency Services Unit.

In Los Angeles, the entire police force of 7,000 officers has been trained to use the taser, said a department spokeswoman, Margie Reid.

Other cities, such as San Francisco, have declined to use the device, however. Detractors cite incidents such as one last week in which a San Diego man suffered a fatal heart attack after being stunned three times with the device by police officers.

The Commissioner Ward said the pressurized-water device could subdue a person from a distance of 15 to 20 feet. "It blinds them, takes them by surprise," said a police spokesman, Deputy Inspector Michael A. Julian.

The taser device, which has been used by the Emergency Services Unit since 1985, would be used against those who are more violent. Both darts from the gun must hit an individual for it to be effective.

Officers have encountered problems in using the taser, Commissioner Ward acknowledged, when the officer jerks his hand while firing or when the darts fail to penetrate heavy winter clothing.

The other stun device, the Nova XR5000, is being mounted on a 5-foot pole so that officers can touch people with it while keeping some distance. Both stun devices deliver a 50,000-volt pulsating charge but only .00006 amps, enough to make an adult fall to the ground.

Allegations of excessive police force and brutality have been made for decades, often by members of minority groups. But the issue drew fresh attention three years ago when Eleanor Bumpurs, an elderly, mentally disturbed woman, was slain by two shotgun blasts from a police officer in her Bronx apartment as she wielded a 10-inch kitchen knife.

Misuse of Devices

In another incident cited by police officials yesterday, three officers shot Nicholas A. Bart-

lett, a Harlem man, last February after he struck a policeman with a 14-inch steel pipe, then raised it at six officers who tried to arrest him.

"I believe that if this equipment had been available in the Bartlett incident on 125th Street," Mr. Ward said, "perhaps the police officers would have been able to continue to dance out of the way of the 14-inch bar Bartlett was swinging if they knew that within seconds a sergeant would respond to the scene with a nonlethal alternative."

Critics of past police actions said that they were encouraged by the department's efforts to find weapons less deadly than guns but were wary about how the devices would be used.

"We need to examine the specific guidelines for the use of the devices before we can make any judgments," said Norman Siegel, executive director of the New York Civil Liberties Union. "But we already have some concerns."

Mr. Siegal said he was concerned that the taser and stun device could be used to torture people, as two officers in Queens did two years ago to force a teen-ager into confessing that he had sold drugs. Mr. Siegal said he was also concerned that the shields and water might be used against those "exercising their First Amendment rights" to demonstrations.

Case 7.1

The Standard Approach

At 1:32 A.M. a man we will call Fred Snyder dials 911 from a downtown corner phone booth. The dispatcher notes his location and calls the nearest patrol unit. Officer Knox arrives four minutes later.

Snyder says he was beaten and robbed twenty minutes before but didn't see the robber. Under persistent questioning Snyder admits he was with a prostitute he had picked up in a bar. Later, in a hotel room, he discovered the prostitute was actually a man, who then beat Snyder and took his wallet.

Snyder wants to let the whole matter drop. He refuses medical treatment for his injuries. Knox finishes his report and lets Snyder go home. Later that day Knox's report reaches Detective Alexander's desk. She knows from experience that the case will go nowhere, but she calls Snyder at work.

Snyder confirms the report but refuses to cooperate further. Knox and Alexander go on to other cases. Months later, reviewing crime statistics, the city council deplores the difficulty of attracting businesses and people to the downtown area.

NONTRADITIONAL POLICING

The Problem-Oriented Approach To Policing

Frequently police officers respond to requests for assistance at locations where they or other officers have been summoned for help on prior occasions. In many cities, officers can usually predict when they may be summoned in response to burglaries, assaults, and robberies. The following examples provide some insight into a fairly typical police response to a robbery associated with prostitution and a second nontraditional response that is termed "problem-oriented policing" (Spolman and Eck 1987, pp. 1–7).[7]

Case 7.2

The Problem-Oriented Approach

Midnight-watch patrol officers are tired of taking calls like Snyder's. They and their sergeant, James Hogan, decide to reduce prostitution-related robberies, and Officer James Boswell volunteers to lead the effort.

First, Boswell interviews twenty-eight prostitutes who work the downtown area to learn how they solicit, what happens when they get caught, and why they are not deterred.

Case 7.2 continued

They work downtown bars, they tell him, because customers are easy to find and police patrols don't spot them soliciting. Arrests, the prostitutes tell Boswell, are just an inconvenience: Judges routinely sentence them to probation, and probation conditions are not enforced.

Based on what he has learned from the interviews and his previous experience, Boswell devises a response. He works with the Alcoholic Beverage Control Board and local bar owners to move the prostitutes into the street. At the request of the police, the commonwealth's attorney agrees to ask the judges to impose stiffer conditions on probation: Convicted prostitutes would be given a map of the city and told to stay out of the downtown area or go to jail for three months.

Boswell then works with the vice unit to make sure that downtown prostitutes are arrested and convicted, and that patrol officers know which prostitutes are on probation. Probation violators are sent to jail, and within weeks all but a few of the prostitutes have left downtown.

Then Boswell talks to the prostitutes' customers, most of whom don't know that almost half the prostitutes working the street are actually men, posing as women. He intervenes in street transactions, formally introducing the customers to their male dates. The Navy sets up talks for him with incoming sailors to tell them about the male prostitutes and the associated safety and health risks.

In three months, the number of prostitutes working downtown drops from twenty-eight to six and robbery rates are cut in half. After eighteen months neither robbery nor prostitution shows signs of returning to its earlier level.

Reacting to incidents reported by citizens—as in the first hypothetical example—is the standard method for delivering police services today. But there is growing recognition that standard "incident-driven" policing methods do not have a substantial impact on many of the problems that citizens want police to help solve. Equally important, enforcing the law is but one of many ways that police can cope with citizens' problems.

Although alternative methods of handling problems have long been available, the police have made relatively little use of them. Or they have been used only sporadically, more often by a special unit or an informal group of innovative officers.

An alternative approach to policing called "Problem-Oriented Policing" has been developed to help solve this problem. It grew out of an awareness of the limitations of standard police practices and responses to criminal incidents. Police officers, detectives, and their supervisors can use the problem-oriented approach to identify, analyze, and respond on a routine basis to the underlying circumstances that create the incidents that prompt citizens to call the police.

Problem-oriented policing is the outgrowth of twenty years of research into police operations that converged on three main themes: *increased effectiveness* by attacking underlying problems that give rise to incidents that consume patrol and detective time; *reliance on the expertise and creativity of line officers* to study problems carefully and develop innovative solutions; and *closer involvement with the public* to make sure that the police are addressing the needs of citizens. The strategy consists of four parts.

1. *Scanning.* Instead of relying upon broad, law-related concepts—robbery, burglary, for example—officers are encouraged to group individual related incidents that come to their attention as "problems" and define these problems in more precise and therefore useful terms. For example, an incident that typically would be classified simply as a "robbery" might be seen as part of a pattern of prostitution-related robberies committed by transvestites in center-city hotels.
2. *Analysis.* Officers working on a well-defined "problem" then collect information from a variety of public and private sources—not just police data. They use the information to illuminate the underlying nature of the problem and suggest its causes and a variety of options for its resolution.
3. *Response.* Working with citizens, businesses, and public and private agencies, officers tailor a program of action suitable to the characteristics of the problem. Solutions may go beyond traditional criminal justice system remedies to

include other community agencies or organizations.

4. *Assessment*. Finally, the officers evaluate the impact of these efforts to see if the problems were actually solved or alleviated.

To test the value of this approach, the National Institute of Justice sponsored the Problem-Oriented Policing Project, conducted by the Newport News (Virginia) Police Department and the Police Executive Research Forum. Results of the project were encouraging:

- Downtown robberies were reduced by 39 percent.
- Burglaries in an apartment complex were reduced 35 percent.

TABLE 7.3
The Problem Analysis Model

Actors
- Victims
  - Lifestyle
  - Security measures taken
  - Victimization history
- Offenders
  - Identity and physical description
  - Lifestyle, education, employment history
  - Criminal history
- Third parties
  - Personal data
  - Connection to victimization

Incidents
- Sequence of events
  - Events preceding act
  - Event itself
  - Events following criminal act
- Physical contact
  - Time
  - Location
  - Access control and surveillance
- Social context
  - Likelihood and probable actions of witnesses
  - Apparent attitude of residents toward neighborhood

Responses
- Community
  - Neighborhood affected by problem
  - City as a whole
  - People outside the city
- Institutional
  - Criminal justice agencies
  - Other public agencies
  - Mass media
  - Business sector

TABLE 7.4
Some Problems Considered by Newport News, Virginia, Police

City-wide
- Assaults on police officers
- Thefts of gasoline from self-service filling stations
- Domestic violence
- Drunk driving
- Repeat runaway youths

In Neighborhoods
- Commercial burglaries, Jefferson Avenue business district
- Heroin dealing, 32d and Chestnut
- Residential burglaries, New Briarfield Apartments
- Residential burglaries, Glenn Gardens Apartments
- Thefts from automobiles, downtown parking area
- Dirt bikes, Newmarket Creek
- Rowdy youths, Peninsula Skating Rink
- Rowdy youths, Marshall Avenue 7-Eleven
- Robbery and prostitution, Washington Avenue
- Vacant buildings, central business area
- Larcenies, Beachmont Gardens Apartments
- Unlicensed drinking places, Aqua Vista Apartments
- Disorders and larcenies, Village Square Shopping Center

- Thefts from parked vehicles outside a manufacturing plant dropped 53 percent.

These findings hold important implications for police administrators and community leaders alike. In any case it is quite clear that new approaches to law enforcement and community problems will be called for in the next decade.

The Baltimore County COPE Project

The police department in Baltimore County, Maryland, provides another example of a nontraditional approach to policing in the 1980s. A unit called Citizen-Oriented Police Enforcement (COPE) was created to identify and reduce citizens' fear within its jurisdiction (Behan 1986 pp. 12–15).[8]

In interviewing hundreds of people, the police department attempted to define "fear." These interviews revealed that citizens were

- Afraid to go out at night
- Afraid to open the door when someone knocked
- Afraid to walk past a stranger
- Afraid to come out of the bank
- Afraid in the grocery store parking lot
- Afraid to leave their curtains open

- Afraid to call the police or to sign a complaint if they saw a crime or had a specific problem

COPE police officers had to be carefully selected and retrained. The traditional ways had to be replaced by new, innovative approaches to problem solving.

COPE officers were equipped with motorcycles and compact cars, which brought them closer to the people. Motorcycles and cars were to be driven slowly and stopped frequently, so officers could greet neighbors and allow youngsters to become acquainted with officers and their equipment.

Police officers were trained to review all facets of a problem while restoring the peace. They were taught to identify specifically the problems that might be causing citizens fear and that might lead to community disruption.

Case 7.3 illustrates how COPE and community-oriented policing in general work in Baltimore County.

Case 7.3

Garden Village Project

On June 7, 1983, a gunfight occurred at Garden Village, a low-income apartment complex occupied predominantly by blacks adjacent to the city of Baltimore. On June 18, a rape took place. Neither crime was reported to police, although one person was wounded in the shooting. Two factions had developed in the community, and they were struggling for dominance. Crime in the area was above normal, with robbery heading the list. The people in Garden Village were living in terror, and their relationship with the government had so deteriorated that they had stopped reporting crimes.

COPE Response

A COPE officer was assigned as project coordinator. His team conducted house-to-house problem identification surveys, which revealed the following characteristics:

- 91 percent black residency
- Low income
- 3–5 years of residency on the average

Case 7.3 continued

- 59 percent of residents under age 29
- 65 percent of respondents calling juvenile crime a main concern
- Area lacking in recreational facilities
- Lighting and alley deterioration in evidence
- No community leadership

Seeing no government commitment to the area, people had a high degree of apathy toward law enforcement. The project team decided on a two-pronged approach : (1) *community interaction*—to open lines of communication and attempt to alleviate community problems, and (2) *criminal intervention*—to gather intelligence information on all criminal activities and to coordinate this information with the patrol and detective forces in the department.

Through community interaction, data were gathered showing a need to upgrade street lighting. The COPE officer arranged meetings with the county lighting supervisor and the local utility company. Using data to show crime patterns related to lack of lighting, the COPE officer was able to convince utility officials to repair and upgrade thirty-one existing lights and to add three new mercury vapor lights.

Although the alleys were private property, COPE got the county roads department to repair the roads. COPE officers learned that the county could not afford to construct a new park facility, so they assisted the community in applying for a federal grant through the community development coordinator's office. When the area did not meet federal guidelines for funding, $70,000 for construction of a multipurpose (volleyball, basketball, tennis) court and tot lot was included in the 1986 county capital improvements budget. Present playground apparatus was repaired and painted, and dilapidated equipment was removed. The overall general maintenance of the park was improved. In the meantime, COPE helped to organize a youth group in the area.

Since crime prevention in Garden Village was nonexistent, the management of the complex

Case 7.3 continued

willingly responded to suggestions by COPE officers. Shrubbery was trimmed, locks upgraded, vacant apartments secured, and a crime-reporting system established.

The interaction group secured a place for the community to meet and organize. With their guidance, the citizens have filed for a charter.

The criminal investigation officers had similar success. Gaining the confidence of the youngsters, they developed information on the burglaries and several arrests were made. High visibility patrols were established and maintained. When an arrest was made in the original shooting, friction between the two groups ceased. One community member was particularly disruptive. Learning that he was on parole, COPE officers had him returned to the penitentiary. Burglaries were reduced 80 percent; auto larceny, 100 percent.

COPE involved eleven agencies in this project. This is a far cry from the traditional police response. A forgotten neighborhood was shown that government cares, and fear was reduced accordingly.

This case is an example of a situation typically defined as merely a "police" problem. Instead, the political and other leaders within the community chose to broaden their scope of defining a problem and work collectively to seek solutions.

LAW ENFORCEMENT'S RESPONSE TO THE ISSUE OF VIOLENCE IN THE 1980s

NCAVC

During the decade of the 1980s all levels of law enforcement were not only increasingly made aware of violent crime in America, but also were actively seeking new methods to solve these serious crimes. In 1981, William French Smith, then U.S. Attorney General, assembled the Attorney General's Task Force in Violent Crime. One of the recommendations of the task force was the formation of the National Center for the Analysis of Violent Crime (NCAVC). The project was originally a joint project of the Department of Justice and the FBI (Depue 1986, pp. 2–5).[9]

The overall goal has been to reduce the amount of violent crime in American society. The NCAVC's role in this regard is to serve as a law enforcement clearinghouse and resource center for the most baffling and frightening unsolved violent crimes, such as homicide, forcible rape, child molestation/abduction, and arson. The NCAVC collects and analyzes violent crime data and provides assistance to law enforcement agencies in their attempts to identify, locate, apprehend, prosecute, and incarcerate the persons responsible for these and other violent crimes and to develop new programs for the prevention of violent crime victimization.

The NCAVC represents a new and powerful weapon in the law enforcement arsenal to combat violent crime. Its research efforts are bringing forth new insights into violent criminal behavior and personality. Its training programs are disseminating the latest violent crime information and investigative techniques. More and more cases are being successfully analyzed, and criminal profiles are being constructed with remarkable accuracy. Imaginative investigative and prosecutive strategies are being developed, resulting in earlier detection and arrest and more certain conviction and confinement.

VICAP

A second innovative program, which stresses cooperation by law enforcement at all levels in resolution of crimes of violence is the Violent Criminal Apprehension Program (VICAP) (Howlett, Hanfland, and Ressler 1986, pp. 14–22).[10]

As envisioned by Pierce Brooks, a well-known expert in the study of violent crime, and eventually implemented by the FBI with Brook's assistance in 1985, VICAP is a nationwide data information center designed to collect, collate, and analyze specific crimes of violence. Cases which meet the following criteria are accepted by VICAP:

1. Solved or unsolved homicides or attempts, especially those that involve an abduction, which are apparently random, motiveless, or sexually oriented, or which are known or suspected to be part of a series.
2. Missing persons, where the circumstances indicate a strong possibility of foul play and the victim is still missing.
3. Unidentified dead bodies where the manner of death is known or suspected to be homicide.

FIGURE 7.6
Demonstration of a nonlethal restraining device. Chester Higgins, Jr., The New York Times.

It is important that cases in which the offender has been arrested or identified are still submitted so that unsolved cases in the VICAP system can be evaluated for possible linkage to known offenders. Also, it is anticipated that the VICAP system will be expanded to include rape, child sexual abuse, and arson cases within the next twelve to twenty-four months.

By analyzing the case-related information submitted by law enforcement agencies, the VICAP staff determines if similar pattern characteristics exist among the individual cases in the VICAP system. The identification of similar patterns is made by analyzing modus operandi, victimology, physical evidence, suspect description, and suspect behavior exhibited before, during, and after the crime.

VICAP's goal is to provide all law enforcement agencies reporting similar pattern violent crimes with the information necessary to initiate a coordinated multi-agency investigation that will lead to the expeditious identification and apprehension of the offender responsible for the crimes.

Criminal Profiling

A third tool developed by law enforcement to aid in solving crimes of violence is called "criminal profiling." The Behavioral Science Unit of the FBI has been providing this form of assistance to local police agencies (Douglas and Burgess 1986, pp. 9–13).[11]

Law enforcement may use criminal profiling to combine the results of studies in other disciplines with more traditional techniques in an effort to combat violent crime.

THE PROFILING PROCESS The profiling process is defined by the FBI as an investigative technique by which the major personality and behavioral characteristics of the offender are identified based upon an analysis of the crime(s) he or she has committed. The process generally involves seven steps:

1. Evaluation of the criminal act itself
2. Comprehensive evaluation of the specifics of the crime scene(s)
3. Comprehensive analysis of the victim
4. Evaluation of preliminary police reports
5. Evaluation of the medical examiner's autopsy protocol
6. Development of profile with critical offender characteristics
7. Investigative suggestions predicated on construction of the profile

DO NOT COMPLETE THIS REPORT WITHOUT FIRST READING INSTRUCTIONS

I. ADMINISTRATION

CASE ADMINISTRATION

FOR VICAP USE ONLY

1. VICAP Case Number: ______ 2. FBI Case Number: ______
3. FBI OO: ______ 4. VICAP Assignment: ______

5. Reporting Agency: ______
6. Address: ______ 7. City: ______
8. County: ______ 9. State: ______ 10. ZIP: ______
11. Reporting Agency's ORI Number: ______
12. Reporting Agency's Case Number: ______
13. NCIC Number If Victim Is 1) Missing or 2) an Unidentified Dead Body: ______
14. Investigator's Name: ______
15. Investigator's Phone Number: ______ - ______ - ______
16. VICAP Crime Analysis Report Type:
    - 1 ☐ Original Submission of This Case
    - 2 ☐ Supplement to Previously Submitted Information
    - 3 ☐ Correction of Previously Submitted Information
17. Investigating Agency's Case Status:
    - 1 ☐ Open (active investigation)
    - 2 ☐ Suspended (inactive investigation)
    - 3 ☐ Open —— Arrest Warrent Issued
    - 4 ☐ Cleared by Arrest
    - 5 ☐ Exceptionally Cleared (by UCR definition)

CRIME CLASSIFICATION

18. This VICAP Crime Analysis Report Pertains to the Following Type Case (check one only):
    - 1 ☐ Murder or Attempted Murder —— Victim Identified (go to Item 19)
    - 2 ☐ Unidentified Dead Body Where Manner of Death Is Known or Suspected to Be Homicide (go to Item 19)
    - 3 ☐ Kidnapping or Missing Person with Evidence of Foul Play (victim still missing) (go to Item 20)
19. Based on Your Experience and the Results of the Investigation of This Case, Do You Believe This Offender Has Killed Before?
    - 1 ☐ Yes (explain in Narrative Summary)
    - 2 ☐ No
    - 99 ☐ Unable to Determine
20. There Is an Indication That This Case Is Related to Organized Drug Trafficking:
    - 1 ☐ Yes
    - 2 ☐ No
    - 99 ☐ Unable to Determine

DATE AND TIME PARAMETERS

21. Today's Date: ____/____/____ (mo) (da) (yr)

	Date	Military Time	Exact	Approx-imate
22. Victim Last Seen:	____/____/____ (mo) (da) (yr)	______	☐	☐
23. Death or Major Assault:	____/____/____ (mo) (da) (yr)	______	☐	☐
24. Victim or Body Found	____/____/____ (mo) (da) (yr)	______	☐	☐

FIGURE 7.7
VICAP crime analysis form. Courtesy of the FBI.

II. VICTIM INFORMATION

VICTIM STATUS

25. This Is Victim _____ of _____ Victim(s) in This Incident.
(number) (total)

26. Status of This Victim:
1 ☐ Deceased (as result of this incident)
2 ☐ Survivor of Attack
3 ☐ Missing

VICTIM IDENTIFICATION

27. Name: ________________________________
(last, first, middle)

28. Alias(es) (including maiden name and prior married names):
____
____

29. Resident City: ____________ 30. State: ________ 31. ZIP: ________

32. Social Security Number: _____—____—_____ 33. FBI Number: ________

PHYSICAL DESCRIPTION

34. Sex:
1 ☐ Male 2 ☐ Female 99 ☐ Unknown

35. Race:
1 ☐ Black 3 ☐ Hispanic 5 ☐ Other
2 ☐ Caucasian 4 ☐ Oriental/Asian 99 ☐ Unknown

36. Date of Birth: ____/ ____/ ____
(mo) / (da) / (yr)
99 ☐ Unknown

37. Age (or best estimate) at Time of Incident: ________
99 ☐ Unknown (years)

38. Height (or best estimate): _____ feet _____ inches
99 ☐ Unknown

39. Approximate Weight: ________ lbs.
99 ☐ Unknown

40. Build (check one only):
1 ☐ Small (thin) 3 ☐ Large (stocky)
2 ☐ Medium (average) 99 ☐ Unknown

41. Hair Length (check one only):
1 ☐ Bald or Shaved 4 ☐ Shoulder Length
2 ☐ Shorter Than Collar Length 5 ☐ Longer Than Shoulder Length
3 ☐ Collar Length 99 ☐ Unknown

42. Hair Shade (check one only):
1 ☐ Light 3 ☐ Neither 1 or 2 Above
2 ☐ Dark 99 ☐ Unknown

43. Predominant Hair Color (check one only):
1 ☐ Gray and/or White 5 ☐ Black
2 ☐ Blond 6 ☐ Other
3 ☐ Red 99 ☐ Unknown
4 ☐ Brown

FIGURE 7.8
VICAP analysts reviewing nationwide data. Courtesy of the FBI.

The process used by the person preparing a criminal personality profile is quite similar to that used by clinicians to make a diagnosis and treatment plan: Data is collected and assessed, the situation reconstructed, hypotheses are formulated, a profile developed and tested, and the results reported back.

Criminal personality profiling has been used by law enforcement with success in many areas and is viewed as a way in which the investigating officer can narrow the scope of an investigation. Profiling unfortunately does not provide the identity of the offender, but it does indicate the type of person most likely to have committed a crime having certain unique characteristics.

PRIVATE SECURITY AND LAW ENFORCEMENT: PARTNERS FOR THE FUTURE

A recent trend in this country is the desire on the part of public law enforcement and private security to examine their respective and interactive roles. Given the increased demands for service made to police agencies coupled with a constant or decreasing tax support base, the need to review critically which services can best be provided by public law enforcement versus the private security industry is an issue being discussed. Politicians, police managers, and private security executives are faced with the same question: How can they serve their constituents in the most cost-effective manner, relative to crime control? (Cunningham and Taylor 1984, pp. 1–5).[12]

Traditionally, society's efforts to prevent and control crime have relied almost exclusively on the police and on other parts of the criminal justice system. Less visible are the private security resources of business, industry, and institutions.

Today, private security plays a major protective role in the nation's life. It employs an estimated 1.1 million persons, and total expenditures for its products and services were estimated at $22 billion for 1980. In 1979, federal, state, and local law enforcement expenditures were only $14 billion.

Private Security Today

To obtain a clear and current picture of the extent and nature of private security efforts, in 1980 the National

Institute of Justice began a comprehensive study conducted by Hallcrest Systems, Inc.

The research included interviews with more than 400 people in law enforcement and all areas of proprietary and contractual security, a survey of state agencies regulating private security and of 1,600 law enforcement and security managers, and an economic analysis and forecast of the private security industry. In addition, field studies were carried out in two urban counties—Multnomah County (Portland), Oregon, and Baltimore County, Maryland.

Major Findings

Private security resources, both expenditures and employment, now exceed those of law enforcement and will continue to increase as resources for public law enforcement stabilize. Business, industry, and institutions together spend more than $20 billion annually for security in their organizations.

Both police and security managers are receptive to the idea that private security should respond to some minor criminal incidents occurring on the property it protects and that some non-crime-related police tasks should be contracted out to the private sector. Thus far, however, there is limited interaction and cooperation between the public police and the private security industry in crime prevention and public safety.

Law enforcement executives tend to view private security as largely ineffective in reducing crime; they rate its performance generally low. The quality of security personnel is a major concern to the police, who favor (as does most of the security industry) state legislation to license and upgrade the quality of security personnel.

Two major problems hamper police-security relationships—off-duty police moonlighting in private security jobs and the excessive number of false burglary alarms to which police must respond.

Crime reporting is a low priority for security managers—sometimes as a policy of the companies for which they work. Partly because of this, the police are rarely called upon to investigate such crimes as internal theft and fraud. Businesses and institutions divert many criminal acts from the public justice system by resolving the incidents internally. Little is known about these "private justice systems."

FIGURE 7.9
Criminal profilers at work. Courtesy of the FBI.

Shift in Protection Resources

The most rapid growth for private security appears to have occurred in the early 1980s, even in the midst of an economic recession; this period of growth corresponded with slowed increases, tending toward stabilization, in police resources. A survey of law enforcement agencies found that 44 percent of police and sheriff's departments reported the same number of or fewer personnel in 1981 as five years earlier. Reductions in force, hiring freezes, and normal attrition contributed to this stabilization or decline in law enforcement jobs.

During this period, growing numbers of Americans undertook self-help measures against crime, increasing the use of locks, lighting, guns, burglar alarms, citizen patrols, and security guards. One National Institute of Justice study found that 40 percent of respondents in ten major U.S. cities had installed some form of security device in their homes.

Such expanded use of private security and increased citizen involvement signal an increasing return to the private sector for protection against crime. The growth and expansion of modern police departments reflected a shift from private policing and security initiatives of the early nineteenth century. Now the pendulum appears to be swinging back. Despite the expanded role of the police in crime prevention in recent years, it appears that the private sector will bear an increased prevention role while law enforcement concentrates more heavily on violent crimes and crime response. Economic realities are forcing law enforcement to seek ways to reduce workloads.

National surveys of proprietary and contract security managers also indicate their willingness to accept more responsibility for minor criminal incidents occurring in their bailiwicks. These new responsibilities could include responding to burglar alarms, investigating misdemeanors and completing official misdemeanor reports, and initiating preliminary investigations of other crimes. The 384 law enforcement agencies surveyed in this study indicated a willingness to discuss such a transfer of responsibilities to private security. They cited a number of police tasks "potentially more cost effectively performed by private security"—among them public building security, parking enforcement, and court security. In some parts of the country, contract security firms already are performing some non-crime-related tasks.

Police and Security Cooperation

Law enforcement executives surveyed rated the overall contribution of private security and its reduction of direct dollar crime loss only "somewhat effective;" private security's contributions to reducing the volume of crime, apprehending criminal suspects, and maintaining order were judged ineffective. In fact, law enforcement gave private security low ratings in ten areas, including quality of personnel, training received, and familiarity with legal authority.

Private security has undertaken some efforts to upgrade the quality of its personnel, including certification programs and a proliferation of academic degree programs. Nevertheless (and although actual contact between police officers and security officers is quite limited), the police are inclined to stereotype private guards as heavy-handed in their use of force and weapons. Research data disputes the accuracy of this image.

Strong criticism of private security by police is not muted despite the fact that an estimated 150,000 police workers work as regular off-duty employees of private security. Their role, in fact, is a source of much of the contention. Some say that the moonlighting police are "hired guns"—that their value to private security is due in part to the fact that they can carry weapons while other security employees might have difficulty obtaining licenses. Other problems occur over the question of liability—is the police force or the off-duty employer legally responsible for the moonlighting officer's acts? Still another criticism stems from the possibility of conflict of interest—particularly when police officers operate their own private security firms as a sideline or when an officer wears his or her uniform and badge while working in private employment.

Another major source of contention between the police and private security is the excessive number of responses to false burglary alarms. False alarms are often reported to make up 10 to 12 percent of all calls for police services; and as public safety personnel struggle to provide current levels of service in the face of declining tax revenues, the accelerated rate at which new alarm systems are being installed threatens to swell police workloads further. An example of how some city police agencies have attempted to deal with frequent false alarms is by having ordinances enacted that penalize citizens and businesses if the problem recurs. See Table 7.5.

False alarms, moonlighting, and negative police perceptions of private security competence have all contributed to a situation in which there is little formal interaction or cooperation between the police and private security. Security managers report some sharing of information, personnel, equipment, and other resources with law enforcement, but most cooperative efforts appear to be initiated by the private sector. Those areas

TABLE 7.5
How Cities Crack Down on False Alarms

City	Population	Burglary Rate per 100,000 Population	First Year of Ordinance	Permit/ Registration	Number of "Free" Alarms	Grace Period	Highest Penalty*	Total Alarm Systems	Total False Alarms
	436,214	2,795	1979	No	4/yr.	No	$50	**	40,000
	573,131	2,001	1982	No	2/yr.	No	$100	2,093	33,000
	997,467	3,154	1982	Yes	2/yr.	Yes	$50	37,000	83,700
	385,892	3,054	1980	Yes	5/yr.	No	$25	7,500	25,434
	495,190	3,284	1972	No	2/6 mo.	No	$50	19,000	20,011
	988,284	1,656	1981	Yes	2/1 mo. 3/3 mo. 4/6 mo. 5/yr.	No	No Fine	**	26,771
	381,473	2,597	1982	No	10/6 mo.	Yes	No Fine	**	**

* does not include fee for reinstatement if license is revoked
** not available

Reprinted by permission of *Security Magazine*, May 1987, p. 52.

in which cooperative efforts have been reported include hazardous materials movement, protection of dignitaries and executives, disaster management, traffic control, crowd control, measures to counter terrorism, and economic crime investigation.

Major Recommendations

How far-reaching will the impact of private security resources and technology on crime prevention and control be? The answer depends on whether law enforcement and private security forge a closer partnership. If greater interaction and cooperation are to take place, a number of actions and strategies are called for. The study made the following recommendations:

- *Upgrade private security.* Upgrading the quality of security personnel was the most frequent recommendation made by both police and security managers who were surveyed. Both groups overwhelmingly agree on the need for statewide regulatory statutes for contract security, plus mandatory criminal background checks and minimum levels of training for both proprietary and contract security officers. In addition, adoption of standards, codes of ethics, and model licensing, certification, and contract performance specifications are recommended.
- *Increase police knowledge of private security.* Seminars, training materials, designation of security liaison officers, inventories of security firms, and other mechanisms are recommended to develop a greater awareness by police of the role and resources of private security in their communities.
- *Expand interaction.* Recommended strategies include identification of specialized investigative resources and equipment of private security that are available to complement police investigations, establishment of joint task forces for investigation of major or recurring losses, and development of official policies for sharing investigative information.
- *Experiment with transfer of police functions.* Research and demonstration programs are recommended to isolate police activities that do not require police authority, identify areas where contracting may be effective, and explore legal mechanisms and special officer status for security personnel. Special attention should be given to contracting burglar alarm response to the private sector, including measuring whether the deterrent value of response rises from police authority or merely from attention that is quick, uniformed, and armed.

If law enforcement is to be relieved of its large workload of minor and non-crime-related calls, some nontraditional approaches are required. Creative use of private security may prove to be a viable option for conserving scarce law enforcement resources and bolstering protection of the public.

Businesses Targeted Among Most Common Crime Venues; Special Police Focus Urged

A new report has found that just 5 percent of a city's occupancies, many of them businesses, produce 64 percent of all 911 calls. The report already is changing the way police treat emergency calls.

"These findings suggest that police should not just treat each call individually. Concentrating police work at the most active locations may be a much more effective way to reduce crime," said Lawrence W. Sherman, president of the Crime Control Institute, Washington, D.C., and author of the report.

The study, which analyzed 312,000 calls to police in Minneapolis, has prompted the police department there to form an experimental Repeat Call Policing unit to focus on 250 of the top dispatch locations.

Findings show that many of the locations deserving special police attention are businesses. Six of the top ten addresses in the city are operated by Fortune 500 companies, each averaging more than one police call per day. Half of the top 50 addresses are commercial locations like retail stores and bars.

Property crime is the most common problem among businesses, the cause of 40 percent of their calls to police, according to the report. Personal disputes prompted 32 percent of the calls, followed by accidents and lockouts at 15 percent and traffic problems with 5 percent.

The report, commissioned by the National Institute of Justice, is titled "Repeat Calls to Police in Minneapolis."

Reprinted by permission of *Security Magazine,* May 1987, p. 14.

TECHNOLOGICAL TRENDS IN POLICING

Numerous technological trends have evolved over the last decade in law enforcement (see the news article, "The Year in Focus: Advances in Technology," on p. 000). Two specific innovations of interest are: computer-aided dispatch (CAD) and fingerprint automation.

Computer-Aided Dispatch

The critical tasks of a police radio dispatcher include obtaining accurate information from members of the public who are in need of assistance and efficiently sending an officer to provide the help necessary. Therefore, the appropriate management of information by the dispatcher may mean the difference between life and death. In a computer-aided dispatch (CAD) system, the police radio dispatcher is assisted by a high-speed digital computer (Larson 1985, p. 2–6).[13]

CAD systems also offer greater options for managing service demands. Dispatchers must manage two lists: the backlog of unanswered police calls for service and the list of available police patrol cars in the dispatch area. Too many police dispatchers (with or without a CAD system) will send a police car to an incident in the dispatch area if at least one police car is available there. This policy often depletes all available police resources by assigning them with equal priority to all varieties of calls for service, stacking them only when all cars in a given area are simultaneously busy.

Guided by an intelligent CAD system, more and more low-priority calls could be deliberately delayed when cars become scarce. Then the remaining cars would be available as "insurance" for high-priority calls that might come in to the dispatcher. Rather than simply acting as an electronic conveyer belt, this system would assist in the correct prioritization and management of demand for police services.

Advanced computer-aided dispatch systems can also assist dispatchers with important details. It is often no trivial task for the operator to obtain the correct address. The caller is often distressed and unable to enunciate the street name and number, much less give the correct spelling of the street name. In some cities and larger multi-jurisdictional CAD systems, two or more streets may have the same name.

Well-publicized tragedies have occurred when incorrect addresses were typed into CAD systems (see Case 7.4).

Case 7.4

A woman residing in a village just outside Buffalo, New York, was brutally murdered by

> **Case 7.4 continued**
>
> an intruder after being assured police assistance was on the way. Unfortunately, patrol units were dispatched to a duplicate address within the city of Buffalo, where the same street and number existed. Police were delayed fourteen minutes, during which the break-in and homicide occurred.

The majority of police calls are of low priority or are noncriminal, but for the 5 or 10 percent that are urgent, police must have correct information and act on it swiftly. An intelligent CAD system would detect an ambiguous address or one that did not exist and could suggest that the operator question the caller to verify the address.

Several currently implemented CAD systems have made major strides in "getting the address right," including the addition of hazardous address files, files containing information on repeat callers, dangerous situations, and the like.

Fingerprint Automation

A second trend in law enforcement technology has been the automation of fingerprints. As the agency that serves as the central repository of this country's fingerprints, the FBI conducted research to find an answer to the ever-increasing problem of accurate, timely fingerprint processing (Neudorfer 1986, pp. 2–8).[14]

In recent years, computer technology is being used as an aid in latent fingerprint work to solve criminal cases. With more and more of the FBI's Identification Division's data placed in computerized files, it is more feasible to let the computer perform tasks too labor-intensive to be performed manually.

In the past, a latent fingerprint specialist would attempt every approach humanly possible to try to identify latent prints submitted as evidence in a case. But, after exhausting all possible suspects or leads without making an identification, the case would be returned to the con-

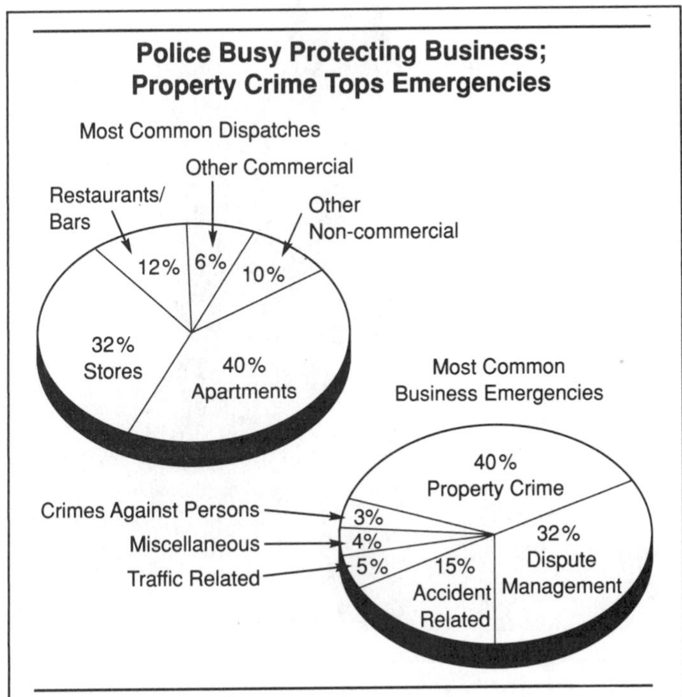

FIGURE 7.10
Half of the top 50 addresses to which police are dispatched are businesses, according to a recent study of police response in Minneapolis. Property crime and disputes comprise about three-fourths of the emergencies.

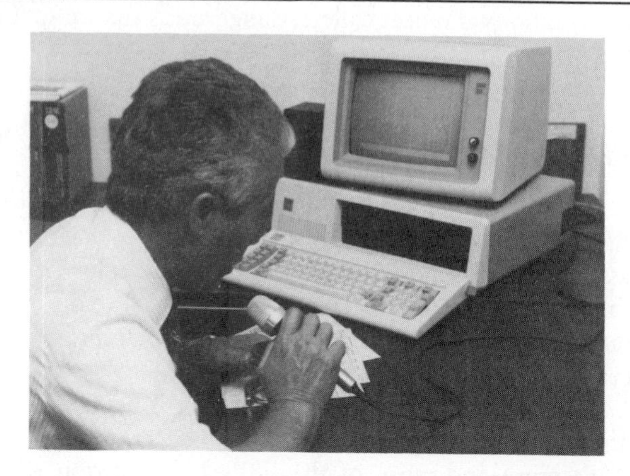

FIGURE 7.11
Automatic voice recognition. FBI examiner orally classifying a fingerprint card using a microphone. Courtesy of the FBI. *FBI Law Enforcement Bulletin,* March 1986, p. 5.

tributing agency unsolved. Due to the millions of criminal fingerprints on file, attempts to develop additional suspects in a case were impractical.

But with the introduction of the computer and with more than 16 million records now in the computerized files, it has become feasible to use new techniques to select logical suspects in cases involving crime-scene latent fingerprints. One program, the Latent Descriptor Index, is currently in operation. Through the use of latent fingerprint pattern types, physical description information, and case information, it can perform a computer search of the FBI's Identification Division's automated files. Since it was instituted, the Latent Descriptor Index has solved cases that would not have been solved otherwise.

A new automated capability, called the Automated Latent System Model, is being developed. This system provides an on-line searching and matching capability against a data base of repeat offenders and criminals categorized by specific crimes. Currently, this data base contains 193,000 records, but expansion to several

FIGURE 7.12
FBI operator utilizing a semi-automatic fingerprint reader to encode a fingerprint manually. Courtesy of the FBI. *FBI Law Enforcement Bulletin,* March 1986, p. 7.

hundred thousand is planned. This system works by entering as much of the personal descriptive information, crime information, and fingerprint data as is available into a semiautomatic fingerprint reader terminal. The Automated Latent System Model selects candidates from the data base that match the personal and crime descriptive information submitted. Then all possible candidates are compared with the latent fingerprint via the matching algorithm.

The Year in Focus: Advances in Technology

While police work remains fundamentally a people-oriented business, there is always more than enough room for advances in a variety of scientific and technical areas. In 1986, whether in terms of speeding up or improving the police job, or increasing officer safety, there were technological breakthroughs by the truckload.

- With drug testing a recurrent theme of 1986, the year saw the first courtroom applications of a procedure that allows scientists to trace personal drug use histories through the examination of a single shaft of hair. As described by Dr. Frederick P. Smith, a pioneer of the process, drug metabolites stay in hair and, like rings on a tree, can prove that a person had used cocaine, amphetamines, barbiturates, heroin and other opiates for an extended length of time.
- The Dallas Police Department's six-month experiment with the use of cellular telephones in squad cars and SWAT team vehicles proved to be a resounding success. The cordless phones, loaned to the Dallas Police Department by a local company, work by automatically transferring calls from a central computer to the nearest transmitter over conventional phone lines. According to Capt. R. D. Stone, who came up with the experiment, police are able to phone in arrest or offense violation information directly to the department's "revolutionary" computerized offense reporting system.
- In mid-December 1985, the Cook County, Ill., Sheriff's Department began testing two different video systems in an effort to improve the safety of officers during traffic stops, and by the middle of last year officers were starting to sing the systems' praises. One of the systems records in color and is mounted atop the car next to a light for filming at night. The system has a videotape recorder attached to the camera. The other system records in black and white and is mounted on the dashboard.
- DNA "fingerprinting," a process developed in England and now under study by the FBI, may eventually revolutionize traditional identification methods. The testing of DNA (deoxyribonucleic acid)—the basic genetic building block that is found in every part of the body—can be done with tiny samples of blood, semen or even hair roots and could be especially helpful in rape cases where it is currently extremely difficult to identify the origins of sperm. With a given individual's blood and semen providing the DNA fingerprint, it would be possible to match a DNA print of sperm from a victim's clothing in a rape case to a sperm sample of a suspected rapist.
- The computerization of fingerprint identification is a revolution in the making, transforming the process of criminal identification by allowing police to identify a suspect within minutes rather than the hours it now takes to match prints manually. Early last year, Los Angeles Mayor Tom Bradley agreed to the purchase of a $6-million system for the city's police department. The system, expected to go on line this year, will help police to clear an estimated 250,000 additional cases a year. The Chicago Police Department recently purchased a system which it hopes will alleviate some of the legal restrictions that last year were put on the time allowed for the fingerprinting of a misdemeanant. The Denver Police Department and the Florida Department of Law Enforcement (FDLE)

have also taken steps to computerize their fingerprinting methods in the very near future.

Reprinted with permission from *Law Enforcement News*, January 27, 1987 edition, p. 5.

SUMMARY

In this chapter we have focused on issues we believe were deserving of special attention: namely, professionalization of the police; affirmative action and equal opportunities in law enforcement; police officer stress; police use of deadly force; nontraditional policing; law enforcement's response to violence in America; the emergence of private security in this country and its interactive role with public law enforcement; and finally technological trends designed to assist police agencies now and in the future.

Police leaders believe that moving towards professionalization of the police would eventually allow them to enjoy the prestige, respect, and high salary normally accruing to those who are considered professionals. Linked to this pursuit of professionalization is the current law enforcement accreditation process and the need for police officers to have a college degree. We have suggested that the acquisition of a college degree by police officers will not necessarily lead to greater productivity or a reduction in the community crime rate. Much of what police officers do, however, is not related to the "crime fighting" function, but rather involves delivering social services, resolving conflicts, and maintaining order. It may indeed be that the greatest benefits police and citizens will derive from the professionalization of the police is not so much improvements in their technical skills, but improvements in their human relations skills.

The affirmative action and equal employment opportunity programs pursued by police departments have met with marginal success. Recruitment of minority men, especially black males, has encountered some resistance, in part because of the negative image some police departments have in their communities. However, some police departments have implemented innovative recruiting programs that have met with considerable success. The recruitment of females has been successful by and large, but the first women to enter traditionally all male organizations have not always been accepted by their male counterparts. Some have even encountered resistance or lack of support from their families and friends. In this chapter, we have outlined some recommendations that should rectify or at least minimize some of the problems that they encounter.

Affirmative action programs engaged in by police departments have not always been met with enthusiasm by all members of the force. White, male officers have alleged that they have been passed over for promotion by less qualified officers because the officers were either members of a minority group or women. These beliefs have resulted in antagonisms between white, male officers and those persons perceived as receiving preferential treatment. There is some evidence that this trend may slow down in the near future.

In our discussion of police officer stress, we tried to identify some of the major features of police work that are perceived by officers and administrators as being the most stress inducing. In addition, we discussed alcoholism among police officers, reviewed the efforts of one police department to help its officers with this problem, and examined some of the benefits derived from these programs by the officer and the police department. We also tried to identify some of the major reasons for the high frequency of suicide among younger and older police officers. Also described were the numerous organizational and individual programs that can be quite useful in helping officers cope with job stress. We also reviewed the use of drug screening of police applicants and current officers. Methods that some departments have used to manage the use of force effectively, the landmark case of *Tennessee* v. *Garner* and the Commission on Accreditation for Law Enforcement Agencies' use-of-force standards were reviewed.

The successful NCAVC and VICAP programs were examined as well as the process called criminal profiling. These efforts by law enforcement are an attempt to curb the rise in violent crime in this country.

In this chapter we also provided an overview of private security and discussed how it may play an essential role as a supplement and partner to public law enforcement.

The last section of this chapter highlighted two of the technological innovations now in use by law enforcement: computer-aided dispatching and fingerprint automation. In the future law enforcement will rely even more heavily on advanced technology for assistance.

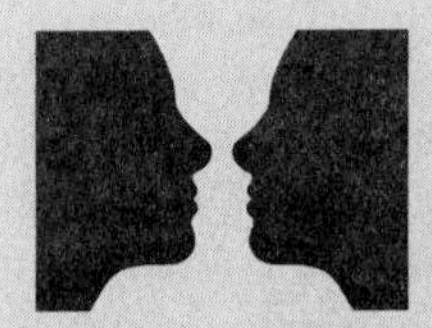

ISSUE PAPER

ACCREDITATION: EXPECTATIONS MET

By K. H. Medeiros

Until recently, an accreditation program for law enforcement had proved to be an elusive goal.

Since the 1930s, law enforcement leaders had talked about it.

In the '60s, key groups made it their goal. Their efforts resulted in praiseworthy reports and recommendations—but no action.

Finally, in 1979, the International Association of Chiefs of Police, the National Organization of Black Law Enforcement Executives, the National Sheriffs Association and the Police Executive Research Forum joined forces in a cooperative effort to establish the Commission on Accreditation for Law Enforcement Agencies (CALEA), Inc. In October of 1983, the commission opened its doors to those who wanted validation of their law enforcement agencies' professional services.

Seed money from the U.S. Department of Justice facilitated each step, leading ultimately to a comprehensive set of standards addressing an agency's role and authority, administration, operations and support services. The standards were promulgated after four years of research and field review by 350 agencies from across the United States. Equally important, the process for meeting the standards—and verifying that they were met—was in place after pilot testing in five agencies of differing sizes and types.

To date, more than 40 agencies have been accredited. They represent varying sizes (from 20 to 3,390 full-time personnel) and types (municipal and county police departments, sheriff's offices, campus and transit police departments, and state police). Another 500-plus agencies in 48 of the 50 states have taken the first step toward accreditation; half of them are immersed in self-assessment.

A philosophy that is sensitive to the unique problems of law enforcement, coupled with practical goals and objectives, provides the foundation for the accreditation program. From the outset, for example, the commission made it clear the program would be voluntary. In fact, CALEA is on record as not just opposing any efforts to mandate participation, but as refusing applications from any agency whose participation is mandated.

Equally important was the desire to develop a financially independent organization—one whose daily operations would be supported by the fees of its participants, with other funding sources tapped only for special projects. This has been achieved, keeping a modest sliding scale fee schedule based on agency size.

The commission's efforts to keep costs down and efficiency up through streamlined program administration have proved successful. One set of standards and one process—both adaptable to different sorts of agencies—keep headquarters operations trim, eliminating the need for separate divisions for accrediting campus police, state police, etc.

Total objectivity—the essence of the accreditation program—is guaranteed in two ways. First, the commission is a private, nonprofit corporation with its own staff of professionals. Second, the on-site assessors for any given agency are selected from outside that agency's state, and confirmation that there is no conflict of interest is required. Thus, the possibility of state or local political influence has been eliminated.

Seeing the accreditation program as a workable management tool for excellence in agencies from coast-to-coast, the commission designed it to provide the framework for "what" is needed to protect the life, health, safety and civil rights of citizens. The "how" is left up to the agency.

In the past, some suggested the standards were too tough and hence unattainable. Until accreditation was achieved by such a wide variety of law enforcement agencies, the former appeared to be a valid concern. But while achievement has been proven possible, experience shows that some agencies may require a longer timeframe for completion of the process.

For those agencies that feel they don't need accreditation—they already are good—the executives of every accredited agency caution they found some areas that required significant attention.

Meanwhile, accredited agencies universally regard their successful completion of the process as both an obligation and a privilege to assist those who would follow suit. An accreditation support network is there for the asking.

Overall, a concern for helping the entire law enforcement community gain the professional respect it deserves provides the major impetus to participate in the accreditation program.

However, important outside pressures to be accredited stem from court, legislative and liability actions. Law enforcement agencies rightly prefer to establish their own plans and activities for professional excellence, rather than reacting to external mandates and decisions. Accreditation places agencies in a proactive stance in the courtroom, the council, the state house, and the liability insurance market.

Underpinning the operational aspects of accreditation is the belief that it is not an end in itself, but rather a beginning. Therefore, the opportunity to keep growing has been built into the process. Both new and revised standards already have been promulgated to reflect the ever-changing nature of law enforcement.

The Commission on Accreditation for Law Enforcement reflects the lessons of the past, cast in the present, always with an eye to the future.

ISSUE PAPER

ACCREDITATION: PROGRESS OR REGRESSION?

by William H. Franks

Many of the standards being promulgated by the Commission on Accreditation for Law Enforcement Agencies (CALEA) are excellent and applicable for many law enforcement agencies in the United States. I would encourage any law enforcement administrator to review the standards prior to revising or writing a manual for his agency, since some standards may be applicable and appropriate for the unique community you serve. However, it is the very uniqueness of our communities that makes one set of national standards inappropriate in the United States. American law enforcement serves a nation comprised of differing, often conflicting cultures within the same political boundaries. We are not a homogeneous people, and one set of standards or written directives will not address all policing demands in the United States' multidimensional urban and rural areas.

Those standards of police performance that should be universal have been dictated by the Supreme Court of the United States. Police standards regarding in-custody situations, prisoners' rights, use of force, etc., will continue to be based upon the law of the land. Other methods of operation, both formal and informal, should be determined by the internal demands of the individual organization and the socioeconomic conditions prevailing in the community it serves.

Professionalism and Accreditation The implication of CALEA appears to be that professionalism is equated with accreditation, which can be achieved by an agency having a series of manuals and written directives that adhere to standards articulated by the commission. Accredited police agencies will, perhaps magically, increase their status within their peer group, enjoy a better reputation with their elected officials, and be more respected by the citizens they serve.

I fail to see any direct relationship between a manual that meets a private organization's standards and the quality of service delivered to the public. Evaluation of the quality of our service and our professional bearing can come only from the community we serve. The citizenry is not concerned whether our agency has one standard or 10,000 standards. I suggest that they are more concerned with the empathy with which we deliver our service and the appropriateness of our interaction with them. Organizations change because of a change in values, not because of rules and regulations. The most successful organizations are those that have not only the fewest rules and regulations, but also a strong sense of identity with an organizational value structure.

Those organizations on the "cutting edge" are not those that develop more manuals, but those that create a value structure encouraging experimentation with new ideas, concepts and values that will better address the needs and demands of 21st century law enforcement. These agencies certainly will not wait for a centralized body to articulate new standards. They will establish, revise and abandon standards as the demands upon their agency fluctuate with the changing problems in urban and rural communities. They will encourage employee risk taking, tolerate failure, and be innovative in their approach to the demands of a changing society. Successful recruitment and development of creative personnel capable of addressing the challenges of the future will be one of the measures of a successful law enforcement agency.

To date, some "nitty-gritty" questions have yet to be addressed either by independent evaluation firms or by the elected representatives of the national law enforcement associations that supported accreditation, i.e. IACP, PERF, NOBLE and the National Sheriff's Association. As a start, I would suggest the following areas for evaluation:

1. Will a cost (hard and soft) benefit analysis, in terms of value received by our clients, justify the cost of accreditation? (Real dollar cost to a 200-person agency may exceed $100,000.)
2. Does the citizenry served by an accredited agency perceive a change in the quality of service?
3. Can an accredited agency demonstrate that there has been a reduction in citizen complaints, alleged civil rights violations, and law suits because of accreditation?
4. Has there been an increase in citizen and employee confidence in the goals, objectives,

policies and practices of the agency? (This was one of the four articulated goals of The Commission on Accreditation for Law Enforcement Agencies in 1979.)

Accreditation may actually be counterproductive to improving law enforcement administrators' stature as leaders in public enterprise. Accreditation merely reinforces techniques, ideologies and methodologies that are over 20 years old—methodologies and concepts that have failed in the past and will most assuredly fail in the future. With the number of talented young men and women entering law enforcement, a rising level of educational attainment and awareness of good organizational development, we are progressing at a rapid rate toward achieving equal status with progressive chief executives in private and public industry. Let's not stop our progress!

■ DISCUSSION AND REVIEW

1. What is the principal motivation for police administrators and officers wanting to achieve the status of a professional?
2. What two factors strengthen arguments to change and expand the responsibility of patrol officers?
3. What have some political departments done to enhance the recruitment of black males?
4. What obstacles not faced by men do women sometimes encounter upon entering police work?
5. Why are minorities, females, and members of certain ethnic groups sometimes given preference in promotional policy?
6. What are the four categories of stress in law enforcement?
7. What benefits do Denver police derive from their alcohol abuse program?
8. What can be done to help police officers reduce stress or learn to cope with it?
9. What are five examples of shooting control techniques that can be used by police departments to control the use of force by officers?
10. What was the significance of the U.S. Supreme Court's decision in *Tennessee* v. *Garner?*
11. What are the seven steps involved in criminal profiling and what is the profiling process?

■ GLOSSARY

CAD Computer-aided dispatch. A technological advance to assist police agencies in handling multiple calls for service.

COPE Citizen-oriented police enforcement program created by the Baltimore County Police Department to identify and reduce citizen's fear.

Job enrichment Steps taken to create an environment in which employees have a highly developed sense of satisfaction about their work.

Job stress Factors associated with police work that may lead to physical disorders, alcoholism, marital disharmony, and suicide.

NCAVC The National Center for the Analysis of Violent Crime. Serves as a clearinghouse and resource center for unsolved violent crimes.

Participative management The involvement of subordinates in making decisions that affect the work environment.

Reverse discrimination Within the context of police work, *reverse discrimination* involves allegations by white male officers that departmental affirmative action policies discriminate against them in assignments and promotions.

Street wisdom Knowledge gained primarily from working the streets as a law enforcement officer.

VICAP A nationwide data information center designed to collect, collate, and analyze specific crimes of violence.

Working-class jobs Jobs that do not require a college degree or any highly developed entry-level skills.

REFERENCES

American Law Institute. *American Law Institute Model Penal Code.* Proposed official draft 3.07. 1962.

Behan, C. J. "Fighting Fear in Baltimore County, The COPE Project." *FBI Law Enforcement Bulletin* (November 1986): 12–15.

Block, P.; Anderson, D.; and Gervais, P. *Policewomen on Patrol: Major Findings,* vol. 1. Washington, D.C.: Police Foundation, 1973.

Commission on Accreditation for Law Enforcement Agencies, Inc. *Accreditation Program For Law Enforcement Agencies.* Information Brochure. Manassas, Va.: 1983.

________. *Accreditation Program Overview.* Information brochure. Fairfax, Va.: 1984.

________. *The Standards Manual of the Law Enforcement Accreditation Program.* Fairfax, Va.: The Commission on Accreditation for Law Enforcement Agencies, Inc., 1985.

Cunningham, W. C., and Taylor, T. H. *The Growing Role of Private Security.* Washington, D.C.: U.S. Department of Justice, 1984.

Danto, B. L. "Police Suicide." *Police Stress* 1 (1978): 32.

Depue, R. L. "An American Response to an Era of Violence." *FBI Law Enforcement Bulletin* (December 1986): 2–5.

Dishlacoff, L. "The Drinking Cop." *Police Chief* 43 (1976): 32.

Douglas, J. E., and Burgess, A. E. "Criminal Profiling: A Viable Investigation Tool against Violent Crime." *FBI Law Enforcement Bulletin* (December 1986): 9–13.

Eisenberg, T. "Labor Management Relations and Psychological Stress." *Police Chief* 42 (1975): 54–58.

Federal Bureau of Investigation. An unsigned letter to Ronald L. Gaines, Acting Deputy Assistant Attorney General, U.S. Department of Justice, 23 November 1979.

Friedman, P. "Suicide Among Police." In *Essays in Self Destruction,* edited by E. Schneidman. New York: Science House, 1967.

Fyfe, J. J. *Readings on Police Use of Deadly Force.* Washington, D.C.: Police Foundation, 1982.

Geller, W. *Deadly Force.* Washington, D.C.: U.S. Department of Justice, National Institute of Justice, 1987, p. 3.

________. "Deadly Force: What We Know." *Journal of Police and Administration* 10 (1982): 151–77.

Heiman, M. F. "The Police Suicide." *Journal of Police Science and Administration* 3 (1975): 267–73.

Henry, A., and Short, J. *Suicide and Homicide.* Glencoe, Ill.: Free Press, 1954.

Howlett, J. B.; Hanfland, K. A.; and Ressler, R. K. "The Violent Criminal Apprehension Program: A Progress Report." *FBI Law Enforcement Bulletin* (December 1986): 14–22.

Hurrell, J. J., and Kroes, W. H. "Stress Awareness." In *Job Stress and the Police Officer: Identifying Stress Reduction Techniques,* edited by W. H. Kroes and J. J. Hurrell, pp. 234–46. Washington, D.C.: U.S. Department of Health, Education, and Welfare, 1975.

International Association of Chiefs of Police. *Training Key*. Gaithersburg, Md.: International Association of Chiefs of Police, 1978.

Kerner, O. *Report of the National Advisory Commission on Civil Disorders*. New York: Bantam Press, 1968.

Kroes, W. H. *Society's Victim—the Policeman*. Springfield, Ill.: Charles C. Thomas, 1976.

Kroes, W. H.; Margolis, B. L, and Hurrell, J. J. "Job Stress in Policemen." *Journal of Police Science and Administration* 2 (1974): 145–56.

Labovitz, S., and Hagedorn, R. "An Analysis of Suicide Rates among Occupational Categories." *Sociology* 17 (1971): 67–72.

Larson, R. C. "The Future of Police Emergency Response Systems." *National Institute of Justice Reports* (March 1985): 2–6.

Lejins, P. P. *Introducing a Law Enforcement Curriculum at a State University*. Washington, D.C.: U.S. Government Printing Office, 1970.

Lester, D. "Suicide in Police Officers." *Police Chief* 45 (1970): 17.

Likert, R. *New Patterns of Management*. New York: McGraw-Hill, 1961.

Lundstrom, R., and Mullan, C. "The Use of Force: One Department's Experience." *FBI Law Enforcement Bulletin* (January 1987): 6–9.

Matulia, K. J. *A Balance of Forces*. Gaithersburg, Md.: International Association of Chiefs of Police, 1982.

McEwen, J. T.; Manili, B.; Connors, E. *Employee Drug Testing Policies in Police Departments*. Washington, D.C.: U.S. Department of Justice, 1986.

McGregor, D. *The Human Side of Enterprise*. New York: McGraw-Hill, 1960.

Milton, K.; Halleck, J. W.; Lardner, J.; and Abrecht, G. L. *Police Use of Deadly Force*. Washington, D.C.: The Police Foundation, 1977.

Nelson, Z., and Smith, W. "The Law Enforcement Profession: An Incidence of Suicide." *Omega* 1 (1970): 293–99.

Neudorfer, C. D. "Fingerprint Automation: Progress in the FBI's Identification Division." *FBI Law Enforcement Bulletin* (March 1986): 2–8.

———. "Officer Restraint in the Use of Deadly Force: The Next Frontier in Police Shooting Research." *Journal of Police Science and Administration* 13 (1985): 153–71.

Police Foundation. "Education and Training Task Force Report." Mimeographed. Report on the Police Foundation, a subsidiary of the Ford Foundation, 1972.

Reiser, M. "A Psychologist's View of the Badge." *Police Chief* 37 (1970): 24–27.

———. "Some Organizational Stress of Policemen." *Journal of Police Science and Administration* 2 (1974): 156–65.

———. "Stress, Distress, and Adaptation in Police Work." *Police Chief* 43 (1976): 24–27.

Reiser, M.; Sokol, R. J., and Saxe, S. J. "An Early Warning Mental Health Program for Police Sergeants." *Police Chief* 29 (1972): 38–39.

Roberts, M. D. "Job Stress in Law Enforcement: A Treatment and Prevention Program." In *Job Stress and the Police Officer: Identifying Stress Reduction Techniques,* edited by W. H. Kroes and J. J. Hurrell. Washington, D.C.: U.S. Department of Health, Education, and Welfare, 1975.

Schwartz, J. A., and Schwartz, C. B. "The Personal Problems of the Police Officer: A Plea for Action." In *Job Stress and the Police Officer: Identifying Stress Reduction Techniques,* edited by W. H. Kroes and J. J. Hurrell. Washington, D.C.: U.S. Department of Health, Education, and Welfare, 1975.

Sewell, J. D. "The Development of a Critical Life Events Scale for Law Enforcement." *Journal of Police Science and Administration* 11 (1983): 109–116.

Sherman, L. W. "Reducing Police Gun Use: Critical Events, Administrative Policy, and Organizational Change." In *Control in the Police Organization,* edited by Maurice Punch. Cambridge, Mass.: MIT Press, 1983.

Skolnick, S. H. *Justice without Trial: Law Enforcement in a Democratic Society.* New York: John Wiley and Sons, Inc., 1966.

Slobogin, K. "Stress." *New York Times Magazine,* 20 November 1977, pp. 48–55.

Somodevilla, S. A.; Baker, C. F.; Hill, W. R.; and Thomas, N. H. "Stress Management in the Dallas Police Department." Dallas, Tex.: Psychological Services Unit, Dallas Police Department, 1978.

Spolman, W., and Eck, J. E. *Problem-Oriented Policing.* Washington, D.C.: U.S. Department of Justice, January 1987.

Stratton, J. G. "Police Stress: An Overview." *Police Chief* 45 (1978): 58.

Territo, L.; Swanson, C. R.; and Chamelin, N. C. *The Police Personnel Selection Process.* Indianapolis, Ind.: Bobbs-Merrill, 1977.

Walinsky, A.; Rubinstein, J.; Deutsch, J.; Kurlander, L.; Price, M.; and Welch, N. *The New Police Corps.* Washington, D.C.: Center for Research on Institutions and Social Policy, date unknown.

Washington, B. "Stress and the Female Police Officer." In *Stress and Police Personnel,* edited by L. Territo and H. J. Vetter. Boston, Mass.: Allyn and Bacon, 1981.

Washington Crime News Service, "Compensation for Police Heart Attacks Allowed." *Crime Control Digest* 9 (1975): 3.

Washington, D.C., Police Department. "Utilization of Police Women on Patrol." *Circular 57,* 17 April 1972.

Wasserman, R., Gardner, M. P., and Cohen, A. S. *Improving Police Community Relations.* Washington, D.C.: U.S. Government Printing Office, 1973.

Wileman, J. A. *Model Policy Manual for Police Agencies.* Institute of Government Affairs, University of Wisconsin, 1968: Sec. 800.

Wilson, J. O. "Police Use of Deadly Force." *FBI Law Enforcement Bulletin* (August 1980): 16–20.

■ NOTES

1. The discussion of the law enforcement accreditation process was adapted with permission from two information brochures entitled, "Accreditation Program For Law Enforcement Agencies," and "Accreditation Program Overview" both published by the Commission on Accreditation for Law Enforcement Agencies, Inc.
2. The information regarding the police corps was adapted from Adam Walinsky, Jonathan Rubenstein, Jan Deutsch, Lawrence Kurlander, Monroe Price, and Neil Welch, *The New Police Corps* (Washington, D.C.: Center for Research on Institutions and Social Policy, date unknown), pp. 1–45.
3. The discussion of police department drug test policies was adapted from J. Thomas McEwen, Barbara Manili, and Edward Connors, *Employee Drug Testing in Police Departments* (Washington, D.C.: U.S. Department of Justice, 1986), pp. 1–5.
4. The discussion of the St. Paul, Minnesota Police Department research on officers use of force in situations was adapted from Ross Lundstrom and Cynthia Mullan, "The Use of Force: One Department's Experience," *FBI Law Enforcement Bulletin* (January 1987): 6–9.
5. The discussion of shooting control techniques was adapted from William Geller, *Deadly Force* (Washington, D.C.: U.S. Department of Justice, National Institute of Justice, 1987), p. 3.

6. The use-of-force standards were adapted with permission from the Commission on Accreditation for Law Enforcement Agencies, Inc., *The Standards Manual of the Law Enforcement Accreditation Program* (Fairfax, Va.: The Commission on Accreditation for Law Enforcement Agencies, Inc., 1985), pp. 1–2, 1–3.
7. The discussion of problem-oriented policing was adapted from William Spolman and John E. Eck, *Problem-Oriented Policing* (Washington, D.C.: U.S. Department of Justice, January 1987), pp. 1–7.
8. The discussion of the Baltimore County Police Department COPE program was adapted from Cornelius J. Behan, "Fighting Fear in Baltimore County, The COPE Project," *FBI Law Enforcement Bulletin* (November 1986): 12–15.
9. The discussion of NCAVC was adapted from Roger L. Depue, "An American Response to an Era of Violence," *FBI Law Enforcement Bulletin* (December 1986): 2–5.
10. The discussion of VICAP was adapted from James B. Howlett, Kenneth A. Hanfland, and Robert K. Ressler, "The Violent Criminal Apprehension Program: A Progress Report," *FBI Law Enforcement Bulletin* (December 1986): 14–22.
11. The discussion of Criminal Profiling was adapted from John E. Douglas and Alan E. Burgess, "Criminal Profiling: A Viable Investigation Tool against Violent Crime," *FBI Law Enforcement Bulletin* (December 1986): 9–13.
12. The discussion of private security and law enforcement was adapted and modified from William C. Cunningham and Todd H. Taylor, *The Growing Role of Private Security* (Washington, D.C.: U.S. Department of Justice, 1984), pp. 1–5. Their discussion was based on the findings of a thirty-month study of private security conducted by Halcrest Systems, Inc., of McLean, Virginia.
13. The discussion of computer-aided dispatch systems was adapted from, Richard C. Larson, "The Future of Police Emergency Response Systems," *National Institute of Justice Reports* (1985): 2–6.
14. This discussion of fingerprint automation was adapted from Charles D. Neudorfer, "Fingerprint Automation: Progress in the FBI's Identification Division," *FBI Law Enforcement Bulletin* (March 1986): 2–8.

■ CASE

Tennessee v. *Garner* 105 S.Ct. 1694 (1985).

CHAPTER

8

Prosecution and Defense

CHAPTER OUTLINE:

The image of prosecutors and defense attorneys in popular television programs, movies, and novels gives a somewhat distorted and oversimplified view of the functions these people perform. There are no real-life counterparts to television's popular defense attorneys Perry Mason or Matlock, who somehow always manage to have their client acquitted ten minutes before the end of the program. Nor are there prosecutors like Perry Mason's protagonist, Hamilton Burger, who manages to lose every case—a fact, incidentally, that would most likely jeopardize the continued employment of even the most charming prosecutor.

Our system of justice and the roles played by attorneys tend to mystify the average citizen, who often has great difficulty understanding why or how anyone could defend certain classes of criminals. There is even greater confusion as to why individuals who have obviously committed crimes are sometimes released on "technicalities." Further, it appears to the layperson that prosecutors and defense attorneys are often more concerned with winning their cases than in seeking truth or justice, and that the final outcome of the criminal trial is affected more by the skills, personalities, and theatrics of attorneys than by the merits of the case.[1]

In this chapter, we address some of the public's concerns and misconceptions and provide the reader with an overview of the rationale underlying our system of criminal justice. Further, we outline the functions and discretion of the prosecutor in the criminal justice system and discuss the implications of this discretion. Lastly, we examine the role of the defense attorney and the pros and cons of various legal assistance programs available to citizens.

THE ADVERSARY SYSTEM

To the layperson, and perhaps even to some social scientists, the role of all lawyers is to see that justice is done. Anyone who has been educated in our legal traditions, however, knows that justice must be done according to law and within the procedures of the adversary system (American Bar Association Project on Standards for Criminal Justice 1974).[2]

The adversary system central to the administration of criminal justice is not the result of abstract thinking about the best way to settle disputes of law and fact. Rather, it is the result of a slow evolution from trial by combat or by champions to a less violent form of testing by argument and evidence. An atmosphere of contention still marks our way to justice, however, and for that reason, the adversary system has received much criticism.[3]

One criticism is that the system does not provide the best setting for discovering the facts of a particular case or for resolving legal policy. However, it must be recognized that the presentation of opposing views in vigorous debate as a prelude to decision is a feature also found in the legislative and executive branches of government. By contention—provided it is kept within proper bounds—a dispute is narrowed, and arguments that appear to be correct and logical, but are not, are exposed in the course of debate. Contest spurs each side to greater intellect and imagination so that, in the words of the nineteenth-century statesman Thomas B. Macaulay, "it is certain that no important consideration will altogether escape notice."

Cross-examination has proved to be an effective means to expose not only false testimony but, more frequently, inaccurate testimony. Two adversaries, approaching the facts from entirely different perspectives and functioning within the framework of an orderly set of rules, will uncover more of the truth than investigators seeking to compose a picture of the event. Scientists may quarrel with this technique for discovering facts, because their approach is properly one of discovering absolute truth. But lawyers know that our legal system is man-made and does not exclusively seek absolute truth. Rather, it is subject to limiting rules directed at higher values and larger purposes than would be a system that guarantees the conviction of every transgressor. Just as we reject, for example, torture and other inhumane techniques, so also we reject certain modes of investigation that, although not inhumane, are incompatible with the values of a free people. Moreover, a man-made system, inevitably finite and fallible, must provide safeguards to account for its fallibility. Because some error is inevitable, the adversary system deliberately chooses to err on the side of the guilty in order to protect the innocent.

Government under law, Lord Coke long ago declared, means that even the king is subject to law. For that reason, in a criminal prosecution in which one adversary is the government, the state is not above the law, but is simply one of the contending parties subject to the law. It is symbolic that, in common-law systems, with rare exception, counsel for the government and for the accused sit in equal positions in the courtroom; prosecutors do not sit at or near the judge's bench as they do in some civil-law courts. As a public officer, the judge has an obligation to do justice "according to law," rather than to decide always "in the best interest of the state."

The neutrality of the judge and jury reflects the historical wisdom of our mode of justice: parties who bring a matter to the attention of the courts are likely to accept the decision of a neutral tribunal. In the context of a criminal case, this means that the victim and the public must accept the finality of an acquittal or a disposition less harsh than they desired. For the defendant, a neutral tribunal provides assurance of fair treatment and establishes confidence that encourages them to stand trial rather than to flee or otherwise seek to subvert the legal process. If found guilty, the defendant must then accept the penalty in a spirit conducive to rehabilitation.

Each adversary in a situation must have ample opportunity to present information relevant to the final court decision. The rules of procedure and evidence are designed to protect that opportunity within the bounds of time and the judge or jury's capacity to absorb information—as well as to preclude (so far as is possible) the introduction of material that does not contribute to the rational disposition of a case.

As limited by rules and procedures, the adversary system is also designed to ensure that the goals of finding the facts and treating everyone justly and fairly are not achieved at the expense of human dignity. Common-law legal institutions long ago decided that the system must permit (but not require) the accused to compel the state to establish their guilt under the rules of procedure and evidence—even though the accused may privately admit facts that, if shown, would warrant a guilty verdict. Thus, lawyers are often asked to defend a person who has admitted guilt.

Traditionally, guilt is something ascertained only at the conclusion of the court process. Our purpose "is not merely to protect the innocent person from the possibility of an unjust conviction, precious as that objective is, but to preserve the integrity of society itself. It aims at keeping sound and wholesome the procedures by which society visits its condemnation on an erring member" (Fuller 1960). The essence of the adversary system is challenge. The survival of our system of criminal justice and the value that it advances depends upon a constant, searching, and creative questioning of official decisions and authority. It is this function that lawyers serve when they secure the acquittal of defendants, undeserving though they may be, when conviction is sought by methods repugnant to basic values protected by the constitution. This is the rationale behind the suppression doctrine, an essentially American invention, by which reliable evidence may be excluded from a trial because of the manner in which it is acquired. In sum, the adversary system seeks to accomplish justice by eliciting facts that can be proven under fixed rules of procedure. This policy, evolved largely by judges, is designed to ensure that trials are conducted fairly in both reality and appearance.

Let us begin our examination by analyzing two of the three main lawyers in the trial phase of the criminal justice system—the prosecutor and the defense lawyer (the third, of course, is the judge). In order to be eligible for these roles, both must first receive a legal education. Although historically a legal education meant many things including an apprenticeship, in order to receive a legal education today prosecutors and defense attorneys must initially obtain an undergraduate degree from a university. Subsequently, they must attend and pass three years of law school. After seven years of formal education, a would-be attorney then must pass the state bar examination before he or she is licensed to practice law. Many young lawyers get their first practical experience in the legal profession by accepting positions as prosecutors or public defenders.

THE PROSECUTOR

In the western world, a prosecuting attorney generally is recognized as the legal representative of the state with sole responsibility for bringing criminal charges. In the

United States he or she is referred to as the "district attorney", "state's attorney", or the "county attorney". The **prosecutor** in the American criminal justice system differs markedly from prosecutors in the systems from which our legal institutions sprang—Roman law and English common law. In continental Europe, prosecutors are appointed career officials who have a close relationship to the court, thus they have, in some respects, certain advantages, and in other respects less autonomy, than American prosecutors. They are generally not considered part of the practicing bar, nor do they participate in lawyer associations. Although like their American counterparts they are key figures in the criminal justice system, their authority stems from being part of a central, rather than a local, government (American Bar Association Project on Standards of Criminal Justice 1974).

Although prosecutors wield a great deal of power in the administration of justice in the United States, their European counterparts are allowed even more extensive powers in certain areas. Some European prosecutors can levy fines without judicial approval; some can even convict defendants without trials; and some can initiate convictions and punishments by written orders instead of trials (Felsteiner and Drew 1978). In England, prosecution is administered by a Director of Public Prosecutions—a career official and subordinate of a cabinet minister. The actual trial of cases is assigned to private-practice barristers designated as Crown Counsel. An English barrister may prosecute for the Crown in some cases and act for the defense in others. However, the Crown Counsel has no part in preliminary decisions about whether to prosecute or what crimes are to be charged; in court, they function as professional advocates. The Crown Counsel's relationship to the Director of Public Prosecutions is essentially like that of a barrister to the solicitor in a civil case. Justices of the Peace and other courts of limited jurisdiction handle the bulk of all criminal prosecutions—95 percent or more; solicitors, private parties, police, or other administrative officials conduct the prosecutions in these courts. The rate of guilty pleas in all courts in England is substantially higher than in the United States, and appeal is not allowed in England as a matter of right.

The Prosecution Function

American prosecutors, representing the executive branch under a system of divided powers defined in a written constitution, are officers of the court only in the same sense as other lawyers are. They are career officials or civil servants, and relatively few of them devote their entire professional lives to this work. Prosecutors are usually elected local officials, largely autonomous and generally having no ties with the state attorney general or the chief officer of the executive branch of which they are a part.[4]

Whatever their precise title and jurisdiction, American prosecutors are invariably drawn from the practicing bar, and they usually return to private practice or seek other public office after a few years. They are generally active participants in **bar associations** and other lawyer groups. Most young lawyers become prosecutors without any significant experience in the criminal justice process. Often, they come in with only a simplistic knowledge of the criminal law. Law school usually requires but one course in the study of criminal law. The National District Attorneys Association discovered that the typical assistant prosecutor is hired after very limited experience in the practice of law and that most of that experience is in civil law. Even most prosecutors who are elected to office often lack substantial criminal law experience. In most respects, including their autonomy, they are more like the English barrister than like the prosecutor in continental Europe. However, they are different from their counterparts in both England and continental Europe in that they are local, elected officials. American prosecutors derive important strengths from this unique characteristic of the office, but also certain weaknesses and burdens that sometimes encumber and impair their function.

In recruiting young attorneys, the prosecutor's office normally attracts two kinds of individuals. In rural communities where the salary of a prosecutor is remarkably low, young lawyers who are struggling economically and with little experience are most likely attracted to the office. They take the position because of the public exposure the office will provide them. They believe that through this experience they will build a clientele who might support them if they become interested in politics at a later date. Most prosecutors' offices experience an alarmingly high turnover. Few elected prosecutors serve for more than two four-year terms. As for the younger attorneys, as Gelber points out, the turnover rate in prosecutors' offices across the country is as high as 33 percent annually (1968).

The political process has played a significant part in the shaping of the American prosecutor. Experience as a prosecutor is a typical stepping stone to higher political office. The **district attorney** has long been glamorized in fiction, films, radio, television, and other media; many political leaders were first exposed to public notice and political life in this office. Many executive and legislative officials, as well as judges, have served as prosecuting attorneys at some point in their careers.

The political involvement of the prosecutor varies with jurisdiction. In some jurisdictions, prosecutors are required to run with a party designation; other prosecutors are elected on a nonpartisan basis. The powers of prosecutors are formidable, and these men and women are important in their communities. If they are not truly independent and professional, their powers can be misused for political or other improper purposes. Perhaps even more than other public officials, the prosecutor's activity is largely open to public gaze—as it should be—and spotlighted by the press.

Election of the Prosecutor

In the United States, prosecutors are either selected or appointed and are consequently political figures in the criminal justice system. Normally prosecutors have a strong party affiliation, which gives them a contingency of voters and supporters. Thus they often respond to the political pressure of special interest groups. This is significant because often the political nature of the prosecutor's office weighs heavily on decisions he or she makes during the course of exercising prosecutorial discretion. The popular election of prosecutors came about as a result of a deep concern that the enormous power of the prosecutor should be vested in a public officer who is directly responsible to the voters. Although ultimate fact finding rests with jurors, the power of prosecutors to institute criminal prosecution vests in them an authority at least as sweeping as, and perhaps greater than, the authority of the judge who presides in criminal cases. In short, the prosecutor is vested with virtually unlimited power in deciding who will be prosecuted.

The prosecutor has a dual role that reflects the ambivalence of public attitudes toward law enforcement. On the one hand, prosecutors are the leaders of law enforcement in the community. They are expected to participate actively in marshaling society's resources against the threat of crime. When a crisis in enforcement arises in the community, the press and others clamor for a "war against crime," and the prosecutor may be drawn into the political controversy by the demand that he or she "stamp out the criminals." Prosecutors are called upon to make public statements, to propose legislative reforms, and to direct the energies of the law enforcement machinery of the community. On the other hand, the office demands—and the public expects—that the prosecutor respect the rights of persons accused of crime. Our nation began with resistance to oppressive official conduct, and our traditions, embodied in national and state constitutions, demand that the prosecutor be fair to all. Often this is referred to as the **"prosecutor's dilemma."** Prosecutors face a dilemma because they are at once lawyers for the state and expected to do everything in their power to win the case, and yet as members of the legal profession they are not expected to win, but instead are ethically required to see that justice is done. Conflicting demands exert pressures on prosecutors that try their sense of fairness as lawyers. Nevertheless, both their public responsibilities and their obligations as members of the bar require that they be something more than partisan advocates intent on winning a case.

Many observers of our criminal justice system who have also studied the English system comment on the importance of the professional independence of the barrister. Because the barrister plays both prosecution and defense—depending on the assignment—traditions have developed that blunt excessive zeal and improve the quality of advocacy. Also, because of its bifurcation, the English system encourages harmony within the bar and is conducive to strong traditions of internal and external discipline, traditions that temper the flamboyant and irrational partisanship so often exhibited in American courtrooms. Thus, American prosecutors might profit by an exchange of roles. For example, experienced criminal defense lawyers might, from time to time, be appointed as special prosecutors. Some younger prosecutors are already moving in this direction by doing private defense work or working on defender programs.

Because prosecutors are lawyers as well as public officers, they must answer not only to the electorate or appointing authority but also to the professional control and discipline of the bar and the courts. Because of the nature of the prosecutor's function and the right to appellate review, the prosecutor's conduct at trial is called into question more often than the conduct of defense counsel. By no means, however, do trials represent the major activity of the American prosecutor. The vast majority of criminal cases are disposed of without trial as a result of negotiated guilty pleas (see Chapter 9).

Power of Discretion

Under American law, criminal litigation generally does not occur until action is initiated by a prosecutor. The prosecutor has the **power of discretion**—the power to investigate citizens, order arrests, present one-sided arguments to the grand jury, and recommend sentences to the court. It is the prosecutor's decision whether a charge shall be pursued, reduced, plea bargained, or dropped altogether—and these choices are made with little or no statutory or case-law guidance (Lewis, Bundy, and Hague 1978).[5] The duties and responsibilities of the prosecutor are generally not specifically defined by law—other than by state statutes and constitutions that require the "prosecutor to proceed with litigation against those who transgress the jurisdiction's laws," or by case law that described the prosecutor's duties in equally general terms (Lewis, Bundy, and Hague 1978).

When a case is brought to the attention of a prosecutor, he or she may simply refuse to proceed. Even after charges are filed or a grand jury indictment is in, the process can be stopped by the principle of ***nolle prosequi,*** the halting of prosecution. A prosecutor may even request the court to dismiss charges. One basis for the

decision to prosecute is whether there is sufficient evidence to proceed with litigation. Beyond this, there are other concerns:

> It is said, for example, that the prosecutor must be allowed to consider whether prosecution will promote the ends of justice, instill a respect for law, and advance the cause of ordered liberty, and to take into account "the degree of criminality," the weight of the evidence, the elements of public opinion, timing and relative gravity of offense (LaFave 1970, p. 532).

Prosecutorial discretion is not a modern-day invention or an accommodation to the stresses of an urban society. This kind of power has always been accorded the prosecutor, as was observed in 1931 by the National Commission on Law Observance and Enforcement: "The prosecutor is the real arbiter of what laws shall be enforced and against whom, while the attention of the public is drawn rather to the small percentage of offenders who go through the courts" (p. 7). Because of the decentralized nature of their office, the low visibility of their decisions, and the incredibly broad power of their discretion of whether to go forward with a case, prosecutors are often able to structure their role so they can play it in ways that are consistent with their political environment. Thus the type and nature of the case that eventually reaches the courtroom often depends on an individual prosecutor's philosophy of crime and criminality within the system as well as the political forces outside that shape that philosophy, rather, than on the dictates of justice. When a prosecutor for whatever reason decides that certain cases should *not* be brought to court, he or she can terminate further proceedings by pleading *nolle prosequi.* This is a formal entry into the record by which the prosecutor declares that he or she will no longer further prosecute the case. Thus the prosecutor has the right not to prosecute further despite sufficient evidence that the defendant is guilty. Prosecutorial discretion is the most powerful example of discretionary authority within the American criminal justice system. Although it is difficult to characterize any particular sequence of the prosecution's dropping cases, a fairly common pattern is found in the overall prosecution's screening throughout the United States. At least with respect to felonies, 30 to 60 percent of all arrestees will be dropped as the result of prosecutorial discretion.

Discretion is not solely the province of the prosecutor, however. Police officers exercise discretion in deciding to write a ticket, make an arrest, issue a warning, or allow an offender to go free. Nevertheless, the police officer's discretionary power is neither as broad nor as well accepted as the prosecutor's. Judges use discretion in dismissing cases, suspending sentences, or sentencing offenders to incarceration. They rule on motions during trial and they play an important role in determining parole dates. Even the jury has discretion—the power to acquit a defendant in spite of his or her guilt.

What makes the prosecutor's discretion so important is that all other segments of the criminal justice system are directly affected by the decisions of this office. On occasion, policy shifts in prosecution are made deliberately to effect change in other areas. For example, prosecutors may dismiss most of some types of cases because they consider police conduct to have gone beyond reasonable limits. Because police efficiency is usually measured by the number of cases closed, the police usually comply with a prosecutor's wishes and redirect their efforts. The prosecutor's decisions also affect the work of the judge. Decisions to proceed with one type of case but not another, to reduce charges and negotiate a guilty plea, or to proceed with an original charge, affect the type and number of cases reaching judges.

Why do we give so much power to one office? For one thing, not every violation of the law needs to be pursued. If every case were prosecuted, the system would be rendered helpless within a short time. Thus, someone has to decide which cases are most important. In addition, wholesale prosecution would not consider individual circumstance and would therefore be arbitrary and unfair in many cases.

The crucial issue to be explored is under what circumstances the prosecutor should choose not to prosecute or to pursue an alternative less than the maximum penalty. As the following example shows, this can be an issue even when a serious crime has been committed:

> A man telephoned the police, reporting in a semihysterical state that his wife had just shot and killed herself. When the police and an ambulance arrived, the victim was dead of a bullet wound in the upper left temple. The husband was holding the gun with which he alleged his wife had shot herself. He stated that he had arrived home from work just prior to the incident, but neither his wife nor their three pre-school children were there. His wife arrived home a short time later and she had been drinking heavily. When he questioned her about the whereabouts of their three children she told him they were at her mother's home. A heated argument then followed about her neglect of their children, her drinking, and her seeing other men. According to the husband, his wife then slapped him in his face and he slapped her back. At that point, she walked over to a nearby desk drawer where he kept a revolver. She removed the revolver from the desk drawer, placed the barrel against her forehead, fired a single shot, and fell to the floor. No one else was home at the time this incident occurred.
>
> The relatives of both the victim and her husband provided the police with the following information.
>
> To their knowledge the victim had not been despondent, nor had she ever previously attempted to discuss suicide.
>
> The victim and her husband had been having serious domestic difficulties because she was seeing other men, spending the house money on liquor, and not properly caring for their three young children.
>
> Both parties were known to have assaulted each other in domestic disputes in the past.
>
> These facts tended to indicate that the victim's death was perhaps not a suicide but a criminal homicide. An interrogation of the husband established what the facts suggested. The husband related that he had been truthful about the events leading up to the argument, but after his wife slapped him, he angrily knocked her to the floor, removed the revolver from the desk drawer, and went back over to his wife, who was now on her knees. Standing over her, he fired a single shot into her head. After shooting her, he became frightened and fabricated the story of his wife's committing suicide (Swanson, Chamelin, and Territo 1981, pp. 205–6).

The investigation of the husband's background by the prosecutor's office revealed several interesting facts. First, he had never before been in trouble with the police (he was in his late forties). Second, he had been steadily employed at the same business for over twenty years, and his employer indicated that he was an honest and hard-working employee. Third, the victim's mother and father testified that their son-in-law was a devoted father, loving husband, and generous provider, and, although they grieved over the loss of their daughter, they felt no good purpose would be served by putting the man in prison. Fourth, the police officers involved felt that the accused would not be a danger to the community when he was eventually released, and, in fact, they were sympathetic about the tragic series of events leading up to the victim's death. After considering all the facts, the prosecutor agreed to accept a guilty plea to the charge of manslaughter and recommended probation for a period of ten years. The judge agreed and the sentence was imposed; the man successfully completed his probation.

Prosecutors often will differ on what weight they will give to a particular factor in determining whether to prosecute the case. The most significant factor across the country is the strength of the evidence. If they believe the evidence insufficient to gain a conviction, then the case normally will be dropped. Prosecutors take keen interest in won and loss records. A case that might not result in a conviction is referred to as a "dog." Most prosecutors run from these "dog" cases. Often, however, when the evidence is sufficient to support the charges, the prosecutors will turn to other factors that might suggest the case is not appropriate for prosecution. Such factors include excessive caseloads in the prosecutor's office, the lack of harm caused by the offense, the victim's attitude toward pressing the case, the arrestee's criminal record, and the adequacy of alternative remedies. These factors are used by almost all prosecutors in deciding when to prosecute cases. The weight given to them, however, varies from jurisdiction to jurisdiction (Kamisar, LaFave, and Israel 1986).

Sometimes, the personality of the person charged may influence a prosecutor's decision. In addition, some categories of crimes and offenses can be more effectively disposed of by some means other than prosecution. In many cases, it is apparent that winning in court is doubtful. By refusing to proceed with a case that does not clearly show the defendant to be guilty beyond a reasonable doubt, prosecutors save themselves and the court expense and time. And prosecutors are aware that a winning record is important for a positive public image at election time.

When theft or property damage has occurred, suspects sometimes agree to pay the victim or take care of the damage in some other way. In such cases, the prosecutor may drop charges. The attitude of the victim is also a factor. Field studies show that in many communities victims consistently refuse to prosecute (Miller 1969, p. 174). In domestic disturbances, for example, few of the original charges made by husbands and wives against each other are ever carried through.

Charges may also be dropped if alternatives to prosecution are sufficient. In the case of an offender who commits a crime while on probation or parole, for example, probation or parole can be revoked instead of charging the offender. If a suspect is mentally ill, it might be better to require commitment under civil procedures; sex deviates and other mentally disturbed persons are often handled in this way. In other cases, suspects (such as drug users) may be persuaded to work as informers for the police. If a suspect agrees to act as a witness against other defendants, charges are often dropped or sharply reduced.

Laws also exist that few citizens expect prosecutors to rigorously enforce. These laws may have been passed long ago and have become meaningless to modern society. Or they may be laws pertaining to fornication or adultery, laws that exist only to maintain the moral tone of the community. Prosecutors would generally lose favor with their communities if they insisted on full enforcement of such statutes: thus, neither the police nor prosecutors usually enforce them. Other types of cases that American prosecutors often seem disinterested in following up in criminal courts are domestic cases, statutory rape where both parties are underage, first offense car thefts involving teenagers who joyride, assaults and petty thefts where the victim and the offender are in the same family or have a significant social relationship, checks that are drawn on insufficient funds, first offender shoplifting when restitution is made, offenses committed by the mentally handicapped, and many drunkenness, vagrancy, and disorderly conduct complaints. See Table 8.1 for other factors that prosecutors consider when deciding whether to take a case to court.

Prosecutorial discretion allows the office to respond directly to the particular requirements of the community. This factor is important, because prosecutors are usually elected. The danger is that in times of severe public pressure a prosecutor may overstep the bounds of legality to satisfy the momentary desires of the community. On the positive side, however, those laws that relate to more serious crimes and areas that the community feels must be dealt with vigorously can be given greater attention.

The prosecutor's office is generally considered a stepping stone to higher political office. Thus, there is obvious benefit to keeping oneself before the public, and how this is done can have an effect on cases. To present their best profile, prosecutors may reduce charges unnecessarily just to gain sure convictions. And cases that would ordinarily be handled expeditiously and quietly are sometimes dredged up for public view. The public interest is not served in either of these instances.

One effective way to control discretion is to make it more visible. Prosecutors should be required to publish policy statements about what circumstances affect their discretion, including which cases and offenders are most likely to be prosecuted and which cases and offenders may expect **plea bargaining.** Circumstances that affect discretion should be spelled out, and guidelines should be written for everything from pretrial screening to sentencing recommendations.

A middle ground between a prosecutor dropping a case and going forward with a full criminal trial is **diversion.** The prosecutors who use diversion often believe the ideals of justice can be better served if they do not seek criminal trial. Traditionally, accused were diverted by requiring them to join the army, join the peace corps, or promise never to come back to town. Today, however, diversion has taken a much more sophisticated meaning. Often the accused receive psychological, social, and medical help to deal with problems thought to be at the root of their criminal behavior. Likewise, if the accused are first-time offenders, these diversions allow them to escape the label of "criminal." This gives them a better chance to reintegrate into society. The Hill Street Mediation program in Cleveland seems to be on the cutting edge of pre-trial diversion programs used by prosecutors in the United States.

The Cleveland Prosecutor Mediation Program

A unique mediation program in Cleveland, Ohio, helps citizens negotiate out-of-court settlements for disputes involving criminal misdemeanor charges. The program is sometimes referred to as "Hill Street mediation" because, like the police of television fame, the Cleveland mediators deal with interpersonal disputes that can erupt into violence. In three years, Cleveland's mediation program has evolved into one of the largest conflict resolution programs in the United States. Forty program staff members process an estimated 14,000 citizen complaints per year. Approximately 60 percent of these complaints are scheduled for mediation hearings.

The Mediation Program is modeled after two other well-established dispute resolution programs in Ohio—the Cincinnati Private Complaint Program and the Cleveland Night Prosecutor Program. In January 1985, the city of Cleveland took over responsibility for the program's funding from the Cleveland Foundation; the program is now a permanent part of the city's Law Department.

How the Program Works

For the most part, cases scheduled for mediation involve interpersonal disputes between neighbors, friends, co-workers, family members, lovers, and acquaintances. For instance: A father and son are drinking together in the father's home when the son, who has a history of drinking problems, loses his temper and threatens his father. The father makes a complaint against the son for menacing.

As a result of mediation, the son apologizes to his father and promises not to drink with him again. After the father leaves, the mediator suggests that the son get help with his drinking problem. The son accepts a counseling referral and joins a treatment program. Mediation is extremely effective in such disputes because the complaining parties usually have strong incentives to find ways to get along peacefully with one another. Mediation defuses hostilities between disputing parties before their conflict escalates into a violent, even life-threatening situation.

The mediator's goal is to have the parties themselves arrive at a mutually acceptable settlement. In the privacy of a room in the prosecutor's office, each party tells his or her side of the case without interruption. The mediator helps the disputants suggest possible solutions to the problem. Once the parties have chosen a solution, the mediator records the settlement, reads it to the parties, and asks for their commitment to it. Two weeks later, the mediator calls to find out if the parties are adhering to their agreement. If they are not, prosecutors determine if warrants need to be issued.

Mediation requires considerable technical skill. Approximately forty staff members, all second- or third-year law students, receive structured training during two intensive weekends.

Evaluation of the Cleveland Program

The success of the Mediation Program in handling disputes was reflected in the Cincinnati Institute of Justice's (CIJ) study of the program, completed in April 1984. This independent evaluation compared a twelve-month period of full operation (June 1982 through May 1983) of the Mediation Program to a baseline study of the Minicipal Court System for the year 1980.

CIJ's analysis indicates that the program not only has met its objectives, but also has provided a beneficial service to the community. In the baseline period, citizen-filed complaints that entered the Municipal Court required more than 105 days and 3 court appearances to reach final disposition. Under the new program, dispositions for cases that required a mediation hearing were reached within 15 days from the date the complaint was originally made.

The number of citizen-filed warrants entering Cleveland's court system on misdemeanor charges was reduced by more than 50 percent during the report period compared to the baseline year.

Citizen Satisfaction High

The CIJ study indicated widespread user satisfaction with both the mediation process and outcome. Approximately 92 percent of the citizens who used the program felt that the mediator had been fair to both sides during the hearing; 85 percent were satisfied with the agreement reached; and 77 percent were still adhering to their settlements a year later.

As CIJ's report has shown, mediation can be a highly effective way of dealing with disputes; it should be one of the many options available when handling criminal as well as interpersonal disputes. The Cleveland Prosecutor Mediation Program has become an essential part of the prosecutor's office and the city of Cleveland's justice system.

By Bradley M. Weiss, National Institute of Justice Reports, SNI 190 (March 1985). Reprinted from the National Institute of Justice's *The Judicial System*, 1987.

DEFENSE

A substantial majority of all lawyers either never take a criminal case or do so only on rare occasions. These lawyers commonly view criminal defense as one of the least desirable fields of specialization. Wice estimates that the total number of lawyers, excluding public defenders, who "accept criminal cases more than occasionally" falls between 6,000 and 16,000. Another study indicates that no more than 1 percent of all private practitioners in Manhattan and the Bronx consider themselves to be criminal lawyers (1978).

The primary responsibility of the **defense attorney** is to represent his or her client, who has the constitutional right to counsel; and if the defendant cannot afford an attorney, the state must provide the cost of legal defense. The defense attorney is responsible for preparing the case and for selecting the defense strategy. In the criminal justice process, the defense attorney is the counterpart of the prosecuting attorney.

Because of the crime explosion, both private and public defense attorneys (especially in urban areas) face immense **caseloads** that severely limit the quality of the services they are able to provide. The "sausage factory" character of many urban criminal courts creates strong pressures on defenders to process cases rapidly. And the interpersonal relationships between prosecutors and defenders combine with court pressures to motivate the defense to "keep the assembly line moving." Thus, the

TABLE 8.1
Other Significant Factors Used by Prosecutors to Determine Whether to Litigate Certain Criminal Cases

Adapted from National Advisory Committee on the Criminal Justice Standards and Goals, *Courts* (Washington, D.C.: U.S. Government Printing Office, 1973), p. 20.

1. Any doubts about the accused's guilt.
2. The impact of further proceedings upon the accused and those close to him or her, especially the likelihood and seriousness of financial hardship or disruption of family life.
3. The value of further proceedings in preventing future offenses by other persons, considering the extent to which subjecting the accused to further proceedings could be expected to have an impact upon others who might commit such offenses, as well as the seriousness of those offenses.
4. The value of further proceedings in preventing future offenses by the offender, in light of the offender's commitment to criminal activity as a way of life; the seriousness of his or her past criminal activity, which he or she might reasonably be expected to continue; the possibility that further proceedings might have a tendency to create or reinforce commitment on the part of the accused to criminal activity as a way of life; and the likelihood that programs available as diversion or sentencing alternatives may reduce the likelihood of future criminal activity.
5. The value of further proceedings in fostering the community's sense of security and confidence in the criminal justice system.
6. The direct cost of prosecution, in terms of prosecutorial time, court time, and similar factors.
7. Any improper motives of the complainant.
8. Prolonged nonenforcement of the statute on which the charge is based.
9. The likelihood of prosecution and conviction of the offender by another jurisdiction.
10. Any assistance rendered by the accused in the apprehension or conviction of other offenders, in preventing offenses by others, in reducing the impact of offenses committed by the accused or others upon the victims, and any other socially beneficial activity engaged in by the accused that might be encouraged in others by not prosecuting the offender.

strongest pressure on a defendant to plea bargain may come not from the prosecutor but from the defense lawyer. In this way, private and public defenders contribute to a decline in the quality of justice dispensed by the criminal courts (Willard 1976).[6]

Even a defendant who can afford private counsel is not guaranteed competent or interested representation. Many lawyers who station themselves outside municipal courtrooms and offer their services to people brought in by officers have a vested financial interest in encouraging their clients to plead guilty. Few such lawyers are willing or able to conduct extensive investigations on behalf of their clients or to engage in intensive pretrial preparation. The best (i.e., most competent and interested) criminal lawyers are more expensive; and there is frequently a direct correlation between a defendant's ability to pay and the quality of representation he or she receives. For the indigent, private counsel is not a viable option, and the only avenue for their defense is through public defenders or court-appointed attorneys.

The Legal Aid System

Prior to the signing of the Constitution, it was not uncommon for criminal courts to deny the right to counsel to some defendants, putting them at the mercy of the judge and the prosecuting agent of the state. In the late 1700s, however, the importance of legal counsel in criminal proceedings came to be widely acknowledged, and many then-independent states acted to provide a legislative guarantee of access to counsel through their constitutions (National Legal Aid and Defender Association 1969, p. 2). This right was extended to criminal defendants in all states by the Sixth Amendment, which states that "in all criminal proceedings, the accused shall enjoy the right . . . to have the assistance of counsel for his defense." By a strict reading, this amendment guarantees only the right to use an attorney in the preparation and delivery of one's defense. A less strict interpretation is needed to guarantee an ability, regardless of wealth, to acquire counsel. Yet to give someone the right to counsel without removing the financial stumbling blocks to the use of that right is really to give nothing at all. (Similarly, freedom of speech can be said to be meaningless without the ability to speak.)

Unfortunately, acceptance of the implied right to afford counsel was long in coming. Until 1932, only New Jersey and Connecticut had provisions for appointing counsel for the poor—and then only for capital offenses (ibid.). The federal government wasn't much more responsive to the needs of the poor; it assigned counsel only in capital cases in which defendants were incapable of defending themselves (ibid., p. 3). Under such arrangements, most poor defendants really had no right to counsel.

In 1932, the U.S. Supreme Court ruled in *Powell* v. *Alabama* (287 U.S. 45) that all states were required to assign counsel to poor defendants in capital cases, thus extending the practice of New Jersey, Connecticut, and the federal government to all states (National Legal Aid and Defender Association 1969, p. 3). The first major step toward expanding the provision of counsel occurred six years later; in 1939, the Court in *Johnson* v. *Zerbst* (304 U.S. 458) expanded the provision of counsel at the federal level beyond capital cases to include all felonies. A similar move on the state level was gaining momentum, but in 1942 the Court ruled in *Betts* v. *Brady* (316 U.S. 455) that the states were not required to extend the provision of counsel beyond capital cases. The *Betts* decision was not unequivocal in its denial of expansion, however; the Court added that the states must provide counsel if it is needed to ensure a fair trial.

Legal scholars generally agree that the *Betts* decision was a judicial mistake; the Court was soon inundated by appeals, all claiming that the denial of counsel in each case was unconstitutional because of complex issues of fact. Essentially, the Court had placed itself as the final arbiter in every felony prosecution on the state level, a task beyond the capabilities of nine justices. Strangely enough, the Court was long in remedying its error; not until 1963, in *Gideon* v. *Wainwright* (372 U.S. 335) did the Court move to change the precedent. In *Gideon*, the Court extended the precedent of *Johnson* v. *Zerbst* to the state level, requiring assigned counsel for indigent accused felons. *Gideon* proved to be the first drop of water over the dam. In the three or four years after the decision, the right to counsel was extended to include delinquency proceedings (*In re Gault* [387 U.S. 1 (1967)]), police interrogations (*Miranda* v. *Arizona* [384 U.S. 436 (1966)]), postindictment lineups (*U.S.* v. *Wade* [388 U.S. 218 (1967)]), and probation revocations (*Mempa* v. *Rhey* [389 U.S. 128 (1967)]).

The defendant also has a right to counsel when he or she is submitting a guilty plea to the court (*Moore* v. *Michigan* [355 U.S. 155 (1957)]). In addition, a convicted offender has the right to counsel at the time of sentencing (*Townsend* v. *Burke* [334 U.S. 736 (1948)]). Even during the Burger years, the Supreme Court was active in extending the defendant's right to counsel. Defendants in state criminal trials have a constitutional right to proceed without counsel when they voluntarily and intelligently elect to do so (*Faretta* v. *California* [422

U.S. 806 (1975)]). The Court has articulated that the preliminary hearing is a critical stage of the criminal prosecution. Thus, a state's failure to provide counsel at that stage may be a violation of the defendant's right to counsel (*Coleman* v. *Alabama* [399 U.S. 1 (1970)]). Also, counsel is required at lineups that take place after indictment or other "adversarial criminal proceedings" (*Kirby* v. *Illinois* [406 U.S. 682 (1972)]). Furthermore a defendant has the right to counsel during an in-court identification at a preliminary hearing after a criminal complaint has been initiated (*Moore* v. *Illinois* [434 U.S. 220 (1977)]). Once any adversary proceeding has begun against a defendant, he or she has the right to the assistance of counsel (*Brewer* v. *Williams* [430 U.S. 387 (1977)]). The only retraction from the right to counsel by the Burger Court came in *Ross* v. *Moffitt* (417 U.S. 600 [1974]), in which the Court held the states are not required to provide counsel for indigents beyond one appeal.

The Supreme Court's 1972 decision in *Argersinger* v. *Hamlin* (407 U.S. 25 [1972]) approached *Gideon* in importance. The *Argersinger* decision provided that, on the state and federal levels, counsel must be provided in all cases where the defendant is threatened with a loss of liberty, whether indicted for a misdemeanor or a felony. The importance of this decision lies largely in the number of defendants it affects: approximately 5,000,000 people a year, or 84 percent of all those arrested, are charged with misdemeanors (Silverstein 1965, p. 1). In 1979 the Court retreated by stating the right to counsel exists only in misdemeanor cases where actual punishment is imposed *Scott* v. *Illinois*.

The legislative contribution to the right to assigned counsel has not been as significant as that of the judicial branch. In fact, the sole legislative contribution is the Criminal Justice Act of 1964 (Cappelletti and Gordley 1972, p. 2). Essentially, the act provides defendants in all federal courts with counsel at all stages of the criminal process. Furthermore, it provides that attorneys for the indigent should be members of the local bar that specialize in criminal law. The practical impact of this act has been to reduce the parameters of discretion in the American criminal justice system. At least in theory, no jurisdiction can now deny a defendant legal advice merely because he or she is indigent. For nearly all categories of offenses, a defendant is accorded an almost absolute legal right to representation.

About three million offenders are given free legal services annually. Programs providing for the assistance of counsel to offenders who are unable to afford private counsel can be divided into three major categories: **public defender systems, assigned (or appointed) counsel systems, and contract systems.** In addition, some jurisdictions use a mixed system, which involves representation by both the public defender and the private bar, law school clinical programs, and prepaid legal services.

The public defender system is the system used most often in large cities and major jurisdictions. The office of public defender may be either private, public-private, or public in sponsorship, depending on the source of funding (Silverstein 1965, p. 46). Newer offices tend to be public, reflecting increased governmental commitment to legal aid (Cappelletti and Gordley 1972). And older offices, most of which were initially private, are becoming increasingly dependent on public sources for support. Attorneys in the public defender's office are full-time employees who, unlike assigned counsel, are helped by office investigators or law students.

A newer system for providing defense services to poor people involves the government entering into a contract with an individual attorney, or more often, a private law firm. The terms of the contract vary. The most common provision, however, is that a private firm agrees to provide representation in all cases for a fixed amount. A majority of the counties that choose this method are rural.

In addition, many private organizations across the country provide legal assistance to poor people, although this is not a formal form of legal aid to indigents. Most of these organizations are financed by private contributions and are staffed by full-time attorneys who earn their living by representing the poor. Examples of such organizations are the Legal Services Corporation, the American Civil Liberties Union, and the Law Center for Constitutional Rights.

Thus we are faced with three fundamentally different systems for providing **legal aid** to the indigent (see Figure 8.1). Is one system preferable over the others?

Strengths and Weaknesses of the Public Defender System

Public defender programs may be either statewide or local programs. Under a statewide system a chief defender is appointed either by the governor or the judiciary. He or she is charged with providing the system of representation for each of the counties in the state. The chief defender usually establishes branch offices staffed by his or her assistants although contractual arrangements with local law firms may be used by some counties. The local branches are subject to supervisory

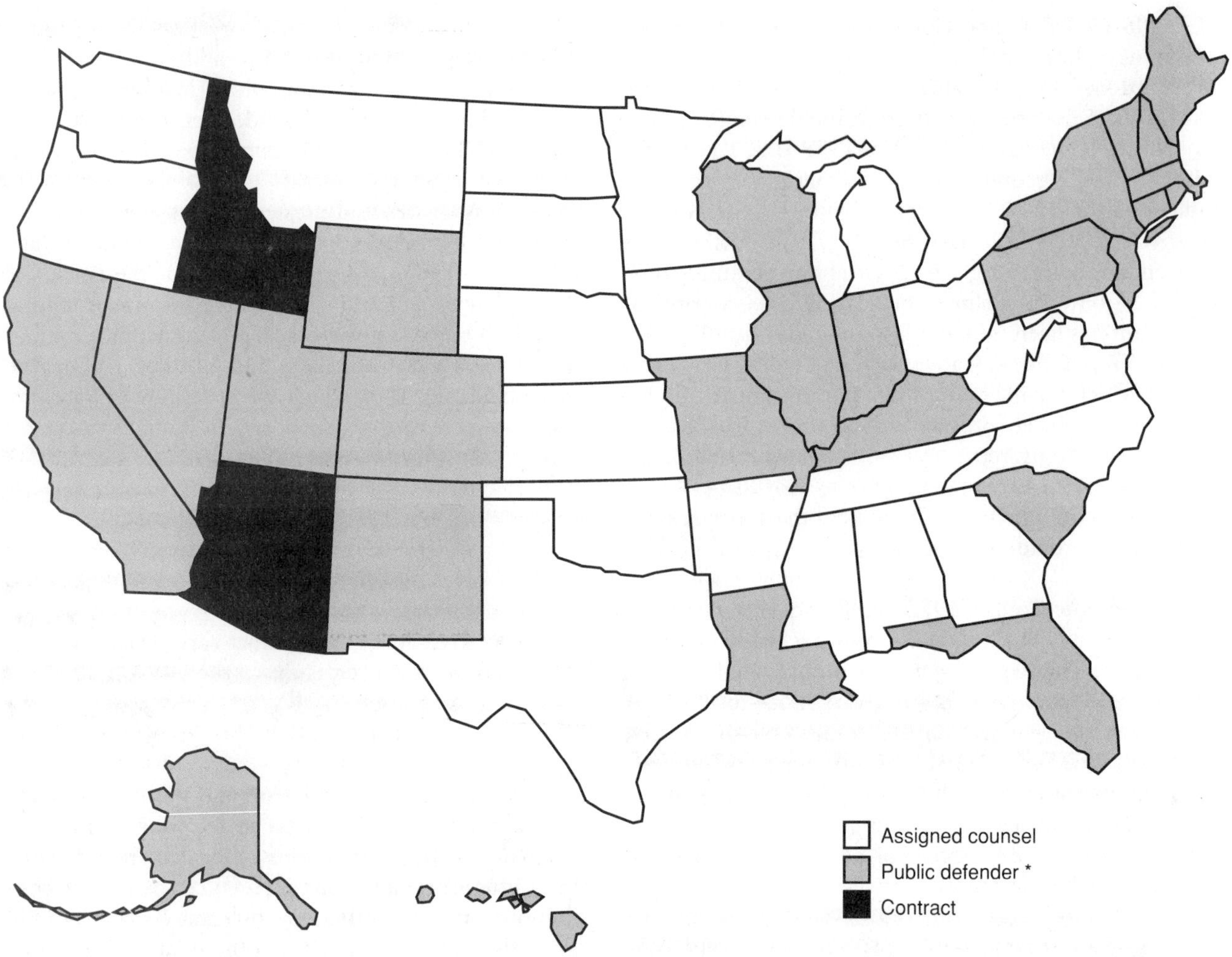

Assigned counsel
Public defender *
Contract

* Indiana and New Mexico have the same number of public defender and assigned counsel counties. Missouri and New Hampshire changed to public defenders around the time of the survey.

FIGURE 8.1
States by type of defense system in majority of counties in 1984. Bureau of Justice Statistics, *Criminal Defense Systems—A National Survey* (Washington, D.C.: U.S. Department of Justice, August 1984), p. 1.

authority of the chief defender and receive support services from the central office. Local defender agencies are organized by the county or judicial district. Most are government agencies, but some are private nonprofit organizations receiving funding from the local courts or the community (Kamisar, LaFave, and Israel 1986). The public defender system offers three benefits to a jurisdiction. First, it ensures that the indigent receive competent legal counsel. Many stories have been told about public defenders depicting them as young lawyers getting experience before they join criminal law firms, or old lawyers not competent enough to support themselves in private practice. But there are good reasons to question these stories: a variety of studies report favorably on the competence of public defenders (Silverstein 1965, p. 47).

Some studies point to statistics showing a higher percentage of guilty pleas for defendants represented by public defenders; however, this percentage is probably related more to the class of defendants that use public defenders than to the competence of the defenders themselves (Wice and Suwak 1974). More often than not, the clients of public defenders are poorly educated, unaware of their rights, and apt to make self-incriminating statements to the police—conditions that might well make a guilty plea the only practical alternative for the defender. Public defenders also handle many clients who are (1) guilty, (2) repeat offenders, and (3) relatively experienced in legal matters. Such individuals may know that the prosecutor has a strong case against them, and, quite intelligently, they regard plea bargaining as the best way to resolve their problems. The high percentage of guilty pleas from the clients of public defenders is directly related to the fact that a higher percentage of persons who plan to plea bargain select public defenders (as opposed to private attorneys). If defendants know they are going to plead guilty, why should they pay for an attorney when equally competent representation may be obtained without cost? As a rule, then, it is unlikely that the percentage of guilty pleas is a serious reflection on the quality of services from the public defender. Rather, public defenders generally provide high-quality legal assistance for indigent defendants.

A second advantage of the public defender system is that public defenders are not strongly motivated to solicit money from the families of their clients. Most or all public defenders are paid fixed salaries, frequently at civil service wage scales. Conversely, appointed counsel is under considerable pressure to secure additional funds, because court fees are relatively nominal. All investigative expenses come out of the court fee, so the margin of profit for an appointed attorney is often small. The public defender, in contrast, pays nothing for office and secretarial support, and expenses for research or investigation come out of a general office fund. Although few public defender offices are sufficiently funded, the financial pressures on the individual defender are not as great as those facing the appointed attorney.

Efficiency is another benefit of the public defender system. As a rule, defenders are able to handle comparatively large caseloads more efficiently and less expensively than private attorneys. Why? First, defenders benefit from group research and investigation. Second, they deal from day to day with similar kinds of cases—cases for which they are well prepared. Thirdly, defenders benefit from an ability to recruit highly motivated and well-qualified law school graduates. Such attorneys are frequently excellent trial lawyers who are motivated to work in a defender's office to gain experience. Because they are fresh out of law school, they are frequently more up-to-date on the state of the law than are their older colleagues. In sum, there are good reasons to believe that public defender systems are the most efficient way—from a financial standpoint—to provide high-quality legal aid to the indigent.

The efficiency advantage, not surprisingly, has been the subject of strong criticism. Some critics argue that efficiency is irrelevant to justice, that it is not a valid criterion for evaluating legal assistance. The best criterion, they say, is the quality of justice attained for the defendant. Thus, critics conclude that public defenders sacrifice justice in the interests of efficiency as they try to deal with their excessive caseloads. Defenders, like all other judicial actors, *are* overloaded; and it is not surprising that they may be as willing as prosecutors to plea bargain, rather than to see a case through in court.

Many critics believe that some public defenders are not sufficiently independent from prosecutors. The public defender and the prosecutor who meet one another in the court day after day form interpersonal bonds that affect their behavior in important ways. One critic compares this relationship to "two professional wrestlers who fight one another every night in a different town, and after a while, get so that they do not want to hurt each other much" (Silverstein 1965, p. 47). And similar bonds may develop between the judge and the defender. The defender learns what kind of behavior the judge approves of and what kind of pleas the judge likes to hear. In this way, the defender serves as a representative of the judge to the client. Defenders gradually acquire a vested interest in keeping the assembly line moving and are loath to "rock the boat" in the interests of one client. To do so might harm their chances in future cases.

Defenders themselves are quick to point out that the personal and professional pride of each public defender may work against a cozy relationship with the prosecutor and the judge. Defenders want to have a successful case record to the same degree that prosecutors do, they are frequently drawn to their positions by a concern about the welfare of indigent defendants, and they are often highly motivated to provide their clients with the best representation possible.[7]

As a practical matter, the central determinant of the quality of a defender's services is the size of his or her caseload. A proper caseload for legal aid attorneys has been set at roughly thirty-five cases per attorney per year (Wice and Suwak 1974, p. 178). By this criterion, many legal aid offices are badly overloaded, and others (by far in the minority) are operating at or below the proper level. When caseloads become unmanageable, public attorneys must accommodate their professional pride to the needs of efficiency. Because plea bargaining is the most rapid way to dispose of cases, defenders must sometimes encourage their indigent clients to plead guilty for reduced sentencing considerations. Too, as caseloads become too large, the ability of public defenders to interview clients properly and to pursue legal research and investigation declines. Thus, the legal advice they give to their clients may be of poor quality (ibid., p. 165).

Low-quality legal representation can have irreparable consequences. For example, the Supreme Court has ruled that guilty pleas incorrectly advised by legal aid attorneys are not grounds for new trials (*Chambers* v. *Maroney* [399 U.S. 52 (1970)]). The victims of incompetent lawyers, then, must bear the burden of that incompetence, often for many years in prison. One legal resource for the convicted defendant may be a **legal malpractice** suit against the attorney to gain financial compensation. Malpractice suits against attorneys are increasing each year for a variety of reasons, although the bulk of these suits stem from civil actions. There is little evidence that the incidence of malpractice suits against criminal lawyers has had much influence on the diligence with which these lawyers work for their clients.

The main impetus for malpractice suits against lawyers is money. Civil cases sometimes involve huge sums of money, and when these cases are handled incompetently, clients are able to claim large financial losses. The financial incentives for criminal cases are not as attractive, however, and there is a natural reluctance on the part of lawyers to sue other lawyers for incompetence (or simple procedural mistakes) on the basis of a small claim. In a sense, however, the field of legal malpractice is "wide open," and it may well have important effects on the future conduct of criminal law.

Strengths and Weaknesses of the Assigned Counsel System

Some jurisdictions prefer the assigned counsel system to the public defender system. In small jurisdictions, for example, the assigned counsel system is less expensive in the long run, because public funds are needed for only a small number of cases that can be parceled out to a variety of private attorneys. These attorneys are customarily chosen from the local bar association's membership rolls. Under most assigned counsel systems, however, a list of eligible and willing attorneys is maintained by the court. Lawyers indicate to the court that they want to be placed on the list. Some jurisdictions require attorneys who want to be placed on the list to qualify by experience and/or training before they are assigned. This is more the exception than the rule, however. In either event, the judge is generally responsible for the actual appointment of the defense counsel in a particular case.

The assigned counsel system places more of the burden for public assistance upon individual lawyers and their staffs. As a general rule, each lawyer is paid a set fee for specific services—a fee that is usually too small even to cover expenses. This benefits the government, which does not have to pay for extensive services.

Cost is not the only benefit of the assigned counsel system, however. Supporters of the system also claim that there are psychological benefits to the defendant. Because one lawyer is assigned for the entire judicial proceeding, the traditional lawyer-client relationship is preserved, even though the defendant may not be able to pay for the services. Thus, defendants feel that they have received the best personal attention, rather than being processed through the public defender's "assembly line." This benefit, of course, is based more on personal feelings than on any real state of affairs. For one thing, the "assembly line" character of the public defender's office cannot be equated with low-quality legal service. Indeed, quite the opposite may be true. And although clients may feel that they have been treated well by an individual lawyer, that lawyer may well have shortchanged the client in terms of research, investigation, and trial preparation. Thus, it is not always true that private attorneys give superior service; it is only true that clients may *feel* better about the service because they have been represented by a single person.

Another advantage frequently claimed for the assigned counsel system is that it involves a wide spectrum of the legal community. But this situation may not be desirable in some cases, especially if corporate lawyers are assigned to criminal cases for which they have no experience. Such a problem can be prevented, however, if judges—as mandated in the federal courts by the Criminal Justice Act of 1964—assign lawyers from a list of attorneys who do have criminal experience.

The strongest claims for the assigned counsel system are usually made on behalf of small jurisdictions. Small jurisdictions often cannot justify a full-time legal aid office: the number of indigent defendants does not war-

rant the spending required to provide office space and support services for a public defender. Thus, for the few indigent defendants in these jurisdictions, it is more cost-effective to assign a lawyer. In addition, many small jurisdictions have local bar associations that view public service as an important part of the organization. Presumably, the members of these associations—as long as they are not terribly overburdened by appointed cases—do not view court-appointed work as too onerous. Thus, they will probably provide high-quality legal assistance to their clients.

The assigned counsel system has been criticized on several grounds. For one thing, there is no guarantee that the assigned attorney will be qualified in terms of training or experience to handle the complexities of the criminal law and criminal procedure in the case. For example, by the luck of the draw one defendant might get an attorney who only knows about wills and trusts. Another problem is that the system does not provide funds to hire investigators, secure expert witnesses, or finance the production of other pieces of evidence for the defense. Another criticism focuses on the fact that since assigned counsel are very seldom repaid out-of-pocket expenses, court-appointed lawyers will not be motivated to do additional tasks in defense of their clients since they will not be reimbursed. Furthermore, many assigned lawyers are either fresh out of law school or "ambulance chasers," both of whom may be incompetent to provide effective legal counsel in a criminal trial. Another problem involves professional assigned counsel. Since they make a life business out of getting assigned cases from the courts, they may be more interested in not rocking the boat from the judge's perspective than in being a forceful advocate for their client's case.

Another important criticism of the assigned counsel system is that lawyer selection is frequently open to abuse. In some cases, judges appoint friends who need income. One such example was noted in Boston:

> [One judge] . . . chose to call on about half a dozen regular lawyers . . . when indigent defendants asked to be represented in court. He parcels out the assignments one-here-one-there so that each lawyer picks up a hundred and fifty to two hundred dollars a week from the state. . . . They get the assignments as long as they do things the way [the judge] . . . wants—with dispatch (Harris 1973, p. 45).

Thus, a judge who is overly concerned with processing a large number of cases might select lawyers who either advise their clients to plea bargain or who do not cause too many problems during trial. To circumvent this situation, some assigned counsel systems use computers to match lawyers and defendants. This approach has already met with success in Houston (National Legal Aid and Defender Association 1969, p. 19).

Some theorists criticize the assigned counsel system for a feature also found in the public defender system: young, inexperienced lawyers frequently assigned as counsel are thought to be less competent than more experienced colleagues. This can be viewed as a positive feature of the system, however, in that it provides opportunities for experience. Yet, as one author remarks, "Experience is valuable only for those who need it" (Silverstein 1965, p. 19). To ask the indigent to serve as human hamsters in legal education may well be to deny the central value of the criminal justice system—equal justice to all.

Another very serious criticism of the assigned counsel system is that it is subject to extralegal pressures. For example, the plea that a defendant is advised to enter by assigned counsel may not be in the defendant's best interests; rather, it may be a reflection of the desires of the counsel. Youthful attorneys may advise a plea of not guilty solely because they desire trial experience. Older attorneys may advise guilty pleas only because they wish to return to their more profitable private practices. In all such cases, the needs of the defendant are essentially irrelevant to the conduct of the case. Private attorneys, it is claimed, sacrifice the best interests of their clients to the administrative or financial needs of their own practices. Of course, there are no reliable statistics to indicate the extent of this problem; and the shortchanging of clients may not be unique to assigned counsel, as the same pressures can bear upon private attorneys who represent paying customers. Yet, the critics say, the pressures to shortchange clients are especially strong for private attorneys representing indigent defendants, simply because the public fees are so low. An obvious solution to this problem is to increase fees, but in some jurisdictions this would be politically impracticable or fiscally impossible.

The financial pressures on private attorneys are often severe; and many of these attorneys are unable to expend large amounts of money for investigation or for expert testimony. In such cases, a defendant may be convicted on erroneous testimony that the defense lawyer could not afford to rebut. In one case, a defendant was cleared of a previous conviction when it was discovered that, contrary to expert testimony, the person the convict was alleged to have killed actually died of a heart attack. Unfortunately, this information came out ten years after the defendant's conviction (Silverstein 1965, p. 29).

Contract Systems

Until recently, the types of indigent defenses were limited to public defender systems and appointed counsel systems. Under the new contract system, individual attorneys, bar associations, and private law firms contract with government to provide specific services for a dollar amount. These awards are usually based on competitive bidding. A selection criteria is integrated as part of the final award. Only 6 percent of all counties in the United States used some form of contract system in 1986. Only two states, Arizona and Idaho, use the contract system as their most significant form of indigent representation. However, this form of legal aid appears to be on the increase. The contract system usually is used in counties that also have public defender offices. These two systems complement each other in instances when a public defender must withdraw from a case due to a conflict of interest with another defendant. If the entire public defender's office has been exposed by the first case, the contract system can take over without damaging the defendant's interests. A study by Houlden and Balkin discovered that contract attorneys were at least as effective as assigned counsel and were more cost effective (1985).

Other disadvantages of the public defender system come from the defendant's point of view. Defense clients often see public defenders as employees paid by the state that is prosecuting them and therefore are suspicious. The article also notes that many defendants believe private attorneys are real attorneys whereas appointed attorneys are not.

Do We Have the Right to an Effective Assistance of Counsel?

In one survey of defendants who had used public defenders, 30 percent reported their attorneys spent less than 10 minutes with them; 32 percent reported their attorneys spent 10 to 29 minutes with them. The remainder reported their attorneys spent 30 minutes or more with them. Forty-nine percent of these clients thought their attorney was on the side of the state (Kamisar, LaFave, and Israel 1986). Early in American history, the Supreme Court held it was the trial court's duty to appoint counsel. However, this did not require the local court to make an effective appointment. At one point the standard for determining whether counsel was competent was the "mockery of justice" standard. Under this standard representation was considered to be ineffective only when it was so poor as to "reduce the trial to a farce" or to render it "a mockery of justice."

In *United States* v. *Deoster* (487 F.2d 1197 [D.C.Cir. (1973)]), a series of minimal requirements for the effectiveness of a defense counsel were announced. An effective counsel is one that generally follows the American Bar Association's standards for "the defense function." Specifically, an effective counsel must confer with his or her client without delay and as often as necessary to elicit matters concerning the defense. Also, he or she must promptly advise his or her client of the client's rights and take all actions necessary to preserve them. And finally, the counsel must conduct appropriate investigations both factual and legal. These rules have been adopted by other jurisdictions to ensure that all defendants have competent legal counsel.

SUMMARY

Our system of criminal law is based upon the adversary system—the presentation of opposing views in vigorous debate as a prelude to decisionmaking. The system is not designed to discover the ultimate truth in the absolute sense, but rather to protect the people against the abuse of governmental power, and to assure that no innocent person is found guilty of a crime he or she did not commit. Cross-examination is used to determine the facts and has historically proved to be the most effective means of exposing false testimony and inaccuracies in testimony. Our system also rejects the practice of torture and other inhuman practices incompatible with the values of free people. In summary, the adversary system seeks to accomplish justice by eliciting provable facts under fixed rules of procedure.

In America, prosecutors represent the executive branch of the government. Their powers are formidable, and they exert considerable influence upon and within the criminal justice system. Their power to institute criminal prosecution vests in them an authority in the administration of criminal justice as large, or perhaps greater than, the authority of the judge who presides in criminal cases. They may initiate criminal charges, stop the charging process, or request that the court dismiss the charges. Thus, the powers within the prosecutor's office in this country are indeed quite formidable.

On the opposing side is the defense counsel. The courts have mandated that counsel be provided at both the state and federal levels, in all cases where the defendant is threatened with loss of liberty, whether the accused is charged with a misdemeanor or felony. Legal assistance may be provided by private counsel, public defenders, counsel assigned by the courts, or counsel under contract. Each alternative has its strengths and weaknesses. For example, hiring a private attorney does not guarantee competent or interested representation. The best criminal lawyers are expensive, and frequently there is a direct correlation between the defendant's ability to pay and the quality of representation received.

The merits of the public defender system include the assurance that the indigent receives competent legal counsel. It avoids some of the worst excesses of the appointed counsel system (such as soliciting money from the families of clients), because most or all are paid constant salaries. Public defenders are able to handle comparatively large caseloads more efficiently and less expensively than private attorneys. Critics of the system contend that public defenders are often not completely independent from prosecutors because of their close day-to-day working relationship. Further, their heavy caseloads reduce public defenders' ability to interview their clients properly and to pursue legal research.

The assigned counsel system also has strengths and weaknesses. It is psychologically beneficial to the client because the defendant sees the traditional lawyer-client relationship preserved. Also, a wide spectrum of the legal community is involved in the process. This method of providing counsel is the most practical and cost effective for jurisdictions too small to justify a full-time legal aid office. Critics of the system claim that it is subject to abuse because judges may appoint their friends who need the income. Others believe that judges concerned with processing large numbers of cases will appoint attorneys who either encourage their clients to plead guilty or do not raise too many difficulties during the trial. In addition, some critics believe that it is the young and inexperienced—and less competent—attorneys who are the ones assigned counsel work. Lastly, the assigned counsel system has been criticized because the pleas that defendants are advised to enter may not be in the defendant's best interests, but rather a reflection of the desires of the assigned counsel.

Contract attorneys appear to be at least as effective as assigned counsel and are more cost effective. Although the contract system is currently used less frequently than either public defenders or assigned counsel, the number of jurisdictions turning to contract attorneys appears to be growing.

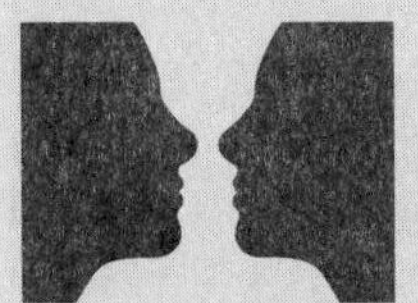

ISSUE PAPER

COURT OF FIRST RESORT—THE NEIGHBORHOOD JUSTICE CENTER

In 1971 in Columbus, Ohio, City Attorney James Hughes and Professor John Palmer (Capital University Law School) developed a dispute-settlement program for resolving citizen conflicts and averting serious crimes. Called the Night Prosecutor Program, the model was intended to provide a means for coping with disputes in which the parties had a long-standing personal relationship with one another (e.g., married couples, relatives, and friends). Hughes and Palmer regarded the courts, with their formal structure and rigid procedures, as more suitable for the adjudication of guilt or innocence in felony offenses than as an appropriate forum for dealing with personal fights, vandalism, petty thefts, wife and child abuse, disputes over parking spaces, barking dogs, loud stereos, and television sets—the kinds of cases the criminal justice system is often nearly powerless to handle effectively. Hughes and Palmer sought to offer an alternative to the courtroom and trial as an approach to conflict resolution.

Although many citizen disputes seem minor or trivial, they represent potential sources of conflict within the home, school, or neighborhood. Assault and homicide frequently occur as the result of petty conflicts between people who are close to each other. And serious juvenile crimes sometimes follow minor abuses that nobody bothers to address.

The procedure adopted by the Night Prosecutor Program has been widely emulated in more than 200 neighborhood justice centers around the country, which together handle over 200,000 cases a year. In a typical case, a hearing officer opens the proceedings by giving a brief explanation of the purposes of the program. Complainants and respondents are then allowed to present their versions of the specific incident without interruption by the other party. After these initial presentations, the hearing officer encourages the two parties to discuss the basic causes of the dispute. Questions are asked of complainants, respondents, and witnesses (who, in many instances, are friends of both parties). The hearing officer's emphasis is to explore the negative and hostile feelings, attitudes, and experiences behind the specific incident, with the goal of arriving at a mutually acceptable resolution of the dispute. If the opponents are unable or unwilling to reach a compromise, the hearing officer may suggest alternatives. Disputants are sometimes nudged toward resolution when the mediator informs them of the possible legal sanctions that could be applied if they fail to resolve the dispute on their own.

Mediation affords direct, face-to-face communication and an opportunity to ventilate pent-up frustrations and anger—activities that formal court proceedings simply do not permit. There are no judgments of guilt or innocence; rather, an agreement is reached that, although it does not have the force of law behind it, is backed up by the pressure of friends, family members, and neighbors. Consider, for example, a case handled by the Milwaukee Mediation Center.

Dispute Resolution: Seeking Justice outside the Courtroom

J. J. McCarthy   Corrections Magazine

A cook had been fired from his job in a Milwaukee chain restaurant. A few days later, he met two of his former supervisors and their district manager in a local bar. The cook threatened to "blow them away," and proceeded to rough them up; he punched one of his ex-bosses in the face before stalking off into the night.

The three men filed a complaint with the district attorney's office. The cook could have been charged with battery, which carries a maximum penalty of nine months in jail and a $10,000 fine. The assistant district attorney, however, strongly suggested that the men take their case to the Milwaukee Mediation Center. This center, and scores of others like it around the country, tries to resolve disputes without expensive and time-consuming litigation. Proponents of this approach aim to reduce court backlogs and even jail populations, for while most of the cases submitted for mediation do not involve criminal matters, they are often the kind of problem that can fester for years. By producing a true solution to a dispute, rather than a mere determination of who is at fault, mediators hope to reduce the tensions that can lead to violence and criminal behavior.

In the Milwaukee incident, the mediator (a trained volunteer who asked to remain anonymous because of the confidentiality of the proceedings) remembered the session well. The restaurant employees were nervous before the meeting, he recalled. "They kept looking out the window," he said. "They even told me I should search the guy when he came."

When the cook showed up, the mediator continued, "his appearance did nothing to calm their fears. He was a big guy in his mid-thirties, with gold chains around his neck and a shirt unbuttoned down to his navel. He wore a huge 'Greek Afro' with a headband and a full black mustache."

The mediator opened the session with an explanation of the process: first the three complainants would tell their stories, without interruption, and then the cook would have his turn. After that, the mediator would try to find a common ground on which both sides could agree.

"The restauranteurs launched into their typed two-page account of the incident, listing the statutes they thought the cook violated," the mediator recalled. "Then the cook spoke. He said his father had died three weeks before and that he supported both his mother and two younger brothers. He hung his head and talked slowly, as he told how the Greeks were a proud people and how his mother had yelled at him when he lost his job, and made him feel not like a man but a little kid. He said he acted like a little kid in the bar. Finally, he said he was sorry, real sorry that the whole thing happened."

Then the mediator met privately with each side to find out what they wanted. One of the restaurant employees said that the ex-cook was dangerous and belonged in jail, but the mediator explained that this might not happen, even if they took the matter to court. Besides, the mediator says, "all of them had been affected by the cook's apology. But when I asked them, 'What do you want out of this?' they just gave me blank looks. They didn't know there was an alternative to sending him to jail. So I said that if the cook would agree to never harass them or even approach them again, would they need anything else from him? They couldn't think of anything."

When he met with the ex-cook, the mediator recalled, "He said he'd never been in this kind of situation and that he felt helpless—this big, macho guy felt helpless. He said he'd been drinking, and apologized again. He said he'd agree to just about anything to resolve this."

The man quickly agreed to the complainant's proposal. The mediator wrote an agreement that neither side would approach or harass the other, and all the parties signed it. The mediator said he stressed that the district attorney would not be happy if the matter returned to his office, and that the center would contact the men in the future to make sure that they stuck to their word. He did not mention that the agreement was unenforceable in court.

Reproduced from J. J. McCarthy, "Dispute Resolution: Seeking Justice Outside the Courtroom," *Corrections Magazine* 8 (1982): 33–34. Copyright 1982 by Corrections Magazine and Criminal Justice Publications, Inc., 19 W. 34th St., New York, N.Y. 10001.

Dispute-settlement programs have been praised by a diverse group, from former Chief Justice Warren Burger of the U.S. Supreme Court to consumer advocate Ralph Nader. Daniel McGillis, a criminal justice researcher who studies neighborhood justice centers, believes that such programs herald a major shift in American jurisprudence (McGillis and Mullen 1977). As an alternative to formal litigation, the neighborhood justice center boasts these following advantages:

1. Cases are handled much faster than in the courts. Hearings are conducted within ten days of referral, as compared with four to five months for court hearings.
2. The settlement process is handled by nonprofessional volunteers; thus, the system is far less expensive than formal legal proceedings.
3. Both parties are able to accept the settlement reached in the mediation process. The settlement is theirs: they participated fully in the decision-making process. As McCarthy points out,

> the most basic distinction between the courts and dispute resolution is that dispute resolution minimizes the differences between the disputants, while the court process exaggerates them. Both parties to a mediation must share responsibility for the dispute and give as well as take, and both sides can't "win." The court's adversary system locks the two sides into their set positions and guarantees a winner-take-all fight to the finish (1982, p. 36).

Neighborhood justice centers are not without their critics, however. For example, some people question the adequacy of training provided for volunteer mediators. It has even been suggested that mediators should be licensed and certified to ensure that they will be properly prepared for their responsibilities. Other questions are directed toward the confidentiality of the proceedings. For example, could the mediator and case

FIGURE 8.2
Two adversaries in a neighborhood dispute agree to settle their difficulties with the assistance of a mediator. Courtesy *Corrections Magazine.*

records be subpoenaed? Most concerns, however, focus on cost-effectiveness and the reduction of case loads in the criminal justice system. Supporters of neighborhood justice centers claim that it is much less expensive to process a dispute through mediation than by adjudication, but there are no data to confirm this contention.

Another hope of Hughes and Palmer was that mediation would significantly reduce the number of misdemeanors jailed before trial. There are no data to indicate that this has been the case, however. And a study conducted by the Brooklyn Dispute Resolution Center indicates that mediation does little to reduce future violence. In that study, selected felony cases were randomly assigned to mediation or court processing. Researchers reported little or no difference between mediated cases and court cases in the stability of agreements or the emergence of new problems between disputants (McCarthy 1982).

Despite such disappointing conclusions, however, enthusiasts of the mediation concept continue to be optimistic. They feel that time will vindicate their hopes and aspirations for dispute-settlement programs throughout the country. They remain confident that neighborhood justice centers will eventually meet their expected goals.

■ DISCUSSION AND REVIEW

1. Why is cross-examination an effective way to expose false or inaccurate testimony?
2. How does the prosecutor in the American criminal justice system differ from prosecutors in continental Europe and England?

3. What factors can affect the decision by a prosecutor to prosecute a case, reduce charges, or dismiss charges?
4. Explain the nature and the significance of the Cleveland Prosecutor Mediation Program.
5. Why is the prosecutor's office a good stepping stone in American politics?
6. What was the significance of the Supreme Court's *Gideon* v. *Wainwright* decision?
7. During which stages of the criminal justice process does a poor defendant have the right to a lawyer?
8. What are the major strengths and weaknesses of the public defender system?
9. What are the major strengths and weaknesses of the assigned counsel system?
10. What are the most frequently cited advantages of neighborhood justice centers?
11. What is the nature of the contracted counsel system? How does it differ from the public defender and assigned counsel systems?

GLOSSARY

Adversary system A system of criminal justice characterized by the testing of propositions by argument and proof.

Assigned control system System in which members of the local bar association are appointed to serve as counsel for indigent defendants for little or no compensation.

Bar association A statewide association that is responsible for licensing attorneys, developing and enforcing ethical standards, and examining and making final decisions about charges brought against attorneys.

Caseload The number of cases being defended or prosecuted by an attorney at a given time.

Contract system of defense representation Local governments contract with individual attorneys, bar associations, or private law firms to represent indigent criminal defendants in their jurisdiction.

Defendant A person charged with a crime.

Defense attorney Attorney retained or appointed to defend individuals charged with committing criminal offenses.

District attorney, state attorney Common titles for the position of prosecutor.

Diversion Instead of taking an accused's case to a full criminal trial, the state elects to give the accused (usually a first-time offender) the option to receive help from social or mediation programs.

Indigent A person who cannot afford legal counsel.

Legal aid Legal assistance paid for by the state and made available at little or no cost to defendants unable to afford an attorney.

Legal malpractice Civil action taken against an attorney, usually for some serious failure in the attorney-client relationship (e.g., dishonesty, incompetence, or other acts of misconduct).

Nolle prosequi A formal entry into the record by the prosecutor declaring the state no longer prosecute the case.

Plea bargaining The interaction of the prosecutor, defense counsel, and judge in negotiating a final charge and sentence without resorting to trial.

Power of discretion The legal power inherent in the position of the prosecutor to decide whether or not to initiate criminal action in a case.

Prosecutor An attorney (usually elected) in public office who presents the state's case against individuals charged with crimes against the state.

Prosecutor's dilemma A contradictory stance assumed by most American prosecutors because they are required to see that justice is done and at the same time try with all their skills to win their case.

Public defender system A publicly funded system with a staff of full-time attorneys available to defend indigent persons accused by the state of committing crimes.

■ REFERENCES

American Bar Association Project on Standards for Criminal Justice. *Standards Relating to the Administration of Criminal Justice*. Washington, D.C.: American Bar Association, 1974.

Cappelletti, M., and Gordley, J. "Legal Aid: Modern Themes and Variations." *Stanford Law Review* (24 January 1972): 347–421.

Felsteiner, W. L. F., and Drew, A. B. *European Alternatives to Criminal Trials: Their Applicability to the United States*. Washington, D.C.: National Institute of Law Enforcement and Criminal Justice, 1978.

Fuller, L. L. "The Adversary System." In Harold J. Berman, ed., *Talks on American Law,* pp. 30–43. New York: Vantage Books, 1960.

Gelber, W. "Who Defends the Prosecutor?" *Crime and Delinquency* 14 (1968): 315–23.

Houlden, P., and Balkin, S. "Quality and Cost Comparisons of Private Bar Indigent Defense Systems: Contract vs. Ordered Assigned Counsel." *Journal of Criminal Law and Criminology* 76 (1985): 176–200.

Kamisar, Y.; LaFave, W. R.; Israel, G. *Basic Criminal Procedure*. St. Paul, Minn.: West Publishing Co., 1986.

LaFave, W. L. "The Prosecutor's Discretion in the United States." *American Journal of Comparative Law* 18 (1970): 532–48.

"Lawyers v. Lawyers." *Time* 12 January 1976, 53–55.

Lewis, M., Bundy, W., and Hague, J. R. *An Introduction to the Courts and Judicial Process*. Englewood Cliffs, N.J.: Prentice-Hall, 1978.

McCarthy, J. J. "Dispute Resolution: Seeking Justice outside the Courtroom." *Corrections Magazine* 8 (1982): 33–40.

McGillis, D., and Mullen, J. *Neighborhood Justice Centers: An Analysis of Potential Models*. Washington, D.C.: U.S. Government Printing Office, 1977.

Miller, F. W. *Prosecution: The Decision to Charge a Suspect with a Crime*. Boston, Mass.: Little, Brown, 1969.

National Advisory Commission on Criminal Justice Standards and Goals. *Courts*. Washington, D.C.: U.S. Government Printing Office, 1973, p. 20.

National District Attorney's Association. *The Presenting Attorneys of the United States*. Chicago: NDAA, 1966, p. 194.
National Legal Aid and Defender Association. *Report to the National Defense Conference*. Washington, D.C.: National Defender Project, 1969.
National Commission on Law Observance and Enforcement. *Report on Prosecution*. Washington, D.C.: U.S. Government Printing Office, 1931.
Silverstein, L. *Defense of the Poor in Criminal Cases in American State Courts: A Field Study and Report*. Chicago: American Bar Foundation, 1965.
Swanson, C. R.; Chamelin, N. C.; and Territo, L. *Criminal Investigation*. 2d ed. New York: Random House, 1981.
Time. See "Lawyers v. Lawyers."
Wice, P. B. *Criminal Lawyers: An Endangered Species*. Beverly Hills, Calif.: Sage, 1978.
Wice, P. B., and Suwak, P. "Current Realities of Public Defender Programs: A National Survey and Analysis." *Criminal Law Bulletin*, 10 (1974): 161–83.
Willard, C. A. *Criminal Justice on Trial*. Skokie, Ill.: National Textbook Company, 1976.

CASES

Argersinger v. *Hamlin* 407 U.S. 25, 92 S.Ct. 2006, 32 L.Ed.2d 530 (1972).
Betts v. *Brady* 316 U.S. 455, 62 S.Ct. 1252, 86 L.Ed. 1595 (1942).
Brewer v. *Williams* 430 U.S. 387, 97 S.Ct. 1232, 51 L.Ed.2d 424 (1977).
Chambers v. *Maroney* 399 U.S. 42, 90 S.Ct. 1975, 26 L.Ed.2d 419 (1970).
Coleman v. *Alabama* 399 U.S. 1, 90 S.Ct. 1999, 26 L.Ed.2d 387 (1970).
Deoster, U.S. v. 487 F.2d 1197 (D.C.Cir. 1973).
Faretta v. *California* 422 U.s. 806, 95 S.Ct. 2525, 45 L.Ed.2d 562 (1975).
In re Gault 387 U.S. 1, 87 S.Ct. 1428, 18 L.Ed.2d 527 (1967).
Gideon v. *Wainwright* 372 U.S. 335, 83 S.Ct. 792, 9 L.Ed.2d 799 (1963).
Hamilton v. *Alabama* 368 U.S. 52, 82 S.Ct. 157, 7 L.Ed.2d 114 (1962).
Johnson v. *Zerbst* 304 U.S. 458, 58 S.Ct. 1019, 82 L.Ed. 1461 (1938).
Kirby v. *Illinois* 406 U.S. 682, 92 S.Ct. 1877, 32 L.Ed.2d 411 (1972).
Mempa v. *Rhay* 389 U.S. 128, 88 S.Ct. 254, 19 L.Ed.2d 336 (1967).
Moore v. *Illinois* 434 U.S. 220, 98 S.Ct. 458, 54 L.Ed.2d 424 (1977).
Moore v. *Michigan* 355 U.S. 155, 78 S.Ct. 191 (1957).
Miranda v. *Arizona* 384 U.S. 436, 86 S.Ct. 1602, 16 L.Ed.2d 694 (1966).
Powell v. *Alabama* 287 U.S. 45, 53 S.Ct. 55, 77 L.Ed. 158 (1932).
Ross v. *Moffitt* 417 U.S. 600, 94 S.Ct. 2437, 41 L.Ed.2d 341 (1974).
Scott v. *Illinois* 440 U.S. 367 99 S.Ct. 1158, 59 L.Ed.2d 383 (1979).
Townsend v. *Burke* 334 U.S. 736, 68 S.Ct. 1252 (1948).
Wade, U.S. v., 388 U.S. 218, 87 S.Ct. 1926, 18 L.Ed.2d 1149 (1967).

NOTES

1. Readers interested in the topics of lawyer training, bar associations, admission to the bar, and so on may wish to review J. J. Bonsignore et al., *Before the Law*, chap. 3 (Boston, Mass.: Houghton Mifflin, 1977), pp. 173–218, and Herbert Jacob,

Justice in America: Courts, Lawyers, and the Judicial Process, chap. 4 (Boston, Mass.: Little, Brown, 1978), pp. 45–78.

2. This discussion of prosecutors and the adversary system was adapted, with permission, from the American Bar Association Project on Standards for Criminal Justice, *Standards Relating to the Administration of Criminal Justice* (Washington, D.C.: American Bar Association, 1974), p. 56. Additional information may also be found in *American Bar Association Standards for Criminal Justice,* 2d ed. (Boston: Little, Brown, 1980).

3. For a more comprehensive treatment of the adversary system and its historical development, see Blair J. Kolasa and Bernadine Meyer, *Legal Systems,* chap. 10 (Englewood Cliffs, N.J.: Prentice-Hall, 1978), pp. 266–301; Gilbert Stuckey, *Procedures in the Justice System,* chap. 2 (Columbus, Ohio: Charles E. Merrill, 1980), pp. 14–33; and Walter F. Murphy and C. Herman Pritchett, *Courts, Judges and Politics,* chap. 1 (New York: Random House, 1974), pp. 355–79.

4. An interesting treatment of the role of the prosecutor may be found in Edward Eldefonso and Alan R. Coffey, *Criminal Law,* app. B (New York: Harper and Row, 1981), pp. 284–89, and Sheldon Goldman and Austin Sarat, eds. *American Court Systems,* chap. 3 (San Francisco: W. H. Freeman, 1978), pp. 92–121.

5. This discussion of prosecutor discretion was adapted, with permission, from the work and references in M. Lewis, W. Bundy, and J. R. Hague, *An Introduction to the Courts and Judicial Process* (Englewood Cliffs, N.J.: Prentice-Hall, 1978), pp. 246–49.

6. This discussion of defense and the accompanying references were adapted, with permission, from the work of C. A. Willard, *Criminal Justice on Trial* (Skokie, Ill.: National Textbook Company, 1976), pp. 111–21.

7. For an in-depth examination of the public defender system, see Jonathan D. Casper, *American Criminal Justice: The Defendants Perspective,* chap. 4 (Englewood Cliffs, N.J.: Prentice-Hall, 1972), pp. 100–125; Abraham S. Blumberg, ed., *Law and Order: The Scales of Justice* (New Brunswick, N.J.: Transaction Books, 1973), pp. 159–72; and Robert Herman, Eric Single, and John Boston, *Counsel for the Poor* (Lexington, Mass.: Lexington Books, 1977).

CHAPTER

9

Pretrial Procedures

CHAPTER OUTLINE:

However important the criminal trial by jury may be to the novelist or dramatist, it occupies a relatively minor position in the administration of justice in the United States.[1] In any given year, less than 10 percent of suspects apprehended for serious crimes go through the formal steps of a criminal trial. Thus, much of the criminal process is administrative rather than judicial. That is, the process flow is accomplished through negotiation rather than adversarial proceedings.

The fact that this administrative model is inconsistent with the traditional model of litigated criminal prosecution should not be viewed with alarm. Given the enormous number of cases that must be processed, particularly in metropolitan areas, the resources of the criminal justice system would be strained beyond the breaking point if most cases were not dropped or carried to a negotiated conclusion. The administration of justice would not merely be slowed, it would come to a complete halt. In addition, the facts in many criminal cases are not disputed. The suspect either clearly did or clearly did not commit the offense with which he or she is charged. If the facts are beyond dispute, there is no need for a time-consuming, expensive, and laborious criminal trial.

Most of the important decisions that affect the disposition of a case and the fate of the accused are made during the pretrial period between arrest and trial or plea. By posting bond or by **release on his or her own recognizance (ROR)**, (i.e., a promise to appear at a later date to stand trial), the defendant may be released from custody pending trial. A defendant who is unable to post bail may face the prospect of remaining in detention until the case is tried—a period of weeks or months. The attorney for the defendant may negotiate with the prosecutor during this period to secure a reduced charge or other advantages for the client. Such negotiations—including the practice of plea bargaining—are the topic of fierce debate and continuing controversy within the criminal justice system.

INITIATING PROSECUTION IN MISDEMEANOR OFFENSES

The process of bringing a criminal offense to justice is put into motion by an arrest. **Arrest** refers to the apprehension or detention of an individual so that he or she is available to answer for an alleged crime. An arrest on a criminal charge can be made upon the issuance of a **warrant**, but a warrant is not absolutely necessary. In fact, most arrests are made without them. A valid warrant may be executed by any law enforcement agent to whom the warrant is directed.

A **misdemeanor**, as we noted in Chapter 2, is a less serious offense that may be punished by a fine or incarceration in a city or county jail for a period of less than one year. Prosecution for a misdemeanor is usually initiated by the issuance of a **complaint.** The complaint is usually made by a victim of, or a witness to, the crime.

Often, the arresting officer is the complaining witness. The purpose of filing a complaint is to make a determination of whether an arrest warrant should be issued. All of the existing evidence and in a few cases the testimony of the complainant is presented by the officer to prove that probable cause exists. Probable cause means that it is reasonable to believe that a crime was committed and that the defendant committed it. If the magistrate determines that probable cause exists, he or she then will issue an arrest warrant. After a suspect is arrested, he or she is brought to the police station, detained, and interrogated. Following interrogation, he or she may be released (for lack of evidence of wrongdoing) or *booked* (pressed with formal charges). Following booking, a suspect may be released on his or her own recognizance with a signed promise to appear in court, released on presentation of bail, or locked up to await trial. The choice is made based on the suspect's reputation and the seriousness of the offense.

The Complaint

As mentioned, the issuance of a complaint is the basis for proceeding with the prosecution of misdemeanors following arrest. The word *complaint* is somewhat misleading, because it suggests an action taken by the injured party or victim of a crime. Although the victim of the crime may be the complainant, the plaintiff is actually the *people of the state* acting through their lawful representative, the district attorney. It is the public prosecutor, therefore, who issues the complaint in a criminal proceeding. The complaint is a written document, which identifies the criminal charge, the place and date of the crime's occurrence, and the circumstances surrounding the arrest. The complaint is sworn to and signed under oath by the complainant, usually a police officer although sometimes a citizen does this. The formal complaint (1) alleges the commission of an offense and the aim of the defendant; (2) identifies the time, place, and jurisdiction of the court involved; and (3) is sworn to and signed by the complainant.

A complaint is essentially a justification for the arrest of a defendant so that he or she can be **arraigned**—that is, allowed to enter a plea. There are four questions a prosecutor must ask to determine if a complaint should be prepared:

1. Has a crime (public offense) been committed?
2. Did a particular individual whose identity is known commit the crime?

3. Is there sufficient legally admissible evidence to ensure a conviction?
4. Are there no adequate alternatives to prosecution available that are preferable to the formal processing of the offender through the criminal justice system?

Unless the answer to all of these questions is yes, a complaint should not be prepared.

The Magistrate

In theory, a suspect should be brought before a magistrate or justice of the peace within a "short time" after the arrest. How short is a "short time"? The President's Commission on Law Enforcement and Administration of Justice (1967) reported that, in 1965 in the District of Columbia, 20 percent of the defendants were detained for more than one day between arrest and the initial appearance in court. A study conducted in 1969 by the American Civil Liberties Union (ACLU) indicates that people at that time were still being illegally detained for excessive periods of time without either formal booking or appearance before an inferior court. Even today, it is difficult to claim with assurance that such practices do not occur. Recognizing that there are sometimes plausible reasons for delays—if the arrest occurs on a weekend or holiday, for example—the President's Commission recommended a *maximum* delay of twenty-four hours between arrest and initial appearance. Extensive delays can be grounds for later actions against the state by defendants.

A magistrate has *summary* jurisdiction; that is, he or she is empowered to determine guilt or innocence and can impose minor sentences for petty offenses. In many states, the accused can request a jury trial. For more serious crimes, the magistrate holds a preliminary hearing to determine if sufficient evidence has been presented to justify holding the suspect for further action. Overall, the setting within which misdemeanor justice is administered is not likely to inspire much respect for law or confidence in the impartiality of justice. As Bloch and Geis remark:

> Misdemeanor justice in its usual form is meted out by magistrates or justices of the peace who as often as not appear to have secured their positions because of their political coloration and activity rather than because of their legal acumen, human compassion, or social insight. Misdemeanor justice usually takes place in rather sordid surroundings and involves in many instances defendants who through considerable exposure to its operation have become familiar as the bailiff with its routine. Guilty pleas are the rule (1962, p. 464).

INITIATING PROSECUTION IN FELONY OFFENSES

Felony offenses are serious crimes that are punishable by incarceration for a year or more in a state prison or by death in the case of capital offenses (see Chapter 2). Some felony offenses are settled by dismissal or by the entrance of a guilty plea at an early stage in the criminal justice process. The initial presentment of the accused to a judge is called the **first appearance.** This is not a fact-finding or probable cause hearing. The sufficiency of the arrest warrant is examined at this stage. At this time the magistrate will note for the record whether the accused is represented by counsel. If the accused suggests that he or she is too poor to afford counsel, the magistrate will make inquiry into the defendant's financial status. Often this is referred to as an indigency hearing. If a finding of indigency is made, the magistrate will require that the accused sign an affidavit swearing to financial impoverishment. This allows the court to appoint a public defender to represent the accused (see Figure 9.1 for a flow chart of the process).

Since a felony is a more serious crime than a misdemeanor, intermediate steps must be taken before the accused can be tried in a felony court. Two different types of objective bodies within the criminal justice system exist to ensure that evidence is sufficient to prove that a crime has taken place and that the accused should be tried on the matter. This proof needs only to be established by the probable cause standard. The two bodies that make these probable cause determinations are the preliminary hearing and the grand jury.

Preliminary Hearing

Following arrest and first appearance, a suspect accused of a felony offense is brought before a lower court for a **preliminary hearing,** which a majority of the states employ rather than the grand jury. A preliminary hearing is conducted before a magistrate and is open to the public. The defendant is present at the preliminary hearing as are attorneys for the defense and prosecution. At this stage only the prosecution needs to present evidence to the judge. The defendant has the right to present evidence at the hearing but seldom does so. This procedure affords the defendant an excellent opportunity to discover the substance of the prosecutor's case, information that he or she can use later as part of the defense strategy in felony court. An interesting aspect of a preliminary hearing is that the defendant has the right to waive the hearing if the prosecutor and the judge agree to the waiver. Usually, the only time defendants waive the preliminary hearing is when they have decided to plead guilty or fear the adverse publicity that the preliminary hearing might bring upon themselves and their families.

At the preliminary hearing, the state is constrained to show "probable cause" for binding the accused over for trial. The expression "probable cause" has the flavor of legal doubletalk, because it is highly *improbable* that a prosecutor would initiate judicial proceedings without a reasonably strong case. Nevertheless, the legal view persists that the preliminary hearing is of benefit to the accused.

On occasion a prosecutor may ask for a ***nolle prosequi,*** which signifies that there will be no further action by the prosecution. A "null pross," as it is known informally, is usually regarded as an acknowledgment that the prosecutor's case has collapsed (perhaps a crucial piece of evidence was lost or stolen, or a key witness died or disappeared before making a deposition).[2] For whatever reason, the prosecutor decides not to pursue the prosecution.

During the final stages of the preliminary hearing, the court also reviews the bail that may have been set at the first appearance. At this time, depending on the authority vested in him or her, the preliminary hearing judge may exercise the option to raise or lower the amount of bail.

After evidence is presented by the prosecution, a judge decides whether there is probable cause to believe that the accused person committed the alleged crime. If the answer is yes, the defendant is bound over for trial; if the answer is no, charges are dismissed and the defendant is released from custody. If the former is the case, the prosecutor files an **information** with the court where the trial will be held. The time period allowed for filing varies from jurisdiction to jurisdiction, but fifteen days from the preliminary hearing is a typical period.

As mentioned earlier, the right of the prosecutor not to prosecute further, even in the face of evidence that seems sufficient to win the case, demonstrates one of the most significant examples of discretionary authority in the criminal justice system. There are many reasons prosecutors "null pross" a case, but the most significant aspect of the decision is that it is seldom reviewed critically by higher authority.

Arraignment

Normally, the arraignment takes place after an indictment or information is filed following a grand jury session or a preliminary hearing. At the arraignment the judge informs the defendant of the charges against him or her. The judge also appoints counsel if counsel has not yet been retained by the defendant. The accused has a constitutional right at this stage of the process to be

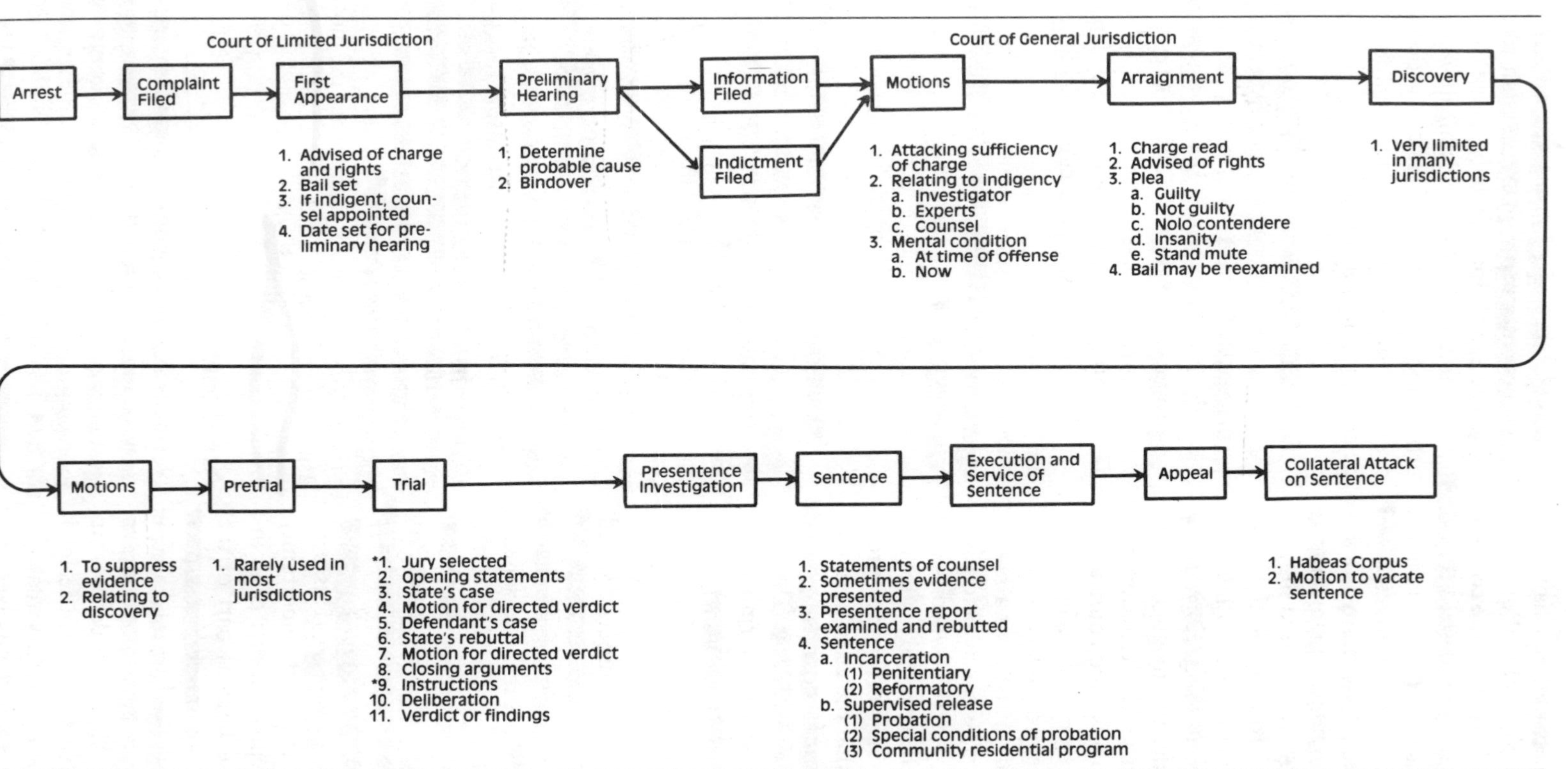

*In jury cases.

FIGURE 9.1
Typical progression of criminal felony litigation.

From THE COURTS; FULCRUM OF THE JUSTICE SYSTEM by H. Ted Rubin. Copyright © 1976 by Newbery Award Records, Inc. Reprinted by persmission of Random House, Inc.

informed of the nature and the cause of the accusations against him or her. The judge accomplishes this by reading the complaint, the information, or the indictment to the accused. The judge must ensure the accused understands the charges. After the charges are read and explained, the defendant is asked to enter a plea. If the plea is not guilty, a trial date is set. If the defendant enters a guilty plea, a date for sentencing is set.

If the defendant pleads not guilty, this places the burden on the state to move forward with the case. After a plea of not guilty, the state is required to prove beyond a reasonable doubt all the charges against the defendant. One of the principles underlining American jurisprudence is that the defendant is morally and legally entitled to make a plea of not guilty. Should the defendant state nothing (stand mute) when asked to give a plea, the court will enter a plea of not guilty for him or her.

In some states, other options in addition to guilty or not guilty may be available: not guilty by reason of insanity, former jeopardy, and ***nolo contendere,*** for example. The plea of *nolo contendere,* in a criminal proceeding is generally regarded as a guilty plea, although in some states it means simply that the defendant does not understand the charges. The chief advantage of a *nolo contendere* plea is that it may spare the defendant from certain civil penalties that might follow a guilty plea. Thus, a *nolo contendere* plea is likely to be entered in situations in which, in addition to criminal sanctions, the defendant is liable to prosecution for civil damages (e.g., cases involving embezzlement or fraud). The *nolo contendere* plea can only be entered at the discretion of the prosecutor and the judge. Another option available to the defendant is "standing mute." However, in many jurisdictions, the court will automatically enter a plea of not guilty if the accused fails to enter a plea.

Before a plea of guilty will be accepted by the court, certain conditions must be met. The plea must be entered voluntarily, and the defendant must be aware of the implications of the plea. *A guilty plea is considered equivalent to a verdict of guilty.* The court may deliver a sentence at the time of the plea or set a date for sentencing.

If the accused enters a plea of guilty during the arraignment, he or she surrenders numerous constitutional rights. These constitutional consequences of a guilty plea have been best articulated by the National Advisory Commission on Criminal Justice Standards and Goals.

> Such a plea functions not only as an admission of guilt but also a surrender of the entire array of constitutional rights designed to protect a criminal defendant against unjustified conviction, including the right to remain silent, the right to confront witnesses against him, the right of trial by jury, the right to be proven guilty by proof beyond reasonable doubt (1973, p. 12).

The U.S. Supreme Court has ruled that "when a guilty plea rests in any significance on the promise or an agreement of the prosecutor, so it can be said to be part of the inducement or consideration, such promise must be fulfilled" (*Santobello* v. *New York* [404 U.S. 257 (1971)]). Hence when a guilty plea is given to a judge, he or she is mandated to ask a certain series of questions to ensure that the method by which the plea bargain was reached adheres to the principles dictated by the Court. Around the courthouse, this series of questions is referred to as the "copping out ceremony."

THE GRAND JURY

The function of the **grand jury** is to investigate criminal charges to determine, or adjudicate, whether a defendant should be brought to trial. When performing this function, the grand jury is supposed to act as the community's conscience in determining whether an unjust accusation has been brought against an accused. The general public is unaware that an equally important function of grand juries in addition to adjudicating probable cause is to investigate. Investigative grand juries are usually impaneled to investigate organized crime or political corruption. As indicated in the "Issue Paper" of this chapter, the combination of investigative and adjudicative grand juries substantially deprives an accused of rights he or she normally would enjoy during a preliminary hearing.

The grand jury system developed early in English common law. It is eight centuries old. The concept of a grand jury was brought to the United States by its earliest settlers and later incorporated into the Fifth Amendment of the United States Constitution, which states that "no person shall be held to answer for a capital or otherwise infamous charge unless on a presentment or indictment of a grand jury." According to Bloch and Geis, "grand juries were intended to allow the defendant to avoid a public accusation and the trouble and expense of a public trial before establishing the likelihood of his having committed the crime. They were also intended to prevent hasty, oppressive, and malicious prosecutions" (1962, p. 481).

The grand jury does not seek to determine guilt or innocence; rather it duplicates in many respects the function of the preliminary hearing. The only major difference is that the defendant has no legal right to be present at grand jury deliberations. Thus, the decision to indict or not to indict is made solely on the evidence presented by the prosecuting attorney.

If a grand jury is convinced by the prosecutor's evidence that a *prima facie* case has been made (i.e., that so far as can be judged on its face value, the evidence will prevail as proof of the facts in issue unless or until it is contradicted or overcome by other evidence) a "true bill" of indictment will be returned, indicating probable cause to proceed to trial. If, on the other hand, the grand jury is not persuaded by the prosecutor's evidence, it can ignore the charges by returning a "no bill" finding, in which case the prosecutor may charge the defendant with a lesser offense. In the majority of indictments, the grand jury follows the inclination of the prosecutor. Most states require a preliminary examination prior to charging in felony offenses. Grand jury indictments are a statutory requirement in about half the states.

PRETRIAL MOTIONS

It is fairly standard for defense attorneys to move for the dismissal of charges against their clients even before a plea is entered. The general strategy is to attack the information or indictment, claiming improprieties in the organization or methods of the grand jury. Other possible grounds for a motion to dismiss are prior jeopardy and the statute of limitations (the latter is used if the law under which the accused has been charged is no longer valid).

A more effective pretrial motion is one requesting the state to reveal information or evidence that the prosecution has gathered against the defendant. This is called a motion for a *bill of particulars*. If the motion for a bill of particulars is upheld by the court, the prosecutor will be ordered to clarify the charges by adding the necessary facts to the original indictment or by adding information in the form of an amendment. This will better allow the defendant to understand the nature of the charges against him or her.

Typical pretrial motions by the defense are a motion to exclude evidence such as a confession, a seizure, or evidence discovered after an illegal arrest; a motion to dismiss because of the state's delay in bringing the case to trial; a motion for pretrial discovery for evidence held by the prosecutor; a motion to change venue because a fair and impartial trial cannot be held in the jurisdiction where the court currently sits; a general motion to suppress illegally obtained evidence; a motion to quash a search warrant; and a motion for severance, which asks for separate trials in cases that have more than one defendant.

If, because of adverse pretrial publicity, the accused and the defense attorney believe it is impossible to receive a fair trial in the area where the crime was committed, the defense attorney may move for a *change of venue*. Despite the attention paid to such motions in media coverage of criminal trials—sensational ones—this motion is made rather infrequently. Equally infrequent are motions seeking a separate trial in cases with codefendants.

Normally, the trial judge has a wide discretion in determining whether to grant a motion to change venue based on pretrial publicity. If the judge decides not to do so, the decision will be reversed only in a rare instance.

Making pretrial motions is advantageous in many ways for the accused. Such motions force the prosecutor to disclose evidence that may lead him or her to consider an early plea bargain. They also force the prosecutor to make certain decisions before the final preparation of his or her case, and they also act as a discovery tool that allows the defense attorney to learn which witnesses are going to testify for the state. Finally, pretrial motions allow the defendant to see his or her attorney in action. This gives the defendant an opportunity to gain more confidence in the lawyer.

A major innovation in the criminal justice system is the advent of the omnibus pretrial hearing. This is a single hearing with a minimum of formalities, held to ensure that discovery has been properly conducted and that the issues are simply and effectively raised. The idea behind this process is to complete all pretrial matters as efficiently and comprehensively as possible in one single hearing before trial. This allows both sides to narrow and sharpen the issues, saves on time and costs and reduces the likelihood of an appeal.

BAIL OR JAIL?

Once it has been determined that there is probable cause to bind a defendant over to the grand jury, it is the function of the lower-court magistrate to set bail. Bail is a legal procedure for securing temporary liberty following arrest through a written promise to appear in court as required. In support of this promise, it may be necessary to provide cash bail, post a surety bond, or supply evidence of equity in real property, together with the written assurance of another person or persons.

Defendants are not quite like other persons in that there is probable cause to believe that they have committed an offense. This may justify some special level of state supervision. Accused defendants have not been convicted and therefore cannot justly be punished. In addition, defendants know that the state intends to prosecute them, and if the case against them is strong enough, they might have reason to flee rather than stand trial.

The basic purpose of bail is to furnish a means for the release of a detained individual while his or her case is pending, provided the accused is ready to give reasonable and sufficient assurance of a willingness to appear in court at the appropriate time. In providing for release on bail, the presumption of innocence goes beyond its well-known place in trial proceedings (i.e., the necessity for proof of guilt beyond a reasonable doubt), emphasizing that, in American criminal jurisprudence, guilt is the decision of the court and is not inherent in prosecution.

Thus bail is a guarantee in return for being released from jail. The accused guarantees his or her future appearance by posting funds or some other form of security with the court. When the defendant's appearance in court is completed, the security is returned. If the defendant fails to appear, the security is forfeited (National District Attorney Association 1977). On the federal level, the release on bail and bond in noncapital cases was considered a constitutional right. However, a 1987 U.S. Supreme Court case declared that this right no longer exists if the government demonstrates by clear and convincing evidence that the defendant in a noncapital crime is considered to be a danger to the community (*United States* v. *Salerno* [____ U.S. ____(1987)]).

Our system emphasizes deliberation and due process to ensure that an accused person is treated fairly and to prevent passions from overwhelming a careful consideration of the facts in an individual case. One aspect of this orientation is the establishment of a reasonable interval between the moment of arrest and the moment of trial. This interval should be neither too long (lest the accused person suffer uncertainty too long) nor too short (lest the development of the relevant facts and careful deliberation be compromised). However valid this interval seems, its existence creates a pool of people who are in an awkward legal status.

Types of Bail

To post bail, an accused is required to give the court some form of monetary surety, most often cash, property, or a bond from a bonding company. However, certain defendants who are highly placed or respected in the community and others considered "good risks" are released on their own recognizance. These forms of bail have been around since colonial times. The so-called schedule of bail contains a list of misdemeanors and the amount of bail required for release. It may also specify a standard amount of bail for release or for all misdemeanor offenses not listed in the schedule.

The bail schedule eliminates disparity in the setting of bail by bail decision makers. It provides judges with a tool that uniformly designs bail criteria while at the same time allowing sufficient flexibility to deal with individual situations. Such schedules define the intensity of an accused's bail risk. The Bureau of Justice Statistics of the federal government has recently released a summary of bail practices among the federal courts. Its findings include:

- The amount of bail is particularly determined by three things: (1) the seriousness of the charged offense; (2) the particular court in which bail is imposed; and (3) the offender's criminal record.
- The bail that was required was somewhat lower for defendants who had lived at the same address for several years as compared to more transient arrestees; somewhat lower for women than for men; and lower for defendants with college and high school educations than for defendants with no high school education.
- Holding other factors constant, there was no relationship between the amount of bail imposed and such factors as race, age, drug use, income, employment history, number of dependents supported by the defendant, and past history of jumping bail.
- As one would expect, the probability of posting bail decreases as the amount of bail increases.
- Certain factors were found to correlate with pretrial misconduct (i.e., arrest for a new crime while out on bail, willful failure to appear for a court date, and violations of the technical conditions of release). These were (1) the longer the person was out on bail before the trial, the greater was the likelihood of some kind of pretrial misconduct; (2) the more extensive the prior criminal record, the greater was the likelihood of misconduct; (3) drug use increased the likelihood of misconduct rates; and (4) the probability of misconduct was higher for males, noncaucasians, and young defendants.

Conditions of Bail

During the post-arrest period of detention, the amount of bail depends upon the severity of the offense, whether the arrest was made with or without a warrant, and whether the defendant has been arraigned. When an arrest is made on a warrant alleging a public offense, bail should be in the amount specified on the warrant's endorsement by the issuing magistrate. When the arrest is for a misdemeanor, the amount of bail should be fixed by the magistrate at the time of arraignment. Prior to arraignment, bail should be set as fixed in the arrest warrant. If arrest is made without a warrant, the amount of bail should coincide with the nationwide schedule of bail for misdemeanors.

Another feature of the bail system, which stands on the periphery of the criminal justice system, is the bail bondsman. He or she is a central figure in the bail system and is normally available twenty-four hours a day. If the defendant delivers a percentage (usually 10 percent) of the amount of the bail to the bondsman, he will secure the remaining obligation. Bondsmen are often viewed as the Achilles' heel in the bail system because even though they are private individuals and hence are not bound by law to the courts and the judicial process, they have the power to overrule a judge's decision concerning the release of the defendant. Bondsmen have an unsavory reputation and are often ex-convicts themselves. Often bondsmen travel intrastate and use criminal methods such as kidnapping and false imprisonment to bring one of their customers to justice. Studies have demonstrated that some bondsmen corrupt the system by offering kickbacks to judges in exchange for a judge's hesitancy to collect on outstanding sureties. Judge J. Skelly Wright stated that:

> Bondsmen hold the key to the jail in their pockets. They determine for whom they will act as surety—who in their judgment is a good risk. The bad risks, in the bondsman's judgment, and the ones who are unable to pay the bondsman's fees, remain in jail. The court and the commissioner are regulated to the relatively unimportant chore of fixing the amount of bail (Burger 1970, p. 6).

For a felony arrest, bail should be fixed by the judge before whom the prisoner is arraigned upon the formal complaint; prior to the arraignment, bail should be set as stated on the arrest warrant. If, without sufficient excuse, a defendant fails to appear as required in the bail agreement, or upon any other occasion when his or her presence in court is required by law, the court will enter the fact in its minutes and will declare forfeited the undertaking of bail or the cash bail deposited. If the amount of the bail or deposit exceeds fifty dollars, the bondsman or depositor must be notified.

Forfeiture of Bail

After a forfeiture of bail, the bondsman or depositor has 180 days in which to adjust the forfeiture. One of three procedures can be followed: (1) the defendant and the bondsman or depositor appear in court and provide an acceptable explanation or justification for the defendant's neglect, or satisfactorily indicate to the court that the absence was not with the connivance of the bondsman or depositor; (2) the bondsman may appear in court and certify that the defendant is dead or physically unable to appear during the time period allowed; and (3) the defendant may be turned over to the court.

Defects in the Bail System

When an accused person lacks financial resources, the bail system adds a discriminatory element to the administration of criminal justice. In his 1964 review of major findings about the bail systems of New York and Philadelphia, Johnson noted that many defendants were unable to furnish bail, especially when bail was set above $1,000. Bail usually was set so high for serious offenses that few defendants in the cases obtained pretrial release. And from 10 to 20 percent of defendants incarcerated pending trial were not convicted. For similar crimes, Johnson noted that jailed offenders were more likely to be convicted and to receive longer sentences than offenders released on bail. Another study by Eric W. Single (1984) found similar results. Why? The indigent defendant is unable to hire a lawyer, locate witnesses, and pay for the investigation necessary to present his or her case adequately, especially when incarceration pending trial interrupts normal earnings. Even when convicted, the bailed defendant has the advantage of showing evidence of steady employment and good conduct while awaiting trial. Such evidence supports a plea for probation.

Another defect in the bail system is that it encourages criminality: bondsmen are willing to set bail for thieves, even if they lack the cash or collateral to pay it back. This puts a thief in the position of having to acquire a large sum of money in a very short time after having been arrested. Thus, bond money is not always come by honestly. For short-term bail bonds, a bondsman is usually permitted to charge an interest rate of 10 to 20 percent, depending on state regulations. Thus, if a person is arrested and bond is set at $25,000, he or she must pay the bondsman between $2,500 and $5,000 for the "loan" (surety) of $25,000. This money may also be raised by illegal means.

And there is yet another way that the bail system encourages crime. Persons arrested, even professional thieves, do not always know where and from whom to get bond. Because jailers, sheriffs, and police officers are in a position to recommend bondsmen, the stage is set for an escalating system of gifts and payoffs for the recommendation of one bondsman over another (Chambliss 1969). However, many progressive law enforcement agencies prohibit this dubious practice.

THE BOUNTY HUNTERS AND THE BAIL JUMPER

Most Americans think that the bounty hunter is a relic of the frontier. However, there is a modern counterpart to this figure from Wild West movies: the bail bondsman in hot pursuit of the bail jumper. On 7 February 1983, CBS's "Sixty Minutes" related the tale of two present-day bounty hunters whose exploits in retrieving a fugitive from Canada caused an international incident.

The story began in Palatka, Florida, where a real estate entrepreneur named Sidney Jaffe was arrested for illegal land dealings. Prosecutors charged him in April 1981 with twenty-eight violations of Florida law for giving quitclaim deeds rather than warranty deeds to people who bought lots in a development in Putnam County near Palatka. The quitclaim deeds were no protection against mortgages that still encumbered the land, as outraged buyers soon discovered. Jaffe's lawyers claimed that the case should have been treated as a civil dispute rather than a crime, especially because Jaffe did not own the real estate company at the outset of the transactions.

Jaffe posted a $137,500 bond and returned to Canada, where he had lived since 1966. (He was granted citizenship not too long after the Florida charges were filed.) He failed to show up for trial in May 1981, sending a physician's statement that he was unable to travel. Circuit Court Judge Robert Perry refused a continuance and declared the bond forfeited. Prosecutors then asked Governor Bob Graham to seek Jaffe's extradition, but the governor's office turned them down twice on the advice of the Florida Attorney General, who stated that the applications for extradition had not been filled out properly.

At this point, according to sworn testimony from a Palatka lawyer named Miller (who was representing the bail firm), two assistant state attorneys encouraged the bondsmen to take the law into their own hands. "Why don't y'all go get him?" was what the prosecutors were supposed to have said. At any rate, the bail firm sent two experienced bounty hunters named Tim Johnsen and Daniel Kerr to Canada to bring Jaffe back.

In Toronto, the bounty hunters grabbed Jaffe at the entrance to his apartment and hustled him into the back seat of a rented Datsun from which the inside door handles had been removed. They then whizzed across the U.S.-Canadian border to a waiting airplane and took off for Orlando, Florida. Jaffe was tried and convicted in February 1982 and was given sentences totaling 145 years, 35 of them to be served consecutively. This is a harsher sentence than is received by many armed robbers. Jaffe's lawyers subsequently argued in federal court, without success, that the state had no right to try Jaffe because of the way he was returned to Florida. According to a traditional tenet of American law, it does not really matter *how* a defendant is dragged into court.

Nevertheless, the issue of Jaffe's guilt or innocence quickly took second place to the fact that he was seized and brought back to the United States in flagrant violation of Canadian law. The Canadian government in Ottawa reacted with understandable indignation and demanded the extradition of the bounty hunters, Johnsen and Kerr, for trial in Canada as kidnappers. U.S. Secretary of State George Schultz asked Florida to release Jaffe from prison, claiming that his incarceration was deleterious to U.S.-Canadian relations. Today, as Florida continues to be the target of bad publicity in the Canadian press, Jaffe languishes in Avon Park Correctional Institution in Avon Park, Florida. And state and federal officials continue to disclaim responsibility for rectifying Jaffe's abduction. In this bizarre affair, Florida justice has managed to make Jaffe look like a martyr.

Apart from the complex tangle of legal issues involved in extradition, the Jaffe case provides a graphic demonstration of the almost complete immunity enjoyed by the bail bondsman in the retrieval of fugitives who flee to avoid prosecution. Incredible though it may sound, the bondsman wields extraordinary powers to arrest a fugitive defendant (bail jumper) and to surrender the defendant to the custody of a law enforcement officer. This power is not based on any authority given to the bondsman by the state in the form of police powers; instead, it derives from the private contract between the accused and the bondsman (in the form of surety on the bail bond). Compared with the severe constraints under which sworn police officers must operate in the retrieval of fugitives, the bondsman's power to arrest, imprison, and transport an accused person across state lines is practically unlimited.

Murphy refers to the arrest and custody power of bondsmen as "a degenerate vestige of a bail relationship between defendant and surety that either perished or never gained footing in this country" (1975, p. 40). Nevertheless, the courts have consistently upheld this power in cases where fugitives have been taken at gunpoint, handcuffed or shackled to the floor of an automobile, beaten severely, and driven long distances without food or water in order to secure the remission of a $100 or $200 misdemeanor bond.

Bondsmen have contended that they perform a valuable service to the state by functioning as custodians of released defendants and hunters of fugitive defendants at no cost to the public. This contention, Murphy claims, is myth. The interest of the bondsman in retrieving fugitives is financial, not judicial. If that interest can be served by some means other than tracking down and returning the fugitive, the bondsman is unlikely to have any strong inclination to see that the defendant appears for trial.

Whenever bail bondsmen are prosecuted for such abuses as fee splitting, bribery, and "fixing" of minor criminal cases, a fine or some other punitive action soothes the public and presumably restores the theoretical purity of the bail system. However, reformers such as Thomas (1976) maintain that it is not abuses in the bail system that constitute the problem: it is the system itself. In Murphy's (1975) view, any reform that leaves the bondsman with undiminished powers of arrest and custody is an exercise in futility. He argues that the answer lies in adjusting the official retrieval system to increase efficiency without causing a corresponding loss of civil liberties—a move that could encourage the final replacement of bondsmen with police officers, a socially acceptable goal.

Bail Reform

In 1961, a wealthy New York businessman named Louis Schweitzer visited the Brooklyn House of Detention, one of the city's largest jails. Appalled by the number of people who were incarcerated pending trial because they were too poor to afford bail, Schweitzer created the Vera Foundation (named in honor of his wife). Using his own money, he set out to provide assistance for defendants who were unable to post bail. Within six months, the Vera Foundation—later renamed the Vera Institute of Justice—launched the Manhattan Bail Project. According to Thomas, "the idea behind the project proved as powerful in practice as it was simple in concept. The project was to provide information to the court about the defendant's ties to community and thereby hope that the court would release the defendant without requiring a bail bond" (1976, p. 4).

Schweitzer's project was administered in cooperation with the Institute of Judicial Administration and student assistants from New York University Law School. Originally, the plan had been to provide a revolving bail fund for indigent defendants; but this plan was soon rejected on the grounds that it merely perpetuated reliance upon money as the criterion for pretrial release. In its place, the Vera Institute sought to expand the idea of release on recognizance by implementing appropriate controls and screening techniques.

The process worked like this: When prisoners were brought in for booking and detention prior to the first court appearance, a staff member of the institute checked their previous records and current charges with the arresting officer to see if bail was possible in the initial arraignment. Crimes considered not bailable included homicide, most narcotic offenses, and certain sex offenses (Sturz 1965). If the offense was bailable, the defendants were interviewed to determine if they were working, how long they had held the job, whether they supported families, whether they had contacts with relatives in the city, how long they had lived in the city, and how long they had lived at their present addresses.

Based on the interview, the accuseds were scored on a point-weighting system. If they appeared to be a good risk for release on recognizance, the rating and a summary of the information were provided to the bench at the initial arraignment. Thus, release rested finally with the judge. (See Figure 9.2 for a sample form granting release on recognizance.) When a defendant was released, a staff member of the institute would notify him or her in writing of the date and location of subsequent court appearances. If the defendant was illiterate, he or she was notified by telephone and a follow-up letter was sent to establish an official record of the transaction.

During the first year of the project, half of the cases recommended for release on recognizance were set aside as a control group and were not recommended to the court. This was to determine how accused persons who met the institute's release standards fared without a recommendation. The court granted release on recognizance in 60 percent of the cases in which an actual recommendation was made and in only 14 percent of the control cases. In the next two years of operation,

IN THE CIRCUIT/COUNTY COURT OF THE SIXTH JUDICIAL CIRCUIT
OF THE STATE OF FLORIDA IN AND FOR PINELLAS COUNTY

COURT NO. ______________

STATE OF FLORIDA

VS.

____

I, ________________________, do hereby request that I be released on my own recognizance with the understanding that I will appear at any time or place the Court or its official may direct. Further, I agree to comply with the following conditions:

(a) I agree not to leave Pinellas County, Florida, or change my residence without first getting permission of the Court Investigator.

(b) I will notify my attorney of my release on my own recognizance immediately upon release.

(c) I will report to the Court Investigator, Room #A-207, Criminal Courts, 5100 144th Avenue North, Clearwater, Florida, as directed on each Monday preceeding a final disposition in all cases. PHONE: 530-6410.

(d) Further, I hereby agree to any and all other conditions that the Court may see fit to impose, as listed below.

(e) Gainfully employed.

(f)

(g)

I understand that any violation of the above conditions of release under this Order will be punishable as a Contempt of Court, and that I will also be subject to being recommitted to custody. I also understand that being arrested while released on my own recognizance may result in my Release on Recognizance being revoked.

I understand that criminal charges arising from and related to my arrest may be prosecuted by the State of Florida in the Circuit and/or County Court in and for Pinellas County, Florida and that I must, and will, appear in either Court as may hereafter be required by either Court.

I have read the above conditions and fully understand them, and agree to abide by them, and to be in Court on the day indicated below.

DUE IN COURT: On Call of Court.

____
DEFENDANT

WITNESS: ____________________

____
DATE

ORDER GRANTING RECOGNIZANCE

The Court after being advised concerning the above matter does hereby Order the above named defendant to be released on the defendant's own recognizance this __________ day of ____________________.

____
CIRCUIT/COUNTY JUDGE

cc: State Attorney
Sheriff
Defendant
Court Investigator

(rev.) 4-82

FIGURE 9.2
Sample order for release on recognizance

the number of releases increased because of two factors: (1) greater proficiency in screening with a more subjective set of standards; and (2) greater reliance by the court upon the institute's recommendations (Sturz 1965).

By 1965, the Manhattan Bail Project was considered so successful that it was transferred to the New York City Office of Probation and made a part of routine court procedure. The work of the Vera Institute generated nationwide interest in bail reform. In 1964, with the endorsement of Attorney General Robert F. Kennedy and Chief Justice Earl Warren of the U.S. Supreme Court, the National Conference on Bail and Criminal Justice was convened in Washington, D.C. On the eve of the conference, Senator Sam Ervin introduced a series of bills intended to reform bail practices in the federal courts. The resulting passage of the federal Bail Reform Act of 1966, the first major change in national bail policy since 1789, led to the revision of bail laws in at least a dozen states within five years. Today, release on recognizance is a standard form of pretrial release in jurisdictions throughout the nation.

In 1963, dissatisfied with the commercial bail system in Chicago, the state of Illinois initiated legislation known as the Illinois Ten Percent Deposit Plan. This legislation retained money as the prevailing form of surety release, but it required that a defendant pay the 10 percent bonding fee directly to the court rather than to a commercial bail bondsman. Upon completion of the case, the money was refunded to the defendant, minus a service fee of only 1 percent. The result, as Thomas (1976) notes, was the complete demise of professional bail bondsmen in the state of Illinois.

The Issue of Preventive Detention

One of the continuing impediments to bail reform is the fear that individuals charged with serious crimes, especially crimes against the person, will be free to commit further crimes if they are released on bail or upon their own recognizance. It was this kind of fear that led Congress in March of 1970 to pass a bill authorizing preventive detention in the District of Columbia—where crime had been depicted by the news media as being "out of control"—for a period of up to sixty days without bond for defendants charged with crimes of violence and "dangerous" crimes. The bill drew the wrathful thunder of Senator Sam Ervin, long recognized as a staunch opponent of preventive detention:

> Preventive detention is not only repugnant to our traditions, but it will handicap an accused person and his lawyer in preparing his case for trial. It will result in the incarceration of many innocent persons.
>
> If America is to remain a free society, it will have to take certain risks. One is the risk that a person admitted to bail may flee before trial. Another is the risk that a person admitted to bail may commit a crime while free on bail.
>
> In my judgment, it is better for our country to take these risks and remain in a free society than it is to adopt a tyrannical practice of imprisoning men for crimes which they have not committed and may never commit merely because some court may peer into the future and surmise that they may commit crimes if allowed freedom prior to trial and conviction (*Hearings on Preventive Detention* 1970, p. 3).

In 1984 the United States Congress passed a series of acts that allowed federal judges the option of considering whether a defendant posed a danger to the community in deciding if, and under what conditions, they would release the defendant before trial. This legislation allowed outright detention of defendants on the basis of presumed danger to particular persons and to the community at large. Hence, at a bail hearing the prosecutor needs to prove one of three things in order to have bail denied: (1) there is a serious risk that the accused will flee; (2) the accused will obstruct justice or threaten to intimidate a prospective witness or juror or a member of the community at large; or (3) the offense is of such a magnitude of violence or is one punishable by life imprisonment or death that preventive detention is justified. In 1987, the U.S. Supreme Court upheld the constitutionality of this act. Many states already had provisions such as these in place.

In a study of Washington's preventive detention law, Bases and McDonald (1974) reported that, during the first ten months of operation, the program resulted in the detention of only 10 of 6,000 felony defendants. And at present, when jails throughout the country are under pressure to reduce overcrowding, it is not likely that many jurisdictions will advocate more such legislation.

Preventive detention should not be confused with the concept **pretrial detention.** Pretrial detention is the status of a criminal defendant who is not eligible for bail due to his or her financial inability to make bail and is not releasable on his or her own recognizance, and is thereby forced to stay in the local jail awaiting trial.

A National Institute of Justice study concluded that public policy in America is cynical. Today the balance can be said to have shifted slightly in favor of public safety whereas in the recent past the interests of the accused person were paramount. Reforms in the bail systems have responded to public concerns and research findings. How you feel about bail and preventive detention may depend on whether you sympathize more with the point of view of the public defenders or the prosecutors. One must ask whether the purpose of bail is to protect the accused or prevent crime. What has yet to be discovered is whether it can do both.

First the Sentence, Then the Trial

The Supreme Court Approves **No Bail** *for Dangerous Defendants*

In one of the most important criminal law rulings of the decade, the U.S. Supreme Court has given a new twist to the first axiom of American justice, that the accused is presumed innocent until proved guilty. In a 6–3 decision, the Court upheld the controversial 1984 Bail Reform Act, by which Congress authorized the "preventive detention" of some federal suspects. For many years federal judges were forbidden to deny bail in most cases, except when there was reason to believe that a defendant might flee before trial. The new law has permitted those judges to refuse bail to thousands of suspects, most of them accused of violent and drug-related crimes, who could be shown to pose a danger to the "safety of any other person and the community." In effect, the accused is presumed to be, if not guilty, at least the guilty type.

The Court's decision was warmly greeted by the law enforcement officials who have used the new law with vigor, typically against accused mobsters and drug dealers who often have the money to meet high bail. Thirty-four states also permit the threat posed by the defendant to figure in some bail decisions. On the federal level, there has been about a 36 percent increase in pretrial detainees since the act was passed from a daily average of 5,383 in 1984 to 7,328 in 1986, or about one-seventh of those in federal lockup. "It puts a burden on us to find jail space," says Georgia U.S. Marshall Lynn Duncan.

Civil libertarians, however, warned that the Court's endorsement of the principle of preventive detention would change the complexion of American justice. Judges faced with potentially dangerous defendants had long practiced a de facto brand of preventive detention: setting bail so high that it could not be met. But the act legitimized what had until then been an unacknowledged purpose of many bail procedures. "This sends a dangerous message that the trial is an afterthought," said Harvard Law Professor Alan Dershowitz last week. New York defense lawyer Alan Silber was reminded of *Alice's Adventures in Wonderland:* "To paraphrase the Queen of Hearts, 'First the sentence, then the trial.' "

The ruling came in the case of mob boss Anthony (Fat Tony) Salerno, head of the Genovese crime family, and Vincent Cafaro, a reputed captain in the same Mafia clan, who were charged with racketeering. A federal appeals court in New York City ruled that to deny them bail would violate constitutional guarantees of due process.

In reversing that decision, the Supreme Court ruled that pretrial detention is not an impermissible punishment forbidden by the Fifth Amendment, because it is not intended as punishment at all. Rather, it was designed by Congress as a "regulatory" act, with the legitimate government goal of public safety. "The mere fact that a person is detained does not inexorably lead to the conclusion that the government has imposed punishment," Chief Justice William Rehnquist wrote for the majority.

The justices also found that the law contained sufficient safeguards for the rights of defendants. A detention decision is made after a hearing in which the government must demonstrate that no conditions of release will reasonably assure the safety of the community. The defendant and his attorney may both be present to challenge evidence, cross-examine, and present witnesses.

These safeguards, however, were not enough to satisfy dissenting Justices Thurgood Marshall, William Brennan, and John Paul Stevens. Marshall charged that laws imposing preventive detention were "consistent with the usages of tyranny and the excesses of what bitter experience teaches us to call the police state." He called the majority's semantic distinction between regulation and punishment an "exercise in obfuscation."

Attorneys already coping with preventive-detention laws complain about preparing a defense for clients imprisoned in distant jails, where private telephone conversations are nearly impossible and where even brief personal meetings are typically conducted in the presence of guards. Moreover, detention can stigmatize the accused in court. "It's pretty hard to get a fair trial after you've been officially declared dangerous," says New York civil rights attorney Richard Emery. Some are also worried that prosecutors may push pretrial detention for less dangerous suspects, small-time burglars, perhaps, or white-collar defendants. "What concerns me is the extremely broad reach of the law," says Phillip Johnson, professor of law at the University of California, Berkeley. "Preventive detention could become routine."

Is an open system of preventive detention better than the wink-and-a-nod method of the past? "The classic civil libertarian argument that everyone is presumed to be innocent is just not a workable principle," says Berkeley's Johnson. "We have given it lip service while in fact doing something else." The demand for tougher enforcement of laws may have made the advent of preventive detention almost inevitable. But the cost to innocent defendants, who sometimes may be unfairly detained for many months, is still to be measured. So is the cost to American justice. Faith in first axioms dies hard.

PLEA NEGOTIATION

Prosecutors are legally empowered to negotiate with defendants and their attorneys. Generally, plea bargaining is a defendant's agreement to plead guilty to a criminal charge with a rational expectation of receiving some consideration from the prosecutor for doing so. Often defendants will plead guilty without a plea bargain and expect to receive some benefit nonetheless. These negotiations are likely to be much more informal during the pretrial period than at a later stage when the court becomes officially involved via the trial. Plea negotiation fulfills various purposes, the most important of which are (1) improving the administrative efficiency of the courts, (2) lowering the costs of prosecution, and (3) permitting the prosecution to devote additional time to more important and more serious cases (Wheatley 1974).

As mentioned earlier, prosecutors prefer to pursue cases that have a good chance for conviction. Thus, because many major crimes include the elements of lesser crimes (e.g., murder and manslaughter), prosecutors with shaky cases may accept a guilty plea to "lesser included offenses" to save the time, money, and risk of a trial for a major crime. They may also offer various incentives to the accused to elicit information about other offenders or to induce them to give testimony that will help the prosecution. One such incentive is an offer to accept a plea of guilty to a lesser charge (called *reduction in charge)*; another is immunity from further prosecution on the incidental charge. Thus, a number of misdemeanors begin as felony charges: drunken driving may be reduced to "reckless driving," or statutory rape may be reduced to "contributing to the delinquency of a minor." At arraignment, the defendant and counsel may attempt to bargain for a ***reduction in sentence***. Other types of plea negotiation or plea bargaining include bargaining for concurrent charges and bargaining for dropped charges.

1. *Bargain concerning the charge*. A plea of guilty was entered by the offenders in exchange for a reduction of the charge from the one alleged in the complaint. This ordinarily occurred in cases where the offense in question carried statutory degrees of severity such as homicide, assault, and sex offenses. . . .
2. *Bargain concerning the sentence*. A plea of guilty was entered by the offenders in exchange for a promise of leniency in sentencing. The most commonly accepted consideration was a promise that the offender would be placed on probation, although a less-than-maximum prison term was the basis in certain instances. All offenses except murder, serious assault, and robbery were represented in this type of bargaining process. . . .
3. *Bargain for concurrent charges*. This type of informal process occurred chiefly among offenders pleading without counsel. These men exchanged guilty pleas for the concurrent pressing of multiple charges, generally numerous counts of the same offense or related violations

such as breaking and entering and larceny. This method, of course, has much the same effect as pleading for consideration in the sentence. The offender with concurrent convictions, however, may not be serving a reduced sentence; he is merely serving one sentence for many crimes. . . .

4. *Bargain for dropped charges.* This . . . involved an agreement on the part of the prosecution not to press formally one or more charges against the offender if he in turn pleaded guilty to (usually) the major offense. The offenses dropped were extraneous law violations contained in, or accompanying, the offense alleged in the complaint such as auto theft accompanying armed robbery and violation of probation where a new crime had been committed. . . . (Reproduced from D. J. Newman, "Pleading Guilty for Considerations: A Study of Bargain Justice," *Journal of Criminal Law, Criminology, and Police Science* 46 [1956]: 787, by permission of the author and the publisher.)

It has been estimated that more than 90 percent of criminal convictions result in negotiated pleas of guilty.[3] Even in serious felony cases many jurisdictions encounter four times as many bargains as requests to litigate the cases in trial. Recent studies indicate that in many lower misdemeanor courts there is a consensus among judges and defense attorneys that there are usual sentences for guilty pleas for certain offenses. The defendant shares this expectation as to what the "going rate" is for guilty plea for a certain offense. This is called implicit bargaining.

The practice of plea bargaining has been both attacked and defended by a wide variety of legal and criminal justice authorities. In 1973, the National Advisory Commission on Criminal Justice Standards and Goals referred to it as a "notorious" practice and recommended that it be completely abolished by 1978.[4] The U.S. Supreme Court, on the other hand—in *Santobello* v. *New York*, 404 U.S. 257 (1971)—held that plea negotiation is a legitimate means to secure a guilty plea from a criminal defendant.

In a more recent decision, the Supreme Court announced in *Blackledge* v. *Allison* (431 U.S. 63 [1977]) that "whatever might be the situation in an ideal world, the fact is the guilty plea and the often concomitant plea-bargain are important components of this country's criminal justice system. Properly administered, they can benefit all concerned." Plea negotiation has defenders among criminal justice personnel and legal authorities for many reasons: society's need to dispose of criminal charges without incurring the expense of a trial; a defendant's willingness to plead guilty; the administrative burden that would be imposed by a large number of trials if plea negotiation were not permitted; the enhanced opportunity for rehabilitation of the offender in the event of an agreed-upon disposition; and the chance to individualize punishment, thus lessening the bitterness felt by many defendants after trial. And plea negotiation is also attractive to the defendant. For a guilty party, a negotiated plea may prevent a long stay in jail awaiting trial, the notoriety and stigma of a criminal trial, and, most importantly, the chance for a minimum sentence. Plea bargaining also reduces the financial costs of legal representation and possible detention during extensive pretrial processing.

The Negotiation Process

Guilty pleas are negotiated in a variety of ways. Often they take place directly between the prosecution and defense counsel without participation by the judge. Some cities such as Detroit have special rooms in the courthouse where the negotiations are conducted. In other jurisdictions the courts fully participate in the process. In Chicago, for example, the judge listens to the facts in each case and determines what type of sentence he or she would impose should a guilty plea be entered. Some prosecutors claim that they never allow a plea to be negotiated until or unless they have decided that the defendant is guilty. This reflects a sense of responsibility on the part of the prosecutor that precludes the use of plea bargaining to coerce or pressure an innocent defendant into pleading guilty. However, because a prosecutor is a lawyer who is responsible for representing the state in its prosecution of criminals, a determination should be made not with regard to a defendant's *guilt*, but with regard to a defendant's *innocence*. If the defendant maintains innocence and the prosecutor believes him or her, plea bargaining should not be used to induce the defendant to take the easy way out.

Inducement for Plea Bargaining

Prosecutors frequently charge the accused with as many offenses as possible. This has been called "horizontal overcharging." Another device, "vertical overcharging," is the practice of charging a suspect with a higher offense than is warranted by the evidence. The practice of overcharging is thought to be widespread, because it allows the prosecutor an advantage: in reality, the prosecutor is not bargaining anything away. If the offense charged does not reflect what the prosecutor really intends to pursue, then it can be argued that the prosecutor is negating the defendant's rights. The defense attorney may be aware that the client is being overcharged, but is nevertheless unable to predict the outcome if he or she decides to recommend that the client stand trial.

Factors in Plea Negotiation

According to Mather (1979), the following variables are most frequently identified as having a significant influence on case disposition:

1. Caseload of the prosecutor
2. Strength or weakness of the case
3. Type of defense attorney
4. Personal characteristics of the defendant (e.g., age, race, prior record, bail status)
5. Type of crime

What is not clear from research is the relative importance of these factors in determining case disposition; nor is it clear how these factors are weighted when seen from the different perspectives of the principals in the negotiations: the prosecutor, the defense counsel, and the defendant.

In 1970–71, in an effort to clarify these issues as they affect the dynamics of plea bargaining, Mather conducted an empirical study of case dispositions in Los Angeles County Superior Court. She found that decisions by prosecutors in Los Angeles were based primarily upon substantive concerns for appropriate punishment or an interest in securing convictions. And she stressed the *un*importance of caseload as a factor in plea negotiation, a finding consistent with the studies of Eisentein and Jacob (1977), Feeley (1975), Heumann (1975), Levin (1977), and Rosett and Cressey (1976). Mather also noted that the type of attorney—whether a public defender or a private lawyer—did not appear to make a difference in the decision to plea bargain or to stand trial. In 1974, Lehtinen and Smith analyzed felony dispositions in Los Angeles and found only marginal differences in sentences. In addition, they suggested that "it does not really matter in the actual results whether convicted offenders are represented by public defenders or private attorneys" (p. 17). (See Chapter 8 for a further discussion of this issue.)

Based on these studies, the two factors that appear to have the greatest influence on case disposition are the seriousness of the case and the strength of the case. "Serious" cases are distinguished from "light" cases on the basis of the likelihood that the defendant will receive a severe sentence. Says Mather:

> There are two attributes by which cases are routinely identified as "serious." First, a mandatory felony offense creates a presumption of seriousness because lenient sentences are less common on these offenses. More specifically, those mandatory felony offenses which *typically* receive severe sentences are generally described as "serious." This includes homicide, robbery, kidnapping, sale of opiates, forcible rape, and lewd acts with child. Second, a bad criminal record for a defendant (particularly a prior felony conviction) indicates that his case is "serious," regardless of his charged offense (1979, p. 40).

In Mather's study, the strength of the prosecution's case was based on the amount and type of evidence in relation to how such evidence would be perceived by the judge and jury with regard to the issue of reasonable doubt. Thus, three kinds of cases were identified based on chance of conviction:

1. *"Dead bang" cases.* Cases in which there was a very high probability of conviction because the prosecution possessed physical evidence such as fingerprints, contraband found on the defendant, stolen goods, and canceled checks (in forgery cases).
2. *"Overfiled reasonable doubt" cases.* Cases in which the defendant was charged in the first degree, but where the evidence was only strong enough to convict in the second degree. For example, a public defender said, "On murder cases, there may be reasonable doubt on first degree, but they're definitely gonna get him on second degree or manslaughter. It's the same with first degree burglary or robbery" (Mather 1979, p. 43).
3. *"Reasonable doubt" cases.* Cases in which there was insufficient evidence to connect the defendant with the crime or to prove that any crime had been committed. Included in this category were cases where the reputation and demeanor of the defendant and victim were crucial to the determination of credibility (e.g., sex offenses [rape, sex perversion, child molestation] and assault cases). Such cases present good prospects of acquittal because the conflict typically is between the testimonies of the victim and the defendant.

Table 9.1 shows the disposition of cases in Mather's study as they were affected by the strength and seriousness of the case—together with the convergence of views between the prosecutor and defense counsel.

In a 1980 study, the U.S. Department of Justice attorneys judged the following eleven factors most relevant in deciding whether to bargain a case: (1) the defendant's willingness to cooperate in the investigation or prosecution of the others; (2) the defendant's history with respect to criminal activity; (3) the nature and seriousness of the offenses charged; (4) the defendant's remorse or contrition in willingness to assume responsibility for his or her conduct; (5) the desirability of prompt certain disposition in the case; (6) the likelihood of obtaining a conviction at trial; (7) the probable effect on the witnesses; (8) the probable sentence or other consequences if the defendant is convicted; (9) public interest in having the case tried rather than disposed of by guilty plea; (10) the expense of the trial or appeal; and (11) the need to avoid delay in the disposition of other pending cases (1980). Finally, it should be noted that a defendant has no constitutional right to enforcement of a proposed plea bargain that the prosecution withdrew before it became official.

Reforming Plea Negotiation

Suggested reforms in plea negotiation—as contrasted with the complete elimination of the practice as recommended by the National Advisory Commission on Criminal Justice Standards and Goals (1973)—generally emphasize the formulation of explicit guidelines for the negotiations. Here is one prosecutor's version of such guidelines:

1. General principles under which plea negotiation is to be conducted should be stated, preferably in writing, and should include how and why plea negotiation is to be carried out.
2. The prosecutor will discuss the possibility of plea negotiation with each defense counsel, recognizing that plea negotiation may not be appropriate in every case.
3. Plea negotiation should be conducted between the defense counsel and the prosecutor without direct intervention of the defendant, except for those rare cases in which the defendant chooses to represent himself or herself.
4. Plea negotiation should be accompanied by full disclosure, with the exception that, in the event that negotiation does not lead to an agreement, the information discovered will not be used subsequently to the detriment of the defendant.
5. Time requirements should be established to encourage negotiation and agreement before a case is set for trial.
6. A prenegotiation report should be prepared by the office of the prosecutor to determine

TABLE 9.1
Recommendations by Defense Attorneys on Method of Disposition as a Function of Strength of Prosecution's Case, Seriousness of Case, and Convergence of District Attorney and Defense Attorney Views

	SERIOUSNESS OF CASE (PREDICTION OF SEVERITY OF SENTENCE)		
		"SERIOUS" CASE	
STRENGTH OF PROSECUTION'S CASE (PREDICTION OF CONVICTION OR ACQUITTAL)	"LIGHT" CASE	IF DISTRICT ATTORNEY AND DEFENSE ATTORNEY VIEWS CONVERGE	IF DISTRICT ATTORNEY AND DEFENSE ATTORNEY VIEWS DIVERGE
"Dead bang" case	Negotiated disposition (implicit bargaining)	Negotiated disposition (explicit bargaining)	Trial
"Reasonable doubt"—chance of conviction on lesser charge	Negotiated disposition (implicit or explicit bargaining)	Negotiated disposition (explicit bargaining—convergence more likely here than above)	Trial
"Reasonable doubt"—chance of complete acquittal	Indeterminate	Negotiated disposition (explicit bargaining)	Indeterminate

Adapted from L. M. Mather, *Plea Bargaining or Trial?* (Lexington, Mass.: Lexington Books, 1970), p. 66, by permission of the author and the publisher.

whether negotiation would serve any useful purpose in the particular case.

7. The prosecutor must determine which charges may be reduced and to what degree.
8. Overcharging to force defendants to enter a guilty plea should be eliminated.
9. Judicial participation in the negotiation process should be prohibited.
10. The defendant must acknowledge his or her guilt in open court before the plea will be accepted.
11. The agreement must be reduced to writing and submitted to the court for acceptance or rejection.
12. Trial court must have available all of its discretion in accepting or rejecting a plea.

Mather feels that most proposals of this kind fail to reach the core of the negotiating process: "the discussions of the defendant's character and the interpretation of his offense to reach decisions on the proper sentence" (1979, p. 146). Efforts to formalize and legalize plea negotiation, as Rosett and Cressey observe, ensure "that defendants are not openly told lies about the consequences of a guilty plea, but [do not] ensure that the punishments they receive are either appropriate or fair" (1976, p. 172).

The Vice President of the United States Cops a Plea

In October of 1973, Vice President Spiro T. Agnew became the first Vice President of the United States to leave office under a cloud of criminal charges. The judicial settlement of the Agnew case was brief but dramatic. At the same time the Vice President's resignation was being announced in Washington, he was appearing in person before U.S. District Court Judge Walter E. Hoffman in a Baltimore courtroom. Mr. Agnew pleaded *nolo contendere*—no contest—to one charge: that he had failed to report some $29,500 of income received in 1967 while serving as Governor of Maryland, and thus evaded paying taxes of some $13,500. In return for that plea, all other charges were dropped.

Judge Hoffman, stating that the plea of *nolo contendere* "is the full equivalent of a plea of guilty," promptly sentenced Mr. Agnew to pay a fine of $10,000 and to be placed under probation—without supervision—for three years. No prison sentence was imposed. It was Attorney General Elliot L. Richardson who formally recommended that the sentence "not include confinement" of the Vice President, and the judge agreed. Usually, the judge commented, he would impose a prison term in a case such as that of Mr. Agnew. "However," Judge Hoffman said, "I am persuaded that the national interests in the present case are so great and so compelling . . . that the ends of justice would be better served by making an exception to the general rule. I therefore approve the plea agreement between the parties." That agreement, the judge said, "provides that the Federal Government will take no further action against the defendant as to any federal criminal charge which had its inception prior to today."

The next day, Maryland Attorney General Francis C. Burch announced that he would recommend no prosecution be undertaken against Mr. Agnew in State courts. Mr. Agnew "has suffered enough," he said. Thus Mr. Agnew was virtually assured that he will never go to prison for any of the charges so far made against him. . . .

Mather advocates any reforms in criminal procedure that might help to lessen the isolation and alienation of defendants in court. She was disturbed by the exclusion of defendants from active participation in the "court culture": "Despite the court's ostensible focus on the 'rehabilitation' of the defendant through extensive use of probation and other alternatives to incarceration, the defendant himself was seen as an outsider" (1979, p. 147). Her recommendation that the defendant should be allowed to participate actively in the plea bargaining process is supported by Norval Morris, who believes that plea bargaining should involve the judge and the victim (1974). Bringing the accused and the victim together has the obvious advantage, according to Morris, of permitting them to see one another as human beings, not faceless entities: He views a pretrial settlement in which the victim takes part as an opportunity for the convicted criminal, in or out of prison, to get an immediate start in the process of self-reformation.

An alternative to plea bargaining in the overcrowded prison situations is *pretrial diversion*. Pretrial diversion programs began in the late 1960s as an alternative to being stigmatized by criminal conviction. An accused participates in a diversion program after an arrest and arraignment but before trial. The decision on whether to place an accused in a pretrial diversion is much like the plea-bargain process. If selected for diversion, an accused is released on a continuance of the diversion program; that is, his or her trial is postponed. Normally, an accused will not be allowed to participate in a pretrial diversion unless the prosecutor, judge, and often the probation officer agrees he or she is a good candidate for the program. During the diversion period, the accused is monitored by the diversion staff's personnel to assess his or her continued suitability to the program. Often these programs include alcohol and drug rehabilitative counseling, job training, and family counseling. After the accused participates in the program, charges may be dismissed entirely. If the program needs to be continued and if staff members are unsure of their client's progress, the trial may be postponed. If the accused fails to participate in the program, however, he or she will be processed through normal court channels. The pretrial diversion reduces court congestion and often gives a first defender a second chance to turn his or her life around. Some critics suggest it is the last arena for the rehabilitative process in the criminal justice system that has the opportunity to become truly effective.

SUMMARY

During the past two decades it has been recognized that the period from arrest to trial (or acceptance of a guilty plea) is perhaps the most crucial phase in the criminal process. This pretrial period is the time when many important decisions are made about what will happen to the defendant. If the grand jury proceeding or preliminary hearing results in sufficient evidence to charge the individual with a crime (i.e., a finding of "probable cause"), the defendant is arraigned and given the opportunity to enter a plea to the charges. He or she is informed of his or her constitutional rights, particularly as to representation by counsel, and may be placed in confinement, freed on bail, or released on his or her own recognizance.

The two critical issues that arise during the pretrial period both involve discretion. The first of these is pretrial release. A defendant who is detained in jail suffers adverse consequences from the experience, but his or her individual plight has to be weighed against the possibility that release will result in further danger to society. The second issue is plea negotiation. Since the criminal justice system lacks the resources to try every person accused of a crime, the practice of plea negotiation—despite its critics and detractors—is seen as an essential element in the administrative disposition of a large percentage of cases.

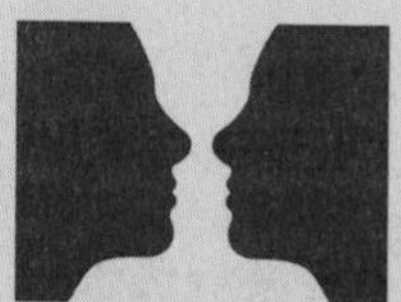

ISSUE PAPER

INVESTIGATIVE GRAND JURIES—THE CONTRA DUE PROCESS PROCESS

A subtle paradox exists between certain rights and privileges of an accused within the American criminal justice system. The federal grand jury system, believed to act as a "buffer" between an accused and an overzealous prosecutor, and constitutional due process rights, which should ensure that the accused receives fundamental fairness during all critical stages of the prosecution against him or her, are canceling each other out.

The grand jury system and due process rights generally are recognized as two of the great "checks" in protecting private citizens from the inherent dangers that may exist should the executive branch of the government be tempted to use the criminal justice system as a vehicle for its own political purposes. These historical checks, however, seem to have dissolved in present practices and procedures implemented by federal prosecutors in their investigations of public officials. Federal prosecutors are using the investigative grand jury system systematically to deny grand jury targets their usual due process rights and then are subjecting them to criminal liability for perjury that is manufactured only because the targets are processed through the grand jury process itself.

Is the Grand Jury a Check?

The American grand jury's historical origins are traced to 1166, during the reign of King Henry II of England. The grand jury is composed of a group of private citizens selected either to review or investigate felony cases for terms lasting various periods of time. Traditionally, the grand jury consists of twenty-three persons and requires a majority vote to indict. Presently, two-thirds of American states do *not* use grand juries (LaFave and Israel 1985).

The grand jury has performed two functions throughout the years: investigative and screening. Concerning the significance of the latter function, the U.S. Supreme Court announced in *United States* v. *Dionisio* (401 U.S. 1 [1973]) that the purpose of the grand jury is to stand between the government agents and the suspect as an unbiased evaluator of evidence. Thus, in theory at least, the grand jury should *shield* a suspect from indictment on an unsubstantiated case presented to it by the prosecutor. Yet, this screening role of the grand jury has lessened over time. Today, most states use a preliminary hearing to serve as this "protective" screen. The *investigatory* role of the grand jury has become stronger than its historical counterpart. This change in the use of grand juries has led to the reversal of its significance over time. As one critic remarked, "The protective function has been trivialized and the investigatory function expanded to the point where the institution is almost precisely the opposite of what the founding fathers intended" (LaFave and Israel 1985, p. 106).

The historical changes in the priorities and functions of the American grand jury have profound due process implications for the rights of grand jury targets. It would seem that since the most celebrated function of the grand jury has been to stand between the government and citizens, it should not abandon its shielding function when it investigates. Unfortunately, this has not turned out to be the case. Investigative grand juries function as a de facto law enforcement agency. Indeed, grand juries may be regarded as perhaps the most effective prosecutorial arm of the executive branch of American government.

One of the primary reasons for the introduction of due process rights in criminal investigatory stages was due to the atmosphere in America at the end of World War II, when there was great fear of the potential use of public force that could be exerted through the criminal justice system (Allen 1975). In addition, due process rights were given to criminal defendants throughout various stages of the criminal justice system due to the fear that fragmentation of the system would give elective prosecutors an independent power base without formal prosecutorial policies (Allen 1975, p. 523). Even the Supreme Court has stated that it cannot tolerate the transfer of the grand jury into an instrument of oppression (*United States* v. *Dionisio*). Yet it seems all these fears and dangers are being realized by the present operations and procedures implemented by the federal prosecutor's manipulative use of investigative grand juries. For whatever the present-day validity of the historical assumptions of neutrality, independence, and the shielding function that underlie the grand jury process, it at least must be recognized that modern grand juries are no longer detached, neutral, nor independent. They have effectively surrendered to the prosecutor. Consequently, the dangers of excessive and unreasonable official interference with personal liberties have increased—exactly the dangers that due process guarantees were intended to prevent.

Grand jury proceedings act to deny their targets due process rights in two ways. First, the target of an investigative grand jury receives fewer due process rights than a subject of a police investigation. Secondly, the defendant in a probable cause investigation conducted at a preliminary hearing receives more due process rights than a target at a probable cause hearing by a screening grand jury.

Due Process Rights: Police Investigations versus Grand Jury Investigations

The constitutional restraints that have been placed on traditional criminal investigation agencies may be the reason investigative grand juries have increased in popularity. In grand jury proceedings, the target of the investigation is not afforded the due process rights that a criminal suspect receives at the station house. Thus investigative grand juries are an attractive investigative tool for prosecutors because they can accomplish what would not be accomplished otherwise (*United States* v. *Dionisio* [410 U.S. 1, 3 (1973)]).

The advantages of using an investigative grand jury rather than traditional law enforcement agencies to probe suspected criminal activity are many. Investigative grand juries have the aid of *subpoena* power; the police do not. This tool allows the grand jury to require the presence of the target's possessions (*United States* v. *Dionisio* [410 U.S. 1, 3 (1973)]). These may be obtained without probable cause, which, of course, is necessary if the police wish to accomplish the same objective by using search warrants (*Warden* v. *Hayden* [387 U.S. 436 (1967)]).

The police generally *warn* a subject that he or she is suspected of committing a crime before interrogating him or her (*Miranda* v. *Arizona* [384 U.S. 436 (1966)]). On the other hand, the grand jury prosecutor need not tell the target that he or she is a target. He or she must only be told of the general subject matter of the subject the grand jury is investigating (*United States Attorney's Manual* 1985).

The police need probable cause to *arrest* or even detain a suspect in order that statements obtained from the suspect through interrogation about his or her suspected criminal activity will not be excluded from evidence (*Dunaway* v. *New York* [442 U.S. 200 (1979)]). The grand jury, on the other hand, can compel a target's appearance by subpoena and thereby do the same thing without having to demonstrate probable cause or even reasonable suspicion that the target is connected to criminal activity (*United States* v. *Dionisio* [410 U.S. 1, 9 (1973)]).

In the station house a criminal suspect has the right to be advised of the right to consult with an *attorney*, the right to have the attorney paid for by the state (if he cannot afford counsel), and the right to have the attorney present during police interrogation (*Miranda* v. *Arizona* [384 U.S. 436, 473 (1966)]). A lawyer may stop a traditional law enforcement interrogation of his or her client at will. On the contrary, only about twelve states allow a target's counsel in the grand jury room (LaFave and Israel 1985, p. 123). In federal grand jury proceedings, a witness is allowed only to *step outside* the courtroom to talk to counsel (National Lawyers Guild 1985). Most targets, however, are afraid to do so because they are afraid they will look guilty before a body that might subsequently indict them. Thus unlike the station house interrogation where defense counsel controls the proceedings, the grand jury prosecutor controls the conduct of defense counsel.

Since all grand jury witnesses are under subpoena, if a witness refuses to cooperate with the investigation, he or she may face a possible jail sentence for contempt (*United States* v. *Dionisio* [410 U.S. 1, 4 (1973)]). At the police station, the same witness could exercise the right to remain silent and then leave the station house with no fear of future jeopardy. The threat of contempt charges is how grand jury investigations obtain testimony from people who ordinarily would not talk to police.

Another way the investigative grand jury secures *evidence* that is otherwise unobtainable through traditional law enforcement methods is by the use of the inherently coercive nature of the grand jury proceeding. Although the Supreme Court has declared that testifying before a grand jury panel is an experience not remotely connected to the coerciveness of a police interrogation (*United States* v. *Mundujano* [425 U.S. 564 (1974)]), experience proves otherwise. One former prosecutor described the grand jury setting as having the feel of the "star chamber" (Keeney and Walsh 1978, p. 579). While testifying before a grand jury, a target is faced with the prosecutorial forces of organized society. "In all the United States legal system, no person stands more alone than a witness before a grand jury," says another critic (Keeney and Walsh 1978, p. 579). In spite of these facts, Miranda warnings are not required to be read to grand jury targets as they are to suspects during custodial interrogation. In spite of the fact that no warnings need be given, a target witness giving false testimony before the grand jury may be prosecuted for perjury.

Another distinct advantage grand jury investigations have over traditional law enforcement investigations is that grand jury proceedings are supposed to be *secret* (*United States* v. *Procter and Gamble Co.* [356 U.S. 677 (1958)]). Yet it is the nonsecrete aspect of this secrecy that proves to be an effective investigative tool. The Supreme Court in *Douglas Oil Company* v. *Petrol Stops Northwest* (1978) declared that the objective of the grand jury's secrecy is to protect the innocence of the accused so that the fact he or she is under investigation is hidden. All jurisdictions prohibit disclosure of grand jury proceedings (Fed. R. Crim. p. 6[e][5]). Contempt orders are threatened for anyone who violates grand jury secrecy. Yet this still has not prevented leaks to the press (Frankel and Naftalis 1975). Diligent reporters come to know who has been subpoenaed to appear before investigative grand juries (although they are sealed) because television cameras often wait outside court room entrances. The faces of all witnesses questioned that day appear on the six o'clock news. This nonsecrecy-secrecy is particularly damaging in grand jury investigations of public figures. Although the Supreme Court announced that being subpoenaed by a grand jury involves "no stigma whatever," public knowledge that a person has been subpoenaed could ruin him or her for life (*United States* v. *Dionisio* [410 U.S. 1, 47 (1973)]).

Due Process in a Probable Cause Determination: A Preliminary Hearing versus a Grand Jury Screening

A citizen suspected of committing a felony has the right to a probable cause hearing to determine his or her guilt before he or she may subsequently be tried for said crime in felony court. The American criminal justice system uses two legal procedures—the grand jury and the *preliminary hearing*—to make the judicial determination of probable cause. Yet in a preliminary hearing an accused is provided with an array of due process rights to ensure that the proceeding is a fundamentally fair one; on the other hand, the grand jury probable cause proceeding provides the target with few of the due process rights he or she would receive in a preliminary hearing. This disparity sometimes results in a fundamental unfairness to the grand jury target.

A defendant in a preliminary hearing has a right to have a detailed *notice* of the charges against him or her; in grand jury proceedings, however, a witness need not even be warned that he or she is a target of the grand jury investigation, let alone the crime being investigated (18 USC 3060).

An accused is afforded the right to consult with *counsel* at post-advisory proceeding line-ups (*Kirby* v. *Illinois* [406 U.S. 682 (1972)]), interrogations (*Miranda* v. *Arizona* [384 U.S. 436, 477 (1966)]), arraignments (*Hamilton* v. *Alabama* [386 U.S. 52 (1961)]), and throughout the preliminary hearing (*Coleman* v. *Alabama* [399 U.S. 1, 9 (1970)]). The grand jury excludes counsel from its proceedings (*United States* v. *Mandujano* [425 U.S. 564, 581 (1974)]).

The accused has the right to be *present* throughout all the proceedings in a preliminary hearing. He or she also has the right to *confront* witnesses against him or her by his or her lawyer through cross-examination. The accused also has the right to *present witnesses* in his or her own behalf (Fed. R. Crime. p. 6[2][d]). Yet a grand jury target does not have the right to be present throughout the proceeding; therefore, he or she does not have the opportunity to cross-examine witnesses against him or her (Fed. R. Crime. p. 6[2][d]). Nor does the target have the right to present witnesses to testify in his or her behalf (*United States Attorney's Manual* 1985).

The rules of *evidence* are generally observed in preliminary hearings (Miller 1970). Grand jury indictments, however, may be based on illegal evidence (*Costello* v. *United States* [350 U.S. 359 (1956)]). Furthermore, grand jury procedures are not subject to objections that the evidence presented is incompetent or irrelevant (*Blair* v. *United States* [250 U.S. 273 (1919)]).

The Fifth Amendment guarantees against *self-incrimination* are exercised during preliminary hearings.

The accused must appear in court, but does not have to take the witness stand and thereby does not have to answer questions by the prosecution. In a grand jury hearing, the target can exercise the right to remain silent, but must personally assert it after every question. Furthermore, a target has no right not to be put on the witness stand and questioned. Once the prosecution has subpoenaed a witness (remember, there is no duty for the prosecutor to tell the witness he or she is the target), the prosecutor has a right to call the witness to the stand and begin to question him or her. In addition, a grand jury target does not have his or her attorney present to help determine whether a question asked by the prosecutor is potentially incriminating (*United States* v. *Dionisio* [410 U.S. 1, 16] (1973)]). Thus, there is no lawyer present to advise the target whether to answer it.

Should an accused receive a favorable judgment from a preliminary hearing judge, the accused will not have to go through such probable cause procedure again unless the prosecution finds additional evidence to present against him or her. On the other hand, the grand jury prosecutor has the power to call a second grand jury if he or she is unsatisfied with the vote of the first one. The grand jury prosecutor has the right to present the same evidence to the second grand jury in hopes of receiving an indictment (*United States* v. *Thompson* 1920).

The problem is obvious. Due process rights are remarkably absent in grand jury proceedings. These dangers can be eradicated only by profound changes. The following are proposed: First, an investigative grand jury target, while being interrogated by a grand jury prosecutor, should receive the same due process rights that he or she would receive if this interrogation were performed by traditional law enforcement. Secondly, whenever a target's actions are being adjudicated for possible indictment by a grand jury, the target should be afforded the same due process rights he or she would have enjoyed had this probable cause determination taken place in a preliminary hearing.

DISCUSSION AND REVIEW

1. How is prosecution initiated in felony cases? How is prosecution initiated in misdemeanor cases?
2. What are the four basic questions a prosecutor must answer to determine if a complaint should be prepared?
3. What is summary jurisdiction?
4. Are there any advantages for the defendant in the preliminary hearing? What are the advantages for the prosecution?
5. What are the major functions and responsibilities of the grand jury?
6. What are pretrial motions and how are they advantageous to the accused?
7. Describe the principal alternatives to pretrial incarceration (such as bail or release on recognizance).
8. What are some of the major inequities of the bail system?
9. Briefly describe the Manhattan Bail Project. What was its significance for bail reform in the United States?
10. What is preventive detention and why do some people think it is inconsistent with the presumption of innocence?
11. What is pretrial diversion?

12. What is a plea of *nolo contendere*? How does it differ in consequence from a guilty plea?
13. What are the four types of plea negotiation described by Newman?
14. What are some of the important advantages of plea bargaining for the prosecutor and the defendant?
15. What are the principal factors that appear to affect plea bargaining? How significant were these factors in the findings of Lynn Mather?
16. Compare and contrast the rights afforded a target by a grand jury to those given to an accused during custodial interrogation and a preliminary hearing.

■ GLOSSARY

Arraignment The event that formally initiates the trial process. The first official occasion in which the accused is given an opportunity to establish his or her identity and enter a plea in response to the accusation. *Arraignment* takes place in the court where the case is to be tried.

Arrest The taking of a person into legal custody for the purpose of holding or detaining him or her to answer to a court of law for an offense with which he or she has been charged.

Bail A system of posting a bond to ensure that a defendant will appear at trial, while allowing him or her to remain free until that time.

Complaint A charge stated before a magistrate that a person named has committed a specified criminal offense.

Felony A criminal offense punishable by death or by incarceration for a year or longer in a state prison.

First appearance A required hearing where the defendant will be brought before a judicial officer within twenty-four to seventy-two hours of arrest to inform the defendant of his or her rights, set bail or other conditions of pretrial release, and appoint counsel if the defendant is indigent.

Grand jury A jury of inquiry whose duties are to receive complaints in criminal cases, to hear the evidence produced by the state, and to indict in situations where a trial is warranted.

Information An accusation against a person for an alleged criminal offense. An *information* differs from an *indictment* in that it is presented by a competent public officer rather than by a grand jury.

Misdemeanor A less serious crime than a felony, which is punishable by a fine or by a period of incarceration of up to one year in a city or county jail.

Nolle prosequi Latin for "I refuse to prosecute." Refers to the discretionary authority of the prosecution to refuse to file a charge against a defendant, even though the evidence supports such a charge.

Nolo contendere Latin for "I will not contest it." A plea in a criminal action that has the same legal effect as a plea of guilty with respect to all proceedings on the indictment and on which the defendant may be sentenced. A plea of *nolo* *contendere,* however, may spare the defendant from certain civil penalties that might follow a plea of guilty.

Preliminary hearing Hearing in which the accused is advised of his or her constitutional rights, in which the *judge* determines if there is probable cause to bind the defendant over to an appropriate court for trial.

Pretrial detention When an accused is incarcerated between the time of arrest and trial due to the fact that he or she is not eligible for bail because of financial inability.

Pretrial motion Motion made by the defense counsel to suppress the introduction at trial of incriminating evidence, alleging the evidence was acquired illegally. Pretrial motions are often made to suppress evidence obtained by police in violation of the Fourth or Fifth Amendments.

Preventive detention A judicial decision to deny an accused bail because of a judicial determination that the accused poses a danger to the safety of some other person and the community.

Release on recognizance (ROR) The release of a defendant, by permission of the court, which permits the defendant to be at liberty upon his or her own agreement and without furnishing sureties for appearance at a pending trial.

Warrant A legal document, issued by a court, that authorizes specific acts by law enforcement officers (e.g., the arrest of a person named in the warrant, or the search of a specific place).

■ REFERENCES

Allen, F. *The Judicial Quest for Penal Justice: The Warren Court and the Criminal Cases.* University of Illinois Law Foundation, 1975.

American Civil Liberties Union. *Secret Detention of the Chicago Police.* New York: Free Press, 1969.

Bases, N. C., and McDonald, W. F. *Preventive Detention in the District of Columbia: The First Ten Months.* New York: Vera Institute of Justice, 1974.

Bloch, H. A., and Geis, G. *Man, Crime, and Society.* New York: Random House, 1962.

Burger, Warren. "Address at the American Bar Association Annual Conference." *New York Times,* 11 August 1970, p. 1.

Chambliss, W. J. *Crime and the Legal Process.* New York: McGraw-Hill, 1969.

Eisenstein, J., and Jacob, H. *Felony Justice: An Organizational Analysis of Criminal Courts.* Boston: Little, Brown, 1977.

Hearings on Preventive Detention Before the Subcommittee on Constitutional Rights of the Senate Committee on the Judiciary. 91st Cong., 2d Sess. (1970) (Statement of Senator Sam Ervin).

Feeley, M. "The Effects of a Heavy Caseload." Paper delivered at the annual meeting of the American Political Science Association, San Francisco, 2–5 September, 1975.

Heumann, M. *Plea Bargaining.* Chicago: University of Chicago Press, 1975.

Johnson, E. H. *Crime, Correction, and Society.* Homewood, Illinois: Dorsey Press, 1964.

Keeney, and Walsh. "The American Bar Association's Grand Jury Principles: A Critique From a Federal Criminal Justice Perspective." *Idaho Law Review* 14 (1978): 45.

Kerper, H. B. *Introduction to the Criminal Justice System.* St. Paul, Minn.: West Publishing Co., 1972.

LaFave, W., and Israel, G. H. *Criminal Procedure.* St. Paul, Minn.: West Publishing Co., 1985.

Lehtinen, M., and Smith, G. W. "The Relative Effectiveness of Public Defenders and Private Attorneys: A Comparison." *Legal Aid Briefcase* 34 (1974): 12–20.

Levin, M. A. *Urban Politics and the Criminal Courts.* Chicago: University of Chicago Press, 1977.

Mather, L. M. *Plea Bargaining or Trial?* Lexington, Mass.: Lexington Books, 1979.

Miller, F. *Prosecution: The Decision to Charge a Suspect with a Crime.* New York: Hill and Wang, 1970.

Morris, N. *The Future of Imprisonment.* Chicago: University of Chicago Press, 1974.

Murphy, J. J. *Arrest by Police Computer.* Lexington, Mass.: Lexington Books, 1975.

National Advisory Commission on Criminal Justice Standards and Goals. *Courts.* Washington, D.C.: U.S. Government Printing Office, 1973.

National District Attorneys Association. *National Prosecution Standards.* Chicago: National District Attorneys Association, 1977. P. 162.

National Lawyers Guild. *Before Federal Grand-Juries,* 3d ed. St. Paul, Minn.: West Publishing Co., 1985.

Newman, D. J. "Pleading Guilty for Considerations: A Study of Bargain Justice." *Journal of Criminal Law, Criminology, and Police Science* 46 (1956): 780–90.

"Plea Offer Not Binding When It's Withdrawn." *New York Times,* 12 June 1984, p. 12.

President's Commission on Law Enforcement and Administration of Justice. *The Challenge of Crime in a Free Society.* Washington, D.C.: U.S. Government Printing Office, 1967a.

_____. *Task Force Report: The Courts.* Washington, D.C.: U.S. Government Printing Office, 1967b.

Rosett, A., and Cressey, D. R. *Justice by Consent.* Philadelphia, Pa.: Lippincott, 1976.

Single, E. W. "The Consequences of Pretrial Detention." Paper presented at the 1984 annual meeting of the American Sociological Association, New Orleans.

Sturz, H. J. *National Conference of Bail and Criminal Justice.* Washington, D.C.: U.S. Government Printing Office, 1965.

Thomas, W. H. *Bail Reform in America.* Berkeley: Universitv of California Press, 1976.

U.S. Department of Justice. *Principles of Federal Prosecution.* Washington, D.C.: U.S. Government Printing Office, 1980. P. 23.

Wheatley, J. R. "Plea Bargaining—A Case For Its Continuance. *Massachusetts Law Quarterly* 59 (1974): 31–41.

■ CASES

Blackledge v. *Allison* 431 U.S. 63, 97 S.Ct. 1621, 52 L.Ed.2d 136 (1977).
Blair v. *United States* 250 U.S. 273, 39 S.Ct. 468, 63 L.Ed. 979 (1919).
Coleman v. *Alabama* 339 U.S. 1, 905 S.Ct. 1999, 26 L.Ed.2d 387 (1970).
Costello V. *United States* 350 U.S. 359, 765 S.Ct. 406, 100 L.Ed. 397 (1956).
Dionisio, U.S. v. 410 U.S. 1, 935 S.Ct. 764, 35 L.Ed.2d 67 (1973).
Douglas Oil Company v. *Petrol Stops Northwest*

Dunaway v. *New York* 442 U.S. 200, 99 S.Ct. 2248, 60 L.Ed.2d 824 (1979).
Hamilton v. *Alabama* 368 U.S. 52, 82 S.Ct. 157, 7 L.Ed.2d 114 (1961).
Kirby v. *Illinois* 406 U.S. 682, 92 S.Ct. 1877, 32 L.Ed.2d 411 (1972).
Mandujano, U.S. v. 425 U.S. 564, 94 S.Ct. 613, 38 L.Ed.2d 561 (1974).
Miranda v. *Arizona* 384 U.S. 436, 86 S.Ct. 1602, 16 L.Ed.2d 694 (1966).
Procter and Gamble Co., U.S. v. 356 U.S. 677, 785 S.Ct. 983, 2 L.Ed.2d 1077 (1958).
Salerno, U.S. v., ___ U.S. ___, 107 S.Ct. 2095, ___ L.Ed.2d ___(1987).
Santobello v. *New York* 404 U.S. 257, 92 S.Ct. 495, 30 L.Ed.2d 427 (1971).
Warden v. *Hayden* 387 U.S. 436, 87 S.Ct. 1642, 18 L.Ed.2d 782 (1967).

■ GOVERNMENT PUBLICATIONS

Federal Rules of Criminal Procedure, Secs. 5, 1(a), 6(d)(2), 6(e)(5).
United States Attorney's Manual, Sec. 9–11.

■ NOTES

1. There are criminal trials by jury and civil trials by jury. This chapter is about the former.
2. A "null pross" may be requested if it is determined that a defendant is not guilty.
3. "Plea Offer Not Binding When It's Withdrawn," *New York Times,* 12 June 1984, p. 12.
4. The commission's recommendation was not followed, however, and plea negotiation continues today.

CHAPTER

10

The Courts

CHAPTER OUTLINE:

The court system in the United States is more complex than any other judicial system in the Western world. Some of this complexity in structure and operations exists because the nation's founders adopted a federal form of government with powers constitutionally divided between two levels of authority. Thus, some arrangement was needed to handle cases that might arise under two distinct sets of laws—the laws of the national government and those of the individual states. To solve this problem, two separate court systems were established, each complete with trial and appellate courts. Each state was free to fashion its own judicial apparatus. As a result, the federal court system is now comprised of 111 district and appellate courts, as well as the individual judicial systems of the fifty states (each with its own organization, personnel, and rules of procedure). The U.S. Supreme Court oversees both systems. The federal Constitution protects the rights of defendants in all criminal cases, although most crimes are processed in state criminal justice systems. Indeed, the trial courts in the state system are the workhorses of the judicial system and handle most of the criminal cases. However, as the result of new federal legislation and a broad interpretation of the power of the federal government to regulate interstate commerce, the federal courts now have the authority for nearly 3,000 federal crimes.

In this chapter, we examine the dual court system and describe the organization and functions of the individual courts at both the federal and state levels. First, however, we look at what a court is and define some of the terms used throughout the chapter.

WHAT IS A COURT?

The term *court* can refer to a particular person (a judge) or a number of persons (a judicial assembly), to a room or building where a tribunal meets to hear the adjudicate cases, or to a session of some judicial assembly. A *judge* is an officer who presides in a court of law. The judge is the senior officer of the court in criminal litigation. His or her duties are varied. During the trial the judge rules on questions of evidence and procedure and guides the questioning of witnesses. During a jury trial the judge instructs the jury members as to which evidence they may properly examine and which they should ignore. In addition, the judge charges the jury by instructing its members on the points of law and evidence they need to consider to reach a verdict in the case. If the defendant waives trial by jury, the judge makes these decisions based on his or her own judicial sensibilities. In some courts (for example, the U.S. Supreme Court), a judge may be called a *justice*. A *magistrate* is a judge who performs a variety of judicial functions other than trial or appellate duties. Magistrates may be regular judges acting temporarily in the capacity of magistrate, or they may be elected or appointed to their positions.

The authority of a court, as established by the legal limits within which it is empowered to handle cases, is referred to as the court's **jurisdiction**. When we speak of the jurisdiction of the trial court, the word "jurisdiction" means that the court in which the prosecution is pending must be competent according to its own standards. This means it must be vested by local law with the power to punish and try the accused for the offense involved. Jurisdiction is a matter regulated by the statutes of each state. Kerper identifies the following courts in terms of their various jurisdictions (1972, p. 210):

1. *Trial court.* A court that has authority to try cases. A trial court impanels a jury, hears the evidence and arguments of counsel, receives the verdict, and sentences the defendant. Such a court has *original jurisdiction* of a case.

2. *Appellate court.* A court that reviews cases that have originally been tried in a trial court. An **appellate court** is also called an *appeals court* and is said to have *appellate jurisdiction.*
3. *Court of record.* A court whose decisions are reviewed *on the record.* This means that an appellate court does not hear the testimony of witnesses and the arguments of counsel. Instead, the court reads the written transcript (or record) of what went on in the original trial and bases its findings and decision on that record.

All courts that try felonies and most that try serious misdemeanors (those that carry possible jail sentences) keep records of court activity in each case, preparing a full transcript of the proceedings in virtually all cases. Thus, the term *court of record* is used to distinguish such courts from *courts of limited jurisdiction* (i.e., courts such as magistrate or justice of the peace courts that do not hold jury trials or handle appeals). Courts of limited jurisdiction also are called minicipal courts or lower courts. These courts are restricted in the types of cases they may hear. Most often these are not jury cases. Usually courts of limited jurisdiction will handle misdemeanors, civil infractions, violations of municipal ordinances, traffic violations, and civil suits where damages involve less than a statutory amount of money. Furthermore, courts of limited jurisdiction often conduct preliminary hearings for felony court cases. Courts of limited jurisdictions can, however, send people to jail in every state.

A *court of original jurisdiction* is authorized to try cases; a **court of general jurisdiction** can hold jury trials, hear the arguments of counsel, examine evidence, and listen to testimony from witnesses; a *court of appellate jurisdiction* has the authority to hear a defendant's appeal to set aside a conviction. Courts with original jurisdiction seldom have appellate jurisdiction, and never with regard to a case they have already tried. Cases can be appealed to a **court of intermediate appeal** in a state, but the highest tribunal to which a case can be appealed is the **court of last resort**—the state equivalent of a supreme court.

It is common practice to refer to "lower" courts, or **inferior courts,** and to "higher" courts, or *superior courts.* The former include courts of limited jurisdiction; the latter include the appellate courts, especially courts of last resort. The status of trial courts (courts of general jurisdiction) in this hierarchy is variable: they are sometimes included among the lower courts, sometimes among the higher courts. Such distinctions are largely the result of custom and usage—a reflection of the prestige accorded to the various courts by the legal profession.

THE FEDERAL COURT SYSTEM

The U.S. Supreme Court is the only federal court specifically mandated by the Constitution. Other federal courts were established by legislative action. Article III, section 1 of the Constitution states that "the judicial power of the United States shall be vested in one Supreme Court, and in such inferior courts as the Congress may from time to time ordain and establish."

The federal court system is a hierarchy with the U.S. District Courts at the base, the U.S. Courts of Appeals at the intermediate level, and the U.S. Supreme Court at the apex. Also a part of the federal judiciary are the U.S. magistrates, formerly called U.S. commissioners, and a variety of specialized courts. Among the latter are the U.S. Court of Military Appeals, the U.S. Court of Claims, and the U.S. Customs Court.

U.S. magistrates are federal judges whose powers are limited to trying lesser misdemeanors, setting bail for more serious cases, and assisting district courts in various legal manners. In 1976 the U.S. magistrates' authority was expanded to include the issuance of search and arrest warrants, the review of civil rights and habeas corpus petitions, and the conducting of pretrial conferences in both civil and criminal hearings. U.S. magistrates can be both full-time and part-time jurists and are appointed by federal district court judges (Institute of Judicial Administration 1971, p. 13).

The U.S. Supreme Court

The U.S. Supreme Court is known also as the Court, High Court, and Highest Tribunal. It is the highest court in the nation. It stands at the apex of the federal judiciary and is truly the court of last resort. The U.S. Supreme Court, often referred to simply as "the Court," consists of nine judges called *justices.* The justices are appointed by the president, subject to confirmation by the Senate. The president also appoints one member of the Court to act as chief justice. As the chair of the Court, the chief justice has no formal powers of coercion over the other justices, but he or she may apportion caseloads or direct the writing of a judicial decision.

The officers appointed by the Court include a clerk to keep records, a marshal to maintain order and supervise the administrative affairs of the Court, a reporter to publish its opinions, and a librarian to serve the jus-

FIGURE 10.1
The Supreme Court Building in Washington, D.C. (Courtesy of the Supreme Court Historical Society)

tices and the lawyers of the Supreme Court Bar. The chief justice is also authorized to appoint an administrative assistant.

There is no formal requirement in the Constitution (or anywhere else) that a Supreme Court justice must have a background of distinguished judicial service. For that matter, a justice is not required to have any legal training whatsoever. Earlier in our national history, appointment to the Supreme Court was a reward for political prominence or party loyalty. Earlier still, nomination to the court was a dubious distinction: George Washington had difficulty finding candidates with suitable qualifications or enthusiasm for the position, and in 1795, Chief Justice John Jay left the Court—firmly convinced that it would never attain equal status with the executive and legislative branches of government.[1] It is fortunate for the nation that in subsequent years the Supreme Court benefited from the wisdom, insight, scholarship, and philosophy of some of the most distinguished legal minds in the country, leaders like Marshall, Brandeis, Cardozo, Holmes, Hughes, and Warren.

Justices hold their tenure for "life or good behavior," as provided by the Constitution. A justice can only be removed by voluntary retirement or impeachment. The Constitution also denies Congress the authority to reduce the salaries of the justices. The term of the Court is variable. Although statutory law requires that the term begin each year on the first Monday of October, it does not set a closing date. Thus, the Court continues in session as long as it has business to transact. The work load has steadily increased with the expansion of the federal and state judiciaries. Although the Supreme Court gets most of its cases on appeal from these courts, the number of justices on the Court has not changed to meet the growing caseload. Each term, the Court handles approximately five thousand cases.

Each year between 200 and 250 cases of great importance and interest are decided on their merits; about one-half of these decisions are announced in full published opinions.

Technically, the Supreme Court has both original and appellate jurisdiction. As specified in the Constitution, it is the **court of first instance** in cases involving diplomatic representatives of foreign powers and in controversies in which a state is a party. Virtually all cases heard under the Court's powers of original jurisdiction relate to disputes between two states—usually over water rights—or between the federal government and a state.

The appellate jurisdiction of the Court accounts for the overwhelming bulk of its business. The Court reviews cases from lower federal courts and from state tribunals when issues are involved that pertain to the Constitution or to laws of the United States. The Court has almost absolute power to control its agenda, thus enabling it to be highly selective and to assume jurisdiction only in cases that raise an issue it wishes to

FIGURE 10.2
The justices of the U.S. Supreme Court. (Courtesy of the Supreme Court Historical Society)

consider. However, the Court must grant its jurisdiction in all instances in which (1) a federal court has held an act of Congress to be unconstitutional; (2) a U.S. Court of Appeals has found a state statute to be unconstitutional; (3) a state's highest court of appeals has ruled a federal law to be invalid; and (4) an individual's challenge to a state's statute on federal constitutional grounds is upheld by the state's supreme court. Over half of the requests for Court time come from losing parties in the U.S. Courts of Appeal; most of the remainder come from disappointed litigants in the state tribunals of last resort.

Only at the level of the Supreme Court is there a bridge between the federal and state judicial structures. No path of appeal exists from a state court to any federal tribunal at lower levels in the hierarchy. If the Supreme Court grants ***certiorari*** (accepts jurisdiction), it will scrutinize the constitutional issue at stake and either sustain the state tribunal's finding or reverse the decision and release the appellant who had the appeal accepted. Prior to granting *certiorari,* the potential case must pass the Rule of Four, that is, a case is accepted for review only if four or more members of the Court feel that it merits consideration by the full court.

A Supreme Court decision that reverses or overturns a defendant's conviction or sentence does not necessarily free the appellant or impose a lighter penalty. Rather, in most instances, the Court *remands* or returns the case to the court of original jurisdiction for a new trial. In those rare instances where the court allows the defendant to go free the case is considered to be reversed and *rendered.* The Supreme Court reverses rulings in about two-thirds of the cases it hears, partly as a result of the careful screening by the Court for cases that have "rightness"—that is, cases that involve the specific issues the Court wishes to address.

When the Supreme Court rules on a case, usually by majority decision (at least five votes), its rule becomes precedent that must be honored by all lower courts. The use of precedent in the legal system gives the Supreme Court the power to influence and mold the everyday operating procedures of the police, corrections departments, and the trial courts.

What They Say It Is

Woodrow Wilson said they were a Constitutional Convention in continuous session, and Charles Evans Hughes observed with only a twist of irony that the Constitution is what they say it is. Each working day—from the first Monday of October until the end of June or early July—the Justices of the U.S. Supreme Court are asked by specific litigants with particular problems, Pray tell me, what does the Constitution mean?

When a major ruling is announced or a Justice resigns, as Lewis Powell did last week, public attention briefly turns to the court. But for the most part the Justices work in a hushed corner of the public arena. An average of 5,000 cases a year are submitted for their review, and they normally select 150 to 180 on which to hear oral arguments and render written decisions. The Justices begin that process at regularly scheduled discussions. Usually just after 3 P.M. on Wednesdays or at 9:30 A.M. on Fridays, they enter a spacious, oak-paneled conference room, located behind the courtroom. Following a century-old custom, they shake hands with one another and then settle around the rectangular conference table, with the Chief Justice at one end and the senior Associate Justice, currently William Brennan, at the other. The most junior, now Antonin Scalia [Anthony Kennedy since 1988], sits to Brennan's right and answers any knocks on the door or hands out any messages necessary. No law clerk or other person is in the room during the conference.

The Chief Justice speaks first, usually outlining the facts and issues in the case and expressing his tentative vote. The other Justices follow with their views in order of descending seniority. The outcome is now provisionally decided, and the majority opinion is assigned by the Chief Justice or by the senior Justice in the majority. Then begins the writing process, for the majority and the dissenters. A Justice produces a draft, or reworks one from a law clerk, and circulates it to colleagues. Changes may be requested or offered to pick up or hold a vote. A coalition can come unraveled; a close initial vote may wind up going the other way. So the first audience a Justice must please is within the court, but the final opinions are directed beyond the litigants to guide lower-court judges, sometimes to instruct the nation, occasionally even to address Congress.

The reasoning is businesslike, lawyerly, as much to the point as the Justices can manage. But frequently an issue will incense or a principle inspire. Their words, which are their deeds, are part of what Americans live by. These selections are from the members of the current sitting Constitutional Convention.

The U.S. Courts of Appeal

The U.S. Courts of Appeal—designated as lower federal courts—were established in 1891 to lighten the Supreme Court's caseload from appeals from federal district courts.[2] Until 1948, the U.S. Courts of Appeal were known as the U.S. Circuit Courts of Appeal. They are characterized as *intermediate appellate courts* because they stand between the U.S. District Courts, the U.S. magistrates, and the specialized federal courts on the one hand, and the Supreme Court on the other hand. They have the principal responsibility for reviewing judicial decisions in the lower courts (Klein 1977).

There are thirteen U.S. Courts of Appeal (including one for the District of Columbia), each with jurisdiction over a particular geographical section of the country—a so-called judicial circuit (see Figure 10.3). The thirteen courts of appeal hear some thirty thousand cases each year involving both criminal and civil matters (Posner 1985). More than 100 judgeships are authorized for the U.S. Courts of Appeal. The number of judges in each court of appeal ranges from three to fifteen, depending on the size and population of the area served.

U.S. Courts of Appeal are essentially what the name implies, appellate courts only. The courts of appeal hear cases that are appealed from the district courts. In only three instances can a case that has been tried in the lower federal courts bypass the particular court of appeal in its circuit and go directly to the Supreme Court: (1) if the case has been decided by a special three-judge district court; (2) if federal statute has been held unconstitutional by a U.S. District Court and the United States is a litigant in the case; or (3) if it can be shown that the case is "of imperative public importance . . . so to require immediate settlement."

At least two judges must sit on each case, but decisions are normally made by a panel of three. The composition of these groups varies from case to case, with the presiding judge in each court making the assignments. On occasion, when disagreement arises among the judges on an important point of law, the matter may be decided by the full court in an ***en banc* decision.** *En banc* means "in bank" wherein the full bench of judges are authorized by the particular court of appeal of the district to hear a specific case. Judges of the U.S. Courts of Appeal, like Supreme Court justices, hold their appointments for "life or good behavior."

The U.S. District Courts

The U.S. District Courts were created by the Federal Judiciary Act (FJA) passed by Congress on September 24, 1789. Originally there were thirteen courts, one for each of the original states. By the early 1980s, there were ninety-five—eighty-nine distributed throughout the fifty

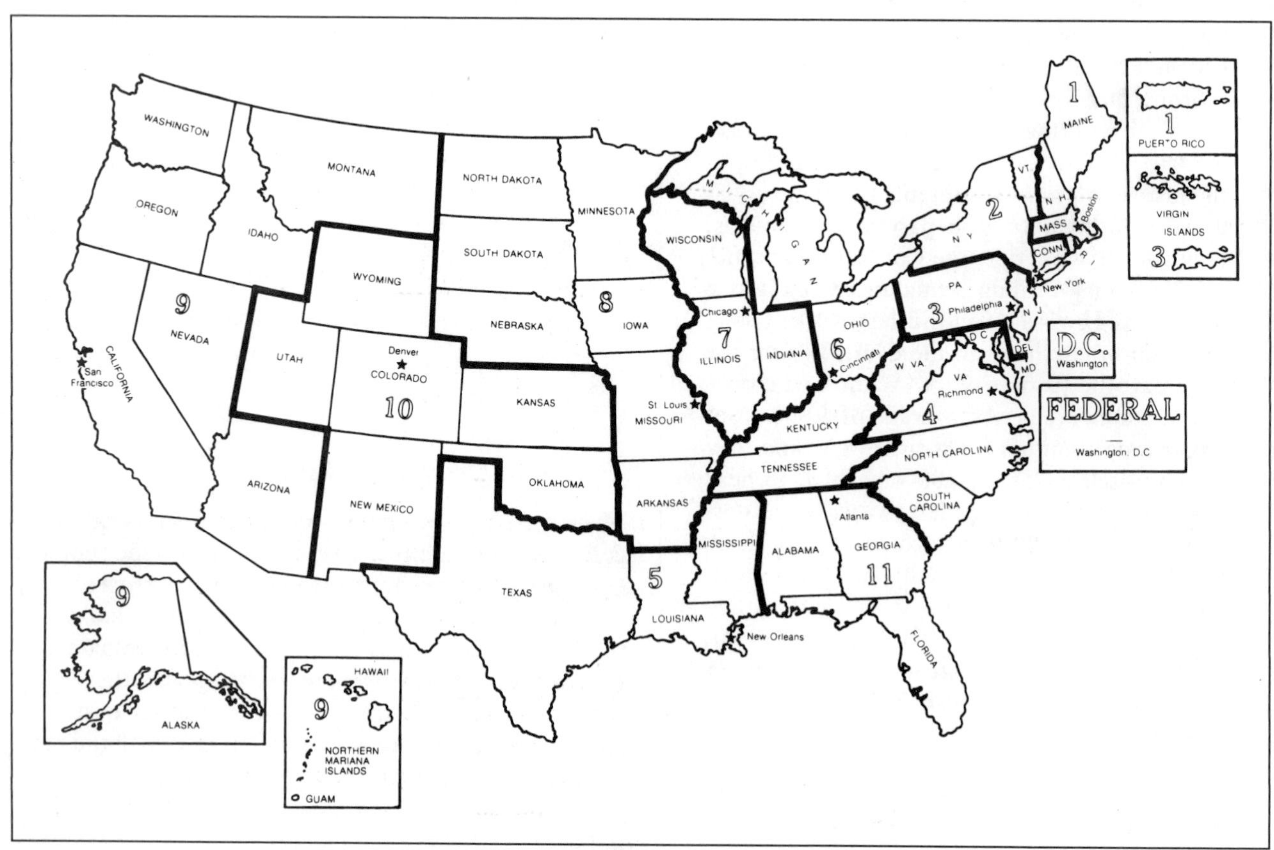

FIGURE 10.3
The thirteen federal judicial circuits.

states and one each in the District of Columbia, Guam, the Canal Zone, Puerto Rico, the Virgin Islands, and the North Marianna Islands. The federal district courts are tribunals of original jurisdiction or first instance. It is in these courts that the majority of noncriminal (civil) suits arising under federal law are initiated and terminated—actions on patent rights, postal problems, copyright violations, bankruptcy, and so on. Here also are tried crimes committed against the federal government (i.e., those that involve conduct prohibited by Congress and that are punishable by the federal government). There are over four hundred authorized judgeships. A federal judge serves on the bench for life. The only way he or she may be removed is by death, resignation, or impeachment by Congress. Each state contains no less than one federal district court (some having multiple divisions); sixteen states have two tribunals, eight have three, and New York and Texas have four each. Every district has at least one judge, depending on the work load, and some districts have as many as twenty-four. A single judge conducts the trials in these lower tribunals, except in cases that involve the constitutionality of national and state statutes. In the latter, three judges must preside at the trial. During 1984 fiscal year the U.S. District Courts processed more than 23,000 cases.

In recent years, the so-called *habeas corpus* jurisdiction of U.S. District Courts has gained importance. The tremendous amount of litigation in this area has become the subject of widespread media attention. Through the *habeas corpus* act, many inmates who have been tried and sentenced in state courts and confined in state correctional facilities have challenged their incarceration by the state authorities. This is a type of post-conviction remedy that is allowed under federal law. The remedy is available for prisoners who can contend that a meaningful factor that caused their confinement violated some aspect of the federal Constitution or the federal statutes. In most cases, however, the petition for a writ of *habeas corpus* claims that some provision of the U.S. Constitution has been violated. The prerequisites for asking the U.S. District Court to intervene in *habeas corpus* cases are that the prisoner must have exhausted all of his or her appellate rights in the state courts and that a "federal issue" is involved in the case such as an alleged violation of the U.S. Constitution.

STATE AND LOCAL COURTS

American state courts are strikingly decentralized. In only a relatively few small states are the court systems completely unified on a state-wide basis, funded by the state government, and centrally administered. In the rest of the country although the state criminal courts operate under the state penal code, they are managed, financed, and staffed by their individual county or city governments. Thus, local politics can be brought to bear on state courts and their local officials. This influence often determines the resources to be allocated to the judiciary. This situation causes a considerable lack of coordination among the courts in a given state, which results in overstaffing in some state courts while others have tremendous case backlogs. Overcrowded courts often are lenient toward offenders while the overstaffed courts are severe. Also, the time for processing criminal cases varies widely depending on local traditions.

No generalizations can be made regarding the jurisdictions, functions, and titles of state and local courts. Although there are structural parallels between state court systems and the federal judicial system, as shown in Table 10.1, the hierarchy in any given state may include two, three, four, or even more levels of courts. To confound matters further, many persons in the criminal justice system often forget that the nomenclature for courts is rather arbitrary. Consequently, courts are often referred to by title rather than by jurisdiction or function.

Courts of Last Resort

Each state has an appellate tribunal that serves as the court of last resort. In New York, Kentucky, and Maryland, the court of last resort is known as the court of appeals. In other states, it is called the supreme court of appeals, supreme court of errors, court of criminal appeals, or supreme judicial court. Whatever its title, the court of last resort is the final authority in cases involving issues of state law.

In almost all states, the courts of last resort are established by the respective constitutions of the states. Judges most often are elected to the court, usually for longer terms of office than the judges of lesser courts in the state. In most states, a candidate for the supreme court bench must have practiced law for a specified number of years to become eligible for this position.

Courts of last resort relate to the lower state courts in much the same way that the U.S. Supreme Court relates to the lower federal courts. As the highest judicial body of the sovereign states, these tribunals have discretionary power to decide which cases they will hear. For this purpose, the court uses a writ of *certiorari*—a writ of review commanding a lower court to "send up

#6)

TABLE 10.1
Parallels between the State and Federal Court Systems

	STATE COURT SYSTEM	FEDERAL COURT SYSTEM
Court of Last Resort	Supreme court, court of criminal appeals, supreme court of appeals, supreme judicial court, etc.	U.S. Supreme Court
Intermediate Appellate Courts	Superior court, district court of appeals, appellate court, supreme court, etc.	U.S. Courts of Appeal
Trial Courts (Courts of general jurisdiction)	Circuit court, district court, state court, county court, etc.	U.S. District Courts
Lower Courts (Courts of limited jurisdiction)	Municipal court, small claims court, traffic court, justice of the peace, etc.	U.S. magistrates and specialized courts (e.g., U.S. Customs Court)

the record" of a case for consideration. (The U.S. Supreme Court uses the writ of *certiorari* in much the same way.) Courts of last resort are presided over by three to nine judges (usually seven).

Intermediate Appellate Courts

Thirty-six of the most heavily populated states have an intermediate level of appellate courts that corresponds to the U.S. Courts of Appeal. As in the federal system, these intermediate courts provide relief for overburdened state supreme courts and serve as courts of last resort for the majority of appeals received from the courts of original jurisdiction. New York was the first state to create a system of appellate courts (it did so shortly before the turn of the century).

Some of the names given to intermediate appellate courts are superior court, appellate court, and supreme court. In some states, courts of appeal may have both original and appellate jurisdiction; in others, jurisdiction may be restricted to particular kinds of cases. Some states assign the defendant the right to appeal, regardless of whether the court wants to hear the case. Following a conviction for a criminal offense, an individual may appeal the decision arrived at by the court.

The U.S. Supreme Court has ruled that convicted defendants who are indigents have a right to a free attorney to represent them in their first automatic appeal of their conviction (*Douglas* v. *California* [372 U.S. 353 (1963)]). In thirty-six states this appeal is to an intermediate appellate court. However, once an appeal is exhausted unfavorably at the intermediate court, a defendant does not have the right to a free attorney to take his or her case to the Supreme Court (*Ross* v. *Moffitt* [417 U.S. 600 (1974)]).

The appeals process is highly fragmented and cumbersome, but there is a basic model that applies to most jurisdictions. The first step in the process is the finding of guilt by some court system at the municipal, county, state, or federal level. In each case, the procedure for appeal is determined by the court of record. Appeals are usually made by the defendant, because the states are highly restricted in their ability to appeal decisions. The effect of an appropriately introduced appeal is a stay in the execution of the original sentence until the appeal is decided. As soon as possible, if not immediately after the sentence is pronounced, the defendant's attorney must either move for a new trial or make an appeal on some grounds. And although appellate courts usually make short work of frivolous appeals, the courts must be careful not to go too far in the other direction:

> Appellate courts . . . do not reverse decisions simply because they disagree with them. Reversal must proceed from error of law and such error must be substantial. But if this account is to be veracious, I must call attention to a fact familiar to every experienced lawyer, yet not apparent in the classical literature of the law, and probably not consciously admitted even to themselves by most appellate judges. By that I mean practically every record contains some erroneous rulings [and] they can

nearly always find some error if they want grounds for reversal (Ullman 1933, pp. 265–66).

In most state systems, courts of appeal review the decisions of the trial courts for judicial error. The facts of a case are not questioned, and all of the trial court's decisions on facts are binding on the appellate court. Thus, evidence is not presented to the court of appeals; rather, the review is accomplished from the trial record. An appellate court cannot reverse the factual findings of the trial court unless they are totally erroneous. In states where there is a second level of review, the trial record and the intermediate court's decision are examined. Usually, the refusal to hear an appeal of a lower appellate court's ruling is the same as upholding the decision; the case stops there unless an appeal is filed separately in federal court on a constitutional issue.

Trial Courts

Trial courts are also known as courts of general or original jurisdiction. They are the courts that have original jurisdiction in most criminal cases, and they are the lowest courts of record at the state level. These courts are referred to as district, circuit, or superior courts, or courts of common pleas, and they are structured differently from state to state (see Table 10.2). Some systems provide for separate criminal and civil divisions; a few retain equity or chancery tribunals; and others have special probate and domestic relations courts. Regardless of how they are structured, however, the trial courts handle the bulk of major litigation under state law. These courts number in excess of three thousand across the nation. All important civil litigation originates in these courts, and persons accused of criminal offenses—other than petty crimes—are tried in them. These tribunals also serve as appellate units for cases instituted in courts of limited jurisdiction. However, because such cases are tried *de novo* (as though they had not previously been heard), further appeal normally lies with a higher court.

Lower Courts

At the bottom of the hierarchy are the lower courts, also known as courts of limited and special jurisdiction. More than thirteen thousand of these courts are in place across the United States. Typically they are the focal point for initiating the criminal justice process. They handle all minor criminal offenses such as drunk and disorderly, DWI, prostitution, petty theft, traffic offenses, and violation of county and city ordinances. These minor tribunals of local character are identified by titles such as justice of the peace, magistrate, municipal, police, and small claims courts. These courts have various duties and jurisdictions. They are not courts of record, so appeals from them are usually appeals for a completely new trial before the next level of courts in the state system. In some states, justices of the peace and magistrates also conduct preliminary hearings in criminal matters to determine whether accused individuals should be bound over for trial in higher tribunals.

Historically, the American experience with lower courts has not been reassuring. It was once common practice (and still is in some areas) for laypersons with no formal legal training and little judicial aptitude to preside over lower courts. Considering this background, the following comment of a justice of the peace about defendants

TABLE 10.2
The State Felony Courts

Circuit Court
Alabama, Arkansas, Florida, Hawaii, Illinois, Indiana,* Kentucky, Maryland, Michigan, Mississippi, Missouri, Oregon, South Carolina, South Dakota, Tennessee, Virginia, West Virginia, Wisconsin

Court of Common Pleas
Ohio, Pennsylvania

District Court
Colorado, Idaho, Iowa, Kansas, Louisiana, Minnesota, Montana, Nebraska, Nevada, New Mexico, North Dakota, Oklahoma, Texas, Utah, Wyoming

Superior Court
Alaska, Arizona, California, Connecticut, Delaware, District of Columbia, Georgia, Indiana,* Maine, Massachusetts, New Hampshire, New Jersey, North Carolina, Rhode Island, Vermont, Washington

Supreme Court
New York

*Concurrent jurisdiction for felonies.

U.S. Department of Justice, U.S. Bureau of Census, *The National Survey of Court Organization (Washington, D.C.: U.S. Government Printing Office, 1973).*

brought before him is hardly surprising: "I don't ever remember having one who *wasn't* guilty. If the sheriff picks up a man for violating the law, he's guilty or he wouldn't bring him in here. Anyway, I don't get anything out of it if they aren't guilty" (Banks 1961, p. 188). The following excerpt from the *Task Force Report: The Courts,* authored by the President's Commission on Law Enforcement and Administration of Justice, conveys something of the atmosphere that characterizes the functioning of the lower courts:

> An observer in the lower criminal courts ordinarily sees a trial bearing little resemblance to those carried out under traditional notions of due process. There is usually no court reporter unless the defendant can afford to pay one. One result is an informality in the proceedings which would not be tolerated in a felony trial. Rules of evidence are largely ignored. Speed is the watchword. . . . Traditional safeguards honored in felony cases lose their meaning in such proceedings; yet there is still the possibility of lengthy imprisonment or heavy fine.
>
> In some cities trials are conducted without counsel for either side; the case is prosecuted by a police officer and defended by the accused himself. . . . Short jail sentences of one, two, or three months are commonly imposed on an assembly line basis . . . (1967, pp. 31–33).

An offender subjected to a process of this kind is not likely to emerge changed for the better. Rather, he or she will return to the streets to begin the cycle again in all of its futility.

THE JUDICIARY

The symbolism and rituals of the judicial process are summarized in the figure of the goddess of justice, Astraea, who stands blindfolded with scales suspended in one hand and a sword in the other. The scales signify the weighing of evidence; the sword implies the power and authority of punitive sanction; and the blindfold indicates that justice is oblivious to temptation or bribery.

This is an inspiring and ideal image, but it has little to do with reality. For one thing, courts are an integral part of the political system and they perform policy-making functions not unlike those of legislative bodies and executive agencies (Peltason 1955). As such, they are often the target of furious controversy, their decisions eliciting both praise and damnation. There is a great contrast between the dignified chambers of the U.S. Supreme Court and the television editorials on the evils of school busing, between the chief justice and the tirades of antiabortionists, between the solemn enclave of the Supreme Court and the vituperation of proponents of school prayer.

Legal realists such as Benjamin Cardozo, Jerome Frank, and Thurman Arnold helped dispel the myths of judges as automatons and of the law as a system of definite and consistent rules readily discoverable by reason alone. When people become judges, they are not suddenly cleansed of all their prejudices or given immunity against social pressures. How they act depends on their personality, background, attitudes, beliefs, and values. In a statistical analysis of the split decisions of the 1960 term of the U.S. Supreme Court, Schubert found that almost all votes could be explained by the justices' attitudes or preferences: "A justice reacts in his voting behavior to the stimuli presented by cases before the Court, in accordance with his attitudes toward the issues raised for decisions" (1962, p. 91).

Other scholars believe that judges make decisions according to conflicting principles and interests because they are guided by what they think will be the decision's impact on society and by what they perceive as its advantages to society. Proponents of this thesis deny that jurists decide questions according to personal preference and point out that, as trained lawyers, judges are influenced by the doctrine of ***stare decisis*** ("let the decision stand") and wish to achieve as much stability in the law as possible (Miller 1965). When societal considerations are reconciled with the doctrine of *stare decisis,* the resulting judicial decisions are, in effect, compromises.

Meet the Judge

Courts and the judicial process usually bring to mind a picture of a judge, draped in a black robe, overseeing a trial. When a judge enters a courtroom, everyone rises and stands quietly until he or she sits behind the elevated bench and raps the gavel to start the proceedings. In courts composed of a number of members, it is common for judges to march in together quickly as if choreographed on cue to take their seats in a flourish of flowing robes. Loud talking or even whispering among court spectators is not permitted. At the U.S. Supreme Court severe-looking ushers holding long sticks roam the aisles, and they poke these sticks at individuals who talk too loudly or distract others from focusing on the front of the large courtroom. Called "the Marble Palace," the U.S. Supreme Court building is very ornate, with high ceilings and decorated walls, polished floors, and long benches that resemble pews in a church. Reverence and respect are expected and enforced. Other courtrooms are less magnificent, but the floor plan, furniture arrangement, and the judge raised above everyone else are similar and clearly show who is in charge and what goes on.

The odds are good that few of us picture a black or a woman presiding over a court. There is an increasing number of female and black judges in the United States, but chances are most of us still envision a middle-aged white man, perhaps slightly overweight, with graying or white hair. Judges are thought to be slightly aloof, but patient, understanding, and unlikely to lose their tempers. They also run their courts firmly but fairly. Judges are not too tall or short or thin or bald, and they do not sport beards or styled haircuts. Of course, judges *do* come in all shapes, shades, and sizes, but [former] Chief Justice Warren Burger *really* looks like a judge.

Reproduced from H. R. Glick, *Courts, Politics, and Justice* (New York: McGraw-Hill, 1983), p. 1, by permission of the author and the publisher.

Selection of Judges

In selecting judges, it is necessary to distinguish between formal procedures and requirements (as specified by constitutional or statutory law) and actual practice. The former provide the legal specifications to be followed in choosing judicial personnel, but leave an undefined area in which informal practices develop. State law may call for the popular election of judges, but who runs may be determined by the political parties. Thus to win a judgeship, the candidate must first secure his or her party's nomination and then campaign on the party ticket. This means that potential state judges normally are embroiled in the same type of partisan politics that are prevalent in the election of legislators, governors, presidents, and other government officials. This system necessarily results in the election of the most politically active candidates rather than possibly the most competent to serve. In other states, the law may provide for gubernatorial appointments, but the choice of candidates may actually be dictated by political leaders or bar associations.

In the judicial system of most European nations, the office of judge is treated as a profession distinct from lawyers. Those who aspire to judgeship must meet rigid qualifications and undergo special training. They usually begin their service as apprentices and are promoted within the judicial hierarchy. This procedure is alien to the United States, where we have opted for what Neubauer describes as "essentially amateurs . . . who have no practical experience or systematic exposure to the judicial world" (1979, p. 168). Judges are chosen from the bar, and there is nothing in law school or in the practice of law that prepares judges to assume their extensive power. A judge may be trained in the rules of evidence and courtroom procedure, but he or she may know little or nothing about criminology, psychology, and the prevailing theories and practices in corrections. Too often, new judges assume their positions with little knowledge of the technicalities of their jobs or the magnitude of their influence on the criminal justice system.

Until recently, few formal requirements—other than those of age, residency, citizenship, and admission to the bar—were prescribed for judicial selection. Candidates with prior experience on the bench do not necessarily have a better chance of appointment or selection than those without such qualifications. For example, since the U.S. Supreme Court was established in 1790, only 40 percent of all nominees to the Court have had prior judicial careers. And the percentage is no higher for the appellate tribunals of most states. Only in the case of the U.S. Courts of Appeal does experience appear to give a candidate a decided advantage; in recent decades, more than 60 percent of the nominees to these courts have had extensive experience on the bench before their appointments.

There are various methods for selecting judges, and each has its own advocates and supporting arguments. The selection procedures used in the United States may be grouped into three general categories: elective, appointive, and appointive with modifications. The method of election prevails in thirty-three states, with nearly equal numbers of partisan (in which the nominee declares a party affiliation) and nonpartisan elections. Appointments are used in the federal judiciary and in somewhat less than one-fourth of the states. The third method of selection, sometimes referred to as the Missouri plan or the nonpartisan court plan, is used in five states—Alaska, Iowa, Kansas, Missouri, and Nebraska. Some of the major features of this method also apply to judicial selections in several other states, including California and Illinois.

Popular election of judicial personnel did not occur in the United States until the rise of Jacksonian democracy shortly before the middle of the nineteenth century. According to those who support this concept, judges should be politically responsible for the conduct of their offices. However, proponents of the appointive system decry the need for judicial candidates to compete with one another for popular favor in partisan, or even nonpartisan, campaigns. They maintain that the average voter is ill equipped to assess the technical fitness and judicial aptitude of the individuals who seek judgeships. Further, they contend that judges who are dependent on popular support for their office incur political obligations that may affect their decisions.

Popular election of state court judges is actually not as predominant as statistics suggest. Numerous vacancies on the bench occur through the death, resignation, or retirement of an incumbent before the expiration of a term. When this occurs, the governor of a state usually has the power to fill the judgeship for the remainder of the term or until the next election. In other words, governors select a substantial number of judges, even in states that have elective systems. Individuals so appointed have a distinct advantage in later elections, because they enter the elections as incumbents.

The modified apppointment plan, developed by the American Bar Association and the American Judicature Society, was first adopted in Missouri in 1940. This plan combines restricted executive selection with popular approval. In Missouri, for example, the governor fills judicial vacancies on the supreme court and on the circuit courts of Jackson County (Kansas City) and St. Louis County (the intermediate appellate tribunals) from lists submitted by nonpartisan nominating commissions. These commissions are composed of gubernatorial appointees, lawyers selected by the state bar, and the presiding judge of one of the appellate courts. The commission in Jackson County, for example, includes two laypersons, two lawyers elected by members of the local bar association, and the presiding judge of the Kansas City Court of Appeals. After newly appointed judges have served on the bench for one year, their names are submitted on ballots to area voters, who determine if the judges should be retained in office. A similar referendum is held every six years thereafter for circuit court judges and every twelve years thereafter for appellate justices.

An examination of the selection process in the federal court system should dispel any illusions about the apolitical character of judicial appointments. When a vacancy occurs on the federal bench, a set procedure is followed. Names of nominees are submitted by senators to the attorney general's office, which serves as a clearing house or screening agency for all appointments to the national judiciary. Informal discussions then take place among members of the Department of Justice, White House staff, senators, and party leaders from the state where the vacancy exists. When the choice is narrowed, the Committee of Federal Judiciary of the American Bar Association is invited to comment on the candidates (this practice was initiated during Eisenhower's administration).

The bar association's committee does not initiate or suggest prospective nominees; it simply makes recommendations on the names submitted by the attorney general. In this capacity, however, the committee exerts its influence by deterring the nomination of individuals it deems unqualified. Simultaneously with the bar committee's review, a full field investigation of the potential nominees is conducted by the FBI. At the conclusion of these activities, the attorney general makes a recommendation to the president. By this time, the acceptability of a candidate to the senators (of the president's party) has been established. Only rarely does a president submit the name of a judicial nominee over the objection of these officials.

Experience has demonstrated the difficulty of excluding politics from the selection process—even under a restrictive appointment method. This was shown in Missouri under the nonpartisan court plan during the plan's first twenty-five years: of the sixty judges appointed during this period, over 70 percent belonged to the same political party as the governor. Charges have been made that governors may attempt to influence the choice of names on the nominee lists through their appointees on the nominating commissions. These allegations have led to proposals to take the appointment of lay members of such commissions out of the governor's hands (Roberts 1965).

To what degree can the selection process be removed from politics? To deny a governor any voice in the composition of the nominating panel would further strengthen the role of the bar associations in the choice of judicial appointees. For example, Hearnes reported in 1965 that over one-half of the members of the Missouri bar believed that the nonpartisan court plan substituted bar politics and gubernatorial politics for the traditional politics of party leaders and political organizations. Few members, however, regarded this development unfavorably, and some suggested removing the element of gubernatorial politics altogether by eliminating the governor's power to appoint part of the nominating panel. If this happened, only bar politics would influence the decision. In the final analysis, any selection method—no matter how it is designed—includes a political decision at some point in the process.

The relationship between the method of selection and the caliber of judges who staff the courts remains more a matter of individual perception than of systematic study. Does the appointive process produce better judges than popular election? Or is the Missouri plan superior to either appointment or election? The subject has been debated for some time. Proponents of executive selection point to the experience of the federal bench, which has traditionally enjoyed a higher reputation for competency than its state counterparts. How much of this relative superiority can be attributed to the mode of selection is not known, however. The greater benefits of federal judgeships—lifetime tenure, better pay, and higher prestige—are probably much more important factors. It can be assumed that the more attractive a position is made because of money, security, and prestige, the more the position will appeal to persons with ability and talent.

Judging the Judges—Dealing with Judicial Misconduct

Clark Mollenhoff, a journalist and Pulitzer Prize winner who spent several years investigating the federal bench, claims that the problems caused by unfit judges amount to a national scandal at present ("Judging the judges" 1979, p. 52). Until October of 1981, when a new system of discipline took effect in the federal courts under an act of Congress, ridding the federal judiciary of unfit judges could only be done by impeachment, a time-consuming and cumbersome procedure. This may help explain why only eight federal judges in our history have been impeached by the House of Representatives and, of these, only four have been convicted by the Senate and removed from office (Mollenhoff and Rushford 1980, p. 39). Following the passage of the new legislation in 1981, 89 grievances were filed in a nine-month period, resulting in corrective action in 11 cases and the retirement of a judge in a 12th case (Gest 1983, p. 42).

A growing number of state judges are being charged with misconduct. Cases range from the California judge who was removed from office after staging a "bargain day" on which those pleading guilty received light sentences, to a Missouri judge who drew a nine-year prison term for conspiring to make illegal drugs (Gest 1983, p. 42). A judge in Ohio was convicted on criminal charges of keeping weapons seized as evidence, seeking sex from female defendants, and attempting to block an investigation of his misconduct. In New York, a judge was removed from the bench after bringing a coffee vendor before the court in handcuffs and bawling him out because he had served "His Honor" a lousy cup of coffee (David and David 1980, p. 105).

Commissions on judicial misconduct have been operating now for about twenty years and can be found in all fifty states and the District of Columbia. They are composed of laypersons, attorneys, and judges, and their mission is to investigate complaints about judicial misconduct on or off the bench. According to Gest (1983), 3,500 complaints were lodged against judges in 1981. During that year, sixteen judges were removed from office; fifty-five were admonished or censured; and seventy judges resigned or retired while under investigation.

It is not surprising that many complaints against judges are made by disgruntled defendants or plaintiffs who are displeased with the decisions made in their cases. About three quarters of these complaints are dismissed, because they are based on judicial rulings rather than on charges of misconduct. For legitimate complaints, however, commission investigators who are, for the most part, lawyers or retired judges, review transcripts and preside over hearings. The commission then either dismisses the charges, issues an informal warning to the judge, or recommends disciplinary action to the state supreme court. Disciplinary matters involving federal judges are dealt with by a panel of peers.

Judges may complain that they are held to a higher standard of conduct than other professionals, but this view is not likely to generate much sympathy. After all, if judges are going to sit in judgment on their fellow citizens, at the very least they should provide a model of intelligence, fairness, and honesty for the rest of us. Thus, if a judge's public behavior discredits the office, people feel entitled to question the fitness of that judge to serve as a member of the judiciary.

Commissions also take actions against judges for medical reasons (alcoholism, for example). When a judge has a drinking problem, a commission may refer him or her to a treatment program rather than recommending removal from office.

Judges who are not alcoholics may do other things on occasion that raise questions about the limits of judicial decorum. Former Los Angeles Municipal Court Judge Noel Cannon painted her chambers pink, kept a pet Chihuahua by her side, and was called the "Dragon Lady." She once threatened to give a traffic officer "a vasectomy with a .38" ("Judging the judges" 1979, p. 49). Brill (1979) describes federal district court judge Irving Ben Cooper, who called Puerto Rican defendants who could not speak English "the slime of the earth" and accused a newly hired bailiff who mistakenly opened a broom-closet door, thinking it led to the judge's chambers, of being assigned to humiliate him because he (the judge) is short (p. 22). The conviction of twenty-four-year-old Eric Michael of New York for robbery, rape, and sodomy was overturned because he had been tried twice for the same crime. According to *Time:*

> The first trial had been terminated by Criminal Judge Arnold G. Fraiman. Why? Because continuing the trial would have interfered with the vacation plans of the judge and some jurors. Judge Fraiman, who had once before ended a trial rather than forgo a holiday, this time offered to postpone his plans, but he did not order the jury to do so; instead, he declared a mistrial ("Judging the judges" 1979, p. 47).

Judge Thomas Wicker, chair of the ethics committee of the National Conference of State Trial Judges, conducted a nationwide survey that indicates that nine out of ten judges across the country believe that judicial commissions protect the rights of the public. Nevertheless, many judges are critical of what they regard as unwarranted intrusions into their personal lives. While acknowledging that their position requires them to conform to more exacting standards than apply to many other professions and careers, they question the kinds of behavior that are labeled misconduct. They maintain that misconduct should be tried directly to what happens on the bench. It was in this spirit that the Montana Supreme Court halted proceedings against a judge, having decided that the judge's wife's sixty unpaid parking tickets had nothing to do with judicial misconduct.

Some judges also complain that they are treated unfairly once misconduct charges are filed against them. Justice Edwin Kassoff of the New York Supreme Court says that judges are not protected by a statute of limitations and do not have adequate opportunities to confront their accusers or present an effective defense. In effect, he says, judges are denied due process.

An especially critical issue is the effect of adverse publicity on a judge's career. Even when a judge is found innocent of misconduct, his or her reputation may already have fallen victim to newspaper and television publicity. In many states and the District of Columbia, misconduct charges are made public either when the judicial commission finds probable cause for misconduct or when the commission makes its recommendations for action to the state supreme court. A remedy for this situation might be to impose penalties for disclosing news about ongoing commission investigations until *after* disciplinary measures have been taken (if, in fact, the commission reaches a decision that misconduct has occurred).

"Courthouse Culture" and the Socialization of Judges

Rosett and Cressey describe the complex of shared values, attitudes, and informal norms of cooperation that make up what they call a "subculture of justice within the courthouse":

> Even in the adversary world of law, men who work together and understand each other eventually develop shared conceptions of what are acceptable,

> right and just ways of dealing with specific kinds of offenses, suspects, and defendants. These conceptions form the bases for understanding, agreements, working arrangements and cooperative attitudes. . . . Over time, these shared patterns of belief develop the coherence of a distinct culture, a style of social expression peculiar to the particular courthouse (1976, pp. 90–91).

Newcomers to the bench undergo a process of on-the-job learning that transforms them into jurists. During this process, judges are exposed to and absorb various aspects of the "courthouse culture" that pertain to organizational goals, preferred means for achieving these goals, role responsibilities, required behavior, and rules for maintaining the court as an organization (Schein 1968).

Alpert (1981) has identified five stages in the occupational socialization of trial court judges: professional socialization, initiation, resolution, establishment, and commitment. Professional socialization is a stage that occurs prior to judicial selection. This period covers both formal legal training in law school and informal training that occurs in legal practice. It also includes experience in public office (e.g., as a prosecutor or city attorney) that may help prepare an individual for the bench. Initiation is described by Alpert as a period of bewilderment and confidence building. The newcomer learns how to behave in court, manage the docket, make proper rulings, and maintain order in trials and hearings. Resolution, which occurs in about years one through four in judicial experience, completes the transformation of the newcomer from advocate to arbiter. The judge reaches a level of comfort in which he or she begins to handle the isolation and the external pressures endemic to the job.

Establishment follows resolution and covers a period of approximately four years. During this time, many judges are susceptible to midcareer crises, as personal and family needs conflict with organizational demands. Judges face the decision of whether to remain on the bench or to seek more lucrative opportunities in nonjudicial pursuits. It is a period of introspection and rumination about the future. Commitment, the final stage in the socialization process, is marked by a deep-seated identification with the court, an increase in personal satisfaction, and a growing sense of dedication to a judicial career.

Carp and Wheeler (1972) note that a judge's colleagues are the foremost training agents in the process of judicial socialization. They accomplish this task through formal meetings and seminars and by informal exchanges during the work day. A second major source of information is attorneys who appear in the courtrooms and persons on the judge's staff: law clerks, secretaries, court administrators, and bailiffs. These people supply the judge with critical advice on procedural and administrative matters (Blumberg 1967). But in the end, as Neubauer (1979) concludes, the judicial socialization process is largely a matter of self-education in which judges spend a lot of time reading in law libraries, seeking out the counsel of knowledgeable people, and learning by doing.

One of the most remarkable changes in the socialization of judgeships has been the introduction of women and minorities to the bench. What previously had been a white-male-dominated institution and consequently an institution dominated by male values and male ways of doing things, particularly those of white males, is undergoing profound changes. Women and minorities have been on the bench for such a relatively short period of time that their impact on the socialization of judges needs to be explored further.

Job Stress and the Judiciary

In chapter 6, we discussed how job stress and anxiety affect the job performance and personal lives of police officers and administrators. In much the same way, occupational and social stresses result from the pressures and conflicts experienced by members of the judiciary.

One source of job stress for judges is the cases they encounter. For example, consider judges who are confronted regularly with jury trials involving gruesome accounts of violent crimes. The judges must try to act impartially, even though they are bombarded with facts that would upset the average person. Judges have direct, meaningful, and unending daily contact with crisis situations that they cannot escape as long as they remain in their jobs.

Another source of job stress for judges is public image. The public traditionally views judges as people equipped to handle situations and make consequential decisions swiftly and correctly. Judges are expected to move from one emotionally charged situation to the next, while remaining aloof and detached. They are expected to be fair and impartial, regardless of the choices they must make. They must have the ability to use emotional control and shut off or suppress emotional responses to provocative situations. To meet these demands, a judge may "keep too tight a rein on his emotions, and over a period of time isolate his feelings or become uncomfortable in expressing them. This can be analogized to a pressure cooker that has its top spout tightened down so that the steam which builds up cannot escape. Eventually with the constant buildup of steam the pressure cooker will explode" (Stratton 1978, pp. 60–61).

People who decide to seek a career as a judge are sometimes attracted by the rewards of independence; thus, they often refuse to admit their dependence upon others, because this dependence is inconsistent with their self-concept. Unless they stay within the confines of their role, they may have feelings of uncertainty about their status as perceived by others. Thus, the job can be a lonely one. This same point has been made about executives with regard to leadership: "I have watched executives curse in desperation the forces which, in moments, vitiated years of their efforts. I have listened to them protest the loneliness of their sometimes opulent offices, the distance from old friends. I have seen them cry out their pent-up fury . . . and disguise their tears with alcohol" (Levinson 1970, p. 127).

Political pressures are another source of stress for the judiciary. Anthony Lewis (1978) describes a regrettable situation that occurred during a Supreme Court election in California in which Judge Rose Bird, who was up for reelection, became the target of an ugly political campaign.[3] Judge Bird's decision to reverse an appellate court decision and provide the possible release of a defendant accused of a brutal rape was based on a point of law, rather than on her personal feelings about the crime. She could not use her repugnance toward the crime and the criminal as a basis for rewriting the statutes—and political conservatives agreed with her. However, unfair publicity and slanted editorializing put the election in jeopardy. The result was a heavily ideological campaign that had a broader target than a single judge: the campaign was designed to exert pressure on all the judges in the state to conform with reactionary views on matters involving criminal law. In 1987 Judge Bird was removed from office by a recall election.

Proposals for sentencing reform have often called for judges to provide reasons in writing for decisions made in difficult, complex, or unusual cases. Judges are pressured to document the reasons for particular sentences because of the "increase in appellate review and reversal, the heightened criticism by the press and the public, and consequent diminution of the judiciary's role" (Robin 1975, p. 201). Robin feels that this pressure is intrinsically threatening and stress producing, because discretion contributes significantly to the self-concept and occupational satisfaction of judges. Further, judges' rejection of sentencing accountability "is rooted in the recognizably human and pervasive aversion to being criticized, countermanded, and sanctioned" (ibid., p. 204). "Viewed publicly, every formalized judicial statement accompanying sentencing is perceived as a justification of action taken and thus invites evaluation and criticism from all sources" (ibid., p. 205).

Most of the stress encountered in an occupation detracts from job satisfaction. However, one study indicates that there are four types of occupational stress that may actually *increase* job satisfaction (Burke 1976). Three of these—too much responsibility, too heavy a work load, and feelings of not being fully qualified—are associated with a demanding, challenging job and the high organizational expectations of the employee. The implication is that a job that can be enlarged or enriched may lead to increased satisfaction, but also to an increase in certain pressures. The fourth occupational stress that Burke found positively related to job satisfaction involves decisions that affect the lives of others. Because all four of these stress factors apply to the judiciary, it may be assumed that not all stresses produce negative effects and that some may lead to greater job satisfaction.

Perhaps the most direct way to understand the stress and anxiety judges experience is to follow a judge through a typical day in court. Judge Lois G. Forer provides such an opportunity in an article entitled "View from the Bench: A Judge's Day" (1975). She allows a glimpse of a routine day through her eyes and the frustrations and anxieties so typical in the life of a trial court judge.

A long day on the bench begins at 9:30 in the morning, and frustrations mount as overloaded public defenders arrive late, witnesses cannot be found, and defendants are forgotten at the jail rather than being brought to court when they are needed. Cases have to be continued, and judges are asked to decide on bail for men and women they cannot see or talk to and who the public defender knows nothing about. They are asked to sentence people using only two alternatives: prison or the streets. What is often needed instead is a drug program or a hospital plan, but these alternatives are seldom available. Judges must sit through five-hour sanity hearings and decide which team of psychiatrists is correct about a defendant. They are frustrated by jail overcrowding, but they face harsh public and self-criticism if they release anyone who commits another crime. They encounter seemingly unsolvable cases in which there are simply no resources to provide for the needs of defendants.

Judges experience the computerization of human beings and the trappings of the bureaucracy when a defendant is "lost in the system" or "forgotten" in a jail for five months without ever appearing before a judge. They must accept negotiated guilty pleas from defendants who have only talked with their court-appointed attorney for five minutes; they wonder if such defendants would have been convicted had they gone to trial. And then there's the "batting average": "Woe betide those who fail to keep pace in getting rid of cases" (Forer 1975, p. 39). Feeling the frustration of being bound by the iron laws of economics, without knowing how to replace the present system, Judge Forer sums up her feelings this way:

> At the end of a day in which as a judge I have taken actions affecting for good or ill the lives of perhaps 15 or 20 litigants and their families, I am drained. I walk out of the stale-smelling, dusty courtroom into the fresh sunshine of a late spring day and feel as if I were released from prison. I breathe the soft air, but in my nostrils is the stench of the stifling cell blocks and detention rooms. While I sip my cool drink in the quiet of my garden, I cannot forget the prisoners, with their dry bologna sandwiches and only a drink of water provided at the pleasure of the hot and harried guard (ibid.).

The judge, then, is seen "not as a cold fish but as a warm-blooded mammal, not as a rational calculator always ready to work out the best solution but as a reluctant decision maker—beset by conflicts, doubts, and worry, struggling with incongruous longings, antipathies, and loyalties, and seeking relief by procrastinating, rationalizing, and/or denying responsibility for his own choices" (Janis and Mann 1977, p. 15).

COURT ADMINISTRATIVE PERSONNEL

The complex and demanding business of the courts could not be conducted without the administrative services performed by the *bailiff,* the *court reporter,* and the *court clerk*. And these criminal justice professionals have been joined in recent years by a specialist who bears the title *court administrator*. In this section, we briefly examine the tasks, duties, and responsibilities of each of these important officers of the court.

The Bailiff

The bailiff is charged with the responsibility of maintaining the order, security, and decorum of the court. In a large metropolitan court that meets daily, the bailiff is generally a permanent employee. In smaller or rural communities, a bailiff may be appointed by a judge to serve only for the duration of a trial. In most rural areas the bailiff is normally a sheriff.

The duties of the bailiff vary. As sergeant-at-arms within the courtroom, he or she keeps watch over defendants and suppresses disorderly behavior among spectators. He or she summons witnesses when they are called to testify and maintains the legal proprieties pertaining to the actions of jurors and witnesses. When the jury is sequestered on the order of the judge, the bailiff accompanies the jurors and guards to prevent violations of trial secrecy—such as making unauthorized phone calls, reading an unedited newspaper, or listening to accounts of the trial on the radio or television. It is also the bailiff's job to see that the jury is suitably housed and fed during a trial.

The Court Reporter

Court reporters take down a verbatim account of the proceedings in all cases conducted within a court of record. Most of these highly proficient reporters use a stenotype recorder—a mechanical device that types shorthand symbols. At the close of each day in court, or at the conclusion of the entire trial, the reporter's notes are transcribed. In most courts, in addition to salary, the court reporter is paid by the page for the preparation of the record. Consequently, as Chamelin, Fox, and Whisenand observe, "it is not rare to find triple spaced, wide margined transcripts" (1979, p. 278).

The Court Clerk

The court clerk keeps all the records of the court. In federal or appellate courts, court clerks are appointed; in lower courts, they are elected. In many areas, the duties of county clerk and court clerk are combined into a single office.

The court clerk has the authority to handle nearly all of the paperwork that accompanies a judicial proceeding. Returns of arrest and search warrants, indictments, informations, all pleadings filed by the prosecutor and defense counsel, instructions to the jury, verdicts, and sentences are filed by the clerk or are transcribed into the permanent court record. Subpoenas for witnesses, notices regarding jury service, and records of all cases filed, dismissed, tried, and appealed are the responsibility of the court clerk.

The task of the court clerk is made unnecessarily arduous and complex by the fact that judicial record keeping is a bewildering hodgepodge of diverse procedures. Despite continuing efforts by professional organizations of court clerks, there is little in the way of uniformity or standardization. It is not unusual to find that a particular criminal justice agency (e.g., a correctional facility) receives more than a dozen different forms of the same document from the various courts within a state, at an annual cost to the taxpayers of thousands of dollars.

The Court Administrator

The new and challenging position of court administrator was mandated at the federal level by the Ninety-first Congress. In H.R. 17906, the court administrator is assigned duties that include exercising administrative control over all nonjudicial activities of the court of appeals in the circuit to which the administrator is appointed; formulating and managing a system of personnel administration; preparing the budget; maintaining a modern accounting system; collecting, compiling, and analyzing statistical data for reports; and other activities relating to the business and administration of the courts. The court administrator—a skilled professional trained in systems analysis, budgeting procedures, the use of computers, and modern techniques of office management and personnel administration—may well prove to be the best hope for bringing efficiency and order to the overburdened courts.

The function of court administrators is certainly not to usurp the judge's authority. Instead, this key court personnel member's task is to develop the court's organizational structures so that it may be more effective. Although the judge remains the policymaker of the court, he or she still relies on the court administrator to assist in the judicial role to a degree that satisfies the judge. The administrator's job is to recommend and implement innovative procedures of executing policy and to help guide the court along appropriate avenues to improve the administration of justice. Despite the obvious advantages of employing court administrators as the overall court managers, some courts continue to refuse to respond to the need for well-centralized administration.

Computers have become an important tool in the administration and management of modern courts. The computer can rapidly retrieve the necessary data that can be used for several court functions. Many courts are employing computer technologies in such areas as videotaped testimonies, new court reporting devices, the installation of computer-based information systems, and the use of data processing systems for the court's docket and jury management. In 1968 only ten states had state-level automated information systems; today all states employ such systems for at least one element in the field. The following areas are likely to undergo expanded computerization in the future: monitoring the schedule of cases; preparing documents; case indexing; maintaining case histories and statistical reporting; notifying witnesses, attorneys, and others of required appearances; and issuing summons.

SUMMARY

The American judicial system is extremely complex. It is more accurate, in fact, to speak of judicial *systems,* because there are courts at the federal, state, county, and municipal levels of jurisdiction. The state operates trial courts, intermediate appellate courts, and courts of last resort (i.e., the highest tribunals to which cases can be appealed). This pattern is repeated at the federal level. Federal appellate courts, however, can rule on state cases, and the U.S. Supreme Court is the court of last resort for all cases involving a constitutional principle that are decided in the United States.

Direct supervision of the courts is the responsibility of the judiciary. Judges are either appointed or elected. As public officials, they are involved in political issues and controversies that are an inseparable feature of public life. Coming from a variety of backgrounds and experiences, newcomers to the bench undergo a process of learning that gradually accommodates them to the role of judge. The human side of judging is nowhere more clearly revealed than in the job-related stresses that affect members of the judiciary.

Other members of the judicial staff include the bailiff, court clerk, court reporter, and court administrator. These members of the judicial team provide expert assistance and counsel, without which the judicial process would barely function. The court administrator, in particular, is beginning to emerge as a focal figure in easing the administrative and management burdens of the judge.

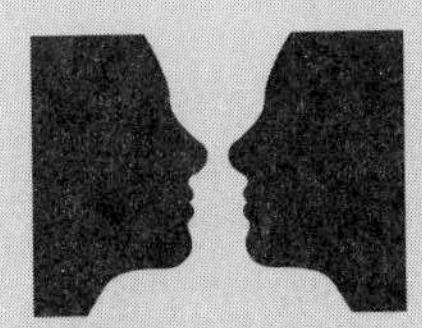

ISSUE PAPER

WOULD YOU SETTLE FOR A ROBOT ON THE BENCH?

Introduction

Amidst all the discussions on the problems and shortcomings of our judicial system there is an area that has not yet received the attention that it may deserve. Calendar congestion, a shortage of judges and courtrooms and many other adverse conditions under which our judicial system operates may indicate a need to examine how, and to what extent, computer technology might help solve some of the problems or at least prevent them from getting worse. Such an examination would need to answer affirmatively a fundamental question: can a computer accomplish the process of judicial reasoning now done by the judicial system—chiefly, the judges aided by their assistants—as it resolves the cases before it? To answer that question, we need to understand the nature of the process our judges employ in deciding what the law is in a particular case.

Sixty-three years ago, a judge of the Court of Appeals of New York State delivered a series of lectures at Yale University on the conscious and unconscious process by which a judge decides a case. The judge was Benjamin N. Cardozo who became chief judge of that Court and later Associate Justice of the Supreme Court of the United States.

The Judicial Process

As Judge Cardozo explained, the primary sources of the law are constitutions and statutes; if in conflict, constitutions override statutes and statutes consistent with the constitution (federal or state) override the law of judges. When both constitutions and statutes are silent, then judges must look to the common law for the rule that fits the case. In this determination the court compares the current case with case precedents and if the current case is the same as a precedent, that determines the matter (unless, of course, the judge overrules precedent or distinguishes the case). But in most cases the precedent is not exactly to the point, and then the judge must fashion the law of the case.

This is where the real work of the court begins. Certain principles of selection are available to the court—none more important than the principle which says nothing is unchangeable; nothing is absolute; everything is fluid and changeable. The court must extract from precedents the underlying principle of such precedents, then determine the path or direction along which the principle is to move and develop. This involves stripping cases of all extraneous, nonessential and accidental facts and features.

In determining the direction or path along which the principle is to move and develop, the court uses one or more of four lines of inquiry: logical progression (the rule of analogy or the method of philosophy); historical development (the method of evolution); customs of the community (method of tradition); and justice, morals and social welfare, the mores of the day (method of sociology).

Explaining each of these paths, Justice Cardozo defines logical progression as the derivation of a consequence from a rule or principle or precedent which contains implicitly within itself the germ of the conclusion. Historical development, the method of evolution, has a tendency to confine precedent within the limits of its history. Concepts relating to corporate personality and real property are examples. Custom, or the method of tradition, is a path not designed to create new rules but to establish tests and standards as to how established rules are to be applied. This is accomplished, among other ways, by consulting usages in a trade or profession, customary morality, and mores of the times. Finally, social justice, or the method of sociology, considers the welfare of society, public policy or the good of the collective body. Examples are the immunities guaranteed by the Constitution; for example, no one shall be deprived of liberty without due process of law.

In making these analyses and comparisons judges must be objective; they may not follow their own ideas of reason and justice, but rather they must adopt those of the community they serve.

In some of these activities judges are called upon to act as legislators, but when so called upon their only function is to fill the gaps in the statutes left by the legislators. In doing so they may use the same yard stick as the legislators use, namely, fitness to achieve an end based on the mores of the community.

In novel situations the judges are called upon to reach decisions regarding what rules may apply, as between many rules abstracted from the precedents, which were determined by following the paths of analogy, convenience, fitness and justice. Which rule or rules will ultimately control will depend on the judge's experience, his study and research and upon his mental processes of reflection, comparison and determination—in a word, from life itself. Such law as results from this process is not found but made. And, in a word, while adhering to precedent and in reaching a determination regarding the application of appropriate rules, the judge must balance all the forces which constitute his individual character: his philosophy and logic; the way he applies analogies, history and customs; his sense of right and justice; and all his other characteristics. He adds a little here, takes something away there and finally determines as best and wisely as he can, where to go—what path to go down and how far. Subconscious forces, likes and dislikes, predilections and prejudices, the complex of instincts, emotions, habits and convictions, all of which make up the person—all are involved in the judicial process. In a word, the judicial process is one of search and comparison and little else.

Computers as a Substitute for the Legal Reasoning Process

With the understanding of how the legal reasoning process is achieved, we need now to consider whether computers are able to accomplish the same objectives in a way acceptable to bench and bar. We know computers are in daily use in many large law offices and are rendering valuable services in doing routine office chores—payroll, time allocation and billings, accounts receivable and payable and many other standard office tasks which busy law firms share in common with all businesses. Further, firms specializing in areas of the law requiring much paperwork of a repetitive nature—real estate, trusts, municipal bonds and securities, admiralty and others—have benefited enormously from the use of word processors. But our question relates to the strictly legal functions which characterize law firms and require legally trained minds to research the law and develop the legal theories upon which the case will be made. How are computers doing in this area?[1] Thus far the attempts made have necessarily been directed to a specific area of the law.[2]

James A. Sprowl, in "Automating the Legal Reasoning Process: A Computer that Uses Regulations and Statutes to Draft Legal Documents," describes a computer operation designed to automatically produce specific legal documents such as a will or trust document.[3] He also indicates other areas of specialization which can be programmed into computers and anticipates further use of computers by attorneys as they become familiar with their possibilities and comfortable with their use. One should not be mislead by the titles to the current articles on computer application to legal reasoning—none which indicate that they do in fact simulate the human process of legal reasoning, mean exactly that. Such language is used merely to indicate something more than word processing.

How should we judge attempts to substitute a computer for the legal reasoning heretofore done by attorneys? Surely they cannot be dismissed out of hand. They do the job they were designed to do. But can a computer really do legal research? Mark Morrise, in *Emerging Computer-Assisted Legal Analysis Systems,* offers a penetrating analysis of the theory and practical uses of these systems. In sum, no computer system thus far developed can reason in the same way that the human mind reasons; it can only act mechanically or electronically on the data put into it and reach conclusions based on that data.

The process of legal reasoning is not an easy concept to translate to computer language. It can be described and defined, but the scope of human intelligence in comparing, analyzing, contrasting statutes, decisions, arguments and principles, in order to come up with the best, strongest, most convincing argument (often a new approach or a unique application or even a novel viewpoint for which authority can be found only by analogy, contrast or otherwise) is so unlimited that a mechanical or electronic process is not ever likely to be found which will adequately substitute for a well-trained, knowledgeable, experienced and able legal mind.

The law book publishers have made considerable progress in offering services that speed up legal research. Typical is West Publishing Company's *Westlaw* service. Its memory base is broad and it operates on a "key-word" system with which lawyers are familiar. However, it required a legal mind to query it. Nor is it held out as anything more than a very useful tool for legal research.

Thus to date we have not seen anything of a mechanical or electrical composition that can begin to replace a trained legal mind, whether at the bar or on the bench. When we consider the marvelous advances that we have experienced in our own time in space exploration, in medicine and in all the sciences, one would be bold to say that it cannot be done. Still from a practical viewpoint, it is a monumental job when we realize that the human body and mind is the most complex mechanism ever created—a self-reproducing organism in which some fifteen billion nerve tracks coordinate one thousand trillion cells, each of which performs a specific function required for the general good of the whole person, who is himself a unique personality, unlike any other of the billions of people who inhabit the Earth. If it is true, as we are told, that computer geniuses thrive on challenges, then the development of a computer that will simulate human legal reasoning should present the ultimate challenge to them. And they may well rise to the challenge. It used to be said of the first generation of computers that the difficult is done immediately; the impossible takes a little longer. Perhaps that will apply also to computerized legal reasoning.

Conclusions

While the law is an ever-changing concept, the nature of the judicial process has remained essentially the same from the earliest days of the common law. Lawyers and judges and all who labor in the judicial system have various philosophies of life, law and morality and all those principles enter into and become part of their own judicial process and affect their approach to the solution of the matters before them for determination. And from all that welter of contrary and sometimes conflicting forces there emerge solutions to the problems our litigious society present. Not everyone is happy with all of them. That is to be expected. But the system works and while at times we need to tinker with it, on the whole it has served us well. The author, for one is not yet ready to settle for a robot on the bench.

From *New York State Bar Journal,* January 1985, pp. 22–26. Reprinted with permission.

Notes

1. Bradford W. Hildebrant, *Impact of Computers in Law Firm of Future, New York Law Journal* (January 11, 1983): 4, C1.
2. *American Bar Association Journal* 66 (1983); *New York Law Journal* (February 15, 1983): 4, C1.
3. 1 *American Bar Foundation Research Journal* 3 (1979).

DISCUSSION AND REVIEW

1. What distinguishes a court of record from a court of limited jurisdiction?
2. Why are state supreme courts sometimes called courts of last resort?
3. What are the principal areas of jurisdiction of the U.S. Supreme Court? How does the Court obtain its cases?
4. In which instances must the Supreme Court grant jurisdiction?
5. What are the areas of jurisdiction of the U.S. District Courts? What kinds of cases reach the U.S. Courts of Appeal?
6. Discuss parallels in the structure and operations of the federal and state judicial systems.

7. What are some of the characteristics of lower courts that earn these courts the reputation of "the weakest link in the administration of justice"?
8. What were some of the major problems in the judicial selection process that the Missouri plan sought to overcome?
9. What are the duties and functions of a trial judge?
10. Describe the duties and responsibilities of the bailiff, the court clerk, and the court administrator.
11. Discuss some of the principal sources of job-related stress that judges encounter.
12. Is it possible to separate effectively the trivial and the important kinds of judicial behavior that lead to charges of judicial misconduct? What, in your opinion, are some types of misconduct that would justify removing a judge from the bench?

■ GLOSSARY

Appellate court A court that reviews cases that have been tried in a trial court. Except in special cases in which original jurisdiction is conferred, an *appellate court* is not a trial court or court of first instance.

Bailiff An officer of the court whose principal duty is to maintain the security and decorum of the court. He or she is responsible for keeping an eye on defendants delivered to the court and for assuring the legality of actions involving witnesses and jurors. He or she summons witnesses when it is their turn to testify, and sees that witnesses and jurors do not discuss cases when they are not supposed to. The bailiff is also responsible for maintaining the secrecy of jury deliberations and for arranging food and lodging for the jury.

Certiorari Latin for "to be informed of, to be made certain in regard to." *Certiorari* is a writ of review or inquiry directed by a superior court to an inferior court, asking that the record of the case be sent up for review. This method of obtaining a review of a case is used by the U.S. Supreme Court.

Court of first instance A court to which a case must originally be brought; usually a trial court.

Court of general jurisdiction The largest jurisdiction a court of first instance can have in a given political unit (i.e., state, federal, district, circuit, county).

Court of intermediate appeal A court of appeals established in several states to lessen the work load of the highest reviewing tribunal. Ultimate review can still be held in the highest court by that court's permission or, in limited cases, as a matter of right.

Court of last resort A court from which there is no appeal to a higher court in the same jurisdiction.

En banc decision Judicial decision rendered by the whole court with all members sitting as a body.

Habeas corpus A post-conviction remedy used by inmates tried and sentenced in state court and confined in state correctional facilities. The petition alleges that his or her confinement violates some aspect of the U.S. Constitution or federal statutes.

Inferior court In the federal system, all courts created under Article III, section 1 of the U.S. Constitution, except the U.S. Supreme Court; in the state systems, all courts of limited original jurisdiction.

Jurisdiction The court in which the prosecution is pending must be vested by its own standards with the power to punish and try the accused for the offense involved.

Stare decisis Latin for "let the decision stand." A doctrine holding that the courts will abide by the rulings of prior court decisions when dealing with cases in which the facts are substantially unchanged.

REFERENCES

Alpert, L. "Learning about Trial Judging: The Socialization of State Trial Judges." In *Courts and Judges,* edited by J. A. Cramer. Beverly Hills, Calif.: Sage, 1981.

Banks, L. "The Crisis in the Courts." *Fortune* 64 (1961): 186–89.

Blumberg, A. *Criminal Justice.* Chicago, Ill.: Quadrangle, 1967.

Brill, S. "Benching Bad Judges: Should It Be Easier Than It Is To Remove Federal Judges?" *Esquire,* 10 April 1979, pp. 20–21.

Burke, R. J. "Occupational Stresses and Job Satisfaction." *Journal of Social Psychology* 100 (1976): 235–44.

Carp, R., and Wheeler, R. "Sink or Swim—Socialization of a Federal District Judge." *Journal of Public Law* 21 (1972): 359–93.

Chamelin, N. C.; Fox, V. B.; and Whisenand, P. M. *Introduction to Criminal Justice.* Englewood Cliffs, N.J.: Prentice-Hall, 1979.

Cohen, M. R. *Law and Social Order.* New York: Harcourt Brace, 1933.

David, L., and David, I. "The Crime of America's Justice." *Good Housekeeping* (August 1980): 105, 191–3.

Forer, L. G. "View from the Bench: A Judge's Day." *The Washington Monthly* (February 1975): 33–39.

Gest, T. "Crackdown on Judges Who Go Astray." *U.S. News and World Report,* 28 February 1983, p. 42.

Hearnes, W. E. "Twenty-Five Years under the Missouri Plan." *Journal of the American Judicature Society* 49 (1965): 100–104.

Institute of Judicial Administration. *A Guide to Court Systems.* New York: Institute of Judicial Administration, 1971.

Janis, I. L., and Mann, L. *Decision Making.* New York: Free Press, 1977.

"Judging the judges." *Time,* 20 August 1979, pp. 48–55.

Kerper, H. B. *Introduction to the Criminal Justice System.* St. Paul, Minn.: West, 1972.

Klein, F. F. *Federal and State Court Systems—A Guide.* Cambridge, Mass.: Ballinger, 1977.

Law Enforcement Assistance Administration. *National Survey of Court Organization, 1971: Preliminary Report.* Washington, D.C.: U.S. Government Printing Office, 1972.

Levinson, H. *Executive Stress.* New York: Harper & Row, 1970.

Lewis, A. "Curious Things a Campaign Brings . . . Including Virulence in California." *St. Petersburg Times,* 31 October 1978, p. 6D.
Miller, A. G. "On the Need for 'Impact Analysis' of Supreme Court Decisions." *Georgetown Law Review* 53 (1965): 365–401.
Mollenhoff, C., and Rushford, G. "Judges who should not judge." *Readers Digest* (February 1980): 39–47.
Neubauer, D. *America's Courts and the Criminal Justice System.* North Scituate, Mass.: Duxbury, 1979.
Peltason, W. J. *Federal Courts in the Political Process.* New York: Random House, 1955.
Posner, R. A. *The Federal Courts, Crises and Reform.* Cambridge, Mass.: Harvard University Press, 1985.
President's Commission on Law Enforcement and Administration of Justice. *Task Force Report: The Courts.* Washington, D.C.: U.S. Government Printing Office, 1967.
Roberts, L. E. "Twenty-Five Years under the Missouri Plan." *Journal of the American Judicature Society* 49 (1965): 92–97.
Robin, G. D. "Judicial Resistance to Sentencing Accountability." *Crime and Delinquency* 21 (1975): 201–12.
Rosett, A. I., and Cressey, D. R. *Justice by Consent: Plea Bargains in the American Courthouse.* Philadelphia, Pa.: Lippincott, 1976.
Schein, E. H. "Organizational Socialization and the Profession of Management." *Industrial Management Review* 9 (1968): 1–16.
Shubert, G. "The 1960 Term of the Supreme Court: A Psychological Analysis." *American Political Science Review* 56 (1962): 90–107.
Stratton, J. G. "Police Stress—An Overview." *Police Chief* (April 1978): 38.
Ulman, J. *The Judge Takes the Stand.* New York: Alfred Knopf, 1933.

■ CASES

Douglas v. *California* 372 U.S. 353, 83 S.Ct. 814, 9 L.Ed.2d 811 (1963).
Ross v. *Moffitt* 417 U.S. 600, 94 S.Ct. 2437, 41 L.Ed.2d 341 (1974).

■ NOTES

1. The lack of enthusiasm was understandable. Supreme Court justices in Washington's administration were required to hear cases in widely scattered and remote locations. To reach these places, they had to endure exhausting trips on horseback and the culinary horrors of wilderness inns and taverns.
2. Federal courts other than the U.S. Supreme Court are often referred to collectively as "lower federal courts." U.S. District Courts are included in this category.
3. A detailed account of Judge Bird's ordeal is given in Preble Stoltz, *Judging Judges: The Investigation of Rose Bird and the California Supreme Court.* (New York: Free Press, 1981). Despite the biased campaign, Judge Bird retained her position on the bench, but later (1987) she was removed by a recall election.

CHAPTER

11

The Criminal Trial

CHAPTER OUTLINE:

The importance of the criminal trial in the criminal justice system has been identified by Kaplan, who refers to the trial as the "balance wheel of the entire process" (1973, p. 337):

> Although . . . relatively few cases are disposed of after full trial, it is the threat of exclusion of evidence at trial that is the basis of the exclusionary rule's effort to control the police; it is the projected result of a trial which influences the exercise of the prosecutorial discretion and it is the chance of success at trial which determines the bargaining positions of the lawyers attempting to dispose of the case through negotiations for a guilty plea (ibid.).

Frank (1949), referring to the adversary nature of American criminal jurisprudence, calls the jury trial a "sublimated brawl" (p. 7). Smith and Pollack seriously question the generality and validity of the public image of the courtroom as a place where "truth is discovered through . . . trial by combat between two equally armed lawyer-gladiators, with the struggle presided over by the judge (as repository of the wisdom of the community)" (1972, p. 137). Despite criticism, however, the adversary model of courtroom procedure is one of the most cherished legacies of English common law and a symbol of the freedoms guaranteed to American citizens under the U.S. Constitution.

The adversary proceeding is the heart of a criminal trial. This is a formal process conducted in an orderly and specific fashion according to the rules of criminal evidence, the Constitution, and the criminal law. In the adversary process, both the prosecution and the defense follow specific requirements in order to argue the merits of their cases in the most favorable light and in the most persuasive manner before the jury. While it cannot be denied that drama is inherent in adversarial proceedings, the jury trial has proven—over centuries of evolution to its present form—to be a reliable means of uncovering the truth. It accomplishes this by following a formal set of rules for presenting evidence, rules that seek to deny advantage to either the prosecution or the defense. Much of what laypersons might regard as a fussy preoccupation with procedural details or interpretations of legal precedent is, in fact, the expression of a painstaking effort to eliminate bias.

RULES OF EVIDENCE

Rules of evidence govern the presentation of evidence at a trial in much the same way that the rules of a game govern the conduct of the players. According to this analogy, the judge acts as impartial referee or umpire. Evidence consists of legal proofs presented to the court in the form of witnesses, records, documents, objects, and other means, for the purpose of influencing the opinions of the judge or jury toward the case of the prosecution or the defense. The four kinds of evidence are:

1. *Real evidence.* Real evidence refers to objects of any kind (weapons, clothing, fingerprints, and so on). Real evidence must be the original evidence, the original objects. Reasonable facsimiles such as photographs, reproductions, or duplicates that are necessitated by practical considerations may also be introduced as real evidence.
2. *Testimony.* Testimonial evidence is the statements of competent, sworn witnesses. All real evidence must be accompanied by testimonial evidence.

3. *Direct evidence.* **Direct evidence** refers to the observations of eyewitnesses.
4. *Circumstantial evidence.* **Circumstantial evidence** involves any information that tends to prove or disprove a point at issue. Circumstantial evidence proves a subsidiary fact from which the existence of the ultimate fact in the criminal trial—the guilt or innocence of the accused—may be inferred.

To be accepted by the court, evidence must be relevant, competent, and material. Relevant evidence is evidence that directly pertains to the issue in question. That is, evidence is relevant not only when it tends to prove or disprove a fact in issue, but also when it establishes facts from which further inferences can be drawn. As Kerper points out,

> . . . if the defendant is charged with murder, and the issue is his ability to commit the offense, his opportunity to commit the offense, and his intention to commit the offense, are all relevant evidence. His fingerprints on the murder weapon, his sudden wealth after the deceased was robbed, the threats he made against the deceased, his attempt to flee or commit suicide, are also relevant evidence, as the proof of these facts would tend to prove the guilt of the defendant. Lawyers often speak of the "chain of evidence," which refers to the fact that evidence tends to develop bit by bit with one piece of evidence supporting and tending to prove another (1972, pp. 306–7).

Relevancy is determined by contrast with the concept of *materiality of evidence.* **Material evidence** is evidence that relates to the crime charged or has a legitimate and effective bearing on the decision of the case (22A C.J.S. § 637., 1961). Evidence is sometimes held to be inadmissible because it does not tend to prove the specific issue (i.e., is immaterial). Evidence may be logically relevant but not necessarily material. For example, evidence that a defendant purchased a .38 caliber revolver and ammunition shows that he possessed a weapon. But if the defendant is accused of burglary, not robbery, evidence that he owns a gun is not material to this trial. The trial judge possesses considerable latitude in the determination of materiality of evidence, and doubts should be resolved in favor of admission of evidence unless some definite rule makes it impossible (22A C.J.S. § 637, 1961).

Competent evidence is evidence supplied by a competent witness. Very young children, mental retardates, and persons classified as mentally disturbed may be considered incompetent witnesses by the court. Competence, however, is a complex and controversial issue. Just how old must children be before they can distinguish between right and wrong? Before they are able to understand the meaning of what they have seen or heard? If a witness has been institutionalized or treated for mental illness, is this incontrovertible proof that he or she is incapable of giving reliable and competent testimony on a specific question?

Competency is no guarantee that the evidence will carry *weight* with the jury. Although a convicted felon may be a competent witness, the mere fact of his or her conviction may discredit the testimony. Similarly, a wife's testimony on behalf of her husband may be competent—but worthless in terms of influencing a juror's opinion. At any rate, *competency* of evidence is a matter for the judge to decide; the weight of the evidence is a matter for the jury.

Competency also concerns the constitutionality of the admissibility of certain evidence. For example, evidence that is gathered in violation of the accused's rights against unreasonable search and seizure, the right to counsel, or the privilege against self-incrimination is incompetent evidence. Furthermore, evidence is incompetent when it is privileged as the next section explains. Evidence based on hearsay is also considered incompetent evidence.

Privileged and Confidential Communications

The distinction between privileged communications and confidential communications is often confused by laypersons. *Privileged communications* are those protected by law (e.g., those that occur between attorney and client or between priest and penitent). The person receiving the communication cannot be compelled to divulge the contents of the communication unless the person making the statement waives the legal right to secrecy. Communications between husband and wife are also privileged. In some states, however, a person may be permitted to testify *for* his or her spouse.

Privileged statements also are ones that occur, in certain cases, between police informers and police, physicians and psychotherapists and their patients, and newspaper reporters and their anonymous sources. *Confidentiality* refers to an ethical obligation on the part of a professional person to safeguard the privacy of communications made by a client within the context of the professional relationship. But confidential communications have no legal protection in the courts. A marriage counselor, for example, is bound by the ethics of the professional relationship to maintain the confidentiality of statements made by the client. Nevertheless, such statements do not constitute privileged communications, and a counselor could be ordered to reveal the statements or risk a citation for contempt of court.

Opinion and Expert Testimony

A cardinal rule of evidence restricts lay (nonexpert) witnesses to testimony based on the direct evidence; their opinions, speculations, or conclusions are not valid. Exceptions to this rule cover situations in which an opinion can be supported by observation of facts that fall within the realm of common experience. Thus, a witness's opinion that a defendant was drunk may be accepted by the court on the basis of testimony that the witness smelled alcohol on the defendant's breath, heard his slurred speech, saw him down several drinks in rapid succession, and observed him walking with an unsteady gait.

Unlike the eyewitness or the alibi witness, **expert witnesses** do not have to have any first-hand knowledge of the crime, nor are they restricted by the rules of evidence from expressing their opinions. In fact, expert witnesses are summoned for the specific purpose of expressing opinions. The court can accept any person as an expert witness whose credentials establish an expertise in a particular field or discipline. Fingerprint specialists, handwriting specialists, crime lab technicians, or criminal investigators may act as expert witnesses. Psychiatrists and psychologists may be asked to give expert testimony on the mental status of the defendant; a ballistics specialist may testify regarding the identification of a murder weapon; an art dealer may be asked to appraise the value of a stolen painting introduced as evidence. Even merchants, artisans, and skilled workers (electricians, plumbers, locksmiths), whose long experience in their field qualifies them as experts among their peers, may be called in specific cases.

Specialists must first be qualified by the court to act as expert witnesses. The side that calls the expert—the prosecution or the defense—must convince the court that the witness is, in fact, an expert and is therefore capable of expressing a valid and reliable opinion. A witness must be an expert by virtue of special knowledge, skill, experience, training, or publication in the pertinent field to which he or she is to testify. Opposing counsel may shorten the inquiry considerably by agreeing that the witness is acceptable as a qualified expert. This is often done when the expert's credentials are well known to both sides. In some instances, the opposing counsel may object to qualifying the witness and may attempt, through cross-examination, to disqualify the individual as an expert. If the witness is discredited, the judge will rule that he or she cannot testify as an expert in the trial.

Hearsay

Another important rule of evidence excludes **hearsay** as admissible evidence in a court of law. Hearsay is knowledge or information that a witness acquires second-hand (i.e., facts he or she is told by someone else). The court views such evidence as a denial of the defendant's right to confrontation, because there is no opportunity to establish the truth of hearsay through the cross-examination of actual witnesses.

One exception to the hearsay rule is the "excited utterance" exception. These are statements made by a person at the time of an exciting event under stimulation of the excitement. What is required is that there be an occurrence startling enough to produce shock and excitement in the observer who makes a spontaneous statement under the stress of the shock and excitement. For example, after hearing a noise a police officer approaches the scene and meets a stranger coming from the scene who exclaims, "A woman's just been shot by a man with a big scar on his face." That witness is never found again. The police officer may testify by repeating the hearsay of the stranger's comments under the excited utterance exception to the hearsay rule.

Other exceptions to the hearsay rule include admissions against interest, confessions, and deathbed statements. An admission ties the defendant to the crime. For example, in a case involving homicide, the accused may tell the investigator, "Yes, I was there in the apartment when the shooting took place." This admission places the accused at the scene of the crime. A plea of guilty may be accompanied by a written confession, which the prosecutor can read to the court. The prosecutor strongly desires a confession, because the Constitution provides safeguards against self-incrimination, and the defendant is not required to take the witness stand. The defense counsel is equally concerned with keeping the confession *out* of evidence. If the defendant is incriminated by his or her own statements, it is obviously difficult to get a **verdict** of not guilty. In any event, the judge carefully examines the circumstances under which a confession is made (i.e., if it was given voluntarily and without coercion) before he or she allows the confession to be read to the jury.

The admissibility of deathbed statements is based on the belief that a person aware of impending death has no motive to lie. Most courts limit these dying declarations to homicide cases. Special requirements must be met in order to admit this form of hearsay evidence.

The dying declaration must be that of a victim and not a third person; the victim's death must be imminent at the time the declaration was made; witnesses who testify about the statement must have the faculties of any other witnesses; and, the statement must pertain to the circumstances surrounding the killing of the victim. Thus, deathbed declarations must include evidence of the declarer's *knowledge* of impending death. In many cases involving deathbed statements, the victim has suffered gunshot or stab wounds and the witness to the statement is a police officer or detective.

Standards of Proof

All prosecution evidence in a criminal trial must present a standard of proof that is higher than in any other trial in the American system of justice. The standard of proof is that of "beyond a reasonable doubt." No defendant may be convicted in this country during the adjudicatory stage of the criminal process without the prosecution meeting this burden of proof. The reasonable doubt standard is the fundamental legal principle of the criminal justice system. It is viewed as the essential instrument for lessening the risk of conviction based on factual errors. The U.S. Supreme Court has announced in many decisions that it is better to release one hundred guilty persons than to convict someone who is innocent.

Civil law, on the other hand, has a standard of proof that is called the "preponderance of evidence" standard. This is a much lower standard than the beyond a reasonable doubt standard. In order to persuade by a preponderance of evidence, one side must merely produce slightly more convincing evidence than the other side in order to win. However, in a criminal trial under the beyond a reasonable doubt standard, if the prosecution only produces slightly more evidence than the defense, then the jury must find the defendant not guilty.

ANATOMY OF A TRIAL

The U.S. Constitution guarantees a defendant's right to a trial before an impartial jury. Unless a defendant waives this right, the trial in a felony case and in many serious misdemeanors is held before a jury. Juries serve several purposes in our criminal justice system. Primarily, juries serve as a check against arbitrary or vindictive law enforcement. In *Duncan* v. *Louisiana* (391 U.S. 145 [1968]), the U.S. Supreme Court recognized that juries also provide a fact-finding process. Additionally, juries provide for public participation in the criminal justice system, which is essential in a democratic society.

The right to trial by jury attaches only to serious, not petty, offenses (*Baldwin* v. *New York* [399 U.S. 66 (1970)]). For purposes of a right to a trial by jury, a serious offense is one for which more than six months imprisonment is authorized. A distinctive feature of the Anglo-American system of justice, dating back more than seven centuries, is the citizen's right to a trial by jury. The English Magna Carta of 1215 contained the provision that no freeholder would be deprived of life or property except by judgment of his peers. This principle was incorporated into the U.S. Constitution. Article III contains the following statement: "A trial of all crimes except in cases of impeachment shall be by jury." The Sixth Amendment holds that "in all criminal prosecutions the accused shall enjoy the right to a speedy public trial by an impartial jury."

In some states, defendants must file a request for a jury trial either when they enter a plea or at some time specified before the beginning of the court term in which a jury will be impaneled. Failure to file a request for a jury trial constitutes a waiver of the right. In other states, an *express* waiver of jury trial is required.

Criminal trials in the United States conform to the following outline (Wells and Weston 1977):

1. Jury selection, impaneling, and administration of oath
2. Opening statements by both sides (facts only)
3. The state's case
4. The defense case
5. Rebuttal (state)
6. Surrebuttal (defense)
7. Closing arguments by both sides
8. Charge to the jury (instructions on law)
9. Deliberations and verdict
10. Judgment

The Jury

A jury is a panel consisting of a statutorily defined number of citizens selected according to law and sworn to determine matters of fact and sometimes matters pertaining to sentencing in a criminal action. The primary process by which the jury produces these results is by a verdict of guilty or not guilty in a specific case.

Within the context of the American judicial system, citizen juries perform a special function. Juries are a symbol of the rule of law, and citizen membership of a jury reinforces the democratic idea that sanctions and justice evolve only from community participation. A convicted person who has been found guilty by a jury of his or her peers provides greater stability for a judicial system than would a guilty verdict that is a product of bureaucratic government action.

Sometimes in a criminal case jury selection is dispensed with altogether. This occurs when the defendant chooses to be tried by a judge alone rather than by a jury of his or her peers. These trials are called **"bench trials."** However, most criminal defendants who choose to litigate their cases choose to have their guilt or innocence determined by a trial by jury.

The jury in a criminal trial is chosen by a complex—and often time-consuming—process. Because the prosecution and the defense both rely upon the jurors for a favorable decision, the factors involved in jury selection are of extreme concern to both parties in the proceedings. So important is the issue of jury selection that the methods of social science and psychiatric research have been applied to the process (with results we consider when we discuss scientific jury selection later in this chapter). When an offense is involved that has acquired great notoriety—such as the case of John Wayne Gacy, the man accused of more than thirty homosexually motivated murders of youths in Illinois—the time required to impanel a jury may stretch into months, and hundreds or even thousands of prospective jurors may be examined.

Eligible voters or taxpayers make up the list from which a group of potential jurors, called the jury panel, or venire, is selected. Ideally, the venire should represent a cross section of the community. For the selection to be constitutional, the original selection must be both randomly and scientifically conducted from an up-to-date list of all adult citizens. Such a group meets the qualifications for jury duty as set by statute in the jurisdiction of the court. (In federal cases, the members of the jury are drawn from the entire jurisdiction of the district court trying the case.)

In 1986 the U.S. Supreme Court ruled in *Turner* v. *Murray* that the racial composition of the jury is particularly acute in cases that might produce the death penalty. The Court ruled in this case that a defendant accused of an interracial crime in which the death penalty is an option can insist on the prospective jurors being informed of the victim's race and being questioned on the issue of their racial bias. Any judge who refuses this line of questioning risks having the death penalty vacated, if not the reversal of the conviction.

State laws may exempt certain categories of individuals from jury duty: people with defective vision or hearing, persons over age sixty-five, and members of particular occupations or professions (e.g., attorneys). Physicians, members of the clergy, and women with infants or small children may also be excluded at their own request.

A venire (sometimes called the **array**) is summoned from the panel of potential jurors to appear in a given case. The members of the venire are sometimes questioned in open court to determine their general qualifications for jury duty. Can they comprehend the English language? Are they citizens of the state? Are there any problems involving health or personal hardship that might interfere with the performance of their duties as jurors? Have they ever been convicted of a felony offense? (This last question is asked in those states in which a felony conviction disqualifies a person from jury duty.) More recently, clerks mail out questionnaires to each person on the venire. In order to be eligible to serve on a jury, the persons must satisfactorily answer on this questionnaire that they are citizens, are at least eighteen, have no felony convictions, have lived within the court's jurisdiction for one year, and do not have a physical or mental handicap that would render them incapable of performing jury service. Lawyers, law enforcement personnel, and doctors are routinely exempted from the jury. Others receive temporary deferments based on time-limited hardships, such as farmers during the harvest season. The trial judge hears requests for exemption and dismisses veniremen with legitimate reasons for being excluded from jury duty.

The names of the prospective jurors are randomly selected from the veniremen who remain after questioning. A fairly common procedure is to write the names on slips of paper and place the slips into a revolving drum; the court clerk then draws names out one by one. As a juror's name is read, he or she takes a place in the jury box and is questioned by both the defense counsel and the prosecutor in the so-called **voir dire.** The voir dire (usually translated as "to speak the truth") is a procedure by which potential jurors are examined as a group and individually with regard to their eligibility as jurors. They are questioned about their knowledge of a case and whether that knowledge might affect their ability to hear the evidence impartially. They are asked about their acquaintance with the participants in the trial (the defendant, judge, attorneys, and witnesses) as a possible source of bias in their judgment of the evidence. And they are asked whether they have already formed an opinion of the facts or issues involved in the case.

A potential juror who is determined to be unfit by either the prosecutor, the defense lawyer, or the judge most likely will be eliminated eventually through a challenge for cause or a peremptory challenge. If the answer to any of the questions is yes, the panel member may be dismissed "for cause" by the judge. The prosecution and the defense each have an unlimited number of **challenges for cause** and the widest latitude in questioning. They may query the prospective juror on almost any matter that bears on that person's ability or willingness to reach an impartial decision. In addition, the judge may exercise an option to examine the potential jurors. (Note that dismissal from a jury panel in one case does not exclude a venireman from selection for service on another trial jury during his or her term of jury duty.)

At this point, each side is allowed a specified number of **peremptory challenges**—requests to the court to exclude a prospective juror without reason. For example, the prosecutor may decide that he or she does not want a woman under forty-five or a man over fifty on the jury; or the defense attorney may feel uneasy about a potential juror on the basis of his or her facial expression, clothing, or demeanor. These reasons, whatever they are, do not have to be justified—or even stated—to the court.

Most criminal lawyers have a "feel" for what makes a good defense witness and what makes a good prosecution witness. These "feels" normally are based on what is believed to be the conservative or liberal leanings of the prospective juror, the juror's capacity for fairness, and the juror's possible bias in favor of whichever side the criminal lawyer happens to be on.

If a defense lawyer feels "bad" about a prospective juror even though the lawyer cannot articulate the reason she feels bad about him, the lawyer may peremptorily challenge that juror during recess. At the same time, the prosecution is doing the same thing about those jurors they do not want on the case for a variety of reasons. Only recently have peremptory challenges been the product of scientific research by social scientists rather than the subjective intuitions of criminal lawyers.

There is a check on the use of peremptory challenges by the prosecutor. In *Swain* v. *Alabama* (380 U.S. 202 [1965]), the U.S. Supreme Court upheld the use of peremptory challenges to exclude jurors by reason of racial or other group affiliation in isolated cases. This policy was extremely troublesome because it allowed what seemed to be a legally condoned discrimination against minority groups. In 1986 the Supreme Court struck down the *Swain* doctrine in *Bastine* v. *Kentucky*.

During the trial of a black defendant (Bastine), the prosecutor used his peremptory challenges to remove four blacks from the venire. Consequently, an all-white jury was selected. Although defense counsel protested that this deprived his client of a fair cross-representation of the community, the trial judge denied his motion. The Supreme Court held that defendants have no right to have a jury composed of members in whole or in part from their own race. However, under the equal protection clause of the Fourteenth Amendment, the Court stated that the state may not exclude jury members on account of race or under a false assumption that members of the defendant's own race cannot render a fair verdict. The Court declared this would discriminate against jury members and undermine public confidence in the jury system. Thus, the state is forbidden to use peremptory challenges to exclude jurors solely on the basis of their race.

Another controversial issue was addressed by the Supreme Court in 1968 when it ruled in a capital murder case, *Witherspoon* v. *Illinois* (391 U.S. 510 [1968]), that general conscientious or religious opposition to the death penalty is not grounds for exclusion of a potential juror, unless the prospective juror can say that he or she would never impose the death penalty or vote for a death sentence if death were a possible sentence.

The following example provides a sampling of the kinds of questions prospective jurors are likely to be asked by the defense during the voir dire.

Typical Questions that the Defense Lawyer Asks All Jury Members during Voir Dire

1. Have any of you been employed by a governmental agency?
2. Have any of you or any member of your family been employed by a *police* department or a *law* enforcement agency or security agency?
3. Have you or any member of your family ever been a *victim* or a witness of a criminal act?
4. Have you or any member of your family ever been a *juror* before?
5. Have you or any member of your family ever been a *witness* in a criminal trial?
6. Are you *related* to anyone present in this courtroom? The judge? Prosecutor? Defendant? Court Reporter? Clerk? Bailiff? Me?
7. Do any of you know, or have dealings, with any of the *other* prospective *jurors?*
8. Before you came into this courtroom today,

did you know any of the persons I've just mentioned?

9. Do any of you know, or have dealings with, any of the following *witnesses?*
10. Do you have any knowledge whatsoever concerning the facts of this case?
11. Have any of you ever been in the *armed service?*
12. *General questions:* Do you have any pressing personal problems that require you to ask to be excused or require your thoughts or attention during the trial?
13. *Burden of proof:* Under the American system of justice the burden of proving the charge rests entirely upon the state, and the defendant is not required to testify or present any evidence whatsoever. Do you agree with this idea? Do you understand that each element of the crime charged must be proved by the state beyond any reasonable doubt and that if any single element is not proved by the state beyond a reasonable doubt that you must return a verdict of not guilty?
14. *Opinion and attitude toward jury duty:* What is the most important quality of a juror?
15. *Presumption of innocence:* Do you believe in the principle of law that each man or woman is presumed innocent until proven guilty? And now, before any evidence has been presented, can you look at Mr. Suspect and truthfully say that at this stage you feel he is absolutely innocent? The law says that Mr. Suspect does not have to prove he is innocent, because the law says that he *is* innocent; he is presumed innocent. The judge will charge you that. Do you agree or disagree with that law? The law in its humanity presumes all persons charged with a crime to be innocent, and you are compelled by your oaths and by human decency to carry this presumption. Do you promise to keep this in mind?
16. *Information or indictment:* Do you understand that the information is no more than an accusation or method by which this matter has been brought to this court's attention?
17. *Two sides to every story:* You believe, do you not, that there are two sides to every story?
18. *Reasonable doubt (How much proof is required):* If, after hearing the evidence, you feel Mr. Suspect is likely guilty or even probably guilty, would you be able to return a verdict of not guilty, knowing that the law requires a stronger showing of guilt, that is, guilt beyond a reasonable doubt? There are two sources of reasonable doubt: (1) from a lack of evidence, or (2) from a conflict in the evidence. Do you have any difficulty accepting this idea? In a civil case the plaintiff must prove his or her case by a preponderance of the evidence, but there is a greater burden in a criminal case; that is, the prosecution must prove Mr. Suspect guilty beyond any reasonable doubt as to each element of the defense. And it must exclude all reasonable hypotheses or other explanations. A reasonable doubt is just what the term implies. It is a doubt founded in reason and for which you could give a reason. If you have such a doubt as to the guilt of the defendant, he is entitled to the benefit of the doubt and should be acquitted. If, after hearing the evidence, you feel Mr. Suspect is likely guilty or even probably guilty, would you be able to return a verdict of not guilty?
19. *Humanizing the defendant:* Mr. Suspect works at Ace Incorporated, belongs to the 39th Street Church, is involved with scouts, and attends night classes. Is there anything in this background that recalls an experience that would prevent you from treating Mr. Suspect fairly?
20. *Police testimony:* Do you believe a police officer can make a mistake like you or me? If the testimony in this case reveals that a police officer made an error or used improper judgment, would you excuse or exempt him or her from the mistake, or lack of judgment, merely because he or she wears a uniform?
21. *Courage to maintain opinion:* If you are convinced, after hearing the evidence, that

the state has failed to prove the guilt of Mr. Suspect beyond all reasonable doubt, will you maintain that opinion if you are in the minority of jurors and even if you find yourself alone in your opinion?

22. *Courage to maintain opinion:* Although it is the duty of each juror to consider the opinions of the other jurors, each juror must decide the case upon his or her own judgment and conscience. Do you promise to decide the case upon your own judgment?
23. *Purpose of cross-examination:* There is a range of human error. Weeding it out to give the jury the truest picture of what happened is the ultimate purpose for cross-examination. Keeping this purpose for cross-examination in mind, will you promise not to penalize Mr. Suspect in the event my cross-examination must be severe on a prosecution witness?
24. *Objections:* Now, ladies and gentlemen of the jury, I want to ask you whether you will think it wrong of me—whether you will hold it against me and my client—if I make objections during the trial to evidence offered by the state and its witnesses that I believe are not legally admissible into evidence? You understand, that this is what I am supposed to do, and that the only way the judge can decide what is proper evidence for the jury to receive under the rules of evidence is if I make objections.

The voir dire can be crucially important to the strategy of both the criminal defense lawyer and the prosecutor during a criminal proceeding, because the voir dire's purpose is more than choosing a jury. Lawyers take this opportunity to argue their cases before the jury in a very disguised and veiled manner. Furthermore, questioning jurors personally helps to develop a sense of bonding between the lawyer and the potential jurors. One district attorney summed up the significance of voir dire as follows:

> There is much more to a voir dire than the simple process of questioning and selecting jurors. In addition to the gamesplay and the psychology, a voir dire is an opportunity for the attorneys to educate the jury about theories of their case. It is also an opportunity to plant the seeds of doubt that they hope will produce a favorable verdict. It is a chance to predispose jurors to be receptive to the attorney's case. (Phillips 1978)

The voir dire examination continues until the required number of jurors has been selected. From any jury panel from which a twelve-person jury is selected, one or two alternate jurors are also chosen. These alternates sit through the entire trial and are available to replace a regular jury member should he or she be forced to withdraw from illness or due to becoming disqualified during the course of the trial.

Alternates do not participate in the deliberations of the jury unless one of the original jurors is unable to continue in the proceedings. When the jurors have been selected, the whole panel is sworn in and one of their members is chosen as foreman.

SCIENTIFIC JURY SELECTION During the 1970s, scientific jury selection attracted a great deal of interest from both the mass media and the legal community. But once the glare of publicity dimmed, skepticism about the success of the method and a concern for ethical issues focused professional interest on the technical details (sampling procedures, questionnaires, and behavior checklists for observing prospective jurors). According to Ellison and Buckhout (1981), one of the factors that limited enthusiasm for this approach to jury selection was cost.

Scientific jury selection is the application of tools and techniques that have long been familiar in social science research—questionnaires, interviews, attitude scales, public opinion surveys, and careful sampling procedures—to the detailed examination of information about prospective jurors. Data obtained from field research are analyzed to identify key variables that may affect the jury's decision-making process. (The methods of attorneys and social scientists in jury selection are compared in Table 11.1.)

Critics of scientific jury selection charge that it represents "sophisticated jury tampering, seeks to identify jurors who are not simply impartial but partial to the defendant, replaces trial by jury with 'trial by social scientists,' and discriminates against the ordinary defendant who cannot even afford the cost of a lawyer, let alone that of consultants and surveys" (Robin 1980, p. 276). Proponents of scientific jury selection claim that it provides a means to detect covert biases among prospective jurors that would not be uncovered during the

TABLE 11.1
Comparison of the Methods of Lawyers and Social Scientists in Jury Selection

Area	*Social Scientists*	*Lawyers*
Jury panel characteristics	Surveys and demographic studies	Experience with previous jury pools
In-court observations	Systematic ratings	Intuition based on experience
Reputations of jury pool members	Information networks	Informal contact
Jury composition	Use of findings from small group research	Selection of key jurors
Follow-up	Systematic interviews of jurors and peremptory challenges	Informal feedback

Reproduced from Katherine W. Ellison and Robert Buckhout, *Psychology and Criminal Justice* (New York: Harper and Row, 1981), p. 177, by permission of authors and publisher.

voir dire examination; thus, the method supports a defendant's constitutional right to a fair trial by an impartial jury.

Indications are that scientific jury selection may spell the difference between conviction and acquittal in cases where the evidence presented in the trial is less important than the attitudes and personalities of the jurors. Also, as Robin states, "whenever there are sound reasons to believe that a defendant would be denied a fair trial by virtue of locale, pretrial publicity, the method of drawing the jury pool, or the identity of the individual jurors, then scientific jury selection is an appropriate tool for responding to the challenge of guaranteeing fair trials in a free society" (ibid.).

JURY SIZE Nothing in the U.S. Constitution expressly mandates that a criminal jury must consist of "twelve good men and true." The significance of the figure twelve has been attributed to the Twelve Apostles, the Twelve Tribes of Israel, and the Twelve Patriarchs, but these theories are purely conjecture. About all we say with certainty is that the jury of twelve is a tradition whose origins are lost in antiquity (Klein 1977).

Although few states have altered the right of a person accused of a serious crime to demand a trial by a jury of twelve, some states have amended their constitutions to permit variations in civil cases and in criminal cases involving misdemeanors. Six-person juries were introduced into the federal court system in 1971. A year earlier, in *Williams* v. *Florida* (399 U.S. 78 [1970]), the U.S. Supreme Court upheld the right of state courts to try individuals charged with serious noncapital felony offenses by juries of six persons. In stating that the main purposes of the jury are to act as a group of fact finders, to exercise commonsense judgment, and to ensure community participation and shared responsibility in the determination of guilt or innocence, the Court indicated that it did not believe that the fulfillment of these purposes depends on the particular number of people that make up the jury:

> To be sure, that number should probably be large enough to promote group deliberation, free from outside attempts at intimidation, and to provide a fair possibility for obtaining a representative cross-section of the community. But we find little reason to think that these goals are in any meaningful sense less likely to be achieved when the jury numbers six, than when it numbers 12—particularly if the requirement of unanimity is retained. And, certainly the reliability of the jury as a factfinder hardly seems to be a function of its size (p. 1906).

In 1973, in *Colgrove* v. *Battin* (413 U.S. 149), the Court extended the six-member jury prerogative to civil suits in federal courts.

As Ellison and Buckhout (1981) point out in their discussion of six-person and twelve-person juries, social scientists and legal scholars have repeatedly criticized the validity and reliability of research that reports no significant differences between the two types of juries. In 1978, the U.S. Supreme Court, in *Ballew* v. *Georgia* (435 U.S. 223) took a closer look at older studies and conducted a thorough review of newer empirical evidence on jury size. In this case, the court rejected the use of a five-person jury in the state of Georgia. The Court concluded that (1) smaller juries are less likely to foster effective group deliberation, (2) twelve-person juries are less likely to reach "extreme compromises" in verdicts that are six-person juries, (3) smaller juries tend to hurt the defense more than the prosecution, and (4) a jury of less than six persons substantially threatens Sixth Amendment and Fourteenth Amendment guarantees. Ellison and Buckhout regard the *Ballew* decision as a "landmark in the application of psychological research to the rendering of a Supreme Court decision that will directly affect policy in the courtrooms of the United States" (1981, p. 163).

In *Burch* v. *Louisiana* (441 U.S. 130 [1979]), the Court ruled that in six-person juries, a unanimous vote is required for conviction, but, with a larger jury, a majority verdict is enough to convict.

Scientific Jury Selection: The Joan Little Case

On 27 August 1974, a young black woman named Joan Little (who was being held in Beaufort County Jail, North Carolina, pending appeal on a conviction for burglary) killed a sixty-two-year-old white jailer and escaped. A little over a week later, she surrendered to the state police and was subsequently indicted for first-degree murder. Her defense was that the jailer had forced her to have oral sex with him by threatening her with an ice pick. According to her account, he dropped the ice pick in the heat of passion, whereupon she grabbed it and used it as a weapon to defend herself.

Psychologists conducted a public opinion survey among the residents of two dozen counties in the Beaufort area to determine attitudes toward race and justice. Results indicated that racial prejudice among the predominantly white inhabitants of this conservative Southern community had already decided the case against Joan Little. A change of venue was granted and the trial was subsequently held in Raleigh (the state capital) in Wake County.

The researchers constructed a psychological profile of the kind of juror who would most likely be sympathetic to the defendant. They also came up with a series of questions for the defense attorneys to use in spotting prejudiced jurors and exercising challenges to remove these persons from the array. Nearly 150 veniremen were examined over a ten-day period before the jury was finally impaneled. The trial jury finally selected included six blacks and six whites. Prior to retiring to deliberate their verdict, the members of the jury were informed by the judge that the charge of first-degree murder was reduced to second-degree murder because the prosecution had failed to prove premeditation.

On 15 August 1975, after seventy-eight hours of deliberation, the jury returned a verdict of not guilty. The circumstantial evidence in the case failed to convince the "scientifically" selected jury of Joan Little's guilt "beyond a reasonable doubt." Chief counsel for the defense credited scientific jury selection with the acquittal.

Opening Statements

After the jury is impaneled, the trial opens with a reading of the indictment or information. Then the prosecution presents its opening statement. (The order in which the defense and prosecution present their cases varies from state to state, but each state follows a legally established procedure. Generally, the prosecution goes first.) The prosecutor, in his or her address to the jury, explains the charge, describes the crime the defendant is alleged

TABLE 11.2
State Provisions on Jury Size in Criminal Prosecutions

Twelve-Member Juries Required	Alabama, Hawaii, Illinois, Maine, Maryland, New Jersey, North Carolina, North Dakota, Rhode Island, Vermont, West Virginia, Wisconsin
Juries of Fewer Than Twelve Members Specifically Authorized	Alaska, Arizona, Colorado, Connecticut, Florida, Georgia, Idaho, Indiana, Iowa, Kansas, Kentucky, Louisiana, Massachusetts, Michigan, Minnesota, Mississippi, Missouri, Montana, Nebraska, New Hampshire, New Mexico, New York, Ohio, Oklahoma, Oregon, South Carolina, South Dakota, Tennessee, Texas, Utah, Virginia, Washington, Wyoming.
Juries of Fewer Than Twelve Members Permitted by Agreement	Arkansas, California, Delaware, Nevada, Pennsylvania.

Based on data from National Center for State Courts, *Facets of Jury System: A Survey (1976), pp. 41–44.*

to have committed, and draws a general picture of what the state intends to prove "beyond a reasonable doubt." The purpose of the opening statement is to provide the members of the jury—who lack familiarity with legal matters and procedures of criminal investigation—with an outline of the major objectives of the prosecution's case, the evidence it plans to present, the witnesses it intends to summon, and what it will seek to prove through the testimony of those witnesses. By the opening statement, the prosecutor tries to show the jury a finished jigsaw puzzle of the case. He or she also explains the nature of each of the pieces of the jigsaw puzzle and how they fit together to produce a whole picture that, he or she will argue, must lead to a guilty verdict. The idea is to make it easier for jurors to grasp the meaning and significance of evidence and testimony, and to keep them from becoming confused by the complexities of the case.

One thing the prosecution must *avoid* doing in the opening statement, however, is to promise evidence that it cannot deliver. Deming points out that in the 1968 murder trial of William Anthony Clinger in Los Angeles, the prosecutor outlined the expected testimony of a witness named Mrs. Dorothy Casto. When the prosecution was subsequently unable to locate Mrs. Casto, the verdict of guilty that the jury returned was set aside "on the grounds that the outline of the expected testimony of the witness who failed to appear had been prejudicial" (1970, p. 115). Furthermore, the prosecutor may make no references to evidence that he or she knows to be inadmissible and may not comment on the defendant's prior criminal record, if any exists. Should the prosecutor make such remarks in the opening statement, it could result in either a mistrial or a reversal of a conviction on appeal.

When the prosecutor concludes his or her opening statement, the defense can either follow with its opening statement or defer its presentation until later in the case. The usual procedure is for the defense to describe how it plans to expose the weaknesses or inadequacies of the prosecution's case and to demonstrate to the jury the defendant's innocence. In no state is the defense *compelled* to make an opening statement.

THE CASE FOR THE STATE After opening statements are concluded, the prosecution calls its first witness. The witness takes an oath or affirmation to tell the truth. The prosecutor then begins the presentation of evidence by **direct examination** of the witness—a question-and-answer procedure designed to elicit information from the witness about the case. According to LeGrande:

> Witnesses are required to respond directly to the question asked, and attempts to avoid the direct thrust of the question or to volunteer additional information beyond the question's scope are strongly discouraged. The basic reason for requiring direct responsiveness is that a witness, if given freedom to do so, might blurt out material which is legally objectionable, and if highly prejudicial might constitute reversible error. The procedural restrictions upon the methods of receiving testimony are designed, insofar as possible, to assure that objectionable material is not received by the jury (1973, p. 128).

Only the prosecutor, the defense counsel, and the judge can ask questions of a witness. Although some states allow jurors to ask questions through the judge, this practice is not prevalent.

On many occasions, the prosecutor's first witness is the arresting officer. In such a case, direct examination might go like this:

PROSECUTOR: Would you please state your name and occupation for the court.

WITNESS: My name is Sergeant James Brown. I am employed as a detective with the Hillsborough County Sheriff's Department.

PROSECUTOR: On the night of 15 January 1983 were you directed to investigate a homicide reported at 10:00 P.M.?

WITNESS: Yes, sir.

PROSECUTOR: Please describe your investigation.

The witness would then describe the details of the investigation as he or she conducted it. Physical evidence is introduced by a witness under oath. It is not enough for the prosecutor to say, "This .38 caliber revolver was found in the defendant's bedroom." The evidence must be validated by a witness who can explain to the court how he or she determined that the evidence is what the prosecutor (or defense counsel) claims it to be.

Usually a logic is present during the state's direct examination of witnesses. Most prosecutors call witnesses either (1) to establish a chronological order of the events leading up to the crime or (2) to establish each and every element of the case. In addition, witnesses can introduce physical real evidence and expert opinions.

When the prosecutor finishes with a witness, the defense attorney has the option to conduct a **cross-examination** of the testimony. Cross-examination is designed to test a witness's powers of observation and recollection, truthfulness, and possible bias against the cross-examiner's side. On cross-examination, the witness can be asked only about things to which he or she testified on direct examination, but the cross-examiner is permitted to ask **leading questions** (i.e., questions that suggest the answers). A skillful cross-examiner attempts to confuse, fluster, anger, or frighten the witness, causing him or her to lose self-control and composure.

Upon completion of cross-examination, the prosecutor may conduct a *redirect examination* to clarify some point or issue raised during the cross-examination. The defense counsel may then carry out a *recross-examination.* These examinations are restricted to matters dealt with in the immediately preceding examination. Subsequent witnesses are called by the prosecution, and the procedure outlined above is followed with each of them. The prosecution presents all of its witnesses before any witnesses are called by the defense. After the last witness for the prosecution has testified, the prosecution rests its case.

During cross-examination of prosecution witnesses, the defense lawyer has two goals in mind. One of the goals is to diminish the effectiveness of a particular witness in demonstrating the guilt of his or her client. This is normally done by showing that what the witness had to say is irrelevant. Another method by which the defense lawyer successfully enhances his or her case is to **impeach the credibility** of the prosecution witnesses. This involves an inquiry of the witness that is distinct from the question of the guilt or innocence of the accused. Impeaching the credibility of a witness implies that a witness is less believable than he or she might appear to be. Showing the following are generally recognized as ways to impeach the credibility of a prosecution witness: other witnesses' testimony is contrary to what the prosecution witness has said; the witness had no knowledge of the facts or that his or her senses were so dulled by sleep or drink that his or her perception was questionable; the witness has a poor character for truthfulness; the witness has a bias about the outcome of the case (e.g., is a relative of the victim); the witness has an interest in the case (e.g., he or she will stand to gain financially from a conviction); the witness has made prior statements that are inconsistent with those he or she made on the stand; the witness has had a valid felony conviction; the witness has committed acts that reflect on his or her honesty (e.g., cheating at cards); or the witness as a poor reputation in the general community for truthfulness and veracity.

During the direct examination of any witness, the opposing attorney has the right and the duty to object to the introduction of evidence or testimony that he or she believes might be immaterial, incompetent, or irrelevant. There is a series of complex evidentiary rules that allow lawyers to object to the testimony. Some of the grounds for objection under these rules include the following: that the other attorney is asking "leading questions" (ones that inherently suggest to the witness how he or she should answer the question) during direct examination; or that the questions asked are argumentative, badgering, or call for the witness's speculations, opinions, or conclusions. If the objection is sustained by the judge, then the attorney asking the question, or the answer elicited, is made incompetent. This is accomplished by the judge ordering the attorney not to ask the same question again or instructing the jury to disregard the answer that was given. If the objection is overruled, the examining attorney may continue along the same line of questions.

MOTION FOR DISMISSAL OR DIRECTED VERDICT At the conclusion of the prosecution's case, the defense attorney asks—almost as matter of routine—for the jury to be sent out of the courtroom while he or she moves for a dismissal of the case or a **directed verdict** of innocence from the judge. Such motions are usually based on one of three grounds:

1. The prosecution failed to show that a crime was committed.
2. The prosecution failed to show that the defendant had anything to do with the commission of the crime.
3. The testimony of the prosecution witnesses was not credible.
4. The conduct of the prosecutor was not proper.

In practice, these motions are rarely granted; the prosecution rarely takes a case to trial if it is not convinced of its own ability to prove the guilt of the defendant beyond a reasonable doubt. If the state fails to meet the burden of proof, however, the judge may grant the motion and acquit the defendant. If the motion is denied, the defense proceeds with its case. A judge cannot direct a jury to convict the accused. Basically, the motion for a directed verdict of not guilty is made by the defense so that a finding of guilt can later be appealed to a higher court. If the judge refuses to grant the motion, the judge's decision can be one of the items for defense on appeal. On appeal the defendant declares the judge did not use proper procedural care in making his or her decision in the case.

THE CASE FOR THE DEFENSE Presentation of the case for the defense is similar to that of the prosecution. The defense counsel calls witnesses and directly examines them, then turns them over to the prosecutor for cross-examination. The following procedural considerations apply to the defense:

1. The defendant is not required by law to present witnesses; instead, the defense can be based entirely on the evidence and testimony presented by the state.
2. The defendant is not required to give personal testimony. A defendant's refusal to take the stand cannot be called to the attention of the jury by either the prosecutor or the judge. If he or she *does* choose to take the witness stand, a defendant faces the same hazards of cross-examination as any other witness.
3. The defense is not obligated to prove the innocence of its client, but merely to show that the state has failed to prove guilt.

If the defendant has a special defense in the case, such as alibi, insanity, or entrapment, he or she has the burden of going forward and proving his or her case. For example, if the defendant claims she was insane at the time of the crime and the defense produces a witness who testifies that the defendant was insane but the witness is not qualified according to the judge, then the insanity defense has not been properly met. Hence, the judge will later instruct the jury to ignore the possibility that the defendant may have been insane at the time of the crime. When the testimony of the last defense witness is completed and all of the evidence has been introduced, the defense rests its case.

Rebuttal and Surrebuttal

At the conclusion of the defense's case, the prosecution is given an opportunity for **rebuttal.** That is, it may summon additional witnesses to buttress its case, which may have been weakened by evidence and testimony presented by the defense. Testimony offered in rebuttal must be limited to matters covered in the defense's case. In addition, if the prosecutor chooses to conduct a rebuttal, the defense may summon surrebuttal witnesses to bolster its case. Defense surrebuttal witnesses are likewise limited to testifying only about matters covered in the testimony of the rebuttal witnesses of the state.

Closing Arguments

Most attorneys consider the closing arguments *the* essential ingredient that determines the skill of a criminal lawyer. Closing arguments, or *summations,* provide the defense counsel and the prosecutor with an opportunity to summarize evidence and testimony and persuade the jury to accept their interpretation of the case. Normally, the state, who has the burden of proof in a case, argues first and the defendant argues second. Under the theory that the state has the burden of proof, some jurisdictions allow the prosecution to rebut the defense argument. In other states arguments from the defense lawyer are the last words spoken from the attorneys in the case. The closing arguments are the opposing lawyers' last opportunity to articulate clearly their theories of guilt or innocence based on the evidence. Closing arguments also give them an opportunity to argue why their evidence is more credible and more believable than the other side's. Finally, closing arguments provide an opportunity for them to attack the opposition's case.

At one time, the summation was a theatrical display of forensic eloquence, as the opposing attorneys sought to influence the emotions of the jury. Hence, the old adage for trial lawyers: If the law is against you, pound the facts; if the facts are against you, pound the law; if both the law and the facts are against you, pound the table. At present, table pounding is considered in poor taste by most judges, and excessive flamboyance on the part of either counsel is apt to draw a rebuke from the bench.

Charging the Jury

When all of the evidence has been presented and both sides have rested their cases, it is the responsibility of the judge to instruct the jury. As already noted, it is the prerogative of the jury to decide the facts, but the court must instruct the members of the jury on those aspects of the law that apply to the case. In instructing the jury, the judge must clearly explain the law arising from the evidence. He or she also instructs the jury on the possible verdicts, the law of the rules of evidence that manifested themselves in the case, and the meaning of the "reasonable doubt" standard. Furthermore, the judge will instruct the jury on the elements of crime alleged, and the fact that each and every element must be proven beyond a reasonable doubt or they must find the defendant not guilty. The judge further instructs the jurors to review all the evidence thoroughly and tells them the procedures they should use during their deliberations.

Both the prosecutor and the defense are given the opportunity to submit instructions for the jurors. These instructions incorporate the theories of the respective attorneys as to the interpretation of the facts of the case. The judge selects from the instructions suggested by the attorneys or prepares his or her own instructions. In the absence of specific instructions, the judge may use a standard set of instructions that apply to cases of a similar nature. After the instructions are prepared, the judge reviews them with both attorneys in the judge's chambers. The final instructions are then prepared, and the attorneys are given the opportunity to enter any objections to them as grounds for possible appeal.

The final instructions read to the jury in open court relate to specific issues of evidence or testimony in the case and traditionally cover the following areas:

1. The definition of the crime with which the defendant is charged.
2. The presumption of the defendant's innocence.
3. The fact that the burden of proof is upon the prosecution.
4. That if, after consideration of all the evidence, there remains reasonable doubt as to the defendant's guilt, he or she must be acquitted.
5. Procedures for electing a foreman and returning a verdict.

Often these instructions are more laudible on paper than they are in practice. Indeed, one Department of Justice study found that in half the cases it examined, jurors were confused and misguided by a judge's instructions (New York Times 1981, p. 25). In many jurisdictions, jurors are given written instructions to take with them into the jury room during deliberations.

Instructions are also offered to the jury concerning the possible verdicts they may render. Guilty and not guilty are the usual alternatives in a criminal case, but the jury may also be given an option to decide on the *degree of the offense* in a particular case (e.g., murder in the first degree, murder in the second degree). The court supplies a written form for each verdict, along with the instruction that the appropriate form be returned to the court as soon as an agreement is reached.

Jury Deliberations

After receiving their instructions, the jurors retire to the jury room to begin their deliberations in an effort to arrive at a verdict. The conduct of jurors and the procedures governing jury deliberations are established by local statutes and court rules. Generally, such rules restrict the members of the jury from communicating with anyone except the bailiff or the judge during their deliberations. And most jurisdictions do not allow the jury to separate once deliberations have begun. If it appears that deliberations might continue for more than several hours, arrangements may have to be made to sequester the jury in an adjacent hotel or motel. During the ensuing deliberations, jurors will be fed and housed together and will be prohibited from reading newspapers or watching television accounts of the trial. Whether they are sequestered or allowed to spend their nights at home, jurors are not allowed to discuss the case with anyone except fellow jurors in the jury room. Until this point, jurors have been passive observers of the trial, unable to question witnesses. During deliberations they become the main actors as they discuss the facts that have been presented.

Early in deliberations, the foreman of the jury may call for a vote. On rare occasions, this first vote may result in a unanimous verdict. More frequently, however, the first vote reveals a three-way split among jurors, with some voting guilty, some voting not guilty, and some undecided. (If the case presents difficult and complex issues, the latter category may include the majority of the jurors.) The jury then discusses the case, with the foreman acting as a moderator or discussion coordinator. Sometimes a jury asks to review a particular piece of evidence or line of testimony or requests further instructions from the court on a point of law.

A unanimous verdict in criminal cases has been a basic requirement of common law since the fourteenth century. The U.S. Supreme Court upheld this requirement in both the nineteenth and twentieth centuries, and most states have endorsed this position in their provisions for jury trials. In *Johnson* v. *Louisiana* (409 U.S. 1085 [1972]), however, the Court held that Louisiana's use of 9–3 verdicts in major criminal cases was constitutional; and a similar decision was made in *Apodaca* v. *Oregon* (406 U.S. 404 [1972]), regarding Oregon's use of 10–2 verdicts in serious criminal cases. More recently, the Court dealt with the issue of less-than-unanimous verdicts in cases involving juries with fewer than twelve persons. In *Burch* v. *Louisiana* (441 U.S. 130 [1979]), the Court held that a 5–1 vote for conviction *does* fail to satisfy the minimum constitutional requirements.

If a jury is hopelessly deadlocked after prolonged deliberations, it may return to the courtroom, where the judge will instruct the members to go back to the jury room for a final effort to arrive at a verdict. The judge usually sets a specific time period for this to be done. If all reasonable methods are exhausted without reaching unanimity—resulting in a hung jury—the judge dismisses the jury, declares a mistrial, and schedules a retrial of the case with a new jury. Sometimes after a hung jury the prosecution decides not to retry the case.

When the jury does return a verdict, the defense counsel or the prosecutor may request that the jurors be polled. Each juror is asked individually by the court clerk or the judge if the verdict announced is his or her verdict. The rationale for this procedure is to determine whether the juror is voting freely according to the dictates of conscience or if he or she is responding to pressure from fellow jurors. If polling discloses a less-than-unanimous verdict where one is required by law, the jury may be instructed to return to the jury room and continue its deliberations, or it may be dismissed and a mistrial declared. A mistrial places the defendant in the same position as if no trial had occurred, and proceedings may be reinstated against that defendant. If the verdict is not guilty, the defendant is discharged.

One of the little-known procedures in criminal trials is **jury nullification.** This occurs when juries do not follow the court's interpretation of the law in every instance or otherwise "nullify" or suspend the force of strict legal procedure: the jurors may have disregarded what they were told about the law or certain aspects of evidence, because they considered the application of certain laws to be unjust, or they may have refused to convict because they considered the penalty too severe. Jury nullification is a twofold process. When a verdict of guilty is returned and, is in the judge's opinion, an erroneous decision, the judge may refuse to abide by the verdict and may direct the jury to acquit the accused. Other times the judge may tell the jury to "arrest" their verdict and enter a judgment of acquittal. However, a trial judge does not have the authority to direct a jury to convict and enter a judgment arresting a verdict of not guilty.

Sentencing and Appeal

Before the sentencing stage of the criminal justice process, the defendant has either pled guilty to, or been found guilty of, a criminal offense. The court must then decide an appropriate disposition for the individual—a decision that is often complex and difficult for the judge. In earlier times, the imposition of sentences was cut and dried. Specific punishments for specific offenses were laid down by the law, and once a verdict of guilty was returned, the judge merely ordered the appropriate sentence to be carried out. The focus of attention was the offense, not the offender. However, this situation has changed as a consequence of societal reaction to crimes and criminals. Sentencing today involves a broader range of alternatives for the offender. Many of these alternatives involve rehabilitation and call for the assistance of professionals in psychology, sociology, education, and social welfare. To effect these goals judges in most jurisdictions require a presentencing investigation. Many states require a presentence report on all felony cases. These usually are conducted by probation officers assigned to the court. The purpose of a presentence investigation is sixfold: (1) to aid the court in determining the appropriate sentence; (2) to aid the probation officer in the rehabilitative effort during probation; (3) to assist the Department of Corrections in its classification and treatment program and its planning for release; (4) to furnish the parole board with information pertinent to its consideration of parole; (5) if parole is granted, to aid the parole officer in his or her supervisory efforts; and (6) to serve as a source of information for systematic research (Administrative Office of the United States Courts 1974, p. 48).

#17

The imposition of a criminal sentence is normally the responsibility of the trial judge. In some jurisdictions the jury may determine a sentence or be called upon to make a recommendation involving leniency for certain offenses. Sentencing is regarded, with justification, as one of the most significant stages in the administration of justice. For criminal offenders, it represents the determination of how they are going to spend the coming months and years, or—as in the case of capital punishment—whether they will face death. For society, as Reid observes, it is "a time of decision that necessitates not only action in a particular case but recognition of that society's philosophy of punishment and rehabilitation" (1982, p. 434). (In Chapter 12, we explore the questions and issues raised by our present philosophical orientation toward punishment and its impact on the entire criminal justice system.)

A basic tenet of the criminal justice process in the United States is that every person accused of a crime is presumed innocent until proven guilty. And the system also requires that the proof be obtained legally. In most jurisdictions a direct criminal appeal to an appellate court exists as a matter of right for all convicted defendants. This means a defendant has an automatic right to appeal his or her conviction based on errors that may have occurred during the trial proceedings. Appellate review acts as a shield for an individual caught up in the processes of criminal trial, incarceration, or supervision in the community. The power of the state is great, and citizens must be protected against the capricious and arbitrary exercise of such power. The right to appeal the verdict in a criminal trial is one of the most important aspects of *due process,* although it is not spelled out in the Bill of Rights.

SUMMARY

Compared with the total volume of cases entering the criminal justice system, relatively few cases are disposed of by trial. Nevertheless, the criminal trial is an indispensable feature of our system. The accused is brought to trial under a presumption of innocence; it is the task of the prosecution to prove beyond a reasonable doubt that the defendant is guilty of the crime with which he or she is charged.

The adversary concept of criminal justice is most clearly exhibited in the trial. The prosecutor uses the authority and resources of the state to gather enough evidence to convince the court and jury of the guilt of the defendant. The defense counsel attacks the weaknesses of the prosecution's case, seeks to impeach the testimony of state witnesses, questions the validity and reliability of the prosecution's evidence, and is alert to any tactics of the opposing counsel that violate the constitutional rights of the defendant.

An extremely important aspect of the trial is the selection of people to serve on the jury. Jurors are chosen by a procedure called voir dire, which assigns the prosecution and defense a number of challenges for cause (stated reason or reasons why a particular person is unfit to serve on a jury) and peremptory challenges (challenges for which no reasons need be given). In recent years, there have been some noteworthy attempts to use the methods of the social scientist to pick jurors who would be inclined to favor the defendant. This process of scientific jury selection has been attacked as "jury stacking" and defended as a guarantor of fairness. Whatever its defects or merits, however, the expenses involved in its use will probably keep it from becoming a routine procedure in criminal trials.

Trials are governed by rules and procedures that have evolved over many years and are enforced by the judge, who acts as an arbiter or referee. The order of a criminal trial may vary somewhat from one jurisdiction to another, but it generally conforms to a standard pattern. After a reading of the formal charges against the defendant, the prosecution presents its case by introducing evidence and witnesses whose testimony is subject to cross-examination by the defense. At the conclusion of the prosecution's case, the defense presents its case, including evidence and testimony, and may call the defendant to testify on his or her own behalf. Following closing statements by both sides, the judge instructs the jury on points of law, and the jury is then sequestered until it reaches a verdict or finds itself hopelessly deadlocked.

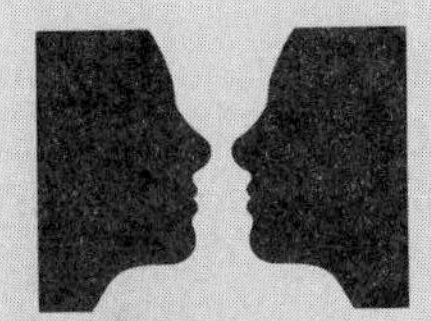

ISSUE PAPER

MAD OR BAD? THE INSANITY DEFENSE

Under our system of criminal justice, there are two methods by which an offender can be absolved of criminal responsibility for his or her behavior. The first method involves being declared incompetent to stand trial; the second method is to be found not guilty by reason of insanity. Both of these defenses grew out of the overuse of the death penalty in England. The issue of competency to stand trial rests upon the common-law criteria that a defendant must be able to understand the charges and be able to cooperate with defense counsel in the preparation of his or her own defense. The insanity defense is based on the proposition that the defendant did not have the capacity to understand the nature of the criminal act or to know that the act was wrong. The common-law development of the insanity plea was a major shift away from the harsh punitive practices of the early nineteenth century.

Laws on competency provide that a person accused of a crime may be tried only if he or she is able to understand the nature of the charge and aid counsel in preparing a defense. As the U.S. Supreme Court ruled in *Dusky* v. *United States* (362 U.S. 402 [1960]), it is not sufficient that the defendant be oriented with regard to time and place or have some recollection of events. The test must be "whether he has sufficient present ability to consult with his lawyer with a reasonable degree of rational understanding—and whether he has a rational as well as a factual understanding of the proceedings against him" (*Dusky* at 402). A defendant found incompetent to stand trial is usually committed to a mental institution (e.g., state hospital) until such time as he or she is certified to be competent by medical or psychiatric authorities. During this period, the defendant remains under the jurisdiction of the court. The significance of the competency issue has generally been obscured, because it is often confused with the insanity defense. Yet far more persons are confined in mental hospitals on the basis of incompetency than as a result of a finding of not guilty by reason of insanity.

The insanity defense raises the issue of criminal responsibility. Is the defendant capable of making distinctions between right and wrong or good and evil, as these terms are defined in codes of social conduct? The general view within the law is that wrongdoing must be conscious to be criminal. The fundamental link between moral knowledge and free choice is indicated by the legal principles that allow for the diminution or elimination of responsibility under certain conditions that lessen or destroy a person's capacity to discriminate between right and wrong and to act in accordance with such discriminations.

A variety of tests or formulas have been developed over the years to help the jury in a case involving the insanity defense. The best known of these tests is the M'Naghten Rule, which is used in about twenty states. This rule is named after Daniel M'Naghten, a psychotic individual who murdered the secretary of Prime Minister Robert Peel in the mistaken belief that he was actually assassinating Peel. M'Naghten was probably a paranoid schizophrenic; he was entangled in an elaborate system of persecutory delusions and believed he was being pursued by government spies. M'Naghten was acquitted on the grounds that he was insane at the time he committed the murder. The basis for the decision is incorporated in the following statement that has come to be known as the M'Naghten Rule:

> Every man is presumed to be sane, and . . . to establish a defense on the grounds of insanity, it must be clearly proved that, at the time of the committing of the act, the party accused was labouring under such a defect of reason from disease of the mind, as not to know the nature and quality of the act he was doing; or if he did know it, that he did not know he was doing what was wrong (*Daniel M'Naghten's Case,* 10 C.&F. 200, 210–211, 8 Eng. Rep. 718, 722–723 [1843]).

As used here, *insanity* is a legal and philosophical term; it is not a synonym for psychosis or mental illness. When psychiatrists or psychologists testify in cases involving the insanity defense, the best they can do is to give evidence or opinions about the possible influence of mental conditions on the capacity of the accused to form criminal intent. The judgment of criminal *responsibility* is a matter for the jury. If the jury decides that a defendant is, in fact, not guilty on the grounds of insanity, the defendant is committed to a mental institution where he or she remains under the jurisdiction of the court until institutional authorities certify a recovery. The subsequent disposition of the individual is up to the court of original jurisdiction.

The intense publicity generated by such cases as that of John W. Hinckley, Jr., the attempted assassin of President Reagan, is out of proportion to the handful of cases in which insanity is actually used as a plea. And as Kaufman (1982) points out, a successful insanity defense is even more rare. In New York, for example, it is estimated that the insanity defense is involved in no more than 1.5 percent of all felony indictments, with success in only about one quarter of the cases. The problem, as Kaufman observes, is that acquittals by reason of insanity tend to undermine public faith in the ability of the criminal justice system to deal rationally and equitably with crime. Many people, he feels, conclude that the insanity defense is a cop-out that allows dangerous criminals to be released to commit further criminal acts after a brief period of psychiatric confinement.

Unfortunately, such cases do occur. As a teenager, Edmund Emil Kemper III murdered his grandparents and was sent to a psychiatric hospital. He was subsequently released, subject only to the requirement that he return periodically for psychiatric examination. After leaving the hospital, Kemper murdered eight more people, including his mother and a fifteen-year-old girl (who he dismembered). A few days later, while driving around with the girl's remains in the trunk of his car, Kemper visited his psychiatrist, who pronounced him "safe."

An issue that came up again and again in the heated discussion that followed the Hinckley case was the inability of psychiatrists and psychologists to predict whether individuals such as Hinckley and Kemper will pose a threat to society if released from psychiatric confinement. (There is the additional issue of whether such persons represent a threat to *themselves,* but this is less likely to trigger public indignation than the danger posed by the homicidal individual.) Research consistently demonstrates that predictions of dangerousness are beyond the capacity of contemporary psychiatric and psychological expertise.

The American Psychiatric Association (APA) issued a policy statement in January 1983 on the insanity defense that recommends a narrower application of the plea. In addition, the APA has criticized a series of legal rulings that authorized findings of insanity for persons with abnormal personalities—such as antisocial individuals who commit crimes of violence with no show of concern or remorse for their victims. The insanity defense, according to the APA, should apply only to persons who are psychotic or who have a severely distorted perception of reality. This limitation, it seems, would exclude President Reagan's would-be assassin, John Hinckley, Jr.

The APA also recommends tighter supervision of persons who commit violent acts but are acquitted by reason of insanity. It is strongly critical of procedures that permit the release of such individuals just because psychiatrists are unable to certify that they pose a danger to themselves or others.

The APA's position is not quite as extreme, however, as a Reagan administration proposal to do away with the insanity plea. The proposal limits the insanity defense to people who do not know what they are doing when they commit an illegal act, and it calls for a verdict of guilty but mentally ill. Several states have already barred the insanity defense or extensively curtailed its use, and the APA's policy statement may offer an acceptable middle ground for legislative action in other states.

DISCUSSION AND REVIEW

1. Why has the jury trial been referred to as a "sublimated brawl"?
2. Discuss the distinctions among real, testimonial, and circumstantial evidence.
3. How does competent evidence differ from relevant evidence? From material evidence? How is the competency of a witness established?

4. Distinguish between privileged communications and confidential communications. Which type of communication is protected by law?
5. What are some of the exceptions to the rules of evidence against the admissibility of hearsay?
6. How does the "guilt beyond a reasonable doubt" standard of proof differ from the "preponderance of the evidence," standard?
7. Briefly describe the selection process for jurors. What are some of the major issues raised by the process of scientific jury selection?
8. Can jurors be excluded from service by peremptory challenges based on race? Why or why not?
9. Name and discuss some typical questions asked during voir dire examination. What role does voir dire play in the case strategy of the prosecution and defense?
10. What do the opposing counsels seek to accomplish in their opening statements? Which side goes first?
11. Distinguish between direct examination and cross-examination. What limitations are imposed on cross-examination?
12. What are some of the major rights enjoyed by the defendant with respect to evidence and testimony in a criminal trial?
13. What are the principal matters covered by the judge in instructions to the jury?
14. What is the significance of the rulings in *Apodaca* v. *Oregon* and *Johnson* v. *Louisiana?* What are the pros and cons of the unanimous jury verdict?
15. Distinguish between incompetency and insanity. Why is the insanity defense so controversial if it is used so sparingly in criminal trials?
16. Who was Daniel M'Naghten and what is the significance of the M'Naghten Rule?
17. What are the purposes of the presentence investigation?

GLOSSARY

Array (Veniremen) The whole body of potential jurors summoned to court as they are arranged or ranked on the panel.

Bench trial A criminal case where jury selection is dispensed with altogether. The defendant chooses to have his or her guilt or innocence tried by the judge alone.

Challenge for cause An attempt by the prosecutor or defense counsel to exclude a prospective juror during the voir dire examination by pointing out to the court why the person in question is unfit to serve or would not be impartial.

Change of venue Moving a trial to a jurisdiction other than the one in which the crime was committed to guarantee the accused a fair trial.

Circumstantial evidence All evidence of an indirect nature; circumstances from which the court or jury may infer a principal fact in a case.

Competency In the law of evidence, the presence of those characteristics that render a witness legally fit and qualified to give testimony.

Cross-examination The questioning of a witness in a trial or in a deposition by the party opposed to the one that produced the witness.

Directed verdict An instruction by the judge to the jury to return a specific verdict.

Direct evidence Proof of facts by witnesses who saw acts done or heard words spoken, as distinct from circumstantial evidence.

Direct examination The first interrogation or examination of a witness by the party (defense or prosecution) who calls the witness.

Expert witness A person who testifies in relation to some scientific, technical, or professional matter (i.e., persons qualified to speak authoritatively by reason of their special training, skill, or familiarity with a subject).

Hearsay Second-hand evidence of which the witness lacks personal knowledge. The witness merely repeats something that someone else said.

Impeachment of witness An attack on the credibility of a witness by the testimony of other witnesses.

Jury nullification The judge believes the jury's "guilty" verdict is erroneous and subsequently causes a judgment of acquittal to take its place.

Leading question A question that suggests to the witness the answer desired. *Leading questions* are prohibited in direct examination.

Material evidence Evidence that is relevant and bears upon the substantial issues in dispute.

Peremptory challenge A challenge that the prosecutor or defense counsel may use to reject prospective jurors without stating a cause for the rejection.

Rebuttal The introduction of rebutting evidence; arguments showing that statements of witnesses are not true; the stage of the trial at which rebutting evidence may be introduced.

Verdict In practice, the formal finding or decision made by a jury, reported to the court, and accepted by the court.

Voir dire French for "to speak the truth." Refers to the examination of prospective jurors by the prosecutor, defense counsel, and (sometimes) the court to determine their fitness to serve as jurors in a trial and to eliminate persons who would not be impartial. Also refers to the questioning of a witness to ascertain potential bias or, in the case of an expert witness, to determine qualifications and competence.

■ REFERENCES

Administrative Office of the United States Courts. "The Selective Presentence Investigation Report." *Federal Probation* 38 (December 1974): 48.

Coffey, A.; Eldefonso, E.; and Hartinger, W. *An Introduction to the Criminal Justice System and Process.* Englewood Cliffs, N.J.: Prentice-Hall, 1974.

Corpus Juris Secundum, vol. 22A. Brooklyn, N.Y.: The American Law Book Company, 1961.

Deming, R. *Man and Society: Criminal Law at Work.* New York: Hawthorn, 1970.

Ellison, K. W., and Buckhout, R. *Psychology and Criminal Justice*. New York: Harper & Row, 1981.
Frank, J. *Courts on Trial: Myth and Reality in American Justice*. Princeton, N.J.: Princeton University Press, 1949.
Kaplan, J. *Criminal Justice*. St. Paul, Minn.: West, 1973.
Kaufman, I. R. "The Insanity Defense." *New York Times Magazine,* 8 August 1982, pp. 16–21.
Kerper, H. B. *Introduction to the Criminal Justice System*. St. Paul, Minn.: West, 1972.
Klein, F. J. *Federal and State Court Systems—A Guide*. Cambridge, Mass.: Ballinger, 1977.
LeGrande, J. L. *The Basic Processes of Criminal Justice*. Beverly Hills, Calif.: Glencoe, 1973.
New York Times. "What They Say It Is." 7 June 1981, p. 25.
Phillips, Steven. *No Heroes, No Villains: The Story of a Murder Trial*. New York: Vintage, 1978.
Reid, S. T. *Crime and Criminology*. New York: Holt, Rinehart and Winston, 1982.
Robin, G. D. *Introduction to the Criminal Justice System*. New York: Harper & Row, 1980.
Smith, A., and Pollack, H. *Criminal Justice in a Mass Society*. New York: Holt, Rinehart and Winston, 1972.
Wells, K. M., and Weston, P. B. *Criminal Procedure and Trial Practice*. Englewood Cliffs, N.J.: Prentice-Hall, 1977.

CASES

Apodaca v. *Oregon* 406 U.S. 404, 92 S.Ct. 1628, 32 L.Ed.2d 184 (1972).
Baldwin v. *New York* 399 U.S. 66, 90 S.Ct. 1944, 26 L.Ed.2d 437 (1970).
Ballew v. *Georgia* 435 U.S. 223, 98 S.Ct. 1029, 55 L.Ed.2d 234 (1978).
Bastine v. *Kentucky* No. 824–6263, 54 LW 4425 (1986).
Burch v. *Louisiana* 441 U.S. 130, 99 S.Ct. 1623, 60 L.Ed.2d 96 (1979).
Colgrove v. *Battin* 413 U.S. 149, 93 S.Ct. 2448, 37 L.Ed.2d 522 (1973).
Duncan v. *Louisiana* 391 U.S. 145, 88 S.Ct. 1444, 20 L.Ed.2d 491 (1968).
Dusky v. *United States* 362 U.S. 402, 80 S.Ct. 788, 4 L.Ed.2d 824 (1960).
Johnson v. *Louisiana* 409 U.S. 1085, 93 S.Ct. 691, 34 L.Ed.2d 672 (1972).
M'Naghten, Daniel, Case of 10 C&F 200, 210–211; 8 Eng. Rep. 718, 722–723 (1843).
Mapp v. *Ohio* 367 U.S. 643, 81 S.Ct. 1684, 6 L.Ed.2d 1081 (1961).
Swain v. *Alabama* 380 U.S. 202, 85 S.Ct. 824, 13 L.Ed.2d 759 (1965).
Turner v. *Murray* ___ U.S. ___ 106 S.Ct. 1683, ___ L.Ed.2d ___ (1986).
Williams v. *Florida* 399 U.S. 78, 90 S.Ct. 1893, 26 L.Ed.2d 446 (1970).
Witherspoon v. *Illinois* 391 U.S. 510, 88 S.Ct. 1770, 20 L.Ed.2d 776 (1968).

NOTES

1. *New York Times,* June 7, 1981, p. 25.
2. Administrative Office of the United States Courts, "The Selective Presentence Investigation Report," *Federal Probation* 38 (December 1974): 48.

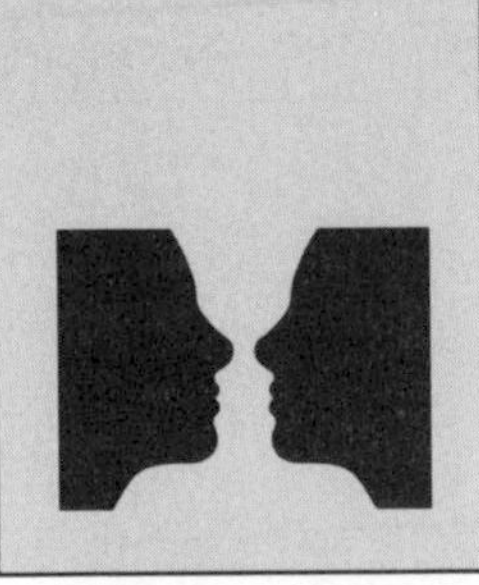

CHAPTER

12

Sentencing and After

CHAPTER OUTLINE:

The traditional role of the criminal justice system has been to apprehend, convict, and punish offenders. Sentencing is the process by which judges impose punishment on persons convicted of crimes. The punishments imposed range from probation without conditions to the death penalty. Other sentences include fines, community service, probation with conditions, and incarceration in jail or prison.

Historically, punishments have involved a full range of effects. Defendants have been sentenced to hard labor, branded, whipped, tortured, and killed. Although many changes have occured in our society in the last century, the orientation of the criminal justice system is still primarily punitive. Based on the historical systems that have shaped our ideas of law and justice, it is difficult to see how it could have been otherwise; and it is almost impossible to imagine any fundamental changes in the administration of justice without sweeping changes in the basic nature of our society and culture. At the same time, it must be emphasized that punishment for the sake of vengeance alone has never enjoyed unqualified support in this country. Since colonial times, a substantial minority has sought the goals of reform and rehabilitation for the criminal offender. And even when these goals have clashed with those of social defense and the maintenance of public order, rehabilitation has remained as an ideal of the American criminal justice system.

Criminologists long accepted the view that an offender's criminal misbehavior was analogous to a disease, which could be cured if the offender was treated in a proper institution. Thus to effect a cure became a major goal of both sentencing and incarceration; when released, the offender would enjoy a more satisfying, productive, and lawful life; he or she would not commit additional crimes, and everyone's interest would have been served. This medical model of disease and cure required that offenders be returned to the free world when the professionals judged them to be "cured."

If sentences were intended merely to mete out punishment to criminal offenders, the task of judges would be much simpler and less controversial than it is. But sentencing—at least in modern times—has also been viewed as the cornerstone of rehabilitation. These broadly divergent objectives constitute part of the dilemma faced by many judges: Is it possible simultaneously to punish and to rehabilitate an offender?

In many jurisdictions, decisions about where and how people may spend years of their lives are made by a judge whose discretion is virtually unchecked or unguided by criteria, procedural constraints, or review. Often a sentence is meted out by a judge who has no information except the offender's name and the crime of which he or she is guilty. The reliability and accuracy of information provided to the court by presentence investigation reports often goes unchallenged. And the laws in many states about the selection of sentences are chaotic. In some states, mandatory "flat-time" sentences allow the court no discretion; in others, judges have full discretion as to the nature and extent of the sentences imposed. Disparity of sentences has been cited as one of the major causes of unrest leading to prison violence.

PUNISHMENT

Punishment is familiar to us in all aspects of life. We are acquainted with its use in the family and in the school; we employ punishment of various kinds with our pets, our children, and with one another; we believe that we understand the operation of punishment, and we can generally foresee its effects when it is employed. Through the use of positive sanctions (such as rewards or reinforcements), groups and societies seek to encourage conformity to various norms; by means of negative sanctions (punishments), attempts are made to discourage deviant behavior.

Reward and punishment, two of the principal techniques or processes for affecting behavior, have been familiar to the philosopher—or indeed to any person with an inquisitive mind—since time immemorial. The notion that people seek to maximize pleasure and avoid pain or discomfort was already ancient when it found its way into Jeremy Bentham's *hedonistic calculus*. Similar ideas had been expressed by the ancient Greek philosophers; and Freud's *pleasure principle* and *reality principle,* and B. F. Skinner's views on reinforcement did little more than restate the idea in a more sophisticated form (Smith and Vetter 1982).

As a technique for modifying behavior, neither reward nor punishment is exact and unvarying in its effect. Punishment is often no more successful in discouraging some kinds of deviation than reward is in encouraging conformity to various norms. The persistence of these techniques in human affairs, however, indicates that they serve an important function other than merely altering behavior.

The use of punishment to deal with norm violators is traditionally justified by one of three rationales:

1. *Retribution.* "You're going to get what's coming to you."
2. *Deterrence.* "We're going to punish you so that you won't do it again." And a variation: "We're going to punish you so that *others* won't do the same thing."
3. *Incapacitation.* "As long as we're punishing *you,* you won't be out doing something to *us.*"

As you might expect, these rationalizations leave considerable room for overlap. For instance, locking a naughty child in his or her room without supper may serve all three functions simultaneously. That is, it may communicate to the child that acting naughty will bring down the wrath of the parents and family; second, that it is no fun being locked up without supper, which gives one something to think about the next time an opportunity to act naughty presents itself; and third, that as long as one is locked up, there is little chance for further naughtiness. If a thoughtful brother or sister draws an appropriate conclusion from watching a sibling being punished in the above manner, the punishment may even manage to serve as a deterrent. These points should be kept in mind when considering the use of punishment for official purposes. The seriousness and magnitude of the punishment may differ, but the principles are the same.

Retribution

The punitive response is rooted in tradition and buttressed by common sense. **Retribution**—which means "something for recompense"—is a rather primitive (one hesitates to call it natural) human reaction: people who get hurt want to hurt back. A retribution theory of punishment means that punishment is inflicted on a person who has infringed the rights and the safety of others. Normally this theory of punishment insists that the severity of the penalty should be equivalent to the seriousness of the crime. It is not difficult, therefore, to understand why this justification for punishment ("the law of just deserts") has received a good deal of popular support throughout the ages. This justification for sentencing considers only the offenders' actual behavior and not what they may do in the future or what others may do unless the offenders are made to suffer. During the Iranian crisis in 1980, for example, practically every newspaper in the country received letters suggesting that the United States round up an equal number of Iranian hostages (from among the Iranians here on student visas) and hold them under exactly the same conditions that U.S. embassy personnel endured in Teheran. And similar messages, some of which verged on the obscene, festooned the bumpers of automobiles from Maine to California.

Deterrence

The most widely held justification for the punishment of individual offenders is to reduce the crime rate. This is why a sentencing philosophy like **deterrence,** which aims in part at reducing the crime rate, is so attractive. The theory of deterrence was developed by reformers in the nineteenth century who were disturbed by the theory of retribution. Furthermore, they argued, by punishing the offender severely, the state demonstrates its determination to control crime. Deterrence has both a *specific* and a *general* aspect. When we punish subject A by imprisonment, we wish to deter A from committing further offenses, not only during A's period of incapacitation, but also following release from confinement. Our desire is reinforced by the belief that punishment brings about beneficial changes in the behavior of the person who is punished. We also believe that punishing A will deter B and C from committing criminal offenses similar to those committed by A. Optimistically, we hope that the example provided by A's punishment will have even broader effects in terms of deterring the commission of offenses *other than* those for which A was punished. Hence, general deterrence by the threat of arrest, conviction, and imprisonment can be thought of as the criminal law and the agencies of the criminal justice system empowered to deter potential offenders from committing crimes.

Psychologists, sociologists, economists, and other specialists have experimented extensively with the deterrent effects of punishment. Psychologists have looked at both animal and human subjects and have generated a large volume of conflicting and often contradictory results. This is quite understandable, given the complexity of even the simplest experiment on punishment; but it offers little help to the judge or correctional administrator. It is particularly difficult to understand how criminal justice authorities can be expected to place much confidence in research involving animal subjects when a crucially important element in deterrence is the human capacity for reasoning about the probable outcome of one's actions (Newman 1978).

Some sociological studies of the effectiveness of punishment as a deterrent deal with variations in recidivism (repeat crimes) in relation to the type and severity of sentencing. Sociologists have also focused on the issue of capital punishment as it affects homicide rates. Economists, too, have devoted considerable attention to capital punishment as a deterrent to violent crime, but they tend to employ extremely sophisticated mathematical models that are beyond the comprehension of almost everyone (except other economists or mathematicians). Despite the sophistication and complexity of the methodology, however, economists' results have not been appreciably different from those reached by psychologists—namely, that some research supports the idea of deterrence, and some does not.

Experts on punishment stress that several factors seem to have a significant effect on the results or outcome of punishment. That is, the factors are related to the success, partial success, or failure of punishment as an approach to deterrence. These factors are the speed, severity, and certainty of punishment. Evidence from both informal anecdotes and laboratory experiments indicates that certainty is a more influential variable than severity or speed, but it is difficult to arrive at an unqualified conclusion. All three factors are rarely present in any real-life situation; and even in the controlled environment of the laboratory, it is nearly impossible to conduct a rigorous and exacting comparison of the relative efficacy of one variable with respect to the others.

According to Grünhut, three components must be present if punishment is to operate as a means for curbing crime. First, "speedy and inescapable detection and prosecution" must convince the offender that crime does not pay (Grünhut 1948, p. 3). Second, after punishment has been meted out, the criminal must have a fair chance for a fresh start. Third, "the state which claims the right of punishment must uphold superior values which the offender can reasonably be expected to acknowledge" (ibid.).

Incapacitation (Restraint)

Punishment that involves imprisonment is justified on the grounds that as long as an offender is being held in confinement he or she is not free to commit more crimes. This rationale is regarded by both supporters and critics of the punitive approach as the most plausible argument in favor of punishment. In everyday language this theory of punishment is known as "lock 'em up and throw away the key."

Extreme forms of punishment, such as execution or life imprisonment, constitute total **incapacitation.** Implicit in incapacitation is the belief that past behavior is the best basis for predicting future behavior. In the case of criminal behavior, the presumption is that a person who commits a particular type of crime is likely to commit more of those crimes or crimes of some other type. As Packer points out:

> This latter justification does not seem to figure largely in the justification for incapacitation as a mode of prevention. To the extent that we lock up burglars because we fear that they will commit further offenses, our prediction is not that they will if left unchecked violate the antitrust laws, or cheat on their income taxes, but we fear further burglaries, or other crimes associated with burglary, such as homicide or bodily injury. The premise is that the person may have a tendency to commit further crimes like the one for which he is now being punished and that punishing him will restrain him from doing so (1968, p. 50).

In every case, Packer reminds us, whether the prediction is valid is something that can only be determined by the subsequent actions of the offender.

Disillusionment with the rehabilitative ideal in corrections has led some influential authorities in criminal justice (e.g.; Van den Haag 1975; Wilson 1977) to argue strongly for swift, certain, and severe punishment to remove habitual and serious offenders (particularly juvenile and youthful offenders) from circulation. This position is supported by research that demonstrates rather conclusively that a small number of offenders account for a large percentage of criminal offenses (Petersilia, Greenwood, and Lavin 1977; Wolfgang, Figlio, and Sellin 1972). What would happen to crime rates if the suggested strategy was followed?

Petersilia, Greenwood, and Lavin (1977) claim that it is counterproductive to incapacitate older habitual offenders when data suggest that individual offense rates decline substantially with age. In a study of a birth cohort by Wolfgang and his associates (Wolfgang, Figlio, and Sellin 1972), approximately 6 percent of 10,000 male subjects in the cohort committed five or more offenses by the time they were eighteen years old; this 6 percent was responsible for about two-thirds of the violent crimes committed by the entire group. The implication is that if these individuals had been removed from circulation at some early point in their criminality, society would have been spared considerable grief and damage.

The principal stumbling block facing proponents of incapacitation is the fact that those who are incapacitated by being placed in confinement do not stay there: they are eventually released from prison or training school, and their subsequent behavior inevitably reflects the consequences of their experience during confinement. Vachss and Bakal (1979), for example, contend that confinement of criminality-prone delinquents has *the effect of increasing,* rather than decreasing, the commitment to a criminal career. Their argument is not directed toward the ineffectiveness of incapacitation, but toward the adverse results of confinement in existing correctional institutions.

There is nothing novel in the discovery that imprisonment has a deep effect upon those who undergo confinement. But it is necessary to point out that a substantial body of opinion within corrections supports the belief that those effects are beneficial for the inmate and society; that those effects are, in fact, the primary purpose for incarcerating an individual in the first place. Based on this theory of punishment, many states have passed **habitual offender laws.** Under habitual offender statutes defendants who have committed two or more serious offenses (in some states, three or more offenses) can be sentenced to extended terms of imprisonment, even for life. The legislators who pass these statutes argue that the criminals have not learned from their past mistakes so all that can be done is to protect society from them.

REHABILITATION: THE TREATMENT PERSPECTIVE

Treatment, according to the general dictionary definition, connotes the manner in which a person or thing is handled, used, or processed. In the context of mental health, the goal of treatment or therapy is to help an individual who has been diagnosed as emotionally disturbed or mentally ill to attain some level of improved functioning. In Chapter 5, we documented some of the problems encountered in the application of the medical model to a wide range of psychological problems, many of which have little or no resemblance to conditions that can reasonably be expedited to fit some model of a disease or illness. If the same is true for much of what psychiatry has claimed for the province of mental illness, the mischief wrought in corrections by the extension of these ideas is well-nigh incalculable.

The idea of rehabilitation in corrections began as a matter of moral redemption of the offender. It was gradually co-opted by psychiatry, however, and transformed into a problem for psychotherapy. The goal of correctional treatment became the changing of the personality of the criminal to achieve improvements in social behavior and personal adjustment. This was a praiseworthy objective; unfortunately, it had to be pursued within a system whose practitioners and representatives are charged with a responsibility for defending society that takes precedence over the rehabilitation of offenders. Consider the issue of incarceration. When the goal of rehabilitation was the predominant philosophy in criminology treatment programs, vocational and psychological training programs were introduced into prisons. This rehabilitative outlook shaped even the vocabulary of criminal punishment. Prisons were often called "correctional institutions"; those for young adults were often called "reformatories."

Reintegration

The newest correctional philosophy for punishing offenders is called **reintegration** into the free community. This philosophy is an extension of the rehabilitative philosophy and attempts to compensate for the weakness of that approach while at the same time adopting more acceptable ideas. Those who advocate the reintegration philosophy of punishment believe that the causes of crime and the functions of corrective efforts are two highways that fail to intersect. These theorists believe the offender does need help, but at the same time they suggest that criminal behavior is often the result of the offender's failure to integrate properly into society. This aspect of the reintegration theory separates it from rehabilitation. Whereas rehabilitation attempts to treat the offender as an isolated entity looking for a medical cause and cure for his or her behavior, the reintegrative model realizes that society and the individual are inseparable and thereby emphasizes particular aspects of the offender's environment as critical. Under this theory, half-way houses and social agencies that assist offenders when they are released from prison receive primary emphasis. Proponents of this theory of punishment believe that contact and interaction with the positive elements rather than the negative elements of society are what is necessary for overall treatment of the offender. This theory has won some acceptance in recent years and seems to enjoy increasing support (Pursley 1987).

The Prison System

Prisons are the most visible manifestation of the corrections component of the criminal justice system. Critics of the penal institution consider the prison a monument to society's failure to devise more effective and humane methods for dealing with criminals. This viewpoint deserves careful consideration, but it is only a part of the story. The righteous indignation directed against prisons is singularly misdirected, especially by critics who fail to offer realistic alternatives for coping with the problems that prisons are compelled to handle.

Prisons today house a disproportionately high concentration of people who are socially deviant, emotionally unstable, psychologically disturbed, mentally retarded, and prone to aggression and violence. No longer are prison populations composed primarily of nonviolent offenders. Our search for alternatives to imprisonment has become focused on probation and other community-based correctional programs for first offenders, minor property criminals, drug offenders, and similar types of persons, leaving behind those who are perceived as a threat to public safety. Thus, we have loaded our prisons with the highest concentration of dangerous offenders in the entire history of penology.

The evidence speaks for itself. In 1974, one American prison witnessed eighty-seven stabbings and twelve inmate fatalities. This was not some backward bastion in the boondocks. It was San Quentin, California—a correctional institution in a state that boasts of having the most progressive correctional system in the country. The following year, ten inmates were slain in Florida prisons in explosive outbursts of violence triggered by some trifle—an argument over a bar of soap, an alleged insult, the theft of a cigarette.

Tensions in prison are elevated by racism. Inmates practice an informal, self-imposed segregation: whites and blacks stand in separate lines for meals, and whites, blacks, and Hispanics rarely sit together in the mess hall. Black convicts with hostile attitudes towards whites and Hispanics band together, and Hispanics with an antiblack or antiwhite bias do likewise. The result is that everyone is constantly struggling over the spoils of prison enterprises and over violations of the prisoner code that constitute slights against each group's honor. This internecine strife creates potentially explosive conditions within the institution that can be fused by a single incident.

Involvement of the New Left in American prisons during the protest years of the late 1960s and early 1970s was reflected in the demands of rioting Attica prisoners for guarantees of "asylum and safe passage to some nonimperialist country" ("Prisons: Uprising in Attica" 1971). Eldridge Cleaver, George Jackson, Huey Newton, and Malcolm X were militants who developed their political consciousness while "doing time." It is not hard to understand how people with a background of social and economic deprivation readily accept the argument that they are political prisoners of a racist, capitalist system that has provided them with no alternative to a life of crime. And it is equally easy to comprehend how such views can make hash out of treatment or rehabilitation. For nonwhite inmates, participation in programs sponsored by "The Man" is the rough equivalent to collaboration with the enemy. For example, George Jackson was contemptuous of the efforts of California prison authorities to turn him into what he called "a good nigger."

The authors of a leading textbook in corrections (Allen and Simonsen 1981) observe that many criminal justice practitioners view any program or institution that is not punitive in its approach as "being soft" on criminals or "operating a country club for cons." These practitioners believe that the implementation of a treatment ideology does not mean coddling inmates or allowing them free run of an institution. In fact, they maintain that some form of treatment can be applied even within the strictest and most custody-oriented institutions.

> The major difference between the treatment and punishment ideologies is that in the former, offenders are assigned to the institution for a correctional program intended to prepare them for readjustment to the community, not just for punishment and confinement. There is room for punishment and for security in the treatment approach, but little room for treatment in the punitive approach. The more humane treatment methods are intended to be used in conjunction with the employment of authority in a constructive and positive manner, but inmates must be allowed to try and to fail. Authoritarian procedures, used alone, only provide the offender with more ammunition to support a self-image as an "oppressed and impotent pawn of the power structure" (ibid., p. 84).

In sharp contrast, Alberta Nassi (1980), on the basis of her experiences within the California prison system, is very skeptical that treatment can be carried out in the punitive context of a state prison. Rather, she sees an almost insurmountable role conflict between the objectives of treatment and custody.

Issues in Correctional Treatment

Three fundamental issues have to be addressed with regard to treatment of the criminal offender: an offender's right to treatment; an offender's right to *refuse* treatment; and the ability of the criminal justice system to provide *effective* treatment. The right to refuse treatment might be alternatively phrased as the right to receive punishment rather than treatment. The first and second of these issues raise significant questions in terms of constitutional law. The third issue involves a searching appraisal of people-changing capabilities as they relate to contemporary intervention techniques.

A series of legal decisions has affirmed the right to treatment on both constitutional and statutory grounds for persons who have been committed to mental hospitals on the basis of a civil commitment rather than a criminal proceeding (*Rouse* v. *Cameron* [373 F.2d 451 (1966)], *Donaldson* v. *O'Connor* [493 F.2d 507 (1974)], *Wyatt* v. *Stickney* [344 F.Supp. 373 (1972)]). The position of the courts has been that confining a person for the primary purpose of securing treatment for that individual in cases where there are unmistakable symptoms of severe psychiatric disturbance carries with it an obligation to provide such treatment. If this obligation is not met—that is, if no treatment is available—the quid pro quo for confinement has been violated, and the individual has been deprived of his or her liberty in violation of due process.

Attempts to extend this right to treatment to incarcerated felons who do *not* exhibit signs of psychiatric disorder raise questions and issues that are different from those that pertain to the civil commitment of mentally disturbed persons. The rationale for confining criminal offenders is punitive rather than therapeutic, despite the belief of many criminal justice practitioners that rehabilitation is a more defensible goal than punishment, deterrence, or incapacitation. A much clearer case can be made for the right of juveniles to treatment, because the doctrine of **parens patriae** (i.e., the juvenile court acting in the role of "kind and loving parent") implies an obligation to provide treatment rather than punishment. As the U.S. Supreme Court pointed out in the Gault decision (*In re Gault* [387 U.S. 1 (1967)]), depriving a juvenile of rights guaranteed to adults under the process can only be justified if the procedural informality of the juvenile court operates in favor of youngsters to secure access to treatment.

Of even greater significance to the incarcerated criminal offender, however, is the right to refuse treatment. When treatment is aimed at changing the mind or thought processes of the recipient, the right to refuse treatment is based on the First Amendment right to free speech. The First Amendment has been interpreted to support an individual's right to "mind freedom" and "privacy of the mind." The right to have private thoughts and ideas is fundamental. The courts have been careful not to interfere in the fundamental rights of individuals except where such interference can be justified—as being in the vital interest of the state, for example. If the right to think, or even to have delusional thoughts, is protected by the First Amendment, the use of coercive treatment to change the mind can thus be justified *only* in cases where there is a clear and compelling state interest.

Case law has held that the more experimental the treatment, the greater the responsibility of the physician to inform patients completely of alternatives and consequences. In *Mackey* v. *Procunier* (47 F.2d 877 [1973]), District Appellate Court Judge Merrill addressed Mackey's contention that he had been subjected to a traumatic administration of succinylcholine, a drug used in aversive therapy, without his informed consent. An inmate of the California prison system, Mackey, contended that he had consented to electroshock therapy, *not* the experimental aversive therapy. Judge Merrill wrote that if Mackey's contention was true, there was a serious question of "impermissible tinkering with the mental processes."

These considerations notwithstanding, however, the most important issue in correctional treatment is whether the state—operating through the formal agencies of the criminal justice system or through the vast informal network of social service and mental health referral agencies—has the *ability* to provide effective treatment for criminal offenders. However "effective treatment" is defined, its objective has to be some demonstrable or measurable decrease in antisocial conduct, particularly as indicated by a decrease in recidivism.

A number of publications have raised the public consciousness with respect to charges that the rehabilitative goals of corrections are a widespread and massive failure. As a result, critics of the treatment approach have been all too simplistically labeled "hardliners," presumably to set them off from those who continue to advocate treatment in corrections. James Q. Wilson, author of the widely read and much-discussed book *Thinking about Crime* (1977), assesses the correctional treatment approach and its results this way:

> It does not seem to matter what form of treatment in the correctional system is attempted—whether vocational training or academic education; whether counseling inmates individually, in groups, or not at all; whether therapy is administered by social workers or psychiatrists; whether the institutional context of the treatment is custodial or benign; whether the person is placed on probation or released on parole; or whether the treatment takes place in the community or in institutions. Indeed, some forms of treatment—notably a few experiments with psychotherapy—actually produce an *increase* in the rate of recidivism (Wilson 1977, p. 159).

Dissent with these negative evaluations has been registered by Glaser (1975), who concluded from a survey of correctional treatment studies that certain programs do have some success with particular categories of offenders. And Adams (1970) reported that an intensive counseling program at a California penal institution—the so-called PICO (Pilot Intensive Counseling Organization) program—appeared to produce positive results with selected offenders. Shireman, Mann, Larsen, and Young (1972), based on a review of a dozen treatment studies conducted in various institutions, conclude that certain types of institutional therapy (e.g., short-term milieu therapy), coupled with high staff morale, can yield results that are sufficiently strong to carry over into the postrelease period. They also found some evidence that positive results are associated with treatment programs aimed at youthful offenders—programs such as intensive milieu therapy, group counseling, and plastic surgery for individuals with psychological problems related to facial deformation or disfigurement.

Further, Gibbons and his colleagues maintain that correctional treatment has not yet been given a fair trial. At the same time, they contend, "it is likely that intervention efforts will need to move away from many of those earlier strategems that were based on psychiatric images of offenders and on efforts to tinker with their mental health through some kind of individual counseling or therapy" (Gibbons et al. 1977, p. 106). This approach seems to be an excellent first step toward divesting corrections of its overload of psychiatric jargon and illness models. Terms such as "treatment" should be reserved for medical procedures, and psychiatrically neutral terms such as "intervention technique" should be used in their place. A meaningful and financially rewarding job or the chance to acquire further education are probably more valuable than short-term or long-term psychotherapy in encouraging prosocial behavior in criminals, because such techniques increase the criminal's stake in conformity.

At present, there is no tried and proven way to "treat" antisocial behavior. Most research that has concerned itself with the durable effects of behavior change has involved relatively stable, reasonably motivated, middle-class patients or clients who have voluntarily sought therapy. Even under these favorable circumstances, it has proven exceedingly difficult to achieve successful therapeutic outcomes, at least in terms of measures for which there is some professional consensus. To extrapolate these findings to some of the clientele of the criminal justice system is out of the question. As Silber reminds us, most of the prisoners in correctional institutions

> . . . are hostile, suspicious, and immature and tend to identify with subcultural values that are legally proscribed. They usually perceive their personality functioning to be acceptable. They are not, in general, likely to clamor for individual psychotherapy and usually are seen on referral. Thus, there is no strong, sustained interest on the part of the prisoners themselves for treatment (1974, p. 242).

SENTENCING

Sentencing reflects a blend of policies and procedures that derive from legislative, judicial, and administrative authorities (Reid 1982). Whatever theory of punishment ultimately guides legislators or judges, the sentencing of the defendant is a series of alternatives including fines, probation, community-based programs, imprisonment, or the death penalty. In some cases, legislatures enact laws that fix penal sanctions for various criminal offenses; in other cases, judges exercise their discretion within limits established by law.

Sentencing Structures

If a legislature fixes the length of a sentence by statute (e.g., a term of fifteen years for armed robbery), the sentence is called a *definite or flat-time* sentence. Thus, neither the trial judge nor administrative agencies (such as the parole board or the department of corrections) are permitted any discretion in assigning such sentences. A flat-time sentence cannot be reduced by parole. This type of sentence lost its popularity in the early part of the twentieth century when those interested in rehabilitation found it to be too rigid and insensitive to the individual prisoners' characteristics and needs.

Other jurisdictions allow judges to fix sentences within a range of minimum and maximum sentences established by the legislature. Thus, armed robbery may carry a sentence of five to fifteen years.The judge imposes a *determinate sentence* within the limits set by statute. In this scheme, administrative authorities have no discretion to reduce the sentence fixed by the court. (The *minimum* term generally refers to the earliest time at which an imprisoned offender can be considered for release.) Under a determinate sentence, at the end of the prisoner's term minus credited "**good time,**" the prisoner is automatically freed. Hence the release is not tied to participation in a treatment program. Determinate sentences are still used in a number of jurisdictions in the United States.

For most of the twentieth century, American jurisdictions have had **indeterminate sentencing** systems in which criminal statutes generally authorize judges to impose sentences from within a wide range. Probation to five years is a common range; probation to twenty-five years is not unknown. The difference between determinate and indeterminate sentencing is that in the former the judge fixes a sentence within the range, whereas in the latter the judge sentences the offender for an indefinite period with only the minimum and maximum being fixed. Under indeterminate sentencing, the judge's decision is final; the appellate court can seldom consider appeals based on sentencing decisions. The penal philosophy supporting the indeterminate sentences is based on a purely correctional model of punishment, which presupposes that the sentence should meet the needs of the defendant. Once the defendant has been rehabilitated, this theory of sentencing sees no reason why he or she should be incarcerated for one more day.

For example, the crime of armed robbery may carry a sentence from as low as one year up to a maximum of life imprisonment, with a ten-year minimum being the most common sentence imposed by judges. Then, as Reid notes,

> the decision to release the inmate is later determined by an administrative agency, usually a parole board. The type of sentence imposed in this model is called the *indeterminate sentence*. The idea is that the offender should remain incarcerated only as long as necessary for rehabilitation, but neither a legislature nor a judge can tell in advance how long a sentence should be for a particular individual (1982, p. 444).

In addition, some states have passed laws that impose *mandatory sentences*. A mandatory sentence is a statutory requirement that a certain penalty shall be set and imposed by *all* criminal offenders upon conviction for a specific offense or a specific series of offenses. Within the past ten years, thirty legislatures have passed mandatory sentencing laws for a selected number of crimes. In essence either offenders convicted of these crimes excluded from probation, or particular offenders who are considered to be recidivists are made ineligible for parole. For example, a Florida law requires a minimum sentence of three years for conviction of any crime involving the use of firearms. Mandatory sentencing statutes usually specify that the offender cannot be considered for probation, parole, or any other form of conditional release until the minimum sentence is completed. Mandatory sentences have been established for crimes such as rape, robbery, murder, and repeated violations of drug laws.

Another approach is *presumptive sentencing*. This came about when legislators found that courts were discovering that the use of mandatory sentences for some crimes led to an increase in plea bargaining as offenders sought to reduce their charges to a different offense that did not carry with it a mandatory sentence. Consequently, the legislatures enacted presumptive sentencing statutes, which set a suggested term as well as a minimum and maximum sentence for a particular crime; the judge then fixes the sentence within the range set up by the legislature. Offenders convicted under this scheme receive the suggested sentence unless there are mitigating or aggravating circumstances that allow the judge to go below or above the suggested sentence. Legislatures in more than a dozen states have integrated presumptive sentencing into their criminal codes.

Earlier in this chapter, we discussed retribution as one of the justifications for punishment. Bayley distinguishes retribution from vengeance as follows:

> Unlike vengeance, retribution is imposed by the courts after a guilty plea, or a trial, in which the accused has been found guilty of committing a crime. Prescribed by the law broken and proportioned to the gravity of the offense committed, retribution is not inflicted to gratify or compensate anyone who suffered a loss but to enforce the law and vindicate the legal order (1976, p. 551).

It is Bayley's view that the primary purpose of sentencing is to punish the offender. Hirsch (1976) believes that punishment is the *only* legitimate goal of sentencing.

A system of law that allows each offender to know what he or she faces is fairer than one based on the offender's social background, personality, or other factors. Bayley calls for the establishment of a range of authorized punishments. For example, a legislature would create a standard or presumptive sentence with a range of authorized variations to guide judges in sentencing. Sentences would be determined by the nature of the crime and the offender's criminal history. Judges could deviate from the presumptive sentence to the extent allowed by the legislation only if there are mitigating factors defined by law. The punishment would be primarily the loss of liberty (i.e., the physical custody of an individual for a substantial portion of every day). This system of presumptive sentencing would still give the court some discretion (Bayley 1976, p. 555).

Bayley also believes that, although there is still a need for rehabilitation, rehabilitation should not be the controlling factor in sentencing. Rather, he feels that the term of a sentence should be fixed in advance so that an offender knows how long he or she will be under state control. In addition, the offender should not have to spend all of his or her time in confinement, but should be offered a graduated release program involving lesser degrees of custody:

> Rehabilitation could be facilitated within the framework of a certainty of punishment model. Defendants would know their exact status at all times and yet be without incentive to engage in the dramatic acts which so often characterize attempts to convince parole boards that rehabilitation has taken place. The opportunity for gradual reentry into society would exist because the defendant is entitled to it, but not because he or she has earned it (ibid., pp. 561–62).

The characteristics of various sentencing structures are summarized in Table 12.1 It must be pointed out, however, that many states employ sentencing procedures that vary from these models and approaches. Senna and Siegel caution that it is difficult to find precise meanings for such terms as "definite sentence," "indefinite sentence," and "determinate sentence": "The situation is further confused because what one state may designate as an indefinite sentence may be called a definite sentence in another state" (1987, p. 424).

Finally, variations in sentencing can occur as a consequence of multiple convictions. That is, if defendants are convicted of more than one offense, or on more than one count of the same type of offense, they may be given either *concurrent* or *consecutive* sentences. When a defendant receives multiple sentences for several crimes and the judge orders that the terms of imprisonment be served concurrently, all of the various sentences are served simultaneously. However, if the judge orders that the various sentences be served consecutively, they are served one after another. Time served for concurrent sentences begins on the same day, regardless of how many sentences are imposed. For consecutive sentences, time served on the second sentence begins *after* the first sentence is completed. When an offender is sentenced to terms that add up to a ridiculous total such as 400 years in prison, media attention may be attracted, and the judge may gain a reputation as being "tough on criminals"; but if the terms are to run concurrently, they will have the same net effect as if the offender had received a single sentence for all of the crimes with which he or she is charged.

Good Time and Actual Time Served

Although good time is not a sentence, its impact on sentencing should be mentioned. In all but four states, days are subtracted from the prisoner's minimum or maximum term for good behavior or for participation in various types of treatment, educational, or vocational programs. Most correctional officials consider these sentence reduction policies as absolutely necessary in order to maintain institutional order. Often they are used as a method to relieve prison overcrowding. The amount of good time that can be earned varies among states. Some states allow five days a month to count for good time; others allow only forty-five days a year to count

TABLE 12.1
Common Sentencing Structures

Sentencing Structure	Characteristics
Indeterminate	Minimum and maximum terms prescribed by legislature; place and length of sentence controlled by corrections and parole; judge has little discretion over time served; goal is rehabilitation; sentence to fit offender; uncertainty and disparity in sentencing is major problem.
Indefinite	Similar to indeterminate sentence in some states; minimum and maximum terms, or only maximum term prescribed by legislature; sentence to match offender's needs; judge has some sentencing discretion; wide disparity in sentences imposed; parole used for early release.
Definite	Fixed period prescribed by legislature and imposed by judge; goal to punish and deter offender from further crime; allows for same sentence to apply to all convicted of particular offenses; eliminates disparity; judge has no discretion over length of sentence, but only over choice of sentence; offender required to serve entire sentence; no parole; inflexibility and rigidity is major problem.
Determinate	Similar to definite sentence; has one fixed term of years set by legislation; offender required to serve entire sentence where no parole exists.
Mandatory	Fixed term set by legislature for particular crimes; sentence must be imposed by judge; judge has no discretion in choice of sentence; goal is punishment and deterrence; contrary to individualized sentence; no sentencing disparity; no parole.
Presumptive	Legislatively prescribed range of sentences for given crimes; minimum and maximum terms with judge setting determinate sentence within these bounds; judge maintains some discretion; guidelines and use of mitigating and aggravating circumstances established by legislature; goal is justice, deterrence and individualization in sentencing; "just deserts."

Adapted from J. J. Senna and L. J. Siegel, *Introduction to Criminal Justice* (St. Paul, Minn.: West, 1981), p. 431, by permission of the authors and the publisher.

for good time. Most often the number of "good time days" are either written into statutes or stipulated by the Department of Corrections.

In *McGinnis* v. *Royster* (410 U.S. 263 [1973]), the U.S. Supreme Court upheld the constitutionality of New York's correction law that did not require the consideration of jail detention time when good time credits were calculated after the inmate was transferred to a state prison. The court held that the purposes of pretrial and posttrial incarceration differ and that offenders waiting in jail should not be granted good time credits because they are not yet participating in a state rehabilitation program.

A distinction should be made between an offender's sentence and the actual time served. What most members of the public do not realize is that there is a great difference between the length of the sentence announced in the courtroom and the amount actually served by offenders. Credit for time spent in jail awaiting sentence, credit for good time, and in many states release into the community on parole greatly reduce the period of actual incarceration. Due to the variations in the sentencing and releasing laws among the states, it is difficult to compare the amount of time served with the actual length of sentences imposed throughout the United States. Some criminals serve 83 percent of the sentence, others only serve 33 percent of the sentence.

Balancing Release Rates and Sentencing

Because the state and federal correctional systems are finite in size, sentencing decisions are affected by the release rates at correctional institutions. If more sentences are imposed than releases are granted, dangerous overcrowding results. Such was the case in Florida in 1972 and in 1974 when Director of Corrections Louis Wainwright refused to admit any more prisoners to the state prison system. His action produced results: the courts diverted prisoners to other facilities, and the parole board went to work to clear out the prisons. Thus, sentencing—unavoidably—is the sum of decisions that affect the number of prisoners in institutions and the balancing of limited resources for handling persons sentenced to serve terms.

Sentencing Disparities

Do offenders who commit similar crimes under comparable circumstances generally receive similar sentences? Impressionistic accounts (Frankel 1973) and systematic research (Partridge and Eldridge 1974; Diamond and Zeisel 1975; Diamond 1981) confirm that they do not. In fact, disparities in sentencing are one of the most serious shortcomings of our criminal justice system. As Kneedler points out, sentencing disparity has adverse effects upon (1) prisoners, who know many of the facts surrounding their fellow prisoners' convictions and do not understand why they are being treated differently; (2) the public, which is more aware of disparities in the sentencing process than is sometimes acknowledged, and which, as a result, questions the integrity of the entire criminal justice system; and (3) judges themselves, who have no guidelines for comparison and who thus find it difficult to remove the disparities (1979, p. 18).

Criticisms of sentencing variations are increasing, and statistical studies show that there is a wide range of dispositions for identical offenses. The judges and parole boards exercise discretion without legislative direction as to which sentencing goals were primary or which factors should be considered in setting sentences or determining parole release. Different judges in the same courthouse may consider the same factor as either mitigating or aggravating the defendant's culpability. Thus, for example, while one judge might consider drug addiction to be a mitigating factor that justified reducing the offender's sentence, another judge or parole board member might consider such information as an indicator of future criminality and a reason to increase the sentence.

The indeterminate sentence, once thought to be a solution to the disparity problem, has been questioned on both philosophical and constitutional grounds. McGee (1974) claims that the only valid arguments remaining for indeterminacy in the sentencing of felony offenders are the injustices and inconsistencies that arise from disparities among judges in the same jurisdictions who administer the same laws and dispose of offenders to the same correctional institutions. Pejorative terms such as "hanging judge," "softy," and "Maximum John" (the nickname given to federal Judge John Sirica of Watergate fame) make the same point: namely, that judges vary considerably along a continuum from leniency to severity in sentencing.

One form of sentence disparity is the minimum sentence that adversely affects the parole eligibility of the offender. Also, some trial judges use consecutive sentences to create minimum terms; this type of sentencing can prevent otherwise eligible offenders from being paroled. Unduly long sentences demoralize offenders and threaten their chances for successful reintegration. Dur-

"Don't worry about it. One day you're feeling down and you dish out twenty years to some poor devil. The next day you feel great and everybody gets a suspended sentence. It all evens out in the end."

FIGURE 12.1
Drawing by Von Riegen; © 1964 The New Yorker Magazine, Inc.

ing the 1980s, the Justice Department conducted a study involving 246 federal judges. All were asked the same question: Under a given set of facts and circumstances, what sentence would each of the judges impose on the same defendant? A major highlight of the finding was that for the same hypothetical offense, the recommended sentences ranged from probation to twenty years in prison (*National Law Journal* 1982).

In daily court business, trial judges often lack sufficient time to consider all of the crucial elements of an offense and the special characteristics of the offender before imposing a sentence. And some judges have a tendency to standardize their decision making, announcing sentences to fit certain categories of crimes without paying too much attention to the particular offender. This is especially true in cases involving minor violations. Although individuals convicted of minor offenses are good candidates for reform, they are frequently sentenced immediately after being found guilty or when they enter a guilty plea. And if counsel requests a presentence report before the sentence is imposed, a defendant may have to remain in jail during the delay, a price many defendants are not willing to pay.

Differences in the sentencing tendencies of judges fascinate social scientists. The disparities may be ascribed to a number of factors: the conflicting goals of criminal justice, the fact that judges are products of different backgrounds and have different social values, the administrative pressures on judges, and the influence of community values. Each of these factors affects, to some extent, the judge's exercise of discretion in sentencing. In addition, a judge's perception of these factors is dependent on his or her own attitudes toward the law, toward a particular crime, or toward a certain type of offender. Gaylin relates an amusing and instructive anecdote on this subject:

> A visitor to a Texas court was amazed to hear the judge impose a suspended sentence where a man had pleaded guilty to manslaughter. A few minutes later the same judge sentenced a man who pleaded guilty to stealing a horse and gave him life imprisonment. When the judge was asked by the visitor about the disparity of the two sentences, he replied, "Well, down here there is some men that need killin', but there ain't no horses that need stealin' " (1974, p. 8).

Kneedler notes that, at a sentencing seminar he conducted, a group of trial court judges from several states listed more than thirty factors (collectively) that they took into account in sentencing decisions. Among the factors identified were prior criminal record, drug history, age, education, economic problems, family problems, attitude toward the offense, health, religious convictions, cultural differences, race, sex, and the judge's personal impression about the defendant's experience as a criminal. Unfortunately, none of the judges took all thirty factors into account, and "the degree to which particular factors influenced their decisions differed widely" (Kneedler 1979, p. 18).

TABLE 12.2

Average Sentences of Federal Prisoners, in Months, by Selected Offense and Judicial Circuit (fiscal year ended June 30, 1972)

Judicial Circuit	Narcotics Laws	Forgery	Robbery
1st (Me., Mass., N.H., R.I., P.R.)	68.0	19.7	133.5
2d (Conn., N.Y.)	58.8	30.4	114.7
3d (Del., N.J., Penna., V.I.)	77.4	27.3	128.3
4th (Md., N.C., S.C., Va., W.Va.)	77.0	36.4	158.8
5th (Ala., Fla., Ga., La., Miss., Tex.)	74.8	36.7	144.0
6th (Kent., Mich., Ohio, Tenn.)	54.0	39.3	134.4
7th (Ill., Ind., Wisc.)	75.6	38.2	114.4
8th (Ark., Iowa, Minn., Mo., Neb., N.D., S.D.)	103.3	36.6	155.8
9th (Alaska, Ariz., Calif., Hawaii, Idaho, Mont., Nev., Ore., Wash., Guam)	70.8	42.9	131.1
10th (Colo., Kansas, N.M., Okla., Utah, Wyo.)	85.7	56.5	134.9
All circuits	69.7	37.3	134.6

U.S. Department of Justice. Federal Bureau of Prisons, *Statistical Report, Fiscal Years 1971 and 1972* (Washington, D.C.: U.S. Government Printing Office, 1973), pp. 96–101.

Sentencing Reforms

Around 1970 indeterminate sentencing came under attack. Some critics claimed that the wide, unreviewable discretion of the judges and parole boards resulted in discrimination against minorities and the poor. Some were concerned about unwarranted sentencing disparities. Because sentences could not be appealed, there was nothing a prisoner could do about a disparately severe sentence. A considerable body of research demonstrated the existence of unwarranted sentence disparities, and many believed them to be inherent in indeterminate sentencing. In addition, a highly publicized review of research on treatment programs concluded that their effectiveness could not be demonstrated; the resulting skepticism about rehabilitative programs undermined one of the indeterminate sentencing's foundations.

Attempts to rectify sentencing disparities follow one of four approaches. The first approach involves legislative overhaul of criminal statutes; the second seeks to establish sentencing guidelines for trial court judges. A third approach seeks to organize sentencing councils or institutions that afford judges an opportunity to meet and discuss the factors that influence their decisions—with the goal of developing sentencing norms for similar offenses and offenders within a given jurisdiction. Finally, some efforts at reform are directed toward the appellate review of sentencing in jurisdictions where sentences have not been subjected to review in the past.

(This approach is discussed later in this chapter under "Appeal and Postconviction Remedies.")

PENAL CODE REFORMS The penal codes of most jurisdictions are a potpourri of social thinking from ages past. Historically, criminal statutes have been enacted as ad hoc responses to specific events, often without relating a crime to similar offenses in the penal code. If an event is particularly heinous or repugnant, the public may pressure legislators to create a new law with a formula for punishment attached. Unfortunately, such laws—with punishments that are often irrationally severe—remain on the books for decades long after the causative event and the legislators are forgotten.

State criminal codes are, at times, illogical in the kinds of sentences they mandate for some offenses. In California, for example, the maximum penalty for breaking into a car to steal its contents is a prison term of fifteen years; stealing the car itself only nets a maximum term of ten years. In two states, bribing a witness, juror, or judge carries with it a maximum sentence of five years, whereas bribing a football player carries a maximum sentence of ten years (National Advisory Commission on Criminal Justice Standards and Goals 1973a, p. 146).

The President's Commission on Law Enforcement and Administration of Justice noted that severe sentences for nearly all felony offenses were characteristic of American penal codes and that "prison sentences in America are, as a general rule, longer than those elsewhere" (1967, p. 142). One reason for such harsh sentences for certain crimes is that many laws imposing extremely long sentences were passed following a criminal incident that shocked the public; a legislature quickly passed a law to protect society by putting the offender away for a long time. Yet only a small portion of the criminal population is responsible for such incidents. The sad fact is that long maximum penalties tend to drive up sentences in cases where long sentences are unwarranted. One judge might choose five to eight years as an appropriate sentence under a twenty-year maximum statute. Others might back away from the minimum end of the range and impose as much as fifteen years for the same offender. Thus, the drafter of penal statutes is in a quandry. He or she must provide a sentence stiff enough to handle the occasional "worst offender," but short enough to be applied to offenders who are not unusual risks.

The American Law Institute's *Model Penal Code: Proposed Official Draft* (1962) addresses the problem of severity and nonuniformity in current penal codes with regard to sentencing. Imprisonment is seen as a last resort and is used only when (1) there is undue risk that during the period of suspended sentence or probation the defendant will commit another crime; (2) the defendant is in need of correctional treatment that can be provided most effectively by his or her commitment to an institution; or (3) a lesser sentence will depreciate the seriousness of the defendant's crimes (ibid., p. 106). These criteria are intended only as a guide to the use of all alternatives to imprisonment before the criteria are applied in a specific case.

The *Model Penal Code* also recommends that all crimes be reduced to five grades, three for felonies and two for misdemeanors. A maximum penalty—shorter than those now used by most states—would be assigned to each grade. Minimum sentences would be set at one year for all felonies and at three years for the most serious felonies. If a particular offense were to strike great fear in the community and if the offender were especially dangerous, a judge would be allowed to extend the maximum sentence. Judges would be granted flexibility to fit a sentence to a particular case. Nevertheless, although the *Model Penal Code* appeals greatly to practitioners in corrections, it has not been widely accepted among legislators—men and women who must face the outcry of enraged citizens when harsh "law-and-order" statutes are struck down.

SENTENCING GUIDELINES Sentencing guidelines are developed empirically by examining past judicial decisions within a jurisdiction. Sentencing guidelines are based on the actual sentencing behavior of judges. The advent of sentencing guidelines represents the frustration of legislatures with sentencing disparities; guidelines are an attempt to develop an instrument to indicate what most judges should usually do in a particular type of case. Guidelines are designed to constrain the discretion of judges and direct the judge to the specific action he or she should take in a given circumstance. In a manner comparable to the development of the actuarial tables used by the Federal Parole Board, a grid is constructed based on two scores. One of these, the *offender score,* is derived by assigning points to such factors as the number of convictions for juvenile crimes, adult misdemeanors, and adult felonies; the number of times imprisoned; escapes from prison; whether probation or parole has been granted; and occupational and educational status. The *offense score* is based on the severity of the crime. As shown in Table 12.3, the scores are arranged so that a judge can consider the likelihood that a given individual will recidivate.

Sentencing guidelines represent a summation of the collective experience of a given city or state in dealing with various kinds of offenders. Although some judges are not compelled to use them, the guidelines provide a means by which a judge can sense how defendants with similar characteristics and offenses were sentenced in the past. Thus, a number of cities and states have already adopted such guidelines. One of the major concerns about sentencing guidelines is that the perceived rigidity of the statute or guidelines enhances the discretion of the pros-

TABLE 12.3
Suggested Sentencing Guidelines for Colorado (felony 4 offenses)[1]

Offense Score (severity of offense)[3]	Offender Score (probability of recidivism)[2]				
	−1 to −7	0 to 2	3 to 8	9 to 12	13+
10 to 12	Indeterminate minimum; 4–5 year maximum	Indeterminate minimum; 8–10 year maximum	Indeterminate minimum; 8–10 year maximum	Indeterminate minimum; 8–10 year maximum	Indeterminate minimum; 8–10 year maximum
8 to 9	Out[4]	3–5 month work project	Indeterminate minimum; 3–4 year maximum	Indeterminate minimum; 8–10 year maximum	Indeterminate minimum; 8–10 year maximum
6 to 7	Out	Out	Indeterminate minimum; 3–4 year maximum	Indeterminate minimum; 6–8 year maximum	Indeterminate minimum; 8–10 year maximum
3 to 5	Out	Out	Out	Indeterminate minimum; 4–5 year maximum	Indeterminate minimum; 4–5 year maximum
1 to 2	Out	Out	Out	Out	Indeterminate minimum; 3–4 year maximum

[1]The Colorado Penal Code contains five levels of felonies (Felony 1 is the most serious) and three levels of misdemeanors. The Felony 4 category includes crimes such as manslaughter, robbery, and second-degree burglary. The legislated maximum sentence for a Felony 4 offense is ten years. No minimum period of confinement is to be set by the court.
[2]The higher the offender score, the higher the probability of recidivism.
[3]The higher the offense score, the more serious the crime.
[4]"Out" indicates a nonincarcerative sentence such as probation, deferred prosecution, or deferred judgment.

Adapted from J. M. Kress, L. T. Wilkins, and D. M. Gottfredson, "Is the End of Judicial Sentencing in Sight?" *Judicature* 60 (1976): 221, by permission of the authors and the publisher.

ecutor, particularly during plea bargain negotiations. The concern here is that the prosecutor will undercharge the crime actually committed in order to receive a plea. Hence, this negotiation reduces the time served for the crime committed.

SENTENCING COUNCILS AND INSTITUTES The sentencing council is a group of judges who sit regularly in a particular court. The work of the council is described by Smith as follows:

> The judges meet in panels of three, each judge having the presentence investigation report from the probation department and having prepared a study sheet, not only for the offenders he must sentence, but also for those who are the primary responsibility of the other two judges. Customarily the one judge will call his first case, merely stating the name of the offender and giving a brief statement of the offense. He will then state to his brother judges the factors, in his judgment, believed to be controlling as to disposition, and will recommend a disposition to be made. Each of the other two judges will then give, in turn, the factors believed by him to be controlling, together with his recommended sentence. . . . It is in the discussion following the recommendation as to sentencing that the Council performs its most useful function. . . . [P]oints are emphasized or subordinated according to the judgment of the individual judges, with the result that there is a close approach to a common meeting ground (1971, p. 551).

According to Senna and Siegel, sentencing councils have three advantages: they make judges aware of their sentencing philosophies; they provide an opportunity for judges to debate their differences; and they provide a forum for periodic evaluation of a court's sentencing practices (1981, p. 437). To date, three U.S. District Courts have used sentencing councils.

Frankel (1973) reports that sentencing councils cause judges to give shorter prison sentences and to make fuller use of probation as an alternative to incarceration. And Kratcoski and Walker claim that such councils are educational: "Judges who serve on them are made aware of the sentencing practices of their colleagues; the council discussions may bring out information from the presentence reports which could well have been overlooked by a judge acting alone" (1978, p. 186). Despite these advantages, however, sentencing councils are still not popular with the states as an approach to resolving sentencing problems.

In several states including Minnesota, Pennsylvania, and Washington, sentencing *commissions* have developed comprehensive "sentencing guidelines," which attempt to standardize sentences primarily on the basis of the offenders' crimes and past criminal records. Of course, even when the legislature delegates the task of setting sentencing guidelines to a commission, it reserves the right to ratify or reject the commission's proposals. The details of the guidelines systems vary substantially as has their impact. In Minnesota, it appears that judges have generally followed the guidelines, and sentencing disparities have been reduced. In 1984 the U.S. Congress established a federal sentencing commission to develop guidelines for the federal system (National Institute of Justice 1987a).

Sentencing institutes, which originated in federal legislation in 1958, provide a mechanism whereby judges can be brought together in a seminar or workshop to discuss sentencing problems. As stated in the American Bar Association's *Standards Relating to Sentencing Alternatives and Procedures,* these proceedings are intended "to develop criteria for the imposition of sentences, to provide a forum in which newer judges can be exposed to more experienced judges, and to expose all sentencing judges to new developments and techniques" (1968, p. 299). Once again, as in the case of sentencing councils, there has been no pell-mell rush on the part of the states to emulate the federal practice. At present, only three states—California, Massachusetts, and New York—use sentencing institutes.

THE DEATH PENALTY

Use of the death penalty has declined dramatically throughout the industrial Western world since the nineteenth century, and nearly every European nation has either formally abolished the death penalty for civil crimes or has abandoned it in practice.[1]

Despite the current American revival of capital punishment, the United States has contributed to the trend toward abolition. Indeed, when Michigan joined the Union in 1847, it had already earned the distinction of being the first abolitionist jurisdiction in the Western world. The U.S. experience in the twentieth century also parallels the long-term, worldwide decline in executions. Since the peak of 1935 and 1936, when the states conducted 199 executions, the number of yearly executions in this country has decreased continuously, culminating in a de facto moratorium between 1967 and 1977. Abandonment of capital punishment appeared complete with the U.S. Supreme Court's decision in *Furman* v. *Georgia* (408 U.S. 238 [1972]). In *Furman,* the Court invalidated the state death penalty statutes, as then administered, because death sentences were "freakishly" and arbitrarily imposed. The Eighth Amendment to the Constitution prohibits a criminal justice system that imposes death sentences with the same consistency as the likelihood of being "struck by lightning."

Contrary to the expectations of many observers, *Furman* did not resolve the death penalty controversy. In *Gregg* v. *Georgia* (428 U.S. 153 [1976]) four years after *Furman,* the Supreme Court opened the door to a revival of capital punishment. The *Gregg* Court held that various state capital punishment laws enacted in response to *Furman* had sufficiently reduced the randomness permitted by the previous statutes. The Court concluded that the "new" death penalty statutes complied with constitutional requirements, and consequently it permitted the states to resume executions. The state statutes approved by the Court differ from prior penal codes in that they permit the imposition of capital punishment only for murder, specify the grounds to be considered by a trier-of-fact in making death penalty decisions, and establish reasonably specific criteria that must be shown to apply if capital punishment is to be imposed.

The Current Situation

The United States is now in transition between enacting the death penalty in the abstract and actually administering the punishment in a manner consistent with society's morals and with constitutional requirements. In the decade following *Gregg,* some states slowly began to implement a policy that had been dormant for the previous ten years and, with the Supreme Court's approval, hesitantly resumed executions. Indeed, the first prisoner executed in the post-*Gregg* era, Gary Gilmore, demanded that the Utah authorities execute him in 1977. The momentum, though negligible at first, eventually increased. There were no executions in 1978, followed by two in 1979, none in 1980, one in 1981, and two in 1982. The rate more than doubled in 1983 to five. Then in 1984, partially due to the Supreme Court's efforts to accelerate the appeals process and diminish Federal oversight, the number of executions increased to twenty-one.

Just as the rate of executions presents an interesting pattern, so too does the distribution of states administering those sentences. Although thirty-nine states currently authorize the death sentence, by mid-1985 only twelve had executed any prisoners. Moreover, of the forty-seven executions since 1976, thirty-four have been performed in four states: Florida (thirteen), Texas (nine), Louisiana (six), and Georgia (six). Executions have also been highly concentrated in the South. Southern states conducted all of the last forty-three executions; and the last execution outside the South occurred in 1981. The South's domination of executions corresponds closely to the distribution of executions in the 1950s. The four states responsible for 72 percent of the post-*Gregg* executions were also among the top six executing states of the 1950s.

Though the South dominates the execution statistics, its share of prisoners sentenced to death is somewhat more modest. Southern states accounted for 62 percent of the 1,540 prisoners under a death sentence as of August 1, 1985. Several other states maintain significant death row populations. For example, 173 prisoners have been sentenced to die in California's gas chamber, the third largest death row population in the country. Illinois and Pennsylvania, each with 77 prisoners on death row, are tied for sixth. Despite the large number of prisoners sentenced to death in these states, none has been executed.

Large death rows are apparently not closely connected to execution policy outside the South. Utah, one of the three non-Southern states to have carried out death penalties, has only 5 prisoners currently on death row. The other two non-Southern states that have executed, Indiana and Nevada, maintain relatively small death rows of 31 and 28, respectively. Even in the South, a small death row population appears to be irrelevant to the state's execution policy. For example, Louisiana's six executions since 1976 rank third among all states, but its death row population of 41 ranks fourteenth. By comparison, the neighboring state of Alabama has 72 prisoners awaiting execution, but has performed only two executions (1983 and 1984). Florida, by contrast, leads the nation in both executions (thirteen) since 1976 and number of prisoners sentenced to death (221).

America is poised at the crossroads in the death penalty controversy. In the long term, it appears to be following the trend of the Western world toward abolition. This conclusion can be demonstrated by the relatively low execution rates and the long-term decline in the death penalty's use. On the other hand, the high numbers on death row and the short-term increase in executions may signal a return to the execution rates of the 1950s if not the 1930s.

The Capital Punishment Debate

There are four major issues in the capital punishment debate: the role capital punishment plans in deterrence; society's need for retribution; the possibility that death sentences will be imposed arbitrarily; and the danger that mistakes will be made.

DETERRENCE A major purpose of criminal punishment is to deter future criminal conduct. The deterrence theory assumes that a rational person will avoid criminal behavior if the severity of the punishment for that behavior and the perceived certainty of receiving the punishment combine to outweigh the benefits of the illegal conduct. Although the accuracy of many of the assumptions behind the deterrence approach is itself a matter of dispute, the deterrent value of a particularly severe punishment, the death penalty, is important in the current controversy.

The deterrence achieved by using the death penalty must be examined in the context of the entire criminal justice system. For the death penalty to deter first-degree (or capital) murders, the killer must know of the penalty's application to the crime and must believe that the certainty of punishment is sufficient to create an unacceptable risk. Without such awareness, the killer will probably not be deterred. One further factor must be considered when assessing a penalty's deterrent impact. Any deterrent value must be judged in the context of alternatives; if a lesser penalty achieves the same or greater level of deterrence, no deterrent justification supports the enhanced punishment.

Possibly because deterrence is ingrained in our lives—for example, children are punished for violating the family rules—a majority of the public support the death penalty because they consider it an effective deterrent. Supporters contend that death sentences and executions heighten the risk of punishment in a potential killer's mind. By threatening to take the killer's life, society "ups the ante" of killing another person.

Studies of the deterrent effect of the death penalty have been conducted for several years, with varying results. As opponents of the death penalty argue, most of these studies have failed to produce evidence that the death penalty deters murders more effectively than the threat of protracted imprisonment. Various reasons might explain this conclusion. First, the weight assigned to the enhanced severity is only marginal since the comparable punishment is, in most cases, life imprisonment without possibility of parole or a very long sentence. Second, the other key element in the deterrence theory, the perceived certainty of imposing the sentence, is rather low for most murders for a number of reasons: many crimes remain unsolved; the defendant may escape apprehension; evidence may be lacking or inadmissible; plea bargaining may enable the defendant to avoid capital punishment; the jury may acquit or may not impose the penalty; and appeals and clemency petitions may delay or preclude execution. The actual probability that a murderer will receive a death sentence is quite low, and the risk of being executed even smaller, about 1 per 1,000 killings in 1984. Even when the certainty of punishment is higher, many killers might refuse to believe they will be apprehended, let alone executed. Third, the assumption of rationality on which deterrence theories are based may not be valid for many killers.

Supporters of the death penalty make two principal arguments about deterrence: that common sense alone suggests that people fear death more than other punishments and that, when studies fail to resolve the issue, executions should continue on the assumption that a small saving of innocent lives will result.

The deterrence issue, important as it is, will not be resolved by statistical studies. Both supporters and opponents agree that the deterrent value of the death penalty is unproved. Furthermore, the practical limits on studies of this type, as well as the complexity of the problem, will probably prevent any definitive "scientific" resolution of the deterrence issue in the future.

RETRIBUTION The central justification for capital punishment is the need for society to express sufficient condemnation for heinous murders. Supporters of the death penalty contend that the only proper societal response to the most vile murders is the most severe sanc-

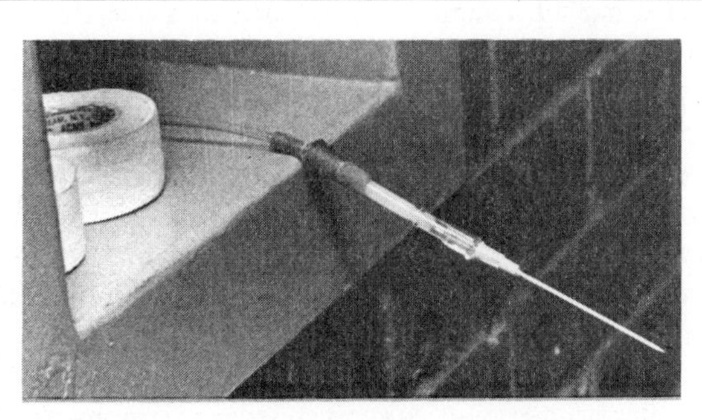

FIGURE 12.2
Convicted murderer Charlie Brooks was put to death with a lethal dose of pentothal injected with this hypodermic needle. Courtesy *Huntsville Item*/Gamma-Liaison.

tion possible. Thus, society should literally interpret the "eye for an eye" principle; when an individual takes a life, society's moral balance will remain upset until the killer's life is also taken.

Although death penalty opponents agree that some punishment, even a harsh one, should be imposed on offenders of society's norms, they disagree with the assumption that society can express its outrage with a vile crime only by inflicting a mortal punishment. Opponents further claim that society's goal of greater morality, rather than being advanced, is actually defeated when its expression of outrage for the taking of one life is the taking of another life. Indeed, opponents argue that the state's act is, in some respects, more calculated and cold-blooded than that of many murderers.

Though individuals must judge for themselves the proper role of retribution in criminal justice, the question is the same for everyone: At what point do we stop trying to match horrible criminal actions with horrible government actions? Taken to the extreme, a retribution theory might require the state to kill the offender in the exact same manner in which the victim was killed. Of course, this position is morally unacceptable to most people; our sense of outrage may be sufficiently expressed by less horrible forms of punishment. The key issue is whether punishment short of killing offenders sufficiently expresses social condemnation of murder in modern America.

ARBITRARINESS The major reason the U.S. Supreme Court invalidated the nation's death penalty laws in *Furman* v. *Georgia* was that death sentences were imposed in an arbitrary and capricious manner. Death penalty opponents claim that the "new" death penalty statutes have failed to reduce the randomness inherent in selecting who shall die. Armed with a decade of experience with the revised statutes, opponents point to the continuing inconsistencies in application. For example, in 1985, of 1,540 death row inmates, 42 percent were black, though blacks constituted only 12 percent of the population at large. Moreover, those convicted of killing white victims are more than four times as likely to receive death sentences as those convicted of killing blacks. An even greater apparent disparity exists between the genders of death row inmates: though 16 percent of those who commit murder are women, they make up only 1.3 percent of the death row population. (This disparity may be less stark than appears when the types of murders committed by men and women are taken into account; murders by men are much more likely to involve predatory crime.)

Supporters of the penalty reply that murder is not evenly committed by both sexes and both races, and that overrepresentation by one group may simply mean that other killers are being improperly spared. Opponents respond that a punishment unjustly administered cannot foster the community's sense of retributive justice or notions of equality. Supporters of the penalty suggest these problems call for greater efforts toward evenhanded administration of the death penalty, not abolition of the penalty. Opponents deny that evenhanded execution is possible in any criminal justice system.

DANGER OF MISTAKE The death penalty's unique character is its finality and irrevocability. Unlike a prison term, which can be commuted at any time, the death penalty, once executed, cannot be recalled. Thus, the irrevocability of the punishment heightens the dangers associated with wrongful convictions.

Opponents of the death penalty argue that the possibility of executing an innocent person necessitates abolishing the penalty. They contend that the likelihood of executing someone who does not deserve to die—that is, one whose crime does not fall within the definition of capital murder—is quite high. And though the person might be guilty of a serious crime, imposing the death penalty in this case would be wrong. The less probable though more morally unacceptable scenario is that a state might execute someone who did not commit the crime. Opponents cite studies concluding that there have been more than one hundred cases of innocent persons wrongly convicted of murder; in at least thirty-one of these, a death sentence was imposed. More important, it is claimed that at least eight innocent individuals have been executed. Opponents argue that the possibility of executing even one innocent person warrants rejecting the penalty.

Supporters, for the most part, argue that the current administration of the death penalty contains adequate safeguards to protect against miscarriages of justice. They cite the numerous levels of review and the scrutiny given to each death sentence. In addition, some supporters claim that the slight possibility of executing an innocent person must be accepted as the price of maintaining a credible criminal justice system.

Minor Issues in the Capital Punishment Debate

Three other issues frequently encountered in the death penalty debate seem of lesser import. These are the question of comparative cost, whether capital punishment plays a crucial role in reducing crime by incapacitating offenders, and the impact of capital punishment on the rate of violent crime.

The debate about cost has curious origins. Some popular sentiment supports the death penalty on the impression that it is less costly to execute prisoners than to maintain them in prison for life terms. Abolitionists, by contrast, have sought to demonstrate that executions in the modern United States are more costly than long prison terms, chiefly because of the cost of special legal processing. The argument is unimportant because the small number of executions or life sentences involved is an insubstantial part of the criminal justice budget. That the alternative to the death penalty is secure confinement for long periods, for life without parole in many states, makes it unlikely that capital punishment decreases crime through incapacitation. Whether executed or not, the offender's dangerousness will not be inflicted on the community.

Furthermore, the small number of candidates for execution under any conceivable regime of capital punishment means that executions cannot be regarded as a way of reducing the incidence of violent crimes in the United States. Violent crimes number in the millions, prison populations in the hundreds of thousands. Executions, even at their twentieth-century peak, were under two hundred per year. The issue of the death penalty is thus largely a symbolic one in the crime control debate, but it is fundamentally important nonetheless (National Institute of Justice 1987b).

APPEAL AND POSTCONVICTION REMEDIES

A few decades ago, very few criminal cases were appealed. Since *Gideon* v. *Wainwright* (372 U.S. 335 [1963]), however, the picture has changed dramatically. The right to counsel for all defendants was secured by the *Gideon* decision, opening the floodgates in appellate courts all across the country. **Collateral attack**—the filing of an appeal in federal court before a state case is decided (a procedure almost unknown prior to the 1960s)—is now almost routine in state courts. As a result, the review system is overloaded, and judges have experienced an unprecedented increase in case loads. And litigation has often been drawn out over a long period of time, thus eroding the public belief in the finality of convictions for criminal offenses.

According to the National Advisory Commission on Criminal Justice Standards and Goals, the major steps in the review process are (1973b, p. 113):

1. A motion for a new trial is filed in the court where the conviction was imposed.
2. An appeal is made to the state intermediate appellate court (in states where there is no intermediate appellate court, this step is not available).
3. An appeal is made to the state supreme court.
4. The U.S. Supreme Court is petitioned to review the state court's decision on the appeal.
5. Postconviction proceedings are initiated in the state trial court.
6. The postconviction proceedings are appealed to the state intermediate appellate court.
7. An appeal is made to the state supreme court.
8. The U.S. Supreme Court is petitioned to review the state court's decision on the appeal from postconviction proceedings.
9. A ***habeas corpus*** petition is presented in U.S. District Court.
10. An appeal is made to the U.S. Court of Appeals.
11. The U.S. Supreme Court is petitioned to review the U.S. Court of Appeals decision on the *habeas corpus* petition.

It is easy to see why the review process can take so long, especially when some steps may be used several times in a single appeal, with review taking place consecutively in more than one court system. Thus, due process may be a long and complicated procedure, and appeals may become part of a long, drawn out, and seemingly endless cycle.

In the 1960s, a series of appellate decisions were made in favor of the incarcerated offender. These decisions had diverse effects on the criminal justice system. On the positive side, the protections of the Fourth, Fifth, Sixth, and Eighth amendments were extended to incarcerated offenders through a series of appeals that were based on the due process and equal protection clauses of the Fourteenth Amendment. The success of such appeals has encouraged more and more defendants to go the appeal route, and the result has been an increase in the appeal rate in some jurisdictions. In some areas, the appeal rate has grown from less than 10 percent to a rate of 90 percent in recent years.

Only fifteen states have some system by which defendants may ask for review of their sentences, while in other states the prosecution may seek a change. In the states authorizing review, two methods are used. In seven states a special panel of trial judges is convened to review the propriety of a sentence in individual cases. On hearing an appeal the panel may increase or decrease the original sentence. In the other eight review states, requests may be brought to a regular appellate court. In all fifteen states, reformers have sought to require trial judges to provide written explanations for each sentence they impose. According to Kratcoski and Walker (1978), review has not been available in many jurisdictions because of fears of increased litigation, concern that appellate judges are less qualified than trial judges to determine appropriate sentences, and the belief that sentencing is a matter of judicial discretion rather than a matter of law. On the other hand, the American Bar Association (through its Committee on Minimum Standards for Criminal Justice) maintains that "judicial review should be available for all sentences imposed in cases where provision is made for review of the convictions" (1968, p. 7).

Sentencing review is one of several *postconviction remedies*—"procedural devices available to a person who, after conviction and sentence, wants to vacate or reduce the sentences imposed, invalidate his pleas of guilty, or set aside his conviction" (Popper 1978, p. 1). For example, consider an individual who is not represented by counsel at trial but has not waived the right of representation; such a defendant might claim that his or her sentence or plea was defective and might seek redress by a postconviction proceeding. Popper notes that petitions filed in U.S. District Courts (including civil rights cases) by state and federal prisoners rose from 2,177 in 1960 to 19,307 in 1975, an increase of nearly 800 percent. Further, he notes:

> As impressive as these figures are, they do not even reflect the number of prisoner petitions filed in state courts. It is this burgeoning post-conviction activity which, in part, accounts for pleas by court administrators, judges, and some communities to put a lid to litigation by cutting back on the chances for post-conviction relief (ibid., p. 4).

The major argument against sentencing reviews are that (1) they will increase litigation; (2) appellate judges are less able to determine appropriate sentences than trial judges because they do not actually see the offenders; and (3) sentencing is generally a matter of judicial discretion and not a matter of law.

In its assessment of the appellate process, the National Advisory Commission on Criminal Justice Standards and Goals expresses doubt that any lasting benefits will result from efforts to speed up the existing review apparatus. Instead, the commission recommends a restructuring of the entire review process: ". . . there should be a single, unified review proceeding in which all arguable defects in the trial proceeding can be examined and settled finally, subject only to narrowly defined exceptional circumstances where there are compelling reasons to provide for a further review" (1973b, p. 113). This unified review would combine into one proceeding all of the issues presently litigated on the basis of motions for new trials, direct appeals, and postconviction proceedings. Thus, the motion for a new trial would be abolished, and the traditional distinction between direct appeal and collateral attack would be abandoned. Unfortunately, the self-evident merits of the commission's proposal have not yet brought the establishment of a unified review. In some states, however, sentencing review has been instituted by means of special panels of trial judges who meet to examine the propriety of sentences in individual cases. After reviewing a case, a panel may decide to decrease or increase the original sentence. In eight states, appeals for sentence review can be brought to a regular appellate court.

SUMMARY

Sentencing is perhaps the most important phase of the criminal process, for it is in this stage that the disposition of the criminal offender is decided. In earlier periods, offenders were subject to retaliation and physical abuse as a punishment for wrongdoing. The contemporary criminal justice system is still punitive in its orientation, but the punishment is justified on several utilitarian grounds, including deterrence and incapacitation. In recent years, support has grown for the position that retribution ("the law of just deserts") is an appropriate objective of sentencing. Traditional dispositions include fines, probation, and imprisonment, with probation being the most common choice.

One of the most significant features of the sentencing process is its tripartite structure involving the legislature, a judge, and correctional agencies. The actions of each of these parties affect the type and length of sentence imposed on the offender. Thus, the system often results in sentence disparity with courts seeking to fit the sentence to the individual offender rather than to the crime. To make dispositions more uniform, some states now allow appellate review of sentences and use sentencing councils and institutes.

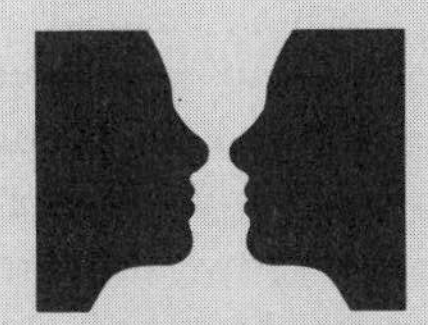

ISSUE PAPER

THE PONY FARM: A TALE OF DISPROPORTIONATE SENTENCING

A few miles from town, to the west, is Fred Bridge's Pony Farm. It lies on a little ridge of sandy and stony ground, surrounded by farms with lush grass and white fences. The buildings are small and in need of repair. They have, with time, weathered, and the boards have twisted so the buildings are, even to the untrained eye, not square. In a little building opposite the house, Fred has set up a tack shop where he sells those articles of harness commonly associated with riding horses. The goods are all covered with a fine dust which filters through the cracks between the boards in the ceiling, a residue from grain which was once stored above.

Fred seems as aged and twisted as the buildings. He walks with a limp and his thin, small frame knows the pains of arthritis. He wears cowboy clothes (chaps, boots, vest, hat) but whether he ever was a cowboy no one knows. One day, about ten years ago, he simply arrived and bought the farm when the old folks who had lived there moved to town.

The name of the farm implies that Fred is in the business of raising ponies, but you would be in error if you believed that. What he does is to buy and sell slaughter horses of any kind, including ponies. At least once a month he starts up the large van which he keeps back of his barn and goes rumbling down the highway to the distant collection points where he picks up his horses. In a few days, he returns and the corrals, patched together with odds and ends of barbed wire, are full until the animal processors come and haul the horses away.

Fred does nothing to dispel the notion that he sells these animals to little children who come with their parents to the farm; but that some child would actually *want* one of the horses or that his parents would actually *let* the child have one would, I think, surprise even Fred. Most of the animals are sick or old, or, having run wild, are genetic accidents, disproportionate assemblages of parts, with necks and legs too long or too short, heads abnormally large or small; and all of them gaunt creatures who look out with dull and frightened eyes upon a world not made for them and to which they will not long belong.

Neglecting The Horses

A few weeks ago, Fred found himself in trouble with the law. He was charged with neglecting his animals. Fred acted as his own attorney and his defense was that the horses were in a bad way when he bought them and that he hadn't had time to fatten them up. But the evidence was the other way and the judge, no lover of horses himself, fined him maximally on multiple counts ("one for each horse," Fred claimed, but that was not true), and threatened him, in lieu of payment, to consecutive terms in jail.

After the event, Fred decided he needed an attorney. He wasn't guilty, he said, but, even if he were, the fines weren't fair and the consecutive jail terms, which Fred had insisted to the court he would sit out, were unreasonable. "You mean," I said, only half listening to him, thinking rather of the strangeness of his farm, "the punishment is disproportionate to the offense?" "That's it," he said, "what you said."

What Fred wanted, of course, was to appeal, even, he said, if it would cost as much as the fines, which he hoped it wouldn't. Maybe, he said, musingly, we would even go all the way to the United States Supreme Court. "You can forget that," I told him. "Well, check it out, anyhow," he said.

The Courts

Well, I did check it out (some might even say "over-checked" it out) and, as he sits across from me now, I tell him there is small comfort for him (there is small comfort for any of us, for that matter) in what I have found. Our own State Supreme Court has said that in order for a sentence to be set aside, it must be so excessive and unusual, and so disproportionate to the offense committed, as to "shock public sentiment and violate the judgment of reasonable people concerning what is right and proper under the circumstances," *State v. Pratt* (36 Wis.2d 312 [1967]) which Fred's sentence surely would not; and as to the United States Supreme Court, whether punishment is disproportionate and whether, being disproportionate, it is prohibited, appears, ultimately, to depend on the Eighth Amendment to the United States Constitution.

There is nothing in the Eighth Amendment itself which prohibits legislated disproportionate punishment, I tell Fred, "but it prohibits 'cruel and unusual punishment' which, the Court has said, disproportionate punishment is." The four major cases on the clause are Weems, Rummel, Davis, and Helm. ("Are they local boys?" Fred asks. "No," I say, smiling, "they aren't local boys.") In *Weems* v. *United States* (217 U.S. 349 [1910]) Weems was convicted in 1909 by the Philippine Islands court of falsifying a public record and was sentenced to twelve years and one day at hard labor, with chains at the ankles and wrists, and no assistance from friends or relatives. He appealed to the United States Supreme Court (the Philippine Islands being a territory of ours, then), claiming cruel and unusual punishment. The majority of the Court, after analyzing the history of the Amendment and not finding much help there, came up with the conclusion that, whatever the history of the clause, the punishment *was* disproportionate to the offense and thus cruel and unusual and, therefore, prohibited. Two justices dissented saying that if the clause were going to be interpreted solely on the basis of compassion for the suffering of the wrongdoer, nothing much would be left of the State's power to punish offenders. The Weems case is important because it establishes that punishment which might not be cruel and unusual under other circumstances is cruel and unusual if it is disproportionate to the offense committed.

"Rummel was convicted in 1975 of obtaining $120 by false pretense *Rummel* v. *Estelle* (445 U.S. 263 [1980]). He had earlier been convicted of passing a forged check and the fraudulent use of a credit card, both involving very small amounts, less than $100 combined. He was sentenced on the 1975 offense, as a recidivist, to life imprisonment. On appeal, the Court said that although the Weems case did prohibit disproportionate punishment, which Rummel's sentence might ordinarily be, Rummel knew of the consequences of his crimes and had been given an opportunity to reform, all to no avail, and, therefore, he could be imprisoned for life. The recidivist statute, Justice Rehnquist wrote, is 'nothing more than a societal decision that when such a person commits yet another felony, he should be . . . subjected to . . . incarceration for life, subject only to the State's judgment to grant him parole.' Four justices dissented claiming the sentence would be viewed as 'grossly unjust by virtually every layman and lawyer.'"

"Davis was convicted in 1974 of possession and distribution of nine ounces of marijuana (*Hutto* v. *Davis* [454 U.S. 370 (1982)]). A jury imposed a fine of $10,000 and a prison term of 20 years on each of two counts, with the prison terms to run consecutively. Upon appeal, the Federal District Court and Court of Appeals agreed the sentence was . . . 'so grossly out of proportion to the severity of the crime as to constitute cruel and unusual punishment in violation of the Eighth Amendment.' The United States Supreme Court, however, said the lower federal courts had no business substituting their judgment for that of the State legislature and the jury, and that Rummel's case prevented the federal courts, including the Supreme Court, from doing anything about the sentence. Three justices dissented, saying *Rummel* applied only to recidivists and that *Davis* had never been adjudicated as one. 'Unfortunately,' the dissenters said, 'it is Roger Trenton Davis who must now suffer the pains of the Court's insensitivity and serve out the balance of a forty-year sentence . . . .'"

"Mr. Helm was convicted in South Dakota in 1979 of writing a 'no account' check for $100 (*Solem* v. *Helm* [463 U.S. 277 (1983)]). He had three prior convictions for burglary, convictions for obtaining money by false pretense, grand larceny, and a third-offense driving while intoxicated, all nonviolent crimes and all, apparently, related to drunkenness. He was sentenced, as a recidivist, to life imprisonment, without the possibility of parole, as South Dakota law allowed. The dissenters in the earlier cases received some help this time from a cross-over justice, thereby becoming a majority, and they wrote the Court's opinion which said: 'In sum, we hold . . . that a criminal sentence must be proportionate to the crime. . . . Helm's sentence is significantly disproportionate . . . and is therefore prohibited.' The dissenters, who had been the majority members in the earlier opinions, said they thought it was 'a curious business for this Court to . . . say that a state legislature is barred by the Constitution from identifying its habitual criminals and removing them from the streets. . . .'"

Conclusion

"So, Fred," I say, "since none of these cases claims to overrule the earlier ones, we are at this interesting point in the law: (a.) Legislatively mandated punishments disproportionate to the offense are constitutionally prohibited as cruel and unusual punishments; but (b.) disproportionate punishments imposed within legislatively mandated limits will not be interfered with by the Court because legislatively mandated punishments are merely societal decisions; and the court will not interfere in societal decisions; however, (c.) the imposition of a disproportionate punishment, even though legislatively mandated and therefore a societal decision, is cruel and unusual punishment and, therefore, is unconstitutional and prohibited."

Fred sits there looking at me, thoughtfully, slowly worrying a toothpick around in his mouth, trying to make sense of what I have said; but there is no sense in it, of course, unless it is looked upon in a certain light.

"What are my chances?" he asks.

"None," I say.

"*None?*" he says, angrily, "and you call that justice?"

"Why, no," I say, surprised that he should even suggest that. "I wouldn't call it *that.* What I *would* call it (and here I brush my hand over my research notes in general reference to them) is an interesting study on the sensitivity thresholds of the individual justices of the Court. I mean, no matter what they may claim to the contrary (and they do claim to the contrary), the cruel and unusual punishment clause is merely a reflection of their consciences. It has no life or warmth or determinable meaning of its own. It merely reflects *them;* it tells us what *they* are like inside."

"No, Fred," I say, warming up to the subject, what *I* would call it is an obvious manifestation of subliminal attitudes cloaked in a patina of juridical objectivity, resulting in paradoxical precedents with an occasional dangling modifier. Or, to put it more simply . . . ."

But, before I can put it more simply, he reaches for his ten-gallon hat, puts the toothpick in his vest pocket, walks stiffly to the door, as if he has been breaking horses all day, and leaves.

"So long, Fred," I say, cheerfully, tossing my charge sheets and research notes into the wastebasket. But he is already gone.

Back to the Pony Farm, I suppose, where things, strange as they are, are nevertheless still to him, I would guess, less . . . what's the word I want? . . . *disproportionate?*

DISCUSSION AND REVIEW

1. Why is sentencing such an important phase of the criminal process?
2. What are some of the factors that significantly affect the success or failure of punishment as an approach to deterrence?
3. How do we distinguish between general and specific deterrence?
4. Does research support the argument that incapacitation or restraint of serious offenders is a sound rationale for imprisonment?
5. On what principle is an offender's right to treatment based? Is there any valid legal basis for claiming a right to *refuse* treatment?
6. What is the distinction between a definite sentence and a determinate sentence? Between a definite sentence and a mandatory sentence?
7. What is the distinction between concurrent sentences and consecutive sentences?
8. What are some of the adverse effects of sentence disparities? What are the major causes of such disparity?
9. How are sentencing guidelines developed empirically for a particular jurisdiction? What is the relationship between offender scores and offense scores in arriving at an appropriate sentence?

10. Discuss the significance of the *Gideon* v. *Wainwright* decision in terms of its impact on the filing of appeals from "behind the walls."
11. What is the current situation in the United States with respect to the administration of the death penalty? Examine the four major issues in the capital punishment debate.
12. How does the National Advisory Commission on Criminal Justice Standards and Goals propose to reform the appellate process?

GLOSSARY

Collateral attack A challenge against the legality of confinement as opposed to an appeal based on the merits of the conviction. A federal writ of *habeas corpus* is the principal method used by state prisoners seeking review of their convictions.

Deterrence A justification for punishment based on the idea that crime can be discouraged or prevented by instilling in potential criminals a fear of punishing consequences. Punished offenders, it is hoped, will serve as examples to deter potential criminals from antisocial conduct.

Good time A correctional scheme by which days are subtracted from a prisoner's minimum or maximum term for good behavior or for participation in various types of treatment, educational, or vocational programs.

Habitual offender laws Statutes that focus on defendants who have committed two (three) or more serious offenses and allow them to be sentenced to extended terms of imprisonment, or even for life.

Habeas corpus Latin for "you have the body." A writ of *habeas corpus* orders a person who is holding another person in confinement to produce the person being detained.

Incapacitation A theory of punishment and a goal of sentencing; generally implemented by imprisoning an offender to prevent him or her from committing further crimes.

Indeterminate sentence An indefinite sentence of "not less than" and "not more than" a certain number of years. The exact term to be served is determined by parole authorities within the minimum and maximum limits set by the court or by statute.

Parens patriae Latin for "father of his country"; a doctrine specifying that the juvenile court should treat youngsters as if it were a "kind and loving parent."

Rehabilitation A rationale for the reformation of offenders based on the premise that human behavior is the result of antecedent causes that may be identified and controlled by objective analysis. The focus in on treatment of the offender, not punishment.

Reintegration A theory of punishment based on the belief that an offender's contact and interaction with the positive rather than the negative elements of society are what is necessary for his or her overall treatment.

Retribution A theory of punishment that maintains that an offender should be punished for the crimes he or she commits because he or she *deserves* the punishment.

Sentencing The process by which judges impose punishment on persons convicted of crimes.

■ REFERENCES

Adams, S. "The PICO Project." In *The Sociology of Punishment and Corrections,* edited by N. Johnston, L. Savitz, and M. E. Wolfgang. New York: Wiley, 1970.

Allen, H. E., and Simonsen, C. E. *Corrections in America.* New York: Macmillan, 1981.

American Bar Association. *Standards Relating to Sentencing Alternatives and Procedures.* New York: Institute of Judicial Administration, 1968.

American Law Institute. *Model Penal Code: Proposed Official Draft.* Philadelphia, Pa.: American Law Institute, 1962.

Andersen, K. "An Eye for an Eye." *Time* 24 January 1983, pp. 28–39.

Bayley, C. T. "Good Intentions Gone Awry—A Proposal for Fundamental Change in Criminal Sentencing." *Washington Law Review* 51 (1976): 529–56.

Diamond, S. S. "Exploring Sources of Sentence Disparity." In *The Trial Process,* edited by B. D. Sales. New York: Plenum, 1981.

Diamond, S. S., and Zeisel, H. "Sentencing Councils: A Study of Sentence Disparity and Its Reduction." *University of Chicago Law Review* 43 (1975): 109–49.

Ellison, K. W., and Buckhout, R. *Psychology and Criminal Justice.* New York: Harper and Row, 1981.

Frankel, M. E. *Criminal Sentences—Law without Order.* New York: Hill and Wang, 1973.

Gaylin, W. *Partial Justice.* New York: Vintage, 1974.

Gaylord, L. C. "The Pony Farm: A Tale of Disproportionate Sentencing." *Case & Comment* 91 (July/August 1986).

Gibbons, D. C.; Thurman, J. L.; Yospe, F.; and Blake, G. F. *Criminal Justice Planning: An Introduction.* Englewood Cliffs, N.J.: Prentice-Hall, 1977.

Glaser, D. "Maximizing the Impact of Evaluative Research in Corrections." In *Criminal Justice Research,* edited by E. Viano. Lexington, Mass.: Lexington, 1975.

Grünhut, M. *Penal Reform.* London: Oxford, 1948.

Keeley, P. A. "Students' Attitudes Toward Capital Punishment as a Function of Training in the College of Their Major." Master's thesis, Department of Criminal Justice, University of South Florida, 1976.

Kneedler, H. L. "Sentencing in Criminal Cases: Time for Reform." *The University of Virginia Newsletter* 55 (1979): 17–20.

Kratcoski, P. C., and Walker, D. B. *Criminal Justice in America: Process and Issues.* Glenview, Ill.: Scott, Foresman, 1978.

Lipton, D.; Martinson, R.; and Wilks, J. *The Effectiveness of Correctional Treatment—A Survey of Treatment Evaluation Studies.* Springfield, Mass.: Praeger, 1975.

McGee, R. A. "A New Look at Sentencing." Part I. *Federal Probation* 37 (1974): 3–8.

Martinson, R. "What Works? Questions and Answers about Prison Reform." *The Public Interest* (Spring 1974): 22–54.

Nassi, A. J. "Therapy of the Absurd: A Study of Punishment and Treatment in California Prisons and the Roles of Psychiatrists and Psychologists." In *Contemporary Perspectives on Forensic Psychiatry and Psychology,* edited by H. J. Vetter and R. W. Rieber. New York: John Jay, 1980.

National Advisory Commission on Criminal Justice Standards and Goals. *Corrections.* Washington, D.C.: U.S. Government Printing Office, 1973a.

National Advisory Commission on Criminal Justice Standards and Goals. *Courts.* Washington, D.C.: U.S. Government Printing Office, 1973b.

National Institute of Justice. "Crime File: Death Penalty." A study guide by F. E. Zimring and M. Laurence. Rockville, Md: U.S. Department of Justice, 1987.

National Institute of Justice. "Crime File: Sentencing." A study guide by R. Singor. Rockville, Md.: U.S. Department of Justice, 1987b.
National Law Journal, April 5, 1982.
Newman, G. *The Punishment Response.* Philadelphia, Pa.: Lippincott, 1978.
Packer, H. *The Limits of the Criminal Sanction.* Palo Alto, Calif.: Stanford, 1968.
Partridge, A., and Eldridge, W. *The Second Circuit Sentencing Study: A Report to the Judges of the Second Circuit.* Washington, D.C.: U.S. Government Printing Office, 1974.
Petersilia, J.; Greenwood, P. W.; and Lavin, M. *Criminal Careers of Habitual Felons.* Santa Monica, Calif.: Rand Corporation, 1977.
Popper, R. *Post-Conviction Remedies.* St. Paul, Minn.: West, 1978.
President's Commission on Law Enforcement and Administration of Justice. *The Challenge of Crime in a Free Society.* Washington, D.C.: U.S. Government Printing Office, 1967.
"Prisons: Uprising in Attica." *Time,* 20 September 1971, pp. 12–14.
Pursley, R. *Introduction to Criminal Justice,* 4th ed. New York: McMillan, 1987.
Reid, S. T. *Crime and Criminology.* New York: Holt, Rinehart and Winston, 1982.
Senna, J., and Siegel, L. *Introduction to Criminal Justice,* 4th ed. St. Paul, Minn.: West, 1987.
Shireman, C. H.; Mann, K. B.; Larsen, C.; and Young, T. "Findings from Experiments in Treatment in the Correctional Institution." *Social Service Review* 46 (1972): 38–59.
Silber, D. E. "Controversy Concerning the Criminal Justice System and Its Implications for the Role of Mental Health Workers." *American Psychologist* 29 (1974): 239–44.
Skinner, B. F. *Science and Human Behavior.* New York: Macmillan, 1953.
———. *Beyond Freedom and Dignity.* New York: Harper and Row, 1971.
Smith, B. D., and Vetter, H. J. *Theoretical Approaches to Personality.* Englewood Cliffs, N.J.: Prentice-Hall, 1982.
Smith, T. "The Sentencing Council." In *The Criminal in the Arms of the Law,* edited by L. Radzinowicz and M. E. Wolfgang. New York: Basic, 1971.
Toomey, B.; Allen, H. E.; and Simonsen, C. E. "The Right to Treatment: Professional Liabilities in the Criminal Justice and Mental Health Systems." *The Prison Journal* 54 (1974): 43–56.
Vachss, A. H., and Bakal, Y. *The Life-Style Violent Juvenile.* Lexington, Mass.: Lexington, 1979.
Van den Haag, E. *Punishing Criminals: Concerning a Very Old and Painful Question.* New York: Basic, 1975.
Von Hirsch, A. *Doing Justice: The Choice of Punishments.* New York: Hill and Wang, 1976.
Wilson, J. Q. *Thinking About Crime.* New York: Vintage, 1977.
Wolfgang, M. E.; Figlio, R. M.; and Sellin, T. E. *Delinquency in a Birth Cohort.* Chicago: University of Chicago, 1972.

■ CASES

Donaldson v. *O'Connor* 493 F.2d 507 (5th Cir. 1974).
Furman v. *Georgia* 408 U.S. 238, 92 S.Ct. 2726, 33 L.Ed.2d 346 (1972).
Gideon v. *Wainwright* 372 U.S. 335, 83 S.Ct. 792, 9 L.Ed.2d 799 (1963).
Gregg v. *Georgia* 428 U.S. 153, 96 S.Ct. 2909, 49 L.Ed.2d 859 (1976).
Hutto v. *Davis* 454 U.S. 370 (1982).

In re Gault 387 U.S. 1, 87 S.Ct. 1428, 18 L.Ed.2d 527 (1967).
McGinnis v. *Royster* 410 U.S. 263, 93 S.Ct. 1055, 35 L.Ed.2d 282 (1973).
Mackey v. *Procunier* 477 F.2d 877 (9th Cir. 1973).
Rouse v. *Cameron* 373 F.2d 451 (D.C.Cir. 1966).
Rummel v. *Estelle* 445 U.S. 263, 100 S.Ct. 1133, 63 L.Ed.2d 382 (1980).
Solem v. *Helm* 463 U.S. 277, 103 S.Ct. 3001, 77 L.Ed.2d 637 (1983).
State v. *Pratt* 36 Wis.2d 312, 153 N.W.2d 18 (1967).
Weems v. *United States* 217 U.S. 349, 30 S.Ct. 544, 54 L.Ed. 793 (1910).
Wyatt v. *Stickney* 344 F.Supp. 373 (D.C.Ala. 1972).

■ NOTES

1. The substance of this section was derived from a publication by the U.S. Department of Justice's division of the National Institute of Justice: Franklin E. Zimring and Michael Laurence, "Crime File: Death Penalty," a study guide (Rockville, Md.: 1987).

CHAPTER

13

Jails and Detention

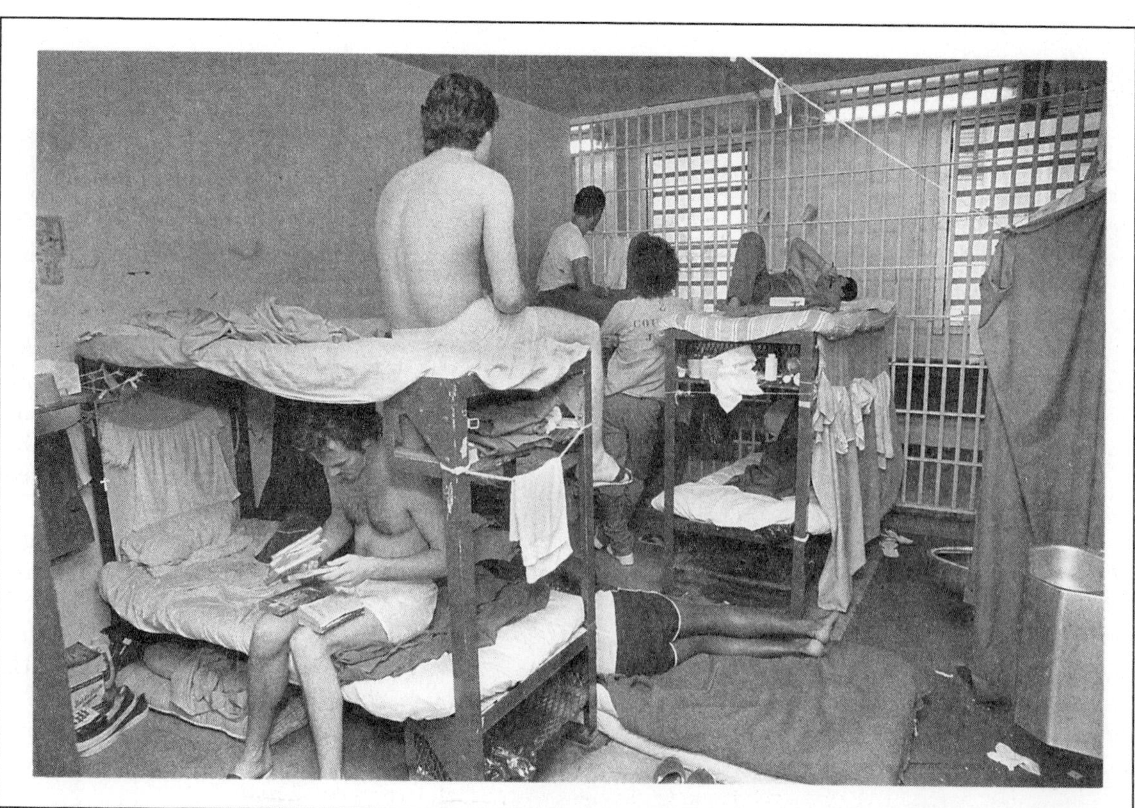

CHAPTER OUTLINE:

Because they are remote from public view, jails have evolved more by default than by plan. Perpetuated without major change from the days of Alfred the Great, these institutions have been a disgrace to every generation. Colonists brought to the New World the concept of the jail as an instrument for confining, coercing, or correcting people who broke the law or were merely nuisances. In the early nineteenth century, with the America innovation of the state penitentiary, punitive confinement became the principal response to criminal acts and removed the serious offender from the local jail. Gradually, with the building of insane asylums, orphanages, and hospitals, the jail ceased to be the repository for all social casualties. But it continued to house minor offenders, the poor, and the vagrant, all crowded together in squalor and misery, without regard to sex, age, or criminal history.

Many European visitors admired the new American penitentiaries. Two observers—de Beaumont and de Tocqueville—also saw, side by side with the new penetentiaries, jails in the old familiar form. They noted that ". . . nothing has been changed; disorder, confusion, mixture of different ages and moral characters, all the vices of the old system still exist" (de Beaumont and de Tocqueville 1964, p. 49). In an observation that should have served as a warning, they continued, "There is evidently a deficiency in a prison system which offers anomalies of this kind. These shocking contradictions proceed chiefly from the want of unison in the various parts of government in the United States" (ibid).

By and large, the deficiencies these two travelers found remain today; the intervening decades have brought little but the deterioration of jail facilities from use and age. Changes have been limited to variations in clientele, and jails have become residual organizations for handling the vexing and unpalatable social problems in each locality. (The most conspicuous additions are the homeless and the drunks.) Thus, "the poor, the sick, the morally deviant, and the merely unaesthetic, in addition to the truly criminal all end in jail" (Mattick and Aikman 1969, p. 114).[1]

THE AMERICAN JAIL SYSTEM

Jails are primarily a function of local government. Approximately 85 percent of our jails are operated by counties, but some large cities do operate their own. And a few cities and counties operate a separate department of corrections. Prisons are operated by the states. A few states—Connecticut, Delaware, Hawaii, Rhode Island, and Vermont—have an integrated jail-prison system. Alaska has a partially integrated jail-prison system with six locally operated jails (United States Department of Justice 1980).[2] (See Table 13.1 for a differentiation of jails and prisons.)

In some major metropolitan areas (Chicago, New York, and San Diego, for example), the Federal Bureau of Prisons operates metropolitan corrections centers for people awaiting trial on federal charges. In places where there are federal courts but no federal detention facilities, the U.S. Marshal's Service arranges for local jails to care for and detain federal prisoners; There are about 800 such arrangements, housing some 5,000 federal detainees (i.e., more than 70 percent of all federal detainees).

TABLE 13.1
The Differences between Jails and Prisons

JAILS	PRISONS
• Usually operated by a local unit of government.	• Operated by the state.
• Holds pretrial detainees and sentenced petty offenders, usually misdemeanants.	• Principally for the confinement of felons.
• The population changes frequently, perhaps as much as 70 percent within seventy-two hours.	• The population is relatively stable.
• Located in population centers.	• Historically located in rural areas.
• Tend to have smaller populations than prisons.	
• Usually have limited inmate programs.	• Have diverse inmate programs.
• Have traditionally been ignored by scholars and researchers.	• Have received considerable attention from scholars and researchers.

Data from Charles Swanson, "Overview of Jails," *Jail Operations* (Athens, Ga.: Institute of Government, University of Georgia, 1983), p. 24.

Types of Jails

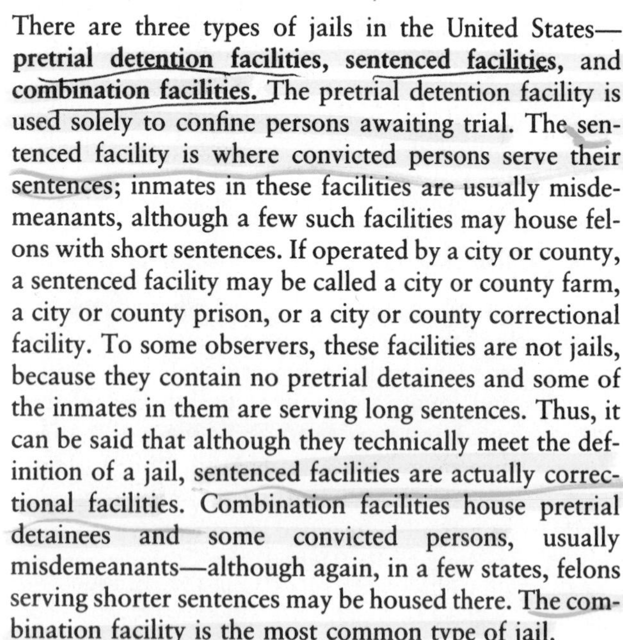

There are three types of jails in the United States—**pretrial detention facilities, sentenced facilities,** and **combination facilities.** The pretrial detention facility is used solely to confine persons awaiting trial. The sentenced facility is where convicted persons serve their sentences; inmates in these facilities are usually misdemeanants, although a few such facilities may house felons with short sentences. If operated by a city or county, a sentenced facility may be called a city or county farm, a city or county prison, or a city or county correctional facility. To some observers, these facilities are not jails, because they contain no pretrial detainees and some of the inmates in them are serving long sentences. Thus, it can be said that although they technically meet the definition of a jail, sentenced facilities are actually correctional facilities. Combination facilities house pretrial detainees and some convicted persons, usually misdemeanants—although again, in a few states, felons serving shorter sentences may be housed there. The combination facility is the most common type of jail.

Purpose of Jails

Jails serve three main functions. First, they enhance public safety by segregating persons deemed a criminal threat to people and property, and then ensure that persons charged with crimes appear at trial. Second, they are expected to effect some measure of positive behavioral-attitudinal change—the rehabilitative function. And third, they serve as a form of punishment.

Most jails in the United States are quite old. At present, 3 percent of the daily jail population is housed in facilities built before 1875. Further, 14 percent of all jail facilities were built between 1875 and 1924; 24 percent were built between 1925 and 1949; 43 percent were built between 1950 and 1969; and only 16 percent were built between 1970 and 1978. It would be inaccurate, however, to say that a jail is inadequate simply because it is old. Obnoxious conditions may exist in a facility of any age, depending on the resources available and the attitudes of jail administrators and jailers.

In general, though it is fair to say that an old facility is more likely than a new facility to have deficiencies. Unrenovated, uncared for, mismanaged, or misoperated jails present problems for the jailers, and persons confined in them are frequently in danger. Such facilities—with their noxious odors, dirty lavatories and dirty floors and walls—are offensive to the eye and nose. In addition, some jails are fire hazards, some have inadequate lighting, ventilation, and bedding, and some are vermin infested and overcrowded.

To a great extent, however, the physical conditions of a jail are affected more by the professional competency and philosophy of the sheriff or the jail director than by the age of the facility (Territo 1983). The following case illustrates this point and also shows that even carefully made plans can take some interesting and unanticipated turns.

As frequently happens every four years there was a hotly contested sheriff's race between a couple of men who were remarkably different in many personal and professional respects. Prior to being elected the incumbent sheriff had very little formal education and no prior administrative experience or professional training to administer the county jail. His opponent had a master's degree in criminology and broad ranging experience in criminal justice. The incumbent was defeated and when the newly elected sheriff took office, one of his first tasks was to conduct a systematic inspection of all parts of the sheriff's department's facilities which naturally included the county jail.

Upon his inspection of the county jail, the new sheriff was shocked at its general state of disrepair and poor sanitary conditions. Puzzled at the obvious long term neglect of the facility the sheriff started questioning some of the jail personnel about it. He learned from them that the former sheriff placed his highest priority on the law enforcement component of the agency and almost no importance on the jail. The former sheriff also believed that jail inmates were criminals, and the jail should be as unpleasant a place as possible to discourage them from ever wanting to return to it.

As a result of this attitude the following conditions existed at the jail:

- No part of the facility had been painted since it opened fifteen years earlier;
- Approximately 25% of all the lights in the cell block area were burned out, in addition, the cell block area was painted black;
- The showers would not drain properly because they were plugged up with human hair and inmates frequently had to stand in at least six inches of dirty water while showering;
- No cleaning material was provided to clean the commodes in the cell block area, thus they were not only stained with human waste but also emitted a very unpleasant odor;
- The jail was overrun by roaches, mice, rats and other vermin;
- The kitchen area, including the stove, had not been cleaned in years;
- The front lobby area where people waited to either conduct some business at the jail or visit inmates contained furniture that was so decrepit and damaged that the chances of being impaled by one of the springs from these worn out couches was considerable.

Interestingly, all of these things existed in a state which is alleged to have very strict state controlled jail inspections, yet the facility was always given a satisfactory rating.

The new sheriff felt that such conditions were intolerable not only for those who were confined in the jail, but also because his employees had to work there, a point the former sheriff seemed to overlook. Thus, a massive housecleaning effort and repairs were undertaken by the county maintenance department at the request of the sheriff. In addition, an exterminator was employed to eliminate all of the unwelcome guests and some decent furniture was purchased, at cost, for the lobby area of the jail.

A couple of months after the cleanup and repairs were underway, some anonymous phone calls were made to the local newspapers and TV stations and complaints were lodged that the sheriff was spending the tax payers' dollars to convert the county jail into a luxury hotel for criminals. Media representatives contacted the sheriff and requested access to the jail to see if in fact it was as elegant and luxurious as some callers had described. There was some speculation that these anonymous phone calls may have been made by some supporters of the former sheriff who were not particularly happy with the defeat of their man. The sheriff agreed, but was concerned that the media might present a distorted or inaccurate picture of what it was that he wanted to accomplish. Nevertheless, the doors were opened and representatives of both the local newspapers and television stations were invited in. When they arrived, the planned changes were approximately half completed thus providing a realistic "before and after" contrast. All employees of the jail and inmates were encouraged to speak freely and openly to the media representatives. A series of totally unplanned but very pleasant side effects occurred as a result of the interviews conducted by the media representatives. For example, they interviewed people in the jail lobby area waiting to visit inmate relatives, attorneys visiting clients, jail officers and inmates. When some of the jail visitors who had witnessed the changes were interviewed their comments were quite favorable. One of them commented that it was unpleasant enough just having to come to the jail to visit a loved one, but when the place looked like a dungeon as it previously had the experience was even more unpleasant. The attorneys who were waiting to see their clients were also quite pleased with the changes. The visitation rooms they used to talk to their clients no longer had broken tables, ripped up floor tiles, broken acoustical tiles, and half of the lights burned out. One attorney commented that the facility now gives the impression that "it was being administered by a professional administrator, and not the Marquis de Sade."

The response from the jail officers was also quite positive, and many commented that it was much more pleasant to come to work in a facility that "looked clean and smelled clean." They also appreciated the special attention that the new sheriff had shown them and the jail and had a renewed sense of pride in their work.

The last group of people to be interviewed were the inmates. This brought to light one of the most startling unplanned side effects of the planned change. Since at that point only half of the cell blocks had been repainted, or had the lights and plumbing repaired, the media was exposed to a vivid "before and after" contrast. The first set of cell blocks visited had been repainted light green, the burned out lights had been replaced and all of the plumbing repaired. As the media representatives walked along the catwalk they would stop and interview some of the inmates. In some cases, the inmates would even call out to the media representatives and request to talk to them. Both inmates and media representatives had access to each other, but the inmates were not permitted out of their cells. The inmates were questioned about their confinement and asked if they had any complaints about the facility. There were some minor complaints about needing more access to a telephone, and there were the normal amount of protestations about their innocence, but all in all, there were no serious complaints.

The second set of cell blocks visited were still in the original state of disrepair, but had basically the same classification of inmates as the previous cell blocks visited. As the heavy steel door to the cell block area was opened, the contrast in lighting and odor was startling. The group entered, and the inmates immediately started complaining about the food, abuse by jail officers, limited recreational opportunities, poor mail service and so forth. These complaints were made even though there was no difference between any of the cell blocks in terms of the quality of food, jail officers, recreational opportunities, mail service, and so forth. The only real difference between these cell blocks were the ones previously discussed. Interestingly, the jail officers also reported far more disciplinary problems in the unrepaired and unpainted cell blocks than in the newly renovated ones.

The cost of these changes were negligible to the taxpayers since all of the work was done by the county maintenance department as part of its regular responsibilities. All of these facts were accurately reported by the media and the criticism subsided (Territo 1983, p. 11–25).

JAIL OVERCROWDING

A comprehensive survey of the nation's jails was conducted in 1978 and again in 1983. This five-year period provides a "snapshot" of the jail crowding problem and permits certain comparisons to be made with the national prison population. As Figure 13.1 shows, the rate of growth for prisons and jails has been approximately the same; both rose more than 40 percent during the five years from 1978 to 1983 (DeWitt 1986).[3]

As Figure 13.2 shows, the rapid increase in jail inmates vastly exceeded the number of beds added to local jail systems. By 1983, the population in local jails had risen by 65,157, while the number of new beds added was only 28,036. Thus, growth in the prisoner population had exceeded new beds by 37,121. Currently, increases in the local jail population are estimated at 21,000 additional inmates each year, the equivalent of two new 200-bed jails every week ("Jail Census" 1983).[4]

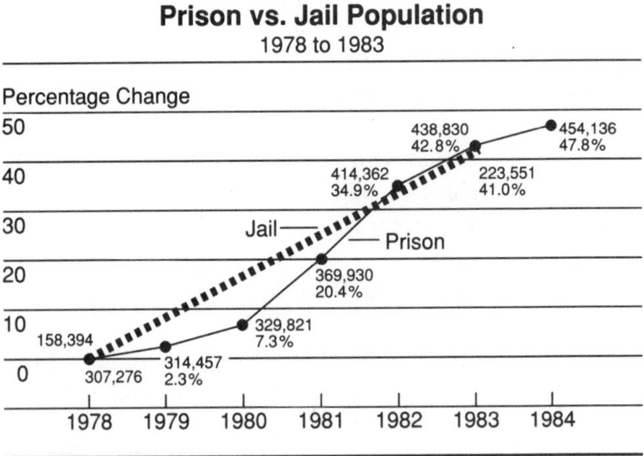

FIGURE 13.1
Prison vs. jail populations, 1978 to 1983. From Charles B. DeWitt, *New Construction Methods for Correctional Facilities* (Washington, D.C.: U.S. Department of Justice, National Institute of Justice, March 1986), p. 3.

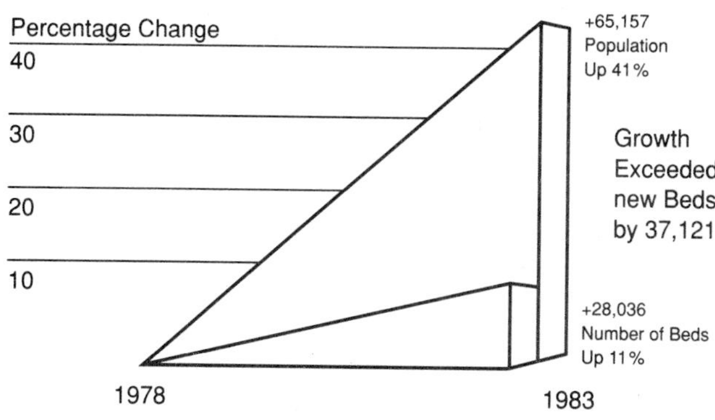

FIGURE 13.2
Jail inmates: population growth vs. new beds, 1978 to 1983. From Charles B. DeWitt, *New Construction Methods for Corrective Facilities* (Washington, D.C.: U.S. Department of Justice, National Institute of Justice, March 1986), p. 3.

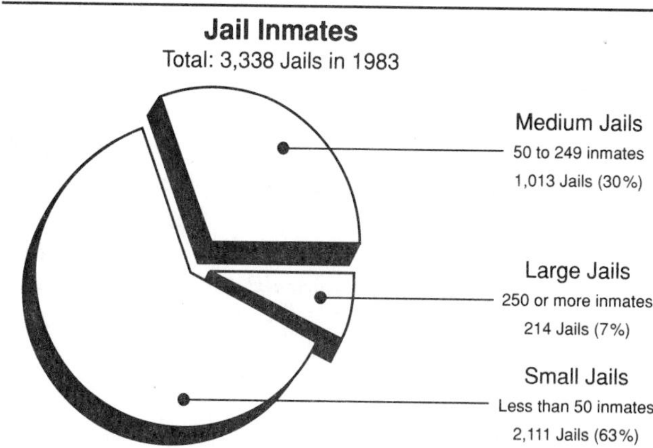

FIGURE 13.4
Jails by size. The total in 1983 was 3,338 jails. From Charles B. DeWitt, *New Construction Methods for Correctional Facilities* (Washington, D.C.: U.S. Department of Justice, National Institute of Justice, March 1986), p. 4.

The problems of crowding have an impact on both large and small jails. As Figure 13.3 shows, crowding appears to be worse in large urban area jails. Between 1978 and 1983, the number of inmates in these facilities jumped 51 percent. Although comparatively few in number (only about 7 percent of all jails hold 250 or more inmates), these large jails house more than half of all local prisoners in this country.[5]

At the same time, most jails in the United States are small and have severe budget constraints. In 1983, 93 percent of local jails housed fewer than 250 inmates, as shown in Figure 13.4. These smaller counties and cities are looking for less costly ways to build and operate new correctional facilities at a pace necessary to avoid crowding and maintain constitutional standards.

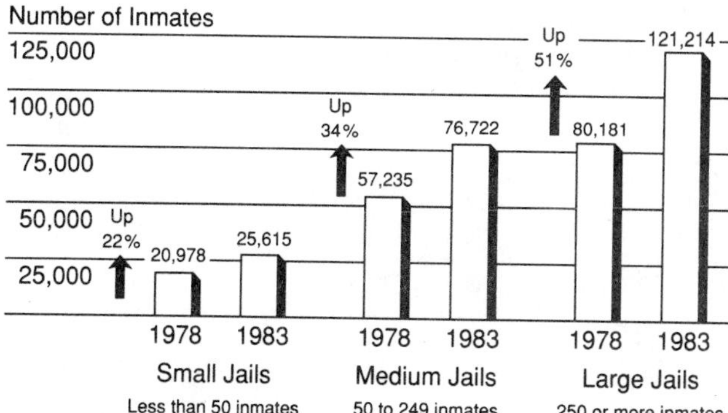

FIGURE 13.3
Jail inmates: growth by size of jails, 1978 to 1983. From Charles B. DeWitt, *New Construction Methods for Correctional Facilities* (Washington, D.C.: U.S. Department of Justice, National Institute of Justice, March 1986), p. 4.

What do these figures mean to state and local officials who must finance new construction? The answer is disturbing. For the nation as a whole, states need to build new facilities at a rate that provides at least 1,000 new beds each week, and counties must expand at a minimum of 400 additional bed spaces weekly. The cumulative figure of 1,400 additional beds each week will only keep pace with the current rate of growth and does not address the shortages described above.

The Advisory Commission on Intergovernmental Relations reviewed the debate about how much construction may be appropriate and whether new facilities may be an effective response to the problem. The commission noted, "Most experts, however, agree on one thing: the costs of correctional facilities—capital and operational—are indeed overwhelming" (Advisory Commission on Intergovernmental Relations 1983, p. 7).

Organizations representing corrections practitioners have come forward to protest the high costs of construction and to encourage new ideas. American Correctional Association President Don Hutto has said ". . . we should encourage a more sensible approach to testing technological innovations. Institutions, approaching $100,000 per bed, are far too expensive. . . ."

It is apparent that many state and local government units will not be able to bear the financial burden imposed by growing construction costs. The National Institute of Justice is conducting a survey of major jail and prison construction completed since 1978. Survey results show that correctional institutions can take up to sixty-two months for construction, and that the average cost per bed of new facilities with single occupancy cells reported to date is approximately $50,000. If one assumes an average cost of $50,000 per cell, the current rate of growth suggests a national building cost of $70 million per week—a staggering expenditure by all standards.

CARE OF SPECIAL PRISONERS

Alcoholics, diabetics, epileptics, the mentally ill, drug addicts, **sex offenders,** and other **special prisoners** present unique problems for the jailer. Such prisoners often require professional attention. And although jail officers are not expected to serve as physician, psychiatrist, or psychologist, they do need to have some knowledge of the problems involved in supervising various types of special prisoners (Pappas 1971).[6]

A jailer deals with people from a wide range of backgrounds, in varying stages of health, and with needs ranging from simple housing with minimal security to tight security with continual supervision and care. The first decision a jailer must make is whether to admit a person brought to jail for detention. This decision is based on the policy of the jail administrator and the laws of the jurisdiction in which the jail is located. If the law requires that every person brought to the jail be admitted, the jail must then assume responsibility for any necessary medical care. And if the jail cannot refuse persons who are ill, injured, or otherwise in no condition to be confined, then the jailer must be able to evaluate the prisoner's condition. In either case, the jailer must be able to recognize the unusual and be aware of the consequences of his or her actions. The safety and wel-

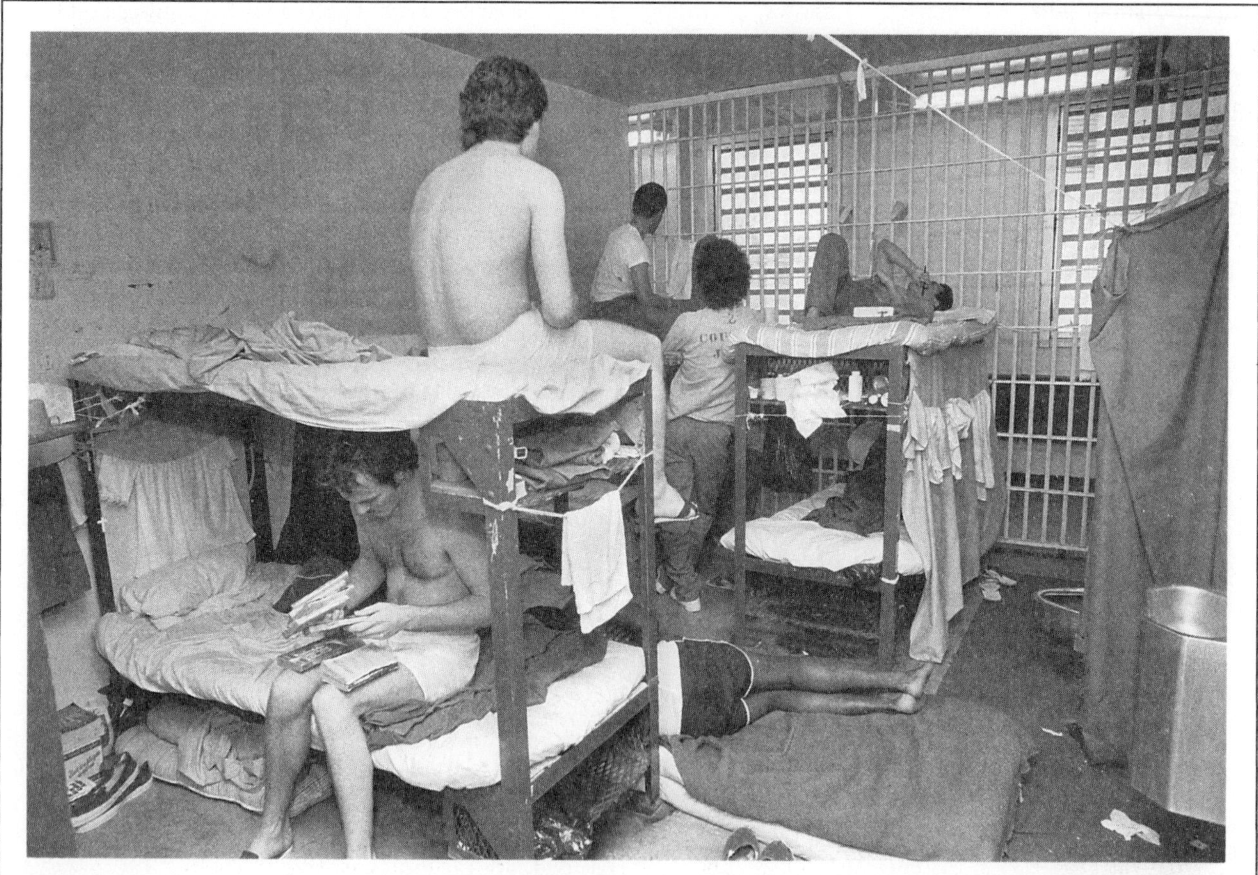

FIGURE 13.5
In some holding cells there are as many as four to six more prisoners than allowed by law. Courtesy Robert Burke/*Tampa Tribune.*

fare of all prisoners may depend on the jailer's ability to recognize illness and injury. Furthermore, the jailer has both a moral and legal responsibility for the health and welfare of prisoners. Increasingly, the courts have recognized the legal rights of prisoners and have, in some instances, permitted civil suits against the jail, its officers, and the municipality when jail personnel have not exercised reasonable care in their duties.

Alcoholics

The special prisoner seen most often by the jailer is the alcoholic. The familiar symptoms of intoxication include shakiness, staggering, thick speech, and a blank, glassy-eyed look. However, because other conditions can produce the same symptoms, it would be a mistake to assume that everyone who exhibits them is drunk. Multiple sclerosis, for example, is a disease that sometimes causes a person to stagger. Persons suffering from this disorder have been arrested for drunkenness despite protests that they have had nothing to drink.

The symptoms of a head injury can also be confused with the effects of excessive drinking. A person who has been hit over the head or who strikes his or her head in a fall may appear intoxicated. Such a person should receive immediate medical attention. And someone in a diabetic coma may resemble a drinker who has passed out; if the diabetes goes untreated, the person may die. Thus, even when jailers are virtually certain that they are dealing with a simple case of intoxication, they should make sure that the prisoner in question is checked regularly. A person who has consumed a large amount of alcohol might first show typical signs of drunkenness, but might later lapse into deep unconsciousness and die.

Jail Blamed for Diabetic's Hospitalization

Cella W. Dugger *Atlanta Journal*

A DeKalb County prisoner who claims jail authorities refused to give him insulin and the special diet he needs was treated for a "critical" diabetic condition at Grady Memorial Hospital and is still listed in poor condition at the hospital.

The jail's physician denies the allegations, saying the inmate, Walter Jones, is lying.

Two doctors who treated Jones at Grady said his condition indicated that he may not have received the insulin.

Jones, 28, of 2369 Columbia Wood Court, Decatur, was arrested Nov. 2 and charged with the armed robbery of a 7-Eleven store at 2381 Columbia Drive, Decatur, and with aggravated assault on DeKalb police officers G. M. Fahey and M. L. Sharkey.

DeKalb police spokesman Chuck Johnson said Jones "fired shots at two officers outside the 7-Eleven as they were attempting to arrest him."

Jones was admitted to Grady Friday morning, five days later, in critical condition with pneumonia and an abnormally high blood sugar level, according to Dr. Mark Goldfarb. Goldfarb said this condition can result from a diabetic not getting enough insulin.

He said he didn't know why Jones—"a young healthy man" despite his diabetic condition—has pneumonia, but said a lack of insulin could have put Jones into a "stuporous state" in which he might have contracted pneumonia. Noting that Jones' blood sugar was 10 times the normal level, Goldfarb said, "I would assume he hadn't been getting his insulin, but I don't know."

Ralph Jackson, the other physician treating Jones, said "either he wasn't getting insulin or he had an infection. If he had been taking his regular dose of insulin, I don't think his glucose (sugar) would have been that high, but I can't be sure."

Jones, a construction worker, told both his brother and the medical student with primary responsibility for his care at Grady that while in custody he had been denied insulin and had been given the same diet as the other prisoners. Diabetics require a special diet to maintain their blood sugar level.

Jones could not be interviewed because of tightened security measures at Grady brought about by the rash of escapes from the hospital this year.

Dr. Charles Allard, who was in charge of the case at the jail, refused to describe the treatment he had prescribed for the patient.

"I don't give any information to anybody over the telephone. He (Jones) is lying. I won't tell you nothing," Allard said.

A doctor and a nurse are on duty 24 hours a day for the jail's more than 500 inmates, according to a DeKalb County Sheriff's Department spokesman. "We feel good about our medical team," Lt. Winston Pittman said.

"We have some people who come in there and don't tell us what's wrong with them and we get the blame," Pittmann said.

Jones' brother Tommy, of the same address, said he received a call from the prisoner on the afternoon of his arrest.

"I called them (the jail) and told them he was a diabetic. He had already told them. And they didn't give him insulin or the right food or anything," Tommy Jones said.

On Wednesday, Tommy Jones said, an inmate called him to tell him his brother was sick. "He said he was out and about to go into a coma," Jones said.

Jones said he then went to the jail, and that the "jailers told me there wasn't nothing wrong with him."

When he got back home, he said, another inmate called telling him his brother was "bad off sick." The inmates must have been passing the phone around.

Thursday morning at about 9:30, Jones said, he went back to the jail to see his brother, and was told that "he was fine." Jones said he hired an attorney, Donald J. Stein, who went to the jail that afternoon.

Stein said those in charge wouldn't let him see Walter Jones because "he was doing too badly and they were giving him a hypodermic to sedate him."

Friday morning, Jones was admitted to Grady.

Ken Dobson, the medical student responsible for Jones' care, said he asked Jones, who Dobson said could not speak coherently until Sunday morning whether he had been getting his insulin and what he had been eating in the jail.

"He said he had asked for it (insulin) and they wouldn't give it to him. And he said, "I'm having to eat the same food as the other men," Dobson said.

Reprinted from the *Atlanta Journal*, 12 November 1980.

The Mentally Ill

Mental illnesses that are least understood are likely to be the most frightening. The behavior of the mentally disturbed person is often strange and alarming. The term **mental illness** is also misleading, because it covers a wide range of complicated emotional disorders that may involve physical, mental, and behavioral disturbances. A disorder may be relatively mild and difficult to detect, and it may not seriously handicap the individual. At the other extreme, conditions may be so obvious and serious that the sufferers require constant care and may even present a danger to themselves and others.

Some behavior that results from mental illness is dramatic and attracts immediate attention. Individuals who insist that they see or hear things that do not really exist are readily recognized as emotionally disturbed. But other signs of mental illness may be difficult to detect; for example, people who assert that someone is plotting against them may sound quite convincing, even though their belief is wholly without basis.

When people hear, see, smell, or taste something that is not really there, they are experiencing **hallucinations.** Hallucinations usually indicate a serious mental disturbance. Continuous heavy use of alcohol, drugs, and other chemical substances may also produce halluci-

FIGURE 13.6
An inmate in the residential unit of the Cook County (Illinois) Jail. The jail provides comprehensive treatment for inmates with mental health problems. Courtesy *Corrections Magazine.*

nations. The most common hallucinations involve hearing. For example, a person might report that a voice is telling him or her to do "bad" things. A person who shows clear signs of mental illness should be referred immediately to a physician (preferably a psychiatrist) or a clinical psychologist.

Drug Addicts

When long-time drug users are brought to jail, they may appear normal and be difficult to recognize as addicts. Nevertheless, cautious jailers should watch for signs of drug intoxication and withdrawal and examine prisoners for needle marks and scars over the blood vessels of the arms and legs. Weight loss and loss of appetite are also signs of drug addiction.

Jail personnel should watch prisoners closely to prevent them from obtaining unauthorized drugs. Jailers are responsible for keeping the addict safe from self-imposed injuries during drug withdrawal and to assist with the medical aspects of the process. The jail physician is responsible for the addicted prisoner's medical care, although most of the care is actually given by the jail staff. If a prisoner becomes seriously ill during withdrawal, the physician may recommend a short period of controlled hospitalization.

Sex Offenders

The jailer also sees a wide variety of sex offenders, including persons accused of indecent exposure, window peeping, child molestation, and rape. Despite popular belief, these offenders are quite different from one another, and each presents unique problems. Not all of them require the same degree of supervision or segregation, for example. Consider a prisoner charged with molesting a child: such a prisoner usually poses no sexual threat to adults, but he (or, rarely, she) may have to be protected from other prisoners. Anger toward the child molester and other sexual criminals is sometimes very intense. In general, most sex offenders are passive persons who pose no major problems in a jail setting; only a few are violent or dangerous. However, because some such offenders become depressed and suicidal, close observation is required.

SUICIDES IN JAIL

The Psychology of the Suicidal Inmate

Bruce L. Danto (1971), a nationally recognized authority on suicide and suicide prevention, concludes that certain types of persons are likely candidates for suicide in jail. One such person is the inmate who has had no previous experience with incarceration. In some cases, such an individual may not have been arrested for a very serious crime, but nevertheless may have strong feelings of depression, shame, and guilt. The following cases present examples of this type of inmate.

Case 13.1

On June 6, 1981, James Kiley was jailed at 3:10 A.M. in the Haverhill, Massachusetts County Jail on charges of drunk driving. He had been drinking with friends at a beach, and his vehicle struck a telephone pole while he was driving home. He was arrested shortly thereafter for drinking and driving. At 4:45 A.M. the police say their television monitor showed him asleep in his cell. Ten minutes later he was found dead—hanged with his shirtsleeves. The victim's mother said, "We just don't understand what happened. He was an easygoing nineteen-year-old boy with a brand new car, a plumbing job he liked, and a girl he loved. He left home whistling that night" (Michaels 1982, p. 4).

Case 13.2

On Thursday morning, August 13, 1981, Risa Boltax was riding her bike to a job interview in Scotch Plains, New Jersey, when she was stopped by the police. They took her into custody in connection with a previous incident involving possession of marijuana. Around lunchtime, Risa's mother, Yetta Boltax, visited her at the Union County Jail in Elizabeth and, she says, found her confused and upset. Some time near midnight, the police said nineteen-year-old Risa stood up on her bunk, twisted the sheet around her neck, tied each end of the sheet around the top bar of her cell, and stepped off the bunk (ibid.).

Some first-time offenders do commit very serious crimes—murder, a highly publicized sex offense, a white-collar crime (such as embezzlement), and so on. This type of inmate, according to Danto, is highly subject to suicide soon after admission to the jail.

Another type of person likely to commit suicide in jail is the inmate who has resided in a holding or postsentence center for weeks, months, or even years and has developed a feeling of hopelessness and futility about the future. This type of person frequently has spent previous time in penal confinement.

Case 13.3

A forty-three-year-old inmate in a county jail who had just been transferred from a federal prison for court proceedings was found dead hanging from the neck by strips of sheets in his cell. The inmate had been serving time in a federal prison for killing a law enforcement officer in a gunfight. The man—a hardened convict experienced in the ways of prisons and jails—soon found himself a niche in the county jail. During his confinement, several inmates heard him say that he was never going back to federal prison, even though his date for transfer was approaching. On the day of his suicide, the inmate received copies of divorce papers from his former wife's lawyer. The man left a note making some practical requests concerning his burial, the disposition of his death benefits, and a note cursing his wife "until my dying breath." His suicide, although quite likely triggered by the receipt of the divorce papers, was merely the culmination of his total loss of hope for the future (Fawcett and Marrs 1973, pp. 93–94).

The third type of person prone to suicidal behavior is the antisocial person who tries to manipulate others. Such inmates choose nonlethal forms of suicide in an attempt to manipulate guards and other officials. They characteristically make superficial cuts on their wrists or swallow glass (or at least say they have). Experience shows that this type of person can, indeed, kill himself or herself if pushed and goaded enough by others (Fawcett and Marrs 1973, pp. 96–97).

Management of the Suicidal Inmate

Jail suicides are not only tragic, but they can also be quite costly to the taxpayer. For example, the parents of James Kiley have notified the city of Haverhill that they intend to file a negligence suit for $100,000 (Michaels 1982, p. 5). As a result of such lawsuits, jail administrators are now training jail personnel in suicide prevention. The following suggestions are becoming a routine part of all such programs:

- The jail officer must take all threats of suicide seriously.
- Inmates who threaten or attempt suicide should not be kept in isolation, but should be housed with inmates who are willing to assist jail officers in watching them.
- Medical treatment for actual or claimed injury is essential.
- If depression and suicidal thoughts or behavior occur in relation to the falling off of contact with relatives or friends, correctional officers should arrange for a quick phone call or a visit between the involved parties.
- If jail doctors prescribe tranquilizers for disturbed inmates, the jail officer must make certain that the medication is taken. Further, efforts should be made to ensure that the inmate does not roll the pill back under the tongue and spit it out later or save it for a suicide attempt.
- Jail officers should be sensitive to inmates who abruptly withdraw from activities, suffer a loss of appetite, have sad facial expressions, or suddenly slow down in their thoughts or actions. Such signs are typical of depression.

The proper training of jail personnel and the use of mental health specialists for the screening and aftercare of suicidal inmates and for the reevaluation of jail directives can go a long way toward reducing the rate of jail suicide. In Los Angeles, for example, drunks are no longer jailed; rather, they are sent to a detoxification center run by the Volunteers of America. This policy change is credited as a major factor in suicide reduction in the Los Angeles County Jail. And the Pima County Jail in Tuscon, Arizona, several years ago adopted a pretrial release program for certain types of nonviolent offenders; as a result, the jail has experienced a 90 percent decrease in both attempted and successful suicides.

FIGURE 13.7
Mr. and Mrs. John Kiley of Methuen, Massachusetts, picket outside Haverhill Jail where their nineteen-year-old son died. Courtesy Lawrence (Massachusetts) *Eagle Tribune.*

JAIL SECURITY

In the real world of jail administration, security is given marked priority over rehabilitation. Although the two goals are often mentioned in the same breath, there is little question that security comes first. In most institutions, virtually all other activities and functions are subordinated to security. The reason is quite simple: no jail administrator has ever been fired for failing to rehabilitate an inmate; but many have been dismissed following prisoner escapes or disturbances (Miller 1978).[7] Some of the common security techniques and procedures used throughout the nation are counts, shakedowns, frisks, tool control, key control, cutlery control, narcotics control, and visitation control.

Counts

During a **count**, institutional activities are temporarily halted and all inmates are counted. It is hoped that the total will equal the number of people who are supposed to be in confinement. If it does not, at least one recount is taken, and an attempt is made to identify and locate the missing inmate or inmates. If the count still comes up short, escape procedures are implemented. In the event an escape does occur, routine counts provide some knowledge of the time frame within which the escape took place.

Shakedowns

A shakedown is a thorough search of a jail or any part thereof for contraband (anything an inmate possesses in violation of institutional rules and regulations). The definition of contraband varies from jail to jail, but weapons, alcohol, and narcotics not prescribed or approved by the jail physician are universally prohibited. Prisoners often employ ingenious methods to conceal contraband and to modify available objects for use as weapons or tools for escape.

Case 13.4

In a county jail in Washington State, U.S. marshals discovered the following items in the inner compartments of a prisoners rubber-soled shoes: two razor blades, five double-edged razor blades, one fingernail clipper (file and case), one

Case 13.4 continued

handcuff key (fabricated from a double-edged razor), and six metal tubes containing a black, paintlike substance.

Case 13.5

Upon searching a cell, officers in a New York State correctional facility found a crude, concealed weapon, handmade from a twelve-inch brass lavatory valve rod. The rod, which normally has a time-release push button at one end, extends downward through the fixture into the wall. The opposite end is linked by a cotter key to internal plumbing. Once the key is broken, however, the rod can be extracted and easily honed to a point by manually rubbing it against an abrasive surface (such as a concrete floor).

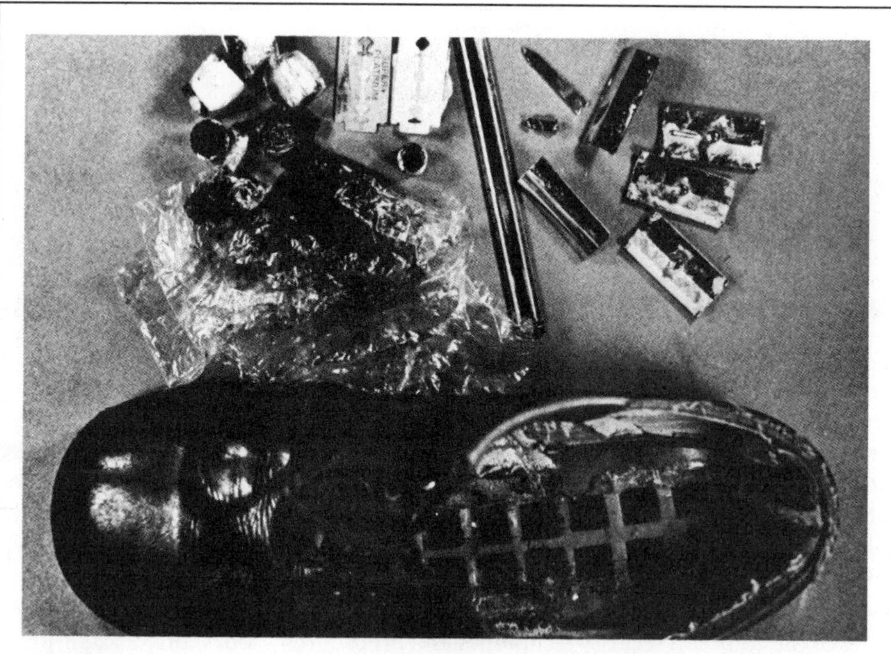

FIGURE 13.8
Shoe containing contraband. Courtesy Pierce County (Washington) Sheriff's office.

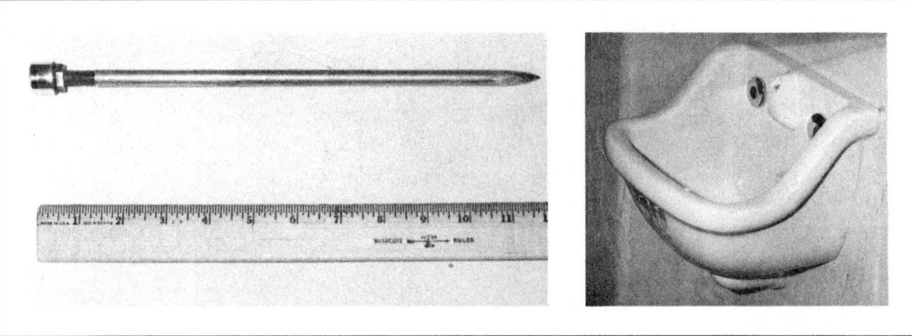

FIGURE 13.9
Weapon, *left,* fashioned from valve rod taken out of a jail cell sink. Courtesy Westchester County Department of Correction, Valhalla, New York.

Case 13.6

Correctional officers in the Westchester County (New York) Jail found a shank—fabricated from a tray—in the possession of a prisoner. The tray had been previously tested and was believed to be unbreakable, but it was discovered that the tray weakened over time.

Frisks

A frisk is a "pat search" of an inmate; officers run their hands along the outside of the inmate's clothing to detect concealed contraband. The frequency of frisks depends upon the security classification of the inmate and the areas to or from which the inmate is coming or going. For example, if a maximum security prisoner is leaving an area where there are usually tools (i.e., potential weapons), a frisk would be an appropriate, if not a mandatory, security procedure. Some jails use metal detectors instead of, or in addition to, standard frisking.

Case 13.7

Officers in an Oregon correctional facility discovered that a prisoner had developed a zipper tab into a screwdriver. The prisoner first worked the tab loose from the zipper, then ground down each side. The result was a custom-made screwdriver that could remove security screws from windows.

Case 13.8

At one jail, only one of sixteen prisoners taken from the jail to court for trial was searched. As a result, the inmates brought a hacksaw blade with them and sawed through one of the bars of their holding cell. Three inmates squeezed through an eight-by-twelve-inch hole, jumped to a lower level outside the building, then dropped to the ground. One inmate broke his ankle and

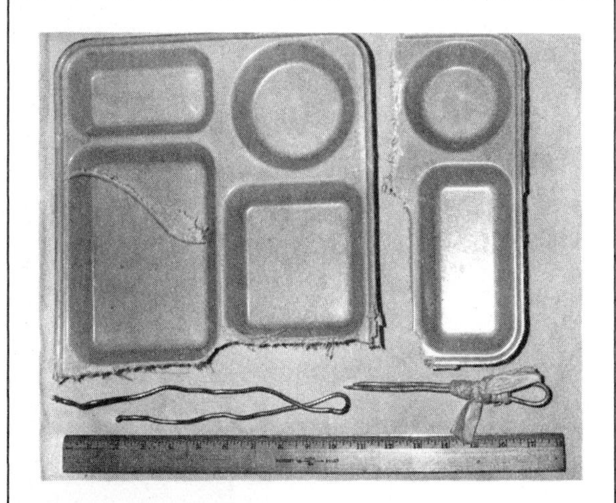

FIGURE 13.10
Shank (a weapon used for stabbing) fabricated from a tray. Courtesy Westchester County Department of Correction, Valhalla, New York.

Case 13.8 continued

was recaptured on the scene. During the next ten hours before recapture, the remaining two inmates murdered six people.

Tool Control

Tool control is a system of accounting for all tools available in a jail. Tight control is essential, because tools can be—and often are—used as weapons or as an aid in escape. Because proper tool control requires up-to-date inventory surveys, all tools should be stored in secure places and be fully accounted for at the end of each workday.

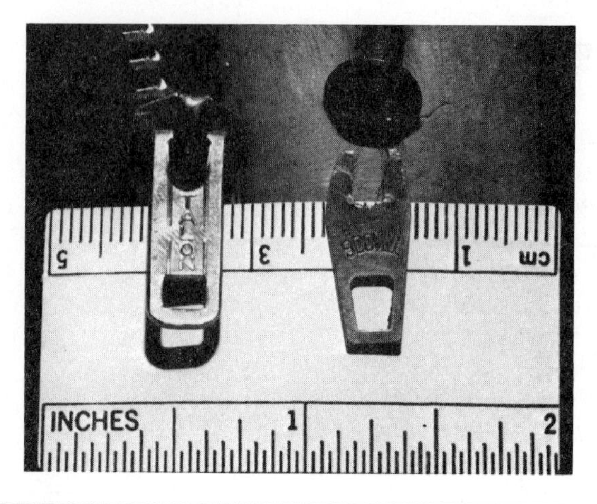

FIGURE 13.11
Zipper screwdriver. Courtesy Douglas Sheriff's Department, Corrections Division, Roseburg, Oregon.

One of the best methods of assuring adequate tool control is the use of a "shadow board" (for tool storage). The outline of each tool is painted on the board, so that a tool-crib operator can tell at the end of the day if tools are missing. When tools are checked out, a receipt is completed and attached to the board in place of the tool to ensure accountability.

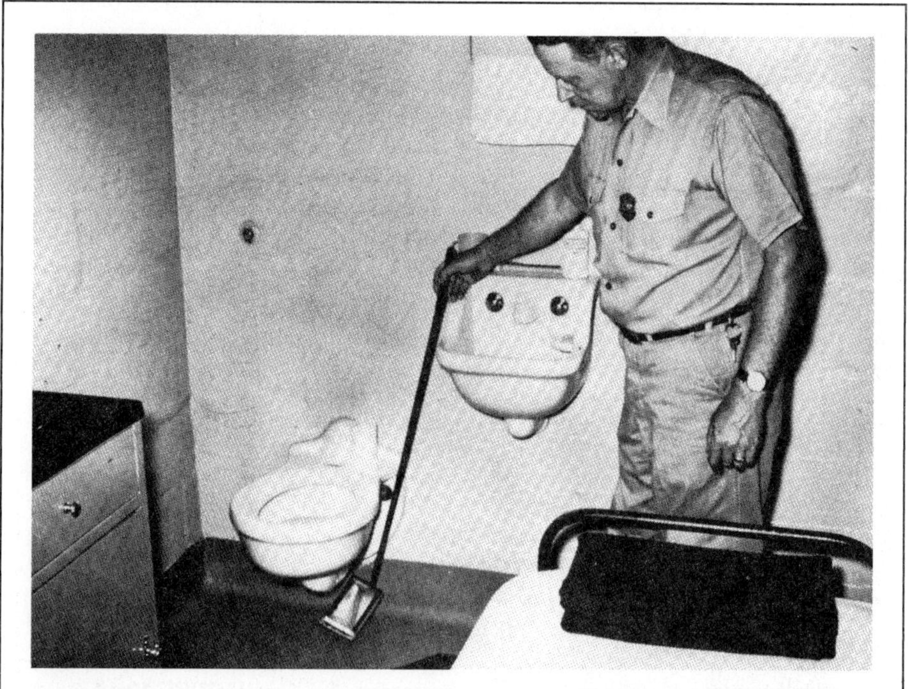

FIGURE 13.12
A guard searching a jail cell for contraband, using a mirror mounted on a rod. Reprinted from Nick Pappas, editor, *The Jail: Its Operation and Management* (Washington, D.C.: U.S. Bureau of Prisons, 1971).

Case 13.9

An inmate escaped from a third-floor rooftop and recreation area, even though the area was completely screened by a heavy-gauge wire fence and cover. A jail officer supervised the area but could not see one corner of the yard from his position. The inmate used a pair of wire cutters inadvertently left behind by a workman, cut through the fence, and climbed down a building drain pipe (National Sheriffs Association 1974, p. 70).

Case 13.10

A jail officer asked an inmate to get cleaning supplies from a furnace room; he gave the inmate the keys to the security door. The inmate got the supplies and returned the keys, but left the door to the furnace room open. Three inmates then simply walked out, because the furnace room was outside the security portion of the jail and led directly to the street. The jail officer was subsequently tried in court and fined for negligence, although the court decided not to give him a jail sentence (National Sheriffs Association, 1974, p. 73).

Key Control #8

Despite its obvious importance, key control is less than effective in many jails. There is often no central control system, and those that do exist may be ineffective because of the casual attitudes of jail officers. Control is particularly difficult in jails that have a different key for every door. A jailer who carries both cell keys and keys to cell blocks risks assault from prisoners attempting to escape. Once prisoners have the keys to their cell block, it is a simple matter for them to get to and open the door leading out of the jail.

Cutlery Control

Cutlery control is a system of accounting for all eating utensils used in a jail. Normally, kitchen equipment such as butcher knives and other potentially dangerous items are monitored under an institution's tool control program. But special measures are needed to ensure that the cutlery used at meals is not "borrowed" and used for illegal purposes. A table knife is an obvious weapon,

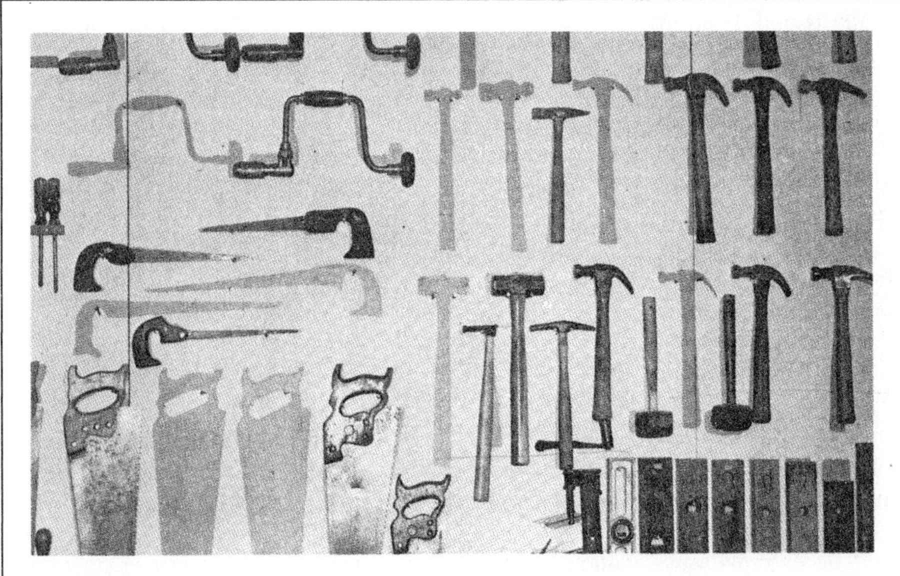

FIGURE 3.13
Shadow board used for tool control. Reprinted from Nick Pappas, editor, *The Jail: Its Operation and Management* (Washington, D.C.: U.S. Bureau of Prisons, 1971).

FIGURE 13.14
Key control board. A metal tag bearing the officer's name is used as a receipt when keys are withdrawn. Reprinted from Nick Pappas, editor, *The Jail: Its Operation and Management* (Washington, D.C.: U.S. Bureau of Prisons, 1971).

and a fork or a spoon that has been sharpened at one end can be equally dangerous.

When inmates eat in communal dining halls, cutlery control is rather standard. When the inmates enter the dining room, they are each handed eating utensils for that meal. At the end of the meal, as the inmates leave via a main exit, they must deposit into a large receptacle under the observation of an officer the same number and type of utensils they were initially issued. If an inmate fails to do this, he or she is detained in the dining hall. After all inmates have deposited their used cutlery as required, the silverware is again counted before it is taken back into the kitchen for washing. If any cutlery is missing at that point, a search or shakedown is conducted to recover the missing items.

When inmates eat in their cells, a common practice in many jails, officers must again be careful to supervise the dispensation and return of silverware. If anything is missing, a search of the area involved should be started promptly. The silverware should also be counted again when it is returned to the kitchen: there is always the possibility that trustees or other inmates will pilfer one or more items during the transit from the cells to the kitchen. Why not use plastic utensils? Because plastic items are difficult to clean properly (given the equipment in most jail kitchens), and it would be extremely expensive and inconvenient to replace utensils after each meal.

Case 3.11

Two prison transportation officers were attacked by an inmate with a knife that was stolen from the jail kitchen by another inmate and concealed in the prisoner-transport vehicle. One officer was killed. The incident occurred on a busy highway, and motorists were in substantial danger because of an exchange of gunfire after the inmate took the gun of the dead officer. Matters worsened when the second officer, already seriously wounded, was shot and wounded again by an off-duty police officer in foot pursuit of the escapee (National Sheriffs Association 1974, p. 73).

Narcotics Control

Narcotics control is a major problem in many jails, particularly in metropolitan areas, because of the high number of addicts confined on criminal charges. This situation creates an immediate and substantial demand for illicit drugs. Again, good control procedures start with an accurate and up-to-date survey of inventory. All narcotics should be stored securely in an area not readily accessible to inmates. And medication prescribed for inmates should be prepared by qualified medical personnel, not by jail officers. In most jails, medication is dispensed in the cell block, because too many problems are involved in moving prisoners to and from an infirmary. Medication should be dispensed personally by an officer, and inmates should be required to swallow the medication in the presence of that officer. A guard should check under the tongue to ensure that the medicine has been consumed and not "saved" for purposes of hoarding or sale within the institution. Certain types of medication can be dissolved in water first to get around this problem. Jail personnel also have to be alert to the possibility that drugs might be mailed or smuggled into the jail.

Visitation Control

Any time people from the "outside" come into or go out of a jail, a threat is posed to the security of the institution. This is especially true today, because of narcotics smuggling. Thus, *visitation control*—the control of visiting procedures and facilities—requires careful attention on the part of prison administrators.

A common form of visitation control is the enclosed booth with a plexiglass or bullet-resistant glass front. Inmates sit in the booth and communicate with their visitors via voice-powered telephone. Some jails use a less structured arrangement and allow inmates to sit across a table from their visitors (with or without a screen between them). A third visitation mode is an informal, quasi-living room setting—sofas, easy chairs, coffee tables—with few, if any, physical barriers. Another type of visit, one that is currently a source of controversy in some jurisdictions, is the "contact" visit. In such visits, the inmate and his or her spouse are allowed to kiss hello and good-bye and to hold hands during the visit. The purpose of this approach is to make visits as normal as possible.

A key to maintaining proper security during visits is the careful screening of inmates. For example, a maximum security prisoner who poses an imminent escape risk or is otherwise considered dangerous should be allowed to visit only in the booth arrangement. On the other hand, a minimum security prisoner who has demonstrated his or her trustworthiness should be allowed to visit in a more relaxed atmosphere. Under any visiting format, however, officers should be present and alert to any sign of trouble or any attempt to pass contraband. To further ensure security, many jails frisk inmates after visits before returning them to their housing or work areas; some jails even perform a complete strip search of every inmate.

Case 13.12

One inventive young woman who visited her boyfriend at a county jail in Florida left a felt-tipped pen and some writing paper for him after each visit. The pen was always checked by correctional personnel before it was turned over to the prisoner, and each time it appeared to be nothing more than a pen. In fact, it *was* a pen, but it was also used as a container to smuggle marijuana into the jail. Before the start of each visit, the woman would remove the pen's plastic top and take out the cartridge. She would then stuff the pen with enough marijuana for two cigarettes. She added black paper on top of the marijuana to block the view of anyone who might remove the top of the pen for inspection. The scheme was discovered only because another inmate informed correctional personnel. The next time the girlfriend visited, she was searched and the marijuana was found. The woman was arrested for attempting to smuggle drugs into the jail.

Case 13.13

A state jail inspector informed a particular jail administrator that his facility had inadequate security procedures and staffing. The jail administrator disagreed with the inspector and released a story to the press that appeared on the front page of the Sunday newspaper. That same Sunday night, the lone officer on duty (for thirty-eight inmates) was called to a cell block area by an inmate, who shot him with a gun smuggled in by a female visitor in a candy box with a fake bottom. (The officer was over seventy years old and had just retired from another job two months before.) The inmate took the

Case 13.13 continued

dying officer's keys and opened his cell door. The jail administrator, who lived in adjacent quarters, heard the gunshot, rushed to the scene and was also shot. The escapee dashed down a stairway into the courthouse lobby, broke a window in the front door, and drove off in a waiting car with an accomplice (National Sheriffs Association 1974, p. 72).

THE ROLE OF THE JAIL IN THE CRIMINAL JUSTICE SYSTEM

As indicated in Chapter 1, the criminal justice system is an arrangement of four working parts: the police, the prosecution, the courts, and corrections. The police force is responsible for criminal investigation and apprehension, the prosecution for the prosecution of offenses against the state, the courts for determination of guilt, and corrections for confinement and rehabilitation. The system will not work at all if any of the parts is missing, and it will work at a low level of efficiency if any of the parts is not operating well (Pappas 1971).

The jail is important as evidence of society's interest in justice, punishment and rehabilitation. Anyone who has been found not guilty by a court has had first-hand experience with our system of law and justice. And anyone who is awaiting trial or serving a sentence will get a long and intensive exposure to the values of society with regard to crime and punishment. The jail has an extremely important place in the criminal justice system, both because it is the most common type of confinement and because more persons pass through the jail than through any other agency in the system.

Jails and the Police

The relationship of jails to the police is one of accommodation and cooperation. Jails must accept any prisoner who is legally detained and who can be legally received. (In some jurisdictions, however, jails cannot admit juveniles, even if the arrest is legal.) Jails are passive, and to some extent, the jail population reflects this. For example, if the police have periodic clean-up campaigns to remove drunks and vagrants from the streets, the jails will soon contain many such persons. And because arrest policies are not a matter of police determination alone, but are a reflection of community attitudes and governmental policy, complaints from local business people may be enough to initiate a clean-up policy.

North Franklin Policing Hit

Ivan Hathaway *Tampa Tribune*

Claiming that panhandlers are running rampant and "women have to walk out into the street to avoid being molested," a group of North Franklin Street merchants charged yesterday that police are not providing adequate protection.

The charge was leveled by a group of about 25 businessmen at a morning meeting at Todd's Restaurant, 208 E. Cass Street, which was attended by City Councilmen Joe Kotvas and Lee Duncan, Deputy Police Chief Allison Wainwright and Police Maj. J. W. Morton.

Making the strongest complaints was Harry Arkus, who told the city officials that customers entering stores on Franklin and its side streets have to make their way past panhandlers begging for money.

"These bums line the sidewalks, alienating customers. I've seen two women who had to walk out into the street to avoid being molested," Arkus said.

One merchant told of being robbed in his store five times in recent years and of being mugged and robbed on the sidewalk only a week ago.

He said, referring to the most recent case, that had there been a policeman on the street the robber could have been caught.

Others complained of "drunks" being allowed to lie on the streets in front of their stores for 30 minutes or longer, saying that police response was slow.

Addressing Wainwright, Arkus said, "We see an officer walking the beat once in a while, and then we don't see him again for a few days and don't know where he is when we need him. We want to be protected."

Responding to the complaints, Wainright said police officials already were aware that downtown merchants "have a problem."

"The only answer to this problem you're having seems to be in assigning more officers to patrol the area. But we just don't have the men to do this," he said.

From *The Tampa Tribune*, 16 January 1973.

Police Crack Down on Panhandlers

Ivan Hathaway *Tampa Tribune*

A crackdown on "nuisance violations," aimed particularly at the growing number of panhandlers in the downtown area, has resulted in 10 arrests within a 24-hour period, Tampa police said yesterday.

Jail dockets indicated the 10 men were charged with "begging." They were held in lieu of $25 bond each.

The arrests came shortly after a meeting in which North Franklin Street merchants criticized the policing in their business area.

Col. Allison Wainwright, deputy chief of police, said the meeting did not bring about the crackdown, "though it may have been a contributing factor."

"We've always been interested in protecting the downtown area. Because of a shortage of officers and the crime rate, we have not had the opportunity to enforce the ordinance as we would have liked to," Wainwright said.

But the panhandling has had a gradual increase and is now a major problem. "People are being pushed around and verbally abused. Panhandlers are even approaching our plainclothes detectives."

To cope with the problem, officers who had been assigned to other Tampa areas have been called in to patrol the "entire downtown area," and policemen are doubling up on their assignments, he said.

"It has been our experience that as soon as we apply enforcement in an area, we begin seeing results and the problem begins decreasing," Wainwright said.

The crackdown will continue "as long as possible," he said.

"With these additional men in the downtown area we have a hairline balance of manpower. We'll keep them there as long as we can. If a need for additional manpower arises in another part of the city, we will have to pull them out for reassignment," Wainwright said.

From *The Tampa Tribune*, 18 January 1973.

The important point here is that the jails feel the effects of community and police policy. They are not independent units in the community, uninfluenced by events around them. Rather, they are part of a larger system, and what the rest of that system does affects them. And the way the jails operate will, in turn, affect the community and the rest of the criminal justice system.

Jails hold the accused until the formal machinery of criminal justice begins to move. While an accused person is in a jail, coordination is often required between the police and jail personnel. Some exchange of information is necessary, particularly when there is a need to keep accomplices separated. When a long-term investigation is required, the police and the jail may need to coordinate efforts to schedule interviews or otherwise make the accused available to the police, the prosecuting attorney, and the defense counsel. The need for information exchange and coordination is equally important when the jail is holding a material witness (a vital service to the police).

Jails and the Courts

Jails and the courts must cooperate closely if both are to complete their work. The courts influence the jail's activity and, in turn, are dependent on the jail's successful handling of the court-imposed work load. And the jail has a scheduling and coordinating function with regard to the courts. The jail must follow trial schedules and be aware of trial results and orders to produce or release prisoners. To a great extent, these functions make the jail a department of the court.

Sentencing decisions clearly demonstrate the extent of interdependence between jails and the courts. The courts can sentence an individual to jail, modify the sentence before its completion, place an offender on probation, and, in some jurisdictions, sentence offenders to work release. These decisions influence the jail population and its composition and the extent of program activity. For example, misdemeanants may be sentenced to jails instead of to workhouses or work farms, thus increasing the number of prisoners in jails. Or the court may decide to sentence prisoners to a county correctional institution, thus reducing the jail population. In some cases, the courts may decide to use probation, a suspended sentence, or a fine. And court decisions against the arrest of drunks may reduce the number of drunks among the jail population.

Although some bail is routine, all bail is a matter of court supervision. Until recently, jails were passive in bail proceedings; if an accused person made bail, he or she was released from jail. Today, however, bail projects have expanded the role of the jail. In addition to detention and confinement, the jail is now involved in selecting persons for release on their own recognizance. The selection may be done by jail personnel, although it is usually done by employees of the probation department. Where such programs do not exist, traditional bail procedures require that the jail work within court and statutory requirements to develop bail procedures.

Because of the need for close coordination, courts and jails are often located in the same building. Although it is possible to operate a jail at some distance from the court, such an arrangement is inconvenient in terms of moving prisoners back and forth to the court. In general, coordination between a court and a jail becomes more difficult as the distance between them increases. A jail outside the immediate vicinity of the court is isolated, and jail personnel may begin to feel that the jail has little to do with the court.

The decisions of the court relative to convicted offenders make it necessary for the jail to serve as a distributor to the system. The jail is the transfer point for prisoners who have been sentenced to a workhouse, county farm, or correctional institution. In some instances, the transfer is a procedural matter handled by notifying the proper agency. Depending on the case, prisoners may be delivered to the receiving institutions either by that institution or by the jail. If large numbers of prisoners are involved in a transfer, the jail may serve as a collection point.

Jails and Corrections

Many people view the jail as primarily a law enforcement operation, probably because the chief administrator of the jail is usually a law officer (namely, a sheriff). However, jails do not have specific law enforcement functions. They are not a base of operations for criminal detection or apprehension, although they may be located in a department where these activities go on. Jail personnel may be formally connected with the law enforcement organization and may, in fact, be deputy sheriffs; but their specific duties in the jail are not in the area of law enforcement.

The jails have more than a passing responsibility for the care of prisoners who are serving sentences. In essence, jails are in the business of corrections. Today there is increased recognition that the jail must serve many functions in the community. And correction is one of these functions. The jail is called upon by the courts and community to become involved in correctional programs and to concern itself with the rehabilitation of prisoners who are serving sentences. Some authorities even recommend that the jail become the focus of the community correctional effort.

The fact that most sentenced prisoners are not felons does not divorce a jail from the rehabilitative effort. Rehabilitation does not begin with the felon; rather, it is needed most for the misdemeanant. And it is an area in which jails have a particular advantage: they are located in the community and can coordinate community resources to develop an effective program.

Aside from their rehabilitative function, jails play a role in the general correctional effort in the state. In this regard, the jail must develop close and effective ties with the state correctional program. This will result in a shared effort between the jail and the larger system—to the benefit of both. In program planning, the jail may be able to benefit by the state's experience with certain rehabilitative techniques. And personnel training can be shared, especially when a jail has too few personnel or resources to develop its own training program. The expert help needed to plan new construction or renovation can also be provided by the state. Finally, local and state facilities can coordinate prisoner statistics to get a statewide picture of jail and correctional needs.

SUMMARY

Jails are the intake point of our entire criminal justice system and are the most prevalent type of correctional institution. They are primarily a function of local government, and they are as diverse in size, physical condition, and efficiency as the units of government that operate them. The three types of jails are pretrial detention facilities for persons awaiting trial, sentenced facilities for persons serving sentences, and combination facilities for pretrial detentions and some convicted persons.

Jails in the United States are quite old and are frequently in need of extensive repair. In addition, many are offensive to the eye and nose because of noxious odors, dirty lavatories, dirty floors, stained walls, and vermin. Many jail facilities also contain fire hazards that endanger both inmates and correctional staff. In all fairness, however, it must be noted that there are also many jails that are clean and well maintained. Often, the major difference between a poorly run and poorly kept jail and one that is well maintained is the attitude, philosophy, and priorities of the local sheriff or jail administrator. For example, it is rarely expensive to keep a jail clean and free of vermin, but if such activity is not viewed as being very important by the person in charge, then poor conditions may not get the attention they need.

Jail overcrowding continues to be a major problem even though jail expansion increased at a rate of more than 40 percent during the five years from 1978 to 1983. In addition, the rapid increase in the number of jail inmates vastly exceeds the number of beds being added to local jail systems. The problems of overcrowding have impacted on both large and small jails. At the same time, most of the smaller jails in the United States are having severe budget constraints and are looking for less costly ways to build and operate new correctional facilities at a pace necessary to avoid overcrowding and maintain constitutional standards. It is apparent that many state and local government units will not be able to bear the financial burden imposed by growing construction costs, which average $50,000 per single occupancy cell.

Special prisoners that present problems for the jailer include alcoholics, the mentally ill, drug addicts, sex offenders, injured persons, and depressed or suicidal prisoners. Jail personnel must be properly trained to recognize and supervise such prisoners, and, when necessary, to provide them with special care. The failure to do so might result in the death of a prisoner and a lawsuit against those responsible for jail administration and operation.

When hard choices must be made between security and rehabilitation in the jail, security is always given priority. This is not surprising, considering that jail administrators can be fired and sheriffs defeated at election time if a dangerous or infamous prisoner escapes. To ensure the integrity of jail security, several measures are employed: shakedowns, which involve a thorough search of a jail or any part thereof for contraband; regular frisking of inmates, especially when they are moved from one part of the jail to another; tool control; key control; cutlery control; narcotics control; and visitation control.

Overall, the jail plays an extremely important role in the criminal justice system. Because of its strategic location, many citizens come into contact with the jail each year and form their first impressions about the quality and fairness of the system. And jail personnel are involved in a close working relationship with the police, the courts, and corrections. The extent to which these other parts of the criminal justice system are effective is sometimes quite dependent upon the quality of the jail and its personnel.

In spite of the bleak picture often presented of American jails, evidence suggests that the quality of jail personnel and jail facilities will steadily improve throughout the 1980s. This will occur in part because of pressure about overcrowding, unsanitary conditions, poor health care, and physical abuse. Other improvements will occur because the states are not taking a more active role in requiring minimum qualifications and training for jail personnel. Finally, there is reason to believe that the chief administrators of our local jails—whether they are sheriffs or civilian administrators—are better educated, better trained, and generally more professional than their predecessors.

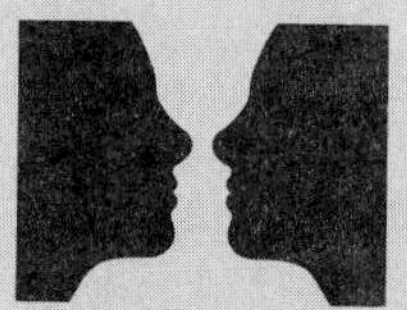

ISSUE PAPER

BUILDING BETTER JAILS

By Richard Wener, William Frazier, and Jay Farbstein

There is an overpowering smell of urine, sweat, stale food and Pinesol. Dirty walls, littered floors of cold, gray concrete and steel-bar doors suggest zoo cages, designed to be washed down with a hose. The noise of blaring television, banging doors and yelling men is deafening. Some of the inmates wander about aimlessly, obviously mentally ill. The few uniformed officers usually stay securely behind the doors. One occasionally hurries in and out, but there is seldom eye contact or personal exchange of any kind with the prisoners.

Movie buffs would recognize this as a scene in the slammer. But how about this one? There are sunlit rooms with carpeted floors. The attractive furniture is covered with fabrics in muted grays contrasted with bright blues and reds. Men joke around ordinary card tables while playing checkers. In a corner, several others watch television from an upholstered couch. A uniformed officer strolls by and stops to chat. An inmate asks her to open the door to his room so he can use the toilet. The room has a bed, sink, desk with desk lamp and a window with a view of the city street below.

The first scene is typical of many of the more than 3,000 jails and 700 prisons in the United States today. The old Tombs, the infamous Manhattan House of Detention, was even worse: a dangerous bedlam of bodies jammed into too-small cages, until it became uncontrollable and was closed in 1974 because it could not meet conditions imposed by a federal court order.

The second scene might be viewed with some variations, in any of a dozen newer jails, including the renovated Tombs, that make use of a new model of management and design known as direct supervision. The officers and inmates in these jails come from the same backgrounds as before. Crime statistics haven't improved, and violence has, if anything, become more common. What has changed is a combination of management and operational philosophy, design features and staff training. The direct-supervision style developed from what the Federal Bureau of Prisons has learned in several prisons and three prototypical jails built during the 1970s. During the past 10 years we have formally evaluated a number of these direct-supervision facilities and found that they work well, far better than most corrections veterans or even psychologists thought possible.

Direct supervision is not for every inmate. Careful classification and screening usually weed out the 5 to 10 percent who are mentally ill or especially violent and assign them to more structured settings. But direct supervision seems to work effectively in almost any jurisdiction and equally well in jails, which are used mainly for pretrial and short-term detention, and in prisons, where sentenced inmates serve longer terms.

The Federal Bureau of Prisons, traditionally the most innovative force in corrections in the United States, developed the direct-supervision model in line with the philosophy that "If you can't rehabilitate, at least do no harm." The bureau built three federal Metropolitan Correctional Centers (MCC's) in Chicago, New York and San Diego in the early 1970s to provide humane, secure detention.

The key concept was direct supervision—placing officers in housing units where they are in contact, direct contact with inmates, rather than in control booths. This is difficult to do in jails designed to keep officers and inmates apart.

The first reaction to this arrangement by traditional wardens, jail officials and most visitors is usually astonishment. They think of public and staff safety in terms of hard barriers between us and them. The new design seemingly places officers at the mercy of inmates. But our research with the MCC's shows that officers in constant contact with inmates get to know them well. They learn to recognize and respond to trouble before it escalates into violence. Staff skills of negotiation and communication become more important than brute strength. As many as 40 percent of the correctional officers in some direct-supervision facilities are women, and there is strong evidence that they do at least as well as male officers there.

Compared to traditional jails of similar size, the MCC's and other direct-supervision jails have much less conflict among inmates and between inmates and staff. Violent incidents are reduced 30 to 90 percent, and homosexual rape virtually disappears.

Vandalism and graffiti take similar dramatic drops. In the new jail at Pima County, Arizona, for example, the number of damaged mattresses dropped from 150 per year to none in two years; from an average of two TVs needing repair per week to two in two years; and

FIGURE 13.15
The watching hour: Inmates at the Contra Costa Detention Facility in Martinez, California, watch TV while an officer watches them. Courtesy *Psychology Today*/photographer Ed Kashi.

from an average of 99 sets of inmates' clothes destroyed per week to 15 in two years.

All this is accomplished in jails that are certainly no more expensive and in some ways cheaper to build than are traditional methods. Because vandalism is so rare, construction money can be saved by using standard materials such as porcelain plumbing and ordinary lighting fixtures instead of more costly vandalproof versions.

It is impossible to compare operating costs directly because the programs provided for inmates vary greatly among direct- and indirect-supervision jails. But in looking at personnel costs, which can account for as much as 70 percent of the operating budget, studies have found that sick leave is generally lower in direct-supervision jails, while job satisfaction among officers is higher.

Another striking finding is the agreement by officers and inmates that direct supervision works better than traditional approaches. Most of the officers acknowledged that what was good for the inmates helped them as well, by improving conditions and reducing tension.

This agreement extended to some joint criticism. Both groups complained about the air quality in sealed, environmentally regulated buildings, a complaint we've also heard from workers in modern office buildings. Inmates and officers also complained that confining all activities to the small housing unit was very monotonous, although they admitted that even constant boredom was better than the constant terror pervading many older jails.

Our studies showed that, overall, the direct-supervision approach produced a string of successes in a field better known for its failures. Curiously, despite this success in the federal system, the approach didn't sell well at first among local correctional officials. They weren't convinced it would work in their systems, with their inmates.

Finally, in the late 1970s, officials in Contra Costa County, California, were sufficiently impressed by the tension-free atmosphere they found at the Chicago MCC to use it as a model for their new jail. They included design improvements based, in part, on recommendations we had made in a report on our earlier study of the MCC's, a document Contra Costa later used for staff training. One major change was adding outdoor recreation yards for each living unit to vary the surroundings for the guards and inmates. In most respects,

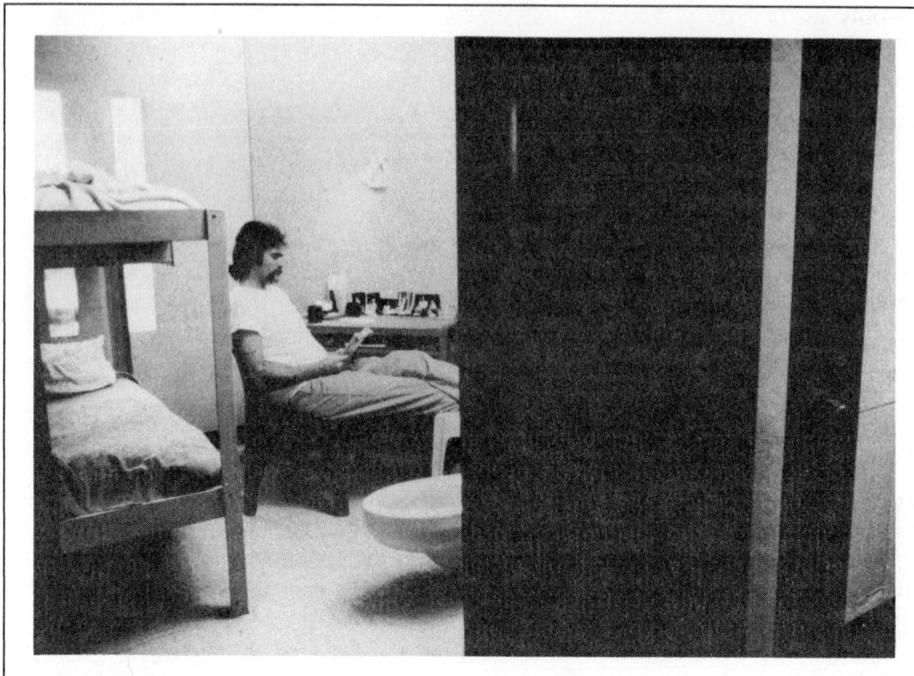

FIGURE 13.16
A Contra Costa Cell. Courtesy *Psychology Today*/photographer Ed Kashi.

however, the design features were the same as in the MCC's. An officer remained inside the living area. Inmates had easy access to television, pay phones and other services in comfortable living areas that provided them with privacy.

In evaluating the Contra Costa jail, we found the same compelling effects seen in the MCC's. Assaults were rare, down 90 percent from the old facility. Homosexual rape had disappeared; vandalism and graffiti were practically nonexistent.

Visiting Contra Costa convinced some correctional officials from around the country that direct supervision really worked. One admitted, "I felt your type of operation was, to say the least, a very liberal approach to incarceration. That was before my tour. It became quite evident that the approach was not necessarily liberal but practical. The lack of tension could be felt . . . Some [of us] thought the prisoners were tranquilized. We soon realized that the prisoners were not drugged, they were simply reacting to the environment."

Officials in many other areas were still not convinced, insisting that the Contra Costa inmates were not as tough as theirs. This argument became harder to support after the transformation at the Tombs in New York City. The new Tombs followed the direct-supervision model, although rather conservatively, as a concession to internal concerns that New York might, indeed, be a tougher case. These concessions included smaller inmate-to-staff ratios (between 22 to 1 and 34 to 1 rather than between 45 to 1 and 65 to 1), eliminating carpeting and using furniture and fixtures of especially durable material to deter vandalism. The exposed officer desks were designed so that they could later be enclosed in glass, if necessary. The partitions have never been used.

In its first two years of operation the Tombs performed better than any other New York City jail. Neither vandalism nor graffiti were found in the living units. (Some visitors only half in jest suggest it may be the only public building in New York without graffiti.) There were no homicides, suicides, sexual assaults or escapes, and only 51 incidents of assault during the first two years—about as many as occur monthly in some other city facilities.

"Violent confrontations were a daily occurrence in the old tombs," says Tom Barry, who as an assistant deputy warden there and the first warden at the new Tombs. "We used to have to fight people to get them on and off the buses." In the new Tombs, inmates rarely make or smuggle in weapons, not because it is hard to do, they told us, but because they don't feel the need for self-protection.

We don't mean to suggest that the Tombs and other direct-supervision jails are problem-free. The worst difficulties, though, are often found in receiving areas, the places most like traditional jails in design and operation. Anxiety levels are at their highest in these areas, where people who hours before were free are now inmates. They stay in hard, bare cells with a dozen or more other inmates, with nothing to do and usually no direct contact with officers. There is also no privacy—toilets are often open stalls in the corner of the cell.

These intake areas have problems with vandalism and graffiti unseen on the living units. Names are etched on walls, stall partitions are broken. Staff and inmates agree these are the most dangerous places in the jail.

The Contra Costa jail has an intake area consistent with the philosophy and design of the rest of the facility. Most inmates wait in an open, carpeted lounge, similar to a doctor's waiting room. Television and magazines are available, and the inmates have access to pay phones, water and toilets. The strategy appears to work. These areas have not suffered the mistreatment dealt out to their counterparts in the Tombs and other jails.

Direct-supervision jails succeed because of a management philosophy that commits the organization to the methods and training needed for direct supervision in such areas as negotiation and communication skills, and a complementary physical design that helps the philosophy function. Barry expressed the point succinctly: "Jail design is to the correctional staff what tools are to the plumber. You can get the job done with out-of-date tools but not as well or as easily."

According to the principles developed by the National Institute of Corrections (NIC) for direct-supervision jails, correctional officers must maintain control of the living areas through personal interaction with the inmates. It is also essential that the system respect the inmates' constitutional rights and assure them of fair and just treatment.

FIGURE 13.17
Mealtime at the new Tombs: no longer feeding time at the zoo. Courtesy *Psychology Today*/ photographer Joe McNally.

FIGURE 13.18
Chess players at the new Tombs. Courtesy *Psychology Today*/photographer Joe McNally.

Our interviews and observations suggest how the philosophy and design work together to mitigate the two biggest jail problems, violence and vandalism. Many people feel that jails are inevitably violent because of the inmates' aggressive nature. What we've learned in direct-supervision jails suggests that "violent personality" is not a sufficient explanation. The physical and social environments are critical in a number of ways.

First, they provide clues to the institution's behavioral norms: what is expected, what will be reinforced and what will be punished. The setting of a traditional jail suggests that animal-like behavior is anticipated. Inmates are placed in hard cages, while the staff maintains a safe distance, separated by steel bars. Direct supervision sends a very different message. The open setting, use of noninstitutional colors and materials, constant presence of an officer in the living area and use of nonsecure furniture and fixtures all suggest that positive behavior is expected. Although no one would mistake it for anything other than a jail, it is a jail with a different set of behavioral norms.

Second, having an officer constantly among the inmates makes for improved safety. Officers can learn of problems in time to head them off before they explode into violence. Their presence also reduces inmates' fear and the macho posturing that often leads to serious fights. Inmates repeatedly told us that they knew "the man" would be there to intervene if they were attacked. In traditional jails, officers often either don't know about an attack or wait until the fight is over to respond.

Third, these facilities typically provide considerably more privacy for inmates than do traditional jails. By being able to go to their own rooms, inmates can cool off rather than have to respond directly to the threatening behavior.

Fourth, the normal look and feel of the surroundings encourage normal use of the facilities. Psychologist Robert Sommer of the University of California, Davis, suggests that institutionally "hard" architecture proclaims its invulnerability to attack and may be viewed as a challenge. Using durable material, the most common response to vandalism, does not really deter it. Destruction of furniture and fittings that might seem impervious to human attack is a common occurrence.

Vandalism is further reduced by giving inmates the ability to move chairs, control TV sets and turn lights on and off—normal adjustments that they are not permitted to make in traditional jails. Much jail vandalism is not so much wanton destruction as it is an accident or an attempt to adjust the environment in the only way possible.

A few design mistakes emphasize this point. In the Chicago MCC, the only living-area lamp that inmates broke regularly was the one without an accessible switch; the lamp's glare made the TV picture hard to see. In the Contra Costa jail, VIP's from around the country slept overnight in the cells before it opened for inmates. The next morning, jail officials found that many of the VIP's had stuffed towels in the vents to keep the draft off their necks, since there were no louver controls. When inmates to the same thing, the maintenance staff usually calls it vandalism.

Making pay telephones, television sets and other resources available in sufficient quantities also lessens violence by reducing competition for them. The Chicago MCC, for example, provided four TV areas for 44 inmates, while there were only two TV areas for 48 inmates in the New York MCC. Conflict over which TV channel to watch was common in New York, rare in Chicago.

The success of direct supervision raises a question: If it has worked so well, why are jails still being built to the old models of operation and design? One reason is size. Administrators of jails with fewer than 50 beds feel that they are too small to afford the staff needed. Another reason is that many decision-makers either don't know about direct supervision or don't know how well it works. Some architectural firms these officials depend upon are equally unknowing or afraid they might lose a contract by suggesting a different approach.

It may also be politically safer to build a traditional jail. Who wants to be accused of coddling criminals, especially if there should later be a killing, riot or escape? This thinking may change as litigation makes jurisdictions financially liable for injuries in unsafe jails.

Some reject direct supervision because they see it as a threat. Its philosophy implies that if a jail doesn't operate well, the responsibility rests with the quality of administration rather than the failings of staff or inmates. Correctional officers are often skeptical at first about direct supervision, especially after years of contract bargaining based on reasonable claims of high job danger. The New York City officers' union, for example, initially opposed direct supervision vigorously; officers at the Tombs now strongly support the concept.

Supporters of direct supervision have no distinctive political leanings. They include old hard-line correctional officers and new criminology Ph.D's, conservatives as well as liberals. Direct supervision is winning favor not simply because it is seen as a way of treating inmates more humanely, although that is critical for some. Supporters see it as a way of making correctional institutions better and safer for the staff as well as inmates.

The hardest and cruelest of jails have not deterred crime, so far as we can tell, any more than public hangings deterred London pickpockets in Charles Dickens's time. However "nice" the direct-supervision jail environment may be, it is still viewed as a jail by the inmates. Loss of freedom is the essential punishment, and there is no evidence anyone finds a jail preferable to being free.

Direct supervision will not directly affect our notoriously high recidivism rates. At the very least, however, it can reduce the harm caused by traditional jails through degradation, terror and assault. At best, it can help provide a setting in which rehabilitative programs have a chance to work.

Aaron Brown of the NIC says that direct supervision "is simply a better way of treating people, and that's who institutions are built for—people, inmates and staff. . . . Correctional institutions can be designed to be people management institutions or hardware institutions." Direct supervision is an attempt at people management.

In our opinion, governments are wasting billions of tax dollars planning and building traditional jails and prisons. We will have to live with these mistakes, which will produce more stressful and dangerous settings for inmates and staff well into the next century, a situation we can't afford economically or socially. As former Chief Justice Warren Burger has said, "To put people behind walls and bars and do little or nothing to change them is to win a battle but lose a war. It is wrong. It is expensive. It is stupid."

DISCUSSION AND REVIEW

1. How did American colonists perceive the function of the jail?
2. What are the three types of jails?
3. What are the three fundamental objectives of jails?
4. What types of custodial problems are typically associated with alcoholics, the mentally ill, drug addicts, and sex offenders?
5. What three types of persons are likely candidates for suicide in jail?
6. What is the purpose of a count?
7. What is one of the best methods for tool control?
8. What is the most basic rule of key control?
9. How are jails affected by community and police policy?
10. What type of coordinating function do jails play in relation to the courts?
11. Why is there considerable support and pressure for jails to get involved in the correctional effort?
12. What type of statistical data was presented in the issue paper that would suggest direct supervision jails are safer than traditional jails?

GLOSSARY

Contraband Anything possessed by an inmate in violation of institutional rules and regulations.

Combination facility A facility that houses pretrial detainees and some convicted persons, usually misdemeanants; the most common type of jail.

Count A method of accounting for all prisoners to be sure that none have escaped; usually conducted on a regular basis.

Cutlery control A system of accounting for all eating utensils in a jail.

Frisks Individual "pat searches" of inmates in which offenders run their hands along the outside of the inmate's clothing to detect concealed contraband.

Hallucinations The hearing, seeing, smelling, or tasting of something that does not really exist.

Key Control A system that assures that no jail officer has keys that would allow inmates to escape if the officer is overpowered.

Mental illness A wide range of complicated emotional disorders that may involve physical, mental, or behavioral disturbances.

Narcotics control A system that involves storing drugs in secure areas not readily accessible to inmates, and keeping an up-to-date record of drug inventory.

Pretrial detention facility A facility used solely to confine persons awaiting trial.

Sentenced facility A facility where convicted persons serve their sentences.

Sex offenders Persons arrested for indecent exposure, window peeping, child molestation, and rape.

Shakedown A thorough search of a jail or any part thereof for contraband.

Special prisoners Jail prisoners that require special care and attention; generally includes alcoholics, diabetics, epileptics, the mentally ill, suicidal persons, drug addicts, and sex offenders.

Tool control A system of accounting for all tools within a jail.

REFERENCES

Advisory Commission on Intergovernmental Relations. *Jails: Intergovernmental Dimension of a Local Problem.* Washington, D.C.: U.S. Government Printing Office, 1983.

Blumer, A. H. *Correctional History and Philosophy.* Washington, D.C.: U.S. Government Printing Office, 1971.

———. *Discipline.* Washington, D.C.: U.S. Government Printing Office, 1971.

———. *Jail Climate.* Washington, D.C.: U.S. Government Printing Office, 1971.

———. *Jail Operations.* Washington, D.C.: U.S. Government Printing Office, 1971.

———. *Special Prisoners.* Washington, D.C.: U.S. Government Printing Office, 1971.

———. *Supervision.* Washington, D.C.: U.S. Government Printing Office, 1971.

Danto, B. "The Suicidal Inmate." *The Police Chief* (August 1971): 64–71.

de Beaumont, G., and de Tocqueville, A. *On the Penitentiary System of the United States and Its Application in France.* Carbondale, Ill.: Southern Illinois University, 1964.

DeWitt, Charles. *New Construction Methods for Correctional Facilities,* Washington, D.C.: U.S. Department of Justice, National Institute of Justice. March 1986.

Fawcett, J., and Marrs, B. "Suicide at the County Jail." In *Jail House Blues* edited by B. L. Danto. Orchard Lake, Mich.: Epic, 1973.

Mattick, H. W., and Aikman, A. "The Cloacal Region of American Corrections." *Annals of the American Academy of Political and Social Science* 381 (1969): 109–18.

Michaels, M. "Why So Many Young People Die in Our Jails." *Parade,* 23 May 1982, pp. 4–7.

Miller, E. E. *Jail Management.* Lexington, Mass.: Lexington, 1978.

National Sheriffs Association. *Jail Administration.* Washington, D.C.: The National Sheriffs Association, 1974.

"1983 Jail Census." *Bureau of Justice Statistics Bulletin* (November 1984): 7.

Pappas, N. ed. *The Jail: Its Operation and Management.* Washington, D.C.: U.S. Bureau of Prisons, 1971.

Territo, L. "Planning and Implementing Change in Jails." In *Jail Management,* edited by C. R. Swanson. Athens, Ga.: Institute of Government, University of Georgia, 1983.

U.S. Department of Justice. *Profile of Jail Inmates.* Washington, D.C.: U.S. Government Printing Office, 1980.

Ward, D. A., and Schoen, K. F. eds. *Confinement in Maximum Custody: New Last-Resort Prisons in the United States & Western Europe.* Lexington, Mass.: Lexington, 1981.

NOTES

1. For a more thorough examination of jail operations and administration, review the following works of Alice H. Blumer: *Correctional History and Philosophy; Jail Operations; Personnel and Fiscal Management; Jail and Community Corrections; Community Relations; Legal Problems;* and *Supervision, Discipline, and Jail Planning.* All of these works were published in Washington, D.C., by the U.S. Bureau of Prisons in 1971.
2. This discussion of demographic data on American jails was obtained and modified with permission from the U.S. Department of Justice, *Profile of Jail Inmates* (Washington, D.C.: U.S. Government Printing Office, 1980).
3. This discussion of jail overcrowding was adapted from Charles B. DeWitt, *New Construction Methods for Correctional Facilities* (Washington, D.C.: U.S. Department of Justice, National Institute of Justice, March 1986).
4. "1983 Jail Census," *Bureau of Justice Statistics Bulletin* (November 1984): 7. Calculations are derived from Table 10. The estimate of 8 percent annual growth is based on the average rate of growth from 1978 to 1983; the 1984 estimate is 241,000 and the 1985 estimate if 260,000. Eight percent growth is approximately 21,000 per year.
5. Ibid. Figure 13.2 and 13.3 are derived from data shown on p. 1, 2, 3 and 7.
6. This discussion of special prisoners and the relationship of the jail to the criminal justice system was obtained and modified from N. Pappas, ed., *The Jail: Its Operation and Management* (Washington, D.C.: U.S. Bureau of Prisons, 1971), p. 9.
7. Much of this discussion on jail security was obtained and modified with permission from E. E. Miller, *Jail Management* (Lexington, Mass.: Lexington, 1978), p. 33.

CHAPTER

14

Correctional Institutions

CHAPTER OUTLINE:

In this chapter, we discuss the development of correctional institutions in the United States, starting with the late 1600s and proceeding through the nineteenth century. This should provide the reader with a historical framework to understand how we got where we are today. We then move into the twentieth century and discuss maximum, medium, and minimum security institutions—even though it is difficult to make clear-cut distinctions. All three classifications may be used (and usually are) in the same institution, and what may be considered maximum security in one state may be considered medium security in another. In general, however, the terms refer to the relative degree of security. We also devote considerable attention to a fourth classification: the maxi-maxi prison designed for the hard-core, violent prisoner. In addition, we discuss a relatively new addition to the corrections scene—the reception and classification center.

Certainly one of the most urgent problems facing the criminal justice system today is our overcrowded prisons. In this chapter, we discuss the three basic approaches to the problem: namely, providing more capacity, diverting convicted people to sentences other than prison, and shortening the time served by those who go to prison. A portion of this chapter is also devoted to a discussion of some of the major features of institutions created for women and youthful offenders (16 to 30 years of age). Lastly, we examine the participation of private industry in prison work programs, the use of private sector alternatives for financing the construction of prison and jail facilities, and the involvement of private organizations in actual facility management and operations.

HISTORICAL PERSPECTIVE

Institutionalization as a primary means of enforcing customs, mores, or laws is a relatively modern practice. In earlier times, restitution, exile, and a variety of corporal and capital punishments—many of them unspeakably barbarous—were used. Confinement was used only for detention (National Advisory Commission on Criminal Justice Standards and Goals 1973).[1]

The North American colonists brought with them the harsh penal codes and practices of their homelands. It was in Pennsylvania, founded by William Penn, that initial attempts were made to find alternatives to the brutality of British penal practice. Penn knew the nature of confinement well, because he had spend six months in Newgate Prison in London for his religious convictions. In the **Great Law of Pennsylvania,** enacted in 1682, Penn made provisions to eliminate to a large extent the **stocks, pillories,** branding irons, and **gallows.** The Great Law directed ". . . that every county within the province of Pennsylvania and territories thereunto belonging shall . . . build or cause to be built in the most convenient place in each respective county a sufficient house for restraint, labor, and punishment of all such persons as shall be thereunto committed by laws." (Dunn and Dunn 1982, pp. 206) In time, Penn's jails, like those in other parts of the New World, became places where the untried, the mentally ill, the promiscuous, debtors, and various petty offenders were confined indiscriminately.

In 1787, when the Constitutional Convention was meeting in Philadelphia (and people were thinking of institutions based on the concept of the dignity of man), the Philadelphia Society for Alleviating the Miseries of Public Prisons was organized. The society believed that the sole purpose of punishment is to prevent crime and that punishment should not destroy the offender. The society, many of whose members were influential citizens, worked hard to create a new penology in Pennsylvania, a penology that largely eliminated capital and corporal punishment as the principal sanctions for major crimes. The penitentiary was invented as a substitute for these punishments.

In the first three decades of the nineteenth century, citizens in New York, Pennsylvania, New Jersey, Massachusetts, and Connecticut were busy planning and building monumental penitentiaries. These were not cheap installations built from the crumbs of the public treasury. In fact, the Eastern State Penitentiary in Philadelphia was the most expensive public building constructed in the New World up to that time (see Figure 14.1). States were proud of these physical plants. Moreover, they saw in them an almost utopian ideal. They were to become stabilizers of society, laboratories committed to the improvement of all humanity (Rothman 1971).

At the time these new penitentiaries were planned and constructed, practitioners and theorists believed that criminal behavior was primarily caused by three factors. The first factor was environment. Report after report pointed out the harmful effects of family, home, and other aspects of environment on the offender's behavior. The second factor was the offender's lack of aptitude and work skills, a problem that led to indolence and a life of crime. The third factor was seen as the felon's ignorance of right and wrong because of a lack of knowledge of the Scriptures.

The social planners of the first quarter of the nineteenth century designed prisons and programs to create an experience for the offender in which (1) there would be no injurious influences, (2) the offender would learn the value of labor and work skills, and (3) the offender would have the opportunity to learn about the Scriptures and the principles of right and wrong. Various states pursued these goals in one of two ways. The **Pennsylvania system** was based on solitary confinement, accompanied by bench labor within the offender's cell. The offender was denied all contact with the outside world except through religious tracts and visits from specially selected, exemplary citizens. The prison was painstakingly designed to make this kind of solitary experience

FIGURE 14.1
Eastern State Penitentiary, Philadelphia, Pennsylvania. Wide World Photos.

possible. The walls between cells were thick, and the cells themselves were large, each equipped with plumbing and running water. Each cell contained a work bench and tools and a small, walled area for solitary exercise. The institution was designed magnificently to eliminate external influences and to provide work and the opportunity for penitence, introspection, and religious learning (Barnes 1972).

New York's **Auburn system** pursued the same goals by a different method. As in the Pennsylvania system, offenders were isolated from the outside world and were permitted virtually no external contact. However, convicts were confined to their small cells only on the Sabbath and during nonworking hours. During working hours, inmates labored in factorylike shops. The "contaminating effect" of the congregate work situation was eliminated by a rule of silence: inmates were not allowed to communicate in any way with one another or the jailers.

The relative merits of these two systems were debated vigorously for half a century. The Auburn system ultimately prevailed in the United States, because it was less expensive and because it lent itself more easily to the production methods of the industrial revolution. But both systems were disappointments almost from the beginning. The solitude of the Pennsylvania system sometimes drove inmates to insanity. And the rule of silence in the Auburn system became increasingly unenforceable, despite regular use of the lash and a variety of other harsh and brutal punishments.

As instruments of reform, prisons were an early failure. But they did have notable advantages. They rendered obsolete a myriad of inhumane punishments, and their ability to separate and hold offenders gave the public a sense of security. Imprisonment was also thought to deter people from crime. But imprisonment had disadvantages, too. For one thing, many prison "graduates" came back. The prison experience often further reduced the offender's capacity to live successfully in freedom. Nevertheless, prisons have persisted, partly because our nation could neither turn back to the barbarism of an earlier time nor find a satisfactory alternative. For nearly two centuries, American penologists have sought a way out of this dilemma.

FIGURE 14.2
Auburn (New York) State Prison cells: 1928, *left,* and today. Courtesy Robert J. Henderson, Superintendent, Auburn State Prison.

MAXIMUM SECURITY PRISONS

For the first century after penitentiaries were invented, most prisons built were in the category of **maximum security prisons**—facilities characterized by high perimeters and internal security and operating procedures that curtailed movement and maximized control. The early zealots who dreamed of institutions that would not only reform the offender but would also cleanse society itself were replaced by a disillusioned and pragmatic leadership that saw confinement as a valid end in itself. Moreover, the new felons were seen as outsiders—Irish, Germans, Italians, and blacks; they did not talk or act like "Americans." The prison became a dumping ground where foreigners and blacks who could not adjust could be held outside the mainstream of society. The new prisons, built in the most remote areas of the country, became asylums—not only for the hardened criminal but also for the inept and unskilled "un-American." Although the rhetoric of reformation persisted, the be-all and end-all of the prison was detention.

From 1830 to 1900, most prisons built in the United States reflected the ultimate goal of security. Their principal features were high walls, rigid internal security, cagelike cells, sweat shops, a bare minimum of recreation, and little else. Prisoners were kept in, the public was kept out; and that was all that was expected or attempted. Many of these prisons were constructed well and lasted long, and they form the backbone of our present-day correctional system.

It is nearly impossible to describe the "typical" maximum security prison. The largest such prison confines more than four thousand inmates; another holds less than sixty. Some contain massive, undifferentiated cell blocks, each housing as many as five hundred prisoners. Others are built in small modules that house less than sixteen inmates each. The industries in some prisons are archaic sweat shops; in others, they are large, modern factories. Many facilities have no space inside for recreation and only a minimum of such space outside; others have superlative gymnasiums, recreation yards, and auditoriums. Some are dark, dingy, and depressing dungeons; others are windowed and sunny. An early warning system in one prison consists of cowbells strung along chicken wire atop a masonry wall, yet other facilities have closed-circuit television and electronic sensors to monitor corridors and fences.

Maximum security institutions are geared to the fullest possible supervision, control, and surveillance of inmates. The architecture of such institutions and the work and recreational programs they provide are largely dictated by security considerations. Buildings and policies restrict the inmates' movements and minimize their control over the environment. The prisons are usually surrounded by masonry wall or a double fence with manned towers. Inside, prisoners live in windowless cells, not rooms. Doors that might afford privacy are replaced by grilles of tool-resistant steel. Toilets are unscreened, and showers are supervised. And control is not limited to structural considerations. All activity—including dining—is weighed in terms of its relationship to custody. Prisoners often sit on fixed, backless stools and eat without forks and knives at tables devoid of condiments. In spite of such control, however, contraband and weapons still find their way into many American prisons.

MAXI-MAXI PRISONS

At present, there are few facilities to house hard-core, violent, and incorrigible prisoners—the group responsible for instigating most of the disruption and damage that occurs in correctional institutions. But there is growing public support for building new facilities of this kind, because the facilities are viewed as investments in community protection. Correctional administrators see such facilities—called **maxi-maxi prisons**—as a solution to the problem of troublesome prisoners in regular maximum security institutions.

To prevent security breaches by intrusions from outside, special devices are built to prevent physical contact with visitors. Relatives often communicate with inmates by telephone and see them through double layers of glass. Contact is allowed only under a guard's watchful eye. And body searches usually precede and follow all visits. Internal movement is limited by bars and grilles that define precisely where inmates may go. Areas of inmate concentration or possible illegal activity are monitored by correctional officers with closed-circuit television. Blind spots—areas that cannot be supervised—are avoided in the building design.

Population

The maxi-maxi prison houses the most dangerous offenders. An individual is usually considered dangerous because of the nature of the offense for which he or she was convicted. Thus, "dangerous" likely refers to persons who have perpetrated violent crimes against the person (such as homicide, forcible rape, robbery, or aggravated assault). It may also refer to individuals involved in persistent property offenses such as residential burglary, racketeering, or the sale of hard drugs. In the

FIGURE 14.3
Weapons confiscated from inmates in an Indiana prison over a period of several months. Courtesy David Agresti, Department of Criminal Justice, University of South Florida, Tampa, Florida.

former case, the heinous nature of the offense may be the deciding factor in making the appraisal of dangerousness; in the latter case, the deciding factor may be the extent of the offender's past criminal activity. The judgment of dangerousness is invoked to support the decision to confine an offender for the purpose of preventing further crimes (that is, to justify incapacitation).

Institutional Models

The structural and procedural controls used at Alcatraz (San Francisco, California), and Marion (Illinois) Federal Correctional Center, the Minnesota Correctional Facility at Oak Park Heights, and the federal correctional facility at Butner, North Carolina, are typical of controls used at maxi-maxi prisons throughout the country. These four facilities are described in the following paragraphs.

ALCATRAZ For thirty years, Alcatraz served as a last resort in the federal prison system. The purpose of the facility—which was closed in 1963—was to punish and incapacitate violent and persistent offenders. In addition to notorious criminals, Alcatraz housed inmates who were management problems at other institutions (i.e., those who were involved in escapes, riots, protests, work stoppages, assaults on staff, and strong-arm gangs). Ward and Schmidt (1981) note that a transfer to Alcatraz was often seen as an honor: in the view of some inmates, Alcatraz housed "the elite" of the system; to be sent there, you had to be among the "baddest." (This attitude suggests that the threat of transfer to a last-resort prison might actually be an *incentive* for further misconduct.)

Security at Alcatraz was multifaceted. Alcatraz is an island in the middle of San Francisco Bay, waters that are swept by treacherous, icy currents and are often enveloped in fog. The island itself was controlled by a system of gun towers connected by overhead walks, and inside security was provided by gun galleries at each end of the cell block (Bates 1936). Despite this rather formidable security system, a major preoccupation of inmates on the "rock" was escape, perhaps because of the long sentences the vast majority had to serve. Only 8 out of the 1,500 inmates who served time on Alcatraz actually succeeded in getting off the island, however; and only three of these inmates were not recaptured. (The story of these three men was portrayed in the Clint Eastwood film *Escape from Alcatraz*.)

In line with the custodial philosophy, the limited programs available at Alcatraz reflected the institution's emphasis on discipline and punishment. Inmates could participate in the work program, but the program was not mandatory. Inmates could stay in their cells all day.

FIGURE 14.4
Maxi-maxi prison: Alcatraz Federal Penitentiary, San Francisco, California. Courtesy Federal Bureau of Prisons.

Communication with the outside world was limited, and inmates were not allowed access to the press, newspapers, and telephones. Not until the 1950s were inmates allowed to have radios. Visits with wives or blood relatives were allowed once a month for one hour, with inmates and visitors separated by bulletproof glass and conversing over guard-monitored telephones. There were no treatment programs or educational and vocational training programs.

Despite the restrictive and punitive atmosphere, however, inmates at Alcatraz generally settled down rather than lashing out at their environment. This response was probably due to several factors, including the constraints of the institutional regimen and the recognition by inmates that Alcatraz was the end of the line (Ward and Schoen 1981). In other words, inmates knew that because they would be in Alcatraz for a long time, acting up would only be to their detriment. They also knew that rule infractions at Alcatraz would be written up and punished. And by the time offenders reached Alcatraz, many had calmed down simply because they had grown older and recognized the futility of troublesome behavior.

Ward and Schmidt (1981) provide some interesting insights into the positive effects of a structured, secure, and predictable prison environment. Alcatraz inmates who were transferred to Atlanta, Georgia, when the institution closed in 1963 regarded Atlanta as a very dangerous environment "full of violence and unpredictable people" (Ward and Schmidt 1981, p. 67). To insulate themselves from such dangers, former Alcatraz inmates organized their lives to avoid as much contact as possible with other inmates. These former Alcatraz inmates felt that Atlanta would be a better place if it was managed more like Alcatraz; at least in a controlled environment, the inmates did not have to worry about living through the day.

MARION (ILLINOIS) FEDERAL CORRECTIONAL CENTER Another model of a super-secure or maxi-maxi prison is the federal prison at Marion, Illinois. The facility was constructed in 1963.

FIGURE 14.5
Exercise yard at Alcatraz. Courtesy Federal Bureau of Prisons.

U.S. Prison not a 'Scout Camp'

By Sharon Cohen of *The Associated Press*

MARION, Ill.—A Two-lane blacktop curves through woods and waters, through a remote refuge for deer, ducks and quail. At the end of the road, a gray concrete fortress looms.

This is the U.S. Penitentiary at Marion, Ill., home to some of America's most dangerous criminals. The squat prison is surrounded by eight bulletproof guard towers and a pair of 14-foot-high fences topped with curling razor wire.

Nowhere in America is there a tougher federal prison. Nowhere is there a place where so many have so little freedom, a prison with such a brutal image it chills even hardened convicts.

Marion "houses the most vicious, unmanageable and manipulative inmates in our penal system today and perhaps in the history of the penal system in the United States," U.S. Magistrate Kenneth Meyers wrote in a 1985 ruling.

Alcatraz, once had such a reputation. Now it's Marion. It gets the inmates who have been in trouble in other prisons. This is the last stop.

For 3½ years, Marion inmates have been locked in their cells up to 23 hours a day. For almost as long, a legal fight has been waged to lift this lockdown that Marion calls its "high-security operation."

The battle enters the 7th Circuit Court of Appeals this week, when lawyers for the inmates challenge a lower court's ruling that prison conditions pass constitutional muster.

At Marion, most inmates live more than 22 hours a day in cells that pace off at 8-foot-4-inches by 6-foot-8-inches. They don't get out to work or to eat. Meals are delivered through a slot and are eaten while sitting on the floor or on beds; there are no chairs or tables.

FIGURE 14.6
U.S. Penitentiary at Marion, Illinois (the New Alcatraz). Wide World Photos.

Most inmates wear handcuffs when they leave their units. Some also wear leg shackles and a black box on their handcuffs to prevent them from picking the lock. Even inmates examined by a doctor or dentist are handcuffed.

This is the only federal prison in America without family contact visits. When relatives arrive, touching is forbidden and glass separates them from the inmates. They talk on telephones.

Marion even has a courtroom, to avoid moving inmates to legal proceedings.

"With such a limited amount of movement . . . and ways for guys to improve themselves . . . the whole place is almost like a hole," said Charles Perry, a bank robber.

The lockdown was ordered after a bloody week in October 1983 in which two guards and an inmate were killed in separate incidents. One guard was stabbed 40 times. But Marion rocked with violence before that.

From February 1980 to June 1983, eight inmates were killed by other prisoners, and there were 14 attempted escapes, 10 group disturbances and 82 serious assaults on inmates or staff, one report said.

In a 1986 sampling of 288 prisoners, Marion found 46.9 percent had histories of escape or attempted escape and almost 40 percent attempted or committed murder while incarcerated.

But the wisdom of Marion's hard-line attitude has stirred debate among penologists, psychologists and others in the outside world.

Critics say it is dangerous.

"If we treat them like animals and call them animals and all they do is sit there and build up hostility and anxieties, what's going to happen when they get out?" asked Michael Mahoney, director of the John Howard Association, a prison watchdog group. "I think they're going to be a walking time bomb."

The National Prison Project of the American Civil Liberties Union also has been critical of Marion.

But prison officials argue this is the only way to keep peace.

"We don't have a better answer right now," said Warden Gary Henman. "I think the model of Marion right now is working. Right or wrong, it's working."

Henman said violence had declined at Marion, with three inmates killed by other prisoners and no escape attempts since the lockdown. He asserted, too, that concentrating the worst inmates here made other federal prisons safer.

Researchers have studied Marion repeatedly. In 1984, two experts working for a congressional committee recommended dispersing the nation's toughest inmates among maximum-security units that would have to be built in prisons around the country and installing a mental-health unit at Marion. Inmates now in need of psychiatric care are commonly sent to other prisons.

A current study seeks to determine the mental effects of the confinement, using inmates at the Leavenworth, Kan., penitentiary as a control group. According to Henman, the study was finding Marion inmates slightly more depressed and anxious than those at Leavenworth, and he said he was not troubled by that.

"We don't want them to be happy here," he said. "This is not a Boy Scout camp. . . We want them to get off their duffs and work themselves out."

Other experts quoted in court records have said that feelings of despair, desperation, anger and frustration are widespread at Marion.

Marion's attention now centers on a class-action suit filed on behalf of inmates, challenging the high security and alleging brutality in the early weeks of the lockdown.

About 50 inmates testified in 1985 hearings they were victims or witnesses of beatings or abuse—some said they were pummeled with riot batons, knocked unconscious or stomped by guards.

But Meyers, the federal magistrate who presided over the hearings, said he saw "no credible evidence to support a pattern and practice of prison abuse."

U.S. District Judge James Foreman accepted Meyers' recommendations in February and ruled prison conditions did not constitute cruel and unusual punishment.

An attorney for the inmates, Nancy Horgan, disagrees.

"What Marion is about is total control—physical and psychological," she said. "It's punishment for the sake of punishment. It tends to make prisoners crazy, violent or depressed. We say no one—even if they are the worst prisoners in the world—should be treated like this. It's dangerous."

Henman, warden since June, conceded that conditions were restrictive, but added, "It's very unfair to project Marion as being no-care, inhumane, hurting inmates . . . We don't make it any more uncomfortable than we have to."

Marion was built in 1963 on the edge of the Crab Orchard National Wildlife Refuge in southern Illinois, 43,000 acres filled with white-tailed deer, Canadian geese and oak, hickory and cedar trees.

That same year, Alcatraz, the fabled fortress in San Francisco Bay, closed. It wasn't until 1979, however, after the Bureau of Prisons created a new classification system, that Marion became its first and only prison at Level 6—most secure.

Marion has been called the new Alcatraz. There are similarities.

The Alcatraz roster of infamous inmates included Al Capone, George "Machine Gun" Kelly, and murderer Robert Stoud, the so-called "Birdman of Alcatraz." Marion houses Christopher Boyce, convicted of selling government secrets to the Soviet Union as the "Falcon" in

"The Falcon and the Snowman," and Edwin Wilson, an ex-CIA agent who shipped explosives to Libya.

Jack Henry Abbott, whose prison letters to writer Norman Maller became the critically acclaimed book "In the Belly of the Beast," did time here.

Escape attempts from Alcatraz became the stuff of Hollywood scripts, but Marion's record could rival them.

In 1978, a woman hijacked a helicopter and tried to free an inmate. The pilot shot and killed her in a gun battle 2,000 feet in the sky, blades whirring.

Months later, her daughter hijacked a plane in a unsuccessful effort to free the same man, Garrett Brock Trapnell.

Three years before that, five inmates fled after building an electronic device that operated like a wireless garage door opener.

Marion now holds about 350 inmates, only 0.8 percent of all 42,000 federal prisoners. The average sentence of a Marion inmate is 43 years, but the average length of stay, usually preceded by time served elsewhere, is 27.2 months.

Horgan contends Marion is the "ultimate warehouse."

Henman said it is "a new beginning. . . Marion is not a dead end."

Henman said of 373 inmates at Marion in October 1983, only 83 remain. Of those who left, 14 returned to Marion.

"Our graduation success is fantastic," Henman said.

Visitors to Marion notice immediately how clean it is—its floors gleam with wax—and how calm. Indeed, it is eerily quiet.

The only sounds on the way to the cell houses are the metallic clanging of blue painted grilles when they shut and the humming motors when they open.

Hallways are empty. So is the chapel, gym and outdoor recreation field.

The two-tiered cell houses, with flesh-colored paint flaking on the bars, look like endless rows of animal cages. Each dimly lit cell has a toilet, small mirror, sink, bed, cabinet and black-and-white TV. Many inmates pass the time watching soap operas.

Marion is divided into nine living units, each designated by a letter of the alphabet. The K unit houses Boyce and six other infamous inmates put there for protection from other prisoners.

The elite unit, B, a pre-transfer area, holds about 50 inmates. Unlike other prisoners, they eat in a dining room and can walk in the unit hallway by day. They also work in Marion's

FIGURE 14.7
U.S. Penitentiary at Marion, Illinois. Inmates are housed in two-tiered cellblocks. Wide World Photos.

only industry, making electrical cables for the military.

The most physically dangerous live in H unit. When they leave their cells, their hands and legs are shackled and they have three guards, two of whom wield 2½-foot batons. They are in their cells 23 hours a day.

Prisoners move to less restrictive units by exhibiting good behavior. But attorneys contend such things as having an extra pair of socks can earn an "incident report" and delay progress.

"They nitpick you to death," said Lawrence Daniel Caldwell, convicted of armed robbery, who said he received reports for having felt-tip pens and a 5-inch ruler.

"It reinforces the attitude (that) if you have the power, absolute power corrupts and it really doesn't matter as long as you don't get caught," added Caldwell, a B-unit inmate who has made three escape attempts.

Marion officials say they use common sense when disciplining inmates, although they conceded having pens can be an infraction.

Prisoners say Marion goes beyond that.

"They don't want anybody that doesn't conform, that doesn't buckle under," said Ronnie Bruscino, a counterfeiter also convicted of conspiring to murder and aiding and abetting a murder in an Indiana prison.

"By the time you get out," he said, "they want you to stand at a green light and look for a guard to say, 'Is it all right to cross now?' They don't like you to have a mind of your own."

From *The Tampa Tribune-Times*, Sunday, April 19, 1987.

MINNESOTA CORRECTIONAL FACILITY AT OAK PARK HEIGHTS The new maxi-maxi prison at Oak Park Heights, Minnesota, is perhaps the most up-to-date, state-of-the-art installation built to date. This all-male facility was developed on the premise that the quality of the prison environment is determined by management, available resources, and the physical facility, rather than by the nature of the offenses committed by its population (Ward and Schmidt 1981).

Designed and conceived specifically to stabilize the inmate population at other Minnesota facilities, the Oak Park Heights facility houses inmates who are chronic management problems, extremely predatory, or high risks for escape. Despite this highly volatile population, the objective is still to create as normal an environment as possible, keeping in mind the need for maximum security. Security is designed to protect the public from these offenders and to provide a safe environment for both staff and inmates.

Community protection is accomplished by a combination of external and internal security measures; but unlike other high security facilities, the institution does not have a system of external towers or an expensive electronic system. Instead, security is based on a system of two fences with coils or razor wire between them and a pit to serve as a vehicle trap. Further, there is an alarm device atop one of the fences to serve as a first warning. However, it is doubtful that an inmate would ever reach the fence. To climb the double fences, an escapee would first have to get out of his room or living area and onto the institution's common green, scale one of the walls of the three-story buildings surrounding the green, and cross an open area of approximately 100 yards. It is estimated that it would take an inmate fifty seconds longer to get out of this institution than to get through the federal government's tightest security system.

The institution's four hundred plus inmates are housed in eight separate units of fifty-two inmates each. This division of the population into relatively small, manageable, and compatible groups improves security, safety, and control, and provides a better climate for communication and interaction between staff and residents. Moreover, because each housing has its own work program and outdoor recreational facilities, the units can be operated separately—although it is not planned that they will be. The housing units themselves are broken down into smaller units of six or seven rooms, each with its own activity area. This provides a defensible space, where staff and inmates can feel a sense of security and control.

A common green large enough for a football field and several baseball fields is located in a central area accessible to all housing units. This area also contains a town center that serves as congregation area for leisure-time activities and provides access to the visiting area. Because of the central location of the green, the staff can allow residents from all or some of the housing units to move freely from one unit to another.

The facility has one special unit designed to handle the most severe disciplinary cases. Following the model of older maximum security facilities, this unit is under

FIGURE 14.8
Minnesota Correctional Facility, Oak Park Heights, Minnesota. Courtesy Frank W. Wood, Warden, Minnesota Correctional Facility at Oak Park Heights.

the supervision of staff specially trained to manage difficult inmates. Unit inmates are allowed to leave their rooms only on a controlled basis. In general, however, the management of inmates in the Oak Park Heights facility does not depend upon segregation and sophisticated electronic devices; rather, it is based on programming.

The institution operates a full day program (sixteen hours) that encompasses both leisure time and working hours and furnishes a full range of program options for inmates. This programming includes industrial work, education, group therapy, and chemical dependency counseling. Although it is not a major focus of the institution, education is available to inmates through both traditional and computer-based approaches.

A major concern of the facility is to enable the offender to earn a legitimate living and to develop a realistic view of the world of "paid work." Inmates experience real work situations such as getting a job, earning wages, and assuming responsibility for on-the-job conduct. They are exposed to hiring and firing, productivity standards, job variety, job progression, and discipline in the work place (Ward and Schoen 1981). Industries include microfilming, commercial sewing, production of office and educational supplies (folders, notebooks, etc.), bookbinding, and general shop. Evening activities include sex offender groups, education, chemical dependency groups, recreation, religion, and organized leisure.

This full-participation program is designed to prepare the inmate for a transfer to one of Minnesota's other adult facilities and to improve his ability to succeed upon returning to the community. It is recognized that some inmates will not participate in any of the programs available. For such inmates, the facility provides the needed supervision and control to ensure that they do not interfere with or obstruct other inmates who want to take advantage of program options.

The construction cost of the Oak Park Heights facility was $32 million, and the annual operating budget is estimated at $12 million. These costs may seem high, but the alternative may be even more costly. Without new prisons, the only option we have is to continue to place violent and unmanageable offenders in archaic, warehouse-type facilities that are already overcrowded. (In some facilities, inmates are confined two or three to a cell, or in tents and trailers.) The result of such a policy is, as Wood suggests, "widespread institutional disturbances, surpassing those of the late 60s and early 70s."[2] Recall the brutality and damage of the riots at the New Mexico State Penitentiary on February 2–3, 1980: thirty-three inmates were killed (see Table 14.1), and the cost of repairing the damage and settling claims from the riot

TABLE 14.1
Inmates Killed in the February 1980 Riots at the New Mexico State Penitentiary

NAME	AGE	ETHNICITY	HOMETOWN	CRIME/ SENTENCE	HOUSING UNIT	WHERE FOUND/CONDITION
Briones, Michael	22	Hispanic	Albuquerque, N. Mex.	Criminal Sexual Penetration, 10–50 yrs.	CB4	Basement, CB4; foreign object through head.
Cardon, Lawrence C.	24	Hispanic	Las Cruces, N. Mex.	Car Theft, 1–5; Failure to Appear, 1–5 yrs.	CB3	CB3, cell 32; multiple stab wounds, neck and chest.
Coca, Nick	30	Hispanic	Taos, N. Mex.	Burglary, 2–10; Kidnapping, life; Criminal Sexual Penetration, 10–50; Aggravated Battery, 10–50 yrs.	CB3	Officer mess hall; carbon monoxide poisoning.
Fierro, Richard J.	26	Hispanic	Carlsbad, N. Mex.	Forgery, 1–5; Possession and Sale of Narcotics, 1–5; Escape, 1–5 yrs.	F1	Carried to Tower 1; stab wounds.
Foley, James C.	19	White	Albuquerque, N. Mex.	Armed Robbery, 15–55; Car Theft, 1–5; Murder (1st) life.	A1	Carried to Tower 1; cranocerebral injuries.
Gossens, Donald J.	23	White	Farmington, N. Mex.	Possession and Sale of Narcotics, 2–10 yrs.	CB4	CB4 basement, cell 35; cranocerebral injuries.
Hernandez, Phillip C.	30	Hispanic	Clovis, N. Mex.	Breaking and Entering, 1–5 yrs.	CB4	CB4 basement; blunt trauma to head, stab wounds.
Jaramillo, Valentino E.	35	Hispanic	Albuquerque, N. Mex.	Possession and Sale of Narcotics, 1–5, 2–10 yrs.	CB4	CB4, mid-tier, cell 23; hanged.
Johnson, Kelly E.	26	White	Albuquerque, N. Mex.	Forgery, 2–10 yrs. 6 mo.	CB3	Gymnasium; burned.
Lucero, Steven	25	Hispanic	Farmington, N. Mex.	Aggravated Battery, 5 yrs.	AD	School corridor; blunt trauma to head, stab wounds.
Madrid, Joe A.	38	Hispanic	Albuquerque, N. Mex.	Possession and Sale of Narcotics, 1–5 yrs.	B1	Near control center; blunt trauma to head, incision in neck.
Madrid, Ramon	40	Hispanic	Las Cruces, N. Mex.	Possession of Burglary Tools, 1–5; Possession and Sale of Narcotics, 1–5; Burglary, 1–5 yrs.	CB4	CB4, cell 25; burned.
Martinez, Archie M.	25	Hispanic	Chimayo, N. Mex.	Escape, 10–50; Violation of Suspended Sentence, 1–5; Escape, 2–10 yrs.	CB3	Carried to Tower 1; trauma to the head
Mirabal, Joseph A.	24	Hispanic	Alamogordo, N. Mex.	Assault and battery on a Peace Officer, 1–5; Receiving Stolen Property, 1–5 yrs.	A2	CB4 basement; blunt trauma to the head.
Moreno, Ben G.	20	Hispanic	Carlsbad, N. Mex.	First-degree Murder, life.	F1	Carried to Tower 1; blunt trauma to head.
Moreno, Gilbert O.	25	Hispanic	Carlsbad, N. Mex.	Robbery, 2–10; Armed Robbery, 50–150; Escape, 10–50 yrs.	F1	Near control center; stab wound in chest, trauma to head.

TABLE 14.1
Inmates Killed in the February 1980 Riots at the New Mexico State Penitentiary—(*continued*)

NAME	AGE	ETHNICITY	HOMETOWN	CRIME/ SENTENCE	HOUSING/ UNIT	WHERE FOUND/CONDITION
O'Meara, Thomas	25	White	Albuquerque, N. Mex.	Armed Robbery, 10–50; Assault and Battery on a Peace Officer, 1–5; Escape, 1–5 yrs; Contempt of Court, 6 mos.	CH2	Gymnasium; burned.
Ortega, Filiberto M.	25	Hispanic	Las Vegas, N. Mex.	Burglary, 2–10 yrs.	B1	Gymnasium; burned.
Ortega, Frank J.	20	Hispanic	Las Vegas, N. Mex.	Second-degree Murder, 10–50; Burglary, 1–5 yrs.	B1	Carried to Tower 1; incised wound to head and neck.
Paul, Paulina	36	Black	Alamogordo, N. Mex.	Armed Robbery, 2–10; Aggravated Battery, 10–50 yrs.	CB4	Brought to front gate; multiple stab wounds; decapitated.
Perrin, James	34	White	Chapparal, N. Mex.	First-degree Murder, life.	CB4	CB4 basement at entry; trauma, burned, stabbed.
Quintela, Robert F.	29	Hispanic	Carlsbad, N. Mex.	Burglary, 2–10; Escape 2–10 yrs.	F1	Near control center; blunt trauma to head, stab wounds.
Rivera, Robert L.	28	Hispanic	Albuquerque, N. Mex.	Burglary, 1–5; Escape, 2–10, 1–5; Theft, 1–5 yrs.	F1	Corridor dorms A–F; stabbed in the heart.
Romero, Vincent E.	34	Hispanic	Albuquerque, N. Mex.	Armed Robbery, 10–50 yrs.	CB4	CB4 basement, cell 41; cranocerebral injuries, wounds in the neck.
Russell, Herman D.	26	Indian	Waterflow, N. Mex.	Rape, 5–10 yrs.	CH6	Dorm A1, bottom floor; burned, carbon monoxide poisoning.
Sanchez, Juan M.	22	Hispanic	Brownsville, Tex.	Aggravated Battery, 2–10 yrs.	CB3	CB3, lower tier, cell 12; shot by tear gas gun, head trauma.
Sedillo, Frankie J.	31	Hispanic	Santa Fe, N. Mex.	Burglary, 1–5 yrs.	CH6	Carried to Tower 1; carbon monoxide poisoning.
Smith, Larry W.	31	White	Kirtland, N. Mex.	Armed Robbery, life.	CB4	CB4, front entry; cranocerebral injuries.
Tenorio, Leo J.	25	Hispanic	Albuquerque, N. Mex.	Contributing to the Delinquency of a Minor, 1–5; Escape, 1–5 yrs.	CB4	CB4, front of cell 76, basement level; stab wound to heart.
Tenorio, Thomas C.	28	Hispanic	Albuquerque, N. Mex.	Robbery, 2–10 yrs.	CB4	CB4, basement, cell 41; stab wounds, neck and chest.
Urioste, Mario	28	Hispanic	Santa Fe, N. Mex.	Receiving Stolen Property, 1–5; Shoplifting, 2 yrs.	CB4	CB4, main entry; blunt trauma to head, rope around neck.
Waller, Danny D.	26	White	Lubbock, Tex.	Credit Card Fraud, 1–5 yrs.	A1	Tower 1; multiple stab wounds, cranocerebral injuries.
Werner, Russell M.	22	Hispanic	Albuquerque, N. Mex.	Armed Robbery, 15–55, 1–5 yrs.	F1	Catholic chapel; carbon monoxide poisoning, burned, blunt trauma to head.

Data are from *Report of the Attorney General on the February 2–3, 1980 riot at the Penitentiary of New Mexico* (Santa Fe, New Mexico: Office of the Attorney General of the State of New Mexico, June 5, 1980), pp. J-1 through J-4.

FIGURE 14.9
The 1980 riot at New Mexico State Penitentiary began on the morning of February 2, when inmates overpowered four officers during a routine inspection of a crowded dormitory floor similar to this one, shown as it appeared after the riot. Courtesy Dennis Dahl.

was $82 million (Bingham 1980). With this in mind, the Minnesota Correctional Facility probably represents a major cost savings.

BUTNER: A NEW FACILITY FOR VIOLENT OFFENDERS The federal correctional facility at Butner, North Carolina, represents much of the new thinking about how facilities for violent offenders should be designed and operated. Butner has a population of four hundred males who are typically multiple offenders with a record of at least one violent offense. The inmates are divided into three groups according to the institution's three major functions: research (150); mental health (100); general population (150).

FIGURE 14.10
This double-sliding security grille, which separates the south wing from the administrative area of the penitentiary, was left open during the morning watch, contrary to prison policy. The open grille allowed inmates to reach the Control Center and take over the entire building. Courtesy Attorney General collection, New Mexico State Record Center and Archives.

FIGURE 14.11
Panels of two-way bullet-resistant glass in the New Mexico Penitentiary Control Center were smashed in minutes by inmates wielding pipes and canister fire extinguishers. The glass had been installed three weeks before, replacing steel grilles and small panes of glass. Courtesy Attorney General collection, New Mexico State Record Center and Archives.

Security at Butner is external. The forty-two-acre site is surrounded by two twelve-foot-high fences with seven rolls of concertina wire between them and barbed wire on top. Mobile patrols of armed correctional officers are present at all times. On the inside, the institution is an open facility that emphasizes a relaxed atmosphere. During the day and early evening, inmates move unrestricted throughout the facility. Inmates are also permitted to wear civilian clothing.

Ingram (1978) reports that most inmates at Butner feel safe and comfortable and want to stay. Thefts are almost nonexistent, and inmates report that they are free of the pressures of homosexuality. Moreover, the buildings are arranged to give the appearance of a small town or a college campus, rather than a prison. The feeling of normality is further enhanced by making inmates responsible for getting to work and school on

FIGURE 14.12
One room of the main penitentiary building destroyed by rioting inmates. Courtesy Attorney General collection, New Mexico State Record Center and Archives.

time. And when not involved in programs, inmates are free to mingle on the common greens between buildings.

Inmates are housed in seven one-story buildings with sun roofs that provide ample light. Each housing unit has several wings that contain either single rooms or cubicles. (Although not as good as private rooms, the cubicles do provide more privacy than dormitories.) Within policy and fire safety limitations, inmates are allowed to decorate their own rooms. However, overcrowding has forced Butner to use double-bunking in many of its housing areas.

As in many other federal institutions, each housing unit at Butner is supervised by a unit team. A team consists of a unit manager, a case manager, a psychologist, a counselor, an educational representative, and several inmates (Lansing, Bogan, and Karacki 1977). Ingram (1981) considers the inmates to be the most important part of the team. This approach to inmate management is designed to provide better control and to improve relationships by dividing large prison populations into smaller, more manageable groups.

Twenty-three percent of the staff, including 15 percent of the correctional supervisors, and two of the lieutenants at Butner are female. Women officers have the same duties as male officers. Only a few inmates object to taking orders from women officers. (One inmate commented, "I have been away from a woman for forty years; I don't want anything to do with women" [Ingram

FIGURE 14.13
Butner Federal Correctional Facility, Butner, North Carolina. Courtesy Federal Bureau of Prisons.

1981, p. 104].) Ingram feels that women officers can maintain the necessary control over male inmates and that they provide a steadying influence in the institution.

The research project at Butner is modeled after the ideas of Norval Morris, as outlined in *The Future of Imprisonment* (1975). Morris contends that forced rehabilitation is unworkable and that inmates should instead be provided with opportunities and resources for *voluntary* self-improvement. To test Morris's approach, all inmates in Butner's research population are told upon admission when they are going to be released. A contract worked out with each inmate includes a graduated release plan that specifies such things as when the inmate will be permitted to go into the community, when he will receive his first furlough, and when he will be released to a halfway house. Participation in self-improvement programs does not affect an inmate's release or his privileges; the latter are influenced only by the inmate's compliance with regulations, his behavior on mandatory work assignments, and his seniority (Ingram 1978). Although inmates in the research experiment do not have any choice as to whether they are sent to Butner, they do have an option to transfer to another institution at the end of their first ninety days. This assures that inmates in the Butner program are there because they want to be. The success of the program is being evaluated by comparing project inmates with a similar group of inmates housed in traditional institutions.

The only difference between inmates in the Butner research project and those in Butner's general population is that the latter cannot transfer to another institution after ninety days. For both populations, participation in self-improvement programs is voluntary, but there are constraints on what inmates have to do. First, all inmates must work for at least half a day, obey institutional regulations, and either participate in available programs or work for an additional four hours; thus, they cannot choose idleness. Ingram (1981) notes that it would be interesting to experiment with a complete voluntary institution in which inmates could choose idleness, work, or program participation.

Inmates in the mental health group at Butner are suicidal or psychotic inmates who are referred from other institutions or who come directly from the courts. An attempt is made to screen out offenders who only *appear* to be disturbed—perhaps because they do not abide by institutional rules and regulations. The primary goal of

FIGURE 14.14
Inmate room at Butner Federal Correctional Facility. Courtesy Federal Bureau of Prisons.

the program is to provide inmates with the treatment they require within the context of a normal routine. This goal is based on the premise that if inmates are *expected* to act normally, they will try to meet this standard. Thus, inmates in the program are all expected to hold regular jobs and to participate in educational and other activities in the company of other inmates. When an inmate can no longer handle a normal routine, he can be placed in a seclusion room—a kind of "time-out" environment for those experiencing difficulties. The mental health program at Butner is intended only as a short-term intervention program; its objective is to return inmates to their regular institutions as soon as possible. And although most inmates do not want to leave the program, Ingram (1981) reports that there have been few repeat referrals.

Butner offers several vocational programs and a range of academic programs for all inmates. Because the institution operates on an optional programming model, a program is only offered if there is sufficient inmate interest to justify it. And like other institutions, Butner has traditional recreational programs, arts and crafts, and facilities for basketball, outdoor track, softball, and miniature golf. Butner has a limited industry program, including a part-time textile products industry that employs 55 men and a glove factory that employs 125. The top wage for inmates in these industries is about $120 a month.

MEDIUM SECURITY CORRECTIONAL CENTERS

Since the early twentieth century, developments in the behavioral sciences, the increasing emphasis on education, the dominance of the work ethic, and changes in technology have led to modified treatment methods in corrections. Parole and probation have increased, and institutions have been set up to handle special inmate populations. Pretrial holding centers, or jails, are now separate from facilities receiving convicted felons, and different levels of security have been developed: maximum, maxi-maxi, medium, and minimum. Most of the correctional construction in the last fifty years has been medium security. In fact, 51 of the existing 110 **medium security correctional centers** were built after 1950.

Today, medium security institutions embody most of the ideals and characteristics of early attempts to reform

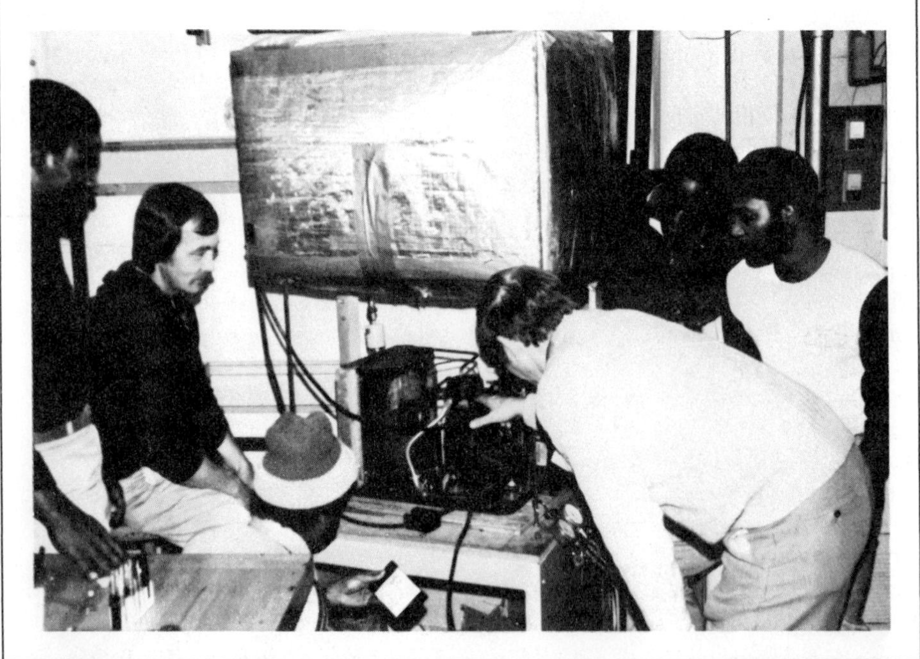

FIGURE 14.15
Vocational training in heating and air conditioning at Butner Federal Correctional Facility. Courtesy Margaret C. Hambrick, Warden, Butner Federal Correctional Facility.

offenders. It is in these facilities that the most intensive correctional and rehabilitative efforts are conducted. Inmates are exposed to a variety of programs intended to help them become useful members of society. The predominant consideration is still security, however, and inmates are confined where they can be observed and controlled. All facilities have perimeter security, either in the form of masonry walls or double cyclone fences. Electronic sensors may also be used. Perimeter towers are staffed by armed guards and equipped with spotlights.

Internal security is usually maintained by locks, bars, and concrete walls; clear separation of activities; defined movement both indoors and outdoors; tight scheduling; head counts; visual observation; and electronic monitoring. Housing areas, rooms for medical and dental treatment, schoolrooms, recreation and entertainment facilities, counseling offices, vocational training and industrial shops, administrative offices, and maintenance facilities are usually clearly separated. Some activities are located in individual compounds complete with their own fences and sally ports. Barred gates and guard posts control the flow of traffic between areas. Central control stations track movement at all times. Circulation is restricted to certain corridors or outdoor walks, with certain areas designated out of bounds. Closed-circuit television and alarm networks are used extensively. Doors are made of steel (and kept locked), and all external windows, and some internal ones, are barred. Bars or concrete walls line all corridors and surround control points.

Housing units in medium security institutions vary from crowded dormitories to private rooms with furniture. Dormitories may house as many as eighty persons or as few as sixteen. Some individual cells have grilled fronts and doors. Variations among medium security institutions are not as extreme as those among maximum security facilities, perhaps because the former developed in a shorter period of time.

In recent years, campus-type medium security facilities have been designed to eliminate the cramped, oppressive atmosphere found in most prisons. Buildings are separated by meandering pathways and modulated ground surfaces to break the monotony. Attractive residences house small groups of inmates in single rooms. The schools, vocational education buildings, gymnasiums, and athletic fields at these facilities compare favorably with the best community colleges. Nevertheless, adequate external and internal security are provided to protect the public.

MINIMUM SECURITY CORRECTIONAL CENTERS

Minimum security correctional centers range from large drug rehabilitation centers to small farm, road, and forestry camps in rural America. The facilities are diverse, but they generally have this in common: they are relatively open, and they house inmates who are considered to be nonviolent and low risk for escape.

Most, but not all, minimum security facilities serve the economic needs of society and institution. Cotton is picked, lumber is cut, livestock is raised, roads are built, forest fires are fought, and parks and public buildings are maintained. Remote facilities have major deficiencies, however. They seldom provide education or services (other than work), and the predominantly rural labor bears no relationship to work skills needed for urban life. The prisoners are separated from their real world almost as much as if they were in a penitentiary.

One unusual minimum security correctional center—a branch of the Illinois State Penitentiary—was opened in 1972 at Vienna, Illinois. Although large, the facility approaches the environment of a nonpenal institution. Buildings resemble garden apartments built around a "town square" complete with churches, schools, shops, and a library. Paths lead to "neighborhoods" where "homes" provide private rooms in small clusters. Extensive indoor and outdoor recreation is provided, and the academic, commercial, and vocational education facilities equal or surpass those of many technical high schools.

RECEPTION AND CLASSIFICATION CENTERS

Reception and classification centers—facilities that examine new inmates and assign them to appropriate institutions—are recent additions to the correctional scene. In earlier times, there were no state correctional systems, no central departments of corrections. Each prison was a separate entity, usually managed by a board that reported directly to the governor of a state. If a state had more than one institution, either geography or a judge determined where an offender would go. As the number and variety of institutions increased, however, classification systems and agencies for central control evolved. Eventually, the need for reception and classification centers seemed apparent.

Not all of these centers operate as distinct and separate facilities, however. In most states, the reception and classification function is performed in an existing institution—usually a maximum security facility. Thus, most new prisoners start their correctional experience in the most confining, most severe, and most depressing part of the system. After a period of observation, testing, and interviewing, an assignment is made that supposedly reflects the best marriage between the inmate's needs and the system's resources.

Security in reception and classification centers is based on the premise that "a new fish is an unknown fish." Nowhere on the current correctional scene are there more bars, more barbed wire, more electronic surveillance devices, more clanging iron doors, and less activity and personal space. All of this is justified on the grounds that the nature of the residents is unknown and that their stays will be short.

A notable exception to this type of security exists at the Reception and Medical Center at Lake Butler, Florida (opened in 1967). This campus-style facility has several widely separated buildings on a fifty-two-acre site enclosed in a double cyclone fence with towers. Inmates circulate freely between the classification building, gymnasium, dining room, clinic, canteen, craft shops, visiting area, and dormitories. Three quarters of the inmates are assigned to medium security units scattered around campus. One quarter are housed in a maximum security building.

FIGURE 14.16
Inmates in corridors at the Lake Butner Reception and Medical Center, Lake Butler, Florida. Courtesy Florida Department of Corrections.

Inmates not specifically occupied by the demands of the classification process at Lake Butler are encouraged to take part in recreational and self-improvement activities. Visits are allowed in an open-air patio and an indoor visiting facility (ordinarily used only in inclement weather). The relationships among staff and inmates are casual, and movement is not regimented. Morale is high, and escapes are rare. However, overcrowding has become a problem in recent years.

Diagnostic processes in reception centers range from a medical examination and a single inmate-caseworker interview (without privacy) to a full battery of tests, interviews, and psychiatric and medical examinations (supplemented by an orientation program). The process can take from three to six weeks.

PRISON OVERCROWDING

Overcrowded prisons may be the most urgent problem facing the criminal justice system today. The number of prisoners in the United States has increased continuously since the early 1970s, and the rate of incarceration (the number of prisoners per capita) has doubled since 1970. By 1984, there were more than 463,000 people in state or federal prisons, which is about 20 percent more than they were designed to accommodate. This represents one prisoner for every 500 persons in the United States. Another 220,000 people were in local jails. Most of these were being held awaiting trial; another large group were serving short sentences, generally under one year, for less serious crimes (Jacobs 1987).[3]

The current situation of prison crowding in the United States stems from the steady growth in prison populations that began in the early 1970s. Until that time, there was a broad consensus that the primary purpose of imprisonment was "correction," that is, rehabilitation of the offender. Evaluations of a wide variety of techniques presumed to be rehabilitative failed to show that any were particularly effective. These results shattered the old consensus and led to a new consensus that changing behavior was extremely difficult. There was no agreement, however, on what to do next.

During the rehabilitation era, parole authorities were empowered to decide when a particular prisoner was "rehabilitated" and ready for release. This role was also well suited for accommodating increases in the inflow of prisoners. Any release of prisoner involves some degree of risk, and so marginal shifts in that risk are barely perceptible—especially in view of the considerable difficulty of estimating future criminality. Thus, when prisons became too crowded, the parole board could become somewhat more liberal in deciding whether an inmate was a good candidate for release. In this way, parole provided an important "safety valve" for adjusting prison populations to their available capacity.

The mid-1970s saw a major reaction to this "indeterminate" sentencing system. Since rehabilitation services were not shown to be effective, it was argued that judgments about a prisoner's state of rehabilitation should no longer influence the length of time served. There came a general shift toward more "determinate" sentences, established by the judge at the time of sentencing, but often within the guidelines established by a legislature or a sentencing commission. The true sentence, as reflected in the time actually served, became more explicit and more public, and pressure grew to increase sentences in response to the public's concern over rising crime rates in the 1970s.

The changing age composition of the U.S. population has exacerbated the crowding problem. The number of people in their mid-twenties, the ages at which people are most likely to be sent to prison, has grown steadily over the last twenty years. That increase reflects the population growth associated with the postwar baby boom, which started in 1947 and peaked in 1961. Thus, even if there had been no change in the fraction of each age group represented in prison, the larger numbers of people in the most prison-prone ages would still have crowded the prisons. This situation, together with the increasing severity of sentences, created the current dramatic increase in prison population.

Alternate Approaches to Relieving Prison Crowding

There are basically three approaches one might use for dealing with overcrowding: providing more capacity, diverting convicted people to sentences other than prison (the "front-door" approach), or shortening the time served in prison by those who do go there (the "back-door" approach).

Additional prison capacity would permit the same number of prisoners (or more) to be kept, but under more acceptable conditions. Providing the additional capacity costs money, however. Construction costs typically range between $50,000 and $75,000 per bed. Additional money is needed each year—about $10,000 to $15,000 per prisoner—to maintain, guard, and manage prisoners. These high costs were undoubtedly influential in the rejection several years ago by New York State voters of a bond issue to provide additional prison space.

Moreover, additional capacity does not become available instantly. Many bureaucratic processes are involved in the construction of any new facility by a state government: deciding to provide the additional capacity, agreeing upon a site (especially gaining acceptance by neighboring residents), authorization and appropriation of funds by the legislature, architectural design, and finally construction. All these processes can take four to seven years or more. Thus, a commitment to provide additional capacity to solve today's crowding problem will not provide the capacity until several years into the future, when the crowding problem may have diminished. By 1990, for example, the earliest date by which new prisons might become available, the number of people in the prison-prone ages will have decreased significantly, and so at least the demographic factor in the overcrowding problem will have begun to diminish.

Many who argue against providing additional capacity are concerned that the imprisoned population will simply expand to fill the available capacity—a variant of "Parkinson's law." One study seemed to show by statistical evidence that this would happen; further studies, however, pointed out errors in those initial studies. It is still possible, of course, that there could be such an effect (even though the initial study failed to demonstrate it). Indeed, some judges are known to inhibit their sentencing when they know prisons are filled. However, during the 1960s, when prison populations were well below the available capacity, there was no pressure on judges to send more people to prison in order to fill that available capacity. Thus, the issue is far from simple.

The "front-door" approach involves finding alternatives to prison for those whom a judge might want to sent there. "Front-door" solutions are not intended for the most serious offenders, for those who commit heinous crimes, or for those who represent a serious continuing risk to the community. They are, however, possibilities for "marginal" offenders who might otherwise be candidates for probation had they not already had one or more prior sentences to probation; these offenders warrant something more severe than probation. The problem is to develop an array of alternatives so that the judge, the victim, and the community can be satisfied that the level of punishment is appropriate and that the alternative might be more successful in reforming the offender. The alternatives most often considered are some combination of intensive probation, restitution, community work, or residence in a group home under tight surveillance but with the right to go to work during the day.

The "back-door" approach involves shortening the time served by imprisoned offenders. Indeed, this is the form traditionally used by parole boards to regulate prison populations. Parole boards hold the key to the "back door" by their authority to release prisoners who have served an appropriate minimum sentence but less than their maximum term. Some states have adopted "emergency release" laws under which some prisoners' eligibility for release is advanced, and some prisoners are released, once the prison population reaches a designated level.

The problem of prison crowding is one of the most vexing dilemmas facing the criminal justice system today. There is widespread agreement that people who commit serious crimes must receive punishment and that people who do so as recidivists must be punished more severely. There is also agreement that the objectives of prison for punishment and crime control (through general deterrence, rehabilitation, and incapacitation) are appropriate, but there is some disagreement as to how effectively they are achieved. There may also be general agreement in ranking convicted offenders in terms of those most and least deserving of prison. There is still significant division, however, over how deeply into that list imprisonment ought to be applied, and for how long. As a richer array of intermediate sanctions is developed to fill the gap between the slap-on-the-wrist referral to an overworked probation officer, at the low end, and a sentence to a state prison, at the high end, and as the cost of imprisonment becomes an important part of the choice, there may emerge greater agreement on how deeply and how broadly the imprisonment sanction should be applied.

INSTITUTIONS FOR WOMEN

The changing role of women may profoundly influence the future of corrections. Women have always been treated differently than men by the criminal justice system, but this now appears to be changing.

Correctional institutions for women are a microcosm of the American penal system. In one state, some women offenders are thought to be so dangerous that they are confined in a separate wing of the men's penitentiary.

Officials Note Steady Growth of Women's Prison Population

By Peter Applebome *New York Times*

HOUSTON—As a criminal court judge well known here for stiff sentences and tough views on law and order, Ted Poe is a keen observer of crime and punishment. Lately, he has been noticing something.

"I think there is a philosophical code of the West that our prisons were built for scoundrels, for outlaws, but not for our women," Poe said the other day. "That code is being changed. Now people are saying there are a lot of Ma Barkers out there."

While women are more likely to be involved in drug offenses, bogus check-writing or domestic violence than armed robbery, increasing attention is being paid to a steady growth in the number of women in the nation's prisons. Every year since 1981 the prison population of women has grown at a faster rate than that of men. In 1986, the rate of increase for women was 15.1 percent, compared to a growth of 8.3 percent for men.

The 26,610 women in the nation's prisons now account for 4.9 percent of the prison population, up from 4.2 percent in 1981 when they totaled 11,212.

"It's only been in the last two or three years that people have begun to talk about it," said Jennie Lancaster, superintendent of the North Carolina Correctional Center For Women in Raleigh. "I've been trying to say the female prison population is growing and they're getting longer sentences for years, but until there were statistically valid figures no one wanted to hear about it."

"It's kind of like out of sight, out of mind," she continued. "And the attitude of the general public has been that if you're a woman and you're in prison, you're just a 25-cent w— anyway and that's far from true."

It is not clear how much of the increase reflects an increase in crime and how much reflects a trend toward more arrests and tougher sentencing of women. Experts say that increasing economic pressures, particularly on the poor, and the spread of drugs through the population are also playing major parts in the increase.

There does not appear to be a major shift toward more violent criminal behavior among women. But experts say that the changing role of women in society is having a noticeable impact on the number of women coming through the justice system and the way they are treated by the courts.

"There is more parity in the criminal justice system today," said Charlotte Nesbitt, co-author of a 1985 American Corrections Association study on women in prison. "Fourteen years ago a woman who was picked up was likely to be dealt with more informally. She was taken home and not arrested. Now the criminal justice system is dealing more strictly with female offenders."

There have been few nationwide studies analyzing the incarceration figures. But experts say the increase reflects two somewhat contradictory social changes in women's lives.

The first is the changing social role of women. Many experts say that as women become more a part of the nation's economy, with jobs, economic pressures and social behaviors more like men, their criminal behavior rises according.

Theresa Johnston, who has twice been convicted of armed robbery and is awaiting trial in Houston on the same charge, said she became involved with drugs in the late 1970s when she worked for a union in New Orleans in which drug use and drug trafficking were widespread. She said she believed economic hard times and drug use were primarily responsible for the rising population of women.

"With the way the economy is, people are just scuffling for a buck," she said. "And when you get a drug habit, it's a bad issue. You can get to the point you don't even care about your children. This is reality, and I see more of it all the time."

In 1978 there were 117 drug offenders in Texas prisons who were women, or 18 percent of the women who were incarcerated. In 1986, there were 535 drug offenders, or 24 percent of the population. But prison officials say those figures understate the role of drugs in crimes by women.

"A lot more of them come in with drug histories than for drug crimes," said Susan Cranford, who is warden of the Texas Department of Corrections women's prison at Gatesville. "A lot of them are in for larceny or shoplifting or hot-check writing, but the real problem is drugs."

A study of women in New York's prison population found that 44 percent had drug or alcohol problems.

But other experts say the increase has as much to do with increased economic and social pressures of women at home. Lancaster, the North Carolina warden said that there had been a dramatic increase in the number of women convicted of child abuse and other kinds of domestic violence in her state. She said that reflected both an increasing tendency of society to intervene in such cases and growing economic and social pressures on women at home.

"We've seen a dramatic increase in domestic violence, particularly crimes involving children," she said. "Domestic violence is a problem that's been with us for a long time, but it's been exacerbated by unemployment, chemical dependence and other problems. Women primarily commit crimes as an emotional response to their environment, and as those pressures grow, women are responding.

"About five or six years ago we began to see a trend toward longer sentences, which means there is less turnover than there used to be," Lancaster said. "A life sentence for a woman used to be unusual. It is not unusual anymore. The courts are going to a more punitive approach and harsher sentences whether you're a man or a woman."

Prison officials agree that women who are prisoners tend to be primarily young, poor and members of minority groups. Most are first-time convicts, because recidivism is much lower among women than men, the officials say. It is estimated that 75 percent are mothers.

Some officials such as Lancaster say that improved education and social-service programs in areas such as child abuse could lead to a slowing of the increased crime among women. But, whether the increase relative to men continues, few officials expect any major changes in the prison trends involving women.

"Chivalry is dead," said Maj. R. L. Greenwood at the Texas Department of Corrections' women's prison at Mountain View. "It's equal rights, dog eat dog, no woman at home with an apron on anymore."

St. Petersburg Times, Sunday, June 21, 1987.

There they are shut up in cells and cell corridors without recreation, services, or meaningful activity. In other states, new (but separate) facilities for women have been built based on the philosophy, operational methods, hardware, and tight security of the state penitentiary. Such facilities are surrounded by concertina fences, and movement is monitored by closed-circuit television. Inmates spend much of their time playing cards or sewing. The contrasts among women's institutions demonstrate our confusion about what criminals are like and what correctional responses are appropriate: in six states, all female offenders are housed in maximum security prisons; at least fifteen other states house them exclusively in "open" institutions.

YOUTH CORRECTIONS CENTERS

With the advent of the penitentiary in the early nineteenth century, corporal punishment for the youthful offender (aged sixteen to thirty) was replaced with the reformatory concept of incarceration with rehabilitation. The keystone of this reform movement was education and vocational training to enable the offender to make a living in the outside world. The concepts of parole and indeterminate sentences were introduced, and inmates who progressed satisfactorily could reduce the length of their sentences.

The physical plant in the early reformatory era was highly secure—perhaps because the first such facility (located in Elmira, New York) was actually a converted maximum security prison. Huge masonry walls, multitiered cell blocks, "big house" mess halls, and dimly lit shops were all part of the model. Several of these early reformatories are still in use. Then, in the 1920s, youth institutions adopted the telephone-pole design developed for adult institutions: in this design, housing and service units pass through an elongated inner corridor. More recently, campus-type plants—some of which resemble new colleges—have been constructed. Most new reformatories, now called **youth correction centers** or youth training centers, provide only medium or minimum security. They emphasize academic and vocational education and recreation, supplemented with counseling and therapy (including operant conditioning and behavior modification).

In terms of physical environment, security, education, and recreation, most youth centers are similar to adult centers of comparable custody classification. The only major difference is that some youth institutions have more space to accommodate more programs. Some youth centers have highly screened populations and only one goal—to increase educational levels and vocational skills. The effectiveness of such centers is highly dependent on inmate selection and classification. Facilities and programs available in youth corrections centers vary widely. Some centers provide many positive programs; others emphasize the mere holding of the inmate, offering few rehabilitative efforts, sparse facilities, inadequate recreational space, and a generally repressive atmosphere.

Youth institutions include at least two types of minimum security facilities—work camps and training centers. Outdoor labor in work camps is useful for burning up youthful energies, but these camps are severely limited in their capacity to meet other important needs of the youthful offender. Moreover, they are usually located in rural America, which is predominantly white; many youthful offenders belong to minority groups. The second type of youth center has complete training facilities, fine buildings, attractive surroundings, and extensive programs; but these, too, are often remote from population centers. And because many states are finding it difficult to choose youthful inmates who are stable enough to handle minimum security facilities, many such centers are operating far below capacity. Because walkaways are a serious problem, some centers have been forced to develop internal controls in addition to visible external controls (such as wire fences).

CORRECTIONS AND THE PRIVATE SECTOR

#12

In an effort to reduce costs and improve services, some states have started contracting with the private sector to administer some of their correctional facilities.

Public service managers face the dilemma of dwindling resources and little public tolerance for cutbacks in services. In their search for solutions, many public managers have looked to the private sector to resolve the dilemma. The corrections field is no exception. Laboring under the burden of outmoded facilities, declining resources, increasing executive and judicial demands for improved services, and public calls for more prisons at half the price, corrections authorities are particularly receptive to an alternative that may offer more responsive, efficient facility construction and management practices. In turn, the private sector has hoped to find new opportunities to apply the concepts and profit motivation of business practice to a field of public service that has all the outward appearances of an industry with significant growth potential as well as social value (Mullen 1985).[4]

To date, the private sector's involvement in facilities for mainstream populations has been relatively modest. The rewards for either the private or the public sector are largely uncertain as yet, and both sides are proceeding with guarded optimism.

The anticipated benefits of many privatization ventures typically include both reduced costs and improved services. Yet, as many observers have suggested, a free lunch may be asking too much. The greatest promise of the private sector may simply lie in its capacity to bring to corrections the vitality and flexibility of a successful business enterprise—to introduce public sector managers to the principles of competitive business; to mobilize facilities and manpower to meet immediate needs; to adapt services rapidly to changing market circumstances; to experiment with new practices; or to satisfy special needs with an economy of scale not possible in a single public sector jurisdiction. From this perspective, the task is not to replace public corrections functions with their private equivalents, but to develop a system that uses both sectors to their best advantage.

"Factories with Fences"

The most logical place to find private sector involvement is in prison industry and work programs. A captive work force, free use of space and utilities, and the opportunity to address a major social problem seem designed to satisfy both the entrepreneurial and public interests of the private sector.

In many states, however, legal restrictions (founded on union opposition and adverse public reactions) continue to act as a barrier to greater private sector participation. In the prison environment, private enterprise must also contend with the costs of transporting materials to and from isolated areas, possible difficulties recruiting skilled supervisors willing to work with prison inmates, and training and scheduling problems imposed by the inherent instability of the prison workforce (whose terms of confinement average about two years, and whose daily routines involve frequent interruption). Population pressures often impose additional constraints, since prison administrators may be unable to welcome new industries if all available space must be converted to living quarters.

Although the private sector initiatives identified in early 1984 were fairly modest in scale, involving selected institutions in only nine states, the movement was clearly gaining momentum. At least seven additional states were exploring private sector projects, and a number of existing efforts had soundly established the feasibility of private involvement. From Arizona, where computer terminals installed by Best Western in a women's facility are used by inmates to make reservations for the hotel chain, to Minnesota, where inmates manufacture disk drives for Control Data Corporation, at least nineteen businesses serve as the owner-operator, key investor, or central purchaser for one or more prison-based industries (Sexton, Farrow, and Auerbach 1984).

All of these efforts assume that prison industries can provide more productive "real world" opportunities and are more likely to function as economically viable enterprises if they are affiliated with the private sector. Reduced idleness, better training and preparation for employment for inmates once they are released, and opportunities to repay victims and generate revenue for the state are the anticipated benefits.

New Financing Alternatives

The second type of privatization effort is no more or less than a straightforward opportunity for the private sector to "sell" construction money, allowing a government to move more certainly or rapidly than it might by following traditional public sector financing routes.

Reported plans to spend $5 billion over the next decade to construct new state prison space, coupled with serious constraints on the use of public funding mechanisms (insufficient cash reserves, limitations on capacity to assume additional public debt, and the refusal of voters to authorize bonds for prison construction) have created a demand for private financing alternatives that are not subject to debt ceilings and referenda requirements. The most widely discussed arrangements are contracts in the form of lease/purchase agreements, which are used to purchase a facility over time, as in an installment sale.

Promoted by investment bankers and brokerage houses, lease/purchase arrangements were being seriously considered in a number of states, and some of the major sponsors (Merrill Lynch, E. F. Hutton, and Shearson Lehman) reported significant activity at the local level. Although some growth in this market seemed virtually assured, no longer term directions could be discerned. The use of lease/purchase financing to avoid the debt ceilings and referenda requirements of general obligation bonds has been challenged by many observers as fiscally imprudent and politically evasive. These challenges could give rise to new regulatory constraints that might dilute the attraction of private financing for state and local governments. At the same time, a viable market for private financing relies largely on the ability of investors to earn tax-exempt income. Any federal legislative action to diminish the tax advantages of financing public projects would also reduce the appeal of this market to the private investor.

Facility Management Contracting

Confinement service or facility management contracts are another way of expanding corrections capacity without imposing any burden for facility construction on the government. Much as if they were running a full-service hotel, private vendors either supply the space or take over an existing public building; room rates are established based on capital investments, operating costs, and expected occupancy; and the government is generally charged by the day for each detainee. Table 14.2 highlights some major developments in this area.

By early 1984, there was an active and somewhat specialized federal market for facility management contracting and a developing market at the local level—both focusing on the provision of fairly straightforward detention services for populations with relatively short terms of confinement (illegal aliens and county prisoners). At the level of state adult corrections, where terms are longer, security requirements are more stringent, and service needs are more elaborate, interest was far more restrained; contracting was generally reserved for secondary placement facilities that closely resembled the halfway house or prerelease model that has been a standard feature of state corrections for many years.

In late 1984, however, the Kentucky Corrections Cabinet announced its intention to contract for minimum security housing for two hundred sentenced felons—a private facility venture that may represent one of the first to deal with a mainstream population of state adult offenders. In early 1985, a number of participants in the National Institute of Justice conference on privatization voiced interest in primary facility management contracts, particularly for offenders with special needs.

Whether these developments will lead to contracts for the management of more secure adult facilities remains unclear. Few proposals in the field of corrections have stimulated such sharply divided opinions as the prospect

FIGURE 14.17
Detention facility in Bay County (Panama City) Florida, administered by Corrections Corporation of America. Courtesy Corrections Corporation of America.

TABLE 14.2
Facility Management Contracting Activity in early 1984[a]

FEDERAL CONTRACTS	STATE CORRECTIONS CONTRACTS	LOCAL JAIL CONTRACTS
Immigration and Naturalization Service • Four facility contracts for aliens awaiting deportation were operating in San Diego, Los Angeles, Houston, and Denver. Capacity: 625 beds. • Three facility contracts were nearing award in Las Vegas, Phoenix, and San Francisco. Capacity: 225 beds. • Two facility contracts were planned in the near term in Laredo and El Paso, Texas. Capacity: 270 beds. U.S. Marshals Service • Two small facilities were operating under contract in California. Capacity: 30 beds. • One contracted facility for alien material witnesses was planned in Los Angeles. Capacity: 100–150 beds. Federal Bureau of Prisons • One contracted facility for sentenced aliens was planned in the Southwest region. (Project delayed due to siting difficulties.) Capacity: 400–600 beds. • One contracted facility for offenders under the Federal Youth Corrections Act was operating in La Honda, California. Capacity: 60 beds.	Secondary adult facilities • A total of 28 States reported use of privately operated prerelease, work-release, or halfway house facilities. Largest private facility networks found in California, Massachusetts, Michigan, New York, Ohio, Texas, and Washington. Primary adult facilities • Kentucky Corrections Cabinet issued an RFP in late 1984 to contract for minimum security housing for 200 sentenced felons. However, no contracts for the confinement of mainstream adult populations were reported in operation. • Two interstate facilities for protective custody prisoners were planned by private contractor. Juvenile facilities • A 1982–83 survey of private juvenile facilities found 1,877 privately operated residential programs holding a total of 31,390 juveniles, of whom 10,712 were held for delinquency. Only 47 institutions were classified as strict security and 426 as medium security. The rest were primarily small, less secure facilities.[b] • An exception was Florida's Okeechobee Training School for 400 to 500 serious juvenile offenders, operated by a private contractor.	• Legislation enabling private jail operations was pending in Colorado and had passed in New Mexico and Texas. • Corporate providers reported significant interest, and there were a number of pending proposals for jail operations in the South and West, in spite of the formal opposition of the National Sheriffs' Association. • In Hamilton County, Tennessee, a private contractor took over operation of a local workhouse for 300 men and women awaiting trial or serving sentences of up to 6 years. Shared facilities • One private organization in Texas was planning to construct and operate a facility to serve both local detention needs and the needs of Federal agencies responsible for confining illegal aliens. • Other proposals called for the development of regional jail facilities to serve multicounty detention needs.

[a]Reported in telephone contacts made in January and February 1984, with additional followup at later points in 1984.

[b]Unpublished tables from *Children in Custody: Advance Report on the 1982–83 Census of Private Facilities,* U.S. Department of Justice, Office of Juvenile Justice and Delinquency Prevention, Washington, D.C.

Source: *Corrections and The Private Sector,* U.S. Dept. of Justice National Institute of Justice May 1985, p. 4.

of enlarging the role of the private sector in corrections management.

SUMMARY

The North American colonists brought with them the harsh penal codes of their homelands. Not until the late 1600s did William Penn take the initial steps that would eventually lead to more humane penal practices and eliminate capital and corporal punishment as sanctions for major crimes.

The monumental penitentiaries still common today in the United States got their start in the first three decades of the nineteenth century. The social planners who designed these prisons had three goals in mind: to remove bad influences; to teach the offender the value of labor and work skills; and to teach the offender about the

Scriptures and the principles of right and wrong. The two systems which emerged for meeting these goals were the Pennsylvania system and New York's Auburn system. The Pennsylvania system was based on solitary confinement with bench labor within the offender's cell. The Auburn system housed inmates in small cells but confined them only during nonworking hours and on the Sabbath. During working hours, inmates labored in factorylike shops. The Auburn system ultimately prevailed in the United States.

The major classifications of correctional institutions are maximum security, maxi-maxi security, medium security, and minimum security. Maximum security institutions employ full supervision, control, and surveillance of inmates. Security is the highest priority, as reflected by the architectural design and the types of work and vocational programs available. Maxi-maxi institutions house the hard-core, violent, and incorrigible prisoners. Most have high perimeter security, high internal security, and operating regulations that curtail movement and maximize control.

Medium security institutions, on the other hand, embody most of the ideals and characteristics of early attempts to reform offenders. Although the top priority in such facilities is still security, intensive rehabilitative efforts are made. Minimum security facilities, although quite diversive in purpose and location, have one common feature: they are relatively open and they house inmates who are considered nonviolent in their actions and low risk for escape.

Reception and classification centers are relatively recent additions to the correctional scene. Some are part of larger facilities, and some are completely separate. Most are maximum security facilities, because the propensity of new inmates for escape or violence is generally unknown. The diagnostic processes in reception centers include medical examinations, psychological testing, and interviews by caseworkers.

Overcrowded prisons may be one of the most urgent problems facing the criminal justice system today. There are basically three approaches that might be used for dealing with overcrowding; namely, providing more capacity, diverting convicted people to sentences other than prison, or shortening the time served by those who go there.

Women's prisons are as diverse in their physical security and philosophy as men's prisons. Yet many have the trappings of maximum security facilities, even though women are generally not considered high risks for escape. In addition, women are less frequently involved in the violent acts characteristic of men's prisons. Thus, the need to house women in maximum security facilities has been questioned.

Youth corrections centers house offenders between the ages of sixteen and thirty. Most such facilities provide medium or maximum security. Some emphasize academic and vocational education and recreation; others emphasize the mere holding of inmates. One of the difficulties some states face with this type of institution is in identifying those youths who are stable enough to handle open facilities: walk-aways are not at all uncommon.

Public service managers face the dilemma of dwindling resources and little public tolerance for cutbacks in services. In their search for solutions, many public managers have looked to the private sector to resolve the dilemma. The corrections field is no exception. Laboring under the burden of outmoded facilities, declining resources, increasing executive and judicial demands for improved services, and public calls for more prisons at half the price, corrections authorities are particularly receptive to an alternative that may offer more responsive, efficient facility construction and management practices. In turn, the private sector has hoped to find new opportunities to apply the concepts and profit motivation of business practice to a field of public service that has all the outward appearances of an industry with significant growth potential as well as social value.

To date, the private sector's involvement in facilities for mainstream populations has been relatively modest. The rewards for either the private or the public sector are largely uncertain as yet, and both sides are proceeding with guarded optimism. The anticipated benefits of many privatization ventures typically include both reduced costs and improved service.

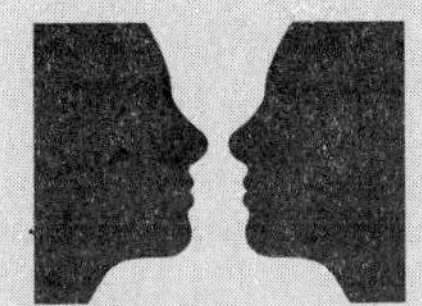

ISSUE PAPER
HOMOSEXUAL RAPE IN CORRECTIONAL INSTITUTIONS

William Laite, a businessman and former Georgia legislator, was convicted in Texas of perjury in connection with a contract he negotiated with the Federal Administration Housing Authority. Laite was sentenced to a term in the Tarrant County Jail in Fort Worth, Texas. The minute he entered the "tank," or dayroom, of the jail, he was approached by five men. Said one of them: "I wonder if he has any guts. We'll find out tonight, won't we? Reckon what her name is; she looks ready for about six or eight inches. You figure she will make us fight for it, or is she going to give it to us nice and sweet like a good little girl? Naw, we'll have to work her over first, but hell, that's half the fun, isn't it?" (Laite 1972, p. 42).

Laite was terrified. "I couldn't move. This couldn't be happening to me," he recalled (ibid., p. 42). But Laite was saved from forcible homosexual rape: a seventeen-year-old youth was admitted to the dayroom just as the five men were about to begin their assault. They were on him at once "like jackals, ripping the coveralls off his limp body. Then as I watched in frozen fascination and horror, they sexually assaulted him, savagely and brutally like starving animals after a raw piece of meat. Then I knew what they meant about giving me six or eight inches" (ibid., p. 42).

But the attack did not end there. While the youth was still unconscious, the attackers jabbed his limp body with the burning tips of pencil erasers, making it twitch—and thereby increasing the sexual excitement of the rapists. In a final sadistic gesture, one of the attackers "shoved his fingers deep into the boy's rectum and ripped out a mass of bloody hemorrhoids" (ibid., pp. 42–44).

It is noteworthy that this homosexual rape occurred in a jail setting. Rape is much more pervasive in jails, detention centers, and training schools than in prisons—where control is tighter and prisoners are subjected to greater physical restraint. Jails typically contain both inmates who are serving sentences of less than one year for misdemeanor offenses and those who are awaiting trial for serious felony offenses such as murder, attempted homicide, robbery, and rape. Also housed in jails are "bound-overs," offenders who have been sentenced to prison terms and are waiting to be transferred. Homosexual rapists in the jails are chiefly found among the latter two categories of prisoners.

Davis (1968) interviewed 3,304 inmates out of 60,000 who passed through the Philadelphia prison system in a two-year period (1966–1968). He also interviewed custodial employees. The study revealed that sexual assaults were epidemic: approximately 2,000 of the inmates interviewed admitted to being victims of homosexual rape. Of this number, only 156 cases were documented; and of those 156 cases, only 96 had been reported to the prison authorities and a mere 26 had been reported to criminal justice agencies outside the prison. Reporting is discouraged by unwritten laws of prison culture and the fear of brutal reprisal.

Davis observes that sexual assaults, as opposed to consensual homosexuality, are *not* caused by sexual deprivation: "They are expressions of anger and aggression prompted by the same basic frustrations that exist in the community, and which very probably were significant factors in producing the rapes, robberies, and other violent offenses for which the bulk of the aggressors were convicted" (1968, p. 16). Rather, as Scacco (1975) points out, racism is the central factor in sexual assaults within correctional institutions. Black aggressors and white victims are found in disproportionate numbers in every study of sexual assault in jails and prisons. Blacks rape whites to humiliate them and degrade them—to give members of the white majority a taste of what blacks experience as members of the minority community. The same pattern is evident with respect to Hispanic minorities and whites. Rarely do blacks and Hispanics rape one another.

Studies also indicate that whites rarely band together to resist attacks or to protect each other. They are also more conscious than minorities of the punishment they are likely to incur from the correctional staff if they fight to defend themselves against sexual aggression. Scacco notes that

> . . . most whites did not have the verbal ability and street savvy to ward off the baiting techniques of their aggressors. The latter were familiar with

> institutional settings and knew how to set up any white they chose for sexual acts. This was true since most of the aggressors had been returned to the same institution for their second or third time. Thus, they knew how to take what they wanted in the form of sexual gratification. The whites usually had little or no experience with institutional subcultures and were at a loss as to how to counteract even the slightest act of intimidation directed against them (1975, p. 55).

Status also plays a major role in rape. Status in prison is a mark of survival. (It was not uncommon in Biblical times for an invading army to sodomize males in the conquered land to demonstrate their dominance.) The higher an inmate's status, the lower the incidence of attack against that inmate. Status in prison is usually related to the type of offense for which the individual was convicted and the length of time he or she has to serve. Lockwood (1980) found that men who were imprisoned for homicide, aggravated assault, and larceny were not likely to be raped. Why? These men commanded respect because they were in for the long term. In contrast, white-collar criminals had more than a 60 percent chance of being raped. Such criminals were usually white, nonviolent, short term, and nonaffiliated. But the inmates most likely to be assaulted (and to be murdered) were sex offenders. These men are at the bottom of the prison totem pole; they are considered scum and are treated accordingly. Sex offenders are usually labeled the minute they arrive in prison.

Thus, it appears that homosexual rape is not committed for sexual relief. Rather, inmates rape each other for the same reason that men rape women—to exert control and dominance and to degrade the victim. Race is a major factor in homosexual rape, and certain types of inmates are more likely to get raped than others. The only practical solution might be to isolate probable victims from the predatory inmates. Because of prison overcrowding, however, such action may be impossible on any wide scale.

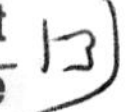

DISCUSSION AND REVIEW

1. What are the basic differences between the Pennsylvania system of corrections and the Auburn system?
2. Why is it so difficult to describe the "typical" maximum security facility?
3. What are the characteristics of maxi-maxi facilities?
4. How did some inmates react when they were transferred to the federal prison in Atlanta after Alcatraz closed in 1963?
5. What is the philosophy behind the Minnesota Correctional Facility at Oak Park Heights?
6. What are the major features of the federal correctional facility at Butner, North Carolina? How does the facility differ from other maximum security prisons?
7. What are the major characteristics of medium security correctional centers?
8. Describe a typical minimum security correctional center.
9. What is the major purpose of a reception and classification center?
10. There are basically three approaches to dealing with prison overcrowding. What are they and how does each work?

11. For what crimes are women typically arrested and convicted?
12. What appears to be the primary motivation for the growing popularity of the private sector becoming involved in corrections?
13. What two inmate characteristics are primary factors in homosexual rape in correctional institutions?

GLOSSARY

Auburn system A corrections system in which inmates labored in factorylike shops during working hours and were confined to their cells on the Sabbath and during nonworking hours; started in about 1830.

Gallows An upright frame with a crossbeam for hanging a condemned person.

Great Law of Pennsylvania Law enacted in 1682 that largely eliminated the use of stocks, pillories, branding irons, and gallows.

Maxi-maxi prisons Facilities characterized by high perimeter security, high internal security, and operating regulations that curtail movement and maximize control; inmates include persistent property offenders, troublesome inmates, and individuals considered to be dangerous because of the nature of their offenses.

Maximum security prisons Facilities geared to the fullest possible supervision, control, and surveillance of inmates; usually surrounded by a masonry wall or double fence with gun towers, electronic sensors, and good lighting.

Medium security correctional centers Facilities in which the most intensive correctional or rehabilitation efforts are conducted. The primary consideration is still security, however, and many centers have the same features as maximum security facilities (i.e., gun towers, masonry walls, and electronic sensors).

Minimum security correctional centers Facilities ranging from large drug rehabilitation centers to small farms, road, and forestry campuses in rural America; inmates are considered nonviolent and low risk for escape.

Pennsylvania system A corrections system based on solitary confinement with bench labor in each inmate's cell; started in about 1830.

Pillory A wooden frame with holes for the head and hands of offenders; offenders were locked in and exposed to public scorn.

Reception and classification centers Facilities (usually maximum security) where most new prisoners are sent for observation, testing, interviewing, and eventual assignment to a state prison.

Stocks A heavy wooden frame with holes to confine offenders' ankles and (sometimes) wrists.

Youth corrections centers Facilities designed to house youthful offenders (ages sixteen to thirty); built to provide medium to minimum security.

REFERENCES

Abt Associates, Inc. *American Prisons and Jails*, 5 vols. Washington, D.C.: National Institute of Justice, U.S. Department of Justice, 1980.

Barnes, H. E. *The Story of Punishment.* Chapter 6. Montclair, N.J.: Smith, Patterson, 1972.

Bates, S. *Prisons and Beyond.* Freeport, N.Y.: Books For Libraries, 1936.

Bingham, J. *Report of the Attorney General on the February 2–3, 1980 Riot at the Penitentiary of New Mexico.* Part 1. Santa Fe, N. Mex.: Office of the Attorney General of the State of New Mexico, 1980.

Blumstein, A. "Prisons: Population, Capacity, and Alternatives." In *Crime and Public Policy,* edited by James Q. Wilson. San Francisco, Calif.: ICS Press, 1983.

Blumstein, A.; Cohen, J.; and Gooding, W. "The Influence of Capacity on Prison Population: A Critical Review of Some Recent Evidence." *Crime and Delinquency* 29 (1983): 1–51.

Blumstein, A.; Cohen, J; and Miller, H. "Demographically Disaggregated Projections of Prison Populations." *Journal of Criminal Justice* 8 (1980): 1–25.

Blumstein, A.; Cohen, J.; Nagin, D., eds. *Deterrence and Incapacitation: Estimating the Effects of Criminal Sanctions on Crime Rates.* Washington, D.C.: National Academy Press, 1978.

Cohen, J. "Incapacitation as a Strategy for Crime Control: Possibilities and Pitfalls." In *Crime and Justice: An Annual Review of Research,* vol. 5, edited by Michael Tonry and Norval Morris, Chicago, Ill.: University of Chicago Press, 1983.

Davis, A. J. "Sexual Assaults in the Philadelphia Prison System and Sheriffs' Vans." *Trans-Action* 6 (1968): 9–17.

Dunn, R. S., and Dunn, M. M., eds. *The Papers of William Penn: Volume II 1680–1684.* Philadelphia: Univ. of Pennsylvania, 1982.

Gaes, G. G. "The Effects of Overcrowding in Prison." In *Crime and Justice: An Annual Review of Research,* vol. 6, edited by Michael Tonry and Norval Morris. Chicago, Ill.: University of Chicago Press, 1985.

Ingram, G. L. "Butner: A Reality." *Federal Probation* 42 (1978): 34–39.

———. "The Federal Correctional Institution at Butner, North Carolina: An Experimental Prison for Repetitively Violent Offenders," In *Confinement in Maximum Security,* edited by D. A. Ward and K. F. Schoen, Lexington, Mass.: Lexington, 1981.

Jacobs, J. B. *Inside Prisons.* Washington, D.C.: U.S. Department of Justice, National Institute of Justice, 1987.

Keating, J. M., Jr. "Public Ends and Private Means." *Accountability among Private Providers of Public Social Services.* New York: National Institute of Dispute Resolution, February 1984.

Laite, W. *The United States vs. William Laite.* Washington, D.C.: Acropolis, 1972.

Lansing, D.; Bogan, J. B.; and Karacki, L. "Unit Management: Implementing a Different Correctional Approach." *Federal Probation* 41 (1977): 43–49.

Lockwood, D. *Prison Sexual Violence.* New York: Elsevier, 1980.

Morris, N. *The Future of Imprisonment.* Chicago, Ill.: University of Chicago Press, 1975.

Mullen, J. *Corrections and the Private Sector.* Washington, D.C.: U.S. Department of Justice, National Institute of Justice, May 1983.

National Advisory Commission on Criminal Justice Standards and Goals. *Corrections.* Washington, D.C.: U.S. Government Printing Office, 1973.

"Our Crowded Prisons." Special issue of *The Annals of the American Academy of Political and Social Science.* Beverly Hills, Calif.: Sage Publications, 1985.

Rothman, D. *The Discovery of Institutions: Social Order and Disorder in the New Republic.* Chapters 3 and 4. Boston, Mass.: Little, Brown, 1971.

Scacco, A. M. *Rape in Prison.* Springfield, Ill.: Charles C. Thomas, 1975.

Sechrest, L.; White, S. O.; and Brown, E. D., eds. *The Rehabilitation of Criminal Offenders: Problems and Prospects.* Washington, D.C.: National Academy Press, 1979.

Sexton, G. E.; Farrow, F. C.; and Auerbach, B. J. *The Private Sector Involvement in Prison-Based Business: A National Assessment.* Washington, D.C.: U.S. Department of Justice, National Institute of Justice, December 1984.

Ward, D. A., and Schoen, K. F., eds. *Confinement in Maximum Security.* Lexington, Mass.: Lexington, 1981.

Ward, D. A., and Schmidt, A. K. "Last-Resort Prisons for Habitual and Dangerous Offenders: Some Second Thoughts About Alcatraz." In *Confinement in Maximum Security,* edited by D. A. Ward and K. F. Schoen. Lexington, Mass.: Lexington, 1981.

■ NOTES

1. Portions of this chapter were adapted from National Advisory Commission on Criminal Justice Standards and Goals, *Corrections.* (Washington, D.C.: U.S. Government Printing Office, 1973), pp. 341–49.
2. F. W. Wood, 16 October 1981; personal communication.
3. This discussion of prison overcrowding was adapted from James B. Jacobs, *Inside Prisons* (Washington, D.C.: U.S. Department of Justice, National Institute of Justice, 1987).
4. This discussion of corrections and the private sector was adapted from Joan Mullen, *Corrections and the Private Sector* (Washington, D.C.: U.S. Department of Justice, National Institute of Justice, May 1985.

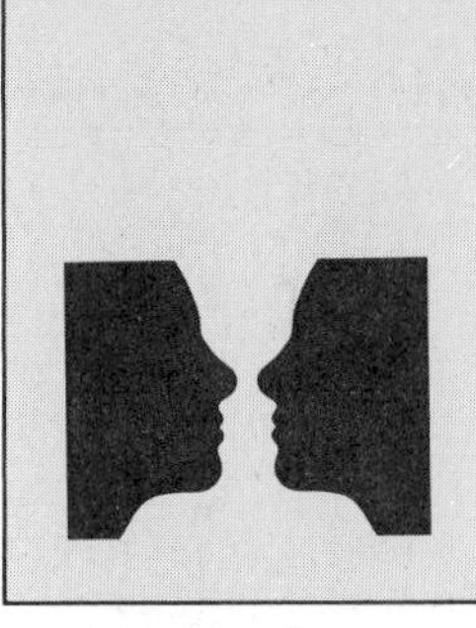

CHAPTER

15

Social, Political, and Racial Forces in American Prisons

CHAPTER OUTLINE:

This chapter focuses on social, political, and racial forces that have been at work in many of our largest and most dangerous prisons since the 1960s. We examine how these forces have changed and how they have impacted correctional administrators, correctional officers, and inmates. Further, we discuss how philosophical changes in prison management have affected the social, political, and racial environment in prisons. We also recommend ways to restore legitimate control in prisons where certain inmates have gained sufficient power to undermine the authority of prison officials. Lastly we discuss the problem of acquired immunodeficiency syndrome (AIDS) in prison and what prison officials are doing to cope with this growing problem.

THE INMATE SOCIAL SYSTEM BEFORE 1960

Because a number of important social and political changes occurred in American prisons in the 1960s and 1970s, it is useful to examine the inmate social system both before and after the 1960s. Starting in the 1970s, and continuing into the 1980s, a substantial number of minorities from lower socioeconomic classes in urban areas entered the prisons, substantially changing the prison environment.

Observers of prison populations prior to 1960 report one common value system among prison inmates: a code of conduct that defined relationships among inmates and between inmates and correctional officers. The code was usually rigidly reinforced by the inmate population, and violators were either ignored by other inmates or subjected to acts of violence (Sykes and Messinger 1960).[1] The chief tenets of the code fall into five categories:

1. *Maxims that caution.* Don't interfere with inmates' desires to serve the least possible time and to enjoy the greatest number of pleasures and privileges possible while in prison. The most flexible directive in this category was concerned with the betrayal of a fellow prisoner to institutional officials: never rat on a con. In general, no qualifications or mitigating circumstances were recognized, and no grievance against another inmate—even though it was justified in the eyes of the inmate—was to be taken to officials for settlement. Other specifics included don't be nosy, don't have a loose lip, keep off a man's back, don't put a guy on the spot, be loyal to your fellow prisoners, and present a unified front against the guard (no matter how great the personal sacrifice).
2. *Injunctions to refrain from quarrels or arguments with fellow prisoners.* Don't lose your head; play it cool; and do your own time. (Exceptions were made for inmates subjected to legitimate provocation, however.)
3. *Assertions that inmates should not take advantage of each other by means of force, fraud, or chicanery.* Don't exploit inmates; don't

break your word; don't steal from cons; don't sell favors; don't be a racketeer, don't welch on debts. Inmates were expected to share scarce goods, rather than to sell to the highest bidder or to selfishly monopolize amenities.

4. *Rules that stress the maintenance of self.* Don't weaken; don't whine; don't cop out (cry guilty); don't suck around; be tough; be a man. Dignity and the ability to withstand frustration or a threatening situation without complaining or resorting to subservience were wildly acclaimed. The prisoner was to be able to "take it" and to maintain his or her integrity. When confronted with wrongfully aggressive behavior, the prisoner was to show courage. And although starting a fight ran counter to the inmate code, retreating from a fight started by someone else was equally reprehensible.
5. *Maxims that forbid according prestige or respect to custodians or the world for which they stand.* Don't be a sucker. Guards were to be treated with suspicion and distrust. In any conflict, officials were automatically considered to be in the wrong. Furthermore, inmates were not to commit themselves to the values of hard work or to submit to duly constituted authority.

FIGURE 15.1
Informers, as this sign in a Rhode Island state prison illustrates, are regarded with contempt by other inmates. *Corrections Magazine* and Criminal Justice Publications.

An inmate who betrayed a fellow prisoner was labeled a **rat** or a **squealer** and was universally scorned and hated. Prisoners who exhibited highly aggressive behavior and who quarreled easily and without cause were often referred to as **toughs.** An individual who used violence liberally was called a **gorilla** (gorillas often used force against other prisoners in violation of the inmate code). The term **merchant,** or **peddler,** was applied to inmates who exploited fellow inmates by manipulation and trickery and who sold or traded goods in short supply. A prisoner who was unable to withstand the general rigors of prison was referred to as a **weakling** or a **weak sister.** An inmate who entered into homosexual activity was labeled a **wolf** or a **fag,** depending on whether the inmate's role was active or passive. An inmate who continued to plead his case was sarcastically known as a *rapo* (from bum rap) or an *innocent.* And an inmate who allied himself with prison officials or expressed the values of conformity was ridiculed as a *square John.*

Inmates who carefully followed the norms of prison society—who *celebrated* the inmate code rather than violated it—were known as **right guys,** *real cons,* and *real men.* These inmates were heroes of the inmate social system, and their existence gave meaning to the prison villains: the rats, the toughs, the gorillas, and the merchants. A right guy was always loyal to his fellow prisoners. He never let them down no matter how rough things got. He kept his promises; he was dependable and trustworthy. He wasn't nosy about other inmates' business, and he didn't shoot off his mouth about his own. He didn't act stuck up, but he didn't fall all over himself to make friends either—he had a certain dignity.

A right guy never interfered with other inmates who were conniving against officials. He didn't look for a fight, but he never ran away from one when he was in the right. Anyone who started a fight with a right guy had to be ready to go all the way. When a right guy got extras in prison—cigarettes, stolen food, and so on—he shared them with his friends. He didn't take advantage of prisoners who didn't have much, and he didn't strong-arm other inmates into fagging for him. Instead, he acted like a man. When dealing with prison officials, a right guy never acted foolishly. When he talked about officials with other inmates, he was sure to say that even the **hacks** (guards) with the best intentions are stupid, incompetent, and not to be trusted; the worst a con could do was to give the hacks information (they'll only use it against you when the chips are down).

A right guy stuck up for his rights and he didn't ask for pity: he could take everything the **screws** (guards) could hand out—and more. He didn't "suck around" the officials, and the privileges he got were deserved. Even if a right guy didn't look for trouble with the officials, he would go to the limit if they pushed him too far. He realized that there were just two kinds of people in the world: those "in the know" and suckers. Those "in the know" skim pleasures off the top; suckers work.

As suggested earlier, the inmate social system that existed before 1960 has undergone considerable change. And the changes are more dramatic in some states than in others. Thus, we focus in the rest of this chapter on two prison systems—California and Illinois—that provide some vivid examples of changes in prison life after the 1960s.

THE BLACK PRISONER MOVEMENT

Racial tensions in prisons began when the number of black prisoners increased and the attitude of black prisoners shifted (Irwin 1980).[2] Although linked to the civil rights movement outside, the latter change had unique qualities. For example, the tactics of civil rights protestors were too gentle to catch the imagination of black prisoners, and the central issue of civil rights—equal treatment under the law—was not critical in prison. Thus, the "black is beautiful" movement and **black separatism** played a more important role in prison than did civil rights.

Black Is Beautiful

After World War II, because of the large migration of southern blacks to northern and western cities (and some measure of educational and occupational progress), many black Americans developed a new sense of worth. This new pride focused on two qualities that blacks in the United States believed were related to the Negro race: **soul** and masculinity. Soul involved spontaneity, the capacity to relate to others with ease, and special expressive abilities—particularly as revealed in music. Masculinity was related to athletic and sexual prowess. Many of the early believers in these new definitions came to prisons in the late 1950s and early 1960s, spreading among black prisoners the idea that "black is beautiful." Not until the late 1960s and early 1970s, however, did the idea really take hold.

Black Separatism

The **Black Muslims** emerged as the major separatist organization in the early 1950s and found their way into the prisons in the mid-1950s. **Malcolm X,** who more than any other individual personified the development of black separatism, describes the growth of Muslim faith in prison:

> You let this caged up Black man start thinking, the same way I did when I first heard Elijah Muhammad's teachings. Let him start thinking how with better breaks when he was young and ambitious he might have been a lawyer, a doctor, a scientist, anything. You let this caged up Black man start realizing, as I did how from the first landing of the first slave ship, the millions of Black men in America have been like sheep in the den of wolves. That's why Black prisoners become Muslims so fast when Elijah Muhammad's teaching filters into their cages by way of other Muslim convicts. "The white man is a devil" is a perfect echo of that Black convict's lifelong experience (1965, p. 183).

Black Muslim prisoners recruited other black prisoners, and the organization grew throughout the 1950s. Members followed a nonviolent, separatist course and clashed with prison administrations only over restrictions of religious practices. They asked to receive copies of the Koran and the Muslim newspaper *Muhammad Speaks,* to hold meetings, to meet with outside representatives of the organization, to be served pork-free meals, and to be segregated from other prisoners. All prison administrations resisted these requests and suppressed the organization, which they perceived as a threat to prison peace and administrative authority. But the Muslims were tenacious: they formed groups of highly disciplined black prisoners who shaved their heads, kept themselves impeccably neat, maintained a cold but polite attitude toward other prisoners, refused to eat pork, congregated whenever possible, and listened to each other deliver the teachings of Elijah Muhammad. Although their rhetoric was hostile, the Muslims seldom precipitated violence. However, they were occasionally involved in violence initiated by someone else—perhaps by a guard firing on a group of Muslims or on a group of Muslims and other prisoners. Eldridge Cleaver describes the aftermath of one such shooting, revealing the essentially nonviolent posture of Muslims:

> After the death of brother Booker T. X., who was shot dead by a San Quentin guard and who at the time had been my cell partner and the inmate minister of the Muslims at San Quentin, my leadership had been publicly endorsed by Elijah Muhammad's West Coast representative, minister John Shabazz of Muhammad's Los Angeles mosque. This was done because of the explosive conditions in San Quentin at the time. Muslim officials wanted to avert any Muslim initiated violence, which had become a distinct possibility in the aftermath of brother Booker's death. I was instructed to impose iron discipline on the San Quentin mosque, which had continued to exist despite the unending efforts of prison authorities to stamp it out (1968, p. 63).

FIGURE 15.2
Wallace Muhammad, standing before a portrait of his father, Elijah, in 1975. Wide World Photos.

Elijah Muhammad's teachings did condemn and vilify whites and white society, however, a situation that antagonized, threatened, and frightened white inmates and prison administrators. As a result, many administrators tried to suppress the organization by introducing rules against membership. One prison even adopted a rule prohibiting more than two black prisoners to congregate. In response, the Muslims carried their fight to the courts, and in 1965 they won the right to exist as a religious organization in prisons.

By the time of their court victories, the Muslims were losing momentum in California prisons. Malcolm X left the outside organization in 1963 and was later assassinated. Malcolm X's departure, his political vision, and his homicide—which many believe was perpetrated by the Muslims—turned many Muslim prisoners in California away from the organization. Some followed Malcolm X's route to political organization. Cleaver responded to Malcolm X's assassination this way:

> What provoked the assassins to murder? It bothered them that Malcolm was elevating our struggle into the international arena through his campaign to carry it before the United Nations. Well, by murdering him they only hastened the process because we certainly are going to take our cause before a sympathetic world. Did it bug the assassins that Malcolm denounced the racist straight-jacket demonology of Elijah Muhammad? Well, we certainly do denounce it and will continue to do so. Did it bother the assassins that Malcolm taught us to defend ourselves? We shall not remain a defenseless prey to the murder, to the sniper, and to the bomber. In so far as Malcolm spoke the truth, the truth shall triumph and prevail and his name shall live; and in so far as those who opposed him lied, to what extent will their names become curses. Because truth crushed to earth shall rise again (1968, pp. 65–66).

In California during the late 1960s and early 1970s, ex-Muslims and other black prisoners followed a variety

FIGURE 15.3
Muslim organizations in many prisons offer Islamic studies to their members. Here an inmate studies the Koran. Tony O'Brien/Criminal Justice Photos.

of courses until the Black Panther Party came into prominence on the outside, supplying black prisoners with the new, dynamic black nationalistic organization. In this phase of separatism, black prisoners who identified with the Black Panthers or similar organizations were more politically radical and more prone to violence than their forerunners (at least they were much more prepared to respond to threats with violence).

RACIAL GANGS IN PRISON

The hate between white and black prisoners is the most powerful source of division in prisons. Gangs of various types—including white, black, and Chicano—inhabit many state prison systems. The gangs in Illinois are generally acknowledged to be the largest.

Black Gangs

Black gangs in Illinois prisons are an extension of Chicago street gangs. The most famous (and probably still the largest) of the street gangs is the Black Stone Rangers, which had 3,000 to 5,000 members in the early 1970s. The Rangers later changed their name to the Black P Stone Nation, and to A Neo-Islamic **El-Rukns** in 1979. Other large gangs are the **Vice Lords**, the **Latin Kings**, and the **Disciples.**

In the 1970s, hundreds of gang members were sent to prison for involvement in drugs and prostitution. Most were sent to the Illinois State Penitentiary at Stateville, near Chicago, and the second largest group went to the state prison at Pontiac. Although these arrests neutralized much of the gang activity on the street, the gangs emerged as a powerful force in prisons (Krajick, 1980, p. 11).[3] Young, militant blacks carried racial hostility with them into the prison system, resulting in clashes among blacks, whites, and custodial personnel. Robinson describes the attitude of black prisoners this way:

> In the prison, the Black dudes have a little masculinity game they play. It has no name, really, but I call it Whup or Fuck a White boy—especially the White gangsters or syndicate men, the bad juice boys, the hit men, etc. The Black dudes go out of their way to make faggots out of them. And to lose a fight to a White dude is one of the worst things that can happen to a Black dude. And I know that, by and far, the White cats are faggots. They will drop their pants and bend over and touch their toes

> and get had before they will fight. So, knowing this, what kind of men did this make us? They told us where, how, and when to shit, eat, sleep (1971, p. 29).

In the face of such treatment, white prisoners tend to reciprocate with racial hostility—regardless of their attitudes *before* entering prison (Irwin 1980, p. 183).

Upon entering the Illinois prison system, black gangs organized massive resistance to prison administration. Prisoners seized hostages, set fires, organized boycotts, refused to be locked up in their cells, and assaulted and intimidated guards. They quickly gathered power by recruiting inmates who had not been gang members on the outside. (Prison officials estimate that at least half of gang members today join in this way.) The advantages of joining up immediately were obvious: anyone who didn't join would be beaten, raped, robbed, or killed, and members would be protected from attack by nonmembers.

The testimony of dozens of prisoners over the last decade indicates that most prisons "offbrand" inmates who are either rejected by the gang or who choose not to join. (Offbrands pay protection money to one or more gangs.) Only the most highly respected offbrands—most of them longtime convicts—escape gang terrorism. For the rest, the complexion of prison life has changed radically. "You used to know what to expect and you could do your time in peace," said one older white prisoner. "Now I don't know what the hell is going to happen next. I'm more afraid of these bangers [the name for the most vicious gang members] than I am of the screws [guards]."

Chicano Gangs

Gang types vary from state to state, depending on the background of the young hoodlums that arrive at adult prisons (Irwin 1980). In California, the gang takeover began in San Quentin in 1967, when a click of young Chicanos—youths who had known each other in other prisons and on the streets of Los Angeles—began to take drugs forcefully from other prisoners (mostly Chicanos). This tough group was labeled the **Mexican Mafia.** According to rumor, Chicano hoodlums aspiring to Mafia membership had to murder another prisoner for initiation. This rumor aroused many "independent" Chicanos to band together to eliminate the Mafia. On a planned day, this group of Chicanos pursued known Mafia members through San Quentin and attempted to assassinate them. Several dozen prisoners were seriously wounded and one was killed in the daylong battle; but the Mafia held its ground and was not eliminated.

After this unsuccessful attempt, some non-Mafia Chicanos—particularly those from Texas and from small towns in California who had been in conflict with Los Angeles Chicanos for decades—formed the counter group **Las Nuestra Familia.** In the ensuing years, the conflict between the two Chicano gangs increased and spread to other prisons and even to the outside, where gangs tried to penetrate drug trafficking. The attacks and counterattacks between members of the two gangs have become so frequent that prison administrators have attempted to segregate the gangs, designating two prisons for the Mafia—San Quentin and Folsom—and two for La Nuestra Familia—Soledad and Tracy.

The escalation of robbery, assault, and murder by Chicano gangs served to consolidate and expand black and white groups, some of which were already involved in violent activities on a small scale. Two gangs, the white-dominated Aryan Brotherhood and the Black Guerilla Family, rose in prominence, and the Aryan Brotherhood eventually formed an alliance with the Mexican Mafia. When the Black Guerilla Family allied with La Nuestra Familia, a very hostile stalemate prevailed (although peace did not return). Racist clicks among black and white prisoners still occasionally attack other prisoners; Chicano gangs still fight each other; and some Chicano gangs fight among themselves. Thus, although the California prisons have passed their peak of violence, the violence and fear that remain are intense.

White Gangs

White gangs in prison are primarily an outgrowth of violence against white inmates by organized blacks and Hispanics. There is little evidence to suggest that white prison gangs are in any way an extension of street gangs in cities. Some white prisoners may belong to the same gang in a city that they belong to in prison, but there is no large-scale white counterpart to the development of black and Hispanic gangs in prisons. Individuals who belong to motorcycle clubs may form coalitions inside prison, but it is doubtful that these gangs recruit individuals who are members of their clubs outside of prison.

White gangs are generally as violent, aggressive, and cohesive as their black and Hispanic counterparts. For example, in the state prison at Menard in southern Illinois on the fringes of Appalachia, half of the twenty-six hundred inmates are white and heavily racist. Many belong to a white gang known as the **White Citizen Council.** Members of the Council, the **Aryan Brother-**

hood, and various offshoots of the Ku Klux Klan have battled with black groups in Menard's yard in recent years. Nevertheless, racial conflict at Menard has declined, probably because of increased security.

Socialization and Recruitment

Gangs are a significant reality behind prison walls. The unaffiliated convict fears that his life may be endangered by gangs and that he will be shaken down for commissary and sex. Unfortunately, the security staff can offer little protection. To survive, a white inmate might become a "punk" for one of the gangs. Some whites also maintain physical security by demonstrating fighting ability or by boasting of connections with organized crime (Jacobs 1977).[4]

The Latin Kings and Vice Lords are skeptical of penitentiary dwellers and do not recruit in the prisons; but the El-Rukns and the Disciples do recruit vigorously in prisons, just as they do on the street. Solicitation is frequently forceful and highly sophisticated. New prisoners are usually confronted by both a "hard" and a "soft" sell.

In contrast to the unaffiliated convict, the gang members that enter prison from the street have no trouble adjusting to their new environment. As the warden of Pontiac (Illinois) penitentiary once said, "When a guy comes up here it's almost a homecoming—undoubtedly there are people from his neighborhood and people who know him." The chief of the Disciples claims that he knew seventy-five Disciples at Stateville Prison when he arrived. And a young leader of the Latin Kings claims that he knew all but two of the Kings at Stateville when he arrived; the first afternoon, he received a letter from the ranking chief welcoming him into the family (Jacobs 1977, p. 152).

B. P., Chief of the Vice Lords, explains that when a young Vice Lord comes into prison, the man is set up immediately with coffee, tea, deodorant, and soap. Visitors and correspondence are arranged for Vice Lords who have been deserted by their families. Normally, the cell-house chief provides an elaborate orientation. The Disciples distribute the following rules to incoming members:

1. Degradation of another Disciple will not be tolerated at any time.
2. Disrespect for any governing body of said cell house will not be permitted.
3. There will not at any time be any unnecessary commotion while entering the cell house.
4. Homosexual confrontation toward another Disciple will not be tolerated.
5. Dues will be paid up on time on any designated schedule.
6. Fighting another Disciple without consulting a governing chief will result in strict disciplining.
7. Upon greeting another Disciple, proper representation will be ascertained.
8. There will never be an act of cowardice displayed by another Disciple, for a Disciple is always strong and brave.
9. There will not be any cigarettes in the hole for those who relentlessly obstruct the rules and regulations of the organization or the institution.
10. Anyone caught perpetrating the above rules and regulations with disorder and dishonesty will be brought before the committee and dealt with accordingly (Jacobs 1977, p. 152).

The parallels between these rules and the general inmate code are striking. In fact, Irwin and Cressey (1964) maintain that the inmate code can be described by reference to the norms of certain criminal subcultures.

Gang Services

The prison gang meets many of the material and psychological needs of its members. In addition to providing physical security, some organizations buffer members from poverty within the institution. At Stateville, for example, each gang has a poor box. Cell-house chiefs in each gang collect cigarettes from members and store them for those who have legitimate need. When a member makes a particularly good "score" or deal, he is expected to share the bounty with the leaders and to donate to the poor box. Although skeptics claim that these boxes are often depleted and that many benefits to not filter down, one observer has seen gang leaders giving cigarettes away. Furthermore, when a gang member is placed in isolation, he can always expect cigarettes and food to be passed in to him.

Gangs also function as communication networks. If McCleery (1960) is correct in asserting that a crucial concern of new inmates is their lack of information about prisons, then gangs function to keep their members informed and to provide guidelines for all situations and events within the institution. By assigning "soldiers" to jobs in the administration building, as runners, as yard workers, and as house help, gangs ensure that information will flow with great precision.

Gangs also provide a distribution network for contraband. One Latin King informant explains that where an independent might hesitate to attempt a score (fearing that he might not be able to hide the stolen items), a gang member knows that he can divest himself of most contraband within minutes. The role of the gangs in organizing illicit activities is unclear, but it *is* clear that no illicit activities operate without the approval of gang leaders. Gang affiliation enables young inmates to establish connections in illegal trafficking and to muscle in on independents who are not already paying off one of the other gangs.

By far, however, the most important function of the Disciples, the Latin Kings, the Vice Lords, and the El-Rukns at Stateville is psychological support. Whether one subscribes to the theories of Cohen (1955) or Miller (1958) to account for the origin of gangs, the important point here is, as Thrasher (1963) notes, that the gang serves as a membership and reference group to provide the delinquent with status and a positive view of himself. As B. P., the leader of the Disciples, explains, "These guys in my branch [of the Disciple Federation] are closer to me than my own family. Anything I do around them is accepted—for stuff that my parents would put me down for, these guys elevate me to a pedestal" (Jacobs 1977, p. 153).

Over and over again, inmate informants, gang members, and offbrands express the opinion that gangs provide an identity, a feeling of belonging, and an air of importance:

> It's just like a religion. Once a Lord always a Lord. Our people would die for it. Perhaps this comes from lack of a father figure or lack of guidance or from having seen a father beaten up and cowering from the police. We never had anything with which to identify. Even the old cons like me—they are looking for me to give them something they have been looking for for a long time (Jacobs 1977, p. 153).

Gang members consistently explain that it is the gang—both on the street and within the prison—that allows you to feel like a man; it is a family with which you can identify. Several informants state that the organization is the only thing worth dying for. With their insignias, colors, salutes, titles, and legendary histories, the group provide the only meaningful reference group for their members. Gang "soldiers" live by specific rules and aspire to successive levels of status.

Impact of Gangs on Prison Systems

According to prison officials and police, gangs are organized into paramilitary hierarchies. Each gang has an identifiable leader or group of leaders who command a chain of "colonels," "enforcers," "ambassadors," "lieutenants," and "soldiers" (also known as "indians"). Gang leaders are revered and often have other prisoners opening cell doors for them, serving them special food, and accompanying them as bodyguards (Krajick 1980).

At the height of their power in the last few years, gangs have controlled cell and job assignments and access to foods at the commissary; some even control certain areas of their prisons. Such control is gained by intimidating poorly trained and outnumbered guards. According to prisoners, officials, and outside observers, much of this control (as well as the extortion of offbrands) has been undermined by better trained and more numerous guards; but this administrative control is tenuous. "We sent a message to the gangs that we were taking back control," says Mike Lane, assistant director of the Department of Corrections in Illinois. "But it is nonsense to say that we can break them up. The gangs are there and they're a hell of an influence." And Marvin Redd, Warden of Stateville, adds, "Things are quiet now, but the gangs can influence and disrupt anything we've got going whenever they want" (Krajick 1980, p. 12).

Administrators have been criticized in the past for not aggressively controlling gangs. "They've been applying traditional methods (lockdowns, informants) to situations where they're not fitted anymore," notes prison authority John Conrad. "The gangs have shown that inmates can trust each other and overwhelm the administration" (ibid.). Conrad suggests punishment and improved living conditions and programs as a way to control gang activity.

Current attempts by prison administrators to regain control of Stateville Penitentiary started with a big shakedown at the prison in February 1979. The most powerful gang leaders were transferred to a federal holding facility in Chicago. Prison officials wanted to transfer the leaders permanently to out-of-state federal prisons, but the gang leaders sued—claiming that they were being denied due process in the transfer. They were held in Chicago pending the outcome of the suit.

Gail Franzen, Director of the Illinois Department of Corrections asked Norman Carlson, head of the Federal Bureau of Prisons, to take more gang members; but he was turned down. "He [Carlson] didn't want them any more than I do," said Franzen. Anyway, Franzen knew that more transfers would not solve the problem. Removing the leaders would not cure gang infestation. A charismatic leader can issue orders (through intermediaries) from wherever he is. Or new leaders might arise. A follower of Disciple leader Dirk Acklin once said, "Sure he was leader. But you get rid of him, somebody else comes up. They can't do nothing to stop us" (ibid. p. 14).

Prison officials in Illinois have tried to recognize and work with the gangs to keep them under control. The Stateville chapel was once set aside on certain days for gang meetings, and leaders were allowed to move freely throughout the institution to collect information and keep order. But the leaders did not keep order, although veteran administrators do credit some of them with trying. Today, administrators avoid officially recognizing gang leaders as representatives of other inmates. They do not give them special privileges, and they do everything they can to prevent organized gang activity.

The El-Rukns are now petitioning the courts for religious status. They claim to be an offshoot of the Moorish Science Temple, a black Islamic sect. This initiative worries prison administrators. Religious status would guarantee the El-Rukns harrassment-free meetings, access to outside clergy, and the right to recruit members openly. In a landmark case in 1964, the U.S. Supreme Court gave the Black Muslims similar rights, recognizing them as a bona fide religious organization.

The El-Rukns and other gangs claim that they are misunderstood and maligned. Members say that the gangs have evolved from criminal enterprise into political and social organizations. One prisoner who joined the Disciples in 1967 when he was eleven asserts: "Sure we were robbing and killing and beating back in the 60s. We all did. I did it. But now we've learned better. . . . We were fighting for justice. . . . We're not a gang any more. We're an organization" (ibid.).

Nevertheless Chicago police say that the gangs are as heavily into criminal activity as ever. Prison officials regularly receive death threats from gang members inside and outside prison, and guards who enforce rules too strictly against the wrong people get phone calls in the middle of the night at their homes. During his first few months as warden at Stateville, Alvin Reed carried a .357 magnum revolver outside the prison because of threats. And Charles Row, director of the Illinois Department of Corrections, stepped down from his post on December 1978 with relief: gang members had threatened to kill his two-year-old daughter unless he gave up efforts to crush a narcotics smuggling ring at Stateville. Because of threats, the family of another high administrator at Stateville is accompanied around the clock by armed guards supplied by the state. One Disciple expresses this attitude about threats: "They beat on us, we'll get back, it doesn't matter whether they're wearing bars or stars on their shoulders, or three-piece suits. We'll get them back. It's only right" (ibid.).

So far, gangs have not made good on any threats against high officials at Stateville. However, guards are periodically stabbed and beaten at the prison, and gang members on the outside have dramatically demonstrated their solidarity with their imprisoned comrades on several occasions. One Sunday morning in August 1979, for example, 150 El-Rukns drove up to the Stateville gates in a caravan of Cadillac limousines. Wearing ceremonial fezes, they supposedly came to visit friends and relatives. Administrators had heard rumors that the El-Rukns planned to take over the visiting room, so guards and state police armed with shotguns tried to turn the caravan away. Many El-Rukns refused to leave, however, and police had to tow their cars away. Several visitors were arrested for carrying guns.

EVOLUTION IN PRISON MANAGEMENT

Dinitz (1980), in a paper presented to the John Vincent Barry Memorial Lecture at the University of Melbourne, Australia, provides an interesting and insightful look into the evolution of prison management.[5] Early in this century (and in the Texas prison system today), the staff of a prison was wholly dependent on the whims of the administrator and was wholly loyal, as in any paramilitary setting, to the maintenance of the system. It helped to have a mentality in which the locking and unlocking of cells and the counting of bodies five or more times a day was considered a "calling"—a quasi-religious experience. It helped to define reality in terms of "good guys" versus "bad guys." It helped to be somewhat paranoid, because the caged were always plotting to escape to contravene the system.

The study of paranoia increased with the introduction of teachers, doctors, nurses, counselors, chaplains, legal aids, and defenders into the prison system. How could a prison be run when every custody decision could be challenged as antitherapeutic or, at the very least, capricious? Treatment and due process became clubs with which to beat underpaid custodial people. Understandably, these workers felt inadequate, demeaned, and powerless in the face of the new penology. Riots in the 1950s and again in the last half of the 1960s were often triggered by custodial losses in this treatment-custody conflict.

Today, the battle is over. Martinson's idea that nothing works (1974), and the writings of Wilson (1975), Van Den Haag (1975), Von Hirsh (1976), and Morris (1974), have buried the ideal of rehabilitation. Even so, a prison staff may feel isolated and unappreciated. Many correctional officers are so poorly paid that their families are on food stamps. Many are overworked and abused and mocked by inmates, and their decisions are scrutinized by lawyers and prison masters appointed by distant judges. As a result, correctional officers desert their jobs and succumb to stress or **burnout** at a high rate.

Recently, correctional officers have joined labor unions and pressed their interests through collective bargaining. In this process, institutional loyalty has disappeared. With a voice of their own, correctional officers in many states are now bargaining, rather than begging, for improved working conditions (Irwin 1980, pp. 220–22). For example, **sick-outs** have been used to close entire institutions to draw attention to staff demands. In such confrontations, the staff is likely to emerge as the power center in the threefold struggle among staff, inmates, and prison administration. What a judge orders in his or her chambers is ultimately obeyed or rejected on the line. Thus, guards have become the final decision makers inside the walls, despite all the due process on the books. The guard is the sovereign—at least until his or her decisions are reversed by riots, hunger strikes, or disturbance, or appealed by jailhouse lawyers or court-appointed overseers (Freeman, Dinitz, and Conrad 1977). Despite the enormity of this power, however, custodial officers still feel isolated, estranged, and embittered. The reason for this is not hard to find. In guard mythology, there is a conspiracy involving do-gooders, defense attorneys, the courts, and spineless prison managers to promote the interests of the inmate—the wrongdoer. These conspirators have tried and failed to turn the prison into an asylum. Yet guards have not promised the public a hospital or offered themselves as attendants. Nor have they promised that prisons, through due process, would be fair communities. Occasionally, a dissident guard, captain, or associate warden will view the prison as a therapeutic community or a lawful community and will try to implement these views. But the rank-and-file officer has no need for such vision. What he or she wants—and is within striking distance of getting—is a quiet day with some overtime pay and no lip from inmates or their defenders.

Dinitz (1980) notes that even wardens have changed dramatically in the past twenty years. Wardens were once full-fledged autocrats endowed with unlimited power and authority over all persons—guards and prisoners—in their territories. Riots or spectacular escapes might topple them, but wardens were generally accountable only to the governor of a state (who was usually interested in other things). Wise wardens mixed terror, incentives, and favoritism to keep their charges fearful but not desperate, hopeful but always uncertain. Their absolute power extended to the guards, who were dependent upon their favor for employment security and advancement. An experienced warden kept some power in reserve, never depending on intimidation alone, and he or she usually atomized the prison community. Groups were never permitted, and silence systems were used to assure that prisoner solidarity did not develop.

After the silence rule went out of fashion, wardens used intelligence systems to maintain control. Stool pigeons were everywhere, and no one could trust anyone else. When uprisings occurred, the warden (or a successor) could regain control by finding and punishing ring leaders. This unregulated authority often led to grotesque abuses of power and privilege by wardens, captains, and con bosses. When a warden boasted that he or she was represented wherever any three prisoners gathered in the prison, the claim was not an exaggeration. A warden had to know how to gather information and use it to achieve the desired degree of atomization (Barak 1978).

After World War II, the centralization of power in the bureaucracy of state prison systems reduced wardens to field managers and made them accountable to a commission of corrections in the state capitol. Through such commissions, wardens were accountable to the governor and the legislature. Many positive results have come from this shift in authority, but there have also been negative consequences. Violence has increased, contraband comes in freely in some prisons, and authorities are often impotent to act.

RESTORING LEGITIMATE CONTROL

Conrad offers six principles of action and three principles of avoidance that can be used to return control now held by gangs to prison authorities (1979, pp. 141–45).[6] The principles of action are to increase work and activity, to increase staff, to reduce unit size, to develop an intelligence system, to encourage a lawful community and to increase program participation by minority group leaders. The principles of avoidance are to avoid recognition of gang leaders, to keep power away from gang members, and to prevent the introduction of contraband.

Increase Work and Activity

Because it serves to relieve boredom and inactivity, the slum gang thrives on unemployment. One participant in a slum gang in Glasgow, (Scotland) reports this experience:

> Life with the gang was not all violence, sex, and petty delinquency. Far from it. One of the foremost sensations that remains with me is the feeling of unending boredom, of crushing tedium, of listening hour after hour to desultory conversation and indiscriminate grumbling. Standing with one's back against the wall, with one's hands in one's pockets . . . was the gang activity. . . . (Patrick 1973, p. 8).

The prison gangster standing with back against a wall and hands in pockets—and sharing complaints with comrades—becomes committed to the gang. The gang promised relief: Narcotics may be on the way, or there may be a punk to rape or a score to settle with a rival gang. The prison provides the basic necessities for survival, but the gang offers life. (Part of this life is the business of waiting; authorities should not mistake the waiting for tranquility.) Full employment in prison will not solve the problem, but without meaningful work and activity, it is inconceivable that gangs will ever be reduced in influence and number.

Increase Staff

The prevailing style at maximum security facilities is to pair off guards so that one can protect the other. This system is necessary, given the hazardous conditions in these prisons, but staff working in pairs have little contact with prisoners. They will see and be seen, but they will be impersonal in their communications. Two officers patrolling together can cover less of a cell block or an activity than can two officers patrolling separately. Correctional officers cannot be everywhere, but the more they get around the more likely it is that violence will be prevented or minimized.

Reduce Unit Size

By their nature, large prisons are limited to reactive control. There are places that must be prepared for the worst—because the worst is certain to happen. Neither correctional officers nor prisoners can know each other or initiate activities to relieve hostilities. Unfortunately, smaller prisons can be terrible places, too: some of the worst prisons are relatively small. The key to preventing violence is to provide units of no more than thirty inmates (and preferably less). This measure can be used in both small and large prisons.

Develop an Intelligence System

It is unlikely that informants can be found to infiltrate prison gangs, and it is not recommended that efforts be made to do so. However, this does not mean that prison officials can or should give up trying to find out what is going on. The patrol guard is around not only to see and be seen, but also to hear and be heard. An officer trained to interact informally but significantly with prisoners will eventually be entrusted with information that can be used for control. This will probably not happen if officers are always in pairs, but it can happen if an officer is in regular contact with a small unit. A decent person who is seen every day and understood by those he works with may become a confidant of some inmates and will at least be respected by most inmates in his charge.

Encourage a Lawful Community

A prison should be lawful, and all persons working in a prison should enforce the law. All violations must be investigated and prosecuted. The unwillingness of district attorneys to add to their work loads, and the reluctance of criminal investigators to engage in the unrewarding work of crime detection in the prison yard, must give way to a rigorous policy of law enforcement. Prisons will become less dangerous only if the consequences of law violations are clear. Wrongdoing must have adverse consequences wherever it occurs, especially in prison. All available resources should be used to increase the effectiveness of investigations and prosecutions. Statutes that set the penalties for felonies committed in prison should be harsh. Incentives to prisoners who supply information leading to convictions must be administered carefully to ensure the safety of the informants.

Increase Program Participation by Minority Leaders

Gang leaders still use the rhetoric of the civil rights movement and the language of the political prisoner. Thus, organizations such as the National Association for the Advancement of Colored People, the Urban League, and the United Farm Workers should be actively encouraged as alternatives to gang activity. It is doubtful that the "hard core" would participate in such groups, but many minority inmates might be drawn in by legitimate minority leadership.

A national prisoners' union has also been suggested as a way to offset the power of gangs. However, the introduction of a union would only complicate the problem. The role of the union would be uncertain, its leaders would be inexperienced, and gangs might even gain control.

Avoid Recognition of Gang Leaders

Prison administrators should never negotiate with gang leaders or make concessions to them. Gang leaders cannot be co-opted, and any attempt to establish a laissez-faire policy toward them is doomed to failure. Gang leaders should not be arrested or held on mere suspicion, but they should be punished when they violate prison rules. In addition, gang insignias should be confiscated, gang meetings should be forbidden, communications should be carefully controlled, and all mail to and from active gang members should be censored.

By necessity, prison management will have to have some contact with gang leaders. These contacts may be unwitting, because the identity of leaders is not always known. However, it a council of prisoners is assembled for management purposes, gang leaders will probably be present. But such a council should not be a forum for negotiations on gang terms. Rather, it should be an occasion for the articulation of community relations acceptable to management.

Keep Power Away from the Gangs

Prison officials must be careful not to assign any advantages to gang members. Rather, it should be made clear that unaffiliated prisoners are favored. Known gang members should not be assigned to privileged jobs, and reports of intimidation should receive intensive investigation. Anyone making threats should be placed under strict control.

Prevent the Introduction of Contraband

The importation of narcotics and other contraband into a prison is undesirable—even without considering the fact that contraband assures the power of gangs. Gang life depends, in part, upon contraband rewards. Current efforts to keep forbidden articles out of the prison should be reviewed to determine their effectiveness. Prosecution of anyone engaged in contraband traffic should be swift, and conviction should automatically bring a prison term. A prison in which narcotics traffic flourishes is a prison with tenuous official control. Gangs have management about where they want it to be—in a condition of relative impotence.

AIDS IN PRISONS

Acquired immunodeficiency syndrome (AIDS) has rapidly become one of the most difficult and complex public health issues facing the United States. The rapid increase in cases, particularly in the past six years, and the continued uncertainties as to the future spread of the disease led former President Reagan to call AIDS "the nation's number one health priority."

In the correctional context, dealing with the problem of AIDS may pose even more difficult problems since inmate populations may include high proportions of individuals in AIDS risk groups, particularly intravenous drug users. Correctional administrators must formulate policies that allow them to manage their institutions effectively, while dealing with a serious health problem that may cause fears among staff and inmates. Administrators face difficult decisions concerning prevention, housing, and the provision of medical care, decisions that are frequently complicated by legal and cost issues (Hammett 1986).[7]

AIDS is a serious communicable disease that undermines the human body's ability to combat infections. In 1983 and 1984, the probable cause of AIDS—variously called human t-cell lymphotropic virus type III (HTLV-III) and lymphadenopathy-associated virus (LAV)—was identified. Thus far, most cases in the United States have been among homosexuals and intravenous drug abusers, with cases primarily concentrated in large metropolitan areas on the East and West coasts.

End-stage AIDS is almost always fatal. However, a range of milder forms of illness, sometimes called AIDS-related complex (ARC), may also appear among those infected with the AIDS virus.

Infection with HTLV-III is transmitted through contaminated blood and semen, primarily during sexual activity and needle sharing related to intravenous drug abuse. The virus is difficult to transmit, and there is absolutely no evidence of its transmission through casual contact, such as coughing, hugging, handshaking, sharing eating and drinking utensils, or using the same toilet facilities.

In 1985, a test was developed and made widely available to detect the presence of antibodies (evidence of the body's attempt to fight off an infection) to HTLV-III. Although the test does not detect the presence of the virus itself, seropositivity (i.e., the presence of antibodies) means that an individual has been infected with the AIDS virus at some time, although the body may have subsequently fought off the infection.

The likelihood that HTLV-III seropositivity means current infection with the virus is considered much greater for individuals in identified AIDS risk groups (e.g., homosexual or bisexual males, intravenous drug abusers). Nevertheless, seropositive individuals may never develop any symptoms, let alone develop end-stage AIDS.

Currently, the Centers for Disease Control (CDC) estimate that 5 to 6 percent of seropositive individuals will develop end-stage AIDS while another 25 percent will develop ARC. However, recent research suggests that the percentage of seropositive individuals who will develop AIDS may be somewhat higher. Moreover, CDC cautions that seropositive individuals may be able to transmit the infection to others, even if they never develop symptoms themselves. Table 15.1 summarizes the relationships among exposure, infection, seropositivity, ARC, and AIDS.

Aids in the Correctional Population

Since 1981, there has been a cumulative total of 455 confirmed AIDS cases in twenty-five state and federal prison systems. Twenty large city and county jail systems reported 311 cases of AIDS among inmates. These figures represent cumulative total cases since the responding jurisdictions began keeping records.

As of the period November 1985 to January 1986, there were 144 cases of AIDS among state and federal inmates in nineteen systems and 35 cases among city and county inmates in eleven systems.

No known AIDS cases have occurred among correctional staff as a result of contact with inmates. The vast majority of correctional AIDS cases, particularly in jurisdictions with large numbers of cases, are believed to be associated with prior intravenous drug abuse. There is substantial debate, but little hard data, on the extent to which the AIDS virus is being transmitted within correctional institutions. The two primary means of transmission are prohibited behavior in all corrections systems. However, logic and common sense suggest that, even in the best-managed correctional facilities, there may be at least some transmission of the infection occurring among inmates.

Correctional Policy Issues and Options

The major policy areas involved in the correctional response to AIDS are education and training; HTLV-III antibody testing; and medical, legal, and correctional management issues.

TABLE 15.1
Relationships among Exposure, Infection, HTLV-III Seropositivity, and Development of ARC or AIDS

Stage	Meaning	Relationship to Previous Stage(s)
Exposure	Individual has contact with HTLV-III in a way that makes transmission possible (e.g., sexual contact or needle-sharing activity)	—
Infection	Individual is infected with HTLV-III. Infection may be permanent or body may successfully combat the virus.	Unknown, although multiple exposures probably increase the risk of infection.
Seropositivity	Individual has antibodies to HTLV-III. Infection has occurred at some time in the past, but date of infection or whether individual remains infected cannot be determined.	CDC considers the HTLV-III antibody test a reliable indicator that infection has occurred at some time. Repeat and confirmatory testing increase reliability.
ARC	A combination of conditions that together give evidence of infection with AIDS virus.	About 25 percent of seropositive individuals will probably develop ARC (CDC estimate). This estimate is uncertain due to the lengthy incubation period.
AIDS	Illness characterized by one or more opportunistic infections at least moderately indicative of underlying cellular immunodeficiency.	About 5 to 6 percent of seropositive individuals will probably develop AIDS. (CDC estimate). Recent studies place the fraction as high as one-third. Again, all estimates are uncertain due to the lengthy incubation period.

Adapted from Theodore M. Hammett, *AIDS in Prisons and Jails: Issues and Options* (Washington, D.C.: U.S. Department of Justice, National Institute of Justice, February 1986), p. 2.

EDUCATION AND TRAINING Because there is no vaccine or cure for the disease, education and training programs are the cornerstone of efforts to curb the spread of AIDS in prisons and jails as well as in the population at large. Education and training programs also provide the opportunity to counteract misinformation, rumors, and fear concerning the disease. For example, the majority of systems responding to a questionnaire reported that inmates and staff worried about the possibility of contacting AIDS; many responses referred to fear of casual contact or types of contact not actually associated with transmission of the virus.

As a result, many correctional administrators feel strongly that education and training are not options but absolute requirements. Ninety-three percent of the responding jurisdictions currently offer or are developing AIDS educational programs for staff; 83 percent offer or are developing such programs for inmates.

Among respondents whose educational programs have operated for some time, the vast majority believe these programs to be effective in reducing the fears of staff and inmates. Several jurisdictions reported that timely educational efforts had successfully averted threatened job actions by correctional staff unions.

Experience suggests that training and education programs should be instituted before deep-seated fears have developed, and should be repeated periodically so that the latest medical information can be presented and new staff and inmates can be reached on a timely basis.

Effective education programs may include live presentations by training teams, printed materials, and videotapes. Program curricula and materials should be brief, clear, and straight forward and tailored to the particular knowledge gaps and concerns of the audience. They should discuss the means of transmission of the AIDS virus and emphasize everyone's responsibility to avoid behaviors known to be associated with transmission. They should also guard against encouraging a false sense of security in any group. At the same time, programs should not create needless fear by advocating unnecessary precautionary measures.

HTLV-III ANTIBODY TESTING There is substantial debate, both in corrections and in society at large, surrounding the uses of the HTLV-III antibody test and the meaning of the test results. The most controversial testing application in corrections is mass screening: the testing of all inmates or all new inmates, regardless of the presence of symptoms or other clinical indications.

MASS SCREENING: THE DEBATE The debate over mass screening for antibodies to HTLV-III in correctional institutions involves the following major questions:

- *Should correctional systems take steps not being taken in the community at large?* Proponents of testing argue that rates of HTLV-III seropositivity are higher among inmates and that the virus is likely to be transmitted within institutions; they believe that screening is necessary to identify infectious individuals and to target prevention programs.

  Opponents argue that there is no proof of higher rates of HTLV-III transmission in prison and therefore there is no legitimate reason to screen.
- *What are the policy implications of identifying seropositive individuals?* Proponents of screening argue that seropositive individuals must be identified so they can be given special supervision, counseling, and other programs.

  Opponents argue that mass identification of seropositives would serve no purposes not better addressed by educational programs and would, in fact, create significant correctional management problems—particularly if large numbers of seropositives were identified and there was irresistible pressure to segregate them.
- *How would mass screening affect education and prevention programs?* Proponents argue that screening is necessary to inform and target education and prevention programs.

  Opponents argue that screening needlessly and misleadingly divides the inmate population into a stigmatized class and a "safe" class, thereby undermining the important educational message that everyone should be careful.
- *Is it possible to develop a reliable and confidential screening program?* Proponents argue that the antibody test is reliable and that confidentiality of results can be maintained.

  Opponents argue that the test results are often unreliable and that real and rumored results would inevitably become known to the inmate population and others outside the institution, potentially subjecting actual or supposed seropositives to threats and intimidation while in prison and to discrimination in housing, employment, and insurability after discharge.
- *What are the legal implications of screening?* Proponents argue that mass screening is legal and proper and, in fact, that failure to conduct mass

screening may result in serious legal liabilities.

Opponents point out that laws and policies requiring subjects' informed consent for HTLV-III antibody testing preclude mandatory mass screening and suggest that liability issues can be effectively managed.

- *What are the costs of mass screening?* Proponents of screening argue that the test can be economically administered.

  Opponents argue that when the costs of repeat and confirmatory tests and the costs of separate correctional programming for seropositives are included, the total price could become prohibitive, particularly for large systems and/or those likely to identify large numbers of seropositive inmates.
- *Will mass screening allay or inflame fears?* Proponents argue that screening could help to calm the concerns of inmates and staff if it found low rates of seropositivity. Moreover, regardless of the seropositivity rates, failure to screen could cause serious public relations problems.

  Opponents argue that mass screening will needlessly inflame fears, particularly if the seropositivity rate is found to be high.
- *Are there feasible alternatives to screening?* Proponents argue that screening is the best method of obtaining the necessary information on HTLV-III seropositivity and transmission.

  Opponents argue that there are better ways to identify high-risk individuals and diagnose AIDS and ARC that avoid the negative consequences of mass screening. These include astute medical surveillance and alternative laboratory work for diagnoses. In addition, anonymous epidemiological studies may permit estimation of HTLV-III seropositivity and transmission rates while avoiding the correctional management and confidentiality problems of mass screening.

Implementation Issues. Correctional administrators who decide to implement any mass or selective testing program face a range of issues, including when and where to administer the test, and whether testing should be voluntary, mandatory, or on request.

Those who oppose mandatory testing argue that, because of the potentially serious negative effects of testing (e.g., discrimination in housing, employment, insurability), medical ethics require that there be a right of refusal, regardless of law or policy.

Some also argue that correctional systems have an obligation to provide the test to any or all inmates who request it. However, if such testing is provided, many physicians believe that inmates should be fully and accurately informed of the potential personal and psychological effects of testing before they make any decisions and that those who are tested be counseled on the meaning and implications of the results.

MEDICAL, LEGAL, AND CORRECTIONAL MANAGEMENT ISSUES Correctional administrators responding to the challenging problem of AIDS in prisons and jails must balance medical considerations and medical advice against complex correctional management factors. Decision-making is further complicated by legal and cost concerns. The following sections discuss these issues.

Medical Issues. Perhaps the highest priority in the correctional response to AIDS is providing timely, professional, and compassionate medical care to inmates who become ill with the disease. As in society at large, prompt detection and diagnosis are needed to minimize spread of the disease and alleviate the suffering of patients.

Whether HTLV-III testing is used or not, appropriate diagnostic workups are necessary to identify immunosuppression, ARC, and AIDS. Also, certain tests may be able to detect early evidence of opportunistic infections typically seen in AIDS patients.

Careful surveillance and regular follow-up are extremely important for patients with AIDS, ARC, and HTLV-III seropositivity, since life-threatening symptoms can develop very quickly. Because AIDS patients experience serious psychological as well as physical problems, counseling and support systems involving correctional staff and family members are also considered important components of care.

Correctional Management Issues. Ironically, the medical treatment of AIDS patients may be the simplest issue confronting correctional administrators. Other questions—where to house and treat the inmate, how to prevent the spread of the disease, and how to pay for medical care—are likely to be even more difficult to resolve.

Housing Policies. One of the most critical and difficult decisions for correctional administrators is where to house and treat inmates with AIDS, ARC, or HTLV-III seropositivity. Of course, medical considerations dictate many of these decisions. Most jurisdictions place inmates with confirmed diagnoses of AIDS in a medical facility either within the correctional system or in the community, although the duration of such hospitalization varies considerably.

Preventing the spread of AIDS within the prison and protecting affected inmates from intimidation and violence are important considerations. Other factors in treatment and housing decisions include availability and location of facilities able to provide appropriate care, costs of any new construction or renovations necessary to prepare special units, and staffing of any special AIDS units (correctional as well as medical).

Correctional administrators have a number of options concerning treatment and housing placements for inmates with AIDS, ARC, or HTLV-III seropositivity. The key options are the following:

1. Maintaining inmates in the general population.
2. Returning inmates to the general population when their illnesses are in remission.
3. Administratively segregating inmates in a separate unit or relying on single-cell housing.
4. Hospitalization.
5. Case-by-case determination of all housing and treatment decision.

Most jurisdictions hospitalize or administratively segregate at least some of the three AIDS-related inmate categories.

The four jurisdictions with almost 75 percent of the correctional AIDS cases (New York State, New York City, New Jersey, and Florida) all follow the same combination of policies:

1. Medical segregation of AIDS patients, but no segregation of inmates with ARC or HTLV-III seropositivity.
2. Careful evaluation and ongoing monitoring of inmates suspected of having ARC or AIDS.
3. No mass screening for antibody to HTLV-III.
4. Extensive staff and inmate educational programs.

All four of these systems report that equilibrium has been reached on the AIDS issue, with no widespread fear among staff or inmates regarding transmission of the virus within the institutions.

Precautionary Measures. Correctional agencies have adopted a wide range of precautionary measures to control the spread of AIDS within institutions; many are based on Centers for Disease Control guidelines for clinical staff. The CDC guidelines advise clinical and laboratory staff "to use the same precautions when caring for patients with AIDS as those used for patients with hepatitis-B virus infection." Specifically, patient-care and laboratory personnel should take precautions to avoid direct contact of skin or mucous membranes with blood, blood products, excretions, secretions, and tissues of persons judged likely to have AIDS.

Several physicians interviewed for this study believe that, since the AIDS virus is less hardy and more difficult to transmit than the hepatitis-B virus, precautions designed to prevent transmission of hepatitis-B should more than suffice to prevent transmission of AIDS.

Some correctional agencies have instituted precautionary measures that go far beyond those recommended by the CDC. Many of these measures are designed to limit exposure under extremely unusual circumstances or to prevent exposure through causal contact. However, all evidence indicates that AIDS cannot be transmitted by a single exposure of any kind or through casual contact. This is a major theme in most AIDS education programs.

Precautionary measures addressing very rare or casual modes of contact, even if implemented in a good faith effort to reduce the fears of staff and inmates, may ultimately increase those fears by encouraging the view that the disease is spread by the very sort of unusual or casual contacts they seek to prevent. Such a conflict between educational messages and practical measures may not only increase fear within the institution, but also may foster suspicion of the correctional system for, in effect, saying one thing about the transmission of AIDS but doing something else.

Costs of Care and Associated Services. Medical care for AIDS patients is extremely expensive, whether it is provided in a correctional medical facility, in another public medical facility, or in a hospital in the community, particularly because correctional inmates are ineligible for Medicaid reimbursement.

Correctional systems should plan on spending anywhere from $40,000 to over $600,000 for hospitalization and associated medical costs of caring for each inmate with AIDS.[8] The costs will vary depending on the amount of acute care required; they will also probably be higher if inmates are placed in hospitals in the community than if they are retained in correctional medical facilities or other public medical facilities.

To the figures for hospitalization and medical care must be added costs of ancillary services such as counseling, possible legal assistance, increased insurance (unless the system is self-insured), and funerals. Obviously, medical care and associated services for inmates with AIDS could have serious budgetary implications for correctional systems.

Legal Issues. There is currently very little law specifically on correctional systems' policies regarding AIDS cases, though several cases have been filed in New York and other states. Otherwise, specific AIDS-related legal concerns remain largely hypothetical. Still, there is substantial case law on correctional medical care in general, which is important for administrators to consider in developing policies regarding AIDS.

Suits on the quality of correctional medical care may be brought on the basis of federal constitutional standards, state law, or common law.[9] There are three constitutional principles relevant to correctional medical care.

First, under the Eighth Amendment, inmates are entitled to a safe, decent, and humane environment.[10] Second, in *Estelle* v. *Gamble* (429 U.S. 97 [1976]), "deliberate indifference to serious medical need" was held to violate the Eighth Amendment protection against "cruel and unusual punishment." Finally, the constitutional guarantee of "equal protection of the laws" applies to correctional medical care cases, and particularly to cases involving AIDS inmates, because of the segregation issues.

Medical care in correctional institutions is usually governed by the same state laws (e.g., medical practice and nursing practice acts) that apply to care in the community at large. Finally, in some states, correctional medical care may be subject to suits for common law torts such as negligence. Medical malpractice suits are also a possibility.

Existing caselaw on AIDS in correctional facilities falls into the following three major categories:

1. *Equal protection.* Cases filed by inmates alleging denial of equal protection based solely on the fact that they had AIDS (e.g., *Cordero* v. *Coughlin* [607 F.Supp. 9 (S.D.N.Y. 1984)]). This case was decided in favor of the correctional department.
2. *Quality of care.* Cases filed by inmates alleging inadequacies in medical care and associated services (e.g., *Storms* v. *Coughlin).*[11]
3. *Failure to protect others from AIDS.* Cases filed by inmates and potentially also by staff alleging inadequate protective measures and seeking additional steps such as mass screening of inmates and segregation of inmates with AIDS, ARC, or HTLV-III seropositivity (e.g., *Mtr La Rocca* v. *Dalsheim* [120 MISC 2d 697 (N.Y. 1983)]).[12] The La Rocca case was decided in favor of the correctional department; other cases on these issues are still pending.

AIDS poses complex and difficult problems for correctional systems. The only certainty is that the problems will not disappear. Every correctional system should develop comprehensive policies and procedures for managing the AIDS problem in its institutions.

SUMMARY

The social, political, and racial forces within America's largest and most dangerous prisons have changed dramatically in the past two decades. The inmate social system and codes of conduct described by Sykes and Messinger (1960) are no longer accurate. A new type of inmate has entered prisons in large numbers since the 1960s, and many political changes have occurred in society since that time.

One of the most significant changes in prison life has been the emergence of gangs. These gangs are generally divided among blacks, whites, and Chicanos. Black gangs emerged in the 1950s as an outgrowth of the civil rights and black movements outside of prisons. White gangs developed largely as a result of violence directed against them by black and Chicano gangs. Chicano gangs were an extension of street gangs operating in the cities and towns of California and Texas; hostilities that existed between these groups on the streets carried over into prison. At one point, the attacks and counterattacks between gangs in California prisons were so frequent that authorities segregated gangs by assigning them to different prisons. Gang affiliation is frequently viewed by inmates as necessary and desirable—necessary for personal safety and desirable because of services provided by the gangs.

Prison management has also changed since the 1960s. People concerned with treatment have come into the system and have been vocal about antitherapeutic or capricious decisions made by administrators. Under strict administrative control, custodial workers felt inadequate, demeaned, and powerless in their jobs, and their decisions were constantly scrutinized by lawyers, prison masters, and others. As a result, officers and guards often dropped out at a very high rate. Recently, however, prison workers have joined labor unions and pressed their claims through collective bargaining. Dinitz (1980) points out that even wardens have not escaped the changes of prison management. They once enjoyed almost limitless power within the walls, but such power has all but disappeared. State bureaucracies have reduced wardens to field managers and made them accountable to legislatures and governors.

Conrad (1979) recommends six principles of action and three principles of avoidance to restore legitimate control in prisons. The principles of action are to increase work and activity for inmates, to increase staff, to reduce unit size in prisons, to develop an intelligence system, to encourage a lawful community, and to increase program participation by minority group leaders. The principles of avoidance are to avoid the recognition of gang leaders, to keep power away from gang members, and to prevent the introduction of contraband into the prison.

Acquired immunodeficiency syndrome (AIDS) has rapidly become one of the most difficult and complex public health issues facing the United States. In the correctional context, dealing with the problem of AIDS may pose even more difficult problems since inmate populations may include high proportions of individuals in AIDS risk groups, particularly intravenous drug users. Correctional administrators must formulate policies that allow them to manage their institutions effectively, while dealing with a serious health problem that may cause fears among staff and inmates. Administrators face difficult decisions concerning prevention, housing, and the provision of medical care, decisions that are frequently complicated by legal and cost issues.

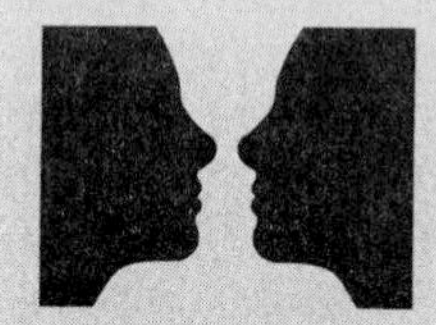

ISSUE PAPER

THE SOCIALIZATION OF MALE AND FEMALE CORRECTIONAL OFFICERS

In the first edition of this book, we focused entirely on the socialization process of male correctional officers. Since that time, there has been a dramatic increase in the use of female correctional officers in all-male correctional facilities. Thus, in this issue paper, we felt that it would be useful and informative to examine the historical, political, and social forces that led up to this change. In addition, we will examine the reactions of both inmates and male correctional officers to this change as well as the ways in which female correctional officers are coping with and adapting to their new working environment.

Staff Culture and the Socialization of Correctional Officers

Even before they finish their first day on the job, new correctional officers are exposed to influences that play an important part in their role conceptions and job orientations. Just as new inmates shape their attitudes and behavior as a consequence of exposure to the convict culture, officer recruits are indoctrinated into the staff culture of the prison by means of their relationships with veteran officers. These veteran guards are the recruit's most important reference group. According to Crouch and Marquart, veterans physically back up the recruit, offer advice and reinforcement, and communicate the values of the guard subculture. They tell the new officer what is expected in three areas: how to perceive inmates, how to anticipate trouble, and how to manage inmates (1980, p. 79). In many prisons, the staff culture depicts convicts as lazy, morally deficient individuals who freely chose crime as a way of life.

The most important message the new officer receives, both from formal training and from veteran guards, is that prisoners must always be controlled and dominated—by words and by behavior. Through observation and imitation of experienced guards, the new officer learns informal strategies for maintaining order and control—such as maintaining social distance from inmates, using profanity and bluster, saying no to inmate requests, and keeping prisoners "off balance." The latter can be done by staring at an inmate, thus keeping him or her wondering what the officer is thinking.

Crouch and Marquart have identified what they refer to as "the several tenets of subcultural wisdom that define acceptable guard behavior" (1980, p. 89). These aspects of the guard role are gradually revealed to the new correctional officer through advice from fellow officers and encounters with inmates. The first of the tenets is that security and control are paramount. Anything that threatens the custodial routine—visits from volunteers, sports figures, or evangelists, or the presence of treatment personnel—should be viewed with suspicion and hostility.

A second tenet is that officers must maintain social distance from prisoners. Recruits are told about officers who made the mistake of trusting inmates and ended up getting "burned." The third tenet is that guards must be tough, knowledgeable, and able to handle prisoners. Veteran guards stress the importance of being authoritative with inmates—even to the extent of using profanity and obscenity when addressing them.

The prison lore transmitted to the new officer—often by a veteran guard (sometimes referred to as a "maggot stomper")—largely consists of stories that emphasize the brutality, depravity, bestiality, or stupidity of convicts. Thus, the recruit hears about the four prisoners who "got loaded" on raisin jack and killed and sodomized the body of a fellow inmate; about the "queen" (male prostitute) who tried to perform a sex-change operation on himself with a razor blade and bled to death; about the inmate who inserted a cola bottle in his rectum and required an emergency operation to remove it; and about the inmate currently in "the hole" (solitary confinement) for knifing a guard with a homemade shank. These stories heighten feelings of solidarity among correctional officers by emphasizing or exaggerating the negative characteristics of convicts.

Learning to anticipate trouble—escapes, attempted escapes, riots, hostage seizures, drug use, or use of homemade intoxicants—is a skill that can take a long time to acquire. Experienced correctional officers, like veteran police officers, insist that the necessary savvy comes only from exposure to inmates and sensitivity to subtle cues. Informal discussions among guards—similar in form and content to "choir practice" among street cops—offer opportunities to share experiences, swap insights and observations, and sharpen the awareness of the new officer. In addition, officers must become familiar with both the formal and informal rules that guide institutional life. They must be able to spot any deviation from the rules, regardless of how well the deviation might be disguised.

Relations with Inmates The most important aspect of prison life for the correctional officer is his or her relationships with prisoners. As already mentioned, recruits are subject to influences from veteran officers and staff culture that stress dominance and authority. In practice, this influence translates not into the development of the hard-nosed, bull-headed James Cagney stereotype, but into an officer who can be described as "firm but fair."

Unlike the police, whose first-hand contacts with crime victims tend to "bring home" society's quarrel with a criminal, correctional officers see criminals under circumstances where they are likely to be perceived as sick, inadequate, stupid, or degenerate. Although the staff culture depicts the inmate population in such terms, exceptions are made in individual cases. "Good" inmates differ from "bad" inmates not on the basis of their instant offense or previous record but on their willingness to conform to authority. The attitude of one correctional officer on Florida's death row is rather typical:

> I don't know anything about what they did that brought them here. And I don't want to know. That might change the way I deal with them. As far as I'm concerned, if they do what they're told and obey the rules, they get a fair shake from me. The ones that make my job tough are the smart asses, the troublemakers. The ones that are always trying to do a number on you. Those are the sons of bitches you have to step on—hard (Personal conversation).

The ultimate show of officer authority was once apt to be a taste of corporal punishment—a rap along side the head. This treatment was often carried out in the privacy of a cell or in a segregation wing. Is such abuse still a problem in American prisons? Do reported beatings or other abuses represent institutional policy, or are they individual acts of brutality?

According to May (1976), overt guard violence is extremely rare. One of the nation's senior prison ombudsmen, Theartrice Williams of Minnesota, investigated about forty-five hundred inmate complaints over a four-year period and found that fewer than six complaints involved correctional officer violence. Similarly, Connecticut's prison ombudsman, James T. Bookwalter, found only a handful of charges of correctional officer brutality in more than one thousand complaints handled over three years. Bookwalter doubts that inmates are taken out and deliberately worked over in today's prisons, but excessive force may sometimes be used: "When there is a physical conflict between an inmate and an officer and force is required to bring an inmate under control, the inmates believe that the officer gets in a few extra licks" (May 1976, p. 40).

The Outcome of Officer Socialization Whatever they bring to the job in the way of personality characteristics, attitudes, and values, officer recruits undergo changes in attitude and behavior once they are on the job. One type of change involves *role conflict,* which is common among recruits who enter maximum security prisons with aspirations of helping prisoners. Rookies discover that inmates regard such aspirations as a sign of weakness, and they are quick to exploit the attitude to their own advantage. Recruits are also frustrated by their inability to operate effectively within the paramilitary structure of the prison system. As a result, new officers either quit and look for a different line of work or they reevaluate their original aspirations in light of the reality of prison life. If they stick it out, recruits are subject to the kind of cynicism that Niederhoffer (1967) identifies as an occupational disease among police officers.

Another useful concept from the study of police officers that can help us to understand the socialization of the correctional officer is the *working personality,* a configuration of attitudes and behaviors that result from learning the police role (Skolnick 1966). As an occupational group, police officers perceive and respond to their work based on two variables—danger and authority. According to Skolnick, "the element of danger isolates the policeman socially from that segment of the citizenry which he regards as symbolically dangerous and also from the conventional citizenry with whom he identifies" (1966, p. 44). Required continually to assert their authority, police officers develop a heightened alertness to potential threats and dangers; thus, they become suspicious persons, always on the lookout for violence and lawbreaking. The same is true of correctional officers.

Prison Guard: Slain Officer Knew the Uniform Wouldn't Save Him from Dangers in "Pretty Sick Environment"

Jon East St. Petersburg (Florida) *Evening Independent*

Steve Dennard, a Union Correctional Institution guard stabbed to death by inmates last week, told of the dangers he faced when interviewed by the St. Petersburg Evening Independent *earlier this year. Here is a condensed version of a March 15 profile of Dennard, who was buried Monday in Jacksonville.*

When Steve Dennard does a good job, the people with whom he works would rather break his hand than shake it.

Dennard is a correctional officer at Union Correctional Institution in Raiford. And his daily companions are some of the most hardened criminals in Florida.

For the past three of his five years at Union, Dennard has been a member of the Inside Security Squad. For officers, it's a position of prestige. The squad members roam the institution each day, acting as trouble shooters. For the inmates, though, the squad represents trouble. To them, it's the "Goon Squad," and the officers on it are targets.

Dennard knows it, too. He knows if he turns his back at the wrong moment, someone is liable to insert a handsculpted dagger into it.

"Okay, let's see the passes. Yeah, that means you. Get over here."

The three men, all in their 20s, stop. One turns his back and shakes his head in disgust. Dennard finds out none is in the proper assigned work area.

"Where are you supposed to be?" he asks.

"The Man sent me to the library," one responds. "He said it was okay."

"That ain't what this says. You know he's supposed to give you a pass."

"Aw, come on, man. Why you want to give me s—?"

"You looking to sleep in the Cage (solitary confinement) tonight? You'd better get all of your a— the hell out of here and back to where you supposed to be. I don't want to see you around here again."

The three walk away, talking to each other as they do. Dennard turns to a companion for the day.

"I guess that sounds kind of harsh to you," he says. "(But) you've got to be that way. When I'm on the yard I will act just as crazy as I need to be. They respect that. They know just how far they can push you."

He pauses, thinking about what he has described. "That sound perverse, don't it? Maybe it is . . . This is a pretty sick environment in here."

Dennard went looking for a job as a correctional officer five years ago, when he found he could get paid tuition for college courses. Since then, he has lived in an environment far different from the academic world. The students on his campus all try to cut class, and he is the teacher they have been trained to hate the most.

To survive in that setting, Dennard, 29, 6 feet tall, 200 pounds, must prove himself. The uniform does not earn respect. His actions must. So Dennard says he is tough with inmates.

He also tries to be fair and reasonable. He could spend his entire day writing disciplinary reports (called DRs) if he wanted to trap every inmate on every infraction. Instead he tries to head off the major problems and help the inmates who are simply trying to do their time and get out.

"I feel like you've got a responsibility to the inmate," he says. "They'll respect you if they know you're tough—as long as you're fair."

Dennard is involved in calming some disturbance nearly every day. That sometimes means approaching two inmates battling with knives and trying to stop them without having a weapon himself. Dennard and the other guards are not even allowed to carry nightsticks.

But after five years, most of his fears have subsided. Most of them—but not all.

"It's not the loud ones . . . They're not the ones that bother me. They're just talk. It's the one who's just sitting there not saying anything. He's the one who scares me."

Like most correctional officers, Dennard is shouted at, hit, and abused almost daily. He sometimes wonders what he's supposed to do about it. He threatens many inmates with the Cage. But some laugh, because they know they still get three good meals there and don't have to work. For some, its even a status symbol.

Dennard himself knows inmates won't stay in the disciplinary confinement cells for more than a few days because overcrowding means they must make way for more discipline problems.

So Dennard just exercises self-control. His fortitude is sometimes tested to its limit.

"Okay, let's say you've got a guy in the Cage and you know you've got to go back there and check every hour. So, the first time you go back there, he spits on you. What do you do? Do you write a DR? He's already in the Cage. That's the worst you can do to the man. So, maybe you wipe if off and walk away. That's professional, right?

"The next time you go back there and he throws a cup of urine on you. So what do you do? Well, maybe you're professional again and you clean yourself up and walk away. So the next time, he's waiting and he throws feces on you. What do you do?

"Let me ask you. What's your limit?"

From the Tampe *Tribune,* 10 May 1983.

The Entry of Women as Corrections Officers*

Women as corrections officers is nothing new. Their early role in this profession reflects their sexual role in society. In the 1800s, women were permitted to guard female inmates. Indiana was the first state to have a women's facility, but before a woman could become an officer, she had to meet some rigid criteria. She had to be virtuous and conduct herself on the job as a lady at all times. She also had to be single and live on the premises. These requirements were deemed necessary because the officer was expected to serve as a role model and provide a home like atmosphere (Pollock 1986).

Despite women's long history in corrections, in the past two decades their roles and status have been challenged in the courts (Pollock 1986; Lombardo 1981). Although women have proved to be successful, they have had to defend themselves against strong male opposition.

The civil rights movement of the 1960s challenged the differential treatment of women and minorities in all professions. Title VII of the Civil Rights Act was the basis for supporting women's rights for mobility within law enforcement agencies. But even in the 1970s women's protection from differential treatment was not evident. Female correctional officers merely searched female visitors and performed administrative duties (Pollock 1986; Jurik 1985). Gradually women's role began to change, and they were assigned posts in the living units of some facilities. Some states, however, for instance, New York, prohibited women in the men's living quarters (Pollock 1986).

The courts played a significant role in helping and restricting women's progress. A significant setback occurred when the U.S. Supreme Court ruled that because of the dangerous conditions at Alabama's maximum security prison, women should be excluded from its workforce. The Court also ordered Alabama to correct the unconstitutional conditions to which inmates were subjected in the maximum security facility (Pollock 1986). A federal district court helped the women's cause by ruling that in Iowa an inmate's privacy rights do not take precedence over a woman's right to promotion. The court ordered the administration to arrange for promotions without compromising inmates' right to privacy (Pollock 1986).

Gains in equal employment opportunity have also presented some problems, specifically, angry male officers and the opposition of administrators. Many male officers are angry because the women who have built up seniority in women's facilities are able to transfer to male prisons and bid for prime positions. They view this as unfair and argue that the women should have to build up their seniority in the same facility before they are allowed to bid for a post (Pollock 1986). Opposition by administrators is evidenced by their unwillingness to assign women to direct contact posts or to let them respond to emergency situations (Zimmer 1986; Pollock 1986).

Younger, more educated male officers, however, appear to be supportive of the women and to view them as an improvement to the prison environment. Perhaps this is related to the general characteristics of the female officers. Jurik (1985) found that women officers tend to be from professional households in urban communities in contrast to the rural, blue-collar upbringing of many male officers. Women officers tend to be better educated overall than the men. More women had bachelor's and master's degrees with specialties in the social sciences whereas the men's degrees tended to be in criminal justice. Women came from jobs unrelated to law enforcement or military service whereas many male officers came from these areas. Hence, the women appeared to be more service oriented and to take a less aggressive approach to supervision.

All areas of prisons had a unique reaction to the hiring of women.

Inmate Reactions Inmates reacted to women officers with mixed emotions. At first there was a kind of amusement, but this soon changed and the concern became, how will it effect me? After an initial period of hostility toward the women, three attitudes developed: neutral, adamantly opposed, and strongly in favor (Zimmer 1986). The inmates who took the neutral stand appeared to believe that one officer was no different from another. The fact that one was female made her no better and no worse than her male counterpart. Those inmates who were adamantly opposed found it humiliating to take orders from a woman. Women as corrections officers appeared to be in direct conflict with these inmates' sense of women's place in society. They perceived the women as being more strict than the male officers. The women, for example, were said to write disciplinary reports on menial infractions, such as an unbuttoned collar. These inmates believed that their rights to privacy were being sacrificed for the women's movement. They complained that it was impossible to take a shower or use the toilet without being watched by the women. Although the inmates claimed they were concerned for their privacy, this did not stop some of them from flashing or masturbating in front of female officers (Zimmer 1986). Peterson (1982) found that the real threat to these inmates was sexual provocation. They saw the women as "teases" rather than as a useful part of the correctional staff. To eliminate this problem, the women wore "unisex" and unrevealing uniforms (Zimmer 1986).

The majority of inmates fell into the strongly-in-favor category. They believed the women were a nice addition to their rough environment. They perceived women officers as more helpful and professional than male officers. These inmates did not see the privacy issue as one of major significance. Instead they made positive adjustments, such as not walking around nude and cleaning up their language. The only disadvantage they reported was the women's inability to protect them in a violent situation. But the inmates considered this insignificant because they realized that not many of the male officers would come to their rescue either. These inmates were concerned for the women's safety and said they would try to control the crazies and troublemakers (Zimmer 1986).

Male Correctional Officers' Reaction The male officers' reaction to women officers took the form of overt opposition. They regarded the women as inferior physically and psychologically. The men believed, for example, that in a crisis, the woman would not respond or would be unable to cope with the situation, which would jeopardize their safety and others in the institution (Pollock 1986; Zimmer 1986; Owen 1985). According to Zimmer (1986), the root of the opposition was male officers' view of the traditional role of women in society. The men saw women officers as becoming less attractive as they became hardened and calloused by the job. Although the basis for acceptance among the male officers was to act like a man, if a woman did, she was openly criticized by both male and female officers. The woman who proved herself to be a "super" officer merely became part of the institution's folklore rather than being accepted as a good officer.

Apparently women in the corrections profession challenges the masculine belief that corrections is a man's job, and men are reluctant to give up this macho ground (Owen 1985). This is a common reaction to women in police work (Horne 1980) and in the military (Segal 1982). Thus, men want to keep these masculine proving grounds as a means of establishing their own maleness (Zimmer 1986). A woman who can do the job has her normality as a woman questioned. She is praised as being masculine, but then becomes the subject of jokes because she is perceived as deviant and abnormal (Zimmer 1986).

Equality in hiring does not ensure equality on the job. Many women found that once they were accepted as officers, the discrimination really began once they were inside the facility. Administrators could not control who came in, but they could determine what training a new recruit would receive or which posts she would be assigned. During the probationary period work assignments for new employees are at the discretion of the supervisor. This period is not governed by the union or grievance procedures; therefore supervisors either put the women in noncontact posts, which some women sought but which male officers viewed as preferential treatment, or gave the women the worst posts in an effort to get them to quit or transfer. Recourse was limited causing the dissatisfied recruits to say nothing, quit, or file a complaint with the Equal Employment Opportunity Commission (EEOC), which would label them as a troublemaker at the beginning of their career (Zimmer 1986). Without protection, the training the women received was not as diverse as their male counterpart.

The union was ineffective in reducing harassment. Although the union is supposed to protect all of its members, it is guided by the majority of its membership—men. Furthermore, the union's purpose is to negotiate with management, not resolve internal strife, but in one study it was found that when management supported the claims of harassment, the union gave its support to the accused (in Zimmer 1986).

Female Correctional Officers' Coping Mechanisms Such opposition and harassment has resulted in several problems for the female officers and the institution. Problems include the coping strategies the women choose, job satisfaction, and physical or psychological illnesses. Without support women build up defense mechanisms and either reject all co-workers or deny that the men really oppose their presence and see the harassment as a form of teasing. These methods of coping help insulate the women from painful personal involvements (Zimmer 1986). Pollock (1986) found that harassment led to significant decreases in job satisfaction, lower career aspirations, and job stress. Harassed women tend to suffer more from physical and psychological illnesses, which contribute to high absenteeism and turnover rates (Zimmer 1986).

Learning to cope with opposition and harassment is a continuing problem, which is compounded by denial of entry into the male officers' subculture. Socialization into the subculture helps cushion the daily frustrations of the officers. Without assimilating the culture, little camaraderie develops, and the female officers find themselves ill prepared to deal with the inmates. Since the academy offers the women no special training to help them deal with the physical and verbal harassment, they must learn to handle it on their own (Zimmer 1986). Therefore, the women develop their own special roles within the institution. These roles include attempting to outdo the men, taking on a mother or little sister role to get preferential treatment from their superiors and co-workers, or using their feminine characteristics to gain inmate compliance (Pollock 1986; Zimmer 1986).

Zimmer (1986) suggested that women's personal style helps them cope with danger, gain inmate confidence, and develop good working relationships. Although men do the same, women must develop defense mechanisms to help them deal with male opposition and testing. It is essential that their role does not conflict with their identity as women. Therefore, role choice is a product of conscious decisions, personality, and predisposition interacting with situational factors within the institution.

Patterns of Adaptation Three patterns of adaptation have been identified: (1) the institutional role, (2) the modified role, and (3) the inventive role (Zimmer 1986). Each pattern has unique qualities for coping with the job pressures as well as problems peculiar to the role.

The woman who chooses the institutional role takes on the characteristics of the "ideal" officer that is portrayed in the academy. She believes that since the administration expects her to perform as a man, she will act like a man. This role is facilitated by being professional and going by the book. By strictly adhering to the organizational policies, she enforces the rules fairly and consistently. She uses a system of rewards and punishments to maintain order. Although she uses the rules successfully, she is not exempt from opposition and harassment from the other officers. Instead, she is viewed as atypical and copes by remaining aloof from her co-workers. As she fights for her own equal rights through law suits and union grievances, she makes inroads for other women to have the same opportunities. However, this is met with opposition from other female officers. Many of the women are happy with a secure job as administrative assistant or other non-contact posts. They see the woman in the institutional role as a troublemaker (Zimmer 1986).

Excluded from socialization into the subculture, she seeks the advice of inmates. This strategy keeps her from seeming incompetent and allows her to learn the rules on her own. By following the rules, she can insulate herself from criticism. An inherent problem within the institutional role, however, is inflexibility in rule enforcement. Without a mechanism for bending or breaking rules, she leaves herself open to criticism by her superiors and fellow officers for not using common sense. Thus, this rule is not effective in solving problems as an officer (Zimmer 1986).

The woman in the modified role realizes her limitations as a woman in terms of her job performance. Therefore, she is content to work any area assigned. Unlike the woman in the institutional role, she insulates herself from harassment by viewing it as teasing and by assuming a dependence on the male officers for protection. The latter believe that women in contact posts jeopardize the security of the facility because they do not have the physical power or the ability to deal with inmates or the administration. The woman in the modified role justifies earning equal pay by viewing her presence in the facility as a necessary contribution to the overall daily functions; she performs such duties as searching women visitors and working posts, such as the control room, that would keep the men from contact posts (Zimmer 1986).

The third method used to adapt is the inventive role. The woman choosing this role uses her femininity to her advantage. To compensate for her inability to compete physically with men, she uses understanding, persuasion, and manipulation to gain inmate compliance. Inmates appear to have a positive reaction to this woman. This is evidenced by their refraining from vulgar language in her presence and protecting her from troublemakers by controlling them. Her relationship with the inmates serves to undermine working relationships with fellow officers. Other officers become hostile because they believe close relationships with inmates facilitate officer corruption, which will ultimately damage the facility's security (Zimmer 1986).

Women must learn to adapt to the male-dominated prison by developing unique methods to cope with the consequences of sexual harassment and opposition by co-workers, administration, and inmates. The problems inherent in the job are a negative environment, adjustment difficulties, and inadequate training. The negative environment and inadequate training result from the friction created by women intruding into a male world. Adjustment difficulties arise due to the polarity of being a woman and a corrections officer. However, none of the roles described here fully insulates women from problems. The institutional role fails because it allows no flexibility. The woman in the modified role has no room for growth in her job because of limited inmate contact and job responsibilities. The inventive role is not successful because it lends itself to dependence upon inmates for assistance and support, which may undermine security (Zimmer 1986).

After almost two decades of Title VII's mandate to provide equal employment opportunities for women, few of the obstacles have been removed. Women are still subjected to opposition and harassment by their male counterparts, discrimination in job assignment by supervisors, and sexual misconduct by inmates. It appears that until there are major disturbances resulting from women's presence, administrators will continue to comply with the law via their personal interpretations (Zimmer 1986).

*This portion of this issue paper was prepared by Bobbie Deck, Indiana University, Indiana, Pennsylvania.

DISCUSSION AND REVIEW

1. What were some of the major features of the inmate social system before 1960?
2. Why did the inmate social system change dramatically starting in the 1960s?
3. When did the black prisoner movement begin, and what was its major impetus?
4. What was the early effect of the Black Muslim movement on white prisoners and prison administrators?
5. What is the connection between prison gangs and street gangs?
6. How did California prison authorities try to neutralize gang conflicts in their system?
7. Why do white gangs develop in prisons?
8. What services do prison gangs sometimes offer their members?
9. How do gangs impact informal and formal prison systems?
10. What are some of the recent changes that have occurred in prison management?

11. Why does the AIDS problem pose even more difficulties within the correctional setting than it does in society generally?
12. What are the tenets of subcultural wisdom that define acceptable guard behavior?
13. What changes in attitude and behavior do new male correctional officers experience as a consequence of their exposure to veteran guards, inmates, and superiors?
14. According to Jurik (1985), what are the general characteristics of female correctional officers as they relate to their socio-economic background, formal education, and previous work experience?

GLOSSARY

Aryan Brotherhood A prison gang of white inmates.

Black Muslims The major black organization espousing the philosophy of black separatism; considered to be responsible for the black prison movement in the 1950s.

Black separatism A movement that gained popularity in the 1950s and 1960s; espouses the political, social, and economic separation of black Americans from mainstream white America.

Burnout A condition of depleted energy; to fail, wear out, and exhaust one's physical and mental resources.

Disciples A black street gang found on Chicago streets and in Illinois prisons.

El Rukns A black street gang found on chicago streets and in Illinois prisons; formerly called the Black Stone Rangers and the Black P Stone Nation.

Gorillas Prisoners who use violence liberally to gain their ends.

Hacks or screws Derogatory terms used by inmates to refer to correctional officers.

La Nuestra Familia A prison gang of Chicanos from Texas and small towns in California; formed to counter the activities of another Chicano prison gang, the Mexican Mafia. Gang members are usually confined at Soledad State Prison or Tracy to avoid conflicts with the Mafia.

Latin Kings A black street gang found on Chicago streets and in Illinois prisons.

Malcolm X A leader of the Black Muslim movement who personified the philosophy of the organization in the 1950s.

Merchant or peddler An inmate who exploits fellow prisoners by manipulation and trickery and who typically sells or trades goods in short supply.

Mexican Mafia A prison gang of young Chicanos who know each other from the streets of Los Angeles and from other prisons. Gang members are usually confined to San Quentin and Folsom to avoid conflict with their chief rivals, La Nuestra Familia.

Rat or squealer An inmate who betrays a fellow prisoner.

Right guy An inmate loyal to fellow inmates who keeps his promises, minds his own business, does not discuss his own business, defends himself, and doesn't look for trouble.

Sick-out A labor tactic in which large numbers of employees fail to report to work because of alleged sickness.

Soul A quality of spontaneity, of having the capacity to relate to others with ease, and of having special expressive abilities (particularly as revealed in music).

Toughs Prisoners who exhibit highly aggressive behavior, quarrel easily, and fight without cause.

Weakling or weak sister A prisoner unable to withstand the general rigors of life in custodial institutions.

White Citizen Council A white inmate gang.

Wolf or fag An inmate unable to endure prolonged deprivation of heterosexual relationships who consequently enters into homosexual activity. The *wolf* plays the active role, the *fag* the passive role.

Vice Lords A black street gang found on Chicago streets and in Illinois prisons.

■ REFERENCES

Barak, I. "Punishment to Protection: Solitary Confinement in the Washington State Penitentiary, 1966–1975." Ph.D. dissertation, Ohio State University, 1978.

Cleaver, E. *Soul on Ice.* New York: McGraw-Hill, 1968.

Cohen, A. *The Sociology of Subcultures,* edited by D. Arnold, pp. 96–108. Berkeley, Calif.: Glendessary, 1970.

Cohen, A. K. *The Culture of the Gang.* New York: Free Press, 1955.

Conrad, J. P. "Who's in Charge? The Control of Gang Violence in California Prisons." In *Correctional Facility Planning,* edited by Robert Montilla and Nora Marlow, pp. 135–47. Lexington, Mass.: D. C. Heath, 1979.

Crouch, B. M., and Marquart, J. W. "On Becoming a Prison Guard." In *The Keepers: Prison Guards and Contemporary Corrections,* edited by B. M. Crouch. Springfield, Ill.: Charles C. Thomas, 1980.

Dinitz, S. "Are Safe and Humane Prisons Possible?" Paper presented to the John Vincent Barry Memorial Lecture, University of Australia, 8 October 1980.

Freeman, R., Dinitz, S., and Conrad, J. P. "The Bottom Is in the Hole." *American Journal of Corrections* 39 (1977): 25–31.

Hammett, Theodore M. *AIDS in Prisons and Jails: Issues and Options.* Washington, D.C.: U.S. Department of Justice, National Institute of Justice, February 1986.

Horne, P. *Women in Law Enforcement.* Springfield, Ill.: Charles C. Thomas, 1980.

Irwin, P. *Prisons in Turmoil.* Boston: Little, Brown, 1980.

Irwin, J., and Cressey, D. R. "Thieves, Convicts and Inmate Culture." In *The Other Side,* edited by Howard S. Becker. New York: Free Press, 1964.

Jacobs, J. B. "Street Gangs behind Bars." In *The Sociology of Corrections,* edited by Robert G. Leger and John R. Stratton, pp. 148–161. New York: Wiley, 1977.

Jurik, N. C. "An Officer and a Lady." *Social Problems* 32 (1985): 377–88.

Krajick, K. "The Menace of Supergangs." *Corrections Magazine* (June 1980): 11–14.

Lombardo, L. X. *Guards Imprisoned: Correctional Officers at Work.* New York: Elsevier, 1981.

Malcolm X. *The Autobiography of Malcolm X.* New York: MacMillan, 1965.

Martinson, R. "What Works? Questions and Answers about Prison Reform." *The Public Interest* 35 (1974): 22–54.

May, E. "Prison Guards in America: The Inside Story." *Corrections Magazine* 2 (1976): 4–5, 12, 36–40, 44–48.

McCleery, R. "Communication Patterns as Bases of Systems of Authority and Power." In *Theoretical Studies on Social Organization of the Prison,* edited by G. M. Sykes and S. L. Messinger, pp. 49–75. New York: Social Science Research Council, 1960.

Miller, W. B. "Lower-Class Structure as a Generating Mileau of Gang Violence." *Journal of Social Issues* 14 (1958): 5–19.

Morris, N. *The Future of Imprisonment.* Chicago: University of Chicago Press, 1974.

Niederhoffer, A. *Behind the Shield.* New York: Doubleday, 1967.

Owen, B. A. "Race and Gender Relations among Prison Workers." *Crime and Delinquency* 31 (1985): 147–59.

Patrick, J. *A Glasgow Gang Observed.* London: Evre-Methuen, 1973.

Peterson, C. "Doing Time with the Boys: An Analysis of Women Correctional Officers in All-Male Facilities." *The Criminal Justice System and Women.* New York: Clark Boardman, 1982.

Pollock, J. *Sex and Supervision: Guarding Male and Female Inmates.* New York: Greenwood Press, 1986.

Robinson, B. "Love: A Hard-Legged Triangle." *Black Scholar* (September 1971): 29–48.

Segal, M. "The Argument for female combatants or noncombatants." *Female Soldiers: Combatants or Noncombatants,* edited by N. Goldman. Westpoint, Conn.: Greenwood, 1988. 267–90.

Sheehan, S. "Annals of Crime: A Prison and a Prisoner." *The New Yorker,* 24 October, 31 October, and 7 November 1977.

Skolnick, J. H. *Justice Without Trial.* New York: Wiley, 1966.

Sykes, G. M., and Messinger, S. L. "The Inmate Social System." In *Theoretical Studies in Social Organization of the Prison,* edited by Richard A. Cloward, et al., pp. 5–19. New York: Social Science Research Council, 1960.

Thrasher, F. M. *The Gang.* Chicago: University of Chicago Press, 1963.

Wilson, J. Q. *Thinking About Crime.* New York: Basic, 1975.

Van Den Haag, E. *Punishing Criminals.* New York: Basic, 1975.

Von Hirsh, A. *Doing Justice.* New York: Hill and Wang, 1976.

Zimmer, L. *Women Guarding Men.* Chicago: The University of Chicago Press, 1986.

■ NOTES

1. This discussion of the inmate social system was adapted, with permission, from G. M. Sykes and S. L. Messinger, "The Inmate Social System," in *Theoretical Studies in Social Organization of the Prison,* edited by Richard A. Cloward, et. al. (New York: Social Science Research Council, 1960), pp. 5–19.
2. The discussions of black and Chicano prisoners, (and the accompanying references) were adapted, with permission, from J. Irwin, *Prisons in Turmoil* (Boston: Little, Brown, 1980), pp. 66–70, 189, 191.
3. Portions of the discussion of black and white gangs in the Illinois prison system and the impact of gangs upon informal and formal prison systems were adapted, with permission, from K. Krajick, "The Menace of Supergangs," *Corrections Magazine* (June 1980): 11–14.

4. The discussion of gang socialization and recruitment and services performed by gangs, along with accompanying references, was adapted, with permission, from J. B. Jacobs, "Street Gangs behind Bars," in *The Sociology of Corrections,* edited by Robert G. Leger and John R. Stratton (New York: Wiley, 1977), pp. 148–61.
5. The discussion of prison management was adapted, with permission, from Simon Dinitz, "Are Safe and Humane Prisons Possible?" Paper presented to the John Vincent Barry Memorial Lecture, University of Australia, 8 October 1980, pp. 13–18.
6. The discussion of restoring legitimate control to prisons was adapted, with permission, from J. P. Conrad, "Who's in Charge? The Control of Gang Violence in California Prisons," in *Correctional Facility Planning,* edited by Robert Montilla and Nora Marlow (Lexington, Mass.: D. C. Heath, 1979), pp. 141–45.
7. This discussion of AIDS in Prisons was adapted from Theodore M. Hammett, *AIDS in Prisons and Jails: Issues and Options* (Washington, D.C.: U.S. Department of Justice, National Institute of Justice, February 1986). This study summarizes the latest medical information on AIDS, presents statistics on the incidence of AIDS in correctional facilities, and enumerates the key issues and options facing correctional administrators as they formulate policy responses to this complex problem. This discussion summarizes the major findings and conclusions of that report.
8. The low figure is from "Special Report: The AIDS Epidemic," *New England Journal of Medicine* (1985): 312, 523; the high figure is based on two years at New York City's annual estimate of $300,000 for patients requiring acute care.
9. This discussion is based largely on the presentation of Clair Cripe, Esq., of the Federal Bureau of Prisons, at a meeting of Correctional Commissioners on AIDS, sponsored by the National Institute of Corrections, Atlanta, Ga., November 6, 1985.
10. See, e.g., *Rhodes* v. *Chapman,* 452 U.S. 337 (1981).
11. *Storms* v. *Coughlin* was filed in the U.S. District Court for the Southern District of New York. Some of the issues may be mooted by new state regulations, but the plaintiff's attorney believes that there are a number of important quality-of-care issues to litigate. See also *Thagard* v. *County of Cook,* unreported opinion: No. 85 C 4429 (N.D. Il., May 20, 1985).
14. 120 MISC 2d 697 (N.Y. 1983). See also *Herring* v. *Keeney* (U.S.D.C., Oregon, filed September 17, 1985): *Sheppard* v. *Keeney* (U.S.D.C., Oregon, filed October 7, 1985): *Malport* v. *Keeney* (U.S.D.C., Oregon, filed October 11, 1985): *Telepo et al.* v. *Keen et al.* Civil Action 85-1742A (U.S.D.C., New Jersey, filed May 1985).

■ CASES

Cordero v. *Coughlin* 607 F.Supp. (S.D.N.Y. 1984).
Estelle v. *Gamble* 429 U.S. 97, (1976).
Herring v. *Keeney* U.S.D.C., Oregon (filed September 17, 1985).
Malport v. *Keeney* U.S.D.C., Oregon (filed October 11, 1985).
Mtr La Rocca v. *Dalsheim* 120 MISC 2d 697 (N.Y. 1983).
Rhodes v. *Chapman* 452 U.S. 337, (1981).
Sheppard v. *Keeney* U.S.D.C., Oregon (filed October 7, 1985).
Storms v. *Coughlin*
Telepo et al. v. *Keen et al.* Civil Action 85-1742A, U.S.D.C., New Jersey (filed May 1985).
Thagard v. *County of Cook* No. 85 C 4429 (N.D.Il. May 20, 1985).

CHAPTER

16

Alternatives to Confinement

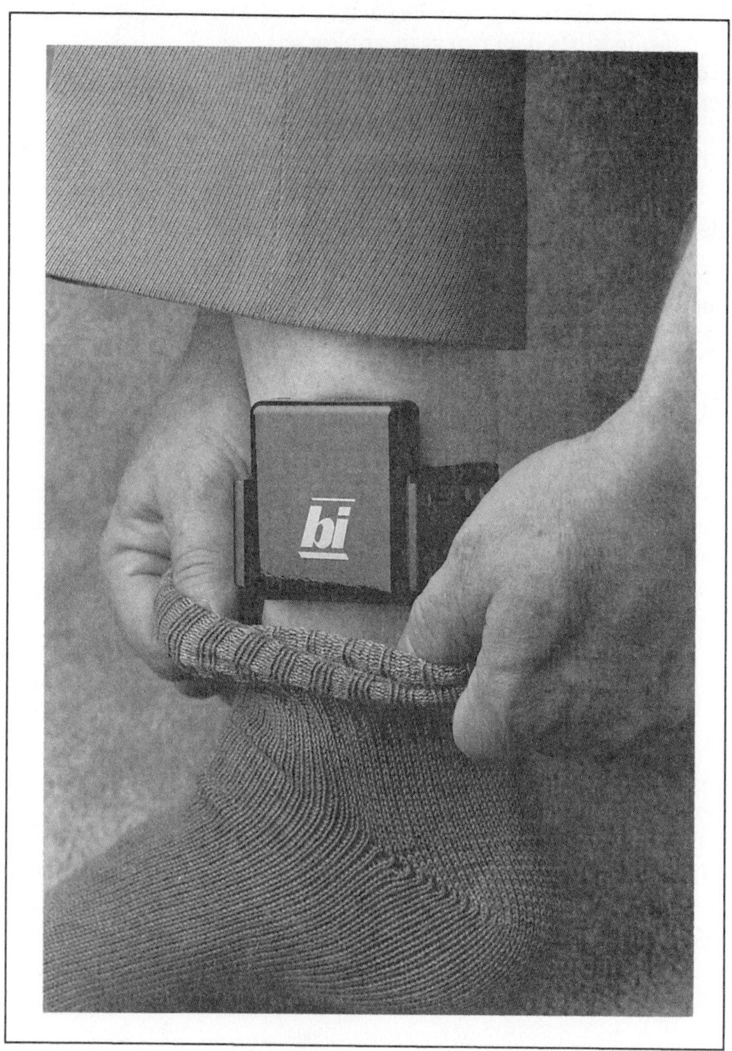

CHAPTER OUTLINE:

Although the law requires that violators receive penalties, it also provides for the mitigation of severe sentences. A person convicted of a crime may be placed on **probation** rather than being incarcerated, may be **paroled** from prison prior to the expiration of his or her sentence, may have his or her prison sentence or fine commuted to a lesser penalty, or may receive a full or conditional pardon (with a restoration of civil rights). A fifth method of mitigating the full force of legal sanctions is called *amnesty*—a group pardon.

Offenders sent away to prison return, sooner or later, to free society. But imprisonment may not only fail to rehabilitate many offenders, it may also exacerbate their criminal tendencies. Criminal justice authorities therefore, have long sought realistic, workable alternatives to confinement. In recent years, the emphasis has been upon involving offenders in programs and facilities based within the community. Such programs allow society to provide offenders with only the amount of supervision they require. And because crime has its roots in the community, it is reasonable that the community assume some responsibility for dealing with offenders. This approach also minimizes the problem of reintegration.

Probation and parole are the two methods most often used to replace imprisonment with community supervision. With rising crime rates, there has come an increasing demand for incarceration, and consequently more felons are being imprisoned than ever before. On the other side, however, the issue of prison overcrowding has become such an enormous problem that the courts are increasingly using probation as one method for dealing with the problem. In this chapter, we examine the results of a Rand Corporation study designed to examine the risks of putting felons on probation as well as alternatives to punishing them.

Strictly speaking, parole is not an alternative to confinement in the same sense as probation; it is actually a form of conditional release for someone already serving a prison term. One of the major concerns of parole authorities is to try to select those individuals who will most likely succeed on parole. In order to remove some of the subjectivity involved in making these decisions, the U.S. Parole Commission has developed a salient factor score to predict recidivism, and considerable discussion is devoted to this topic.

In addition to probation and parole, we briefly consider **work release,** study release, home **furloughs, halfway houses,** detoxification and drug abuse programs, and **diversion** as alternatives to incarceration. Considerable discussion is also devoted to electronically monitored home confinement. This innovative and sometimes controversial means of diversion seems to have captured the imagination of the judiciary. We also discuss the concept of the community correctional center as a multipurpose facility that can provide human services in a community setting.

PROBATION

Probation has been called "the least visible, least studied, most diffuse and most underfunded part of the criminal-processing apparatus" (Krajick 1980, p. 7). Yet probation is the sanction that a criminal court is most apt to impose on offenders. Between 60 and 80 percent of sentences meted out by the courts involve probation, and on any given day, there are about one million persons on probation in the United States. This figure, at best an estimate, because probation services are spread among many agencies and facilities, from the municipal level to the federal level. According to a count by the National Council on Crime and Delinquency (1981), there are about twenty-four hundred probation offices administering adult probation services in the United States. But the authors of the report acknowledge that the actual figure is probably much higher. Some jurisdictions practice "postcard probation," in which clients report their activities once or twice a month by sending in preaddressed postcards.

Probation is intended as a combination of treatment and punishment. An offender is actually serving time on probation, but he or she is also supposed to be treated in the context of community-based supervision. Ideally, probationers receive counseling and guidance to ensure they adjust to free society. But probation is also punitive, because restrictions are placed on the probationer. (Many authorities deny the punitive aspects of probation and claim that their policies are strictly rehabilitative.)

Liberal and conservative critics of the criminal justice system agree that placing an offender on probation without using private community services is equal to doing nothing. Such action is neither treatment nor punishment. As a criminal court judge observes, "The offender continues with his life style . . . . If he is a wealthy doctor, he continues with his practice; if he is an unemployed youth, he continues to be unemployed. Probation is a meaningless ritual; it is a sop to the conscience of the court" (Krajick 1980, p. 7).

A major problem in probation is the built-in role conflict experienced by probation officers. Are they police officers or counselors? Is their responsibility primarily surveillance, or should they be agents of active social change? Many of the other difficulties that plague probation—high staff turnover, low morale, and burnout—stem from this basic conflict. There are also critical problems in trying to evaluate the effectiveness of probation as an alternative to confinement. However, some innovative and experimental approaches have been proposed to augment traditional probation programs in an attempt to deal with these problems.

The Suspended Sentence: Birthplace of Probation

Probation is derived from the suspended sentence, handed down indirectly from our judicial past. Both a suspended sentence and probation are a form of mitigating punishment through judicial procedure. Their earliest antecedent is the Right of Sanctuary, which is frequently cited in the Bible; holy places and certain cities were traditionally set aside as places of sanctuary.

The practice of Right of Sanctuary was written into Mosaic law. To escape the vengeance of a victim's family, a killer could go to a sanctuary and find refuge. In the Middle Ages, many churches offered sanctuary to persons hiding from harsh secular laws. The practice of santuary disappeared in England in the seventeenth century and was replaced with "benefit of clergy." This practice, originally reserved for clerics, was eventually extended to those who could pass the "Psalm 51" test, which required the ability of the offender to read the verse beginning "Have mercy upon me . . . ." The result was a form of suspended sentence that allowed offenders to move about in society without undue fear of retribution.

The suspended sentence differs from probation, even though the terms are sometimes used interchangeably. The suspended sentence does not require supervision and usually does not specify a particular set of goals for the offender. It is merely a form of quasi freedom that can be revoked at the discretion of the court. The practice of suspended sentence, like the right of sanctuary, has outlived its usefulness in the United States and has generally been replaced by supervised probation.

John Augustus: Father of Probation

A nineteenth-century Boston cobbler named John Augustus is regarded as the father of probation. Augustus spent much of his leisure time in the courts and was distressed that common drunks were forced to remain in jail because they had no money to pay their fines. A humane, sympathetic man, he convinced authorities to allow him to pay offenders' fines; after their release, he provided offenders with friendly counsel and supervision. From 1841 to 1848, Augustus bailed out nearly two thousand men, women, and children. Barnes and Teeters describe his approach:

> His method was to bail the offender after conviction, to utilize this favor as an entering wedge to the convict's confidence and friendship, and through such evidence of friendliness as helping the offender to obtain a job and aiding his family in various ways, to drive the wedge home. When the defendant was later brought into court for sentence, Augustus would report on his progress toward reformation, and the judge would usually fine the convict one cent and costs, instead of committing him to an institution (1959, p. 554).

Augustus's efforts encouraged his home state of Massachusetts to pass the first probation statute in 1878. Five more states followed suit before the turn of the century. In 1899, with the creation of the first juvenile court, probation was established as a legitimate alternative to penal confinement. The need to supervise troubled youths and to keep them out of adult prisons provided strong motivation toward developing probation in the United States.

Imposing Probation

Probation can be implemented in three ways. First, the law may allow the trial judge to suspend the execution of sentence and to place the offender on conditional probation. Second, a state statute may require sentencing but may permit suspension. Finally, sentencing and probation may be left to the discretion of the trial judge. If a probationer violates the conditions of his or her probation, the trial judge usually orders the execution of the sentence originally imposed. If a judge has suspended sentencing, a probation violation might result in a stiffer prison sentence than would have been imposed earlier.

PROBATION WITHOUT ADJUDICATION Once the court has decided to grant probation, the sentencing judge must decide whether the offender should be adjudicated guilty and labeled a convicted felon, or whether he or she should be placed on probation without adjudication. This decision is outlined by Murchek:

> Although adjudication of guilt may provide certain safeguards to society such as: requiring criminal registration, serving notice to prospective employers that the applicant has been convicted of a criminal offense, preventing the offender from voting, holding public office, serving on a jury and perhaps making it more difficult to obtain firearms, it appears to provide very little appreciable effect in providing protection to society. It does, in fact, seriously hamper the offender's chances of rehabilitation.
>
> The withholding of adjudication of guilt, on the other hand, is consistent with the philosophical concepts of probation which combine community-based treatment with the full utilization of available community resources as a viable alternative to imprisonment and the accompanying degradation and stigma associated with same (1973, p. 27).

Actually, probation without adjudication was practiced at the time of John Augustus. Augustus convinced judges to withhold sentencing on offenders released to him for a period of three weeks, after which the offenders returned for sentencing. This procedure gave offenders a chance to prove themselves, and it usually resulted in offenders being fined rather than imprisoned. This system of delayed or postponed sentencing kept the offender in the community, under supervision and without the handicap of a criminal record. The ability to function in the community without the stigma of a criminal conviction often provides a psychological uplift to the offender that may contribute to a desire for self-improvement and reform.

PRESENTENCE INVESTIGATION REPORTS To determine which offenders are good candidates for probation, sentencing judges rely heavily upon presentence reports. Information secured in presentence investigations can be used at almost every stage in the criminal justice process: by the courts in deciding the appropriate sentence; by the prison classification team in assigning custody level and treatment; by the parole board in determining when a offender is ready to be returned to the community; by probation and parole officers in helping offenders readjust to free society; and by correctional researchers in identifying the characteristics of successful probation (Carter and Wilkins 1976). The primary purpose of presentence investigations is not to determine the guilt or innocence of defendants, but rather to give insights into their personalities and lives.

Some type of a presentence investigation report should be made in every case. Objectivity is essential in the preparation of this document; probation officers must see things as they are, not as they would wish them to be. Under our adversary system of justice, the district attorney and the defense counsel are committed to particular points of view, but the preparer of the presentence investigation report is free to include all facts pertinent to the case. The report should include a description of the offense, including statements of co-defendants; the defendant's own version of the offense; prior record; family and marital history; description of the neighborhood in which the defendant was reared; and facts about the defendant's education, religion, interests, mental and physical health, employment history, and military service. Optional information might include the attitude of the defendant toward arresting officers, the amount of bond, and the attitude of arresting officers.

The evaluative summary is the most difficult and important part of the presentence report. It is this summary that separates professional probation officers from fact-gathering clerks. Probation officers need considerable analytic skills and an understanding of human behavior to interpret the facts in a presentence report and to make a meaningful recommendation to the court. Many judges ask these officers to recommend sentencing alternatives, or, if the defendant is placed on probation, to recommend a plan of treatment.

CONDITIONS OF PROBATION AND PAROLE

Although probation is usually managed by the courts and parole by an executive department of government, the conditions of both alternatives are simple. These conditions are generally fixed jointly by the legislature, the court, and the probation and parole departments. Some general regulations—such as requirements that probationers live law-abiding lives, that they not leave the state without the court's consent, that they report periodically to their probation or parole officer, and that they pay court costs—may be fixed by statute; no allowances are made for discretion by the trial court or the parole board. However, unique conditions may be applied in individual cases. For example, probationers may be required either to stay home or leave home, to support their parents, to get a steady job working days, to make restitution to their victims, or to attend church regularly.

Some conditions of probation and parole have been unfair and unrealistic. When this occurs, a probation officer may choose to enforce the conditions selectively, thereby muting their effect in the interest of common-sense justice. The concerned probation officer should ask, Are these rules reasonable? Are they effective? Do they serve the best interests of the individual and the community?

Revocation of Probation

There are no uniform criteria for revoking probation throughout the country—not even among judges in the same district courts. Conditions of probation should be realistic, and they should be applied fairly. Unrealistic conditions frustrate the offender and may lead to further violations. For example, it is pointless to fine a probationer if financial problems caused the original violation. Similarly, compulsory church attendance might create resentment on the part of the probationer. Thus, conditions of probation should be guidelines to assist the probationer in leading a law-abiding life—not rigid vows of chastity and obedience that only the most disciplined can endure.

When probationers violate the conditions of their probation, care must be taken to determine whether the violation is the result of unrealistic probation rules or the attitude of the probationer (DiCerbo 1966). The probation officer must ask, To what extent is this violation a reflection of deep-seated hostility? To what extent is the behavior symptomatic of a person trying to find himself or herself? Revocation of probation is justified only when probationers defy the courts or when they become a threat to the community. In cases involving restitution, if a probationer is sentenced to prison, the crime victim loses out. No violation should result in automatic revocation. Probation officers should ask themselves how they would respond to the probationer's acts if he or she was *not* on probation. For example, we do not sentence people to prison for losing or quitting their jobs. Thus, all violations should be judged in light of the probationer's total adjustment to society.

Probation and Felony Offenders

Over the last two decades, several trends have converged to change the nation's probation population. Rising crime rates have led to public demand that criminals get harsher treatment; "just deserts" and incapacitation have displaced rehabilitation as the primary aim of corrections. Consequently, more felons are being imprisoned than ever before in our history. But at the same time, budget limitations have made it impossible for prison construction to keep pace with felony convictions. Prison crowding has become so critical that the courts have increasingly used probation to catch the overflow (Petersilia 1985).[1]

Probation sentences for adult felons have become so common that a new term has emerged in criminal justice circles: felony probation. Today, over one-third of the nation's adult probation population consists of persons convicted in superior courts of felonies (as opposed to misdemeanors).

This phenomenon raises some serious questions. Probation was originally intended for offenders who posed little threat to society and who were believed to be capable of rehabilitation through a productive, supervised life in the community. Given its intent and structure, can probation accommodate more serious offenders, supervise them properly, and keep them from committing more crimes? Understanding how well probation works for felons is a compelling public safety issue.

A recent Rand Corporation study, funded by the National Institute of Justice, used data from California to look at basic assumptions about probation and its mission, to examine the public risks of putting felons on probation, and to consider alternative means of punishing them.[2]

California's probation system is one of the largest in the nation and was once regarded as the most innovative. Most probation systems across the country have experienced budget cuts because of fiscal limitations and the shift from rehabilitation to punishment. With Proposition 13 and other fiscal constraints, California's probation agencies may have suffered the most severe cuts of all. Since 1975, the state's probation population has risen 15 percent, while the number of probation officers has fallen by 20 percent. In the same time period, the state has spent 30 percent more on criminal justice in general, but 10 percent less on probation. As a result, probation staffs have had to take on greater caseloads, often at the cost of supervising probationers less carefully. Its experiences should be instructive for other states.

In California, 70 percent of all convicted offenders are granted probation. By the mid 1980s, about 1 percent of the state's total population was on probation. The group's size alone places a tremendous burden on probation agencies, and that burden is made heavier by the increasing number of serious offenders it includes.

As Figure 16.1 shows, a significant proportion of all persons granted probation in 1983 had been arrested and convicted of serious crimes. This situation requires that policymakers look closely at probation, at the public risks of probation for convicted felons, and at possible alternative sanctions. In anticipation of the problems and questions a policy may raise, Rand's study was designed to answer some basic questions about probation (Petersilia 1978):

- How well do felons fare on probation, measured in terms of rearrests, reconvictions, and incarcerations?
- What criteria do the courts use to decide whether convicted felons go to prison or get probation?
- How accurately can statistical models predict which felons will recidivate and which will not?
- If the answers to these questions indicate that probation is not appropriate for most felons, can the criminal justice system devise workable alternatives?

The Rand study performed several types of statistical analyses of data for over 16,000 felons convicted in California's superior court during 1980, and of recidivism data on a subsample of 1,672 convicted felons who received probation in Los Angeles and Alameda Counties.

Because these two counties have experienced severe budget constraints and growing caseloads, their recidivism rates may differ from those in counties that have

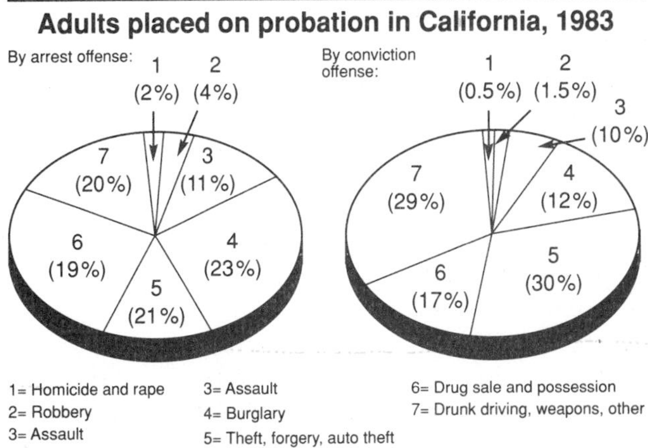

FIGURE 16.1
Adults placed on probation in California, 1983. From Joan Petersilia, *Probation and Felony Offenders* (Washington, D.C.: U.S. Department of Justice, National Institute of Justice, March 1985), p. 2.

more adequate budgets. Nevertheless, Los Angeles and Alameda supervise 43 percent of the California probation population, and their data provide a good base for examining the issues surrounding probation as a sentencing alternative for adult felons.

PUBLIC RISKS OF FELONY PROBATION Felony probation does present a serious threat to public safety. Figure 16–2 suggests just how serious. Only 35 percent of the probationers managed to "stay clean," as far as official records indicate. During the forty-month period following their probationary sentence, 65 percent of the total sample were rearrested and 53 percent had official charges filed against them. Of these charges, 75 percent involved burglary/theft, robbery, or other violent crimes—the crimes most threatening to public safety.

Fifty-one percent of the total sample were reconvicted. Eighteen percent were convicted of homicide, rape, weapons offenses, assault, or robbery; and 34 percent eventually ended up in jail or prison.

The data also showed that offenders originally convicted of property crimes (burglary, theft, forgery) were the most likely to recidivate, followed (at some distance) by those who were convicted of violent and drug offenses. Only 33 percent of the property offenders had no subsequent arrests, while about 40 percent of the drug and violent offenders managed to stay clean.

The study found two other important facts about the probationers. First, with the exception of drug offenders, probationers were most often rearrested and convicted of the same crimes for which they had originally been convicted. Second, property offenders tended to be rearrested more quickly than those originally convicted for violent crimes or drug offenses.

The median time to first *filed* charge (not necessarily the first arrest) was five months for property offenders, eight months for violent offenders, and fifteen months for drug offenders. However, as Figure 16.3 shows, both property and violent offenders either committed new crimes or "retired" within two years, while drug offenders continued to recidivate at a linear rate—that is, a roughly equal number returned to crime each month. Consequently, it was not known what the rate of recidivism for drug offenders would be beyond forty months, nor could it be determined if the recidivism rate for drug offenders would, in the long term, remain lower than the rates for property and violent offenders.

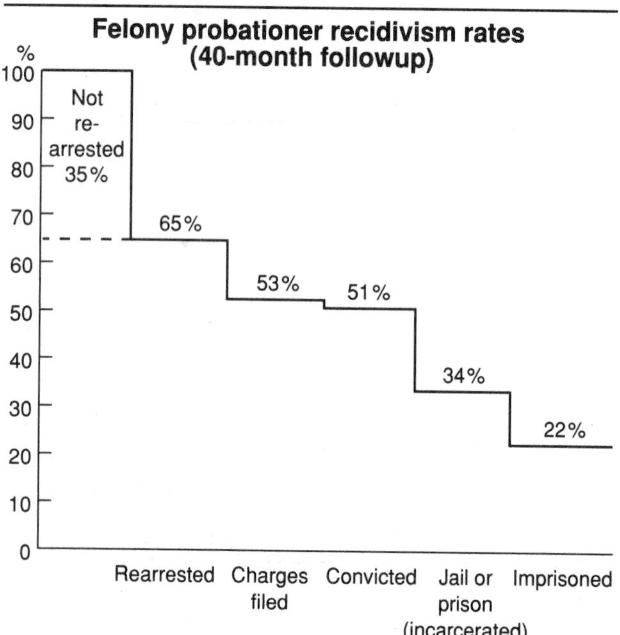

FIGURE 16.2
Felony probationer recidivism rates (40-month followup). From Joan Petersilia, *Probation and Felony Offenders* (Washington, D.C.: U.S. Department of Justice, National Institute of Justice, March 1985), p. 3.

MAKING THE PRISON/PROBATION DECISION These high recidivism rates naturally raise questions about what criteria the courts use to decide whether a convicted felon receives a prison or probation sentence. Statistical analyses indicate a high correlation between prison sentences and certain basic factors of the case:[3]

- Having two or more current conviction counts
- Having two or more adult prior convictions
- Being on parole or probation when arrested
- Being a drug addict
- Being armed
- Using a weapon
- Seriously injuring the victim

The California Penal Code (Section 1202d) states that such factors should be weighed before an offender is granted probation, and the courts do appear to consider them. For all offenses except assault, offenders who had three or more of these characteristics had an 80 percent probability of going to prison, regardless of the type of crime for which they were currently convicted. Because correctional facilities are strained to capacity, prisons appear to be increasingly reserved for "career criminals."

However, when the study attempted to "predict" which sentence specific offenders would receive, 20 to 25 percent of the sample received sentences at odds with their

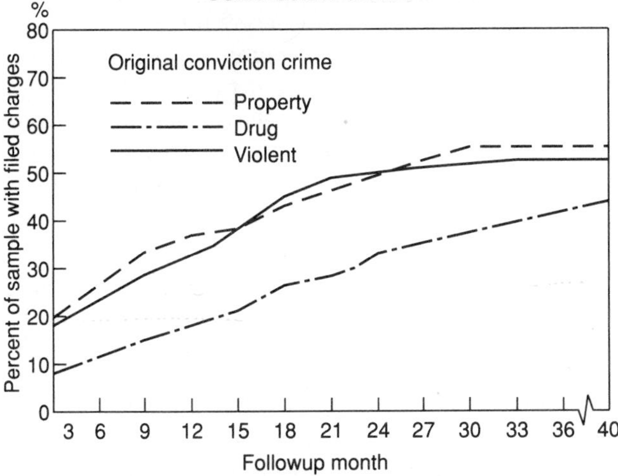

FIGURE 16.3
Cumulative percent of probationers with filed charges during followup months, by original conviction crime. From Joan Petersilia, *Probation and Felony Offenders* (Washington, D.C.: U.S. Department of Justice, National Institute of Justice, March 1985), p. 3.

"statistically predicted" sentence. These findings suggest that—in terms of their crimes or criminal records—many of the felony probationers cannot be distinguished from their counterparts who went to prison.

PREDICTING RECIDIVISM To determine what factors were associated with rearrest, reconviction, and conviction for violent crime, the study used a hierarchy of information levels similar to that used by the court in the prison/probation decision.[4] The factors included (1) type of conviction crime; (2) prior record, drug and alcohol abuse, and income; (3) sentence recommendation and special circumstances from the presentence investigation (PSI); and (4) demographics (age, race, education) and living situation.

Regression analyses identified the following factors as most significantly related to recidivism:

- *Type of conviction crime.* Property offenders had the highest rates of recidivism.
- *Number of prior juvenile and adult convictions.* The greater the number, the higher the probability of recidivism.
- *Income at arrest.* Regardless of source or amount, the presence of income was associated with lower recidivism.
- *Household composition.* If the offender was living with a spouse and/or children, recidivism was lower.

These factors were equally strong predictors of rearrest, reconviction, and reconviction for violent crime. Nevertheless, as Figure 16.4 shows, knowing these factors still did not make the statistical prediction of rearrest a great deal better than chance.

For the total probation sample, knowing the type of conviction crime improved over chance by only 2 percent. Considering information on prior criminal record, drug and alcohol use, and employment made the prediction 11 percent more accurate than chance. However, adding demographics increased accuracy only 2 percent more—for a total of 69 percent in predicting rearrests. The study's predictions for reconvictions were only 64 percent accurate, while those for violent crime reconvictions were 71 percent accurate. Thus, using the best statistical models and a wealth of information on offenders, recidivism could not be predicted with more than 71 percent accuracy.

It is interesting to compare the factors that predict the prison/probation decision with those the study used to predict recidivism. There was not as much correspondence as one might expect. The only factor used that

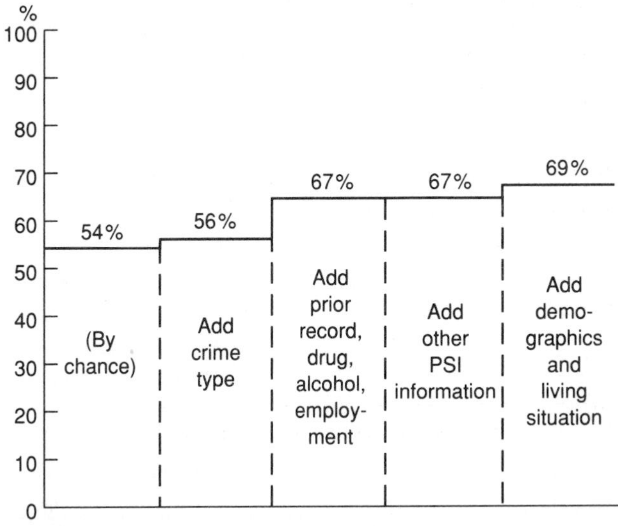

FIGURE 16.4
Statistical ability to predict rearrests correctly. From Joan Petersilia, *Probation and Felony Offenders* (Washington, D.C.: U.S. Department of Justice, National Institute of Justice, March 1985), p. 3.

strongly predicted both the decision to imprison and recidivism was prior adult criminal convictions. Prior juvenile convictions, while a very strong predictor of recidivism, were not particularly influential in the sentencing decision.

Most of the other factors important to the imprisonment decision, such as weapon use and victim injury, failed to predict recidivism significantly. Likewise, factors that did predict recidivism, such as living situation and monthly income, failed to influence the imprisonment decision. These differences undoubtedly reflect the trend in the California sentencing system toward a "just deserts" model, where sentencing is based primarily on the crime and prior criminal record, and not on factors necessarily associated with recidivism.

The study also discovered some important facts about presentence investigations (PSIs) reflected in Figure 16.4. Like many of their counterparts across the nation, probation agencies in Los Angeles and Alameda Counties spend almost half their time and resources preparing PSIs.

In California, PSIs routinely include very detailed offender and offense information, plus judgments made by the probation officer concerning special aggravating or mitigating factors (e.g., offender is remorseful, has health problems, or testified against accomplices). The study found that this additional information did not improve the recidivism prediction, once the analysis controlled for the offender's background and criminal history (which did come from the PSI).

Moreover, the study found that, contrary to common belief, the courts do not necessarily follow the PSI's sentence recommendation. In the two counties, the PSI had recommended prison for 31 percent of the offenders who got probation. Although this tendency to override the PSI recommendation merits more study, it may reflect the courts' awareness that PSIs are not necessarily accurate in predicting recidivism.

In the probationer sample, 63 percent of the people recommended for probation were rearrested, compared with 67 percent of those recommended for prison (see Figure 16.5).[5] Similar results were obtained for reconvictions and reconvictions for violent crimes. In general, there were no statistical differences in the recidivism rates of those persons probation agencies recommended for probation and those they recommended for prison.

The problems with predicting recidivism prompted the study to approach the prison/probation decision from the opposite direction: to try to identify convicted felons who have a relatively high chance of succeeding on probation, and to determine if there are enough of them to reduce the prison population significantly without jeopardizing public safety.

The study created a statistical model, based on regression analyses, of "good prospects" for probation. This model used known factors common to probationers who had no new convictions to predict how many prisoners would have had a 75 percent chance of successful probation. Unfortunately, only about 3 percent of California's 1980 "incoming" prisoner population qualified. This result reinforces the study's general finding that very few adults convicted of felonies in Los Angeles and Alameda Counties are good candidates for probation, as it is now administered.

The conclusion is not intended as an indictment of the probation departments. With their reduced budgets and mountainous caseloads, they cannot supervise probationers much more closely. However, even if they could, routine probation was not conceived or structured to handle serious offenders. And, what is worse, these of-

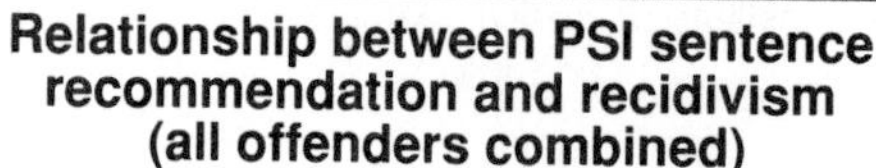

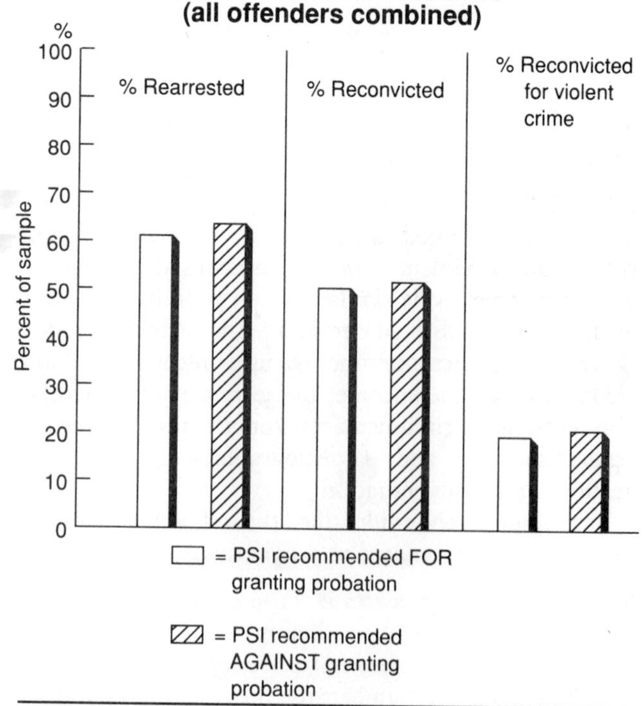

FIGURE 16.5
Relationship between PSI sentence recommendation and recidivism (all offenders combined). From Joan Petersilia, *Probation and Felony Offenders* (Washington, D.C.: U.S. Department of Justice, National Institute of Justice, March 1985), p. 5.

fenders seem to have crowded out the traditional probationer population—first offenders, petty thieves, drug offenders, and disrupters—many of whom evidently see the system's "indifference" as encouragement to commit more serious crimes. Prior Rand research has shown that believing they can "get away with it" is characteristic of career criminals (Petersilia 1978).

FINDING ALTERNATIVES The criminal justice system is facing a severe dilemma. Probation caseloads are increasing at the same time that budgets are shrinking. Nevertheless, probation will probably be used for still more convicted felons because of prison crowding and the lack of funds to build more prisons. Most of the felony probationers in the Rand study failed on probation, and it seems unlikely that the courts can improve their ability to predict recidivism, given current information and methods. Further, very few offenders now entering prison are good prospects for traditional probation.

The situation demands that the criminal justice system rethink its response to felony probationers. Without alternative sanctions for serious offenders, prison populations will continue to grow and the courts will be forced to consider probation for more and more serious offenders. Probation caseloads will increase, petty offenders will be increasingly "ignored" by the system (possibly encouraging recidivism), and recidivism rates will rise.

The criminal justice system has never developed a spectrum of sanctions to match the spectrum of criminals. Some believe that the system overutilizes imprisonment because it is virtually the only severe punishment available. There is a critical need to establish a greater array of sentencing options. However, the new options must be restrictive enough to ensure public safety.

One promising approach, being tried in Georgia and New Jersey, is intensive surveillance programs. The New Jersey program keeps offenders under strict curfew, requiring them to be in their homes from 10 P.M. to 6 A.M. Participants must also maintain employment, receive counseling, provide community service, submit to random urine testing for drugs, and make restitution to their victims.

The National Institute of Justice is sponsoring an evaluation of the New Jersey program, and preliminary results are encouraging. Of the 226 persons who have participated in the program during the past fourteen months, 29 (13 percent) have been returned to prison—only 1 for an indictable offense. Most of the violations were curfew and drug related (Pearson 1985).

Intensive surveillance programs cost $3,000 to $5,000 per offender per year, compared to about $1,600 for each person on probation and $14,000 for each offender in prison. To help pay for these programs, some states have begun to collect probation supervision fees from the felons themselves. Georgia's program is basically self-supporting; during its first year of operation, it collected about $650,000 in probation supervision fees (Erwin 1983). Other states are attempting to develop risk-prediction models that identify "low-risk" probationers needing minimal supervision; this allows more resources to be applied to high-risk individuals.

Given the existing problems of prison crowding and the risks of felony probation, intensive surveillance may well be one of the most significant criminal justice experiments in the next decade. If such programs prove successful, they will restore probation's credibility and reduce imprisonment rates without significantly increasing crime. Most important, since such programs require that the offenders be gainfully employed and functioning members of a community, the programs offer the prospect of rehabilitating some of the offenders who participate.

Role Conflict and the Probation Officer

Probation and parole both involve community supervision of the offender. The offender is required to conform to certain conditions as a basis for securing an alternative to imprisonment. The probation officer is the person who must see to it that the offender lives up to and carries out the terms imposed by the court or by probation authorities. Thus, the probation officer has the task of surveillance, which is basically a police function.

However, the probation officer is also expected to provide a variety of human services to the probationer or parolee. That is, the officer is expected to perform as a social caseworker. The influence of social work has had a profound effect on the development of probation services. In the past, an overemphasis on casework and the medical model—which conceived of the criminal offender as a "sick" person—resulted in a narrow focus on the relationship between the probationer and the probation officer. This led, in turn, to a tendency to overlook the connection between crime and contributing factors such as poverty, racism, unemployment, poor health, substandard housing, and poor education.

One drawback in the model of the probation officer as a caseworker is that officers may have to assume functions not related to probation. Placement in foster homes, operation of shelters, alcoholism, drug addiction, and mental illness may be more properly handled by community mental health agencies. No one probation officer has the background required to deal with all the problems of probationers. Yet probation officers are accountable for probationers who get into trouble again. The first question asked by the court in this situation is usually, When did you last see your client? As a result, probation officers tend to overextend themselves to prevent or justify client failures. For many officers, the role conflict of "cop or counselor" is a major source of job stress.

CONDITIONAL AND GRADUATED RELEASE

As noted earlier, all offenders except those who are executed or committed to prison for "life certain" terms will eventually be released. How well they fare once they return to society—whether they successfully reintegrate or commit further offenses that lead back to prison—depends on many complex factors, one of which is the length of time they spend in prison. Reid cites the case of Ralph Lobaugh, who was released in 1977 after spending thirty years in an Indiana prison:

> The freedom for which he had fought during 14 years, however, was too much for him. After two months, Lobaugh decided he could not cope with life outside the walls and went back to prison. According to Harold G. Roddy, director of the work-release program in Indiana, Lobaugh "just wanted to live in a cell again and be with his old friends" (1981, p. 282).

The Lobaugh case may be extreme, but the problem of readjustment to free society for a released prisoner is not unusual.

Parole

Parole is the conditional release, under supervision, of offenders from correctional institutions after they have served part of their sentences. It is the way in which the majority of incarcerated felons are released from prison each year. The concept of parole has its roots in military history; the practice of releasing a captured officer on his word of honor that he will not take up arms against his captors is called *parole d'honneur*. Similarly, inmates are released to free society on their word of honor that they will not again violate the law. Parole differs from probation, because it implies that the offender has served time. Administratively, parole is a function of the executive branch of government, and probation is a judicial act of the court. Selection, supervision, regulations, revocation, and release procedures are similar for parole and probation, however, and the two kinds of release are often confused by the public.

Prisoners have always been released on their *mandatory release date*—that is, on the termination date of their sentence. In inmate terms, this is referred to as serving "flat time" or "day to day." Parole is conditional release. Inmates who make genuine progress toward rehabilitation are selected to serve a final part of their sentence under some form of community supervision.

PAROLE SELECTION Prisoners seeking to be released on parole must follow a procedure of recommendation and review to determine their readiness. Review and selection are subject to the decision-making authority of a *parole board,* which generally includes representatives from the prison, the state department of corrections, and other professionals qualified to assess an inmate's eligibility for parole.

Most parole boards assign cases to individual board members who review the cases in detail; the members then make recommendations to the full board when it meets. The recommendations of board members are usually accepted, but sometimes the full board will ask for more details. Some states even send parole board members into the prisons to interview inmates and institutional staff; other states convene their entire boards at individual institutions on a regular schedule. If inmates do not meet board criteria, their sentences are continued and they are "flopped." If parole is granted, the inmate is prepared to be turned over the adult parole authority for the period of supervision determined by the parole board.

A major problem with parole decisions is that offenders often do not know the criteria they are expected to meet and the reasons that parole might be denied. Porter comments on this aspect of the decision-making process:

> It is an essential element of justice that the role and processes for measuring parole readiness be made known to the inmate. This knowledge can greatly facilitate the earnest inmate toward his own rehabilitation. It is just as important for an inmate to know the rules and basis of the judgment upon which he will be granted or denied parole as it was important for him to know the basis of the charge against him and the evidence upon which he was convicted. One can imagine nothing more cruel,

> inhuman, and frustrating than serving a prison term without knowledge of what will be measured and the rules determining whether one is ready for release. . . . Justice can never be a product of unreasoned judgment (1958, p. 227).

Correctional staff should also be told the "rules of the game" so that they can guide inmates toward desirable behavior.

Four inmates at the Indiana State Penitentiary have described three aspects of parole decisions that candidates resent. First, most parole boards emphasize a candidate's prior record:

> What is so frustrating to men who keep getting rejected for parole because of "past record" is that there is obviously nothing that the individual can do about it. It cannot be changed, it cannot be expunged. It therefore generates a feeling of helplessness and frustration, especially in men who take seriously what they are told about rehabilitation and perfect institutional records. These men cannot understand the rationale behind parole denials based on past records if the major goal of the correctional system is rehabilitation and if they have tried to take advantage of every rehabilitation program offered by the institution. The men know that merely serving another two or five years is not going to further the "rehabilitation" process (Griswold et al. 1970).

Second, many parole boards believe that their principal responsibility is to protect society, not to rehabilitate the offender. With this attitude, boards are reluctant to release offenders who are considered poor risks. Rather, they prefer to let such offenders serve their full sentences and return to the community without supervision. This practice may reduce the recidivism rate for offenders on parole, but it may not affect nonparoled inmates' chances for successful reintegration. For some, the wait might be positive: the sheer passage of time seems to mature some people. For most inmates, however, the longer they remain in prison, the more likely they are to absorb the values, techniques, and rationalizations of the criminal subculture. Finally, inmates believe that parole boards are more responsive to public opinion and political pressure than to the record and behavior of the individual applicant. This feeling adds to cynicism about the entire parole process.

Another aspect of parole that has come under attack is the inmate's inability to appeal an unfavorable decision. Parole decisions are often subject to question, especially when an inmate is denied knowledge as to why he or she was denied parole. Future parole selection *must* include self-regulating and internal appeal procedures. If such procedures are not provided, case after case will be sent to court, and the U.S. Supreme Court will eventually step in and establish rules and procedures based on the Fourteenth Amendment. Some states have seen the handwriting on the wall and have started to formalize selection criteria and to develop appeal procedures.

CONDITIONS OF PAROLE Many of the first parole procedures imposed unreasonable restrictions on the released offender. Too often the rules were simply an convenient pretext for returning the parolee to prison—which was often done if the parolee created even the slightest fuss for the parole officer. As recently as twenty years ago, it was not uncommon for the conditions of parole to require the parolee to "only associate with persons of good reputation." Rules of this type gave the parole officer great discretionary power. Offenders knew that their parole could be revoked for a technical violation at almost any time—a situation not conducive to reform and respect for the law. The parolee's attitude was often, "If I'm going to get busted for a technical violation, I might as well do something *really* wrong." Today, however, the rules of parole are much more reasonable and realistic.

Enhancing Parole Prediction

Criminal justice officials increasingly use statistical methods to predict whether an individual will commit future crimes. These methods sometimes take the form of sentencing and parole guidelines that classify people into groups on the basis of their likely future behavior. Individuals in high-risk groups generally receive longer prison sentences or are held in prison longer before parole release (Hoffman 1987).[6]

Sentencing and parole decisions generally involve consideration of two matters: the seriousness of the offense and the characteristics of the offender. Most people believe that both should be taken into account; it is difficult to imagine a system in which differences among offenders are totally ignored (for example, a system in which first offenders and habitual offenders are treated identically).

In this context, predicting criminality means attempting to assess the likelihood that a convicted offender will commit another offense when released into the community. Researchers distinguish between the generic definition of recidivism—simply the act of reoffending—

FIGURE 16.6
An example of a parole agreement.

STATEMENT OF PAROLE AGREEMENT

The members of the parole board agree that you have earned the opportunity of parole and eventual release from your present conviction. The board is therefore ordering a parole release in your case.

Parole status has a twofold meaning: first, it is a trust status in which the parole board accepts your word that you will do your best to abide by the conditions of parole set down in your case; second, by state law, the Adult Parole Authority has the legal duty to enforce the conditions of parole even to the extent of arrest and return to the institution.

The following conditions of parole apply to your parole release:

1. Upon release from the institution, report as instructed to your parole officer (or any other person designated), and thereafter report as often as directed.
2. Secure written permission of the Adult Parole Authority before leaving the [said] state.
3. Obey all municipal ordinances and state and federal laws, and at all times conduct yourself as a responsible, law-abiding citizen.
4. Never purchase, own, possess, use, or have under your control a deadly weapon or firearm.
5. Follow all instructions given by your parole officer or other officials of the Adult Parole Authority.
6. If you have any problems with the conditions or instructions of your parole, you may request a meeting with your parole officer's supervisor. The request should state your reasons for the conference, and it should be in writing if possible.
7. Special conditions.

I have read, or have had read to me, the foregoing conditions of my parole. I fully understand them and I agree to observe and abide by them.

Witness

Parole Candidate
Date

and recidivism rates, which tell us the percentage of any group of offenders that is likely to commit a new offense within a specified period.

There is no standard approach to calculating recidivism rates. In a given context, the calculation depends on what kind of behavior is to be counted—arrests, violation of parole conditions, convictions, incarcerations—and for how long. Generally, the broader the definition of reoffending or the longer the follow-up period, the higher the reported rate of recidivism will be. For example, if recidivism is measured by any arrest within two years, the frequency of recidivism will be higher than if recidivism is measured by a new conviction for a serious crime within the same time period. Or if reoffending is looked at for twelve months, the recidivism rates will be lower than if the follow-up period were twenty-four months.

THE SALIENT FACTOR SCORE The experience of the U.S. Parole Commission illustrates how predictions of recidivism are used in the criminal justice system. In the early 1970s, the U.S. Parole Commission developed an objective scale, based on empirical research, that is used to assess a prisoner's likelihood of recidivism. This scale, called the "Salient Factor Score," is similar to the actuarial tables that insurance companies develop and use. If people in one category of life insurance applicants, nonsmokers, for example, are likely to live longer than those in another category, smokers, life insurance companies may require higher premiums from smokers, whose average life expectancy is lower. So it is with the Salient Factor Score: members of groups having a higher likelihood of reoffending are likely to be held in prison longer.

The U.S. Parole Commission's Salient Factor Score contains six items:

- The offender's prior criminal convictions.
- The offender's prior criminal commitments for longer than thirty days.
- The offender's age at the time of the new offense.
- How long the offender was at liberty since the last commitment.
- Whether the prisoner was on probation, parole, or escape status at the time of the most recent offense.
- Whether the prisoner has a record of heroin dependence.

These items, individually and collectively, have been demonstrated to be associated with the likelihood of recidivism. For each item with a favorable response, the offender receives a fixed number of points. The points scored on each of the six items are added together to produce a total score that can range from 0 to 10. The higher the total score, the lower the predicted likelihood of recidivism. By taking these scores into account when deciding when to release prisoners on parole, the Parole Commission can release low-risk offenders sooner than high-risk prisoners.

The Salient Factor Score and the seriousness of the current offense are combined in a grid to determine a guideline range of total time to be served. The examiner establishes the seriousness of the offense and identifies the horizontal "offense severity" row that applies to the prisoner. Then the examiner calculates the prisoner's Salient Factor Score and finds the vertical column that applies to that category of offenses. The cell where the applicable row and column intersect shows the presumptive time to be served by that prisoner. An example of the grid for an offender who has committed a Category Five seriousness offense is shown in Table 16.1. This example shows that an offender with a very low Salient Factor Score may serve two to three times as long for the same offense as an offender with a very high Salient Factor Score.

The period of confinement set by the guidelines is "presumptive" (i.e., the guidelines have legal authority and a sentence consistent with them must be imposed or an explanation must be provided if it is not). The commission may depart from the guidelines if it finds aggravating or mitigating factors that are not already reflected in the guidelines, but it must provide specific reasons in writing for such a departure. In this way, the commission can try to be consistent and evenhanded while taking unique individual circumstances into account.

TABLE 16.1
Guidelines for Decision Making: Customary Total Time to Be Served before Release (Including Jail Time)

Offense Characteristics: Severity of Offense Behavior	Offender Characteristics: Parole Prognosis (Salient Factor Score 1981)			
	Very Good (10–8)	Good (10–6)	Fair (5–4)	Poor (3–0)
		Guideline Range		
Category Five	24–36 months	36–48 months	48–60 months	60–72 months

Adapted from Peter Hoffman, *Predicting Criminality* (Washington, D.C.: U.S. Department of Justice, National Institute of Justice, 1987), p. 2.

How well does the Salient Factor Score predict recidivism? Using one standard definition of recidivism (any new commitment of sixty days or more including a return to prison for parole violation within a two-year follow-up period), research showed that federal prisoners with the highest Salient Factor Score (a score of 10) had a recidivism rate of 6 percent. Offenders with the lowest Salient Factor Score (a score of 0) had a recidivism rate of 59 percent, nearly ten times as high. For the four risk categories defined by the Parole Commission for use in its guidelines, research has shown recidivism rates as follows:

SALIENT FACTOR SCORE CATEGORY	RECIDIVISM RATE
Category A (scores of 10–8)	12 percent
Category B (scores of 7–6)	25
Category C (scores of 5–4)	39
Category D (scores of 3–0)	49

As noted, different research studies have used different definitions of recidivism and different follow-up periods. Regardless of the definition of recidivism or the follow-up period used, the Salient Factor Score has shown clear differences in recidivism rates between categories. Yet within a given category nothing like perfect prediction is possible.

OTHER PREDICTION EFFORTS How do these results compare with other efforts to predict recidivism? The Salient Factor Score's predictive power is representative of the imperfect quality of predictions found by others who have conducted research in this area. Considerable effort has been devoted by the criminal justice research community to improving the predictive power of such devices, but the effort has thus far not been notably successful.

"Selective incapacitation," a sentencing strategy also based on prediction, has received substantial attention in recent years. The goal is to learn how to identify high-rate offenders in advance, before they commit many offenses. If these offenders can be accurately identified and incarcerated, the crimes they would have committed will not occur, and other offenders who present less risk of recidivism can be incarcerated for shorter periods or not at all. A recent major research report from the Rand

Corporation has given impetus to selective incapacitation efforts (Greenwood 1982).

Rand Corporation researchers found substantial variations in the rates of crime among offenders. The researchers questioned more than two thousand inmates in state prisons in California, Michigan, and Texas about their past criminal conduct. Some admitted to having committed one or two crimes per year; a small proportion said they had committed hundreds per year. The following factors were associated with the differences between high- and low-rate recidivists:

- Prior conviction for the same charge
- Incarcerated more than 50 percent of the preceding two years
- Served time in the state juvenile facility
- Drug use in the preceding two years
- Drug use as a juvenile
- Employed less than 50 percent of the preceding two years.

The Rand Corporation study is unusual because it is based on prisoners' admissions of the crimes they committed. Most recidivism research, by contrast, is based on arrests or convictions and, because many crimes do not result in arrests and fewer result in convictions, provides a less complete picture of offending.

Although the Rand Corporation demonstrated that offenders' rates of committing crimes vary dramatically, the Rand study cannot yet serve as the basis for actual decision-making. First, some of the information required for the predictions is not routinely and reliably available to judges and other officials. Second, because the Rand scale was developed on the basis of information about prisoners, it is not known how it would operate when applied to all convicted persons (many of whom have never been prisoners). Third, the research was based on past, not future, criminality. Predictions must deal with future behavior. It is yet to be seen whether prediction devices can be developed for operational use that will identify highly active recidivists with even modest accuracy.

The primary alternative to using statistical approaches to predictions relies on the clinical judgments of psychiatrists, psychologists, judges, or parole board members. The research evidence to date indicates that predictions based on statistical devices are usually better than the judgments of clinicians.

It is plausible to speculate that clinical judgments coupled with statistical predictions may provide better predictions than either alone. This combined approach is used by the U.S. Parole Commission. As noted earlier, its hearing examiners may override the decisions indicated by the Salient Factor Score when they can set forth substantial research evidence that documents whether combined clinical and statistical judgments actually improve predictive accuracy over that obtained by statistical approaches alone.

CRITICS AND JUSTIFICATIONS Critics of the use of predictions of future crime as the basis for parole and sentencing decisions have raised a number of ethical objections. They argue that prediction methods are far from perfect and that many of those who are classified as poor risks will not in fact commit additional crimes. Further, they argue that it is unfair to increase a person's current punishment because of what that person might do in the future.

Critics also question the legitimacy of relying on certain kinds of information in making predictions. Most people would agree that neither race nor sex should be used as a basis for increasing sentence lengths even if this information were shown to be statistically related to recidivism rates. Similarly, critics argue, "status items" such as employment and marital status should not be considered in predicting future crime even though they have been shown to have predictive power. Because low-income people are especially likely to score poorly on these status items, critics argue that using them constitutes a form of class and income bias. In addition, these items of information are not related to the offender's prior criminal record, are not "illegal in themselves," and may in some cases not be within the offender's control. For example, even if unemployed or unmarried offenders were found to have higher recidivism rates, would it be fair to punish them with longer sentences than are received by employed or married offenders who have committed the same offense?

Advocates of the use of criminological predictions generally agree that certain items may be ethically inappropriate to use even if they prove to be predictive (just as some law enforcement techniques, such as coerced confessions, are legally impermissible notwithstanding their effectiveness). But they point out that the best predictive items tend to be those concerning prior criminal record, and that valid prediction devices have been developed that do not use race, education, employment, or marital status.

Advocates also argue that most judges and parole officials do in fact take an offender's "dangerousness" into account, but they do it subjectively and based on their own intuition. Statistical prediction devices, even if imperfect, are more reliable than intuition. In addition, if the prediction device applies to all sentencing or parole decisions, it constitutes a single consistent set of standards and is therefore fairer than a system in which each judge or parole examiner applies his or her own idiosyncratic or intuitive standards.

Advocates of prediction acknowledge that criminological predictions are far from perfect and that a significant number of offenders who will not commit new offenses will be misclassified. But they argue that the offenders have made themselves vulnerable by committing the crimes for which they have been convicted. They maintain that a balance must be struck between the rights of the offenders and the right of the community to be protected from further crimes by the offenders.

These proponents of prediction point out that the use of prediction is advocated only for those who are convicted and then only within the range of what would otherwise constitute fair punishment for the offense. That is, advocates of prediction generally agree that the seriousness of the offense should set the upper and lower boundaries of what constitutes "just" punishment. Within these outer limits, they argue, it is both desirable and ethically appropriate to use predictive considerations to attempt to protect society, at least temporarily, by giving prison terms to those most likely to commit additional offenses.

Innovations in Parole

In 1965, the state of Ohio introduced a program of shock probation, or shock parole, that allowed the courts to impose a brief sentence of incarceration, followed by probation. The rationale for the program was to impress offenders with the seriousness of their crimes (thus, the prison sentence), but to release them for community supervision before they became "prisonized." (As Reid [1981] points out, "shock parole" is actually the better term: probation is technically an *alternative* to confinement; parole is a conditional release following a period of incarceration.)

Encouraged by its experience, Ohio passed a shock parole statute in 1974 that permitted shock parole for many prisoners after a six-month prison sentence. Eligibility criteria included the following:

1. The offense for which sentence was imposed must not be aggravated murder or murder.
2. The prisoner must not be a second offender.
3. The prisoner must not be dangerous.
4. The prisoner must not appear to need future confinement as part of his or her correction or rehabilitation.
5. The prisoner must give evidence that he or she is not likely to commit another offense.

The number of inmates released on shock parole in Ohio reached a high of 691 in 1974. That number has since declined because of an adverse Ohio Supreme Court decision, negative publicity, and the adoption of newer and more stringent guidelines for parole eligibility. Ironically, as shock parole was eclipsed in Ohio, several other states began to look at it as a possible way to reduce prison overcrowding.

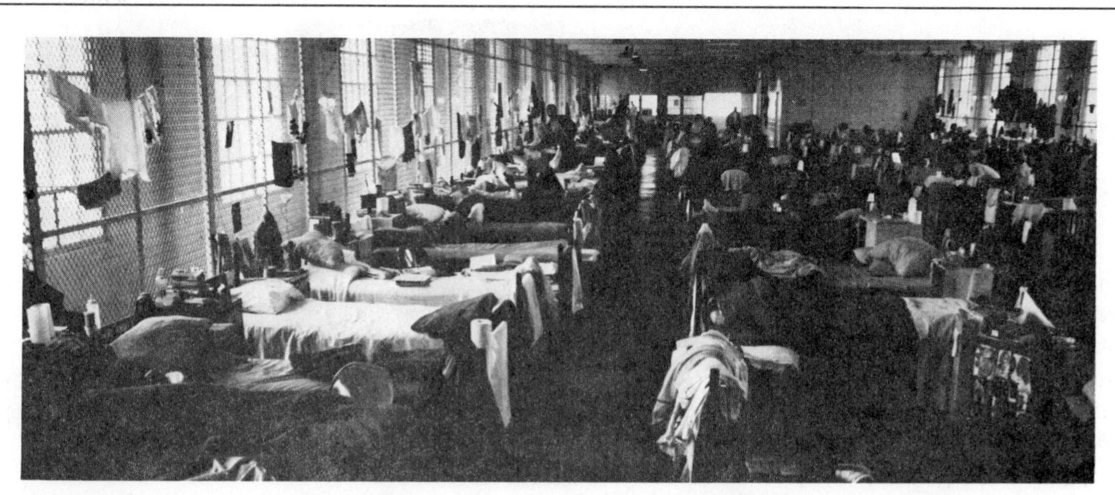

FIGURE 16.7
Overcrowding at Maryland House of Corrections. Courtesy *Corrections Magazine.*

Another approach to conditional release involves a three-way contract between the inmate, the parole board, and correctional authorities. This approach, designated as **contract parole** or Mutual Agreement Programming (MAP), lays out, in a legally binding contract, a series of specific activities that the inmate agrees to undertake for self-improvement. The parole board, in turn, agrees to a fixed parole date contingent upon the inmate's successful completion of the program. It is the responsibility of correctional authorities—the third party in the contract—to provide needed services and resources to inmates and to monitor their progress.

As Reid has noted, the contract parole arrangement "is aimed not only at giving the inmate more participation in the decision with regard to his or her future, but also at providing a mechanism by which parole boards will have to be more definite and more articulate about their decision making and give more thought to the reasons for their decisions" (1981, p. 340). The contract agreement also promotes long-range planning by both the inmate and the institution. However, a MAP program is difficult to implement and "requires persistence and determination on the part of administrators" (Keve 1981, p. 317). Many institutions simply lack the training and counseling services necessary to permit the inmate to fulfill MAP objectives.

An even more serious flaw of contract parole is that the various parties in the contract are not equals. Because prisoners are fully aware that their involvement in a MAP program is a crucial factor in determining how long they will stay in prison, they can scarcely be considered free agents in the negotiation (Morris 1974). But despite its drawbacks, contract parole is a worthwhile and progressive pursuit.

OTHER FORMS OF CONDITIONAL RELEASE

Work Release

The pioneering reform efforts of Crofton in Ireland in the nineteenth century provided prisoners with a chance to work within the community prior to release. This idea has been revived in recent years, and work release has become an important part of institutional programs. Under work release, offenders are allowed to work at jobs in the community and still receive the benefit of programs and services at the institution.

The first legislation of work release was a 1913 Wisconsin statute that allowed misdemeanants to work at their jobs while they served short sentences in jail. Then in 1957, North Carolina applied the principles of the Wisconsin statute to felony offenders under limited conditions; Michigan and Maryland soon followed suit with similar acts. In 1965, Congress passed the Federal Prisoner Rehabilitation Act, which provided for work release, furloughs, and community treatment centers for federal prisoners. Many states shortly took similar action.

Work release is not really an alternative to incarceration. Rather, it provides a chance for offenders to test their work skills, to control their own behavior in the community, and to spend the major part of the day away from the institution. Because the inmate is required to return to the institution, work release is actually only a *partial* alternative to incarceration.

The benefit of work release is more than allowing inmates to be outside the prison walls for part of each day. If an inmate has a family, his or her earnings can be used to keep the family off welfare or to augment public assistance. Income might also be used to reimburse victims or to acquire a modest savings account. One of the major advantages of work release, however, is that private citizens can observe offenders working in the community without creating problems for themselves or others. Association with fellow workers who enjoy stable lives in freedom may also give offenders support and guidance that they cannot gain inside prison walls. In the American tradition, the ability to produce a day's work is highly valued, and an inmate's return

FIGURE 16.8
A resident of Milwaukee's Baker House, a pre-release center, goes to work. Courtesy *Corrections Magazine.*

to normal work may instill a needed feeling of self-worth.

Study Release

Study release is a recent innovation in corrections. Before 1960, only Connecticut had an operational study release program. As of 1974, however, forty-one states had programs of some kind, most of them open to both male and female participants (Smith, McKee, and Milan 1974). The range of educational services offered by such programs is extremely broad, ranging from vocational training and basic adult skills to college education.

Variables involved in the screening of offenders for study release are comparable to those used for work release: severity of offense, time served, custody grade, educational needs, and attitudes of the offender. Because education is so important in our achievement-oriented society, programs that seek to increase the marketability of offenders are plausible alternatives to imprisonment. We are not in a position, however, to make broad statements about the value of such programs, because we are still waiting for reliable information on study release outcomes.

Furloughs

Furloughs are another form of partial incarceration. Work release, study release, and furloughs extend the limits of confinement by allowing unsupervised absences from prison. Furloughs and home visits have been used informally for many years. The death of a family member or some other crisis situation has been the most common reason for furloughs. States have passed legislation to make furloughs a legal tool of corrections, so their use has been expanded. Most furloughs are granted for home visits during holidays. They are also used just prior to release to ease the transition from confinement to freedom. It is probable that furloughs will be granted more and more frequently as correctional administrators gain experience in their use.

Graduated Release

An offender who serves a long sentence in an institutional setting may suffer culture shock when he or she is suddenly returned to the community. Just as astronauts must reenter the atmosphere in a series of steps, so too the offender needs to reenter society gradually. Thus, *graduated release programs* have been developed to ease the culture shock experienced by institutionalized offenders. Any preparation for release is better than none, but preparation that includes periods of nonincarceration is even more effective.

The periods immediately before and after the release of an offender are especially critical to the social readjustment of the offenders. Most ex-offenders know that they will have serious problems trying to reestablish a life for themselves outside the institution. Their fears and apprehensions build as they approach the time for release. In fact, some inmates even commit minor infractions of prison rules to postpone their release. These deliberate offenses allow them to remain in the total dependency of the institution. In recognition of this phenomenon, many correctional administrators have established prerelease and postrelease programs to assist offenders through these critical periods. Topics covered in such programs include how to get a driver's license, how to open a savings account, how to use credit, how to fill out an employment application, and how to adjust to sex and family.

The Sam Houston Institute of Contemporary Corrections provides some pointers for prerelease and graduated release programs (Frank 1973, pp. 228–29):

1. Prerelease preparation should begin as early as possible in the sentence, and inmates should know in advance the purpose and intention of the program.
2. Reliance must be placed on a sound program and not upon the use of special privileges as an enticement to participation.
3. The program should be organized with realistic goals in mind and should be part of the total treatment process.
4. The counseling program should deal with the immediate problems of adjustment, rather than with underlying personality problems.
5. Participants should be carefully selected on an individual basis, rather than according to predetermined arbitrary standards.
6. Employee-employer relationships, rather than custodian-inmate relationships, should exist between staff and inmates.
7. Every effort should be made to enlist the support and participation of the community, and family contact should be encouraged.
8. Whenever possible, work release should be included.
9. The center itself should be minimum security and should encourage personal responsibility. If prerelease programs are to be part of the

treatment process, there should be some provision for determining their effectiveness.

Graduated release and prerelease programs are not either-or alternatives to incarceration, but they do recognize the destructive and dependency-producing effects of imprisonment.

Halfway Houses

Although halfway houses were originally conceived as residences for homeless offenders released from prison, they have also been used for other purposes. Small residences that provide shelter have been managed by prison aid societies for over a century. And in recent years, halfway houses have been viewed as possible nuclei for community-based networks of residential treatment centers. There is also a move to use halfway houses as prerelease guidance centers.

FIGURE 16.9
Baker House, a pre-release center in Milwaukee. Opposition to new halfway houses in Wisconsin and many other states has intensified in recent years. Courtesy *Corrections Magazine.*

In 1961, the Federal Bureau of Prisons established prerelease guidance centers in several metropolitan areas. Offenders are sent to one of these centers several months before they become eligible for parole. Center personnel are selected based on their treatment orientation and their aptitude for counseling. While at a center, the offender is allowed to work and attend school in the community without supervision, and he or she may participate in a number of programs at the center. This approach has been copied by many states, and it appears to be worthwhile with adequate staff and supervision.

The PORT Program

The Probated Offenders Rehabilitation and Training (PORT) program in Rochester, Minnesota, was developed in 1979 to fill the gap between probation and institutionalization. PORT is a live-in, community-based treatment program for young adult and juvenile offenders who defy conventional correctional practices. Located on the grounds of the Rochester State Hospital, PORT offers a combination of group therapy and behavior modification. Some twelve to fifteen counselors of both sexes, most of them college students, reside in the building and help provide a healthy culture for program participants. Offenders work up a scale from one (minimal freedom) to five (maximum freedom) by demonstrating their ability to handle responsibility in school and work situations. Backsliding is recognized as a normal occurrence, and appropriate measures are taken to deal with it. Because of PORT's success, the Minnesota Department of Corrections has used it as a model for several other halfway houses in the state.

Electronically Monitored Home Confinement

Interest in the electronic monitoring of offenders goes back at least to 1966, when Ralph K. Schwitzgebel described a telemetry system in the *Harvard Law Review.* A prototype of "Dr. Schwitzgebel's machine" was tried in 1968, using multiple receivers to trace the wearer's movements through a building. More recently, the concept of electronic monitoring has expanded to include active and passive systems. Such systems are intended to monitor an offender's presence in a given environment—usually the home or a community corrections center—where the offender is required to remain for specified periods of time. This discussion focuses on active systems but concludes with a brief discussion of the passive alternatives (Ford and Schmidt 1985).[7]

By 1983, workable active monitors had been developed by Michael Goss in Albuquerque, New Mexico, and Thomas Moody in Key Largo, Florida. Each consisted of three elements:

- A miniaturized *transmitter,* strapped to the offender's ankle and broadcasting an encoded signal at regular intervals over a range of about two hundred feet.
- A *receiver-dialer,* located in the offender's home, to detect signals from the transmitter and to report periodically to a central computer.
- A *central computer* to accept reports from the receiver-dialer over the telephone lines, compare them with the offender's curfew schedule, and alert correctional officials to unauthorized absences.

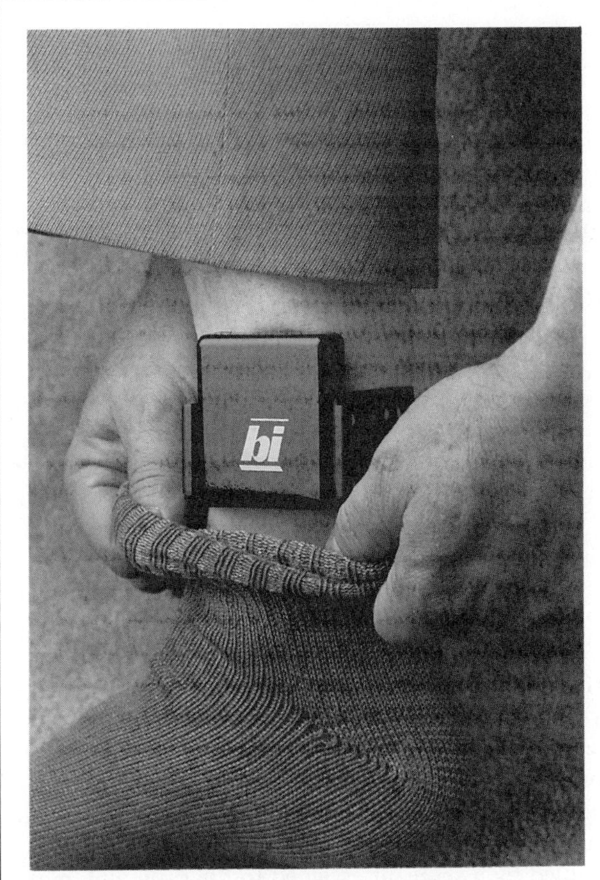

FIGURE 16.10
Miniaturized transmitter strapped to offender's ankle. Courtesy BI Incorporated, Boulder, Colorado.

In Albuquerque, a judge ordered a Goss transmitter attached to the ankle of a thirty-year-old probation violator for a one-month period starting in April 1983. He later sentenced four other offenders to monitored home confinement. An appraisal funded by the National Institute of Justice concluded the following:

- The equipment operated successfully.
- Monitored home confinement appeared to be acceptable to the local criminal justice community.
- The concept did not appear to pose legal problems when used as an alternative to detention.
- As compared to detention, monitoring resulted in "substantial savings" to the criminal justice system.

Meanwhile, a Florida judge tried new equipment, the Moody system, in Monroe County (Key West). The program involved twelve offenders over a six-month period, who were serving house-arrest sentences ranging from two days to four months.

THE PALM BEACH COUNTY FLORIDA EXPERIENCE On December 1, 1984, the Moody device—now called the In-House Arrest System—was adopted by Palm Beach County, Florida, in two programs, one involving probationers and the other involving work-release offenders from the county stockade, a minimum-security facility.

Probation. The probation program is administered by Pride, Inc., a nonprofit corporation that had supervised traffic and misdemeanor probation cases for the county since 1977. Pride had fifteen monitors and receiver-dialers in May 1985, with a few kept in reserve in case of breakdowns. Thus, no more than thirteen offenders were on home confinement at any given time. These were individuals who would otherwise have been incarcerated; their sentences were calculated on the basis of three or four days of home confinement for each day they would have spent in jail. Most were drunk-driving offenders, who were given a choice between thirty days on monitored home confinement or ten days in jail, the latter being the mandatory minimum sentence under Florida law for a second drunk-driving conviction.

In the program's first six months, the presiding Judge sentenced all candidates for the program. In each case, the sentence and conditions had to be acceptable to the prosecutor, the defendant, the defense attorney, and a probation officer from Pride, Inc.

While on home confinement, the offender is required to do the following:

FIGURE 16.11
Receiver-dialer located in the offender's home. Courtesy BI, Incorporated, Boulder, Colorado.

- Pay $5 per day for the monitoring equipment in addition to Pride's standard probation fee.
- Maintain a working telephone, installing one if necessary or making arrangements to live with a friend or relative who has a phone.
- Remain at home during the established curfew hours.
- Report weekly to the Pride office to have the transmitter straps inspected, pay probation and monitoring fees, and discuss any problems with respect to probation or home confinement.

In the Pride office, the probation officer fastens the transmitter to the offender's ankle with plastic straps, pop-riveted by a hand tool. The offender takes a receiver-dialer home and plugs it into the electrical and telephone circuits. The probation officer programs Pride's computer with the individual's curfew schedule, the computer receives a test signal, and any installation problems are worked out by telephone.

Pride's offices are unstaffed at night and on weekends, but a telephone answering machine is available so offenders can leave messages for the probation staff. Each weekday morning, the probation officer plays back these messages and scans a summary printout of the transmission from each offender's unit. If appropriate, the probation officer telephones the offender to check on his or her whereabouts. In addition, the printouts are reviewed with the offender at the weekly inspection and counseling session.

Under the program's policy, a major violation of curfew results in a return to court and probable incarceration. The violator would thereafter be ineligible for monitored home confinement. If an individual fails to return Pride's equipment, he or she will be charged with grand theft.

Work Release. In June 1985, the Palm Beach County stockade had a population of 325, of whom 45 were on work release. They were required to return to the stockade after work and to pay the county $9 per day from their earnings. After a month or two, selected work-release inmates were allowed to complete their sentences on monitored home confinement. Individuals convicted of sex offenses or crimes against persons were not eligible for the program. In May 1985, the program had 22 offenders on monitored home confinement, and 11 others had completed their sentences in the program.

The transmitter is fitted to the offender at the stockade office, and a sergeant accompanies the individual home to install the receiver-dialer. At the end of the work week—Friday evening or Saturday—the offender reports to the stockade gate guard, who inspects the straps and accepts the $63 weekly fee. All other communication between the offender and the stockade division is handled by a sergeant assigned to the case, who makes regular unannounced visits to the individual's job site and to the home.

The division had one violator in the first six months of the program. He was considered to have escaped from the stockade, an offense involving a possible five-year sentence.

Observations. Although no formal assessment of the Palm Beach County experience has been undertaken, some observations can be drawn from anecdotal accounts:

- Because of the county's geographical area, an incoming WATS line was necessary for the Pride program. In the first two months, telephone charges averaged about $22 per month for each offender.
- The typical room has "dead space" in which the receiver-dialer cannot pick up the transmitter's signal. In particular, metal tends to limit the range of the transmitter; kitchens are therefore an especially difficult environment. Transmission breaks have also been attributed to metal furniture, waterbeds, and even certain sleeping positions. Mobile homes constitute a problem for offenders trying to do yard chores: the range outside the building is as little as ten feet, compared to as much as two hundred feet from a woodframe building. All interference problems have been resolved by having the offender move the receiver-dialer, change his or her routine, or (in one instance) move in with a friend or relative.
- A few offenders complained about irritation from the transmitter or its straps. They reduced the chafing by wearing a cutoff tube sock under the monitor or an elasticized sock over it to hold it in place.
- The transmitter, of course, was visible when the offender wore shorts or a skirt. Some offenders coped by telling questioners that it was a heart-monitoring device.

TOWARD A FORMAL ASSESSMENT By spring 1985, electronic monitoring devices had been acquired by at least seven U.S. jurisdictions. The National Institute of Justice is planning a field assessment of some of these programs. Among the issues to be studied are the functioning of the equipment, the costs to the criminal justice system and to the wearer, the experience of offenders sentenced to monitored confinement, and the reactions of the criminal justice system and the community to this form of penalty.

Programs are now operating or under consideration in Kentucky, Oregon, Michigan, and Utah.

Kenton County, Kentucky. The Kentucky legislature debated a home confinement bill in 1984. The bill did not pass, but the legislature recommended a pilot program in anticipation of a similar bill in 1986. Kenton County (Covington) agreed to underwrite the $32,000 cost of installing the In-House Arrest System for up to twenty offenders. The first units arrived on April 15; the first offender was placed on the system on May 2.

Candidates for the program were misdemeanants who posed a minimum risk to the community, yet needed a restricted environment. These qualifications, officials feel, apply to an estimated 42 percent of Kentucky's prisoner population. After finding that the first offenders in the program had alcohol problems and could not comply with the program, officials began to screen candidates for alcohol dependency.

If an offender seemed appropriate, the judge deferred sentencing and instructed the individual to report to the state probation and parole officer in Covington. The officer explained the equipment, the conditions of home confinement, the consequences of violations, ways to deal with difficulties, and any special requirements such as restitution, community service, or participation in a counseling or treatment program. If the defendant agreed to the program and the probation officer regarded him or her as an appropriate risk, the judge entered a formal order confining the individual to house arrest.

Officials sent pictures of the transmitter to hospital emergency rooms and police stations, so personnel would recognize the device on an injured or arrested offender. They also involved the media at an early stage in the program, emphasizing that participants were in the program voluntarily, that the device could not eavesdrop, and that the offender was permitted to go to church as well as to his or her place of employment.

Rental fees were based on income and length of time in the program. Defendants with net weekly household incomes under $100 were provided the equipment without charge; a sliding scale was applied thereafter. An offender with a net household income of $400 per week, for example, would pay about $45 per week up to a maximum fee of $700 for four months on the monitor.

As with the other programs, offenders were fitted with the transmitter and returned home to install the receiver-dialer. The offender returned to the county jail each Thursday for a visual check of the transmitter straps and to pay the rental fee.

A county liaison officer checked the printout each morning, notifying the state probation officer whenever the computer failed to receive a signal or indicated a violation, the equipment malfunctioned, the offender failed to report for inspection or to pay the rental fee, or there was any evidence of tampering with the equipment. The probation officer investigated violations and made a weekly check of arrest records to ensure that the offender remained arrest-free. When the home confinement term was successfully completed, the judge put the offender on routine probation.

Clackamas County, Oregon. Clackamas County (Oregon City) had about two thousand individuals on probation or parole. To ease caseloads, it too adopted the In-House Arrest System. The central computer was installed in a community corrections center and was supplemented by an electronic monitoring system.

Officials say they plan to use monitored home confinement with both misdemeanants and felons, with pretrial releasees, and with offenders on furlough from residential centers.

Washtenaw County, Michigan. The Michigan Department of Corrections is planning a test in Washtenaw County (Ann Arbor) to determine if home confinement is a feasible alternative to incarceration in its crowded prisons and jails. In this jurisdiction, the target population will consist of felony offenders. The pilot project involved twenty monitors and support equipment for a period of six months.

Persons who had been charged with assault or escape or who had a history of assault or flight will not be candidates for the program. Narcotics dealers are also to be excluded. When an offender seems an appropriate candidate for home confinement—and a prison commitment would otherwise have been called for—the case will be referred to the Probation Sentence Panel. If the offender agrees to take part, the panel will recommend to the judge that the offender be placed on delayed-sentence status and ordered to participate in the home-confinement program.

Participants in the program will have to be able to support themselves; if not working, they will have to provide evidence that they are engaging in a job search. They will not be charged for the equipment. The expected maximum term of home confinement is ninety days.

After the delay order is entered, the defendant will be assigned to a probation agency, which arranges for the transmitter to be placed on the offender and the receiver-dialer to be placed in his or her residence. The offender will sign an agreement to maintain an operating telephone, respond to telephone calls, report malfunctions, and return for visual inspection of the transmitter if required.

In the first phase of the program, a small number of offenders will be confined to their homes during non-working hours, with monitoring from 4 P.M. to 6 A.M. weekdays and around the clock on Saturdays and Sundays. The central computer is monitored by community corrections staff. If an inappropriate signal is received, an officer attempts to telephone the client and reports the incident to the probation agent.

The probation agent can return the offender to jail if the conditions of home confinement are violated or if the individual is arrested for any crime. Once removed from home confinement, the offender will no longer be eligible to take part in the program.

State of Utah. In 1983 the Utah legislature passed a bill giving courts authority to sentence people to home confinement for prescribed periods of time. A year later, the legislature appropriated $60,000 to support a pilot program; it authorized $200,000 more in 1985. Meanwhile, the state attorney general's office held in an informal opinion that, "where the appropriate procedural safeguards are followed and the use of electronic surveillance is related to the rehabilitation of the offender and the protection of society, given the nature of the offense and the character of the offender, the resulting limitation on the exercise of constitutional rights will be upheld."

In Utah, electronic monitoring was intended to enhance an intensive supervision program already in place. The clientele was to be drawn from individuals whose parole or probation would otherwise be revoked, and the maximum period of home confinement was expected to be six months, with a likely average of four months. The first phase involved about thirty monitors and clients, with the first equipment received in November 1984.

In January 1985, corrections officials began to experiment with the system in halfway houses and other locations. By April, the first two clients were on the monitors in Salt Lake City. The central computer was located in the Bonneville Community Corrections Center with staff available round the clock. Probation and parole agents on duty in the community were equipped with beepers, so that an agent could be dispatched immediately if a violation was signaled.

PASSIVE MONITORING SYSTEMS In addition to the active devices just described, there are passive systems on the market that can monitor individuals in the homes. For example, an automated caller can be programmed to deliver one of several prerecorded messages to the probationer; this device can be used in tandem with a wristlet that, when inserted into a verifier box, sends a signal identifying the recipient of the call. The offender may also be asked to respond to a question, with the response recorded as an additional means of identification. (Officials in Clackamas County, Oregon, who used this system in addition to an active system, found that the recording could reveal that the offender was having difficulty inserting the wristlet into the verifier—a possible indication that he or she had been drinking.)

A limitation of such passive systems is that telephoning the offender in the middle of the night or the early morning hours can be disruptive and annoying. However, the systems offer the advantages of simplicity, lower cost, and the absence of false signals.

Diversion

Diversion refers to organized efforts to use alternatives to the criminal process. To qualify as diversion, efforts must be made *following* a violation of the law and *before* adjudication. This definition may include some traditional conceptions of *prevention*. For instance, the exercise of discretion at some point in the criminal justice process may result in the *informal* diversion of an offender. Only about 30 percent of reported property offenses in the United States result in arrest, and only about one-third of those arrests result in conviction.

Police agencies practice informal diversion by using their extensive powers of discretion at the time of arrest. Police have been reluctant to formalize their discretion practices because they fear the public will regard the practice as a weakness, or believe they are assuming responsibilities that are rightly those of prosecutors and the courts. As a result, most formalized programs are aimed at the youthful offender in an effort to prevent the start of a crime career. Another example of diversion at the police level is the family crisis intervention approach. By identifying conflict situations early on, police officers trained to intervene in family disturbances can prevent the escalation of violence. If they are unable to resolve the conflict on the scene, they may refer the antagonists to a community agency. This kind of training is now a standard part of professional development in many law enforcement agencies.

The judicial system is also engaged in diverting offenders. Diversion efforts of the prosecutor typically involve the exercise of discretion to "nol pros" (i.e., *nolle prosequi)*—the suspension of formal prosecution against a suspect when the prosecutor feels that a judicial proceeding would not serve the best interests of the community or the offender. The courts become involved with diversion when they use civil commitment for individuals who might benefit from hospital treatment. However, the constitutionality of civil commitment procedures is currently being questioned, and their continued use is in doubt. A more common and reasonable use of diversion by the courts is the pretrial intervention program. These programs use both paid workers and community volunteers to provide counseling, employment services, and education to defendants who are eligible based on such factors as sex, age, residence, employment status, present charge, pretrial release status, and prior record.

Diversion programs all have the same goal—to provide a reasonable alternative to incarceration in large, punitively oriented prisons. Most programs now in effect are informal responses to ambiguous legislation. Thus, the value of such programs is difficult, if not impossible, to estimate. For the programs to succeed, the goals, methods, and procedures of diversion must be articulated and integrated into the rest of the criminal justice system, and procedures for operating and evaluating diversion programs must be developed.

Diversion programs are most effective when they are integrated into a community-based correctional system with alternative levels of supervision and custody. Converting informal programs into formalized, accountable programs must be done without creating rigidity and inflexibility. If controls over community-based programs are too restrictive, the programs will become "institutions without walls." Diversion should be seen as the threshold of the community corrections system and should be designed to remove as many offenders as possible from the criminal process *before* conviction and criminalization occur.

Alcohol and Drug Abuse Programs

DETOXIFICATION CENTERS In *Robinson* v. *California* (370 U.S. 660 [1962]), the U.S. Supreme Court held that a California statute making it a criminal offense to be addicted to a narcotic drug was unconstitutional because it amounted to cruel and unusual punishment. The decision was based on a view of addiction as an illness rather than a crime. The argument of cruel and unusual punishment was also applied in the lower court cases of *Driver* v. *Hinnant* (356 F.2d 761 [1966]) and *Easter* v. *District of Columbia* (361 F.2d 50 [1966]). In the latter case, chronic alcoholism was allowed as a defense to a charge of public intoxication.

In *Powell* v. *Texas* (392 U.S. 514 [1968]), the U.S. Supreme Court upheld the conviction of a chronic alcoholic charged with public intoxication. However, the vote in the case was 5–4, and the opinions indicate that the Court might decide differently in a future case involving the same constitutional questions. At any rate, the trend has been set by these cases and by the findings and recommendations of several commissions, including the President's Commission on Law Enforcement and Administration of Justice (1967).

The recognition of alcoholism as a disease rather than a crime was furthered in 1973 by the drafting of the Uniform Alcoholism and Intoxication Treatment Act by the National Conference of Commissioners on Uniform State Laws. Guided by this model, several states passed laws to decriminalize public intoxication and to remove its control from the criminal justice system. As in the case of Florida's Myers Act (also known as the Comprehensive Alcoholism Prevention, Control, and Treatment Act), these laws treat alcoholism as a disease rather than as a crime and seek to provide treatment for the alcoholic.

The rationale behind these laws was put into action in 1966 when the St. Louis (Missouri) Police Department opened the nation's first *civil detoxification center*. A federal demonstration grant provided the financing, and a standing order from the chief of police codified the new procedure. An arrested drunk is now offered the choice between criminal processing and "voluntary" detoxification (Nimmer 1971). If a qualified offender chooses detoxification (a person who requires hospitalization for a physical disease or someone charged with a serious crime does not qualify), he or she is transported to the detoxification center for a seven-day stay. A summons charging the "patient" with public drunkeness and setting a court date is left with the center's staff. If the person completes the seven-day program, the summons is torn up on his or her release. If the person leaves the center against medical advice, the criminal process is resumed and the patient-offender is prosecuted for drunkenness.

FIGURE 16.12
Public drunkenness is seen increasingly as a problem for civil detoxification rather than arrest. Courtesy Harry Wilkes/Stock Boston.

The St. Louis program continues to operate under these guidelines. It offers emergency medical care of the highest quality, but it reaches only a fraction of those who could benefit from it. In addition, it provides no effective aftercare for the patient-offender following detoxification. This program has succeeded in conserving court time and jail space—but that is about all. No convincing evidence has been produced to show that the program has intervened successfully in the degenerative, repetitive life cycles of most of its patients.

DWI OFFENSES Public drunkenness is primarily a public nuisance; offenders are rarely violent, and their prosecution is often a matter of aesthetic, rather than criminal, concern. Drunk driving, on the other hand, is a serious offense. More than 50 percent of the nation's traffic fatalities in a given year (25,000 to 30,000) occur in accidents that directly or indirectly involve alcohol consumption. Although the official designation of "driving while under the influence" does not distinguish between alcohol and narcotics, alcohol consumption accounts for the overwhelming majority of DWI arrests.

To cope with the highway carnage caused by the drunk driver, the U.S. Department of Transportation, through the National Highway Safety Administration, initiated the Alcohol Safety Action Project (ASAP) in 1966. ASAP is a series of twenty-one countermeasures that involve law enforcement agencies, courts, schools, and the media in an effort to enlist support for various programs. Included in ASAP is DWI Counterattack, an eight-hour course for drunk drivers enrolled by the court. The course teaches about the effects of alcohol on the body and attempts to change attitudes about drinking while driving. In some jurisdictions, people arrested for DWI offenses are given the option to have adjudication withheld on the condition that they attend a DWI Counterattack course.

ADDICTION TREATMENT The National Advisory Commission on Criminal Justice Standards and Goals (1973) suggests a multimodality approach to drug treatment. The commission recommends crisis intervention and drug emergency centers; facilities and personnel for methadone maintenance; facilities and personnel for narcotics antagonist programs; therapeutic community programs staffed entirely or largely by ex-addicts; closed and open residential treatment facilities; and halfway houses staffed primarily by residents.

Crisis Intervention and Emergency Treatment Programs. Crisis intervention and emergency treatment programs supply addicts with emergency medical aid and psychological services—such as hot-line telephones and counseling.

Methadone Maintenance. Addicts treated by methadone maintenance receive a daily oral dose of methadone, usually in a controlled clinical setting (Nelkin 1973). Addicts receive increasing amounts of methadone until they reach a dose regarded as sufficient to provide a cross-tolerance that will block the euphoric effects of heroin. However, because methadone does not dull depression or anxiety (as heroin does), this treatment is only successful if addicts are highly motivated to give up heroin.

The commission considers methadone maintenance to be a more satisfactory method of treatment than the heroin maintenance system used in Great Britain. As Nelkin points out, "Unlike heroin, methadone is absorbed effectively through the gastrointestinal tract and is effective for a full 24 hours. It is, therefore, administered orally only once a day" (1973, p. 38). Also, the addict does not require increasingly larger doses of methadone to remain comfortable, and the symptoms of methadone withdrawal are less intense than the symptoms of heroin withdrawal. The possibility of complete withdrawal from methadone remains uncertain, however. One study claims that methadone withdrawal is harmless, with little danger of severe physical reaction; but many programs have had only limited success withdrawing patients who were stabilized on methadone.

Methadone maintenance has been criticized because it offers only a medical solution to a complex social, political, and psychological problem. It has also been argued that, because methadone does not produce euphoria, addicts will seek other drugs. Another problem is the illegal use of methadone: if a stabilized addict is allowed to take home a small supply, the drug may fall into the hands of addicts not participating in the maintenance program.

Narcotic Antagonist Treatment Programs Narcotic antagonist treatment programs use chemotherapy to block the effects of heroin and other narcotics. The goal is to create a pharmacological state, whereby the effect of any narcotic is nullified. The ultimate aim is to stop all drug use.

Therapeutic Communities In the drug-free environment of therapeutic communities, the drug user is viewed as an underdeveloped, immature personality. Residents are expected to remain in therapeutic communities for extended periods of time, ranging from eighteen months to two years or more. These communities have been criticized on the grounds that only a small number of their residents are successfully rehabilitated.

Residential Treatment Facilities The commission recommends that residential treatment facilities include both closed and open centers and halfway houses. Closed facilities provide a therapeutic environment in which an addict can live free of drug use—with the help of constraints such as locked doors. Open centers have the same basic services as closed centers, but they lack physical (and other) restraints to keep residents inside. Halfway houses provide lodging and support services for residents making the transition from an institutional setting to the open community. These houses are also available to persons already in the community who require temporary support.

Community Correctional Centers

The essential element in successful community-based corrections is the coordination of activities and services for *all* offenders. Presently, most programs function as separate entities under separate branches of government. However, there are a number of community-based facilities that approach an integrated community correctional center. Such centers are generally open institutions located in the community and using community resources to provide services. The centers can be used for a variety of purposes, including detention, treatment, holding, and prerelease. One type of facility that can be developed into an integrated center is the jail.

A community correctional center derived from an existing jail would provide residential care to four major categories of inmates: persons awaiting trial, persons serving sentences, persons leaving major institutions, and short-term returnees. These inmates would use the center only after the court has taken advantage of all diversionary and alternative procedures—such as release on personal recognizance, release under supervision, and use of summons and warrants by the police. In the treatment of pretrial inmates, it must be remembered that these individuals have not been found guilty of a crime. Thus, no phase in their treatment should imply guilt. In a jail census taken several years ago it was determined that 52 percent of the jail population had not been convicted but was awaiting arraignment or trial. This indicates the magnitude of the problem in providing services and programs to this group. Nonconvicted detainees should be separated from convicted offenders and from persons who are mentally or physically ill. And various types of security and treatment should be provided.

The community correctional center can also benefit the sentenced offender. Jails traditionally confine misdemeanants, and felons are sentenced to state prisons. However, there is reason to believe that it might be effective to treat nondangerous felons the way misdemeanants are treated. But this theory is probably too advanced for most jurisdictions, and it is probable that most community correctional centers will continue to handle only minor offenders and misdemeanants. Nevertheless, some jurisdictions have tried more imaginative methods of handling the convicted offender—methods such as work release, study release, and weekend sentencing. Jurisdictions with small halfway houses might consider using these facilities for some categories of jailed offenders.

The community correctional center permits programs that are found in many contemporary halfway-*out* and halfway-*in* houses. Offenders preparing for release from state institutions may be transferred to community centers, where they can be gradually reintegrated into the mainstream. Released ex-offenders might also use the centers to obtain help and guidance instead of reverting to criminal behavior. This two-way function is in line with attempts to reduce involuntary returns to control. The model is used widely in the mental health field, where outpatient service and temporary voluntary recommitment have helped some offenders to avoid major problems and to receive more effective treatment.

The community correctional center is a reasonable alternative to the traditional jail and it is an important move toward the integration of all correctional services within a state or region. For these centers to be effective, they must include accurate observation of the individual, intensive staff-client interaction, opportunities for reality confrontation and reality testing, discussions, some element of choice, positive leisure-time options, optimal living and constructive learning situations, and community and group interaction.

SUMMARY

In this chapter, we have examined some of the more traditional alternatives to confinement as well as some newer ones. Certainly, one of the older and more common forms is the concept of probation, which can be implemented in three ways. First, the law may allow the trial judge to suspend the execution of sentence and to place the offender on conditional probation. Second, a state statute may require sentencing but may permit suspension, and third, sentencing and probation may be left to the discretion of the trial judge. If a probationer violates the condition of his or her probation, the trial judge usually orders the execution of the sentence originally imposed. If a judge has suspended sentencing, a probation violation might result in a stiffer prison sentence than would have been imposed earlier.

In order to determine which offenders are good candidates for probation, sentencing judges rely heavily upon presentence investigation (PSI) reports. The primary purpose of the PSI is not to determine the guilt or innocence of defendants, but rather to give insights into their personalities and lives. Such reports should include a description of the offense including statements of codefendants; the defendant's own version of the offense; prior record; family and marital history; description of the neighborhood in which the defendant was reared; and facts about the defendant's education, religion, interests, mental and physical health, employment history and military service.

As a general rule, revocation of probation is justified only when probationers defy the courts or when they become a threat to the community.

Over the last two decades, several trends have converged to change the nation's probation population. Rising crime rates have led to public demand that criminals get harsher treatment; "just deserts" and incapacitation have displaced rehabilitation as the primary aim of corrections. Consequently, more felons are being imprisoned than ever before in our history. But at the same time, budget limitations have made it impossible for prison construction to keep pace with felony convictions. Prison crowding has become so critical that the courts have increasingly used probation to catch the overflow.

Probation sentences for adult felons have become so common that a new term has emerged in criminal justice circles: felony probation. Today, over one-third of the nation's adult probation population consists of persons convicted in superior courts of felonies (as opposed to misdemeanors).

Parole is the conditional release, under supervision, of offenders from correctional institutions after they have served part of their sentences. It is the way in which the majority of incarcerated felons are released from prison each year. Parole differs from probation, because it implies that the offender has served time. Administratively, parole is a function of the executive branch of government, and probation is a judicial act of the court. Selection, supervision, regulations, revocation, and release procedures are similar for parole and probation, however, and the two kinds of release are often confused by the public.

Considerable research has been conducted to determine what can be done to enhance parole prediction. One of these is the Salient Factor Score, which was developed in the early 1970s by the U.S. Parole Commission to assess a prisoner's likelihood of recidivism. This scale is similar to the actuarial tables that insurance companies develop and use. If people in one category of life insurance applicants, nonsmokers, for example, are likely to live longer than those in another category, smokers, life insurance companies may require higher premiums from smokers, whose average life expectancy is lower. So it is with the Salient Factor Score: members of groups having a higher likelihood of reoffending are likely to be held in prison longer.

The U.S. Parole Commission's Salient Factor Score contains six items: the offender's prior criminal convictions; the offender's prior criminal commitments for longer than thirty days; the offender's age at the time of the new offense; how long the offender was at liberty since the last commitment; whether the prisoner was on probation, parole, or escape status at the time of the most recent offense; and whether the prisoner has a record of heroin dependence.

Among the other forms of conditional release are work release programs; study release; graduated release; halfway houses; and home confinement. Certainly one of the more interesting and innovative devices utilized in conjunction with home confinement is the chance monitoring of offenders to assure that they do not violate the conditions of their probation.

Within the past twenty-five years, the criminal justice system has been forced to assess the ways in which it deals with alcoholics and drug addicts. A number of important U.S. Supreme Court decisions have provided the impetus necessary for the creation of alcohol and drug abuse programs.

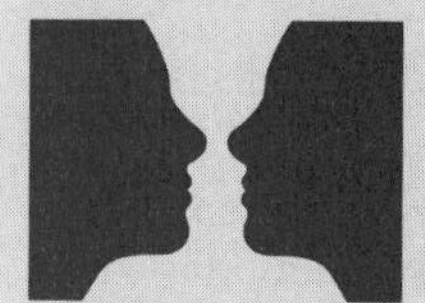

ISSUE PAPER

CASTRATION FOR SEX OFFENDERS: PUNISHMENT OR VENGEANCE?

ANDERSON, S.C.—With big steel pots of grits gurgling on the burners behind her, waitress Judy Kay dropped her dishrag to engage in debate with the retired tobacco salesman sipping coffee at the counter. The topic: the castration of rapists.

"It won't stop them. They can still have sex," the waitress said, "they just can't have no children."

"Unh unh," the man said, shaking his head and smiling. "They can't have no sex, honey."

"Can too," the waitress said emphatically.

"You're wrong. I've raised cattle, and there ain't no difference between people and cattle," the customer replied as the waitress went back to work. "You castrate a bull and he can't do anything. Right? Am I right? Tell her I'm right."

It was pretty much a draw, this late-night countertop point-counterpoint at the Waffle House in Anderson, a sprawling South Carolina textile town not far from the Georgia border. It was here that a judge on Nov. 17 ordered an unusual choice of punishments to three convicted rapists: 30 years in prison or freedom through castration.

The sentence—or rather, the choice—has been criticized by medical, correctional and constitutional experts as ignorant, illegal, impractical and inhumane. This, some of them say, is gut-level justice—the type that satisfies the public's growing desire for vengeance but does little to address the problem of rape.

Criminologists say that rape most often is a crime of violence, not of lust. Castration—removal of the testicles—might reduce or eliminate a man's sex drive but it does not eliminate the violent personality, psychiatrists say. And they say that less-drastic measures are being used successfully to treat some rapists.

Those states with established specialized therapy programs—Oregon, Connecticut, New Jersey, Maryland, Washington and Minnesota, among them—are reporting impressive success rates in their work with rapists, child molesters, exhibitionists and voyeurs. Such programs are based primarily on group and individual therapy aimed at reshaping the deviant sexual behavior that most experts believe was learned in the person's childhood.

In Anderson, though, the reaction has been one of resounding support from a citizenry fed up with crime. Yes, most say, it is a last resort; and yes, it might sound a little barbaric; and yes, it might not work on everybody. But, they say, it is high time criminals stop being coddled.

On a recent edition of the "Matt and Bev Talk Show," 152 listeners called radio station WRIX-FM in neighboring Honea Path to give their views on the subject: 148 said castration was an appropriate sentence for a convicted rapist. The other four said castration was a start, but by itself was not a severe enough penalty.

"It shocked us so much," said co-host Beverly Brandon. "We're right in the middle of the Bible Belt, but even the ministers who called in thought it was a just punishment."

"I thought it was great," state Rep. D. L. "Woody" Aydlette Jr. said of the sentence. Aydlette introduced a bill in the legislature in November to make surgical castration a mandatory punishment for rapists in South Carolina. Of the 200 letters he has received about his bill, only two have been in opposition.

"This is not simply a Southern thing, either," said Aydlette, a Republican. "The intellectuals in the North would like everybody to think that, but if they get out in the street and questioned people, they'd find out different."

The idea of castrating rapists—particularly violent ones—is probably more popular, less Southern and more common than many people think.

Only 10 years ago, Richard R. Milo, a Denver, Colo., gas-station attendant facing 40 years for rape and child molesting and having already been beaten in jail (as child molesters often are), volunteered for and underwent castration, with a prior agreement that the judge would grant probation in exchange.

In the 1930s and 1940s scores of sex offenders were castrated in California, and thousands more have gone under the knife in Denmark, Sweden and other countries in Europe and the Middle East. It is still a common practice in some Muslim countries.

New Jersey and Oklahoma are among the states in which bills similar to Aydlette's have been introduced in the last three years, only to die because of questions about their constitutionality. In the case of Oklahoma, however, the bill got through one chamber of the legislature, passing 50–35 in the House.

At Temple University in Philadelphia, criminal justice Professor Sharon Brown says that when she asks her students whether they favor castration for convicted rapists, about half of them—generally the females—raise their hands.

And on the Jan. 9 "Donahue" television show, taped in Chicago and featuring the victim and other principals in the gang-rape case in Anderson, a member of the audience said that not only does she favor castration, she thinks the operation should be performed without the benefit of anesthesia.

(Between 1930 and 1970, 455 rapists, 89 percent of them black men, were executed in the United States, mostly in Southern states. The death penalty for rapists was declared unconstitutional by the U.S. Supreme Court, ruling on a Georgia case, in 1977.)

Here in Anderson, what little opposition there is to Judge C. Victor Pyle's sentence comes from those who think he was not stern enough, considering the violence of the crime. The victim lost four pints of blood during the rape, though she has since recovered physically.

"I believe in an eye for an eye," said Carl Parker, 21, the manager of a fast-food restaurant. "I'm all for this castration. I think it would stop them completely. Guys would think twice before they did it. I know I would. People don't mind going to prison, but cutting something off, that's what scares people."

"If they can still have sex, cut the penis off, too. Cut off the whole damn works. It they need to go to the bathroom, make them wear a little bag on their sides that everyone can see."

Lawyer Glenn Thomason is familiar with the mood. He has received letters advocating that he be castrated for even representing Roscoe J. Brown and Mark Vaughn, two of the three convicted rapists who are still weighing their options in the Perry Correctional Center in Pelzer, S.C.

One of Thomason's clients, Brown, had chosen castration but said in an interview that he was reconsidering his choice because it would require that he drop his appeal. Of the other two, one has said he is leaning toward castration.

Although Brown said he would like to try to prove his innocence, both he and his wife say castration will be their choice if the option remains 30 years in prison.

"It's possible that it (castration) could happen but not probable," Thomason said. "I don't know what it would accomplish, though. I don't know if Judge Pyle's intent was to punish these people, to deter others, or alleviate the possibility of these people ever doing this again. I have no earthly idea. If he wanted to scare the hell out of people, I think he did. If he wanted to address the problem of rape, he didn't."

Civil libertarians, echoing the concerns of many criminologists and even some advocacy and counseling groups for rape victims, agree.

Chances are that taxpayers such as Carl Parker, who would "cut off the whole works," would not think much of the Oregon Correctional Treatment Program at Oregon State Hospital.

They probably would not want to see their money spent on devices such as the penile plethysmograph, which is attached to a prisoner's penis while he is shown erotic pictures. The machine determines, in layman's terms, what turns the inmate on. When aroused by a deviant theme, the inmate is given a slight electrical shock or a whiff of ammonia.

They probably would find little use either for the group-therapy sessions or for the requirement that inmates keep masturbatory logs, recording their fantasies daily.

They definitely would not want to read about how those inmates are being taught about dating and sex education or about how they go on river rafts or ski trips as part of their training in socialization.

And that may have something to do with why there are so few programs around specializing in the treatment of sex offenders.

Most state prison systems offer no such specialized programs. Some that once did have cut them from the budget in what many prison-reform groups see as a national shift away from the ideal of rehabilitation.

Similarly, funding has decreased for scientific and sociological research into the behavior of sex offenders.

"Many sex offenders, including many rapists and child molesters, can, in fact, be rehabilitated through soundly planned, staffed and administered treatment programs," said a 1978 report of the Law Enforcement Assistance Administration. But "nothing in particular is being done about the vast majority of them, and little or no attention is being paid to the particular factors which make those sex offenders," the report said.

That conclusion still holds true, many experts maintain.

"We're missing the boat, putting all the money into bricks and mortar," said Faye Honey Knopp, who has written several articles on sex offenders and is director of a Vermont prison-research organization. "My feeling is this should go under crime prevention. Instead, they put the money after the fact, building prisons."

At a Johns Hopkins University clinic, where some participants receive injections of Depo-Provera, a controversial drug that lowers the sex drive by reducing the body's production of the male hormone testosterone, program officials boast of a 90-percent success rate.

In Oregon, 19 inmates have "graduated" since that state's sex-offenders program began in 1979. There has been one case of recidivism: An inmate was returned to prison after violating his parole by stealing women's undergarments.

At the Adult Diagnostic and Treatment Center in Avenel, N.J., the only state prison in the country exclusively for sex offenders, 31 of the 233 inmates released since the program began in 1976 have been returned for new offenses, according to William Plantier, assistant superintendent.

Roger Smith, Oregon's manager of correctional treatment programs, said about 85 percent of the prisoners in the 33-member sex-offenders program at a state mental hospital there had been victimized as children.

"We don't think people are born rapists or born child molesters; instead, an event happened in their lives that shaped them," said A. Nicholas Groth, author of the book, "Men Who Rape," and director of a Connecticut program for sex offenders that operates out of a maximum-security prison in Somers. "The majority were sexually abused as a child. Like battered children, the victim usually becomes the victimizer."

Groth, like many experts, does not see sex as the primary motivation in most rapes. "We see rape as the sexual expression of aggression, rather than aggressive expression of sexuality," he said.

"It's like the alcoholic," Groth said. "He is not drinking because he's thirsty." And for the sex offender, like the alcoholic, there is no cure, Groth said. The goal, instead, is learning to control the behavior.

Behavior modification is frequently used in the programs. An inmate might be required, for example, to listen to a tape-recorded story. At first, the story—written to fit his particular deviancy—arouses him. At the height of arousal, its tone changes, with the inmate getting arrested, perhaps beaten by police or divorced by his wife.

The cornerstone of all the programs, however, is therapy. The Oregon program, for example, requires each inmate to undergo five hours a day of group therapy, six days a week.

In the Johns Hopkins program, that therapy is coupled with the use of Depo-Provera, a drug used by women in more than 80 countries as a birth-control agent. In men, because it lowers the sex drive by suppressing production of the sex hormone, it is referred to as chemical castration.

In this country, the U.S. Food and Drug Administration has approved the drug only for use on certain inoperable cancers. However, doctors may legally prescribe it for other purposes when a patient volunteers and is aware of the risks involved.

Critics of the drug say it has been shown to cause cancer in laboratory animals, that its side effects include hot and cold flashes, weight gain, headaches, fatigue and high blood pressure and that even when a prisoner volunteers for it, he is, in effect, being used as a human guinea pig.

Dr. Fred Berlin, co-director of the Johns Hopkins program, said the program is not an experiment. "We're giving medicine to the inmates that we are very hopeful will help them in an immediate and practical way."

The drug is given only to volunteers, who are made aware of its side effects, he said. About half of the 150 participants in the program at Johns Hopkins, and about five of the 25 prisoners enrolled in another branch of the program at the Maryland State Penitentiary, receive regular—usually weekly—injections of the drug.

Other prison systems and some community programs for sex offenders have decided against prescribing the drug. A Connecticut Department of Corrections Task Force that studied Depo-Provera and recommended in October that it not be used cited "very real concerns about the safety of this drug," including concerns about the possibility of its recipients developing "atypical sperm capable of producing malformed offspring."

Complaints also were raised in Connecticut about the use of aversive therapy, in which inmates receive electric shocks when aroused by deviant themes. In the mid-1970s that therapy was ceased after the Connecticut ACLU took the matter to court.

While the treatments used in some states have been questioned, the lack of any treatment in most states is of greater concern to many.

In Pennsylvania, a task force formed by Philadelphia's Women Organized Against Rape, one of the oldest rape-crisis centers in the country, has recommended to the state Bureau of Correction that a statewide treatment program for sex offenders be developed.

The task force concluded that with the exception of a few weekly group-therapy sessions, no programs exist to change the behavior of sex offenders, who account for about 10 percent of Pennslyvania's prison population.

John Woestendiek. "Castration for Sex Offenders: Punishment or Vengeance." From *The Tampa Tribune-Times*, 22 January 1984.

DISCUSSION AND REVIEW

1. What is meant by the contention that probation is a combination of treatment and punishment? Can such a combination be expected to work?
2. How does probation differ from a suspended sentence? What is "probation without adjudication"?
3. Discuss the process of revocation of probation. What are some of the issues raised by revocation?
4. According to the Rand study performed in Los Angeles and Alameda Counties, which type of offender is most likely to recidivate?
5. Statistical analyses indicate a high correlation between prison sentences and certain basic factors of a case. What are they?
6. To determine what factors were associated with rearrest, reconviction, and conviction for violent crime, the Rand study used a hierarchy of information levels similar to that used by a court in the prison/probation decision. What are these factors?
7. What is an intensive surveillance program, and how does it work?
8. What are some of the major problems in parole selection?
9. Sentencing and parole decisions generally involve consideration of two matters. What are they?
10. The U.S. Parole Commission's Salient Factor Score contains six items. What are they?
11. What is selective incapacitation?
12. What are some of the advantages of contract parole?
13. What are some of the more common forms of conditional release?
14. What is the purpose of electronically monitored home confinement?
15. What are the three elements of the electronically monitored home confinement units developed by Goss and Moody?

16. Diversion programs all have the same goal. What is it?
17. What is the drug Depo-Provera used for, and has it accomplished its intended purpose in regard to sex offenders?

GLOSSARY

Contract parole (Mutual Agreement Programming) System in which the parole board, correctional department, and inmate agree to a three-way contract in which the prisoner assumes responsibility for his or her own rehabilitation program, with the goal of obtaining parole release on a specific date.

Diversion Removal of offenders from the criminal justice system by channeling them into alternative programs; also describes the process of sentencing offenders to a community-based correctional program rather than to prison.

Furlough Temporary leave of absence given to an inmate housed in an institution; usually consists of a brief visit to the home or the community.

Halfway house A community correctional facility that provides a residence for convicted offenders who do not require the secure custody of a prison; also a transitional setting for prisoners being released from a correctional institution.

Parole Supervision of an offender in the community before expiration of his or her sentence. If parole conditions are violated, parole may be revoked and the offender may be returned to the institution for the remainder of the sentence.

Probation A form of sentencing that allows the offender to remain free in the community under supervision and subject to conditions set by the court; violation of these conditions may lead to revocation.

Shock parole (Probation) System in which an offender is imprisoned for a brief period of time (to acquaint him or her with the rigors of incarceration), after which he or she is released under supervision.

Work release Temporary release from prison to work in the community. Persons on work release may reside at a facility within the community or they may commute from the prison to their work site.

REFERENCES

Barnes, H. E., and Teeters, N. K. *New Horizons in Criminology*. Englewood Cliffs, N.J.: Prentice-Hall, 1959.

Carter, R. M., and Wilkins, L. T. *Probation, Parole, and Community Corrections*. New York: Wiley, 1976.

DiCerbo, E. C. "When Should Probation Be Revoked?" *Federal Probation* 30 (1966): 11–17.

Epstein, R., et al. *The Legal Aspects of Contract Parole*. College Park, Md.: The American Correctional Association, 1976.

Erwin, B. S. *Evaluation Design: Georgia's Intensive Probation Supervision Program.* Office of Research and Planning, Georgia Department of Offender Rehabilitation, 1983.

Ford, D., and Schmidt, A. K. *Electronically Monitored Home Confinement.* Washington, D.C.: U.S. Department of Justice, National Institute of Justice, 1985.

Frank, B., ed. *Contemporary Corrections.* Reston, Va.: Reston, 1973.

Greenwood, P. W., with Abrahamse, A. *Selective Incapacitation.* Report to the National Institute of Justice, August 1982. Santa Monica, Calif.: Rand Corporation, 1982.

Griswold, H. J., Misenheimer, M.; Powers, A.; and Tromanheiser, E. *An Eye For an Eye.* New York: Holt, Rinehart and Winston, 1970.

Hoffman, P. *Predicting Criminality.* Washington, D.C.: U.S. Department of Justice, National Institute of Justice, 1987.

Keve, P. W. *Corrections.* New York: Wiley, 1981.

Krajick, K. "Probation: The Original Community Program." *Corrections Magazine* 6 (1980): 7–13.

Monahan, J. "The Case For Prediction in The Modified Desert Model of Criminal Sentencing." *International Journal of Law and Psychiatry* 5 (1982): 103–13.

________. *The Clinical Prediction of Violent Behavior.* Washington, D.C.: U.S. Government Printing Office, 1981.

Morris, N. *The Future of Imprisonment.* Chicago: University of Chicago Press, 1974.

Morris, N., and Miller, M. "Predictions of Dangerousness." In *Crime and Justice: An Annual Review of Research,* vol. 6, edited by M. Tonry and N. Morris. Chicago: University of Chicago Press, 1985.

Murchek, P. "Probation without Adjudication." Paper delivered at the 18th annual Southern Conference on Corrections, Tallahassee, Florida 25–27 February 1973.

National Council on Crime and Delinquency, Research Center West. "National Probation Reports Feasibility Study on *NPR National Aggregate Probation Data Inquiry." Probation in the U.S.: 1979.* San Francisco: National Council on Crime and Delinquency, 1981.

Nelkin, D. *Methadone Maintenance: A Technological Fix.* New York: George Braziller, 1973.

Nimmer, D. *Two Million Unnecessary Arrests.* Chicago: American Bar Association, 1971.

Pearson, F. "New Jersey's Intensive Supervision Program: A Progress Report." *Crime and Delinquency* (forthcoming 1985).

Petersilia, J. *Criminal Careers of Habitual Felons.* The Rand Corporation, R-2144-DOJ, June 1977 (coauthored); also published as GPO document, July 1978.

________. *Probation and Felony Offenders.* Washington, D.C.: U.S. Department of Justice, National Institute of Justice, March 1985.

Porter, E. M. "Criteria for Parole Selection." *Proceedings of the American Correctional Association.* New York: American Correctional Association, 1958.

President's Commission on Law Enforcement and Administration of Justice. *Task Force Report: Corrections.* Washington, D.C.: U.S. Government Printing Office, 1967.

Reid, S. T. *The Correctional System: An Introduction.* New York: Holt, Rinehart and Winston, 1981.

Smith, R. M.; McKee, J. M.; and Milan, M. A. "Study-Release Policies of American Correctional Agencies: A Survey." *Journal of Criminal Justice* (1974): 357–63.

Smykla, J. O. *Community-Based Corrections: Principles and Practices.* New York: Macmillan, 1981.

von Hirsch, A. *Doing Justice: The Choice of Punishments.* New York: Hill and Wang, 1976.

CASES

Driver v. *Hinnant* 356 F.2d 761 (4th Cir. 1966).
Easter v. *District of Columbia* 361 F.2d 50 (D.C. Cir. 1966).
Powell v. *Texas* 392 U.S. 514, 88 S.Ct. 2145, 20 L.Ed.2d 1254 (1968).
Robinson v. *California* 370 U.S. 660, 82 S.Ct. 1417 (1962).

NOTES

1. This discussion was adapted from Joan Petersilia, *Probation and Felony Offenders* (Washington, D.C.: U.S. Department of Justice, National Institute of Justice, March 1985).

2. Complete results are contained in Joan Petersilia, Susan Turner, James Kahan, and Joyce Peterson, *Granting Felons Probation: Public Risks and Alternatives* (R-3186-NIJ, The Rand Corporation, January 1985). The report can be obtained by writing Rand, 1700 Main Street, Santa Monica, CA 90406.

3. After controlling for the basic factors of each case, researchers also performed analyses to determine whether the manner in which the case was officially processed by the courts made a difference in the prison/probation decision. The analyses revealed that having a private attorney and obtaining pretrial release could reduce a defendant's chances of imprisonment, whereas going to trial (as opposed to plea bargaining) generally increased that probability. These "process" variables significantly affected the prison/probation decision even after all the basic factors had been statistically controlled—that is, when all the offenders were statistically "interchangeable" except for their court handling.

4. The Rand data contained information over 235 factors, including extensive information about the offenders' criminal, personal, and socioeconomic characteristics.

These findings on PSIs should be interpreted cautiously. The PSIs examined were prepared in counties where officials admit to having less than adequate time to prepare proper reports. Under these conditions, it is not surprising that the PSI information does not adequately distinguish recidivists. In less burdened counties, the "predictive" quality of the PSI might be higher.

5. This discussion of "Enhancing Parole Prediction" along with accompanying references was adapted from a study guide written by Peter Hoffman, U.S. Parole Commission, *Predicting Criminality,* (Washington, D.C.: U.S. Department of Justice, National Institute of Justice, 1987).

6. This discussion was adapted from Daniel Ford and Annesley K. Schmidt, *Electronically Monitored Home Confinement,* (Washington, D.C.: National Institute of Justice, 1985).

CHAPTER

17

Juvenile Justice

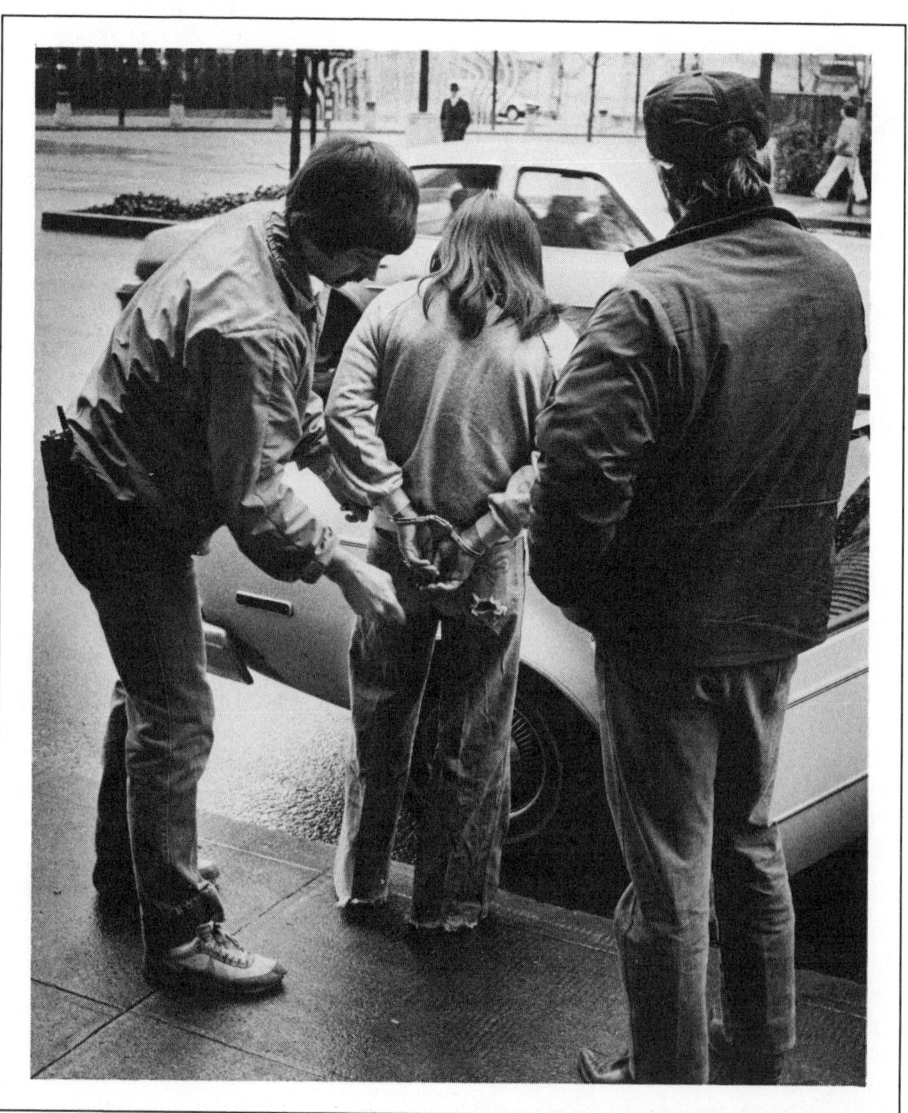

CHAPTER OUTLINE:

During the five-year period, 1982–1986, total arrests in the United States increased 7 percent (Uniform Crime Reports 1987). The arrests of juveniles (persons under eighteen years of age) dropped 1 percent. However, this is not to say that juveniles in this country are not responsible for a substantial number of violent and serious property offenses.

For example, in 1986 17 percent of all persons arrested nationwide were under eighteen. That same year the total number of persons under the age of eighteen was 1,747,675. Juveniles were arrested for selected serious crimes in the following numbers: murder, 1,396; rape, 4,798; robbery, 27,987; burglary, 134,823; and larceny, 378,283 (see Table 17.1). As the table shows, juveniles accounted for the following percentages of the total number of persons arrested in 1986: robbery, 22.5 percent; burglary, 35.7 percent; and motor vehicle theft 39.2 percent (Uniform Crime Reports 1987).

The juvenile offender is generally handled in a system distinct from the rest of the criminal justice system. Until recently, the courts that dealt with juvenile cases had few of the features generally associated with a judicial tribunal. The orientation of the courts was toward treatment; there was relatively little concern for determining guilt or innocence of the juvenile through traditional court procedures. Under a guiding philosophy called

TABLE 17.1
Total Arrests of Persons under Fifteen, Eighteen, Twenty-One, and Twenty-Five Years of Age, 1986

Offense Charged	Total All Ages	Number of Persons Arrested				Percent of Total All Ages			
		Under 15	Under 18	Under 21	Under 25	Under 15	Under 18	Under 21	Under 25
Total	10,392,177	536,609	1,747,675	3,216,752	5,072,761	5.2	16.8	31.0	48.8
Murder and nonnegligent manslaughter	16,066	156	1,396	3,717	6,641	1.0	8.7	23.1	41.3
Forcible rape	31,128	1,514	4,798	8,634	14,148	4.9	15.4	27.7	45.5
Robbery	124,245	6,615	27,987	51,168	76,923	5.3	22.5	41.2	61.9
Aggravated assault	293,952	10,816	37,528	71,758	124,394	3.7	12.8	24.4	42.3
Burglary	375,544	47,080	134,823	206,908	267,406	12.5	35.9	55.1	71.2
Larceny-theft	1,182,099	156,033	378,283	549,190	710,016	13.2	32.0	46.5	60.1
Motor vehicle theft	128,514	11,961	50,319	74,788	94,447	9.3	39.2	58.2	73.5
Arson	15,523	3,837	6,271	7,959	9,767	24.7	40.4	51.3	62.9
Violent crime[1]	465,391	19,101	71,709	135,277	222,106	4.1	15.4	29.1	47.7
Property crime[2]	1,701,680	218,911	569,696	838,845	1,081,636	12.9	33.5	49.3	63.6
Crime Index total[3]	2,167,071	238,012	641,405	974,122	1,303,742	11.0	29.6	45.0	60.2
Other assaults	593,902	30,411	85,905	153,596	265,718	5.1	14.5	25.9	44.6
Forgery and counterfeiting	76,546	1,101	7,234	19,341	35,760	1.4	9.5	25.3	46.7
Fraud	284,790	6,722	17,727	42,141	94,110	2.4	6.2	14.8	33.0
Embezzlement	10,500	52	696	2,268	4,429	.5	6.6	21.6	42.2
Stolen property; buying, receiving, possessing	114,105	7,613	28,739	51,054	71,484	6.7	25.2	44.7	62.6
Vandalism	223,231	45,247	95,479	129,034	160,278	20.3	42.8	57.8	71.8
Weapons; carrying, possessing, etc.	160,204	6,394	25,170	49,876	79,981	4.0	15.7	31.1	49.9
Prostitution and commercialized vice	96,882	247	2,192	14,804	42,464	.3	2.3	15.3	43.8
Sex offenses (except forcible rape and prostitution)	83,934	6,110	13,753	21,625	33,470	7.3	16.4	25.8	39.9
Drug abuse violations	691,882	9,374	68,351	177,864	335,212	1.4	9.9	25.7	48.4
Gambling	25,839	105	610	1,859	4,626	.4	2.4	7.2	17.9
Offenses against family and children	47,327	1,255	2,521	6,403	14,141	2.7	5.3	13.5	29.9
Driving under the influence	1,458,531	456	22,749	156,143	442,984	([4])	1.6	10.7	30.4
Liquor laws	490,436	10,163	132,335	310,193	372,022	2.1	27.0	63.2	75.9
Drunkenness	777,866	3,283	26,589	96,341	223,570	.4	3.4	12.4	28.7
Disorderly conduct	564,882	22,517	82,986	173,800	292,630	4.0	14.7	30.8	51.8
Vagrancy	32,992	539	2,550	7,100	12,184	1.6	7.7	21.5	36.9
All other offenses (except traffic)	2,272,589	70,918	276,876	614,253	1,068,934	3.1	12.2	27.0	47.0
Suspicion	7,455	846	2,595	3,722	4,809	11.3	34.8	49.9	64.5
Curfew and loitering law violations	72,627	19,260	72,627	72,627	72,627	26.5	100.0	100.0	100.0
Runaways	138,586	55,984	138,586	138,586	138,586	40.4	100.0	100.0	100.0

Note: 10,743 agencies; 1986 estimated population 198,488,000.

[1]Violent crimes are offenses of murder, forcible rape, robbery, and aggravated assault.
[2]Property crimes are offenses of burglary, larceny-theft, motor vehicle theft, and arson.
[3]Includes arson.
[4]Less than one-tenth of 1 percent.

Data from the U.S. Department of Justice, *Uniform Crime Reports in the United States, 1986.* (Washington, D.C.: U.S. Government Printing Office, 1987), p. 180.

parens patriae, judges were expected to act as "kind and loving parents" and to do whatever they could to direct juvenile offenders toward socially acceptable conduct. The approach was designed to spare the youngster the punishment and stigma of criminality.

Some critics point out that, although the original objectives of this approach were laudable in theory, they simply could not be achieved in practice. Thus, the juvenile court was doomed to failure because it assumed responsibilities that far exceeded its resources: it tried to take the place of a failed educational system, a broken home, or the collapse of informal social control formerly carried out by the neighborhood.

Other critics are concerned with the inability of the juvenile justice system to deal with juveniles who commit serious felony offenses such as murder, rape, robbery, assault, and arson. Juvenile court authorities like Judge Seymour Gelber of Dade County, Florida, maintain that the juvenile court is no longer relevant to today's juvenile criminals, especially those charged with crimes against the person. When one encounters a hulking fifteen-year-old in juvenile detention who is charged with forcible rape and homicide and learns that this is the "child" named in the juvenile court petition—the juvenile court equivalent of indictment—it is difficult to believe that this is the kind of client the founders of the juvenile justice system had in mind. And it does not help much that the terms *delinquent* and *criminal* are widely used as though they were synonymous.

Fortunately, the juvenile courts now appear to be moving in a new direction (for reasons we explore later in this chapter). An increased emphasis on due process safeguards for the accused juvenile is helping to shape the juvenile court into something resembling a "junior criminal court." At the same time, in response to public demands for community protection, growing numbers of juveniles are being placed for community protection, growing numbers of juveniles are being placed under the jurisdiction of the adult criminal justice system; many groups believe that the juvenile justice system can no longer handle serious youthful offenders. In the issue paper at the end of this chapter, we examine some of the problems raised by the certification or *transfer* of juveniles to the jurisdiction of adult criminal courts.

THE CREATION OF DELINQUENCY

Delinquency is a relatively new concept. Throughout the Middle Ages, and even as late as the seventeenth century, youths engaged in behavior that today would probably result in their adjudication as **delinquent**—and their parents would probably be charged with contributing to the delinquency of minors. Many children, as soon as they could talk, used obscene language, drank without restriction in taverns and at home, had sexual experiences freely or under duress, rarely attended school and, when they did, carried arms and fought duels (Empey 1976). Today, however, most people feel that this kind of behavior should be curbed among juveniles.

This change in attitude toward youthful behavior resulted from a change in the conception of childhood and children. In the late sixteenth and early seventeenth centuries, it was widely believed that children require distinctive preparation to become productive members of the community. This view influenced the development of schools, whose function was to assist parents in providing both intellectual and moral training. If children were to attend school, the period of childhood had to be extended, a circumstance that justified restricting children's behavior on the grounds that they were too immature or too naïve to engage in certain behaviors. Initially, this conception of childhood influenced mostly the middle class: lower class and minority children were not affected until the nineteenth or early twentieth century.

During the early 1800s, institutions for children called "houses of refuge" were established to combat the negative influences of inadequate families and disorganized communities. Designed to serve as family substitutes, these facilities supplied the discipline, affection, and training that parents were not able, or available to provide. At the New York House of Refuge,

> . . . the first bells rang at sunrise to wake the youngsters, the second came fifteen minutes later to signal the guards to unlock the individual cells. The inmates stepped into the hallways and then, according to the manager's description, "marched in order to the washroom . . . from the washroom they are paraded in open air (the weather permitting), where they are arranged in ranks, and undergo a close and critical inspection as to cleanliness and dress." Inmates next went in formation to chapel for prayer . . . and afterwards spent one hour in school. At seven o'clock the bells announced breakfast and then, a half hour later, the time to begin work. The boys spent until noon in the shops, usually making brass nails or cane seats, while the girls washed, cooked, and made and mended the clothes. "At twelve o'clock," officials

> reported, "a bell rings to call all from work, and one hour is allowed for washing . . . and dinner. . . . At one o'clock a signal is given for recommencing work, which continues to five o'clock in the afternoon, when the bell rings for the termination of the labor day." There followed thirty minutes to wash and eat, two and a half hours of evening classes and, finally to end the day, evening prayers. "The children," concluded the Refuge account, "ranged in order, and are marched to the Sleeping Halls where each takes possession of a separate compartment, and the cells are locked, and silence is enforced for the night" (New York House of Refuge, *Seventh Annual Report,* pp. 253–55, as cited by Rothman 1971, pp. 225–26).

Although these child-saving institutions were thought by reformers to hold great promise for changing the behavior of wayward youth, they became—in reality—places to house the youthful misfits of society. In light of the discipline, regimen, and living conditions that characterized these institutions, it is not surprising that they did little to change the conduct of their charges. (Punishment included increased work loads, loss of play periods, a diet of bread and water, solitary confinement, wearing a ball and chain, and whippings.) By 1850, these institutions were not producing children who would become upstanding members of the community, but instead were turning out children who—at best—thought, marched, and otherwise behaved like robots.

But other conditions overshadowed these negative results, making the need for child-saving facilities even more critical. The latter part of the nineteenth century brought rapid urban growth, an influx of immigrants, and a marked increase in social instability (Empey 1978). Immigrants who arrived in the United States were generally poor and lived in deteriorated areas with high rates of crime and delinquency. Their patterns of behavior—sexual, marital, and liguistic—were viewed as deviant, thus providing a rationale for treating them as inferior and as threats to the social order. Further, the theories of Charles Darwin, as applied to social life, provided justification for regarding immigrants as *biologically* inferior.

Out of these views on the immigrant community emerged two major themes that had important implications for the continued institutionalization of children. One focused on the "disruptive" conditions of life in industrial urban slums; the second, heavily influenced by Darwin's ideas, attributed crime to biological factors. If crime could be ascribed to social conditions such as poverty and family instability, then these factors could possibly be changed—or at least their more adverse influences could be mitigated—by subjecting affected persons to countervailing influences. Thus, despite the contention by some authorities that crime is rooted in biological factors, human behavior was still considered to be susceptible to environmental influence. Nevertheless, these two themes underscored the need for institutions designed to counter adverse biological and social influences.

During this same era, groups of middle-class women became preoccupied with the so-called child-saving movement. Appalled by the depraved conditions of life in urban slums, these women sought to establish institutions to reverse negative influences and give youngsters a chance to become conventional members of society. At this point, an interesting paradox existed: While it was recognized that the houses of refuge had failed to meet their objectives as "superparents," they were still seen as the only substitute for a natural home providing the education, discipline, and benign environment needed to counteract adverse biological and social factors. This issue was resolved by blaming the failure of these institutions on the methods they employed, rather than on the objectives themselves. This view required that new institutions be built.

The new facilities thus established were called industrial schools and reformatories. Industrial schools, which replaced the houses of refuge, were organized along the cottage or family system. Reformatories, originally intended to replace prisons, came to be used as institutions for youthful offenders convicted of crimes (their philosophy and programs were consistent with the views of the day on how youths should be handled).

Both the reformatory and the industrial school failed miserably. Although their objectives were sound, the methods employed were, in most cases, no better than those employed by the houses of refuge. Discipline was repressive and ranged from benevolent despotism to tyrannical cruelty (Teeters and Reinemann 1950). Floggings were common, but were among the less cruel punishments inflicted on youngsters. The regimen was rigid: mass formations and military drills were emphasized. The main program of reform involved long hours of tedious work. At industrial schools, the principal work was farm labor, which was of doubtful value to youngsters who returned to the city. In essence, these facilities differed from houses of refuge only in name and location.

The failure of these institutions after a century of experimentation with various juvenile facilities may be surprising, but a valuable lesson was learned; our experiences in the nineteenth century demonstrated the futility of trying to use institutions as a method of social control in periods of rapid social and ideological change. These early facilities provided only a temporary means of incapacitating dangerous offenders; they were not up to the task of socializing or redirecting youthful criminals. As Empey (1976) observes, even if there had been reformatories on every street corner, it is doubtful that they would have been able to do much to moderate the effects of industrialization, immigration, and urbanization, or to have served as surrogate parents and produced the same kind of person as would a nuclear family in a small rural community. Almost a century has passed since we first tried to devise urban institutions to provide justice and opportunity and to offset the problems faced by children in a pluralistic society. Unfortunately, time seems to have done little to improve our ability to deal with the situation, and we are far from encouraged about the future.

Despite the ineffectiveness of nineteenth-century methods of dealing with children, it must be noted that childhood had been recognized by the close of the century as a status distinct from adulthood—one that afforded its occupants exemptions from certain kinds of behavior expected of adults. Children were acknowledged as a distinct group that required not only different correctional facilities, but also regulations and laws to protect them against exploitation by our economic system. The recognition of these needs helped bring about the establishment of the juvenile court. (See Table 17.2 for a summary of developments in juvenile justice from 1646 to the present. Table 17.3 lists various stages in the creation of the juvenile court.)

TABLE 17.2
Juvenile Justice Developments: 1646 to the Present

SYSTEM (PERIOD)	MAJOR DEVELOPMENTS	INFLUENCES	CHILD-STATE RELATIONSHIP	PARENT-STATE RELATIONSHIP	PARENT-CHILD RELATIONSHIP
Puritan (1646–1824)	Massachusetts Stubborn Child Law (1646).	Christian view of child as evil; economically marginal agrarian society.	Law provides symbolic standard of maturity; support for family as economic unit.	Parents considered responsible for and capable of controlling child.	Child considered both property and spiritual responsibility of parents.
Refuge (1824–1899)	Institutionalization of deviants, New York House of Refuge established (1824) for delinquent and dependent children.	Enlightenment; immigration and industrialization.	Child seen as helpless, in need of state intervention.	Parents supplanted as state assumes responsibility for correcting deviant socialization.	Family considered to be a major cause of juvenile delinquency.
Juvenile court (1899–1960)	Establishment of separate legal system for juveniles—Illinois Juvenile Court Act (1899).	Reformism and rehabilitative ideology; increased immigration, urbanization, large-scale industrialization.	Juvenile court institutionalizes legal irresponsibility of child.	Parens Patriae doctrine gives legal foundation for state intervention in family.	Further abrogation of parents' rights and responsibilities.
Juvenile rights (1960–present)	Increased "legalization" of juvenile law—*Gault* decision (1966). Juvenile Justice and Delinquency Prevention Act (1974) calls for deinstitutionalization of status offender.	Criticism of juvenile justice system on humane grounds; civil rights movements by disadvantaged groups.	Movement to define and protect rights as well as provide services to children.	Reassertion of responsibility of parents and community for welfare and behavior of children.	Attention given to children's claims against parents. Earlier emancipation of children.

Adapted from U.S. Department of Justice, Reports of the National Juvenile Assessment Centers, *A Preliminary National Assessment of the Status Offender and the Juvenile Justice System* (Washington, D.C.: U.S. Government Printing Office, 1980), p. 29, by permission of the U.S. Department of Justice.

TABLE 17.3
Antecedents of the Juvenile Court

1825	New York House of Refuge was opened, followed by houses in Boston (1826), Philadelphia (1828), and New Orleans (1845).
1831	Illinois passed a law that allowed penalties for certain offenses committed by minors to differ from the penalties imposed on adults.
1841	John Augustus inaugurated probation and became the nation's first probation officer.
1854	State industrial school for girls opened in Lancaster, Massachusetts (first cottage-type institution).
1858	State industrial school for boys in Lancaster, Ohio, adopted a cottage-type system.
1863	Children's Aid Society founded in Boston. Members of the organization attended police and superior court hearings, supervised youngsters selected for probation, and did the investigation on which probation selection was based.
1869	Law enacted in Massachusetts to direct State Board of Charities to send agents to court hearings that involved children. The agents made recommendations to the court that frequently involved probation and the placement of youngsters with suitable families.
1870	Separate hearings for juveniles were required in Suffolk County, Massachusetts. New York followed by requiring separate trials, dockets, and records for children; Rhode Island made similar provisions in 1891.
1899	In April, Illinois adopted legislation creating the first juvenile court in Cook County (Chicago). In May, Colorado established a juvenile court.

DEVELOPMENT OF THE JUVENILE COURT

The first juvenile court was created in Chicago, Illinois, in 1899. In many respects, this court represented the dawn of a new era for our legal system. Previously, our court processes had the objectives of retribution and deterrence, and they gave little attention to individual differences. By the turn of the century, however, the teachings and research in the new area of social science began to impact on the legal system. It was recognized that differences existed between offenders, regardless of whether they had committed the same offense. This recognition implied that differences in physical and mental conditions, as well as in environmental influences, should be taken into account in judicial decisions. The result was the birth of "individualized justice."

To put the concept of individualized justice into operation, the courts had to examine a wide variety of psychological and social factors that had nothing to do with guilt or innocence in a strict legal sense. Consideration was given to the economic, social, cultural, and emotional factors that shape the individual and to data regarding the offender's education, career, family, employment record, and community environment. The purpose of this diagnosis was to provide information that could be used to determine the type of treatment needed by the offender.

The First Courts: 1899 to 1967

The establishment (by statute) of the first juvenile court in Illinois in 1899 marked the beginning of an era of "social jurisprudence" (Faust and Brantingham 1979). Although the juvenile court was a bona fide court, its procedures were dramatically different from adult court proceedings. The court's major objective was to help the wayward child become a productive member of the community. The determination of guilt or innocence, using standard rules of evidence, was not of primary importance. Instead, the purpose of the court hearing was to determine "What is he, how has he become what he is, and what had best be done in his interest and in the interest of the state to save him from a downward career" (ibid., p. 112). In other words, court procedures were to be more diagnostic than legal in nature, giving major consideration to the information obtained on the youngster's environment, heredity, as well as his physical and mental condition (Mack 1979).

The aim of the Illinois juvenile court was prevention and rehabilitation, not punishment. And youngsters who violated the law were called juvenile delinquents, not criminals; this term implied that the juveniles were wayward children in need of assistance from the court, their new "superparent." The juvenile court judges were to assume the "parental" role in an atmosphere less threatening than that of the adult criminal court—reviewing the behavior of youngsters, disciplining them when appropriate, and devising a course of action to prevent further delinquent behavior. To aid in these tasks, the court hired psychologists, psychiatrists, and social workers to prepare comprehensive reports on youngster's backgrounds and psychological characteristics. The goals and methods of the juvenile court remained essentially unchanged until 1967.

Where We Are Today

Given the basic commitment to rehabilitation rather than punishment, juvenile courts developed along the lines of social casework. Hearings were conducted in an informal atmosphere, and testimony and background data were introduced without regard to rules of evidence. In addition, the juvenile was denied many of the rights guaranteed by due process—including representation by counsel, confrontation with one's accuser, cross-examination, and the right to invoke the privilege against self-incrimination.

In *Kent* v. *United States* (383 U.S. 541, 546 [1966]), Justice Abe Fortas of the U.S. Supreme Court expressed concern that the guiding philosophy of the juvenile court—parens patriae—had not been realized. Youngsters were getting the worst of both worlds: they were denied the rights accorded adults, and they did not receive the care and treatment promised under the parens patriae doctrine.

The *Kent* decision raised many issues and paved the way for the Supreme Court to come to grips with these problems in the Gault decision (*In re Gault,* 387 U.S. 1 [1967]). Gerald Gault, a fifteen-year-old, was sentenced to confinement for the "remainder of his minority" (six years) for an offense that carried a maximum *adult* penalty of only two months. During hearings, Gault was deprived of most of the procedural rights afforded his adult counterparts. His appeal was heard by the U.S. Supreme Court on the following issues: right to notice of the charge, right to counsel, right to confrontation and cross-examiation of witnesses, privilege against self-incrimination, right to a transcript of the proceedings, and right to an appellate review.

As a result of the *Kent, Gault,* and subsequent decisions (e.g., *In re Winship* [397 U.S. 358 (1970)]), the juvenile court process now has two distinct phases: an *adjudication phase,* which accords juveniles the same due process rights as adults, with the exception of a jury trial; and a *disposition phase* in which, following a determination of guilt, a treatment or rehabilitation plan is drawn up.

Language of the Courts

The terms used in criminal courts have been changed to apply to juvenile justice. For example, "petition" replaces "complaint," "summons" replaces "warrant," "finding of involvement" replaces "conviction," and "disposition" replaces "sentencing." The words "child," "youth," and "youngster" are used synonymously to denote a person of juvenile court age. Juvenile court laws define a child as any person under a specified age no matter how mature or sophisticated he or she may seem. Juvenile jurisdictions in at least two-thirds of the states define persons under eighteen as children; the other states also include youngsters between the ages of eighteen and twenty-one. The most significant terms used in the juvenile system are defined in Table 17.4

Types of Juveniles Handled by the System

As noted earlier, youngsters who break laws are not the only concern of juvenile authorities. Some children need the protection of the state just to fulfill the most basic needs of life. Such youngsters—referred to as **dependent children**—often come to the attention of the juvenile or family court because their parents have died and they cannot receive adequate support from other family members. In other cases, children have to be taken away from parents or relatives for their own protection and welfare. For example, children may be subjected to sexual or physical abuse—the typical circumstances of the battered child. These **neglected children** (as they are referred to by the juvenile court) usually become the concern of authorities as a result of reports from neighbors, friends, or relatives. Even when they are severely abused, children tend to remain loyal to their parents; thus, neglect is seldom reported by the children themselves.

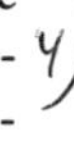

Delinquency itself takes two different patterns. The first type of delinquency includes those offenses that would be considered crimes if they were committed by adults. Burglary, larceny, and motor vehicle theft are examples of property crimes that fall into this category. The second category is **status offenses**—violations of statutes that apply exclusively to juveniles. Legislation for status offenses is often worded ambiguously. Phelps

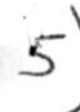

TABLE 17.4
The Language of Juvenile and Adult Courts

JUVENILE COURT TERM	ADULT COURT TERM
Adjudication: decision by the judge that a child has committed delinquent acts.	Conviction of guilt
Adjudicatory hearing: a hearing to determine whether the allegations of a petition are supported by the evidence beyond a reasonable doubt.	Trial
Adjustment: the settling of a matter so that parties agree without official intervention by the court.	Plea bargaining
Aftercare: the supervision given to a child for a limited period of time after he or she is released from training school but while he or she is still under the control of the juvenile court.	Parole
Commitment: a decision by the judge to send a child to training school.	Sentence to imprisonment
Delinquent act: an act that if committed by an adult would be called a crime. The term does not include such ambiguities and noncrimes as "being ungovernable," "truancy," "incorrigibility," and "disobedience."	Crime
Delinquent child: a child who is found to have committed an act that would be considered a crime if committed by an adult.	Criminal
Detention: temporary care of an allegedly delinquent child who requires secure custody in physically restricting facilities pending court disposition or execution of a court order.	Holding in jail
Dispositional hearing: a hearing held subsequent to the adjudicatory hearing to determine what order of disposition should be made for a child adjudicated as delinquent.	Sentencing hearing
Hearing: the presentation of evidence to the juvenile court judge, his or her consideration of it, and his or her decision on disposition of the case.	Trial
Juvenile court: the court that has jurisdiction over children who are alleged to be or found to be delinquent. Juvenile delinquency procedures should not be used for neglected children or for those who need supervision.	Court of record
Petition: an application for a court order or some other judicial action. Hence, a "delinquency petition" is an application for the court to act in a matter involving a juvenile apprehended for a delinquent act.	Accusation or indictment
Probation: the supervision of a delinquent child after the court hearing but without commitment to training school.	Probation (with the same meaning as the juvenile court term)
Residential child care facility: a dwelling (other than a detention or shelter care facility) that is licensed to provide living accommodations, care treatment, and maintenance for children and youth. Such facilities include foster homes, group homes, and halfway houses.	Halfway house
Shelter: temporary care of a child in physically unrestricting facilities pending court disposition or execution of a court order for placement. Shelter care is used for dependent and neglected children and minors in need of supervision. Separate shelter care facilities are also used for children apprehended for delinquency who need temporary shelter but not secure detention.	Jail
Take into custody: the act of the police in securing the physical custody of a child engaged in delinquency. The term is used to avoid the stigma of the word "arrest."	Arrest

cites an example from section 601 of the California Welfare and Institutions Code:

> Any person under the age of 18 years who persistently or habitually refuses to obey the reasonable and proper orders or directions of his parents, guardian, custodian, or school authorities, or who is beyond the control of such person, or any person who is a habitual truant from school within the meaning of any law of this state, or who from any cause is in danger of leading an idle, dissolute, lewd, or immoral life, is within the jurisdiction of the juvenile court which may adjudge such person to be a ward of the court (1976, p. 37).

How does a youngster prove that he or she is not leading "an idle, dissolute, lewd, or immoral life"?

Juvenile justice authorities are sharply divided on the issue of who should have jurisdiction over status offenses. Those who wish to leave jurisdiction with the juvenile court argue that today's status offender is tomorrow's adult criminal, and that further acts of delinquency cannot be prevented unless such juveniles are discovered. Their opponents maintain that "the processing of juveniles in the formal authoritarian agencies is likely to reinforce the pattern of delinquency which the system proposes to eradicate" (Phelps 1976, p. 38). These critics emphasize that the social services usually required to deal effectively with the problems of the status offender can be made available without formal adjudication.

POLICE CONTACT AND INTAKE

As noted in Figure 17.1, the police officer is usually the first representative of societal authority and the criminal justice system to come in contact with a youthful offender. According to the President's Commission on Law Enforcement and the Administration of Justice, "Contacts with police are the gateway into the system of delinquency and criminal justice," (1967, p. 420). Over a million youngsters have contact with the police each year, one-third of whom appear in juvenile court.

Police contact with juveniles may result from juvenile involvement in serious offenses, disturbances, or status offenses. A substantial number of contacts occur just because juveniles are out and about—which brings them to the attention of officers on patrol. Because juveniles often move in groups, they seem more suspicious and more difficult to control. And because they tend to congregate at shopping plazas, street corners, fast-food operations, and the like, they may be the object of complaints requiring police attention.

Police have a variety of alternatives available to them in making dispositions in juvenile cases: #6

1. *Warn and release.* In the case of a minor offense, a police officer may simply warn a youth not to engage in the same type of behavior again. The youth may be further advised that future violations will result in official action.
2. *Release and report.* The juvenile may be released, but an official report will be prepared detailing the incident.
3. *Release to parents.* A juvenile may be placed in the custody of his or her parents with just a warning or an official report. The Task Force on Juvenile Justice Delinquency Prevention (1976) recommends that the primary criterion for release to parents should be whether the juvenile is a threat to public safety. Another important consideration is the parents' ability to control and discipline their child (Kobetz and Bosarge 1973). This type of disposition is not suitable when the parent or guardian is indifferent to the youngster's criminal behavior or is unable to provide the concern and supervision the youngster needs to stay out of further difficulty.
4. *Agency referral.* Depending on departmental policies, the availability of appropriate programs, and police awareness of community resources, juveniles may be referred to community-based social service agencies or welfare agencies. Police are in an ideal position to divert youths from the juvenile justice system to community agencies, where they can receive the help they need without the stigma associated with processing by the juvenile court. Typical police referrals are to youth service bureaus, special school programs, boys clubs, the YMCA, community mental health agencies, and drug programs.
5. *Juvenile court referral.* Depending upon the jurisdiction, a police officer can use several methods to bring a juvenile offender to the attention of the juvenile court. Rather than taking a youngster into custody, for example, an officer can issue a citation or make a formal report to juvenile intake or the juvenile court and release the youngster to the custody of parents or guardians. The National Advisory

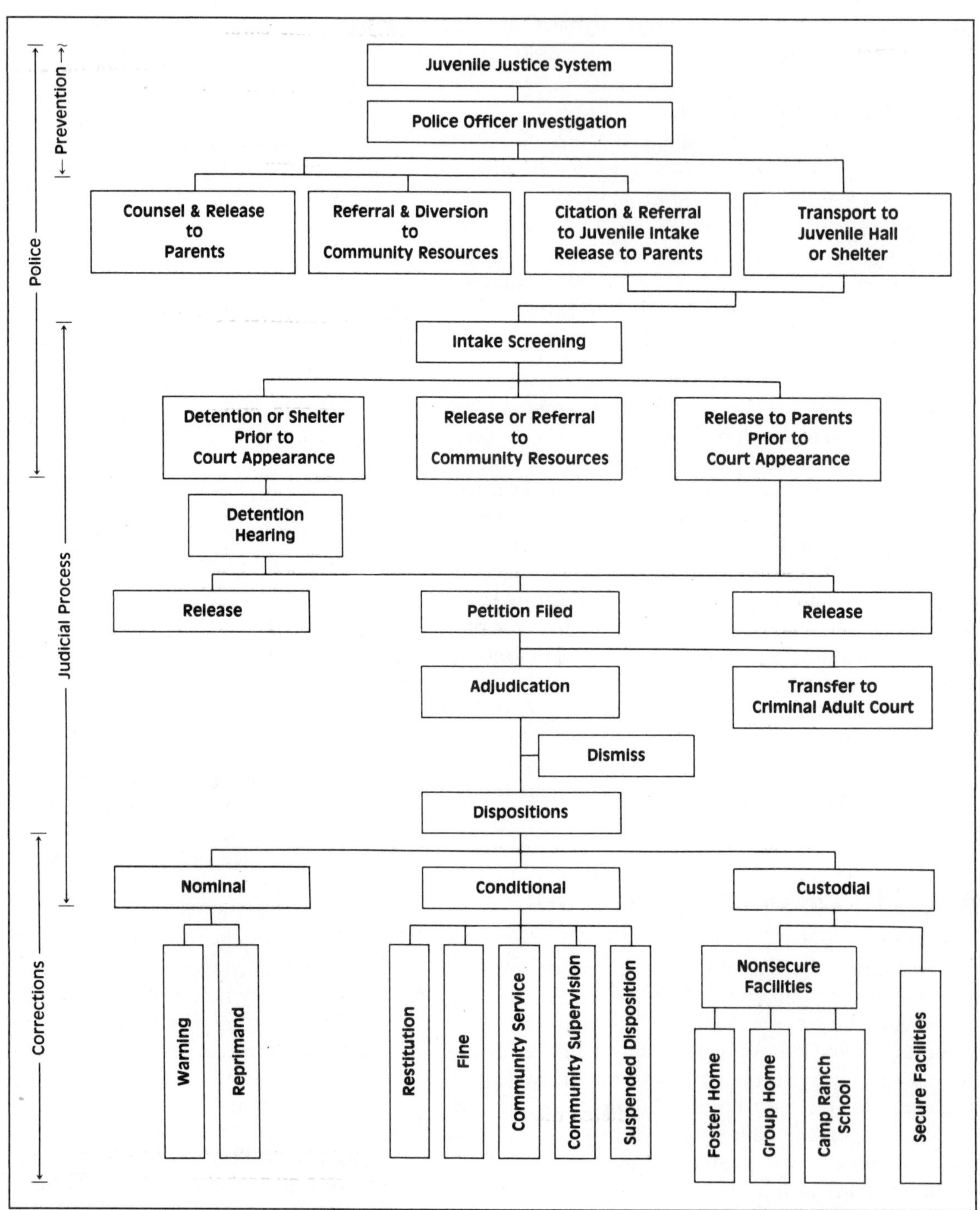

FIGURE 17.1
Procedures of the criminal justice system. Reprinted from the National Advisory Committee on Criminal Justice Standards and Goals, Task Force on Juvenile Justice and Delinquency Prevention, *Report of the Task Force on Juvenile Justice and Delinquency Prevention* (Washington, D.C.: U.S. Government Printing Office, 1976), p. 9, by permission of the U.S. Department of Justice.

> Committee on Criminal Justice Standards and Goals (1976) recommends that police departments make maximum use of state statutes that permit police agencies to issue written citations and summons in lieu of taking the juvenile into custody. This recommendation is consistent with the committee's philosophy of using the least coercive alternative available to preserve public order, safety, and individual liberties. The police may also take a youngster into custody and deliver him or her to juvenile intake or detention.

Research conducted in Flint, Michigan, further illustrates the various options police officers can utilize in dealing with juvenile offenders. The research focused on the officers' role in resolving complaints about a group of rowdy juveniles as part of their neighborhood Foot Patrol Program.

In resolving the rowdy teenager situations, Flint police officers mentioned various actions they took: (1) made a referral to social services, (2) counseled the teenagers, (3) counseled the parents, (4) reassured the complainants, (5) tried to get people to empathize with each other and see each other's side, (6) gave orders, (7) made an arrest, and (8) threatened arrest (Belknap et al. 1986, p. 16).

The research in Flint also identified five role identity orientations assumed by police officers in dealing with rowdy juvenile encounters: peacekeeper and problem solver, competent law enforcer, authority figure, friend or peer, and knight in shining armor (Belknap et al. 1986, p. 9). The following statements by officers in the Flint, Michigan, study illustrate these five role identity orientations and indicate how the officers view their interactions with rowdy juveniles:

> *Problem solver and peacekeeper:*
>
> I would like my supervisor to picture me as having solved the problem, that is, having quieted the people involved and satisfied the neighbor to the best of my ability and hopefully prevented a recurrence, without any type of arrest or negative police enforcement.
>
> I could have saved time by just making an arrest, but that wouldn't have solved anything. It was talking to the man, the kids, to the parents—trying to get everybody to see where everybody was coming from.
>
> *Competent law enforcer:*
>
> I'll be professional, won't cuss out the kids. Handle [the situation] within the realm of the law. Efficient, won't be blasé, won't play fun games.
>
> I understand the problem. As a police officer I will have to obtain proper evidence to be able to make a case.
>
> *The authority figure:*
>
> Very authoritative. Possibly intimidating. This is all I have working for me.
>
> I advised them [the teenagers] that they should leave when told, and if necessary we would show them that we were the "baddest gang" in town.
>
> *Friend or Peer:*
>
> I go home at 3:30 every day and watch cartoons. I let them [the teens] understand I'm human with needs. I jog a lot with the kids after work.
>
> I found the head honcho, ring leader, and talked to him man to man. I don't want to talk down to him. I explained the situation he was putting me in.
>
> *Knight in shining armor:*
>
> I'm there to save the day. "Don't worry sir, I'll take care of it; I'll talk to the boys and if necessary the parents." [I'm] the perfect public servant because these situations are easy if kids are reasonable. They can call again if the problem recurs.
>
> Even if it can't [I] want the victim to feel something can be done. They start talking about how things used to be here. Before you know it, you make a friend. When you leave: "Hey, he was the greatest cop there ever was!" (Belknap et al. 1986, pp. 9–12)

Juveniles diverted from the system by the police are referred to the juvenile court intake unit, which is frequently staffed by probation officers. The primary purpose of intake is to determine if youngsters accused of criminal acts or status offenses should be diverted from the juvenile court. Intake officers consider a variety of factors in making this decision. First, they must decide if the juvenile falls within the jurisdiction of the court by virtue of his or her age, the place where the offense took place, and the nature of the offense itself. For example, a juvenile can be beyond a court's jurisdiction if he or she is above juvenile court age, has committed the offense in another jurisdiction, or is involved in behavior considered deviant but not prohibited by law.

In many jurisdictions, intake workers must also ascertain the legal sufficiency of the referred offense and determine if there is sufficient evidence to support the allegations of delinquent conduct. Following this, a decision is made whether to refer the case to the juvenile court. In making this decision, intake workers consider the seriousness and time of day of the alleged offense; the type of neighborhood where the youth lives; and the youth's age, attitude toward authority, involvement in religious activities, prior court and police contacts, home environment, school record, reaction to sanctions previously imposed, and present interests and activities. In recent years, the intake function has taken on increasing importance because of the dual emphasis on diverting as many youths as possible, while at the same time protecting the community.

After an assessment of the legal and social factors associated with the case, the intake worker must decide on an appropriate disposition: outright dismissal, informal adjustment, informal probation, consent decrees, or filing of a petition. Complaints are dismissed if the intake worker determines that the alleged violation is not within the jurisdiction of the juvenile court. Informal adjustment involves a decision to close the case after the youngster is warned or on the provision that the youngster meet certain conditions (such as restitution, private treatment, involvement in a diversion program, or an agreement by the parents to improve supervision).

Informal probation generally involves a period of informal supervision during which the youngster is required to fulfill certain requirements such as attending school or obeying his or her parents. To ensure equity and the protection of the juvenile's rights, the National Advisory Committee on Criminal Justice Standards and Goals (1976) recommends that four procedural safeguards be followed: (1) that the facts of the case against the juvenile be undisputed; (2) that all parties, including the juvenile, agree to the informal probation disposition; (3) that a reasonable time limit—three to six months—be placed on the informal probation; and (4) that no petition should be filed following the agreement of all parties involved to the conditions of the probation.

A consent decree is a midpoint between informal supervision and a formal disposition. It involves a formal order for treatment or supervision to be provided by the court staff or another agency. The decree requires the approval of the judge and the consent of the child and his or her parents. The advantage of this disposition is not only that is eases the case load of the court, but also that it protects the community while enabling the juvenile to avoid the stigma of formal adjudication. To protect the rights of the juvenile, the advisory committee recommends that decrees not be issued unless there is sufficient evidence that the juvenile committed the alleged offense; that they be limited to a period of six months, or at the most a year; and that they do not require the juvenile to be removed from the family. In this way, staff members can provide juveniles with supervision or services without requiring them to go through formal adjudication.

JUVENILE DETENTION CENTERS

For a variety of reasons some juvenile offenders must be formally detained prior to eventual release or court appearance. Variables considered in making the decision whether to detain a juvenile offender include the following:

1. Child is alleged to have committed an act that would be a felony if it were committed by an adult.
2. Child is an alleged escapee from a juvenile justice facility or control program.
3. Child is wanted in another jurisdiction for committing a misdemeanor or felony.
4. Child has committed an act of violence.
5. There are reasonable grounds to believe that the child, if not detained, will fail to appear at subsequent hearings.
6. There are reasonable grounds to believe that the child, if not detained, will be a threat to witnesses, victims, or other persons.
7. Prior record indicates the child has committed other acts of delinquency.
8. There is no parent, guardian, or responsible adult relative to release the child to.

Juvenile Detention Center Security

Although the average length of stay in a juvenile detention facility is only about 10 days in a given year, the detention centers, nationwide, process about 80% of all juvenile justice admissions to detention centers and training centers. Numerically, this percent translates into over 450,000 admissions

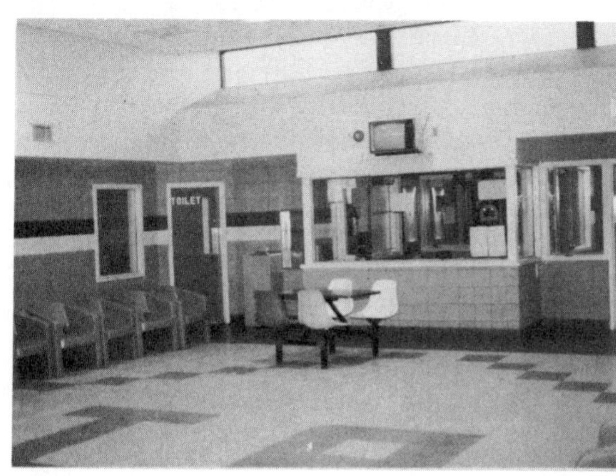

FIGURE 17.2
A juvenile detention center facility. *Top left,* facility entrance; *bottom left,* master control for facility; *top right,* inside dorm area; *bottom right,* outside facility recreation area. Photos courtesy of Florida Department of Health & Rehabilitative Services.

each year. The detention facility, furthermore, is usually the juvenile's first contact with the correctional system and this initial stay impacts seriously on the juvenile (American Correctional Association 1984).

The juvenile detention center serves a function parallel to that of the adult jail.[1] As with the adult jail, security and peacekeeping within the juvenile detention facility are critical. Therefore, many of the same security techniques must be employed within a juvenile detention facility. These include perimeter security, supervision of movement, counts, searches, key control, tool control, control of firearms and other security equipment, and use of force. The following provide some examples of juvenile detention center policies concerning security techniques and procedures.

PERIMETER SECURITY All security perimeter entrances and designated doors are kept locked except when used for admission or exit of staff, detained juveniles, or visitors and in emergencies. Prior to taking the juveniles outside, a juvenile careworker should make a security check of the outdoor area including the fence and the ground along the fence, which should be checked for contraband.

Complete records are maintained on all persons entering or exiting the facility.

SUPERVISION OF MOVEMENT Close supervision of movement is utilized to ensure juvenile and public safety. Juveniles should never be left unattended in any area inside or outside the facility. Intensive staff supervision is intended to reduce reliability on security hardware and to promote a positive relationship between staff and juveniles as the primary means of control. The juvenile careworkers must be aware of the location of all juveniles at all times. At least one of the juvenile careworkers should have visual contact with each juvenile.

COUNT The process called "count" is used to ensure around-the-clock accountability of all juveniles within the facility. A system of physically counting the juveniles is usually established. The facility director usually informs the county juvenile/family court judge when the facility has reached its design capacity. In the event that the resident count exceeds design capacity, caseworkers initiate a review of each case to determine if conditions warrant a transfer to a nonsecure program or a recommendation for conditional release pending final disposition of the case(s).

Informal, irregular counts, or census checks, are made by all staff supervising juveniles to verify that all juveniles are present. Typically, counts of this kind are made while juveniles are working, engaged in daily activities within the housing section, and the like. These counts are reported only when a juvenile is missing.

SEARCHES Most juvenile detention centers have policies governing searches of persons in their custody. Searches are conducted to prevent the introduction of weapons or other dangerous contraband into the detention facility. Contraband in a juvenile detention center may include matches, alcohol, drugs, or money or any item not authorized. Searches may also be conducted to discover and suppress the "trafficking" of contraband between facility staff and juveniles. In juvenile detention centers, strip, frisk, and body cavity searches may be employed. These policies are usually implemented after review by legal counsel to ensure the adequate protection of all parties. In general, searches may only be conducted when there is sufficient reason to believe the security of the detention center is endangered or that contraband is present.

KEY CONTROL All detention centers must have an adequate system to control all keys for the facility. The system of control requires simple and daily checks of all keys and locks within the detention center. Tight controls are maintained on the issuance, duplication, and return of all keys (see Figure 17.3).

TOOL CONTROL All detention centers utilize various kinds of tools and culinary equipment for their daily operation. Tools generally fall into one of two categories:

- *Restricted tools.* Tools that may be useful to effect escape or cause serious death or injury. These may include ice picks, bolt cutters, and files.
- *Less restricted tools.* General mechanical tools, such as nonsecurity screwdrivers and wrenches.

Tight controls are maintained on the issuance (by category), storage, and retrieval of tools within the detention facility. Inventory controls on all tools may be conducted on a daily, weekly, or monthly basis.

FIREARMS, RESTRAINING DEVICES, AND USE OF FORCE In most juvenile detention facilities, firearms or other weapons are strictly prohibited. The issuance, storage and staff use of security equipment such as handcuffs, chains, and other restraining devices are closely controlled. In many facilities staff who find it necessary to use restraining devices during their shifts are required to submit a written report. Generally, detention facility staff may only utilize the minimal amount of force necessary to control a juvenile or situation. Restraining devices are not to be employed as punishment and may be used only when absolutely necessary. From time to time restraining devices or minimal force may be necessary to protect a juvenile from self-injury. When physical restraints or force are utilized by staff, written reports of the incident usually must be completed (see Figure 17.4 on page 546).

Recent Research on Juveniles in Detention

One of the areas of interest regarding juveniles who end up in detention centers relates to the various problems they've experienced. Two specific areas of concern are the relationship between juvenile detainees' drug use and crime, and the association between detainees' physical abuse and sexual victimization experiences and their delinquent behavior.

Dembo and his associates (1987a, 1987b, forthcoming) conducted significant research regarding these issues.[2] Their work involving urinalysis revealed that approximately 40 percent of the youths entering a southeastern detention center had recently used marijuana or cocaine. The researchers also found that juveniles who test positive for marijuana use have higher rates of referral to juvenile court for nondrug property felonies. Although a specific cause-and-effect relation-

KEY CONTROL SIGNATURE SHEET

Date	Departing Staff Signature	# of Keys	Accepted By

FIGURE 17.3
A signout sheet used for key control. Adapted from American Correctional Association, *Guidelines for the Development of Policies and Procedures—Juvenile Detention Facilities* (College Park, Md.: American Correctional Association, 1984), Chapter 11.

ship could not be established, high frequency of marijuana use needs to be regarded as a sign that a youth may be in need of some form of intervention service. Cocaine or heroin users usually require special intervention/treatment to reduce the likelihood of continued personally and socially harmful patterns of behavior.

Dembo's research also revealed high rates of physical abuse and sexual victimization among juvenile detainees. A relationship was also found to exist between the detainees' physical and sexual abuse experiences and their use of illicit drugs. Many of the cases of physical or sexual abuse took place within the youths' households. Again, this information has implications for intensive intervention efforts. Although the majority of juvenile detention centers are not equipped to deal with issues such as drug abuse or physical and sexual abuse, if detention center staff are fully informed, they can make appropriate referrals to other public or private resources for intervention and follow-up.

JUVENILE COURT CASELOADS

Juvenile courts typically handle both delinquency and dependency/neglect cases within their jurisdiction. A

FIGURE 17.4
A form for reporting the use of physical force. Adapted from American Correctional Association, *Guidelines for the Development of Policies and Procedures—Juvenile Detention Facilities* (College Park, Md.: American Correctional Association, 1984), Chapter 11.

Sample Juvenile Detention Facility
PHYSICAL RESTRAINT REPORT

Date: ____________

Name of Juvenile ____________

Unit: ____________

Place Where Incident Occurred: ____________

____

Incident Requiring Juvenile to be Restrained (Describe Fully): ____________

____

____

____

____

____

____
Signature of Staff Member

summary of a multi-year study of juvenile court cases follows (Nimick et al., 1987).[3]

Delinquency Cases

Courts with juvenile jurisdiction disposed of an estimated 1,275,600 delinquency cases in 1983. Between 1957 and the mid-1970s, delinquency caseloads increased from 440,000 to over 1.4 million cases annually (see Table 17.5). From the mid-1970s through 1980, caseloads remained relatively constant, but began decreasing thereafter with 1983 being the lowest level since 1974. Changes in annual delinquency caseloads have to some extent paralleled the changes in the juvenile population in the United States. Some of the increase between 1957 and the mid-1970s and much of the decrease thereafter can be explained by these population trends. The impact of the changing youth population on the volume of delinquency cases handled by juvenile courts can be assessed through a study of delinquency case rates. In 1983 the juvenile courts processed 43.5 delinquency cases for every 1,000 youths aged ten through seventeen years living in the United States (see Figure 17.5). While the 1983 delinquency case rate was equal to the average rate of the previous seven years, during the twenty-seven-year period from 1957 through 1983 the rate of delinquency cases increased by 120 percent. Therefore, only a part of the overall increase in delinquency caseloads can be attributed to the growth in the youth population. As the growth pattern of delinquency case rates implies, juvenile courts in 1983 were seeing a larger percentage of the nation's youth for delinquency matters than were courts in the late 1950s; but in the years since the mid-1970s, this proportion has remained relatively constant.

Males were involved in 77 percent of the delinquency cases the courts processed in 1983. In 1983 for every 1,000 males aged ten through seventeen years in the general population, the juvenile courts handled 66 male cases compared to 21 female delinquency cases for every 1,000 females in the same age range. Between 1957 and 1983, the number of male cases increased by 174 percent while the number of cases involving females increased 260 percent. Once again, only a portion of these increases can be attributed to population growth. Differences between the male and female delinquency case rates decreased between 1957 and 1983; although both male and female rates increased, the increase in the female rate was proportionally greater.

Dependency and Neglect Cases

Children can be referred to juvenile court because they may be dependent and/or the victims of abuse and ne-

TABLE 17.5
Estimated Number and Rate of Delinquency Case Dispositions: 1957–1983

YEAR	ESTIMATED NUMBER OF DELINQUENCY CASES[1]	CHILD POPULATION 10–17 YEARS OF AGE[2]	RATE[3]
1957	440,000	22,173,000	19.8
1958	470,000	23,433,000	20.0
1959	483,000	24,607,000	19.6
1960	510,000	25,368,000	20.1
1961	503,000	26,056,000	19.3
1962	555,000	26,989,000	20.6
1963	601,000	28,056,000	21.4
1964	686,000	29,244,000	23.5
1965	697,000	29,536,000	23.6
1966	745,000	30,124,000	24.7
1967	811,000	30,837,000	26.3
1968	900,000	31,566,000	28.5
1969	988,500	32,157,000	30.7
1970	1,052,000	33,141,000	31.7
1971	1,125,000	33,643,000	33.4
1972	1,112,500	33,954,000	32.8
1973	1,143,700	34,126,000	33.5
1974	1,252,700	34,195,000	36.6
1975	1,317,000	33,960,000	38.8
1976	1,432,000	33,482,000	42.3
1977	1,389,000	32,896,000	42.2
1978	1,359,000	32,276,000	42.1
1979	1,374,500	31,643,000	43.4
1980	1,445,400	31,171,000	46.4
1981	1,350,500	30,725,000	44.0
1982	1,292,500	29,914,000	43.2
1983	1,275,600	29,345,000	43.5

[1] Estimates for 1957–1969 are based on data from a national sample of juvenile courts. Estimates for 1970–1983 are based on data from all units reporting consistently for two consecutive years.

[2] Based on estimates from the Bureau of the Census, U.S. Department of Commerce Current Population Reports, Population Estimates and Projections, Series P-25, No. 965, Issued March, 1985 and the data file entitled "County Population Estimates (Provisional) by Age, Sex and Race: 1980–1982 prepared in 1985." Also included are population figures for Puerto Rico and the Virgin Islands.

[3] Rate is the number of delinquency cases per 1,000 children 10 through 17 years of age.

Adapted from Ellen H. Nimick et al., *Juvenile Court Statistics* (Washington, D.C.: U.S. Department of Justice, 1987), p. 10.

glect. Dependency/neglect cases involve charges against parents or guardians of neglect or inadequate care, abandonment or desertion, abuse or cruel treatment, or improper or inadequate conditions in the home. In 1983 courts having juvenile jurisdiction handled the largest number of dependency/neglect cases in their history; these courts disposed of an estimated 196,200 dependency/neglect cases. A quick comparison of the delinquency and dependency/neglect caseloads shows that this figure is only a small fraction of the number of delinquency cases courts handled in 1983, which might imply that juvenile courts devote less court time and resources to dependency/neglect matters. However, due to the nature of the dependency/neglect cases, periodic reviews over many years can commit a court to a long-term involvement with a particular case, and the typical dependency/neglect case, in fact, consumes a larger amount of court time and resources than the typical delinquency case.

Between 1957 and 1983, dependency/neglect caseloads increased by 72 percent, much less than the 190 percent increase in delinquency caseloads. But unlike the delinquency pattern, most of this variation can be attributed to the growth and decline in the youth population. The dependency/neglect case rate remained relatively constant from 1957 until the late 1970s when the rate of dependency/neglect cases brought before the

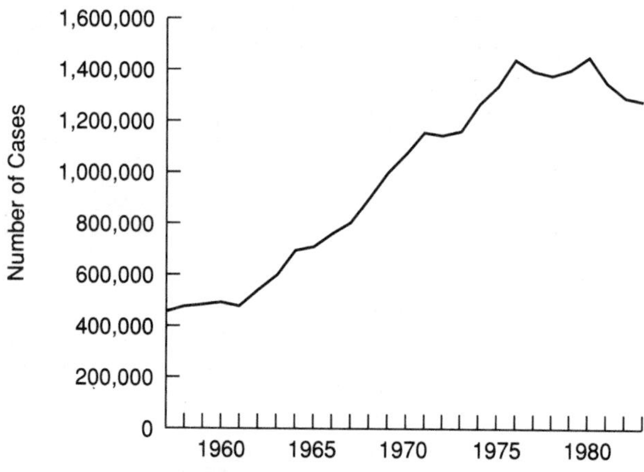

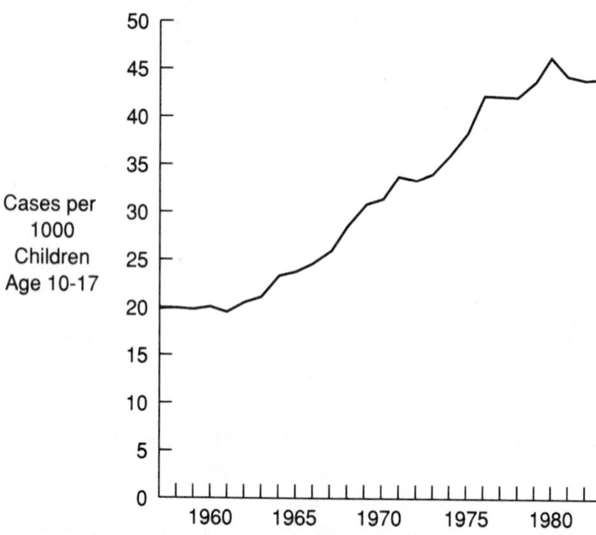

FIGURE 17.5
Adapted from Ellen H. Nimick et al., *Juvenile Court Statistics* (Washington, D.C.: U.S Department of Justice, 1987), p. 10.

juvenile courts began to increase. In 1983 juvenile courts processed 3.07 dependency/neglect cases for every 1,000 children below the age of eighteen, the largest annual rate ever observed. Therefore, it appears that in the last few years the juvenile courts have been seeing a growing proportion of their youth population for dependency/neglect matters.

In 1983 juvenile courts handled slightly more female than male dependency/neglect cases. This roughly equal representation of males and females sharply contrasted with the predominance of males in delinquency cases.

It appears that if the current caseload trends hold true, the importance of the juvenile courts will continue to be significant in the criminal justice system during the next decade.

POSTADJUDICATION ALTERNATIVES

In deciding on a disposition for adjudicated juveniles, judges can exercise considerable discretion and are limited only by available resources and statutory requirements. The options open to them include probation, warning the youngster, placing the youngster in the custody of his or her parents, levying a fine, ordering restitution, assigning work, placing the youngster in a foster home, group home, or halfway house, or—as a final resort—committing the youngster to a training school.

Juvenile Program Census

The 1986 census of juvenile detention and correctional facilities reports that as of February 1, 1983 there were 63,221 juveniles housed in 2,277 public and private long-term juvenile facilities (U.S. Department of Justice 1986). This report also indicates that the average length of time a juvenile stays in a long-term facility is 157 days for public facilities and 188 days for private facilities.

Juveniles in both detention centers (short term) and correctional institutions (long term) are included in the census report. When these two populations are combined, the 1986 report indicates violent juvenile offenders comprised 17.1 percent of those in custody and property offenders amounted to 34.6 percent. The remainder of those in custody reflect nondelinquent categories, such as status offenders and abused and neglected juveniles. The demographic and adjudication status of juveniles held in custody is reflected in Table 17.6.

Juvenile Restitution Programs

Restitution is one of the postadjudication alternatives available to juvenile judges. It is defined as repayment by the offender, in money or services, of the losses suf-

TABLE 17.6
Demographic Characteristics and Adjudication Status of Juveniles Held in Public and Private Juvenile Facilities, 1979 and 1983

	1979			1983		
	PUBLIC AND PRIVATE FACILITIES	PUBLIC FACILITIES	PRIVATE FACILITIES	PUBLIC AND PRIVATE FACILITIES	PUBLIC FACILITIES	PRIVATE FACILITIES
Total	71,922	43,234	28,688	80,091	48,701	31,390
Sex						
Male	57,679	37,167	20,512	64,424	42,182	22,242
Female	14,243	6,067	8,176	15,667	6,519	9,148
Race						
White	47,707	26,053	21,654	50,182	27,805	22,377
Black	19,595	13,752	5,843	25,842	18,020	7,822
Other*	2,141	950	1,191	2,020	1,104	916
Not reported	2,479	2,479	0	2,047	1,772	275
Ethnicity						
Hispanic	6,301	4,395	1,906	7,844	5,727	2,117
Non-Hispanic	65,621	38,839	26,782	72,247	42,974	29,273
Age						
9 years and under	...	...	...	661	42	619
10–13 years	...	...	...	8,523	3,104	5,419
14–17 years	...	...	...	63,808	39,571	24,237
18–20 years	...	...	...	5,890	4,804	1,086
21 years and over	...	...	...	115	86	29
Not reported	...	...	...	1,094	1,094	0
Average age	15.1 yrs.	15.3 yrs.	14.9 yrs.	15.2 yrs.	15.4 yrs.	14.9 yrs.
Adjudication status						
Committed	53,128	31,381	21,747	59,590	35,178	24,412
Detained	12,289	11,552	737	14,376	13,156	1,220
Voluntarily admitted	6,505	301	6,204	6,125	367	5,758

Note: Data are for December 31, 1979 and February 1, 1983.
... Not available.
* American Indians, Aleuts, Asians and Pacific Islanders.

Data from the U.S. Department of Justice, Bureau of Justice Statistics, *Children in Custody: 1982/83 Census of Juvenile Detention and Correctional Facilities, 1986* (Washington, D.C.: U.S. Government Printing Office, 1986), p. 5.

fered by the victim or society as a result of the offender's criminal/delinquent act.

One of the most profound changes in juvenile justice during the past decade has been the phenomenal growth in the use of restitution as a sanction for juvenile offenders. (Warner and Burke 1987).[4] Every state and the District of Columbia has at least one of the programs described here (see Table 17.7). Most offer both community service restitution and financial restitution (see Table 17.8), while smaller numbers provide for victim-offender mediation or other victim services. Financial restitution and community service restitution are almost equally common; 84 percent of the programs responding to a national survey handle monetary restitution orders and 90 percent handle community service. Seventy-five percent have both types. Victim service components are offered by 28 percent of these programs; 23 percent offer victim-offender mediation.

The oldest financial restitution program identified through the Warner and Burke survey was established

TABLE 17.7
Restitution Programs by State

Alabama	2	Missouri	2
Alaska	1	Montana	5
Arizona	5	Nebraska	3
Arkansas	2	Nevada	1
California	15	New Hampshire	3
Colorado	6	New Jersey	5
Connecticut	3	New Mexico	1
Delaware	1	New York	8
District of Columbia	1	North Carolina	9
Florida	6	North Dakota	1
Georgia	5	Ohio	17
Hawaii	1	Oklahoma	12
Idaho	3	Oregon	7
Illinois	7	Pennsylvania	23
Indiana	9	Rhode Island	1
Iowa	9	South Carolina	3
Kansas	4	South Dakota	3
Kentucky	4	Tennessee	1
Louisiana	5	Texas	16
Maine	1	Utah	5
Maryland	6	Vermont	2
Massachusetts	5	Virginia	14
Michigan	8	Washington	9
Minnesota	7	West Virginia	3
Mississippi	2	Wisconsin	24
		Wyoming	1

Adapted from Jean S. Warner and Vincent Burke, eds., *National Directory of Juvenile Restitution Programs, 1987* (Washington, D.C.: U.S. Government Printing Office, 1987), p. 3.

in 1945 in Bartow, Florida. The oldest community service program, located in Pierre, South Dakota, traces its origin to 1965.

In the research conducted by Warner and Burke, juvenile programs were asked to identify the administrative unit in which the restitution program was located. As has been true throughout the history of restitution programming in the United States, there are many different kinds of administrative and organizational arrangements. The most common is for the restitution program to be administered by probation (35 percent). Twenty-six percent report to the court itself. Another 8 percent report to the court as well as to probation.

Nonprofit organizations operate a surprisingly large percentage of the restitution programs. Nonprofits describing themselves as "private" nonprofits operate twelve of the programs; an additional 9 percent are administered by nonprofits describing themselves as "public" nonprofits (see Table 17.9).

MODEL RESTITUTION PROGRAMS Several juvenile restitution programs were designated by the Department of Justice's Office of Juvenile Justice and Delinquency Prevention as being national models. Three of the models are described below:

- *Quincy, Massachusetts.* Established in 1975, the "Earn-It" program is a multifaceted concept, involving community work service, victim-witness mediation, tourniquet sentencing, and job development. This program is an intricate part of the Probation Department within Quincy District Court, with its major goal focusing on defendant accountability. In its eleven years of operation, the "Earn-It" program has collected thousands of dollars from its defendants. In 1984–85, over $350,000 in restitution was collected and paid back directly to victims, and 45,235 hours of community work service were performed by 831 juvenile and adult offenders. The Victim Services Program includes face-to-face meetings between victims and offenders, focusing on the determination of restitution. The Job Development Program enables unemployed defendants to make

TABLE 17.8
Types of Restitution Programs

COMPONENTS OFFERED	NUMBER	PERCENTAGE
Community service only	45	15
Financial/monetary only	29	10
Community service and financial	221	75
Victim-offender mediation	67	22
Other victim services	82	28

Adapted from Jean S. Warner and Vincent Burke, eds., *National Directory of Juvenile Restitution Programs, 1987* (Washington, D.C.: U.S. Government Printing Office, 1987), p. 3.

monetary restitution by means of job placement in the private sector, while the Tourniquet Sentencing Program incorporates an intensive supervision alternative sentencing measure for high-risk juvenile offenders.

- *Charleston, South Carolina.* The Juvenile Restitution Program, Inc., (JRP) began in 1978 as part of a federally funded nationwide initiative and was incorporated as a private nonprofit organization in 1981. Offenders between the ages of ten and seventeen are referred to JRP from Family Court for completion of unpaid community work service or paid restitution to their victims. Since 1978, youngsters have performed 87,000 hours of community service as symbolic restitution, and have earned $35,000 in order to repay their victims. Community service clients are placed at one of a hundred public agency job sites. Monetary restitution clients are responsible for finding their own paying jobs. Seventy-five percent of the youngsters referred complete their restitution successfully. Each youngster completes a seventeen-hour preemployment skills curriculum before beginning the restitution job. The South Carolina Department of Youth Services (DYS) provides major funding for JRP through a contractual agreement. All other juvenile restitution programs in South Carolina are administered by the DYS through its probation department. Additional funding for JRP is provided by Trident United Way and Charleston County.
- Ventura, California. The Ventura County, California Juvenile Restitution Program started in 1978 as part of the National Restitution Program (RESTTA). In 1985, RESTTA selected the program as one of six outstanding programs in the country. As a Host Site, the program provides intensive onsite training. One unique feature is a residential program for chronic juvenile offenders. The agency also provides intensive probation supervision for offenders leaving the institution and for those placed directly on probation by the court. The program is operated by the Corrections Services Agency, offers both financial and community service restitution, and helps victims

TABLE 17.9
Organization of Programs

PROGRAM ADMINISTERED BY	PERCENTAGE	NUMBER
Probation located in the judicial branch	29	82
Probation located in the executive branch	6	17
Court	26	73
Court and probation in both judicial and executive branch	8	22
Private nonprofit organization	12	33
Public nonprofit organization	9	26
Other	10	44

Adapted from Jean S. Warner and Vincent Burke, eds., *National Directory of Juvenile Restitution Programs, 1987* (Washington, D.C.: U.S. Government Printing Office, 1987), p. 4.

develop financial loss statements. The institutional program focuses on job readiness and job search preparation. The school program emphasizes emancipation and independent living skills. The total program focuses on juvenile accountability. Reimbursements to individual victims and community service work are vital to symbolize that the victim and the community need to be repaid for the youth's delinquent act(s). In 1985, $85,000 was paid to the victims, and 55,000 hours of community work were completed.

Community-based Programs

Community-based programs for juveniles developed on two premises: (1) that traditional institutional programs are ineffective at best, and at worst actually reinforce delinquency, and (2) that alternative environments are needed to help youths who do not require institutionalization in order to protect the community (President's Commission on Law Enforcement and Administration of Justice 1967; National Advisory Committee on Criminal Justice Standards and Goals 1973). These programs take place in both residential and nonresidential facilities. Residential programs include foster homes, group homes, and halfway houses; nonresidential programs range from those that provide sporadic supervision (e.g., probation and aftercare) to those that supervise youngsters for all or part of the day.

RESIDENTIAL PROGRAMS Foster homes board neglected, dependent, and delinquent youngsters. Foster parents are paid by the state to provide supervision within the home. Delinquent and status offenders are placed in foster homes when it is believed that unsuitable circumstances in the parental home may have contributed to the problem behavior. Misbehavior by juveniles is sometimes a result of parent-child conflicts, child abuse, the inability or unwillingness of parents to provide appropriate support and supervision, and parental problems—alcoholism, mental illness, or criminal behavior. Foster parents can provide the juvenile with the supervision and support lacking in the real family and can do so in a more sustained manner than a probation officer. Also, this type of placement removes the juvenile from the neighborhood and companions with whom he or she previously engaged in deviant behavior. At an average cost of $2,500 per year per juvenile, the foster home is the least expensive alternative to institutionalization.

Group homes, group residences, and group foster homes are all terms used to describe programs that provide residential care for groups of four to twelve youngsters. The residences may be owned or rented by the state, a private agency, or the house parents. Typically, they are operated by a husband and wife assisted by one or more staff members. The objective is to provide a family environment for youngsters who cannot adjust to a one-to-one relationship with foster parents, but who can benefit from and adjust to a family environment in the company of their peers.

Halfway houses are small facilities that serve as few as five residents but typically have populations of between ten and twenty-five. Standing somewhere between the community and training schools, these facilities serve youngsters released from an institution as part of a reintegration program, as well as those who come directly from the juvenile court. One of the advantages of these programs is that they provide an alternative placement for youngsters who require more supervision than they can receive in nonresidential programs, yet do not require the level of supervision and security provided by training schools.

NONRESIDENTIAL PROGRAMS Day treatment programs provide supervision for juveniles for all or part of the day, but they do not require that a youngster live at the facility housing the program. Juveniles in these programs require more supervision than can be provided through probation or aftercare, yet they are judged to be capable of living at home during their involvement. Thus, these youngsters are forced to confront the problems that contributed to their delinquency: school problems, adverse community influences, family difficulties, and work problems. Counseling and group sessions focus on problems that the youngsters encounter in their daily lives. Also, because youths usually live near the program facility, staff members can work closely with the parents to achieve successful home adjustment. Day treatment programs usually cost less than halfway houses because they use community resources and services and do not provide housing, meals, and clothing for their clients.

Long-Term Institutional Facilities

Juveniles in custody are usually housed in facilities classified as "institutional" or "open." These categories are based on existing security arrangements and the extent to which the juvenile offender has access to community resources. Training schools usually fall into the designation of institutional. Training school populations are also usually classified as "long-term" as opposed to the detention facilities discussed earlier in this chapter.

FIGURE 17.6
A, Outside view of a halfway house (a converted motel). A halfway house provides a structured, residential environment for twenty to twenty-five committed youth, boys or girls. The program is budgeted for a length of stay of three to six months. Youths from fourteen to eighteen years of age who have been convicted of a felony or first-degree misdemeanor can be placed in a halfway house following court commitment. Each halfway house program uses the resources available in the community to enhance its own program services and give the residents an opportunity for interaction outside the confines of the halfway house.
B, Juvenile Short-Term Offender Program (STOP) camp cabins and laundry; **C,** STOP camp cabins; **D,** STOP camp cabin inside view. One of the community-based alternatives to sending delinquent youths to an institution is the Short-Term Offender Program (STOP). The program consists of various campsites located in state parks and forests. Through the combination of rigorous outdoor work, counseling, wholesome recreation and educational activities, youth have an opportunity to change behavior patterns. Educational services are provided by the local school district at the camp site. Efforts are made to integrate the work project activities into the educational curriculum. The length of stay is generally two months although it may vary from thirty to ninety days. Photos courtesy of Florida Department of Health and Rehabilitative Services.

In 1983 juveniles housed in public, long-term institutional facilities numbered 24,527, while those in public, long-term open facilities were estimated to be 8,971 (U.S. Department of Justice 1987, p. 8). In 1982, to house a juvenile in a public, long-term institutional facility cost $61 per day. The cost per day to house a juvenile in a public, long-term open facility was $50. The average length of stay for a juvenile in a public, long-term institutional facility was 172 days versus 122 days for juveniles in a similar facility with an "open" environment (U.S. Department of Justice 1987, pp. 7, 11).

In the final analysis, long-term institutional facilities such as training schools are expensive to operate. Yet, despite the efforts of many, long-term institutional facilities still outnumber and hold more juveniles than open environment facilities such as halfway houses and group homes.

CONTEMPORARY INSTITUTIONS Today's training schools are self-contained, relatively large, confinement facilities for youngsters removed from the community. The programs vary according to the extent to which they emphasize their dual goals of custody and rehabilitation. Compared with adult institutions, these facilities most closely resemble minimum security institutions. Most are located in rural areas, so security is provided primarily by their isolation. Some of the institutions—those located near populated areas—have fences or security patrols on their perimeters; few have guard towers. Many resemble small colleges or boarding schools in design.

The cottage concept is the predominant housing model for most contemporary schools. Residents live in cottages that house up to sixty youths (although many house fewer than twenty). Cottage staff are frequently called house parents, and married couples are sometimes recruited for these positions—with the goal of providing a homelike atmosphere.

Education, both academic and vocational, is the principal type of program offered at training schools. Academic programs fit three categories of students: those who will return to a conventional school; those who will go to work; and those who want to earn a high school equivalency diploma before going to work. Many youngsters require extensive remedial help because of previous school failures. Youths performing at a level far below their age require nontraditional school programs that emphasize basic skills and use interesting learning materials. Computer-based instruction is sometimes used to provide immediate feedback to youngsters who have difficulty deferring gratification.

The education curriculum may include survival skills, budgeting, contracts, sex education, nutrition, and drug education. The quality of the curriculum depends on such factors as funding, staffing, and state standards. In general, however, educational programs at training schools are far more effective than casework and counseling at other institutions, because the teaching role is better understood and there is a well-established training program for teachers.

TRAINING SCHOOLS OF THE FUTURE A decline in the juvenile population, the removal of status offenders from training schools, and the emphasis on community-based alternatives to institutionalization will undoubtedly contribute to a future reduction in the training school population. Countering this trend will be the concern over protecting the public from the dangerous or violent juvenile offender. Thus, we can expect a policy that refers status offenders and youths engaged in less serious delinquent acts to community-based treatment programs, while potentially dangerous youths will be committed to training schools. As a result, training schools of tomorrow will probably house a higher percentage of older, minority, and serious offenders than ever before (Wilson 1978).

PREVENTION AND DIVERSION

As Ward (1978) suggests, the concept of delinquency prevention has probably been with us as long as we have sought to differentiate juveniles from adult offenders. *Prevention* refers to any attempt to forestall anticipated delinquent behavior. *Diversion,* on the other hand, deals with delinquent behavior that has already occurred; thus, it falls within the province of control. Diversion had antecedents within the child-saving movement. Recall that separate institutions for juveniles and the juvenile court itself were originally developed to divert youth from the harsh and punitive orientation of the adult criminal justice system.

Prevention

Prevention encompasses programs ranging from those intended to reduce criminal opportunities to those directed at ameliorating adverse conditions presumed to cause (or contribute to) delinquency. Most programs focus on community reorganization, education, employment, and recreation.

COMMUNITY REORGANIZATION Community reorganization programs—also known as area projects, inclusive neighborhood programs, and social action programs—assume that delinquent behavior results from social and cultural conditions, rather than from individual disturbances, pathologies, or inadequacies (Stratton and Terry 1968). Moreover, because delinquency rates and cultural and social conditions vary from community to community, the type of program developed depends to a great extent on the nature and composition of the particular community or neighborhood.

The Chicago Area Projects, which have been operating since 1934, are among the most well-known community reorganization programs. Another prominent program is Mobilization of Youth, started in 1962 and based on the delinquency and opportunity thesis of Cloward and Ohlin (1960). Following the pattern of the Chicago Area Projects, this program emphasizes the involvement of local residents in delinquency prevention. It includes more than thirty separate action programs in the areas of work, education, services to individuals and families, and group and community organization.

EDUCATION Prevention programs can also focus on general public education and the education of at-risk youths. Public education might include programs on drug and alcohol abuse or parent effectiveness training. Programs for youth often involve school activities.

Theories and research on delinquency suggest that delinquent behavior is partly a result of negative school experiences (Schafer and Polk 1967). School occupies a strategic place in the lives of youths, because it provides the skills and values needed to structure legitimate alternatives. Thus, school has the potential to offset or neutralize some of the pressures toward delinquency created by adverse family or community conditions. On the other hand, an unsatisfactory school experience can push a youth toward delinquency. Programs such as Head Start and Higher Horizons, as well as less academically oriented career education programs, are designed to strengthen the positive aspects of a school experience.

EMPLOYMENT Unemployment and underemployment are also thought to be major contributors to delinquency (Fleisher 1966; Cloward and Ohlin 1960; and Singell 1965). A job serves to integrate the individual into the dominant structure of society by providing a legitimate way to achieve success, by giving the individual a stake in legitimate social order, and by serving as a check on behavior. Unemployed youths have little at stake if they disobey the laws; thus, they may turn their efforts toward achieving success by illegitimate means. In contrast, employed youth may decide that they would lose more as a result of being apprehended for delinquent behavior than they would gain by the perpetration of such acts.

Comprehensive employment programs seek to expand the number of employment opportunities, to create job training and manpower development opportunities, and to break down the barriers that unjustly exclude persons from productive employment (National Advisory Committee on Criminal Justice Standards and Goals 1976). A number of these programs offer juveniles on-the-job training in industry; others, like the National Youth Corps, provide both academic and business education.

RECREATION The idea that recreation can prevent delinquency is reflected in the proverb "The Devil makes mischief for idle hands." This simplistic view was the rationale for the hundreds of playgrounds built in our major cities in the early 1900s, and it was also used to some extent to justify settlement houses in lower income areas. Some delinquency is probably related to the misuse of leisure time, but recreational activities alone cannot prevent delinquency. Following a survey of available research on recreation, Beck and Beck concluded that "these studies neither demonstrated in any conclusive fashion that recreation prevented delinquency, nor were they able to demonstrate conclusively that recreation was without value in delinquency prevention" (1967, p. 334).

Recognizing the limitations of conventional approaches to using recreational programs in delinquency prevention, youth organizations such as the Boy Scouts and Girl Scouts developed special programs to deal with these shortcomings. Other organizations developed detached worker programs for youngsters involved in gang delinquency. Developed in response to research showing that gang members do not participate in traditional recreation programs, detached worker programs send workers into the community to seek out work with gangs "on their own turf."

Diversion

The idea of diversion, as already noted, dates back to the beginning of the juvenile justice system. The recent emphasis on diversion can be credited to the President's Commission on Law Enforcement and Administration of Justice (1967), which recommends the increased use of alternatives to the juvenile justice system.

The following discussion on diversion focuses on the police, the courts, and probation departments. However, many diversion programs are *administered* by schools, juvenile welfare boards, and other community agencies, or by special organizations established for that purpose. Many school, employment, and recreation programs are also used by communities to divert youth from the juvenile justice system. These programs are discussed in chapter 18.

THE POLICE As the law enforcement agents of our social system, the police must often make discretionary judgements as to how a juvenile should be handled. In fact, police discretion accounts for as much as 90 percent of all diversion. Patrol officers have always had to make decisions as to whether to ignore an accident, to handle a juvenile informally, or to take him or her into custody for further processing. Prompted by the availability of funds and frustration with existing community programs, some police departments have established and operated diversion programs. Some departments operate youth service bureaus, even though such programs were originally intended to be independent of the juvenile justice system.

INTAKE AND THE COURTS Intake workers—who are usually probation officers, juvenile court personnel, or state youth service counselors—are in a strategic position to reduce the penetration of juveniles further into the juvenile justice system. "Penetration" is a term used to characterize a youngster's contacts with the formal agencies of the system. Intake workers can warn and release juveniles, refer them to outside programs, place them on informal probation, or file a petition with the juvenile court. Pressures on juvenile court intake units have led them to develop their own diversion programs to minimize penetration.

PROGRAMS OUTSIDE THE JUVENILE JUSTICE SYSTEM Diversion programs that operate outside the juvenile justice system are in the best position to fulfill the goals of diversion. That is, they can provide a juvenile with assistance without the stigma of involvement in programs associated with official agencies of social control. These programs are sponsored by a variety of community organizations, including departments of children's services, welfare departments, mental health departments, religious organizations, and nonprofit organizations established to provide services to children and young people.

YOUTH SERVICE BUREAUS Youth service bureaus are a hallmark of the diversion movement. Although the first such bureau was started in Chicago in 1958 and others were estabished in the mid-sixties, the real growth in these programs resulted from a recommendation by the President's Commission on Law Enforcement and Administration of Justice (1967) for the establishment of neighborhood agencies to provide services to youths.

Bureaus obtain their referrals from schools, the police, juvenile courts, parents, neighbors, and young people and their friends. They assist youngsters and their families in identifying problems that underlie delinquent behavior, and act to ensure that youngsters get the services they need. By accepting only voluntary referrals and by making referrals only to programs agreed to by the youngster and his or her parents, the bureaus attempt to avoid stigmatizing their clients.

Realizing that they would be of little value without outside resources, youth service bureaus work with citizens to develop needed services that are not available. Bureaus contract for services, encourage existing agencies to expand their programs or develop special services, and develop programs of their own to fill voids in available services.

To prevent further difficulties on the part of their clients and other juveniles, bureaus also attempt to deal with some of the conditions within the community that contribute to the problems of youngsters. An effort is made to change attitudes and practices that discriminate against problem youth and exacerbate their antisocial behavior. The bureaus have the responsibility to educate, consult, demonstrate, and—when necessary—resort to political pressure to ensure that resources and institutions are responsive to the needs of their clients.

RUNAWAY AND MISSING CHILDREN ISSUES

Recently there has been an increase in the public's concern for runaway and other missing children. Accounts of missing children becoming homicide or sexual abuse victims as well as being involved in street crimes or drug and alcohol abuse have attracted public attention (Burgess 1986).[5]

It is useful to consider missing children in terms of four major categories: (1) runaways, (2) stranger or acquaintance abductions, (3) parental kidnappings, and (4) lost or accidentally injured children.

In general, when a child is not where he or she is supposed to be, that child is labeled *missing*. To be labeled missing, however, means that someone cares enough about the child to report the incident. When more about the child's whereabouts is learned, he or she may fall into one of the following categories.

- *Runaways.* Runaway children make up the largest category of missing children. Sometimes called "voluntary missings," runaways are usually defined as those who have left their parents or other caretakers without permission. Although their departure may appear voluntary, not all runaways wish to leave their homes. Instead, they may feel they are being pushed out because they are troublesome or unemployed. Adolescents who are forced out of their homes or ignored by their families and who find their way to the streets are often called "throwaway children." Children who are allowed to come and go as they please also fall into this category.

- *Abducted children.* Abducted children may be taken by either a family member or by a person who is not part of the child's family. Circumstances of family member abduction—often called "parental kidnapping"—include a divorced or separated parent's failing to return a child to the child's guardian or taking the child without the knowledge or permission of the child's guardian. Children abducted by nonfamily members (sometimes called "stranger abductions") are also taken without the knowledge or permission of the child's caretaker.
- *Homeless youth.* Runaways, throwaways, or abducted youth eventually may be come homeless, although the term generally applies to the runaway group. It implies that either the family has abandoned the youth completely or the youth has voluntarily exiled himself or herself from the family group.
- *Lost or accidentally injured children.* This category refers to those situations in which, for example, a child wanders into the woods, becomes injured or trapped, and is unable to contact others for help. The child's intention was not to run away; rather, the situation occurred in the context of daily childhood activities.

The Runaway

Contemporary U.S. studies have found that in addition to being adventurous, rebellious, and stubborn, the "typical" runaway is often a victim of a troubled family environment and of multiple abuses. The youth is without employment skills or plans, and by the act of running away becomes vulnerable to the dangers of survival in the unprotected environment of the street. The runaway, denied the opportunity to live in a safe and stable environment, is a youth at risk of physical and emotional injury, of sexual and other criminal exploitation—and even death. Frequently, a pattern of runaway may develop as depicted in Figure 17.7.

Clearly, runaways are often the victims of some sort of abuse and, behind their defensive demeanor, many of them are frightened. Although they have positive potential as members of society, they do not feel important to their families and are not valued by family members or by society. Many of them have been kicked out, forced out, or never allowed into the spotlight of the family or the community.

Running away exacts a high price on the adolescent. Life on the street frequently means learning tactics, often criminal, for survival. This perpetrates further the public's image of the runaway as an outcast of society rather than as a member of a troubled family.

The System's Response to Runaway Youth

Agencies have responded to runaways in a number of ways:

- *Runaway shelters.* To provide runaways with a safe haven, communities and agencies have established shelters, halfway houses, and crisis centers throughout the country. Some runaways—lonely, terrified, and hungry—come to these places of their own accord, while others are left there by police to await return to their homes or placement elsewhere. Nevertheless, the so-called freedom of life on the streets still has a powerful attraction for many runaways. Some choose not to use the crisis centers at all and instead stay with friends or literally live on the streets. In addition, many runaways who do use or are placed in shelters run from these havens, despite the risks of living on the streets.

  Runaways as a group present critical questions for social service agencies that provide them with food and shelter. Many agencies adhere to conventional policies of returning runaways to their homes. This approach, however, simply allows the chronic runaway to continue in the cycle of leaving home. Many runaways avoid or leave the various agencies set up to keep them. When the runaway's reasons for leaving home are not adequately addressed, the running continues. Although many local communities do attempt to help runaways with their problems, a lack of resources may affect these programs.
- *Law enforcement.* Law enforcement personnel also experience obstacles in dealing with runaway youth. Because a runaway cannot be detained, the police officer who brings a runaway to a shelter may, within a few hours, see the same runaway out on the street again. In addition, many police departments may place runaways low on their lists of priorities, particularly in view of the fact that many youths reported as missing or runaway return home of their own accord within a relatively brief period of time.

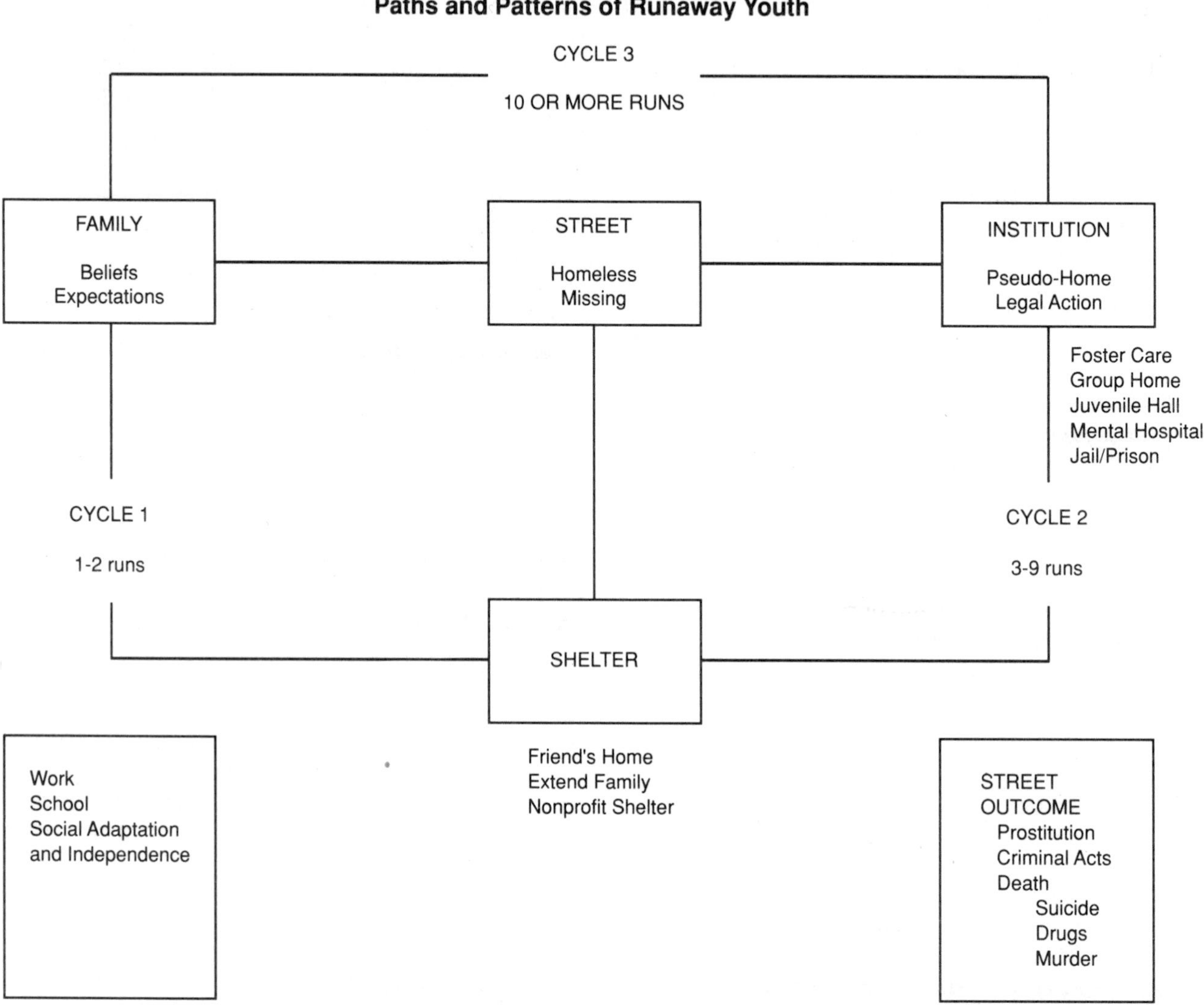

FIGURE 17.7
Paths and patterns of runaway youths. Adapted from Ann W. Burgess, *Youth at Risk: Understanding Runaway and Exploited Youth* (Washington, D.C.: National Center for Missing and Exploited Children, 1986), p. 43.

- *Health and mental health.* Runaways often turn to health clinics and emergency rooms for medical attention. Nurses and physicians, in attending to immediate health concerns, may not be able to inquire about the safety of the youth's living environment. Mental health professionals, who may detect a history of running away during an intake evaluation, may not always connect the running behavior with the youth's psychological problems.

It is clear that immediate efforts at intervention for the youth on the street and the families in crisis deserve the priority attention of existing service and legal agencies. The public health dimensions of the problem as a symptom of deeper conflicts and disturbances, however, require national attention.

The U.S. Congress highlighted this problem and took important steps to resolve it by passing the Missing Children Act in 1982 and, later, the Missing Children Assistance Act of 1984. Establishment of the National

Center for Missing and Exploited Children is another example of the federal government's commitment to solving the problem of missing and exploited children.

Much more can be done on the state level, however. Comprehensive state legislation is critically needed to address the particular needs of missing and exploited children and to help solve problems that are unique to the state level (National Center for Missing and Exploited Children 1985, p. 1).

An example of a poster suggested for use by private citizens or law enforcement agencies in missing children cases is illustrated in Figure 17.8.

COMMUNITY SUPERVISION

Community supervision of juveniles includes probation and aftercare services. Probation is viewed as a desirable disposition for youths who need some supervision but do not require the level of control supplied by nonresidential day treatment programs or residential community-based programs. Aftercare, in the form of supervision and services, is frequently required for juveniles released from training schools or community-based facilities.

Juvenile Probation

Juvenile probation actually preceded the first juvenile court. Probation is a legal status, imposed by the juvenile court, that permits a youth to remain in the community under the guidance and supervision of a probation officer. It typically involves "(a) a judicial finding that the behavior of the child has been such as to bring him within the purview of the court; (b) the imposition of conditions on his continued freedom; and (c) the provision of means for helping him to meet these conditions and for determining the degree to which he meets them" (National Council on Crime and Delinquency 1967, p. 231).

Probation involves much more than merely giving a youngster another chance; it is also intended to enable the youngster to adjust to the free community. From a variety of standpoints, probation represents the most desirable formal alternative to the juvenile court. While on probation, juveniles are able to (1) live at home and maintain family ties; (2) remain in school or retain their jobs; (3) maintain their involvement in community activities; and (4) avoid the stigma of being removed from their home and placed in a residential program. The alternative also costs less than placing youth in residential programs. Probation is the most frequent disposition used by the juvenile court.

Juvenile Aftercare

Aftercare is the juvenile equivalent of parole. It involves "the release of a child from an institution at the time when he can best benefit from release and from life in the community under the supervision of a counselor" (President's Commission on Law Enforcement and Administration of Justice 1967, p. 149). The term "aftercare" was proposed in an effort to dissociate juvenile programs from the legalistic language and concepts of adult parole.

Historically, juvenile aftercare in the United States can be traced to the system of indenture employed by houses of refuge in the early nineteenth century. The superintendents of these facilities were authorized to bind as apprentices youngsters they believed were reformed. Total control of the children was invested in their guardians, who could supervise boys until the age of twenty-one, girls until the age of eighteen. Within these limits, the employer made the decision as to when a youth had earned the right to be discharged. Females were usually indentured as domestics, and males were placed on farms, on ships, in stores, or in factories.

The problem with indenture was that there was initially no follow-up to determine how youths were being treated. Thus, the youngsters depended upon the goodwill of their employers, who could treat them either as slaves, employees, or foster children. States did not assume responsibility for supervising the youngsters until the middle of the nineteenth century, when New York appointed an agent to supervise indentured children and guard them against abuse. Despite this early development, however, aftercare did not become an integral part of the juvenile rehabilitation system until the 1950s (National Council on Crime and Delinquency 1967). Even today, aftercare in most states is considered to be the least developed aspect of corrections and is viewed by many observers as being less effective than adult parole.

According to a national study, there were 53,347 juveniles involved in aftercare programs in 1976 (Vinter 1976). The purpose of aftercare is to aid the juvenile in the transition from the restricted institution to the relatively free environment of the community. Implicit is the belief that the youth's institutional experience represents only the first phase of the treatment process, the second phase being completed in the community under the guidance and supervision of aftercare workers. Planning for aftercare should be an essential part of all institutional programs and should begin immediately after a youth is committed to the institution (National Council on Crime and Delinquency 1967). A wide range of placement options is required because of differences in

POSTER FORMAT

MISSING

CHILD'S PHOTO

Date of Photo

CHILD'S PHOTO,
different angle

Date of Photo

NAME OF CHILD

Date of birth: Age: Height: Weight:
Color of hair: Color of eyes: Complexion:
Physical characteristics: (braces, glasses, pierced ears, scars, marks, tattoos, etc.)
Clothing description:
Circumstances of disappearance: (last seen where, with whom, hitchhiking, etc.)

IF YOU HAVE INFORMATION, PLEASE CONTACT:

Name of police department: Police telephone number:
Officer assigned to case: Police case number:
Parents' telephone number: (optional)

Personal message to runaway: (We all love you. We want to work this out. Please call. Love, Mom and Dad.)

NATIONAL CENTER FOR MISSING AND EXPLOITED CHILDREN
1-800-843-5678

FIGURE 17.8
A poster suggested for use in missing children cases. Adapted from Ann W. Burgess, *Youth at Risk: Understanding Runaway and Exploited Youth* (Washington, D.C.: National Center for Missing and Exploited Children, 1986), p. 45.

age, experience, community conditions, and medical and psychological problems.

Consideration must also be given to the impact of institutionalization on youth. Some youngsters become more sophisticated and antisocial as a result of their training school experience; others become dependent and timid. There are also vast differences in the community settings to which these youngsters return. Most juveniles return to their old communities and are therefore exposed to the same conditions (e.g., peer influences) that originally contributed to their delinquency. And many youngsters must overcome the stigma of confinement in a juvenile institution. Thus, each youngster has specific needs that require the use of all available resources both within and outside the institution.

The advantages of good aftercare more than justify the required investment of time and money. First, aftercare provides a transitional period in which youths can adjust to the community with the assistance and support of a parole officer. The parole officer can help youngsters and their families to cope with problems that may have contributed to prior delinquency, to readjust to school, or to secure employment. A good aftercare program can also minimize a youth's length of stay at an institution: Authorities are likely to expand the number of early releases if they know that released youths will be supervised by aftercare workers. Another advantage is that it costs less to keep a youth on parole than to retain him or her in a juvenile training school. Based on a national survey, the National Council on Crime and Delinquency (1967) estimates that aftercare costs less than one-tenth as much as institutional care. And although the council suggests that this cost difference reflects, to a large extent, the inadequacy of aftercare programs, these programs would still be vastly cheaper than institutional care even if their funding was increased substantially. Many of the inadequacies exist simply because aftercare workers are assigned caseloads of two hundred or more adolescents. (Optimum caseloads for community supervision are discussed in the next section.) Given the adverse effects of institutionalization, as well as the potential benefits of good aftercare, it appears that increased funding of aftercare programs would be a wise investment.

The Quality of Supervision

Youths on probation are under the jurisdiction of the juvenile court; as a rule, youths on aftercare are under the jurisdiction of an agency or a state system. Youths on probation are more likely to have less serious and less extensive records than youths involved in aftercare; and youths on aftercare have to readjust to the community after their period of institutionalization. In spite of these differences, however, probation and aftercare are based on many of the same principles and considerations, and they have similar requirements.

First, there is a need for the development of a comprehensive services plan based on the youth's needs and the availability of community programs and resources. This plan should be developed by the aftercare or probation worker in conjunction with the youth, his or her significant others (e.g., parents), and representatives of programs in which the youth will participate. It is recognized that certain constraints have to be placed on a youth's freedom while under supervision, but these constraints should not interfere with the juvenile's regular employment, schooling, or other activities needed for normal development and growth (National Advisory Committee on Criminal Justice Standards and Goals 1976). If juveniles are not subjected to unreasonable restrictions, it is more likely that they will not violate the conditions of their supervision.

The major elements of effective supervision are surveillance, service, and counseling. Thus, the probation or aftercare worker must perform both police and counseling functions. Counseling requires trust between counselor and client, but the police function—the duty to ferret out client violations—makes the establishment of trust difficult or impossible. In surveillance, the worker is required to maintain contact with the youngster, his or her parents, school, and other persons directly concerned with the youth's adjustment to community life. It is the worker's responsibility to determine not only the extent to which the youth is meeting his or her commitments, but also how well the family, school, and others are conforming to their responsibility as agreed upon in the comprehensive plan.

In performing the service function, the worker must assess the extent to which the problems confronting the youth and his or her family may be ameliorated by available community resources—including community mental health centers, state employment agencies, health departments, vocational training programs, drug and alcohol abuse programs, and recreational programs. Based on that assessment, the worker must then develop a plan to use these services effectively for each child and family.

The counseling function is the most important and demanding of the aftercare or probation worker's responsibilities. For counseling to be effective, the worker must establish a relationship with a youth based on mutual confidence, trust, and understanding. In the course of individual or group sessions, the youngster, his or her family, and other persons directly involved must be helped to confront and comprehend the personal or environmental problems that contribute to delinquency.

The extent to which a worker can provide a juvenile with effective supervision depends largely on the size of the worker's caseload. The National Advisory Committee on Criminal Justice Standards and Goals (1976) argues that community supervision workers should carry no more than twenty-five active cases at any time. This figure was derived from various projects and studies that demonstrate conclusively that a worker with twenty-five cases spends only an hour and a half each month in face-to-face contact with each youth. While this may be enough for some juveniles, it is marginal for most, and woefully inadequate for a few. Thus, a caseload management system should be developed based on the recognition that not all juveniles require the same level of supervision and not all respond to the same approach.

Revocation

Probation revocations are generally handled by the juvenile court; the aftercare agency typically has the authority to revoke aftercare. Although juveniles are not *legally* entitled to a hearing prior to aftercare revocation, many jurisdictions do voluntarily provide due process hearings to avoid subsequent legal action. As a rule, parole or probation should be revoked only if the youths engage in behavior that would have brought them to the attention of the juvenile court were they not already under supervision (National Advisory Committee on Criminal Justice Standards and Goals 1976). However, there are some cases in which the conditions of probation or aftercare are so critical to the integrity of supervision that any violation necessitates a hearing.

Evaluating the Programs

The success of probation aftercare is difficult to assess because authorities do not agree as to how success should be defined. Research indicates that some programs are effective within certain limitations (Scarpitti and Stephenson 1968). Some studies show that more intense supervision relates to program success, but other studies refute this conclusion.

DEINSTITUTIONALIZATION OF STATUS OFFENDERS

Deinstitutionalization (DSO) refers to the removal of youths whose only infractions are status offenses (such as running away, incorrigibility, truancy, and curfew violation) from secure institutions and detention facilities. Serious efforts to deinstitutionalize status offenders (youths whose offenses would not be crimes if committed by an adult) began in most states after Congress established the Office of Juvenile Justice and Delinquency Prevention (OJJDP) in 1974 and issued a strong mandate for the removal of these youths from secure confinement (Schneider 1985).[6]

The Rationale of Deinstitutionalization

Several different rationales have been put forth to support a policy of deinstitutionalization. First, and perhaps most common, is the argument that deprivation of liberty for persons who have not violated the criminal code is unjust and unwarranted. This was the position taken by Congress in 1974.

Another argument is that decreasing coercive contact between status offenders and the juvenile court will have a positive impact on recidivism. Labeling theorists contend that a juvenile develops a fixed self-image as a delinquent primarily in response to being treated as a delinquent by persons in authority. This result may occur through subtle psychological pressures or through learning delinquent behavior from confinement with delinquents who have committed more serious offenses.

The third argument hinges on costs and priorities within the juvenile justice system. According to this argument, it is too expensive to institutionalize juveniles who are not committing crimes and too expensive for the court to continue expending a large portion of its resources on these nonoffenders. Instead, the court should devote its attention to serious and violent offenders and leave the nonoffenders in the hands of the social welfare system.

Experiences with deinstitutionalization, however, have not been overwhelmingly positive. In fact, much of the discussion and writing about deinstitutionalization has focused on potential or actual negative effects. These include the following:

1. A possible failure to reduce the number of status offenders in secure confinement (especially local detention).
2. Net-widening effects (i.e., pulling into the juvenile system youths who would not have been involved before).
3. Relabeling (e.g., adjudicating youths as delinquent or as emotionally disturbed who, in the past, would have been handled as status offenders).

4. Negative impacts or no impact on recidivism.
5. Service delivery problems including inadequate services, or nonexistent services or facilities, or the inability to provide services in a voluntary system.

Strategies of Deinstitutionalization

Deinstitutionalization brought with it the problems of finding nonsecure placements for status offenders and of devising new methods of enforcing compliance with court-ordered treatment, services, and out-of-home placements. The primary strategies adopted at the state and local levels fall into one of three categories: decarceration, diversion, or divestiture.

In some jurisdictions, the changes have not gone beyond prohibitions on institutional commitment and restrictions on local detention. In this approach, usually referred to as "decarceration," status offense cases are handled in much the same way as before: Juveniles charged with status offenses are brought before the court; a petition is filed alleging "delinquency" or "dependency" or "child in need of supervision" (depending on the state); a hearing is held and, if the facts of the petition are upheld, the youth is given a disposition by the court. This can include out-of-home placement in nonsecure facilities, probation, attendance at specified treatment or service programs, and so forth.

In other jurisdictions, the change has been much more substantial. Many areas established diversion programs that receive status offense cases directly from law enforcement officers, schools, parents, and even self-referrals. By providing crisis intervention services, these programs seek to return many of the juveniles to their own homes; and, for those cases with more serious problems, referrals are made to shelter homes, group homes, or foster homes.

The primary characteristics of full divestiture are that all services are provided on a strictly voluntary basis by a nonjustice agency, and the juvenile court cannot detain, petition, adjudicate, or place a youth on probation for the behaviors previously identified as status offenses. The juvenile court simply does not take these cases at all.

Reviewing the Impact of DSO

The National Center for the Assessment of the Juvenile Justice System conducted a review to assess the impact of the deinstitutionalization movement on recidivism and confinement of status offenders. The study produced the following findings.

Deinstitutionalization was expected to reduce the number of status offenders held in secure confinement. It was hoped that removing these youngsters from confinement would have a positive impact on recidivism, reduce the costs of the juvenile system, and permit more attention to be given to the serious and violent juvenile offenders.

The impact of deinstitutionalization on recidivism can be summarized very briefly: there does not appear to be any. There has not, however, been an adequate test.

Secure commitment and detention of youths for misbehavior designated as status offenses clearly has significantly declined in the aftermath of the federal legislation, but it has not been ended. Further, the significance of the increase in commitments to private institutions is not clear at this writing. If the increase reflects the availability of resources, utilized on a voluntary basis by status offenders and their families, then most would agree the increase is appropriate. If it simply represents a shift from one type of secure and involuntary confinement to another, or if behavior has inappropriately been relabeled for such purposes, then the goals of deinstitutionalization are being thwarted by shifts to the private sector. In a similar way, the significance of the increase between 1979 and 1983 of youths in long-term correctional settings also is not clear. This could reflect a one-time only phenomenon that will be followed by a continued downward trend, or it could reflect a return to increased commitments permitted by the valid court order amendments (discussed below). Although there are no definitive answers, available data on the juvenile justice system suggest a continued recognition of the need to provide services to juveniles whose behavior is troublesome, though noncriminal, but that these services should be provided in less restrictive environments than was common a decade ago.

The impact of deinstitutionalization on jailing juvenile status offenders has been more pronounced perhaps due to the additional thrust of the federal government to effect the removal of all juveniles from adult jails. As with the secure confinement of status offenders in secure juvenile institutions, there is still need for substantial progress.

Finally, the debate continues regarding the desirability of prohibiting secure confinement for status offenders under all circumstances. Particularly troublesome to some observers is the difficulty in enforcing out-of-home placements. The 1980 amendments to the Juvenile Justice Delinquency Prevention Act that permit contempt of court charges to be levied against juveniles who have run away from valid out-of-home placements were a response to intense pressure generated by those who opposed the deinstitutionalization movement. These amendments, however, are in turn opposed by those who believe that individuals should not be held against their will for behavior that, no matter how troublesome to the parents, is not a violation of any criminal code and represents no immediate danger to the individual or the community.

VIOLENT JUVENILE OFFENDERS

Adults often observe that kids can "get away with murder." Actually, this is sometimes literally true. Few violent juveniles are ever institutionalized. Trojanowicz refers to a study by the Office of Juvenile Services in New York, which indicated that less than 5 percent of over five thousand juveniles arrested in New York City for violent crimes (murder, kidnapping, forcible rape, assault, and arson) from July 1973 to June 1974 were sent to an institution (1978). Andrew Vogt, executive director of Colorado District Attorneys Association, says that, "in effect, we have created a privileged class in society" ("The Youth Crime Plague," *Time,* 11 July 1977, p. 19).

Most juvenile violence is random, casual, and purposeless—not for profit or even vengeance, but strictly for kicks. The victims are the elderly and the young, the handicapped and the helpless; the perpetrators are indifferent to the people they have slashed, shot, and beaten into insensibility. Remorse is so rare that a fifteen-year-old boy in New York who murdered a high school girl so he could steal her bicycle received a sentence of only eighteen months in an unlocked rehabilitation center because the judge was impressed by the boy's "repentance" ("Fifteen-year-old draws Probation for Murder," *Tampa Tribune* 1978).

Children Who Kill: Should They Be Treated and Punished as Adults?

As small children, Yvette and Janet Weaver were model sisters. But as they grew older, they grew apart. Yvette became a star pupil, the ambitious bearer of her family's dreams. Janet was a tomboy, slow in school and hot-tempered. The normal rivalry ended tragically last March when an argument between them led to murder. According to police in Savannah, Ga., Janet, 15, and her brother's fiancée, 22-year-old Renee Thomas, cornered 17-year-old Yvette in her bedroom and reportedly stabbed her 51 times. Then they allegedly dumped her body on a neighbor's property.

For three days Janet remained silent, watching cartoons while police scoured the house for clues of the mysterious intruder. Finally confronted with questions, both Janet and Renee broke down, describing the murder in gory detail but each insisting that the other was the actual killer. Police don't know who wielded the weapon, so they charged both with murder; Renee's trial begins this week. Whatever the outcome, hanging over this case and too many others like it is the last question Yvette asked her sister as she stared up from the blood-spattered floor: "Why?"

They are the youngest killers, adolescents and preteens who poison the innocence of childhood by murdering a stranger, a parent or a sibling. The wantonness of their crimes inspires a grim fascination: are they examples of human nature unbound or products of lives as depraved as their acts?

According to FBI statistics, 1,311 kids under 18 were arrested for murder nationwide last year. That's a slight drop over the last eight years and still represents less than 10 percent of total homicide arrests; most of those arrested were youths of 16 and 17. Nonetheless, each case presents an agonizing problem: what's to be done with an adolescent killer? Twenty-six states now permit underage executions, and death rows hold 37 teen killers. But many of the condemned will never face an executioner, and for most young killers the legal system prescribes punishments far short of death. A Justice Department study commission has recommended that youths under 14 who kill be held for at least seven years in a juvenile facility and that those over 15 be treated just as adult killers.

The law has responded in an erratic fashion to these difficult cases. Most states have long permitted the transfer into adult courts of juveniles charged with particularly heinous murders. In recent years many states have expanded those provisions to include lesser crimes such as manslaughter and armed robbery and also expedited the necessary procedures, sometimes automatically sending a youth arrested for murder to adult court. But legislatures tend to be more concerned with mandating get-tough sentences. Predictably, states have lagged behind in designing and funding facilities to hold violent youngsters. According to a 1985 survey, 6,300 juveniles (out of roughly 49,000 in custody nationwide) were held in adult facilities, a practice that neither reforms nor protects the young prisoners.

While legislatures and lawyers struggle with one more problem they can't truly solve, cases keep coming. Here is a look at two of them and the issues they raise:

Fourteen-year-old Arthur Bates didn't set out to kill: he was looking for a house to burgle. Once inside Lillian Piper's home, however, he proceeded to strangle her and then rape her. Having ravaged a 60-year-old woman who ran a popular day-care center, Bates stepped to the freezer and helped himself to some butter-pecan ice cream. Then he drove off in Piper's Cadillac. When the police caught him an hour later, he immediately confessed and added, matter-of-factly, "You can't do anything to me. I'm just 14."

The state had been trying to "do" something, anything, for Bates for a decade and had failed miserably. Before he turned four his mother was asking a welfare caseworker for help with her troubled son. By the age of 10 he was an abused child (authorities don't know by whom) taken by the state and treated as a pinball ricocheting between detention centers and mental hospitals. Doctors at a Houston hospital concluded he needed treatment but refused to admit him because he was not "out of touch with reality." After two months at a center in Waco, doctors decided they couldn't help and cut him loose. The state sent him to a private psychiatric facility for two years—at a cost of $113,000. It, too, gave up on his case. So, after a judge rubber-stamped the decision, he was sent to his stepmother. "When we went to court on that day, we knew that this child was not well," says Judy Hay of the Harris County (Houston) Childrens Protective Services. "We ran out of possibilities. No one would accept him."

'Multihandicap kid':

On the street, Bates got in trouble, moving through the juvenile courts on charges of auto theft, trespass and burglary. He did seven months in a reform school and was sent home just three months before Piper's murder. Arrested again, Bates was still treated as a child: in Texas, juveniles can't be treated as adults until they are 15. Now he's back in the custody of the Texas Youth Commission, which still isn't quite sure what to do with him. Bates is what the TYC's chief counselor, Matthew Ferrara, calls a "multihandicap kid," with legal, emotional and behavioral problems. "Multihandicap spells trouble," Ferrara says frankly. "It also means no treatment," because neither the staff nor the holding centers are equipped to deal with such kids. That's an ominous admission that is made worse by the fact that Bates may be getting out sooner than anyone wants. Last year the state legislature gave the TYC authority to hold juveniles like Bates until the age of 21 but neglected to come up with extra money for more beds. The lawmakers apparently did not appreciate the gravity of the problem. As Hay of Protective Services says: "I don't think people realize this, but Arthur is not the most severely disturbed kid under our care. I would put him somewhere in the middle."

David Joseph, 16, is a child of Silicon Prairie, the sprawl of suburbs west of Chicago that bustles with high-tech prosperity. Although he came from a broken home, he still made good grades and dreamed of law school. In the last year he seemed to go through a rebellious stage, opting for a modified punk hairdo and a jacket festooned with safety pins that spelled out "HELP" on the back. His father, Larry, didn't object and continued to lend David his Corvette and provide him with a set of credit cards. Police say that arrangement came to an abrupt halt in September when David, as part of a complicated plot hatched with two friends, allegedly shot his father to death in cold blood.

Police say that at 6:30 on a Friday morning, David, awakened by his alarm, pulled on a pair of rubber gloves, took a pistol from his father's collection and fired one bullet into Larry Joseph's head. Then, determined to feign a burglary, he and a friend allegedly loaded the family Corvette with audio and video equipment. Before he drove off, David had one more chore: he went back to his father's room and allegedly fired another bullet into his chest.

As police piece the tale together, the next three days were bizarre. Using his father's Corvette, David took a date to the homecoming dance and picked up a $147 tab for dinner with friends. At shopping malls he spent $6,000 and made the punk-club scene. Finally, on Monday evening, he called his mother and reported that he had found his father dead in bed. Police say that all of his careful artifice quickly came apart under questioning. Now he and his two friends are in custody awaiting trial as adults; if convicted, David could be sentenced to life imprisonment.

Help me:

What was the motive? "We don't know," says Hanover Park Police Chief Robert Sauer. David's mother, Susan, is also mystified—and angry. When the Josephs divorced 10 years ago, the judge separated their two sons, giving one to each parent. Susan says she worried about David but her ex-husband didn't listen. "I didn't know about the jacket that said HELP," she says. "When they signal like that, they're screaming. Larry's answer when we argued was, 'David's getting good grades.' So now he is in the county youth home, getting good grades."

The young killers are as different as their crimes. Research remains sparse, but a few tentative findings have emerged. Youngsters are most likely to kill strangers; intrafamily violence, despite recent publicity, is a relatively rare event. Also, older teens tend to be more dangerous. One reason: they are more likely to have access to handguns.

Since juvenile crime became a major public issue a decade ago, scholars have been laboring to develop a taxonomy of young killers. Kathleen M. Heide, a criminologist at the University of South Florida, interviewed 59 male adolescents convicted of homicide and attempted murder in Florida during a 25-month period. She found they could be divided into seven categories, ranging from the fearsome nihilist who killed because he wanted to hurt people (thankfully, a small part of her sample) to the action seeker who regards crime as good sport and homicide as a random event in an otherwise businesslike robbery. Her group also divided along one basic question: did the killer feel remorse: About 40 percent did not, she reports, preferring to blame the victim for not responding appropriately to a demand or, incredibly, for failing to duck. A stunning statistic—and one that underlines Yvette Weaver's last question: Why?

From *Newsweek*, November 24, 1986, pp. 93, 94, Newsweek, Inc.

Juvenile gangs have undergone a revival in recent years in our nation's largest cities. Today, urban gangs are responsible for roughly one-quarter of all juvenile crimes committed each year. Gone are the knives, clubs, bicycle chains, and homemade "zip" guns used as weapons in yesterday's "rumbles." The gang wars of today (fought over the possession of "turf") feature sophisticated weaponry—AR-15s, M-16s, grenades, and plastic explosives—that would do credit to a military assault troop.

In addition to being better armed, today's gangs, or "clicks," have a tighter, more cohesive, and more durable structure. At the top is the "prez," who gains his or her position by being the most ruthless and violent member of the gang—and who remains on top only as long as he or she meets every challenge of authority. Under the "prez" is the "veep," who collects dues, supervises the recruitment and initiation of new members, and manages internal affairs. The "war counselor" serves as general; he or she plans "gang hits" and "rip-offs" and commands "gestapo squads" composed of "enforcers." Weapons are the responsibility of the "armorer," who maintains them and stashes them in a safe place.

Miller (1976) reports that there may be as many as twenty-seven hundred gangs in the nation's six largest cities: New York, Los Angeles, Chicago, Detroit, Philadelphia, and San Francisco; the membership in these gangs may be as high as 81,500. According to Trojanowicz,

> In some cities, gangs have gotten out of control to the point where regular activities in the community are disrupted. Armed bands of young gang members board buses and physically force passengers to give up wallets and other personal items. Gang members are getting so bold that not only do they show total disregard for their fellow man, but they have no fear of police or any formal consequence for their actions (1978, p. 402).

In Detroit, Michigan, gang violence prompted the governor to order state police to patrol the city's highways and freeways.

Violence in the Schools

Schools have always had discipline problems, but it is only recently that they have taken on some of the properties of maximum security prisons. At one time the U.S. Senate Subcommittee on Juvenile Delinquency (chaired by Senator Birch Bayh) reported that in 747 school districts across the country (out of a total of 16,600), there are annually over seventy thousand assaults on teachers, more than a hundred student murders, and $500 million in property losses from vandalism—a figure equal to the cost of the entire supply of textbooks for all schools in the country.

Disturbing as these figures are, they only begin to indicate the gravity of the situation in many school districts. In some cases, the educational process is threatened with extinction. Approximately two hundred thousand pupils are truants on an average school day in New York City; and in some areas, the only way schools can get through the motions of providing educational services is to have armed guards patrolling the corridors. Teachers in these schools develop symptoms of "battle fatigue" and joke bitterly about asking for "combat pay."

Intervention

The decision to use (or not use) correctional treatment or intervention assumes greater urgency when the juveniles involved have committed violent crimes rather than delinquent acts not involving persons. Dale Mann (1976), a Rand Corporation consultant to the National Institute for Juvenile Justice and Delinquency Prevention, has conducted an extensive study of correctional intervention programs with violent juvenile offenders. Two questions were addressed in the study: (1) What interventions are used with serious juvenile offenders? (2) How well do these interventions work? "Serious" juvenile offenders were defined as those who had been adjudged delinquent (i.e., convicted of nonnegligent homicide, armed robbery, forcible rape, aggravated assault, or arson).

The first problem Mann encountered was in trying to determine the number of juvenile offenders in custody who could be classified as serious offenders. Based on the *Uniform Crime Reports of the United States* (1975), seventy-three thousand juveniles were arrested in 1974 for violent crimes. One might reasonably expect that a substantial number of these juveniles were dealt with by placement in a reasonably secure institution. If such was the case, these offenders would have added to the population already incarcerated. But such was *not* the case. By the time Mann tracked the seventy-three thousand offenders through the various stages of the juvenile justice system and subtracted those who had been "processed out," he found that only *six thousand* of the offenders were undergoing some type of treatment in an institutional or extrainstitutional setting; and the total institutional population of juvenile offenders in the country was only forty thousand.

Mann's findings reinforce the view that juveniles can get away with almost anything, including murder. And it supports the contention that serious juvenile offenders usually continue to commit crimes of violence—despite repeated arrests and juvenile court appearances—until they are old enough to be handled in an adult criminal court. Mann insists that the serious offenders identified in his study are more important than their number indicates:

> Because of the crimes they have committed, they are regarded as dangerous. Because they are young, they are thought to deserve opportunities to change themselves or to be rehabilitated. The two perceptions merge into one aspiration for successful treatment when it is recognized that a successful intervention also *reduces the danger* posed to society by this group (1976, pp. 10–11).

Intervention with violent juvenile offenders takes place within settings that range from secure correctional facilities to community-based facilities. Mann identifies the following modes of intervention that can be used:

1. *Intervention based on clinical psychology and psychiatry.* This type of intervention relies on psychotherapy, transactional analysis, Gestalt therapy, and other types of therapy on a group or individual basis.
2. *Intervention based on sociology and social work.* This type of intervention emphasizes the restructuring of the social environment and the positive use of the peer group (e.g., an approach called Guided Group Interaction).
3. *Intervention based on schooling.* According to Mann, "the use of schooling as a behavior-changing treatment for offenders is based on two facts: (1) the vast majority of juvenile offenders experienced failure in school, and (2) social and vocational advancement for such juveniles is blocked without academic training" (ibid., pp. 12–13).
4. *Intervention based on vocational education.* This type of intervention stresses the acquisition of job skills to gain access to legitimate opportunities for reinforcing the "stake in conformity."

Mann also identifies what might be called a "non-intended-treatment" situation that involves "doing time" in an institution without exposure to any kind of treatment or intervention. Just because treatment programs are not provided, however, there is no reason to assume that institutionalization *by itself* will not have some effect on the subsequent behavior of the offender. Unfortunately, Mann's study did not address this issue.

In summarizing his findings, Mann stresses two considerations that are not specific to the evaluation of intervention techniques with violent juvenile offenders, but that are endemic to the whole enterprise of assessing behavior-change approaches. First, Mann notes that treatment outcomes in most programs are defined in terms of behavior within the institution—not with reference to the characteristics of the offense for which the offender was adjudicated (convicted). Thus, behavior change that is accomplished within the institutional or program setting may not carry over into the postrelease period. Second, the absence of agreement on just what *are* the salient behavioral characteristics of the serious juvenile offender makes it nearly impossible to locate and evaluate programs that concentrate exclusively on changing the behavior of these offenders.

In response to the general question, What works?, Mann's survey reports that each of the four intervention modes described herein attained limited success in the treatment of serious juvenile offenders: "While these positive effects were not as well documented, as dramatic, or as long-lasting as might be wished, each of the four treatment modalities could legitimately claim to have changed some behavior on the part of some juvenile offenders" (ibid., p. viii). Among the characteristics of successful programs, Mann lists such factors as client choice (i.e., discretion about whether or not to enter a program), involvement in and commitment to the program, availability of a wide range of techniques to the program or institutional staff, the readiness of the staff to profit from their own failures and a variety of standard features associated with successful practice in learning situations—clear goals and tasks, behavior models, early and frequent successes, rewards for appropriate behavior, and credible training relevant to the demands of the real world.

Lock'em up—Give up—Try Harder

In Dale Mann's (1976) view, serious juvenile offenders can be dealt with in one of three ways:

1. By making a vigorous attempt to implement the punish-deter-incapacitate policy, the basis of the "lock'em up and throw away the key" approach.
2. By giving up and doing nothing, which means that the problem will be deferred until the juvenile is no longer a juvenile but a problem for the adult criminal justice authorities.
3. By making more use of available approaches toward correctional intervention (while recognizing the absence of a panacea, a universally effective approach to treatment). This "try harder" alternative requires that improvements be made elsewhere in the juvenile justice system and that efforts be pursued to develop new and more effective intervention strategies.

Mann believes that his findings strongly support the third alternative. He sides with the Indian guru, maintaining that it is better to light a single candle than to curse the darkness.

Most of the violent juveniles in the programs that Mann studied are in the category of "life-style violent juveniles" (as characterized by Vachss and Bakal [1979]).

These juveniles are born and reared in a subculture of violence, are socialized into patterns of exploitative aggression, and are prone to chronic violence. A much smaller number of youths who come to the attention of the juvenile court exhibit a propensity for occasional outbreaks of impulsive violence related to severe personality disturbances, including psychosis. The latter juveniles are really a problem for the mental health system rather than the criminal justice system, but the provisions for their care and treatment are even sketchier than the provisions for the life-style violent juvenile.

Vachss and Bakal present a detailed proposal for a secure treatment unit that realistically combines custody and treatment within a single facility. The unit would feature a multifaceted program intended to resocialize the life-style violent juvenile into more acceptable, prosocial behavior. Treatment would be carried out within a secure context specifically designed to eliminate or drastically reduce the adverse effects of confinement. Although the proposal does not detail the programs that would be used, the concept of the secure treatment unit represents a quantum leap in correctional planning for the serious juvenile offender. The critics of the concept undoubtedly object to the cost of the needed facilities, but Vachss and Bakal point out that the cost of continuing with present approaches and facilities is even more prohibitive. Further, human cost is impossible to measure in dollars and cents.

PROGRAMS FOR REPEAT JUVENILE OFFENDERS

Some communities and their criminal justice agencies have attempted to target their resources in the direction of juvenile offenders who repeatedly commit serious offenses. In Towson, Maryland, the Baltimore County Police Department, in conjunction with other criminal justice agencies, became involved in a juvenile repeat offender program experiment (JROPE). Behan (1986, p. 92) described the efforts of the program.

> The department recognized the need for incapacitating juveniles who repeatedly commit delinquent acts. It is imperative that the department work closely with the Juvenile Services Administration (JSA) and the State Attorney's Office (SAO) to carry out the following general objectives:
>
> - To ensure that the police department, the JSA and the SAO identify and give maximum attention to those juveniles who have become a danger to themselves and the general public as defined by the Juvenile ROPE definition.
> - To remove juvenile repeat offenders from the community as soon as possible after being taken into custody for a delinquent offense, and detain them in a strictly governed environment (e.g., the Maryland Training School or Montrose School) until the detention hearing the next court day.
> - To seek continued detention until the time of adjudicatory or waiver hearings through the authorization of the juvenile court.
> - To obtain waivers to adult court on repeat offender juveniles who are taken into custody for a violent offense (i.e., offense listed under Article 27, Sections 643B/441e), for the purpose of obtaining a conviction for the instant offense and incapacitation.
> - To ensure that all cases involving juvenile repeat offenders are complete and legally sufficient, in order to obtain a conviction if waived to adult court, or a finding of delinquency by the juvenile court.
>
> The procedures require that, when handling juvenile repeat offender cases, the department must: identify and target juvenile repeat offenders and flag their cases and histories for special attention; search these juvenile records whenever a juvenile is taken into custody for a delinquent act; request detention from JSA for all verified juvenile repeat offenders; make every effort to ensure that the juvenile court has all the juvenile's prior delinquent/criminal history records to justify continued detention of the juvenile; work with JSA and SAO and seek waivers to adult court on each juvenile identified as a repeat offender; keep accurate records on juvenile repeat offenders, including records with other juvenile justice agencies; and assure that each juvenile repeat offender case has been thoroughly investigated and is ready for prosecution.

During the initial phase of the JROPE study, 9 percent of the juvenile contacts for felony delinquent acts fulfilled the program's definition of repeat offender. However, this small group of juvenile felony offenders were found to be responsible for a disproportionate amount of crime, 19 percent of all charges filed during the initial study (Behan 1986, p. 92). It would appear that criminal justice agencies in the future may be required to consider the impact of crimes committed by a small number of juvenile offenders, just as has been the case in the adult criminal justice system.

TRAINING FOR JUVENILE JUSTICE PRACTITIONERS

Traditionally, an area that has not received enough attention in the field of juvenile justice is the provision of adequate training for the individuals responsible for carrying forth the services. Probation officers, case workers, detention center personnel, and institutional staff were often hired and placed in their positions of significant responsibility with little or no formal training. Topics such as delinquency problems, mental health issues, behavioral management of juvenile offenders, and client aggression were often left to "informal" or on-the-job types of training for new staff.

Ironically, other segments of the criminal justice system recognized the need for formalized training for entry-level practitioners years ago. Police officers, correctional officers, and others serving in the criminal justice arena have long been required to attend academies in order to be properly certified prior to assuming their critical responsibilities. However, it appears as if the need for training juvenile justice personnel has been recognized. As the following article indicates, one state has developed and implemented a formalized system.

New Era Begins for Juvenile Justice Training

By Irma Rubin

The University of South Florida made history March 9 when the state's—and probably the nation's—first Juvenile Justice Training Academy (JJTA) was opened at the Florida Mental Health Institute (FMHI).

"As far as we know, Florida has developed the first statewide juvenile justice system with specifically planned and evaluated curriculum and organized monitoring on the training's effectiveness," said James P. Doyle, charter director for the JJTA.

Before JJTA was initiated, no specific training or experience in dealing with delinquency problems, mental health difficulties, client aggression or client behavior management was required for job entry into the juvenile services system.

Until now, according to Doyle, there was nothing for personnel working with delinquent children that was equivalent to the academies and training for other branches of the Florida Criminal Justice System such as police, county sheriffs, correctional officers, highway patrolmen and even fire fighters and emergency medical service technicians.

"Youngsters' first experience with the law has a major determining effect on their future attitudes and actions," said Doyle. "It is urgent that Florida's first-line workers in this area be trained, and trained well. With the opening of the first JJTA, Florida is taking a giant step in the right direction and providing leadership in this area to the nation."

In 1984 alone, over 100,000 cases were referred to the youth services system and over half of these were delinquency related. On any day, there are more than 10,000 children and adolescents under the supervision of Florida's delinquency system.

In a 1985 study of direct-care staff in Florida's public youth services programs, USF-FMHI researchers Dr. Joseph H. Evans and C. Matthew Tynes, Jr. found that, if trained at all, the typical first-line juvenile worker had received less than 25 hours of formal instruction.

In most cases, *even the worker* considered the amount of training inadequate. Given the insufficient training, the worker has a realistic fear of being injured by the clients (this happens in 40 percent of the cases), especially when two to three times a week he must use physical intervention to manage the clients' behavior.

According to the research, the lack of training, job risks and low salary were factors contributing to a fast turnover of workers—91 percent in detention centers and 68 percent in community residential programs.

The curriculum set up for the JJTA includes critical training related to its actions between staff and clients:

- behavior management;
- conflict resolution;

- communication and counseling skills;
- crisis management and
- suicide prevention.

A 15,000 square foot area of FMHI was made available to meet the housing and classroom needs of the students who will be attending the academy. The facilities include two spacious residence wings, a large conference area, several conventional classrooms, social and recreational sections, a kitchen, a coin laundromat, a mock courtroom and offices for the JJTA training, clerical and support staff. Although part of the FMHI complex, the JJTA is exclusively a training unit and is separated from the general activity of the institute.

A select group of HRS staff was invited to attend and critique the charter session designed for 48 participants. A system of five or six regional academies will be in place by 1988, providing both pre-service and in-service training to more than 3,000 people working with all aspects of the Juvenile Justice System in Florida.

Reprinted with permission from USF MAGAZINE 29 (March 1987): p. 36.

SUMMARY

The juvenile justice system evolved as an attempt to deal constructively with the problems of dependent, neglected, and delinquent youngsters within an informal, nonadversarial setting. The first juvenile courts operated as a blend of the social casework agency and the criminal court. However, the procedural informality of these courts often resulted in the denial to juveniles of rights guaranteed to adults under the Constitution. Thus, in a series of important decisions in the 1960s, the U.S. Supreme Court eventually extended due process and equal protection rights to juveniles.

The police and the courts make a strong effort to divert as many youths as possible from the juvenile justice system. Once a juvenile is adjudicated delinquent, a variety of postadjudication alternatives are available to the court in the form of residential and nonresidential programs. As many delinquents as possible are handled in community-based correctional programs, but the training school continues to house most adjudicated delinquents. Release from training school may allow a youngster to remain in the community under aftercare supervision, a status that roughly corresponds to parole for adult offenders.

In the 1980s and 1990s the issues of missing and exploited children will continue to receive a great deal of attention on the part of the juvenile justice system and the public in general.

Large U.S. cities are experiencing a resurgence of gang violence. Juveniles who participate in gang activity often belong to the category of "life-style violent juveniles"—youth born and reared in a subculture that reinforces exploitative aggression. Thus far, the juvenile justice system has been unable to deal effectively with these offenders. Many juveniles who commit violent crimes are shuttled in and out of the system until they become the responsibility of the adult criminal courts.

Some critics of the current juvenile justice system call for additional reforms that would make the system more closely parallel to the adult process. Juvenile justice practitioners will continue to examine repeat juvenile justice offenders in relationship to the resources available in the system.

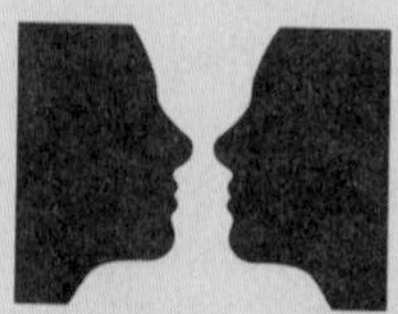

ISSUE PAPER

TREATING JUVENILE OFFENDERS AS ADULTS

By Peter Greenwood, U.S. Department of Justice: Crime File Series

Current Dissatisfaction with the Juvenile System

The juvenile system does not lack critics. Conservative critics, focusing on public safety, fault the system for giving serious offenders too many chances on diversion or probation and for imposing terms of confinement that are too short. These critics often characterize juvenile facilities as country clubs and argue that some juveniles should be confined in more punitive settings.

Liberal critics, concerned with the problems of juveniles and anxious to protect them from unwarranted State intrusions, fault the system for being too tough. Where conservative critics use the evidence of "no rehabilitative effect" to argue for more explicitly punitive sanctions, liberals use the same evidence to argue for less State involvement altogether. Liberals generally support the view that subjecting juveniles to confinement only further criminalizes them, no matter how benign the treatment.

Another liberal group, heavily represented by defense attorneys and other youth advocates, deplores the lack of adequate procedural protections for juveniles. This group argues that many young people are "railroaded" through a system that offers no adequate protection of their rights.

Among practitioners, criticisms and suggestions for reform tend to reflect individual agency biases. In general, police and prosecutors want tougher sentencing. Probation officials want to preserve some group of juveniles over whom they can employ their traditional authority to focus on the "needs" of the child, perhaps through a special court set up to handle the less serious delinquents. Corrections officials, interested in controlling the behavior of juveniles in their charge, want to play a greater role in deciding whom they must accept and how long they are to be kept.

Proposals for Reform

The movement toward treating juvenile offenders more like adults began with the "due process" reforms in the late 1960's and included, in the 1970's, the Federal effort to deinstitutionalize status offenders, juveniles who had not committed crimes but were "beyond the control of their parents" or otherwise in apparent need of supervision. The current trend toward sentencing serious and chronic juvenile offenders like adults is a reflection of the same movement.

The first major attack on the body of juvenile court law, which had developed without much controversy during the first half of the 20th century, was aimed at the lack of procedural protection. Supreme Court decisions in the cases of *In re Gault* and *In re Winship* struck down the juvenile court's reliance on informal factfinding. They provided juveniles charged with crimes all the procedural protections held by adults, except the rights to bail and jury trial. For instance, juveniles were provided notice of charges, right to counsel and to cross-examination of witnesses, protection against self-incrimination and unlawful searches.

The next major wave of reform, reflecting the liberal agenda of the 1967 President's Commission on Law Enforcement and the Administration of Justice, involved efforts to keep status offenders out of juvenile justice institutions. Prior to this movement, many detention centers and juvenile training schools contained a substantial proportion of youths whose only "crimes" were their inability to get along with their parents. The movement to deinstitutionalize status offenders in a sense granted adolescents the same rights to leave home or to ignore their parents' wishes as adults have; it helped further the notion that children should be treated legally as if they were adults.

The removal of status offenders and minor delinquents from juvenile institutions resulted in dramatic shifts in the perceived role of the institutions and in the characteristics of the people within them. No longer concerned with "out of control" youths whose most offensive behavior was talking back to adults or disobeying their orders, juvenile institutions became increasingly filled with hardcore, chronic offenders for whom rehabilitation and community readjustment were seen as highly optimistic goals. These perceptions about the futility of treatment were given added emphasis by a number of critical reviews of the "treatment" evaluation literature purporting to show that most treatment programs had negligible effects on recidivism rates; and by a line of research, started by Wolfgang, Figlio, and Sellin in their Philadelphia Cohort Study, showing that a small nucleus of chronic offenders (18 percent of all those arrested as juveniles) accounted for a disproportionate share of all juvenile arrests (52 percent).

Comparisons between the disposition patterns of juvenile and adult courts are often misleading because the two courts deal with such different types of individuals. Most juvenile cases, which involve first or second time offenders accused of minor offenses, are settled informally. Adult cases are usually more serious. Fewer than 20 percent of all juvenile arrests result in findings of delinquency, compared to a 50-percent conviction rate for adults, but these percentages can be misleading. Studies that take into account such things as age, prior record, and offense find that, for the more serious offenders, juvenile and adult courts have similar conviction and incarceration rates. The major difference between the two systems is in the length of the terms imposed; criminal courts occasionally impose very long terms.

Theoretically, criminal courts should sentence more harshly than juvenile courts, but there are reasons to believe this may not happen in every case that could be waived. Juveniles who are subject to waiver are the most serious offenders that a juvenile court judge sees and therefore may receive the harshest available sentence. However, the same offenders appearing in a criminal court may look much less serious when compared to the older, more hardened offenders with whom a criminal court judge must typically deal.

Studies of the impact of recent waiver statutes have produced inconclusive results. Some juveniles whose cases are waived to criminal court are sentenced more leniently than they would have been in juvenile court. Since the criminal court prosecutor must make an independent evaluation of the strength of evidence, some cases are dropped after the decision has been made to waive them.

In many States, even when juveniles are tried in criminal court and convicted of the charges, they may still be sentenced to a juvenile or youthful offender institution rather than to an adult prison. The laws may allow them to be transferred to an adult prison when they have reached a certain age.

Aside from the waiver or age-jurisdiction issue, there is movement within the juvenile justice system to treat juveniles more like adults. Some of this activity is clearly in response to the pressures for waiver reforms, including a call for more frequent use of waiver. One of the steps is toward the use of sentencing guidelines in making placement and in determining time to be served. Sentencing guidelines, such as those developed by the State of Washington, constitute a move away from a focusing on the needs of the minor toward the more modern concept of just deserts—that the punishment should fit the crime. The introduction of punishment considerations into juvenile sentencing is an attempt to hold juveniles accountable in the same way adults are held accountable.

Records and confidentiality constitute another area in which traditional distinctions between juvenile and adult criminal proceedings are breaking down. Because of heightened interest in chronic offenders, better juvenile criminal history systems are being established. The information thus generated is increasingly being made available to criminal court officials when juveniles are charged as adults.

Why Do Many Critics Think Juveniles Should Be Treated More Like Adults? #16)

There are several reasons:

1. Juveniles as a group account for a large fraction of the crime rate—40 percent of all felonies in 1980, at least as measured by arrests.
2. Some juveniles continue to commit serious or frequent crimes in spite of extensive efforts to rehabilitate them.
3. The juvenile justice system is limited in its capacity to punish and to incapacitate.
4. Officials in the adult criminal justice system are more visibly accountable to the public for their action than those in the juvenile justice system.

What Kinds of Reforms Have Been Proposed?

Proposals range from instituting more adult-like procedures in the juvenile system, such as removing confidentiality restrictions on media accounts of juvenile proceedings, to removing whole categories of offenders from the system and treating them as adults.

The maximum age jurisdiction of juvenile courts is set by State laws and varies from the 16th to the 19th birthdate, with the 18th the standard. Although many suggest lowering these age limits in States where they are the highest, there is little serious movement in this direction.

The more typical method for moving juvenile offenders to criminal courts is through "waiver" or "removal" procedures. For some categories of offenses, if certain conditions are met, jurisdiction over juvenile offenders can or must be waived to criminal courts. Typically, in States where the maximum age jurisdiction of the juvenile court ends at the 18th birthdate, jurisdiction can be waived only over juveniles who have passed their 16th birthdate. The types of offenses eligible for waiver include homicide, rape, aggravated assault, arson, and robbery with a firearm. If waiver is not mandatory, most waiver statutes require the court to consider whether the youth is "amenable to treatment" within the juvenile system and whether the system will have jurisdiction over the juvenile for long enough for treatment to be practicable. The recent trend in many States is to increase the list of offenses subject to waiver, to decrease the age limit for cases in which waiver can be applied, and to make the waiver decision presumptive or mandatory.

What Do You Accomplish by Treating Juveniles More Like Adults?

At a bare minimum, juveniles who are prosecuted in criminal courts can be sentenced to longer terms in more secure and punitive institutions. They have the right to a jury trial. And records of the proceeding are more open to public scrutiny.

The trend to treat serious juvenile offenders more like adults is a natural reaction to some of the outmoded concepts of the original juvenile courts and to the much higher levels of violence exhibited by some modern youth. Because juvenile and criminal court systems are both responding to some of the same new theories or concepts, the two systems are tending to become more closely aligned. Rehabilitation, the principal point of departure for the original juvenile system, now plays a far less critical role. Notions of deserved punishment, incapacitation of chronic offenders, and sentencing guidelines have become the common concerns of both systems.

Adapted from Peter Greenwood, *Crime File: Juvenile Offenders*, Crime File Study Guide (Washington, D.C.: U.S. Department of Justice, National Institute of Justice, 1985), pp. 2–3.

DISCUSSION AND REVIEW

1. What were the principal objectives of the child-saving movement? How influential was this movement in the development of the juvenile court?
2. Discuss the concept of "individualized justice" and the role it played in the emergence of the juvenile court in the United States.
3. Discuss the implications of the *Gault* case for the juvenile justice system.
4. In addition to delinquents, what other types of youngsters are handled by the juvenile courts?
5. How do status offenses differ from crimes?
6. What alternative dispositions are available to the police and the intake worker in handling juvenile cases?
7. In the Flint, Michigan, study of police officers and their handling of juvenile encounters, what were five role identity orientations assumed by police officers?

8. Describe the postadjudication alternatives available to the court in the disposition of juvenile cases.
9. What are the five types of juvenile restitution programs? Which is the most common?
10. It is useful to think of missing children in four major categories. What are the categories?
11. Identify and discuss the advantages and disadvantages of community-based residential and nonresidential programs for juveniles.
12. Describe the goals and methods of youth services bureaus.
13. What are the essential elements in effective community supervision of delinquent youngsters?
14. What are the implications of Mann's finding that only a small percentage of serious juvenile offenders arrested each year for violent crimes participate in treatment programs?
15. Describe the modes of intervention outlined by Mann for dealing with the serious juvenile offender. How do Vachss and Bakal propose to deal with the life-style violent juvenile?
16. Why do many critics think juveniles should be treated more like adults?

■ GLOSSARY

Delinquent A juvenile who violates the criminal law or commits a status offense.

Dependent children Juveniles placed under the jurisdiction of a juvenile or family court because of a court finding that the care provided by the parent, guardian, or custodian falls short of the standard of proper care.

Diversion The removal of an offender from the criminal justice system by channeling him or her into a social casework, mental health, or other type of agency. The term has also been used to describe the handling of juveniles in a system separate from the adult criminal justice system and the sentencing of offenders to community-based correctional facilities rather than to prison.

DSO Deinstitutionalization of Status Offenders. This refers to the removal of youths whose only infractions are status offenses from secure institutions and detention facilities.

JROPE The Juvenile Repeat Offender Program Experiment begun in Maryland.

Juvenile A person subject to the jurisdiction of the juvenile court based on an age limit imposed by statute. Jurisdiction is based on the age of the juvenile at the time the misconduct occurred; thus, a person twenty years of age would be tried in juvenile court for a crime committed when he or she was seventeen.

Neglected children Children subjected to sexual or physical abuse by parents or other family members.

Parens patriae Historical doctrine holding that the state is the ultimate parent of the child. The doctrine provided the rationale for the jurisdiction of the juvenile court as a substitute parent to guide, train, care for, and maintain custody of juveniles.

Status offense The violation of a statute that applies only to juveniles and that has no counterpart in the adult criminal code (e.g., truancy, running away from home, "incorrigibility").

REFERENCES

American Correctional Association. *Guidelines for the Development of Policies and Procedures—Juvenile Detention Facilities.* College Park, Md.: American Correctional Association, 1984.

Beck, B. M., and Beck, D. B. "Recreation and Delinquency." In *Task Force Report: Juvenile Delinquency and Youth Crime* by the President's Commission on Law Enforcement and Administration of Justice. Washington, D.C.: U.S. Government Printing Office, 1967.

Behan, C. J. "Innovative Police Practices—Repeat Offender Program Experiment." *Police Chief* (March 1986): 92.

Belknap, J.; Morash, M.; and Trojanowicz, R. *Implementing a Community Policing Model for Work with Juveniles—An Exploratory Study.* East Lansing, Mich.: National Neighborhood Foot Patrol Center, School of Criminal Justice, Michigan State University, 1986.

Burgess, A. W. *Youth at Risk: Understanding Runaway and Exploited Youth.* Washington, D.C.: National Center for Missing and Exploited Children, September 1986.

Cloward, R. A., and Ohlin, L. E. *Delinquency and Opportunity: A Theory of Delinquent Gangs.* Glencoe, Ill.: Free Press, 1960.

Dembo, R.; Washburn, M.; Wish, E.; Young, H.; Getre, A.; Berry, E.; and Blount, W. R. "Heavy marijuana use and crime among youths entering a juvenile detention center." *Journal of Psychoactive Drugs* 19 (1987a): 47–56.

Dembo, R.; Dertke, M.; LaVoie, L.; Borders, S.; Washburn, M.; and Schmeidler, J. "Physical abuse, sexual victimization and illicit drug use: A structural analysis among high risk adolescents." *Journal of Adolescence* 10 (1987b): 13–33.

Dembo, R.; Washburn, M.; Wish, E.; Schmeidler, J.; Getre, A.; Berry, E.; Williams, L.; and Blount, W. R. "Futher examination of the association between heavy marijuana use and crime among youths entering a juvenile detention center." *Journal of Psychoactive Drugs* (forthcoming).

Empey, L. T. "The Social Construction of Childhood, Delinquency, and Social Reform." In *The Juvenile Justice System,* edited by M. W. Klein. Los Angeles, Calif.: Sage, 1976.

———. *American Delinquency: Its Meaning and Construction.* Homewood, Ill.: Dorsey, 1978.

Faust, F. L., and Brantingham, P. J., eds. *Juvenile Justice Philosophy: Readings, Cases, and Comments.* St. Paul, Minn.: West, 1979.

Feld, B. C. "References of Juvenile Offenders for Adult Prosecution: The Legislative Alternative to Asking Unanswerable Questions." *Minnesota Law Review* 62 (1978): 515–618.

"Fifteen-year-old Draws Probation for Murder." *Tampa Tribune,* 9 May 1978, p. 8A.

Fleisher, B. M. *The Economics of Delinquency.* Chicago: Quadrangle, 1966.

Greenwood, P. W.; Abrahamse, A.; and Zimring, F. *Factors Affecting Sentence Severity for Young Adult Offenders.* Santa Monica, Calif.: The Rand Corporation, 1984.

Greenwood, P. W.; Lipson, A. J.; Abrahamse, A.; and Zimring, F. *Youth Crime and Juvenile Justice in California*. Santa Monica, Calif.: The Rand Corporation, 1983.

Hamparian, D. M.; Estep, L. K.; Muntean, S. M.; Priestino, R. R.; Swisher, R. G.; Wallace, P. L.; and White, J. L. *Youth in Adult Courts: Between Two Worlds*. Washington, D.C.: U.S. Department of Justice, Office of Juvenile Justice and Delinquency Prevention, 1982.

Kiersh, E. "Minnesota Cracks Down on Chronic Juvenile Offenders." *Corrections Magazine* 7 (1981): 21.

Kobetz, R. W., and Bosarge, B. B. *Juvenile Justice Administration*. Gaithersburg, Md.: International Association of Chiefs of Police, 1973.

Lanning, K. V. *Child Molesters: A Behavioral Analysis*. Washington, D.C.: National Center for Missing and Exploited Children, 1986.

Mack, J. C. "The Juvenile Court." In *Juvenile Justice Philosophy: Readings, Cases, and Comments*, edited by F. L. Faust and P. J. Brantingham. St. Paul, Minn.: West, 1979.

Mann, D. *Intervening with Convicted Serious Juvenile Offenders*. Washington, D.C.: U.S. Government Printing Office, 1976.

Miller, W. B. *Violence by Youth Gangs and Youth Groups as a Crime Problem in Major American Cities*. Washington, D.C.: U.S. Government Printing Office, 1976.

National Advisory Committee on Criminal Justice Standards and Goals. *Report of the Task Force on Juvenile Justice and Delinquency Prevention*. Washington, D.C.: U.S. Government Printing Office, 1976.

National Center for Missing and Exploited Children. *Selected State Legislation: A Guide for Effective State Laws to Protect Children*. Washington, D.C.: National Center for Missing and Exploited Children, 1985.

National Council on Crime and Delinquency. "Corrections in the United States." *Crime and Delinquency* 13 (1967): 1–281.

Nimick, E. H.; Snyder, H. N.; Sullivan, D. P.; and Tierney, N. J. *Juvenile Court Statistics 1983*. Washington, D.C.: U.S. Department of Justice, Office of Juvenile Justice and Delinquency Prevention, National Institute for Juvenile Justice and Delinquency Prevention, 1987.

Nold, J., and Wilpers, M. "Wilderness Training as an Alternative to Incarceration." In *A Nation Without Prisons*, edited by C. R. Dodge, Lexington, Mass.: Lexington, 1975.

Phelps, T. R. *Juvenile Delinquency: A Contemporary View*. Pacific Palisades, Calif.: Goodyear, 1976.

President's Commission on Law Enforcement and Administration of Justice. *Task Force Report: Corrections*. Washington, D.C.: U.S. Government Printing Office, 1967.

Rothman, D. *The Discovery of the Asylum*. Boston: Little, Brown, 1971.

Rubin, H. T. "Retain the Juvenile Court? Legislative Developments, Reform Directions, and the Call for Abolition." *Crime and Delinquency* 25 (1979): 281–98.

Scarpitti, F. R., and Stephenson, R. M. "A Study of Probation Effectiveness." *Journal of Criminal Law, Criminology, and Police Science* 54 (1968): 361–69.

Schafer, W. E., and Polk, K. "Delinquency in the Schools." In *Task Force Report: Juvenile Delinquency and Youth Crime*, by the President's Commission on Law Enforcement and Administration of Justice. Washington, D.C.: U.S. Government Printing Office, 1967.

Schneider, A. L. *Reports of the National Juvenile Justice Assessment Centers—The Impact of Deinstitutionalization on Recidivism and Secure Confinement on Status Offenders*. Washington, D.C.: U.S. Department of Justice, Office of Juvenile Justice and Delinquency Prevention, National Institute for Juvenile Justice and Delinquency Prevention, 1985.

Singell, L. "Economic Opportunity and Juvenile Delinquency: A Case Study of the Detroit Labor Market." Ph.D. dissertation, Wayne State University, 1965.

Stratton, J. R., and Terry, R. M. *Prevention of Delinquency: Problems and Programs.* New York: Macmillan, 1968.

Tetters, N. K., and Reinemann, J. O. *The Challenge of Delinquency.* Englewood Cliffs, N.J.: Prentice-Hall, 1950.

Trojanowicz, R. C. *Juvenile Delinquency: Concepts and Control.* Englewood Cliffs, N.J.: Prentice-Hall, 1978.

U.S. Department of Justice. *Children in Custody: 1982/83 Census of Juvenile Detention and Correctional Facilities.* Washington, D.C.: U.S. Government Printing Office, 1986.

———. *Uniform Crime Reports in the United States.* Washington, D.C.: U.S. Government Printing Office, 1975.

———. *Uniform Crime Reports in the United States.* Washington, D.C.: U.S. Government Printing Office, 1982.

———. *Uniform Crime Reports for the United States.* Washington, D.C.: U.S. Government Printing Office, 1987.

Vachss, A. H., and Bakal, Y. *The Life-Style Violent Juvenile: The Secure Treatment Approach.* Lexington, Mass.: Lexington Books, 1979.

Vinter, R. D. *Time Out: A National Study of Juvenile Correctional Programs.* National Assessment of Juvenile Corrections. Ann Arbor: University of Michigan Press, 1976.

Ward, F. W. "Prevention and Diversion in the United States." In *The Changing Faces of Juvenile Justice,* edited by V. L. Stewart. New York: New York University Press, 1978.

Warner, J. S., and Burke, V, eds. *National Directory of Juvenile Restitution Programs, 1987.* Washington, D.C.: U.S. Government Printing Office, 1987.

Wilson, R. "The Long-Term Trend Is Down: Diversion into Community Programs Has Continued—Despite Public Reaction to Youth Crime." *Corrections Magazine* 2 (1978): 3–11.

Wolfgang, M.; Figlio, R.; and Sellin, T. *Delinquency in a Birth Cohort.* Chicago: University of Chicago Press, 1972.

"The Youth Crime Plague." *Time,* 11 July 1977, pp. 18–19.

■ CASES

In re Gault 387 U.S. 1, 87 S.Ct. 1428, 18 L.Ed.2d 527 (1967).
Kent v. *U.S.* 383 U.S. 541, 546; 86 S.Ct. 1045, 1049–50; 16 L.Ed.2d 84 (1966).
In re Winship 397 U.S. 358, 90 S.Ct. 1068, 25 L.Ed.2d 368 (1970).

■ NOTES

1. Much of this discussio. .. juvenile detention center security was adapted and modified from American Correctional Association, *Guidelines for the Development of Policies and Procedures—Juvenile Detention Facilities* (College Park, Md.: American Correctional Association, 1984), p. 3, and Chapter 11.

2. This discussion on recent research regarding juveniles in detention centers was provided courtesy of Dr. Richard Dembo, University of South Florida.

A more complete review of this research appears in the following articles: R. Dembo, et al., "Physical abuse, sexual victimization and illicit drug use: A structural analysis among high risk adolescents," *Journal of Adolescence* 10 (1987): 13–33; "Heavy marijuana use and crime among youths entering a juvenile detention center," *Journal of Psychoactive Drugs* 19 (1987): 47–56; and "Further examination of the association between heavy marijuana use and crime among youths entering a juvenile detention center," *Journal of Psychoactive Drugs* (forthcoming).

3. The information regarding juvenile court statistics was adapted from Ellen H. Nimick, Howard N. Snyder, Dennis P. Sullivan, and Nancy J. Tierney, *Juvenile Court Statistics 1983* (Washington, D.C.: U.S. Department of Justice, 1987), pp. 7–11.

4. The information regarding juvenile restitution programs was adapted and modified from Jean S. Warner, and Vincent Burke, editors, *National Directory of Juvenile Restitution Programs, 1987* (Washington, D.C.: U.S. Government Printing Office, 1987), pp. 1, 3, 4, 5, 28, 69, 130.

5. Much of this discussion of missing and runaway children was adapted from Ann W. Burgess, *Youth at Risk: Understanding Runaway and Exploited Youth* (Washington, D.C.: National Center for Missing and Exploited Children, September 1986), pp. 2, 5, 29, 43, 45. This report was prepared under Cooperative Agreement #86-MC-CS-K003 from the Office of Juvenile Justice Assistance, Research, and Statistics, U.S. Department of Justice.

6. The majority of the information regarding the impact of deinstitutionalization on status offenders was adapted from Anne L. Schneider, *Reports of the National Juvenile Justice Assessment Centers—The Impact of Deinstitutionalization and Recidivism and Secure Confinement on Status Offenders* (Washington, D.C.: U.S. Department of Justice, Office of Juvenile Justice and Delinquency Prevention, National Institute of Juvenile Justice and Delinquency Prevention, December 1985), pp. v, vi, 1, 2, 19.

CHAPTER

18

Crime Control and Crime Prevention

CHAPTER OUTLINE:

All societies impose sanctions to protect lawful members of society from individuals or groups that engage in deviant behavior. The sanctions imposed and the means employed to control or prevent such behavior are as diverse and complex as human nature itself. In this chapter, we look at some of the recent developments in crime control and prevention and examine the recommendations of several highly respected national commissions. We also examine some of the social factors that lead to crime—such as unemployment, poor education, and lack of recreational opportunities. Further, we discuss what action citizens can take to reduce the crime that emanates from these factors. We also discuss the fear of crime that many Americans share as well as some of the crime prevention tactics that law enforcement agencies have initiated in cooperation with their communities. We examine how citizens can work with police, courts, and corrections to make each component of the criminal justice system more efficient, more effective, and more responsive to the needs of society. Recent citizen-oriented national crime prevention programs are reviewed. Finally, we discuss the evaluation of crime prevention programs.

HISTORICAL OVERVIEW

Great Britain is the world leader in modern crime prevention. Impetus was provided early on by Oliver Cromwell, Thomas deVeil, Henry Fielding, and Sir Robert Peel. Fielding, better known as a novelist and political satirist, is credited with initiating the first crime prevention measures in the mid-1700s. He had two goals: to stamp out existing crime and to prevent future outbreaks of crime (Duncan 1980).[1]

Fielding's emphasis on crime prevention was revolutionary among criminologists of the day. He felt that three steps were needed to ensure achievement of his goals: (1) development of a strong police force; (2) organization of an active group of citizens (a body of citizen householders); and (3) initiation of action to remove some of the causes of crime and the conditions in which it flourishes.

Although developed in the eighteenth century, these steps remain basic to crime prevention and still serve as a model for many contemporary crime prevention programs. When Henry Fielding died in 1754, his half-brother, John Fielding, took over his work. John Fielding is reported to have said "... it is much better to prevent even one man from being a rogue than apprehending and bringing forty to justice" (Texas Crime Prevention Institute 1978, p. 3).

But Fielding's emphasis on crime prevention did not last. Law enforcement officials soon found their time taken up by investigation, apprehension, and prosecution of criminals. Thus, efforts to prevent crime decreased until the 1950s, when Great Britain launched a national crime prevention campaign. By 1963, the Home Office Crime Prevention Training Center had been established in Stafford, England. The center offered formal training in crime prevention to all British police. The principles taught there have become an integral part of the British police function today.

Modern prevention concepts were formally developed in the United States in the early 1960s. Although crime prevention had been the primary focus of private security firms for more than a hundred years, early attempts by law enforcement officials were sporadic. In 1968, John C. Klotter of the University of Louisville (Kentucky) School of Police Administration began studying the British concept of crime prevention and its potential for the American criminal justice system. Klotter's efforts led to the establishment in 1971 of the **National Crime Prevention Institute (NCPI)**, sponsored jointly by the Law Enforcement Assistance Administration (LEAA) of the Department of Justice, the Kentucky Crime Commission, and the University of Louisville. Nearly five thousand criminal justice personnel have been trained in the principles and practices of crime prevention at NCPI.[2]

The field has grown significantly since 1971, and several other crime prevention training centers have been established (the Texas Crime Prevention Institute is a prime example). Hundreds of law enforcement agencies, community organizations, and private groups have undertaken crime prevention programs, and new programs are being developed in communities every day. Sponsorship of these programs by the LEAA, state and local governments, and private sources has increased the acceptance of crime prevention practices.

In 1978, LEAA established the **National Center for Community Crime Prevention** within the Institute of Criminal Justice Studies at Southwest Texas University in San Marcos, Texas. The center was established to teach crime prevention skills to citizens representing community-based organizations across the United States. It is committed to dispelling the notion that crime control is the sole responsibility of the criminal justice system.

CITIZEN RESPONSIBILITY IN CRIME PREVENTION

Citizen involvement in crime prevention is not only desirable, but also necessary (National Advisory Commission on Criminal Justice Standards and Goals 1974).[3] The President's Commission on Law Enforcement and Administration of Justice (1967) emphasizes that direct citizen action is needed to improve law enforcement and that crime prevention should become the business of every American and every American institution. Police and other specialists alone cannot control crime: they need all the help the community can give them.

A task force of the National Commission on the Causes and Prevention of Violence notes that

> government programs for the control of crime are unlikely to succeed all alone. Informed private citizens, playing a variety of roles, can make a decisive difference in the prevention, detection and prosecution of crime, the fair administration of justice, and the restoration of offenders to the community (1969, p. 278).

But these and other pleas for citizen action are heeded by few. Most citizens agree that crime prevention is everybody's business, but, as indicated previously, few accept crime prevention as their *own* duty.

The idea that crime prevention is the duty of each citizen is not new. In the early days of law enforcement—well over a thousand years ago—the peace-keeping system encouraged the concept of mutual responsibility. Individuals were responsible not only for their own actions, but also for the actions of their neighbors. Citizens who observed a crime were obligated to rouse their neighbors and pursue the criminal. Thus, for the most part, peace was kept not by officials but by the entire community.

With specialization in law enforcement, citizens began to delegate their personal responsibilities to paid officials. Law enforcement became a multifaceted specialty, as citizens relinquished more and more of their crime prevention activities. But such specialization has its drawbacks: in the absence of citizen assistance, neither manpower, nor improved technology, nor money can enable law enforcement to shoulder the monumental burden of combating crime in America.

The need today is for a more balanced allocation of law enforcement duties between specialists and citizenry—for citizens to reassume many of their former responsibilities.

> Community leadership appears all too willing to delegate (or default) its responsibility for dealing with anti-social behavior. Eventually that responsibility is assumed by large, public agencies. . . . [The extremely expensive services of these agencies] never seem to catch up with the need. They come too late to be "preventive" in the most desirable sense of the word. Moreover, the policies are controlled from political and administrative centers far removed from the "grass roots" . . . where delinquency and crime originate through obscure and complex processes."[4]

And in its report *State-Local Relations in the Criminal Justice System,* the Advisory Commission on Intergovernmental Relations notes that

> the distance between city hall or county courthouse and neighborhoods is often considerable. As a result, the delivery of services may be slow, communication channels may be cumbersome, and policy-makers may be unaware of the real needs of neighborhood areas. Moreover, highly centralized decision-making may deter citizens from participating in crime prevention efforts (1971, p. 269).

Many crime prevention authorities believe that the responsibility for planning and implementing some anticrime programs should be placed at the lowest level consistent with sound decision making—that is, in the neighborhood with the individual citizen. Some also advocate that neighborhoods receive financial and technical assistance from the government to spur grass-roots citizen involvement. And in response to recommendations for government decentralization issued by the Advisory Commission on Intergovernmental Relations, the National Advisory Commission on Civil Disorders, and the National Commission on Urban Problems, many people now advocate neighborhood citizen councils that would exercise substantial control over the delivery of neighborhood services, including those related to crime prevention.

Getting Involved

The typical citizen response to the crime problem is to demand greater action by the police, the courts, correctional institutions, and other government agencies. Citizens seldom ask what they can do themselves. And when the public finally does decide to act, its activities often are short-lived, sporadic outbursts in response to particularly heinous crimes or crimes that occur too close to home. Fortunately, such limited and frequently counterproductive actions are yielding to more informed citizen involvement in crime prevention.[5]

One role that citizens can play within the criminal justice system is a preventive one of reducing the circumstances and situations in which crimes are likely to be committed. In recent years, for example, citizens have banded together in programs like "neighborhood watch" through which participants combat crime by marking property to make it more secure, increasing surveillance of public areas, and promoting behavior that increases citizen safety (for example, avoiding walking alone after dark).

Essential to the effectiveness of these crime prevention measures is enhanced willingness on the part of citizens to call the police about suspicious criminal activity. Even when police take no action other than answering a citizen observation of suspicious behavior, police presence can serve as a warning that citizens and police are vigilant to the possibility of crime and are willing to take additional steps, if necessary.

Citizens can also play a role after the fact by reporting actual crimes to the police. In calling the police, victims and others introduce crimes to the criminal justice system. Contacting the police activates the process through which society seeks to apprehend and punish wrongdoers and thereby to promote a peaceful and orderly existence for its members. If criminal incidents are not made known to the police, they are likely to remain outside of, or hidden from, the system that has been established to deter wrongdoing (Harlow 1985).[6]

Before citizens take preventive action, however, they should be aware of the many approaches possible for any given problem. For example, an individual who wants to prevent illicit gambling in the community might inform neighbors that the proceeds from such activities help finance the importation of hard drugs by organized crime. The same goal might also be pursued through a block or neighborhood crime prevention organization. In one case, members of a neighborhood association followed numbers runners to determine the neighborhood gambling network. This information was then turned over to local police.

In addition, members of churches, social clubs, fraternal groups, or civic associations can exert pressure on their officers and other organization members to discontinue limited and informal—but nonetheless illegal—gambling that occurs on the premises. Slot machines, sports pools, and punchboards may provide enjoyment for a club's membership, but they may also supply funds to criminal elements. Finally, as an employer or employee, a citizen can be alert for signs of inplant gambling. As recommended by the Committee for Economic Development, "Individually, businessmen can clean their own houses. Organized gambling need not be tolerated on business premises. . ." (1972, p. 62).

Concerned citizens can also combat crime through regional or national crime prevention organizations, trade associations, educational institutions, political parties, unions, charities, foundations, and professional societies. For example, the executive vice president of the American Institute of Certified Public Accountants once issued this call to action:

> There are already cases on record where publicly traded companies have become dominated by hoodlums. CPA's should be watchful of changes in ownership and management of their clients.
>
> If they find a once solid company taken over or influenced by unsavory elements, they may have to make a difficult decision. They may decide to withdraw from the engagement or may feel obligated to remain on the scene to protect innocent investors and creditors.
>
> Auditors are expected to have absolute integrity. Any evidence of organized crime coming their way should trigger prompt and drastic action to discharge their professional responsibilities. It should also bring forth cooperation with authorities to discharge their civic duties (Savoie 1969).

No one is asking any organization to make extraordinary sacrifices on behalf of crime prevention. What is suggested is that decisions relating to daily operations be reviewed in terms of their crime prevention impact: Are crimes that come to the attention of the organization reported to the police? Are community crime prevention efforts considered for the organization's charitable donations? Is time off for jury duty or court testimony granted grudgingly? Are management controls so loose that they invite crime?

Even if crime prevention is not the main purpose of an organization, crime prevention opportunities probably still exist. Such opportunities need not focus directly on specific crimes. Tenant patrols may help prevent burglaries in apartment buildings, and cargo security councils formed and supported by local transportation companies may reduce the incidence of cargo theft. But so also will programs aimed at increasing the employability of the jobless, furthering the education of the dropout, supplying adequate medical treatment to the alcoholic and the drug addict, and providing recreational and other constructive activities for youth.

Almost any organization can support and engage in the latter crime prevention activities—which, in the long run, are far more effective than tenant patrols or cargo security councils. Studies reveal that more than 80 percent of prison inmates are high school dropouts, and that the majority of inmates in correctional facilities are functional illiterates (Chamber of Commerce of the United States 1970, p. 62). And research indicates a high correlation between unemployment (or lack of salable job skills) and crime; in some penal institutions, as many as 40 percent of the inmates have no previous sustained work experience. There is also a high correlation between drug addiction and robbery.

Collective efforts by citizens may be directed at strengthening the crime prevention activities of government agencies (e.g., courts, corrections, and law enforcement agencies), or at bolstering anticrime measures undertaken within the private sector. For instance, a block crime prevention association may focus on self-help measures to increase the safety of persons and property over and above the protection afforded by local police. Other citizen groups, such as local chambers of commerce, might sponsor surveys of police effectiveness, propose more effective ways to select judges, or promote community-based correctional facilities.

Citizens may participate in the crime prevention efforts of government agencies by attending community relations meetings conducted by the local police department, by volunteering for probation and programs administered by the city court, by serving as parole volunteers under the supervision of a state parole commission, or by volunteering to help a social or rehabilitative agency improve the delivery of its services. Voluntary service by citizens *within* government agencies is also possible. Citizen volunteers may act under the close supervision of an agency, or they may be involved in an advisory capacity—their role being to react to plans and decisions of the agency. Finally, citizens may share planning and decision-making powers with the agency.

Many organizations play important crime prevention roles as a result of initiative taken by their members. Organized efforts to reduce crime do not *replace* individual action; they result *from* it. And organizations do not relieve citizens of their crime prevention duty; rather, they offer citizens excellent reasons and opportunities for exercising that duty.

A Sense of Community

Important as it is, individual action in crime prevention is not enough. Our society is built upon the premise that people are responsible both for themselves and for the general welfare of others. Exclusive reliance on a self-oriented or family-oriented approach to crime prevention can only isolate individuals and families from one another. If that happens, the crime prevention effectiveness of a community as a whole becomes considerably less than the sum of its parts. Indeed, with citizens looking out for themselves only, there is no community and no strength in numbers—only a fragmentation that will embolden criminal elements. Burglars, for example, are encouraged if they know that they do not have to contend with the eyes and ears of an entire neighborhood, but only with the immediate obstacles in an apartment or house intended for entry.

A self-centered approach to crime prevention also causes individuals to transform their residences into fortresses. This action, in turn, increases social isolation and the inability of the block or neighborhood to present a united front against crime. Thus, without a sense of community, the crime prevention potential of mutual aid and mutual responsibility remains unfulfilled.

ATTACKING THE INFRASTRUCTURE

As mentioned earlier, citizens can prevent crime by focusing on the social factors that lead to crime: poor education, unemployment, a lack of recreation, and a lack of adequate counseling and treatment. These factors are the infrastructure, or foundation, of crime.

Education

Many citizens are involved in encouraging school dropouts to complete their education. For example, the "Keep a Child in School" program in Charleston, West Virginia, works with students on a one-to-one basis and makes sure that they have adequate clothing and supplies. Tutors are provided for students who fall behind in their work or need special help.

Other groups offer alternative educational opportunities, such as street academies or vocational programs. New York City's Harlem Prep is one of the best-known and most successful street academies in the country. It is supported by contributions from foundations and industry, and its purpose is to prepare high school dropouts for college. The Philadelphia Urban Coalition runs a vocational program for inner-city high school youths who have poor reading skills and are planning to drop out. The school system and the business community cooperate to give youths the training they need for specific jobs in specific industries. In some areas, citizens are instrumental in familiarizing students with the law and how it affects them. A sixteen-page booklet, "You and the Law" is produced by Kiwanis International and distributed to teenagers to help them understand the concept of freedom under the law.

Many parents donate their time to schools on a daily basis, preparing instructional materials and helping teachers in the classroom. Citizen action has also contributed to the establishment of community schools and neighborhood councils that advise school administrators. Individuals also assist schools in counseling youths on drug use, pregnancy, family breakdown, employment, and various forms of antisocial behavior. Citizens can also get involved by establishing scholarship funds.

Employment

Many business people are working to place disadvantaged youths in summer jobs and in part-time jobs during the school year. The National Alliance of Businessmen's JOBS program has placed almost a million youths in jobs in private business and industry. At the urging of the Urban Coalition and other citizen organizations, some companies are filling a certain percent of new jobs with the hard-core unemployed, and they are setting up new eligibility standards in this regard. In Riverside, California, a group of employers founded the Job Opportunities Council to recruit the hard-core unemployed.

Some citizen groups promote "hire first, train later" programs, in which applicants undergo a two-week orientation program prior to placement with an employer; the employer then provides on-the-job training and other support. But job training and counseling may also come through the citizen organization. Project Bread—a nationwide jobs training program—started in Salem, Massachusetts, as one individual's idea to teach ex-addicts how to earn a living as cooks. Other groups are active in disseminating job information to people who live in areas of high unemployment.

Recreation

Some citizen organizations finance or operate summer camps for disadvantaged youth, and organize sports activities and tournaments. "Send a Kid to Camp" programs sponsored by many local newspapers solicit funds to provide young people with new experiences and recreational opportunities. And some individuals, acting in a "big brother" capacity, regularly take youths to sporting, entertainment, and cultural events.

Some groups finance youth centers or spearhead drives for better parks and other municipal recreational facilities. Current interest in ecology has spurred citizens to develop nature trails in the city and to take teenagers for hikes or camping trips in nearby rural areas. To reach urban youth, the National Audubon Society has established nature demonstration centers at wildlife sanctuaries; three of these centers are located on the outskirts of large cities.

A special program in Washington, D.C., teaches inner-city children about the ecology within the city and encourages them to discover nature trails within their own communities. A top priority for many citizens is to develop additional forms of organized recreation—such as talent shows, arts and crafts classes, and special interest programs that focus on car repair, aviation, weather, motorcycle safety, music, and dancing.

In some cities, citizens have established neighborhood councils that hire gang members to build small parks. Others have organized adventure clubs that feature mountaineering and trips to wilderness areas. One citizen group, in an effort to channel youthful energy into constructive pursuits, has authored a booklet on volunteer opportunities for teenagers.

Counseling and Treatment

Citizens can counsel and advise youths and adults within a variety of organizational frameworks. For example, counseling might occur in the context of a hot line established to help persons with drug-related problems. There are now over three hundred hot lines in the country for various types of problems. Counseling might also occur at a local YMCA, which refers persons with serious problems to community agencies that supply medical and mental health services, drug abuse rehabilitation, contraceptive counseling, juvenile aid, and legal and psychological services. The Listening Post in Bethesda, Maryland, is a telephone hot line and center for young people who need advice and help. Volunteers at the center create a warm, accepting environment and provide constructive alternatives for troubled youth.

Citizens also volunteer at counseling centers that work to develop better and more secure relationships between children and their parents. Other volunteers at clinics or treatment centers assist professionals who treat drug or alcohol problems. The Cincinnati (Ohio) Free Clinic, which offers detoxification and medical services to drug-involved individuals, has about four hundred professional and nonprofessional volunteers on staff. In addition to medical aid, these volunteers offer telephone counseling and crisis intervention services.

Educational campaigns against drug abuse are often supported and conducted by citizen groups. At Auburn University in Auburn, Alabama, twenty-two pharmacy students developed a drug abuse program for Alabama high schools. Traveling in teams of two or three, the students show films, lecture, and distribute literature about drug use. In some companies, businesspeople and union officials have embarked on a joint program of education, referral, and follow-up for persons with alcohol problems.

In some cities, citizen groups provide the bulk of financial support for treatment centers. One group supplies over two-thirds of the operating funds for a facility offering residential care for addicts and heavy drug users—the Memphis House in Memphis, Tennessee. This facility also offers at-home teaching and helps residents find jobs and housing before they return to the community.

NEIGHBORHOOD ACTION

As you have seen, the three components of the criminal justice system—the police, the courts, and corrections—are supplemented and strengthened by a wide range of citizen activities. In the rest of this chapter, we examine some of the more important of these activities in detail. This section focuses on neighborhood action.

Prior to starting a neighborhood crime prevention program, systematic information should be gathered on the characteristics of the particular neighborhood. Table 18.1 depicts information that a program should have in order to target the crime prevention activities properly.

TABLE 18.1
Relevant Neighborhood Characteristics for Targeting Crime Prevention

RESIDENT CHARACTERISTICS	
DEMOGRAPHIC	**SOCIOECONOMIC**
Age mixture (esp. youth, elderly)	Income
Race and ethnicity	Education
Household composition	Housing tenure mix (owners and renters)
	Mobility (turnover)
PHYSICAL CHARACTERISTICS	
HOUSING	**LAND USE**
Type of structure (size, configuration)	Boundary characteristics
Density	Commercial or industrial activity
	Major thoroughfares
OVERALL CONDITION	
Residential trends	
Local business trends	

Adapted from Judith D. Feins et al., *Partnerships for Neighborhood Crime Prevention* (Washington, D.C.: National Institute of Justice, U.S. Department of Justice, 1983), p. 10.

Block Clubs

A survey of urban area crime prevention programs found that "Block Watch" programs were a popular neighborhood action tactic. **Block clubs** may well be the best starting point for organized citizen response to crime. At the block level, citizens can see what is going on in their neighborhoods and can recognize suspicious people or behavior. Citizens also have a vested interest at the block level (e.g., property values, neighborhood safety). And the organizer's task is simplified at the block level, because it is easier to bring together a limited number of people in a specific geographic area than to arrange a community-wide effort (Minnesota Crime Prevention Center 1978, p. 3).

Block security programs improve citizen awareness and concern about public safety by assigning street surveillance or assistance responsibilities to block mothers, block parents, or other individuals (Yin 1976, p. 121). Early contact with the police is important when these programs are implemented. Table 18.2 lists some of the tactics used most frequently by block groups.

Neighborhood Watches

Neighborhood watches are typical in citizen crime prevention activity. Such programs attempt to improve the reporting of crimes or suspicious activity in the neighborhood. Neighborhood residents are urged to be sensitive to any signs of criminal activity and are often given special telephone numbers to call in case of emergency (Yin 1976).

Information about neighborhood watches has been widely disseminated by the National Neighborhood Watch Program, which was established in 1972 under a grant to the National Sheriffs' Association from the Law Enforcement Assistance Administration. The programs concludes that

> after 4 years of continued growth and refinement, the National Neighborhood Watch Program is a highly effective, nationally based effort reaching millions of citizens. It is efficiently administered by the National Sheriffs' Association and promoted by a balanced, sound program of news media and special audience coverage. The program has gained and maintained major momentum which is currently reflected by the enthusiasm of program participants and by a level of demand, for new or resupply materials, which exceeds supply (Midwest Research Institute 1977, p. 4).

An inmate-interview project involving admitted burglars revealed that a neighborhood watch program is the most effective deterrent against burglary. The majority of burglars interviewed said that merely being noticed by a neighbor was enough to deter them. All indicated that they would leave an area if challenged by a neighbor (Palmer 1978, pp. 7–8).

TABLE 18.2
Tactics Used by Crime Prevention Programs in Twenty-Two Cities

TACTIC	TEN COMMUNITY-BASED PROGRAMS	TWELVE POLICE-BASED PROGRAMS	TOTAL
Block and apartment watches	9	12	21
Operation identification	8	10	18
Home security surveys	7	10	17
Street patrols	8	5	13
Crime reporting projects	5	8	13
Physical environment changes	6	6	12
Police/community boards	4	7	11
Home security improvements	5	4	9
Building patrols	5	2	7
Escort services	4	3	7
Crime prevention education	3	2	5
Victim/witness services	2	2	4
WhistleSTOP	2	2	4
Court watch	2	1	3

Adapted from Judith D. Feins et al., *Partnerships for Neighborhood Crime Prevention* (Washington, D.C.: National Institute of Justice, U.S. Department of Justice, 1983), p. 16.

The positive impact of neighborhood watches seems to relate to the number of participants and the degree of personal interaction. Large groups with low involvement have little success in reducing crime or improving the sense of security. In contrast, smaller, more intensive programs can have a positive impact, resulting in improved crime reporting and an eventual reduction in crime and the *fear* of crime (National Institute of Law Enforcement and Criminal Justice 1978, p. 6).

FIGURE 18.1
Roadside sign at DeKalb County, Georgia, border announces block parent crime prevention program. Courtesy DeKalb County (Georgia) Police Department.

Citizen Patrols

Disturbed by crime in their neighborhoods, some citizens have initiated citizen patrols to protect neighborhood residents. In some cases, the residents themselves patrol; other neighborhoods hire security guards to do it. Some vehicle patrols cover neighborhood sections and maintain contact through citizen-band radios. Others concentrate on specific buildings or housing areas. More than two hundred resident patrols in sixteen urban areas were identified by the National Evaluation Program in a 1977 report on citizen patrol projects (Yin 1977, p. 111). The National Evaluation Program report is an executive summary of a more extensive report published by the Rand Corporation. The Rand study defines residential patrols as groups that (1) have specific patrol or surveillance routines; (2) have the principal purpose of preventing criminal acts; (3) are controlled by a citizens' organization or a public housing authority; and (4) are directed primarily at residential—rather than commercial—areas (ibid., p. 1).

FIGURE 18.2
Block parent assists neighborhood children. Courtesy DeKalb County (Georgia) Police Department.

The Rand study's main contribution to the knowledge of residential patrols was more descriptive than evaluative. For example, research in representative cities involving more than a hundred patrols led to the following conclusions (ibid., pp. 29–31):

1. Contemporary patrols emphasize residential crime prevention. This emphasis is in contrast to the riot-pacification functions highlighted in most literature from the early 1960s.
2. It is estimated that more than eight hundred resident patrols are currently active in urban areas in the United States—in neighborhoods of varied income and racial composition.
3. Contemporary patrols vary widely in cost, but most operate on a small budget on a voluntary basis.
4. Patrols may be divided into four types: building patrols, neighborhood patrols, social service patrols, and community protection patrols.
5. Contemporary resident patrols are susceptible to occasional vigilantism, but not as frequently as the mass media suggests.
6. Building patrols in public housing differ from other building patrols in that the crime problem in public housing may be partially attributable to the residents themselves.
7. Several factors influence a patrol's ability to operate and achieve its goals: personnel, organizational affiliation, and bureaucratization.

BUILDING PATROLS The main objective of **building** (or tenant) **patrols** is to protect specific buildings and the adjacent grounds (Yin 1976, pp. 55–56). Buildings protected may vary from high-income, high-rise dwellings, to low-income housing for the elderly, to detached houses with private access. Building patrols are distinctive in four ways: (1) they operate in areas with minimal local police activity; (2) they are usually supervised by an official organization that in some way represents the tenants of the buildings being protected; (3) the principal duties of the patrol are to prevent crime and to keep unwanted strangers out of buildings or the immediate area; and (4) patrol members, except in public housing projects, are usually paid guards.

NEIGHBORHOOD PATROLS **Neighborhood patrols,** in contrast to building patrols, usually have a poorly defined area of surveillance (Yin 1976, p. 61). The area may cover several blocks, may not have strict boundaries, and may not be patrolled as intensively as buildings. Few neighborhood patrols operate twenty-four hours a day, and because they mainly cover streets and other public areas rather than buildings, they frequently coordinate their activities with the local police. Finally, because it is difficult for neighborhood patrols to distinguish between area residents and strangers, such patrols can only focus on observed behaviors that appear undesirable or suspicious. In contrast, building patrols can screen strangers and deny them access to the premises.

Neighborhood patrols are used in areas of all income levels and ethnic compositions. They may be conducted on foot or in cars, and they may cover certain areas related to activities such as children walking to and from school. When a patrol observes a suspicious incident, it usually reports the observation by radio to a base station or to the police.

SOCIAL SERVICE PATROLS **Social service patrols** are building or neighborhood patrols that perform social service functions (Yin 1976, p. 69). The main reason for distinguishing social service patrols is that they tend to have functions other than crime prevention that transcend the immediate objectives of other types of patrols. The social service patrol may be organized around a variety of community responsibilities, of which patrolling is only one. For instance, a patrol might be involved in escorting senior citizens or in providing employment opportunities for youths. There may be a purposeful attempt to recruit youths suspected of causing some of the neighborhood's crime problems to serve as patrol members.

FIGURE 18.3
Badge identifies volunteers who accompany elderly persons on errands. Courtesy Wilmington, Delaware, Police Department.

COMMUNITY PROTECTION PATROLS **Community protection patrols** serve as either building, neighborhood, or social service patrols, but they also monitor police activities (Yin 1976, p. 74). The monitoring is carried out because of a fear of police harassment based on previous incidents or on a generally antagonistic relationship with the police. The emergence of community protection groups is associated with the civil rights movement and the urban riots of the 1960s. In particular, several black patrols were formed in the South—often in connection with urban disorders—to protect black residents from the white community.

Environmental Design

A widely recognized crime prevention program in the North Asylum Hill area of Harford, Connecticut, combines many of the neighborhood security activities discussed herein with a redesign of the neighborhood's traffic patterns. The goal was to decrease burglaries, robberies, and purse snatchings. Streets were closed and traffic was rerouted to diminish through-traffic, to enhance the area's residential character, and to increase residents' use of public space. This well-researched and successful application of the theories of crime prevention through environmental design underscores the importance of neighborhood cohesion in crime control (U.S. Department of Justice, Law Enforcement Assistance Administration, National Institute of Law Enforcement and Criminal Justice 1978, pp. 1–2). The following "Tale of Two Projects" (Newman 1978, pp. 39–48) illustrates the importance of environmental design in crime prevention.

A Tale of Two Projects

Brownsville and Van Dyke are strikingly different in physical design, while housing comparatively identical populations in size and social characteristics. The high-rise towers at Van Dyke are almost totally devoid of defensible space qualities, while the buildings at Brownsville are comparatively well-endowed with such qualities. It should be mentioned, even before beginning the comparison, that Brownsville, the better of the two projects, is still far away from answering all defensible space design directives.

Review of the objective data on the physical characteristics of the two projects reveals many striking parallels. The projects are almost identical in size, each housing approximately 6,000 persons, and are designed at exactly the same density: 288 persons per acre. Major differences arise in the composition of buildings and the percentage of ground-level space they occupy. Brownsville buildings cover 23 percent of the available land, whereas Van Dyke buildings cover only 16.6 percent of the total land area—including nine, three-story buildings which occupy a large percentage of space but house only 24 percent of the total project population. In addition, the two projects differ in design in that Brownsville is comprised of low, walk-up and elevator buildings, three to six stories, while the latter is comprised of a mix of three-story buildings and fourteen-story high-rise slabs (87 percent of the apartment units at Van Dyke are located in the high-rise slabs). The two projects are located across the street from one another and share the same Housing Authority police and New York City police services.

Differences in physical design of the Brownsville and Van Dyke projects are apparent even to the casual observer. Van Dyke Houses has the appearance of a large, monolithic project. The most dominant buildings are the thirteen, fourteen-story slabs. In less evidence are the nine, three-story structures. Each of the buildings at Van Dyke sits independently on the site, with large open spaces separating it from its neighbors. At the center of the project is a single, large open area, used for a Parks Department playground and for automobile parking. By means of its design, this large open area has been distinctly separated from and is unrelated to the surrounding buildings.

None of the buildings at Van Dyke may be entered directly from the public street. Entrance requires that tenants leave the public street and walk onto project paths that wind into internal project areas, blind to street surveillance. The only areas of the project grounds which relate somewhat to buildings are the small seating areas in the channel of space between the double row of buildings. The functional entrance to the high-rise buildings is a small door shared by 112 to 136 families. This door is located directly off the project paths, with no gradation or distinction indicated by the design of the grounds in front of the building lobby.

Two low-speed elevators carry families to their living floors in each of the high-rise buildings. Elevators are placed directly opposite the building entrances, as mandated by the Housing Authority, to improve surveillance from the outside. Full benefit is not derived from this

FIGURE 18.4
The fourteen- and three-story Van Dyke Houses *(left side of street)* and the smaller building clusters of the Brownsville Houses *(right side)*. Although tenant populations are identical, crime and vandalism rates are 40 to 150 percent higher in Van Dyke Houses. Courtesy Oscar Newman, Institute of Planning and Housing, New York University, New York, N.Y.

arrangement, however, since entrances face the interior of the project rather than the street.

The housing floors of the high-rise buildings are each occupied by eight families. The elevator stops in the middle of the corridor, and the apartment units are reached by walking left or right down a dead-end corridor with apartments positioned on both sides (a double-loaded corridor).

In contrast, Brownsville Houses presents the appearance of being a smaller project, due to the disposition of units in smaller and more diverse clusters of buildings. It might be said that the buildings and the way in which they were placed on the site has been used to divide the project into smaller, more manageable zones. The ground areas have been humanized through their relationship with the individual residential buildings. Activities that take place in small project spaces adjoining buildings have become the business of the neighboring residents, who assume a leading role in monitoring them.

All residents and police who have been interviewed at Brownsville perceive the project as smaller and more stable than Van Dyke. All intruders, including police and interviewers, feel more cautious about invading the privacy of residents at Brownsville. By contrast, their attitude toward the invasion of the interior corridors at Van Dyke is callous and indifferent.

This emphasis on space division carries over into the design of the buildings interiors of Brownsville Houses. Individual buildings are three- and six-story structures with six families sharing a floor. The floor is further divided, by an unlocked swinging door, into two vestibules shared by three families each. In the six-story buildings there is an elevator which stops at odd floors, requiring residents of upper stories to walk up or down one flight, using an open stairwell around which apartment doors are clustered. Vertical communication among families is assured by this relationship of elevators to apartments, and also by the presence of open stairwells connecting the floors.

At the ground level, the building lobby leads up a short flight of stairs to several apartments that maintain surveillance over activity in this small entryway. On all floors, tenants have been found to maintain auditory surveillance over activity taking place in the halls by the device of keeping their doors slightly ajar. These features of the building have allowed occupants to extend their territorial prerogatives into building corridors, hallways, and stairs. Those mothers of young children at Brownsville who allow their children the freedom to play on landings and up and down the stairwells monitor their play from within the apartment. A mere interruption in the din of children at play was found to bring mothers to their doors as surely as a loud scream.

By contrast, most young children at Van Dyke are not allowed to play in the corridors outside their apartments. The halls of Van Dyke and other high-rise buildings are designed solely for their corridor function and are inhospitable to the fantasy-play of children. In addition, too many families utilize a typical high-rise hall for a mother to comfortably leave her child there unsupervised. For the same reason, mothers are reluctant to leave their door ajar for surveillance—too many people, including strangers and guests of neighbors, wander through the Van Dyke halls unchecked and unquestioned. Finally, to give children real freedom in the use of the building would require their using the elevator or fire stairs to gain access to other floors. But both these areas are frightening and would take the children out of the surveillance zone of the mother and other tenants. The elevator cab is sealed by a heavy metal door that cannot be opened manually. The fire stairwells are designed to seal floors in the event of a fire. A by-product of their fireproofing is that noises within the stairwells cannot be heard in the corridors outside. Criminals often force their victims into these areas because the soundproofing feature and low frequency of use make the detection of a crime in progress almost impossible.

The sense of propriety which is apparent in the way tenants of Brownsville Houses use their halls to monitor and maintain surveillance over children and strangers appears to have carried over to the grounds adjacent to the building entrances. Because of the unique construction of the buildings, there are areas on the ground level just outside the front door of the building where parents can allow their children to play, while maintaining contact with them through their kitchen windows. Interviews have revealed that the range of spaces into which young children are permitted to roam is greater in Brownsville than in Van Dyke.

Finally, where entries to Van Dyke high-rise buildings serve 130 families, Brownsville buildings are entered through different doors, each serving a small number of families (nine to thirteen). The ground area adjacent to these entries has been developed for use by adults, and for play by young children. Parents feel confident about allowing their children to play in these clearly circumscribed zones. Frequently, these entry areas are located just off the public street, and serve to set off the building from the street itself by acting as an intervening buffer area. The placement of entrances just off the street avoids the dangers created by Van Dyke: forcing tenants to walk along blind interior project paths to get to their buildings.

[Tables 18.3 and 18.4 reveal] that the tenants of Brownsville and Van Dyke are rated similarly on overall indexes of socio-economic status, family stability, and ethnic, racial, and family composition. It is also clear that these rough similarities are consistent from year to year. Comparison of demographic data over the period 1962 to 1969 reveals few exceptions to this overall pattern of identity between the projects.

It was a widely held belief that many so-called "problem families," displaced by the Model Cities renewal programs, were among recent move-ins to Van Dyke. Many people drew an immediate correlation between the higher crime rate at Van Dyke and this change in population. Information was therefore obtained on a representative sample of families who have moved into the two projects over the past three years. Sample data on one of every five move-ins reveal no striking differences in the social characteristics of residents in both projects.

The total number of move-ins in the past three years in any case constituted fewer than 5 percent of the project population in both Van Dyke and Brownsville. To blame problems of the Van Dyke project on a small number of "bad seeds" is clearly gratuitous. However, to insure that these mean figures were not misleading, frequency distributions were plotted for each variable which permitted such treatment. For example, the frequency of each family size varying from one to fifteen was plotted separately for Brownsville and Van Dyke and reveals no apparent reason to doubt the representativeness of these summary statistics. . . .

Crime and vandalism are major problems at both Van Dyke and Brownsville Houses. The problem has become serious over the past ten

TABLE 18.3
Tenant Statistics

CHARACTERISTIC	VAN DYKE	BROWNSVILLE
Total population	6,420	5,390
Average family size	4.0	4.0
Number of minors	3618 (57.5%)	3.047 (57.8%)
Percentage families black	79.1%	85.0%
Percentage families white	5.6%	2.6%
Percentage families Puerto Rican	15.3%	12.4%
Average gross income	$4,997	$5,056
Percentage on welfare	28.8%	29.7%
Percentage broken families	29.5%	31.7%
Average number of years in project	8.5	9.0
Percent of families with two wage earners	12.2%	11.0
Number of children in grades 1–6	839	904

Source: New York City Housing Authority Records, 1968.

TABLE 18.4
A Comparison of Physical Design and Population Density

PHYSICAL MEASURE	VAN DYKE	BROWNSVILLE
Total size	22.35 acres	19.16 acres
Number of buildings	23	27
Building height	13–14 story 9–3 story	6-story with some 3-story wings
Coverage	16.6	23.0
Floor area ratio	1.49	1.39
Average number of rooms per apartment	4.62	4.69
Density	288 persons/acre	287 persons/acre
Year completed	1955 (one building added in 1964)	1947

Source: New York City Housing Authority Project Physical Design Statistics.

years, with the decline of the old Brooklyn community and the failure to create renewal opportunities. The area surrounding both projects is severely blighted; store owners conduct business in plexiglass booths to protect themselves from addicts. The local library requires two armed guards on duty at all times. The local hospital claims it records fifteen teen-age deaths per month due to overdoses of drugs.

[Table 18.5] presents data on major categories of crime for both projects as collected by housing police. Data are presented on specific crimes, including robbery, possession of drugs, and loitering. A comparison of 1969 crime incident rates (see [Table 18.5]) and maintenance rates (see [Table 18.6]) for the two projects was quite revealing. In summary, Van Dyke Homes was found to have 50 percent more total crime incidents, with over three and one-half times as many robberies (384 percent), and 64 percent more felonies, misdemeanors, and offenses than Brownsville. Another measure of security can be understood from examination of the rate of decline of facilities. Even though Brownsville Houses is an older project, beginning to suffer from natural decay, Van Dyke annually required a total of 39 percent more maintenance work. It is interesting to note that the average outlay of time and funds for upkeep of Van Dyke is significantly higher than that of Brownsville. Not only is there less need of repair at Brownsville, but tenants themselves play a greater role in seeing to the cleanliness of buildings either through insistence on the upkeep of janitorial services or by individual effort.

One of the most striking differences between the two projects concerns elevator breakdowns. The far greater number of breakdowns at Van Dyke is primarily a function of more intensive use. However, more breakdowns are due to

TABLE 18.5
Comparison of Crime Incidents

CRIME INCIDENTS	VAN DYKE	BROWNSVILLE
Total incidents	1,189	790
Total felonies, misdemeanors, and offenses	432	264
Number of robberies	92	24
Number of malicious mischief	52	28

Source: New York City Housing Authority Police Records, 1969.

TABLE 18.6
Comparison of Maintenance

MAINTENANCE	VAN DYKE (CONSTRUCTED 1955)	BROWNSVILLE (CONSTRUCTED 1947)
Number of maintenance jobs of any sort (work tickets) through 4/70	3,301	2,376
Number of maintenance jobs, excluding glass repair	2,643	1,651
Number of nonglass jobs per unit	1.47	1.16
Number of full-time maintenance staff	9	7
Number of elevator breakdowns per month	280	110

Source: New York City Housing Authority Project Managers' bookkeeping records.

vandalism at Van Dyke than at Brownsville. This form of vandalism is especially diagnostic, showing that adolescents who tamper with Van Dyke elevators do not have a sense of identity with the people they inconvenience.

As a measure of tenant satisfaction, Brownsville Houses, with smaller room sizes in similarly designated apartment units, has a lower rate of move-outs than Van Dyke Houses. To avoid historical accident and subsequently limited conclusion, results were tabulated annually over an eight-year period, including sampling of move-ins to the two projects. These data have provided additional confirmation of the differences in crime and vandalism between the projects that cannot be assigned to differences in their tenant populations.

It is unwarranted to conclude that this data provide final and definitive proof of the influence of physical design variables on crime and vandalism. It is equally misleading to assume, as management officials initially did, that the differences can be explained away by variations in tenant characteristics in the two projects. The project manager assumed that Van Dyke Houses had a larger number of broken families and that these families had a larger number of children than those at Brownsville. The statistics do not bear out this assumption, but the image described by the manager and other public officials suggests the extent of the problem and may in turn contribute to it.

There are some elementary differences in the physical construct of the projects which may contribute to the disparity of image held by officials. Police officers revealed that they found Van Dyke Houses far more difficult to patrol. To monitor activity in the enclosed fire stairs requires that a patrolman take the elevator to the upper floor and then walk down to the ground level, alternating at each floor between the two independent fire-stair columns.

Police express pessimism about their value at Van Dyke Houses. About Brownsville they are much more optimistic and, in subtle ways, respond to complaints with more vigor and concern. All these factors produce a significant positive effect in Brownsville. At Van Dyke the negative factors of anonymity, police pessimism, pessimism about police, and tenant feelings of ambiguity about strangers (caused by large numbers of families sharing one entrance) conspire to progressively erode any residual faith in the effectiveness of community or official response to crime.

In summary, it seems unmistakable that physical design plays a very significant role in crime rate. It should also be kept in mind that the defensible space qualities inherent in the Brownsville design are there, for the most part, by accident. From a critical, defensible space viewpoint, Brownsville is far from perfect. The comparison of the crime and vandalism rates in the two projects was made using gross crime data on both projects. Twenty-three percent of the apartments at Van Dyke consist of three-story walk-up buildings serving a small number of families. It is likely that comparative data on crime rates in the low buildings versus the towers at Van Dyke would reveal significant differences. This would make the comparison of crime rates between Van Dyke and Brownsville even more startling.

CRIME REPORTING PROJECTS

Many civic organizations, in cooperation with law enforcement agencies, sponsor area-wide campaigns to encourage the public to report crimes or information about suspected crimes. Some citizen crime reporting projects operate independently, whereas others are integral components of comprehensive programs. Some typical crime reporting projects are described in the following paragraphs.

WhistleStop

WhistleStop is a community signal system that facilitates the reporting of in-progress crimes by victims and witnesses. Citizens are urged to carry whistles and to use them if they are victimized, if they observe a crime, or if they hear another whistle. Persons who hear the whistles are supposed to telephone the police and then "sound the alarm" in an effort to disrupt the crime (Gibbs 1977, pp. 89–90).

Radio Watches

Participants in radio watches must have access to two-way, citizen-band, or ham radios in personal, company, or taxi vehicles. They are urged to report suspicious activities through dispatchers or directly to police departments that monitor emergency frequencies (Bickman 1977). The Civilian Radio Taxi Patrol in New York City was started in spring of 1973 as a result of cab drivers' concern about street crime and the lack of public cooperation with the police. Cab owners formed an association and obtained training and support from local police. These volunteer patrols have been a significant factor in preventing crime on the streets (Washnis 1976, pp. 78–79).

Crime Stoppers

Crime Stoppers programs provide special telephone lines to facilitate anonymous reporting of suspicious or criminal activity. Some of the programs offer monetary rewards for information leading to convictions, with the amount of the reward often determined by citizen committees. The Albuquerque (New Mexico) Crime Stoppers, established in 1976, is funded by public contributions and controlled by an eighteen-member civilian board of directors. The project issues select case reports to newspapers and sixty-second public service announcements to radio stations. A local television station films a two-minute reenactment of the "crime of the week." The Albuquerque project is just one of many similar programs across the country.

Educational Programs

A variety of educational approaches can be used to encourage witnesses to report crimes. For example, presentations can be made before civic and service groups, schools, parent-teachers associations, church organizations, and other community groups (see Figure 18.5 & Figure 18.6). Another approach involves membership projects, which are similar to group presentations except that they usually demand greater involvement because of membership requirements. A third approach is home presentation.

A unique educational approach to the specific crime problem of black communities has recently been attempted. It is well documented that blacks are frequently the victims of serious crimes of violence and property crimes. Garry Mendez of the National Urban League offers the following description of a variation of community crime prevention.

> Street crime disproportionately involves African Americans. In recent years, most governmental responses to street crime, such as prison building, have stressed law and order. They have failed. A newer approach has been to organize local communities, especially in white and middle-class neighborhoods. It has been said that African Americans in low-income communities do not care about reducing crime and cannot organize themselves. However, most of what is called community crime prevention is defensive, in effect locks up the community, and does not address the causes of crime. Block watches and patrols are

SEXUAL ASSAULT

Every Female Is A Potential Victim !

Regardless of age, dress or race!

Find out how to protect yourself from criminals.

DATE:__________ **TIME:**__________

PLACE:____________________

FIGURE 18.5 Poster announcing an educational program on rape prevention. Courtesy of the Florida Attorney General's Office Help Stop Crime Program.

HELP! STOP CRIME

SHOPLIFTING IS A CRIME!

SHOPLIFTERS WILL BE PROSECUTED Fla. Statute 812.015

DON'T RISK A PERMANENT CRIMINAL RECORD

OFFICE OF THE ATTORNEY GENERAL

FIGURE 18.6
A sample poster for preventing shoplifting. Courtesy of the Florida Attorney General's Office.

> illustrative. By contrast, the national Crime Is Not a Part of Our Black Heritage program opens rather than closes African American communities. Through informal schools that teach African American heritage and culture, as well as through organizing with the help of the media, blacks in communities take ownership of the program. Preliminary evaluation results are promising, but it is important to recognize that the goals of the program, to change attitudes and behavior, will require time and commitment (1987, p. 105).

An example of a brochure used in this program is displayed in Figure 18.7.

FEAR OF CRIME

We know that fear of crime results from many causes besides crime itself. Some kinds of people and people in some kinds of neighborhoods probably fear crime more than they need to, given their low risk of actually becoming victims. What makes them fearful is seeing things they associate with crime.

The "signs of crime" associated with higher levels of fear are both social and physical. The social signs include prostitutes soliciting for customers, drug dealers conducting visible transactions, rowdy teenagers loitering on corners, derelicts panhandling or lying in the street in a stupor, and mentally ill persons shouting at the tops of their lungs at unseen enemies. The physical signs include broken windows, garbage littered on sidewalks, abandoned cars, and broken bottles and glass.

Both physical and social signs of crime indicate disorder in the neighborhood and convey a sense that things are "out of control." Ultimately, disorder may attract such predatory violent crimes as robbery; a neighborhood that can't control minor incivilities may advertise itself to potential robbers as a neighborhood that can't

EVERY THREE MINUTES A BLACK PERSON IS A VICTIM OF BLACK CRIME...

ARE YOU NEXT?

Photography by John Pinderhughes

Blacks are more likely to be the victims of murder, rape, assault, robbery and force-able burglary. And in 9 out of 10 cases, the offenders in these crimes are also Black.

For more information on how you can help,

contact:

Crime...Is not a part of our Black heritage.

FIGURE 18.7 A brochure used in the Crime Is Not a Part of Our Black Heritage program. Courtesy of Garry A. Mendez, Jr., Director, Criminal Justice Program, National Urban League.

control serious crime either. But long before serious crime develops, the residents of disorderly areas suffer undue fear. Neighborhood businesses suffer loss of patronage due to that fear. Property values may decline. People who have sufficient resources may move elsewhere. Thus the fear of crime is an important problem in itself.

It is tempting to describe disorder as an inner-city problem, which is especially concentrated in minority and poor neighborhoods, and unprotected, low-density residential areas as a middle-class suburban problem, but that would be an oversimplification. Although there are some differences of degree, middle-class suburbs often suffer disorder problems at shopping centers and even on residential street corners. Poor inner-city neighborhoods in many cities are often quite low in density, with many houses empty during the day. Both problems pose a challenge to almost all kinds of police departments. Many have developed a variety of programs to deal with these problems.

These programs share the goal suggested by some experts of "breaking down the barriers" between the police and the public that are created by the low-density, automobile-based life-style. Other programs address problems of disorder and the causes of fear of crime. To the extent that these programs are successful, the better quality of life may leave people better off than they were before, even if crime is not reduced. If police can help foster a sense of community in an anonymous, atomized residential neighborhood, there are good reasons to believe the neighborhood will be a better place to live in (Sherman 1987).[7]

Several general types of programs have been initiated to reduce the fear of crime and the amount of crime itself:

- *Community organizing*. Efforts at community organizing, such as "Neighborhood Watch" programs, attempt to mobilize citizen involvement in local crime prevention efforts.
- *"Storefronts."* These and other local police facilities have been established to replace some of the precinct headquarters that were closed in earlier periods.
- *Neighborhood foot patrol*. Greatly reduced in earlier periods, this activity has been reinstituted as a means of increasing citizens' contact and constructive interaction with police.

Some police agencies have utilized methods such as community newsletters to demonstrate their concern and to attempt to reduce citizen fear to the extent possible. These newsletters serve a variety of purposes for police departments and frequently provide citizens with a clear set of expectations regarding the police role in crime prevention (see Figure 18.8).

Police Tactics for Neighborhood Crime Prevention

In this section we present examples of crime prevention programs and methods utilized by police departments across the United States in cooperation with their communities (Feins et al. 1983).[8]

NEIGHBORHOOD BEATS Although patrol officers have traditionally been rotated by shift or beat, the stable assignment of officers to neighborhood beats is important for neighborhood crime prevention. This gives citizens a chance to get to know the officers in their neighborhood, which can increase their sense of safety and their willingness to report suspicious activities or crimes. Officers on neighborhood beats can gain a sense of involvement with, and responsibility for, the neighborhood. Their familiarity with the area and knowledge of trouble spots may facilitate crime detection and apprehension. Officers may spend an entire shift on foot patrol, or they may intersperse car and foot patrols. Some potential problems can be avoided if officers on neighborhood beats receive special training (for example, in working with residents or in utilizing any special environmental design tactics on their beats), and if dispatchers are required to learn and respect neighborhood boundaries so that officers are not dispatched outside their patrol areas.

POLICE MINI-STATIONS Police mini-stations or storefronts are a way to bring police into the neighborhood outside the precinct structure, either for special purposes or for added patrol resources. As the Detroit Police Department states, "Mini-stations can most readily be viewed as analogous to parked scout cars. They are fixed positions from which officers may reach out within certain prescribed geographic limits to render police service." For crime prevention, this service can include scheduling block watch formation meetings, loaning out Operation ID engravers, arranging for home security surveys, and other proactive efforts (see Figure 18.8 and 18.9). Personnel for these twenty-four-hour-a-day stations can be supplemented by trained community service officers, interns, or volunteers (including bilingual staff as necessary); use of volunteers can free sworn officers for patrolling or crime prevention organizing.

CRIME ANALYSIS UNITS Crime analysis units within police departments compile information on types, times,

Community Policing Exchange

PUBLISHED BY THE HOUSTON POLICE  OFFICERS SERVING YOUR NEIGHBORHOOD

Vol. 1, No. 2 DECEMBER

Urgent calls handled first

It is 11:00p.m., and all appears calm in Houston. Sam Smith, a retired plumber, arrives home after vacationing in Mexico with his family. Upon arriving home, the family discovers that their home has been burglarized. Meanwhile, in another section of the City, a local store owner is being held up by an armed assailant.

Within seconds of one another, the calls are received by the Department's Dispatch Division at 222-3131. Both individuals are victims of crime. Which of the two victims does the police department respond to first?

This type of circumstance is not uncommon for a police department the size of Houston's. Your police department serves an area covering over 565 square miles and receives about 4,500 calls for service daily. While all requests for service are given immediate police attention, some calls have priority over others - based on the "urgency" of the call.

To provide the most efficient police service to your neighborhood, the Department uses a response prioritization system. This system has been used for some time and has proven to be effective.

Under response prioritization, requests for police services are categorized into three designated levels:

- CODE 1 Responses. An officer will proceed to a call, but the assignment involves no emergency or urgency, and the situation will not deteriorate because of delayed police action. Examples of CODE 1 assignments are parking violations, speeding cars, and abandoned vehicles.
- CODE 2 Responses. An officer will proceed directly to the call, as it requires immediate response and could deteriorate if prompt police action is not initiated. Examples of CODE 2 assignments are traffic accidents, criminals in custody and report calls.
- CODE 3 Responses. An officer will proceed to the call using red lights and siren, as the situation is an emergency that poses a threat to human life. Examples of CODE 3 assignments are a felony crime in progress, a crime endangering life in progress, or an immediate threat to life is imminent.

Going back to our example of Mr. Smith and the local store owner, who both requested police service at almost the same time, we can now determine, of the two, whose situation requires the priority response.

Since the local store owner's situation is a felony crime in progress - CODE 3 - this would be the priority call. Failure of the police to respond immediately could result in the situation deteriorating and becoming life threatening. Whereas, in Mr Smith's case - CODE 2 - the crime has already occured; and a police officer is needed to take a report.

The Houston Police Department responds to every citizen call for service; but, we do so using common sense. We want to keep citizens informed of our services, and how we operate as a Department, so that we can continue to serve this exciting and expansive city.

Community Comments

Lee P. Brown, Chief of Police

On behalf of the Houston Police Department, I would like to thank you for your continued support for helping us to make Houston a safer city. Also, all the members of the Houston Police Department, especially your neighborhood beat officers, would like to extend to you and your family warm wishes for the Holiday Season and a sincere hope for prosperity in the New Year.

Holiday joys & fears

The holiday season always brings with it an increase in home burglaries and thefts - and this year will be no exception. The display of gifts, coupled with the probability of an empty home while families are shopping or visiting with friends, provides more temptation than most burglars can resist.

If you are planning to be away from home during the holidays - for a short or extended time - keep these safety precautions in mind:

- Keep all doors and windows locked, including the garage.
- Keep gifts out of view from windows or entryways.
- Leave on a light or two or invest in a timer to automatically turn lights on and off.
- Don't let daily deliveries accumulate. Ask a neighbor to collect the newspaper or milk bottles.

Continued on pg./2

FIGURE 18.8 Example of a police/community newsletter. Courtesy of the Houston Police Department.

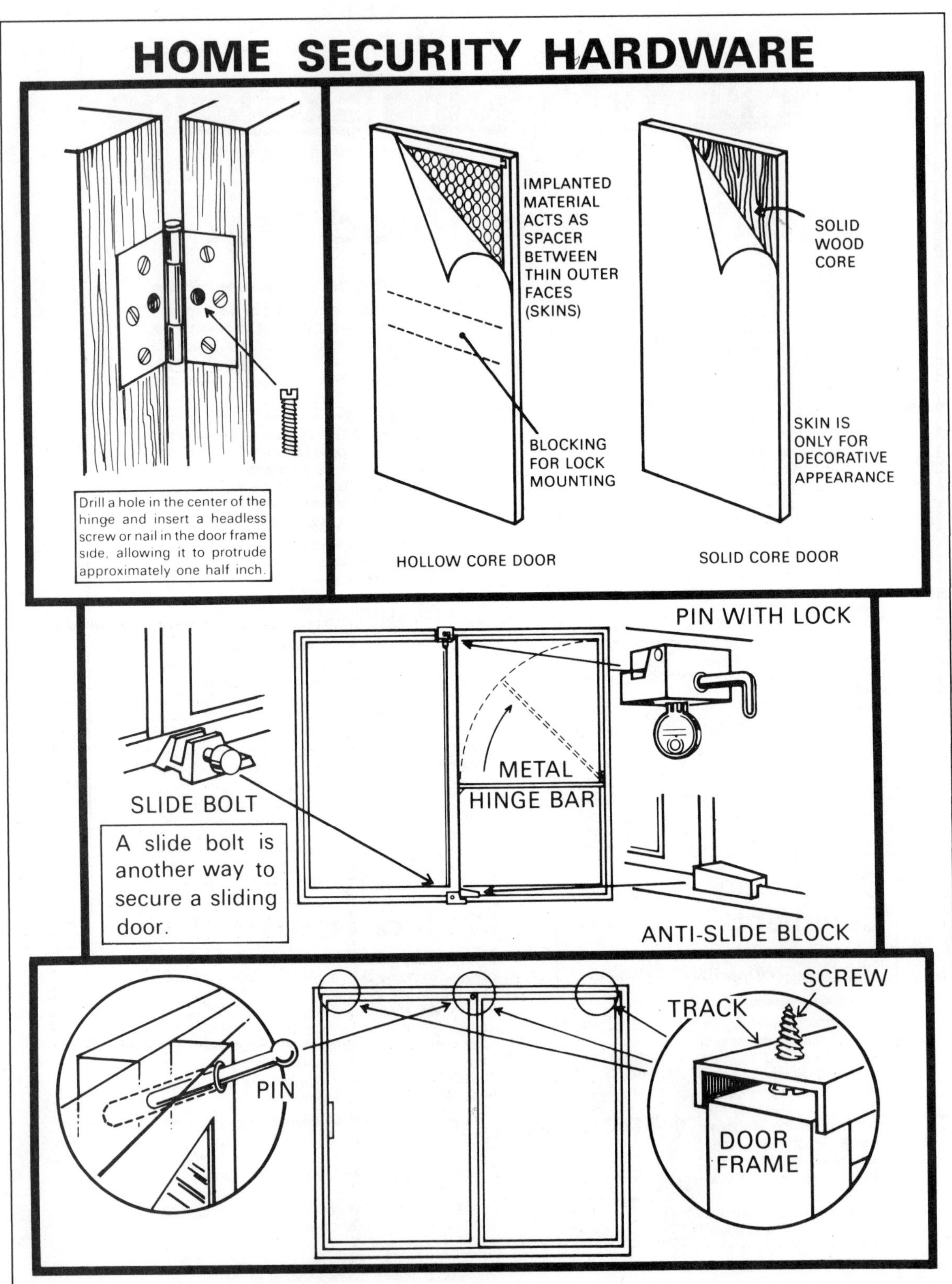

FIGURE 18.9 Information on locks available as part of a police home security program. Courtesy of the Florida Attorney General's Office Help Stop Crime Program.

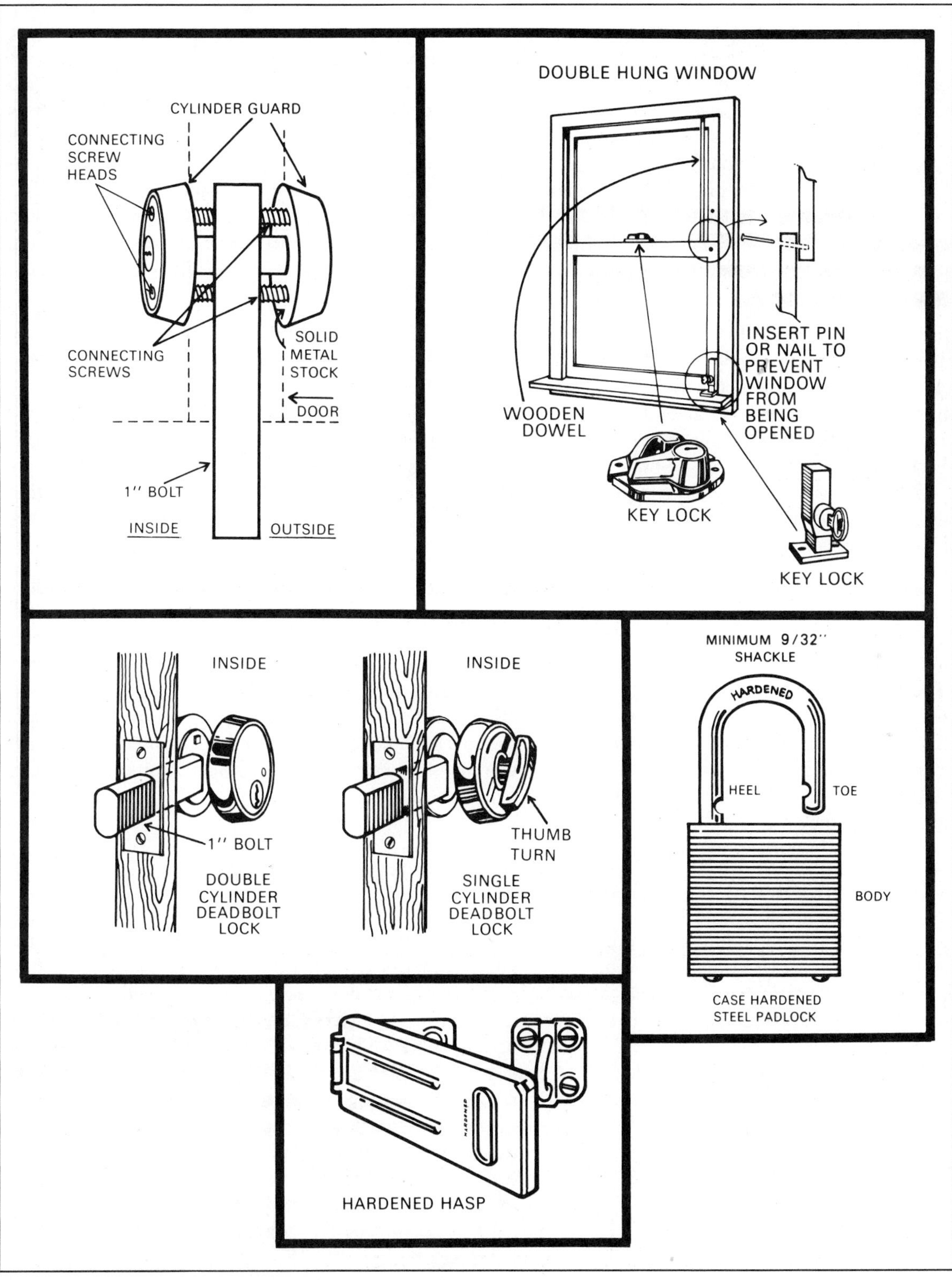
CYLINDER GUARD
CONNECTING SCREW HEADS
CONNECTING SCREWS
SOLID METAL STOCK
DOOR
1" BOLT
INSIDE
OUTSIDE
DOUBLE HUNG WINDOW
INSERT PIN OR NAIL TO PREVENT WINDOW FROM BEING OPENED
WOODEN DOWEL
KEY LOCK
KEY LOCK
INSIDE
INSIDE
1" BOLT
THUMB TURN
DOUBLE CYLINDER DEADBOLT LOCK
SINGLE CYLINDER DEADBOLT LOCK
MINIMUM 9/32" SHACKLE
HARDENED
HEEL
TOE
BODY
CASE HARDENED STEEL PADLOCK
HARDENED HASP

and locations of crimes in a given area, on trends in area crime over time, and on case status and resolution. Crime evaluation, crime maps, and monthly or six-month reports can usually be generated routinely or by request. Crime prevention groups may arrange for routine information and special reports on crime in their area. Groups should realize, however, that certain information is confidential and cannot be provided to civilian organizations. By recognizing the nature and patterns of crimes and offenders, police and residents can build crime prevention strategies more effectively and monitor the impact of anti-crime activity.

POLICE DEPARTMENT ENVIRONMENTAL DESIGN REVIEW Some police departments have a review procedure for checking the security aspects of new construction or public works projects. In San Diego, the police department's Public Affairs Unit reviews designs for planned parks and residential and commercial developments. Their review covers street design, building security, lighting, and other crime prevention components and pinpoints any needed changes before construction starts.

COMMUNITY SERVICE OFFICERS Some police departments hire and train neighborhood youth, senior citizens, or other civilians to do police/community liaison work. These community service officers can staff mini-stations, give educational presentations, assist with Operation ID services, perform home security surveys, and help set up block patrols. They are also a way to supplement sworn personnel and relieve them of certain support functions, but they are not a substitute for the participation of officers in crime prevention programs.

POLICE/COMMUNITY BOARDS A police/community board, or chief's advisory committee, increases contact between the police and community leaders and helps ensure the full support of crime prevention programs by both essential participants. Citizens present their priorities and concerns, police representatives share information on departmental resources and services, and joint crime prevention efforts can be planned.

POLICE/COMMUNITY RELATIONS PROGRAMS Programs that enable citizens to ride in officers' cars, walk along on their beats, and visit police communications centers can provide a better understanding of police duties and capabilities, although they do not increase the citizens' role in crime prevention.

STREET OBSERVATION Street observation is a simple technique for identifying and closing off opportunities for crime. Police officers or residents, while walking or driving in the neighborhood, note systematically where they see vulnerability to crime: open garage doors, keys left in cars, overgrown shrubbery, lobby doors propped open. They inform residents of trouble spots and how to improve them. In Detroit, police officers on patrol leave Courtesy Security Awareness "Tickets," maintaining a copy for the Crime Prevention Section. When followed by more information, observation reports can introduce residents to other crime prevention activities, from home security surveys to block or apartment watching.

POLICE TELEPHONE PROJECTS Special telephone lines or services may increase crime reporting and help police officers use their time most effectively. Crime reporting lines, with a number different from that for regular emergency calls, can utilize a twenty-four-hour staff (perhaps civilians) or recording devices that are frequently checked. A separate number for reporting crimes no longer in progress helps dispatchers free police officers for emergencies.

POLICE DIRECTIONAL AIDS Large, clear house numbers facing the street and legible at night, as well as painted house numbers at the back of a building or in an alleyway, can help police officers find what they are looking for faster. In Oakland, California, "Operation Roof-top consists of painting addresses on roofs to aid police helicopters. Numbers painted on truck or van roofs can help police spot stolen commercial vehicles from the air.

COURT VOLUNTEERS

According to some estimates, most of the volunteers within the criminal justice system are found within the court component. Some one hundred thousand volunteers are estimated to be affiliated with well over a thousand courts. Most are volunteers in probation, but volunteers are involved in all of these capacities: advisory council member, arts and crafts teacher, home skills teacher, recreation leader, coordinator or administrator of programs, employment counselor, foster parent (group or individual), group guidance counselor, information officer, support services worker, neighborhood worker, office worker (clerical, secretarial), volunteer for one-to-one assignment to probationers, professional skills volunteer, public relations worker, community education counselor, record keeper, religious guidance counselor, tutor, and educational aide.

FIGURE 18.10
Officers providing crime prevention tips to neighborhood resident. Courtesy Detroit (Michigan) Police Department.

One of the first court volunteer programs began in Royal Oak, Michigan, with eight volunteers. This program, Volunteers in Probation, is now a nationwide organization associated with the National Council on Crime and Delinquency. Studies at Royal Oak indicate that volunteers and professionals working together can provide intensive probation services that cannot be supplied in any other way. When probationers from Royal Oak were compared with probationers from nonvolunteer courts, it was found that those from Royal Oak were not only less hostile, but also that their recidivism rates were drastically lower (15 percent for Royal Oak probationers, 50 percent for the other group).

Court watching is an activity in which citizens monitor the performance of judges and prosecutors, the reasons for delays and continuances, the presence of bail bond solicitors, and the consistency of sentences for comparable offenses. As a result of their court-watching experience, a group of women in Montgomery County, Maryland, published a detailed report on juvenile court and care procedures.

Many citizens concerned about extensive pretrial detention have launched studies and reforms to minimize its use (consistent with public safety). The Washington (D.C.) Pretrial Justice Program shares these concerns and has conducted three studies on the pretrial period.

FIGURE 18.11
Officers on neighborhood foot patrol. Courtesy of Detroit (Michigan) Police Department.

The program helps persons who have been detained in jail by reporting and attempting to resolve cases of error and delay and by securing admission of some defendants into community programs.

Other citizen groups have implemented innovative projects to divert defendants from the criminal justice system at a point between arrest and trial—thereby reducing caseloads. And improved communication between lawyer and client is the objective of other citizen efforts. Businesspeople have volunteered their time to study how court systems can effect speedier justice without adding to the court staff. The judicial process in New York City has been accelerated due to the work of the Economic Development Council, a coalition of 130 businesspeople. The council found that court backlogs could be reduced by applying businesslike methods to court procedures, a plan that did not require additional public funds.

In a court-administered program, volunteers counsel delinquent youths and their parents in an attempt to strengthen family ties. Court volunteers in Kalamazoo, Michigan, spend several hours a month with their court-assigned families. In addition to listening sympathetically to the families' problems, the volunteers help them find medical and other aid and provide transportation. Citizen organizations also finance court studies and propose improved methods for selecting judges. Under a court referral program in Alameda County, California, community agencies receive over a hundred misdemeanants each month who have agreed to contribute several hours of their time to a nonprofit agency in lieu of a fine or imprisonment.

Finally, family courts employ liaison referral workers—that is, volunteers who explain the court process to apprehensive parents, gather information about the family to assist the judge, and help families obtain aid from appropriate community agencies. In some jurisdictions, courts use volunteers to assist the families of delinquents to meet immediate needs and to resolve pressing problems.

CORRECTIONAL VOLUNTEERS

The corrections component of the criminal justice system is receiving increased attention from both professionals and citizens. Citizen effort in corrections may pertain to prisoners, to ex-prisoners, or to persons in transition to or from prison.

Qualified citizens volunteer medical and legal aid to inmates and conduct inspections and surveys of jails, prisons, and juvenile institutions. The Osborne Society has found these surveys useful in encouraging reform and reorganization of state institutions. The society is a national, nonprofit organization that helps juvenile and adult correctional institutions prepare offenders for useful and successful lives in society. Members of other citizen organizations work with prisoners on a one-to-one basis, offering service such as tutoring and recreational activities. Amicus, Inc., in Minneapolis, Minnesota, matches volunteers with inmates upon request. The volunteer, acting as a friend, visits an inmate at least once a month and writes letters regularly while the inmate is in prison.

Through a program of study and discussion, volunteers can also help inmates prepare for release from the institution. The volunteers act as counselors and listeners, and as intermediaries between inmates and their families. Some citizen programs attempt to improve the self-confidence of inmates, who frequently are convinced that they are losers who cannot change their lives. This is the purpose of Project Self-Respect, which uses over two hundred volunteers at the Shelby County (Tennessee) Penal Farm. The volunteers help inmates improve their attitudes toward themselves and others so they will be better equipped to function in the community.

Friends Outside, based in Los Altos, California, is a community organization that works to meet the immediate needs of inmates and their families by providing friendship, support, recreation, transportation, food, furniture, and clothing. Other organizations provide education and job training to offenders, and still others press for needed correctional legislation and try to educate the public about the problems of offenders and correctional institutions.

Recall that many convicted persons are in halfway houses or on parole—rather than in prison. Here again, citizens can help. Homes for runaways and other children in trouble frequently are funded or staffed by citizens. These residences may be group homes housing fifteen to twenty youths, or they may be foster homes. Group homes usually have regular counseling sessions, study periods, housekeeping chores, and recreational opportunities. In other residential programs, offenders work or attend school in the community while they progress through stages of increasing responsibility prior to release. A group home in Little Rock, Arkansas, offers an alternative to incarceration for delinquent and predelinquent girls. And the Women's Prison Association and Home in New York City houses women making the transition from institutional supervision to community life.

Upon release, ex-offenders frequently need services that can be supplied by concerned citizens. One organization publishes a guide to services for ex-offenders. Many citizens actively help ex-offenders find jobs and obtain welfare, medical and legal aid, and adequate clothing and housing. Ex-offenders with alcohol or drug problems are referred to appropriate community agencies. Some business associations—including many Jaycee chapters—have job training programs for ex-inmates.

TRENDS IN CITIZEN INVOLVEMENT

Citizen-oriented crime prevention programs continue to provide an effective means to involve a cross-section of society in self-protection. There is general agreement on the part of criminal justice practitioners that they have neither the human nor fiscal resources to provide the level of community safety desirable. The following sections highlight several citizen-based innovations.

The McGruff Campaign

The McGruff, "Take a Bite Out of Crime" campaign was initiated in 1979 as a collaborative effort on the part of groups such as the Crime Prevention Council and the U.S. Department of Justice. The program was developed in an effort to encourage citizens to join in making their communities safer places to live. The campaign uses a "spokesdog" (see Figures 18.12 and 18.13) to give helpful crime prevention tips through a variety of techniques—television sports, posters, newsletters, and brochures. The McGruff figure is easily recognized by children and adults and is strongly identified with the crime prevention movement.

FIGURE 18.12
A McGruff Campaign poster. Courtesy of National Crime Prevention Council.

American Association of Retired Persons

The American Association of Retired Persons (AARP) has been very active in supporting law enforcement by developing a sophisticated program of volunteers to assist in a number of activities. A recent survey, conducted by AARP regarding the nature and extent of volunteers utilized in police and sheriffs' departments, found general support for the concept and some have even predicted a growth in this trend (American Association of Retired Persons 1986).

The AARP survey of law enforcement agencies also revealed the following (American Association of Retired Persons 1986, pp. 2–3):

> Citizens are formally involved as volunteers in law enforcement agencies in greater numbers than was previously assumed. It appears likely that more than 600,000 citizens are serving police and sheriffs' departments of every size in all parts of the nation.
>
> Volunteers assist in nearly every aspect of police work, including crime prevention, law enforcement and internal support. The variety of roles open to volunteers appears to be related to an agency's philosophy and knowledge about volunteers rather than to the number or capabilities of specific individuals.
>
> No precise data is available on the number of law enforcement agencies that sponsor volunteer programs. However we can safely estimate that at least one in every seven agencies does involve citizen volunteers in one or more of its activities. The total number probably exceeds 2,000, but may be considerably higher.
>
> Volunteer recruitment is most successful when undertaken by individuals and community organizations rather than through general promotion and the media. Half the volunteers surveyed reported they were recruited by another volunteer or through an organization of which they were already a member. Thirteen percent were recruited through the media.
>
> Many agencies use volunteers primarily to maintain services within budget constraints. Others use volunteers primarily to improve police/community relations. In either case, *both* cost-savings and improved citizen support are achieved.
>
> The law enforcement officials surveyed predicted substantial future growth in volunteer numbers, the number of agencies providing volunteer opportunities and the number of functions in which volunteers will be allowed to serve.

Volunteer programs are not a new concept. However, in the criminal justice system, there is every reason to believe that volunteers will continue to be utilized in an effort to involve and educate citizens as well as to supplement limited resources available.

Keep the Holidays Happy and Safe

When Shopping and at Home, McGruff's Got Lots of Tips For You.

- √ Even though you are rushed and thinking about a thousand things, stay alert to your surroundings and the people around you.
- √ Stop before dark if possible. Coordinate shopping trips with a friend if you plan to be out late.
- √ Park in a well-lighted area. Don't walk to your car alone if it's parked in a dark area.
- √ Lock your car and close the windows, even if you are only going to be gone for a few minutes. Lock your packages in the trunk. Have your key in hand when you return.
- √ Wait for public transportation or rides from friends in busy, well-lighted areas.
- √ Teach your children to go to a store clerk and ask for help if you become separated while shopping. Tell your children never to go into the parking lot alone.
- √ Avoid carrying large amounts of cash and don't carry it all in one place. Pay for purchases with a check or credit card when possible.
- √ Be extra careful with purses and wallets. Carry your purse tightly under your arm and don't leave it unattended, even for a minute.
- √ Help keep the holidays happy for everyone. Get together with your co-workers and their families to go caroling in a children's hospital. Teenagers can wrap packages for elderly neighbors or help decorate their homes.

YOU CAN MAKE A DIFFERENCE THIS HOLIDAY SEASON!!!

Happy Holidays from McGruff

FIGURE 18.13
A McGruff Campaign poster provides tips for safe Christmas shopping. Courtesy of National Crime Prevention Council.

National Organization for Victim Assistance Programs

The National Organization for Victim Assistance (NOVA) has also been involved in the development and implementation of citizen-oriented crime prevention efforts. In recent years, NOVA and other groups have been very active in sponsoring and encouraging specific programs such as rape prevention. These seminars provide potential victims with information regarding particular forms of victimization (such as rape) and specific suggestions on how to avoid being victimized. For example, considerable attention has been given to the problem of "date or acquaintance rape." Most experts feel that it is important to educate *men* and *women* regarding this problem if the problem is to be dealt with effectively. Openness, mutual respect, and the rights of both men and women are emphasized in these sessions. They also stress the right of women to say "no" to unwanted sexual advances.

The National Organization for Victim Assistance also gives additional advice regarding the problem of date rape:

- Be wary when your relationship seems to be operating along classic stereotypes of dominant male and submissive female. Some men, particularly in late adolescence, are very domineering, putting the woman in a poor position to assert herself. If a man orders for you in a restaurant, plans all date activities, and always gets his way, chances are that he will do the same thing in an intimate setting.
- Be wary when a date tries to control your behavior in any way—for example, trying to restrict the people you meet or forcing you to do something you don't want to do. Be especially wary of men who pressure you, knowing that you would be too embarrassed to tell mutual friends or that you would not be believed. All these things make you more vulnerable.
- Be very clear in communicating what you feel, beyond just saying "no." If a date wants to go further sexually than you are willing, insist that he leave. Or *you* leave.
- Avoid giving ambiguous messages. For example, don't engage in petting, then say you don't want to go any further, then return to petting.
- When dating someone for the first time, try to do it in a group. This is particularly important for young people.
- Don't go somewhere so private that there is nowhere to get help. Parking in a remote spot is not a good idea at any age.
- If it is clear in your mind that you don't intend to have sex with someone you are dating, discuss that at the outset. Communicating your intentions openly can diffuse a possibly dangerous situation.

Campus Crime Prevention

College campus communities have been very active over the last decade in developing and implementing crime prevention programs. The campus environment is generally vulnerable to both property and personal crimes. Today proactive crime prevention programs are found on campuses both large and small. Usually, they involve campus law enforcement officials, students, and college staff members in a variety of efforts such as educational workshops, lighting surveys, operation identification, dorm watch programs, and personnel escorts. These programs stress public education and a high degree of campus community participation. Publicity campaigns, including posters and brochures, are often utilized effectively (see Figure 18.14).

EVALUATING CRIME PREVENTION PROGRAMS

Monitoring and evaluating are two ways to examine a crime prevention program's efforts to reduce crime, disorder, and fear in the neighborhood. Monitoring means keeping track of the crime prevention activities being carried out. Evaluation means asking whether the activities are having the effect that was intended and are meeting the program's goals—either formal goals or the informal goals implicit in its work. The information gathered from monitoring and evaluation can pinpoint trouble spots and suggest more effective ways to run the program. Together with a clear description of goals, that information also provides the details necessary for obtaining resources, especially funding (Feins 1983, p. 51).

Unfortunately, most crime prevention programs—even some of the most widely praised—put little effort into monitoring and evaluation. Although police crime prevention units routinely report on their activities to the departmental chain of command, it is still rare to see a unit take advantage of its crime analysis capabilities and other resources to evaluate the program's effects. In community-based programs, good record keeping is the exception, not the rule. Evaluations are widely viewed as expensive to carry out, and they are not usually attempted except under grant requirements. But there are some less resource-intensive ways to find out which parts of a program are working and how to improve the parts that need help. The effort that goes into monitoring and evaluation is amply rewarded by the program's greater effectiveness and credibility—its ability to convince others that the crime prevention program deserves their help.

Monitoring and evaluation are essential tools for mobilizing new resources and making better use of existing resources. They help mobilize resources in several ways:

- They provide documentary evidence of what is being done already.
- They measure the value of volunteer time and other in-kind resources that can be used to obtain matching grants.

UNIVERSITY of LOUISVILLE

Department of Public Safety

ESCORT SERVICE

The Department of Public Safety offers an escort service after the hours of darkness 7 days a week. You can reach the escort service by calling:

588-6111

State Your Name and Location, and an Officer will be dispatched to meet you.

Your Safety is our FIRST CONCERN

FIGURE 18.14 A poster used in a campus crime prevention program. Courtesy of the University of Louisville Department of Public Safety.

- They show which goals are being met and, where necessary, help in making goals more realistic.
- They establish the crime prevention program's overall track record.

The following report highlights an attempt to evaluate the Crime Stoppers program mentioned earlier in this chapter.

Crime Stoppers: A National Evaluation

From the Director

Research over the past decade has revealed what many practitioners are now realizing—citizen cooperation and participation in solving crimes is crucial. Law enforcement officials alone cannot control crime.

Information is the lifeblood of a criminal investigation. In gathering information about a crime, the criminal investigator seeks as primary sources eyewitnesses or people with knowledge about the crime to provide essential details that will lead to its solution.

One of the goals of the National Institute of Justice is to make people aware of the important role they play in preventing and controlling crime. To this end, the Institute has translated research findings into a series of four public service announcements. This series, *Report—Identify—Testify,* uses the influential medium of television to encourage citizens to cooperate with the criminal justice system by reporting crimes, identifying criminals, and testifying in court. The product of a cooperative effort between the public and private sectors, the announcements are being shown nationally on all major networks.

Despite increasing awareness of the role of citizens in crime control, there are many who, for whatever reason, are reluctant to provide information known about a crime that has been committed. "Crime Stoppers" was developed as a way to open investigative doors that would otherwise remain closed and to assuage citizen anxieties when "official" procedures cannot.

Creative use of the local media and other resources in Crime Stoppers programs enables the criminal investigator to obtain often critical information about a case, including those that have defied solution through traditional investigation.

By participating in Crime Stoppers programs, local media are sending the message that fighting crime is not a responsibility of law enforcement alone—community cooperation and support is needed. At the same time, local media help reduce fear of crime in the community by providing tangible assistance in solving crime.

The National Institute of Justice sponsored the first social-science inquiry into whether Crime Stoppers as a policy strategy works to accomplish the described goals.

One indicator of the success of the Crime Stoppers concept is the substantial public support it has received. From its inception in Albuquerque, New Mexico, in 1976, Crime Stoppers programs have increased to an estimated 600 throughout the United States, and a steady growth of new programs continues.

However, simply establishing a Crime Stoppers program is no assurance of its effectiveness. The evaluation found that the success of programs varies.

Crime stoppers has emerged as a significant "grassroots" movement, locally funded and controlled, It has arisen because our justice process has become narrowly focused, often unbalanced, and less able to handle anonymous leads.

Perhaps more important, it provides all participants—the media, contributors, volunteers, people with information about a crime—with a positive, productive way to help solve terrifying crime.

James K. Stewart
Director
National Institute of Justice

Adapted from *Crime Stoppers: A National Evaluation* (Washington, D.C.: U.S. Department of Justice, 1986), p. 1.

SUMMARY

The idea of crime prevention started in England in the mid-1700s. Three objectives set forth by Henry Fielding laid the foundation for our current concepts of crime prevention: development of a strong police force; organization of active citizen groups; and initiation of action to remove some of the causes of crime and the conditions in which it flourishes.

Modern crime prevention concepts were not formally adopted in the United States until the 1960s, when the National Crime Prevention Institute was founded with joint funding from the U.S. Department of Justice, the Law Enforcement Assistance Administration, the Kentucky Crime Commission, and the University of Louisville (Kentucky). Since that time, other crime prevention centers have been established, and many police departments now have units created specifically to address the issues of crime prevention and to set up liaisons with citizen groups.

Citizen involvement in crime prevention is not only desirable, but also necessary. Citizen efforts should be aimed at the infrastructure of crime—toward problems such as unemployment, poor education, and lack of recreation activities.

Citizens can take many actions to supplement and strengthen the various components of the criminal justice system. For example, they can institute neighborhood security activities, citizen patrols, and crime-reporting programs. They can work with the courts as volunteers in probation, as court watchers (monitoring the perforances of judges and prosecutors), as volunteers in intervention programs to divert defendants from the criminal justice system at a point between arrest and trial (thus reducing caseloads), and as volunteer counselors for delinquent youth and their parents. In corrections, citizens can volunteer medical and legal aid to inmates; inspect and survey jails, prisons, and juvenile institutions; counsel and listen to inmates and serve as intermediaries between them and their families; and provide job training programs for inmates (through business associations).

The monitoring and evaluation of crime prevention programs, whether initiated by the criminal justice system or citizen groups, is a critical factor in achieving long-term success and overall credibility.

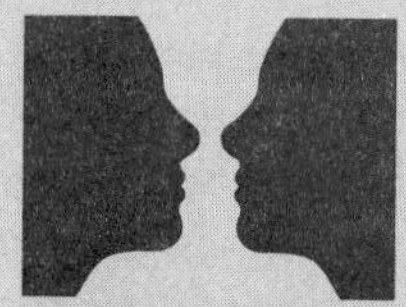

ISSUE PAPER

THE GUARDIAN ANGELS—GOOD SAMARITANS OR VIGILANTES?

Citizens and the police have many opportunities to cooperate in crime prevention. However, if citizens lack confidence in prevention programs, or if they have lost faith in the ability of the police to protect them, they may act *on their own* to protect themselves, their families, and their property. Whether other citizens and the police view such groups as realists looking out for their own welfare or as vigilantes may depend upon the group's membership and the extent of its activities. Since 1979, no other group has so dramatically captured the attention and imagination of citizens, the police, and the media as New York City's Guardian Angels.

Who Are They?

The Guardian Angels were founded in 1979 by a twenty-five-year-old high school dropout, Curtis Sliwa, out of a growing concern about crime in his neighborhood and a belief that the police were unable or unwilling to do anything about it. He originally formed a small group called the Magnificent 13. Today, the Guardian Angels number nearly a thousand and have chapters in such cities as Pittsburgh, New Orleans, Los Angeles, Newark, and Boston (Edelman 1981).[9]

Most of the Angels come from the poorer sections of the city. Almost 65 percent are Hispanic, 20 percent are black, and 5 percent are Oriental. Two dozen are female. Sliwa says that his mission and the mission of the Angels—beyond the immediate issue of crime and fear—is to provide "role models for the young ones committing the atrocious crimes, young guys hanging out, smoking dope, and drinking wine. Even the hardest of the hard will try to do something good if only given the opportunity."

Sliwa is articulate. He can shift his speech from gutteral slang laced with street expletives, which he uses often when talking to the Angels, to well-reasoned answers and polished anecdotes during interviews with the press.

How Do They Operate?

The Guardian Angels board a subway en masse in the rear car before advancing through the train. They check for trouble in each car and scan each platform by craning their necks out of the doors when the train pulls into a station. They are continually checking on each other's safety using whistles and shouts. They are always moving, shuttling from car to car and train to train along a designated route that often transports them halfway across the city in a four-hour tour. They will unceremoniously kick graffiti scribblers off the trains after confiscating their magic markers and spray paint. Angels are not allowed to carry weapons, and they are frisked by a team leader before going out on patrol.

The Guardian Angels have been described as a cross between a special-forces military squad and a street gang. In groups of ten or more, they patrol the New York City subways day and night looking for "bad guys." Some of them wear martial-arts uniforms or jungle fatigues with spit-shined combat boots and red berets (often embossed with studs, pins, patches, raccoon tails, and long strings of colored beads).

Reaction of the Criminal Justice System

Many people in New York City's criminal justice system speak with high regard of Sliwa and his Angels. For example, Robert Keating, the city Coordinator for Criminal Justice, says, "He's a tough kid; someone the Angels respect. Most of the kids come from such bad areas that Curtis might be the first real leader they've encountered. He's also their conduit to something outside the ghetto."

"To call them vigilantes is nonsense," says Mario Merola, the Bronx district attorney. "The municipal and state governments have not met their obligation to provide the kind of security that's needed on the subway. It's true they're not trained, but the mere presence of a uniform is the kind of deterrence we're looking for."

In contrast, however, leaders of the New York City Transit Police Patrolman's Association say that the Angels are publicity mongers whose role comes dangerously close to vigilantism. They also question the exploits of the angels, who claim to have stopped more than a hundred crimes—including an assault on a transit police officer. The association president, William

McKechnie, while not denigrating the motives of most Angels, believes that what they represent is dangerous: "They act far beyond the scope of the ordinary citizen. They don't have training in when to use and not to use force. What happens if they are injured or if they injure a commuter in their over-zealous pursuit?"

Citizen Reactions

According to one free-lance writer in New York, most people in the city, especially subway riders, are enchanted with the Angels. One Manhattan resident wrote to the *New York City Post* and said, "The Guardian Angels are very much appreciated by commuters who must take the subway every day. I'd like to thank them for making me feel safe for a change." Another citizen, writing to the *Sunday News Magazine,* said, "I am truly impressed with their courage and initiative. If the judicial system and the police can't stop crime, maybe the Angels can."

Nonaffiliation with Police Departments

Thus far, the Angels have rejected any formal affiliation with the New York City Transit Police Department. Sliwa once rejected a department request that he submit to the city the names, addresses, and phone numbers of his members. "It is something the police can use to harrass us," he said.

In October 1981, Chief Meehan of the Transit Police Department offered a program to the Angels that would recognize them as auxiliary police officers. The police would provide Angels with identification cards and develop a training program on subway safety, laws governing citizen arrests, lawful use of force, and communication techniques and procedures. Sliwa rejected the proposal, insisting that the Angels remain independent.

The National Network

Today, the Angels claim to have twenty-two hundred members, with eighteen hundred more in training in cities across the country. In the process of expansion, the Angels hope to shed their image as a squad of reformed ghetto toughs. In the Midwest and West, many volunteers are middle-class whites. Says Sliwa, "In Los Angeles I was astounded to see blond-haired, blue-eyed boys drive up in cars with surfboards, park, and go on patrol."

FIGURE 18.15
Curtis Sliwa, *left,* founder of the Guardian Angels. Courtesy Bernard Edelman.

The Angels' effort to forge a national network has had mixed success. In New Orleans, Angels nabbed a knife-wielding robber with a record of fifty-seven previous arrests and a pickpocket who turned out to be a murder suspect wanted by police. But in other cities, their impact has not been so evident. A police spokesman in Pasadena, assessing the Angel patrol at the Tournament of Roses Parade, summed up the verdict of many observers: "No runs, no hits, no errors." In Boston, the Angels predicted that there would be 250 volunteers on patrol by the end of 1983; there are only 60 so far. "They attracted a lot of attention," says Paul DiNatale of the Massachusetts Bay Transit Authority, "and now the question is, Where are they?"

A bigger problem than numbers, however, may be the quality of the protection offered. *Chicago Sun-Times* reporter Michael Codtes, who went undercover and became a Guardian Angel recruit, drew a disturbing picture of his three-month training period. He charges that recruits were poorly trained in citizens' legal rights, that two violence-prone youths were graduated simply to bolster the size of the chapter, and that the group was wracked by a power struggle between co-leaders dubbed by the rank and file as "Mr. Ego" and "Mr. Mouth."

Sliwa calls reports of problems "exaggerated," but some Angels are less reluctant to acknowledge troubles. Admits Rahni Fiduccia of Chicago: "Most applicants think the Guardian Angels are a glorified Bruce Lee squad and they just want to go out there and smash heads." Says Boston chapter leader Susan Piver: "The idea never should have been to blitz Boston. We are limited by manpower and we are limited by funds." Growing pains are inevitable, but if the Guardian Angels fall short on their promises, they will undermine their own effectiveness. Says Piver, "We've got to build from the ground up, and that takes time" ("Guardian Angels Growing Pain," *Time,* 18 January 1982, p. 21).

Conclusion

The Guardian Angels were certainly not the first group of citizens—nor will they be the last—to mobilize outside the formal structure of the criminal justice system for self-protection or the protection of others. The formation of similar groups will depend directly on the public's perception of the ability of the formal structure of the criminal justice system to protect citizens and their property and to dispense justice even-handedly and swiftly.

DISCUSSION AND REVIEW

1. What were the three steps identified by Henry Fielding for stamping out existing crime and preventing future outbreaks of crime?
2. What role did citizens play in crime prevention before the specialization of law enforcement?
3. What dangers are associated with self-centered approaches to crime prevention?
4. What are some of the major features of crime prevention programs directed at education, employment, and recreational opportunities?
5. Discuss the Crime Is Not a Part of Our Black Heritage program.
6. What are some of the major features of block clubs, neighborhood watches, citizen patrols, building patrols, neighborhood patrols, social service patrols, and community protection patrols?
7. How can environmental design affect the incidence of crime?
8. Describe some typical crime-reporting projects.

9. What are some of the "signs of crime" associated with higher levels of citizen fear? What are three general types of programs that have been initiated to reduce the fear of crime and crime itself?
10. How can citizen volunteers get involved in correctional activities?
11. How does monitoring and evaluating crime prevention programs help to mobilize new resources and make better use of existing ones?
12. Why were the Guardian Angels formed?
13. How would you describe the Guardian Angels—as Good Samaritans or as vigilantes?

GLOSSARY

AARP The American Association of Retired Persons. This group has been very active in developing citizen volunteers to aid law enforcement in crime prevention.

Block club A group of persons who live in the same general vicinity and work together to improve citizen crime awareness and to educate citizens about public safety.

Building patrol A citizen patrol whose major objective is to protect specific buildings and adjacent grounds.

Citizen patrol Citizens who patrol their neighborhoods in vehicles and maintain contact with each other through citizen-band radios; may concentrate on specific buildings in housing areas.

Community protection patrol A citizen patrol that monitors the police—in addition to serving as a building patrol, a neighborhood patrol or a social service patrol. The monitoring is done because of fear of harassment by the police based on previous incidents or on a generally antagonistic relationship with the police.

McGruff Campaign A collaborative effort on the part of the Crime Prevention Council and the U.S. Department of Justice to encourage citizens to join in making their communities safer.

National Center for Community Crime Prevention A center established to teach crime prevention skills to citizens representing community-based organizations across the United States; part of the Institute of Criminal Justice Studies at Southwest Texas University in San Marcos.

National Crime Prevention Institute One of the best-known and highly regarded crime prevention training programs for law enforcement officers; located at the University of Louisville, Louisville, Kentucky.

Neighborhood patrol A citizen patrol that usually has a poorly defined area of surveillance. Patrols may be conducted in cars or on foot and may cover specific areas related to such activities as children walking to and from school.

Neighborhood watch A program aimed at improving citizen reporting of crimes or suspicious events and people in their neighborhoods.

Radio watch A program that involves the use of two-way citizen-band or ham radios in personal, company, or taxi vehicles. Participants are urged to report suspicious activities through dispatchers or directly to police departments that monitor emergency frequencies.

Social service patrol A citizen patrol that performs a variety of community functions—from senior citizen escort services to private protection for older citizens.

WhistleStop A community signal system that facilitates the reporting of in-progress crimes by victims and witnesses.

REFERENCES

Advisory Commission on Intergovernmental Relations. *State-Local Relations in the Criminal Justice System.* Washington, D.C.: U.S. Government Printing Office, 1971.

American Association of Retired Persons. *AARP National Study on Volunteers Augmenting Law Enforcement Agencies.* Washington, D.C.: American Association of Retired Persons, 1986.

Bickman, L. *Citizen Crime Reporting Projects.* Washington, D.C.: U.S. Government Printing Office, 1977.

Chamber of Commerce of the United States. *Marshalling Citizen Power against Crime.* Washington, D.C.: Chamber of Commerce of the United States, 1970.

Committee for Economic Development. *Reducing Crime and Assuring Justice.* New York: Committee for Economic Development, 1972.

Duncan, J. T. *Citizen Crime Prevention Tactics: A Literature Review and Selected Bibliography.* Washington, D.C.: U.S. Government Printing Office, April 1980.

Edelman, B. "Does New York Need the Guardian Angels?" *Police Magazine* (May 1981): 51–56.

Feins, J. D.; Peterson, J.; and Rovetch, E. L. *Partnerships For Neighborhood Crime Prevention.* Washington, D.C.: National Institute of Justice, U.S. Department of Justice, 1983.

Gibbs, L. A. *Fourth Paper in the Balance: Citizen Efforts to Address Criminal Justice Problems in Cook County, Illinois.* Chicago, Ill.: Chicago Law Enforcement Study Group, 1977.

"Guardian Angels Growing Pain." *Time,* 18 January 1982, p. 21.

Harlow, C. W. *Reporting Crimes to the Police.* Washington, D.C.: Bureau of Justice Statistics, U.S. Department of Justice, 1985.

Mendez, G. A. "Crime and Policy in the African American Community," *The Annals of the American Academy of Political and Social Science* 494 (1987): 105–110.

Midwest Research Institute. *Evaluation of the National Sheriffs' Association National Research Watch Program.* Kansas City, Mo.: Midwest Research Institute, 1977.

Minnesota Crime Prevention Center. *Block Club Organizing for Crime Prevention.* Minneapolis, Minn.: Minnesota Crime Prevention Center, 1978.

Murray, C. A. "The Physical Environment and Community Control of Crime." In *Crime and Public Policy,* edited by J. Q. Wilson. San Francisco: Institute for Contemporary Studies, 1983.

National Advisory Commission on Criminal Justice Standards and Goals. *A Call for Citizen Action: Crime Prevention and the Citizen.* Washington, D.C.: U.S. Government Printing Office, 1974.

National Advisory Commission on Criminal Justice Standards and Goals. *A National Strategy to Reduce Crime.* Washington, D.C.: U.S. Government Printing Office, 1973.

National Commission on the Causes and Prevention of Violence. *Staff Report: Law and Order Reconsidered.* Washington, D.C.: U.S. Government Printing Office, 1969.

National Institute of Law Enforcement and Criminal Justice. "Community Security Research and Development." Mimeographed. Washington, D.C.: U.S. Government Printing Office, 1978.

Newman, O. *Defensible Space.* New York: Collier, 1978.

Palmer, P. W. *Burglar Prevention: Inmate Interview Project.* Lakewood, Colo.: Lakewood Department of Public Safety, 1978.

President's Commission on Law Enforcement and the Administration of Justice. *The Challenge of Crime in a Free Society.* Washington, D.C.: U.S. Government Printing Office, 1967.

Rosenbaum, D. P.; Lurgio, A. J.; and Lavrakas, P. J. *Crime Stoppers—A National Evaluation.* Washington, D.C.: National Institute of Justice, U.S. Department of Justice, 1986.

Savoie, L. M. "What Issues Will Challenge CPA's in the 1970's?" Paper read at the 1969 convention of the Ohio Society of CPAs.

Sherman, L. W. "Patrol Strategies for Police." In *Crime and Public Policy,* edited by J. Q. Wilson. San Francisco: Institute for Contemporary Studies, 1983.

———. *Crime File—Study Guide: Neighborhood Safety.* Washington, D.C.: U.S. Department of Justice, National Institute of Justice, 1987.

Texas Crime Prevention Institute. "History and Principles." In *Principles and Practices of Crime Prevention: An Introduction.* San Marcos, Tex.: Southwest Texas University, 1978.

U.S. Department of Justice, Law Enforcement Assistance Administration, National Institute of Law Enforcement and Criminal Justice. *Research Bulletin.* Washington, D.C.: U.S. Government Printing Office, June 1979.

Washnis, G. J. *Citizen Involvement in Crime Prevention.* Lexington, Mass.: D. C. Heath, 1976.

Wilson, J. Q. 1983. *Thinking about Crime,* revised ed. New York: Basic Books, 1983.

Wycoff, M. A.; Skogan, W.; Pate, A.; and Sherman, L. W. *Personal Contact Patrol: The Houston Field Test.* Washington, D.C.: The Police Foundation, 1985.

Yin, R. K. *Patrolling the Neighborhood Beat: Residents and Residential Security.* Santa Monica, Calif.: Rand, 1976.

———. *Citizen Patrol Projects.* Washington, D.C.: U.S. Government Printing Office, 1977.

———. *Police Community Stations: The Houston Field Test.* Washington, D.C.: The Police Foundation, 1985.

NOTES

1. This discussion of the historical overview of crime prevention activities, along with the accompanying references, was adapted from J. T. Duncan, *Citizen Crime Prevention Tactics: A Literature Review and Selected Bibliography* (Washington, D.C.: U.S. Government Printing Office, 1980), pp. 2, 3, 21–25.
2. Students in the NCPI course are exposed to such topics as environmental criminology; crime risk management; intrusion detection devices; crime and the older person; armed robbery prevention; rape prevention; lighting for crime prevention; crime analysis; locks and hardware; and community planning for crime prevention.
3. This discussion of crime prevention and citizen action, along with the accompanying references, was adapted from the National Advisory Commission on Criminal Justice Standards and Goals, *A Call for Citizen Action: Crime Prevention and the Citizen* (Washington, D.C.: U.S. Government Printing Office, 1974), pp. 1–10.

4. Statement by E. K. Nelson, quoted in Kenneth Polk, *Non-Metropolitan Delinquency: An Active Program* (Washington, D.C.: U.S. Department of Health, Education, and Welfare, 1969), p. 11.

5. For more information on the role of citizens in crime prevention programs, see National Advisory Commission on Criminal Justice Standards and Goals, A National Strategy to Reduce Crime (Washington, D.C.: U.S. Government Printing Office, 1973).

6. This discussion of the citizen's role was adapted from Caroline W. Harlow, *Reporting Crimes to the Police* (Washington, D.C.: Bureau of Justice Statistics, U.S. Department of Justice, 1985), p. 2.

7. This discussion of the causes of the fear of crime was adapted from Lawrence Sherman, *Crime File—Study Guide: Neighborhood Safety* (Washington, D.C.: U.S. Department of Justice, National Institute of Justice, 1987), pp. 2, 3.

8. The discussion of police tactics for neighborhood crime prevention was adapted from Judith D. Feins, Joan Peterson, and Emily L. Rovetch, *Partnerships for Neighborhood Crime Prevention* (Washington, D.C.: National Institute of Justice, U.S. Department of Justice by Abt Associates, Inc. under contract #5-LEAA-011-81, 1983), pp. 60–63. Readers interested in obtaining further information may also wish to refer to the following sources: George L. Kelling, Tony Pate, Duane Dieckman, and Charles E. Brown. *The Kansas City Preventative Patrol Experiment: A Summary Report* (Washington, D.C.: The Police Foundation, NCJ 42537, October 1974); Lawrence Sherman, Catherine H. Milton, Thomas V. Kelly, *Team Policing: Seven Case Studies* (Washington, D.C.: The Police Foundation, NCJ 11430, August 1973); U.S. Department of Justice, Law Enforcement Assistance Administration, National Institute of Law Enforcement and Criminal Justice, *Issues in Team Policing: A Review of the Literature—National Evaluation Program* by William G. Gay, Jane P. Woodward, H. Talmadge Day, James P. O'Neil, and Carl J. Tucker (Washington, D.C.: U.S. Government Printing Office, NCJ 34480, September 1977); U.S. Department of Justice, Law Enforcement Assistance Administration, National Institute of Law Enforcement and Criminal Justice, *Neighborhood Team Policing: National Evaluation Program Phase 1 Report* by William G. Gay, H. Talmadge Day, and Jane P. Woodward (Washington, D.C.: U.S. Government Printing Office, NCJ 35296, February 1977); Detroit Police Department, "Mini-Station Handbook" (Unpublished, n.d.); San Diego Police Department, Crime Prevention Unit, "City of San Diego, Neighborhood Crime Prevention Program, Final Report," (September 1979); National Crime Prevention Institute, *Community Crime Reporting Programs: Information Package* (Louisville, Ken.: National Crime Prevention Institute, NCJ 51116, n.d.).

9. This discussion of the Guardian Angels was adapted, with permission, from B. Edelman, "Does New York Need the Guardian Angels?" *Police Magazine* (May 1981): 51–56.

INDEX